# The *SNL* Companion

# The *SNL* Companion

## An Unofficial Guide to the Seasons, Sketches, and Stars of *Saturday Night Live*

Stephen Tropiano
Steven Ginsberg

**APPLAUSE**
**THEATRE & CINEMA BOOKS**
Bloomsbury Publishing Group, Inc.
ApplauseBooks.com

Distributed by NATIONAL BOOK NETWORK

Original material copyright © 2013 Stephen Tropiano

New material copyright © 2024 Stephen Tropiano and Steven Ginsberg

*All rights reserved.* No part of this book may be reproduced in any form or by any electronic or mechanical means, including information storage and retrieval systems, without written permission from the publisher, except by a reviewer who may quote passages in a review.

Some of the material in this book was previously published in 2013 as *Saturday Night Live FAQ: Everything Left to Know about Television's Longest-Running Comedy* by Stephen Tropiano, in the series "FAQ" conceived by Robert Rodriguez and developed with Stuart Shea.

All photographs from the authors' collection

**Library of Congress Cataloging-in-Publication Data**
Names: Tropiano, Stephen author. | Ginsberg, Steven, 1955- author. | Tropiano, Stephen. Saturday night live FAQ.
Title: The SNL companion : an unofficial guide to the seasons, sketches, and stars of Saturday Night Live / Stephen Tropiano, Steven Ginsberg.
Description: Essex : Applause Press, 2024. | "Some of the material in this book was previously published in 2013 as Saturday night live FAQ: every thing left to know about television's longest-running comedy by Stephen Tropiano"–Title page verso. | Includes bibliographical references and index.
Identifiers: LCCN 2024017512 (print) | LCCN 2024017513 (ebook) | ISBN 9781493072606 (paperback) | ISBN 9781493072613 (epub)
Subjects: LCSH: Saturday night live (Television program)
Classification: LCC PN1992.77.S273 T766 2024  (print) | LCC PN1992.77.S273 (ebook) | DDC 791.45/72–dc23/eng/20240520
LC record available at https://lccn.loc.gov/2024017512
LC ebook record available at https://lccn.loc.gov/2024017513

To my older brothers, Michael and Joseph,
who stayed up with me to watch *SNL* in the '70s.
To Steven Ginsberg, who has been watching *SNL*
with me for the past thirty-six years;
and to Lorne Michaels, for giving all of us
something to watch on Saturday night.—ST

For Deb Silberberg, who taught me how to laugh,
and to Stephen Tropiano, who keeps me laughing.
And to *SNL*, which has somehow managed to do both.—SG

# Contents

| | | |
|---|---|---|
| Prefaces | | ix |
| Acknowledgments | | xiii |
| Introduction | | xv |
| 1 | "A Major Show in Television That People Will Talk About": The Birth of an American Institution | 1 |
| 2 | "A Show That I Would Watch": Lorne Michaels and *SNL*'s Creative Team | 7 |
| 3 | "No Television Experience Required": The Not Ready for Prime Time Players | 14 |
| 4 | "Live from New York—It's *Saturday Night*": October 11, 1975, 11:30 p.m. (EDT) | 27 |
| 5 | Breaking New Ground: *SNL*'s Television Comedy Roots | 47 |
| 6 | One Samurai, Two Wild and Crazy Guys, and Three Coneheads: *SNL* in the 1970s (1975–1980), Seasons 1–5 | 54 |
| 7 | Season 6—The Worst Season (So Far): The 1980s, Part 1 (1980–1981) | 75 |
| 8 | Starting Over (and Over): The 1980s, Part II (1981–1985), Seasons 7–10 | 86 |
| 9 | Getting Into Character: The 1980s, Part III (1985–1990), Seasons 11–15 | 102 |
| 10 | Saturday Night Alive (and Dead): The 1990s, Part I (1990–1995), Seasons 16–20 | 119 |
| 11 | Resuscitating *SNL*: The 1990s, Part II (1995–2000), Seasons 21–25 | 131 |
| 12 | Laughing Matters: Memorable Characters, Sketches, and Moments (2000–2013), Seasons 26–38 | 144 |
| 13 | *SNL* Goes Digital (2013–2024), Seasons 39–49 | 156 |
| 14 | A New Era in Political Comedy | 170 |
| 15 | Politics and the Presidency, Part 1: Richard Nixon to George W. Bush (1970s–2000s) | 181 |
| 16 | Politics and the Presidency, Part 2: Barack Obama to Joseph Biden (2000s–present) | 205 |
| 17 | Repertory and Featured Players: An *SNL* Cast Directory (1980–2024), Seasons 6–49 | 228 |
| 18 | "No Comedy Experience Required": Hosting *SNL* | 263 |
| 19 | Keeping Live Music Alive: *SNL*'s Musical Guests | 285 |
| 20 | An Unexpected Surprise: *SNL*'s Late-Night Cameos | 296 |

| | | |
|---|---|---|
| 21 | "A Nonexistent Problem with an Inadequate Solution": *SNL*'s Commercial Parodies | 311 |
| 22 | "And Here's a Short Film By . . .": *SNL*'s Original Shorts | 328 |
| 23 | *Weekend Update*: "Our Top Story Tonight . . ." | 343 |
| 24 | "Yeah, That's the Ticket!": *SNL*'s Catchphrases | 361 |
| 25 | "Well, Isn't That Special?": *SNL*'s Objectionable, Offensive, and Controversial Moments | 376 |
| 26 | From the Small Screen to the Big Screen: *SNL* Goes to Hollywood | 391 |

| | |
|---|---|
| Appendix A: Episode Guide | 411 |
| Appendix B: Awards | 577 |
| Selected Bibliography | 593 |
| Index | 603 |

# Prefaces

One very cold Saturday afternoon in January 1978, a week after my sixteenth birthday, my brother Joe and I took a train from Croton-on-Hudson, New York, into "the city" to watch a rehearsal of *Saturday Night Live*. The tickets I mailed away for a year before were for the 8:00 p.m. "dress rehearsal," which meant we could take the 10:00 p.m. train back home to see the live broadcast of the show at 11:30 p.m. (The Tropiano family didn't get their first VCR until 1982.)

I had never been in a television studio before, nor had I ever seen a television star in person. I also remember being nervous because "No one under seventeen will be admitted" was printed on the ticket. Fortunately, no one was paying very close attention, and after waiting for two hours in the halls of 30 Rockefeller Center, the NBC pages ushered us into the balcony of Studio 8H.

We lucked out—season 3, episode #10 was great. Comedian Robert Klein was the host, and Bonnie Raitt, who at the time I only knew as the daughter of Broadway star John Raitt, was the musical guest (she sang "Runaway" and "Give It All Up or Let Me Go" with Klein on the harmonica). The original cast members were all there (minus Chevy Chase, plus Bill Murray). We saw the first "Olympia Café" sketch ("Cheezburger, Cheezburger, Cheezburger") and the debut of nerds Lisa Loopner (Gilda Radner) and Todd DiLaMuca (Murray), and heard Nick the Lounge Singer (Murray) sing the "theme song" from *Star Wars*. The episode ended with the studio being taken over by atomic lobsters. The invasion was orchestrated by head writer Michael O'Donoghue, who stood with a bullhorn directing the audience to look scared even though there were no lobsters—atomic or otherwise—in the studio.

The following year I attended another rehearsal with my friend Heidi Jensen, whose father was a correspondent for NBC News. We entered the studio on the VIP line and sat in the first row in front of one of the tiny stages where they perform the sketches. The host was actress Margot Kidder (4.15), who played Lois Lane in the original film version of *Superman* (1978). The show wasn't as funny as the first, except for one clever sketch in which newlyweds Lois Lane (Kidder) and Superman (Bill Murray) are throwing a party, and she is concerned her friends won't mix with his friends, who are all superheroes, like the Flash (Dan Aykroyd) and the Incredible Hulk (John Belushi).

As we were exiting the studio, members of the cast were milling around thanking the audience. As we passed by John Belushi, who had a scowl on his face, the comedian said, "You should have laughed more." He wasn't talking directly to me, but without thinking I replied, "It should have been funnier." Belushi looked at me and flashed me a smile.

# Prefaces

*Saturday Night Live* is one of the reasons I entered college as a television and radio major. Four degrees and many years later, I am now teaching television studies to undergraduates who are pursuing careers in television and film. As I grow older and the generation gap between my students and me widens, it has become increasingly difficult to explain why *Saturday Night Live* was considered groundbreaking when it debuted on October 11, 1975. I imagine it's like Woodstock. The people I've met who were there (and can actually remember being there) say you had to have been at Woodstock and experienced it for yourself to fully understand why it was a milestone in our cultural history.

*Saturday Night Live*'s contribution to American culture and, more specifically, American comedy, is immeasurable. I never imagined back when I was a teenager sitting in Studio 8H that forty-six years later I would not only still be watching *SNL* but writing a book about the show. For this opportunity, I am truly grateful.

*Stephen Tropiano*
*Los Angeles, California*

I was born at the tail end of the baby boomer generation. So when *Saturday Night Live* first aired in 1975 it felt like being invited into one of those mysterious parties an older sibling got to attend that you were never allowed to go to. Of course, I didn't have any older siblings, and I didn't know much, or really anything, about the kind of parties I imagined I was missing. All I knew was that watching *Saturday Night Live* meant I was finally hanging out with the cool kids.

I was nineteen and living with my divorced mom and younger sister in Flushing, Queens. I had just become a senior in college and had a job after school and on weekends. Academically I was, well, precocious. Plus, I was saving money and on the fast track to attend law school or grad school or some school. But all of this is easy to do when you've living someone else's version of life. The latter was becoming very apparent thanks to George Carlin, Paul Simon, Candice Bergen, and "The Not Ready for Prime Time Players." For three straight Saturday nights in a row, they were nudging me, making me laugh, and whispering directly into my ear, "What the f–k are you doing with your life?"

I knew I wanted to be in show business and probably as a writer, but it all seemed too preposterous. Then, the beginning of an answer came when my dad, who was a gambler and a bookie living in LA, found out I liked *SNL*. On one of our weekly phone calls, he said, "You wanna go to the show? I know a guy who can get you in." Seriously, I think he really did say, "I know a guy."

The guy turned out to be an *SNL* cameraman, and soon my friend Rich and I were in Studio 8H, watching the rehearsal of a show hosted by Lily Tomlin. I was a little disappointed it wasn't the actual show, but Lily was a huge win. What was not huge was the studio or the limited bleacher seating. Not to mention the actors and crew were really close. It all felt like a slightly larger version of the room at school where they taught drama class. A room where I'd meet my friends to hang out and watch improv, scenes, and backstage school drama play out.

"That's all there is to this?" I thought. "And you get paid, too? Well, this seems . . . doable." Then I looked around, and there was the *SNL* cast hanging out on the side, Lily in the center of the stage area talking with a tech guy, and someone scribbling on some pages near a camera indulging in some drama. It all felt soooo homey to me. Maybe it was or maybe it wasn't, but one thing was for sure: I was no longer nervous.

I don't remember much about the actual show, just Lily being funny, Chevy Chase's *Jaws* bit consisting of half a shark puppet dangling through the facade of a partially built door, and "The Not Ready for Prime Time Players" in bee costumes for no reason at all running under a camera to center stage near the end of the show and looking slightly embarrassed. Turns out I was right about all three. And wrong about everything I thought I would wind up doing with my life up to that point.

Years later, when I would first meet my coauthor and longtime partner/husband, Stephen Tropiano, it was on a Saturday night. We went to a party, took a long walk around the neighborhood (where I told him a story that turned out to be a screenplay I got made about me and my gambler father), and wound up back at his grad school apartment watching Sean Penn (then married to Madonna) hosting this late-night comedy show where he joked about beating up paparazzi. We, though sadly not they, have been together ever since. As for that late night show, it's lasted even longer and is still going strong.

And we wrote a book about it.

*Steven Ginsberg*
*Los Angeles, California*

# Acknowledgments

We wish to thank Faith Ginsberg and Steve Kerem; our agent, June Clark; Chris Chappell, Barbara Claire, Naomi Minkoff, Della Vache, and Emily Burr at Rowman & Littlefield; and Karen Herman, former archivist for the Television Academy. We are also greatly indebted to the late Herbert S. Schlosser, former president and CEO of NBC, for allowing us to reprint portions of his memo outlining his idea for a new late-night variety show to air live from New York on Saturday night.

This project was made possible in part by a James B. Pendleton Grant from the Roy H. Park School of Communications at Ithaca College.

# Introduction

**S**aturday Night Live is an American institution.
It is the longest-running sketch comedy show on television—a total of 968 episodes over forty-nine seasons (through May 2024), which, if you do the multiplication and the division, equals approximately 1,117.5 hours of original programming.

Since its debut on October 11, 1975 (under its original title, *NBC's Saturday Night*), certain elements of the show have remained consistent: a repertory cast of players, a new guest host and musical guest each week, an opening monologue, *Weekend Update*, commercial parodies, and, except for a period in the early 1980s, someone opening the show with "Live from New York, it's *Saturday Night!*" But when you start to take a closer look at the show and begin to break it down by decade and season, it's evident that in an effort to stay relevant and maintain its fan base, plus deliver respectable ratings, *SNL* had to evolve. Change is not necessarily a good thing, and it certainly isn't always the answer. Then again, just when you think *SNL* has fallen off America's radar and is on a creative downward spiral, the public's interest in the show is suddenly energized and expanded thanks to a talented new cast member, or a digital short that goes viral, or a female governor running for vice president, or a New York real estate developer who gets elected president.

Before you begin reading, let's get a few points out of the way, beginning with what this book is *not*. It is not a "tell-all" book about what *really* went on behind the scenes of the show, nor is it a "set the record straight" book in response to what has already been written about *SNL*. There are three informative and entertaining books on the history of the show: *SNL: Saturday Night: A Backstage History of* Saturday Night Live (1986), by Doug Hill and Jeff Weingrad, which deals with its early history; *Saturday Night Live: The First Twenty Years* (1994), an "authorized" coffee-table book edited by Michael Cader with terrific photos of the show's early years by Edie Baskin; and the updated edition of *Live from New York: An Uncensored History of* Saturday Night Live (2015), an oral history by Tom Shales and James Andrew Miller. Shales, a Pulitzer Prize–winning critic for the *Washington Post*, started writing about *SNL* from day one and has since been one of the show's harshest critics and biggest fans.

Speaking of fans—this book is written from the perspective of a "critical fan," someone who has remained loyal to the show over the years—warts and all—and is willing to put up with all those naysayers who love to go on about how the show is "less funny now" than it used to be. Maybe it's out of a sense of nostalgia, or the satisfaction we get knowing someone younger missed out on

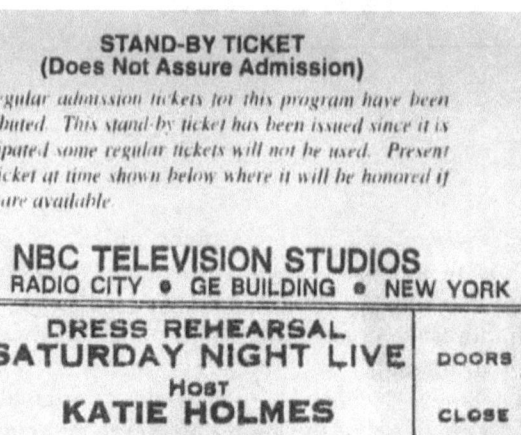

After attending the 7:30 p.m. dress rehearsal of *Saturday Night Live*, audience members can go home and watch the broadcast of the live show at 11:30 p.m., though it's possible some sketches were cut for the final show.

something really special because he or she was born in the wrong decade, but we all have a tendency to romanticize the past, and, in the case of *SNL*, believe that the show was better back in the day "when I watched it." But as a genre, sketch comedy shows, particularly one that airs late in the evening, are by their very nature uneven.

Within a single episode, there are typically one or two or more hilarious sketches, a few jokes or moments that warrant a chuckle, and portions of the show that signal that it's bedtime. The first five seasons of *SNL* are commonly referred to as the show's "Golden Age." The early episodes were stellar, but by no means perfect.

The fact that *SNL* is uneven should not detract from its unique and significant contribution to American culture. As this book demonstrates, the show has been a cornerstone in popular culture for six decades with its endless supply of recurring characters, catchphrases, and memorable comedic and musical moments. At the same time, through satire, parody, and a fake newscast, *SNL* has also provided a running commentary on American culture, politics, and society.

*SNL* has done this by literally becoming the door many of the biggest comedy names in the business have passed through in order to hone their craft, get seen and heard, or simply gain the kind of wider audience that being on a weekly network television series allows. It's not the only way to it do, but over the years it has become one of the undeniable boot camps for the next generation of comedy talent.

What is not always noted is that these people have then left and gone on to write, create, and/or star in some of the most successful television and movies of our times. Readers can view our credits list of cast members from seasons 1–5, as well as the directory of cast bios for those who followed them. But consider the popularity over the last fifty years of films starring Bill Murray, Adam Sandler, Eddie Murphy, Will Ferrell, Chevy Chase, John Belushi, Dan Aykroyd, and Mike Myers.

Or the impact on TV made by shows created by, produced by, or starring Tina Fey, Larry David, Amy Poehler, Jane Curtin, Julia Louis-Dreyfus, Conan O'Brien, Seth Meyers, Jimmy Fallon, Bill Hader, Jason Sudeikis, Maya Rudolph, Andy Samberg, and Will Forte.

Not to mention writers and directors, like Adam McKay, Michael Schur, Greg Daniels, and Bob Odenkirk.

Or stand-up comedy stars, like Chris Rock, John Mulaney, Sarah Silverman, and Leslie Jones.

Or already-known performers in the cast, like Billy Crystal, Martin Short, and Christopher Guest.

Or comedy talents so unique they had sold-out evenings of their sketch characters on Broadway, like Gilda Radner, or at Carnegie Hall, like Andy Kaufman.

That's only a very partial list, but you get where we're going with this.

A single name that repeatedly appears in the pages that follow is the show's creator, Lorne Michaels. Television is a collaborative medium, and while some critics are hesitant to assign authorship of a television series to a single individual, there is no denying that despite all the limitations imposed on a producer, from budget constraints to network interference, throughout television history there have been producers (most of whom are also writers) who have served as a show's primary creative force: Norman Lear (*All in the Family* [1971–1979]), Dick Wolf (*Law & Order* franchise), David Chase (*The Sopranos* [1999–2007]), Rod Serling (*The Twilight Zone* [1959–1964] and *Night Gallery* [1969–1973]), and Larry David and Jerry Seinfeld (*Seinfeld* [1989–1998]).

Lorne Michaels produced forty-four of *SNL*'s forty-nine seasons. Over his fifty-six-year career in television, he has been the recipient of twenty-one Primetime Emmys, the Mark Twain Prize for American Humor, and an individual Peabody Award. But awards are only a part of a much larger story. His contribution to American television comedy is unparalleled, and his influence is immeasurable.

A brief word on how to use this book: In appendix A you will find a list of every episode of *Saturday Night Live* along with the name(s) of the guest host(s) and musical guest(s) and other pertinent information. The episodes are numbered according to the season and the order in which the episode appeared (for example, 32.4 = season 32, episode 4). A reference to a host, sketch, character, musical performance, cameo, or guest appearance in the book will include the corresponding episode number in parentheses.

# "A Major Show in Television That People Will Talk About"

## The Birth of an American Institution

The story of *Saturday Night Live* begins with the "King of Late Night" himself—Johnny Carson. In the 1970s, Carson was NBC's biggest star, and the highly rated *The Tonight Show Starring Johnny Carson* (1962–1992) was one of the network's top moneymakers. Since January 1965, NBC affiliates had the option of airing a rerun of *The Tonight Show* after the local 11 p.m. news on either Saturday or Sunday night. Nine years later, at Carson's request, NBC pulled the show from its weekend late-night schedule. Carson may have decided America didn't need to hear "Heeeeere's Johnny!" six nights a week, or perhaps he was just thinking ahead. In December 1977, *New York Times* media critic Les Brown reported that Carson negotiated a new contract with the network raising his annual salary to $3 million and cutting his work schedule down to three shows a week for half the year. A guest host subbed for Carson on Monday nights, but on his second night off NBC aired a repeat of *The Tonight Show*.

Whatever Carson's reasons, Herbert S. Schlosser, president and CEO of the National Broadcasting Company, agreed it was a good idea. Keeping the network's highest-paid star happy was certainly a priority, and giving America a break from Carson over the weekend would certainly not affect the show's stellar ratings. Schlosser expressed this point in a memo dated February 11, 1975, to NBC Network president Robert T. Howard: "There is a question in my mind whether or not telecasting the Saturday/Sunday 'Tonight Show' repeats may not in the long run begin to hurt us. The 'Tonight Show' has now reached an all-time peak. Certainly overexposure of a repeat on the weekend can't help what we have going Monday through Friday."

Like most programming decisions, the primary reason NBC agreed to the schedule change was financial. The hole in the weekend schedule provided the network with the opportunity to generate additional revenue by creating a brand-new show that affiliates could air either on Saturday or Sunday night.

The show also fit into the NBC family of shows that began with *Today* and *The Tonight Show* in the 1950s and continued with *Tomorrow* and *The Midnight Special*.

At the time, *The Tonight Show* was on weeknights from 11:30 p.m. to 1:00 a.m. On Mondays through Thursdays, Carson was followed by *Tomorrow* (1973–1981), a talk show hosted by Tom Snyder and launched by Schlosser in 1973. On Friday nights, *The Midnight Special* (1973–1981), a taped concert series, aired after *The Tonight Show* from 1:00 a.m. to 2:30 a.m. As Schlosser explained in a 2007 interview for the Archive of American Television (AAT), "I thought it was kind of a no-brainer. If you can get people to watch on 1 o'clock on Friday night, what's wrong with Saturday night? And at 11:30—an earlier hour—I really thought that would work." To develop the new late-night Saturday show, Schlosser hired twenty-six-year-old Dick Ebersol as NBC's director of weekend late-night programming. At the time, he was working as an assistant to Roone Arledge, president of ABC Sports.

The original model for *Saturday Night Live*'s format was *The Colgate Comedy Hour* (1950–1955), a 1950s variety series that had not one but several hosts who rotated each week. In a 2009 interview for the AAT, Ebersol recalled how he was happy and surprised when Richard Pryor, whose edgy brand of stand-up comedy was hardly censor friendly, accepted his offer to be one of the hosts. As a result of landing Pryor, Ebersol was also close to signing George Carlin and Lily Tomlin. But Pryor suddenly dropped out at the urging of his new manager, who told him that he could never do his own material on network television. Losing Pryor was a setback for Ebersol, and the idea of rotating hosts was eventually dropped.

In the same February 11 memo to Robert T. Howard, Schlosser outlined his vision for "a new program concept called 'Saturday Night.'" The memo, consisting of eleven "considerations and questions" (excerpts of which are included below in italic), served as the blueprint for a "new and exciting program" that would one day become an American comedy institution.

*1. This program would play from 11:30 PM to 1:30 AM Saturday night in place of the Saturday/Sunday "Tonight Show," each Saturday except when "Weekend" is on. What arrangements would we make with stations to help get maximum clearance on Saturday night? (Note: the program would be two hours long.) To the extent that we do not affect clearance on Saturday night stations could play it on Sunday night while we work towards greater Saturday night clearance. But under what title would the show play on Sunday night? Would we have separate titles for those stations who play it on Sunday night?*

According to Ebersol, the Saturday vs. Sunday scheduling time was still an issue at this point because only one rerun of *The Tonight Show* aired each weekend: on Saturday night for 65 percent of the NBC affiliates and on Sunday night for the remaining 35 percent. But the affiliates would no doubt recognize that the new show's major selling point is that it was live (and had *Saturday* in the title).

The length of the show was cut down from two hours to ninety minutes (same as *The Tonight Show*, which Carson trimmed to sixty minutes in 1980). *Weekend* (1975–1979), the other program mentioned in the memo, was a Peabody

Award–winning late-night news magazine show hosted by Lloyd Dobyns that combined investigative reporting with light feature stories. The show continued to air on Saturday nights on the weeks *SNL* was "dark" (meaning not airing live) until 1978 when it was added to NBC's prime-time schedule.

*2. This would be an effort to create a new and exciting program. "Saturday Night" should originate from the RCA Building in New York City, if possible live, from the same studio where we did the "Tonight Show" or perhaps from [Studio] 8H.*

The RCA Building (30 Rockefeller Center, or, thanks to Tina Fey, better known today as "30 Rock") has been *SNL*'s home since 1975. The show is broadcast from Studio 8H (on the eighth floor), and the writers' offices occupy the seventeenth floor. Studio 6-B, home to *The Tonight Show* from 1957 until the show relocated to Burbank in 1972, is the future home of *The Tonight Show with Jimmy Fallon*.

*3. It would be a variety show, but it would have certain characteristics. It should be young and bright. It should have a distinctive look, a distinctive set and a distinctive sound.*

From Edie Baskin's title sequences, to the imaginative production and costume design of Eugene and Franne Lee, to the jazz theme song by musical director Howard Shore, *Saturday Night Live*, from the very beginning, had a very distinctive youthful, and for want of a better word, "hip" look and sound. The comedic sensibility of the cast and the writers, most of whom were under thirty, would also be a major factor in capturing the show's young target audience.

*4. We should attempt to use the show to develop new television personalities. We should seek to get different hosts who might do anywhere from one to eight shows depending on our evaluation of each host. It should be a program where we can develop talent that could move into prime time, either in the summer, as a January replacement, or even in the fall. It would be a great place to use people like Rich Little, Joe Namath, and others. If we give the show sufficient style and promotion it could attract certain guest stars because of the uniqueness of the show.*

*5. The show should not only seek to develop new young talent, but it should get a reputation as a tryout place for talent.*

The idea of rotating hosts was part of the original concept, but the network settled on the idea of a new guest host each week. While it made *SNL* unique, it was not exactly an original idea. *The Midnight Special*, for most of its run, also had a different host each week. Singer Helen Reddy hosted for one season (1975–1976), but for the other five years *The Midnight Special* was hosted by a singer or comedian, including three of *SNL*'s early hosts: George Carlin, Richard Pryor, and Lily Tomlin. (Frequent *SNL* guest Andy Kaufman and original cast members Chevy Chase and Laraine Newman guest hosted during its final season in 1980–1981.) During the six-year period (1975–1981) when *SNL* and *The Midnight Special* were both on the air, they also showcased some of the same musical talent.

In terms of guest hosts, producer Lorne Michaels took a unique approach by not limiting hosting duties exclusively to comedians and musical performers. During seasons 1–5, *SNL* boasted an eclectic list of guest hosts that included television legends Desi Arnaz (1.14) and Milton Berle (4.17), White House press secretary Ron Nessen (1.17), *Playboy* publisher Hugh Hefner (3.3), activist Ralph Nader (2.11), veteran character actors Broderick Crawford (2.16) and Strother Martin (5.17), athletes O. J. Simpson (3.12) and Bill Russell (5.3), and television producer Norman Lear (2.2).

*SNL* certainly did live up to Schlosser's original concept in regard to using the show to "develop new young talent," yet Michaels didn't necessarily see *SNL* as a training ground for future prime-time stars. Rich Little and the New York Jets' star quarterback Joe Namath, who had recently signed a contract with NBC, never hosted or even made a cameo appearance on *SNL*. Rich Little briefly had his own comedy-variety series on NBC (*The Rich Little Show*) in 1976. Namath, who made frequent guest appearances on talk shows (he even guest hosted *The Tonight Show*), was given his own sitcom, the short-lived *The Waverly Wonders* (1978), in which he played a high school basketball coach. According to Doug Hill and Jeff Weingrad's *Saturday Night: A Backstage History of Saturday Night Live*, Little's name was brought up again to Michaels and Ebersol during a meeting. Schlosser added the name of another NBC favorite to the talent list—Bob Hope. Keeping his young target audience in mind, Little and Hope were exactly the kind of performers Michaels wanted to avoid.

*6. As indicated, if possible the show should be done live. If it were done live at 11:30 PM it would permit people from Broadway shows to appear on it on Saturday night. However, if not done live it should be taped earlier in the evening the same day it goes on the air to maintain its freshness and topicality.*

A live weekly variety show was certainly a novel idea in 1975, yet *SNL* was not the only live show to be added to the fall 1975 television schedule. On September 20, 1975, nearly one month before the premiere of *NBC's Saturday Night*, *Saturday Night Live with Howard Cosell* debuted in prime time on ABC. Broadcast live from the Ed Sullivan Theatre in New York City with live remotes from around the world, the premiere episode featured singers John Denver, Paul Anka, and Shirley Bassey; from London, the Scottish pop group the Bay City Rollers; and from Las Vegas, entertainers Siegfried and Roy.

*Saturday Night Live with Howard Cosell*'s executive producer (and Dick Ebersol's former boss), Roone Arledge, managed to book A-list performers like Bill Cosby, Roberta Flack, Frank Sinatra, and George Burns; star athletes, including Walt Frazier, Willie Mays, and O. J. Simpson; and an assortment of B-list celebrities and comedians. But Arledge came from the world of sports and knew nothing about putting on a live, weekly variety show. The same can be said for Cosell, who was his usual irritating self. It was no surprise when the show was a critical and ratings failure. In his interview with the AAT, the show's director,

# "A Major Show in Television That People Will Talk About"

"Live from New York... It's Howard Cosell!" *Saturday Night Live with Howard Cosell* premiered three weeks before *NBC's Saturday Night* at the start of the 1975–1976 TV season. Unfortunately, Cosell was no Ed Sullivan, and the show was canceled four months later.

Don Mischer, admitted the Cosell show was "chaotically produced," dubbing it "one of the greatest disasters in the history of television."

Once ABC yanked Cosell from their Saturday-night lineup in January 1976, NBC obtained the rights to the title, which was officially changed on March 26, 1977, to *Saturday Night Live*. This was not the only connection between the two shows. Cosell's show featured three comedy performers, billed as "The Prime Time Players," which is how *SNL* arrived at the name "The Not Ready for Prime Time Players" for their original cast. Better yet, the three Cosell regulars—Bill Murray, Christopher Guest, and Brian Doyle-Murray—would all eventually become *SNL* regulars. According to Chevy Chase's biographer, Rena Fruchter, Chase originally wanted to call the show *Saturday Night Live Without Howard Cosell*, but NBC wouldn't allow it (no surprise there).

After the first episode, the show's official title was *NBC's Saturday Night*—only to be shortened toward the end of season 1 to *Saturday Night*. Once NBC secured the title rights of Howard Cosell's canceled variety series from ABC, the show's title was changed on March 26, 1977 (2.17) to *Saturday Night Live*.

7. *All of this sounds like a very expensive, high budget show. It should not be that. Based on sales and other projections we would have to determine a reasonable budget. Could we make out if it cost $85,000 to $125,000? What are the parameters? We should set a goal and hire a producer who can do it for the parameters we establish.*

8. *We should not look upon this effort in terms of a short term financial evaluation. We undertook "The Tomorrow Show" knowing that we might only break even for some period of time.*

Schlosser understood that it took time and money to create a hit television show. According to Hill and Weingrad, in the early days *SNL* cost far more than it was making. The cost per episode was initially estimated at $134,600, but the show was going approximately $100,000 over budget per episode, and the network was only getting $7,500 for a thirty-second commercial spot. Once *SNL*'s status as a hit show was established, NBC was spending $406,000 per episode (season 4), which rose to $553,000 per episode (season 5, the first season the show came in under budget). According to Shales and Miller's *Live from New York: An Uncensored History of* Saturday Night Live, the ratings for season 4 were at an all-time high of 12.6 and 39 percent share (that's the percentage of homes with their television sets on that were watching *SNL*). In the plus column, the show was earning the network somewhere between $30 and $40 million a year.

9. *Saturday night is an ideal time to launch a show like this. Those who now take the Saturday/Sunday "Tonight Show" repeats should welcome this and I would imagine we could get much greater clearance with a new show.*

Schlosser concludes on an optimistic and foretelling note: "With proper production and promotion, 'Saturday Night' can be a major show in television that people will talk about." When asked about his contribution to the making of *Saturday Night Live*, the NBC executive quite humbly admits he didn't really meddle in the content of the show, only fielded the weekly complaints from the head of standards and practices. In his interview for the AAT, he credited producer/creator Lorne Michaels for giving him more than what he outlined in his memo: "What he gave me was not only more than I thought, it was really a new kind of show, it was a breakthrough . . . nobody was doing what he was doing on television. Nobody."

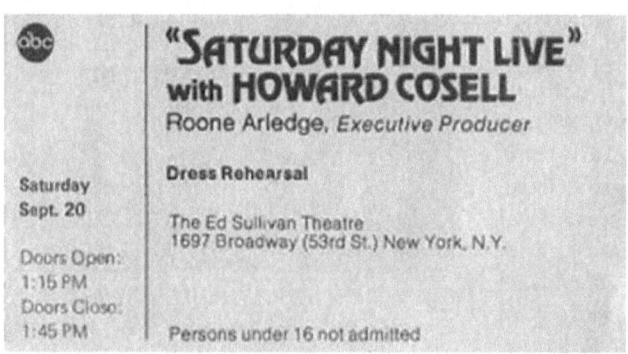

A ticket to the dress rehearsal of the premiere episode of *Saturday Night Live with Howard Cosell* (1975–1976).

# "A Show That I Would Watch"

## Lorne Michaels and *SNL*'s Creative Team

To translate NBC president Herb Schlosser's three-page memo into a hit television series, Dick Ebersol, director of weekend late-night programming, hired thirty-one-year-old Lorne Michaels, whose experience in television as a comedy performer and writer/producer made him the ideal producer to get the new series off the ground. In a 1992 interview with *Playboy* magazine, Michaels explained why he was hired: "The head of NBC then, Herb Schlosser, said, 'We're looking for a show for young urban adults.' Yuppies weren't invented yet. I was a young urban adult. I knew that television had changed everything. There was no difference in what people knew whether they lived in New York, Los Angeles, or the heartland. So if I could bring what was already popular in records and movies to television—if I just did a show that I would watch—well, there were lots of people like me. There was nothing cynical about it; no clever scheme of outsmarting anyone."

The eldest child of Florence and Henry Lipowitz, Lorne Lipowitz grew up in Toronto, Canada, where his first exposure to show business was the College Playhouse, a movie theater owned by his grandparents on College Street near the University of Toronto. After earning his bachelor's degree in English from University College, University of Toronto, he pursued a career in broadcasting at CBC (Canadian Broadcasting Corporation) Radio. He also performed on the air with his writing partner, Hart Pomerantz. The pair were then hired as staff writers on the short-lived NBC variety show *The Beautiful Phyllis Diller Show* (1968), and for a season on *Rowan & Martin's Laugh-In* (1968–1973), for which Michaels received his first of many Emmy nominations. Michaels and Pomerantz also starred on their own sketch comedy series on Canadian television, *The Hart & Lorne Terrific Hour* (1971–1972). After going their separate ways (Pomerantz became an attorney), Michaels's career took off when he was hired to write and produce three successful Lily Tomlin television specials, winning Emmys for writing in 1974 and 1976, the same year he took home statues for writing and producing season 1 of *Saturday Night Live*.

In his interview with the AAT, Ebersol recalled how he and Michaels spent February through mid-March of 1975 developing *SNL* while living at the Chateau Marmont, the same Los Angeles hotel where John Belushi would die of a drug overdose seven years later. When it was time to pitch their idea to the NBC brass, they wouldn't allow Michaels in the boardroom because he was a producer for hire and not an NBC employee. So Ebersol gave them a rundown of the show and explained there would be a repertory company of players with a new guest host each week (he dropped the names of some of the people they had in mind—George Carlin, Richard Pryor, and Lily Tomlin). Two names had also been added as regular contributors to the show: comedian Albert Brooks, who was signed to make a short film each week, and puppeteer Jim Henson, who would be introducing a new breed of Muppet characters. Incidentally (and certainly not coincidentally), Henson and Michaels had the same manager, Bernie Brillstein, who, over the years, handled the careers of many *SNL* cast members, including Dan Aykroyd, John Belushi, Gilda Radner, Martin Short, Dana Carvey, Adam Sandler, and David Spade.

As Ebersol recalled, his pitch to the executives played to "total silence." When Herb Schlosser asked if anyone had anything to say, there was no response. Schlosser then turned to the head of research and asked for his opinion. He said the show would never work because its target audience would never come home by 11:30 p.m. on a Saturday night. Fortunately, he was wrong.

When it was time to hire talent for both behind and in front of the camera, Michaels assembled a group of performers, writers, and artisans who were relatively young by television standards. Most of them were under the age of thirty (the youngest cast members, Dan Aykroyd and Laraine Newman, were twenty-three when *SNL* debuted) and had an irreverent, subversive comedic style compared to the crop of family friendly prime-time variety shows like *Cher* (1975–1976), *Tony Orlando and Dawn* (1974–1976), and the long-running *The Carol Burnett Show* (1967–1978). Their comedic roots were in sketch and improvisational theater, and in the pages of *National Lampoon* magazine. Michaels appointed former *Lampoon* editor Michael O'Donoghue, better known to early *SNL* fans as "Mr. Mike," as the show's first head writer. Anne Beatts, the *Lampoon*'s first female editor, was one of three women hired as staff writers.

Many of the writers and cast members had worked together on *National Lampoon*–related projects. O'Donoghue was also the creator of *The National Lampoon Radio Hour*, a half-hour, syndicated weekly sketch comedy radio show that ran from November 1973 through December 1974 and featured Chevy Chase, Gilda Radner, Bill Murray, and John Belushi, who succeeded O'Donoghue as the show's creative director. *SNL* cast members also appeared off Broadway in two *Lampoon* stage shows in the early 1970s: *National Lampoon's Lemmings* (1973) with Chase and Belushi, and *The National Lampoon Show* (1975) with Radner, Belushi, Murray, and his older brother, Brian Doyle-Murray, who joined the *SNL* family in 1979 as a featured player.

While *Lampoon*'s subversive sense of humor certainly influenced *SNL*'s comedic style, Michaels admitted he was not much of a *Lampoon* fan. In a 1979 *Rolling Stone* interview with Timothy White, Michaels stated, "there was a kind of male-ego sweat socks attitude" in *Lampoon*'s humor that "[I] never have really been a part of." In the same interview, Michaels explained that Second City, the sketch comedy and improvisation theater troupe founded in 1959 in Chicago's Old Town neighborhood, had a more profound influence on *SNL*'s brand of humor. Most of the cast members had training in stage sketch comedy and improvisation: Dan Aykroyd and Radner were graduates of Second City in Toronto; Belushi and Murray hailed from Second City in Chicago; Jane Curtin was a member of the Boston improv group the Proposition; and Laraine Newman was one of the founding members of the Los Angeles–based improv group the Groundlings, whose alums boast a long list of *SNL* cast members, including Will Ferrell, Will Forte, Ana Gasteyer, Phil Hartman, Chris Kattan, Taran Killam, Jon Lovitz, Cheri Oteri, Chris Parnell, Maya Rudolph, Julia Sweeney, and Kristen Wiig.

## The Creative Team

- **Anne Beatts** (1947–2021) (writer) was the first female editor of *National Lampoon* and editor of two women's comedy anthologies, *Titters* (1976) and *Titters 101* (1984). She, along with Rosie Shuster, created characters like "the nerds," Todd and Lisa (Bill Murray and Gilda Radner), perverted babysitter Uncle Roy (Buck Henry), and the sleazy entrepreneur Irwin Mainway (Dan Aykroyd). After her five years on *SNL*, for which she won an Emmy and a Writers Guild Award, Beatts created the CBS situation comedy *Square Pegs* (1982–1983), starring an unknown Sarah Jessica Parker, and was responsible for revamping *The Cosby Show* (1984–1992) spin-off *A Different World* (1987–1993). Beatts continued to work in television and taught writing at the University of Southern California and Chapman University.
- **Al Franken** and **Tom Davis** (1952–2012) (writers) began their twenty-year-plus comedy partnership when they met in prep school in Minneapolis, where after college they joined Dudley Riggs's Brave New Workshop. They performed comedy in Los Angeles and Reno before being hired as writing apprentices by Lorne Michaels, splitting a single salary of $350 a week. They also appeared semiregularly on *SNL* under the title *The Franken and Davis Show*. They departed the show after season 5, only to return together and separately several times beginning in the mid-1980s through the 2002–2003 season. They both received multiple Emmys for their work on the show and an Emmy for writing *The Paul Simon Special* (1977). Franken wrote and starred in *Stuart Saves His Family* (1995), a film vehicle for his popular recurring *SNL* character Stuart Smalley (see chapter 26) and created and starred in the NBC sitcom *Lateline* (1998–1999). He is also the author of several books, including *Rush Limbaugh Is a Big Fat Idiot and Other Observations*. Franken was elected to the U.S. Senate from his home state of Minnesota in 2008 and 2014. He resigned on January 2, 2018, due to allegations of sexual misconduct. In 2019, Franken launched *The Al Franken Show* on SiriusXM. Davis, who cocreated the Coneheads with Dan Aykroyd, collaborated on

the screenplay for the 1993 film. He later hosted *Trailer Park* (1995–2000) on the Sci-Fi Channel and in 2009 published his memoir, *Thirty-Nine Years of Short-Term Memory Loss: The Early Days of* SNL *from Someone Who Was There.* Davis died of cancer on July 19, 2012.

- **Eugene Lee** (1939–2023) and **Franne Lee** (1941–2023) (production and costume designers) are a former husband-and-wife design team best known for their work on Broadway. They both won a pair of Tony Awards for scenic and costume design for the 1974 revival of *Candide.* Eugene Lee was the scenic designer for over twenty Broadway productions, winning Tony Awards for *Sweeney Todd* (1979) and *Wicked* (2003). He was the production designer on over six hundred episodes of *SNL* (seasons 1–5, 11–47). Franne Lee, who also won a Tony for her costumes for *Sweeney Todd*, left *SNL* after five seasons and continued to work in the theater.

- **Marilyn Suzanne Miller** (writer) had no professional writing credits when the recent college grad made a cold call to writer/producer James L. Brooks (she doesn't know why he took the call) and pitched her idea for an episode of *The Mary Tyler Moore Show* (1970–1977), which led to a job as a junior writer on *The Odd Couple* (1970–1975). In addition to her five years on *SNL*, she wrote episodes of *The Mary Tyler Moore Show, Rhoda* (1974–1978), *Maude* (1972–1978), and *Welcome Back, Kotter* (1975–1979). Her post-*SNL* credits include *Cybill* (1995–1998), *Murphy Brown* (1988–1998), and *The Tracey Ullman Show* (1987–1990), for which she won her third Emmy. Miller's profile for the Paley Center for Media describes her work on *SNL* as "Marilyn pieces"—sketches that focused on character, rather than jokes, and infused "humor with poignancy." Some of her most memorable sketches include "Slumber Party," in which Gilda, Jane, Laraine, and host Madeline Kahn are young girls having a late-night talk about where babies come from (1.19); a sketch from an Emmy-winning episode in which host Sissy Spacek plays a newlywed whose husband (John Belushi) can't perform in the bedroom (2.15); and "The Judy Miller Show," in which Radner plays a hyperactive tween alone in her room who entertains herself. Miller returned to *SNL* as a writer for seasons 18–20.

- **Michael O'Donoghue** (1940–1994) (head writer), a.k.a. "Mr. Mike," began his writing career as the author of dark, absurdist plays and illustrated books, including *The Adventures of Phoebe Zeit-Geist* (1968). He was one of the founding writers and later the editor of *National Lampoon* magazine. Lorne Michaels hired him as the show's head writer, earning him two Emmy Awards for writing. O'Donoghue stayed with *SNL* for three years, but returned in 1981 when he was hired by the show's new executive producer, Dick Ebersol, to save *SNL* after its disastrous sixth season. He only lasted eight shows. According to his biographer, Dennis Perrin, author of *Mr. Mike: The Life and Work of Michael O'Donoghue*, he was fired over creative differences, though he was rehired for the 1985–1986 season when Lorne Michaels returned to the show. As Mr. Mike he told "Least-Loved Bedtime Tales" like "The Enchanted Thermos" (2.6), "The Blind Chicken" (2.7), and, to fourteen-year-old guest host Jodie Foster, "The Little Train That Died" (2.9). During his tenure at NBC, O'Donoghue wrote, directed, and starred in a special for NBC, *Mr. Mike's Mondo Video* (1979). Although it was slated to air in *SNL*'s time slot, the network demanded too many cuts, so it was released (and bombed) in theaters. His other acting credits include featured roles in *Manhattan* (1979), *Head Office* (1985), *Wall Street* (1987), and *Scrooged* (1988), which he cowrote with Mitch Glazer. O'Donoghue died in 1984 from a cerebral hemorrhage at the age of fifty-four.

- **Don Pardo** (1918–2014) (announcer) has been one of the voices of NBC since 1944. Prior to *SNL* he was best known as the announcer on several game shows, including the original *Jeopardy!* (1964–1975). Pardo has served as *SNL*'s announcer for all but one season (season 7, when he was replaced by Mel Brandt with Bill Hanrahan sitting in for Brandt for two episodes [7.7, 7.8]), and while viewers are more familiar with his voice than his face, Pardo did occasionally appear on camera. He participated in NBC's "Save the Network" telethon (6.8) and came out from his announcer's booth in 2008 to blow out his candles on his ninetieth birthday cake (33.5). In what is certainly an unusual collaboration, Pardo lent his voice to three Frank Zappa recordings, including "I'm the Slime," which was performed on *SNL* (2.10). At the age of ninety-two, he was inducted in the Academy of Television Arts & Sciences' Hall of Fame. Pardo appeared onstage when *SNL* celebrated his ninetieth birthday on February 23, 2008 (33.5). He died on August 18, 2014, at the age of ninety-six. Pardo was memorialized in the season 40 opener (9/27/14) with a photo that appeared on-screen after *Weekend Update*.
- **Herb Sargent** (1923–2005) (writer) was a veteran television writer whose credits dated back to the mid-1950s when he wrote for Steve Allen (*The Steve Allen Plymouth Show* [1956–1960], *The New Steve Allen Show* [1961]) and *The Tonight Show Starring Johnny Carson* (1962–1992) early in its run. He was also a staff writer on the American version of one of *SNL*'s predecessors, *That Was the Week That Was* (1964–1965) (see chapter 5) as well as other comedy-variety shows and specials. Sargent also wrote numerous network specials, winning two of his six Primetime Emmys for writing and producing Lily Tomlin's 1973 special, *Lily*. Sargent was on the writing staff of *SNL* as a writer and "script consultant" for a total of seventeen seasons (1975–1980, 1983–1995). In his interview with the Archive of American Television, Dick Ebersol described Sargent as one of the few "adults" involved in the show in its early years (director Dave Wilson and associate producer Audrey Peart Dickman were the two others). Sargent is credited as the one responsible for developing the *Weekend Update* segment with its first anchor Chevy Chase. At the time of his death from a heart attack in 2005, Sargent was president of the Writers Guild of America, East. Since then, an award bearing his name, the Herb Sargent Award for Comedy Excellence, has been given to James L. Brooks (2006), Lorne Michaels (2007), Judd Apatow (2012), Steve O'Donnell (2017), *30*

*Rock* creators Tina Fey and Robert Carlock (2018), *SNL* writer Paula Pell (2020), Paul Simms (2023), and Wanda Sykes (2024).

- **Tom Schiller** (writer) is the son of veteran television comedy writer Bob Schiller (*I Love Lucy* [1951–1957], *The Carol Burnett Show*, *Maude*, and *All in the Family*). Before *SNL*, he wrote and directed a short documentary about the writer Henry Miller, *Henry Miller Asleep & Awake* (1975). During *SNL*'s first five seasons, he was a staff writer and contributed a series of memorable short films to *SNL*, including *Don't Look Back in Anger* (3.13), *La Dolce Gilda* (3.17), and *Java Junkie* (5.8). His association with *SNL* as a writer and filmmaker continued through the 1980s into the early 1990s, winning him three Emmys. Schiller also wrote and directed the 1984 feature *Nothing Lasts Forever*, featuring Bill Murray, Dan Aykroyd, and Zach Galligan.
- **Howard Shore** (musical director) first collaborated with Lorne Michaels when they were campers and later counselors at Camp Timberlane in Ontario. Shore was the musical director of *The Hart & Lorne Terrific Hour* and for the first five seasons of *SNL*, returning in season 11 as the show's music producer. He composed the score for over fifty films, frequently collaborating with directors David Cronenberg, Martin Scorsese, and Peter Jackson. He is the recipient of three Academy Awards for *The Lord of the Rings: The Fellowship of the Ring* (2001) (Original Score), and *The Lord of the Rings: The Return of the King* (2003) (Original Score and Original Song, cowritten with Fran Walsh and Annie Lennox).
- **Rosie Shuster** (writer) is a Toronto native and a second-generation comedy writer. The daughter of Frank Shuster, of the legendary Canadian comedy duo Wayne and Shuster, she was on the writing staff of *The Hart & Lorne Terrific Hour*. In 1971, she married one of its stars (and longtime friend) Lorne Michaels. They next worked together on several Lily Tomlin specials and then on *Saturday Night Live*, where she was a staff writer for the first seven seasons and again in 1986–1988. Her other television writing credits include episodes of *Square Pegs*, *The Larry Sanders Show* (1992–1998), and the animated series *Bob and Margaret* (1998–2001).
- **Dave Wilson**'s (1933–2002) (director) affiliation with NBC dates back to the 1960s when he worked on variety shows like *The Bell Telephone Hour* (1959–1968) and *The Kraft Music Hall* (1967–1971). Over the course of seventeen seasons (1–11, 15–20), he directed over three hundred episodes of *SNL*, winning an Emmy for directing the second episode (1.2), hosted by Paul Simon. Wilson (affectionately known as "Davey") was sometimes featured in cold openings and monologues that spilled over into the control room, where we saw him dressed as a bee (2.9), drunk with his crew on St. Patrick's Day (4.15), and dead, only to miraculously wake in time to signal the engineer to roll the opening credits (2.15).
- **Alan Zweibel** (writer) was a joke writer for stand-up comedians when he was hired by Lorne Michaels to write for *SNL*. He is best known for writing the samurai sketches and for Gilda Radner's alter egos Roseanne Roseannadanna

and Emily Litella. His friendship with Radner was the subject of his best-selling book *Bunny Bunny: Gilda Radner—A Sort of Love Story*. He was also executive producer on the 2018 documentary *Love, Gilda*. Zweibel was the cocreator and producer of *It's Garry Shandling's Show* (1986–1990) and cowrote the screenplays for *Dragnet* (1987), *North* (1994) (based on his novel), and *The Story of Us* (1999). He also collaborated with former *SNL* cast members Billy Crystal on his one-man Tony Award–winning show *700 Sundays* (2004), and Martin Short on his autobiographical musical revue *Martin Short: Fame Becomes Me* (2006).

# 3

# "No Television Experience Required"

## The Not Ready for Prime Time Players

Most of the original creative team of *SNL* had one thing in common: relatively little, if any, experience working on a weekly television show (let alone a *live* weekly television show). But it was their lack of experience, particularly of the cast, that fueled the raw creative energy that gave *Saturday Night Live* its edge in the early days.

Two weeks before the show's debut, Lorne Michaels and the seven original cast members appeared on NBC's late-night talk show *Tomorrow*, hosted by Tom Snyder (the interview is included as an extra on the season 1 DVD set). During the five-minute segment, Michaels introduces the cast one by one. "We're hoping for two [cast members] to really work," he drily explains. "Not all of these people will become stars." Chevy Chase jokingly adds that he will be one of the two. He was right—he did become a major star—but not at the exclusion of his castmates, who, in time, would become household names and after *SNL* would continue to work in television and films.

### Dan Aykroyd (Seasons 1–4)

The youngest member of the Not Ready for Prime Time Players, twenty-three-year-old Ottawa-born Dan Aykroyd performed in comedy clubs and was a member of the Toronto's first Second City cast, which also included Gilda Radner, Brian Doyle-Murray, Joe Flaherty, and Valri Bromfield, who performed on the premiere of *SNL*. At the time he was invited to audition for *SNL*, Aykroyd was playing a building superintendent on a Canadian sitcom, *Coming Up Rosie* (1975–1977).

While most of the first *SNL* cast members played characters that are variations of their own personas (bad boy John Belushi, smart and snide Jane Curtin, smarmy Bill Murray, etc.), Aykroyd is a human chameleon. You never have a handle on who the real Dan Aykroyd is, which allows him to simply disappear into his characters. In Timothy White's 1979 *Rolling Stone* profile of Aykroyd,

Michael O'Donoghue described how Aykroyd's characters "seem to leap out of nowhere. It's utterly startling because you think he can do anything; he can just make it up, fully realized, on the spot." Aykroyd was also *SNL*'s resident impressionist, portraying presidents (Richard Nixon, Jimmy Carter) along with movie stars and television personalities (Clark Gable, Orson Welles, Rod Serling, and *Tomorrow* talk show host Tom Snyder).

Over the four seasons in which he appeared as a regular, Aykroyd was the body and voice behind some of *SNL*'s most iconic original characters: family patriarch (and driving school instructor) Beldar Conehead; sleazy talk show host E. Buzz Miller; the equally sleazy entrepreneur Irwin Mainway; pretentious public television host Leonard Pinth-Garnell; and one-half of the "wild and crazy" Festrunk brothers and the Blues Brothers.

A former member of Second City in Toronto and Chicago, Dan Aykroyd played a wide range of recurring characters, including sleazy toy manufacturer Irwin Mainway, who sold dangerous toys for kids.

Aykroyd left *SNL* at the end of season 4 and enjoyed a successful film career as an actor and cowriter of such films as *The Blues Brothers* (1980), *Ghostbusters* (1984), *Spies Like Us* (1985), and *Ghostbusters II* (1989). He received an Academy Award nomination for Best Supporting Actor for his portrayal of Boolie Werthan in *Driving Miss Daisy* (1989). He continued working in films and on television and has remained loyal to *SNL*, hosting the show in 2003 (28.20) and making numerous guest appearances in the late 1990s impersonating presidential candidate Bob Dole. More recently, Aykroyd was an executive producer on the female reboot of *Ghostbusters* (2016) and on *Ghostbusters: Afterlife* (2021) and *Ghostbusters: Frozen Empire* (2024), sequels to *Ghostbusters 1* and *Ghostbusters 2* in which he costarred with many of the original cast members.

## John Belushi (Seasons 1–4)

John Belushi was the last cast member to be hired—and it almost didn't happen. In Judith Belushi Pisano and Tanner Colby's *Belushi: A Biography*, Lorne Michaels admits he wasn't "knocked out" by John's performance in *The National Lampoon Show*, but Chevy Chase and Michael O'Donoghue were pressuring him. "At our first meeting," Michaels recalled, "he said he didn't do television. It was all terrible and so forth. And I couldn't afford that kind of attitude. . . . I think, looking back, what he meant to say was that he didn't do television, but he'd heard that I was different." After seeing his screen test, Michaels, at the urging of everyone in the cast who knew and worked with him, hired Belushi.

Belushi joined Second City in his native Chicago in 1971 at the age of twenty-one. Two years later, he was cast in *National Lampoon's Lemmings*, where he perfected his Joe Cocker imitation, which he performed several times on season 1 of *SNL* (1.3, 1.18, 1.20) and once again on season 2 (2.3). Belushi took over as creative director of *The National Lampoon Radio Hour* after Michael O'Donoghue quit, and he appeared onstage in *The National Lampoon Show* alongside Bill Murray, Brian Doyle-Murray, Gilda Radner, and Harold Ramis. Although *New York Times* critic Mel Gussow found much of the show's satirical take on New York City, President Gerald Ford, and Patty Hearst weak, he singled out Belushi with his "bearlike presence and his malleable voice" to be the "funniest actor" in the show.

Another Second City alum, John Belushi was *SNL*'s "class clown" who put his comedic spin on historical figures like Napoleon, Franklin D. Roosevelt, Nehru, and Ludwig van Beethoven (pictured).

Belushi could make us laugh by simply raising his bushy, black eyebrows (he performs "eyebrow calisthenics" on his audition tape). As an impressionist he was not in the same league as Aykroyd, but he did have a talent for mimicking famous people with a distinctive voice (Truman Capote, Humphrey Bogart, Marlon Brando), speech pattern (William Shatner), or accent (Henry Kissinger). He was also a physical comedian who showed no restraint when swinging a sword as Samurai Futaba, turning cartwheels as Jake Blues, or delivering a rant on *Weekend Update* about the "luck of the Irish" (2.16), the weather (2.19), and the Muhammad Ali–Leon Spinks fight (3.11)—all of which were punctuated by his signature "But noooooooooo."

His rants were an extension of his off-screen persona as a rebellious and at times difficult cast member. In the third episode (1.3), Belushi and the cast, dressed as the Bees, interrupt a sketch with host Rob Reiner and his then wife Penny Marshall. Reiner stops the sketch and insists that he made it clear he didn't want to work with the Bees, which sets off Belushi. "Do you think we like this?" Belushi asks, "No, no, Mr. Reiner. But we don't have a choice." After the departure of Chevy Chase, who was clearly the first breakout star of *SNL*, Belushi was finally given the first opportunity to open the show (2.17), but instead of saying, "Live from New York," he decides to take advantage of the situation. Knowing they can't start the show until he says the words, he delays the opening and reads his list of demands to NBC (showers for the male and female cast members, beer for the crew, etc.).

After the success of *Animal House* (1978), Belushi pursued a film career full-time, leaving *SNL* at the end of season 4. He had a supporting role in director Steven Spielberg's *1941* (1979) and starring roles in *The Blues Brothers* (1980), *Neighbors* (1981), and a romantic comedy, *Continental Divide* (1981). His last appearance on the stages of Studio 8H was a cameo on *SNL*'s 1981 Halloween show (7.4) in which he inexplicably emerges during the cold open from a bathroom stall while the show's nervous host, Donald Pleasence, is "vomiting for luck" in another stall. He looks into the camera but doesn't speak, and then walks off. Less than four months later, Belushi died of a drug overdose in the Chateau Marmont hotel in West Hollywood at the age of thirty-three.

## Chevy Chase (Seasons 1–2 [10/30/76])

During his relatively short stint as an *SNL* cast member, Chevy Chase was often photographed in a shirt that read: "Yes, it's my real name."

Born Cornelius Crane Chase, he was nicknamed "Chevy" by his paternal grandmother, though according to his authorized biography, the aptly titled *I'm Chevy Chase . . . and You're Not*, he is unsure about the source of his nickname. Chase's association with *SNL* began on a movie line for a midnight screening of *Monty Python and the Holy Grail* (1975) in Hollywood, where he was introduced to Lorne Michaels by their mutual friend Rob Reiner. Chase and Michaels then had what's known in Hollywood as a "meeting," which resulted in an offer for Chase to be a staff writer on *SNL*.

Chase's credits were a perfect match for the kind of show Michaels and Dick Ebersol were developing. His pre-*SNL* writing credits included *The Smothers Brothers Show* (1975) and the 1974 satirical television special *Alan King's Energy Crisis: Rising Prices and Assorted Vices* (1974). He appeared in *National Lampoon*'s *Lemmings* and *Radio Hour*, and was a writer/performer on Channel One Underground Television (1967–1972), a stage show that satirized television and was the basis for the 1974 comedy film *The Groove Tube*, in which Chase also appeared. Chase also performed in one of *SNL*'s predecessors, the acclaimed PBS series *The Great American Dream Machine* (1971–1972) (see chapter 5).

Although he appeared in front of the camera, Chase was initially hired as a writer only. He wanted to be in the cast, and, according to Dick Ebersol, he made that clear late one night when Ebersol, Chase, and Michaels were coming out of a downtown club in the middle of a rainstorm with no umbrellas and raincoats. In his interview for the AAT, Ebersol described how Chase volunteered to get a cab and ran down the block. "He's running down the street and he gets about two-thirds of a block away from us. . . . And he begins this whole fall, as the cab is coming up the street. . . . And he made this unbelievable sort of slip and slide and tumble and all that and he actually ended up partially submerged in a rather large puddle. And I turned to Lorne, I said, 'I give up. If he's going to go to these lengths, I ought to at least let him have a shot.' And that led to the first time he fell down."

Chevy's signature fall, combined with his movie-star good looks, made him an instant fan favorite. Frucht points out that, as the first anchor of *Weekend Update*, Chase was also the only cast member to say his name every week as part of his famous introductory catchphrase, "I'm Chevy Chase, and you're not." The

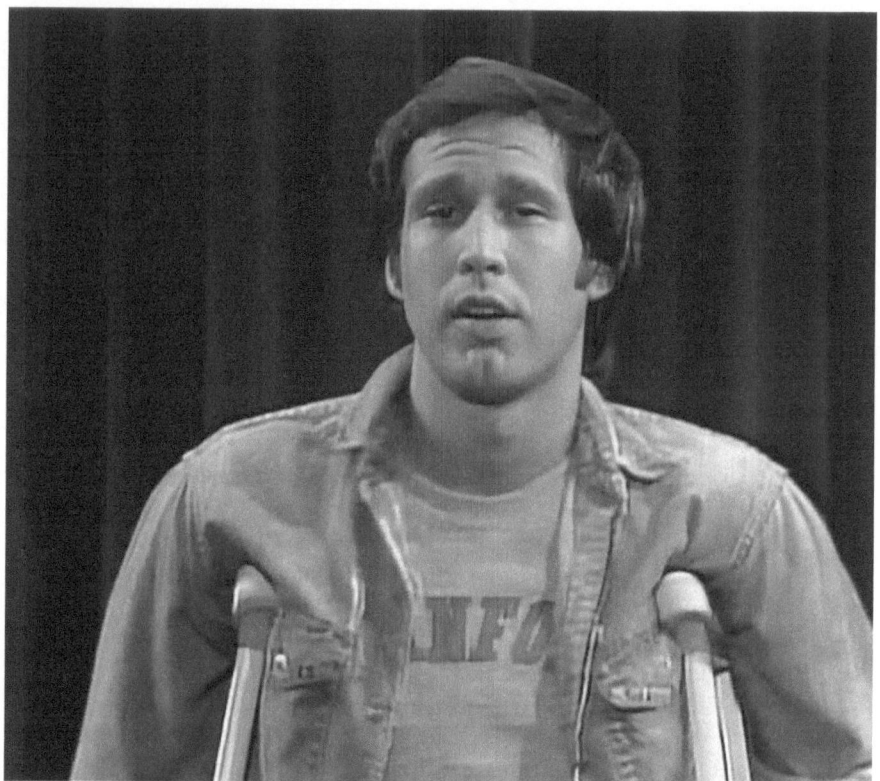

During his short tenure on *SNL*, Emmy-winner Chevy Chase opened each episode with a pratfall. After taking a tumble while accepting his Emmy for Best Supporting Actor in Variety or Music, Chase, pretending he was injured, appeared on crutches in the opening of the next episode (1.21).

fact that his name is so unusual certainly helped. In the short time he was on the series (a total of thirty episodes), Chase never created recurring characters like Aykroyd, Belushi, and his replacement, Bill Murray. The closest he came was a "land shark" who tricked his female victims into opening their apartment doors and his "impersonation" of President Gerald Ford. While all of the presidents that followed Ford, from Carter to Obama, would be imitated in terms of their appearance, manner, and speech, Chase made no attempt to look and sound like President Ford.

Chase's rise to stardom was meteoric. He quickly became the face of *SNL*. A little over two months after the show's debut, he graced the cover of *New York* magazine. The accompanying profile by Jeff Greenfield deemed him a "hot property" and the guy network executives were looking to as "the first real potential successor to Johnny Carson when he gives up *The Tonight Show*." But Chase only had a one-year contract, and much to everyone's surprise, he decided to walk away from the show, taking with him two Emmys—for "Outstanding Writing in a Comedy-Variety Music Series" and "Outstanding Continuing or

"No Television Experience Required"

Single Performance by a Supporting Actor in Variety or Music"—and a deal to headline three prime-time comedy specials (two of which were made, in 1977 and 1979). Years later, in an interview with Larry King, Chase explained why he left six episodes into season 2 (2.6): "I never really wanted to do any show for more than year. I felt we had done what I wanted to do, which was basically subvert television and parody it and lampoon it, and that was one reason." The second reason was more personal—he was in love with a woman who lived in Los Angeles who would soon become his second wife. His subsequent career was a mixture of hits (*Foul Play* [1978], *Caddyshack* [1980], *National Lampoon's Summer Vacation* [1983]) and misses (*Oh! Heavenly Dog* [1980], *Under the Rainbow* [1981], *Caddyshack II* [1988]), and a short-lived talk show. In 2009, he returned to television as a member of the ensemble cast for the first four seasons of the NBC sitcom *Community* (2009–2015).

Chase always remained loyal to his *SNL* roots. He's a member of the Five-Timers Club (see chapter 18) and has made numerous cameo appearances, the last in 2007 (33.2), when he once again sat behind the *Weekend Update* desk as a senior political correspondent and delivered an editorial on the current Democratic and Republic presidential candidates.

## Jane Curtin (Seasons 1–5)

In a short 1976 interview aptly entitled "Curtin Finds New Horizon," Jane Curtin observed how "people don't believe that if you look like Middle America you can do comedy. Unless you're kind of kooky-looking they don't hire you."

Curtin's long career in television, beginning with her five-year stint on *SNL*, and continuing with two long-running sitcoms, *Kate & Allie* (1984–1989) (for which she received two Emmys) and *3rd Rock from the Sun* (1996–2001), proved otherwise. Dick Ebersol admitted in his 2009 AAT interview that Curtin was "the easiest hire because we clearly had a cast of people who by 1975 standards were going to be quite different from the way anything looked on American television up to that point. And here was this woman who was so remarkably funny. And certainly more sophisticated not only than the cast, but also almost of all of us. And very serious about life. . . . But she had a biting wit that could be as hip and as wry as anybody in the world."

As anchor of *Weekend Update* for seasons 2–5, Jane Curtin's comic persona combined an icy demeanor with a snide attitude.

Prior to making her television debut on *SNL*, Curtin was a member of the Boston improvisation group the Proposition, which took their show to New York in the early 1970s. Curtin next coauthored the book and appeared in an off-Broadway musical revue *Pretzels*. *New York Times* critic Clive Barnes praised the "blonde Miss Curtin" for showing "just the kind of range one hopes for in a revue performer, moving easily from a snob cosmetics lady to a Ninth Avenue harridan."

Over the course of five seasons, Curtin did impressions of celebrities and stars (Anita Bryant, Dolly Parton, Joan Crawford, Rose Marie) and former, current, and future First Ladies (Eleanor Roosevelt, Pat Nixon, Betty Ford, Nancy Reagan), along with a handful of recurring characters like Prymaat Conehead and Enid Loopner. Curtin is best remembered for her portrayal of hard-edged, often sarcastic women, like talk show host Joan Face and the impatient anchorwoman at *Weekend Update*. When she was on *SNL*, Curtin was relatively guarded about her private life (she was also the only cast member who was married when the show debuted). When *Rolling Stone* magazine published a collection of interviews with the cast in book form, Curtin's profile consists of some photos, vital statistics, and the headline: "Jane Curtin does not give interviews."

Curtin continues to work in films, including roles in *Godmothered* (2020), *Queen Bees* (2021), and *Jules* (2023), and on television, most recently on the short-lived sitcom *United We Fall* (2020) and in episodes of *The Librarians* (2014–2018), *The Good Fight* (2017–2022), *The Conners* (2018–present), and *Bupkis* (2023–present).

## Garrett Morris (Seasons 1–5)

The oldest and most experienced performer in the original cast, Garrett Morris's list of credits prior to joining the cast of *SNL* included Broadway (*Hallelujah, Baby* [1967] and *Ain't Supposed to Die a Natural Death* [1971]), television (*Roll-Out*, a short-lived 1973 World War II sitcom from the creators of *M*A*S*H*), and feature films (*The Anderson Tapes* [1971], *Cooley High* [1975]).

Morris was also a playwright who was initially hired by Lorne Michaels as a writer. As Morris recalled in his interview for the Archive of American Television, Michaels screened *Cooley High* and told Morris he should audition to be a performer on the show. His audition was an improvised scene with Gilda Radner in which he played a cab driver and Radner his passenger, whom he cheats out of her cab fare by taking the long route from the JFK Airport to Manhattan. Compared to the other cast members, Morris received less airtime

Garrett Morris was most underutilized original cast member. His résumé included film, television, and five Broadway shows. He occasionally had a chance to showcase his singing talent, as in this classic sketch playing an inmate on death row auditioning for the prison follies.

and as the only African American, he was often cast in stereotypical roles and played fewer recurring characters.

When he was given the opportunity to sing, *SNL* audiences were always blown away by his beautiful tenor voice. In his interview with the AAT, he revealed that when opera lover Walter Matthau guest hosted the show, he had it put in his contract that there would be no musical guest and Morris would sing "Dalla sua pace" from Mozart's *Don Giovanni* (without the usual comic crawl over the screen!).

Since leaving *SNL* in 1980, Morris has remained active in television on situation comedies with roles on *Martin* (1992–1995), *Cleghorne!* (1995–1996), *The Jamie Foxx Show* (1996–2001), and, most recently, *2 Broke Girls* (2011–2017). He had a recurring role in season 2 of *This Is Us* (2016–2022) and has appeared in episodes of *A Black Lady Sketch Show* (2019–2023), *Station 19* (2018–present), and *How I Met Your Father* (2022–2023).

## Bill Murray (Seasons 2–5)

After replacing the departing Chevy Chase in the middle of season 2, "new guy" Bill Murray offered a tongue-in-cheek on-camera apology for not being funny enough. "I'm a funny guy," Murray admitted, "but I haven't been so funny on the show."

Toward the end of season 2 (2.16), Bill Murray delivered a monologue in which he shares his concern that as the "new guy" he's not making it on the show: "I'm a funny guy, but I haven't been so funny on the show. . . . It's not that I'm not funny, it's that I'm not being funny at the right time. Honest." He then asks the viewers at home for their support: "If you could see it in your heart to laugh whenever I say something. I don't care what it is . . . I just want to make it as a Not Ready for Prime Time Player."

It's always hard to know when Murray is joking and when he's being sincere. He auditioned for *SNL* along with the other Not Ready for Prime Time Players, but he didn't make the cut (he appeared instead on Howard Cosell's short-lived *Saturday Night Live*). But the decision to add him to the cast gave the show a shot in the arm during season 2 and kept it going despite the absence of Chevy Chase. Murray is a live wire whose style of comedy is cheeky and impromptu. Whether he is giving noogies to Lisa Loopner or singing in the shower with a soap-on-a-rope microphone or in a ski lodge lounge, Murray always give the impression that he is making it all up as he is going along. It was also hard to take anything he said seriously.

Murray was able to make the transition to the big screen, appearing in a string of hit comedies, including *Caddyshack* (1980), *Ghostbusters* (1984), *Ghostbusters II* (1989), and *Groundhog Day* (1993). He also appeared in indie films directed by Sofia Coppola (*Lost in Translation* [2003], for which he received an Academy Award nomination, and *On the Rocks* [2020]), and Wes Anderson (*Rushmore* [1998], *The Royal Tenenbaums* [2001], *The Life Aquatic with Steve Zissou* [2004], *Darjeeling Limited* [2007], *Moonrise Kingdom* [2012], and *The French Dispatch* [2021]. In 2016, he received the Mark Twain Prize for American Humor.

As a member of the Five-Timers Club (see chapter 18), Murray has remained loyal to *SNL*. In 1995 he paid tribute to *SNL*'s first head writer, Michael O'Donoghue (20.5), and, more recently, did a cameo as Trump political strategist Steve Bannon (43.10).

Like Chevy Chase, Murray has remained loyal to *SNL*. He's a member of the Five-Timers Club (see chapter 18) and, in 1994, he made a special appearance to pay tribute to his friend and *SNL*'s first head writer Michael O'Donoghue (20.5).

## Laraine Newman (Seasons 1–5)

Laraine Newman, who was discovered performing at the Groundlings in Los Angeles, falls victim to the land shark at her front door.

Laraine Newman is a Los Angeles native whose performing career began as a student at Beverly Hills High School, where she directed and appeared in the school's first improv show ("It was probably the first time 'shit' was said on that stage," she told *Rolling Stone* reporter Maryanne Vollers). After studying mime in Paris with Marcel Marceau, she returned to Los Angeles to study acting and improv at the Gary Austin Workshop, which evolved into the Groundlings, where she was seen by Lorne Michaels and Lily Tomlin, who cast her in Tomlin's 1975 television special.

Newman was not only one of the youngest cast members, she was the hippest in terms of her appearance and attitude. She did offbeat impressions and had her own repertoire of recurring characters: Christy Christina, girlfriend of sleazoid E. Buzz Miller (Dan Aykroyd); Connie Conehead, daughter of Beldar and Prymaat; Sherry, the stewardess from the San Fernando Valley; and the droll *Weekend Update* correspondent. Her "little girl" characters—Shirley Temple (1.22); Dr. Schiffman (4.13), the child psychiatrist who is a child; and Penny (3.15), who has a late-night chat with Mr. Death (guest host Christopher Lee)—were some of her best work. In a 1989 *People* magazine article commemorating the show's fifteenth anniversary, Newman candidly admitted that she was "terribly jealous of Gilda. Terribly. I knew she'd earned it. The audience loved her. But it hurt so much." While Radner did emerge as the show's female star, the contribution the talented Newman made to the show as a comedian and an actress was significant and has been unfortunately overlooked and undervalued by critics.

Newman's post-*SNL* work includes dramatic and comedic roles on television (*St. Elsewhere* [1982–1988], *Ellen* [1994–1998], *Curb Your Enthusiasm* [2000–2024], and *Brothers & Sisters* [2006–2001]) and in feature films (*Perfect* [1985], *Invaders from Mars* [1986], *Problem Child 2* [1991], and *The Flintstones* [1994]). She has also lent her voice to animated TV series (*Metalocalypse* [2006–2013]) and features (*The Lorax* [2012], *Toy Story 3* [2010], *WALL-E* [2008], and *Wreck-It Ralph* [2012]).

## Gilda Radner (Seasons 1–5)

Gilda Radner was the first cast member to be hired by Lorne Michaels, who knew her in Toronto. During her five seasons on the show, she created some of *SNL*'s most memorable characters: Roseanne Roseannadanna, Emily Litella, Lisa Loopner, Judy Miller, Rhonda Weiss, Candy Slice, and Baba Wawa. Her versatility made her a favorite of both the show's fans and *SNL*'s writing staff.

Her show business career began in Canada, where she appeared in a Toronto production of *Godspell* that also featured Eugene Levy, Andrea Martin, Martin

Gilda Radner's comedic repertoire consisted of off-the-wall characters, including the hyperactive Judy Miller, a little girl pretending to star in her own TV show.

Short, and Victor Garber. She was a member of the original Second City Toronto cast and appeared in *National Lampoon*'s radio and stage shows before *SNL*. Like Dan Aykroyd, the secret to her talent lies in her ability to lose herself in a character to the point that you forget that Emily Litella, Roseanne Roseannadanna, and Judy Miller are all the same person. As *Rolling Stone*'s Roy Blount Jr. observed, "Gilda's characters are people you enjoy knowing." Her characters were also women who were happy and unapologetic for being who they are, even though their behavior may be perceived as peculiar or inappropriate.

Gilda was one of the show's breakout stars early in the show's run. During *SNL*'s first season, she was one of the few Not Ready for Prime Time Players who appeared as herself on camera. In the segment "What Gilda Ate," the comedian tells the audience what she ate that day (1.3) and recalls how she overate last Christmas (1.8). (Gilda later went public about her struggle with bulimia.)

In the summer before her final season on *SNL*, Gilda took her menagerie of characters to the Broadway stage, appearing in *Gilda Radner Live* (see chapter 26). After *SNL*, she teamed with her future husband, actor/writer/director Gene Wilder, in three films: *Hanky Panky* (1982), *The Woman in Red* (1984), and *Haunted Honeymoon* (1986). Her career was cut short when she was diagnosed with ovarian cancer in 1986 and died three years later at the age of forty-two. Gilda's Club, a community organization for people living with cancer and their family and friends, was named in her memory.

In 2002, Radner's autobiography, *It's Always Something*, was adapted into a made-for-television movie starring Jami Gertz as Radner and Tom Rooney as Gene Wilder.

## Regular and Featured Players

Two names that appear on the bottom of the cast list in the opening credits of the first episode—Michael O'Donoghue and George Coe—would be gone by episode 1.2. Head writer O'Donoghue would continue to make appearances, most memorably in season 2 as his alter ego, the very twisted "Mr. Mike."

George Coe (1929–2015), a character actor with a long list of stage, television, and film credits to his name (he supplied the voice of Woodhouse the Butler on the animated series *Archer* [2009–2023]) appears in the premiere episode as the judge in the "Trial Sketch." Although he is no longer officially a Not for Ready Prime Time Player, he continued to make occasional appearances in prefilmed commercials (for "Golden Needles" [1.3], "Jamitol" [1.5]) and a few live sketches. His best moment is in the opening of episode 1.21 in which he plays a 30 Rock security guard who won't let Buck Henry upstairs to do his monologue ("The host of the show is a star, this man is not a star . . . have I ever heard of you?").

When John Belushi and Dan Aykroyd departed *SNL* at the end of season 4, there were only two male cast members remaining (Bill Murray and Garrett Morris). Consequently, over the course of season five, seven members of the

## "No Television Experience Required"

"The Not Ready for Prime Time Players": (clockwise from top right) Bill Murray, Laraine Newman, Garrett Morris, Jane Curtin, Gilda Radner, John Belushi, and Dan Aykroyd.

writing staff—Peter Aykroyd, Jim Downey, Brian Doyle-Murray, Don Novello, Tom Schiller, Harry Shearer, and Alan Zweibel—and Paul Shaffer, who contributed "special musical material," joined Al Franken and Tom Davis as featured players.

- **Peter Aykroyd** (1955–2021), the younger brother of Dan Aykroyd, was a member of Second City in Toronto who joined the show as a writer and featured player in season 5. He later cocreated the syndicated sci-fi Canadian series *PSI Factor: Chronicles of the Paranormal* (1996–2000) hosted by his brother Dan, with whom he cowrote the screenplay for *Nothing but Trouble* (1991). Aykroyd died at the age of 65 on November 6, 2021, in Spokane, Washington.

- **Jim Downey** (season 5), writer and actor, was a former president of *Harvard Lampoon* who wrote for *Saturday Night Live* for more than thirty seasons (1977–1980, 1984–1998, 2000–2013) and served as head writer of *Late Night with David Letterman* (1982–1984). In 1998, Downey was reportedly fired from *SNL*, along with *Weekend Update* anchor Norm Macdonald, over jokes about O. J. Simpson, who was a friend of NBC executive Don Ohlmeyer (see chapter 23). Downey is best remembered for coining the word *strategery*, which was introduced into the American lexicon by George W. Bush (Will Ferrell) in an *SNL* parody of the first Bush-Gore presidential debate (26.1; see chapter 15). In addition to commercial parodies on *SNL*, Downey appeared on the big screen as the principal/decathlon judge in Adam Sandler's *Billy Madison* (1995) and in a bit part in Paul Thomas Anderson's *There Will Be Blood* (2007).
- **Brian Doyle-Murray** (see chapter 17).
- **Don Novello** was best known to *SNL* fans as Father Guido Sarducci, a character he first introduced on *The Smothers Brothers Show* (1975). He was a featured player in season 5 (1979–1980) and again in season 11. In addition to being a staff writer on *SNL*, he was a writer/producer on *SCTV Network* (1981–1983). Novello's acting credits include supporting roles in *Tucker: The Man and His Dream* (1988) and *The Godfather Part III* (1990).
- **Paul Shaffer** began his affiliation with *SNL* as a member of the house band, though he also contributed special musical material and, as a featured player in season 5, appeared in sketches. He earned a place in *SNL* history when he dropped the first official f-bomb on the show (5.14) (see chapter 25). In addition to his two solo albums and collaborations with a long list of artists that reads like a who's who of the music business, Shaffer served as musical director for *Late Night with David Letterman* (1982–1993) on NBC and the *Late Show with David Letterman* (1993–2015) on CBS.
- **Harry Shearer** joined the cast of *SNL* as a regular player during season 5 and returned for three months at the start of season 10. Shearer was a cocreator of *Spinal Tap* (1984) and is a longtime cast member of *The Simpsons* (1989–present), supplying the voices for Mr. Burns, Waylon Smithers, Ned Flanders, and Principal Skinner. In 2014, he won a Primetime Emmy for Outstanding Character Voice-Over Performance. Since 1983, Shearer has hosted the weekly syndicated public radio comedy/music radio program *Le Show*.

# "Live from New York— It's Saturday Night"

## October 11, 1975, 11:30 p.m. (EDT)

The premiere episode of *SNL*, hosted by comedian George Carlin with musical guests Billy Preston and Janis Ian, was comprised of many of the same segments still featured on the show today: the cold open, an opening monologue, commercial parodies, short films, musical performances, and, of course, *Weekend Update*. While the mixture of comedy and musical performances, live sketches, and filmed segments is uneven by current show standards, on the whole it has a "rough-around-the-edges" quality one expects from a live television show. By mid-season, the show's general format was established, the transitions between segments were smoother, and the Not Ready for Prime Time Players were on their way to becoming household names.

### Cold Open: "I would like to feed your fingertips to the wolverines."

The episode (and series) opens with an absurdist sketch by head writer Michael O'Donoghue, who is seen in the first shot reading a newspaper. John Belushi walks in with a bag of groceries and sits in the chair next to him. O'Donoghue opens a book and begins what sounds like an

Original ad for the premiere episode hosted by George Carlin. Unfortunately, the dress rehearsal ran too long and comedian (and future cast member) Billy Crystal was cut from the show at the last minute.

The cold open of the first episode most likely confused many viewers: an absurdist sketch featuring head writer Michael O'Donoghue (right) giving English lessons to a foreigner (John Belushi) (left), who repeats a series of nonsensical sentences.

English lesson. He instructs Belushi to repeat each sentence, which he does in a thick foreign accent with obviously no understanding of what he's saying. The sentences make no sense:

> "I would like to feed your fingertips to the wolverines."
>
> "I am afraid we are out of badgers. Would you accept a wolverine in its place?"
>
> "'Hey,' Ned exclaimed, 'let's boil the wolverines.'"

O'Donoghue suddenly clutches his heart and falls dead to the ground. Belushi, unsure of what to do, imitates O'Donoghue and clutches his heart and falls to the floor.

Chevy Chase, wearing a headset and holding a clipboard, appears, smiles into the camera, and says, "Live from New York, it's *Saturday Night!*"

Popularized in the 1960s, a "cold open" is when a show begins with a piece of action, in this instance a sketch, rather than the opening credits, in order to hook the audience. In Shales and Miller's oral history of *SNL*, Lorne Michaels revealed that he decided on the Thursday night before the premiere to "open cold" with the wolverine sketch. It was risky because the sketch, like the sentences Belushi is instructed to repeat, is totally nonsensical. The first appearance by Chase, who walks into the scene as if he is a television

Chase, wearing a stage manager's headgear, breaks "the fourth wall," declaring, "Live from New York—it's *Saturday Night*

stage manager, brings everything back to reality and reminds us that what we are watching is a sketch on a television show. More importantly, the wolverine sketch signaled to the audience that *SNL* was like nothing they've ever seen before on television.

In 1989, on the occasion of *SNL*'s fifteenth anniversary, O'Donoghue shared with *People* magazine how he felt that night: "I did the first line on the show. I was terrified. If I close my eyes I can see that moment as they were counting off 30 seconds, 15 seconds, as if a roller coaster is just at the top of the big hill and hasn't quite been caught by gravity and gone screaming into the valley yet. I had that feeling when time stops and a big yawning abyss is below me."

For the remainder of season 1, *SNL*'s cold opens featured Chevy Chase doing his signature pratfall—sometimes, but not always, playing President Gerald Ford. He took his first official fall in the second episode (1.2), when he stumbles in the background holding a guitar after Paul Simon opens the show singing "Still Crazy After All These Years."

## Opening Title Sequence

The show's opening title reads *NBC's Saturday Night*. The title was shortened to *Saturday Night* beginning with episode 1.16. The title did not officially change to *Saturday Night Live* until season 2 (2.17).

Edie Baskin (daughter of Burt Baskin, cofounder of Baskin-Robbins) contributed the photographs of New York City nightlife for the opening titles: a couple eating pizza, a cabbie eating watermelon, two cops on a street corner, and a couple [writers Michael O'Donoghue and Anne Beatts] having dinner, etc. As Baskin recalled in Shales and Miller's *Uncensored History*, publicity photos of George Carlin were used during the "bumpers" (that's television lingo for the images that appear between the show and the commercial or vice versa). In the second episode (1.2), they used photos Baskin had taken of Paul Simon (she did the album cover for Simon's *Still Crazy After All These Years* [1975]). Lorne Michaels decided that Baskin should take the photos of the host every week—her photographs, the faces or backgrounds of which were often painted in pastel colors, along with the work of graphic artist Bob Pook, earned an Emmy nomination for "Outstanding Achievement in Graphic Design and Title Sequences" for episode 1.10, hosted by Buck Henry.

During the opening title sequence, announcer Don Pardo mistakenly introduced "The Not Ready for Prime Time Players" as "The *Not for* Ready Prime Time Players." In an interview for the Archive of American Television, he recalled: "I said it correctly . . . in the dress rehearsal . . . Herb Sargent [a writer on the show] came to me after the show. He says, 'You know what you said? You said, '*Not for ready.*' I said, 'I did? I don't remember it.'" But he shouldn't have felt too bad. When George Carlin says good night, he refers to the cast as the "Not *Quite* Ready for Prime Time Players." Pardo would eventually begin reading the cast members' names (1.11), and individual photos by Baskin were added to the opening credits the following March (1.16).

## Opening Monologue: "Ladies and Gentlemen ... George Carlin."

Carlin delivers the first of four monologues—a classic routine in which he explains why football, not baseball, is the real national pastime because it reflects American values ("Football's a ground acquisition game. You knock the crap out of eleven guys and take their land away from them. . . . That's what we did to the Indians.")

Carlin does not appear in any sketches. As he explained in an interview for the AAT, he told Michaels he didn't feel "comfortable" and "competent" as an actor to perform in comic sketches. In the same interview, he also admitted that he was "full of cocaine" that week, which makes it difficult for him to watch the episode. He was disappointed he was never asked back by Michaels

While future guest hosts will appear in sketches, counterculture comedian George Carlin's stint as host consisted of four monologues that touched on issues like American values, God, and religion.

or to participate in the anniversary shows, though he was invited to host again by producer Dick Ebersol in November 1984 (10.5). This time around he did appear in sketches alongside cast members Billy Crystal, Christopher Guest, and Harry Shearer.

## New Dad: "Tops in Pops" (Commercial #1)

*SNL*'s first official fake commercial is a parody of insurance ads that speak directly to the "man of the house" about the necessity of making sure your family is provided for after you've gone. Only this insurance policy will cover your family's "emotional and physical" needs if you "were suddenly out of the picture" by supplying your widow and children with a "New Dad." The widow is played by the future Mrs. Chevy Chase, Jacqueline Carlin, who appears as an extra in several filmed segments during season 1.

The first episode introduces a popular show segment that continues to this day: a commercial parody that lampoons an actual commercial, or, as in this case, advertises an absurd product, like an insurance policy that replaces your late husband with a new dad for your kids.

SNL's debut kicked off with two performers with different musical styles: R&B singer Billy Preston ("Nothing from Nothing," "Fancy Lady") (left) and folk-rock singer-songwriter, Janis Ian ("At Seventeen," "In the Winter").

## Billy Preston Sings "Nothing from Nothing"

The show's first musical performance is Billy Preston singing "Nothing from Nothing," from his 1974 album *The Kids and Me*. The song reached #1 on the *Billboard* Chart in October 1974.

## "The Trial" (Sketch #1)

The first official *SNL* sketch is not characteristic of the type of comedic sketches that would become the show's trademark. It is essentially a setup for a single punch line delivered at the end. Jane Curtin plays a rape victim on the witness stand who cannot bring herself to repeat out loud what her rapist said to her when he pulled her into an alleyway. She writes it down on a piece of paper and gives it to the judge. He reads it and hands it to the attorneys, who then give it to the jurors who read it and pass it along. Juror John Belushi nudges dozing juror Gilda Radner and passes her the note. She reads it and, thinking he wrote it, she delivers the punch line (actually it's a "punch gesture" because it's communicated nonverbally) by winking at him and giving him an "A-OK" gesture.

## Guest Performance by Andy Kaufman: "Here I come to save the day..."

American audiences are introduced to the bizarre world of Andy Kaufman, who performs one of his most memorable routines. He turns on an old-fashioned record player, and we hear the theme song to *Mighty Mouse*, a cartoon superhero who first appeared in theatrical shorts (1942–1961) and then on Saturday mornings in the late 1960s. While the record is playing, Kaufman simply stands

"Live from New York—It's *Saturday Night*"

Andy Kaufman's appearances on *SNL* were more performance art than stand-up. In his debut, Kaufman played the theme song of the animated series *Mighty Mouse* on a phonograph and lip-synched the superhero's watch cry: "Here I come to save the day!"

silently until the line "Here I come to save the day . . ." is sung, during which he mouths the words while making a broad waving gesture with his left hand. The song continues and he goes back to place (and at one point he even drinks some water from a glass). And then the song is over and he takes a bow. Two weeks later (1.3), Kaufman and his record player return—and this time he mouths the voice of a father singing, "Pop Goes the Weasel" to his child. The song is interrupted with some dialogue between the two, during which the father suggests they make up some words that rhyme with "weasel" (like "sneeze").

His appearances over the next five seasons are equally bizarre. In a thick foreign accent he tells a joke (1.4), and then imitates Archie Bunker (in the same foreign accent, which he also used as Latka Gravas on the sitcom *Taxi* [1978–1983]). He does a little dance and then gets flustered and begins to cry and starts to bang on a conga drum." I don't know if you are laughing at me or with me?" he asks the audience. We're not sure either. But all is well in the end when he walks off only to return to take a bow. He also gets audience members to lip-synch to a recording of "Old MacDonald Had a Farm" (1.15), does an impression of Elvis (2.11), sings "Oklahoma" (3.3), and attempts to read *The Great Gatsby* to a confused and restless audience (3.13) (fortunately Lorne Michaels appears and puts an end to it).

## George Carlin: "What do dogs do on their day off?" (Monologue #2)

Carlin's second monologue consists of a series of questions posed to the audience: "Do you ever look in the crowds in old movies and wonder if they're dead yet?," "Have you ever tried to throw away an old wastebasket?," and "What do dogs do on their day off?"

## Janis Ian Sings "At Seventeen"

Ian's haunting lament of teenage angst, as told by a self-proclaimed "ugly duckling," appeared on her 1975 album, *Between the Lines*, and reached #3 on the *Billboard* Pop Singles Chart the week of September 13, 1975 and ranked #19 on *Billboard*'s Top 100 Songs of 1975. The song won Ian a Grammy for Best Female Pop Vocal Performance in 1976. According to Jay Warner's *On This Day in Music History*, Ian also received 461 Valentine's Day Cards in 1977 in response to the lyrics in the song saying that she had never received one.

## Victim of Shark Bites (Sketch #2)

This is the first in a long line of talk show parodies with Jane Curtin (as host Phyllis Crawford) interviewing shark bite victim Martin Gresner (John Belushi), who claims he had his arm bitten off—until he accidentally reveals he has an arm concealed under his jacket. The sketch capitalizes on the hysteria surrounding shark sightings and attacks sparked by the 1975 summer blockbuster *Jaws*. Sharks or, more specifically, a "land shark" would make several appearances during the first and second seasons. The absurdity of the premise is reminiscent of the talk show sketches performed on *Monty Python's Flying Circus* (1969–1974).

## Jamitol: "My wife. She's quite a gal. And I love her for it." (Commercial #2)

Geritol was a dietary supplement containing vitamin complexes and iron marketed to consumers through the early 1970s as a remedy for tiredness, loss of strength, rundown feeling, nervousness, and irritability caused by a deficiency in vitamins or iron. According to a January 1973 *New York Times* story ("Geritol Ads Result in Fines of $812,000"), a federal judge found the makers and advertisers of Geritol to be guilty of deceptive advertising because the tonic is not a remedy for any of those symptoms, and those who have them are not necessarily suffering from a deficiency in vitamins or iron. Although it was not a factor in the judge's decision, the company was also guilty of first-degree sexism with what seemed at the time were an endless stream of annoying commercials in which a husband patronizingly attests how much he loves his wife, who takes care of herself, eats right, and takes Geritol every morning.

In the *SNL* version, it's a male couple, one of whom (Chase) introduces the second (Michael O'Donoghue) as "my best friend, my business partner, my advisor, my companion, my wife." The dialogue is lifted almost directly from the commercial, and it's delivered straight (pun intended) without a wink or a nod or any acknowledgment that it's two men. Considering most gay characters on television in the early 1970s were negative stereotypes, there was something, albeit perhaps unintentionally, progressive about Chase and O'Donoghue posing as a gay male couple. In a 1977 interview with *Playboy* magazine, Chase partially credited the fact that "he came off well" in this commercial convinced Lorne Michaels to add him to the cast.

The Jamitol commercial is repeated later that season (1.9) in the middle of *Weekend Update*. When we cut back to the anchor desk, O'Donoghue has joined Chase and the two are bickering like a married couple (O'Donoghue, tired of staying home by himself every Saturday night, accuses Chase of not caring).

A second Jamitol commercial (1.5), no doubt shot at the same time, featured single-episode cast member George Coe as a husband who sings the praises of his wife (Curtin) by sharing the long list of things she manages to do in a single day. She looks drowsy, and right after giving her pitch for Jamitol, she falls asleep. The husband says, "My wife—I think I'll stuff her."

## Paul Simon Promo

Simon does a promo for next week's *NBC's Saturday Night* when he'll be hosting and joined by Randy Newman, Phoebe Snow, and his ex-partner, Art Garfunkel, for "a little Simon & Garfunkel reunion." Early in the show's run, a cast member would usually announce the name of next week's host and musical guest.

## *Weekend Update* with Chevy Chase

In what is perhaps the shortest edition of *Weekend Update* on record (approximately four minutes, not including the Triopenin commercial below), most of the jokes were topical and about real people: Union leader Jimmy Hoffa, who disappeared on July 30, 1975, and was presumed to have been killed by the mob (he was declared legally dead on that date seven years later); Japanese Emperor Hirohito and the Empress, who attended a state dinner at the White House a few weeks earlier on October 2, 1975, and then flew to California to meet Mickey Mouse and John Wayne; and President Ford and his new campaign slogan, "If he's so dumb, how come he's President?" Chase is interrupted by a remote report by Laraine Newman at the Blaine Hotel, where another in a long string of murders has occurred. The report was actually the setup to a joke made later in the broadcast when Don Pardo announces, "Guests of *Saturday Night* stay at the Blaine Hotel in midtown Manhattan."

During his short stint as a series regular (thirty episodes, 1.1–1.24, 2.1–2.6), Chase showcased his comic timing and irreverent sense of humor anchoring *Weekend Update*, which continues to be the centerpiece of each episode.

*Weekend Update* worked in the early days because the punch line to each joke was funny, and Chase's comic timing coupled with his boyish goofiness made it all the funnier. He was clearly the best choice for delivering the news, but not necessarily the first. Up until a few weeks before the show's debut, Lorne Michaels was going to sit behind the news desk as he had done in a recurring skit on *The Hart & Lorne Terrific Hour*. In his academic study of *SNL* and *Weekend Update*, Aaron Reincheld revealed that Michaels was concerned about "being in an awkward situation when cutting other people's material from the show while performing and maintaining his own segment."

## Triopenin: "Get your hands working again." (Commercial #3)

The funniest and simplest commercial to air during the premiere episode is a homage to those medicine bottles with the childproof lids that are impossible to open (thus the name, Tri-open-in). The piece was written by writer Tom Schiller, who would contribute a series of short films (under the title *Schiller's Reel*) between the years 1977 and 1981. For the record, those are Chase's hands trying to open the bottle.

## The Muppets: "The Land of Gorch"

Lorne Michaels signed puppeteer Jim Henson when *SNL* was in its development stage to contribute a weekly segment featuring a new breed of adult-oriented Muppets designed by Henson and Michael Frith specifically for the show. At the time, Henson was best known as the creator of Kermit the Frog and Miss Piggy, along with Big Bird, Grover, Oscar the Grouch, and the other residents of *Sesame Street*, the children's television show that debuted on PBS on November 10, 1969, and is still on the air today. Including *The Muppets* on the bill certainly seemed like an unusual move for Michaels, who was so intent on creating a show that would appeal to a certain demographic that might not consider puppets, even if the material is written for an adult audience, their idea of late-night entertainment.

In the series' debut, Henson, along with his talented band of puppeteers, introduced America to the bubbling tar pits known as the Land of Gorch and its inhabitants:

- **King Ploobis** (performed by Henson), who is described by Henson in his notes on the characters (posted on henson.com/jimsredbook) as "loud/angry/dominant/King/boisterous/violent/dumb."
- **Queen Peuta** (Alice Tweedie), the king's wife, who Henson described as "haughty/pretentious/shallow."
- **Wisss** (Richard Hunt), the hippie son of the king and queen, who discover their son is a "crater head" who likes to sniff the smoke out of craters and blow it out through his snout (1.3).

Jim Henson created a whole breed of Muppets for *SNL* who, according to Lorne Michaels, could stay up late. Set in the mythical Land of Gorch, the sketches, which were meant to appeal to older audiences, simply did not work.

- **Scred** (Jerry Nelson), the king's "loyal" assistant, who has been having a four-hundred-year affair with the queen, who forces him to come clean with Ploobis or risk losing her (1.9).
- **Vazh** (Rhonda Hansome/Fran Brill), the king's servant and mistress.
- **The Mighty Favog** (spelled "Fuvog" in the original scripts) (Frank Oz), an all-knowing, talking statue from whom King Ploobis seeks advice.

The sketches were written by the writers on the show, and apparently it was not an assignment anyone enjoyed. According to writer Alan Zweibel, he and Al Franken and Tom Davis, who were the rookie writers, were assigned to write the Muppet sketches. Head writer O'Donoghue hated the Muppets. Zweibel recalled in Shales and Miller's *Live from New York* the first time he met O'Donoghue he was in the middle of taking a stuffed Big Bird and wrapping the cord of the Venetian blinds in Lorne Michaels's office around its neck. Even after the Muppets were long gone, O'Donoghue couldn't contain his disdain for what he described to *Playboy*'s John Blumenthal and Lindsay Maracotta as "those fucking Muppets, those little hairy facecloths. I'd deep-six them in a second." Although the material (sex, adultery, drugs) was adult by *Sesame Street* standards, the audience never quite warmed up to Scred and company. In a 1998 interview with Judy Harris, Henson said he respected Michaels and really loved what he was going for on *SNL*. "But somehow what we were trying to do," he added, "and what his writers could write for it never jelled. . . . When they were writing for us, I had the feeling they were writing normal sitcom stuff, which is really boring and bland." The critics recognized this from the start. Tom Shales, critic for the *Washington Post*, said the Muppet sketches were not working and tended to "flounder." *Los Angeles Times* critic Dick Adler agreed, admitting he liked the Muppets on children's shows and musical specials, but "they are as out of place on *Saturday Night* as a 5-year-old listening to Lenny Bruce albums."

The moments that worked were the interactions between the characters and the guest hosts: Scred sings "I Got You Babe" with Lily Tomlin (1.6) and joins King Ploobis and Candice Bergen in a rendition of "Have Yourself a Merry Little Christmas" (1.8). In a later episode (1.11), Scred dons a bee outfit hoping to play Aunt Bee in a Bee parody of *The Andy Griffith Show*, but when Gilda tells him the sketch was cut, she lets him introduce tonight's musical guest, Neil Sedaka. Once the Muppets know their days on the show are numbered, they ask Anthony Perkins (1.16) and Chevy Chase (1.19) to help them get their jobs back. Their last appearance is in the season 2 opener, in which the Muppets, who have been asleep in filing cabinets, wake up and join Lily Tomlin in "Whistle a Happy Tune" despite their inability to whistle.

The Muppets would soon have an opportunity to interact with some of the biggest names in show business when they moved to London to star in their own weekly series, *The Muppet Show* (1976–1981), which debuted in September 1976. The guest list included Gilda Radner and several former *SNL* hosts (Candice Bergen, Madeline Kahn, Steve Martin, Paul Simon, Raquel Welch).

## George Carlin: "Did you ever . . . ?" (Monologue #3)

Carlin offers more observations about blue food, traveling with vitamins, and jumbo shrimp.

## "A Film by Albert Brooks": *The Impossible Truth*

In August 1975, *Time* magazine called Albert Brooks, twenty-eight, "the smartest, most audacious, comic talent since Lenny Bruce and Woody Allen." Between the years 1970 and 1973, he was on sitcoms and variety shows, including eighteen appearances on *The Tonight Show Starring Johnny Carson* (1962–1982). He also contributed a comedy short to the PBS series *The Great American Dream Machine* (1971–1972), "Albert Brooks' Famous School for Comedians," which was based on an article he contributed to the February 1971 issue of *Esquire* that looked like a real brochure for a comedians' school.

According to a July 1983 *Playboy* interview, Brooks was asked to be the permanent host of *SNL* but contributed short films instead, beginning with the series opener, which features a mockumentary of impossible but true stories—a blind cabdriver continues to drive, the countries of Israel and the state of Georgia change places, and Oregon lowers the age of consent from eighteen to seven. According to Shales and Miller, Brooks recalled the total budget for the six films he made was $50,000. The five remaining untitled shorts written and directed by Brooks are:

- Brooks shares home movies from his childhood (1.2), which show how he was traumatized by his father, who was always filming him at the most inopportune times, and scenes from Brooks's failed attempts at "candid camera."
- The second, thirteen-minute short (1.3), in which Brooks performs open-heart surgery despite his lack of medical training, was interrupted by commercials. In Shales and Miller, Brooks credits his longtime friend and this week's host Rob Reiner for insisting that it air despite its length.
- Brooks parodies a preview of "NBC's Super Season" (1.4)—three series to air as midseason replacements: *Medical Season* (a parody of medical dramas), *The Three of Us* ("the wildest new comedy you've ever seen" about a married couple who live with her best female friend), and *Black Vet* (a black veterinarian in a small Southern town).
- Brooks is sick in bed this week (1.7). His doctor verifies over the phone that he is ill and also recommends that he doesn't fulfill his six-film contract. A delivery boy who stops by plugs Brooks's Grammy-nominated comedy album, *A Star Is Bought*.
- In his final film, Brooks pays researchers at the National Audience Research Institute to find out what people like and don't like about his comedy (1.9). The results confirm that Brooks is not funny (1.9). Director James L. Brooks (no relation), who would later direct Albert in *Broadcast News* (1987), has a cameo as one of the researchers.

## Bee Hospital: "Congratulations, it's a drone!" (Sketch #3)

This nonsensical soap opera parody written by Rosie Shuster features the cast dressed up in bee costumes. Gilda, Laraine, and Jane (as bee nurses) appear one at a time holding a baby and informing the anxious daddy-to-bee his wife has given birth. The first two are ecstatic to hear the nurse say, "Mr. Bee? Congratulations, it's a drone!" But the third expectant father (John Belushi) is disappointed when he's told, "Congratulations, it's a worker!" The sketch concludes with a scene from next week's episode of *Bee Hospital*, in which a nurse informs a very proud papa, "Congratulations, it's a queen!"

In Shales and Miller's *Live from New York*, Michaels said, "The only note we got from the network on the first show was, 'Cut the bees.' And so I made sure to put them in the next show." Maybe the executives at NBC were uncomfortable with the *Bee Hospital* sketch because they didn't get the joke—because there really was no joke to get. Then again, maybe they were not familiar with the caste system within the colony of the honeybee in which the queen bee sits at the top, followed by the drones (the males, whose only function is to mate with the queen bee), with the workers (all females) at the bottom.

One of the staples of *SNL*'s brand of comedy were recurring characters, beginning with "The Bees," which debuted in "Bee Hospital" and returned for fifteen sketches through season 4.

The bees did return the following week (1.2), only to be told by host Paul Simon that the bee number was cut because it didn't work last week.

In the next episode (1.3), the bees appear during a sketch in which Rob Reiner and guest Penny Marshall are talking in a restaurant. Suddenly, the place fills up with bees. When Reiner sees John Belushi dressed as a bee, he gets upset: "I was told when I came on the show that I would not have to work with bees!" Speaking on behalf of the cast/colony, Belushi shames Reiner for his attitude: "Do you think we like this? No, Mr. Reiner." With "The Battle Hymn of the Republic" playing in the background, Belushi continues: "You see, we're just like you were five years ago, Mr. Hollywood, California, number-one-show big shot. That's right. We're just a bunch of actors looking for a break, that's all." Reiner feels bad—end of show. Apparently there was some truth to Belushi's anger. In Pisano and Colby's biography of Belushi, Shuster (and others) agree that Belushi did not like being a bee because he felt it was beneath him. Costume designer Franne Lee recalled how much Belushi hated wearing the costume. "A lot of his performance in that costume was so good because he hated it so much," she observed. "He felt that it was so humiliating, and all of that really came through in the character."

And the Bees kept coming:

- Chevy Chase swats a bee (Belushi) away from host Candice Bergen (1.4) during her monologue. Later in the show, Bergen dresses as a bee so she and Chase can demonstrate the Polaroid Deluxe SX-70 camera. When Bergen returns later that season for *SNL*'s first holiday episode (1.8), she appears in the "Bee Capades," a two-minute filmed segment shot on the ice rink at Rockefeller Plaza with the cast in their bee costumes doing various tableaux, including the Nativity, and spelling out "Noel" on ice.
- In a "Bee Centennial Minute" (1.15), a bee in Revolutionary War attire (Garrett Morris) tells the story of a bee named Henry who was crushed by a napping soldier in the tent of General George Washington.
- Host Lily Tomlin (1.6) ends her first appearance on the show performing "Bee Scat" with the cast dressed as bees.
- Host Elliott Gould (1.9) stars in the best of the bee sketches in which a couple (Chase and Radner) and their Aunt Betty (Curtin) are terrorized by a swarm of South American Killer Bees, who break into the house demanding their pollen. In the middle of the sketch, in which the leader of the Killer Bees (Gould) is giving a dramatic speech, Belushi notices the camera is not on Gould and interrupts the sketch. Lorne Michaels makes his first on-camera appearance when he comes out to investigate, only to discover that director Dave Wilson is drunk. Gould and the cast decide not to continue with the sketch. The Killer Bees returned in season 2 to invade a Swine Flu Innoculation Center (2.3) to steal the vaccine, though Eric Idle's British accent ruins the sketch.
- America's first introduction to the Blues Brothers (1.10), Jake (Belushi) and Elwood (Aykroyd), is when the duo—dressed as bees—sing Slim Harpo's

swamp blues song, "I'm a King Bee" accompanied by Howard Shore and the All-Bee Band. The audience loves it. In their next appearance (3.18), they perform "I Don't Know" sans the bee costumes.
- Muppet Scred appears dressed as a Bee (1.11), only to be told by Gilda Radner that the sketch has been cut.
- Sherry (Laraine Newman) complains to her professor (Anthony Perkins) about getting a Bee (Belushi) on her philosophy paper (1.16). He gives her a B+ (the plus being a child who begins to cry in Belushi's arms).
- Bees play an integral role in parodies of *One Flew Over the Cuckoo's Nest* (1975) (*One Flew Over the Hornet's Nest* [1.18]), featuring Raquel Welch as Nurse Ratched, and the all-bee version of *The Honeymooners* (1955–1956) (1.22).
- In a tag-team wrestling match (1.13), a pair of bees (Belushi, host Peter Boyle) take on a pair of WASPs (as in White Anglo-Saxon Protestants) (Radner and Chase).
- Host Shelley Duvall (2.21) was prepared to open the show with a love scene from "Flight of the Bumblebees," but it was cut due to NBC's new rule that all shows must make up for the network's losses for airing the Duane Bobick–Ken Norton fight, which lasted only fifty-eight seconds, by airing the fight footage at the start of every NBC program.
- After a long absence, the bees return in a parody of *The Bad News Bears* (4.7). On the night before a big game, one of the players, Alan (Belushi), is taunted for reading a *Playbee* magazine and "buzzing off," prompting the Coach (host Walter Matthau) to explain that it's perfectly normal to "bend their barb" once in a while and how a great ballplayer named Reggie Jackson buzzed off five, six, seven times a day.
- On the 2011 Christmas show, host Jimmy Fallon, along with the cast and guests, said their "good nights" on the Rockefeller Center skating rink with Fallon dressed as a bee (it must have brought him good luck as he won an Emmy for "Outstanding Guest Actor in a Comedy Series").

## Academy of Better Careers: "Don't let life put you on hold!" (Commercial #4)

During the 1970s recession, when America was battling high inflation and unemployment, viewers of late-night television were bombarded with ads for trade schools promising an exciting new career as a computer programmer, air conditioner repairman, or truck driver. The ads end with a phone number flashing on the screen and the message, "Operators are standing by to take your call." In this parody of those cheesy commercials, a woman (Radner) receives a phone call from the Academy of Better Careers, which promises to train you in only six weeks for a high-paying new career (up to eight dollars a day!) as a skilled standby operator. We see footage of students repeatedly picking up a phone and saying "hello" and there's a shot of one of their experienced instructors giving a lecture on area codes. The salesman urges the woman, "Don't let life put you on hold. Become a standby operator! Call now for a free booklet. . . . Operators are standing by to take your call."

## Guest Comedy Performance by Valri Bromfield

Bromfield was in the first Toronto Second City cast with Gilda Radner, Dan Aykroyd, and Brian Doyle-Murray. Her long list of television comedy credits includes supervising producer on *The Kids in the Hall* (1988–1994), writer/performer on Lorne Michaels's short-lived prime-time variety series *The New Show* (1984), and a supporting role on the sitcom *Grace Under Fire* (1993–1998).

In her solo bit, Bromfield pretends to be a schoolteacher preparing her all-girl volleyball team for a big match. She suddenly morphs into team captain Debbie, who tells her teammates they have to go out there and be "really, really cute, okay? Cause we are really cute."

## Public Service Announcement (PSA): "Show Us Your Guns!"

This comedy short sends a not-so-subtle message about the need for stronger gun laws in the United States. The narrator tells us: "We at *Saturday Night* wanted to see what kind of people carry guns. So we took our camera crew into the streets to find out." With the "William Tell Overture" playing on the soundtrack, we see the truck traveling through small-town America (actually suburban Westchester County) with a film camera and a sign reading "Show Us Your Guns." Everyone is happy to oblige: the dad barbequing in his backyard, the guy mowing his lawn, a woman who comes out of her house with a submachine gun, a mother who keeps her pistol in her baby's carriage, the little old lady in the park, and the bride and groom carrying a pistol and a machine gun, etc. Ironically, the cop directing traffic can't find his.

In his autobiography, *Thirty-Nine Years of Short Term Memory Loss*, writer Tom Davis explained the film short was a parody of an ad for Lark cigarettes in which a roving camera and an off-camera voice asked people to "show us their Larks."

## George Carlin on God and Religion (Monologue #3)

Saving his edgiest material for later in the show, Carlin addresses two of his favorite subjects: God ("Maybe he's only a semi-Supreme Being because he's like us and we're not perfect") and religion (which "has a way of relieving yourself of any responsibility for your acts.").

Meanwhile, the NBC switchboard in New York received complaints from Roman Catholics over Carlin's material. Ebersol recalled in his AAT interview that one caller informed NBC that Cardinal Cooke, the archbishop of New York, was furious and implied there were going to be repercussions on Monday.

He didn't tell anyone about the call, and after the show he walked over to St. Patrick's Cathedral and sat outside of the residential entrance wondering if he should wake up the cardinal and talk to him. He realized this was crazy and went home. On Monday, he discovered it was a prank call. Ebersol said he learned a valuable lesson. He realized the "whole thing was ludicrous that anybody who cared enough to call isn't necessarily a typical viewer." So in order to skew the number of calls in his favor, for the next two months he had the three female cast members call the NBC switchboard, disguise their voices, and tell the operator how much they were enjoying the show.

## Billy Preston Sings "Fancy Lady"

Preston sings "Fancy Lady," from his tenth studio album *It's My Pleasure*, which was released in June 1975.

## "Trojan Horse Home Security" (Sketch #4)

In this sketch, Kenny Vorstrather (Dan Aykroyd), a salesman from the Trojan Horse Home Security Company, and his assistant Harvey (Garrett Morris), break into a couple's home (John Belushi and Gilda Radner) and scare and intimidate them into buying a home safety security policy for $499.99 (the deal is sealed when the couple learn that Vorstrather is holding their son Ronnie hostage). The sketch showcases the talent of Aykroyd, who for the next four seasons specialized in playing fast-talking salesman, pitchmen, and law enforcement officers.

## Triple Track: "Because you'll believe anything." (Commercial #5)

The double-edged razor had only been on the market since 1971 (Gillette's Trac II) when this commercial parody by Chevy Chase was originally written for *The Smothers Brothers Show* (1975). The irony is that the product it's advertising—the "Triple Track" razor—would eventually become a reality when Gillette introduced the first triple-blade razor cartridge (the Mach3) in 1998. In this parody, Al Franken plays a caveman trying to get a close shave at the start of the commercial. His partner, Tom Davis, recalled in his autobiography how the one-minute spot was a nightmare for Franken, who passed out from the spirit gum used to glue the hair to his face, sliced his hand on a shard of glass that was in the pool of water, got stung by a bee, and had to be taken to the hospital to get a tetanus shot.

## Janis Ian Sings "In the Winter"

Carlin introduces Ian, who sings another track from her 1975 album *Between the Lines*.

## George Carlin Says "Goodnight"

Carlin stands alone onstage to say "good night," but not before holding up the cover to his brand-new album, *An Evening with Wally Londo Featuring Bill Slaszo*. He thanks his guests and mistakenly refers to the cast as the "Not Quite Ready for Prime Time Players."

## The Closing Credits

The nickname "Bud" is inserted in everyone's name in the closing credits because Lorne Michaels found it amusing when people included their nicknames in parentheses. Perhaps he was inspired by the closing credits of *Monty Python's Flying Circus* (1969–1974), which occasionally had some fun with the names of the cast and crew (like the time they inserted the word "Spam" in the middle of the cast's names, along with the occasional "egg," "chips," and "sausage"). At the very end, the *SNL* credits read "Executive Producer for NBC Dick 'Bud' Ebersol." It is the only time this credit would appear.

## The Reviews

In reading the reviews of *NBC's Saturday Night*, it's evident that there was a cultural (and perhaps generational) divide among critics in regard to how they responded to the show's brand of humor and loose format. The first episode of *Saturday Night Live* caught the attention of some critics, though most of the reviews of the show did not appear in many of the major newspaper and magazines until a few episodes into the first season. David Cuthbert of the *Times-Picayune* called the new show "free-wheeling in concept and consistently fresh and sophisticated in execution." The *Washington Post*'s Tom Shales, who would become a longtime fan of the show, recognized *NBC's Saturday Night* as "the first network series produced by and for the television generation—those late-war and post-war babies who were the first to have TV as a sitter." While some people might find some of the sketches in questionable taste, Shales found the "show's audacity . . . refreshing in a medium obsessed with the fear of offending anybody."

John J. O'Connor of the *New York Times* waited to publish his review because he missed the first half-hour of the first episode due to inclement weather and "an unusually good dinner on Long Island." He watched episode 1.2, which consisted mostly of musical performances, including a reunion of Simon & Garfunkel. "The reunion was, it should be stressed," O'Connor writes, "nice while it lasted. The same cannot be said, unfortunately, for the rest of 'Saturday Night,' either the final half-hour of this one or most of the 90 minutes of the previous week's premiere, with the increasingly pretentious comedy lectures of George Carlin. . . . Even an off-beat showcase needs quality, an ingredient conspicuously absent from the dreadfully uneven comedy efforts of the new series."

Over a month and four episodes later, O'Connor wrote a second review of the show in which he estimated that when the show debuted, "about 75 percent of the surrounding material seemed to meander pointlessly. In more recent weeks, however, at least 75 percent has proved to be sharply and sometimes wickedly on target." O'Connor praised the most recent episode hosted by Lily Tomlin (1.6), with whom the critic admits he is "helplessly in love," though he felt that host Robert Klein (1.5) was good and Candice Bergen even better (1.4) because she blended "easily and attractively into the company." O'Connor praised the cast for "proving incredibly adept at using liveness to full advantage." "For however long it lasts, 'Saturday Night' is the most creative and encouraging thing to happen in American TV comedy since 'Your Show of Shows.'" By the end of the year he was hooked, calling *Saturday Night* "the most significant and welcome TV development of the year."

It would take a little time—but America would soon become hooked as well.

# Breaking New Ground

## SNL's Television Comedy Roots

In the beginning, *Saturday Night Live*'s special brand of humor combined the comedic antics of Second City improv and sketch comedy with the envelope-pushing irreverence of *National Lampoon*. But satirical commentary, topical parody, and absurdist tomfoolery were not exactly new to television. *SNL*'s comedic roots can be traced to several American and British variety and sketch comedy shows, some of which still managed, despite varying degrees of interference from the networks, advertisers, irate viewers, and the Nixon administration, to break new ground in the 1960s and 1970s. They raised the bar for television comedy and in the process occasionally lowered its standards in pursuit of a laugh.

### Your Show of Shows (1950–1954)/Caesar's Hour (1954–1957)

The description of *Your Show of Shows* sounds awfully familiar: an original, ninety-minute sketch comedy show broadcast live on NBC every Saturday night from 30 Rockefeller Plaza featuring a repertory of comic actors. Sid Caesar, with his company of players (Imogene Coca, Carl Reiner, and Howard Morris) and a team of young, talented, and mostly Jewish comedy writers (including Reiner, Mel Brooks, Neil Simon, Danny Simon, and Mel Tolkin), were the true pioneers of live television comedy. Caesar's blend of verbal and physical comedy, which consisted of parodies of television shows and films, musical sketches and pantomimes, and something that would become a staple on *SNL*, recurring character sketches (The Professor, The Hickenloopers, etc.) had a profound and lasting influence on all the sketch comedy shows that followed. In his memoir, *Laughing Matters*, Larry Gelbart, a staff writer on Caesar's second series, *Caesar's Hour*, recalled how the material "sprang from our collective backgrounds, our tastes in literature, in film, in theatre, music, ballet, our marriages, our psychoanalyses." And their comedic targets? "Everything, every subject, was fair game. Nothing was too hip for the [writers'] room." The *SNL* writers, particularly in the beginning, followed a similar credo. Consider the overdose of drug humor in the early days and the attention *SNL* paid to Chevy Chase's meteoric rise to stardom and his hasty departure during the second season.

The best part of *Your Show of Shows* was that it was performed live in front of an audience (and, unlike *SNL*, without cue cards!). Audiences cherished the moments when something went wrong, like a problem with a costume or a wig, or an actor forgetting his or her lines, or the host forgetting the name of this week's guest star. That's exactly what happened when Caesar totally blanked for a minute on the name of his guest, British actor Basil Rathbone, who got back at his host by referring to him as "Mr. Sid Silvers."

In his autobiography, *Caesar's Hours: My Life in Comedy with Love and Laughter*, Caesar acknowledges the influences his show had on television comedy: "Our work has been credited for setting the stage, figuratively and literally, for almost every variety show and sketch and parody-driven program from *Saturday Night Live* to *Monty Python's Flying Circus*. We made the rules, broke new ground, and had a lot of fun and interesting times." Although Caesar admits he gets more enjoyment today watching the History Channel than television comedy, he acknowledged in his interview for the AAT that he has watched *Saturday Night Live* and that they "had some very good stuff on there."

On February 5, 1983, thirty-three years after the debut of *Your Show of Shows*, Caesar hosted *Saturday Night Live* (8.12). When he appeared onstage during the cold open, the audience gave him a standing ovation as the cast joined in the applause. In his heartfelt monologue, he shared how happy he was to be hosting the show. Later in the show, he revisited one of his most popular characters, the Professor, and in the final credits he received a plaque making him an honorary *SNL* cast member.

## That Was the Week That Was (BBC: 1962–1963; NBC: 1964–1965)

There haven't been many comedy shows on television that are as timely as *Saturday Night Live* when it comes to satirizing current events. For example, if something newsworthy happens on a Thursday night (let's be more specific and say, for instance, during a Republican presidential debate), *SNL* can present their comic take on what happened two days later.

One British program that devoted an entire fifty minutes each week to political satire was the groundbreaking series *That Was the Week That Was* (also known as *TW3*), which aired late on Saturday nights on BBC. The program, which was part of the British "satire boom" in the early 1960s, took a satirical look at current events and politics in Britain through a mixture of songs, sketches, and running commentary provided by its host, David Frost. No topic or public figure was off-limits. The show's team of writers, which included future Monty Pythoners Graham Chapman and John Cleese, comedian Peter Cook, novelist Roald Dahl (*James and the Giant Peach, Charlie and the Chocolate Factory*), and dramatist Dennis Potter (*The Singing Detective*), didn't shy away from controversial subject matter (race relations in the United States, apartheid in South Africa) and reveled in exposing government hypocrisy. Along the way they slung barbs at Prime Minister Harold Macmillan, the British monarchy, the military, and, in one episode, thirteen members of Parliament who hadn't made a speech in three years (the latter prompted a parliamentary debate). The show ran for two seasons (or what the Brits call a "series") on BBC, but was not brought back for a third because of all the controversy it stirred and the fact it was an election year.

*TW3* took a serious turn on Saturday, November 23, 1963, the day after the assassination of President Kennedy, who was honored with a twenty-minute tribute that included cast member Millicent Martin singing "In the Summer of His Years." The special aired in the United States on NBC the following day.

A few weeks before, NBC aired an American version of *TW3* as a special, which led to a half-hour weekly series beginning in January of 1964. According to historians Tim Brooks and Earle Marsh, the show used a similar format and tackled controversial topics (religion, race, and, of course, politics), but it was preempted during the first half of the 1964–1965 season due to the election (ironically, often by paid political announcements for Republican candidates). By the time the show returned in the spring, it couldn't compete with *Peyton Place* (1964–1969) and *Petticoat Junction* (1963–1970) and was canceled.

*TW3* should also be noted for its extensive use of an "open studio" in which the camera and the show's crew could be seen by the home audience as the performers moved freely about through the studio. Although it doesn't use this method during sketches and musical performances, *SNL* often previews what's coming up next with a long shot of the set or the musical stage as everyone's getting ready. Sketches also typically end with a quick long shot of the set where we see the performers and the crew racing to the next sketch.

In *Frost on Satire*, a 2012 special for BBC4, *TW3* host David Frost sat down with Lorne Michaels in Studio 8H, which was also the former home of the American version of *TW3* back in 1964–1965. Michaels explained that when *SNL* debuted in the mid-1970s, there was a distrust and opposition to authority in the air due to Watergate. "*Weekend Update* is a direct descendant of *That Was The Week That Was*," he added, "so we came on with somehow the right to question."

## The Smothers Brothers Comedy Hour (1967–1969)

In 1967, CBS gave comedy duo Tom and Dick Smothers their own hour variety show on Sunday evenings from 9 to 10 p.m., immediately following *The Ed Sullivan Show* (1948–1971), now in its nineteenth season. When *The Smothers Brothers Comedy Hour* debuted on February 5, 1967, Sullivan did the introduction: "Now I'd like to kick off the premiere of an exciting new comedy show which we're all going to enjoy for a long, long time." The show, a mixture of musical performances, comedy sketches, and verbal sparring between Tom and Dick, was popular with critics and audiences (it ranked #16 in its freshman season). At the time, CBS's highest-rated shows were long-running comedy and variety shows that were popular among older viewers in Middle America: *The Red Skelton Hour* (1951–1971), *The Andy Griffith Show* (1960–1968), *The Lucy Show* (1962–1968), and *The Jackie Gleason Show* (1966–1970). While the Smothers Brothers aimed to appeal to older folks with guest stars like Kate Smith, Carol Burnett, Bette Davis, Carl Reiner, Mickey Rooney, and George Burns, they also managed to attract younger viewers, a highly desirable demographic for advertisers, with guests like Jefferson Airplane, the Beatles, the Doors, Simon & Garfunkel, and the Who.

Young people (now known as "baby boomers") were also tuning in because *The Smothers Brothers* was the first show on network television to "speak their language" and express their left-of-center political views. Their political commentary in the form of sketches and the comical exchanges between Dick and Tom tackled the Vietnam War and the draft, gun control, and religion—hot-button topics, especially for Middle America, which happened to be CBS's core audience. There was also drug-laced humor about marijuana and LSD, but unlike *SNL*, drugs were never explicitly mentioned. A popular segment called "Share a Little Tea with Goldie," in which comedian Leigh French plays the hippie TV host who gives advice to housewives, was laden with double entendres (like "high" and "roaches"), most of which went straight over the heads of CBS executives and the network's core audience in Middle America.

The tension between the Smothers Brothers and CBS escalated during the show's third and final season, beginning with the network's refusal to air singer/political activist Harry Belafonte singing "Don't Stop the Carnival" against footage of the antiwar protests that broke out at the '68 Democratic Convention in Chicago. By the end of season 3, CBS pulled the plug on the show.

On June 8, 1969, the writing team of *The Smothers Brothers Comedy Hour* received the Emmy for "Outstanding Writing Achievement in Comedy, Variety, or Music." Although he received writing credit on the show, Tom Smothers did not submit his name for consideration for fear that all the controversy surrounding him would prevent his fellow writers from winning. Forty years later, Steve Martin, a member of the show's Emmy-winning writing staff, presented Tom Smothers with the Emmy he deserved. In his acceptance speech, he thanked his fellow writers "for all the great writing that got me . . . fired" and reminded us of the importance to speak the truth: "There's nothing more scary than watching ignorance in action, so I dedicate this Emmy to all people who feel compelled to speak out, to speak to power and won't shut up and refuse to be silenced."

## *Rowan & Martin's Laugh-In* (1968–1973)

This Monday night comedy free-for-all was the #1 show in America during its first two seasons (1968–1969, 1969–1970) and put "beautiful downtown Burbank" (where it was taped) on the map. When *Rowan & Martin's Laugh-In* premiered on January 22, 1968, there was nothing like it on television in terms of both its comedic style and format. Along with *The Monkees*, American television's version of the 1964 Beatles film *A Hard Day's Night*, which aired in an earlier time slot on the same night, *Laugh-In* was the closest NBC ever came to successfully capitalizing on the counterculture and the changing political climate of the late

1960s. Compared to *The Smothers Brothers*, *Laugh-In*'s political content was tamer and less in-your-face, though it managed to take jabs at elected officials and comment on political and social issues. They also bestowed the "Flying Fickle Finger of Fate Award" (a statue of a hand with an extended winged finger) to such dubious recipients as the City of Cleveland (the Cuyahoga River was at one point so polluted it caught fire), L.A. chief of police Ed Davis (for suggesting installable portable gallows in airports so hijackers could be immediately tried and hanged), and California governor Ronald Reagan ("There's no reason right now, but we're sure he'll come up with one"). There was also a news segment, "*Laugh-In* Looks at the News," which was in the same spirit as *That Was The Week That Was*. As Hal Erickson observed in his revealing critical history of *Laugh-In*, *From Beautiful Downtown Burbank*, "political commentary was treated with the same comic impiety as everything else on the program." Still, it's doubtful the Smothers Brothers would have invited Republican presidential candidate Richard Nixon on their program two months before the election, as *Laugh-In* did, to utter one of the show's most famous catchphrases (in the form of a question)—"Sock it to *me*?" Nixon no doubt scored some votes with the younger set that night. Head writer Paul Keyes, a Nixon supporter who quit after two seasons, went to work for the president.

*Laugh-In* catered to audience members with impaired attention spans with its rapid-fire editing techniques and weekly surge of blackout sketches, sight gags, running jokes, musical numbers, and a grab bag of corny, bawdy, topical (yet cheap) jokes. If a joke wasn't funny it didn't matter because they were delivered at warp speed. In addition to "Sock-it-to-Me," *Laugh-In* was also the birthplace of many popular catchphrases: "Here comes the judge," "Say good night, Dick," "You bet your sweet bippy" (what is a bippy, exactly?), "Look that up in your Funk & Wagnalls," and "Verrrry Interesting."

Hosted by the comedy team of Dan Rowan and Dick Martin, *Laugh-In*, like *SNL*, featured an ensemble cast of eight to ten unknown players, several of whom emerged as the show's breakout stars: Judy Carne, Goldie Hawn, Ruth Buzzi, Henry Gibson, Arte Johnson, Lily Tomlin, and Joanne Worley. *SNL* creator Lorne Michaels was a staff writer on the show (along with his partner Hart Pomerantz) during the 1968–1969 season, but he didn't care for the writing process because it involved submitting jokes to the head writer, who then compiled them into a script. In George Plasketes's profile of Michaels, the producer recalled, "It was very confusing to me because at the end of it, I didn't know what I'd done. Everyone was sitting around, congratulating the writers, saying what a great script it was." The show was taped without a studio audience, so there was no real feedback from an audience. In the same article, Michaels reflected further on this time on *Laugh-In*: "What I did learn from there was the structure and sort of industrial way in which television shows were produced. The show's producer, George Schlatter, was brilliant, as were the editors. They were the real 'stars' of that show. The writers were only a part of it and the audience was less a part of it. It was all electronics, but very innovative for its day."

## Monty Python's Flying Circus (1969–1974)

Two Oxford graduates (Terry Jones, Michael Palin), three Cambridge grads (Graham Chapman, John Cleese, and Eric Idle), and one American (Terry Gilliam) wrote a new chapter in the annals of television comedy with this inventive British sketch comedy series that premiered on BBC One in 1969 and later aired on PBS in the United States, where it developed a cult following. This postmodern romp comprised of filmed segments, sketches performed in front of a live studio audience, and bits of animation by Gilliam lived up to its catchphrase, "And now for something completely different." It was unlike anything audiences on both continents had ever seen before. Their unique brand of humor ranged from the absurdist ("Spam, Spam, Eggs, Spam") to the sometimes shocking ("The Prejudice Game") to the downright silly ("The Lumberjack Song"). The show was smart, original, and hyperconscious about the fact that it was a sketch comedy show, often reminding the audience by calling attention to a sketch's lack of an ending or a punch line. The show was also media conscious. One of its favorite targets was television and the BBC in particular with spoofs of the news, talk shows, game shows, and children's programming. The Pythoners also hated pretension and enjoyed poking fun at the upper class (especially Britain's "twit" population).

Two Pythoners, Eric Idle and Michael Palin, made regular appearances on *SNL*. Lorne Michaels served as executive producer on Idle's mockumentary of the Beatles, *The Rutles: All You Need Is Cash*, which was codirected by *SNL* filmmaker Gary Weis and featured Bill Murray, Gilda Radner, John Belushi, Dan Aykroyd, and Franken and Davis in bit roles. The special aired in prime time on March 22, 1978.

John Cleese never hosted, but he did make an appearance alongside Palin to explain *SNL*'s new sketch ratings system and to recreate the famous "Dead Parrot" sketch (22.10). In *Autobiography of the Pythons*, Cleese recognized the influence Python had on American television. "In America," Cleese observed, "of course, *Saturday Night Live* was influenced by it in a very positive way, in fact what was so funny was that kids who watched *Saturday Night Live* and then watched *Python* thought that we'd stolen from *Saturday Night Live*."

## The Great American Dream Machine (1971–1972)

Public broadcasting in the United States during the 1970s conjures up images of British costume dramas, Big Bird, science and nature documentaries, and roundtable discussions on the state of the world. But amid all the programming aimed to expand our minds, NET (National Education Television), the predecessor of PBS (Public Broadcasting Service), briefly ventured into original comedy programming with the innovative series *The Great American Dream Machine*. The show, which ran from October 1971 through February 1972, had no host, and each episode was comprised of twelve to twenty segments of various lengths in the form of comedy sketches, documentary shorts, musical performances, dramatic readings, play excerpts, and social and political commentary on different aspects of American life. Some episodes revolved around a specific theme, like death, war, and attaining success in America. Authors Kurt Vonnegut and Studs Terkel provided social commentary, and humorist Marshall Efron offered his perspective on American consumerism. There were musical performances by pianist Eubie Blake, singer Joan Baez, Broadway star Elaine Stritch (singing "Ladies Who Lunch" from the musical *Company*), Carly Simon (singing her hit single "That's the Way I've Always Heard It Should Be"), and Don McLean. Writer/director Ken Shapiro (*The Groove Tube* [1974]) and two future *SNL*ers, Chevy Chase and Albert Brooks, appeared in comedy segments.

The critics praised the show. *Time* magazine's Richard Burgheim dubbed *Great American Dream Machine* an "ambitious series . . . [that] combines elements of the CBS newsmagazine *60 Minutes* and NBC's *Laugh-In*, with a useful admixture of iconoclasm." Fred Ferretti began his review for the *New York Times* with a declaration: "Television, real television, came at last to television last night in *The Great American Dream Machine*. It's been a long time coming."

The response from the White House was less than enthusiastic. In an interview with the Archive of American Television, director Don Mischer claimed the Nixon administration, which did not appreciate that public money was funding a show that was critical of the president and his policies, was responsible for the show's cancellation: "We were a thorn in the establishment's side. We were always raising issues that questioned decisions made by the administration. Nixon had a man named Clay Whitehead, who was director of communications at the White House. And at that time public television had quite a bit of government funding. And if we made fun of Nixon or made fun of one of his policies, or whatever, the more we did that—but we were fairly balanced, we were not like just Democratic vs. Republican, we kind of made fun of everybody. . . . They just got so upset they put so much pressure on them [NET], that they had to take them off the air."

# One Samurai, Two Wild and Crazy Guys, and Three Coneheads

## SNL in the 1970s (1975–1980), Seasons 1–5

Seasons 1–5 of *SNL* showcased a menagerie of off-the-wall characters, ranging from a family of aliens, to a pair of Czech wannabe playboys, to a couple of teenage nerds. When a certain character clicked with the audience, he or she was certain to become a permanent part of the show's repertoire of recurring characters. Here are the most memorable characters, sketches, and moments from seasons 1–5. In the case of recurring characters, the number in parentheses indicates the episode in which he or she debuted.

### Land Shark: "Candygram" (1.4)

Nineteen seventy-five was the year of the shark due to the release of director Steven Spielberg's *Jaws*, which became Hollywood's first summer blockbuster, earning over $100 million by mid-August and becoming the biggest moneymaker of all time. In season 1, *SNL* first parodied *Jaws* (1.4) with a sketch (titled *Jaws II*) in which a "land shark" (Chevy Chase) knocks on the apartment doors of young, unsuspecting single females as the *Jaws* theme plays in the background. When they ask who it is, the shark mumbles a series of answers in a low tone ("Plumber" . . . "Flowers" . . . "Candygram"). The land shark made subsequent appearances, including a visit to host Louise Lasser's dressing room door when she won't come out (1.23), on Halloween night posing as a trick-or-treater (2.6), at the door of *The Spirit of St. Louis* when Charles Lindbergh (Buck Henry) gets too close to the water during his transatlantic flight to Paris (2.22), in the middle of a sketch that had no ending when Chase returned as host (3.11), at a woman's door via a video monitor (when Chase hosted from Burbank) (8.1), and on the set of *Weekend Update* where he eats Tina Fey (27.2).

## Emily Litella: "Never mind." (1.5)

In her memoir, *It's Always Something*, Gilda Radner revealed that Emily Litella was based on Mrs. Elizabeth Clementine Gillies (affectionately known as Dibby), who was her nanny for eighteen years. Throughout her life, Radner stayed in touch with Dibby, who, in March 1989, two months before Radner died of cancer, turned ninety-six years old.

Emily Litella debuted on *SNL* (1.5) as a guest on a talk show, *Looks at Books*, hosted by Jane Curtin. She is there to discuss her new book, *Tiny Kingdom*, which is part of her "Tiny Book" series. Two shows later (1.7), she delivers her first editorial reply on *Weekend Update*, speaking out against "*busting* schoolchildren" (as opposed to "busing schoolchildren"). Once anchorman Chevy Chase (or as Emily called him, "Cheddar Cheese") corrected her and she realized her mistake, she smiled into the camera and simply said, "Never mind." Jane Curtin (or as Emily called her, "Miss Clayton'), who anchored *Weekend Update* when Chase departs the show, is far less patient with Litella, who, after apologizing profusely, utters one final word—"Bitch." Playing the role of the serious newscaster, "Miss Clayton" eventually demotes Emily to appearing as a dancing red and blue "N" (the current NBC logo) (3.8), though she returned to *Weekend Update* when "Cheddar" came back to guest anchor the news (3.11).

From the death penalty to the environment to television violence, Miss Litella came close to addressing some of the more important national and international issues of the 1970s:

### "What is all this fuss I've been hearing about . . ."

- "Busting" (busing) schoolchildren (1.7)
- "Firing" (hiring) the handicapped (1.8)
- "Saving Soviet 'jewelry'" (Jewry) (1.11)
- "Eagle" (Equal) Rights Amendment (1.12)
- "Canker" (Cancer) research (1.13)
- The "deaf" (death) penalty (1.15)
- Preserving natural "race horses" (resources) (1.16)
- The 1976 presidential "erection" (election) (1.17)
- "Violins" (violence) on television (1.19)
- "Crustaceans" (Croatians) hijacking a plane (2.1)
- Collecting money for "unisex" (UNICEF) (2.10)
- Making Puerto Rico a "steak" (state) (2.11)
- Endangered "feces" (species) (2.15)
- The "Sssssst" (SST—Super Sonic Transport) (3.8)

When actress Ruth Gordon hosted the show (2.12), she appeared as Emily's equally eccentric sister, Essie Litella, who suggested burning tissues [issues] for Emily's next editorial: "transcendental medication [meditation]" and equipping cars with "air fags [bags]."

## "Word Association Test" (1.7)

The most memorable sketch of the early days of *SNL* was not written by a member of the writing staff but comedian Paul Mooney, who wrote for guest host Richard Pryor. It involves a human resources interviewer (Chevy Chase) giving a word association test to a job applicant for a janitor position (Pryor). The test starts off with word pairs one would expect on such a test. Chase says "fast" and Pryor says "slow." But the test takes an unexpected turn when Chase begins to spout a series of racial epithets like "tarbaby," "colored," "jungle bunny," "spade," until he gets to the word "nigger" (which he says). For every epithet, Pryor throws back white slurs like "redneck," "cracker," and "honky." The sketch delivers a powerful statement on institutionalized racism, something Mooney revealed in his autobiography, *Black Is the New White*, that he experienced during his week at *SNL* when he was cross-examined all week regarding his qualifications to write for the show.

As for Pryor, his manager's advice not to accept a position as a rotating host on *SNL* was right on the money in light of the treatment he received from the network when he was given his own show after his successful appearance on *SNL*. *The Richard Pryor Show* (1977) was canceled after four episodes over creative differences between its star and the network, which is a polite way of saying standards and practices wouldn't allow his material on the air.

## Samurai Futaba: "And now, another episode of Samurai [*fill in profession here*]." (1.7)

In addition to his rants on *Weekend Update*, John Belushi was given the chance to let loose by inhabiting the body of a Japanese samurai, one of the elite warriors who served the feudal lords of preindustrial Japan. The samurai practiced a strict code of conduct known as *Bushido* ("the way of the warrior") that valued chivalry, loyalty, and honor. A samurai who was dishonorable, or may have brought shame upon himself, or would rather die with honor than fall into enemy hands performed a form of ritual suicide known as *seppuku* or *hara-kiri* by sticking a sharp blade in his abdomen. The samurai was popularized by Japanese cinema, particularly in the films of director Akira Kurosawa such as *Seven Samurai* (1954), *Throne of Blood* (1957), and *Yojimbo* (1961), all of which starred Toshiro Mifune.

According to Judith Belushi Pisano, Mifune was the inspiration for her husband's Samurai Futaba character. She told Michael Streeter, author of *Nothing Lasts Forever: The Films of Tom Schiller*, that John started to imitate Mifune after watching a Japanese film festival on television. "John would sit so close to the television," Belushi Pisano recalled, "that when there was a close-up of Mifune, it appeared as if he was looking in a mirror—John would reflect what he saw." She gave him a robe, a rubber band to put his hair up, and a clothes bar from a closet to use as a sword. Belushi auditioned for the show with the samurai character playing pool, which is how writer Tom Schiller got the idea of "Samurai Hotelier." Lorne Michaels, who worked on the sketch with Schiller, Chevy Chase, and Alan Zweibel, thought some people wouldn't know what a "hotelier" is, so they changed the title of the sketch to "Samurai Hotel." Zweibel wrote the remaining sketches, though Schiller provided him with a list of possible occupations for Samurai Futaba.

Each sketch works off the same premise: Samurai Futaba, who is dressed in traditional samurai garb and has a limited understanding of the English language, has a different profession that's incongruous with being a samurai warrior. In his sketch debut (1.7), Samurai Futaba faces off with a bellboy samurai (host Richard Pryor) over who is going to take a guest's (Chase) bag up to his room. Belushi enjoys playing with his sword, using it to mime a golf putter and, like his audition, a pool cue. After some swordplay, Futaba insults the bellboy with the Japanese version of the traditional maternal insult ("Your momma-san"). The bellboy reacts by splitting the front desk in two with his sword. Samurai Futaba responds with the only English words we ever hear him speak—"I can dig where you're comin' from . . ."—as he takes the guest's bag up to his room.

From season 1 to his final episode in season 4, Belushi repeated the role in a series of sketches featuring Buck Henry or another guest host as his customer or patient, who seems oblivious to the fact he's a samurai as he engages in small

"Samurai Tailor": John Belushi's Samurai Futaba was inspired by repeated viewings of Japanese director Akira Kurosawa's samurai drama *Sanjuro* (1962), starring Toshiro Mifune. But instead of fighting corruption, Samurai Tailor Futaba uses his sword to make adjustments to his customer's (Buck Henry) suit.

talk, which Futaba at times seems to understand. Belushi comically responds with grunts and Japanese gibberish, along with the raising of his bushy eyebrows and his sword. When the customer is displeased, Futaba kneels on the floor and pulls out his sword as if he is about to commit *hara-kiri* (at that point the customer usually assures him it's all right). The sketch ends with Futaba raising his sword—with a freeze-frame and Don Pardo inviting us to "Tune in next week, for another episode of Samurai _____." Some of the later episodes include:

- **"Samurai Delicatessen"** (1.10): When Henry orders a sandwich, Futaba is happy to cut it in half.
- **"Samurai Psychiatrist"** (3.6): When Henry calls him a quack, Samurai Futaba threatens to kill himself—and does.
- **"Samurai TV Repairman"** (3.20): Henry needs his television fixed to watch the basketball playoffs tomorrow. Futaba is ready to kill himself with a dagger because the person who inspected the defective machine, Inspector #68, is his momma-san. Futaba is relieved when Henry discovers the tag was upside down—it was Inspector #89.
- **"Samurai Optometrist"** (4.5): Henry breaks his glasses on a Sunday and needs a new pair. Futaba reaches for his sword when Henry calls him an optician instead of an optometrist.
- **"Samurai Bakery"** (4.20): Best man Henry needs a last-minute wedding for his brother's wedding.

In "Samurai Stockbroker" (2.6), Belushi accidentally cut Henry's forehead with the sword. Henry seems a bit dazed, but he continues the sketch by jumping out the window as if he is committing suicide. The next time we see Henry, he's the moderator in a '76 debate sketch between Jimmy Carter (Aykroyd) and President Ford (Chevy Chase), which is conducted like a beauty contest. Henry has a large bandage on his head—as does Chase when he comes out, and later Jane Curtin on *Weekend Update*. In Belushi Pisano and Colby's biography of Belushi, Henry said he found it ironic that Belushi's doctor happened to be in the audience. By the end of the show, almost everyone has a Band-Aid or bandage on his or her head (even Belushi).

Samurai Futaba also makes appearances during musical performances by Gordon Lightfoot (1.21) and Frank Zappa (2.10). Perhaps Samurai Futaba's oddest and most unexpected appearance was in the pages of a *Marvel Team-Up* series comic book (#74) featuring Spider-Man and the Not Ready for Prime Time Players! vs. Silver Samurai. It's set in Studio 8-H during a broadcast of *SNL* with Spider-Man creator Stan Lee as the guest host and Peter Parker and Mary Jane Watson in the audience.

## Godfather Group Therapy (I.9)

Participants in group therapy share their problems and feelings with each other in a "safe" environment under the supervision of a licensed therapist (played here by Elliott Gould). This group includes two people who live in very different worlds: *The Godfather*'s Vito Corleone (John Belushi, channeling Marlon Brando) and Sherry (one of Laraine Newman's few signature characters), a girl from the San Fernando Valley who really loves being a stewardess "'cause she loves people." When Vito starts talking about the grief the Tattaglia family is causing him, Sherry accuses him of blocking his true feelings and the group gets him to act them out, which he does—and performs Corleone's heart attack at the end of the film. Belushi appeared again as Brando in a parody of *The Godfather* (3.5) and alongside another Brando imitator, host Peter Boyle. As the "Dueling Brandos," they recite the actor's most memorable lines from his movies (1.13).

## Baba Wawa: "Not for Wadies Only" (1.18)

Gilda Radner's imitation of Barbara Walters, better known as Baba Wawa, was first performed onstage in *The National Lampoon Show*. At the time, Walters was the host of a daily morning show, *Not for Women Only* (1968–1979), and Radner would watch the show before going to rehearsals. During a 1976 appearance with Lorne Michaels on a Canadian talk show, *90 Minutes Live*, she told host Peter Gzowski that she noticed how she and Walters have "the same speech impediment and then all we had to do was change the L's and R's to W's." Radner perfected her impersonation with some help from some of the hair and makeup people at *SNL* who worked with Walters and told her "how to sit and all those secret things."

In *Gilda: An Intimate Portrait*, biographer and friend David Saltman described the awkward first meeting between Gilda and Walters at a cocktail party in November 1976 at the Canadian consulate in honor of the Bicentennial. Gilda was nervous about meeting Walters, who seemed not to recognize Radner or her name. The comedian explained that she imitated her on *Saturday Night*. Walters said she had never seen it, but then said, "Oh, yeah, that's right. Someone told me about that—that someone did an imitation of me."

Walters proceeded to draw Radner into another room and asked her to do her imitation. She did and Walters responded, "I don't see what so funny about it." Radner managed to get a laugh out of her when she explained how she changed the L's and R's to W's. Radner was still upset by the exchange and was worried she had perhaps damaged Walters's credibility. David F. Smith, the former consul who introduced the two, later told Saltman, "Gilda . . . [was] so young and unworldly back then. Gilda was trying so hard to be kind. Barbara Walters did not have to be so cold, so rude to her." "It was one of the few times Gilda, with her winning way," observes Saltman, "did not bring out the best in people."

Apparently the awkward meeting didn't deter Gilda from imitating Walters. Baba Wawa made her *SNL* debut in April 1976 (1.18) with an appearance on *Weekend Update* to explain that she didn't leave NBC for ABC because of her $5 million deal, but because of "Tom Snyduh. I simpwy cannot see his eahs" (1.18). Her later appearances were interviews with people from politics and entertainment, including "wiving wegend" Mahwena Dietrich [Marlena Dietrich] (Madeline Kahn) (1.19), Italian director Wena Wertmuller [Lina Wertmüller] (Laraine Newman) (1.21), Indian prime minister Indiwa Gandhi [Indira Gandhi] (Laraine Newman) (2.4), First Wadies Betty Fowd [Betty Ford] (Jane Curtin) and Woslyn Cawter [Rosalynn Carter] (Laraine Newman) (2.6), Henwe Kissingew [Henry Kissinger] (John Belushi) (2.8), Wichard Buwton [Richard Burton] (Bill Murray), (2.21), and Godziwa [Godzilla] (John Belushi) (2.16). Baba Wawa also appeared in a parody of *My Fair Lady*, in which Henry Higgins (Christopher Lee) and Colonel Pickering (Dan Aykroyd) try to help her with her R's.

## Super Bass-O-Matic '76: "Wow, that's terrific bass!" (1.17)

Dan Aykroyd played the perfect fast-talking television pitchman, who, in this in-studio commercial for a kitchen appliance known as the Super Bass-O-Matic '76 demonstrates how you can prepare a bass "with no fish waste, and without scaling, cutting, or gutting." You just put the whole bass (that's right, the whole bass!) into what looks like an ordinary blender and turn it on. Then pour it into a glass like a milkshake. The Super-Bass-O-Matic '76 also comes with ten interchangeable rotors, a nine-month guarantee, and a booklet, *1,001 Ways to Harness Bass*. It also "works great on sunfish, perch, sole, and other small aquatic creatures."

As one satisfied customer (Laraine Newman) attests, "Wow, that's terrific bass!"

On the season 2 Halloween show, Aykroyd did a commercial for Bat-O-Matic (2.6). It's the perfect alternative to a mortar, pestle, or cauldron because it can cut, chop, slice, dice, mix, and blend anything, including plants, herbs, skin, hair, limbs and organs of all kind, and toads, lizards, newts, mice, rats, and bats!

As one bat lover attests, "Wow! That's great bat! And a great potion, too. I'm in love and my hives are cured!"

## The Last Voyage of the Starship *Enterprise* (1.22)

*SNL* takes another jab at NBC in this popular and, for the time, ambitious, hilarious parody of *Star Trek* in which NBC executive Herb Goodman (Elliott Gould) comes aboard the Starship *Enterprise* and announces to the cast that they have been canceled due to poor Nielsen ratings (Mr. Spock [Chevy Chase] defines the Nielsens as a "primitive system of estimating television viewers once used in the mid-twentieth century"). When everyone admits that they have been defeated (even Mr. Spock gets emotional), Captain Kirk/William Shatner (John Belushi) refuses to abandon his ship and is left sitting alone on the dismantled set when he makes his final entry in his Captain's captain's log: "We have tried to explore strange new worlds, to seek out civilizations, to boldly go where no man has gone before. And except for one television network, we have found intelligent life everywhere in the galaxy. [He gives the Vulcan salute.] Live long and prosper. Promise. Captain James T. Kirk, SC 937-0176 CEC."

The *Saturday Night Live* book published in 1977 includes a letter from *Star Trek* creator Gene Roddenberry to Elliott Gould, telling him that the sketch was "delicious": "That is the proper word for it—imaginatively conceived and ably carried out with the kind of loose good humor that an entertaining parody demands."

## "The Right to Extreme Stupidity League" (2.10)

There's nothing like live television—especially when a simple line flub can make a funny sketch even funnier. In this PSA for "The Right to Extreme Stupidity League," two friends—Fern (Candice Bergen), the smart one, and Lisa (Radner), the stupid one—defend every American's God-given right to be stupid. Lisa uses the expression "I'm so thirsty I could drink a horse" and pours her milk inside of her purse and says she is still thirsty. When Fern observes that she's not too bright, she inadvertently calls Lisa by her name ("Fern . . . or whatever your name is"). Lisa then admits she is extremely stupid and proud of it. "You know," tells the camera, "we all can't be brainy like Fern here. . . ." Bergen can't stop laughing (and neither can we). The flub, Bergen's "deer-in-headlights" reaction to what she just said, and the way Gilda improvises around it without missing a beat, reminds us what we love most about live television.

## The Coneheads: "We're from France!" (2.11)

Created by Dan Aykroyd and Tom Davis, the Coneheads were inspired by the giant head statues carved from rock (better known as *moai*) that they saw on their holiday vacation to Easter Island. When Davis and Aykroyd returned to work in January, they wrote a sketch that eventually evolved into the Coneheads. In a 1978 Q&A with Franken and Davis, "Saturday Night Writers Strive for 'Bad Taste,'" Davis credits Lorne Michaels with the idea of having Beldar Conehead (Aykroyd), his wife Prymaat (Jane Curtin), and their daughter Connie (Laraine Newman) live in suburbia (Parkwood, New Jersey, to be exact).

The Coneheads were an instant hit when they first appeared on the show (2.11). In "The Coneheads at Home," Beldar and Prymaat explain to their teenage daughter Connie that twenty years ago the five high Masters of Remulak dispatched a fleet of Starcruisers to the earth's solar system. They were instructed to land on Earth, take control of all the major radio and television communication centers, and introduce themselves: "People of Earth, we are the timekeepers of the planet Remulak. Your weapons are useless against us." But Beldar lost the rest of the speech (containing the instructions, times, dates, places, and orders for the UN), and their flying saucer ended up in the bottom of Lake Michigan.

So they bought a house in Parkwood, New Jersey (2130 Pineway Drive), changed their names to Fred and Joyce Conehead, and tell people they're from France. Beldar now works as a driving school instructor. But the Coneheads sometimes had trouble concealing that they were from another planet, which is why they scare off an IRS agent (Steve Martin) (2.14) and run in horror themselves from their next-door neighbors' house, the Farbers', at the sight of a hairdryer (2.17).

The humor in the Coneheads sketches lies in how no one seems to notice they are not from this world coupled with their inability to fully assimilate, which is evident by the names they give to objects used by humans (a vacuum cleaner is a "particle collector," the kitchen is a "food preparation chamber") and the foods we consume like bacon and eggs ("shredded swine flesh and fried chicken embryos") and pizza ("starch disks with vegetable matter and lactate extract of hoofed mammals"). Still, they somehow manage to win on *Family Feud* (3.9).

The Coneheads were also featured in *Cone Encounters of the Third Kind*, a parody of *Close Encounters* (1977) with host Richard Dreyfuss playing Roy Neary (his role in the film). Neary constructs a cone-shaped object, which leads him to the Coneheads' house and then on to Remulak with the High Master (John Belushi).

Fourteen years after their debut on *SNL*, the Coneheads landed on the big screen with Aykroyd and Curtin reprising their roles as Beldar and Prymaat (see chapter 26).

The Coneheads are contestants on a parody of *Family Feud* hosted by Richard Dawson (Bill Murray, left), who welcomes (left to right), Beldar (Dan Aykroyd), his wife Prymatt (Jane Curtin), and their daughter Connie (Laraine Newman).

One Samurai, Two Wild and Crazy Guys, and Three Coneheads        63

## Mardi Gras Prime-Time Special: "Mardi Gras is just a French word meaning 'No Parade.'" (2/20/77)

At the start of the second season, Lorne Michaels announced that he would be taking *SNL* on the road and broadcast from Princeton University on October 16, 1975, and Georgetown University's gymnasium two weeks later on Saturday, October 30, 1976, two days before the November 2 presidential election. "This will be our last chance to influence the November 2 election," Michaels told Tom Zito of the *Washington Post*, "Basically our audience is college anyway, so the decision was made to try some shows on the road that rely on new video techniques—mini-cameras and a lot of hand-held stuff." Less than two weeks later, the *Post* reported that all remote broadcasts from college campuses were called off. The unofficial reason was "technical problems," though costs were most likely a factor.

The following February, Michaels did take his show on the road to New Orleans for a live, prime-time special from Mardi Gras, which aired on NBC on Sunday, February 20, 1977. The episode opened with Dan Aykroyd as President Jimmy Carter sitting on the top of a statue of Andrew Jackson in Jackson Square while First Lady Rosalynn Carter (Laraine Newman) stands below begging the president to come down. The segments that followed, shot both inside and outside at various locations around the city, featured musical performances by Randy Newman ("Louisiana 1927" and "Marie") and the New Leviathan Oriental Fox Trot Orchestra ("Rebecca Came Back from Mecca") from the Theatre of the Performing Arts; *Laverne and Shirley* stars Penny Marshall and Cindy Williams reporting from the Krewe of Apollo drag ball; Eric Idle reporting on the crowd's reaction to the festivities from an empty café; two films by Gary Weis, and comedy bits by Radner as Emily Litella and Baba Wawa, who interviews this year's King of Bacchus, Henry Winkler; Aykroyd as Tom Snyder; John Belushi as Marlon Brando as Stanley Kowalski in *A Streetcar Named Desire*; and Paul Shaffer singing "The Antler Dance" while Mr. Mike shows the crowd how it's done. Surprisingly (or maybe not), Garrett Morris, a New Orleans native, received minimal airtime. He hoped Gary Weis would shoot a segment in which he sang a song he had written, "Walking Down Bourbon Street," about returning to his hometown, but it was never shot. Still, Morris was a hospitable host; the cast and crew were all invited over to his Aunt Audrey's house for dinner.

The Mardi Gras episode was a great idea in theory, but as Lorne Michaels recounted to Mark Lorando in a 2008 article for the New Orleans newspaper the *Times-Picayune*, logistical difficulties, particularly with millions of drunken revelers in the streets, caused transportation problems that prevented everyone getting to and from where they needed to be.

But perhaps the biggest snafu was the last-minute rerouting of the Bacchus Parade due to an emergency on the route, leaving Buck Henry and Jane Curtin, who were sitting above the crowd at Canal Street and St. Charles Avenue, ready to provide the commentary as the parade went by, with nothing to do. Michaels considered them the show's safety net. If a sketch wasn't ready to start, they could always cut back to Henry and Curtin, which they did anyway. The pair were seated on the top of shaky scaffolding, and the revelers down below were hurling beads, doubloons, and bottles at them. "We had a writer, we had a sound guy, and we had a camera man, and we had a production assistant," Curtin told Lorando, "and we had no security. So getting down off the scaffolding was almost as much fun as being on the scaffolding. They had to call in retired detectives ... a lovely older gentleman came and literally carried Buck and me through the crowd. It was terrifying. Just terrifying. *The Day of the Locust.* And everybody chanting your name. It was scary." Curtin did manage to deliver the evening's punch line before the credits rolled: "The parade has not been delayed. It doesn't exist. It never did. 'Mardi Gras' is just a French word meaning 'No parade.' Good night."

With the exception of Newman and the New Leviathan Orchestra, who were far from the chaos outside, the show's entertainment value had less to do with its comedic content and more to do with the fact it was live and you really didn't know what was going to happen. There was the occasional technical mistake when the show was broadcast on its home turn in Studio 8H, but these tended to be very isolated moments. In this instance, the whole entire show felt like you were watching a powder keg that could blow at any minute.

The following day, the *Times-Picayune*'s Sandra Barbier reported that both the newspaper and the local NBC affiliate, WDSU, received phone calls complaining about the episode. "Everyone was expecting so much, it was a disappointment," observed one New Orleans native. "People in other parts of the country probably didn't understand what it was all about." One caller to the *Times-Picayune* sounded more like a New Yorker than a Southern when she told the paper "NBC raped New Orleans."

## Leonard Pinth-Garnell: "That really bit it!" (2.15)

So-called high culture was skewered in a series of sketches that featured really bad plays, musicals, films, and short performance pieces. Our host is tuxedo-clad Leonard Pinth-Garnell (Dan Aykroyd), who introduces the evening's presentation and assures us that what we are about to see is "Stunningly bad!" Bill Murray, featured as a regular player in each piece, is introduced as "our very own, Ronnie Bateman." Pinth-Garnell usually ends each episode with his one-line review, an introduction of the players, and, finally, the ceremonial tossing of his program into the garbage can. Some of the exceptionably bad performances include:

- *Bad Playhouse* presents *The Millkeeper* (2.15) by Dutch writer, Jan Worstraad ("one of the worst of the new breed of bad Dutch playwrights of the Piet Hein School")

    The scene depicts the inner torment of a bride who lives in a windmill with her husband and sister, who is the literally in the clutches of Death (played by Ronnie Bateman [Murray]).

One Samurai, Two Wild and Crazy Guys, and Three Coneheads   65

- *Bad Cinema* presents *Ooh-la-la! Les Legs* (2.18) by Henri Heimeau

    Pinth-Garnell assembles a distinguished panel that includes Italian director Lina Wertmüller (Newman) and Truman Capote (Murray) to comment on this terrible film that consists of footage of a couple doing the twist in the streets of Paris. At the start of the sketch, Aykroyd appears to be looking around for Newman, who arrives late for the sketch and apologizes (in character).

- *Bad Opera: Die Goldenklang* (The Golden Note) by Friedrich Knabel (3.2)

    A maiden named Mazda (host Madeline Kahn) is chosen by the gods to sing the golden note, which, if she sings, she will die. The opera is seldom performed because once Mazda reaches the "Golden Note," she gets larynx lock (she sings the note forever), and must be taken away by the paramedics.

- *Bad Musical: Leeuwenhoek* by Hans Van der Scheinen (3.7)

    Performed by the service staff of the Glendale Hospital for Wrist Disorders, this awful old-fashioned musical is about Antonie Philips van Leeuwenhoek (Pinth-Garnell refers to him as "Frederic Leeuwenhoek"), the Dutch scientist (played by Belushi) who contributed to the development of the compound microscope. The show originally ran "very Off-Broadway" in 1953 and closed in two and a half minutes.

- *Bad Conceptual Art: Pavlov Video Chicken I* by Helen Trouva (3.20)

    A 378-hour conceptual piece first performed in 1965 at the Lifespace Galleries in Los Angeles. Written by and featuring Helen Trouva, it juxtaposes Zen poetry on video (a close-up of Newman's lips as she recites poetry) and a woman (Radner, as Trouva) dancing like a chicken for 378 consecutive hours. There is a close-up of an eye (of Garrett Morris) on a second video screen. "Stunningly pointless," Pinth-Garnell concludes. "Absolutely no meaning whatsoever. Really sucks."

Twenty-nine years later, Leonard Pinth-Garnell (Aykroyd) returned to Studio 8H to present a new installment of *Bad Conceptual Theatre,* written by a group of chimpanzees. Anyone familiar with the *Bad* series got the joke when Chris Kattan was introduced as Ronnie Bateman Jr.

## Nick the Lounge Singer: "Ah . . . *Star Wars!* Nothing but *Star Wars!*" (2.19)

Bill Murray revived a character from his Second City days, an untalented singer named Nick who performed in out-of-the-way, hole-in-the-wall lounges. Nick overcompensates for his lack of talent by trying to make each song his own by doing his variations of the lyrics to songs or inventing lyrics to movie theme songs with no lyrics.

Nick's last name also changes with every sketch depending on the season and/or the venue. Here are some of his most memorable gigs:

- **Nick Summers** (2.19), from the Zephyr Room, at the beautiful Breezy Point Lodge at Lake Minnehonka, sings "I Write the Songs," "Happy Anniversary" (to Mr. and Mrs. Gunnar Alquist [John Belushi and Gilda Radner] from Fond du Lac, Wisconsin), and "Sing."
- **Nick Winters** (3.10), from the Powder Room, at a ski lodge on beautiful Meatloaf Mountain, sings the themes to *2001: A Space Odyssey* and *Star Wars*, "Don't It Make My Brown Eyes Blue," and "That the Way (I Like It)."
- **Nick Springs** (3.19), from the Honeymoon Room at the Pocomount resort sings "Love to Love You Baby," "Poison Ivy," "Hava Nagilah," and the "Theme from *Close Encounters of the Third Kind*."

## American Dope Growers Union: "Look for the union label" (2.20)

Founded in 1900 in New York City, the International Ladies Garment Workers Union (ILGWU) was one of the country's largest labor unions and the first to be comprised of a majority of female members. In the 1970s, the ILGWU released an ad campaign in which its members sing "Look for the Union Label," a song that urges consumers to buy American at a time when manufacturing jobs were being lost to shops overseas. The commercials featured actual members of the ILGWU, mostly female and of all ages and races, who would come together and sing the song as an expression of solidarity.

In 1977, while the ILGWU commercials were airing, *Saturday Night Live* did their own version in support of another union that suffers whenever someone buys foreign over American-made. A representative of the American Dope Growers Union (Laraine Newman) tells us that every time you buy pot from Mexico or Colombia, you are putting an American out of work. "We have had a pretty hard time on our own," she says, "but with the union we can lead decent lives and stay off welfare. That's MY union, and that's what our union label stands for." She holds up a bag of pot with the Union's sticker on it and begins to sing. She is soon joined by an enthusiastic group of pot growers (played by the cast members, members of the writing staff, and assorted extras). They begin to sing: "So look for, the Union label, when you are buying your joint, lid or pound."

This is an example of what certain critics like to refer to as "drug humor." After all, this was the 1970s, and most of the cast, the writers, and everyone else associated with the show both above and below the line, along with the audience were getting stoned (probably before, certainly during, and most likely after the show). As Hill and Weingrad so eloquently put it, "The image of a bunch of heads on *Saturday Night Live* putting together a show for the heads out there in TV land was definitely a large part of the show's appeal. *Saturday Night* became in many respects, a passing of the communal joint around a circle that spanned, through television, the entire country."

The comic bits about dope (mostly marijuana as cocaine would not become the drug of choice until the 1980s) were common, yet they never really

One Samurai, Two Wild and Crazy Guys, and Three Coneheads

dominated the show's humor. The basic joke was that drugs were prevalent backstage. During host Eric Idle's monologue (4.8), he wanders backstage to the writer's lounge where sitar music is playing and the writers are either unconscious or smoking a hookah. John Belushi, who is at the center of most of the jokes, gives an editorial on *Weekend Update* (3.1) about the decriminalization of marijuana. He returns from Durango, Mexico, where he awarded a $2,500 scholarship on behalf of *Weekend Update* to a young aspiring journalist who is illiterate—but has some good connections (3.1). In another sketch, Belushi, dressed in a Cub Scout uniform, sits with host Minnesota Vikings quarterback Fran Tarkenton (2.13), who does a PSA for "Community Appeal," which is helping unfortunates like John whose mind has been destroyed by drugs. Belushi later shares one of his killer joints with the "Anyone Can Host" contest winner, eighty-year-old Miskel Spillman (he told her it was a French cigarette) (3.8). When she appears onstage for her monologue, she's flying and clutching a bowl of fruit from her dressing room.

## The Festrunk Brothers: "Two wild and crazy guys." (3.1)

Dan Aykroyd paired up with Steve Martin for a series of sketches in which they played the Festrunk Brothers from Czechoslovakia, from which, as Georg (Martin) explains it in their debut (3.1), he and his brother Yortuk (Aykroyd) escaped "during the '75 riots, by throwing many rocks at a Russian tank." "A Wild and Crazy Guy," was one of Steve Martin's popular catchphrases and the title of his 1978 Grammy Award–winning comedy album. According to writer Marilyn Suzanne Miller's bio for the Paley Center for Media (she was honored, along with Anne Beatts and Rosie Shuster, as part of their "She Made It: Women Creating Television and Radio" series), Aykroyd was inspired by Martin's catchphrase and collaborated with her to create this pair who had successful careers back at home (Georg claims they had medical degrees) and were now selling decorative bathroom fixtures. The joke is that they are totally clueless when it comes to attracting American women (sorry, American "foxes") because they look so ridiculous in their mismatched tight plaid shirts and slacks ("which give us great bulges!") and the way they toss around American expressions like "You and what army?"

In his book Saturday Night Live: *Equal Opportunity Offender*, William Clotworthy, who worked for NBC's Broadcast Standards Department, recalled that NBC received a letter from a Czechoslovakian special-interest group who "were very displeased and insulted by the presentation of two men as being refugees from Czechoslovakia. These individuals were two characters of a very low capability, skill, and moral values. They did not know how to dress properly and how to behave. Their English was very poor and what was presented to the TV audience as the Czech language was nothing but a mockery of our native tongue." They demanded an apology and threatened to boycott the network. In their response, NBC explained that the Festrunk brothers "had never been recognized as insulting" and "the humor derived not from ethnicity but from their

"Two wild and crazy guys"—a catchphrase popularized by Yortuk (Dan Aykroyd) and Georg (Steve Martin), two brothers from Czechoslovakia who come on a little too strong when trying to pick up "American foxes" played by (left to right) Gilda Radner, Laraine Newman, and Jane Curtin.

unfamiliarity with American customs and slang. Thus the satire was directed at the *American* character; i.e. the male breast emphasis, sexual emphasis, and the like."

Twenty years after Georg and Yortuk were first seen swinging across their bachelor pad, the Festrunk Brothers appeared alongside the Roxbury Guys (Will Ferrell and Chris Kattan) (24.1), which coincided with the release of the feature film, *A Night at the Roxbury*. Their most recent appearance (38.16) was a game show parody, *It's a Date*, in which contestant Judy Peterman (Vanessa Bayer) had to choose between Bachelor #1 (Bobby Moynihan), an ordinary guy; the "Dick-in-a-Box" guys (Justin Timberlake and Andy Samberg); and Georg and Yortuk Festrunk (Steve Martin, Dan Aykroyd). She rejects Bachelor #1, but is charmed by the others and decides to choose all four of them.

## Things We Did Last Summer (10/28/78)

This odd collection of short documentaries (actually more like "mockumentaries") directed by Gary Weis and written by Don Novello shows us what the Not Ready for Prime Time Players did over their summer, including Gilda Radner giving tours of her apartment, the Blues Brothers (John Belushi and Dan Aykroyd) going on tour, Garrett Morris posing for lawn jockeys, Laraine Newman taking a tropical vacation, and Bill Murray playing minor-league baseball. The special is included on the *SNL* season 3 DVD set.

## Roseanne Roseannadanna: "It's always something!" (3.9)

Like Emily Litella, frizzy-haired Roseanne Roseannadanna did not make her *Saturday Night Live* debut on *Weekend Update* but in a "graveyard sketch" (the last sketch of the night)—a PSA for "Hiring the Incompetent" (3.4). Roseanne gives a short testimonial about how she was fired from her job making burgers at Burgerland because customers complained about human hair in the burgers ("What was I supposed to do, wear a bathin' cap to work? . . . Besides, there's a lot worst things that could be in burgers!")

Later that season, Roseanne Roseannadanna joined *Weekend Update* as a correspondent. She began each report with a letter, usually from Mr. Richard Feder from Fort Lee, New Jersey, who asked questions about UFOs ("Do you believe in UFOs? Have you ever seen a UFO?") (3.19), Studio 54 ("Why is it so hard to get in?") (4.1), quitting smoking ("I'm cranky and I have gas. What should I do?") (4.6), and depression over the holidays (". . . I feel like hell! What

"It's always something"—Roseanne Roseannadanna (Gilda Radner) is the direct opposite of most female newscasters, who Radner observed always looked like they were in fear of losing their job. She is uninhibited, and her reports always go off on tangents and focus on gross minutiae.

should I do?") (4.9). After making a crack about Mr. Feder and New Jersey ("Mr. Feder, you ask a lot of questions for someone from New Jersey!"), she answered the question by launching into a long diatribe that was completely off the topic and always included something disgusting, like warts and fever blisters (3.11) or toilet paper stuck to the bottom of Princess Lee Radziwill's shoe (4.9) or a wet spot on Yves St. Laurent's white pants (5.2). When an exasperated Jane Curtin tells her she's making her sick, Roseanne delivers her catchphrase: "Well, Jane, it goes to show you—it's always something."

Roseanne Roseannadanna's monologues were written by Alan Zweibel, who worked closely with Gilda Radner during their time together on the show. Mr. Richard Feder was also the name of Zweibel's brother-in-law, who did live in Fort Lee, New Jersey. At the time, many people believed Roseanne was named after a local ABC New York newscaster, Rose Ann Scamardella, who was nothing like Roseannadanna in her demeanor. But in his profile of Radner for *Rolling Stone*, Roy Blount Jr. said the comedian's name grew out of the rhyming song "The Name Game." As Radner explains it, Roseanne Roseannadanna was meant to counteract "all these women reporting the news on TV; they always look like they're so frightened to lose their job. You know they're saying, 'We're women

## Live from Studio 8H: The 1970s

Simon & Garfunkel (1.2) reunite to sing "The Boxer," "Scarborough Fair," and their new single, "My Little Town" ... America's favorite Cuban entertainer Desi Arnaz (1.14) appears in a parody of *I Love Lucy* and performed his signature songs, "Babalu" and "Cuban Pete." He closes the show by leading the cast in a conga line ... In a rare television appearance, Carly Simon (1.19) pretapes her performances of "Half a Chance" and "You're So Vain" ... In his first of six appearances, Simon's husband, James Taylor (2.1), sings "Shower the People" and "Sweet Baby James" ... A week before their farewell concert appearance, captured on film by director Martin Scorsese as *The Last Waltz*, The Band (2.6) performs "Life Is a Carnival," "The Night They Drove Old Dixie Down," "Stage Fright," and "Georgia" ... Ray Charles (3.5) sings "I Can See Clearly Now," "What I'd Say," "Oh! What a Beautiful Morning," and "I Can't Stop Loving You." Two years later he appears with Dan Aykroyd and John Belushi in *The Blues Brothers* (1980) ... Elvis Costello (3.8) is (temporarily) banned from *SNL* when he makes a last-minute change and sings "Radio, Radio" instead of "Less Than Zero" ... Long Island's favorite son Billy Joel (3.11) sings "Only the Good Die Young" and "Just the Way You Are" (1978 Grammy winner for "Record of the Year" and "Song of the Year") ... Rolling Stones host the season 4 opener (4.1) and perform "Beast of Burden," "Respectable," and "Shattered" ... Deadheads converge in Studio 8H to hear the Grateful Dead (4.5) perform "Casey Jones," "I Need a Miracle," and "Good Lovin'." They make a second appearance in season 5 (5.15) and perform "Alabama Getaway" and "Saint of Circumstances"... David Bowie (5.7) makes a fashion statement when he wears a skirt and sings "TVC-15."

and have credibility to report the news, we don't go number two, we don't fart' . . . And Roseanne, she's a *pig*."

The character is also the author of *Roseanne Roseannadanna's "Hey, Get Back to Work!" Book*, published in 1983 by Long Shadow Books. The preface to the book is one hundred pages long, and, like her reports on *Weekend Update*, it has nothing to do with the topic suggested by the title. Instead, it's filled with personal information and stories of her family history. By the time she's ready to discuss how to get, keep, lose, and get back the job you lost, she's run out of pages. A letter from her publisher appears on page 11 in which he explains that due to "rising production costs" it would be "financially impractical" to allow her book to go beyond one hundred pages. "As disappointed as I am," he adds, "I can't help but feel that had more thought been given to the body of the book than to the compelling, yet indulgent, preface, this situation would have never arisen."

As Roseanne Roseannadanna would say, "It's always something."

## Lisa Loopner and Todd DiLaMuca: "Noogie Patrol" (3.10)

If you felt like a nerd, were called a nerd, or were a nerd in high school, you probably felt a little better about yourself when you first laid eyes on Lisa Loopner (Gilda Radner) and Todd DiLaMuca (Bill Murray). The way they dressed (Lisa with glasses, Todd with his pants pulled up high over his waist), the expressions they used ("Pizza face!" "Noogie Patrol"), and their awkward behavior were all nerdy to the nth degree, yet there was something endearing about this pair—maybe because they seemed quite content with their own nerdy existence and didn't seem to care what other people thought of them. Or maybe it was the chemistry between Radner and Murray, who were apparently romantically involved sometime during their years on *SNL*. Todd teased and pursued Lisa, who was saving herself for her one true love—composer Marvin Hamlisch, whom she paid tribute to in her piano recital onstage at the Winter Garden Theatre in New York during her 1979 one-woman show, *Gilda Radner—Live from New York* (see chapter 23).

Todd and Lisa were first introduced (3.10) as "Pizza Face" (Todd) and "Four Eyes" (Lisa), respectively, who, along with their friend Spazz (guest host Robert Klein), appeared on a radio show to promote their newly released "nerd rock" album, *Trying Desperately to Be Liked*. ("We're an idea whose time has come," Lisa tells DJ Larry Duggan [Dan Aykroyd].) Unfortunately, no one calls in to claim a free copy. Lisa and Todd next appear as authors on the talk show *Looks at Books* (3.13) to discuss their new book, *Whatever Happened to the Class of '77?* Inspired by the 1976 nonfiction best seller *What Really Happened to the Class of '65?* in which authors Michael Medved and David Wallechinsky traced what happened to members of their high school class, Todd and Lisa's book traced what's happened to their graduating class *since last June*.

The next time we see Todd and Lisa they are inexplicably back in high school, entering their "Dialing for Toast" experiment at the science fair (3.18)

It's prom night for *SNL*'s resident nerds, Lisa Loopner (Gilda Radner) and her boyfriend, Todd DiLaMuca (Bill Murray), who gives her a wrist corsage and some "prom noogies."

and going to the prom (3.20). Todd even borrows his equally nerdy older brother Milt's (Richard Benjamin) apartment in order to seduce Lisa (4.16). Fortunately, Mrs. Loopner's "Parents Without Partners" was canceled and she arrives in time to interrupt the festivities. (Mr. Loopner, who invented the Slinky, was dead—"he was born without a spine, so it was just a matter of time.") The sketch was one of the comedy highlights of the fourth season. Lisa can't stop laughing, though it's not entirely clear if it's Lisa or Radner who is laughing at Todd's attempt to get her drunk on Mateus Sparking Rosé.

## The Olympia Café: "Cheezburger, Cheezburger" (3.10)

The setting is a greasy spoon diner owned by an impatient Greek named Pete Dionasopolis (John Belushi) with only three items on the menu—cheeseburgers, chips, and Pepsi. His staff are all members of his family: George Dionasopolis (Dan Aykroyd), his first cousin, whom he treats like a brother, grills the cheeseburgers; Sandy (Laraine Newman), his only waitress, is his second cousin, whom he treats like a first cousin; and Niko (Bill Murray), who works behind the counter, is his third cousin, whom he treats like a fourth. Niko only knows one word of English—cheeseburger. According to Pete, Niko is *vlahos* (that's Greek for *stupid*).

Gilda Radner plays a loyal customer who seems totally unfazed by the goings-on (and she usually orders a cheeseburger, Pepsi, and a bag of chips to go).

Writer Don Novello, who plays Pete's brother, Mike Dionasopolis, who works in the back, modeled the Olympia Café after the Billy Goat Tavern, a real restaurant in Chicago established in 1934. In *Live from New York*, Novello recalled, "I used to go down there all this time . . . just to hear these guys going, 'Cheezburger cheezburger cheezburger.'" In Judith Belushi Pisano and Tanner Colby's *Belushi: A Biography*, Novello explained how "the owner was an old Greek guy who would hit you in the head with a cane when you walked in and yell 'Get a haircut!'." He had also brought his cousins over from Greece one at a time to work for him. The proprietors of the Billy Goat are grateful to *Saturday Night Live* for putting them on the map.

Novello believed that Belushi, the son of an Albanian immigrant, "really understood the working-class immigrant mentality." The name of the restaurant was also changed from the Pyreaus Café because Belushi's father owned a restaurant named the Olympia.

It's basically a "one idea" sketch—the Olympia only serves cheeseburgers, and every time someone says the word (pronounced "cheezburger"), George thinks it's an order and throws another patty on the grill. A customer comes in and orders something only to discover there's no tuna, just cheezburgers; no fries, only chips; and no grape, orange, or Coke—just Pepsi. If they run out of cheeseburgers (3.10), they might serve you eggs, but scrambled, not "over lightly." Over the course of seasons 3 and 4, the Olympia hires a new waitress (Jill Clayburgh), who has a meltdown her first day on the job (3.14); gets a makeover when Pete is away in Greece (the new waitress is Garrett Morris in drag) (4.1); and switches from Pepsi to Coke when he gets a good deal from a Coca-Cola salesman (Walter Matthau) (4.7). In our final visit (and Belushi's final show), a suspicious fire (caused by "sparks") has destroyed the Olympia Café and, unfortunately, his insurance policy is void because Niko had been living in the back room. A despondent Pete says the only thing they can do now—because they are Greeks—is dance!

## Chico Escuela: "Baseball been berry, berry good to me." (4.5)

Compared to his castmates, Garrett Morris didn't play many recurring characters, but he is best remembered for playing former all-star for the New York Mets Chico Escuela (he was originally introduced as a former Chicago Cubs shortstop and second baseman). Although he has been playing ball in the United States for many years, Chico, who hails from Santo Domingo, has yet to master the English language. He's best known for two phrases he would utter over and over, "Baseball been berry, berry good to me" and "Keep your eye on the ball." Created by writer Brian Doyle-Murray for a sketch about a meeting of St. Mickey's Knights of Columbus (4.5), Chico Esquela was based on Manny Mota from Santo Domingo in the Dominican Republic, whose career spanned twenty years (1962–1982), twelve of which were playing for the Dodgers (1970–1982). In an interview with the AAT, Morris explained that Chico was actually "a compilation of a whole lot of those guys" but he was really trying to capture the "whole energy" of Brazilian footballer Pelé, who had retired in 1971 but maintained a high public profile throughout the 1970s.

For the remainder of season 4 and continuing into season 5, Chico was added to the *Weekend Update*, in which he gave the sports report, which consisted mostly of his two favorite phrases.

## Julia Child: "I've cut the dickens out of my finger!" (4.8)

In what is considered his most memorable moment on *SNL*, Dan Aykroyd donned drag as Julia Child (4.8) in a takeoff of her cooking show *The French Chef*. While preparing a holiday feast, Child slices her finger and the blood starts to heavily gush out ("Oh, God, it's throbbing!"). She instructs her audience on what to do in such an emergency ("If you are too woozy to tie the tourniquet, you might call emergency help!"), but eventually loses consciousness as the blood continues to drain from her hand. The sketch is shocking because there is such an excessive amount of blood and hilarious because of Aykroyd's performance, particularly as Child begins to lose consciousness and begins to mutter about her childhood.

## Lord and Lady Douchebag: "Just some salt and vinegar, thank you." (5.20)

It's the final show of the season and the final show for the writers and cast, so it was one final opportunity to push the limits of good taste with a Monty Python–esque sketch set in 1730 in Salisbury Manor. Lord Salisbury (Harry Shearer) is hosting a party for aristocrats, all of whose names, like their host's, would one day be part of the English vernacular: Lord and Lady Wilkinson (Jane Curtin and Tom Davis) (he is carrying two swords, like the stainless steel razor blades made by Wilkinson Sword); the Earl of Sandwich (Bill Murray); Lord Worcestershire (Jim Downey); and, finally, Lord and Lady Douchebag (Buck Henry and Gilda Radner). You can tell Harry Shearer, Bill Murray, and Buck Henry are having fun repeatedly saying "Douchebag" on television ("Spoken like a true Douchebag!").

The sketch concludes with Lord Douchebag walking outside into the garden with Lord Salisbury and the Earl of Sandwich to explain his new invention inspired by his wife that will immortalize the Douchebag name.

# Season 6—The Worst Season (So Far)

## The 1980s, Part I (1980–1981)

*"The new version—new cast, writers, and producer—had no compensating satirical edge. It was just haplessly pointless tastelessness."*
—Tom Shales, critic, *Washington Post*

*"[T]he shows were just not watchable."*
—Fred Silverman, former NBC president, as quoted in Shales and Miller

*"We did suck. I can't blame it all on the press. The show sucked."*
—Gilbert Gottfried, *SNL* season 6 cast member, as quoted in Shales and Miller

On March 7, 1981, in the cold open of episode 6.12 of *Saturday Night Live*, the show's seven new cast members—Denny Dillon, Gilbert Gottfried, Gail Matthius, Eddie Murphy, Joe Piscopo, Ann Risley, and Charles Rocket—visit guest host Bill Murray in his dressing room to commiserate over the negative press the show and the cast have been receiving since the season 6 opener back in November. In his signature half-joking manner, Murray quotes from some of the show's actual reviews (the critics are not identified): "*Saturday Night Live* is *Saturday Night Dead*" (*Newsday*'s Marvin Kitman); "From Yuks to Yeccch" and—Murray's favorite—"Vile from New York" (both by the *Washington Post*'s Tom Shales).

Murray offers each cast member some constructive criticism. He tells Rocket he's funny, but warns him to watch "his mouth" (Rocket dropped an f-bomb during the "good nights" the previous week [6.11]). Murray pats sad-eyed Gottfried on the back and tells him to "cheer up"; recommends frizzy-haired Dillon comb her hair; suggests Piscopo change his last name; and compliments Risley and Matthius on their looks, but admits he can't tell them apart. Finally, he turns to nineteen-year-old Murphy, who was promoted to a regular player a few weeks back, and says, "You're black . . . that's beautiful. You can do whatever you want."

Murray then launches into the same "anti-motivational" speech he delivered in the summer camp comedy *Meatballs* (1979) to the kids at North Star Camp, who were the underdogs going into a competition against a rival camp. Murray leads them in a chant: "It just doesn't matter! It just doesn't matter!" Suddenly, he realizes if he goes out there, he risks humiliating himself in front of millions of people. He panics and reaches for a drink, but the cast stops him. Together they open the show with "Live from New York, it's *Saturday Night*!"

It's understandable why Murray panicked. The reviews were abysmal, and while there was plenty of finger-pointing going on both inside and outside the walls of 30 Rock, it was producer Jean Doumanian, the cast, and the writers who, deservingly so, bore the brunt of the blame by the critics. Gary Deeb, critic for the Field Newspaper Syndicate, called the new season of *Saturday Night Live* "embarrassing" to the network. "The new cast of *Saturday Night Live* is pretty

Advertisement for the premiere of season 6 of *SNL* highlighted the show's six new cast members.

# Season 6—The Worst Season (So Far)

Season 6, episode 1, scene 1: The new cast members and tonight's host wake up to start a new season: Denny Dillon (center front) and (left to right) Charles Rocket, Gail Matthius, host Elliott Gould, Ann Risley, Joe Piscopo, and Gilbert Gottfried. Piscopo and Eddie Murphy, who joins the cast in episode 4, are the only cast members invited back for season 7.

terrible, so are the dozen new 'comedy' writers who dredge up the rotten material to be performed." In his review of the season opener, *Los Angeles Times* critic Howard Rosenberg directed his remarks to the writers: "For much of *Saturday*'s debut, the writing was sophomoric, or even banal, either close to the vest or crude rather than creative. The writers (they're all new, too) sought security in cheap targets: Anita Bryant, Jimmy Carter." Rosenberg also felt the show only "regained its old zest" with the short films (*Foot Fetish* and "Gidgette Goes to Hell"). The harshest review, "Yuk to Yeccch," was by Shales, who found the new *SNL* to be "a snide and sordid embarrassment."

Thanks to Murray, the next ninety minutes was a major improvement over the first ten episodes. The sketches even managed to generate some genuine "yuks" from the studio audience. In the first (and best) sketch, Murray is a writer whose characters come to life in the background as he composes his next novel. Unfortunately for them, the writer keeps changing his mind, so the characters are scrambling around trying to keep up, resulting in some very funny bits of physical comedy. In *Altered Walter*, a parody of the film *Altered States* (1980), Murray impersonates the recently retired Walter Cronkite, who now spends all of his time holed up in a sensory-deprivation tank in search of "the big story." Murray also revisits some of his old characters. He sings up a storm as Nick Rivers, who performs in the Paddlewheel Lounge aboard the Riverboat Queen during a Mardi Gras cruise (his musical selections include "Proud Mary" and "Celebrate Good Times"). It's too bad the boat never made it to New Orleans due to engine trouble, and the passengers had to celebrate Mardi Gras on a dock in Cincinnati. On the revamped *Weekend Update* (renamed *Saturday Night Newsline*), Murray does his annual Oscar predictions, but throws out all the nominees and predicts all of his former castmates will win: Best Supporting Actress: Laraine Newman in *Wholly Moses!* (1980); Best Supporting Actor: Chevy Chase in *Oh Heavenly Dog* (1980); Best Actress (it's a tie): Jane Curtin in *How to Beat the High Cost of Living* (1980) and Gilda Radner in *Gilda Live* (1980) and *First Family* (1980), etc. Best Picture goes to Murray's film *Caddyshack* (1980).

Later, at approximately 12:58 a.m, Murray stands center stage, surrounded by the cast, ready to say good night. But before he does, he looks into the camera and addresses his former castmates directly: "Danny, John, Gilda, Laraine, Garrett, Jane . . . I'm sorry for what I've done." The current cast bursts into laughter. Murray gives the audience a half smile and waves. Once again, it's not clear if he really meant what he said. As the cast moves in for a group hug, Murray looks very uncomfortable.

So what was Murray really thinking at that moment? Did he really feel the need to apologize for trying to salvage what the critics and NBC executives already considered a sunken ship? In Shales and Miller's *Uncensored History*, Murray revealed that he contacted the show's new producer, Jean Doumanian, and offered to host. "It was a tough week," he recalled. "We worked really hard writing and rewriting, and the show turned out good, and I thought, 'This could work.'" But even the talented Bill Murray couldn't prevent NBC from giving Doumanian the axe, bringing her twelve-episode stint as *SNL*'s second producer to an abrupt end.

Doumanian, who had been with the show since 1975 as a talent coordinator (her title was changed to "Associate Producer" beginning with episode 2.2), was hired to succeed Lorne Michaels at the end of season 5. At that time, the remaining cast's five-year contracts were up, and the writers were ready to move on, although director Dave Wilson and some members of the production staff stayed with the show. Lorne Michaels reportedly would have stuck around if NBC had met his terms.

On June 17, 1980, Tony Schwartz did a *New York Times* story on Michaels's departure from the show and the hiring of Doumanian as his successor. According to Schwartz, Michaels decided to quit after long negotiations and settled for a one-year deal with NBC to develop shows for prime time and late night. He spoke candidly to Schwartz about how the "spirit" of *SNL* had changed over the years: "As everyone became more and more successful, and got other offers, it was harder to do. The show was purer in the first three years. I don't think it became decadent, I just think it became successful." He added that he wanted to do something different and felt he couldn't create that by the start of the next season in September.

Meanwhile, Doumanian shared her "vision" for the future of *SNL*: "I want to keep the elements that have made 'Saturday Night' great, the repertory company, the guest host, showcasing music, and to add new dimensions. I feel as if we're beginning a new show, because there will be an entirely new cast and I'll bring my own ideas to it. The challenge is to see if we can grow and still keep our audience." Doumanian was a surprise choice—especially for Michaels. When he created the show, he was an experienced television comedy performer, writer, and producer with an Emmy on his shelf (for writing Lily Tomlin's 1973 special). As Michaels explained to *People* magazine's Richard K. Rein, Doumanian was a booker (the person responsible for booking the hosts and musical acts): "The job was important, but it had nothing to do with the spirit, the improvisation, what the show should be about. The writers and performers were a family, but Jean was never a part of that group."

Four months later, in mid-October 1980, Schwartz wrote another piece for the *New York Times* in which he revealed the names of the six new cast members. *Variety* later reported that Doumanian leaked their names to Schwartz after a "disgruntled ex-staffer" gave them to the New York *Daily News* (ironically, the *Times* published them first). Consequently, a big press conference NBC had planned to introduce the new cast was canceled, and Doumanian's bosses, NBC president Fred Silverman and president of NBC Entertainment Brandon Tartikoff, were not pleased she leaked the names to Schwartz without their knowledge.

Like the Not Ready for Prime Time Players, the six new cast members all had limited television experience:

- **Denny Dillon** appeared on Broadway in the 1974 Angela Lansbury revival of *Gypsy*, a short-lived 1975 revival of *The Skin of Our Teeth*, and a stage adaptation of *Harold and Maude*. She also had a small role in the film *Saturday Night Fever* (1977) and was a regular on NBC's *Hot Hero Sandwich* (1979–1980), a Saturday morning television show featuring comedy sketches and musical performances shot in Studio 8H (sound familiar?).
- **Gilbert Gottfried** was a stand-up comic in New York.
- **Gail Matthius**, an actress from Sioux Falls, South Dakota, had been performing in comedy clubs in Los Angeles.
- **Joe Piscopo**, a New Jersey native, appeared in regional theater productions and on *The Merv Griffin Show* (1962–1986).
- **Ann Risley** was a character actress who had small roles in several Woody Allen films (*Annie Hall* [1977], *Manhattan* [1979], and *Stardust Memories* [1980]).
- **Charles Rocket** was a former news anchor in Providence, Rhode Island; Pueblo, Colorado; and Nashville, Tennessee; and a front man for a number of bands before pursuing a career in comedy.

Rounding out the cast were three featured players—Yvonne Hudson, Matthew Laurance, and Eddie Murphy, who was the only one promoted to a full cast member (6.8).

Doumanian was smart to play it safe and ask Elliott Gould, who had hosted *SNL* five times, to host the season opener (at this point, Buck Henry held the hosting record with ten). She told the Associated Press's Tom Jory that she "thought it would be a good idea to have someone who had done the show before." Granted, Doumanian was aware of the challenges she was about to face. "It's really like it was starting the show five years ago. But it's tougher because the audience has a preconceived idea of what the show should be like. I have to sell it all over again."

Season 6, episode 1 of *Saturday Night Live* opens with a funny bit: Gould wakes up in a large bed with the six new cast members, each of whom introduces himself or herself as a cross between two of the show's original cast members: Matthius is Gilda + Jane, Rocket is Chase + Murray, Risley is Gilda + Laraine, and Gottfried is Belushi + "that guy from last year . . . nobody could remember his name" (Harry Shearer). When Piscopo, who apparently isn't a cross between anyone, asks Gould about drug use backstage on the old show, the host tells him "cocaine was everywhere" and everyone used it, even Tom Snyder, Roger Mudd, Tom Brokaw, Edwin Newman—"they all snort a few lines" before they go on. Finally, the sixth cast member, Denny Dillon, appears from under the covers and officially opens season 6 by saying, "Live from New York, it's *Saturday Night!*"

Even to this day, *SNL*'s season opener is not necessarily one of the better episodes of the season. The writers and the cast usually need a few episodes to find their comedic footing. Those involved in season 6 were also under the added pressure of trying to live up to the show's legacy (even if season 5 was not the strongest due to the absence of Belushi and Aykroyd) and, at the same time, to some extent, reinvent the wheel. Season 6 failed to do either. There's no question that as producer, Doumanian was the one who was ultimately responsible for what goes on the air. But television is a collaborative medium, so it is only fair that everyone involved bear some of the responsibility as well, and in the case of *SNL*'s season 6, there was certainly enough blame to go around.

In the early years of *SNL*, political satire was one of *SNL*'s strong points, thanks to Chevy Chase's hilarious portrayal of President Ford as a clumsy idiot and Dan Aykroyd's dead-on impersonation of President Carter. Season 6 debuted eleven days after the 1980 presidential election. The Carters would soon be returning to Georgia, while Nancy and Ronald Reagan were heading east to Washington, D.C. But the new *SNL* floundered in both its comedic treatment of the transition and the Reagans' first few weeks in the White House.

In the first official sketch of season 6, Rosalynn Carter (Risley) convinces her depressed husband that losing the election was a good thing because now they can resume their sex life. The characterization of the First Lady as undersexed comes out of nowhere, though there is an allusion to Carter's admission in a November 1976 interview with *Playboy* that he "looked on a lot of women with lust." ("And now honey," Rosalynn says, "you can release all those lustful thoughts.") The sketches about the Carters were not satirical pieces. They had very little to say about the public image of the outgoing president and his family. A few weeks later, right before Reagan's inauguration, Carter is seen sitting in a Washington bar drowning his sorrows, while the guy next to him, who doesn't recognize the president, tries to cheer him up (6.6). In the cold open of the following week, the Carters spend President Reagan's Inauguration Day dismantling the interiors of the White House (6.7).

The early Reagan sketches also didn't work due to in part to Charles Rocket's weak impersonation of Ronald Reagan, who is portrayed as a clueless, doddering old man. In a speech to the American people about the state of the economy, Reagan uses what look like a child's drawings to illustrate his points (6.9). The saving grace of two other sketches is Joe Piscopo's impersonation of Frank Sinatra, who, along with Nancy Reagan (Gail Matthius), is really running the show (6.7). In the last sketch (6.10), Reagan addresses the nation and publicly clears Sinatra's name in regard to his alleged ties to the mob. After denying he knows Manny the "Horse" and Louie the "Squid," Sinatra asks Reagan to pose for a picture with Sinatra's buddies, who all look like hoodlums.

Rocket was better suited to play the role of anchor on *Weekend Update*. He not only looked the part, but before he became a comedian he was a professional news anchorman. But the writing was simply not as strong as past seasons, and there were problems with his delivery. Instead of playing the part of an anchorperson, something Chase and Curtin did so well, he delivered the news like he was doing stand-up by changing the intonation of his voice, putting unnecessary emphasis on certain words, and then reacting to what he just said. Rocket's smug persona was much better suited for the *Rocket Report*, his filmed man-on-the-street interviews and reports. At one point he even travels down to Washington, D.C., to give a rundown of Reagan's daily schedule, substituting unrelated film footage for what we are supposed to believe is actual footage of the president. Overall, he appeared more comfortable out in the field than behind the *Weekend Update* desk, where he occasionally stumbled over words while reading the news. But it didn't matter because the jokes were often flat, and one too many punch lines were greeted with mild chuckles or dead silence from the studio audience.

Matthius, Piscopo, and Dillon were the most adept at creating characters, many of whom were recurring over the course of twelve episodes. Matthius introduced teenage valley girl Vickie in a sketch on the first episode in which she's on a date with a forty-year-old businessman (Elliott Gould) ("Do you have a job or some junk?" she asks him). She really wants him to take her to the Homecoming Dance at school. Of course, he can't, and she tries to hide that she's upset by saying another guy is going to take her who is a Marine and "sort of black." He reacts because he knows she's lying. She calls him a racist and storms out, leaving this pathetic guy all alone.

Critic Randal McIlroy of the *Winnipeg Free Press* singled out Matthius as "the only new player with any flair for a line" and the sketch for its blend of "dark humor with pathos in the best *Saturday Night Live* tradition. It was funny in a bitter way and suggested that the new show may have a chance after all." Critic Tom Shales, who was not amused by the season opener, remarked, "it was one of the few sketches with any sort of resonance or subtlety." In later sketches we see Vickie and her best friend Debbie (Denny Dillon) pay a visit to Planned

Parenthood (6.3), hang out at the Cedar Mall (6.5), go to a club to meet punk rocker Tommy Torture (host Ray Sharkey) (6.6), and talk to a girl (host Deborah Harry) who dropped out of high school (6.10).

Denny Dillon, who was a guest performer on *SNL* during season 1 (1.3), was by far the most enthusiastic and energetic member of the cast—the kind of performer who was up for anything. She specialized in brassy female characters, including kids like Amy Carter and Mary Louise, a nasty little British girl whose best friend is a sock puppet named Sam. Both she and Matthius certainly deserved to be asked back for season 7.

On the whole, the cast was also trapped in some really awful sketches. The second episode of the season (6.2), hosted by British actor Malcolm McDowell, included one misfire after another. In "The Leather Weather Report," a leather-clad dominatrix named Thelma Thunder (Dillon) gives the weather forecast while beating a man (Rocket) who is tied horizontally across a map of the United States. The next sketch, "Commie Hunting Season," is not only a season low point, it's a candidate for the single worst sketch in the history of *Saturday Night Live.* The sketch opens with a bunch of southern hicks with their rifles in hand gathering for the opening day of "Commie Hunting Season." The sketch was a response to a jury's recent acquittal in Greensboro, North Carolina, of six members of the Ku Klux Klan and the American Nazi Party who were accused of shooting and killing five protest marchers, members of the Communist Workers Party, during a "Death to the Klan" rally on November 3, 1979. On November 17, a week prior to the airing of this sketch, the jury returned a not-guilty verdict on all five counts of murder. The sketch is in poor taste, and the studio audience responds with uncomfortable laughter and silence—especially when Uncle Lester (Charles Rocket) answers first-timer Jim-Bob's (Joe Piscopo) question, "How can you spot a Commie if they ain't demonstrating?" "All you got to do is shoot yourself a Jew or a Nigger," Uncle Lester explains. Silence—ten seconds' worth to be precise—though on live television it feels more like ten hours. The viewers at home obviously had the same reaction. According to the United International Press, the NBC switchboard in New York received 150 telephone calls complaining about the sketch in addition to complaints registered directly with the NBC affiliates in South Carolina. The sketch is intended to be satirical, but its use of racist language to combat racism is problematic. Unlike the Chase-Pryor "Word Association Sketch," in which the audience is aligned with Pryor, no one in this sketch has a negative reaction to what's being said.

There were also some missed opportunities. For example, in her monologue, Jamie Lee Curtis (6.4), whose reputation as a horror film scream queen was well established, treats the audience to her trademark scream. This was 1980—the height of the slasher film craze (*Friday the 13th, Terror Train,* and *Prom Night,* the latter two starring Curtis, were all released that year). But in *SNL*'s attempt at a horror parody, "The Attack of the Terrible Snapping Creatures," Curtis and her roommate (Matthius) move into a new apartment inhabited by "snapping creatures" or as my mother like to call them—clothespins. *Clothespins? Really? This was the best they could do?*

## Season 6—The Worst Season (So Far)

Some of the best moments of season 6 were not live from Studio 8H. In the season opener, Elliott Gould introduces two shorts (he calls them "Short Shots") by established directors: *Foot Fetish*, a stop-motion animated film by Randal Kleiser (*Grease* [1978]), and "Gidgette Goes to Hell," a music video directed by Jonathan Demme (*Silence of the Lambs* [1991]), featuring the post-punk group the Suburban Lawns. Episode 6.4 included a truncated version of director Martin Brest's film short from his days as a film student at NYU, *Hot Dogs for Gauguin* (1972), starring Danny DeVito. *SNL* also aired the pre-MTV cult music video "Fish Heads," written and sung by Barnes and Barnes, a pair of fictional twins named Art and Artie Barnes, who are actually former child actor Billy Mumy and his childhood friend Robert Haimer. The song, recorded in 1978, was inspired by a meal at a Chinese restaurant during which an actual "roly poly fish head" was served. The song developed a cult following thanks to radio show host Dr. Demento, who appears in the video along with its director, actor Bill Paxton. Although they are more entertaining than the sketches, the inclusion of these films also contributes to the general unevenness of the season 6 episodes, which, from cold open to the "Good nights" consisted of approximately twenty segments, as opposed to the average of fifteen segments that comprised the season 5 episodes. More importantly, most shorts featured on *Saturday Night Live* are produced by *SNL*'s resident filmmakers or members of the writing staff and cast, so their tone and style are in sync with the overall comedic tone of the show.

The highlight of season 6 was the addition of nineteen-year-old cast member Eddie Murphy. His first appearance is as an extra in a sketch, a spoof of *Mutual of Omaha's Wild Kingdom*, in which host Marlin Perkins (Charles Rocket) sends Jim Fowler (Joe Piscopo) out into the wild in search of a "Negro Republican" (6.1). Over the next few shows he begins to have speaking roles in sketches and introduce some of his characters like Raheem Abdul Muhammed and Mr. Robinson of *Mr. Robinson's Neighborhood*. Neil Levy, the talent coordinator responsible for bringing the comic to *Saturday Night Live*, helped Murphy get an even bigger break when an episode was running five minutes short (6.6) and he suggested to Doumanian to let Murphy do part of his stand-up about "black people fighting." Three shows later, Murphy's name appears in the opening credits between Matthius and Piscopo as a cast member.

Eddie Murphy as Mr. Robinson in "Mr. Robinson's Neighborhood," a takeoff of the long-running children's TV series, *Mister Rogers' Neighborhood*, set in the ghetto.

After the season 6 opener, the show's ratings declined steadily. The first three programs averaged a 10.2 Nielsen rating and 30 percent share. The episodes that aired in comparable time periods the previous year (season 5) averaged a 14.2 rating and 40 percent share. Adding insult to injury, ABC's *Fridays* (1980–1982), a sketch comedy airing late on Friday nights that was mostly dismissed as an *SNL* rip-off when it debuted in April 1980, was finding an audience. Although it was not in direct competition with *SNL*, the fact that *Fridays* was more popular than the show on which it was modeled was a kick in the teeth for NBC.

By December 1980, the problems *SNL* was facing were hardly an industry secret. A December 17 *Variety* article by John Dempsey, "'Saturday Night Live' Just Ain't" outlined the "behind the scenes turmoil" involving Doumanian (who Dempsey predicted would be "gone by midwinter or sooner") and the writers. What his sources describe sounds like a perfect storm of "creative dysfunction." According to Dempsey's anonymous sources, Doumanian was unqualified to be producer and needed to be in total control, which ultimately affected the content of the show, including her choice of hosts. Instead of choosing "strong comic performers" like Chevy Chase and Steve Martin, she chose actors who were less likely to question the material. With the exception of Elliott Gould (his sixth and final time hosting the show), former cast member Bill Murray, and Robert Hays, the guest hosts (Ellen Burstyn, Jamie Lee Curtis, David Carradine, Deborah Harry, Charlene Tilton) were not known for their comedic talents. She seemed to be more concerned with the quantity than the quality of sketches. Instead of writing a few sketches and devoting the rest of their time polishing and rewriting what they'd written, they were expected to continue to churn out more sketches. The writers also objected to Doumanian's reliance on associate producers Letty Aronson and Michael Zannella for advice. Ironically, Aronson, younger sister of Woody Allen, who was a close friend of Doumanian's, later replaced Doumanian as executive producer of her brother's films after Allen sued Doumanian for allegedly cheating him out of an unspecific amount of profits for eight films (the suit was settled out of court for an undisclosed amount).

One individual who voiced his criticism of Doumanian was Irv Wilson, senior vice president of programming at NBC. Speaking on the record, Wilson told Dempsey that Doumanian "needs help badly. There's a major writing problem, and the actors are not getting the proper staging. The show has no bite—it should be providing intelligent irreverence but instead it's mostly taking cheap shots." When a television executive criticizes a show on his or her own network, you know it's just a matter of time before heads will roll.

In yet another *New York Times* article by Tony Schwartz about the current state of *SNL*, aptly titled "Whatever Happened to TV's 'Saturday Night Live'?" former head writer Michael O'Donoghue identified one of the show's chief problems—"the absence of an identifiable point of view." "Good humor exploits real tensions that are upsetting people," O'Donoghue explained. "Ten years ago, sex and drugs were big issues, but now there are plenty of other things to be upset about: Iran, the hostages, the oil situation, Reagan. That's where the humor ought to be coming from."

## Season 6—The Worst Season (So Far)

On March 10, 1981, three days after her last show (6.12), Doumanian told *Variety* that she *resigned* "because the show had not attained the high standards I set for it. . . . By stepping aside, I hope the network will be successful in realizing the full potential of the show." The article also announced that Dick Ebersol was hired by NBC to take over the show, which would go on a one-month hiatus.

Season 6 both resumed and ended with episode 6.13 due to the Writers Guild strike. One strategy Ebersol employed was something he felt should have been done with the first episode of season 6—an "on-air" transition between the old guard and the new. "The first show of the season was a repeat of the very first *Saturday Night* with all the original members," Ebersol told the *Los Angeles Times*' William K. Knoedelseder Jr. "The next week it was an entirely different show with all new people and no similar writers, so there was no familiarity for the audience out there."

To bridge the past and the present, Ebersol enlisted Chevy Chase, who opens episode 6.13 with a trip down memory lane as he goes into a storeroom and finds remnants from the 1970s—his land shark costume, the Coneheads' cones, and Mr. Bill, who Chase saves from a trash can and then accidentally step on him. Chase is not the official host (there is none), so there's no monologue. As for the cast, Gottfried, Risley, Rocket, and featured player Matthew Laurance were gone. Piscopo and Murphy remained, as did Dillon, Matthius, and Hudson, though this would be the last show for all three women (Hudson later appeared uncredited in sketches during seasons 7 and 8). The new players included two cast members from television's *SCTV*—Robin Duke and Tony Rosato—and a member of Second City, Chicago, Tim Kazurinsky. There were two additional featured cast members: Chicago stage actress Laurie Metcalf and *National Lampoon* alum Emily Prager. Metcalf appeared in a filmed segment during *Weekend Update* in which she asked people on the street who they would take a bullet for and if they would take one for the president. Prager's sketches were all cut in dress rehearsal, so she doesn't appear in the show at all. Consequently, she is the only performer credited as a cast member to never appear on the show.

To really experience season 6 of *SNL*, you should hunt down bootleg copies of the thirteen episodes, though you can still get a sense of how bad it really was by watching the heavily edited, shortened versions available on Peacock.

# Starting Over (and Over)

## The 1980s, Part II (1981–1985), Seasons 7–10

In an interview with the Archive of American Television, producer Dick Ebersol, reflecting on the four seasons he spent producing *Saturday Night Live*, said he would like to be remembered for saving the show. He suggested that if anyone were to write about his association with *SNL* on his tombstone, it should read: "When it was almost dead, he revived it."

Ebersol is not exaggerating. He managed, with the help of former head writer Michael O'Donoghue, to pull a decent show together for what would be the final episode of season 6 (6.13) due to the Writers Guild strike. At that point, NBC could have easily justified pulling the plug on the show.

Meanwhile, the ratings for ABC's late-night sketch comedy show *Fridays* (1980–1982) were steadily climbing and at one point even surpassed *SNL*. With the cancellation of *The Midnight Special* in May 1981, NBC was also now concerned that they had nothing to put on Friday nights against *Fridays*. They even asked Johnny Carson to extend *The Tonight Show* a half hour on Friday night, but he refused. According to Carson's attorney, the talk show host felt it would "confuse his audience," and he had spent a year negotiating with the network to cut the show down to an hour.

Although the shows were not in direct competition for viewers, *SNL* and *Fridays* were competing for advertisers interested in reaching the 18- to 34-year-old demographic. As *SNL*'s ratings declined, so did its profits. In March 1981, the Associated Press's Peter J. Boyer reported that *SNL* slashed their commercial rates in half, from $60,000 to $30,000 per half-minute.

In an effort to revive *SNL* after its near-death experience, Ebersol's plan was not to so much revamp the show but restore it to its former glory. He started by hiring the show's original head writer, Michael O'Donoghue, who would also serve as the show's supervising producer with Bob Tischler. What little edginess the show exhibited during season 7 was due mostly to O'Donoghue, though his time with the show would be cut short when he was canned midway through the season. The writing staff also included veterans Rosie Shuster and Marilyn Suzanne Miller, who was credited for providing "special material."

# Starting Over (and Over)

Like the Not Ready for Prime Time Players, the majority of the new cast members had their roots in improvisational theater. Mary Gross, Tim Kazurinsky, and Jim Belushi were Second City Chicago alums. Tony Rosato and Robin Duke were former cast members of the Canadian-produced television show *SCTV* (1976–1981). Julia Louis-Dreyfus, Brad Hall, and Gary Kroeger, who all joined *SNL* in season 8, were members of the Practical Theatre Company in Chicago, where they appeared together in an improvisational revue called *The Golden 50th Anniversary Jubilee*. For his final season (#10), Ebersol brought in seasoned performers like Harry Shearer, Martin Short, Rich Hall, Billy Crystal, and Christopher Guest.

The changes Ebersol made over the course of seasons 7–10 suggest he was being pulled in two different directions. On the one hand, he wanted to erase all memory of season 6 so season 7 would seem as if it is a continuation of seasons 1–5. As Chevy Chase had done, Ebersol wanted the original cast members to make brief appearances, but they declined the invitation. At the same time he also did not want to revert back to what had been done before. Consequently, he made several changes—both major and minor—though most of them would

The season 8 cast was a mixture of new and familar faces: (from left to right) Joe Piscopo, Robin Duke, Brad Hall, Tim Kazurinsky, Mary Gross, Eddie Murphy, Gary Kroeger, and Julia Louis-Dreyfus. *NBC/Photofest*

not be permanent. For season 7, Ebersol eliminated the traditional "Live from New York" greeting from the opening of the show, though it would be restored in season 8. He also cut the traditional monologue. After the opening credits, the announcer says, "Ladies and gentlemen—[the host's name] and the cast of *Saturday Night Live!*" The host and the cast members assemble on the center stage and stand for a moment for the camera (as if they were posing for a picture). Then everyone would break, presumably to run to their respective marks or finish getting dressed backstage for their first sketch.

As a way to distance itself from the first eleven episodes of season 6, Ebersol changed the name of the news for episode 6.13 from *Saturday Night Newsline* back to *Weekend Update*. When the show returned in season 7, the name was changed again to *SNL Newsbreak*. Then, for seasons 8–10, it was called *Saturday Night News*. When Lorne Michaels returned as producer in season 11, it would once again be *Weekend Update*.

In what seemed for die-hard *SNL* fans like a sacrilegious act, Ebersol fired the official voice of *SNL*, Don Pardo, who was replaced for one season (1981–1982) by Mel Brandt. Fortunately, Ebersol had the sense to hire him back for season 8. When Piscopo gives him a warm welcome back (8.2), Pardo shares with the audience, in his best game show announcer voice, how he spent his year away feeling sorry for himself in the Lazy Palms Motor Court motel in Florida, drinking Jack Daniels, and thinking about putting his head in an Amana oven.

## Memorable Moments, Characters, and Sketches

### "Prose and Cons" (7.1)

"Where are tomorrow's Hemingways and Faulkners coming from?"

*Rolling Stone* editor Terry McDonell poses this question in the comedy short about how the American prison system has replaced colleges and universities as the source of a generation of American writers. Famed literary agent Swifty Lazar agrees: "Without a doubt, anything by a prisoner is an automatic bestseller. I tell aspiring writers, if you commit a crime, we'll talk." The short piece profiles Rockland Prison, which its warden tells us has "a sterling literary tradition." We meet killer Bobby Glover (Joe Piscopo), who is into haiku; and this year's winner of Rockland's poetry festival, Tyrone Greene (Eddie Murphy), whose poem "Images" contains the immortal lines, "Kill my landlord, kill my landlord ... *C*-I-L-L my landlord."

The end credits identify this as a "Norman Mailer Film" produced, directed, and written by Mailer. According to the *New York Times*' Tony Schwartz, Mailer apparently had his lawyers write a protest letter to NBC's legal department stating that he "strongly resents" NBC's use of his name "as the creator of a skit with which he has nothing to do."

Mailer's connection to the American penal system is a sensitive issue that dates back to the 1979 publication of his Pulitzer Prize–winning book *The*

Eddie Murphy as Tyrone Green, a black prisoner and author exploited by the white literary world.

*Executioner's Song*, a profile of convicted murderer Gary Gilmore, who was executed by a firing squad (at his request) at Utah Prison on January 17, 1977. Gilmore was the first person executed in the United States since the death penalty was reinstated in 1976. In the season 2 Christmas show (2.10), *SNL* addressed America's enthusiasm around the execution. Apparently the prison received calls from people volunteering to kill Gilmore, the three major television networks asked to film the event, and Gilmore's lawyer was negotiating with film studios for the book and movie rights to his story. "And so it is in this spirit that *Saturday Night* has prepared a very special Christmas song"—and host Candice Bergen and the cast serenade the audience with: "Let's Kill Gary Gilmore for Christmas" (written by none other than Michael O'Donoghue).

After the publication of *The Executioner's Song*, Mailer helped a convicted killer, Jack Abbott, to get out on parole in 1981 and get his letters to Mailer published. Abbott's book, *In the Belly of the Beast*, was well reviewed by the *New York Times*, but the ex-con was never able to enjoy his literary success. On July 19, 1981, he stabbed an East Village waiter, Richard Adan, when he refused to let him use the café's bathroom that was for staff only. In a 1982 interview with talk show host Dick Cavett, Mailer admitted, "I have a very large responsibility for the death of Richard Adan. If I tend to get irritable about it, it's because I'm always going to be living with it."

"Prose and Cons" is a satirical short about the exploitation of the "angry black man" in prison by the white literary world. The short also introduced a new Eddie Murphy character, Tyrone Green, who appeared in a series of sketches in seasons 7 and 8. Green—artist, poet, and felon—is first seen outside of prison breaking into the house of two sisters, only to discover that one of them is poet Ariel Feely, an eccentric woman (played convincingly by Mary Gross) who speaks in verse and lives in her own world (7.15). Ariel is familiar with Tyrone's work as well and begins to recite his most famous poem, "Kill My Landlord."

We follow Green as he continues to turn his anger toward the white man into art. The white patrons of an upscale art gallery, who he refers to as "boogie white trash scum," marvel at his conceptual paintings, *Sleeping Security Guard at the A&P* and *Smart Ass White Boy Blue* (8.1). He recites a new poem, "I Hate White People," much to the delight of his audience. Green next performs "Kill De White People!" with his reggae band in a talent show at a VFW Hall. The single black man in the audience is the only one who claps along (8.1). He also appears as a contestant on a game show, *I'll Be the Judge of That*, hosted by Dick Cavett (Rick Moranis), who asks his cultured contestants (and Tyrone) a series of meaningless, pretentious questions about himself (8.11).

### Christine Ebersole Sings "Single Women" (7.2)

New cast member Christine Ebersole sits alone at a piano in a bar called Lonely Hearts and sings "Single Women," a somber country song written by Michael O'Donoghue about the lonely women who sit in bars each night hoping to meet that someone special. Although she is not a country singer by trade, Ebersole has an amazing voice (her Broadway credits prior to *SNL* included Ado Annie in the 1979 revival of *Oklahoma!* and Guenevere opposite Richard Burton in the 1980 revival of *Camelot*). The song is one of those rare musical sketches on *SNL* when a cast member is allowed to sing without a comical "crawl" scrolling over the screen. When Dolly Parton recorded the song for her 1982 album *Heartbreak Express*, it reached #8 on the U.S. Country Singles chart. The song also inspired a made-for-television movie, *Single Bars, Single Women* (1984), starring Tony Danza, Paul Michael Glaser, Christine Lahti, and Shelley Hack.

### William Burroughs Reads a Story (7.5)

A highlight of *SNL* in the 1980s was the television debut of American novelist William S. Burroughs. One of the most influential and prolific writers of the Beat Generation, a literary circle that included Allen Ginsberg and Jack Kerouac, Burroughs's novels, such as *Junkie* (1953) and *Naked Lunch* (1959) were literary canons of the American counterculture. Michael O'Donoghue succeeded in booking Burroughs to appear on *SNL* to read an excerpt from *Lunch* and "Twilight's Last Gleaming" from *Nova Express*. But after the dress rehearsal Ebersol told O'Donoghue to cut the segment down to four minutes. According to O'Donoghue's biographer, Dennis Perrin, he only pretended to have told Burroughs, so the reading went on as rehearsed.

## President Reagan Makes a Movie (7.5)

In this first in a series of sketches set in the Oval Office, President Ronald Reagan (Joe Piscopo) is portrayed as a doddering old man who lacks the intelligence and attention span to be president. Consequently, he is being controlled by Ed Meese (Tony Rosato) and his team of advisors, who all have the former movie star believing he is actually shooting a film in which he is playing the president. As they prepare for a press conference, they grow frustrated with Reagan because he hasn't studied his script and doesn't know all of his lines. The sketch is effectively shot using a subjective camera from Reagan's point of view, which creates an eerie effect as the actors look directly into the camera at you. The same technique is employed in subsequent sketches as Reagan hires Dr. Strangelove as a military advisor (7.14) and directs British prime minister Margaret Thatcher (Mary Gross) and Argentine general Leopoldo Galtieri, who are there to talk about the Falklands War, in a love scene (7.17). The outgoing President Jimmy Carter (8.3) also recalls in his memoirs the day Reagan visited him in the Oval Office and tried to fill him on foreign affairs, but was unable to get his attention. As Michael O'Donoghue had stated in his critique of season 6, "good humor exploits real tensions that are upsetting people." *SNL*'s depiction of Reagan as intellectually incompetent to run the country, which was actually in the control of his handlers, did just that.

## Two Sketches That Never Happened: "The Good Excuse" and "The Last Ten Days in Silverman's Bunker"

On the 1981 Halloween show (7.4), hosted by Donald Pleasence, with the punk rock group Fear as the musical guest, journalist Roger Director was in Studio 8H at 30 Rock researching a story on the state of *SNL* for *New York* magazine. In his article, "Fear and Laughing at 'Saturday Night Live,'" published in the November 23, 1981, issue, Director describes the ongoing tension between Executive Producer Dick Ebersol and head writer Michael O'Donoghue over the content of the show. While Ebersol was visibly upset over Fear's slam-dancing fans getting out of control in the studio, he was glad that he had vetoed a sketch written by O'Donoghue about a Nazi concentration camp. "As long as I'm with the show," Ebersol told Director, "[T]here's not gonna be comedy about the Holocaust."

According to O'Donoghue's biographer, Dennis Perrin, the sketch in question, "The Good Excuse," was to be presented as part of a dramatic program, *Scripts the Dog Ate the Ending to Playhouse.* Introduced by playwright Neil Simon, "The Good Excuse" is set during the liberation of Auschwitz by the American troops. One soldier, Private Turner, asks an SS colonel, Rudolph Franz Hoess, how they could have committed such atrocities. When Colonel Hoess whispers the reason in his ear, Turner admits he had jumped to the wrong conclusion and apologizes. A Jewish camp survivor has the same reaction when Colonel

Hoess whispers the same thing in his ear. When the Russians enter the camp and are about to kill him, Turner tells Colonel Hoess to say the reason out loud. Suddenly, a sheepdog runs across the stage with the script for "The Good Excuse" in his mouth. Neil Simon, who can't catch the dog, says "What a shame. Now we'll never know what that good excuse was." The point of the sketch is fairly obvious (there could never be a "good excuse" for such atrocities), thought its questionable taste would have most likely overshadowed its message.

Ebersol got his way—"The Good Excuse" was cut.

A second O'Donoghue sketch never saw the light of day. In Director's piece for *New York* magazine, O'Donoghue described the most ambitious sketch he has ever undertaken, "The Last Ten Days in Silverman's Bunker." Set to air on December 5, the sketch ran sixteen minutes and had four sets. "It should offend Fred pretty much," O'Donoghue told Director.

According to a 1983 interview with Charles M. Young for *Mother Jones* magazine, the sketch was going to trace the final days of Silverman as the Hitler-like head of the "Nazionale Broadcasting Network." But the sketch was pulled because the network feared a libel suit, and O'Donoghue was later fired. Apparently someone mailed copies of the sketch to several television writers with a cover letter criticizing the "gross act of corporate censorship" carried out by the "sleazy and cynical men who determine our lives."

"The lawyers said the main thing was that we compared Fred Silverman to Hitler," O'Donoghue told *Rolling Stone*'s Christopher Connelly. "Somebody asked me if I thought it would offend Fred and I said, 'Yeah. Most Jews don't like being called Nazis."

By this time jokes about Silverman and bad NBC TV shows had grown tiresome anyway—and how much did viewers really care about the downfall of a TV network president?

### Larry the Lobster Meets His Maker (7.16)

In the episode's cold open, Tony Rosato plays an Italian chef who is about to boil a live lobster, only to be interrupted by Eddie Murphy, who breaks the fourth wall and shames the audience for taking delight in what they are about to see (and at the same time admits it might be fun to watch him throw it into the pot). Murphy explains that the lobster has a name—Larry—and it's going to be up to the viewers to decide his fate. Two numbers appear on the screen: Dial 1-900-720-1808 to save Larry. To kill Larry, dial 1-900-720-1809 (Murphy reads the second number very slowly). It's 50 cents a call. What made this early form of interactive television possible was the introduction in 1980 of the 900 number as a premium-rate special area code. Apparently AT&T employees, unaware of the sketch, were surprised by the sudden spike in call volume. In 1998, *USA Today*'s Mark Lewyn reported that the heavy phone use was actually a record or near-record for many years.

Viewers were invited to call a 900 number and cast their vote to "save" or "kill" Larry the Lobster. Eddie Murphy and Brian Doyle-Murray reveal Larry's fate by enjoying a lobster dinner.

The show's announcer, Mel Brandt, later tells the audience what Larry will win if he lives (a ride in a limo, two tickets to see the musical *Sugar Babies*, and a chance to go backstage and meet its stars, Ann Miller and Mickey Rooney). Then it's late-night dancing at the Rainbow Room, located on the sixty-fifth floor of the GE Building.

Midway through the show, host Daniel J. Travanti appears to announce the results so far: 56,893 (save Larry) vs. 65,743 (kill Larry). A few sketches and a musical performance by John Cougar Mellencamp later, the score is reversed: 184,316 (save Larry) vs. 171,717 (kill Larry). In the end, Larry received 239,096 votes in favor of saving him vs. 227,452 votes to kill him.

But that was not the end of Larry's story. The following week, Eddie Murphy appeared on *SNL Newsbreak* to share a letter he received from a woman claiming to be a member of the Oklahoma University Chapter of Citizens Concerned for the Life of Larry the Lobster. She wanted proof that Larry was actually alive. "If he hasn't died from over exposure, surely Eddie Murphy has murdered him or at least maimed him. That man is sick—and I thought *those people* don't like seafood." Murphy goes on to explain that he was going to let Larry live, but after receiving her racist letter, he's changed his mind. He proceeds to pull him apart and share him with anchors Brian Doyle-Murray and Christine Ebersole.

### Doug and Wendy Whiner: "We have diverticulitis!" (7.16)

Doug and Wendy Whiner's (Joe Piscopo and Robin Duke) constant whining are a reminder of why the 1980s was dubbed "The Me Decade." The Whiners were not materialistic yuppies but a middle-class couple from New Jersey who whined incessantly about absolutely everything because nothing was ever to their liking. They go into a restaurant, but they don't like their table and there's nothing on the menu they can eat ("We have diverticulitis!") (7.16). They don't like their seats on an airplane (7.19) and are not happy when they arrive late at a taping of *SNL* (8.17) because there's only standing room, and the host, Joan Rivers, is "so loud." When they have trouble conceiving (8.3), they end up adopting a little girl named Wanda (Drew Barrymore), who fits perfectly into the Whiner family after being rejected by 3,000 couples (8.7).

The Whiners don't go unnoticed. Everybody is willing to volunteer to get off the airplane when they announced that it's overbooked. Doug's roommate in the hospital (Sid Caesar), who is deathly ill, manages to get out of bed and walk across the room with the intention of killing him (8.12). In their final appearance (9.18), Wendy and Doug win a free tour of New York City ("We hate New York! We wanted to go to Toledo!"), but they find it's crowded and the hot dogs are difficult to digest. By the end of the tour, their guides, *2 On the Town* hosts Robb Weller (Gary Kroeger) and Melanie Anderson (Julia Louis-Dreyfus), are so annoyed with them, they arrange for the Whiners to be mugged. But the muggers can't take it either and give them back their money—and even hand over their gun (9.18).

### Andy Kaufman Is Banned from SNL (8.2)

In the show's fifth season (5.2), Andy challenged a woman from the audience to a wrestling match onstage in order to prove the point that women are not physically and mentally able to defeat a man. He starts talking smack about women to the audience and offers $500 to any woman who can pin his shoulders in three minutes. In *Andy Kaufman Revealed! Best Friend Tells All*, Kaufman's friend and biographer Bob Zmuda revealed the challenger, Mimi, was an audience member, and while they were rolling around on the mats, he started whispering "love talk" in her ear. Kaufman won the match. A few shows later, Andy takes on another challenger, a woman named Diana Peckham, who doesn't win the $1,000 purse. The angry letters (and photographs) Kaufman received from women accepting his challenge were published in an appropriately titled coffee-table book *Dear Andy Kaufman, I Hate Your Guts!*

In 2001, Stephanie Desmon profiled Peckham in the *Baltimore Sun*. The article revealed that Peckham was the granddaughter of wrestler Alex "Iron Legs" Peckham, and her father, James Peckham, wrestled in the 1956 Olympics and coached the 1972 and 1976 Olympics. Peckham had seen Kaufman's first match and was encouraged by her friends to take on Kaufman. In a preliminary round (scenes of which are shown prior to the *SNL* match), she wrestled and beat three other female contestants. Peckham was (and still is) an English teacher in Maryland and according to the article, she would begin each class by showing her students the video.

Kaufman started wrestling women in nightclubs around the country (he called himself the "Intergender Heavyweight Champion"), and on April 5, 1982, he ended up in the ring with professional wrestler Jerry "the King" Lawler, who sent Kaufman to the hospital in an ambulance. Their subsequent feud erupted into an altercation on July 29, 1982, on *The David Letterman Show*. Lawler slapped Kaufman, who threw his coffee at him.

"Andy Kaufman vs. *SNL* Producer: Real or Fantasy?" The question was posed by a New York *Daily News* headline for a story by critic Kay Gardella.

The same call-in gimmick that was used to decide Larry the Lobster's fate was used again to decide the future of Andy Kaufman on *Saturday Night Live*. There are different versions of what really happened in the fall of 1982 between Kaufman and producer Dick Ebersol that led to the comedian's banning from *SNL*. In Phil Berger's *The Last Laugh: The World of Stand-up Comics*, Ebersol gives a detailed account of the events. According to Ebersol, Kaufman was cut from the live show on October 23, 1982, because the producer felt his routine didn't work. They had a fight, which was reported in the press. "He was infuriated," Ebersol recalled, "We had a falling out about it. But we agreed to have fun with it." Kaufman was booked for the next show, but he didn't make it to the dress rehearsal on time because he was traveling from a gig at the University of Florida. Ebersol looked over what Kaufman had prepared for the night before he was scheduled to go on. "He handed me two, three pages—an attack on me. . . . It was just a diatribe. I said to Andy: 'Where's the comedy?' Told him: 'It's okay to rag me, but there's got to be comedy.'" There was another screaming match. Kaufman didn't go on and he later told the press he was cut for no reason.

In his interview with the Archive of American Television, Ebersol explained that it was Kaufman who approached him with the idea in the summer of 1983 and laid out the entire scenario. At that point in his career, Kaufman had pulled one stunt too many, including a staged fight that broke out in the middle of a sketch on the ABC sketch comedy show *Fridays* (2/20/81) between him and Michael Richards when Kaufman refused to read his lines.

All of the so-called backstage drama between Ebersol and Kaufman, which nobody saw but ended up in the newspapers, led to another viewer vote to decide whether Kaufman should be allowed to return to *SNL*. As they had done with Larry the Lobster, viewers were given the option of calling a number (8.7) and casting a vote to decide Kaufman's future on the show. The final vote was 195,544 (Dump Andy) vs. 169,186 (Keep Andy). Ebersol later received word that the stunt was damaging Kaufman's career because he was losing bookings. He knew he couldn't just put Kaufman on because they had sworn this was real and would be accused of fraud. The comedian did appear in a filmed message a few weeks later (8.10) to thank the fans that voted for him, which Ebersol arranged in hope that if it was well received, he could put him back on the air. According to Ebersol, the studio audience booed—so he wasn't able to do it.

Sadly, Kaufman was diagnosed with a rare form of lung cancer and died in 1984 at the age of thirty-five.

## "Live, from New York, it's *The Eddie Murphy Show!*" (8.9)

During season 6, when ratings were at a longtime low, Eddie Murphy was a welcomed addition to the cast. The comedian was originally hired as a featured player, but he was bumped up to series regular in episode 6.9. Murphy stood out because unlike the other cast members (Joe Piscopo being the exception), who were beaten down by all the negative press, he looked like he was actually having a good time. Murphy was confident, totally at ease in front of the camera, and, above all, funny. His comedic sensibility was also more in sync with younger audiences. He was also no doubt aware that during his five seasons on the show, the African American cast member who preceded him, Garrett Morris, was marginalized on the show.

Murphy was undoubtedly the show's breakout star, and the amount of airtime he received increased steadily as he continued to add characters to his repertoire. The funniest by far was Mr. Robinson, star of *Mr. Robinson's Neighborhood*, the ghetto version of *Mr. Rogers' Neighborhood*, who educates his young audience on the harsh realities of his neighborhood. He teaches his viewers new words like "scumbucket" (his landlord, who gave him an eviction notice) (7.3); "pyromaniac" (who he hired to torch the landlord's apartment); "pain" (what his neighbor [guest star Mr. T] is going to inflict on Mr. Robinson because his drum playing is disturbing him) (8.2); and "bastard" (what Juanita left in a basket by his door) (9.2). His other characters included Velvet Jones, a pimp, founder of the Velvet Jones School of Technology and author of the book *I Wanna Be a Ho*; and Dion, a swishy hairdresser who owns his own salon.

In an unprecedented move, producer Dick Ebersol chose Murphy to host the show while he was still a regular as a replacement for actor Nick Nolte, who was booked to host season 8's Christmas show (8.9). He and Eddie Murphy had appeared together in the buddy action comedy, *48 Hrs.*, which opened to strong box office on December 2. But in the cold open of episode 8.9, Murphy, alone in his dressing room, turns to the camera and explains that when Nick arrived in New York, he was too sick to do the show (word on the street was that he was partying too hard the night before at Studio 54). "I know you folks tuned in to see one of the stars of *48 Hrs.* host the show, and, damnit, you're gonna see it. 'Cause I'm gonna host the show. Live from New York, it's *The Eddie Murphy Show!*"

Like many hosts, Murphy opened his monologue with the usual clichés expressed by hosts (how much fun it was working with these kids, how hard they work, etc.). He then launched into a comic monologue about haunted houses and his impression of Stevie Wonder.

In his first sketch, he appears as one of his characters, the cantankerous Gumby in his own Christmas special (*Merry Christmas, Damnit!*), featuring Frank Sinatra (Joe Piscopo), Donny and Marie Osmond (Gary Kroeger and Julia Louis-Dreyfus), who end their song with a passionate, creepy kiss, and the King Family (not the large white singing family that appeared on television in the 1960s and 1970s, but three men who look like boxing promoter Don King). In other sketches, Murphy appears as a member of the Kensington Dance Theatre for the Blind (the dancers are terrible, but they're not blind, the audience is); as gay hairdresser Dion, who is a guest on *Hairem Scarem*, a talk show about women with badly damaged hair; and in what is certainly one of the most bizarre sketches of the season, as a human Herpes Simplex II virus.

At the end of the show, Murphy is upstaged by none other than guest star Steve Martin, who interrupts Murphy's good nights to rant about how Murphy was taking a hosting job away from him.

The resentment some of the cast members may have felt about Murphy being elevated to host was addressed in the next episode hosted by Lily Tomlin, who warns the comedian about being on a destructive star trip and reminds the cast that comedy is all about team spirit.

## "Otay!": The "Assassination" of Buckwheat (8.15, 8.16)

*The Eddie Murphy Show* essentially continued when one of Murphy's characters was given what is called in scripted television a "story arc" (a story that continues over a series of episodes). This was not unprecedented. The plight of the Coneheads was followed over a series of sketches as they tried to find a way back to their home planet, Remulak, which became the plot of the 1993 film.

Buckwheat was a character in Hal Roach's *Our Gang* series played by African American actor William "Billie" Thomas. In *Toms, Coons, Mulattoes, Mammies, and Bucks: An Interpretive History of Blacks in American Films*, critic Donald Bogle classifies Buckwheat as a pickaninny: a Negro child character who was "a harmless, little screwball creation whose eyes popped out, whose hair stood on end with the least excitement, and whose antics were pleasant and diverting." The *Our Gang* series had two similar characters—Farina (Allen Hoskins) and Stymie (Matthew Beard)—though as Bogle observes, "each individualized his performances through his own unique personality. . . . With a round chocolate moon face and enormous eyes, Buckwheat always came across as a quiet, odd-ball type, the perfect dum-dum tag-along."

As impersonated by Eddie Murphy, Buckwheat is still an "odd-ball" and a "dum-dum." Wearing his signature striped shirt and suspenders, the adult Buckwheat has the same incoherent speech pattern as little Buckwheat, which makes the idea that he's making a comeback as a recording star all the more ridiculous. His first appearance (7.2) is a commercial for his album *Buh-Weet Sings* (with the real Buckwheat's photo on the cover), which includes such hits as "Munce, Tice, Fee Tines a Mady" ("Once, Twice, Three Times a Lady") and

"Wookin Pa Nub" ("Looking for Love"). He returns in a few weeks to promote his album on Mick Jagger's (Tim Curry) first network special (7.7) and a new children's album *Buh-Weet Sings por de Tids* on *The Uncle Tom Show* starring Tom Snyder (Joe Piscopo) (7.10). For his monologue, guest host Robert Urich (as Burt Reynolds) (7.14) introduces Buh-weet and de Dupweems, who perform some of the Supremes' greatest hits.

The problem with Murphy's resurrection of Buckwheat is that it's all done strictly for laughs. He talks funny—that's the joke. There is no commentary on race and the fact that the character is based on an outdated, offensive stereotype. As critic Jim Whalley, in his book Saturday Night Live, *Hollywood Comedy, and American Culture*, observes, "Murphy's character finds humor only in Buckwheat's absurd dialect and appearance without addressing their implications."

But poor Buckwheat's success is cut short when he's assassinated outside of 30 Rock while getting into his limousine (8.15). The tragic shooting of Buckwheat and the aftermath turns into a biting and topical piece of satire of how the media reports and sensationalizes such events and turns killers into media stars. *Nightline*'s Ted Koppel (Joe Piscopo) breaks the big story of Buckwheat's death and, as the news organizations had done back in 1981 with the assassination attempt on President Ronald Reagan by John Hinckley Jr., he keeps showing the video footage of the shooting over and over again. With each new development in the story, a new title appears across the screen ("Emergency Surgery: America Waits and Worries,"). The next episode (8.16) opens with Koppel's special *Nightline* report ("Buckwheat Dead: America

*SNL* satirized the media's sensationalistic coverage of the assassination attempt on President Ronald Reagan with *Nightline* host Ted Koppel (Joe Piscopo) reporting on the assassination of the Little Rascals' Buckwheat (Eddie Murphy).

Mourns") where we meet Buckwheat's killer, John David Stutts (played by Murphy), who is clearly crazy. Then Buckwheat's bodyguard, Burger Johnson (Murphy once again), goes on *The David Susskind Show* (1958–1987) (the talk show host plays himself in a cameo) to promote his new tell-all book, *Buckwheat Was a Sleezeball* (8.17). We learn that Buckwheat was no saint—a home video shows him burning a caterer with a cigarette, shooting out his television, and engaging in a ménage à trois with two ladies.

Eddie Murphy left *SNL* in February 1984, though he did make one final appearance when he returned to host in December (10.9). He brought along all of his friends—Mr. Robinson, Gumby, and Buckwheat, who Alfalfa (Mary Gross) discovers is still alive after faking his own "tilling" (killing). Buckwheat claims he had to do it because he was receiving death "trets" (threats) even though he had never "dun nubbin" to nobody. But that's not true. He once put a frog down Alfalfa's pants just as he was about to sing. Alfalfa then takes out a gun and shoots his former costar dead. Bye, bye, Buckwheat.

## *SNL's* Comedy Trio—Billy, Marty, and Chris

The departure of *SNL's* leading cast member, Eddie Murphy, in February 1984 (9.14), followed by the exits of Joe Piscopo, Robin Duke, Tim Kazurinsky, and Brad Hall at the end of season 9, left four remaining cast members: Jim Belushi, Mary Gross, Gary Kroeger, and Julia Louis-Dreyfus. Instead of adding a class of unknowns to the cast, Ebersol hired more experienced performers: Billy Crystal, who had hosted (9.15) and cohosted (9.19) with a guest appearance (as Fernando) in between (9.18); Christopher Guest, who appeared in season 9 as his alter ego, Nigel Tufnel, when Spinal Tap was the musical guest (9.18); Martin Short, who was coming off two seasons on *SCTV*; comedian Rich Hall, who spent seven years on HBO's *Not Necessarily the News* (1983–1990), where he coined the term "sniglet"; and Pamela Stephenson, who appeared on the British comedy show *Not the Nine O'Clock News* (on which HBO's *Not Necessarily* was based) (1979–1982) and in *Superman III* (1983).

As many of the new cast members specialized in celebrity impressions (like Crystal's Sammy Davis Jr., Fernando Lamas, Howard Cosell, Muhammad Ali, and Joe Franklin; Shearer's Mr. Blackwell and Robin Leach; Martin's Katharine Hepburn) and fictional characters that are entertainers (Short's Irving Cohen, Jackie Rogers Jr.), many season 10 sketches revolved around show business. One of the most popular was Ed Grimley, a hyperactive childlike man with a cowlick who plays the triangle; loves popular culture, especially *Wheel of Fortune* (1983–present) and its host, Pat Sajak; and often breaks into a hyperactive dance.

The biggest change in season 10 was the increase in the number of prerecorded segments included in each episode. At the end of season 9, Dick Ebersol decided the way to "update the show" and keep it fresh was to produce more content outside of the walls of Studio 8H. A year later, in May 1985, the *New*

The cast continues to expand. The season 10 cast includes Pamela Stephenson (center) and clockwise (from top left): Billy Crystal, Gary Kroeger, Rich Hall, Harry Shearer, Christopher Guest, Julia Louis-Dreyfus, Jim Belushi, Martin Short, and Mary Gross.

York Times' Nancy Sharkey reported that 40 percent of the show in season 10 (1984–1985) was prerecorded, and the network was pleased with the results and the ratings, which were up a little from the previous season.

Initially, at the start of the tenth season, *Washington Post* critic Tom Shales thought the show returned looking "healthier" and "funnier." In his review of the season opener (10.1), he was pleased that it "contained more Class-A sketches than clinkers, and the quality of writing was noticeably improved, to say the least." He also observed how many of the sketches, perhaps the majority of them, were either pretaped or contained pretaped or filmed elements, suggesting that the time may have come to rename the program "Saturday Night

Nominally Live." "It's too early to proclaim, yet again, the rebirth of *Saturday Night Live*," Shales concluded, "but not too early to say that the 10th season premiere was Gem City."

Six months later, Shales weighed in on the state of *SNL* after season 10. He offered his final impressions of a season he thought started off with a promising premiere, which had "lots of bright, smart, funny stuff in it." "But much of that was on film," he added, "and the whole notion that 'live' combustion between gifted performers and cheeky material seemed gone. Once the season got rolling, the show lulled off into stasis." Shales was not only pessimistic that Crystal and Short would return, he wasn't sure NBC would renew it for the fall: "Once a tremendously high-rated profit center for the network, the show's merely passable ratings now translate into only marginal profits. . . . If they decide to dump the show, there isn't likely to be weeping in the streets. To kill 'Saturday Night Live' is to kill a ghost."

At the end of season 10, Ebersol decided it was time to leave. He fell in love with actress Susan Saint James when she hosted the show at the start of season 7 (7.2). Six weeks later they were married, and together they were now raising a family while Saint James was starring in the CBS sitcom *Kate & Allie* (1984–1989). When Ebersol resigned, he said that NBC came back to him and asked what it would take to get him to come back. In his interview for the Archive of American Television, Ebersol recalled how he told NBC president Grant Tinker that he would come back if the show was taped on Friday nights, which would allow him to spend his entire weekend at home with his family. He also told him that if they agreed to this, they were a "fool" because "you're basically killing the part about the show they like the most." Ebersol insists he was only humoring them and they never took his proposal seriously.

There was a possibility that *SNL* would be canceled, but NBC allowed the show to continue once Lorne Michaels agreed to return as producer. The start of a new decade would also be the beginning of a new era in *SNL*'s history.

# Getting into Character

## The 1980s, Part III (1985–1990), Seasons 11–15

*"I've returned because (NBC) asked me to return and because the show was in danger of being canceled. When I left the show, I think I wanted it to die. As it stayed on, I began to take it as a compliment, and as time went by, it seemed to me that it belonged on the air. I just didn't want to see it go off."*
—Lorne Michaels, as quoted in the *Los Angeles Times* (10/21/85)

When Brandon Tartikoff, the head of NBC's Entertainment Division, asked Lorne Michaels to return to *Saturday Night Live* as executive producer, Michaels was advised by some of his friends not to return to the show. In a 1992 interview with *Playboy* magazine, he recalled how someone he identifies only as "a very powerful guy in the industry" told him, "*You* don't do *Saturday Night Live*, somebody who *wants* to be you does it." Michaels thought, "I didn't mind being me. I liked doing it."

Season 11 (1985–1986) was another transitional season for *SNL*. The talent slate was wiped clean in terms of the cast, and like his predecessors, Jean Doumanian and Dick Ebersol, Michaels was faced with the arduous task of reinventing the wheel. The one major difference is that Michaels *invented* the wheel, and he had a clear plan as to what needed to be fixed. In August 1985, Michaels told the *New York Times* he was busy hiring writers and a new cast. He assured fans of the show that the basic format would not be changed. "It's nice that it has lasted 10 years," he admitted, "It needs to be spruced up with fresh and energetic people. One of the things that got lost was the ensemble feeling."

Another major change was Michaels's decision to serve as the show's executive producer. As Susan Orlean reported in an article for *Rolling Stone* at the end of season 11, Michaels still had the final say on all matters pertaining to the show, but he would leave the "daily decisions" to his two producers, *SNL* alums Al Franken and Tom Davis, despite the fact that the pair had no producing experience. In addition to Franken and Davis, Michaels rehired former staff writer Jim Downey to be head writer; Eugene Lee, the show's original production designer, who would share credit with his successor, Akira Yoshimura, who had remained with the show since the beginning; and Howard Shore as the show's music producer. Michaels also moved the band, which in the past few years had been off-camera, back onto the main stage. *Saturday Night News* reverted back to its original title, *Weekend Update*. Michaels also planned to restore the show's satirical edge. In an interview with the *Los Angeles Times*' Clarke Taylor, Michaels said he anticipated the show would deal with some serious social and political subjects, such as President Ronald Reagan's policies of the last five years, along with some questioning of current American values.

Putting the "live" back into *Saturday Night Live* was another priority for Michaels, who, without pointing fingers, was quite candid about how the show suffered during the past few seasons because they relied far too much on pre-recorded material. Prior to the debut of season 11, Michaels explained in a *Los Angeles Times* interview with Morgan Gendel why the show was no longer faithful to his original vision: "The illusion we created—which is true—is that from 11:30 when it starts till 1 o'clock this thing is happening in New York. As it got into more prerecorded tapes and got more into videos, it lost what is magic about it. I think 'Saturday Night Live' is about a contact with another group of humans coming through this tube. . . . It became a television show. There's nothing wrong with it being a television show, but I think it was something more."

As for the new cast, Michaels took a few chances and, in the process, broke some new ground. The most conventional choices were the three cast members—Nora Dunn, Jon Lovitz, and Dennis Miller—who had a background in improvisation and/or stand-up comedy. Dunn and Lovitz stayed for five seasons, while Miller remained for six, during which he anchored *Weekend Update*. The remaining cast members, all of whom lasted one season, were unconventional by comparison:

- Seventeen-year-old **Anthony Michael Hall**, the youngest cast member in the show's history, played Chevy Chase's son in *National Lampoon's Vacation* (1983) and a geeky teenager in three John Hughes films—*Sixteen Candles* (1984), *The Breakfast Club* (1985), and *Weird Science* (1985).
- Twenty-year-old **Robert Downey Jr.**, son of filmmaker Robert Downey and nephew of *SNL* writer Jim Downey, was another young actor who appeared alongside Hall in *Weird Science* and in other supporting film roles.
- **Danitra Vance**, an actress who performed with Second City in Chicago and off-Broadway, was the first female African American repertory cast member.
- **Terry Sweeney**, a comedian and stage actor who was on the *SNL* writing staff during season 6, was the first (and so far only) openly gay male cast member.
- **Randy Quaid**, a film actor who had appeared in over twenty-five made-for-TV movies and films, earned an Academy Award nomination in 1975 for *The Last Detail*.
- **Joan Cusack**, a trained actress from Chicago, had a background in improvisation with some film credits (including *Sixteen Candles*).

Their combined lack of television and sketch comedy experience certainly posed a problem for the show's producers. In a 2008 interview with Terry Keefe, Anthony Michael Hall described the environment at *SNL* as "very competitive"

When Lorne Michaels returned in season 11, he assembled a new cast comprised of mostly character actors: (front row, from left to right) Nora Dunn, Danitra Vance, Anthony Michael Hall, Terry Sweeney, and Jon Lovitz, and (back row, from left to right) Randy Quaid, Robert Downey Jr., Joan Cusack, and (not pictured) Dennis Miller.

and "cutthroat." "I think the people who found the most success came from a stand-up background where they had their own material," he added, "and they had a competitive nature."

## Season 11: A Work in Progress

First-time host Madonna Louise Ciccone was chosen to kick off the 11th season on November 9, 1985. At the time, the Material Girl's star was on the rise after the success of her second studio album, *Like a Virgin* (1984), and subsequent tour, and her indie comedy *Desperately Seeking Susan* (1985). She made headlines with the publication of nude photos, taken back in 1978, in the September 1985 issues of *Penthouse* and *Playboy*. There was also the media frenzy surrounding her wedding to actor Sean Penn in Malibu on August 15, 1985 (her twenty-seventh birthday). The latter was parodied in her monologue. Madonna, who didn't take herself so seriously back then, narrates fake home movies of her wedding, which is interrupted by a windstorm created by the swarm of helicopters.

The remaining sketches were the usual mixed bag: an overlong *Who's Afraid of Virginia Woolf?* parody in which the president (Randy Quaid) and Nancy Reagan (Terry Sweeney) host Prince Charles (Jon Lovitz) and Princess Diana

(Madonna) for a nightcap; Madonna as Marika, the star of a cheesy Spanish-language variety show; and an episode of *National Inquirer Theatre* that suggests John and Bobby Kennedy (Anthony Michael Hall and Randy Quaid) murdered Marilyn Monroe (Madonna), which some critics and viewers found offensive. *Washington Post* staff writer John Carmody reported the NBC switchboard in New York logged 140 complaints about the sketch.

Michaels kept his promise and did include some social commentary in the mix. What at first appeared to be a slick parody of a beer commercial celebrating the yuppie lifestyle of its drinkers turns out to be a message from Almighty God about where their self-indulgence and materialism are leading them: "Where you're going, you're going to pay.... Yes, you're going to hell!" But the edgiest sketch addressed the paranoia in Hollywood surrounding the AIDS crisis and the "pinklisting" of gay actors who were forced back into the closet.

When Rock Hudson appeared with his former costar Doris Day at a press conference to launch her new television cable show, it was clear he was sick. His publicist later confirmed that he did have AIDS. The actor died at his home on October 2, 1985, about a month before the Season 11 opener aired. Hudson's last acting gig was a recurring role on *Dynasty* as Daniel Reece, a horse breeder who falls in love with Krystle Carrington (Linda Evans). On February 6, 1985, Hudson and Evans shared an on-screen kiss. Once the truth about Hudson's condition was exposed, the press had a field day, suggesting that Hudson may have transmitted AIDS to Evans, despite the fact there was no evidence that HIV can be transmitted through casual contact. In August 1985, *Los Angeles Times* TV critic Howard Rosenberg criticized KABC, the *Orange County Register*, and Knight-Ridder of fueling the hysteria surrounding AIDS with their "hysterical reporting" of what was essentially a nonstory.

*SNL* satirized the hysteria in a sketch that begins with an opening crawl explaining that like the blacklisting of Communists in the 1950s, Hollywood is once again "gripped by paranoia, this time provoked by the tragic AIDS outbreak. Actresses refuse to do romantic scenes with unknown actors. Gay actors are forced back into the closet, leading double lives, wearing wedding bands, riding motorcycles—living in fear that they will fall victim to Pinklisting." In the sketch, Madonna plays Melinda Zoomont, a temperamental television actress who initially refuses to do a love scene with her new costar, Clint Weston (Terry Sweeney), a closeted actor who tries to act like a hetero. His secret is out when a studio light falls and he lets out a girlish scream, but that's okay because it turns out the director and everyone else working on the film is gay. But when Melinda comes out as an intravenous drug user, Clint refuses to kiss her. Although the irony of the twist at the end seems to have been lost on the studio audience, the sketch was bold and broke new ground because no other comedy program was even close to touching the subject of AIDS and the homophobia the disease was generating (the first made-for-TV movie about AIDS, *An Early Frost*, aired two nights later). Unfortunately, the satire on *SNL* did not consistently tackle such controversial subject matter, and when it did, it was not so direct, nor did it always take a clear position.

The season 11 opener posted the highest ratings the show had in years (9.5 with a 28 share). The first three shows averaged 8.8 with a 25 share, significantly higher than last season's average of 7.4 with a 22 share. As Leslie Bennetts pointed out in a critical piece on the show for the *New York Times* in December 1985, these numbers still pale in comparison to the show's highest season average of 13.6 with a 38 share in 1979–1980 (season 5).

The season opener also received terrible reviews. *Los Angeles Times* critic Howard Rosenberg wrote that the new show "is for people who get their kicks tearing wings off flies. . . . This was comedy the way Hiroshima was comedy." He was not amused by the Marilyn Monroe–Kennedy sketch: "Bobby was there, and so was Jack, who murdered her by putting a pillow over her face. I mean, you just can't get any funnier than that." The Associated Press's Fred Rothenberg accused the show of violating "the first and only rule for political satire: It didn't make it funny." This was especially true of the Monroe-Kennedy sketch. Unfortunately, the backlash didn't end with episode 11.1. As in season 6, the press continued to criticize the show along with reporting on the morale problem plaguing the cast and the writers behind-the-scenes.

Michaels appeared to take it all in stride, characterizing the reaction of the critics to the season opener as "extreme." He explained to Bennetts that the show did not get great reviews when it debuted in back in 1975 and for the next five years the phrase "Saturday Night Dead" was used repeatedly by critics. He also waxed philosophical about the show's relevancy in the 1980s. *Saturday Night Live* "came of age as an expression of the counterculture movement," but rather than appeal exclusively to the same audience that watched in the 1970s, he decided to "redefine it as an '80s show and let a new generation create it in its own image." Michaels was aware that the comic sensibility had changed and this might not sit well with fans of the show who had been watching since the beginning. He said, "It's still evolving, but it's different, and I think we're getting better as we shake down."

One individual who did not make Michaels's job any easier was Michael O'Donoghue, who was hired as a writer and grew frustrated because he couldn't get any of his material on the air. In that same December 12 *New York Times* article, O'Donoghue, who was on the NBC payroll at the time, told Bennetts the show was an "embarrassment." "It's like watching old men die," he said, "It's sad, sluggish, old, witless and very disturbing. It lacks intelligence and it lacks heart, and if I were grading it I'd have to give it an F." In a *Rolling Stone* article published at the end of season 11, Susan Orlean reported that O'Donoghue was fired one last time a few hours after the *New York Times* article appeared in print.

## The President's Son Dances (11.9)

Twenty-seven-year-old Ronald Prescott Reagan, the son of President Ronald and First Lady Nancy Reagan, is the first and only member of a "First Family" to appear on *SNL*. A former member of the Joffrey Ballet's junior corps, Ron got a chance to show America some of his dance moves in the show's cold open, which begins with Ron on the phone with his parents (Randy Quaid and Terry Sweeney, in drag, as Nancy), who are away at Camp David. They remind him that being in charge of the White House while they are away is a big responsibility. He promises to behave. We then hear the first few bars of Bob Seger's "Old Time Rock and Roll," and, like Tom Cruise in *Risky Business* (1983), Ron, wearing a pink button-down shirt, white briefs, and Ray-Ban sunglasses, starts dancing, jumping around, and playing air guitar to the music. For the son of the current president, and a conservative one at that, it was a bold move. But Ron, who at the time was pursuing a career as a journalist, which would eventually lead to his current gig as a Seattle-based radio show host, was never politically on the same page as his parents.

Two days after it aired, the Associated Press reported the president and First Lady's response to their son's performance (apparently 11:30 p.m. is past their bedtime, so they watched a copy on VHS the following evening). Assistant White House press secretary Mark Weinberg released a statement from the Reagans: "We always knew Ron was a good writer, and we were delightfully surprised to see what a good performer he is." When asked by the press at a news conference for his reaction, President Reagan said he was "very surprised" and "Well, you know, like father, like son." What he meant by "surprised" is certainly open for interpretation. When asked the same question, Nancy Reagan said she was not embarrassed by his performance, adding, "I guess that's what they did in the picture [*Risky Business*]." There was, of course, no mention that Nancy was being played by a gay man in drag. In Shales and Miller's *Live from New York*, Sweeney said Ron shared with him that his mother "did not care" for his impression of her, "but he thought it was eerily accurate."

Quaid and Sweeney were back in another funny but clunky sketch, a parody of *Back to the Future* (1985) in which Ronald and Nancy Reagan are poor Democrats. Doc Brown (Jon Lovitz) invents a time machine (it's actually a blender) that transports son Ron back to the set of *Hellcats of the Navy* (1957), where his parents met and fell in love. Like the plot of the film, young Ron is forced to get his parents together by convincing his father, a Democrat, he should be a Republican, which is a total turn-on for Nancy. One can only imagine the looks on the faces of the president and First Lady while they were watching that sketch.

## A Wayans Brother Swishes (11.12)

Comedian Damon Wayans was apparently less than pleased with the limited roles he was getting in sketches, and he made it known by breaking one of Lorne Michaels's cardinal rules—no ad-libbing on the air. In this sketch, Jon Lovitz plays "Mr. Monopoly," who arrives at the police station to help his client (guest host Griffin Dunne) who has been arrested. There's a series of Monopoly-related jokes about real estate, free parking, and getting out of jail free.

The two policemen who arrested Dunne are played by Randy Quaid and Damon Wayans. When the show went live, Wayans decided to play the cop as a flamboyant gay man (as he would often do on *In Living Color* [1990–1994]). It made no sense because it had absolutely nothing to do with the rest of the sketch, leaving his fellow actors and the audience very confused.

In recounting the story in Shales and Miller's *Live from New York*, Wayans admitted, "I was angry, I basically wanted them to fire me. I wanted to quit, but I thought they would sue me." Michaels did fire Wayans and then, in an odd turn of events, invited him back for the season finale (11.18) to perform stand-up. Wayans would return one more time in 1985 (20.17) to host the show.

The story of Wayans's firing in the middle of the season, which was an *SNL* first for Michaels, has been told many times in books and interviews. The one point that no one seems to address, as it apparently was not perceived as a problem, was the fact that at the height of the AIDS crisis he was portraying a gay cop in such an offensive manner to get laughs, particularly when it had absolutely nothing to do with the sketch. In a 1992 *Playboy* interview, Michaels described Wayans's "caricature gay voice" as a "funny voice, but it was completely inappropriate for the scene." How about it was just completely inappropriate—*period*.

## Cast Members Are Burned Alive (11.18)

The cohosts for the season finale were Angelica Huston and former New York Yankees manager Billy Martin (don't look for a connection—there isn't any). Martin was once again fired in 1985 after an altercation with one of his pitchers, Ed Whitson, in a hotel bar in Baltimore. During a sketch at the end of the show, Martin pretends to be drunk, forcing Michaels to fire him on the air. A bitter Martin gets revenge by setting the cast on fire, though Michaels manages to save the season's star player, Jon Lovitz, before the room is engulfed in flames. This parody of a prime-time cliff-hanger, popularized in the 1980s by shows like *Dynasty* and *Dallas*, ends with two questions: "Who Will Survive? Who Will Perish? Tune in October 11th." There's also a question mark at the end of every name as the credits roll (Lorne Michaels? Al Franken? Tom Davis? etc.) The cast members whose fate was sealed that night were Joan Cusack, Robert Downey Jr., Al Franken, Anthony Michael Hall, Randy Quaid, Terry Sweeney, Don Novello, and Danitra Vance. One factor that sealed their fate was that, unlike two of the surviving cast members, Nora Dunn and Jon Lovitz, none of them created any strong breakout characters (or, to be fair, were given the chance). During season 11, Nora Dunn's model-turned-talk show host Pat Stevens made eight appearances, while Jon Lovitz made multiple appearances as Tommy Flanagan (11), Master Thespian (6), and Mephistopheles (3). The third survivor, Dennis Miller, was popular anchoring *Weekend Update*.

So what exactly went wrong with season 11? That's the question Susan Orlean posed in her June 1986 *Rolling Stone* article. Producer Al Franken suggested there was not "one walloping problem" with the show that could account for its "humble ratings, hostile reviews, and hardly any of the cachet that it enjoyed in

## Live from Studio 8H: '80s Musical Guests

Aretha Franklin injects some soul into season 6 (6.3) performing "United Together" and "Can't Turn You Loose" . . . The following week (6.4), the "Godfather of Soul" himself, James Brown, in his only *SNL* appearance, performs "Rapp Payback" and a medley of his hits . . . Late-night audiences are introduced to hardcore punk when Fear (7.4) performs "Beef Bologna," "New York's Alright If You Like Saxophones," and "Let's Have War," accompanied by a group of moshing fans . . . British imports include Queen (8.1) ("Crazy Little Thing Called Love," "Under Pressure") and the Clash (8.3) ("Straight to Hell," "Should I Stay or Should I Go") . . . New Wave bands and artists dominate the decade with single or, in some instances, multiple appearances by Men at Work (8.4, 9.3) ("Who Can It Be Now," "Down Under"/"Doctor Heckyll and Mr. Jive," "It's a Mistake"), Duran Duran (8.16) ("Hungry Like the Wolf," "Girls on Film"), the Cars (9.19, 13.3) ("Magic," "Drive"/"Strap Me In," "Double Trouble"), the Thompson Twins (10.1) ("Hold Me Now," "The Gap"), John Waite (10.10) ("Saturday Night"), Simple Minds (11.1) ("Alive and Kicking"), the Pretenders (12.7) ("Don't Get Me Wrong," "How Much Did You Get for Your Soul?," and "Rockin' Good Way"), and the Eurythmics (15.5) ("Angel," "Baby's Gonna Cry") . . . Run-DMC (12.2) are the first rap artists to appear ("Walk This Way," "Hit It, Run") . . . The Saturday Night Band is under the direction of Tom Malone, followed by codirectors Cheryl Hardwick and G. E. Smith.

---

the past." Among the many reasons he cites are competition with cable television and the video rental boom, a shortage of comedic talent because "great young comedians are being gobbled up by movies and other television shows," and the rise of neoconservatism that has politically splintered America's youth, who are the show's core audience. "And it doesn't help," Franken joked, "when we do bad shows." Orlean added another reason to the list: the tension between Franken and Davis (the producers) and the writers, who complained about the cast, who, in turn, complained about the writers.

In a 1993 interview with *Spin* magazine editor Bob Guccione Jr., Michaels reflected back on the 1985–1986 season, which he said was "very difficult" because everything had to be replaced from the previous season. "You find yourself going with what you think would be safe because the new thing hasn't emerged," Michaels explained, "And then you come on the air and realize it's not what you want it to be, and you get beat up in the press . . . By the end of '85, I was able to see: Wait a minute, we need . . . we don't have enough of this." Michaels's solution was to bring in "two or three performers who could balance what I already had" and "a couple of writers who were better writers for them." Joining the three cast members who survived last season's cliffhanger—Nora Dunn, Jon Lovitz, and Dennis Miller—were Jan Hooks, Dana Carvey, Phil Hartman, Kevin Nealon, and Victoria Jackson. Compared to the previous 1984–1985 cast, they were all seasoned comedy performers with more television experience. More importantly, they specialized in "character comedy," meaning most of them excelled at playing a range of characters. Jackson was the one exception. Her characters were mostly variations of her dumb blonde persona. Michaels also hired writers who could write for them, like Terry and Bonnie Turner and Conan O'Brien, who joined the staff in 1987.

For the first time in *SNL* history, all eight cast members would remain on the show for four seasons (with Mike Myers added as a feature player in 1988–1989 and then bumped up to a regular cast member the following season).

## Seasons 12–15: Staying in Character

Madonna, who headlined the underwhelming season 11 opener, appeared on-screen at the start of season 12 to deliver a message: "As you may remember, one year ago tonight I hosted the premiere episode of *Saturday Night Live*. Therefore, NBC has asked me to read the following statement, concerning last year's entire season. Ready? [Reading from a piece of paper] 'It was all a dream, a horrible, horrible dream.' And now, to confuse you even further, 'Live from New York—It's Saturday Night!'" The idea that all of last season was a dream was based on a cheesy stunt the producers of the popular prime-time soap opera *Dallas* (1978–1991) played to get actor Patrick Duffy back on the series. In the season 9 cliff-hanger and season 10 opener, Pam Ewing (Victoria Principal) sees her late husband, Bobby Ewing (Patrick Duffy), come out of the shower. Bobby was struck by a car and died at the end of season 8. Pam realizes that everything that had happened on the show since Bobby's death (in other words, all of season 9!) was a dream.

Asking the audience to forget about *SNL*'s season 11 like a bad dream doesn't seem quite fair because it's asking us to forget about the creative contributions made by the talented cast members like Joan Cusack, Randy Quaid, Terry Sweeney, and Danitra Vance. Season 11 wasn't perfect, but it certainly wasn't the worst. Compare it to season 6 and you'll see.

There were some early signs that the so-called nightmare had ended with the introduction of several new characters early on in season 12, who were soon be joined by some carry-overs from season 11 by returning cast members Nora Dunn and Jon Lovitz, and later additions from Mike Myers when he joined the cast in 1989. While some of the characters were one-note, season 11 marked the return to character-driven comedy.

## Memorable Moments, Characters, and Sketches

### Dana Carvey as the Church Lady

Her name is Enid Strict, but she refers to herself as "the Church Lady." In an interview with Ryan Murphy for the *Washington Post*, Dana Carvey explained that the Church Lady was originally a schoolteacher who was condescending to little kids. His mother told him the character reminded her of the ladies at their church who made her feel inferior when she brought a casserole to potluck dinners and turned their heads when the Carvey family walked into church after missing a few Sundays. The Church Lady debuted on Carvey's first episode of *SNL* (12.1), but he felt like his recognition factor "went through the roof" when he sang a duet of "You Don't Bring Me Flowers" with guest Willie Nelson (12.12).

Then there was her interview with ex-PTL Club leader evangelist Jim Bakker (Phil Hartman) and his wife, Tammy Faye (Jan Hooks) (12.15). She prefaced it by assuring the couple that they can just relax "because on my show no one is going to mention adultery, blackmail, missing funds, drug induced psychosis, or getting booted from the PTL. So, what else is going on?"

The holier-than-thou Church Lady had no difficulty booking guests for her show because there were plenty of scandals in the late 1980s to make her feel superior. She usually prefaced an interview by stating that she was not going to judge her guests, but allow them to tell their story. But she enjoyed bringing up the sordid details and liked to "break down" what may have happened in those fifteen minutes

On *Church Chat*, the self-righteous Church Lady (Dana Carvey) enjoyed passing judgment over "sinners" like televangelists Jim and Tammy Faye Bakker (Phil Hartman and Jan Hooks) and Jimmy Swaggert (Phil Hartman), and actors Danny DeVito, Sean Penn, and Rob Lowe.

spent in a cheap motel room. Between 1996 and 2000, the Church Lady judged and scolded Jessica Hahn (Jan Hooks) (13.6), Jimmy Swaggart (Phil Hartman) (13.13), Donald Trump (Phil Hartman) and Marla Maples (Jan Hooks) (15.14), Leona Helmsley (Jan Hooks) (15.9), Saddam Hussein (Phil Hartman) (16.7). O. J. Simpson (Tim Meadows) (22.4), and Madonna (Molly Shannon) (22.4). Several guest hosts, like Sean Penn (13.2) and Rob Lowe (15.15), were brave enough to discuss their bad behavior. When Carvey hosted the show in 2011 (36.14), the Church Lady had a few choice words for Nicole "Snooki" Polizzi (Bobby Moynihan) and the Kardashian sisters—Kourtney (Vanessa Bayer), Khloé (Abby Elliott), and Kim (Nasim Pedrad). She ended each episode by cueing her organist Pearl and doing the "superior dance."

The Church Lady will also be remembered for an assortment of catchphrases, like "Isn't that special?," "Now who could it be? Could it be . . . Satan?," and "How conveeeenient!"

## Nora Dunn and Jan Hooks as the Sweeney Sisters

Liz (Nora Dunn) and Candy (Jan Hooks) Sweeney, better known as the Sweeney Sisters, made their *SNL* debut as guests on *Instant Coffee with Bill Smith* (their original names were Franny [Hooks] and Mary Ann [Dunn]). They are a "lounge act" with limited talent, so they never get to play the "big room" (the closest they come is a ski lodge lounge (13.8) and a hotel lobby [14.15], where, in their final *SNL* appearance, the duo are joined by their older sister Audrey [Mary Tyler Moore]). Wearing tacky pastel gowns, they hit the stage and sing a medley of songs tailored for their audience with lots of patter and corny jokes in between. They entertain the residents of the Baycrest Jewish Retirement Home with traditional Jewish songs and selections from *Fiddler on the Roof*. They celebrate the Chinese New Year in a Chinese restaurant with songs about the Far East (like "Tea for Two" and "Have an Egg Roll, Mr. Goldstone"). At the Brookfield Zoo Banquet, which is a benefit for the Primate House Renovations, they break into "Yes! We Have No Bananas" and "The Lion Sleeps Tonight." The highlight of their *SNL* appearance is when they spot Paul Simon in the audience at the ski lodge and serenade him with a medley of his hits—"50 Ways to Leave Your Lover," "Mrs. Robinson," "The 59th Street Bridge Song (Feeling Groovy)." But to hear the Sweeney Sisters sing (or rather, try to sing) "Bridge over Troubled Water" was worth the price of admission.

Liz Sweeney (Nora Dunn, left) and her sister Candy (Jan Hooks) spread yuletide cheer with their patter and a medley of holiday tunes.

## Dana Carvey and Kevin Nealon as Hans and Franz

Arnold Schwarzenegger was the inspiration for this pair of Austrian bodybuilders who had their own show, *Pumping Up with Hans and Franz* (a cutout of Schwarzenegger appeared in the background of the set). "We're going to pump you up" was their catchphrase, but the irony is they never actually did anything to help viewers get into shape. They spent their time showing off their muscles and insulting viewers for being weak and "girlie men." When the real Schwarzenegger appeared on their show, he called them the same thing.

The irony of the term "girlie men," which one can only assume is the opposite of a "he-man" or a "man's man," was lost when Schwarzenegger began to use it publicly, beginning with the 1988 presidential election. While campaigning for George H. W. Bush, Schwarzenegger said of his opponents, "They all look like a bunch of girlie men, right?" As governor of California he used the term in a 2004 speech to mock his opponents in the California Legislature: "They cannot have the guts to come out in front of you and say, 'I don't represent you. I want to represent those special interests: the unions, the trial lawyers.' . . . I call them girlie men. They should get back to the table and finish the budget." He also encouraged voters to "terminate" his opponents at the polls in the upcoming election.

There was talk of turning Hans and Franz into a feature film, but the project (thankfully) never materialized.

## Jon Lovitz as Master Thespian, Mephistopheles, and Tommy Flanagan

Lovitz's specialty was over-the-top characters—"big talkers" with inflated egos who commanded your attention when they walked into the room.

- **Tommy Flanagan:** America's favorite pathological liar popularized the catchphrase "That's the ticket!" (see chapter 24).
- **Master Thespian:** "Another page from the diary of the world's greatest actor!"

    His real name is Jonathon Yankonvichi, and, in his own mind, he is *the* greatest actor of all time, which is why he prefers to be called by his stage name—Master Thespian! Onstage and offstage he is a major ham with a penchant for overacting, exaggerating every word and gesture. He attributes everything he says and does to his talent ("Acting!" "Genius!" he constantly cries, raising his hand in the air, as if ready to take a bow).

    Too bad Master Thespian's greatness (and talent) is all in his head. He drives a Hollywood director (host Robin Williams) crazy when he can't remember his single line (12.5) and his costar (host Jerry Hall) in a film he's directing can't stand him. When he's "cast" by W. H. Macy (Phil Hartman) as Macy's Santa (13.8), he doesn't seem to understand the role that Santa *likes* children and the store *doesn't* give children whatever they want for free.

- **Mephistopheles:** Wearing his signature red cape and horns and carrying a pitchfork, Mephistopheles, a.k.a. the Devil, shows up in some of the most unexpected places. He's the defendant in a case on *The People's Court* when Vonda Braithwaite (host Rosanna Arquette), a beautician who tries to nullify a contract she made with the devil in exchange for success in her hairdressing business (12.3). He also pays the Church Lady (Dana Carvey) a visit in her home on Christmas Eve (14.9) and cheers up Andrew Dice Clay (15.19), who is depressed over all of the negative publicity surrounding his invitation to host the show.

- **Tonto:** Three popular fictional characters—Tonto (Lovitz), Tarzan (Kevin Nealon), and Frankenstein (Phil Hartman)—all of whom have limited command of the English language first appeared as guests on a talk show, *Succinctly Speaking* (13.8), hosted by Kathleen Fulmer (Nora Dunn), who asks each of them their opinion on such topics as "Bread" and "Fire" (Tarzan and Tonto say, "Fire good," but Frankenstein says, "Fire bad."). The third topic is the 1987 Intermediate-Range Nuclear Forces (INF) Treaty, signed by President Reagan and General Secretary Mikhail Gorbachev on December 8, 1987, which eliminated the United States' and USSR's nuclear and conventional ground-launched ballistic and cruise missiles with intermediate ranges. Just as the entire sketch makes no sense to the audience, the question is lost on Frankenstein. In a rare moment on the show, Phil Hartman breaks character and begins to crack up. "Fire bad," is his only response as he gets up from his chair and crashes through the back of the set.

On *Saturday Night Live 25*, cast members from seasons 12 and 13 (front row, left to right) Dennis Miller, Jan Hooks, Jon Lovitz, Victoria Jackson, Jan Hooks, and (back row, left to right) Mike Meyers and Kevin Nealon pay tribute to their late friend and beloved fellow cast member, Phil Hartman, who appeared on *SNL* for ten seasons (1986–1994).

The trio returned for *As World Turn*, a soap opera parody in which Frankenstein has an affair with Tarzan's Jane (Victoria Jackson) (14.11) and, in another episode, has an evil twin played by Mel Gibson (14.16). They also have their own classic Thanksgiving special, *Thanksgiving Good, Fire Bad* (15.6), and appear on-screen together around various holidays to wish us Halloween, Thanksgiving, and Season's Greetings.

## William Shatner at a *Star Trek* Convention (12.8)

Some thought it was a case of biting the hand that feeds you, but Trekkies and non-Trekkies alike no doubt found some truth in this hilarious sketch by Bob Odenkirk and Judd Apatow. In his monologue, host William Shatner expresses his amazement at the influence *Star Trek* has had worldwide. "All the Trekkies and Trekkettes and the Trek-kores . . . they're truly incredible," he adds, "and I hope they have a sense of humor about this show tonight or I'm in deep trouble." Shatner then gives us a glimpse into what it's like at a *Star Trek* convention, where we see an assortment of Trekkies assembled around a podium waiting to hear from Captain Kirk himself. He takes questions from the audience that are essentially minutiae about the show (like what was the combination you used to open a safe in episode 25). At one point, Shatner stops and tells them all to "Get a life, will you people? I mean, for crying out loud, it's just a TV show! . . . You've turned an enjoyable little job, that I did as a lark for a few years, into a *colossal waste of time*." At the end of his tirade, Shatner and the emcee exchange words, prompting Shatner to return to the microphone and say that his speech was a "re-creation" of the Evil Captain from episode 37. The Trekkies applaud.

The sketch was a brave move on the part of Shatner considering that *Star Trek* was the highlight of his career and *Star Trek IV: The Voyage Home* was currently playing in theaters (by then it was already cleaning up at the box office). At the same time, there were no doubt some Trekkies tuning in to *SNL* that night just to see Captain Kirk who were less than pleased with his message to his fans.

## Introducing Dieter and *Sprockets* (14.17)

Dieter (Mike Myers), host of a West German television show from Berlin, *Sprockets*, made his first public appearance on the stage in Second City in Toronto before moving to television. Myers and his collaborator, actor Dana Anderson, appeared together on the Canadian summer series *It's Only Rock 'n' Roll* (1987) as Kurt and Dieter, a German avant-garde musical duo. During their interview, where they are joined by their pet monkey that they love to touch, they show clips from their 1977 music video, "Kunst Und Zeitgeist" ["Art and Zeitgeist"] (you can watch the segment on YouTube under the title "Kurt & Dieter"). Another one of Myers's characters, Wayne Campbell, also debuted on *It's Only Rock 'n' Roll*.

Myers brought the character to *SNL* and gave him his own talk show, *Sprockets*, which focuses on German and American art and *kultur*. Wearing all black and round wire-rimmed glasses, Dieter welcomes an odd assortment of guest like actor Butch Patrick, who played Eddie Munster (Ben Stiller) (14.17); art critic Heike Mueller (Nora Dunn) (14.20), who is also his lover; and actor James Stewart (Dana Carvey) (15.1), who is there to plug his new book of poems. Dieter also hosts a German dating game show, *Love Werks*, where bachelor Wolfie Schreiber (Jason Priestley) chooses a she-male named Susan (Phil Hartman) who was recently released from prison (17.13). Dieter bores easily and often interrupts his guests to tell them, "Your story has become tiresome." Like Myers's other characters, Dieter's banter is peppered with many catchphrases like "Would you like to touch my monkey?" and "Now is the time on *Sprockets* when we dance!"

In 1998, Mike Myers made a $20 million deal with Universal Pictures to turn *Sprockets* into a film. Myers, who was not pleased with his own script, wanted to delay the filming, stating, "I cannot, in good conscience, accept $20 million and cheat moviegoers who pay their hard-earned money for my work by making a movie with an unacceptable script." Universal sued Myers, who countersued. The case was settled out of court, and Myers agreed to appear in another Universal film as the title character in Dr. Seuss's *The Cat in the Hat* (2003).

## Steve Martin Pays Tribute to Gilda Radner (14.20)

On May 20, 1989, the final episode of the fourteenth season (14.20), an emotional Steve Martin honored the memory of Gilda Radner, who died that day at the age of forty-two after a long battle with ovarian cancer. Without mentioning her name, Martin stated, "[T]he thing that keeps bringing you back is the people you get to work with . . . and I would like to show you something we recorded on this stage in 1978." In the sketch, "Dancing in the Dark," Martin is sitting at a bar; Radner is at a table with two friends. Their eyes meet, and everyone else freezes as we hear "Dancing in the Dark," the song Fred Astaire and Cyd Charisse danced to in the park in the MGM musical *The Band Wagon* (1953). He stands up, takes her hand, and the two engage in a choreographed dance (by Patricia Birch) that is both graceful and comical, with Martin occasionally doing one of his signature "happy feet" moves.

"You know, when I look at that tape," Martin concludes, "I can't help but think how great she was, and how young I looked. Gilda, we miss you."

On *SNL*'s fifteenth anniversary special, Jane Curtin and Laraine Newman also paid tribute to their former costar with clips of some of her best moments.

## *Saturday Night Live*: 15th Anniversary Show (9/24/89)

On Sunday, September 24, 1989, *Saturday Night Live* celebrated its fifteenth anniversary in style with a two-hour prime-time special. It's a star-studded black-tie affair with an audience of VIPs and former hosts. Past and current cast members and past hosts including Charlton Heston, Steve Martin, Mary Tyler Moore, O. J.

Simpson, and Robin Williams. In addition to the tribute to Gilda Radner, John Belushi's "little brothers" Dan Aykroyd and Jim Belushi honor John's memory with some of his best moments. In their introduction, they take a jab, without mentioning any names, at Bob Woodward, author of the 1984 Belushi biography *Wired: The Short Life and Fast Times of John Belushi*, which focused primarily on the comedian's drug use.

One cast member who was a no-show was Eddie Murphy, though his entourage showed up (and they are billed in the opening credits as "Eddie Murphy's Entourage"). They appear onstage with Mary Tyler Moore, who introduces past sketches that were in questionable taste.

## *Wayne's World* Welcomes Aerosmith (15.13)

Wayne Campbell (Mike Myers) and Garth Algar (Dana Carvey)—the most excellent hosts of *Wayne's World*—welcome their idols Aerosmith to *Wayne's World* thanks to Garth's cousin, Barry (Tom Hanks), a roadie for the band. While interviewing Barry, Wayne checks the upstairs camera and discovers Aerosmith is sitting in his breakfast nook talking to his mother (Nora Dunn), who then

*Wayne's World*, which airs on Cable 10, a community access channel in Aurora, Illinois, has two excellent hosts, Wayne Campbell (Mike Myers, left) and his best friend, Garth Algar (Dana Carvey).

takes them on a tour of the house. The band eventually made it downstairs and Wayne asks them three questions: (1) Is it true you don't do drugs and alcohol any more? Answer: Yes. (2) (to Steven Tyler) Are those your real lips? Answer: Yes. (3) With the recent developments in Eastern Europe, do you think Communism is on the decline, or is this just a temporary setback? Tyler and his bandmate Tom Hamilton disagree on this one. The segment ends with Wayne fulfilling his dream of playing with Aerosmith. Together, they play and sing the *Wayne's World* theme song.

# Saturday Night Alive (and Dead)

## The 1990s, Part I (1990–1995), Seasons 16–20

Between the years 1986 and 1990 (seasons 12–15), *SNL* boasted a stellar cast consisting of Dana Carvey, Nora Dunn, Phil Hartman, Jan Hooks, Victoria Jackson, Dennis Miller, and Kevin Nealon, who was promoted from featured to regular player in season 13. Mike Myers, who joined the cast as a featured player in the middle of season 14 (14.10), was bumped up to a regular at the start of season 15. A second featured player, some guy named Ben Stiller, started in March 1989 (14.15), but he only stuck around for six episodes. Three years later, Stiller and Judd Apatow created *The Ben Stiller Show* (1992), a one-camera sketch comedy show on the Fox Network featuring Janeane Garofalo, Andy Dick, and Bob Odenkirk. Although Fox pulled the plug after twelve episodes, the show won a Primetime Emmy for "Outstanding Achievement in Writing in a Variety or Music Program," beating the writing staff of *Saturday Night Live*. Stiller did return to host *SNL* in 1998 (24.4) and 2011 (37.3).

As to be expected, some members of *SNL*'s cast decided it was time to move on. Jon Lovitz and Nora Dunn, who had both been there for five seasons, departed at the end of season 15. Dunn left amid the controversy surrounding her public refusal to share the stage with host Andrew Dice Clay (15.19), though she did return for the season finale hosted by Candice Bergen (15.20). Lovitz later admitted in a July 1997 interview with *Playboy* that at the time he wasn't sure if he had made the right decision. "Should I have left? I did that for about two years," he said, "Then I got a job and I was OK." At the end of season 16 (1990–1991), *SNL* lost two more major players: Dennis Miller, who had anchored *Weekend Update* for the past six seasons, and Jan Hooks, who headed to the West Coast to join the cast of *Designing Women* (1986–1993).

To prepare for the inevitable loss of the five remaining cast members (Carvey, Hartman, Jackson, Myers, and Nealon), Michaels started to stack the deck with new talent. Over the course of season 16 (1990–1991), he added seven featured players to the remaining two (A. Whitney Brown and Al Franken), bringing the total to nine. Three of them were from improvisational theater: Julia Sweeney was a Groundling, while Chris Farley and Tim Meadows worked together at

Second City in Chicago. The remaining four—Chris Rock, Adam Sandler, Rob Schneider, and David Spade—were stand-up comics. All but Sweeney were in their mid- to late twenties, which was significantly younger than the outgoing and remaining "veteran" cast members with the exception of Mike Myers, who was twenty-five when he started on the show.

The fact that seven out of the eight newcomers were males under the age of thirty would have a significant effect on the show's comic sensibility in the early 1990s. Their brand of humor appealed more to viewers like themselves.

Adam Sandler epitomized a brand of humor popular among the same demographic that watches Comedy Central, who *Wired* magazine's Frank Rose describes as "white, college-educated, post-frat-boy males." On *SNL*, Sandler's specialty was mostly mentally challenged men who act like children and speak in odd voices, like Canteen Boy, Cajun Man, and the Herlihy Boy. Since leaving *SNL*, Sandler has had a lucrative movie career playing adult males suffering from arrested development in comedies like *Billy Madison* (1995), *The Waterboy* (1998), and *Big Daddy* (1999). But on the show, Sandler was at his best when he was singing the news headlines as "Opera Man" on *Weekend Update* or original holiday songs like "The Thanksgiving Song" (18.7), "Santa Don't Like Bad Boys" (19.9), and "The Chanukah Song" (20.7). As for the others, all but Chris Farley, a fearless physical comedian with improvisational experience, were stand-up comedians, so there was a learning curve before they seemed entirely comfortable doing sketch comedy. Chris Rock used his voice as a stand-up comic to create his most popular recurring character, an angry black talk show host named Nat X. David Spade raised the bar on snide humor as the receptionist at Dick Clark Productions, a flight attendant on Bastard Airlines, and an entertainment reporter doing "The Hollywood Minute." Rob Schneider took the longest to stand out, though his character, Richard Laymer, introduced one of the most popular *SNL* catchphrases of the 1990s ("Makin' copies.").

Their humor was not sophisticated, but then again it wasn't trying to be, though at times it was too crass and sophomoric for *SNL*. In December 1993, *New Yorker* magazine James Wolcott wrote a scathing review of the show, accusing each cast member of being "issued a single shtick, which he or she beats to death": David Spade ("practices nasal one-upmanship"), Adam Sandler ("does the annoying Opera Man"), Rob Schneider ("never broadened beyond his copymachine kibbitzer"), and Chris Farley ("the most overindulged one-note"). "As for the women in the cast," Wolcott quipped, "they could stage a work stoppage and who would know?"

Wolcott was right about the female cast members. In season 16 (1990–1991), there were three women in the cast (Hooks, Sweeney, and Victoria Jackson). After Hooks's departure at the end of season 16, Jackson and Sweeney were joined by four new female featured players: Beth Cahill and Siobhan Fallon, who both lasted only one season; Melanie Hutsell; and Ellen Cleghorne, bringing the total number of cast members to an all-time high of eighteen. At the time of Wolcott's review (during season 19), there were four women—Cleghorne, Hutsell, Sweeney, and newcomer Sarah Silverman—and twelve men.

Consequently, between seasons 16 and 20, the majority of recurring characters were male. By comparison, you can count the number of prominent recurring female characters during that time on a six-fingered hand: Zoraida the NBC Page and Queen Shenequa (both played by Ellen Cleghorne), Jan Brady (Melanie Hutsell), and the three sisters of Delta Delta Delta (Hutsell, Siobhan Fallon, Beth Cahill). Then there's androgynous Pat (Julia Sweeney), who falls somewhere in the middle, raising the count to six and a half.

Allegations that *Saturday Night Live* is a "boys' club" were nothing new, but the show was certainly low on estrogen. Between the years 1985 and 1990, the male-to-female cast member ratio was 3:1. In a February 1992 piece for the *New York Times*, "Women in the Locker Room at *Saturday Night Live*," Eve Kahn addressed *SNL*'s gender politics both behind and in front of the camera. Lorne Michaels admitted that in trying to replace Jan Hooks, he got carried away when he hired four women who are all different types at the same time, calling it an "accident" (was it an "accident" that he added *six guys* in 1990 to a cast that already had five male regulars and two male featured players?). He also makes the point that he would not run a woman's sketch for its own sake. "If it's not funny," he explains, "it doesn't matter if it's well intentioned." But according to Kahn, the reality is that the female cast members get less airtime, which is why "all the new women are now frantically trying to write skits for themselves . . . but for the moment, they still appear only briefly on each show, and they may never dominate skits, the way the tenured male comics—Phil Hartman, Kevin Nealon, Dana Carvey—do."

Whatever they were doing seemed to be working. In December 1992, *Entertainment Weekly* named the cast of *Saturday Night Live* "Entertainers of the Year." "In its 18th year," Mark Harris wrote, "*Saturday Night Live* has, with the buoyant rudeness that made its reputation in 1975, reclaimed its status as the show of the moment, and refashioned itself as something big enough to embrace both *Wayne's World* and *Wayne's parents*." Harris cites the mixture of political and celebrity impersonations, which he says "coexist, immortalized in mockery, along some slightly less real but no less famous names" like Wayne and Garth, Hans and Franz, Dieter, Nat X, Mr. Subliminal, etc. In addition, there were some surprises over the past few years, like a visit by none other than Barbra Joan Streisand to *Coffee Talk* (17.14), and the ending of Sinéad O'Connor's rendition of "War" in which she tore up the pope's picture (18.2) (see chapter 19).

Two years after praising the show and its cast, a headline in *Entertainment Weekly* posed this question: "Is *Saturday Night* Dead?" The March 1994 article by Bruce Fretts offered *SNL* "20 helpful ideas" in honor of the show's upcoming twentieth anniversary. The list of complaints and personal attacks sounded like something David Spade would read in his "Hollywood Minute" segment (as Spade would say, "It's called backlash. Get used to it."). In fact, Spade is the subject of their first suggestion, which is to have him replace Kevin Nealon because he "could bring the same snide sensibility to current events that he does to showbiz." Other suggestions that made the list were to retire the Gap girls (Farley, Sandler, and Spade in drag) because the women on the show have "little to do," produce new commercial parodies each week (and stop rerunning the same ones over and over), stop booking athletes as hosts, book hipper musical guests, teach cast member Melanie Hutsell a new facial expression, and tell Chris Farley to keep his shirt on.

So what happened between December 1992 and March 1994 that prompted *Entertainment Weekly* to do a complete 180° about *Saturday Night Live*? Answer: season 19 (1993–1994), which according Doug Hill was "generally considered" by the critics to be "a disaster." Hill wrote an extensive piece for the *New York Times* at the start of season 20 that tried to put what was going on with the show in perspective and some of the possible causes for the decline in the ratings last season. The list included the loss of five veteran writers, which left head writer Jim Downey with "a nervous group of neophytes on both sides of the camera"; behind-the-scenes tension and "internal feuds" involving writers, production staff, and cast members; and interference by top brass at NBC, who Lorne Michaels characterized as a "much more activist management." Although changes had been made, including the addition of seasoned comedic performers, like Chris Elliott, Michael McKean, and *Kids in the Hall*'s Mark McKinney, the criticism launched against the show only continued with reviews that featured headlines like "After Two Decades, How Much Longer?" (John J. O'Connor, *New York Times*), "Dear *Saturday Night Live*: It's Over. Please Die." (Rich Marin, *Newsweek*), and "Saturday Night Moribund" (Craig Tomashoff, *People*). One major loss to the show was the departure of the beloved Phil Hartman, whose impersonation of President Bill Clinton was prominently featured at the end of season 19. Darrell Hammond would eventually fill that gap when he joined the cast in season 21.

The negative press just kept coming, and Warren Littlefield, president of NBC Entertainment, was not helping by publicly criticizing the show. On March 8, 1995, Littlefield told Bill Carter on the record in a *New York Times* story that some of the "major changes" suggested by the network were "accomplished" but "there are a lot of things left undone." He added that there was no question the show needed "sharper writing and a new batch of stars" and that "both those areas are being addressed." Carter pointed out that it was not a decline in ratings that caused NBC to make changes in the show, which was still making money for the network. Although the show had reach a 9 rating in the 1992–1993 season, the current (1994–1995) 7.6 rating is the same as it was back in 1990–1991 (at the time, one rating point equaled 954,000 households). Also adding fuel to the fire that same month was a devastating thirteen-page cover story in *New York* magazine by Chris Smith, "Comedy Isn't Funny: *Saturday Night Live* at Twenty—How the Show That Transformed TV Became a Grim Joke." Smith spent a significant amount of time behind the scenes, observing and talking to the cast and writers. The article captures the turbulence, dysfunction, and discontent that permeated the seventeenth floor of 30 Rock. Some of the people Smith spoke to were not identified by name. One new cast member, Janeane Garofalo, was unhappy with the fraternity atmosphere and the limited roles she was getting to the point that she got out of her contract to go do a movie. The article ends with Garofalo waving goodbye during the "good nights" on her final show (20.14).

## Memorable Characters and Sketches (Seasons 16–20)

### Simon (16.5)

Simon (Mike Myers) is the British boy who hosts his own show on BBC 1 from his bathtub. He's neglected by his father, with whom he travels, and lives in hotels because his mummy is "living with the angels" (16.5). He likes to do "*drawerings*" and shares them with us—but you better not look at his bum, "you cheeky monkey." Sometimes he has other children in the tub with him whose fathers work for the same big American company: Trevor (Macaulay Culkin) (17.7), who shares his cowboy drawings; Vinnie Esposito (Danny DeVito) (18.10), a crude little Italian lad ("Were you lookin' at my ass?"); and Kelly Clayton (Sara Gilbert) (19.11), whose mother is dating Simon's father.

### The Dark Side with Nat X (16.5)

Live from Compton, California, Nat X (Chris Rock) is a militant African American with a large afro and the only 15-minute show on TV "because the man would never give a brother like me a whole half-hour!" He gives his top five list (reasons why white people can't dance) and insults his white guests like

*The Dark Side with Nat X*: "The only show on TV written by a brother, produced by a brother, and starring a brother [played by Chris Rock]!"

Vanilla Ice (Kevin Bacon) (16.12), and then has his sidekick Sandman (Chris Farley) sweep them off the stage with a broom.

## Bill Swerski's Super Fans (16.10)

*Bill Swerski's Super Fans* is a television show broadcast from Ditka's Restaurant in Chicago, Illinois, home of a "certain football team, which has carved out a special place in the pantheon of professional football greats. . . . Da Bears!" In the first of five sketches, which aired in the 1990–1991 season (16.10), Bill Swerski is played by Chicago native Joe Mantegna, though in subsequent sketches his brother Bob (George Wendt) has taken his place due to Bill's heart attack. Bill/Bob are joined by fellow Chicago Bears fans Todd O'Connor (Chris Farley), Pat Arnold (Mike Myers), and Carl Wollarski (Robert Smigel), who wear dark glasses and have mustaches—just like Coach Mike Ditka. They sit around drinking beer and eating sausage and predicting the score of the next game. Depending on the time of year, they also discuss Chicago's other team—"Da Bulls!" In September 1991, they are joined by host Michael Jordan (17.1), who gives a short on-air plug for "the Michael Jordan Foundation."

## Richard Laymer, a.k.a. the Richmeister (16.11)

Richard Laymer (Rob Schneider) is the annoying guy in the office near the photocopier who likes to give his coworkers nicknames every time they walk by and narrate what they were doing ("makin' copies") ("Stevester, Steve-man, Sandy the Sandstress," "The Great Randino"). At one point, the copier has to be taken away (16.12), and his coworkers (Phil Hartman and Julia Sweeney) are concerned about the Richardmeister, who moves the coffeepot over to his desk. We also learn via a flashback that Richard (Macaulay Culkin) has been doing this since grade school when his desk was next to the

"Makin' copies!": Richard Laymer (Rob Schneider), a.k.a. the Richmester, has a front-row seat to the office photocopier.

pencil sharpener (17.7). In later sketches we see Richard in other office locations, such as *L.A. Law*'s (1986–1994) McKenzie, Brackman, Chaney, and Kuzak (17.12), and on the Branch Davidian Compound (18.15) where David Koresh (the "Christ-meister") is "makin' copies."

## Daily Affirmation with Stuart Smalley (16.12)

The television host Stuart Smalley (Al Franken) is introduced as a "caring nurturer, but not a licensed therapist" though he seems a little more focused on himself and his own issues than other people (his mantra is "I'm good enough, I'm smart enough, and doggonit, people like me"). He does try to help a couple, John and Lorena B. [Bobbitt] (Rosie O'Donnell and Mike Myers) (19.6), who have filed for divorce, to share their feelings (Smalley gets Lorena to apologize for cutting off John's penis). He also shows viewers the meaning of true love when he chats with a pair of newlyweds, Michael J. [Jackson] and Lisa Marie P. [Presley] (Tim Meadows and Marisa Tomei), who can't keep their hands off one another. (See also chapter 26.)

## Chippendales Audition (16.14)

Chris Farley blew the needle off the laugh meter in this sketch in which he competes with Patrick Swayze to be a Chippendales dancer. Before they get

## Live from Studio 8H: The 1990s

The eclectic choice of musical guests in the 1990s suggest that SNL was trying to hold on to its loyal baby boomer fan base, yet at the same time appeal to a younger audience by featuring new talent. SNL continued to showcase artists like Bonnie Raitt (15.11, 17.4, 20.2), Elvis Costello (16.20), Billy Joel (19.4), Mick Jagger (18.12), Paul Simon (16.6, 18.20, 20.4), Tom Petty and the Heartbreakers (17.3, 20.6, 22.1, 24.17), and James Taylor (17.9, 19.6), all of whom debuted on the show in the 1970s . . . Nirvana's *Nevermind* was the #1 album on the *Billboard* Chart when the band introduced America to grunge with their SNL debut in January of 1992 (17.10) and sang "Smells Like Teen Spirit" and "Territorial Pissing." Their second appearance (19.1) followed the release of their third and final studio album, *In Utero*, from which they sang "Heart-Shaped Box" and "Rape Me" . . . SNL also continued to feature artists whose albums landed at the top of the *Billboard* Chart as the best-selling album of the year, including Alanis Morissette (21.4) ("Hand in My Pocket" and "All I Really Want" from *Jagged Little Pill* [1996]), and commercial pop groups like the Spice Girls (22.17) ("Wannabe" and "Say You'll Be There" from *Spice* [1997]), and the Backstreet Boys (23.16, 24.19) ("As Long as You Love Me" from *Backstreet's Back* [1997] and "I Want It That Way" and "All I Have to Give" from *Millennium* [1999]) . . . There were also debut performances by Public Enemy (17.1) ("Can't Truss It," "Bring the Noize"), the Beastie Boys (20.8) ("Sure Shot," "Ricky's Theme," "Heart Attack Man"), and R.E.M. (16.17) ("Losing My Religion," "Shiny Happy People").

In one of his most memorable sketches on the show, the fearless Chris Farley (right) squares off with guest host Patrick Swayze during a Chippendales audition.

started, the head judge (Kevin Nealon) tells them that either of them would make a wonderful addition to the Chippendales family. The music, Loverboy's "Working for the Weekend," begins. The handsome and lean Adrian (Swayze, a former dancer) has all the right moves. Barney (Farley) also has the moves, but when he takes off his shirt, he reveals his large belly. In the end, Nealon explains that the job goes to Adrian because Barney's body is "fat and flabby."

According to Farley's biography, *The Chris Farley Show*, *SNL* writers and cast members had mixed reactions to the sketch, ranging from "fantastic" to "lame" and "mean." The sketch, written by Jim Downey, appeared in Farley's fourth show. In the same biography, Downey recalled giving Farley the note that what's important here is that he is not at all embarrassed when he's told by the judge that the audience prefers a "more sculpted, lean physique as opposed to a fat, flabby one." Whatever you may think about it, the sketch was definitely a turning point in Farley's career. One of his agents, Doug Robinson, recalled that the sketch was key to getting the other agents at CAA to sign him as a client. "All we had to do was show everyone a video of the 'Chippendales' sketch, and it was done," Robinson explained, "We signed him right then."

## *The Chris Farley Show* (17.2)

On a rare occasion, Chris Farley got the chance to play a character who was not loud and overbearing. In this case it was himself as the host of his own talk show. Only he wasn't very good at asking his guests Jeff Daniels (17.2), Martin Scorsese (17.6), and Paul McCartney (18.13) questions. All he could think of to ask Sir Paul is, "You remember when you were with the Beatles . . . that was awesome." When he brings up McCartney's recent arrest in Japan for pot possession, Paul says he would like to forget all that. Farley reacts by hitting himself and saying, "Idiot! That's so stupid! What a dumb question." It was a pleasure just to watch

Farley sit still in a chair for five minutes and demonstrate his skill as a comedian with great timing. The name of the sketch was used as the title of Farley's biography by his older brother Tom and Tanner Colby. Head writer Jim Downey remembered the idea came from Farley himself, a "comedy nerd," who would ask him about old sketches and essentially recite the entire thing for him. "Yes, Chris," Downey would ask, "What about it?" "That was awesome," Farley replied.

## Coffee Talk with Linda Richman (17.3)

Modeled after Mike Myers's first wife's mother, Linda Richman (Myers) was a middle-aged Jewish woman, complete with Liz Taylor hair and large eyeglasses, who spoke in a heavy New York accent. She occasionally threw in a Yiddish word (or a word that was close enough), her favorite being "I'm a little verklempt" (*verklempt* means choked up or speechless). At that point she usually threw out a topic for her viewers to discuss, like "The New Deal was neither new nor was it a deal" or "The chickpea is neither a chick nor a pea." But her favorite discussion topic was Barbra Streisand, who made a surprise appearance on the show (17.14). Richman loved *The Prince of Tides* (1991) and Streisand's nails, which were "like buttah." Myers also did an impersonation of Streisand on *SNL* in a parody of President Clinton's Inaugural Gala (18.11) and as one of the many performers who records a duet with Frank Sinatra (Phil Hartman) (19.6).

## Dick Clark Productions Receptionist (17.8)

This simple sketch lets David Spade do what he does best: be snide and condescending, cut people off mid-sentence, and then tell them to "take a seat." He has no idea who rapper Hammer is, nor does he allow Kremlock, an alien from Planet Orton 5 (Dana Carvey), to see earthling Richard Clark so he can go on the "television airwaves to warn people of this planet of imminent doom and destruction" (17.8). He irritates Roseanne Arnold because he's never heard of her or her show ("I only watch PBS."), tells a women claiming to be Clark's long-lost biological mother (Julia Sweeney) to "be a dove" and keep the area clear in front of his desk, and doesn't recognize Jesus Christ—from the Bible ("I'm not a big reader. If you could just have a seat.") (17.14). The last time we see Spade as the receptionist he's working for the chief of the Los Angeles Fire Department during the Malibu fires (19.6), which gives him the chance to pull the same attitude on celebrities like Charlton Heston (Phil Hartman), Sean Penn (Jay Mohr), Penny Marshall (Rosie O'Donnell), and Marla Gibbs (Ellen Cleghorne), who are all desperately trying to get past his desk to see their ravaged homes.

## "Tonight Song," Sung by Steve Martin and Cast (17.9)

Backstage before the show, Chris Farley shows Steve Martin his old King Tut costume, which makes the host realize that back then he used to care—when the show meant something. And that's his cue to launch into one of the more elaborate opening numbers sung by Martin and the season's sixteen cast members in which they all vow to do their best tonight.

### Debate '92: The Challenge to Avoid Saying Something Stupid (18.3)

The three contenders for the Democratic nomination in the 1992 presidential election—former California governor Jerry Brown (a.k.a. Governor "Moonbeam," a nickname given to him by onetime-girlfriend singer Linda Ronstadt); former U.S. Senator from Massachusetts Paul Tsongas; and governor of Arkansas Bill Clinton—were not high-profile candidates. The public knew little about them, which accounts for their *SNL* debut in a cold open in March 1992 (17.15), in which all three candidates (Dana Carvey as Brown, Al Franken as Tsongas, and Phil Hartman as Clinton) address a *Star Trek* convention as part of C-SPAN's coverage of "Road to the White House." Once Clinton is declared the Democratic nominee, he joins a three-way debate between incumbent President George H. W. Bush and the independent candidate, a short, bossy Texas billionaire named Ross Perot. Dana Carvey, who had spent the last four years perfecting his George H. W., is forced to do double duty and impersonate the diminutive Perot. In the first presidential debate, which *SNL* dubs "Debate '92: The Challenge to Avoid Saying Something Stupid," Carvey plays both Bush and Perot, whose answers to questions were previously recorded. At one point Perot led the polls, but his popularity stalled due to a variety of factors, including his decision to exit and then reenter the election and his questionable campaign tactics. With his small size, heavy Texan accent, and bigger-than-life personality, he was the ideal target for parody. After the poor performance of his running mate, Vice Admiral James Stockdale, a highly decorated, navy hero and former Vietnam POW, in the vice presidential debate, Perot tries to ditch him on a country road (18.4). Stockdale, who was unprepared to be a political candidate, is portrayed by Phil Hartman as a shell-shocked old man.

### Clinton Visits McDonald's (18.8)

On the same episode that opened with a *Wayne's World* sketch in which derogatory remarks were made about First Daughter–elect Chelsea Clinton (for which Lorne Michaels and Mike Myers later apologized; see chapter 25), there was a funnier, less-than-flattering sketch about her father. President-elect Clinton (Phil Hartman) jogs about three blocks with the Secret Service in tow and makes a pit stop at McDonald's. At the time, Clinton's bad eating habits were no secret. He gained thirty pounds on the campaign trail, and, according to a December 1992 *New York Times* story, he made a "solemn vow" to eat right. Clinton starts to mingle with the people, and as he does, he begins to eat their food, even using it as props to explain his position on sending troops to Somalia. He even gets an Egg McMuffin on the house (and puts barbecue sauce on it). When Hartman

# Saturday Night Alive (and Dead)

exited *SNL* at the end of the 1993–1994 season, he left the show without a Clinton impersonator. The following season opens (20.1) with cast members Chris Farley, Chris Elliott, David Spade, and Tim Meadows auditioning to be the show's new Bill Clinton (they all get rejected). Consequently, the president was MIA during season 20, though new cast member Michael McKean impersonated him for two sketches in which he outlines his health care bill (20.2) and delivers his Christmas message with Mrs. Clinton (Janeane Garofalo). In the following season, Darrell Hammond takes over the role for the remainder of Clinton's years in the White House.

## Matt Foley, Motivational Speaker (18.19)

A popular character on *SNL* in the early 1990s, Matt Foley (Chris Farley) was developed on the Second City stage in Chicago by Chris Farley and writer Bob Odenkirk. According to Farley's biography, *The Chris Farley Show*, he was named after a classmate at Marquette University who became a priest. Farley's Foley is a big, loud, overbearing, hyperactive motivational speaker who tells his audience about the harsh realities of life, including his own, which is meant to serve as a warning that if they don't wise up, they might end up like him: "thirty-five years old, eating a steady diet of government cheese, thrice divorced, and living in a

Happy Mother's Day!: The season 17 cast members and their moms celebrated the day in style in a prime-time special that aired on Sunday, May 10, 1992.

van down by the river!" It doesn't matter if the people he's talking to are young or old or if someone has a great life and/or a successful career—he will mock them and tell them to shut up. In the process he throws his large frame around, sometimes breaking furniture in the process.

In his first appearance (18.19), concerned parents (Phil Hartman, Julia Sweeney) hire Foley to talk to their kids (David Spade, Christina Applegate) after they find a large bag of weed in the family room. Foley was downstairs in the basement drinking coffee for four hours before he comes upstairs and starts going off on the kids, during which both Spade and Applegate can barely contain themselves. In later episodes he's hired to straighten out Halloween pranksters (19.5), works as a motivational Santa in a mall and tells kids there is no Santa Claus (19.9), and speaks to juvenile delinquents in a Scared Straight program (19.14). When Farley returned to host the show in October 1997, Foley made his last appearance (23.4), in which he is working for a fitness instructor to motivate his spinning class and, in the process, destroys the bike he's using for a demonstration.

### "So Long, Farewell" to Phil Hartman (19.20)

On the final show of season 19, the entire cast bid the audience adieu by singing Rodgers and Hammerstein's "So Long, Farewell" from *The Sound of Music* with most of the cast dressed as their recurring characters (Mike Myers as Linda Richman, Julia Sweeney as Pat, etc.). At the end of the song, Hartman sits down on the stage next to a sleepy Chris Farley (dressed as Matt Foley) and puts his arm around him and says, "I can't imagine a more dignified way . . . to end my eight years on this program." In retrospect, seeing the two of them together in that final moment is touching and very sad as both of them died within the next four years—Chris Farley in 1997 at the age of thirty-three and Phil Hartman in the following year at the age of forty-nine.

During his final week on the show, the much beloved Hartman was given a bronze stick of glue because his castmates considered him "the glue" of the show.

# Resuscitating *SNL*

## The 1990s, Part II (1995–2000), Seasons 21–25

"Barely Alive, It's Saturday Night!: Can Lorne Michaels Revive *SNL* Before It's Too Late?" is the question Tom Shales posed in an article that appeared in the *Washington Post* on August 20, 1995, a little over a month before the season 21 opener. Shales is generally sympathetic toward Michaels due to the bad press he received during season 20 (1994–1995) coupled with the interference by NBC executives (which Michaels downplays) and pressure to essentially reinvent the show. The article publicly eased some of the tension between Michaels and NBC, and, more specifically, Don Ohlmeyer, president of the network's West Coast division, who expressed his support and faith in Michaels. At the same time, Ohlmeyer was equally candid in expressing his displeasure over certain *SNL* cast members who were in a "mad race to make movies" and treating *SNL* as "a part-time job between theatrics."

The issue regarding cast members using the show as a springboard for their own film careers was addressed in the revised contract that went into effect with the new cast members for the 1999–2000 season. Previously, they were given a standard five- to six-year contract. According to the *New York Observer*, the new contract also gives NBC the power to take a cast member off a show after two years and put him/her into a sitcom. While a performer can pass on the first two show offers, he/she must accept the third. The contract for the sitcom can be up to six years. Technically, a performer could be under contract for a total of twelve years (six years on *SNL* + six years on a sitcom).

The second major change also gives NBC more control of a cast member's film career. Cast members now have a three-movie option with *SNL* Films, a production company co-owned by Michaels, Paramount Pictures, and NBC. They will receive a nonnegotiable salary of $75,000 for the first film, $150,000 for the second film, and $300,000 for the third. The network can also pay a star a similar rate to say no to a movie being made by another studio. In the same article, Lorne Michaels didn't seem to think the contractual changes were significant, describing *SNL* as still very "talent friendly," and was optimistic that NBC would not be pulling cast members from his show to star on a sitcom. Still, anyone auditioning for the show for the coming season had to sign the contract, despite the protests of their agents.

Ohlmeyer also assured Shales that Michaels would be devoting less time to producing movies and be more focused on *SNL*. At the moment, he had two films in production: *Black Sheep* (1996) starring Chris Farley and David Spade and *The Kids in the Hall: Brain Candy*. Between 1992 and 1995, Michaels produced a total of six feature films: *Tommy Boy* (1995), starring Chris Farley and David Spade; *Lassie* (1994) (yes, that's right, *Lassie*), and four comedies based on recurring *SNL* characters: *Wayne's World* (1992), *Coneheads* (1993), *Wayne's World 2* (1993), and *Stuart Saves His Family* (1995). The glut of films based on *SNL* sketches, along with comedies starring *SNL* cast members, did not go unnoticed by the critics. In April 1995, *Rolling Stone* critic Peter Travers wrote: "With all the bile being spewed at *Saturday Night Live* for lowering its comic aim after 20 years on the air, one key act keeps getting lost: The movies featuring *SNL* cast members are much, much worse."

To get back to the question posed by the title of Shales's article, the answer is "yes." Michaels was able to retool and revive *SNL* by making some changes and bringing in new writers and cast members. Surprisingly, two popular current cast members—Chris Farley and Adam Sandler—were both fired from the show. Many years later, Adam Sandler appeared on the final week of *The Tonight Show with Conan O'Brien* to share the story of his exit from *SNL* and commiserate with O'Brien, a former staff writer on *Saturday Night Live*, who was recently given his walking papers from NBC along with a $33 million settlement and a $12 million severance package for his staff. Other cast members from season 20 who did not return include Morwenna Banks, Ellen Cleghorne, Chris Elliott, Al Franken, Laura Kightlinger, Michael McKean, Jay Mohr, plus two who left in the middle of the season, Mike Myers and Janeane Garofalo. Several of the new cast members—Will Ferrell, Cheri Oteri, and Chris Kattan—were Groundlings, while two others—Dave Koechner and Nancy Walls—were from Second City in Chicago. Jim Downey, who had been the show's head writer since 1986 (season 12) and co-head writer with Fred Wolf for season 20, remained on the show as a staff writer, while Steve Higgins joined Wolf as the show's new co-head writer. Ginia Bellafante reported in *Time* magazine that there was a major turnover in the writing staff—twelve out of seventeen writers were newcomers.

In the late 1990s, *SNL* also faced some late-night competition with the premiere of another sketch comedy show, *MADtv* (1995–2009), which aired on the Fox Network opposite *SNL* but started one half hour earlier. *MADtv* earned respectable ratings and enjoyed a fourteen-year run, yet it never posed a major threat to *SNL*'s ratings. Fox decided to pull the plug at the end of the 2008–2009 season when the show became too expensive to produce. Another competitor was shock jock Howard Stern, who claimed his new television *The Howard Stern Radio Show* (1998–2001) on CBS and in some areas on UPN was going to beat *SNL* in the ratings. Midway through its first season, the *New York Times* reported that while Stern did manage to attract more male viewers between the ages of eighteen and thirty-four in seven or eight big-city markets, ultimately the self-proclaimed "king of all media" did not pose a threat because while *SNL* was available in 99 percent of homes in the country, Stern could only be seen in 61 percent.

*SNL*'s ratings did improve steadily between 1995 and 2000. According to the *Hollywood Reporter*, *SNL* posted its biggest May sweep audiences in six years, an average of 8.5 million viewers (May, along with November and February, are the most important months for ratings because they determine the rates charged for ads). The season finale on May 20, 2000 (25.20), hosted by Jackie Chan with musical guest Kid Rock, drew 9.4 million viewers.

The improvement in the show's ratings over time can be attributed to improvement in the writing and a core group of talented cast members who started with the show during season 20, 21, or 22, many of whom remained with the show for five years or more: Will Ferrell (seven seasons), Ana Gasteyer (six seasons), Darrell Hammond (fourteen seasons), Chris Kattan (eight seasons), Cheri Oteri (five seasons), Tracy Morgan (seven seasons), Colin Quinn (five seasons), Molly Shannon (seven seasons), and Tim Meadows (ten seasons), who would leave at the end of the 1999–2000 season. This group, along with Jim Breuer (three seasons) and Norm Macdonald (five seasons), who were both gone after season 23, seemed more like a repertory company than a group of individual performers, much like the cast of the late 1980s (Carvey, Dunn, Hartman, Hooks, Jackson, Lovitz, Miller, Myers, and Nealon). A steady stream of ex-*SNL* cast members were invited back to host (in season 22 alone, seven out of twenty), plus Five-Timers Club members Alec Baldwin, John Goodman, and Tom Hanks.

One performer who was certainly a catalyst for breathing new life into *SNL* was Will Ferrell, whose comic persona is that of an immature, oversized kid who hasn't reached that age yet when he becomes self-conscious and begins to care what others think of him. This is best illustrated by a classic sketch broadcast on the second show after 9/11 (27.2) in which Ferrell walks into a business meeting at work wearing a red, white, and blue Speedo and half shirt as an expression of his patriotism.

Ferrell's success can also be attributed to his creative collaboration with the other performers on the show, especially the women, with whom he played a series of loopy characters: the Spartan Cheerleaders, Arianna (Cheri Oteri) and Craig (Ferrell); hosts of *Morning Latte*, Tom Wilkins (Ferrell) and Cass Van Rye (Oteri); the Lovers, Virginia (Rachel Dratch) and Roger Klarvin (Ferrell); singing duo Bobbi Mohan-Culp (Ana Gasteyer) and her husband and accompanist, Marty Culp (Ferrell); hosts of *Dog Show*, Miss Colleen (Molly Shannon) and her husband, David Larry (Will Ferrell).

Another welcome addition to the cast was master impressionist Darrell Hammond, who filled a void left by Phil Hartman with his departure in 1994. For eight seasons, from the mid-1980s through the mid-1990s, Hartman was the go-to guy for impressions, including President Bill Clinton, from his 1992 election campaign to the middle of his first term. Hammond took over in time for the reelection campaign and played Clinton throughout his second term in office (1996–2000), which included the Starr Report, the Monica Lewinsky scandal, and the impeachment hearings.

## Memorable Moments, Characters, and Sketches

### Mary Katherine Gallagher Auditions (21.4)

Mary Katherine Gallagher, the very nervous Catholic high school girl, made her *SNL* debut when she auditioned for St. Monica High School's talent show. She recited a monologue from her favorite made-for-TV movie, *A Woman Scorned: The Betty Broderick Story* (1992), starring Meredith Baxter, and sang "You Ask Me If I Love You." When she attempts a back flip, she crashes into chairs. But all her stumbling and falling down never stops little Mary Katherine from achieving her goal of being the center of attention.

In later sketches she competes to be *Seventeen* magazine's Fresh Face (and wins by default) (21.14), and Clean Teen Deodorant Spokesman (24.7) (she sticks her hands under her arms and smells her fingers when she's nervous, so there was no contest). When she's not performing, she is upstaging her classmates in St. Monica High School's production of *West Side Story* (21.18) and the St. Monica Christmas Choir's holiday pageant (22.9). (See more in chapter 26.)

### Arianna and Craig Buchanan Do the Perfect Cheer (21.5)

Arianna (Cheri Oteri) and Craig Buchanan (Will Ferrell) are wannabe cheerleaders who didn't make the East Lake Spartan Spirit cheerleading squad, so they take it upon themselves to attend school functions involving competitions that don't have cheerleaders.

They cheer at a high school chess tournament (21.11), a math competition (21.18), and ping pong (22.1) and bowling (22.6) tournaments. They are eventually seen cheering off campus at the local Hickory Farms (22.9) and in the maternity ward, where Arianna's nemesis Alexis (Jennifer Love Hewitt) is giving birth (24.7). Their cheers are off-the-wall, and each sketch ends with "the perfect cheer."

Oteri told *Rolling Stone* in a 1997 profile of the cast why she likes Arianna and Craig: "One thing I like about them is, they're losers, but they don't know it. I would feel sorry for them if they knew they were outcasts. They have no clue, thank God."

### Joe Pesci Hosts a Talk Show (21.7)

One of the underrated performers of the late 1980s was comedian Jim Breuer, who unfortunately played third banana to Will Ferrell and Darrell Hammond. One of his memorable impressions was of Italian character actor Joe Pesci, who won an Academy Award for playing mobster thug Tommy DeVito in *Goodfellas*

They may not be members of East Lake High School's Spartan cheerleading squad, but that doesn't stop Craig (Will Ferrell) and Arianna (Cheri Oteri) from cheering at the school's swim meet, chess tournament, math competition, and other events where they are not wanted.

(1990). In his autobiography, *I'm Not High*, Breuer recalled how he used to make one of the interns at *SNL* laugh by imitating Pesci. He and staff writer Steve Koren envisioned Pesci as a talk show host who would invite actors, including some of his costars, onto his show. But Pesci acts just like Tommy DeVito. He is easily agitated (he shoots the kid holding the cue cards) and is abusive toward his guests, twisting their words around if they describe Pesci's characters as "irritating" or a "lunatic." He orders them offstage or gets violent, even smashing "pretty boy" Brad Pitt's (David Spade) head in with a baseball bat. In his first appearance (21.7), Pesci welcomes two of his costars: Macaulay Culkin (played by guest host Anthony Edwards) from *Home Alone* (1990) and Sharon Stone (Nancy Walls), with whom he was currently starring in Martin Scorsese's *Casino* (1995). In later episodes he welcomes best friend Robert De Niro, played by Alec Baldwin (21.11) and, in a later sketch, by John Goodman (21.15); Frank Sinatra (Phil Hartman) (22.7); and Al Pacino (Kevin Spacey) (22.10). But a major coup for Breuer was to have the real Pesci and De Niro interrupt a sketch and show Breuer and Colin Quinn (as De Niro) how to hit someone with a bat. Equally entertaining is Breuer's description of his meeting with the real Pesci, who was extremely intimidating as he started to question him about the racial slurs he was using in the sketch, etc. Breuer was apologetic and promised not to do the sketch again. Finally, Pesci said to him, "I'm just playing games with you, Jimmy. Busting your balls, sheesh."

## March 23, 1996: The Roxbury Guys Go Clubbing (21.16)

The song "What Is Love" by Haddaway blares in the background as two brothers, Steve (Will Ferrell) and Doug Butabi (Chris Kattan), in shiny suits stand by the bar thinking they look cool—and totally clueless. For more about the Butabi Brothers, see chapter 26.

## Goat Boy Remembers the '80s (22.1)

As his name suggests, Goat Boy is half boy, half goat—the product of an experiment conducted in a University of Chicago lab and Jim Breuer's fertile and warped imagination. In his autobiography, *I'm Not High,* Breuer explained that the character of Goat Boy was a persona he created to get free drinks in a bar. In the middle of ordering a drink, he would start "bleating and rutting like a goat" (in his stand-up, Breuer describes how he was traumatized as a child by the goats at a petting zoo). The bartender figured he had Tourette syndrome and did not charge him. When Breuer mentioned the character to some of the writers at *SNL*, he was greeted with blank stares. But one writer, Tom Gianas, thought it would be funny if Goat Boy was a singer and pitchman for a CD of hit songs from the 1980s. Goat Boy's debut (21.19) is in a commercial for a CD in which he bleats and ruts through songs like "Safety Dance," "Let's Dance," and "I Can Dream About You." In the season 22 opener (22.1), Goat Boy is the host of his own MTV show, *Hey, Remember the '80s,* which featured celebrities from that decade like *Family Ties*' Tina Yothers (Cheri Oteri) and Andrew Ridgeley (Tom Hanks) from Wham!. When he starts braying excessively, scientists standing nearby calm him with electric prods. In addition to his own show, Goat Boy is interviewed by Charlie Rose (Mark McKinney) (22.13) and is reunited with his long-lost brother (David Duchovny) by Oprah (Tim Meadows) (22.20).

## Mr. Peepers "Eats" an Apple (22.1)

The missing link between *Homo sapiens* and the animal kingdom, seventeen-year-old Mr. Peepers (Chris Kattan) has some physical characteristics of a human, but he moves and acts like a baby chimpanzee. He always appears to be in a frenzied state, which becomes even more frantic when he gets nervous or scared. His favorite things are apples, though he doesn't eat them like a human; instead, he plows through them at rapid speed with his teeth and spits them out.

His *SNL* debut was with his trainer (Tom Hanks) on a parody of *The Tonight Show with Jay Leno* (2009–2014). Mr. Peepers later pops up in a series of parodies: Peepers and Trent (Vince Vaughn) try to get lucky in Vegas in *Swingers* (1996); *Sex and the City*'s (1998–2004) Carrie Bradshaw (Jennifer Aniston) picks up Mr. Peepers in a bar; and in an episode of *Dawson's Creek* (1998–2003), Joey (Katie Holmes) falls for the new international student from the Amazon, Mr. Peepers. The best of the Peepers sketches involves his reunion with the father, Papa Peepers (Dwayne "The Rock" Johnson) (25.15)—it's worth watching if only to see "The Rock" in red overalls sitting on top of a table plowing through an apple.

## Marty Culp and Bobbi Mohan-Culp Serenade Us (22.5)

According to a chart of the most frequently seen *SNL* recurring characters (political impersonators not included), published on Vulture in November 2011, topping the list for the years 1995–2002 are the married musical duo Marty Culp (Will Ferrell) and Bobbi Mohan-Culp (Ana Gasteyer). The couple made a total of twenty-one appearances (Mary Katherine Gallagher came in second with eighteen appearances, followed by the Spartan Cheerleaders with seventeen). The Culps are music teachers at Altadena Middle School (outside of Los Angeles) who also perform as a musical duo. Their clothes are out of style, and their medley of inappropriate songs tailored for a specific occasion is painfully

Middle school music teachers Marty Culp (Will Ferrell) and Bobbi Mohan-Culp (Ana Gasteyer) moonlight as performers specializing in song medleys tailored for any specific occasion like a renaissance fair, drug awareness assembly, Lamaze class, an alternative prom, or snowed in at an airport waiting for your plane.

bad. Bobbi sings every song in the same high-pitched operatic voice along with Marty, who accompanies her on the keyboards. At a Renaissance Faire, they sing "Medieval Woman" (25.20) (a parody of Electric Light Orchestra's "Evil Woman") and Sisqó's "Thong Song." For a Martin Luther King Jr. assembly (26.9), it's a funk medley that includes Sly and the Family Stone's "Everyday People," Wild Cherry's "Play That Funky Music," and DMX's "Party Up." Their other gigs include a Gore–Lieberman rally (26.5), O'Hare Airport during a blizzard (24.10), and, in their final appearance, an alternative prom for LGBT youth (37.21), with a medley that includes Adele's "Rumour Has It," "Super Gay" (Nicki Minaj's "Super Bass"), Justin Bieber's "Boyfriend," and the gay anthem "YMCA" but with the initials "LGBT."

## Let's Play *Celebrity Jeopardy!* (22.8)

Created by Merv Griffin, *Jeopardy!* debuted on March 30, 1964, remained on NBC's daytime schedule through 1975, and was revived again in 1978–1979 (as the *All-New Jeopardy!*). A nighttime syndicated version aired in 1974–1975. The current syndicated version debuted in 1984 with host Alex Trebek. The Game Show Network ranks *Jeopardy!* #2 in its list of the 50 Great Game Shows (*Match Game* is #1).

The first *Jeopardy!* parody was *Jeopardy 1991* (2.5), a futuristic version of the show hosted by Art F-114 (Steve Martin), with the show's real announcer, Don Pardo, and contestants Danny M-125 (Dan Aykroyd), Laraine A-270 (Laraine Newman), and Lee P-413 (Chevy Chase). The categories include the standard subjects like "Medicine," "Movies," and "TV," along with "Mutant Viruses" and "Nuclear Accidents." The question and answers are absurd predictions about the future: name of the original Tidy Bowl man who won eight Oscars (Fred Miltonburg—that was his real name); legalized in 1983, it eased population (baby-killing); and with the recent news of Chase's departure: "Comedian whose career fizzled after leaving *NBC's Saturday Night*." (No one knows the answer or seems to have heard of him.)

Twenty years later, *Jeopardy!* was revived by *SNL* in a series of sketches that were based on *Celebrity Jeopardy!*, a special edition of the show in which actors, writers, and television personalities compete to win money for their favorite charity. The concept actually dates back to the 1960s, though the first *Celebrity Jeopardy!* tournament with host Alex Trebek aired on October 26, 1992, and featured contestants Carol Burnett, Donna Mills, and Regis Philbin (Trebek assured the audience that the celebrities had not been briefed and did not even know the categories). For the record, Burnett won, but $10,000 was awarded to each celebrity's respective charities. In 2010, former *SNL* cast member Michael McKean won the *Jeopardy! Million Dollar Celebrity Invitational* tournament, beating Cheech Marin—and Jane Curtin!

The winnings on *SNL*'s version of *Celebrity Jeopardy!* are rarely in the plus column as host Alex Trebek (Will Ferrell), with all the patience he can muster,

A fan favorite with Will Ferrell as *Celebrity Jeopardy!* host Alex Trebek (left front), who must contend with dumb contestants like Burt Reynolds (Norm Macdonald) (behind Ferrell, wearing an oversized cowboy hat) while actor Sean Connery (Darrell Hammond) hurls an endless stream of insults.

tries to get through the game despite the stupidity of celebrity guests like Burt Reynolds (also known as Turd Ferguson) (Norm Macdonald) (22.8, 22.19, 23.2, 25.3, 34.22) and the vicious insults hurled at him and his mother by the salty-tongued Sean Connery (Darrell Hammond), who likes to purposely mispronounce the categories ("Famous Titties" instead of "Famous Titles"). Other *SNL* cast members who impersonated celebrity guests include Jimmy Fallon as Adam Sandler (24.4), French Stewart (25.3), and Hilary Swank (25.17); Amy Poehler as Sharon Osbourne (30.19); and Molly Shannon as Minnie Driver (23.20). Guest hosts have also contributed celebrity impressions of Marlon Brando (John Goodman) (22.19), Michael Keaton (Matthew Perry) (23.2), Jeff Goldblum (David Duchovny) (23.20), Tom Cruise (Ben Stiller) (24.4), Calista Flockhart (24.16), Tobey Maguire (Keanu Reeves) (25.17), Catherine Zeta-Jones (Lucy Liu) (26.8), Anne Heche (Reese Witherspoon) (27.1), and Björk (Winona Ryder) (27.20). The man himself—Alex Trebek—even made a very brief cameo on Will Ferrell's last show to commiserate with Ferrell's Trebek over the stupidity of the contestants and to tell Hammond's Sean Connery, "Back off, Connery, I don't have to take that from you" (27.20).

## Attorney General Janet Reno Hosts a Dance Party (22.10)

Janet Reno was the first female United States Attorney General, serving during President Clinton's first and second terms (1993–2001). She had a high profile during that time due to a series of events involving the Department of Justice, including the 1993 standoff between the FBI and the Branch Davidians in Waco, Texas; the 1995 Oklahoma City bombing; and the Centennial Olympic Park bombing during the 1996 Summer Olympics. Reno's mannish looks and deep voice made her an easy target for female impersonators, including Will Ferrell, who first appeared as Reno alongside President Clinton (Darrell Hammond) (22.10). In the next episode, Reno hosted her own show, *Janet Reno's Dance Party*, from her basement. Like *American Bandstand*, teenagers danced while Reno welcomed guests like President Clinton and Secretary of Health and Human Services Donna Shalala (Kevin Spacey) (22.11), and New York City mayor Rudy Giuliani (23.7). Reno herself proved to America she's a good sport when she appeared on the final episode (26.10). When Ferrell asks Reno what she does when she's depressed, she says, "dance!" "It was all her idea to come on the show," Ferrell told Jeffrey Zaslow in an interview for *USA Weekend* magazine, "and I was impressed with her. She talked about how important humor is to our political process. She said that when she speaks at schools, the first question she's asked is, 'Have you seen the guy who plays you on *Saturday Night Live*?' She tells them she loves [being lampooned]; it lets all the tension out of the room."

## *Goth Talk*: "Stay Out of the Daylight!" (22.17)

Goth culture, which originated in Great Britain within the postpunk music scene of the 1980s, spread to the United States, where its influence could be seen in fashion and youth culture. A stereotypical Goth teenager dresses in black and wears pale white makeup, black mascara and lipstick, and silver jewelry. Goths listen to punk, death rock music, and Gothic rock; read eighteenth- and nineteenth-century Gothic and horror literature, and watch horror movies. Like *Wayne's World*, *Goth Talk* is a public-access television cable show broadcast on Sunshine State Cable Access (Channel 33) in Tampa Bay, Florida (hardly a Goth setting!). Hosted by Azrael Abyss (Chris Kattan) and Circe Nightshade (Molly Shannon), the show is shot in Abyss's basement, though the dark mood is usually disrupted when Azrael's older brother, Glenn (Jim Breuer), turns on the light. Azrael, who identifies himself as the "Prince of Sorrow," welcomes viewers "to the show that explores the moody depths of the Goth lifestyle here in Tampa, Florida." Their guests are fellow Goths with names like "The Beholder" (Rob Lowe) (22.17), Countess Cobwella (Sarah Michelle Gellar) (23.11), Baroness Blackbroom (Lucy Lawless) (24.3), and Hezabiah of the Dusk (Christina Ricci) (25.7).

## Everybody Loves the Mango (23.3)

Another bizarre character from Chris Kattan is Mango, a male exotic dancer who becomes an obsession of everyone who comes in contact with him. His demeanor is effeminate, and he wears tight-fighting gold hot pants and a beret—but he is a heterosexual who dances to support his wife (Molly Shannon) and children. He speaks with a pseudo-Hispanic accent and refers to himself in the third person ("If you start out using Mango, it will only lead to more Mango"). Everyone who sees Mango—male and female, gay and straight—becomes obsessed with him, including a gang leader (Samuel L. Jackson) (23.10), Garth Brooks (23.14), David Duchovny (23.20), Cuba Gooding Jr. (24.18), and Ellen DeGeneres (27.9). Like Will Ferrell, Kattan is fearless and will go to extremes to get a laugh.

## The Delicious Dish, with Special Guest Pete Schweddy (24.9)

Viewers received an early holiday surprise this season when Margaret Jo McCullin (Ana Gasteyer) and Terry Rialto (Molly Shannon), hosts of the National Public Radio talk show *The Delicious Dish*, welcome their guest, Pete Schweddy (Alec Baldwin), owner of his own holiday bakery, Season's Eatings. Pete was on the show to talk about all the delicious treats sold at his bakery. "Well, there are lots of great treats this time of year—zucchini bread, fruitcake," he explains, "but the thing I most like to bring out this time of year are my *balls*." At this point all semblance of good taste goes out the window as the two hosts and their guest have an innuendo-laden discussion about Schweddy's balls. This sketch appears on many "Top 10 *SNL* Sketches of All Time" lists because of lines like "They're bigger than I expected" and "I can't wait to get my mouth around his balls" delivered in that mellow, conversational NPR-style delivery by Baldwin, Gasteyer, and Shannon.

A sketch featured on every *SNL* holiday special: NPR's *The Delicious Dish* with hosts Margaret Jo McCullin (Ana Gasteyer) and Terry Rialto (Molly Shannon), who welcome baker Pete Schweddy and sample his holiday treats, including his specialty—"Schweddy balls."

To honor the sketch's place in American popular culture, Ben & Jerry's named a new flavor of ice cream "Schweddy Balls," which contains fudge-covered rum balls. But apparently not all women are fans of Schweddy Balls. Stephanie Reitz reported in the *Huffington Post* that supporters and members of the One Million Moms were pressuring Ben & Jerry's to keep Schweddy Balls away from their children. Monica Cole, director of the organization, didn't want to call the ice cream manufacturers out publicly because they didn't want to give them any free publicity. The group also disapproved of another flavor, a variation of "Chubby Hubby" called "Hubby Hubby" to mark the legalization of same-sex marriage in Vermont.

Pete Schweddy returned to *The Delicious Dish* in spring of 2001 (26.16) to discuss his love of baseball stadium cuisine: popcorn, pretzel bread, and—his weiner.

Betty White (35.21) also joined in the fun when she appeared as Florence Dusty to show off her "Dusty Muffin."

Good times.

## *Brian Fellow's Safari Planet* (24.19)

Tracy Morgan played few recurring characters—and his most popular was a guy named Brian Fellow, who hosted a show called *Brian Fellow's Safari Planet*. Like Stuart Smalley, who is not a licensed therapist, Brian Fellow is not an accredited zoologist nor holds an advanced degree in the environmental sciences. As the show's introduction tells us, Brian "is simply an enthusiastic young man with a sixth-grade education and an abiding love for all God's creatures." In his autobiography, *I Am the New Black*, Morgan describes him as a "gay, self-centered, paranoid host of an *animal talk show*" (emphasis his). He only has a sixth-grade education, so he's hardly qualified to host a talk show (well, actually . . .). The "gay" aspect of his character is downplayed, though he is certainly a paranoid and a nitwit, thinking a bald-headed cat is going to shave him (28.19) and that seals like to go clubbing (29.7).

## *Saturday Night Live 25* (9/26/99)

*SNL* celebrated twenty-five years on the air with a prime-time special that followed the same format as its *15th Anniversary Special*. Past and present cast members along with popular hosts like Tom Hanks, Candice Bergen, Paul Simon, and Lily Tomlin introduce clips from past shows. There are musical performances by the Eurythmics, Al Green, and, with an introduction by the Culps (Will Ferrell and Ana Gasteyer), the Beastie Boys and Elvis Costello (who sing "Radio, Radio"). The evening also includes moving tributes to Gilda Radner, John Belushi, and two additional beloved cast members—Chris Farley (by his friend David Spade), and Phil Hartman (by his castmates who started with him in 1986).

The special won a Primetime Emmy for "Outstanding Variety, Music or Comedy Special" and a Writers Guild of America Award.

## Nick Burns, Your Company's Computer Guy: "Move!" (25.6)

In a "20(ish) Questions" interview with *Playboy* magazine's Eric Spitznagel, Jimmy Fallon revealed he was a computer science major until his senior year at the College of St. Rose in Albany, New York. His grades were low, so he switched to communications but never finished. He admits that he was pretty close to being like Nick Burns, the nerdy, snide company computer guy who is constantly annoyed at having to fix stupid computer problems caused by stupid people who don't know how to do simple things like upgrade their software (25.6) or change the font on a spreadsheet (25.20). He has zero patience for the "dimwits" he works for so when he tells them how to do something and they can't do it, he tells them to "Move!" from their desk so he can sit down at their computer. You need his help, but he is so condescending it's hard to have him around.

In his final appearance, we learn that Nick is a chip off the old block when his dad (host Billy Bob Thornton) joins him on his rounds and enjoys insulting the employees.

On his way out the door, Nick stops and makes one last sarcastic comment: "Oh, by the way, you're welcome!"

# 12

# Laughing Matters

## Memorable Characters, Sketches, and Moments (2000–2013), Seasons 26–38

Saturday Night Live's political content, combined with the fact that it's broadcast live, keeps the show's humor timely and relevant. The longevity of the popular cast members and their continued loyalty to the show and producer Lorne Michaels helped keep SNL toward the top of its fans' DVR record list. SNL may no longer have the "appointment TV" status it once enjoyed back in the 1970s. Still, "Who's on SNL tonight?" remains a question often heard on Saturday afternoons.

The quality of the show greatly benefited from the extended stay of some performers, which, in some seasons, made the transition between the outgoing and incoming cast members much smoother. Many of the regulars, most of whom started off as featured players, stuck around for as long as seven (Jimmy Fallon, Will Ferrell, Rachel Dratch, Andy Samberg, Molly Shannon, Kristen Wiig) or eight (Chris Kattan, Chris Parnell, Horatio Sanz) seasons. The three cast members who departed at the end of the 2013 season—Fred Armisen, Bill Hader, and Jason Sudeikis—also enjoyed an eight-season run. Seth Meyers, who would leave in the middle of season 39 to host *Late Night*, was on SNL for twelve seasons, and Kenan Thompson for ten.

When a cast member leaves, it sometimes feels as if he or she never actually left because of their frequent guest appearances on the show. Jan Hooks departed in 1991, but made nine appearances between 1992 and 1994. After his departure in 1990, Jon Lovitz has made eight appearances and hosted the show in 1997. Since then it seems that more cast members are stopping by more often in a cameo or as the host. Between 2005 and 2012, Will Ferrell and Tina Fey have both hosted the show three times. Fey has also made twelve cameo appearances, while her former castmates Jimmy Fallon, Amy Poehler, and Maya Rudolph all took a turn at hosting and have each made nine cameos. Other SNL alums who have made frequent guest appearances include Rachel Dratch, Darrell Hammond, Tracy Morgan, and Chris Parnell.

No one ever seems to make a clean break from SNL or Lorne Michaels. In addition to the SNL "sketch films," his name either has been, or currently is, or will be on a list of projects starring or featuring one or more past and/or current SNL cast members: *Mean Girls* (2004), *Hot Rod* (2007), *Baby Mama* (2008), *Up*

*All Night* (2011–2012), *Bridesmaids* (2011), *The Skeleton Twins* (2014), *Ghostbusters* (2016), *30 Rock* (2006–2013), *Portlandia* (2011–2018), and *Late Night with Jimmy Fallon* (2009–2014).

Then there are the non–cast members who appear on the show, sometimes in a cameo, but often as host. In the 1970s, it was Elliott Gould, Candice Bergen, Buck Henry, and Steve Martin. Now it's Alec Baldwin, Jon Hamm, and Justin Timberlake, plus holdovers from past decades like Martin and Tom Hanks. They appear on the show so frequently as either a host or in a cameo, they should have "recurring" status.

Between 2000 and 2013, the show's ratings have were not high, but that did not necessarily translate into lower advertising revenues. As *Variety*'s Brian Sternberg reported, season 28 (2002–2003) ended with an average of 7.1 million viewers, 4.5 million of whom are between the ages of eighteen and forty-nine. According to the Nielsen ratings, season 38 ended with an average of 5.2 million overall viewers and an average of 2.4 million between eighteen and forty-nine. Despite the drop, the amount of money advertisers spent increased from $94.4 million in 2008 to $110 million in 2012.

One thing the ratings don't account for is how many people are watching *Saturday Night Live*—or at least parts of it—on something other than their television set. A show like *SNL* comprised of a series of short segments (each with a beginning, middle, and end), is a beneficiary of technological advancements like the smartphone and the creation of video websites like YouTube, Vimeo, and Daily Motion and on-demand streaming sites like Hulu. If you missed last week's show, you could find the sketch on Peacock (and until it's taken down, an unauthorized site like YouTube). *SNL* also caters to the YouTube generation with their library of short films, particularly Robert Smigel and his "Saturday TV Funhouse"; Adam McKay, who did the first digital shorts before cocreating the comedy shorts channel Funny or Die; and the Lonely Island (Andy Samberg, Jorma Taccone, and Akiva Schaffer), which created over one hundred shorts and music videos (including "Lazy Sunday" and "Dick in a Box," which went viral) that were usually written, shot, and edited in five days, much like the videos posted on YouTube (see chapter 22).

## Memorable Moments, Characters, and Sketches

### Tribute to 9/11 First Responders (27.1)

On September 29, 2001, New York City mayor Rudolph Giuliani opened season 27 of *Saturday Night Live* with a moving tribute to the first responders of 9/11. Standing with members of the New York City Fire Department, the New York Police Department, and the Port Authority Police Department, along with Fire Commissioner Tom Von Essen and Police Commissioner Bernard Kerik, Giuliani reminds us that on September 11, more lives were lost than on any other day in America's history, and it was the heroism of these brave men and women that

At the start of the season 27 opener, New York City Mayor Rudolph Giuliani led a tribute to the brave first responders on 9/11.

saved more than 25,000 lives. "Our hearts are broken," Giuliani added, "but they are beating, and they are beating stronger than ever. New Yorkers are unified. We will not yield to terrorism. We will not let our decisions be made out of fear. We choose to live our lives in freedom." Cut to Paul Simon, who sings "The Boxer" as the camera pans over the faces of these brave men and women. At the end, Lorne Michaels joins them onstage and thanks everyone for being there. Giuliani thanks him and calls *Saturday Night Live* "one of our great New York City institutions, and that's why it's important for you to do your show tonight." "Can we be funny?" Michaels asks. "Why start now?" Giuliani replies, "Live, from New York! It's *Saturday Night!*"

As one would expect, episode 27.1 is short on political content. During host Reese Witherspoon's monologue, she tells a joke about polar bears. The punch line is "because I'm freezing my balls off!" According to a story in *New York* magazine's tenth anniversary issue commemorating 9/11, Michaels wanted Witherspoon to say the original punch line to the joke: "Because I'm *fucking* freezing." He explained to her that "because what happened to our country was profane, and he felt it deserved profanity. I think he also thought it was funny to have this tiny young blonde girl tell a joke whose punch line is "fuck." He also assured her that the network would pay the FCC fine. But Witherspoon changed her mind at the last minute in case any of her young fans were tuning in that night.

### Farewell to Ferrell (27.20)

It was time for Will Ferrell to say goodbye—and he gets a heartfelt send-off from his castmates. They each confirm he's a nice guy and a good friend with whom they love sharing the stage. Chris Parnell reveals (and this is a true story) that he was fired from the show at the end of 2001 and was rehired again in 2002, and it was all because of Ferrell. The segment ends on a comical note with Tracy

Morgan sharing about Ferrell: "He a cold, thievin', selfish, evil dude" and a racist who stole his Walkman, is cheating on his wife, and gave Tracy's eight-year-old son a cigarette. Morgan backs down when Ferrell joins him onstage. The two walk off together, but not before Ferrell admits to stealing his Walkman and that he does hate black people.

## Debbie Downer (29.18)

Jimmy Fallon and Horatio Sanz are notorious for cracking up during sketches, but they were not alone in this sketch introducing a new character named Debbie Downer (Rachel Dratch). The premise is simple. It's a happy occasion, in this case a family reunion in Disney World (29.18) (in future sketches it's a birthday party [30.1], Thanksgiving dinner [30.6], even the Academy Awards [30.13])—and Debbie always manages to ruin everyone's good time by bringing up subjects like mad cow disease, a tsunami, political assassinations, and feline AIDS. When she makes a negative comment, the camera moves in for a close-up and a trombone makes a "wah wahhhh" sound. Every time it happened in the first sketch, Dratch found it more difficult to keep a straight face, let alone speak her lines.

In her book *Girl Walks into a Bar . . . Comedy Calamities, Dating Disasters, and a Midlife Miracle,* Dratch explained that the idea for Debbie Downer came to her when she went on vacation in Costa Rica. At the lodge where she was staying there were communal tables. Someone asked Dratch where she was from, and

Debbie Downer—the character's name not only reflects the bad news she delivers about mad cow disease and global warming, but her facial expressions as well.

## Breaking Character

Sometimes a funny (or even a not-that-funny) sketch is funnier when a performer breaks character and starts laughing. On the stage, "corpsing" (the British slang term for an actor unintentionally breaking character that originated when an actor playing a corpse started laughing) is a cardinal sin, but on a sketch comedy show it's almost expected. Here are a few moments from *SNL* in which one or more of the actors broke character:

- In a PSA for the "Right to Extreme Stupidity League," Candice Bergen blows a line that sends the entire sketch into a downward spiral (2.10; see chapter 6).
- Gilda Radner (as Lisa Loopner) loses it as Todd (Bill Murray) keeps making her drink a glass of wine (4.16; see chapter 6).
- Frankenstein (Phil Hartman) appears on a talk show, *Succinctly Speaking*, with Tonto (Jon Lovitz) and Tarzan (Kevin Nealon). Hartman, who rarely broke character, appears to have a sudden realization that the sketch is ridiculous (13.8; see chapter 9).
- David Spade can't look at Matt Foley (Chris Farley) as he accuses him of "rolling doobies" (18.19; see chapter 10).
- Jimmy Fallon can't look at Gene Frenkle (Will Ferrell) playing the cowbell (25.16; see chapter 24).
- Bill Hader as Stefon, who cracks up thanks to his writing partner John Mulaney's last-minute changes.

Here are some of the best moments from *SNL* when one or more cast member and/or host lost it:

- Black History Month (10.9): When host Eddie Murphy (as Shabazz K. Morton) continually stumbles over some words ("soul" instead of "soil," "pastes" instead of "tastes"), he breaks character and tells the audience, "Stop clapping before y'all make me smile!"
- Massive Headwound Harry (17.6): Dana Carvey is "Massive Headwound Harry," whose gaping bloody wound spoils a couple's (Linda Hamilton, Kevin Nealon) party. A dog that was supposed to lick Harry's wound almost ruins the sketch when it starts to tear and eat off Carvey's fake wound. The moment is actually funnier than the sketch itself.
- Rude clerks (Sean Hayes and Jimmy Fallon) at Jeffrey's (26.12), a pretentious clothing store, begin to fall apart when their supervisor (Will Ferrell) enters on a scooter. The version used in reruns is reportedly the dress rehearsal during which Hayes and Fallon laugh uncontrollably at Ferrell.
- Janet Jackson (29.17) seemed to fit right in when she appeared in a sketch in which she is on a tour of a winery where she learns all about the art of "cork soaking" (a sexual euphemism). She starts off taking it very seriously, but as the discussion about cork soaking intensifies, she starts to giggle as she tries to get her lines out. It doesn't help that she's talking to Horatio Sanz and Jimmy Fallon, who crack the occasional smile but are relatively subdued compared to their other sketches.
- In *The Californians* (37.19), a parody of a soap opera airing on SoapNet, the characters talk in affected Southern Californian (especially Fred Armisen) and crack each other up.

when she replied, "New York," someone else asked, "So were you there for 9/11?" "The question hung awkwardly in the jungle air," Dratch writes, "and sort of screeched things to a halt." When she returned home, the name "Debbie Downer popped into my head" and she wrote the sketch with writer Paula Pell. During rehearsal, Fallon and Sanz were cracking up, but when it was time to go live, Dratch flubbed a line and it was all downhill from there. She described what happened as a "'church laugh,' where you know you should not be laughing but you can't help yourself." Dratch admits that she tries not to break character because it can become a "cheap tool to get the audience on your side," yet the first Debbie Downer sketch was her "favorite moment" of her time at *SNL*.

## Wiig's Women

When Kristen Wiig joined the cast in season 31 (2005–2006) as a featured player, there were four strong women in the cast of twelve regular players. By season 35, all four—Rachel Dratch, Tina Fey, Amy Poehler, and Maya Rudolph—were gone, leaving Wiig as the only female regular for season 35 (featured player Abby Elliott joined her as a regular for seasons 36 and 37). Additional women were added to the cast as featured players, but most of them only remained for one or two seasons (Casey Wilson, Michaela Watkins, Jenny Slate). Wiig was given an opportunity traditionally afforded mostly to male cast members who became the show's breakout stars: John Belushi, Mike Myers, Dana Carvey, and Will Ferrell (and one female, Gilda Radner). The lack of women worked in Wiig's favor, giving her more airtime to develop a whole repertoire of bizarre characters—nervous, sometimes hyperenthusiastic women with no social barometer. Wiig specializes in over-the-top oddballs. Their lack of self-awareness is problematic because many of them want to be the center of attention. Wiig's women are at times overbearing to the point of being obnoxious or annoying, though she has said that's not her intention. "I never think of them as annoying," she explained in a 2011 *New York Times* interview with Susan Dominus. "If I had to put them in a category like that, I would just say a lot of my characters are that person at a party you don't want to talk to, because maybe they're talking too much. It's fun for me to play people that are just kind of odd."

Here is a partial list of Wiig's women (and the episode in which she first appeared):
- **Target Lady** (31.7): She's not only excited about being a cashier at Target, but she seems to go crazy over every product she rings up. Instead of paying attention to the customer, she will think nothing of running off and finding one for herself.
- **Penelope** (32.16): No matter the topic of conversation, Penelope engages in an ongoing game of one-upmanship. Whatever you've done, know, or have, Penelope (twirling her hair as she speaks) says she's done, knows, and has more.
- **Sue** (33.8): Everybody loves surprises, especially Sue. She really, really, really loves surprises. The excitement is just too much for her to handle. Just don't expect Sue to keep it to herself.

Wiig's women (left to right): the overly enthusiastic Target Lady, mischief-maker Gilly, and the odd-looking, inappropriate performer Dooneese.

- **Dooneese** (34.4): When she and her sisters sing on *The Lawrence Welk Show* (1955–1982), Dooneese is easy to spot—she has doll-size hands (which she uses to catch bubbles), a large forehead, and nothing she sings makes any sense.
- **Gilly** (34.13): She's a maker of mischief with a large bow in her frizzy hair. If someone throws a milk carton against the blackboard, stabs another student with a pencil, or lights another student's tie on fire, you can bet it was Gilly. And if you ask her, she'll admit it and say her catchphrase: "Sorry."
- **Mindy Gracin** (35.7): She's a B actress and a panelist on *Secret Word*, an old game show airing on the Game Show Network. Gracin is very grand and thinks she's a big Broadway star. She is also the worst player, who screws up every time it's her turn.

While she did a great impression of financial advisor/author/talk show host Suze Orman, Wiig specialized in impressions of right-wing ladies like Republican U.S. representative and 2008 presidential candidate Michele Bachmann, Second Lady of the United States/author Lynne Cheney, Callista Gingrich, former talk show host Elisabeth Hasselbeck, Delaware Republican senatorial candidate Christine O'Donnell (who is not a witch), Ann Romney, and Fox News host Greta Van Susteren.

## *SNL* and America's Talkfest

*Saturday Night Live*'s role within media culture is complex. On the one hand, the show is a major supplier of media culture in the form of digital shorts, popular catchphrases, and recurring characters. At the same time, the very culture to which *SNL* contributes is media saturated. We are bombarded by all types of media (television, radio, print, etc.), all competing for our attention, simultaneously transmitting too many messages for us to attend to. Consequently, the media continues to be the primary target of *SNL*'s satirical sketches and parodies, from political debates, to commercials, to news shows. Talk shows include parodies of actual shows and fictional shows, the latter of which suggests that anyone—meaning *anyone*—is a potential talk show host. The episode on which the sketch first aired is in parentheses next to the title.

Talk show parodies: (top left, clockwise) *Bronx Beat* with Betty Caruso (Amy Poehler, left) and Jodi Deitz (Maya Rudolph); *What's Up with That?* hosted by Diondre Cole (Kenan Thompson); *The Barry Gibb Talk Show* hosted by singer Barry Gibb (Jimmy Fallon) and his brother Robin (Justin Timberlake); and Italian talk show *La Rivista dell Televisione* hosted by Vinny Vedecci (Bill Hader).

### *The Barry Gibb Talk Show* (29.2)

It's called *The Barry Gibb Talk Show*, but it actually features two of the three Bee Gees—Barry (Jimmy Fallon) and Robin (Justin Timberlake)—who, as their theme song goes (to the tune "Nights on Broadway"), are there to talk about real important issues. Their guests have included Nancy Pelosi (Cameron Diaz) and Ann Coulter (Drew Barrymore) (30.16), as well as Jimmy Carter (Darrell Hammond) and Sandra Day O'Connor (Kristen Wiig) (32.9). Too bad the brothers are more interested in harmonizing than asking their guests any questions.

### *Prince Show* (29.12)

It's a talk show hosted by the eccentric singer who doesn't talk much, so Beyoncé Knowles (Maya Rudolph) does most of the talking to the guests (when Prince does say something, he usually sings it). Beyoncé tells guest Paula Abdul (Janet Jackson) that Prince wants to paint her picture while she stands in a giant clam holding a pearl (29.17). Jessica Simpson (Lindsay Lohan) is asked to play a harp on a cloud (30.20). Tobey Maguire (Shia LaBeouf) agrees to sit on a giant cupcake holding a cherry. Oddly enough (or maybe not), a *Prince Show* sketch was included when he was a musical guest on the show (31.12), but he did not appear in it.

### Deep House Dish (31.6)

This music talk show devoted to the club music scene, which airs on MTV 4 ("the alternative to the alternative"), is hosted by DJ Dynasty Handbag (Kenan Thompson) and his sidekick Tiara Zeeee (Rachel Dratch), who is replaced by T'Shane (Andy Samberg) (32.7). It features performances by alternative artists like Tres Latraj (Amy Poehler) ("I Killed Couture") and—for the very first time—a duet by Madonna and Lady Gaga (35.2)

### Bronx Beat (32.10)

This no-budget morning show is hosted by two ladies from the Bronx (you can tell from their accents), Betty Caruso (Amy Poehler) and her best friend, Jodie Deitz (Maya Rudolph). They are more interested in complaining about their husbands, kids, and how bad New York City smells than talking to their guests. Their first guest is Frank O'Connor (Jake Gyllenhaal), who wrote a book about bike trails. He's "gorgeous," so they are only interested in asking him questions about his nationality ("What are you? Part Indian? You Cherokee? You Chippewa?"), his Zodiac sign ("What are you? Leo? Aries? Taurus?"), and if he is good to his mother (he is). Their other guests included a hunky zookeeper (Peyton Manning) (32.16), a fireman (Brian Williams) (33.4), and a young volunteer who reads to children at a local library (Katy Perry) (36.1).

### The Dakota Fanning Show (32.12)

Dakota Fanning is two years younger than Miley Cyrus, but in movies like *I Am Sam* (2001), *Man on Fire* (2004), and *War of the Worlds* (2005), she seems like she's ten going on thirty-five. Dakota (Amy Poehler) has her own show, which she describes as "a forum for child actors to discuss cinema, theater, politics, philosophy, and the cultural zeitgeist-at-large!" But there's a culture gap that separates Dakota from her peers. She tells Daniel Radcliffe (Bill Hader) she's not familiar with the Harry Potter series (it's children's literature), and she tries to hide that she's jealous of Abigail Breslin's (Drew Barrymore) Oscar nomination. Dakota is also condescending to her bandleader, Reggie (Kenan Thompson), who she constantly reminds is not her intellectual equal.

### La Rivista Della Televisione, Hosted by Vinny Vedecci (Bill Hader) (32.15)

Italian talk show host Vinny Vedecci first appeared on *SNL* as a hotel owner who welcomes three young Americans (Kenan Thompson, Amy Poehler, and Jason Sudeikis), whose bus has broken down. Vedecci is excited they are here, though his English is limited to pop-culture sayings and references, mostly from the 1970s like "Where's the beef?," *WKRP in Cincinnati* (1978–1982), and *Welcome Back, Kotter* (1975–1979). Two seasons later, he was given his own

## Live from Studio 8H: 2000–2013

Radiohead (26.2) debuts two songs from their new album *Kid A* ("The National Album" and "Idioteque") and returns again in 2011 (37.1) to perform "Lotus Blossom" from *King of Limbs* and their single "Staircase" ... In his sixth appearance on the show, Beck (32.4) performs "Clap Hands," which features a percussion section sitting at a dinner table playing dinnerware, which is intercut with puppet versions of Beck and company ... Arcade Fire's Win Butler ends "Intervention" with an old-fashioned guitar smashing (32.14) (and they were asked back in 2010 [36.6] and 2012 [37.22]) ... Young artists featured on the show as either host, musical guest, or both include Taylor Swift (35.5), Miley Cyrus (36.16), and Justin Bieber (38.13) ... Lady Gaga added more "Little Monsters" to her fan base with her performance of "Paparazzi" and a medley of her songs (35.2) ... Paul McCartney performs "Cut Me Some Slack" with Nirvana's David Grohl, Krist Novoselic, and Pat Smear (38.10). This marked the twelfth appearance for Grohl, who appeared as a member of Nirvana (17.10, 19.1), the Foo Fighters (21.7, 25.4, 28.13, 31.5, 33.3, 37.22), and Them Crooked Vultures (35.14, 36.19). Grohl also performed with Tom Petty and the Heartbreakers (20.6), who made their eighth appearance ... Artists with the #1 album on the *Billboard* Chart were represented by 'NSYNC (25.14) ("Bye, Bye, Bye" and "I Thought She Knew" from *No Strings Attached* [2000]), Eminem (26.1) ("Without Me," *The Eminem Show* [2001]), 50 Cent (28.18) ("In da Club" and "21 Questions," *Get Rich or Die Tryin'* [2003]), Usher (29.18) ("Yeah" and "Burn," *Confessions* [2004]), and Lil Wayne (34.1) ("Got Money" and "Lollipop," *The Carter III* [2008]), and Eminem (and Lil Wayne) (26.10) ("No Love" and "Won't Back Down," *Recovery* [2010]) ... Adele's performance of "Chasing Pavements" and "Cold Shoulder" on a high-rated episode featuring Sarah Palin (34.5) boosted U.S. sales of her album *19* ... Kanye West delivers a high-powered performance (38.21) as he introduces two new songs, "Black Skinheads" and "New Slaves," from his forthcoming album, *Yeezus*.

talk show about television in which he sits down with American stars like Julia Louis-Dreyfus (32.15), Zach Braff (32.20), Jon Bon Jovi (33.3), Shia LaBeouf (33.11), and Drew Barrymore (35.3) and proceeds to talk to them—in Italian. He then becomes frustrated and starts to yell at his crew, who are always seen off camera eating spaghetti. When he talks to LaBeouf, he is under the impression that "transformer" refers to a sex change he's had from a woman to a man and pronounces the film Barrymore starred in when she was a child as "Et" instead of *E.T.* (1982). Hader is very convincing as an Italian talk show host, smoking cigarettes and talking at breakneck speed.

## What Up with That? (35.4)

Like *The Barry Gibb Talk Show*, *What Up with That?* is another show on BET (Black Entertainment Television) in which the guests are never given a chance to talk because host Diondre Cole (Kenan Thompson) and his entourage suddenly get the urge to start singing and dancing. His guests—an assortment of actors and celebrities—have included Ernest Borgnine, Chris Colfer, Samuel L. Jackson, Mindy Kaling, Bill O'Reilly, and Frank Rich.

### The Miley Cyrus Show (36.2)

It's possible the former Disney Channel tween queen may one day have a show of her own—so let this sketch serve as a warning. Vanessa Bayer plays the plucky singer/actress who made a fortune as the star of Disney's long-running sitcom *Hannah Montana* (2006–2011), which was at the center of a mega-franchise complete with two feature films, live concert appearances, an endless stream of CDs and DVDs, and a lifetime supply of merchandising. Guests have included Johnny Depp (Paul Brittain) (36.2), Katie Holmes (Anne Hathaway) (36.7), Nick Nolte (Jeff Bridges) (36.10), and Whitney Houston (Maya Rudolph) (37.8). Cyrus's father, singer Billy Ray Cyrus, who plays her father on *Hannah Montana*, was first played by guest host Bryan Cranston in the first episode and later by Jason Sudeikis. In each episode, Miley attempts to tell a joke, asks her guests a series of questions all at once, and then tells them they are cool. When Miley hosted *SNL* (26.16), she showed America she has a sense of humor by appearing as a guest on the show—as Justin Bieber!

## In Memoriam: Victims of Sandy Hook School Tragedy (38.10)

On Friday, December 14, 2013, twenty-year-old Adam Lanza fatally shot twenty schoolchildren and six adults at Sandy Hook Elementary School in the village of Sandy Hook in Newtown, Connecticut. He then killed himself. While the nation was in shock over these tragic events, *Saturday Night Live* offered a subtle, emotional tribute at the start of its annual holiday show with the New York City Children's Chorus singing "Silent Night." Afterward they gave the traditional opening, "Live from New York, it's *Saturday Night*!" The Children's Chorus returned later in the show to join musical guest Paul McCartney in "Wonderful Christmastime."

## Stefon Gets Hitched (38.21)

In his final appearance as *Weekend Update*'s City Correspondent (Bill Hader, in his last episode as a cast member), Stefon gives his usual inappropriate suggestions for places for people who are headed to New York City and are looking for a classic New York Weekend. When anchorperson Seth Meyers tells Stefon that his recommendation (the hottest club in New York . . . *Pannnnttts*) is not what they're looking for, Stefon lashes out and says, "You never respect me, Seth . . . I've met someone else! And he's a lot like you . . . except he likes me for me . . . and we are getting married! Bye, Seth Meyers!" Stefon runs out, and Seth eventually goes after him. Seth ends up in a church where we see Stefon is about

In a somber opening to the 2012 Christmas episode (33.10), the New York City Children's Choir sings "Silent Night" in memory of the twenty children and six adults who died in the mass shooting at Sandy Hook Elementary School in Newtown, Connecticut.

to be married to Anderson Cooper, but Seth steals him away and brings him back to the studio. Inside of the church we see some of the people who are included in the description of the club that are introduced by the phrase "This club has everything...": a Black George Washington; HoboCops (homeless RoboCops); Jewpids (Jewish cupids); Gizblow, the coked-up gremlin; Furkels (fat Urkels), Germfs (German smurfs); a screaming geisha; DJ Baby Bok Choy; and the Hanukkah cartoon character Menorah the Explorer. Also in attendance is Ben Affleck, who played Stefon's brother, David, in that character's first appearance on the show (34.7). Stefon was created by Hader and writer John Mulaney, who prior to airtime would add things to the list of what's in a club, which Hader would not actually see until he was on the air.

# SNL Goes Digital

## (2013–2024), Seasons 39–49

Over the course of five decades and 950+ episodes, there have been relatively few changes to *Saturday Night Live*'s format. The show still begins with a cold open, followed by the credit sequence and a monologue delivered by the guest host. There are an assortment of sketches (in studio and on film) and two performances by the musical guest—one before *Weekend Update* and the other in the last fifteen minutes, usually before a short (and often odd) sketch. In the show's final moments, everyone is assembled on the main stage of Studio 8H. The guest host thanks the musical guest, the cast, Lorne Michaels, and so on, and everyone exchanges hugs as the production credits roll.

Early in the show's run, there were the occasional, albeit then temporary, minor changes, including episodes with no official host (5.14, 6.13, 7.1, 10.1) or no musical guest (1.3, 4.7, 8.10, 12.1). In one instance, a current cast member—Eddie Murphy—hosted the show (8.9) to fill in for his ailing *48 Hours* costar Nick Nolte.

Although the format has remained relatively the same, *SNL* has undergone some significant changes that have had an impact on the show's content and when and how we are able to enjoy *SNL*.

## Cast Diversity

On November 2, 2013 (39.5), Kerry Washington appeared in the cold open as First Lady Michelle Obama opposite Jay Pharoah as President Obama. The sketch opens with Obama's press secretary Jay Carney (Taran Killam) telling the president some of his favorite supporters are going to be at the state dinner that evening. When Michelle (Washington) enters, the president laments he hasn't seen her in years (presumably because there are no Black women in the cast to play her). Carney (Taran Killam) interrupts to tell the president that Oprah Winfrey has arrived, and she wishes to come in and say hello. Carney asks the First Lady if she'd like to leave and get changed. When she asks why, Carney pauses, looks at her, and signals, "*So Oprah can come in.*" Washington suddenly realizes what he means and asks, "Oh, because of the . . . ? . . . and Keenan won't [wear a dress] . . . ?" There is silence, and she (and we) soon realize the actress is expected to exit the sketch and return dressed as Oprah.

# SNL Goes Digital    157

*SNL* responds to the criticism launched against the show for the lack of Black female cast members with a sketch that requires guest host Kerry Washington to play both First Lady Michelle Obama (left) and Oprah Winfrey.

She leaves, and there is an awkward silence, during which a word crawl appears on the screen:

> The producers at *Saturday Night Live* would like to apologize to Kerry Washington for the number of black women she will be asked to play tonight. We made these requests both because Washington is an actress of considerable range and talent and also because *SNL* does not have a black woman in the cast. As for the latter reason, we agree this is not an ideal situation and look forward to rectifying that in the near future . . . unless, of course, we fall in love with another white guy first."

Washington appears as Winfrey for a few seconds, but she has to leave because, as Carney announces—Beyoncé is here! Washington rushes out, and Carney ushers in not one—but five—Matthew McConaughys, played by five of the eight White male cast members.

The sketch concludes with a cameo appearance by Reverend Al Sharpton, who puts what the viewers just witnessed in perspective. Speaking directly to the audience, he asks, "What have we learned from this sketch? As usual, nothing. . . . Live from New York . . . it's *Saturday Night!*"

This metasketch is a direct response to the criticism launched at *SNL* when the show announced they are adding six new feature players to the cast (five men and one woman)—all of whom are White. For critics and longtime viewers of the show, this was not surprising. Between 1975 and 2013, only four of the 138 cast members were women of color, two of whom were only on the show for a single season: Yvonne Hudson (season 5); Danitra Vance (season 11); Ellen Cleghorne (seasons 17–20); and Maya Rudolph (seasons 25–mid-season 33). It is seldom *SNL* makes fun of its internal workings in such an apologetic, self-reflexive, on-air moment, but the show had received a lot of justified criticism and felt the need to respond.

To remedy the situation, *SNL* hired the talented Sasheer Zamata, who joined the cast in early 2014 as a featured player (39.11), and the hilarious Leslie Jones, who made her debut on *Weekend Update* on May 3, 2014 (39.19), and was officially added to the cast in the early fall (40.4). Zamata left at the end of season 42, and Ego Nwodim, a former cast member of The Upright Citizens Brigade in Los Angeles, was added as a featured player in season 44. By season 47, *SNL* had the most diverse cast to date: sixteen repertory players and five featured players that included five Black performers (Michael Che, Ego Nwodim, Punkie Johnson, Chris Redd, and Kenan Thompson); Melissa Villeseñor, who is of Spanish, Basque, and Indigenous Mexican descent; Australian-born Bowen Yang, who is of Chinese descent and gay; and two lesbians, Johnson and Kate McKinnon. The latest hires include Molly Kearney, the first nonbinary cast member; Marcello Hernandez, who is of Cuban Dominican descent; and Devon Walker, a Black stand-up writer/comedian. A more diverse cast (and writing staff) doesn't automatically guarantee the show's humor will more inclusive (and less straight, White, male-centric), yet based on the memorable sketches and music videos discussed in this chapter, there is some indication that *SNL* is slowly heading in the right direction.

It's worth noting there was another major change in the cast when a record number of performers, some of whom had been on *SNL* for many years, exited the show at the end of season 47 (2021–2022): Kate McKinnon (eleven seasons), Aidy Bryant (ten seasons), Kyle Mooney (nine seasons), Pete Davidson (eight seasons), Alex Moffat (six seasons), Melissa Villeseñor (six seasons), and Chris Redd (five seasons). One new featured player, Aristotle Athari, was also let go after one season when his contract was not renewed. Cecily Strong also said goodbye in the middle of her eleventh season in December 2022. Kenan Thompson, who joined *SNL* in 2003, continues to hold the record as the show's longest-tenured cast member.

## Live from New York—Coast to Coast

The fact that *SNL* is broadcast live has given the show's producers the opportunity to immediately respond to national and international tragedies, which over the past decade seem to be happening more frequently. In lieu of the traditional cold open, several episodes started on a serious note with a musical tribute to 9/11 first responders (27.11 [9/29/01], Paul Simon singing "The Boxer"); the twenty children and six adult victims of the mass shooting at Sandy Hook Elementary School in Newtown, Connecticut (38.10 [12/15/12], the New York City Children's Choir singing "Silent Night"); and the people of Ukraine, who were invaded by the Soviet Union (47.13 [2/26/22], the Ukrainian Chorus Dumka of New York singing "Prayer for Ukraine"). In her tribute to the victims of the terrorist attacks in Paris (41.5 [11/14/15]), Cecily Strong declared in English and in French, "We stand with Paris!" In the season 49 opener (49.1 [10/14/23]), host Pete Davidson personally reflected on the Israeli victims of the Hamas-led attacks. *SNL* took a more unconventional approach and responded to the tragic school shootings in Parkland, Florida, on February 14, 2018, with a sketch (an episode of *Anderson Cooper 360*) that addresses gun control and mental health (43.14 [3/3/18]).

April 15, 2017 (42.18), marks an important milestone in the history of *Saturday Night Live* and live-entertainment programming. For the first time, *SNL* was broadcast live in all four time zones. Since its debut in 1975, *SNL* had been airing live in the Eastern and Central time zones and tape-delayed in the Mountain and Pacific time zones. Now the show would air at 11:30 p.m. (ET), 10:30 p.m. (CT), 9:30 p.m. (MT), and 8:30 p.m. (PT). *Deadline*'s Denise Petski reported that season 42 was the show's highest-rated season in eight years in the coveted eighteen-to-forty-nine-year-old demographic and the most-watched season in twenty-four years (since 1992–1993). Since last season (Season 41), viewership increased 26 percent. NBC Entertainment Chairman Robert Greenblatt expressed his excitement over the show's success and the time-zone changes: "That way, everyone is in on the joke at the same time."

## More SNL, Fewer Commercials

In April 2016, *SNL* announced that in the fall (season 42), the sketch comedy show would have two fewer commercial breaks. By decreasing the amount of time devoted to national and local commercials and NBC's promos, there would be more programming content. In a statement issued by Lorne Michaels, the show's longtime producer explained, "As the decades have gone by, commercial time has grown. This will give time back to the show to make it easier to watch the show live." In an article for the *Los Angeles Times*, staff writer Stephen Battaglio explains that approximately one-third of the ninety-three-minute show consists of commercials. To compensate for the loss of advertising revenue, "viewers will see more program content with an addition of original sponsored content from advertisers that partner with the show." The "sponsored content" are advertisements produced in conjunction with *SNL* writers and talent. In 2009, Pepsi produced three such commercials featuring the character of MacGruber, a parody of TV's *MacGyver*, played by Will Forte, that featured the star of TV's *MacGyver*, Richard Dean Anderson. In the same year, Anheuser Busch purchased all the national ad time to advertise its new beverage, Bud Light Golden Wheat. The commercial incorporated vintage clips from *SNL* dress rehearsals (35.4). In a 2014 Jeep commercial, Cecily Strong and a crew member zoom around the city looking for a brown bear costume and head back to 30 Rock in time for dress rehearsal. *Variety*'s Brian Steinberg reported in 2017 that *SNL* also collaborated with Apple and Verizon.

According to NBC, "sponsored content" does not refer to product placement, though viewers might be skeptical, as more sketches seem to focus on actual products, such as Cheetos (42.14, 45.1), Blue Bunny Ice Cream (47.19), and Sara Lee (45.6), or incorporate a brand into the sketch's setting, like Olive

Garden (42.16) and, in the same episode (48.7), the Hello Kitty store and Arby's. The oddest insertion of a brand was in a segment in which the cast bid farewell to Cecily Strong (48.9). It ends on an emotional high note when guest host and *Elvis* star Austin Butler (and cast members) sing the Elvis Presley tune "Blue Christmas." The segment inexplicably begins in a RadioShack, with the featured players dressed as employees with their supervisor (Kenan Thompson), who, to emphasize the absurdity, repeatedly and deliberately enunciates the store's name: "Ra-dio Shack." Incorporating real products does add a degree of realism to the sketch, but the writers, who must clear it through NBC's legal department, understand they cannot represent the product or service in a bad light. As Lorne Michaels explains, "'You can't *make fun* of it, and be *with* it' simultaneously." In a rare instance (42.20), a sketch in which an Apple computer is prominently displayed was preceded by the announcement: "Promotional Consideration for *SNL* Furnished by Apple."

## "40 Seasons. One App."

If you were going out on a Saturday night in the late 1970s through the 1990s, you could tape *Saturday Night Live* on your videocassette recorder (VCR)—provided you figured out how to set the timer and had a spare VHS tape in the house). Beginning in the 2000s, you could record the show on the digital video recorder (DVR) you were renting from your cable or satellite television provider. An episode of *SNL* recorded on your VCR or DVR and watched the next day or a week later may lack the immediacy and spontaneity of live television because it's not happening now, yet it gives the viewer one important advantage. With the touch of a button on their remote control, the viewer has the power to fast-forward past the actual commercials (as opposed to the commercial parodies), the recurring sketches and characters you didn't find funny the first time, and the musical guests you've never heard of and/or who don't spark your interest.

Fortunately for *SNL*, advancements in digital technology were equally beneficial for the show because its format, which consists of a series of approximately fourteen to seventeen live or filmed/taped segments of usually no longer than seven minutes each, is perfectly suited for watching on a computer or a mobile app. In 2015, in honor of *SNL*'s fortieth anniversary, NBC released a new free mobile app with a page for each season and a menu consisting of photos of each season's cast members that you can click on to watch your favorite sketches and see the ones you might have missed. NBC kept the app updated for five years until it was finally discontinued.

As Josef Adalian and Megh Wright recount in a 2020 article about the *SNL* library on Vulture, prior to the launching of Comcast's (NBC's parent company) official streaming service, Peacock, which is now the permanent home of the *SNL* library, episodes were made available over the years on different streaming platforms: Hulu and Netlix (2010–2013), Yahoo (2013–2016), and NBC's short-lived internet comedy platform Seeso (2016). In addition to past episodes, Peacock also posts new *SNL* episodes the day after they air.

Some sketches from the *SNL* library, along with content from current episodes, is also available on *SNL*'s official YouTube channel (https://www.youtube.com/@SaturdayNightLive). For die-hard fans, there is also a YouTube channel where you can access more than ninety sketches that were "cut for time" prior to the live show, though time constraints might not be the only reason these sketches did not make it on the air.

## Cut for Time

- **"Gus Chiggins, Old Prospector" (27.3):** A military unit getting ready to deploy to Afghanistan includes an old gold prospector named Gus Chiggins (Will Ferrell), who looks and sounds like he just stepped out of an old Hollywood western. The overall comic timing is a bit off because most of the male cast members (Jimmy Fallon, Chris Kattan, Tracy Morgan, Seth Meyers, etc.) struggle to keep a straight face, especially when the prospector uses expressions like "Oh, cinnamon and gravy!" and "Oh, pickle shoes!"
- **"Alan" (40.3):** A husband and wife (Taran Killam and Vanessa Bayer) receive an unusual gift: Alan—"the future of casual entertainment in a box"—a remote-controlled, life-size robot (Bill Hader) who dances in a plastic case. She reads through the directions and tries the different settings while her perplexed husband tries to figure out the benefits of owning "an Alan."
- **"Morning News" (40.8):** It's time for "Rise and Smile with Kip and Jenny!" Hosts Kip (Kenan Thompson) and Jenny (Cecily Strong) are finding it difficult to host their happy live morning show in the Greater St. Louis area. It's the Monday after the Ferguson unrest broke out in the Missouri city on August 10, 2014, the day after a White police officer, Darren Wilson, gunned down an eighteen-year-old Black man, Michael Brown.
- **"My Little Stepchildren" (43.13):** "Most girls like dolls, but not every girl wants to be a mommy." Introducing My Little Stepchildren, the perfect doll set for the little girl who enjoys playing the role of the evil stepmother. She locks up her stepchildren's birth certificates, burns letters from their birth mother, and sends them off to boarding school.
- **"New Cast Member" (44.15):** It's ironic that this short film—one of Kyle Mooney's best—was cut. Mooney plays a new cast member named Adam Zigman (Mooney in makeup), who gets cut from sketches and finds it difficult to fit in with the cast, who avoid him.
- **"Cast List" (45.7):** Will Ferrell is the overly theatrical, sadistic high school drama coach who enjoys creating chaos as his anxious students wait for him to post the cast list of the school's upcoming production of *Bye, Bye Birdie*.

Will Ferrell is the sadistic high school drama coach who enjoys watching his anxious students suffer as they wait for the cast list of the spring musical to be posted.

## *Saturday Night Live*'s 40th Anniversary Special

Admittance to *SNL*'s *40th Anniversary Special*, which aired on Sunday, February 15, 2015, was by invitation only. According to Lorne Michaels, the guest list included everyone who had hosted the show, most of the musical guests, and cast members who lasted more than one season. The special is a three-and-a-half-hour extended version of the show's standard ninety-minute format, starting with a cold open (Jimmy Fallon and Justin Timberlake perform a rap recounting the history of the show) to the "good nights" (Steve Martin pulls Lorne Michaels up onstage). Like an *SNL* episode, many of the sketches are hit or miss because they are overstuffed with cameos and are surprisingly under-rehearsed. The best parts are the prerecorded clips of show highlights, political humor, audition tapes, sports moments, shorts, and an "in memoriam" montage introduced by Bill Murray. All the effort put into a live telecast paid off. The special was watched by 23.1 million viewers.

## Memorable Characters, Sketches, and Moments

### *Black Jeopardy!* (2014–2019)

From the late 1990s through the early 2000s, the celebrity edition of *Jeopardy!* was a popular game show parody featuring Will Ferrell as the frustrated host, Alex Trebek, who is forced to deal with a verbally abusive Sean Connery (Darrell Hammond) and clueless contestants like Burt Reynolds (Norm Macdonald), who likes to sign his name "Turd Ferguson."

Hosted by Darnell Hayes (Kenan Thompson), *Black Jeopardy!* is essentially the same game except, instead of knowledge-based questions, the categories are snippets of Black vernacular, such as "It's been a minute," "I don't know you," "You better," "I'm gonna pray on this," and "They out there sayin'," which

Wearing a MAGA hat, Doug (Tom Hanks) is an unlikely contestant on *Black Jeopardy!* whose correct answers suggests there may be some common ground between the races.

contestants have to incorporate into their answers. Another category that is always included is "White People." Two of the three contestants are Black and excellent players, but the third contestant typically has a difficult time, at least initially, playing the game because they do not share the same Black culture. White contestants like Mark (Louis C.K. [39.16]), a professor of African American studies, and Allison (Elizabeth Banks [41.5]), who thinks she is ready to play the game because she once dated a Black guy, are essentially clueless. Two Black contestants also struggle with their answers because of geographic and cultural differences. Jared's (Drake [41.20]) frame of reference is limited to Canada, and T'Challa (Chadwick Boseman [43.17]), revisiting his *Black Panther* role, is from Wakanda. Another episode features host Tom Hanks as Doug (42.4), who, based on his red "Make American Great Again" hat, one can assume is a stereotypical racist redneck. But this smart sketch takes a surprising turn when Doug starts to answer the questions correctly, demonstrating that there might be some common ground between the races. In his positive review of the sketch for *Paste* magazine, Ben Gran found the sketch to be "funny and well worth watching—it was also sneakily profound, quietly subversive and sweetly optimistic."

## Music Videos

In addition to commercials and short films, *SNL* also added original musical videos to the weekly lineup on a more regular basis. The *SNL* Digital Shorts (2005–2018) produced by the Lonely Island (Jorma Taccone, Akiva Schaffer, and Andy Samberg) include music videos, two of which became viral hits on YouTube: in December 2005, "Lazy Sunday" (31.9), cowritten by Chris Parnell, who appears with Samberg, and one year later, the "holiday" R&B classic "Dick in a Box" (32.9). The latter song, cowritten by the Lonely Island, Katreese Barnes,

Original music videos that carry a political message: (top left, clockwise) Chris Redd (left), Chance the Rapper (center), and Kenan Thompson sing the Emmy-winning original song, "Come Back, Barack" (43.6); Black voters can't find a place to cast their ballots in "Strollin' to the Polls" (46.6); Kate McKinnon (left) and Ariana Grande and the female cast sing "This is Not a Feminist Song" (but maybe it is?) (41.15); and (left to right) Cecily Strong, guest host Saoirse Ronan, Kate McKinnon, and Aidy Bryant remind us that sexism is part of their everyday lives in "Welcome to Hell" (43.7).

and Justin Timberlake, won a Creative Arts Emmy Award for Outstanding Original Music Lyrics, and several videos that followed received nominations: "Motherlover" (34.21), "Shy Ronnie" (35.8, featuring Rihanna), "Jack Sparrow" (36.20, featuring Michael Bolton), and "3-Way (The Golden Rule)" (36.22, featuring Lady Gaga).

In the Lonely Island music videos, guys sing mostly about "guy stuff" (mostly sex-related themes). The music videos produced in the "post–Lonely Island era" were a welcomed change because they dealt with gender issues (some sex-related) and social and political themes from a distinctly female, Black, and LGBTQ perspective. Women and Black cast members, conspicuously absent from Lonely Island's videos, now have the opportunity to raise their singing voices.

### Music Video Play List

- **"Boy Dance Party" (39.3):** When the women go out dancing, the men (including guest host Bruce Willis) stay home to watch an "important game" on television. But as soon as the coast is clear, the men cut loose and start singing and twerking, swaying their "tater skins" (butts) and "chicken wings" (arms) and "shaking their shack" (male anatomy).

- **"(Do It on My) Twin Bed" (39.10):** In the first music video featuring all the female cast members, the women bring their boyfriends home and force them to sleep—and do it—in their old bedroom on their twin bed. The song, with music by Eli Brueggemann and lyrics by Aidy Bryant, Kate McKinnon, Chris Kelly, and Sarah Schneider, was nominated for an Emmy for Outstanding Original Music and Lyrics.
- **"Back Home Ballers" (40.7):** "Your girls are back!" Cecily, Kate, Sasheer, Vanessa, Leslie, guest host Cameron Diaz, and Lil' Baby Aidy are home for Thanksgiving. Their mother is happy to see them, but these ladies won't be lifting a finger and expect to be treated like queens. The fridge is stocked with food from Costco, Mom does their laundry, and there's free Wi-Fi (if they can type in their parents' long password, which starts with seventeen *O*s).
- **"A Thanksgiving Miracle" (41.6):** In her November 2015 appearance as a musical guest, Adele proved she has a sense of humor by allowing *SNL* to use her hit song "Hello" from her recently released album *25* in a sketch that demonstrates how music can unite everyone at the Thanksgiving table, despite their different opinions and beliefs. When family members start spouting their racist views, a little girl turns on a recording of "Hello," and suddenly they all begin to lip-synch the song while mirroring her highly emotive singing style and appearance in the "Hello" video, including the black nail polish, a faux fur car coat, and the wind blowing through their hair.
- **"This Is Not a Feminist Song" (41.15):** In this smart, self-reflective music video, the female cast members and guest host Ariana Grande want to sing an anthem "for all womankind"—until they realize they can't put everything they want to say into a single song. So what they are singing is *not* a feminist song. Yet the fact they are women—and they are singing—doesn't that make it a feminist song? In her review of *SNL*'s best music videos, Brittany Delay describes "This Is Not a Feminist Song" as the "most genuinely intellectual *SNL* music video every made. That it holds this title while also maintaining the show's classic brand of humor makes it especially impressive."
- **"Jingle Barack" (42.10):** In a parody of Run-DMC's 1987 "Christmas and Hollis," Kenan Thompson and Chance the Rapper, along with Leslie Jones and DMC himself—Darryl McDaniels—mourn Barack Obama's final Christmas as president and contemplate what life will be like next year without Barack in the White House. Eli Brueggemann (music) and colyricists Chance the Rapper, Will Stephen, and Kenan Thompson received an Emmy nomination for Outstanding Original Music and Lyrics.
- **"Come Back, Barack" (43.6):** Eli Brueggeman, Will Stephen, Kenan Thompson, and cast member Chris Redd collaborated the following year on a 1990s-style R&B ballad that could easily be mistaken for a song from that era. In an oral history of the writing of "Come Back, Barack" compiled

by Mandi Bierly for *Billboard*, Brueggeman explains the song is an "amalgam of three or four K-Ci & JoJo and Boyz II Men songs." But angst-ridden Redd, Thompson, and Chance the Rapper are not asking an ex-girlfriend they miss to come back to them. It's the middle of the Trump presidency, and they are pouring their hearts out to former President Barack Obama. Even though they know it's not possible, they still want him to come back to run the country. In 2018, the songwriters took a well-deserved Emmy for Outstanding Original Music and Lyrics.

- **"Welcome to Hell" (43.7):** In response to the habitual sexual predators making headlines (like film executive Harvey Weinstein), the female cast members and guest host Saoirse Ronan sing this catchy pop song and share a "little secret every girl knows": sexual harassment is nothing new but has been part of women's daily lives throughout history.
- **"It's Pride Again" (46.20):** Gay Pride was canceled the prior year due to COVID-19, so the LGBTQ+ cast members (Punkie Johnson, Kate McKinnon, and Bowen Yang), along with host Anya Taylor-Joy and musical guest Lil Nas X, are happy to be celebrating that "It's Pride Again." ("This is our St. Patty's Day, acting sloppy cuz we're gay.") But not much has changed. Pride month still means plenty of boyfriend and girlfriend drama, overpriced drinks—and too many straight people. Thanks to having more than one "out" cast member, it's refreshing to see *SNL* tackle subject matter that is relevant specifically to the queer community.

## Live from Studio 8H: The 2010s

Seven years after her first appearance on *SNL* and a month after the release of her album *25*, Adele returned (41.6) to sing "When We Were Young" and "Hello," which would take home the Grammy for Record of the Year, Song of the Year, and Best Pop Solo Performance. One month later, her television special executive-produced by Lorne Michaels, *Adele Live in New York City*, aired on NBC. The Foo Fighters' multiple appearances as a musical guest (43.9, 46.6, 49.3) raised the group's total to nine and guitarist David Grohl's total to fifteen. Prince made his last *SNL* appearance with 3RDEYEGIRL singing "Clouds," "Marz," and "Another Love." On April 24, 3026, two days after his death, *SNL* aired a retrospective of his appearances on the show hosted by Jimmy Fallon. Bruce Springsteen and the E Street Band returned for the holiday shows in 2015 (41.9) and 2020 (46.8). Many performers did double duty as both the host and musical guest, including Bad Bunny (49.2), Miley Cyrus (39.2, 41.1), Drake (39.11, 41.20), Chance the Rapper (45.4), Donald Glover (43.19), Billie Eilish (47.9), Ariana Grande (41.15), Halsey (44.12), Jack Harlow (48.4), Nick Jonas (46.14), Lady Gaga (39.6), Lizzo (47.18), Megan Thee Stallion (48.3), and Blake Shelton (40.12). The *40th Anniversary Special* included musical performances by Paul McCartney ("Maybe I'm Amazed"), Miley Cyrus ("50 Ways to Leave Your Lover"), Paul Simon ("Still Crazy after All These Years"), and Kanye West ("Jesus Walks," "Only One," and "Wolves" with Sia and Vic Mensa).

- **"Strollin' to the Polls" (46.6):** The purpose of the 1965 Voting Rights Act was to prevent racial discrimination in voting. In 2013, the U.S. Supreme Court struck down in a 5–4 decision a portion of the 1965 Voting Rights Act that prohibited the individual states from changing their voting laws without getting clearance from the federal government. This opened the doors for states to pass restrictions like voter ID laws and close polling locations, thereby making it more difficult for some Black and Latino voters to cast their ballots. "Strollin'" is sung by a quartet of Black voters, who identify themselves as Crazy Legs Jimmy (Kenan Thompson), Rubber Band Ronnie (Chris Redd), Pitty Pat Patricia (Punkie Johnson), and Michelle (just Michelle) (Ego Nwodim), who are strollin' to the polls "to get their voices heard." But all the polling places are closed, forcing them to stroll down the middle of a busy highway to get to the closest one. This political point is crystal clear in this timely music video, which Vulture's Rebecca Alter observes "would be funny if it wasn't so sad."

## McKinnon's Women (and Men)

The breakout star of *SNL* in the 2010s was Kate McKinnon, who won two consecutive Emmy Awards for Outstanding Supporting Actress in a Comedy Series in 2016 and 2017. Like Kristen Wiig, McKinnon is a talented character actress who specializes in portraying eccentrics who are more three-dimensional (and less annoying) than Wiig's women (see chapter 12). McKinnon is also known for her impressions of powerful women on the political left (Hillary Clinton, Supreme Court Justice Ruth Bader Ginsburg, Representative Nancy Pelosi, Senator Elizabeth Warren); conservative pundits and commentators (Kellyanne Conway, Kayleigh McEnany, Laura Ingraham); and actresses/entertainers (Frances McDormand, Jane Lynch, Shakira, Tilda Swinton). Her list of impressions is not limited to women. She made frequent appearances as singer Justin Bieber, and during the Trump era, her repertoire included Dr. Anthony Fauci and caricatures of Attorney General Jeff Sessions; Senator Lindsay Graham; and former New York City mayor Rudy Giuliani, who served on President Trump's legal team. Some of McKinnon's characters appear in recurring sketches:

- **Barbara DeDrew:** a lesbian volunteer at a cat adoption center, Whiskers R' We, who appears in local commercials alongside a different woman, who is presumably her new girlfriend, each time played by the guest hosts. As the pair hold up each kitten in need of a home and tell their story, the girlfriend flirts and touches Barbara, who is uncomfortable with PDA on camera. Their exchanges contain an endless number of cat puns, beginning with the names of Barbara's girlfriends: Cat Muller (Charlize Theron [39.20]), Purr-sula (Reese Witherspoon [40.20]), Tabby-tha (Melissa McCarthy [41.13]), and Furonica (Kristen Wiig [42.7]).
- **Sheila Sovage:** It's "last call" at the local singles bar, which means it's time for barfly Sheila to make her move on any guy (or woman or male-female

Kate's women: (starting at top, clockwise) At "Last Call," Sheila Sovage (McKinnon) (right) flirts with Sue Seal (Amy Schumer) (43.20); Whiskers R We owner Barbara McDrew (left) and Furonica (Kristen Wiig) (42.7); and alien abductee Colleen Rafferty describes her latest close encounter.

couple), played by the week's guest host, who has not paired up with anyone for the night. Their drunken exchanges are as bizarre as their names: Vernon Crotcher (John Goodman [39.9]), Ace Chuggins (Larry David [41.12], Sue Seal (Amy Schumer, [43.20]), and Bernie Letzman and Melba Letzman-Toast (Kristen Wiig). Anthony (Kenan Thompson), the bartender, is also a recurring character in this sketch, which appropriately closes out the show.

- **(Miss) Colleen Rafferty:** An alien abductee who is being questioned by a pair of NSA agents about her repeated close encounters with space aliens. She is joined by another pair of abductees, a woman named Sharon (Cecily Strong) and a third abductee, who speak about their experience. When they share details about their encounters, Sharon and the third abductee describe their close encounter with visitors from another planet as spiritual, mystical and magical ("like being enveloped by this warm, blue light"). Colleen can't believe what she is hearing. Besides always losing her pants ("so my yeasty and my beasty are in full view"), she is transported up to a spaceship where the "little Grays start batting my knockers." While Sharon's and the third abductee's return to earth is serene, Colleen gets dropped out of the spaceship and lands in a baseball field or in the middle of a twelve-year-old's birthday party. Ryan Gosling makes three appearances in this sketch (41.7, 43.1, 49.17), and both times he and the NSA agents can't contain their laughter over Miss Rafferty's ramblings (and McKinnon's performance).

# 14

# A New Era in Political Comedy

For the last half-century, *Saturday Night Live* has been an enduring part of the cultural zeitgeist of American politics. That's fifty years' worth of being "really the voice of adolescence," as Lorne Michaels put it in a 2021 talk on comedy and politics at the University of Delaware. "It's just badly behaving and questioning things, endlessly so."

Michaels's remarks took place at the university's Biden Institute, and the moderator of the event was Valerie Biden Owens, longtime close advisor to and younger sister of President Joe Biden, as well as Biden Institute Chair.

That alone would be grist for the tired old chestnut that *SNL* has a liberal agenda it is determined to foist onto the rest of America, most especially red-state America, as well as anyone else on even the slightly purplish of fences.

Yet, as Michaels contends and a look at *SNL* history supports, the impressions it does of real-life politicians are indeed "not personal," and its representation of politics is, for the most part, "nonpartisan."

When President Gerald Ford was portrayed by Chevy Chase as a clumsy lummox, Ford's own press secretary Ron Nessen was invited to be the first, and to this day only, presidential press secretary to host the show back in 1976 (1.17). New York City's Republican mayor Rudolph Giuliani not only hosted the show on November 22, 1997 (23.7), but also made what became an iconic appearance on *SNL*'s first live broadcast following 9/11 (27.1).

Tina Fey's first viral impression of then Republican vice presidential candidate Sarah Palin (34.1) was one month later, followed by a live appearance by the real Sarah Palin alongside Fey and again, as herself, in her own comedy segment on *Weekend Update* (34.5).

Donald J. Trump hosted the show twice, the first time as a New York real estate developer (29.16) and the second almost five months *after* he famously came down the escalator of Trump Tower and declared his candidacy for the Republican nomination for U.S. president (41.4). Though many presidential candidates and subsequent U.S. presidents have appeared on the show, Trump is thus far the only one to serve as host.

Like any television series, *SNL* certainly has a point of view, but overall it's one of prodding irreverence rather than an insurgent political agenda. In a 2011 interview with *Vanity Fair*'s Todd Purdham, a former White House correspondent for the *New York Times*, the show's creator and longtime producer Lorne Michaels explained the origins of *SNL*'s attitude in dealing with politicians and the political arena in general:

I think coming on right after Watergate was crucial. I was 30. We just lived through all that, and because of that and Vietnam, politics was something everyone knew and talked about. I think we defined ourselves as a generation in that way. I think we were playing to an audience that was really under 30. We didn't expect anyone else to know the music or to get the jokes. We weren't deliberately thinking that way. It was just the truth.

What could be considered *SNL*'s version of youthful cynicism in 1975 has evolved over the years, along with both the world and the coverage and lampooning of affairs of state. But because the show has been on for so long and in the process has become a familiar staple of American television, critics and sometimes even fans often seem confounded these days about how to explain the way it deals with politics; politicians; and most particularly, U.S. presidents.

It feels topical, but it's not hard-edged, breaking news—political comedy in the vein of *The Daily Show* or *The Colbert Report* in the early 2000s. It frequently has real-life elected officials and newsmakers as guests or hosts, but they don't engage in discussion in the way that they do on programs like *Real Time with Bill Maher* or *Late Night with Seth Meyers*. *SNL* can be broad and silly, like a comic set piece on *The Tonight Show with Jimmy Fallon*, or slyly funny in the style of a filmed side bit that might be featured on *Jimmy Kimmel Live!*, but neither quite captures its tone or mission.

The fact is that *SNL* is a bit of all of the above and yet none of the above. It is first and foremost a sketch comedy show where guest hosts and a troupe of comic actors portray characters in live skits or short films and music videos. But it also has set pieces, like a host monologue where a real public figure talks to the audience, often about timely events. More importantly, at least as far as political coverage is concerned, in the middle of each episode is *Weekend Update*, a ten- to fifteen-minute comic take on the news with an often-heavy dose of politics. It is in this segment that political figures often appear as themselves—or at least a comic version of whom they want to be seen as. That is unless they decide to go big and appear as a fictional character in a traditional sketch:

- President Gerald Ford (1.17), portrayed each week by Chevy Chase as a clumsy lummox, made a filmed cameo and opened the episode hosted by his press secretary Ron Nessen.
- After his four-year term ended, President George H. W. Bush (20.4) made a filmed cameo, opened the show, and also appeared on film in the monologue alongside his doppelgänger, guest host Dana Carvey.
- Senator John McCain hosted the show in 2002 (28.3), made cameos as a presidential candidate prior to the 2008 election (33.12, 34.7), and appeared right before Election Day on *SNL*'s *Presidential Bash '08* (11/3/08).
- Before he became the Democratic presidential nominee, Senator Barack Obama proved he could take a joke when he appeared in a Halloween sketch wearing an Obama mask (33.4).

- Hillary Clinton (41.1) as Val, the bartender, talked to candidate Hillary Clinton (as played by Kate McKinnon), in a sketch during her presidential campaign.

Part of the show's secret is that, while certain segments remain constant, the rotating cast of actors and writers, all of whom bring different strengths to the creation and presentation of material, cause it to morph how it chooses to interpret and showcase lawmakers and the news they make and enable along with the times. Irreverence in the 1970s is different from irreverence in the 2020s. But is it really? In the end it depends who is doing the interpreting, the viewing, and the judging.

## A Changing TV Landscape

When *SNL* premiered, it followed what was then a very small group of American network TV comedy and variety series that dared to address politics in any significant way. Its closest counterpart in lampooning American political figures and events in the news was NBC's American version of *That Was the Week That Was* (1963–1965), based on the controversial British satire series on BBC Television that ran from 1962 to 1963. The U.S. offshoot was broadcast as a half-hour show each week near the end of the NBC Friday night prime-time schedule.

Among the cutting-edge writers on the British *TWTWTW* were Roald Dahl and future Monty Python troupe members John Cleese and Graham Chapman, just as the American *TWTWTW* writers included such U.S. intellects as Gloria Steinem and Calvin Trillin. But also among the recurring cast of players on the American show was actor-writer Buck Henry, who would later become a key component in *SNL*'s early years, serving as its host for a then record ten times from 1976 to 1980.

There were only two other big-three network prime-time entertainment series that dared to consistently touch the political rail in subsequent years prior to *SNL*.

The first was CBS's *The Smothers Brothers Comedy Hour* (1967–1969), a critically acclaimed but continually controversial series that did well in the ratings but infuriated its network brass. Featuring singers like Joan Baez and Pete Seeger, who performed and spoke out against the Vietnam War, as well as sketches lampooning religion and drug use, the show also created a fake presidential candidate (Pat Paulsen) to run against Richard Nixon, a stunt that became a national phenomenon. Though it drew a sizable audience, particularly among young people, the more traditional CBS network finally had enough and abruptly canceled the show before its third season could conclude in 1969.

Nevertheless, the show won the Emmy that year for Outstanding Writing for a Comedy, Music, and Variety Series. And notably, one of the winning writers on the staff picking up an award was the young Steve Martin, another future *SNL* staple who would not only become a major film and television star in his own right but also over the next five decades an almost de facto *SNL* cast member, hosting the show a near-record sixteen times (topped only by Alec Baldwin, a seventeen-time host).

The other series in that era was the baby boomer–beloved NBC's *Rowan & Martin's Laugh-In* (1968–1973). It was a fast-paced hour-long comedy show that on the surface played as a broad burlesque-like series of comic bits and sketches through the lens of hippie culture but underneath, mostly through its writing and performers, often tweaked the establishment on political issues like war and civil rights, as well as with references to many of the more staid elected officials at the time.

Perhaps due to its lighter, more jokey presentation, *Laugh-In* soon became the most popular show on television and lured the likes of then presidential hopeful Richard Nixon, a friend of head writer Paul Keyes. Keyes persuaded Nixon, against the advice of his advisors, to do a cameo in which he uttered the show's four-word catchphrase as a question: "Sock it to *me?*" Less than two months later, Nixon would win the presidency by a narrow popular vote margin, forging debate to this day whether appearing on a network sketch comedy somehow humanized the notoriously stiff Nixon and put him over the finish line.

What is not debatable is that a little more than a month after Nixon's win, a young comedy writer named Lorne Michaels officially joined the *Laugh-In* writing staff for the 1968–1969 season and during that time had a behind-the-scenes seat to an even more popular television show that almost every well-known political and pop culture figure now clamored to, and often did, appear on.

Late-night talk shows, such as NBC's *The Tonight Show Starring Johnny Carson* (1962–1992), or syndicated ones, such as *The Merv Griffin Show* (1965–1969, 1972–1986) also addressed politics. But they would limit current events talk to either soft jibes in their monologues or guest spots where an elected official or political columnist or occasional satirist (the word *pundit* was not yet a thing) would sit on the designated couch and answer some prescreened questions covering a few key issues. And competitors, like ABC's *The Dick Cavett Show* (1969–1975), a prime-time and late-night talk show that was a bit more serious and intellectual than its competitors, were no longer on the air by the midseventies.

So when *SNL* arrived during the post-Watergate era of 1975, the time was ripe for a new series run by a group of young comedy writers and performers who could test just how far a series could go in lampooning both pop culture *and* politics on a weekly basis.

Still, no one expected that show would kick open the door for so many other subsequent series in the next fifty years—programs whose main focus would be to mine comedy from electoral politics and hot-button political issues, particularly of the presidential kind. Nor was there a thought that *SNL* could also remain on the air all those years later, still capturing a significant chunk of the key eighteen-to-thirty-five-year-old audience demographic right alongside them.

## The Political Comedy Revolution

As any fifty-year-old with even the slightest bit of insight will confess, they are not exactly who they were when they were younger. Nor could they be. Nor, perhaps, would they want to be. We are all molded by the world we live in and our experiences in it. Yet who we are at our core remains pretty constant.
It's not much different for a late-night TV series that has been on the air for a comparable amount of time.

SNL has covered nine U.S. presidencies over six decades of American life with a gigantic range of domestic and foreign events, as well as political ups and downs. Different demographic groups will have their favorite moments, often depending on their ages and backgrounds. They will also have their most regrettable ones. But there is no denying that revisiting them through those sketches, impressions, and guest appearances provides a unique cultural touchstone of ourselves and Washington, DC, in particular—a sort of time capsule of who we are, what we thought, and how we reacted, shown by what we chose to make fun of.

Still, it's important to acknowledge a few key factors in how the show parodied politics, politicians, and news through its innately American lens.

## The Lure of the POTUS

We Americans tend to identify politics through our presidents and more often than not use them to define an era. Even historical scholars will often define the seventies as the Nixon-Ford-Carter era, the eighties as the Reagan years, and the nineties as the time of the Clintons.

The explosion of cable news, the internet, and social media platforms found a greater array of politicians becoming household names in the aughts, making designations a bit stickier. Still, in all the years *SNL* has been on the air, no impression of any single political figure recurred more in a season than the person who was serving as president or at least running for president.

Jimmy Carter was portrayed on the show a total of thirty-nine times, more than two-thirds of which occurred when he was in the Oval Office. George W. Bush impressions appeared seventy-two times in the eight years he served as POTUS, with the breakout performance of Will Ferrell accounting for nearly half of them. Even *no-drama* Barack Obama, who *SNL* writers and actors agree was the most difficult of them all for impressionists, was done sixty-two times, while either serving or running in an election cycle.

A year after leaving *SNL*, Ferrell created and performed a one-man show on Broadway as George W. Bush, *You're Welcome, America.* He recalled to *U.S. News & World Report* (12/4/13) that he never planned on impersonating W on *SNL*, but because resident impressionist Darrell Hammond was already playing Al Gore, Michaels asked him to try doing the Republican nominee in a 2000 debate sketch because they were "both tall." So he agreed to give it shot. Ferrell explained,

"I just find one thing I can hang my hat on, and for Bush, for instance, I knew he squinted his eyes a lot. . . . And then I got more comfortable with the voice. So if you can find one little tick you can build on it."

That follows in a long tradition of *SNL* presidential impressions: Chase stumbling across the stage as Gerald Ford; Dan Aykroyd's can-do attitude and sly-southern Jimmy Carter smile; Jay Pharoah's almost too cool-for-school Barack Obama, complete with the halting phraseology he often employed in his speeches.

Still, none embody the kind of larger-than-life, sometimes-scandalous traits that make for the most popular and repeated *SNL* impressions, political or otherwise. So it should come as no surprise that the number 1 spot for the most impersonated U.S. president on the show is actually . . . a tie.

Through season 49, the fictional versions of Bill Clinton and Donald Trump each hold the record with approximately 115 appearances apiece.

Each has survived impeachment, sexual scandals, and multiple investigations. As president both men had voracious appetites for . . . well, many things, as well as distinctive regional accents. And most importantly, both were funny in real life, even if they didn't always have a sense of humor about themselves.

It also helped that each have endured as pop culture figures either before and/or after their presidencies, with massive notoriety that makes them continual fodder for parody. In President Clinton's case, it is as the naughty, untamed spouse of former presidential candidate, New York senator, and U.S. secretary of state Hillary Clinton (the most impersonated political figure in *SNL* history aside from her husband, Trump, and George W. Bush). As for Trump, take your pick from morally questionable New York real estate mogul, reality TV show host, defendant in multiple criminal indictments across the country, and leader of the purposefully button-pushing Make America Great Again (MAGA) movement.

Bill Clinton and Donald Trump are the most impersonated because they somehow managed to transcend the presidency and become twenty-first-century American icons, in part with *SNL*'s help, but in greater part by how easy it has become for fame, or infamy, to endure in our postmillennium 24/7 news cycle.

## Casting Characters

Finding the right person to portray the right politician at the right time is an essential part of how *SNL* manages to capture a political moment. The quintessential example is Tina Fey's resemblance to and performance as the 2008 Republican vice presidential candidate Sarah Palin. Fey admits she herself didn't see any similarity in their looks when her husband first casually mentioned to her early on there was a resemblance. But when her doorman, Lorne Michaels, and countless others in her personal and work life pointed it out, she finally gave in, and with the help of the sketch writers and a few friends, including former *SNL* writer Paula Pell, who helped her with the "accent," the impression became an international moment.

Impersonations of major party candidates for U.S. president and vice president and the ultimate winners of those elections are requirements for a weekly sketch comedy show to stay timely. But on *SNL* over the years, it's been often nothing more than educated guess work about whom and what will work and whom or what won't.

Chase as Ford and Dan Aykroyd as Carter scored instantly in the early seasons when the expectations, if there were any at all, were different. Chase didn't bother with Ford-like hair, makeup, or even voice. He simply grabbed onto a single trait, the president's stumbling in public a handful of times, and made it the basis for the entire character. In Aykroyd's case it was Carter's attitude, accent, and smile. In his early appearances, the actor didn't even bother to cover or shave his own moustache.

This would not be the case as time went on and hair and makeup techniques evolved, as did audience demand for something a little deeper but no less funny. By the time Alec Baldwin got around to playing Trump, he was wearing a wig that took fifty hours to construct ("each hair was sewn in," hairstylist Jodi Mancuso told the *Hollywood Reporter* in 2017); wild, pasted-on eyebrows glued into small peaks; and carefully curated orange-hued makeup whose shade

## Live from New York . . . the President of the United States

- **President Gerald R. Ford (1974–1976):** Chevy Chase (1975–1976, 1978, 1980, 1985)
- **President Jimmy Carter (1976–1980):** Dan Aykroyd (1976–1979); Joe Piscopo (1980–1982); Michael McKean (1994); Darrell Hammond (2002–2009)
- **President Ronald Reagan (1980–1988):** Chevy Chase (1976); Harry Shearer (1980, 1984); Charles Rocket (1980–1981); Joe Piscopo (1981–1984); Randy Quaid (1985–1986); Robin Williams (1986); Phil Hartman (1986–1991)
- **President George H. W. Bush (1988–1992):** Jim Downey (1980); Dana Carvey (1987–1993, 1996, 2000); Fred Armisen (2005)
- **President William Jefferson Clinton (1992–2000):** Phil Hartman (1992–1994); Michael McKean (1994); Darrell Hammond (1995–2009); Dana Carvey (1996)
- **President George W. Bush (2000–2008):** Will Ferrell (1999–2002, 2008, 2009, 2012); Chris Parnell (2002–2003); Darrell Hammond (2003); Will Forte (2004–2006); Jason Sudeikis (2006–2008, 2010)
- **President Barack Obama (2008–2016):** Fred Armisen (2008–2012); Jay Pharoah (2012–2016); Chris Redd (2021)
- **President Donald Trump (2016–2020):** Phil Hartman (1988–1990); Darrell Hammond (1999–2016); Jason Sudeikis (2012); Taran Killam (2015); Alec Baldwin (2016–2020); John Cena (2016); James Austin Johnson (2021–2023)
- **President Joe Biden (2020–2024):** Kevin Nealon (1991); Jason Sudeikis (2007–2021); Woody Harrelson (2019); Jim Carrey (2020); Alex Moffat (2020–2021); James Austin Johnson (2021–2022); Pete Davidson (2022); Mikey Day (2023)

changed depending on the actor's mood. The visual itself became so convincing that when the Dominican newspaper *El Nacional* published an article about Israeli settlements in 2017, it mistakenly ran a photo of Baldwin made up as Trump instead of Trump himself, alongside a photo of Israeli prime minister Benjamin Netanyahu.

Michaels's only requirement for political impersonations is to capture something real about the person and the moment. As he explained in his Biden Institute talk, "The character has to embody something that people believe is true. . . . You can't play a villain by repeatedly pointing out how awful they are. . . . You find the thing about them that's true, that seems like them."

The show has leaned into doing a far greater amount of politically related impressions over the last several decades as government officials have become more recognizable, and sometimes infamous, thanks to our 24/7 news cycle. If it can find a cast member or guest star to make a timely moment work or simply an original take on a person in the political arena, then some of the show's most popular and most repeated political "appearances" of non-POTUS figures carry on far beyond where they would have gone during *SNL*'s first few decades.

For instance, *SNL* barely paid attention to a member of the U.S. Supreme Court (even Clarence Thomas's controversial confirmation hearings were only done a handful of times) before Kate McKinnon's unique take on the late Justice Ruth Bader Ginsburg became a hit on *Weekend Update* in 2015. Justice Ginsburg gladly embraced the wilder, more effervescent version of herself (McKinnon played her on the show ten times) and once admitted to NPR's Nina Totenberg there are moments she'd like to say McKinnon's catchphrase, "Gins-burned!" to some of the other justices.

McKinnon also scored heavily with sinister renditions of Trump consigliore Kellyanne Conway (she impersonated her twenty-three troubling times from 2016 to 2019) and Trump lawyer Rudy Giuliani. Hers was a fresh take on a whole new version of other *SNL* performances of the former New York City mayor that have thus far shown up twelve times, almost as many as all the other Giuliani impressions combined. Though, in fairness, the current real-life Giuliani also feels like a whole new and definitely very, very, very fresh version of his past self.

Similarly, guest host Melissa McCarthy's 2017 appearance as comically belligerent Trump press secretary Sean Spicer helped win her a 2017 Emmy as Guest Actress in a Comedy Series, and she came back to do it three more times.

Also notable have been Will Ferrell's bizarre portrait of Clinton-era Attorney General Janet Reno as a tough, deep-voiced bully who held her own private dance parties (thirteen appearances from 1997 to 2001); Cecily Strong's soused take on Fox News personality Judge Jeanine Pirro (fifteen appearances from 2015 to 2022); Darrell Hammond's two dozen sketches (2000–2020) as a fast-talking, unhinged, and uncensored version of MSNBC's former *Hardball* host Chris Matthews; and Bill Hader's unique take on political pundit and former Clinton campaign manager James Carville as a slap-happy, loveable know-it-all.

Interestingly, Carville had only been done once during the entire Clinton administration but made ten appearances from 2009 to 2013 when Hader took him on.

## Cable News, Partisan News, and "Fake" News

For its first two decades, *SNL*'s political coverage emphasized the top echelon of the White House, those who ran for election against them, a few key foreign leaders, and a small handful of congressional names. *Weekend Update* dealt with some of these political figures but also spoke equally on social issues. Otherwise, it was rare for anyone else in politics to recur so many times. A political journalist like Ted Koppel, who hosted the popular ABC late-night news series *Nightline* from 1980 to 2005, was an exception, as were a few other journalists. But Koppel, as well as other reporter "characters," tended to not so much be the center of a sketch but rather portrayed in relation to the person they were covering.

This all began to change in the mid- to late nineties with the rise and audience reach of 24/7 cable news networks. Their broadcasting shone the spotlight on a lot of previously under-the-radar, even odd types who previously would have gone unnoticed. This in turn fostered the breakout popularity of comedy shows lampooning Washington, as well as the news and all these new "celebrity" newsmakers, with those programs frequently and boldly offering their own version of "fake news" before the Trump campaign tried to coin the phrase as his own.

That explosion has now become its own genre of programming across television, streaming platforms, and the internet, making it increasingly difficult to separate fact from fiction for those of us still interested in that sort of thing.

The first significant change in political news reporting actually began in 1980, when CNN's twenty-four-hour news service launched, albeit with only a small fraction of the approximately 80 million subscribers it now has. But because its ratings were barely a blip at that time, it didn't have the ability to boost any political figure or event onto the broader cultural landscape (thus making them ripe for parody) until much later.

Similarly, HBO in 1983 launched one of its first scripted series, *Not Necessarily the News* (*NNTN*, 1983–1990), a half-hour spoof of a news program inspired by the BBC2 series *Not the Nine o' Clock News* (1979–1982) that featured a *Weekend Update*–like segment. But despite some critical acclaim, it also didn't have anything close to the viewer base to make a solely political comedy show into a crossover hit (though *NNTN* did have future *SNL* stalwart Jan Hooks in its cast and Conan O'Brien on its writing staff). Little did HBO realize, it would attain the status to do that and a lot more by the end of the nineties with the debut of *The Sopranos* (1999–2007) and later several other series that, on a good day, could outdraw any other broadcast network show.

On the news side, it took the launch in 1996 of both Fox News and MSNBC and the rapid expansion, popularity, and influence of both in their first five years to make so many political figures beyond the Oval Office into the type of well-known and spoofable characters they are today. As Seth Meyers, former

*SNL* head writer and *Weekend Update* host, noted of the breakout success of *SNL*'s political sketches in the 2008 election year and the amount of coverage they received from so many networks, "It's the best for a writer when 70 million people see a debate because everyone knows the lines. We did 11.5 minutes on [a] debate sketch last week. We couldn't do that if everybody hadn't watched it."

Fox and MSNBC prime-time cable newscasts began attracting anywhere between an average of 1 to 2.5 or 3 million viewers nightly. Often they were not casual viewers but devoted (some would say rabid) fans who were motivated to engage with news and politics via shows that shared their specific political points of view (and later repost clips from their broadcasts all over social media, thus enabling many more millions of multiple views). Fox News was specifically launched by media mogul Rupert Murdoch to appeal to what he and Roger Ailes, the Republican political consultant and TV producer he hired to run it, believed was a vast untapped and underrepresented conservative audience. MSNBC, a cable offshoot of NBC, would not fully embrace its liberal lens until the rise of the Fox News machine began far outpacing its programming.

But once they did, the growth of the big three cable news channels opened the door to the growth and frequency of political comedy. The sheer number of politically related impressions in sketches and bits on *SNL* more than doubled beginning in the late 1990s and early 2000s through today, with the show portraying many prime-time cable news hosts like Fox's Greta Van Susteren, Bill O'Reilly, Laura Ingraham, Brian Kilmeade, and Steve Doocey numerous times and often as personalities in their own right. Ditto CNN's Larry King and Wolf Blitzer, as well as MSNBC's Chris Matthews and Rachel Maddow.

The exposure they enabled also caused an explosion of impressions of outspoken people they had on their shows and helped make well known across the country and even the globe. These included community activists, such as Al Sharpton (twenty-five impressions from 2001 to 2016); fringe members of Congress suddenly made famous for outrageous sound bites, like former Minnesota congresswoman Michelle Bachmann (nine appearances from 2009 to 2013) and Representative Marjorie Taylor Greene (seven times from 2021 to 2024); or others unwittingly caught in a hurricane scandal of news, such as Monica Lewinsky (sixteen appearances from 1998 to 2000 and 2002) and Linda Tripp (John Goodman played her five times from 1998 to 1999). Some began wondering aloud whether all the information and parody was helping to create the widening political divide that would fester and become even more amplified by an ad infinitum amount of 24/7 talking heads.

A large part of political comedy is observing and reflecting what's going on in the world, so given the growing divides and changes in how news was being delivered and consumed, it was only natural that *SNL* would focus on and expand the political aspect of its show. Also recognizing the change were a whole new brand of young writers and comics who would go on to create a slew of their own news comedy shows on emerging and existing cable networks that would join in and expand the genre.

In 1996, Comedy Central premiered the half-hour series *The Daily Show* (1996–present), and in its first three years, it spent more time on pop culture than it did on politics (despite cocreator Lizz Winstead's objections). But when Jon Stewart took over in 1999 and launched it into *The Daily Show with Jon Stewart*, he made the focus political satire and news and in less than five years doubled the ratings. A few years later, the ratings tripled and pretty much remained that way until he left in 2015.

Stewart's take on the news was a bit more pointed and activist than *SNL* but, like the show, also skewed decidedly toward younger audiences in the eighteen-to-thirty-five-year-old range. If anything, it proved there was additional room for political comedy with another kind of edge on television, much the way *SNL* did when it premiered twenty-five years prior to Stewart. Its popularity no doubt fueled even more interest in and attention to *SNL*'s *Weekend Update* segment, and some of the show's most popular "anchors," including Tina Fey, Amy Poehler, and Seth Meyers, emerged in the years it was on.

Stewart had a specific style of delivering his version of the news, much like the *Weekend Update* anchors did over the last fifty years. And like *SNL*, his show was also an incubator for a new group of comic performers, as *SNL* continued to be, but usually as news correspondents for a "pretend news show." When many went out on their own to create and star in still newer successful series, they in turn expanded the political comedy genre and pushed the boundaries even further.

Among them are Comedy Central's *The Colbert Report* (2005–2014), starring Stephen Colbert as a loveable blowhard, semiclueless news bigot in the vein of former Fox News host Bill O'Reilly; TNT's *Full Frontal with Samantha Bee* (2016–2022), a more frenetic and freewheeling take on the news with Bee's signature feminist slant; and HBO's *Last Week Tonight with John Oliver* (2014–present), a well-researched presentation of topical events where an often-outraged Oliver snidely comments on hot-button issues and humorously but fiercely advocates for overlooked stories in the news. Another *Daily Show* correspondent, South African–born Trevor Noah, took over hosting duties from Stewart from 2015 to 2022, and his point of view made for a more nuanced, expanded focus on racial issues.

Rather than limit the field of comic political discourse, these shows, like *SNL* before it, have expanded it for the next group of "good troublemakers" yet to come. And as of this writing, it looks as if yet another version of *SNL* writers, producers, and cast will continue on the road alongside them. That said, it still leaves room for the once-a-week, Monday-night return of Jon Stewart as *The Daily Show* host (there are alternating hosts the other nights of the week) in early 2024 to cover the presidential campaign. Not to mention the real Stephen Colbert taking over as the new host of CBS's retitled *The Late Show with Stephen Colbert* (2015–present) and Seth Meyers assuming the top spot on NBC's revamped *Late Night with Seth Meyers* (2014–present), platforms that both frequently lead with topical political humor.

# 15

# Politics and the Presidency, Part I

## Richard Nixon to George W. Bush (1970s–2000s)

Fifty years of U.S. presidents and the *SNL* cast members who portrayed them provide either a fun-house or haunted-house reflection of our White House. Like anything, it depends on one's perspective. For the majority of Americans, it's probably a combination of both, landing somewhere in the middle.

With each decade, the lens shifts a bit depending on who occupies the Oval Office. Presidents don't dictate all of our politics, but they steer the country in a specific direction during the time they serve and help define the era.

Political comedy has a similar task, but it's an easier lift. All it has to do is make fun of everyone in charge and mock everything they do just enough to make us laugh and perhaps think. On second thought, maybe that's not so easy.

The following is how *SNL* told us the news and our history through the presidents it covered.

### The 1970s: Post–Richard Nixon, Gerald Ford, and Jimmy Carter (1975–1980)

Richard Nixon resigned the presidency on August 8, 1974, more than a year before *SNL*'s premiere. Still, it wouldn't be accurate to talk about *SNL*'s coverage of presidents without including the Nixon factor, especially after Watergate reporters Bob Woodward and Carl Bernstein's *The Final Days*, a dishy and disturbing book chronicling the ex-president's last few somewhat-mad months in the White House that was published toward the end of the show's first season. Nixon and Watergate cast a giant shadow on Washington, DC, and not so silently haunted the coverage of politics for everyone, including *SNL*, which devoted six sketches to him in its first two seasons. The first, "Remembrance of Things Past" (1.13) featured a TV interview of a monkey-masked Mr. X, billed as a "distinguished ex-statesman" but speaking in a Nixon-like voice, referencing new age religion and repentance while musing about moving to "Red China" in the future. The second, far darker, funnier, and more troubling was the classic "Nixon's Final Days" (1.19; see details later). A tour de force of writing and acting, it is based on moments literally lifted from Woodward and Bernstein's account of the ex-president wandering the halls of the White House talking to oil paintings of some of the country's most renowned presidents in hopes they can help him sort out his troubles.

But like any new series, *SNL* was just finding its footing when it made its debut on October 11, 1975, and for the vast majority of its initial season, its political coverage was defined by one of the most experienced politicians in Washington, DC. He also happened to be the man occupying the Oval Office at the time—President Gerald R. Ford.

Ford was (and still is) the only individual to hold both the first- and second-highest offices in the land without winning a national election. A twenty-five-year member of Congress, including the last seven serving as House Minority Leader, in 1973 he was appointed by Nixon to replace his elected vice president, Spiro Agnew, who had been forced to resign in disgrace due to an impending bribery scandal. Less than a year later, Vice President Ford automatically became the next in succession to assume the presidency when Nixon himself was forced into giving up his elected office, also in disgrace, albeit for different reasons. Compared to Nixon's second term, which only lasted two and a half years due

Chevy Chase didn't attempt to impersonate Gerald Ford, but relies instead on his own physical comedic skills to portray the thirty-eighth president of the United States as a clumsy fool.

to the Watergate scandal, Ford's tenure in the White House was subdued. He was a relatively drama-free POTUS both politically and personally who devoted most of his time in office to dealing with the country's economic crisis and encouraging Americans to join him in his fight against inflation by wearing a WIN (Whip Inflation Now) button.

Chevy Chase's "portrayal" of President Ford (it was more of a portrayal than an impersonation because he made no attempt to look or sound like him) had nothing to do with Ford's politics or the policies of his administration. Chase's Ford is essentially a klutz who has a tendency to fall down—a lot. He also has trouble performing the simplest tasks, like standing behind a podium or pouring himself a glass of water. Ironically, the real Ford was an athlete who happened to take a few tumbles in public, including the time he fell down the stairs of Air Force One during a visit to Austria in June 1975. He blamed it on his bum knee, an old college injury from his days playing football for the University of Michigan. Whatever the reason, Ford's spills were not, as *SNL* suggested, a daily occurrence. However, the one in Austria occurred several months before the series' first show was to air and provided a rare silly giggle in a politically dark time. It also gave Chase the basis for a portrayal that would publicly define Ford for the rest of the time he was in office and beyond.

Fortunately Ford had a sense of humor. He allowed his press secretary Ron Nessen to host *SNL* in April 1976 (1.17; see chapter 18) and even made a filmed cameo appearance on the show. A month prior he also invited Chase to a White House dinner (perhaps for a trial *SNL* run), stealing the show himself when he turned to the comic and said, "I'm Gerald Ford, and you're not," a riff on Chase's self-referential *Weekend Update* catchphrase, "I'm Chevy Chase, and you're not."

Since Chase took his first tumble over the presidential podium (1.4), *Saturday Night Live* has been at the forefront of American political satire. Studio 8H is a national stage for the weekly public skewering of the American political system—its two major parties, its major players, and the media's role in the political process. In a 2020 interview with *New York Magazine*'s pop culture site Vulture, Michaels reflected on *SNL*'s take on political discourse and how it has evolved:

> Going back to Ford/Carter, we've had a voice, and we will try as hard as possible to maintain that voice. If anybody talks about "truth to power" or any of that, it's tedious because everybody says they're doing it, and power seems to be unaffected by it entirely. So, we'll give our point of view. There are lots of writers, a lot of differing points of view. And the show's tried really hard to not just be a partisan voice, but to be clear-headed about it. Over the years, I've had, obviously, complaints from both parties. People feel things are unfair, and I understand that. But if we're taking shots, I hope we're taking clean shots.

Ford's presidency ended after two-plus years, when he was defeated in 1976 by Jimmy Carter. The contrast between the two men was sharp. Carter was a southerner known for his affable manner and wide smile. A former governor of Georgia, he was a Washington outsider and fifty-two years old when he was elected president. Though Ford was only eleven years older, Carter seemed a lot younger, hipper, and, most importantly, not a part of the DC establishment that many in the country felt had almost done them in.

This played into Dan Aykroyd's portrayal of him on *SNL* as both candidate and president, in part helped along by the famous *Playboy* interview published a month before the election where Carter admitted that he had "looked at women with lust" and "committed adultery in my heart many times." Carter was a decorated naval officer and Annapolis graduate, came from a religious family, and had been happily married to his childhood sweetheart Rosalynn for many years. His admission of "lust" in *Playboy*, of all places, was unexpected and added a dose of sexuality to Aykroyd's take on him as an extremely smart but kind man of faith who could bring honesty, humanity, and now even a bit of swag back to the Oval Office.

"We think of Jimmy Carter as this older statesman, peanut farmer, evangelical Christian and (building houses for) Habitat for Humanity," observed *Pod Save America* cohost Tommy Vietor (who was also spokesperson for the U.S. National Security Council under President Obama) on a 2023 podcast.

> When he ran for president, it was post-Watergate, so everyone was looking for this anti-Washington breath of fresh air. But also, he was "boys" with the Allman Brothers Band, so that made him seem cool. And the Allman Brothers Band, at the time, were rowdy, did drugs, was multiracial. . . . [T]hey had Black members, White members. So it was seen as this really hip, counterculture-type thing.

In various sketches, Aykroyd's Carter could riff on foreign policy in one moment and then talk a constituent down from an acid trip in the next. His military background allowed the President Carter "character" to be comfortable on a nuclear reactor, so much so that when a worker spills a soft drink on the control board, Aykroyd's Carter could be the kind of guy who could step up and disarm it (See "The Amazing Colossal President" [4.16] later). Or could he? Since the sketch aired at the end of his presidency, Carter's "superpowers" were no longer quite what they were cracked up to be.

Unfortunately, rising inflation, American hostages held captive in Iran, and gas lines around the block due to an energy crisis plagued his can-do image. It also didn't help that he gave a speech (in his third year in office) where he talked about American malaise and a "crisis of the American spirit," observing that "human identity is no longer defined by what one does but by what one owns." He went on to lecture Americans that "owning things and consuming things does not satisfy our longing for meaning." Those words may have been ahead of their time, but it didn't square with his good-guy savior image, one that had been partially magnified by one of the few sketch comedy shows on the air doing political comedy. Carter would go on to lose his reelection in a landslide to Ronald Reagan, another former governor and also former actor.

## Notable Sketches

### Cold Open: "Ford Speech" (1.4) and Cold Open: "Oval Office" (1.6)

These sketches, broadcast two weeks apart on *SNL*'s fourth and sixth episodes, were the debut of Chevy Chase as Gerald Ford. But in just over two minutes apiece, they established what would be the show's fifty-year tradition of often using its opening segment, along with its version of the current president of the United States, to comment on political events of the day.

In the first, Ford, while delivering a speech, immediately bumps into an American flag and drops the papers he is holding, only to flub words, mispronounce names, and stumble and tumble around the podium during an "appearance" on *SNL*. It ends with the president face-planting on the floor after he trips over two chairs and then raising his head to the camera to utter the inimitable words, "Live from New York, it's Saturday Night!" The second ends the same way but instead places Ford at a desk, this time giving a speech to the American public. The president's bumbling becomes even bigger, as he picks up a full glass of water and puts it to his ear, thinking it's a ringing phone; tries to connect separate calls with Egyptian president Anwar Sadat and his secretary of state Henry Kissinger by putting their two phone receivers together; and accidentally banging his head on the desk between addressing New York City's then impending financial crisis before once again falling on his face. The result of those four minutes was the creation of an *SNL* Ford persona that would stick around much longer than the one year Chevy Chase remained as a cast member of the show.

### Nixon's Final Days (1.19)

*SNL* writer and performer (and former Minnesota senator) Al Franken, who wrote the sketch along with his frequent writing and performing partner Tom Davis, recalled in a 2016 article he penned for the *Washington Post* that he and Davis had tried out an earlier version of this piece at a local theater in Minnesota. Perhaps that is why it feels like a scene from a really smart black comedy play and has held up for so long.

The premise is simple and taps into what at the time were several well-publicized anecdotes from *The Final Days* about an inebriated Nixon losing his grip on reality before resigning the presidency. First Lady Pat Nixon, played by that week's guest host Madeline Kahn, writes remembrances in her diary of "those stormy final days" as the sketch cuts back and forth between her and her troubled husband.

As a distraught Nixon is being talked down by family members and the likes of Henry Kissinger and Sammy Davis Jr., Nixon has none of it and laments about what went wrong to oil paintings of former presidents John F. Kennedy (who defeated Nixon in the 1960 presidential election), Franklin Roosevelt, and Abraham Lincoln (Lincoln's portrait actually talks back and calls him a "dip," though Franken reveals it was supposed to be "schmuck" until the NBC censors made them change it because they insisted the word *schmuck* meant *penis* in Yiddish).

Aykroyd's hunched-over mannerisms and pitch-perfect vocal intonations of Nixon are so vivid that the fact that he refused to shave his own moustache for the performance becomes moot. Nixon's opening speaking line also helped him along when he proclaims to Lincoln's portrait, "You were lucky they shot you!"

By far the most controversial moment in the sketch by today's standards is Nixon dragging down Kissinger, expertly played by John Belushi, onto the floor to "pray with me, Henry." When Kissinger says he needs to get back and take care of matters of state, the president pouts, then turns to him and blurts out, "You don't want to pray, Jew boy?" Kissinger exits and Nixon angrily repeats with disdain, "Jew boy."

The moment addresses what were by then well-publicized stories in the Woodward and Bernstein book about Nixon's secret anti-Semitism (he also expresses his disdain for Roosevelt's liberal policies in the sketch by calling him "Rosenfelt") and an anecdote where he actually wanted Kissinger to join him when he got down on his knees to pray in the Lincoln sitting room and the Jewish Kissinger felt obliged to go along with him. In the sketch Pat Nixon tries to explain away her husband's behavior to her diary by noting, "Dick wasn't

In the final days of his presidency, Richard Nixon (Dan Aykroyd) (left), who is losing his grip on reality, forces a reluctant Henry Kissinger (John Belushi) to get on his knees and pray with him.

anti-Semitic. He hated all minorities." Whether a sketch that pointed could get on the air these days is debatable. But it certainly broke boundaries at the time and remains a telling piece of satire to this day.

## Ask President Carter (2.15)

Jimmy Carter did a much-publicized call-in radio program with journalist Walter Cronkite, *Ask President Carter*, in March 1977 that served as the jumping-off point for this *SNL* parody a week later. It played off Carter's image as a smart, keyed-in man of infinite knowledge by portraying him as a guy who was equally adept at helping a confused Kansas postal worker with the intricacies of the new automatic sorting system at her workplace as he was with talking down a young listener from a bad acid trip by discerning he had taken "orange sunshine" and simply needed to relax; perhaps listen to some Allman Brothers music; and remember he was a "living, breathing organism" and was safe.

It concludes with the barely disguised voice of Nixon posing as a caller who claims he was previously employed at the White House and left an envelope of several thousand dollars in small bills taped to the bottom of the dresser in Carter's bedroom. He asks Carter if can send it to him at his home address in San Clemente, California (the city where Nixon lived at the time), and the ever-affable Carter agrees. Aykroyd's grounded competence as Carter was a reminder that he was the clear moral choice for the Oval Office compared to the disgraced, exiled, and still manipulative voice of a predecessor such as Nixon.

Walter Cronkite (Bill Murray, left) hosts President Carter (Dan Aykroyd), who answers questions about minutiae and "talks down" a caller on a bad acid trip.

## "The Pepsi Syndrome" (4.16)

In this zany takeoff of the quite serious Three-Mile Island nuclear power plant partial meltdown in Pennsylvania, President Carter shows up to try and save the day but instead becomes exposed to nuclear material himself and increases in size to ninety feet. It is notable in that it shows the president, who in real life was a trained nuclear engineer, able to diagnose the problem in the plant (another engineer, played by Bill Murray, had spilled a large Coke on the control board) but, despite his best efforts, was unable to fix it. Well into the third year of his administration, it is a metaphor for all the issues Carter had thus far been unable to solve for the country in spite of his vast knowledge and unwavering commitment. In one of the sketch's best moments, a doctor tries to explain to the still in-the-dark First Lady her husband's now enormous size. To do so she introduces real-life comedian Rodney Dangerfield, who makes a cameo appearance. When posed with the question, "How big is he?" in reference to the fictional Carter's current dimensions, he retorts with lines like, "He's so big, he could have an affair with the Lincoln Tunnel." Rim shot!

## The 1980s (and a Little Beyond): Ronald Reagan (1980–1988) and George H. W. Bush (1988–1992)

Considering how far to the right his conservative politics moved the country, President Ronald Reagan got off relatively easy during his eight years in office (1980–1988) because the show shifted away from edgy political humor during Dick Ebersol's tenure as producer (1981–1985). In the Ebersol years, Reagan was played by a variety of cast members, including Harry Shearer, Charles Rocket, Joe Piscopo, and Randy Quaid (and once by Robin Williams when he hosted [12.5]), but none of the bits were particularly memorable or insightful. Ironically, the exceptions were a handful of early sketches where Reagan was heard but never seen (only his hand, mirror image, and/or shadow were) that toyed lightly with his age, competence, and background as an actor.

The conceit of the send-ups, under the title "Hail to the Chief" (7.5, 7.11, 7.14, 7.17), is that the unseen president was being talked to by staff and "directed" by cabinet members, like Ed Meese (presidential counselor and later secretary of state), as if he were merely an actor *playing* the president in a film they are shooting rather than actually being president. Piscopo voiced Reagan as a clueless performer asking questions about character motivation or making suggestions for possible changes to the "script," the latter usually being the daily itinerary he was handed or copy for a speech he was scheduled to make that day. In one sketch he impatiently asks, "How much longer are we going to be making this movie?" to which Meese smugly replies, "Three or four years." Later he complains that he's confused about his motivation in a speech, questioning, "Why would a president try to take money away from old people and poor people and kids? I just don't understand it." The latter reference to Reagan's cuts to social programs and his trickle-down economics policy was about as tough as it got for a while.

Michaels returned to produce the show in 1985 and added more and stronger political content. The undisputed highlight during the Reagan era was the sketch "Mastermind" (12.6; see later), which is widely regarded as one of the show's best political sketches. The picture it paints of Reagan is the complete opposite of how he was portrayed in previous sketches—as a doddering old fool who has no idea what's going on.

Dana Carvey's impersonation of Reagan's successor, President George H. W. Bush, was more popular than the president himself, especially after the latter reneged on his 1988 campaign promise of "no new taxes." Carvey relied heavily on catchphrases Bush used, like "wouldn't be prudent" (as in "Not gonna do it. Wouldn't be prudent at this juncture.") and "a thousand points of light," which Bush first referenced when accepting the presidential nomination at the 1988 Republican National Convention regarding American clubs and volunteer organizations ("a brilliant diversity spread like stars, like a thousand points of light in a broad and peaceful sky"). In James Andrew Miller and Tom Shales's book *Live from New York: The Complete, Uncensored History of Saturday Night Live*, Lorne Michaels observes that Carvey's impression of Bush was so resonant and so on point that, "after a while when you saw George Bush on television, he wasn't enough like George Bush."

Unfortunately for Carvey, Bush was a one-term president. But like Gerald Ford, Bush also had a sense of humor and even invited Carvey and his wife for an overnight stay at the White House. When Carvey returned to host the show in 1994 (20.4), Bush graciously agreed to appear in the cold open to introduce him. In addressing the American people, he admits that he *does* have hard feelings about how *SNL* made fun of him and will seek revenge, but not at this time—"wouldn't be prudent." He also critiqued Carvey's imitation of him during the monologue. It's by far the funniest appearance on the show by a real-life former U.S. president. (Side note: George H. W. Bush is the only *former* U.S. president to appear on *SNL*. Ford, who was still in office when he filmed his cameo, is the only president to say, "Live from New York" [1.17], while in office. When Senator Barack Obama said it in 2007, he was still seeking the Democratic nomination [33.4]).

## Notable Sketches

### "Mastermind" (12.6)

Most of the Reagan White House sketches paint the president as an old fool who lacks the intellect and the mental capacity to run the country. This brilliant sketch, written by Jim Downey and Al Franken, begins with a kindly Reagan (Phil Hartman) being interviewed about the Iran-Contra scandal, claiming he had no knowledge of the operation. But once the reporter leaves, it's revealed that

In this classic sketch, Ronald Reagan (Phil Hartman) is a doddering old fool in public, but behind closed doors he is the mastermind of his administration.

Reagan's doddering old-man persona is all an act. He is not only the man in charge, but he's also the only one who knows what's going on (he speaks Arabic and German fluently and quotes the French political thinker Montesquieu ["Power without knowledge is power lost!"]).

Reagan calls his staffers into his office and becomes a taskmaster, rapidly barking orders to CIA director William Casey (Jon Lovitz) that he's in charge of his new operation to fund the Contras and to Chief of Staff Don Regan that he's going to have to resign. In between all this, he keeps getting interrupted—first for a photo op with a Girl Scout and then by his old Hollywood friend Jimmy Stewart (Dana Carvey), whom he brushes off so he can get back to plotting the cover-up, as well as the next part of his plan. After seeing so many impersonations of Reagan as a clueless senior citizen, the reversal comes as a complete shock. Franken credits Robert Smigel, who is known for *SNL*'s "TV Funhouse" cartoon shorts, for coming up with the original idea for the sketch, and George Meyer, who went on to become a top writer on *The Simpsons*, for doing some of the rewriting. Whatever the combination of writers, it is not only insightfully written but also perfectly staged in the theatrical farce tradition of characters constantly entering and exiting like a scene out of a Marx Brothers film.

### "ABC Campaign 88: Presidential Debate" (14.1)

This is one of the early and more successful parodies of the kind of presidential debate sketch that would become an *SNL* staple as the years went on. Carvey plays George H. W. Bush for only the second time, but it's easy to see him beginning to master Bush's various catchphrases when he is up against the more intellectual but much more unemotional and detached Democratic nominee, Massachusetts governor Michael Dukakis. The sketch is remembered for three very funny moments. The first is in the candidates' entrance, when Bush, who towered over the much shorter Dukakis, pats him on the head like a child. This leads Dukakis to go over to his podium and push the button on what sounds like a hydraulic lift to bring him up past, then down, to the level of his microphone, a bit that Franken, one of the cowriters, credits to then *SNL* writer Conan O'Brien.

The second and at the time most remembered bit occurs when Bush is flummoxed in answering a question about homelessness and children going hungry and launches into a series of meaningless bromides, falling back on his usual canned slogans. Thinking he's used up his allotted three minutes, moderator Diane Sawyer (Jan Hooks) tells him, "You still have a minute-twenty," to which Bush replies, "That can't be right. I must have spoken for at least two minutes." It goes back and forth for a while (with Bush just trying to fill the time with anything), and when he finally gets his chance at rebuttal, an exasperated Dukakis turns to the camera and says, "I can't believe I'm losing to this guy." The line and Lovitz's tone was an apt reflection on both the poll numbers and the clear fact that Bush would be the likely victor despite his word salad.

The third moment was when ABC news anchor Peter Jennings (played by host Tom Hanks), does postdebate analysis, and Bush's vice presidential running mate Dan Quayle, widely considered to be much too youthful and inexperienced for the number 2 spot, is invited to give his thoughts. Quayle enters and is played by child actor Jeff Renaudo, the image of Quayle if Quayle were six years old. Renaudo would go on to play the senator a total of five times during the Bush administration.

## "Barbara and Nancy" (14.10)

Like her husband, First Lady Nancy Reagan was an actor before entering the political arena. She was not particularly popular there, often seen as the protective, tough-as-nails "power behind the throne" that smiled on the outside but was ruthless and controlling behind the scenes. Primarily two cast members portrayed her nineteen times on *SNL*. Terry Sweeney (1985–1986), an openly gay man, played her in drag and as a bit theatrical. But Jan Hooks (1987–1991) brought out her more elitist side, the latter as a result of real-life moments, like the First Lady demanding all the White House china had to be replaced when the country was in the middle of a recession (it cost more than $200,000, which she said was covered by "private donations") or her endless array of free designer clothes, which she claimed she either returned or donated to museums after she wore them. In this sketch, new First Lady Barbara Bush, white-haired and decidedly unglamorous (cast member Phil Hartman in drag), has Mrs. Reagan (Hooks) over to tea on what will presumably be the latter's last day in the White House.

The new First Lady, Barbara Bush (Phil Hartman, right), has moved into the White House, yet outgoing First Lady Nancy Reagan (Jan Hooks) isn't ready to leave.

After Mrs. Reagan passes a number of passive-aggressive remarks about Mrs. Bush using the old Roosevelt China ("I so prefer the ones donated by Barbara Sinatra and Frank Sinatra") and moves *her* Limoges vase back to a more prominent place on a side table ("Let's great rid of that picture of George and the grandchildren"), tensions escalate, and it becomes clear Mrs. Reagan has no intention of leaving the White House. Finally, when Mrs. Bush has to wrap up the tea, she must call in two aides to "escort" Mrs. Reagan, who wants to remain and Mrs. Bush now clearly can't trust, out of the room. Hooks grabs onto furniture and door handles and topples over chairs as the aides have to literally pick her up and carry her sideways out of the room. The sketch hilariously encapsulates what much of the public was secretly thinking about the former First Lady through the years and served as a perfect transition to what would be the more staid and patrician Bush administration.

### "Bush Presidential Address" (15.1)

Yet another of what were now numerous spoofs of a Bush presidential address, this season's opener takes place in the fall of 1989 and is partly based on a real speech the president made from the White House, where he held up an actual bag of crack cocaine to emphasize how his administration was cracking down on the country's drug problem (which ironically was in decline by

1989). Carvey had honed his impression of Bush to where he was hard not to like, despite his bottomless pit of incomplete sentences and repeat phrases. At the same time, the sketch was a subtle skewering of what was then recognized as his very privileged Ivy League perspective, with Bush referencing vacationing in Kennebunkport, Maine, at the family compound; enjoying doing "loop-the-loops" on his speedboat; and denying any responsibility for the recent Hurricane Hugo "down there" because, since it was a natural disaster, that's "not my fault."

From a contemporary lens, the section of the sketch about drugs and the very real public threats to his family from a drug cartel is fascinating. Carvey's version of the president mentions how his sons Neil Bush and Jeb Bush are well prepared for any possible killers and that his daughter just graduated from a basic driving course. However, there is no mention of his older son and future president George W. Bush, who very publicly admitted during his presidential campaign ten years later to using cocaine and other drugs, in addition to excessive drinking, before getting sober. It is not likely the *SNL* writers knew this, but it is a good example of how time and the oncoming amount of requisite public disclosures about the famous (and in this case rich) adds and/or subtracts from the true reality of our presidents and First Families and how they are portrayed through comedy.

Dana Carvey punctuated his impression of President George H. W. Bush with hand gestures and catchphrases like "No new taxes," "Wouldn't be prudent," and "A thousand points of light."

## The 1990s: Bill Clinton (1992–2000)

The Clinton years provided the show's writers with a wealth of material due to a series of personal scandals that plagued his presidency, from Whitewater to Paula Jones to Monica Lewinsky, the latter of whom appeared on the show in May 1999 (24.18). Between 1995 and January 20, 2001, the day of President George W. Bush's inauguration, Darrell Hammond made approximately sixty appearances as Bill Clinton, plus an additional thirty-eight since he's been out of office (Phil Hartman played him in his first few years, and Dana Carvey and Beck Bennett each played him once, in 1996 and 2013, respectively). When the Clinton-Lewinsky sex scandal was at its peak during season 23 (1997–1998), *SNL* ratings climbed significantly, especially among adults ages eighteen to forty-nine. Lewinsky's appearance on the show followed a special *SNL* (2/27/99) devoted to the Clinton scandal, featuring a compilation of clips from the best sketches, and the publication that same year of *SNL Presents: The Clinton Years*, which contains all the best *Weekend Update* jokes and lines from Clinton sketches, should be enough to silence those on the right who complain about the left-wing media and *SNL*'s liberal bias.

Looking at the arc of the Clinton years through the comic lens of *SNL* gives a broad but fairly accurate picture of his shifting image in the country and perhaps throughout the world during his time in office. As the first baby boomer president, his "images" also became somewhat reflective of how the public began to reassess boomers generally.

Clinton was elected to the presidency in a three-way race against the incumbent Bush and Texas business billionaire Ross Perot, a third-party candidate. The contrast between the three men was funny on its own and barely needed much exaggeration, but the cold-open sketch "Debate 92" (18.3) tweaks their personas just enough to highlight the differences. Franken's recollection of his favorite moment is a good comic barometer of the change America was contemplating. At one point the candidates glance at each other, and we, the audience, get a look at what in their minds they are really viewing. Bush sees Clinton as a hippie with long hair and a headband; Clinton sees Bush as a prim, elderly lady in a silly hat and shawl; and when Bush and Clinton look at Perot, they see grainy film footage from *The Wizard of Oz* (1939) of a munchkin politician in a little suit speechifying in front of Dorothy. (Side Note: Carvey portrays both Bush *and* Perot in the sketch. Because he was already doing Bush and previously appeared several times as Perot, the decision was made to pretape Carvey's single shots as the Texas billionaire and use cast member David Spade, in Perot makeup, for a wider shot when the candidates make their entrance.)

Clinton represented a generational point-of-view change about presidents and what American leadership could now be. He campaigned as an "I feel your pain" everyman who actually liked to mix it up with the "real people" and would spend hours talking to everyday voters at campaign stops. He also famously appeared on *The Arsenio Hall Show* (1989–1993), wearing sunglasses and playing the saxophone, and spoke to niche groups about issues mostly ignored by recent administrations (e.g., about economic and educational opportunities with Black voters in their neighborhoods; at big public LGBTQ events about the raging AIDS epidemic, etc.). Though his vice president, the Tennessee senator Al Gore, was a bit more conservative, Gore was also an early advocate of the environmental issues that concern many young people today.

One of the major changes in the Clinton administration, something that no one at the time knew would become continuous comic fodder for *SNL* (and many others) over the next thirty-plus years, was his partnership with his wife, First Lady Hillary Clinton. An accomplished lawyer in her own right who did pro bono work in child advocacy, Bill Clinton publicly stated across the country his election was a "two-for-one" proposition in that voters would get him but also his wife in the executive hive mind. The opportunity for a First Lady to do more than "stay at home and bake cookies" (a remark Mrs. Clinton got in a bit of trouble for in more traditional circles but skillfully managed to overcome) spoke directly to the evolving roles of men and women in society. This, of course, would become a double-edged sword as rumors and then confirmation of Clinton's various sexual infidelities began to form one of the key traits in his comic persona.

The classic Bill Clinton sketch was early in his administration. "President Bill Clinton at McDonald's" (18.8; see more details later) shows Hartman playing the president as a down-to-earth, engaging good old boy who, like many Americans, struggles with his love of fast food and lack of exercise. Loosely based on a real incident, Hartman, in jogging attire and with Secret Service agents in tow, stops at McDonald's for some food and talks up the patrons while eating and explaining the issues in simple, digestible sound bites. It's a very sympathetic portrait overall, but the beginning of the sketch signals the more ominous dark comedy of the Clinton to follow in the next eight years.

When a Secret Service agent agrees to let him stay at McDonald's but implores, "Please don't tell Mrs. Clinton," Hartman turns to him and retorts, "Jim, let me tell you something. There's going to be a who-oole bunch of things we don't tell Mrs. Clinton." Six years later Clinton's affair with young White House intern Monica Lewinsky was an international scandal and millions were discussing whether the country might see its first presidential divorce or at least separation. Clinton's moral image was in the doghouse, even though his policies remained popular with the majority of American voters, and at that time the cold open "Bedtime at the White House" (24.2; see more details later) of Bill and Hillary (Darrell Hammond and Ana Gasteyer) and the tension between them was an about-face dark-comedy portrait addressing the status of their partnership. It also began to cement the satirical images of their marriage dynamic for quite a while in the public mind.

From a comedic perspective, Clinton's political achievements were thoroughly overshadowed by the various personal scandals and lawsuits that plagued him over eight years. Still, it's not unusual for *SNL* to steer away from the wonky in favor of the broad overview where the Oval Office occupant is concerned. As Seth Meyers summed up the issue several decades later in 2011 to *Vanity Fair*, "It helped when the D.C. characters are bigger because, as actors, we have to play those people, and just like with any impression, it helps if the target is just bigger, with funnier things about them. We don't do policy pieces well. We do sort of big character pieces well."

## Notable Sketches:

### "President Bill Clinton at McDonald's" (18.8)

Phil Hartman said, in doing his impression, he watched Bill Clinton debate tapes, made drawings of his hand gestures, and focused on his allergies to evoke the famous scratchy voice. But it was how he captured the Clinton ease, humor, and intellectual swagger through the words and actions he was given to do that allows this sketch to endure as the quintessential version of first-term Clinton. On a jog with Secret Service agents the out-of-shape-but-trying-to-stay-healthy POTUS stops at McDonald's to "maybe get a Diet Coke" and "talk with the real folks." But as he makes the rounds, he begins asking for and then slowly out and out starts grabbing food off the plates of unsuspecting constituents. After he compliments a young Black woman on her baby ("Shakira, that means African princess"), he asks if she's going "to finish those fries." He then sits with a small business owner and asks about his son's leftover pickles (which he grabs), and then orders an Egg McMuffin and "those greasy sausage patties" from an admiring Mickey D manager (who agrees to get them all for him, even though "it's after 11 a.m."). He continues making the rounds with a student worried about the cost of college and a young guy inquiring about sending troops into Somalia, all the while grabbing barbecue sauce, a Filet-O-Fish, an apple pie, and a McDLT, among other items, off everyone's plates, barely able to stuff down all the food into his mouth (at one point Hartman has to pause as he begins to choke, but cast member Rob Schneider quickly offers him a sip from his drink). The message of the sketch mirrors the loveable Clinton image of "I can talk with you about your issue and offer solutions, but like you, I like to eat fast food and don't really love to work out." How do you not identify with a guy like that?

## "*The Real World* with Bob Dole" (21.15)

Bob Dole was a tough-talking World War II veteran and Senate Majority Leader who became the Republican presidential nominee and was decisively defeated by Bill Clinton in his 1996 reelection. Dole was a straight talker who pulled no punches, and aside from wanting to make cuts in social security, he was known for blunt pronouncements, like saying the baby boomers were a "spoiled" generation.

Norm Macdonald, who at the time was anchoring *Weekend Update*, personified a hilarious, confrontational Dole in a whole series of *SNL* moments where the politician talked about himself in the third person. Among the most bizarrely entertaining is a short film where Dole appeared as a cast member of the then very popular pioneering MTV reality show *The Real World*. In the sketch (and series) young inhabitants from varied backgrounds live in a big house and have to learn to get along despite their many differences. Usually there is one person the rest of the group can't seem to get along with, and in this case it's Dole, who is seen enraged that someone has eaten his peanut butter sandwich ("Nobody eats Bob Dole's peanut butter without asking," he bellows) or sitting in a chair in the house that he believes is only his chair ("Get out of my chair! That's Bob Dole's chair, and everyone knows it!"). The sketch ran in March of the election year and was an example of how, despite Clinton's troubles, he was more in tune with key voting demographics of the American public. Interestingly, the sketch does end with Dole laughing and frolicking with a puppy he brought into the house, albeit one who peed on the coat of one of his roommates.

## "Janet Reno's Dance Party" (23.7)

There were multiple versions of this sketch in the nineties, and Will Ferrell's "interpretation" of Janet Reno, Clinton's choice as the nation's first female U.S. attorney general, became one of Ferrell's most popular characters at the time. In real life, the quiet and hardworking 6'1" Reno was involved in a series of tough cases, including a federal raid of a deadly religious cult in Waco, Texas; the custody battle of young Cuban refugee Elián González; and even her boss's relationship with Monica Lewinsky. But she didn't have much of a public image until this comic take on her took hold.

Ferrell played Reno as a tough-talking, deep-voiced, take-no-prisoners strongwoman who just so happens to like to blow off steam by hosting dance parties in her basement, where she cuts a rug with choppy dance movements. Wanting to do a character that was "broad and physical," Ferrell told the *Washington Post* in 2016 that he originally imagined Reno as Clinton's bodyguard, but then he and cowriter Scott Wainio came up with Reno hosting a dance party in her signature blue dress.

During this version of the sketch, in an *SNL* episode hosted by then New York City mayor Rudolph Giuliani, she interviews teenage attendees at her "party" about their school activities but doubts they are telling the truth and often stops them midsentence with signature retorts like, "Shut your mouth, you dirty liar," or simply, "I'm sick of all your lies." She then goes totally off-the-wall after she introduces them to Giuliani, who she is convinced is jealous of her job as the leading law officer in the country, which he denies. To prove the rivalry, she challenges Giuliani to a boxing match (with gloves and all) and by the end pins him and gets him to say, "Janet Reno is the boss of me!" The real Reno grew to love the sketches even though the Farrell impression was nothing like her. On her last day in office, she appeared as herself with Ferrell at the final dance party and even had him appear with her at a campaign event a few years later when she ran for governor of Florida against Jeb Bush.

## Cold Open: "Phone Chat" (with Bill Clinton, Saddam Hussein, Monica Lewinsky; 23.14)

By this time, Darrell Hammond was playing Clinton, and he and the writers leaned into black comedy to portray a somewhat darker time in his administration. In trying to distract the public from his sex scandal with Lewinsky, Hammond's Clinton puts a call in to his "buddy" Saddam Hussein (a hilarious, beret-wearing Farrell) to convince the dictator to publicly say he was not going to let UN weapons inspectors into Iraq (even though Saddam had publicly said at the time he would), admitting he is desperate to get sex out of headlines.

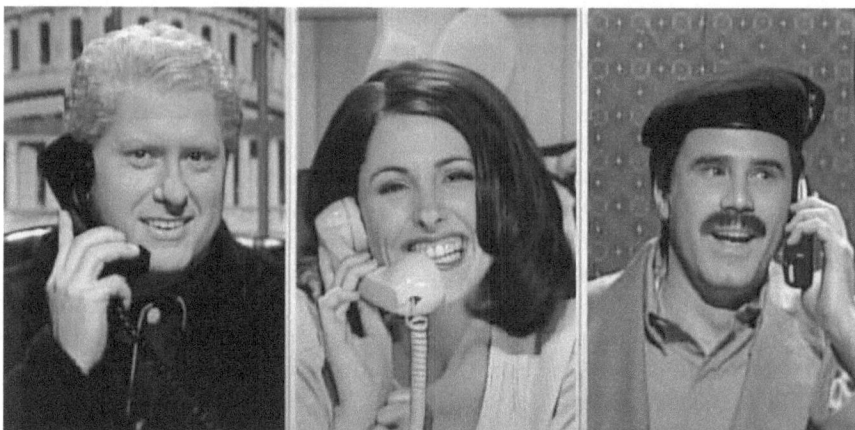

An international party line: A three-way conversation between (left to right) President Bill Clinton (Darrell Hammond), Monica Lewinsky (Molly Shannon), and Saddam Hussein (Will Ferrell).

Clinton then has to put Saddam on hold to take another call, which turns out to be . . . Lewinsky (Molly Shannon's take is that of a dreamy, in-love teenager). Clinton's first line to her is "I was just going to call you," to which Monica replies, "It's like we have the same brain!" The president then connects Saddam into the conversation, and it's implied he and Monica have somehow met through Clinton because he thanks her for the beret (a reference to a famous still photo of beret-wearing Lewinsky), at which point she laments that Bill "won't wear his." The conversation gets stranger from there, with both Monica and Saddam laughing at Clinton's public statement that he has never had a sexual relationship with her.

It ends with Clinton plugging in a fourth caller, *SNL* cast member Tim Meadows; Clinton promising Saddam a spot on *SNL*; and the three of them urging the dictator to say the show's signature, "Live from New York . . ." The hesitant Saddam finally agrees with the mangled words, "Lifetime from New York, it's Saturday Fun Hour!" Given our historical perspective on Hussein and the Iraq War, the bit plays as an uncomfortably weird but still funny take on where we were in the final years of the Clinton administration and how little we knew of what would unfold internationally in the future.

## Cold Open: "Bedtime at the White House" (24.2)

The enduring power here is how it captures the national awkwardness over the Clinton marriage vis-à-vis what were now the very public details of the Clinton-Lewinsky affair in the last few years of his second term. With not a lot of dialogue, Hammond's Bill Clinton and Ana Gasteyer's Hillary Clinton must navigate sleeping in the same bed together. At the outset, Bill is on the phone jocularly vowing to "kick ass" on the international stage, when Hillary enters, and he immediately deflates and hangs up. The tension is palpable, as Hillary pulls her robe tighter and icily gets into bed next to him. There's a long silence, and he starts to tell her a joke to break the tension but thinks better of it. Then there's more silence, and he decides to begin reading a book, the Holy Bible, at which point Hillary finally speaks to him, blurting out, "Yeah, right."

Bill then picks up the remote, turns on the television, and begins channel surfing, but all he can get is commentary, jokes, or comments about him and Monica, even on the weather report. He turns it off, and there's more silence until he makes a decision to try and gingerly move toward his wife, at which point she gives him a resounding, "No!" Finally getting the message, he then turns away to his side of the bed and sheepishly stage-whispers to the camera, "Live from New York, it's Saturday night."

## George W. Bush (2000–2008)

Since George W. Bush entered the White House in 2000 through Joe Biden's election and first term, politics has remained high on *SNL*'s comedy agenda. In the wake of 9/11, the show took its time to find its comedic footing when it came to political content, but it didn't necessarily go easy on President George W. Bush. As he had been doing since Bush entered the 2000 presidential race, Will Ferrell continued to impersonate him as an inarticulate dimwit whose speeches to the American people consisted of mindless jabber that lacked substance or relevance regarding national and world affairs.

It all started with the first of three parodies of the Bush-Gore 2000 presidential debates (26.1; see more details later), in which Bush can't answer any of the questions posed to him (his response to one question is to "pass," though Gore doesn't come off much better, as he drones on and on about his "lockbox"). When at the end of the sketch moderator Jim Lehrer (Chris Parnell) asks both candidates "to sum up, in a single word, the best argument for his candidacy," Governor Bush responds, "Strategery." Credit writer Jim Downey with introducing the term—a Bushism for the word *strategy*—into the American lexicon. It even became an inside joke in the Bush White House. Ironically, Bush, rather than Downey, is often credited with coining the term (the president himself some years later told Lorne Michaels he thought he *had* actually said it), but it's not surprising considering he's the man who, after being elected president, said, "They misunderestimated me."

On Sunday, November 5, 2000, two days before Election Day, NBC aired the *Saturday Night Live: Presidential Bash 2000*. When the last "Presidential Bash" aired in 1992, none of the presidential candidates (Bush Sr., Clinton, or Perot) appeared on the show, which was comprised of political sketches from over the years. Eight years later, in her review of the *Saturday Night Live: Presidential Bash 2000*, *New York Times*' Caryn James observed how the "line between show business and presidential politics has never been thinner." George W. Bush and Al Gore, whom the show had been targeting since the season 26 opener (26.1), both made pretaped appearances. Using a split screen, they stand side by side. Bush, showing that he could take a joke, admitted that he was "ambilavent" about appearing on the show because some of the material was "offensible." Gore pokes fun at his large ego and brags, "I was one of the very first to be offended by material on *Saturday Night Live*." James's review offers some valuable insight into why these two candidates would agree to participate: "By joining in, Mr. Bush and Mr. Gore can try to defuse criticism by embracing it. And because satire deflates pretensions, they can appear to the public on a regular-guy level, engaging in the campaign's all-important personality contest." She also observes how shows like *Saturday Night Live* have an important role in defining the "cartoon outlines that stereotype politicians, from Reagan-the-empty-headed to Clinton-the-womanizer" (which is probably why neither president ever graced the stages of Studio 8H). This would certainly be true in the 2008 election, with Tina Fey's classic impersonation of Sarah Palin, and even more so in 2016, when Alec Baldwin first took on Donald Trump.

The eight years of the George W. Bush administration were a seesaw between partisan politics and an overall truly "United" States but ended with an even greater distance between blue and red America than ever before. Initially, the 2000 election between Bush and Gore was so close that a recount was demanded via the famous *Bush v. Gore* lawsuit that went to the U.S. Supreme Court. Electoral College votes were split down the middle, so the slim Electoral College victory that would determine the eventual winner rested with the razor-thin vote margins in Florida (where Jeb Bush, brother to George W., was governor) and its remnants of several thousand disputed ballots. It wasn't until it was finally determined George W. was ahead by five-hundred-plus votes that Gore would concede on December 13, making for a lot of controversy but, more than a month after Election Day, also the assurance that the now even more divided country would at least have a president-elect.

With the presidency now in the hands of George W. Bush, an office his father had been elected to more than a decade before, it also meant that it was the first time a father and a son would each occupy the Oval Office since John Adams and John Quincy Adams almost two hundred years ago. This type of perceived dynastic rule didn't help much in bringing people together, but it was certainly great comic material. In fact, *SNL* writers had already jumped on the nepotism angle more than six months prior to the election in a cold open, "Capitol Building" (25.16), set in the Austin, Texas Capitol Building where then Texas governor George W. is getting campaign advice from his former-president father. In this early version of Ferrell's W., he is played like a dim, goofy frat boy, drinking a glass of beer on tap in his office and saying things like, "I'm gonna be president! That's wicked!"

But when his father enters (Dana Carvey returns as the senior Bush), he cautions his son to watch his language and proceeds to talk to him about "that dance to the middle," warning him not to commit to a position on anything because Gore and his ilk are "crafty." The younger Bush just doesn't get it and admits to being insecure, and Dad pushes, prods, and comically slaps him a couple times to get him into shape. It still doesn't work, and finally the exhausted younger Bush is invited to sit on his daddy's lap. The elder Bush says to him, "I know you're not a bright man," but assures him that "when you get to the White House, my friends will tell you what to do. . . . Just work hard to be a shining monument to vagueness."

This characterization of George W. as the ultimate nepo baby continued through the beginning of his presidency and reinforced what the half of America who didn't vote for him was already thinking. In the first sketch of 2001, a cold open "Vice President Address" (26.9), we see the POTUS seal and an announcement of an "important special address" from the president-elect. But at the desk is not George W.; rather it's Dick Cheney, George W.'s vice president and a well-known close colleague of his dad's who had served as his secretary of defense. The *SNL* version of Cheney, played with heart-of-darkness humor by Darrell Hammond, states to those watching he is "thrilled" to be elected your new vice president, but then he knowingly winks, raises his hands in quotation marks, and sticks out his tongue in laughter. It's an inside joke between him and, well, everyone but George W., confirming the long-held rumor through the second Bush presidency that it was really Cheney who was in charge and pulling the strings. The new president's image is not helped any when Farrell's George W. Bush enters and refers to Cheney as "Uncle Dick" and then proceeds to crack himself up at the idea that a guy's name could be Dick.

Not only does the sketch reinforce the new president's privileged family connections, but it then goes a step further in foreshadowing what would cause the final death knell of his eight years in the Oval Office: large tax cuts and favored financial favors for the rich, all of which would lead to the Great Recession and economic collapse of the U.S. economy in 2008. Early during Cheney's "speech," he brashly warns those listening who "make less than $264,000 a year" to "please change the channel" and later insists everyone who makes less than $7.8 million to do the same, crowing to the few theoretically remaining, "Good, now let's get into the sweet-ass tax breaks I lined up for you all."

Ferrell's tenure as a cast member at *SNL* ended in 2002, while Bush remained in office through 2008. Steve Ryfle, in an article for *Netscape Celebrity*, reported that *SNL* wanted to keep Ferrell on the show for the 2001–2002 season, so they upped his salary to $350,000, making him the highest-paid cast member in the show's history at the time. Creatively, it turned out to be a good investment. In 2002, the *SNL* writing team, under the supervision of co–head writers Tina Fey and Dennis McNicholas, won an Emmy for Outstanding Writing in a Variety or Music Program, the first win since 1989. When Ferrell departed, George W. Bush was played by Chris Parnell (2002–2003), Darrell Hammond (2003), Will Forte (2004–2006), and Jason Sudeikis (2006–2010).

The 2004 presidential race between George W. Bush and John Kerry posed even more challenges, as neither the incumbent nor his mild-mannered Democratic challenger were dynamic candidates. Seth Meyers, who played

Kerry, later admitted to *Vanity Fair* that the 2004 election was simply "less interesting." This was especially true in relation to Bush's smaller status in light of the troubling U.S. war in Iraq. And Forte, who began playing him at the time, confessed in *The Complete Oral History of Saturday Night Live* that he "did not want to do Bush" because he was not an impressionist and thought Will Ferrell was "so good at it." He tried his best but preferred more absurd characters, noting that in the end, "I didn't think I was that good. . . . Seth Meyers did a great John Kerry but I just didn't give him anything great to play off of." Perhaps Michaels summed it up best to the *New York Times*: "So much of it is casting. If Will Ferrell plays George [W.] Bush they like Bush more. 'Strategery' was entirely forgivable because he seemed like a guy they liked."

## Notable Sketches

### Cold Open: "First Presidential Debate" (26.1)

This is considered one of best presidential debate sketches in the show's history because it deftly and equally captures the foibles of the Republican (Will Ferrell as Bush) and Democrat (Darrell Hammond as Al Gore). George W. Bush already had the image of being not particularly quick and not very good at expressing himself, which becomes crystal clear in this *SNL* version when he pretty much can't answer any question coherently. But Al Gore, the incumbent vice president, comes across as too smart—a pompous policy wonk who sighs at his opponent's shortcomings and speaks in complicated and obtuse references that are difficult to understand, even if you're not George W. Bush. Using phrases from the

Al Gore (Darrell Hammond, left) vs. George W. Bush (Will Ferrell): In a satire of the first presidential debate, Gore oversells his "lockbox" metaphor and Bush introduces a new word into the English lexicon: "strategery."

actual 2000 debate such as the "lockbox" where *SNL*'s singsong talking version of Gore keeps endlessly insisting he is going to put the funds for Social Security, it becomes a comic volley for the heart of the country.

Who do you want as president: the guy with the southern drawl who isn't very smart but seems like a decent enough joe or the uptight Ivy Leaguer who is smarter than you and doesn't seem like he'd be much fun? Says *Pod Save America*'s Tommy Vietor, "This debate between Bush and Gore was lost in the spin room. Gore lost in the spin room because it became about sighing; it became about his demeanor. The *SNL* version I think cemented that existing narrative where Bush was the guy you wanted to have a beer with and that Gore was a little uppity and sort of a snob and maybe you didn't want to vote for him."

## Cold Open: "Presidential Address" (27.13)

Airing post-9/11 in the second year of the Bush administration, Will Ferrell once again plays his version of the president but this time dealing with foreign policy and what would turn out to be a costly war in Iraq. Using the real Bush's "axis of evil" phrase about America's post-9/11 enemies, Ferrell comically describes them as "Iraq, Iran, and one of the Koreas." When he goes on to talk about the billion-dollar accounting scandal at the Enron Corporation, which cost tens of thousands of people their pension money at the time, he also places them in the axis of evil—along with America's flailing economy; politicians who don't agree with him; and the countries of France, Germany, Italy, and Japan. He ends his speech by telling Americans not to listen to what the economists say "because economists like math and math is very much a part of the axis of evil." Ferrell's take still painted Bush as a comically endearing dumbbell, but given the gravity of the issues the real president was facing, some of that endearment was beginning to fade and become a tad less funny.

## Cold Open: "NBC Special Report" (28.1)

NBC's Tom Brokaw (a spot-on Chris Parnell) is to interview Dick Cheney (Darrell Hammond at his hilarious best) on an overseas feed about the debate over the potential war in Iraq. But when we see the vice president, he is already high in the sky, gleefully riding on top of a missile toward Iraq with the words *Hi there, Saddam* painted on its side. When Brokaw questions, "Wasn't the plan to wait until Congress debated the issue?" the omnipotent Cheney replies, "That was one plan. I had another plan." It doesn't get much better when he receives a call on his cell phone from George W. Bush (whom he rolls his eyes at) and tells him, "Yeah, I'm on a missile, a mission to Baghdad. Instant regime change, sir. . . . No, no, I'm not gonna say to Saddam, 'Dude, you're getting a Dell'" (a reference to the popular commercial at the time for Dell Computers). When the sketch aired, it seemed apparent America was likely headed to war and that the vice president was more than comfortable being the behind-the-scenes instigator who would get us there. That notion is confirmed when the sketch concludes with *SNL*'s power-loving version of Cheney growling that all his enemies can "suck on it," before he announces the "Live from New York . . ." catchphrase.

# Politics and the Presidency, Part 2

## Barack Obama to Joseph Biden (2000s–present)

*SNL*'s engagement in the political process deepened in the 2008 presidential election. From the primary season through the election itself, both the Democrats and the Republicans provided writers with ample material to skewer the candidates, their respective campaigns, the debates, and, finally, *SNL* also extended its coverage with *Saturday Night Live: Weekend Update Thursday*, which aired in October 2008 on three consecutive Thursday nights in prime time before Election Day. Installments of *Weekend Update Thursday* also aired in 2009 (a nonelection year) and in 2012 before the election in September.

In the 2008 election, Senator John McCain's choice for his running mate, Alaska governor Sarah Palin, was like manna from heaven (not only for late-night comedians but Democrats, as well). On August 29, 2008, in Dayton, Ohio, McCain introduced Americans to Palin, who at the time was a relatively unknown figure in national politics. Less than a month later, former *SNL* cast member Tina Fey, who was busy working on her own TV series *30 Rock* (2006–2013) at the time, made her first appearance as Palin (34.1; see more later). Hillary Clinton (Amy Poehler), no longer a Democratic presidential candidate, and Palin (Fey) delivered a nonpartisan message regarding the sexism that had permeated the media's coverage of the female candidates over the past few months. Although Clinton was characterized in a much more negative light (one commentator described her voice as "nagging") than Palin, the point of the sketch is that the media's focus has been on gender rather than their qualifications. But Fey's Palin repeatedly demonstrated just how unqualified she was to be running for the second-highest office in the land. As Fey observed in her book *Bossypants*, "Amy's line [as Clinton in the sketch] 'Although it is never sexist to question female politicians' credentials' was basically the thesis statement for everything we did over the next six weeks."

This point is more evident in Fey's second appearance as Palin, a parody of her disastrous interview with CBS news anchor Katie Couric, who is played by Amy Poehler (34.3). When it came to the question about the bank bailout, Fey actually used Palin's long, rambling answer verbatim. With each appearance as

Alec Baldwin interrupts Tina Fey (as Sarah Palin) during a press conference (left) and replaces her with the real Governor Palin.

Palin, it was becoming increasingly difficult not to think of Fey as Palin when listening to the real Palin complain about the "mainstream gotcha media."

The highlight of the season (which also gave *SNL* a huge jump in the ratings) was the real Sarah Palin's appearance on the show. It seems ironic that Palin would agree to appear on a show that had been devoting airtime to demonstrating how she was not a viable candidate for the vice presidency, especially compared to the Democratic vice presidential candidate Joe Biden, who had been a U.S. senator from Delaware for twenty-five years. In her memoir *Going Rogue: An American Life*, Palin said it was a "bit surreal" seeing Tina Fey impersonating her on television. (Palin revealed that she had actually dressed up as Tina Fey for Halloween before Fey started imitating her.)

During her appearance on the show (34.5), she interacted with staunch Democrat Alec Baldwin, who mistakes Palin for Tina Fey, and appeared on *Weekend Update* where a very pregnant Amy Poehler performed a rap song with two Inuit (Andy Samberg and Fred Armisen), a Todd Palin imitator (Jason Sudeikis), and a moose (Bobby Moynihan). Fey later returned as Palin, appearing in an episode of *Weekend Update Thursday* (10/23/08), in which Palin and John McCain (Darrell Hammond) get President George W. Bush's (Will Ferrell) endorsement, and on the last show before the election featuring a cameo by John McCain (hosted by staunch Democrat Ben Affleck). In that episode, Palin (Fey), McCain, and his wife Cindy appear on a parody of QVC (it's all he can afford), in which he makes a last-minute pitch to the American people and hocks some souvenirs from their campaign.

In the latter, the best moment is when Fey's Palin whispers to the viewers and tells them to listen up. She announces she's going rogue and holds up a "Palin in 2012" sign. While McCain's appearance certainly showed he has a lighter side, the idea that he would go on *SNL* with a Sarah Palin imitator the Saturday before the election suggests he knew the race was over before the polls even opened.

On the last show before the 2008 election, Sarah Palin (Tina Fey) and John McCain make a last-minute pitch to the American people—and hock souvenirs from their campaign—on QVC.

Over on the Democratic side, there were only two candidates: Hillary Clinton (Amy Poehler) and Barack Obama (Fred Armisen). *SNL* was accused of playing favorites in a parody of the "CNN Univision Democratic Debate" (33.5; written by Jim Downey), in which the audience and news anchors John King (Jason Sudeikis) and Campbell Brown (Kristen Wiig) fawn all over Obama and ask if he's comfortable but are rude to Clinton and ask questions that emphasize her losses in the primary.

In the next debate sketch (33.6), also written by Downey, Obama is once again the favorite son. Moderators Brian Williams and Tim Russert are also rude to Clinton and are critical of her long-winded answers. They ask questions she doesn't know the answers to, give the answers, and then ask Obama the same questions. After the sketch, the real Hillary Clinton appeared on the show to clarify that the sketch they just saw was not meant to be an endorsement of her candidacy, which was the accusation made by the press and Obama supporters against *SNL*, Lorne Michaels, and Jim Downey. The two men did agree that Clinton benefited from being portrayed by Amy Poehler, whom Downey refers to as their "charm machine." In fact, in a March 13 *New York Times* story, Bill Carter

Campbell Brown (Kristen Wiig, right) introduces the Obama-Clinton CNN debate in which the moderators clearly favor Barack Obama (Fred Armisen) over Hillary Clinton (Amy Poehler).

reported that some commentators have credited the sketches for Clinton's primary victories in Texas and Ohio. Carter also cited a study by Pew Research that reported an increase in critical coverage of Obama in the news media.

Palin, or rather Fey as Palin, was missed during the 2012 presidential election, though the Republican primary was more entertaining than a circus sideshow. There was one GOP debate too many and an excessive number of candidates, giving almost all the *SNL* cast a chance to participate in the democratic process: Rick Perry (Alec Baldwin, Bill Hader); Ron Paul (Paul Brittain); Jon Huntsman (Taran Killam); Newt Gingrich (Bobby Moynihan); Rick Santorum (Andy Samberg); Mitt Romney (Jason Sudeikis); Herman Cain (Kenan Thompson); and Michele Bachmann (Kristen Wiig). Once Romney was declared the nominee, the multimillionaire worked hard at proving he was an "ordinary guy," but it's a hard sell when you are rich and lack the one thing that's necessary to be a successful candidate: charisma.

## Notable Sketches

### Cold Open: "A Nonpartisan Message from Sarah Palin and Hillary Clinton" (34.1)

This cold-open message is consistently rated one of the top, if not number 1, political comedy moments in *SNL* history. It also marks the debut of Tina Fey as Sarah Palin, which is considered *SNL*'s standout political impression (certainly it is the one most viewed), airing two months before Obama won the election for president.

The brilliance of the sketch, written by Seth Meyers, with some jokes provided by Fey and Poehler, is that not only is it funny and balanced in how it takes its

VP candidate Sarah Palin (Tina Fey, left) and a frustrated Hillary Clinton (Amy Poehler), who is now a surrogate for Obama, deliver a nonpartisan message about sexism in the presidential campaign.

punches, but also it does it in a way that plays on the very real differences between the two woman and what we perceive, based on their personalities, histories, and political beliefs, is a beneath-the-surface utter disdain for each other—all the while talking about the "ugly role sexism has played in this campaign."

Hillary Clinton (Amy Poehler), who was an active Obama surrogate even though she lost the Democratic nomination for president to him in a contentious race, and current Republican vice president nominee Sarah Palin (Fey) are addressing the nation about how all women should be treated fairly despite their differences.

Poehler's Clinton evokes smarts and grace under pressure with a barely contained rage underneath. Fey's Palin is that good-looking, jovial, but hopelessly dim person you remember growing up who unfathomably succeeded far, far, far beyond their abilities. They are polar opposites in everything but their gender.

As the ostensible public service message goes on, both women begin to expose whom they really are. With Palin this comes early on when they start to talk policy:

PALIN: You know, Hillary and I don't agree on everything—
CLINTON (overlapping): Anything. I believe that diplomacy should be the cornerstone of any foreign policy.
PALIN: And I can see Russia from my house!

The Russia line is the most famous and most quoted moment, and many assume Palin actually did say it. The latter isn't unreasonable because huge chunks of *SNL*'s sketch dialogue for Palin were lifted directly from her sound bytes. But in this case it's comedic license based on the truth. Two days prior, Palin did her first major interview for ABC News, and when asked what insight she gained living so close to Russia (a subject she herself raised), she responded, "They're our next-door neighbors, and you can actually see Russia from land here in Alaska, from an island in Alaska."

Later in the sketch, it's Clinton's turn to show what we believe to be her true self when Palin blithely (or perhaps intentionally) says, "Just look at how far we've come—Hillary Clinton, who came *so close* to the White House and me, Sarah Palin, who is *even closer*. Can you believe it, Hillary?" At this point, Hillary finally loses it and goes on a diatribe of how there is no comparison between them and how hard she had to work compared to the former beauty queen, proclaiming, "I scratched and clawed my way through barbed wire and you just glided in on a dogsled wearing your pageant sash and Tina Fey glasses," while all the while Palin strikes glamour poses and plays to the crowd. Of course, they never settle their differences, but they do manage to smile as they say "Live From New York . . ." together.

## The Late 2000s and Early to Mid-2010s: Barack Obama (2008–2016)

*SNL* almost doubled its overall ratings in 2008 over the previous year and also saw a significant increase among those eighteen to thirty-four years old. This was due in part to the Fey/Palin of it all and also to yet another generational shift with the "hope and change" election of America's first Black president, forty-seven-year-old Barack Obama. One would think the Obama years would usher in an endless array of irresistible *SNL* political takes, but this would not be the case. The United States was trying to crawl out of the economic collapse the Bush administration left behind, and as great of an orator as Obama is, he was not particularly controversial.

*SNL* struggled with how to make hay of a president who was happily married with two well-behaved children, had no political or personal scandals past or present, never lost his temper publicly despite many provocations, and was basically a professorial workhorse. He made public appearances, but nothing much happened other than what was supposed to. So *SNL*'s political humor in the Obama years primarily concentrated not so much on the man but on the resistance he met from a resentful Congress, as well as portions of the electorate who would never get behind the historic nature of his candidacy despite how many olive branches he offered amid the unprecedented passing of near-universal health care (a.k.a. Obamacare); the rescue of the American auto industry; and the resuscitation of the crumbled U.S. economy.

Fred Armisen was tasked with what turned out to be the thankless task of playing Obama in his first term, and ironically the standout sketch in that period turned out to be not so much due to his performance of the president as we knew him but of a surprise guest midway through—Dwayne (the Rock)

American rarely saw President Obama get angry, but when he does the President transforms into "The Rock Obama" (played by Dwayne Johnson).

Johnson as "The Rock Obama" (35.4). The setup has Obama meeting with his famously volatile chief of staff Rahm Emanuel (Andy Samberg), who tells him he sometimes thinks he's "too calm" and needs to get angry. The ever-cool Obama replies, "Getting angry is *your* thing, Rahm," and tells him to send in the senators holding up his spending bill.

Three Republican senators—John McCain (Darrell Hammond), Kay Bailey Hutchinson (Kristen Wiig), and Tom Coburn (Will Forte)—enter and let loose a barrage of condescending, stinging criticism of Obama and how he's been president seven weeks and hasn't fixed the economy, ending with McCain's cutting jibe about his job performance ("My friend, I fear you may not be up to it"). Obama tries to contain his annoyance, then anger, and eventual seething rage (egged on by Emanuel, who keeps whispering, "Get angry"), until finally he bursts out of his suit à la the Hulk, his body expanding with huge muscles, and the impossibly large Johnson emerges in Armisen's place as "The Rock Obama."

Noting he is like Barack Obama "only stronger and more impulsive," the Tarzan-like Johnson briefly questions the pols opposite him and, when he doesn't like their answers, begins throwing them out the window or smashing the phone when a corporation calls asking for billions more in bailout money. In the end, McCain volunteers to show himself out and follows his colleagues through the window, at which point Armisen's mild-mannered Obama appears, waking Emanuel from what turned out to all be a dream as he once again asks him to send the opposing senators in the room. The sketch plays on the president's maddeningly effective but almost-inhuman ability to stay calm and not play dirty, though two future iterations of the sketch jettison the Emmanuel setup and simply have Obama become the perilous "superhero" when he's made too angry.

During Obama's first term, *SNL* also subtly addressed the president's rock-solid popularity in the Black community with a series of sketches called "How's He Doing?" (the best being 37.5), a talk show where Black intellectuals discuss Obama policies. There is some back-and-forth debate, but when met with hypothetical scenarios where Obama betrays them or advocates positions they find particularly abhorrent, each panelist either makes excuses for him or ultimately admits they'd vote for him anyway.

Impressionist and new cast member Jay Pharoah began appearing as Obama in his second term and fared a bit better, but with the president still scandal free and simply doing his job, it remained an uphill climb. Nevertheless, there was a memorable appearance with Seth Meyers on *Weekend Update* (38.7) right after he wins the White House again, where Pharoah plays a swag, loosened Obama, popping his shoulders up and down and getting Meyers to join him ("Bounce with me") as he jovially notes how, from now on, "we are going to do things my way."

Two cold-open sketches from 2014 (39.16, 40.6) are also especially entertaining and silly, even if they don't rise to being classic. The first features Obama bowing to social media marketing in the aftermath of the real president's viral appearance on Zach Galifianakis's faux talk show on Funny or Die, *Between Two Ferns*, to promote Obamacare. In the *SNL* sketch, two young aides convince him to participate in posed photos for them to post online, including one of him with Kim Kardashian (Nasim Pedrad) and Harry Styles (Brooks Whelan), another with Justin Bieber (Kate McKinnon), and a single as himself wearing Pharrell Williams's "Happy" hat.

The second, more edgy sketch has him at the White House trying to bond with about-to-be-reinstalled Republican Senate Majority Leader Mitch McConnell (Taran Killam) over what turns out to be an entire bottle of Kentucky bourbon (the real Obama actually did offer to have a drink with the senator after the Republicans took the majority in the house a week before). Though it starts out a little contentious, four drinks in, Obama is laughing when McConnell makes a phony phone call to his former secretary of state Hillary Clinton. After six drinks, he even counterpunches. When McConnell drunkenly blurts out, "You're Black! And you are the president of the United States! That's crazy! You ever think about that, a Black U.S. president with this country's history! No one would've ever thought that!" To which an inebriated Obama tartly counters,

"And no one would have ever thought that the Senate Majority Leader would be a redneck who lost his lips in a fire." After nine drinks it's even sloppier and more real, but unlike real life, the two actually wind up as friends.

## Notable Sketches

### Cold Open: "Hillary Election Video" (Kate McKinnon; 40.18), "Hillary Clinton and Hillary Clinton" (41.1)

In the third year of Obama's second term, Hillary Clinton finally announced she was once again running to be the Democratic Party's nominee for president, which she eventually won, only to famously lose to Republican nominee Donald Trump in the general election. These two sketches mark her campaign at its beginning in April 2014 and then, six months later, with *SNL*'s emerging star cast member Kate McKinnon making her debut in the role.

Clinton had teased for months she was considering a run, and by the time the cold open "Hillary Election Video" was broadcast, word had leaked several days before of her "official" campaign announcement video release the following day. This gave the show a jump on its version of the potential content, which turned out to be far more entertaining than the real thing. *SNL* and McKinnon's take was that the ambitious, "smartest person in the room" Hillary had been preparing this moment for a lifetime and wanted it more than anything.

Her version of taking her aides' advice to appear more personable and natural while filming the video on her phone is to take off her blue power jacket (only to reveal an exact duplicate underneath) or get too close to the camera and overemphasize every word in a deep, frightening manner. It's not that she wants to come across harsh; it's that she is so amped she can't help herself. She tries again more sincerely, saying she "wants to be a voice for women everywhere," when suddenly a cardigan-wearing Bill Clinton (Darrell Hammond) ambles by, inquiring suggestively, "Did someone say, 'Women everywhere'?" Hillary is affectionate but tries to contain Bill (he jokes he's thankful phones didn't have videos in the nineties), guffawing her signature laugh, making a joke about his past, and then hinting he should leave, which he does, wanting to give her the spotlight. The sketch ends with a more sincere Hillary promising Americans that, with her in charge, it will be a "brand-new White House," only to have Bill reenter the frame behind her, playing his sax, and Hillary finally admitting, "The Clintons are back!"

McKinnon somehow managed to give *SNL*'s Hillary more of a knowing sense of playful humor amid the determination, which feels appropriate when the real Hillary Clinton shows up six months later in a different sketch beside McKinnon's Hillary ("Hillary Clinton and Hillary Clinton" [41.1]). The real Hillary here is a lot funnier and willing to goof around than we've ever seen her on the campaign trail (perhaps she enjoyed McKinnon's impression and took notes), but instead of appearing as herself, she plays Val, a bartender at a

Hillary Clinton (Kate McKinnon) complains to Val the bartender, played by the real Hillary Clinton, about "media hog" Donald Trump.

local pub where McKinnon's Hillary pays a visit with an aide. Bummed when she overhears patrons talking about the Republican field and noting how fun Trump was at a rally, she stays for one more drink after her aide leaves. When the bartender Val turns around, it's the real Hillary.

What proceeds are a series of postmodern exchanges between Val and McKinnon's Hillary that play on the real Clinton's slow but finally positive acceptance on legal gay marriage (the openly gay McKinnon as Hillary keeps saying, "I could have supported it sooner," and Val, who defends her at first, admits, "That's a fair point") and McKinnon's Hillary complaining to Val about media hog Trump, at which point Val (a.k.a. the real Hillary) does a Trump imitation ("Isn't he the one who's like, 'Uh, you're all losers'?"). There's also a funny cameo by Darrell Hammond as a freaked-out Bill Clinton seeing the fake and real Hillary together and running out of the bar ("Oh my God, they're multiplying!").

The final postmodern moment comes when McKinnon's Hillary says to Val, "I wish you could be president," to which Val, admits, "Yeah, me, too," to the cheers and applause of the *SNL* audience. That didn't happen, but before the sketch ends, Hillary and Val do sing a duet of "Lean on Me" together, arm in arm.

### "Bern Your Enthusiasm" (41.12)

Obama would still be president for eight more months, but this hilarious take on a Bernie Sanders campaign short film features Larry David for the first time playing the aspiring Democratic presidential nominee (he would return to do it numerous times) and previewed a long line of well-known names outside of *SNL* who would soon visit Studio 8H to impersonate so many of the over-the-top figures in the Trump administration.

David stars here as Bernie Sanders as if Sanders was really the curmudgeonly, argumentative version of the Larry David character that viewers are familiar with from his hit HBO series *Curb Your Enthusiasm*. Due to the physical similarity between the pair, their Brooklyn-accented cadences, and the fact that some of the major supporting players in the *SNL* cast are literally playing some of the regulars on *Curb*, it quickly becomes difficult to tell Larry from Bernie, which is clearly the point. Through the film, Larry/Bernie won't shake the hand of an enthusiastic supporter ("You specifically coughed [in your hand]. I don't shake germ-infested hands.") and is scolded by the characters from the *Curb* cast for refusing to drink coffee with 2 percent milk a campaign aide offers ("What's wrong with you?" yells Cecily Strong, voicing the whine of *Curb* cast member Susie Essman).

When another supporter on her way to vote for him gets in a small car accident and asks Larry/Bernie to pop her injured shoulder back into place, he refuses ("We don't pop in Brooklyn!"), and she curses him out. Larry/Bernie finally returns to his headquarters to watch the returns from the Iowa primary, only to find that he loses by a mere five votes, and on TV, the small group of people (a.k.a. voters) he offended are waving at the camera to him, clearly having turned on him. The sketch actually plays on the close vote between the real Bernie Sanders and Hillary Clinton in the recent Democratic primary in Iowa, when he lost to her by the smallest margin in state history (49.8 percent to 49.6 percent).

"Bern Your Enthusiasm": Host Larry David impersonates Senator Bernie Sanders. David is seen here with staffer Kyle Mooney (right), as if Sanders is the star of David's *Curb Your Enthusiasm*.

## "Racists for Trump" (41.14)

This satire of a filmed ad for Donald Trump is darkly funny but blunt and hard-edged, prompted by what was Trump's blatant embrace of racial divisions during his presidential campaign. The ad begins with images from Middle America and asks, "What are real Americans saying about Trump?" Among the people we hear from are an upper-middle-class man at a desk, a suburban mom ironing, a housepainter, a suburban dad stoking embers in his fireplace, and a rural guy hauling wood outside. They speak about Trump in complimentary phrases like, "The guy's a winner," "He's authentic," "He's the only one who's creating jobs," and "He's not some cautious politician. The country needs that." The big reveal comes when they are later viewed in wider shots, and we see the upper-middle-class man wears a swastika arm band, the suburban mom has ironed a KKK robe, the housepainter has painted in big letters "White Power" on the side of a house, the suburban dad is burning a book on Mexico in his fireplace, and the wood-hauling guy is walking toward a group of men in hoods dancing around the fire of a huge burning cross. The ad ends with this voiceover of on-screen words: "A message from Racists for Donald Trump."

What is effective about the piece, aside from everything, is that the beginning takes the form of many political ads geared toward the heartland. Plus, the fact that all the people we see are White (which some White viewers might not pick up on) does not seem particularly unusual until it's revealed just how casually they reveal their outward racism on camera. The parody was a brash pushback against the feverish blue-versus-red-state battle (some might say race war) Trump was fomenting as he traveled across the country campaigning toward the end of the Obama era and portended how gut-wrenchingly controversial Trump's four years in the Oval Office was soon to be.

## The Late 2010s: Donald J. Trump (2016–2020)

Coverage of the Donald Trump presidency actually started eighteen months before he took office when he was tapped to host an episode of *SNL* (41.4). Sure, Trump the motormouth New York real estate magnate had already hosted one other time more than eleven years before and since then was frequently imitated by Darrell Hammond in the context of his stint as host of NBC's hit reality series *The Apprentice* (2004–2015). But once he descended his golden escalator at Trump Tower to announce his candidacy for the Republican Party's nomination for president of the United States on July 16, 2015, calling for an immigration ban on Muslims and spitting out notions that Mexico is also "not sending its best.... [T]hey're bringing drugs; they're bringing crime; they're rapists," it was an entirely different situation. Trump was now an extremely polarizing figure who fell under television's "equal time" rule, meaning U.S. broadcast and radio stations were required to devote an equal amount of time to other candidates running against him (if asked).

Former cast member Taran Killam spoke about the week Trump hosted on a 2018 episode of Matt Gourley's popular *I Was There Too* podcast, recalling that the cast could hear anti-Trump protesters outside the studio days before the show aired: "We could hear protests during our table read. As we're reading forty mediocre sketches, we just hear, 'No Trump! Donald Trump!'" He said, "It was not enjoyable at the time and something that only grows more embarrassing and shameful as time goes on."

Numerous cast members agreed, and the actual episode was somewhat of a comedic disappointment. Trump was actually only on-screen for just under twelve minutes, about half the time of prior hosts that year, perhaps due to "equal time." (Hillary Clinton was on-screen almost as long in the season opener that year, and she only appeared in one sketch.) On the Trump episode, Ivanka Trump made a cameo in a sketch of how her father might behave in the Oval Office, but it didn't generate many laughs and was certainly not nearly as memorable as when the real thing happened in the next four years.

Killam was there for much of *SNL*'s ensuing coverage of the campaign (he left the show in August 2016) and remembers Michaels specifically telling the cast not to "vilify" Trump and to consider "he's like any New York cab driver.... He just says whatever it is he's thinking. You have to find a way in that makes him likeable." In truth, the likeable mantra has always been the producer's philosophy for political impressions. At his post-Trump administration talk about comedy at the University of Delaware in 2021, he reiterated, a political character "won't work unless you make them likeable, and likeable doesn't mean you're endorsing them. Likeable means some level of charm."

Whether the producer would still use the cabdriver analogy regarding Trump or finds the ex-president himself charming is another story. Still, there are a few clues. Michaels did say at the talk that Trump was "really angry we used a woman" (Melissa McCarthy) to play his former press secretary Sean Spicer: "He thought it was disrespectful." And in reflecting on what he learned covering Trump over four years, he told *New York Magazine* in 2020, "So much of news coverage is, 'Do you believe he [Trump] did this? Do you believe he said this?' And somehow or another, he ends up being the thing everyone's talking about, which I have a feeling, on a show business-level, is part of his plan." This was borne out by the *SNL* episode Trump hosted, garnering the show's best ratings in almost four years and creating a bonanza of viewership once Alec Baldwin first began playing Trump (42.1) once his administration began. (Baldwin would go on to win one Emmy among three nominations for his more than fifty-three appearances, including a classic debate sketch [42.3; see details later] based on the real Trump physically stalking opponent Hillary Clinton across the stage.) Not since the Tina Fey/Sarah Palin days was a presidential impersonation that popular.

The *SNL* Trump years were controversial, exhausting, and over the top, just like the man himself. But it was also a comedy goldmine, especially when so many actors and former cast members began clamoring to play (some would say skewer) the ever-multiplying number of colorful characters in the Trump era. In terms of comedy, it was as if there was a perfect storm of events enabling the show to operate at optimum speed. There was scandal (sexual, constitutional, and political); controversy; corruption; and a multitude of larger-than-life, eccentric, and downright borderline offensive figures being amplified in the twenty-four-hour cable news cycle, as well as in the constant national and international coverage the Trump administration was receiving with its often-rule-breaking, outrageous behavior and policies.

There had never been as many American right-left, blue-red fissures, but all the conflicts were an opportunity for scads of relevant material. A potential war with North Korea, among others; the Russian disinformation campaign; racial animus fomenting a backlash against Blacks, the LGBTQ community (especially trans people), Muslims, Mexicans, Jews, Asians, and pretty much most ethnic and/or immigrant minorities; and Trump's countless gaffes and pronouncements about other world leaders on the international stage all made it difficult for *SNL* to keep up with the political news—to say nothing of the ongoing Trump investigations, firings, and/or resignations from his administration and his own impeachments before his four years in office were over. The following is a partial list (in no particular order) of the variety of guest actors playing politically related characters on the show during that time:

Alec Baldwin (Donald Trump), Melissa McCarthy (Sean Spicer), John Goodman (Rex Tillerson), Scarlett Johansson and Margot Robbie (Ivanka Trump), Matt Damon (Brett Kavanaugh), Brad Pitt (Dr. Anthony Fauci), Jimmy Fallon (Jared Kushner), Bill Hader (Anthony Scaramucci), Ben Stiller (Michael Cohen), Matthew Broderick (Mike Pompeo), Maya Rudolph (Kamala Harris), Robert De Niro (Robert Mueller), Martin Short (Trump's doctor Harold Bornstein), and Bill Murray (an unmasked Steve Bannon). (Note: Actors Zack Braff and Michael Kelly each desperately wanted to play Trump speechwriter and anti-immigration zealot Stephen Miller, but the show chose to go with the image of a snake in a basket instead.)

Michaels bridles at the idea that any of these choices were stunt-casting celebrity cameos because most of the actors were either former cast members themselves or had hosted the show. After so many years on the air, *SNL* has a huge repertory of performers to choose from that only keeps growing. Current cast members during that time playing Trump administration–related characters included Kate McKinnon (Kellyanne Conway, Jeff Sessions, Rudy Giuliani, Betsy DeVos, Dr. Anthony Fauci, and Amy Coney Barrett); Cecily Strong (Melania Trump, Kimberly Guilfoyle, Jeanine Pirro, and Stormy Daniels); Aidy Bryant (Sarah Huckabee Sanders and Bill Barr); Beck Bennett (Vladimir Putin and Mike Pence); Mikey Day (Steve Bannon [as the Grim Reaper], Donald Trump Jr., and Michael Flynn); Alex Moffat (Eric Trump and Paul Manafort); and Leslie Jones (Omarosa Manigault Newman).

After a series of campaign debates, as well as postelection "trauma" sketches over Trump's unexpected win (see more details later), Alec Baldwin had a field day playing Trump in the Oval Office making offensive statements, double-talking on issues he didn't understand, and placing phone calls to his counterparts around the globe just so he could feel superior to them. Of particular note is a cold-open sketch at the beginning of his administration (42.13), when, under the supervision of then White House chief strategist Steve Bannon (Mikey Day dressed as the Grim Reaper in a long black robe and skeleton hood and speaking in a spooky engineered electronic voice), he calls world leaders in Australia, Mexico, and Germany. Trump has a tantrum the moment he doesn't like their questions about his presidency or stance on an issue he raises, then quickly tells them, "We're going to war," and hangs up on them. That is until he gets an African dictator who is unafraid and says he will eat him alive. Terrified, Trump ends the call, gets up from his desk, sits on a side chair, and plays with a toy, referring to Bannon as Mr. President. It's an early, stinging evaluation of the Trump presidency based on the lukewarm reception he and his policies received from long-standing U.S. allies around the world.

It was no less stinging than the cold open (42.15) a few weeks later, when his attorney general Jeff Sessions was played by Kate McKinnon as Forrest Gump sitting on a park bench and eating a box of chocolates as he confesses to meetings with unsavory Russians (the first of many Trump figures to do so over the years) to total strangers. Also in that episode is one of many scathing appearances on *Weekend Update* by Trump's "sons" Eric and Don Jr. The kindergartner-like Eric (Alex Moffat) speaks in non sequiturs and is corralled by his brother Don Jr. (Mikey Day), a poser with shiny, slicked-back hair who touts the Trump Organization he and Eric now "run," reinforcing his father's claim he no longer has a role in the company, even as infantile Eric blurts out that he does as he plays with the cereal and juice box his brother provides him.

The following week was the much-written-about parody of daughter Ivanka Trump, who actually was working in the White House (her official title was advisor to the president, focusing on the education and economic empowerment of women and their families) and taking a lot of heat in relation to her father's policies, especially on illegal immigration when he began separating babies and young children from their parents, sometimes locking them in cages. In the gauzy video "Complicit" (42.16), shot like a bougie perfume commercial, the adult First Daughter (Scarlett Johansson) is seen in a gold evening gown, making the rounds at a fancy party as a sultry-voiced female announcer says things like, "She's Ivanka. She deserves her own scent because she's beautiful, she's powerful, she's . . . complicit." The voice then goes on to tell us, "She doesn't crave the spotlight, but *we* see her," and touts that the Complicit fragrance is for the "woman who could stop all this but won't."

The powerful takedown was the comic articulation of a raging resentment across the country toward the Trump family, who had gained power and profit working for their father but accepted none of the responsibility for his policies or actions. The next few years went on like that, with sketches where Baldwin's Trump would fast-talk/defend one outrageous worldview, action, back-door connection, or relationship with strongman leaders and dictators, especially his bromance with Russian president Vladimir Putin (Beck Bennett in snakelike menace) after another. There were also sketches or videos of others in his administration, most hilariously "Kellywise" (43.3), where Anderson Cooper (Alex Moffat) has a run-in with Kellyanne Conway, the Trump senior counselor who defended a myriad of lies from the Oval Office as simply "alternative facts." In that filmed sketch, Conway appears as herself in a sewer with clown-white foundation and red lipstick, then periodically morphs into a Kellyanne version of Pennywise, the ghoulish clown from the popular *It* horror film franchise, as she haunts him.

Also notable is *SNL*'s take on Trump's actual gun-control symposium (43.14), when an incredibly uncomfortable Mike Pence (Beck Bennett) and Diane Feinstein (Cecily Strong) must maintain their composure amid the president's self-indulgent blathering and tangential talking points (his segue to how other countries are "beating us" references China; Japan; and Wakanda, the fictional country in *Black Panther*) in the aftermath of the tragic mass shooting at Marjory Stoneman Douglas High School in Parkland, Florida. It's funny and ridiculous and hits close enough to home that it also made more than a few viewers uneasy.

The last year of the Trump administration was engulfed by the COVID-19 pandemic, which caused an almost-worldwide shutdown, tens of thousands of deaths in the United States, and a substantial economic collapse. Consequently, *SNL* ended its forty-fifth season two months early, in mid-March 2020 (with the exception of some home-filmed segments), and resumed season 46 in the first week of October, a month before Joe Biden decidedly defeated Trump in both the popular and Electoral College vote to become the next, and quite different, president of the United States.

## Notable Sketches

### Cold Open: "Donald Trump vs. Hillary Clinton Town Hall Debate" (42.3)

What makes this sketch resonate is that it's outrageous but barely exaggerated. In their second presidential town-hall debate, Trump was stalking Hillary Clinton, at different points literally looming behind her onstage and trying to be intimidating by casting a huge, ominous, lingering presence while shadowing her no matter where she went.

In her subsequent book on the 2016 election *What Happened*, the real Mrs. Clinton said it made her "skin crawl." But that's only part of the story. Like the actual debate, the sketch also has Trump refer to a group of women he has brought with him to the studio who have accused Bill Clinton of sexual harassment, making it seem like Hillary is trying to silence them. This was done in real life in order to counteract an *Access Hollywood* tape released days prior, where Trump himself bragged about grabbing women by their private parts, a sexual-harassment accusation Baldwin's Trump never quite answers. It all goes downhill from there. No wonder when the town hall first starts, hosts Anderson Cooper (Alex Moffat) and Martha Raddatz (Cecily Strong) drink shots and say to the audience, "Now let's get this nightmare started."

In this parody of a Clinton-Trump town hall, Clinton (Amy Poehler) tries to stay focused while Trump (Alec Baldwin) exhibits disuptive, childish behavior.

## Cold Open: "Election Week—Hillary Sings 'Hallelujah'" (42.6)

An *SNL* bit becomes classic by capturing a truth and running with it. A majority of the country was reeling election week 2020 when Hillary Clinton lost the Electoral College vote and hence the presidency to Donald Trump while beating him in the popular vote by almost three million votes. So that night, the show chose a simple cold open, where Kate McKinnon's Hillary, clad in a version of the suffragette white pantsuit she wore on election night, sits playing the piano, singing Leonard Cohen's iconic "Hallelujah" (a tribute also to Cohen, who died days earlier). It was a bold, unusual, and emotional way to open the show, but as she continued it became difficult not to associate the lyrics of the introspective song with the battle Mrs. Clinton and her supporters had fought and thought they had won until that fateful night, especially when she got to the new double meaning of Cohen's actual as-written final verse: "I couldn't feel, so I tried to touch, I told the truth, I didn't come to fool ya. And even though it all went wrong, I'll stand before the lord of song, with nothing on my tongue but hallelujah." The song concludes, and the sketch ends with McKinnon's final encouraging spoken words as Hillary: "I'm not giving up and neither should you," at which point she launches into, "And live from New York . . ." and the Trump years officially begin.

## "Election Night" (42.6)

Dave Chappelle and Chris Rock insightfully let us know that, while a lot of White people on election night 2020 were shocked and depressed at Donald Trump's win, many members of the Black community were not as surprised. A group of friends huddle together watching the returns, sure of Hillary's win, while their friend Chappelle tells them not to get ahead of themselves and celebrate too soon. As the sketch cuts from 6:00 p.m. to various times through the evening and then the wee hours of the morning, the results get worse and worse, but the White friends try to remain hopeful with bromides like, "She got Vermont"; "If we can get Pennsylvania and North Carolina, we don't even need Ohio"; and "Early returns are always going to be Republican because they go to bed early," while Chappelle rolls his eyes and makes sarcastic remarks. By the time Rock arrives and asks what he missed, one of the women turns to him, shaken, and says, "Larry, Trump actually might win!" Rock, like Chappelle, isn't shocked, all to the chagrin of their White friends, who begin blurting out at the end of the evening when Trump is announced as the victor, "Oh my God, I think America is racist," and "This is the most shameful thing America has ever done." At which point, Chappelle and Rock just look at each other and break up laughing, and the sketch ends. The routine simultaneously takes on intellectuals who live in the blue states and the even bigger bubble one lives in being a White Democrat in America.

### "Press Conference" (42.13)

This is the first of four sketches where Melissa McCarthy played Trump press secretary Sean Spicer. It is fascinating to watch McCarthy in full "Spicey" makeup at the podium, belligerently addressing reports in much the style the real Spicer did, partly because it's clear the studio audience does not realize it's the comic actress until about thirty seconds in, at which point the hoots and laughs grow thunderous. McCarthy throws her entire self into the role, unmercifully dressing down the press ("I came to apologize on behalf of *you* to *me* because of how you've treated *me* these past two weeks!"), using dolls and props to explain Trump's Muslim ban to these simpletons, and shooting soapy water through a large Super Slider toy at one reporter to "wash that stupid lying mouth out" when he asks if Trump's statement released on Holocaust Remembrance Day is anti-Semitic because it does not mention Jews. (In fact, Trump's real Holocaust Remembrance Day statement the week prior did not mention Jews *or* anti-Semitism.) It concludes with "Spicey" picking up his podium and moving it across the room to taunt and threaten still another reporter whose question he doesn't like. *SNL* quickly had McCarthy return for her next Spicer appearance the following week, this time with a motorized podium she uses to chase the entire gaggle of reporters around the room.

### "Michael Cohen Wiretap" (43.19)

Then Trump lawyer Michael Cohen (Ben Stiller) is trying to cover up the president's lying about financial payoffs made to adult porn star Stormy Daniels (who appears at the end of the sketch playing herself) over their alleged affair, and Cohen phones Trump (Alec Baldwin) in a panic. What ensues is a series of interconnected two-, three-, and four-way calls, some of which Trump is on, where Cohen either seeks advice or secretly dials the wrong number on one of his burner phones. Populating the quick, back-to-back comic conversations is a who's who of Trump's inner orbit at the time, including Rudy Giuliani (Kate McKinnon), Trump's New York physician Dr. Harold Bornstein (Martin Short), press secretary Sarah Huckabee Sanders (Aidy Bryant), Ivanka Trump (Scarlett Johansson), Jared Kushner (Jimmy Fallon), Melania Trump (Cecily Strong), Mike Pence (Beck Bennett), and Omarosa Manigault (Leslie Jones).

Cohen and Trump finally get the woman at the center of the scandal, the real Stormy Daniels, on the line, and it turns into yet another stranger-than-truth moment, with Baldwin's Trump hanging up on Cohen so he can speak to Stormy privately. He asks her what she needs "for this to all go away," and she slyly answers, "A resignation," to which he memorably replies, "Being president is like doing porn. Once you do it, it's hard to do anything else." The Stormy cameo and all that came before and after it capture an era in presidential politics where even *SNL* had difficulty separating fact from fiction.

## The 2020s: Joe Biden (2020–present)

Americans voted for a return to normalcy with the election of Joe Biden, which isn't necessarily great for comedy. The United States was still recovering from the COVID-19 pandemic, and voters made a bet on a dependable, pretty much scandal-free politician with decades of experience in Washington, DC, to lead the country out of it and through a number of increasing international and economic challenges. Coverage of Biden has so far centered on his age ("Folks, I'm on the Peloton every morning, tempting fate," he says in one midterm election cold open [48.5]); unforced gaffes; or his long history in the House, Senate, and as Obama's vice president. On that note, there have been nine *SNL* Biden impersonators since 1991. The most notable includes Jason Sudeikis, who played him as energetic middle-class Joe from Delaware, to Jim Carrey's zany and a bit strange Biden during his presidential race with Trump, to current resident *SNL* impressionist James Austin Johnson, an older, folksy, and slightly desperate Biden though still one with a twinkle in his now-squinting eyes as he makes grandpa-like jokes and outdated references. But because Johnson also does *SNL*'s pitch-perfect Trump, who is the front-runner for the 2024 Republican nomination for president, Mikey Day's more deliberate but even older-seeming Biden debuted in the last months of 2023 (49.3), likely so Johnson would not have to portray both men if 2024 means yet another Biden-Trump showdown.

The start of season 46 began with the Carrey version of Biden debating Baldwin's Trump and was in part based on their actual Fox News debate earlier that week. The cold-open sketch (46.1; see more later) had a promising beginning where Biden takes out a tape measure to make sure their podiums are distanced enough to adhere to COVID-19 protocols, especially after Trump says to moderator Chris Wallace (Beck Bennett) he did indeed take a COVID-19 test prior to the debate but crosses his fingers while he answers. Still, Carrey's entrance as an overly energetic Biden, who becomes an imaginary gunslinger firing shots out of a mimed six-shooter, didn't seem like the version we know of him today (though wearing his signature aviator shades was a good touch). Nor did a somewhat off-the-wall moment toward the end of the sketch where Biden uses a remote control to freeze-frame Trump and imply a fantasy about his competitor's demise. That interpretation is at odds with Biden's well-known decency. Carrey milked this and other appearances for some humor, but in the following season, the Biden torch was passed to Johnson.

*SNL* struggled with what to do with the president because he was mostly busy working off-camera, leaving not much controversy to be mined during his first year in office. Instead, it focused on the bizarre antics of the Trump-led attempted insurrection at the Capitol, the subsequent Senate investigation and hearings, and coverage of topical events on news shows like the Republican-leaning *Fox and Friends* and others, which gave them an opportunity to present a variety of loony politicos who were a lot more comically colorful than Biden. Speaking of which, there was still a constant flow of Trump himself. He made it clear he was not going away, refusing to concede he was not president and shouting the election had been "stolen" from him. It was unfortunate but prompted a whole new slant in covering him, best highlighted in a cold open right after midterm Election Day (48.6). The predicted Republican blowout at the ballot box didn't happen, and on *SNL* even the *Fox and Friends* hosts thought Trump was the reason, holding up unfavorable coverage such as the *New York Post*'s front-page headline, "Trumpty Dumpty," and trying to rush an oblivious Trump off the air when he calls into the show.

*SNL* continued to find opportunity to parody the president through the rest of that year, especially on a pre-Halloween episode where Mikey Day debuted his Biden walking toward a ladder to hang decorations in the Oval Office in the cold open (49.3). Admitting that the world is a scary place right now with wars, shootings, and climate change, he wanted to put everyone at ease, "and nothing puts people at ease like an eighty-year-old man hanging Halloween decorations." The self-deprecating humor felt a lot more like 2023 Biden, especially when, climbing the wobbly ladder, he tries to assure us ("Relax, I'm not going to fall") and then thinks the better of it, noting, "On second thought, let's do that later."

The Biden portrayal evolved a bit in 2024 partly due to the reemergence of Trump as a defendant in multiple court cases across the country where he monopolized the news. In the process, he also managed to capture the Republican nomination for president and, whenever he could, forcefully attacked and linked the Biden administration "witch hunt" to his misfortunes, aggressively making the downfall of the sitting president a part of his campaign. That tactic seemed to reenergize the real Biden and led to his renewed public image as an energetic and quite active warrior for decency, culminating with a barnstorming State of the Union speech represented in the cold open "CNN Special Report" (49.14).

Intercutting audience response from the real speech, Biden whoops it up at the podium, nailing his "predecessor" (he never refers to Trump by name) and his political party for tanking his proposed bill for dealing with the border crisis, all to the chagrin of ultraconservative Speaker of the House Mike Johnson, who is stuck sitting behind him shaking his head in disapproval. When members from Johnson's party begin to shout back at him from the House chamber, Biden teases back, "Oh, you don't like that?" and smiles the trademark Biden grin as he continues on, more jazzed than ever. But rather than address any more policy issues, he says he's going to cede the floor to the Republican response to his speech, which he's "seen clips of" and claims will help him "more than anything else" he can say. CNN then cuts to the rebuttal from Representative Katie Britt, but it's Scarlett Johansson standing behind a kitchen counter in the middle of nowhere doing a scathing though barely exaggerated portrayal of the junior congresswoman from Alabama, disastrously delivering her thoughts on why the American dream has "turned in a hellscape" in full-on, barely suppressed suburban-mom rage.

Because the sequence stuck so close to the basic facts of the real Biden appearance, which had already captured worldwide attention and the news cycle away from his "predecessor," the "doddering Biden" was put to rest publicly and for the rest of *SNL*'s 49th season. This left season 50 to deal with the volatile real life events in June and July of 2024 that would make history and radically change the dynamics of the upcoming U.S. presidential election.

Biden's disastrous first debate performance in June, and the growing pressure for Biden to bow out as his party's nominee due to shrinking poll numbers that cratered even further after an assassination attempt on Trump, led to Biden withdrawing as a candidate and endorsing Kamala Harris, his vice-president, to run against Trump.

At this writing, Harris has accrued more than enough delegates to become the official nominee of her party by mid-August, raised several hundred million dollars for her campaign in less than two weeks, and is now in a statistical tie with Trump in the polls. All of this, and perhaps more, promises to make *SNL*'s golden anniversary political season the very definition of "must see TV."

## Notable Sketches

### Cold Open: "The Presidential Debate" (46.1)

This is the first of Jim Carrey's six appearances as Biden and takes place during his first debate with Trump. But what is most memorable about the sketch is that, even though the antics of the real and *SNL* Trump are not much different from prior years, the country is after four years of his presidency. His constant interruptions, boastful rants, and stream of untruths are still funny during this debate but in a more pathetic way, as if what passed for an alpha male four years ago is now a tired carnival act.

That's why it's particularly appropriate when Maya Rudolph makes a surprise appearance as Biden vice presidential running mate Kamala Harris. In full mom mode (or, as she puts it, "Mamala," a reference to the nickname Harris's real stepchildren have for her), she dresses down a misbehaving Trump after he uses a laser pointer to distract Biden, who gets flustered and mimes a roar at him. Stopping the debate entirely, she puts both candidates in a time-out and says to Trump sternly, "You look at me, Donald. You do not treat my Joe like that. He's a nice boy. . . . Now I want you to apologize to Joe." When Trump protests and lies ("He started it!"), she will hear none of it (much to "son" Biden's embarrassment) and reiterates the request, at which point Trump finally verbalizes a word never uttered from his lips: "Sorry." She then looks at the audience and proclaims what we learned tonight is America needs a woman president but that for now she will settle for the number 2 spot, promising the two "boys" onstage "PB&J and apple slices." It's the major moment in the routine because it shows just how juvenile presidential politics have now become.

### Cold Open: "Ghost of Biden Past" (47.4)

Jason Sudeikis shows up as charismatic, jokey Joe Biden from 2013 in a very clever premise that contrasts the present Biden with who he was when he was Barack Obama's vice president and Sudeikis was playing him. It begins with press secretary Jen Psaki (Chloe Fineman) informing the president (James Austin Johnson) that no one watched his recent town hall, and his poll numbers are in the dumpster.

Press secretary Jen Psaki (Chloe Fineman) delivers the bad news to President Biden (James Austin Johnson) that his poll numbers are down.

When she exits he wonders aloud where the old "Uncle Joe" went and how people used to like him, when suddenly the door to the Oval Office flies open and through smoke enters Sudeikis, smiling from ear to ear and dressed in the old Biden casual attire—blue flight jacket, baseball hat, and aviator glasses. The president asks who he is, and a disbelieving Sudeikis finally blusters, "I'm you! From eight years ago, the ghost of Biden past. Boom!" The routine continues with jokes about Biden's lucidity and how sad he is compared to how he used to be. It even references questionable moments from the real Biden's past where he put his hands on people's shoulders or embraced them and, with women, apparently smelled them. Sudeikis actually does this to the current Biden and then tells him, "Hope this doesn't sound sexist sweetie, but you gotta smile more." At one point, the March 2021 Biden (Alex Moffat) makes a brief appearance but leaves quickly. Sudeikis then says to the president he should also go but urges him to crack a smile with those "100 percent natural choppers we got"; stand tall; and always remember, "We may be from different eras, but at the end of the day, we're both Joe Freakin' Biden!" For just a moment, the president and even the audience feel hopeful again.

## 2020, Part 2: 2024 (48.4)

This aired a few weeks before the midterm elections and is done exactly like a trailer for a horror film. The conceit is that the horror of the film is Joe Biden running for reelection in two years and how panicked a group of his young supporters are that he will lose because he is too old. A young woman (Chloe Fineman) sees on the news that Biden says he intends to run, and suddenly she, her boyfriend, and their friends panic. It's not that they don't like him. It's more "What if he isn't able to . . . win?"

Complete with voice-overs like, "You trusted him once. Can you trust him again?" and "Just when you thought the terror is over, you realize it's just beginning," the short touches on most every trope of modern horror films and modern horror movie trailers. There are slasher music cues, reverberating images of someone becoming possessed, blood dripping from people's mouths, and then the walls, all while a bunch of innocent young people run around the room trying to figure a way out. One of the best sections is when they count down alternative choices, and each one becomes worse to them ("Kamala . . . Wake up!" "Cory Booker . . . He's corny!" "Mayor Pete . . . Listen to yourself!"). They scream bloody murder after there's a knock on the door and a "Beto 2024" flier slides in. They stare at the wall in disbelief when blood drips with the word *Bernie* ("Not again!") and save their worst horror for when one of their now possessed friends says in a weird mechanical voice that they have the perfect candidate, a superstar who can go all the way: "Hillary." It also has a resonant ending when the group, which also includes Mikey Day, Punkie Johnson, Bowen Yang, and Heidi Gardner, circle back to Biden as their choice, realizing that despite his age he truly is their best option. A must see—for many reasons.

# Repertory and Featured Players

## An *SNL* Cast Directory (1980–2024), Seasons 6–49

The abbreviation "RP" denotes the years in which a cast member was billed as a "Repertory Player."

"FP" denotes the years in which a cast member was billed as a "Featured Player."

For bios of the Not Ready for Prime Time Players and Featured Players during seasons 1–5, see chapter 3.

**ARMISEN, Fred** (FP, 2002–2004; RP, 2004–2013): Armisen is a professional drummer who played for the Blue Man Group and in the punk band Trenchmouth. Armisen joined *SNL* in 2002 and was promoted to repertory player two years later. By the time he left in 2013, he was one of the longest-tenured cast members in *SNL* history, often playing memorably bizarre characters. The prolific Armisen also cocreated and starred in both the Peabody Award–winning comedy show *Portlandia* (2011–2018) and the Spanish-language series *Les Espookys* (2019–2023). He was the bandleader and frequent drummer for the *Late Night with Seth Meyers* (2014–present) house band, the 8G Band until NBC discontinued the show's house band in 2024 due to budget cuts. Best Impressions: President Barack Obama, *The View*'s Joy Behar, and Queen Elizabeth. Best Characters: Regine, Ferecito, and Stuart from "The Californians."

**ATHARI, Aristotle** (FP, 2021–2022): Athari was the first Middle Eastern male *SNL* cast member and second (after Nasim Pedrad) of Iranian descent. He began his career in standup and collaborated with Muslim American comedians Hasan Minhaj, Asif Ali, and Fahi Amwar in the sketch comedy quartet Goatface. He also had a recurring role on the HBO series *Silicon Valley*. Best Characters: Angelo, Laughintosh 3000.

**BANKS, Morwenna** (RP, 4/8/95–5/13/95): The British actress/writer appeared in the last four episodes of season 20. Since then she has supplied voices to several animated series in the UK, including *Stressed Eric* (1998–2000), and has appeared in several British series, including *Saxondale* (2006–2007) and *Skins* (2007–2013). In addition to providing one of the voices for *The Adventures of Paddington* (2019–present), she wrote the acclaimed play *Goodbye* about a woman diagnosed with breast cancer, which was broadcast on BBC Radio 4 in 2013 and starred Olivia Colman.

BAYER, **Vanessa** (FP, 2010–2012; RP, 2012–2017): A former intern on *Sesame Street* (1969–present) and *Late Night with Conan O'Brien*, Bayer appeared in the all-Jewish cast of Second City's *Jewsical: The Musical* before landing on *SNL*. She cocreated, starred in, and co–executive produced the Showtime comedy series *I Love That for You* (2022) based on her experiences as a survivor of childhood leukemia. Best Impressions: Miley Cyrus, Khloé Kardashian, and Rachel from *Friends*. Best Character: Jacob, the Bar Mitzvah Boy.

BELUSHI, **Jim** (RP, 1983–1985): Like his older brother John, Jim Belushi was a member of Second City in Chicago before joining the cast of *SNL* in 1983. In the late 1980s/early 1990s, he appeared in over a dozen films, including *"About Last Night . . ."* (1986), *Salvador* (1986), and *K-9* (1989), and later starred in his own long-running sitcom, *According to Jim* (2001–2009). More recently, he has starred in all three seasons of the Discovery Channel reality series *Growing Belushi* (2020–2023), about life on his Oregon cannabis farm.

BENNETT, **Beck** (FP, 2013–2015; RP, 2015–2021): Bennett began his comedy career alongside fellow *SNL* cast member Kyle Mooney as part of the improv/sketch comedy groups Commedus Interruptus and Good Neighbor, which eventually led to them joining *SNL*. He is also known for doing voices on the animated series *Duck Tales* and *Hamster & Gretel*, and the animated film *The Mitchells vs. the Machines* (2021). Best Impressions: Vladimir Putin, Wolf Blitzer. Best Characters: Office Boss Baby, Brothers (along with Kyle Mooney).

BREUER, **Jim** (RP, 1995–1998): Breuer is a stand-up comic best remembered for his impression of actor Joe Pesci and the character Goat Boy, host of the fictional MTV show *Hey, Remember the '80s*. He recounted his experiences on *SNL* in his 2010 autobiography, *I'm Not High: But I've Got a Lot of Crazy Stories About Life as a Goat Boy, a Dad, and a Spiritual Warrior*. Since 2002, he has starred in four comedy specials—*Hardcore* (2002), *Let's Clear the Air* (2009), *And Laughter for All* (2013), and *Comic Frenzy* (2015)—and currently hosts *The Jim Breuer Podcast*.

BRITTAIN, **Paul** (FP, 2010–2012): Brittain trained at iO Chicago (along with castmate Vanessa Bayer) before joining *SNL* as a featured player. The nephew of legendary comedian Bob Newhart, Brittain departed the show in the middle of the 2011–2012 season, but left a lasting impression as the foppish man-child Lord Cecil Wyndemere ("I want sweets!"). Currently, he plays the character Dr. Richard Bunn on the podcast *Comedy Bang! Bang!*

BROWN, **A. Whitney** (FP, 1985–1991): Brown was a writer and featured player best known for his *Weekend Update* commentaries ("The Big Picture"). After *SNL*, he was one of the original correspondents on *The Daily Show* (1996–present). He won an Emmy in 1987 as part of the *SNL* writing staff and in 2004 briefly worked for the liberal network Air America Radio.

**BRYANT, Aidy** (FP, 2012–2013; RP, 2013–2022): Bryant is a graduate of Columbia College who trained at iO Chicago and was an ensemble member of the Second City's E.T.C. stage. She joined *SNL* as a featured player at the start of season 38, became a repertory performer the following year, and stayed with the show for ten seasons, receiving an Emmy nomination for Best Supporting Actress in 2018. During that time she also made guest appearances on the TV series *Girls* (2012–2017) and *Horace & Pete* (2016) and voiced the main character on the animated series *Danger & Eggs* (2017). In three of her last four years on *SNL*, Bryant starred in and served as cowriter and co–executive producer of the Hulu series *Shrill* (2019–2021). She was encouraged to work on both shows by producer Lorne Michaels, who also supported her decision to remain with SNL one more year for its first post-COVID-19 season (2021–2022). She voiced one of the principal characters on the adult animated comedy series *Human Resources* (2022–2023). Best Impressions: Senator Ted Cruz, Adele, and Hannah Gadsby.

**CAHILL, Beth** (FP, 1991–1992): Prior to her season on *SNL*, Cahill did improv at the Annoyance Theater in Chicago and played Marcia in *The Real Live Brady Bunch*. She was hired for *SNL* along with Melanie Hutsell, who played Jan Brady. Today Cahill is a dress designer who continues to perform in Chicago and Los Angeles.

**CARVEY, Dana** (RP, 1986–1993): Carvey's versatile talents made him one of SNL's leading players in the late 1980s/early 1990s. He became best known for his impersonations of President George H. W. Bush and Ross Perot, along with original characters like the Church Lady, Austrian bodybuilder Hans, and Wayne Campbell's (Mike Myers) sidekick, Garth Algar, a role Carvey played in the films *Wayne's World* (1992) and *Wayne's World 2* (1993). Carvey is one of four performers in *SNL* history to win an Emmy as a series regular (the other three were Chevy Chase in 1976, Gilda Radner in 1978, and Kate McKinnon in 2016 and 2017). In 2022, he began cohosting the *Fly on the Wall* podcast with fellow *SNL* alum David Spade, where they take you behind the scenes and share *SNL* memories along with other former cast members.

**CHE, Michael** (FP, 2014–2015; RP, 2015–present): A stand-up comic, Che joined *SNL* as a writer in 2013. The following spring he became an on-air correspondent for *The Daily Show* (1996–present), where he quickly established himself as a breakout performer covering the Ferguson protests. In the fall of 2014, he was hired back by *SNL* to coanchor *Weekend Update* alongside Colin Jost, becoming the first African American in history to permanently host that segment. In his third season, Che became an official cast member, performing in sketches, and at the end of 2017, he was named co–head writer, with Jost, through 2022. During that time he released a Netflix comedy special, *Shame the Devil* (2021), showcasing his stand-up act, and starred in the sketch comedy series *That Damn Michael Che* (2021–2022) on Max.

**CLEGHORNE, Ellen** (FP, 1991–1993; RP, 1993–1995): Cleghorne is a New York–based comic whose appearances on the sketch comedy show *In Living Color*

(1990–1994) led to her being cast as a featured player in 1991. She stayed through 1995, becoming the first woman of color to appear in the main cast more than a single season. She left the show to star as a single mother in her own WB sitcom *Cleghorne!* (1995), which lasted one season. She has since appeared in supporting roles in film and TV and in 2014 earned a PhD in performance studies at New York University. Best Impressions: Anita Baker, Mary J. Blige, Natalie Cole, Patti LaBelle, Tina Turner, and Whoopi Goldberg. Best Characters: Queen Shenequa and Zoraida, the NBC Page.

**CRYSTAL, Billy** (RP, 1984–1985): Prior to joining the cast as a regular in season 10, Crystal appeared on *SNL* as a guest performer (1.17) and a host in season 9 (9.15, and as a cohost, 9.19). In the late 1970s, he played one of television's first gay male regular characters on the sitcom *Soap* (1977–1981). Crystal starred in a string of hit movie comedies (*When Harry Met Sally . . .* [1989], *City Slickers* [1991], *Analyze This* [1999]), and has won a total of six Emmy Awards and a Drama Desk Award, as well as a Tony Award for his 2005 one-man show, *700 Sundays*. In 2022, he cowrote and starred in the Broadway musical *Mr. Saturday Night*, based on his 1992 feature film. Crystal hosted the Oscars nine times from 1990 to 2012, winning two Emmys in the process. Memorable Impressions: Fernando, Joe Franklin. In 2023 he was recognized at the 46th Annual Kennedy Center Honors.

**CUSACK, Joan** (RP, 1985–1986): Cusack is a character actress from Chicago who appeared in teen films like *My Bodyguard* (1980) and *Sixteen Candles* (1984) before joining *SNL* for a single season. She went on to a successful career in television and film, receiving Oscar nominations for supporting roles in *Working Girl* (1988) and *In and Out* (1997) and winning, after five consecutive nominations, an Emmy in 2015 for Outstanding Guest Actress in a Comedy Series for her recurring role as Sheila Jackson on the Showtime comedy-drama *Shameless* (2011–2021). She also provided the voice of Jessie in the animated films *Toy Story 2, 3,* and *4* (1995, 1999, 2010).

**DAVIDSON, Pete** (FP, 2014–2016; RP, 2016–2022): Davidson joined *SNL* as a featured performer several months before he turned twenty, became a repertory player in 2016, and stayed for a total of eight seasons. During this time he also starred in and cowrote a film loosely based on his life, *The King of Staten Island* (2020); was featured in or starred in four Netflix comedy specials; and developed and later launched a comedy-drama TV series for Peacock, *Bupkis* (2023), where he plays a fictionalized version of himself. Davidson has openly struggled with mental illness, which he has incorporated into his comedy and addressed in his commentaries on *Weekend Update*. Memorable Characters: Chad, Pete Davidson.

**DAY, Mikey** (FP, 2016–2018; RP, 2018–present): Day began his comedy career as a member of the LA-based improv group the Groundlings and was originally hired as a writer for *SNL* in 2013. He became a featured player in 2016 and two years later was promoted to repertory status, where he remains as one of the show's most versatile male performers. He cowrote the sixth of the *Home*

*Alone* franchise, *Home Sweet Home Alone* (2021), on Disney Plus, and hosts the popular game-show-style cooking competition *Is It Cake?* (2022–present) on Netflix. Best Impression: Donald Trump Jr. Best Characters: David S. Pumpkins' dancing skeleton and Nico Slobkin, one-half of an Insufferable Instagram Couple.

**DILLON, Denny** (RP, 1980–1981): After her one-season stint on *SNL*, Denny Dillon returned to Broadway and received a Tony nomination for her performance in the 1983 Gershwin musical *My One and Only*. She has also made numerous television appearances, including a regular role on the HBO comedy *Dream On* (1990–1996). She works frequently in regional theater and teaches at SUNY Ulster and Primary Stages.

**DISMUKES, Andrew** FP, 2020–2022; RP, 2022–present): Dismukes is a graduate of the University of Texas at Austin and as a freshman became active in the local stand-up scene. Upon graduation, he performed as part of the Just for Laughs New Faces Festival, which landed him an *SNL* audition. Dismukes was hired as a staff writer for the show and after three years became a featured player in 2020. He was promoted to the main cast in 2022.

**DOWNEY, Robert, Jr.** (RP, 1985–1986): The talented, charismatic actor was only twenty years old when he joined the cast in season 11. He went on to have a distinguished acting career in films, receiving Academy Award nominations for *Chaplin* (1992) and *Tropic Thunder* (2008). He became a worldwide superstar playing the action hero Tony Stark/Iron Man in ten films in the Marvel Universe, including *Iron Man* (2008), Iron Man 2 (2010), *The Avengers* (2012), *Iron Man 3* (2013), and *Avengers: Endgame* (2019). Most recently, he costarred in the critically acclaimed box-office hit *Oppenheimer* (2023), for which he won the Oscar for Best Supporting Actor. Downey Jr. is the son of the late film director Robert Downey Sr. (*Putney Swope* [1969]), and in 2022 Netflix released the documentary *Sr.*, which he produced and starred in along with his father. He is also the nephew of longtime *SNL* writer Jim Downey.

**DOYLE-MURRAY, Brian** (FP, 1979–1980, 1981–1982): The older brother of Bill Murray, Doyle-Murray was a staff writer on the show for three and a half seasons, two of which he also spent in front of the camera as a featured player. Doyle-Murray has since had a successful career as a writer and character actor, appearing in dozens of television shows and films and supplying voices for such animated series as *Spongebob Squarepants* (1999–present), *The Goode Family* (2009), and *Family Guy* (1999–2002, 2005–present), as well as video games.

**DRATCH, Rachel** (FP, 1999–2001; RP, 2001–2006): Dratch came to *SNL* via Second City in Chicago, where she performed with Tina Fey and former *SNL* writer Adam McKay. On *SNL*, Dratch did impressions and created a host of memorable characters, ranging from ancient film studio owner Abe Scheinwald (29.6) to Wakefield Middle Schooler Sheldon (30.15) to the human dark cloud, Debbie Downer (29.18). Since leaving the show, Dratch has made dozens of guest appearances on numerous TV series. In 2022, she received a Tony nomination for Best Featured Actress in a Play for her Broadway debut in *POTUS: Or, Behind Every Great Dumbass Are Seven Women Trying to Keep Him Alive.* Best Character: Debbie Downer, c'mon!

**DUKE, Robin** (RP, 1981–1984): Duke was a member of Second City in Toronto and a regular on *SCTV* during the 1980–1981 season before she was recruited to join the cast of *SNL*. She continues to appear on American and Canadian television, most recently alongside other SCTV alums in such projects as Martin Short's autobiographical film, *I, Martin Short, Goes Home* (2012) and on the Emmy-winning *Schitt's Creek* (2016–2019).

**DUNN, Nora** (RP, 1985–1990): One of *SNL*'s leading female players in the late 1980s, Dunn brought a much-needed feminist sensibility to *SNL*. She is best known for her impressions of strong, outspoken women like Ann Landers, Leona Helmsley, Pat Schroeder, and Cokie Roberts, and original characters, like model-turned-talk-show-host Pat Stevens and Liz Sweeney, one half of the singing Sweeney Sisters. Dunn continued her acting career in films and on television, with recurring roles on *Sisters* (1991–1996), *The Nanny* (1993–1999), *Entourage* (2004–2011), and *Home Economics* (2021–2023). She is the author of *Nobody's Rib: Pat Stevens, Liz Sweeney, Babette, and Some Other Women You Know.* Best Characters: Liz Sweeney, Pat Stevens.

**EBERSOLE, Christine** (RP, 1981–1982): A graduate of the American Academy of Dramatic Arts, Ebersole appeared on the ABC soap opera *Ryan's Hope* (1975–1989) before joining the cast of *SNL* in season 7. She frequently sang in musical sketches and coanchored *SNL Newsbreak*. Ebersole is a two-time Tony winner, for Best Actress in a Musical for the 2001 revival of *42nd Street* and in 2007 for *Grey Gardens.* Recently, she had a recurring role on the CBS sitcom *Bob Hearts Abishola* (2019–2024).

**EDWARDS, Dean** (FP, 2001–2003): Edwards is best remembered on *SNL* for his impressions of Chris Tucker, Colin Powell, Denzel Washington, and Michael Jackson. He replaced Eddie Murphy as the voice of the Donkey in the television special *Scared Shrekless* (2010) and the six-minute short *Thriller Night* (2011). More recently, he has voiced characters on Robert Smigel's Fox puppet series *Let's Be Real* (2021) and appeared on the Netflix comedy series *Tiffany Haddish Presents: They Ready, Season 2* (2021).

**ELLIOTT, Abby** (FP, 2008–2009; RP, 2010–2012): Elliott is the daughter of former *SNL* cast member Chris Elliott (see below) and granddaughter of comic legend Bob Elliott (of Bob and Ray fame). She is an alumna of The Upright Citizens Brigade in Los Angeles and in addition to her work on *SNL*, she's appeared in films and on television, including guest appearances on several situation comedies (*2 Broke Girls* [2011–2017], *How I Met Your Mother* [2005–2014], and *Happy Endings* [2011–2013]). She is currently a regular on FX's breakout hit comedy-drama series *The Bear* (2022–present).

**ELLIOTT, Chris** (RP, 1994–1995): Elliott recently gained acclaim for his costarring role on the Emmy-winning comedy series *Schitt's Creek* (2015–2020).

Before that, he was best known for his frequent appearances on *Late Night with David Letterman* (1982–1993) as well as big-screen roles in *There's Something About Mary* (1998) and *Groundhog Day* (1993). In 1990, he starred in his own Fox sitcom, *Get a Life* (1990–1992).

**FALLON, Jimmy** (FP, 1998–1998; RP, 1999–2004): Prior to joining *SNL*, Fallon took comedy classes at the Groundlings and performed at the Improv in Los Angeles. In addition to coanchoring *Weekend Update* for four seasons, he played several recurring characters, like Nick Burns, Your Company's Computer Guy; Pat Sullivan; and Jarret, who does a live webcast from his dorm room at Hampshire College. Fallon left *SNL* to host his own show, *Late Night with Jimmy Fallon* (2009–2014), and succeeded Jay Leno as host of NBC's *The Tonight Show* (2014–present), which is now named *The Tonight Show Starring Jimmy Fallon*. He also hosts the musical game show *That's My Jam* (2021–present) for NBC. In 2012 and 2014, Fallon won Primetime Emmys for Outstanding Guest Actor in a Comedy Series for hosting *SNL*.

**FALLON (HOGAN), Siobhan** (FP, 1991–1992): Character actress Siobhan Fallon (no relation to Jimmy) received her theater training at the Atlantic Theater Company in New York, and is still a member of their repertory company. After a season as a featured player on *SNL*, she embarked on a successful career in films and on television, including a three-episode arc as Elaine's annoying roommate on *Seinfeld* (1989–1998). Her movie credits include *Men in Black* (1987), Forrest Gump (1994), and Lars Von Trier's *Dancer in the Dark* (2000). In 2021, she wrote and starred in the film *Rushed*, coproduced by Von Trier.

**FARLEY, Chris** (FP, 1990–1991; RP, 1991–1995): Farley was another Second City graduate who specialized in over-the-top, outrageous characters, like motivational speaker Matt Foley and Bill Swerski fan Todd O'Connor. Farley starred opposite fellow *SNL* cast member David Spade in two films—*Tommy Boy* (1995) and *Black Sheep* (1996). His last film, *Almost Heroes* (1998), directed by Christopher Guest and costarring Matthew Perry, was released after his death from a drug overdose in 1997. A biography, *The Chris Farley Show*, coauthored by his older brother Tom Farley Jr. and Tanner Colby, was published in 2008.

**FERRELL, Will** (RP, 1995–2002): One of *SNL*'s breakout stars in the late 1990s, Ferrell was a Groundling in Los Angeles, along with Chris Kattan and Cheri Oteri, all of whom joined the cast in 1995. Ferrell was best known for his impressions of President George W. Bush, Attorney General Janet Reno, *Inside the Actors Studio* host James Lipton, and *Jeopardy!* host Alex Trebek. His film roles have included *A Night at the Roxbury* (1998), *Elf* (2003), and *Anchorman: The Legend of Ron Burgundy* (2004), and Ferrell was also cofounder, along with writer/director Adam McKay, of the renowned comedy website Funny or Die. Farrell has since become a bona fide movie star, appearing in such movies as *Talladega Nights* (2006); *Blades of Glory* (2007); *Step Brothers* (2008); *Anchorman 2* (2013); *The Lego Movie 1* and *2* (2014, 2019); and *Barbie* (2023). Best Impressions: George W. Bush, Alex

Trebek. Best Characters: Spartan Cheerleader Craig Buchanan, Marty Culp (lounge singer), Steve Butabi (Roxbury Guy).

**FEY, Tina** (FP, 2000–2001; RP, 2001–2006): Fey was a member of Chicago's Second City when she was hired in 1997 as a writer for *SNL*. She became a featured player in 2000 and coanchored *Weekend Update* for six seasons. Known for her sharp wit and intelligence, Fey became the show's first female head writer in 1999, and with Rachel Dratch, Amy Poehler, and Maya Rudolph, infused *SNL* with some much-needed female energy and points of view. Fey returned frequently in front of the *SNL* cameras during the lead-up to the 2008 U.S. presidential election due to her uncanny resemblance to Republican vice presidential candidate Sarah Palin, an impression that became an international phenomenon. On the big screen, Fey wrote and appeared in the feature film *Mean Girls* (2004) and starred opposite Amy Poehler in *Baby Mama* (2008), Steve Carell in *Date Night* (2010), and Paul Rudd in *Admission* (2013), among others. After *SNL*, Fey created and starred in *30 Rock* (2006–2013), winning a total of six Primetime Emmys for producing, writing, and acting (plus three more for writing and guest starring on *SNL*). She also wrote a *New York Times* best-seller about her life, *Bossypants* (2011) and the book to the Broadway musical *Mean Girls* (2017), and cocreated and produced the Netflix comedy series *The Unbreakable Kimmy Schmidt* (2015–2019). In 2010, forty-year-old Fey became the youngest recipient of the Mark Twain Prize for American Humor. She wrote and produced the movie musical *Mean Girls* (2024), adapted from the hit Broadway show. Best Impression: Sarah Palin, obviously!

**FINEMAN, Chloe** (FP, 2019–2021; RP, 2021–present): Fineman was equally adept in both drama and comedy in high school, college, and drama school (NYU and Stella Adler Studio), but upon graduation, she moved to LA and focused on comedy, performing at both the Groundlings and The Upright Citizens Brigade Theatre. She gained attention at the Just for Laughs Festival and appeared on such TV series as *Jane the Virgin* (2014–2019) and *Search Party* (2016–2022), all the while creating a growing online presence with a myriad of celebrity impressions she posts on YouTube and Instagram. This led to her joining *SNL* as a featured player in 2019, and she was promoted to the repertory cast two years later. She voiced Delilah on *Big Mouth* (2021) and on the big screen played Marion Davies in Damien Chazelle's *Babylon* (2022). Best Impressions: Jennifer Coolidge, Nicole Kidman.

**FORTE, Will** (FP, 2002–2003; RP, 2003–2015): Forte is a West Coast native who, prior to *SNL*, was a Groundling and also wrote for *The Late Show with David Letterman* (1993–2015) and for several sitcoms, including *Action* (1999), *3rd Rock from the Sun* (1996–2001), and *That '70s Show* (1998–2006). Forte also cowrote and starred in *MacGruber* (2010), a film parody of the television action series *MacGyver*, based on a character he originated on *SNL*. In 2021 he rebooted *MacGruber* as a streaming series on Peacock. Forte gained wide acclaim after leaving *SNL* for starring in the big-screen drama *Nebraska*

(2013) and for creating and starring in the postapocalyptic comedy series *The Last Man on Earth* (2015–2019). Best Character: MacGruber.

**GARDNER, Heidi** (FP, 2017–2019; RP, 2019–present): Gardner was working for nine years at an LA hair salon when she was urged by a friend and member of the LA Groundlings Theatre to take an improv class there. She did and soon became a member of the main company, which led to work as a voice actress on such animated shows as *Bratz* (2005–2008) and *Supermansion* (2015–2019). She became an *SNL* featured player in 2017 and joined the repertory cast two years later, creating such characters as teen film critic Bailey Gismert and Angel, the distressed girlfriend of every movie boxer. She has appeared in such films as *Life of the Party* (2017) and *Hustle* (2021) and has a recurring role on the Apple TV series *Shrinking* (2023–present).

**GAROFALO, Janeane** (RP, 1994–1995): The talented, edgy comedian did not last an entire season when she joined the male-dominated show in 1994 (at the time, she and Ellen Cleghorne were the only female cast members). Her numerous television appearances during and after leaving the show included roles on *The Larry Sanders Show* (1992–1998), for which she received two Emmy nominations; *The West Wing* (1999–2006); and *24* (2001–2010). She also starred in the films *Reality Bites* (1994), *The Truth about Cats and Dogs* (1996), and *Wet Hot American Summer* (2001), among many others. Garofalo became prominent for her liberal political views in the early 2000s, frequently appearing as a cable news guest opposing the Iraq War and standing up for women's rights. She cohosted a radio show on the Air America Network in 2004 and has continued to tackle contemporary issues in her stand-up act and TV appearances since then. She has also continued as an actress on such series as *Girlfriends' Guide to Divorce* (2014–2015), *Broad City* (2015–2019), and *Billions* (2021).

**GASTEYER, Ana** (RP, 1996–2002): Gasteyer was a member of the Groundlings who had small television roles on *Seinfeld* (1989–1998), *Party of Five* (1994–2000), and *N.Y.P.D. Blue* (1993–2005) before joining the cast of *SNL*. Her signature characters include *Delicious Dish* host Margaret Jo McCullen and singer Bobbi Mohan-Culp. After *SNL* she appeared on Broadway in productions of *The Threepenny Opera*, *The Royal Family*, *The Rocky Horror Show*, and *Wicked* (as Elphaba). She costarred on the ABC comedy *Suburgatory* (2011–2014) with another *SNL* alum, Chris Parnell; *The Goldbergs* (2014–2020); and *American Auto* (2021–2023). A trained singer, Gasteyer released an album of jazz standards, *I'm Hip*. Best Impressions: Martha Stewart, Barbra Streisand.

**GOTTFRIED, Gilbert** (RP, 1980–1981): Before he became known for his screechy voice and squinty eyes, stand-up comic Gottfried played it straight on *SNL* as a sketch comedian. He also lent his voice to commercials, animated television series (*The Ren & Stimpy Show* [1991–1996], *Superman: The Animated Series* [1996–2000]), and the Disney animated feature *Aladdin* (1992); and, more recently, *Cyberchase* (2002–2022) and *Family Guy*

(2007–2023). He was also well known for his hilarious comic appearances on dozens of television talk shows and celebrity roasts. Gottfried died on April 12, 2022, at the age of sixty-six.

**GROSS, Mary** (RP, 1981–1985): Recruited to join the cast in season 7 from Second City in Chicago, Gross is the only female cast member to stay with the show during Dick Ebersol's four-season tenure as *SNL*'s producer. With her big eyes and high-pitched voice, she played a variety of characters ranging from *Our Gang*'s Alfalfa to Dr. Ruth Westheimer to Nancy Reagan and spent a season (1981–1982) behind the *SNL Newsbreak* desk. Since the mid-1980s, Gross has worked steadily in television and films and has been the voice of numerous animated characters. She is the younger sister of *Family Ties* (1982–1989) star Michael Gross.

**GUEST, Christopher** (RP, 1984–1985): Actor/writer/director Christopher Guest spent a season on *SNL* with his good friends Billy Crystal, Martin Short, and *Spinal Tap* bandmate Harry Shearer. British-born Guest (his father was an English lord) cowrote and costarred in the hit mockumentary *This Is Spinal Tap!* (1984) and is best known for his work behind the camera as the prolific director, writer, or cowriter of such other films as *The Big Picture* (1989), *Waiting for Guffman* (1996), *Best in Show* (2000), *A Mighty Wind* (2003), and *For Your Consideration* (2006), some of which he also appears in. Guest also cocreated the British comedy series *Family Tree* (2013) and directed the documentary *Loudon Wainwright III: Surviving Twin* (2018).

**HADER, Bill** (FP, 2005–2006; RP, 2006–2013): Prior to joining the cast of *SNL* in 2005, Hader did improv at Second City in Los Angeles. His specialty is iconic stars like Clint Eastwood, Vincent Price, Alan Alda, and Al Pacino; eccentric public figures like Julian Assange, James Carville, and Richard Branson; and characters who live in their own world, like *Weekend Update* correspondent Stefon. Hader won an Emmy as a producer on *South Park* and has appeared in several cult comedies like *Hot Rod* (2007), *Pineapple Express* (2008), *Tropic Thunder* (2008), and *Adventureland* (2009), and costarred with Kristen Wiig in the independent dramedy *The Skeleton Twins* (2014). Post *SNL*, Hader achieved wide success for cocreating, producing, cowriting, directing, and starring in HBO's dark comedy *Barry* (2018–2023), receiving twelve Emmy nominations and two wins as Best Lead Actor, as well as three DGA and three WGA Awards. In addition, he is a producer and star of IFC's mockumentary series *Documentary Now!* (2015–present), along with Seth Meyers and Fred Armisen. Best Characters: Stefon, Vinny Vedecci. Best Impressions: Al Pacino, Keith Morrison, Vincent Price.

**HALL, Anthony Michael** (1985–1986): Prior to joining *SNL* as the show's youngest cast member, the seventeen-year-old actor played Chevy Chase's son in *National Lampoon's Vacation* (1983) and a geek in three teen comedies written and directed by John Hughes—*Sixteen Candles* (1983), *The Breakfast Club* (1985), and *Weird Science* (1985). After *SNL*, Hall appeared in films and starred on *The Dead Zone* (2002–2007) on the USA Network. He had minor roles in *The Dark Knight* (2008) and *Halloween Kills* (2021) and appeared in the TV series *The Goldbergs* (2013–2023) and *Bosch: Legacy* (2022–present).

**HALL, Brad** (RP, 1982–1984): Hall was a member of Chicago's Second City, along with Gary Kroeger and Julia Louis-Dreyfus, when he joined the cast of *SNL* in 1982. He spent most of his screen time during his two seasons on the show anchoring *Saturday Night News*. Hall created the sitcom *The Single Guy* (1995–1997), and prior to that was a producer, writer, and director on *Brooklyn Bridge* (1991–1993). He was also creator-writer on *Watching Ellie* (2002–2003) and a director on *Veep* (2016–2019), the latter two starring Louis-Dreyfus, whom he married in 1987.

**HALL, Rich** (RP, 1984–1985): Hall is a popular stand-up comedian who was a writer and a performer on ABC's sketch comedy show *Fridays* (1980–1982) before beginning a seven-year run on HBO's sketch comedy series *Not Necessarily the News* (1983–1990), on which he coined the term "sniglet" (words that should appear in the dictionary, like *doork*, which is someone who pushes on a door marked "pull"). As a cast member on *SNL*, he did impressions of Paul Harvey, magician Doug Henning, and New York "subway vigilante" Bernhard Goetz. In 2000, he won a Perrier Comedy Award (now the Edinburgh Comedy Award) and has since created and starred in several comedy and documentary series for the BBC.

**HAMMOND, Darrell** (RP, 1995–2009; Announcer, 2014–present): Comedian and master impressionist Hammond has one of the longest cast member tenures on *SNL* (fourteen years), during which he impersonated politicians (President Bill Clinton, Vice President Al Gore, Vice President Dick Cheney, Governor Arnold Schwarzenegger), celebrities (Donald Trump, Regis Philbin), actors (John Travolta, Sean Connery), and journalists (Chris Matthews, Ted Koppel, Geraldo Rivera). After his departure from the show, he continued to make appearances on both *SNL* and *Weekend Update Thursday*. In 2011, he published his memoir, *God, If You're Not Up There, I'm Fucked*. He took over as *SNL* announcer in 2014, after longtime announcer Don Pardo passed away at the age of ninety-six. As an actor, he has appeared on numerous commercials and episodes of *Law & Order: SVU* (1999–present), *Law & Order: Criminal Intent* (2001–2011), and *Criminal Minds* (2005–2020).

**HARTMAN, Phil** (RP, 1986–1994): Prior to joining the cast of *SNL* in season 12, Phil Hartman was a member of the Groundlings, where he collaborated with comedian Paul Reubens on the development of the character of Pee-wee Herman. Hartman cowrote *Pee-Wee's Big Adventure* (1985) and appeared as Captain Carl in the first season of *Pee-Wee's Playhouse* (1986–1990). During his eight seasons on the show, Hartman was the "go-to guy" for impressions (the list includes over seventy-five), not to mention characters like Keyrock, the Unfrozen Cave Man Lawyer, and hammy actor Johnny O'Connor. After *SNL*, Hartman played egocentric newscaster Evelyn William "Bill" McNeal on the NBC sitcom *NewsRadio* (1995–1999). In 1998, during the show's run,

Hartman was tragically killed by his wife in a murder-suicide. He was forty-nine years old.

**HERNÁNDEZ, Marcello** (FP, 2022–present): Hernández moved from his native Miami to New York to pursue a stand-up career in 2019 while also performing short pieces on various social media channels, including TikTok. In 2022, he was chosen for Just for Laughs New Faces of Comedy and that same year joined *SNL* as a featured player, where he has done numerous comic riffs on his Cuban Domincan heritage. He was upped to repertory player for season 50.

**HOLT, Lauren** (FP, 2020–2021): Holt began her comedy career with The Upright Citizens Brigade in LA and was a featured player in *SNL*'s forty-sixth season. She has appeared on episodes of *The Fifth* (2019–present) and plays a mom in *Barbie* (2023).

**HOOKS, Jan** (RP, 1986–1991): Hooks was a member of the Groundlings and appeared on the Atlanta-based sketch comedy show *Tush* (*The Bill Tush Show*) (1980–1981) and HBO's *Not Necessarily the News* (1982–1990). On *SNL*, Hooks was one half of the popular singing duo the Sweeney Sisters (with Nora Dunn) and impersonated First Ladies (Betty Ford, Nancy Reagan, Hillary Clinton), actresses (Bette Davis, Jodie Foster), and personalities (Tammy Faye Bakker, Kathie Lee Gifford). After *SNL*, she joined the cast of *Designing Women* (1986–1993) for the show's final two seasons. She continued to work in episodic television, receiving an Emmy nomination for *3rd Rock from the Sun* (1996–2001), and voiced characters for *The Simpsons* (1989–present) and *Futurama* (1999–2023). Hooks died on October 9, 2014, at the age of fifty-seven. Best Impression: Tammy Faye Bakker. Best Character: Candy Sweeney.

**HUDSON, Yvonne** (FP, 1980–1981): A featured player during season 6, Hudson was the first African American female in the cast of *Saturday Night Live*. She had appeared uncredited in sketches from 1978 to 1980 and continued to do so off and on through October 1984.

**HUTSELL, Melanie** (FP, 1991–1992; RP, 1992–1994): Prior to joining *SNL*, Hutsell was best known for her portrayal of Jan Brady in the stage show *The Real Live Brady Bunch*, which started at the Annoyance Theatre in Chicago and later played in New York. In addition to Jan Brady, Hutsell did memorable impressions on *SNL* of Tori Spelling and Tonya Harding. She appeared alongside fellow *SNL* alums Kristen Wiig and Maya Rudolph in the hit comedy *Bridesmaids* (2011) and had recurring roles on the streaming series *Lady Dynamite* (2016) and *Transparent* (2014–2019).

**JACKSON, Victoria** (RP, 1986–1992): The daughter of a gymnastics coach, Jackson made several appearances on *The Tonight Show Starring Johnny Carson* (1962–1992), where she did a handstand while reciting poetry) before joining the cast of *SNL*. On *SNL* she was typecast in ditzy blonde roles, though she also did impressions of Roseanne Barr, Tipper Gore, and Zsa Zsa Gabor. After leaving *SNL*, Jackson did small TV and film roles and many years later returned to the spotlight as a Tea Party activist and the host of her own web show.

**JOHNSON, James Austin** (FP, 2021–present): After joining *SNL* in 2021 as a featured player, Johnson became instantly known for his breakout comic portrayal of former U.S. president Donald J. Trump. He also portrayed President Joe Biden, as well as a host of other celebrities. Originally from Nashville, Johnson landed a small part in the Coen Brothers' film *Hail, Caesar!* (2016), shortly after relocating to LA. He has since appeared on *Better Call Saul* (2015–2022) and provided voices for such animated series as *Tuca & Bertie* (2019) and *Fairview* (2022–present).

**JOHNSON, Punkie** (FP, 2020–2022; RP, 2022–2024): Johnson is a stand-up comedian who appeared at the Comedy Store and Just for Laughs before joining *SNL* as a featured player in 2020. She is the second Black LGBTQ cast member (following Danitra Vance, who was not publicly out in her lifetime) and has performed several comic routines on *Weekend Update* that reference her personal life. She has also appeared on such TV series as *Love Life* (2020–2021) and *Ghosts* (2021–present), as well as voicing a character on the animated show *Crank Yankers* (2002–2022). In 2022, she became part of the *SNL* repertory cast.

**JONES, Leslie** (FP, 2014–2016; RP, 2016–2019): Jones was a veteran stand-up comedian prior to joining *SNL* in 2014 as a writer and, later in the year, as a featured player. At forty-seven, she became the oldest person to become a cast member. The six-foot-tall Jones had instant breakout success on the show in her first appearance on *Weekend Update* (39.19), where she did a controversial and hilarious routine on her dating life and her potential effectiveness as a "breeding slave." She was promoted to repertory player in 2016 and received two nominations for Primetime Emmy Awards in 2017 and 2018 as Outstanding Supporting Actress in a Comedy Series for her work. On the big screen, Jones costarred in *Ghostbusters* (2016) alongside Melissa McCarthy and *SNL*'s Kristen Wiig and Kate McKinnon, as well as in *Coming 2 America* (2021). An avid sports fan, Jones's live Tweets and social media video commentaries of the 2016 summer Olympics went viral, prompting NBC to fly her to Rio de Janeiro and join the network's other Olympics commentators. She provided on-and-off Tweets and commentary of the 2018, 2020, and 2022 games, and is scheduled to be part of the NBC team in Paris covering the 2024 Summer Olympics as "chief superfan commentator." Jones also hosted the reboot of the competition show *Supermarket Sweep* (2020–2022) for two seasons.

**JOST, Colin** (FP, 2014–2015; RP, 2015–present): Jost had been editor of the *Harvard Lampoon* and a writer for the animated Nickelodeon series *Kappa Mikey* (2002, 2006–2008) prior to sending a writing packet into *SNL* and getting hired as a writer in 2005. He rose through the ranks and became co–head writer from 2012 to 2015. During that time, he was approached by Lorne Michaels to take over as cohost of the *Weekend Update* anchor desk when it was announced Seth Meyers would soon be leaving the show. Jost officially became cohost of the segment, joining Cicely Strong, in spring 2014 and then became a permanent cohost at the start of season 40 with Michael Che. During the 2021–2022 season, Jost and Che officially became the longest-running anchor team in the show's history, and Jost became the anchor with the longest tenure (Jost also served as co–head writer during the 2017–2022 seasons). Prior to *SNL*, Jost worked as a stand-up comedian, and in 2020, he published his memoir, *A Very Punchable Face: A Memoir*, which landed on the *New York Times* Best-Seller List. In 2024, he also served as host of the annual White House Correspondents' Dinner. Fun Fact: Jost was dormmates with U.S. Transportation Secretary Pete Buttigieg when they were both students at Harvard and did an impression of him during *SNL*'s forty-sixth season.

**KATTAN, Chris** (FP, 1995–1996; RP, 1996–2003): Kattan is a California native who followed in his father's footsteps and joined the Groundlings (his father was one of the original members). He spent eight seasons on *SNL*, where he introduced bizarre characters like Mango, Mr. Peepers, and Gay Hitler. He is best known for his portrayal of Doug Butabi, one of "the Roxbury Guys," a role he repeated in the film *A Night at the Roxbury* (1998), costarring Will Ferrell, with whom he wrote the screenplay. He was a regular on the sitcom *The Middle* (2009–2018), appeared in several episodes of *How I Met Your Mother* (2005–2014), and has since appeared on several reality competition shows. Kattan briefly united with former *SNL* castmates Jimmy Fallon, Horatio Sanz, and Tracy Morgan on December 17, 2018, in the cold-open sequence of *The Tonight Show Starring Jimmy Fallon*. Best Characters: Doug Butabi, Mango, Mr. Peepers.

**KAZURINSKY, Tim** (RP, 1981–1984): Kazurinsky, who specialized in playing nebbishy characters, was one of the new cast members introduced in the final episode of season 6 (6.13) of *SNL*. During his three seasons on the show, he shared a stage with a live chimp in a soap opera parody (*I Married a Monkey*) and played a series of eccentric characters, like *SNL Newsbreak/Saturday Night News* science editor Dr. Jack Badofsky, and Havnagootiim Vishnuuerheer, a wise old Hindu man. He was also part of the *SNL* writing team nominated for an Emmy for Outstanding Writing in a Variety or Music Program in 1984. Kazurinsky has guest-starred on numerous comedy and drama series over the last four decades and frequently performs in Chicago theater. Fun Fact: He filmed Prince's impromptu performance of *Let's Go Crazy* at the *SNL40* after-party in 2015, and the video went viral after Prince's death the following year.

**KEARNEY, Molly** (FP, 2022–2024): Kearney joined *SNL* as a featured player in 2022 and was announced as the show's first nonbinary cast member, a subject Kearney has referred to on several segments of *Weekend Update*. Prior to the show, they performed stand-up in Chicago and LA and in 2019 were chosen for Comedy Central's *Next Up* showcase. They have appeared on such series as *A League of Their Own* (2022–2023) and *Mighty Ducks: Game Changers* (2021–2022). Kearney was upped to repertory player in season 50.

**KIGHTLINGER, Laura** (FP, 1994–1995): Kightlinger is a stand-up comic who wrote and performed on *SNL* during season 20, which led to a prolific career as a writer and/or consulting producer on several situation comedies, including *Will & Grace* (1998–2020), *$#*! My Dad Says* (2010–2011), and *2 Broke Girls* (2011–2017). From 2019 to the present, she has also made guest appearances on *Pen15* (2019–2021), *Will & Grace*, *Curb Your Enthusiasm* (2000–2024), and *The Goldbergs* (2013–2023).

**KILLAM, Taran** (FP, 2010–2012; RP, 2012–2016): Killam first appeared on television as a teenager in dramatic roles on *Judging Amy* (1999–2005), *Touched by an Angel* (1994–2003), and *Roswell* (1999–2002). A member of the Groundlings, he was the youngest cast member of that other sketch comedy show *MADtv* (1995–2009). More television roles followed before he joined *SNL* as a featured player in season 36, and was then promoted to repertory player in 2012, becoming a key cast member for the next four years. On the big screen, Killam appeared in *12 Years a Slave* (2013) and *Teenage Mutant Ninja Turtles* (2014) and directed, wrote, produced, and starred in the comedy-action film *King Gunther* (2017) alongside Arnold Schwarzenegger, who served as executive producer. He also played King George in the musical *Hamilton* on Broadway, starred in the ABC half-hour comedy *Single Parents* (2018–2020), and recently costarred in the action-thriller *The River Wild* (2023). Best Character: Jebidiah Atkinson, 1860s Newspaper Critic. Next!

**KOECHNER, David** (RP, 1995–1996): Koechner's comedy career began at the ImprovOlympic and Second City West, where he worked with fellow *SNL* cast member Nancy Walls and writer/director Adam McKay. He is best remembered on *SNL* for playing Fagan, the British Fop (alongside Mark McKinney as Lucien), and Norm Macdonald's little brother, Gary. Koechner is also known to comedy fans for his recurring role as Michael Scott's obnoxious buddy, Todd Packer, on *The Office* (2005–2013). On the big screen, Koechner costarred in both *Anchorman: The Legend of Ron Burgundy* (2004) and *Anchorman 2: The Legend Continues* (2013), among others. He has also appeared in numerous TV series, including a recurring role on *The Goldbergs* (2013–2023) and the reboot of *Twin Peaks* (2017).

**KROEGER, Gary** (RP, 1982–1985): Kroeger arrived at *SNL* with his Second City Chicago castmates Brad Hall and Julia Louis-Dreyfus. He played Democratic presidential candidate Walter Mondale during the 1984 election season, and did impressions of Paul Shaffer, Donny Osmond (with Louis-Dreyfus as Marie), and Carl Sagan. After *SNL* he made numerous television appearances and starred in the made-for-TV movie *The Return of the Shaggy Dog* (1987). In the 1990s and early 2000s, he worked in the game show world as the host of revivals of *The Newlywed Game* (1996–1997) and *Beat the Clock* (2002–2003). He currently lives in his home state of Iowa, where he works in advertising and acts in local theater. Fun Fact: Kroeger ran in the Democratic congressional primary in Iowa in 2016 but dropped out of the race. Later that year, he ran for a seat in the Iowa State House but lost to the Republican.

**LAURANCE, Matthew** (FP, 1980–1981): Before his short stint as a featured player on *SNL* during season 6, Laurance was an assistant director on the show from season 3 to 5. He continued to pursue an acting career, landing roles in the feature films (*Prince of the City* [1981], *Eddie and the Cruisers* [1983], *Streets of Fire* [1984], and *St. Elmo's Fire* [1985]). He later starred on the situation comedy *Duet* (1987–1989) and played David Silver's father, Mel, on *Beverly Hills, 90210* (1990–2000). Laurance is currently the cohost of *The Sports Huddle* on ESPN Radio.

**LONGFELLOW, Michael** (FP, 2022–present): Prior to joining *SNL*, Longfellow appeared at comedy clubs across the country, as well as in the *Netflix Is a Joke* comedy showcase. He also appeared on *Conan* (2010–2021), as well as *Bring the Funny* (2019), an NBC reality show competition where *SNL*'s Keenan Thompson served as one of the judges. Longfellow's first appearance on *Weekend Update* focused on antivaccination relatives, and in his stand-up act he often refers to his parents' divorce (his father is a divorce lawyer) and his many stepparents. He had a breakout performance on *Weekend Update* playing an old-fashioned cigarette (49.6) and in season 50 has been upped to repertory player.

**LOUIS-DREYFUS, Julia** (RP, 1982–1985): Louis-Dreyfus was the youngest female cast member of *SNL* when she dropped out of Northwestern University to join the cast in season 8. She had a supporting role on the NBC sitcom *Day by Day* (1988–1989), but her real success came in 1990 when she was cast by former *SNL* writer Larry David as Elaine Benes on *Seinfeld* (1990–1998), for which she received a Primetime Emmy and a Golden Globe. She received seven more Emmys for two series that followed— one for *The New Adventures of Old Christine* (2006–2010) and six for *Veep* (2012–2017). She has starred in the independent films *Enough Said* (2013), *You Hurt My Feelings* (2023) and the Netflix comedy *You People*, and had a supporting role in the blockbuster *Black Panther: Wakanda Forever* (2022).

**LOVITZ, Jon** (RP, 1985–1990): An alumnus of the Groundlings (where he befriended fellow cast member Phil Hartman), the Emmy-nominated comedian created an array of characters during his five seasons on *SNL*, including pathological liar Tommy Flanagan, Master Thespian, Tonto, and Mephistopheles. After *SNL*, he was the voice of New York film critic Jay Sherman on *The Critic* (1994–1995, 2000–2001) and did guest spots on sitcoms and supporting roles in films, including *A League of Their Own* (1992), *Happiness* (1998), and *The Producers* (2005). He continues to perform in TV series and films as an actor and voice actor and appears frequently on talk shows and podcasts. Best Impression: Michael Dukakis. Best Characters: Tommy Flanagan, Master Thespian.

**MACDONALD, Norm** (FP, 1993–1994; RP, 1994–1998): The Canadian-born stand-up comic was twenty-four when he landed a stint as a featured player on *SNL*. From 1994 to 1997, he anchored *Weekend Update* until he was shown the door by NBC executive Don Ohlmeyer. Macdonald was also known for his impressions of David Letterman, Senator Bob Dole, and Burt Reynolds. He later starred in his own ABC sitcom, *Norm* (1999–2001), and hosted season 7 of *High Stakes Poker* (2006–2007, 2009–2011) on the Game Show Network. He was a prolific voice actor and frequent talk show guest on such series as *Late Night with David Letterman* (1982–1993) and *The Tonight Show with Conan O'Brien* (2009–2010). Macdonald died of leukemia on September 14, 2021, at the age of sixty-one.

**MATTHIUS, Gail** (RP, 1980–1981): During her brief time on *SNL*, Matthius played Vickie, an annoying Valley girl character, and coanchored *Weekend Update* with Charles Rocket. She has since appeared in commercials and guest-starring TV roles, and supplied the voices for dozens of animated characters on shows like *The Chipmunks* (1984), *Tiny Toon Adventures* (1990–1992), *Bobby's World* (1990–1998), and *Animaniacs* (1993–1998). Today she is a member of the Los Angeles–based improv group the Spolin Players and works as a voice acting coach.

**McKEAN, Michael** (RP, 1994–1995): McKean was a regular on *Laverne and Shirley* (1976–1983), and while on *SNL* he was concurrently on the HBO sitcom *Dream On* (1990–1996). He also starred in and cowrote *This Is Spinal Tap* (1984) and *The Big Picture* (1989) and appeared in *Coneheads* (1993). Like Billy Crystal, McKean hosted *SNL* (10.4) before becoming a cast member. After his season on the show, he continued to appear on television and in films. He received an Academy Award nomination for the song "A Kiss at the End of the Rainbow," which he cowrote with his wife, actress Annette O'Toole, for the comedy *A Mighty Wind* (2003). He has since performed numerous roles in film, TV, and on the Broadway stage and received an Emmy nomination in 2019 as Outstanding Guest Actor in *Better Call Saul* (2015–2022).

**McKINNEY, Mark** (RP, 1995–1997): Prior to joining the cast of *SNL*, Canadian-born McKinney was a member of the sketch comedy troupe The Kids in the Hall, who had their own show (1988–1995) produced by Lorne Michaels that aired on CBS and HBO for five seasons. During his two and a half seasons on *SNL*, he did impressions of Vice President Al Gore and Republican presidential candidate Steve Forbes. McKinney also appeared in three films based on *SNL* characters: *Superstar* (1999), *The Ladies Man* (2000), and *A Night at the Roxbury* (1998). He was also the cocreator of the critically acclaimed Canadian comedy series *Slings and Arrows* (2003–2006), for which he won four Gemini Awards for writing and acting. In 2022, he appeared in an eight-episode sixth season of *The Kids in the Hall* for Amazon Prime along with his other castmates, twenty-seven years after the last original season had aired.

**McKINNON, Kate** (FP, 2012–2013; RP, 2013–2022): Prior to *SNL*, McKinnon was a regular on *The Big Gay Sketch Comedy Show* (2007–2010) and performed at The Upright Citizens Brigade in New York City. On *SNL* she's done such varied impressions as Hillary Clinton, Ellen DeGeneres, Ruth Bader Ginsburg, Rudy Giuliani, Edie Falco, Jodie Foster, and Scarlett Johansson. She is the second openly gay cast member of *SNL* to appear on the show (Terry Sweeney was the first) and its longest-running female cast member, along with Cecily Strong. McKinnon won two consecutive Primetime Emmys for Outstanding Supporting Actress in a Comedy Series in 2016 and 2017, the only cast member to do so in the acting category. She has guest-starred and voiced characters on numerous TV series and costarred in such films as *Ghostbusters* (2016), *Bombshell* (2019), and *Barbie* (2023). Best Impressions: Hillary Clinton and Ruth Bader Ginsburg. Best Characters: Olya Povlastsky, Colleen Rafferty, and Dabette Goldry.

**MEADOWS, Tim** (FP, 1991–1993; RP, 1993–2000): Meadows was a member of Second City in Chicago and followed his castmate Chris Farley to *SNL*, where he would remain for what was then a record ten seasons. Meadows is best remembered for his impressions of Michael Jackson, Tiger Woods, Oprah Winfrey, and his own creation, Leon Phelps, host of the late-night radio talk show *The Ladies' Man*. Meadows recreated the role in the 2000 film and was featured in other *SNL*-related film projects, including *Coneheads*, *It's Pat* (1994), *Wayne's World 2*, and *Mean Girls*. He has had recurring roles on the sitcoms *The Goldbergs* (2013–2023) and *Brooklyn Nine-Nine* (2013–2021) and recently guest-starred in the Peacock series *Poker Face* (2023). Best Character: Leon Phelps, Ladies' Man.

**METCALF, Laurie** (FP, 4/11/1981): Best known to television audiences as Roseanne Connor's sister, Jackie, on the long-running sitcom *Roseanne* (1988–1997), for which she won three Emmy Awards, as well as on *The Connors* (2018–2025). Metcalf was a featured player for a single episode at the end of season 6 (6.13), in which she appeared in a filmed segment during *Weekend Update*. She is an acclaimed stage actress with two Tony Awards out of six nominations, and on the big screen, she received an Oscar nomination for Best Supporting Actress in *Ladybird* (2017).

**MEYERS, Seth** (FP, 2001–2003; RP, 2003–present): A graduate of Northwestern University, Meyers performed in Chicago at iO before joining *SNL* in 2001, where he moved up the ranks to co-head writer with Tina Fey and Andrew Steele. When Fey left *SNL*, he also took over as coanchor of *Weekend Update* with Amy Poehler. He was the show's head writer and coanchor or sole anchor of *Weekend Update* from 2006 to 2014. In 2014, Meyers moved on to host *Late Night with Seth Meyers* (2014–present) when Jimmy Fallon took over as host on *The Tonight Show*. Meyers created, cowrites, and coproduces the mockumentary series *Documentary Now!* along with Bill Hader and Fred Armisen (the latter served as bandleader of *Late Night*). He has the third-longest run on *SNL* of any cast member, behind Darrell Hammond and Kenan Thompson.

**MILHISER, John** (FP, 2013–2014): Milhiser was part of The Upright Citizens Brigade sketch comedy group Serious Lunch before joining *SNL*. Since then, he has appeared on the big screen in *Camp Takota* (2014) and *Ghostbusters* (2016) and in such network and streaming series as *2 Broke Girls* (2011–2017), *Other Space* (2015), *Love* (2016–2018), and *Adam Ruins Everything* (2015–2019).

**MILLER, Dennis** (RP, 1985–1991): Miller was a stand-up comedian when he was reportedly discovered by Lorne Michaels at the Comedy Store. He joined the cast in 1985 and took over as anchor of *Weekend Update*, where he developed his snarky anchorman persona that he continued in other formats in network and cable TV. After *SNL*, Miller hosted several television talk shows, including *Dennis Miller Live* (1994–2002), for which he won five Emmys. He was host of a self-titled syndicated radio show, *The Dennis Miller Show* (2007–2015), and a half-hour interview show for RT America, *Dennis Miller + One* (2020–2022).

**MINOR, Jerry** (FP, 2000–2001): Minor is a stand-up comic who had performed at Second City in Detroit, Chicago, and Toronto. During his season on *SNL*, he was known for impressions of Al Sharpton, Jimi Hendrix, and Cuba Gooding Jr. Minor has also appeared on *Mr. Show with Bob and David* (1995–1998) and *Lucky Louie* (2006–2007) on HBO and had a recurring role as Officer Carter on *Arrested Development* (2003–2006; 2013, 2018–2019). He guest-stars frequently in series television and had a recurring role in season 2 of *Abbott Elementary* (2021–present).

**MITCHELL, Finesse** (FP, 2003–2005; RP, 2005–2006): Mitchell was a former college football player turned comedian who appeared on late-night talk shows before being signed to *SNL*, where he is best remembered for playing Starkisha, a black girl from the ghetto. After being dropped from the show in 2006 due to budget cuts, he continued to perform in comedy clubs and appeared as a guest correspondent on *Today* (1951–present). In 2007, he published a dating guide for women, *Your Girlfriends Only Know So Much: A Brother's Take on Dating and Mating for Sistas*. He has appeared on numerous TV series, including a supporting role in *Outmatched* (2020) and on *Kenan* (2021–2022).

**MOFFAT, Alex** (FP, 2016–2018; RP, 2018–2022): Prior to joining *SNL*, Moffat was a comedy improv performer in Chicago at such venues as Second City, and an actor who appeared in the dramatic-thriller film *Uncle John* (2015). Moffat was a particularly reliable cast member who appeared in numerous sketches and *Weekend Update* segments. He also briefly took over the role of then President-Elect Joe Biden from Jim Carrey in the last show of 2020. Moffat recently appeared in the films *Christmas with the Campbells* (2022) and *80 for Brady* (2023), as well as on the TV series *The Bear* (2022–present). He also appeared on Broadway in the comic play *The Cottage* (2023). Best Impression: Eric Trump. Best Character: Guy Who Just Bought a Boat.

**MOHR, Jay** (FP, 1993–1995): In Mohr's honest account of his time on *SNL*, *Gasping for Airtime: Two Years in the Trenches of* Saturday Night Live (2004), he revealed his struggle with panic attacks and the competitive atmosphere behind the scenes at the show. Since then, Mohr has appeared in films and continued to work in television as the creator and producer of *Last Comic Standing* (2003–2010), which he hosted for the first three seasons. Mohr also starred in the sitcom *Gary Unmarried* (2008–2010), which ran for two seasons on CBS. He became active in sports radio with his own show, *Jay Mohr Sports* (2013–2015). Since leaving *SNL*, Mohr has worked as an actor in TV series and films, the latter spanning everything from *Jerry Maguire* (1996) to *Air* (2023). Best Impression: Christopher Walken.

**MOONEY, Kyle** (FP, 2013–2015; RP, 2015–2022): Mooney was part of the sketch comedy group Good Neighbor, along with future *SNL* castmate Beck Bennett and future *SNL* segment director Dave McCary, prior to being hired as a featured player in 2013. Mooney became known for a series of oddball, off-the-wall characters, including Baby Yoda, bad comedian Bruce Chandling, and a fictional version of himself that was having a romance with fellow *SNL* performer Leslie Jones. On the big screen, Mooney cowrote and starred in *Brigsby Bear* (2017), and he cocreated, cowrote, and executive-produced the streaming adult cartoon series *Saturday Morning All-Star Hits!* (2021), also voicing some of the characters. Most recently, he appeared in the Jennifer Lawrence film *No Hard Feelings* (2023) and as Snap (of Snap, Crackle, and Pop) in the Jerry Seinfeld–directed comedy *Unfrosted*. Best Character: Baby Yoda.

**MORGAN, Tracy** (RP, 1996–2003): Before joining the cast of *SNL*, Tracy Morgan appeared on the sketch comedy show *Uptown Comedy Club* (1992–1994) and the HBO series *Snaps* (1995). His seven seasons on *SNL* were followed by his own short-lived sitcom, *The Tracy Morgan Show* (2003–2004), in which he played the owner of an auto repair garage. Three years later, he was cast as comedian Tracy Jordan, a character loosely based on himself, on *30 Rock* (2006–2013). In 2014, Morgan was a passenger in a serious six-vehicle car crash, and his long recovery prompted his stand-up comedy special *Tracy Morgan: Staying Alive* (2017). In that period of time, he also returned to host *SNL* (41.3). He continues to make appearances in film and TV, most recently in *Coming 2 America* (2021) and as a voice actor in *Spirited* (2022) and *Squidbillies* (2005–2021). Best Characters: Brian Fellow, Astronaut Jones.

**MOYNIHAN, Bobby** (FP, 2008–2010; RP, 2010–2017): Moynihan is a longtime member of The Upright Citizens Brigade in New York City, and has performed with the internet sketch comedy group Derrick Comedy, including appearing in their 2009 film *Mystery Team*. He had a supporting role in the acclaimed web series *The Line* (2008), written and directed by *SNL*'s Seth Meyers, which led to him joining the show that fall. His repertoire of characters on *SNL* includes Drunk Uncle and secondhand news reporter Anthony Crispino, along with impressions of Food Network personality Guy Fieri, *Fox and Friends*' Brian Kilmeade, and *Jersey Shore*'s (2009–2012) Nicole "Snooki" Polizzi. He has voiced characters in such films as *Monsters University* (2013) and *The Secret Life of Pets* (2017) and in numerous animated series, including the reboot of Disney's *Duck Tales* (2017–2021), *We Bare Bears* (2015–2019), and *Nature Cat* (2015–present). He was also a series regular on the NBC sitcom *Mr. Mayor* (2021–2022). He reprised his Drunk Uncle character on *Weekend Update* in *SNL*'s 2022 Halloween episode (48.4). Best Impression: Snooki. Best Character: Drunk Uncle. Authors' Favorite Impression: Snagglepuss (34.8).

**MURPHY, Eddie** (FP, 1980–1981; RP, 1981–1984): Murphy made his *SNL* debut in 1980 at the age of nineteen as a featured player and for the next three seasons was the show's breakout performer, introducing a host of popular characters like Buckwheat, Dion, Gumby, and Mr. Robinson, as well as impressions of Bill Cosby and Stevie Wonder. He is credited with giving the show back its edge after the departure of the original cast. While he was still on *SNL*, Murphy starred in *48 Hrs.* (1982), the first in a string of box-office hits, which continued with *Trading Places* (1983), *Beverly Hills Cop* (1984), *Beverly Hills Cop II* (1987), *Beverly Hills Cop III* (1994), and the 1996 remake of *The Nutty Professor*, as well as *Nutty Professor 2: The Klumps* (2000). He has also supplied the voice of the Donkey in three *Shrek* films (2001, 2004, 2007) and received an Academy Award nomination for Best Supporting Actor in *Dreamgirls* (2006). More recently, Murphy starred in *Dolemite Is My Name* (2019) and *Coming 2 America* (2021). He received a Primetime Emmy for Outstanding Guest Actor in a Comedy Series for hosting *SNL* in 2019. Best Impression: Bill Cosby. Best Characters: Mr. Robinson, Gumby.

**MYERS, Mike** (FP, 1988–1989; RP, 1989–1995): Canadian-born Mike Myers did improv in Toronto, Chicago, and London before joining the cast of *SNL*. During his eight seasons, he created such memorable characters as German talk show host Dieter, *Coffee Talk* host Linda Richman, and TV cable access host Wayne Campbell, who made the leap to the big screen in *Wayne's World* (1992) and *Wayne's World 2* (1993). After *SNL*, Myers wrote and starred in the *Austin Powers* trilogy (1997, 1999, 2002) and supplied the voice for the title role of *Shrek* (2001) and its two sequels (2004, 2007). More recently, Myers played supporting roles in *Terminal* (2018), *Bohemian Rhapsody* (2018), and *Amsterdam* (2022). Best Impression: Judge Lance Ito. Best Characters: Wayne Campbell, Linda Richman.

**NEALON, Kevin** (FP, 1986–1987; RP, 1987–1995): Nealon joined *SNL* the same year as close friend Dana Carvey and remained with the show for nine seasons, three of which he spent behind the *Weekend Update* anchor desk. On *SNL*, Nealon was also known for playing one-half of the fitness duo Hanz and Franz (Nealon was Franz, and Carvey was Hanz), two breakout characters that lampooned Arnold Schwarzenegger and the bodybuilding craze. Since *SNL* he's appeared in feature films and has done guest appearances on sitcoms, plus a supporting role on Showtime's *Weeds* (2005–2012). He was also a regular on the comedy series *Man with a Plan* (2016–2020). When he is not making people laugh, Nealon is a serious animal rights activist. Best Impression: ABC newsman Sam Donaldson. Best Character: Franz.

**NULL, Luke** (FP, 2017–2018): Null is an actor, comedian, musician, and singer who performed at the iO Theatre with the improv sketch group Newport Hounds prior to appearing on *SNL* during its forty-third season. Though he did not get a shot at doing much musical comedy on *SNL*, in 2019 he released an album, *Guitar Comic*, and he frequently tours doing comedy and music in live shows.

**NWODIM, Ego** (FP, 2018–2020; RP, 2020–present): Nwodim received a biology degree from USC before taking classes at and becoming part of the regular cast of Upright Citizens Brigade, where she eventually performed a one-woman show, *Great Black Women . . . and Then There's Me*. Nwodim appeared at the Just for Laughs Comedy Festival and had a three-episode arc on *Law & Order True Crime: The Menendez Brothers* (2017) before joining *SNL* as a featured and then repertory player. Her breakout character on the show is Lisa from Temecula, a plain-talking lawyer who is a no-nonsense disrupter at a restaurant dinner table. Nwodim has continued to make guest appearances on such TV series as *Love Life* (2020–2022) and *Roar* (2022). Best Impression: Dionne Warwick. Best Character: Lisa from Temecula.

**O'BRIEN, Mike** (FP, 2013–2014): O'Brien was hired as a staff writer for *SNL* in 2009, became a featured player four years later for a season, and then left the cast but continued as a writer for the 2014–2015 season. He still contributes short films to the show under the title "A Mike O'Brien Picture." O'Brien created and wrote the half-hour comedy *A.P. Bio* (2018–2021), which ran for two seasons on NBC and then moved to Peacock. He occasionally guest-stars or works as a voice actor on TV and appeared in the movie *Booksmart* (2019).

**OTERI, Cheri** (RP, 1995–2000): An alumna of the Groundlings, Oteri is best remembered for her impressions of Barbara Walters and Debbie Reynolds, along with an array of loopy characters like Arianna, the Spartan cheerleader; Cass Van Rye, the not-too-bright host of *Morning Latte*; and Nadeen, whose only response to customers' questions and complaints is the catchphrase "Simmer down now!" Since leaving *SNL*, Oteri continued to play offbeat, hyperactive female characters in films and on television and frequently works as a voice actor. Recent credits include *Inside Job* (2021), *Scooby-Doo Where Are You Now!* (2021), and the YouTube series *PBC* (2022–present). Best Impression: Barbara Walters. Best Characters: Arianna, Nadeen.

**PARNELL, Chris** (FP, 1998–1999: RP, 1999–2001, 2002–2006): A graduate of the University of North Carolina School of the Arts, Chris Parnell was performing with the Groundlings in Los Angeles when he was hired in 1998 as a featured player on *SNL*. After three seasons, he was let go due to budget cuts, but was rehired toward the end of the 2001–2002 season and stayed for four more seasons. He contributed impressions of *American Idol* (2002–present) judge Simon Cowell and journalist Jim Lehrer, and showed off his singing talent when he collaborated with Andy Samberg on the rap music video "Lazy Sunday." The latter became a viral sensation and ushered in a whole new era of *SNL* video parodies. Parnell appeared in films (*Anchorman 2: The*

*Legend Continues* [2014]) and on television (*30 Rock* [2006–2013], *Suburgatory* [2011–2014], *Grown-ish* [2018–2024]). He is also a notable voice actor, playing core characters on the iconic animated series *Archer* (2009–2023) and *Rick and Morty* (2013–present).

**PEDRAD, Nasim** (FP, 2009–2011; RP, 2011–2014): Born in Tehran, Iran, Pedrad's family moved to the United States when she was two. She grew up in Southern California, where she graduated from UCLA, joined the Groundlings, and performed her one-woman show, *Me, Myself and Iran*, at The Upright Citizens Brigade Theatre. She also had a recurring role as Nurse Suri on *ER* (1994–2009). During her time on *SNL*, Pedrad became best known for her impressions of Arianna Huffington and Barbara Walters. She left the show to become a regular on *Mulaney* (2014), then joined the cast of *New Girl* (2011–2018) for three seasons and later went on to create, write, and star in her own series, *Chad* (2021–2024), where she convincingly played an adolescent boy. She frequently works in film and on TV as an actress and voice actor. Best Impressions: Kim Kardashian, Arianna Huffington.

**PHAROAH, Jay** (FP, 2010–2012; RP, 2012–2015): Virginia-born Pharoah was twenty-two when he joined the cast of *SNL*, where he has done uncanny impressions of Denzel Washington, Will Smith, Kanye West, Jay-Z, and former *SNL* cast members Eddie Murphy and Chris Rock. In season 38, he took over for Fred Armisen as the show's resident President Barack Obama impersonator. He works frequently as a voice actor on such animated TV series as *Bojack Horseman* (2014–2020), *Family Guy* (1999–present), and *American Dad!* (2005–present). He even did a 2021 episode of *Robot Chicken* (2012–present), where he once again voiced Barack Obama. Best Impression: Barack Obama (duh!).

**PISCOPO, Joe** (RP, 1980–1984): Piscopo was one of the surviving cast members from season 6 who emerged, along with Eddie Murphy, as one of the show's breakout performers. His resume includes a long list of celebrity impersonations, ranging from *60 Minutes*' Andy Rooney and Dan Rather, to Ted Koppel, to his all-time favorite, Frank Sinatra. Since *SNL* he has performed in clubs and appeared in commercials and films, most recently in the indie musical *How Sweet It Is* (2013) and in several episodes of *Law & Order: Special Victims Unit* (1999–present). Best Impression: Frank Sinatra.

**POEHLER, Amy** (FP, 2001–2002; RP, 2002–2009): Poehler studied improv at Chicago's Second City and went on to cofound Upright Citizens Brigade. She and the troupe then moved to New York and performed in a self-titled half-hour Comedy Central sketch series (1998–2000) before she joined *SNL*. During her eight seasons on the show, Poehler became a breakout cast member with a repertoire of impressions that ranged from Hillary Clinton to Sharon Osbourne to Dennis Kucinich. She also spent five seasons behind the *Weekend Update* anchor desk as coanchor with Tina Fey (2004–2006) and Seth Meyers (2006–2009). Poehler went on to star in the Peabody Award–winning NBC sitcom *Parks and Recreation* (2009–2015) and co–executive produce/

cohost the reality competition show *Making It* (2018–2021). She was also an executive producer on such successful TV series as *Broad City* (2014–2019), *Difficult People* (2015–2020), and *Russian Doll* (2019–2022), and she directed *Lucy and Desi* (2022), a documentary about *I Love Lucy* and the relationship between the two stars, as well as the features *Wine Country* (2019) and *Moxie* (2021). She also famously provided the voice of Joy in the acclaimed animated films *Inside Out* (2015) and *Inside Out 2* (2024). Poehler and friend/former *SNL* castmate Tina Fey frequently appear in each others' projects and together have cohosted the Golden Globe Awards multiple times, as well as appeared on tour as a comedy duo. Best Impression: Hillary Clinton. Best Characters: Kaitlin, Betty Caruso from "Bronx Beat."

**PRAGER, Emily** (4/11/81): Prior to her one-episode stint on *SNL*, Prager appeared on the soap opera *The Edge of Night* (1956–1984) and was a contributing editor of *National Lampoon*. She is the only cast member to have never actually appeared on the show. She was added for the last show (along with Laurie Metcalf) of season 6 (6.13), but her sketches were cut at the last minute, so although her name is in the opening credits, she never appeared on camera.

**QUAID, Randy** (RP, 1985–1986): Prior to *SNL*, Randy Quaid was an accomplished character actor who had featured roles in several Peter Bogdanovich films (*The Last Picture Show* [1971], *What's Up, Doc?* [1972], and *Paper Moon* [1973]), and received Academy Award and Golden Globe nominations for his role as a sailor in the 1973 comedy *The Last Detail*. His post-*SNL* career has included both films and television, most notably *Brokeback Mountain* (2005) and the television miniseries *Elvis* (2005).

**QUINN, Colin** (FP, 1995–1997; RP, 1997–2000): Prior to *SNL*, the Brooklyn-born stand-up comic performed in clubs and cohosted the MTV game show *Remote Control* (1987–1990) and *Caroline's Comedy Hour* (1989) on the A&E Network. He brought his special brand of observational humor to *Weekend Update* (which he anchored from 1998 to 2000), and then to Broadway, when he starred in his one-man show, *Colin Quinn Long Story Short*, directed by Jerry Seinfeld, which aired as an HBO special in 2011. He has written and starred in seven one-man shows, including *Unconstitutional* (2015) and *Red State Blue State* (2019), both Netflix specials. He continues to act in TV and film, including supporting roles in *Girls* (2012–2017) and *Trainwreck* (2015).

**REDD, Chris** (FP, 2017–2019; RP, 2019–2022): Redd was briefly a rapper, a sketch comedian with the Second City touring company, and an actor who was a regular on Netflix's *Disjointed* (2016–2017) before joining *SNL* in season 43. His celebrity impressions included New York City mayor Eric Adams, Cory Booker, and former U.S. president Barack Obama. Redd won a Primetime Emmy for Outstanding Music and Lyrics for cowriting the song "Barack Come Back" on *SNL*'s November 18, 2017 episode hosted by Chance the Rapper. He was a regular on the half-hour comedy series *Keenan* (2021–2022), recently appeared in the film *Spinning Gold* (2023), and cocreated and starred in the Peacock series *Bust Down* (2022). Best Impressions/Characters: Eric Adams, Steve Urkel.

**RICHARDS, Jeff** (FP, 1995–1997; RP, 1997–2000): Stand-up comic Richards had a short stint as a featured player on *MADtv* (1995–2009) before joining *SNL*. He's best remembered for the character Drunk Girl and his impressions of politicians and talk show hosts like Howard Dean, Rush Limbaugh, Karl Rove, and Bill O'Reilly. After *SNL*, Richards returned to performing in comedy clubs and has appeared on television. He hosts his own podcast series *The Jeff Richards Show* (2020–present).

**RIGGLE, Rob** (FP, 2004–2005): A former lieutenant colonel in the U.S. Marine Corps who served in Liberia, Kosovo, and Afghanistan, Riggle was a correspondent for *The Daily Show* (1996–present) in Iraq and in China for the 2008 Beijing Olympics. On *SNL* he did impressions of Howard Dean, Larry the Cable Guy, and Rick Sanchez. He has appeared in numerous films and TV series, including *The Hangover* (2009), and in a recurring role over multiple seasons of *Modern Family* (2009–2020).

**RISLEY, Ann** (RP, 1980–1981): Risley had small roles in the classic Woody Allen films *Annie Hall* (1977) and *Manhattan* (1980) prior to joining *SNL*. She continued to work in films and television and on the stage, originating the role of Martha in the original Broadway production, and later film of *Come Back to the 5 & Dime Jimmy Dean, Jimmy Dean* (1982). In 1984, she opened the Studio for Actors in Tucson, Arizona, where she taught for more than three decades while continuing to do voice work.

**ROBINSON, Tim** (FP, 2012–2013): Robinson performed at the Second City, iO, and the Just for Laughs comedy festival in Montreal before he became one of three Chicago-trained comedians (along with Aidy Bryant and Cecily Strong) who joined the cast in season 38. He went on to wider acclaim as the cocreator, cowriter, and costar of Comedy Central's *Detroiters* (2017–2018) and the Netflix sketch series *I Think You Should Leave with Tim Robinson* (2019–present).

**ROCK, Chris** (FP, 1990–1991; RP, 1991–1993): Raised in Brooklyn, Rock performed at Catch a Rising Star in New York, which led to bit parts on television and, thanks to Eddie Murphy, a part in *Beverly Hills Cop II* (1987). On *SNL* he is best remembered for the recurring character Nat X, the black militant host of the talk show *The Dark Side*, who insults his guests and is always complaining about "the man." Since leaving *SNL*, Rock has become one of the most successful, cutting-edge stand-up comedians in the world and also often works as an actor, writer, and director. He hosted his own show, *The Chris Rock Show* (1997–2000), on HBO, for which he won one of four Primetime Emmys. He was also the executive producer of *The Hughleys* (1998–2002) and *Everybody Hates Chris* (2005–2009), which he cocreated and is based on his childhood growing up in Bedford-Stuyvesant. He has done six comedy specials, and his most recent, *Selective Outrage* (2023), was broadcast live on Netflix. He has also costarred in numerous films in the last four decades and voiced Marty, the eccentric zebra, in *Madagascar 1, 2,* and *3* (2005, 2008, 2013). Rock took a dramatic turn as the star of the 2020 season of the TV series *Fargo* and directed, wrote, and starred in the features *I Think I Love My Wife* (2007) and *Top Five* (2014). Fun Fact: He recommended Leslie Jones to *SNL* and had to convince the very independent comic into auditioning. Best Character: Nat X.

**ROCKET, Charles** (RP, 1980–1981): Rocket's dropping of the f-bomb in season 6 (6.11) may have contributed to his departure from *SNL*, but it wasn't the end of his career. Rocket had a string of supporting roles in film comedies in the 1980s and the 1990s, including *Earth Girls Are Easy* (1988), *It's Pat* (1994), *Hocus Pocus* (1993), and *Dumb and Dumber* (1994) as well as a small dramatic role in *Dances with Wolves* (1990). On television, he played Bruce Willis's brother on *Moonlighting* (1985–1989) and had featured roles on several series, including *Max Headroom* (1987–1988), *Touched by an Angel* (1994–2003), and *The Home Court* (1995–1996). In 2005, Rocket tragically committed suicide in a field near his home. He was fifty-six years old.

**ROSATO, Tony** (RP, 1981–1982): After appearing on season 3 of *SCTV*, the Naples-born Canadian comedian joined the cast of *SNL* on the last show of season 6 and stayed through season 7. He later returned to Toronto, where he appeared as a street informant on the Canadian police drama *Night Heat* (1985–1989), and continued to do voices for animated series over the next few decades. Rosato died of a heart attack on January 10, 2017, at the age of sixty-one.

**RUDNITSKY, Jon** (FP, 2015–2016): Rudnitsky performed with the Groundlings prior to joining *SNL* in season 41. After leaving the show, he costarred in the film *Home Again* (2017) opposite Reese Witherspoon and had a role in the Netflix comedy *Set It Up* (2018). He was a regular on the musical dramedy series *The Big Leap* (2021–2022) and tours the country as a stand-up comic.

**RUDOLPH, Maya** (FP, 2000–2001; RP, 2001–2007): Rudolph is the daughter of composer/music producer Dick Rudolph and singer Minnie Riperton ("Lovin' You"), who died at the age of thirty-one (ten days before Rudolph's seventh birthday), Rudolph was a member of the Groundlings in Los Angeles before joining the cast of *SNL*. She became one of the most popular performers on the show during her tenure, known for spot-on comic impressions of Beyoncé, Whitney Houston, and Oprah Winfrey and for the character Jodi Deitz on *Bronx Beat*. Although she left the show in 2007, she has returned for numerous guest appearances (playing Vice President Kamala Harris, among others) and has hosted three times. Rudolph starred in the romantic dramedy *Away We Go* (2009); costarred in the ensemble cast of *Bridesmaids* (2011); and has appeared in numerous other films as an actress and voice performer, including the recent *Teenage Mutant Ninja Turtles: Mutant Mayhem* (2023). In 2020 and 2021, Rudolph won back-to-back Emmy Awards as Guest Actress in a Comedy Series for performances on *SNL*. She also won two additional Emmys in those years in the Character Voice Performance category for her work in *Big Mouth* (2017–2025). Currently, Rudolph stars in her own Apple

TV comedy series *Loot* (2021–present), produced by a company she ran with actress Natasha Lyonne, Animal Pictures. The company also produces Lyonne's series *Russian Doll* (2019, 2022) and *Poker Face* (2023–present), as well as the animated series *The Hospital* (2023–present), which both actresses provide voices on.

**SAMBERG, Andy** (FP, 2005–2006; RP, 2006–2012): Samberg's entry into show business was on YouTube, where he posted videos he made with his friends Akiva Schaffer and Jorma Taccone, who are known collectively as the Lonely Island. The trio was hired as writers on *SNL* with Samberg doubling as a cast member. Together they contributed over 100 digital shorts to *SNL*, and their second, "Lazy Sunday" (2005), a hip-hop song featuring Samberg and castmate Chris Parnell singing about trying to see *The Chronicles of Narnia* (2005), was an international viral sensation and ushered *SNL* into a whole near era. The trio went on to win an Emmy for another song in a viral video that aired the following season, "Dick in a Box," performed by Samberg and Justin Timberlake. After leaving *SNL*, Samberg starred as a modern-day hippie with a conservative father-in-law in the British situation comedy *Cuckoo* (2012) and costarred in the long-running comedy series *Brooklyn Nine-Nine* (2013–2021), for which he gained wide acclaim. He continues to work on TV and in movies as an actor and voice actor and was coproducer and star of the sci-fi romantic comedy *Palm Springs* (2020).

**SANDLER, Adam** (FP, 1990–1991; RP, 1991–1995): Prior to joining the cast of *SNL*, Sandler performed in comedy clubs in New York and had a recurring role as Theo Huxtable's friend Smitty on *The Cosby Show* (1984–1992). On Dennis Miller's recommendation, he was hired as a featured player on *SNL*, where he specialized in playing offbeat and juvenile characters and appeared as himself on *Weekend Update* singing original novelty tunes, like "The Chanukah Song." After being fired from the show, he embarked on one of the most successful film careers in *SNL* cast history as an actor/producer, initially starring in a string of successful comedies, including *Happy Gilmore* (1996), *The Waterboy* (1998), *The Wedding Singer* (1998), *Big Daddy* (1999), *Anger Management* (2003), and *50 First Dates* (2004). He then branched into dramatic acting with acclaimed performances in *Punch-Drunk Love* (2002), *The Meyerowitz Stories* (2017), *Uncut Gems* (2019), and *Hustle* (2022) while continuing to do mainstream comedies like *You Don't Mess with the Zohan* (2008), *Grown Ups 1* and *2* (2010, 2013), and *Murder Mystery* (2019). Sandler's films have grossed more than $2 billion worldwide, and in 2023 he was awarded the Kennedy Center's Mark Twain Prize for American Humor. He recently produced the Netflix comedy *You Are So Not Invited to My Bat Mitzvah* (2023), costarring along with his two daughters, Sunny Sandler and Sadie Sandler; his wife, Jackie Sandler; and *SNL* cast member Sarah Sherman. Best Characters: Opera Man, Canteen Boy.

**SANZ, Horatio** (FP, 1998–1999; RP, 1999–2006): Born in Santiago, Chile, Sanz is one of the founding members of The Upright Citizens Brigade and also performed at Second City in Chicago before joining the cast of *SNL*. Sanz made numerous appearances as Elton John and Ozzy Osbourne and played stoner Gobi, cohost of *Jarret's Room*. After leaving *SNL*, he costarred with former castmate Chris Parnell on the Comedy Central series *Big Lake* (2010). Since then, Sanz has done numerous guest spots as both an actor and as the voice of various animated characters. Best Impressions: Elton John, Billy Joel, Ozzy Osbourne. Best Character: Carol.

**SCHNEIDER, Rob** (FP, 1990–1991; RP, 1991–1994): Schneider began his stand-up career in the San Francisco Bay Area and appeared on *HBO's 13th Annual Young Comedians Special*, which led to him being hired as a writer and featured player on *SNL*. His breakout character was Richard Laymer, better known as "The Richmeister." Schneider's post-*SNL* career included an American version of the British TV comedy *Men Behaving Badly* (1996–1997), as well as the title role in such films as *Deuce Bigalow: Male Gigolo* (1999), *The Animal* (2001), and *The Hot Chick* (2002). He also plays small parts in many of his former *SNL* castmate Adam Sandler's comedies, often shouting the catchphrase, "You can do it!" Schneider created and starred in two sitcoms loosely based on his life, *Rob* (2012) and *Real Rob* (2015–2017).

**SHANNON, Molly** (FP, 1995; RP, 1995–2001): Shannon made her television debut with a minor role on the original *Twin Peaks* (1990–1991), which was followed by appearances on sitcoms before beginning her six-and-a-half-year tenure as an *SNL* cast member. She created a series of spirited and off-the-wall characters, including joyologist Helen Madden, Sally O'Malley ("I'm 50!"), *Dog Show* cohost Miss Colleen, *Delicious Dish* cohost Terry Rialto, and, of course, Mary Katherine Gallagher, who she brought to the big screen in *Superstar* (1999). Her other film work includes supporting roles in *Happiness* (1998), *A Night at the Roxbury* (1998), *How the Grinch Stole Christmas* (2000), and *Marie Antoinette* (2006). She's appeared in dozens of half-hour comedies over the years, costarred on *Kath & Kim* (2008–2009) and had a recurring role as Val Bassett, the crazy neighbor on *Will & Grace* (1998–2006). Shannon received an Independent Spirit Award for Best Supporting Actress for the dramedy *Other People* (2017), a film written and directed by former *SNL* co-head writer Chris Kelly loosely based on his life and his relationship with his mother (played by Shannon). Recently, she costarred in season 1 of *The White Lotus* (2021) and on the series *I Love That for You* (2022), cocreated by and starring *SNL* alum Vanessa Bayer. Best Impressions: Monica Lewinsky, Ann Miller. Best Characters: Mary Katherine Gallagher, Sally O'Malley.

**SHERMAN, Sarah** (FP, 2021–2023; RP, 2023–present): Also known under the stage name Sarah Squirm, Sherman's surreal, unique comic style was developed as an opening act for alternative musicians and as a writer on Adult Swim's *The Eric Andre Show* (2012–present). She joined *SNL* in its forty-seventh season and quickly gained a following for her *Weekend Update* "Sarah News" segments, where she appears in front of a small, brightly colored backdrop; relates news stories to her personal life; and intermittently teases coanchor Colin Jost for innuendos about her that he never made. Sherman was a writer on *Jackass Forever* (2022) and has a supporting role as a hip female rabbi in the Adam Sandler comedy *You Are So Not Invited to My Bat Mitzvah*. Best character: Sarah Sherman.

**SHORT, Martin** (RP, 1984–1985): Prior to his season on *SNL*, Canadian-born Short had appeared in two short-lived American sitcoms, *The Associates* (1979–1980) and *I'm a Big Girl Now* (1980–1981) and spent a season on *SCTV* (1981–1983). On *SNL*, he brought along many of his *SCTV* characters, including Jackie Rogers Jr. and Ed Grimley, and did impressions of Katherine Hepburn and Jerry Lewis. Short's impressive post-*SNL* career has spanned television, films, and the stage. He starred in the Broadway musicals *The Goodbye Girl* (1993) and *Little Me* (1999), winning a Tony Award for the latter. On film, he is known for his scene-stealing performances in *Father of the Bride 1* and *2* (1991, 1995), and on television he was nominated for multiple Emmys for his comedy/variety series *Primetime Glick* (2001–2003), as Guest Actor in a Drama for *The Morning Show* (2019–present), and as Lead Actor in a Comedy Series for *Only Murders in the Building* (2021–present), among others. Over the years, Short has made multiple guest appearances on TV, animated series, and talk shows and recently did a comedy tour with his *Only Murders in the Building* costar and frequent *SNL* host Steve Martin.

**SILVERMAN, Sarah** (FP, 1993–1994): As a comedian and writer, Silverman proved to be too much of an iconoclast for the male-dominated world of *SNL*, a situation she later parodied on *The Larry Sanders Show* (1992–1998). She had her own series, *The Sarah Silverman Program* (2007–2010), which ran on Comedy Central for three seasons, and later hosted the late-night Hulu talk show *I Love You, America with Sarah Silverman* (2017–2018). Silverman won a Creative Arts Emmy for writing the song "I'm Fucking Matt Damon," the video of which debuted on *Jimmy Kimmel Live* (2003–present) during the time she and Kimmel were dating. In 2020, she launched *The Sarah Silverman Podcast*, where she discusses social issues, and her most recent one-hour comedy special, *Someone You Love* (2023), became the first stand-up special to debut on the streaming service Max and won a Writers Guild of America Award for Outstanding Comedy/Variety Special.

**SLATE, Jenny** (FP, 2009–2010): Prior to *SNL*, Slate appeared on *Late Night with Jimmy Fallon* (2009–2014) and had a recurring role on the HBO series *Bored to Death* (2009–2011). On *SNL* she impersonated Ashley Olsen, Kristen Stewart, and *Today* show host Hoda Kotb opposite Kristen Wiig's Kathie Lee Gifford. Post-*SNL*, Slate made guest appearances on several TV series, but her breakout role was as the star of the indie dramedy *Obvious Child* (2014). This led to supporting roles in numerous films, including *Everything, Everywhere All at Once* (2022). Slate cowrote and provided the voice for the stop-motion animated short *Marcel the Shell with Shoes On* (2010), which was adapted into a children's book in 2011. In 2021, Slate produced, cowrote, and once again voiced the title character in a full-length film of the same name that went on to receive an Academy Award nomination as Best Animated Feature.

**SMIGEL, Robert** (FP, 1991–1993): For over twenty seasons, the talented Robert Smigel wrote for *SNL*. During part of that time he appeared as a featured player and contributed animated shorts under the segment title "Saturday TV Funhouse." Smigel's numerous credits include *Late Night with Conan O'Brien* (1993–2009), for which he created Triumph, the Insult Comic Dog; the short-lived *The Dana Carvey Show* (1996)), where he first launched his cartoon *The Ambiguously Gay Duo*, an *SNL* hit a few months later and over the years; and cowriter of the feature films *You Don't Mess with the Zohan* and *Hotel Transylvania 1* and *2* (2012, 2015).

**SPADE, David** (FP, 1990–1993; RP, 1993–1996): Spade performed on *HBO's 13th Annual Young Comedians Show* hosted by Dennis Miller, who recommended him to Lorne Michaels. On *SNL*, Spade specialized in playing snide characters, like the airline attendant on Bastard Airlines and the dismissive receptionist at Dick Clark Productions. Spade costarred in two comedies with his friend and former *SNL* castmate Chris Farley (*Tommy Boy* [1995] and *Black Sheep* [1996]). He also appeared with former castmates Adam Sandler, Chris Rock, and Rob Schneider in the hit comedies *Grown Ups 1* and *2* (2010, 2013); starred in two long-running sitcoms, *Just Shoot Me!* (1997–2003) and *Rules of Engagement* (2007–2013); and hosted *The Showbiz Show with David Spade* (2005–2007) for three seasons on Comedy Central. Currently, Spade and Dana Carvey cohost the *Fly on the Wall* podcast, which takes viewers behind the scenes at *SNL* and shares reminiscences with others who appeared on the series. He also continues to make appearances in episodic TV. Best Catchphrases: "And you are?" "Buh-bye."

**STEPHENSON, Pamela** (RP, 1984–1985): Prior to her season on *SNL*, New Zealand–born Pamela Stephenson appeared on the British sketch comedy show *Not the Nine O'Clock News* (1979–1982). On *SNL* she did impersonations of Madonna, Billy Idol, Joan Collins, and Cyndi Lauper. She later became a clinical psychologist specializing in human sexuality. She has authored a number of books, including a biography of her husband, comedian Billy Connolly; an autobiography; and several on mental health and sex.

**STILLER, Ben** (FP, 3/25/1989–4/22/1989): The son of husband-and-wife comedy team Stiller and Meara, Ben has had a successful career as an actor, writer, and director. His short film *The Hustler of Money*, in which he impersonated Tom Cruise, aired on *SNL* in 1987 (12.15). He joined the show as a featured player, but remained for only four episodes during season 14. He later had his own sketch comedy show, *The Ben Stiller Show* (1992–1993), that lasted only one season on FOX, but won a Primetime Emmy that season for writing. His directing credits include *Reality Bites* (1994), *Zoolander 1* and *2* (2001, 2016), *Tropic Thunder* (2008), and a remake of *The Secret Life of Walter Mitty* (2013). On TV, he won a Directors Guild of America Award for the miniseries *Escape at Dannemora* (2018) and is director and executive producer on the Apple TV series *Severance* (2022–present). Stiller has hosted *SNL* twice and over the years has popped up in several short films and guest spots, most recently in recurring appearances in 2018–2019 as Donald Trump's former attorney Michael Cohen.

**STRONG, Cecily** (FP, 2012–2013; RP, 2013–2022): The actress and comedian is a graduate of the California Institute of the Arts and studied and performed improv at Second City and iO Chicago. Her breakout character on *SNL* was the aptly named "The Girl You Wish You Hadn't Started a Conversation with at a Party." She also became known for impressions of former Fox News host Jeanine Pirro and Melania Trump, as well as a brief stint cohosting *Weekend Update*, and received two Emmy nominations as Best Supporting Actress for the 2019–2020 and 2020–2021 seasons. Her eleven years on the show make her the longest-running female cast member, along with Kate McKinnon. Strong also costarred in and produced the Apple TV musical parody series *Schmigadoon!* (2021–2023) and starred in an off-Broadway revival of Jane Wagner's one-woman play *The Search for Signs of Intelligent Life in the Universe* (2022). Best Characters: Cathy Anne, the Girl You Wish You Hadn't Started a Conversation with at a Party. Best Impression: Jeanine Pirro.

**SUDEIKIS, Jason** (FP, 2004–2006; RP, 2006–2013): Sudeikis's improv background includes the ImprovOlympic, the Second City's National Touring Company, and The Upright Citizens Brigade Theatre. He was initially hired on *SNL* in 2003 as a writer and made occasional on-screen appearances until he was hired as a featured player in 2005 and then promoted to repertory cast member the following year. His long list of characters and impersonations includes the Devil, Dane Cook, Joe Biden, Mitt Romney, and Wolf Blitzer. During that time, Sudeikis's acting credits included recurring roles on *30 Rock* (2006–2013) and *Eastbound & Down* (2009–2013), and in the feature films *A Good Old Fashioned Orgy* (2011), *Horrible Bosses* (2011), and *We're the Millers* (2013). He was also the voice of Holt Richter and Terry Kimple on the animated series *The Cleveland Show* (2009–2013). Sudeikis has since become well known as the cocreator, cowriter, and star of the Apple TV comedy series *Ted Lasso* (2020–2023), a character he first played in promotional videos for NBC Sports beginning in 2013. For his work on the series, he won four Emmys, two for Outstanding Lead Actor in a Comedy Series and two for Outstanding Comedy Series. Best Character: the Devil. Best Impression: Joe Biden.

**SWEENEY, Julia** (FP, 1990–1991; RP, 1991–1994): Comedian, actor, and author Julia Sweeney was cast on *SNL* while appearing at the Groundlings in Los Angeles, where she first performed her most famous character, the androgynous Pat. She wrote and starred in the feature film *It's Pat* (1994) and had supporting roles in *Pulp Fiction* (1994), *Stuart Little* (1999), and *Clockstoppers* (2002). For the stage, she has, from 1995 to the present, written and performed four critically acclaimed, autobiographical monologues—*God Said Ha!*, *In the Family Way*, *Letting Go of God* and *Julia Sweeney: Older and Wider*. She has also had featured roles in the comedy series *Work in Progress* (2019–2021), *Shrill* (2019–2021), and *American Gods* (2021). Best Character: Pat.

**SWEENEY, Terry** (RP, 1985–1986): Sweeney's first association with *SNL* was as a writer in season 6, though he returned as a performer in season 11. He is the first openly gay cast member in *SNL* history and is best remembered on the show for his impersonation of Nancy Reagan (though he also donned drag as Diana Ross, Patti LaBelle, and Joan Collins). After *SNL*, he was a writer on *MADtv* (1995–2009) and the adult CGI science-fiction series *Tripping the Rift* (2004–2007). He also acted on-screen in the limited TV series *The Assassination of Gianni Versace: American Crime Story* (2018) and *The Politician* (2019).

**THOMPSON, Kenan** (FP, 2003–2005; RP, 2005–present): Thompson is the longest-running *SNL* cast member at twenty-plus seasons and counting. His television career began in 1994 when he was on Nickelodeon's sketch-variety show *All That* (1994–2005), which led to a starring role on the Nick sitcom *Kenan & Kel* (1996–2000). On *SNL* he's best known as Diondre Cole, host of the BET talk show *What Up with That?*, along with impersonations of a long list of African American men and women, including Steve Harvey, Reverend Al Sharpton, Bill Cosby, Charles Barkley, CeeLo Green, Aretha Franklin, and Whoopi Goldberg. He has made numerous appearances as an actor in film and TV over the years, as well as a voice actor on many animated series. He starred in his own network sitcom, *Kenan* (2021–2022), for which he received an Emmy nomination as Outstanding Lead Actor in a Comedy Series. Thompson was also Emmy-nominated four other times for his work on *SNL*, three as Outstanding Supporting Actor in a Comedy Series and one win for cowriting the song "Come Back, Barack" for a 2017 episode hosted by Chance the Rapper.

**TROAST, Chloe** (FP, 2023–present): Troast, who did improv, stand-up, and sketch comedy in New York City, was season 49's only new cast member. A graduate of New York University, she is a frequent collaborator with the comedy trio Do Not Destroy and appears in their feature film, *Please Don't Destroy: The Treasure of Foggy Mountain* (2023). She gained attention on *SNL*'s season 49 for doing an uncanny impression of Mama Cass Elliot singing her signature song "Make Your Own Kind of Music" in a sketch of the same title opposite guest host Emma Stone (49.6).

**VANCE, Danitra** (RP, 1985–1986): Vance was the first African American woman to be a regular on *SNL*, appearing as Latoya Marie in *That Black Girl*, a parody of *That Girl* (1966–1971) and as Cabrini Green Jackson, a teenage mother. Vance's New York stage credits include her Obie Award–winning performance in *Spunk* and George C. Wolfe's *The Colored Museum*, a satire on racial stereotyping, which was broadcast on PBS's *Great Performances* in 1991. Vance died of breast cancer in 1994 at the age of forty.

**VILLASEÑOR, Melissa** (FP, 2016–2018; RP, 2018–2022): Villaseñor was a stand-up comic and impressionist who was a semifinalist on *America's Got Talent*

(2006–present) and featured in the New Faces Just for Laughs Comedy Festival prior to joining *SNL* in 2016. She is the second Latina cast member and the first to achieve repertory status. Her first impression on the show was of fellow comedian Sarah Silverman, and over the years she was known for being able to deftly impersonate people as varied as Gwen Stefani, Alexandria Ocasio-Cortez, Owen Wilson, and Rachel Maddow. Villaseñor voices characters on numerous animated series and films, including Disney Channel's *Primos* (2023).

**VITALE, Dan** (FP, 1985–1986): As a featured player in the mid-1980s, Vitale appeared in only three episodes, usually as a guard, police officer, or firefighter. He appeared on *Grace Under Fire* (1993–1998) and *Tough Crowd with Colin Quinn* (2002–2004), and wrote and starred in a one-man show, *Live from Rehab, It's Dan Vitale*. Vitale died in May 2022 at the age of sixty-six.

**WALKER, Devon** (FP, 2022–present): Walker joined *SNL* as a featured player after working as a stand-up comic in Austin and doing his act on Comedy Central, as well as creating and appearing in various digital shorts for the network. He was also a writer for Freeform's comedy series *Everybody's Trash* (2022), as well as for the 2022 season of *Big Mouth* (2017–present).

**WALLS, Nancy** (FP, 1995–1996): Walls, who now goes by "Nancy Carell," met her future husband, actor Steve Carell, when they were both performing in Second City in Chicago. During her season on *SNL* she specialized in impersonations of journalists (Bobbie Battista, Cokie Roberts, Diane Sawyer, Judy Woodruff). She had a recurring role on *The Office* (2005–2013), playing Carol Stills, Michael Scott's onetime love interest, and has a small role in the film *Bridesmaids* (2011). She and her husband cocreated the cult TBS comedy series *Angie Tribeca* (2016–2018), which had a four-season run.

**WATKINS, Michaela** (FP, 2008–2009): After graduating from Boston University, Watkins was active in theater in Portland, Oregon, and Los Angeles. During her season on *SNL*, she impersonated *Today Show* host Hoda Kotb, Barbara Walters, Arianna Huffington, and Julia Louis-Dreyfus. She also had recurring roles on *The New Adventures of the Old Christine* (2006–2010), *New Girl* (2011–2018), and *Enlightened* (2011–2013) but is best known as one of the stars of the Hulu comedy series *Casual* (2015–2018). Watkins is also a prolific voice actor who has worked on such shows as *American Dad!* (2006–2023) and *Big Mouth* (2017–2025), as well as in numerous films, most recently *You Hurt My Feelings* (2023).

**WAYANS, Damon** (FP, 1985–1986): A member of the famed Wayans family, Damon started his career as a stand-up comedian. His time on *SNL* was cut short when he was fired for improvising during a sketch. Wayans would later team up with his brother Keenen Ivory Wayans to create a groundbreaking sketch comedy show with a mostly black cast that originally ran on Fox TV, *In Living Color* (1990–1994). Wayans later cocreated and starred in his own sitcom, *My Wife & Kids* (2001–2005) and costarred in the one-hour action-comedy-drama series *Lethal Weapon* (2016–2019).

**WEATHERS, Patrick** (FP, 1980–1981): Weathers was a featured player during *SNL*'s rocky sixth season. His career since then has been long and varied. A former bathroom attendant at Studio 54, he wrote for *National Lampoon*, played Elvis on Broadway in *Rock and Roll: The First 5000 Years*, and toured the country performing his own music, releasing three albums in the process.

**WELLS, Noël** (FP, 2013–2014): Wells was a member of The Upright Citizens Brigade sketch team New Money and a popular YouTube comedy performer prior to her brief stay on *SNL*. She has since gone on to costar with Aziz Ansari in his comedy series *Master of None* (2015, 2017, 2021) and is one of the lead voice actors on the animated series *Star Trek: Lower Decks* (2020–2024).

**WHEELAN, Brooks** (FP, 2013–2014): Iowa-born and raised, Wheelan was a stand-up comic in LA and worked as a biomedical engineer before joining *SNL*. He was originally hired as a writer but a week before the season began was made a featured player who periodically appeared on *Weekend Update* doing commentary on himself and his life. He now works in stand-up and as an actor and voice actor and hosts the podcast *Entry Level with Brooks Wheelan* (2017–present).

**WIIG, Kristen** (FP, 2005–2006; RP, 2006–2012): One of *SNL*'s post-9/11 breakout stars, Wiig was a Groundling in Los Angeles and appeared as Dr. Pat, the quack marriage counselor in season 1 of Spike TV's faux reality show, *The Joe Schmo Show* (2003), prior to joining *SNL*. During her seven-season run, she received four Primetime Emmy nominations for Outstanding Supporting Actress in a Comedy Series (2009, 2010, 2011, 2012). Wiig also branched into feature films, earning an Academy Award nomination for Best Original Screenplay (with cowriter Annie Mumolo) for the 2011 hit comedy *Bridesmaids*, in which she also starred. Wiig has gone on to have an eclectic career in movies of many different genres, with leading roles in *The Secret Life of Walter Mitty* (2013), *The Skeleton Twins* (2013), *Ghostbusters* (2016), *Downsizing* (2017), *Wonder Woman 1984* (2020), and *Barb and Star Go to Vista Del Mar* (2021), the latter of which she cowrote and starred in with Mumolo. She has been a voice actor, most recently on *Big Mouth* (2017–2025), and costarred opposite former *SNL* cast member Will Forte on the Peacock series *MacGruber* (2021), which began as an *SNL* parody sketch and later became a 2011 feature film. She starred in the Apple TV series *Palm Royale* (2024) opposite one of her comedy idols, Carol Burnett. Best Impressions: Kathie Lee Gifford, Elisabeth Hasselbeck, Nancy Pelosi, Liza Minnelli. Best Characters: Dooneese, Gilly, Aunt Linda, the Target Lady, Penelope.

**WILSON, Casey** (FP, 2007–2009): Wilson is an alumna of New York University and The Uprights Citizens Brigade Theatre in New York and Los Angeles, where she performed with her comedy partner June Diane Raphael, with whom she cowrote the 2009 comedy *Bride Wars* and *Ass Backwards* (2013), in which they both also starred; and several television pilots. Wilson spent two seasons as an *SNL* featured player but became better known after leaving the show as star of the ABC comedy *Happy Endings* (2011–present) and, more recently, costar of the miniseries *The Shrink Next Door* (2021). Currently, she appears on HBO's *The Righteous Gemstones* (2019–2023) and voices characters on various animated shows.

**WOLF, Fred** (FP, 1995–1996): Wolf joined the *SNL* writing staff in 1992, became co–head writer from 1994 to 1996, and was a featured player in the 1995–1996 season. He went on to collaborate with *SNL* alums as a cowriter on several comedies, including Black Sheep (1996), *Dirty Work* (1998), *Joe Dirt 1* and 2 (2001, 2015), *Dickie Roberts: Child Star* (2003), and *Grown Ups 1* and *2* (2010, 2013). He also directed the comedy films *The House Bunny* (2008), *Drunk Parents* (2019), and *40-Love* (2021).

**YANG, BOWEN** (FP, 2019–2021; RP, 2021–present): Yang performed improv at The Upright Citizens Brigade (after graduating from NYU with a degree in chemistry) and cohosted the popular podcast *Las Culturistas* (2016–present) before joining *SNL* as a writer in 2018. The following season he was promoted to on-air featured player, where he remained for two years before joining the repertory cast. Yang became the first-ever *SNL* featured player to receive a Primetime Emmy Award nomination for Outstanding Supporting Actor in a Comedy Series in 2021, largely for his breakout performance on *Weekend Update* as the Iceberg That Sank the *Titanic*. He has since gone on to do memorable impressions of Kim Jong-un and Andrew Yang and oddball characters, like Chinese trade representative Chen "Trade Daddy" Biao, as well as one-half of a trend-forecaster team (along with Aidy Bryant). Yang is the first Chinese American and third openly gay male *SNL* cast member. He is a regular on the comedy series *Awkwafina Is Nora from Queens* (2020–2023) and costarred in the LGBTQ romantic comedy films *Bros* (2022) and *Fire Island* (2022). He also can be seen in the big screen musical *Wicked* (2024).

**ZAMATA, Sasheer** (FP, 1/18/2014–2015; RP, 2015–2017): Zamata was a sketch performer at The Upright Citizens Brigade for "CollegeHumor" and was a popular YouTube impressionist before joining *SNL* in 2014. She played a variety of celebrities and characters on the show but has since become better known as a series regular on the comedy series *Woke* (2020–2022) and *Home Economics* (2020–2023), and for the five-part Showtime drama *Waco: The Reckoning* (2023). She is also a celebrity ambassador for the ACLU, working with its Women's Rights Project to break down socioeconomic and educational gender biases, especially among women of color.

# "No Comedy Experience Required"

## Hosting *SNL*

WANTED: Actor, singer, comedian, athlete, politician, or celebrity for a temporary hosting gig for a long-running late-night network sketch comedy–variety television show. Must be available for six consecutive days (Monday–Saturday) and willing to work long hours. No comedy experience required. Sense of humor and ability to read cue cards are a plus. Compensation: $5,000 plus an opportunity to plug your current television series and/or recently released film, book, or CD. No phone calls, please.

No such ad exists. The opportunity to host *Saturday Night Live* is by invitation only—like an exclusive club you have to be asked to join. Once you gain entrance, it poses a series of challenges, particularly if you've never worked in television, performed in front of a live audience, or appeared in front of millions of people as yourself.

Still, today's hosts have it much easier than the talented people who hosted season 1 of *NBC's Saturday Night* back in 1975–1976. There were no reruns on cable, episodes on VHS and DVD, or video clips on nbc.com for a future host to watch and study. The show was still a work in progress, and the first hosts were flying blind, which explains why producer Lorne Michaels chose mostly seasoned performers like George Carlin, Rob Reiner, Robert Klein, Lily Tomlin, Richard Pryor, and Elliott Gould to host the first half of the season.

So what makes a good *Saturday Night Live* host? Personality and talent are certainly two important factors. Based on the past 49 seasons, a general set of criteria has emerged that distinguishes a "great host" from a "good host" from one who is "just okay" to one who turned out to be a "bad idea":

*Be comfortable performing on live television.* If you have a theatrical background, play professional sports in front of millions of fans, or sing in a 15,000-seat arena, you are probably better prepared to host *SNL* than a trained film or television actor with little or no experience working in front of an audience (and used to doing multiple takes of a scene). Hosting a live television show may prove challenging for an athlete because trying to make people laugh is not part of his or her professional training. Through no fault of their own, some athletes, like Olympic figure skater Nancy Kerrigan (19.15), swimmer Michael Phelps (34.1), and cyclist Lance Armstrong (31.4), simply lack acting talent. But that doesn't mean nobody will be watching. Kerrigan's appearance posted the highest overnight ratings in six seasons. When Phelps, the most decorated Olympian of all time, hosted the season 34 opener, it was the most watched *SNL* episode since former Vice President Al Gore hosted in 2002 (28.8).

In May 2012, Lorne Michaels told *Entertainment Weekly* that athletes make good hosts because they are "used to being in front of large groups of people and not knowing how it's going to turn out." He was defending his recent choice of New York Giants quarterback Eli Manning to host the show (37.20): "I think he's both charming and radiates a certain kind of intelligence," Michaels explained. "You sort of believe that he doesn't take himself too seriously." The same can be said about his older brother, Peyton, a quarterback for the Denver Broncos, who hosted in 2007 (32.16). Athletes who have also shined as *SNL* hosts (and, in some instances, generated laughs even when they weren't trying) include Joe Montana (12.9), Michael Jordan (17.1), Tom Brady (30.17), and three-time host Charles Barkley (19.1, 35.11, 37.11, 43.14).

*Be a team player who trusts the show's writers and producers.* In an interview that appeared in the February 1993 issue of *Spin* magazine, guest edited by the folks at *Saturday Night Live*, Lorne Michaels told Bob Guccione Jr. that the worst hosts are "people who are obsessed with control and don't want to give it over to us. They're not used to being part of a team." It would take them awhile, usually after the dress rehearsal, until they understood that "we know what we're doing. We made this up. This is our business, this is what we do. You would think people understand that coming here."

Michaels is too much of a gentleman to "name names," but over the years he and others affiliated with the show have revealed there have been uncooperative hosts in the past, including one who broke the cardinal rule of "no ad-libbing."

- "Mr. Television" himself, **Milton Berle** (4.17), seemed like a good choice for hosting a live comedy-variety show. But one of the comedy pioneers of television's Golden Age was prone to ad-libbing and upstaging other actors, and his material—jokes about Arabs, Puerto Ricans, Dolly Parton's breasts, and his sex life—were better suited for the Friars Club. Michaels told *Spin* magazine it was "incredibly aggravating" because anytime he'd say to Berle, "We don't do that here," the seventy-year-old comedian would dismissively reply, "Yeah—satire."
- In May 2003, a few months after winning an Academy Award as Best Actor for his role in *The Pianist* (2002), **Adrien Brody** hosted *SNL* (28.19). In an uncharacteristically candid 2006 interview with Howard Stern, Tina Fey said Brody was one of those hosts who came in with ideas for sketches that weren't too great—and he wasn't happy when they didn't use any of them.

That may explain why when Brody appeared on camera to do a ten-second introduction of musical guest Sean Paul, a Jamaican reggae artist, he was sprouting dreadlocks and talking incoherently in a Jamaican accent for about forty seconds, thereby breaking the "no ad-lib" rule. The rumor circulated around the web that he had been banned by Michaels from appearing on *SNL* (he hasn't been on since), but when Brody was questioned about it by Eric Larnick at the *Huffington Post*, he said he had heard about the rumor and added that Lorne said nothing about it to him backstage.

*Have a sense of humor—especially about yourself.* You don't necessarily have to be a good joke teller or have comic timing, but it certainly helps if you can put your ego aside and allow the writers to poke fun at your public image, personal life, and/or past and present film and television roles. Here are some examples:

- Sixteen years after the role of Norman Bates in Alfred Hitchcock's *Psycho* (1960) made him a star, **Anthony Perkins** appeared in a commercial parody for "The Norman Bates School of Motel Management" (1.16).
- **Susan Dey** returned to her first television role as Laurie Partridge in a hilarious parody in which the Brady Bunch kids challenge the Partridge Family in a "battle of the bands" (17.12).
- In an "*SNL* Digital Short," NBC news anchor **Brian Williams** reveals his true egotistical and narcissistic self when he lets a camera crew follow him around for the day (33.4).
- **Daniel Radcliffe** appeared in a sketch as Harry Potter, who ten years after graduation is still hanging around Hogwarts Academy (37.12).
- The same rule applies for musical guests. The group **Hanson** performed their number one hit "MMMBop" on *SNL* (23.9). Later in the episode, the song's excessive airplay in 1997 is the focus of a sketch in which Hanson is taken hostage in an elevator by a pair of terrorists (Helen Hunt and Will Ferrell) who force the three brothers to listen to "MMMBop" over and over. Zac and Isaac Hanson start to go crazy, but lead singer Taylor is unaffected. When Ferrell starts to enjoy it, Hunt has no choice but to put him out of his misery. Apparently Hanson has retained their sense of humor. In 2005, a high school in Pennsylvania raised money for Hurricane Katrina victims through its "Stop the Bop." The song "MMMBop" was played over the loudspeakers at school until they met their fundraising goal. Hanson not only matched their goal but gave a copy of their new album, *Underneath*, to every student.

Some hosts, particularly those who are no stranger to tabloid headlines, are even willing to make fun of their own bad behavior.

- Bad boy **Sean Penn** spent some time in the hoosegow for assaulting a photographer in 1987. In that same year, he hosted *SNL* and appeared on *Church Chat* (13.2). The Church Lady (Dana Carvey) provokes him by trying to take his picture, and they discuss his marriage to Madonna ("So, she's named after the mother of our Lord"). The interview ends with Penn punching the

Church Lady in the nose and strangling the other guest, an Iranian diplomat (Jon Lovitz) who offers to buy Madonna. The Church Lady hits Penn over the head with a vase and jumps on his back.

- **Rob Lowe** first hosted the show (15.15) two years after a sex tape scandal tarnished his image. When he walks out onstage, the audience is quiet and a nervous Lowe says he's glad to be there. Members of the audience start shouting, "You've got a lot of nerve!" and "I've got a daughter!" Lowe later sits down with the Church Lady, who paddles his behind ("Get out of his buttocks, Satan! Leave his buttocks!") as punishment for his sins.

## A Week in the Life of an *SNL* Host

### Monday
On Monday, the research department provides everyone with a bio of the week's host. Writers assemble in Lorne Michaels's office along with the host to pitch sketch ideas for the upcoming week.

### Tuesday
The writers work all day and night writing sketches for the next day's read-through. Meanwhile, the host shoots a series of promos with one or two members of the cast that will be posted on nbc.com and air on the network.

### Wednesday
The cast, writers, crew, and host pile into a conference room for a three-and-a-half-hour session and read aloud thirty-five to forty sketches. Lorne Michaels plays the role of the narrator. After the read-through, the host gives his or her input on the sketches to Michaels, the head writers, and the producing team. The number of sketches is narrowed down to around eleven. After the meeting, the cast and writers go into Lorne's office to look at the corkboard on his wall and see what sketches have been chosen.

### Thursday
The selected sketches are rewritten (and rewritten) to produce a final draft of the sketch. Meanwhile, rehearsals begin for the nonsketch parts of the show, and the sets and costumes for the week's sketches are designed and assembled.

### Friday
The rewriting of sketches continues, and the process of blocking the sketches for the camera begins.

### Saturday
The dress rehearsal begins at 8:00 p.m. (ET) in front of a studio audience. Before the dress rehearsal, performers who submitted pieces to *Weekend Update* are told which pieces will be rehearsed. After the dress rehearsal, sketches that didn't work are cut from the final show. A new audience arrives for the show that airs from 11:30 p.m. to 1:00 a.m., followed by the after-party.

- In December 2001, **Winona Ryder** was arrested for shoplifting in Beverly Hills. Once her legal problems were settled, she accepted an offer to host *SNL* (27.20). During her monologue, she learns that in anticipation of her hosting the show, they recently installed security cameras around the studio. We also see footage from the previous night in which she thanks Lorne Michaels for inviting her to host, after which he checks his pockets to make sure she didn't pick them.
- Due to her run-ins with the law and the stories of her alcohol and substance abuse, **Lindsay Lohan**'s monologue (37.16) is interrupted by members of the cast who check to make sure she's clean and sober, while Jon Hamm sits in the audience as the "backup host."

## *SNL*'s Most Popular Hosts: The Five-Timers Club

On December 8, 1990, Tom Hanks hosted *SNL* for the fifth time (16.8). During his monologue, he shows the audience his new membership card to "one of the most exclusive clubs in the world"—the Five-Timers Club. He's greeted by Sean the Doorman (played by Conan O'Brien, at the time an *SNL* staff writer), and inside he meets some of the other five-timers—Paul Simon, Steve Martin, and Elliott Gould. Since then it's become a running joke that when someone hosts for the fifth time, they're admitted to the club, where we see former cast members Dan Aykroyd, Jon Lovitz, and Martin Short, tending bar and waiting tables.

On November 11, 2006, Alec Baldwin (32.5) is invited by Steve Martin into the even more exclusive Platinum Lounge, whose membership is reserved for twelve-time hosts like himself and John Goodman.

Although it's all a big joke, there is something to be said for the relatively small number of hosts (twenty-six) who have qualified for membership to the Five-Timers Club as of the forty-ninth season. There are many people who have hosted the show two or three times, but it definitely says something about these hosts, most of whom still occasionally return to host the show.

### Ben Affleck (Five-time host, member since 38.21)

The two-time Oscar winner has had more success in dramatic films (*Good Will Hunting* [1997], *Armageddon* [1998], and *The Town* [2010]) than comedies (*Jersey Girl* [2004], *Gigli* [2003]). Over the course of his career, *SNL* has served as a creative outlet for comedy. He's fallen in love with Mango (Chris Kattan) (25.13); impersonated James Carville (30.1), Alec Baldwin (34.7), and Keith Olbermann (34.7); and had a recurring role as Donnie Bartolotti, best friend of Boston teens Pat "Sully" Sullivan (Jimmy Fallon) and Denise "Zazu" McDonough (Rachel Dratch). In his final appearance, Donnie invites Sully and Denise to his wedding, which turns out to be a commitment ceremony

268  The *SNL* Companion

between Donnie and "Smitty" (Seth Meyers) (29.15). Affleck also has a sense of humor about himself, poking fun at his nickname with former girlfriend Jennifer Lopez ("Bennifer"), explaining what he meant by his remark "marriage is work" in his 2013 Oscar speech (with some help from wife Jennifer Garner), and appearing in parodies of his bomb movie with Lopez, *Gigli* (29.15), and Oscar-winner *Argo* (2012) (38.21).

### Alec Baldwin (Seventeen-time host, member since 20.8)

In his first *SNL* monologue (15.18), Alec Baldwin tells the audience he's going to use his movie-star looks to charm the audience and win them over. As a recurring *SNL* host for sixteen years, he's proven time and time again he doesn't need to rely on his handsome face to win anyone over. Baldwin's feature film career has been a mixed bag, though he's made a greater impression with audiences and critics in dramatic roles in films like *Glengarry Glen Ross* (1994), *The Cooler* (2003), *The Aviator* (2004), and *The Departed* (2006). That's one reason his work on both *SNL* and its sister show, *30 Rock* (2006–2013), for which he won two Emmys, took everyone by surprise. Another thing—there's something entertaining about a handsome guy who does comedy (Jon Hamm will no doubt be joining the Five-Timers Club sometime soon). *Baldwin's best moments*: As Scoutmaster Armstrong seducing Canteen Boy (Adam Sandler) (19.13), Pete Schweddy promoting his "balls" on *The Delicious Dish* (24.9), and imitating Charles Nelson Reilly on *Inside the Actors Studio* (26.16), and Tony Bennett interviewing the real Tony Bennett on *The Tony Bennett Show* (32.5).

Baldwin was impersonated by Ben Affleck in a parody of *The View* (34.7). *Baldwin on hosting SNL*: "Most people who come on [*SNL*] and do a good show, you become a member of a company and make an ass of yourself, just like they do," explained Baldwin in an interview with examiner.com. "That's what comedy is: to make a fool of yourself."

### Drew Barrymore (Six-time host, member since 32.12)

Barrymore still holds the record as *SNL*'s youngest host. She was seven and a half years old when she made her first appearance on *SNL* in November 1982, the year *E.T.: The Extra-Terrestrial* was released in theaters. In one sketch, she reprises her role of Gertie, who kills E.T., only to discover he's the son of Mr. T. (Eddie Murphy). Her second hosting gig was seventeen years later. Being funny seems to come naturally to Barrymore, who doesn't take herself too seriously and always seems like she is having fun when hosting the show. Over the years she's impersonated Cher at the Academy Awards Pre-Show (24.16), Calista Flockhart on *Jeopardy!* (24.16), and Courtney Love (29.12). Barrymore has been impersonated on *SNL* by Jan Hooks (16.15), Kate Hudson (26.2), Rachel Dratch (26.5), Katie Holmes (26.13), and Kristen Wiig (31.12, 37.9, 37.18).

### Candice Bergen (Five-time host, member since 15.20)

The daughter of ventriloquist Edgar Bergen, she was a former model who up to that point appeared mostly in dramatic films, such as *The Sand Pebbles* (1966), *Soldier Blue* (1970), *T. R. Baskin* (1971), and *The Wind and the Lion* (1975). Her hosting gigs in season 1 (1.4, 1.8) gave her the chance to show America she's a talented comedian, which led to her being cast as Burt Reynolds's ex-wife in the romantic comedy *Starting Over* (1979) and the title role on the long-running sitcom *Murphy Brown* (1988–1998), for which she won five Emmys. *Bergen's best moments*: A PSA for "Right to Extreme Stupidity League," in which she screws up royally by accidentally calling Gilda Radner's character the wrong name (2.10); and a Thanksgiving sketch in which she plays Priscilla Biddle Barrows, the original Mayflower Madam (13.5).

### Chevy Chase (Eight-time host, member since 12.6)

Although Chase departed *SNL* in the fall of season 2 to move to Los Angeles and pursue a film career, it seemed like he never left. In addition to numerous cameo appearances, he's hosted the show eight times. His most unusual appearance was when he was forced to host the show from Burbank, California, via a monitor because he didn't make it back to New York in time (8.1).

### Danny DeVito (Six-time host, member since 18.10)

DeVito's first appearance on the show was not when he hosted for the first time in May 1982 (7.19). In December 1980 (6.4), he appeared in a short film, *Hot Dogs for Gauguin*, directed by Martin Brest when he was a film student at New York University. Two years later, DeVito hosted *SNL* (7.19) while he was starring as Louie De Palma on the situation comedy *Taxi* (1978–1983). In 1983, he cohosted with his wife, Rhea Perlman (9.2). *DeVito's best moments*: DeVito, as De Palma, blows up ABC's headquarters (7.19) when the network cancels *Taxi* (NBC picked up the show for its final season); DeVito's guest appearance on *Church Chat*

(13.6) to promote his new film, *Throw Momma from the Train* (1987) ("Well, that's a charming little title, Daniel," observes the Church Lady [Dana Carvey]). The sketch ends with DeVito and the Church Lady singing "Here Comes Santa Claus."

### Will Ferrell (Five-time host, member since 45.7)

When Will Ferrell returns to host *SNL*, he never disappoints his fans and revisits some of the impressions and characters he created during his seven-season tenure, like *Jeopardy!* host Alex Trebek (30.19, 34.22); singer Robert Goulet (30.19); George W. Bush (34.22, 37.21, 43.12); and Marty Culp, who performs with his wife Bobbi Mohan Culp (Ana Gasteyer), at an alternative prom (37.21).

### Tina Fey (Six-time host, member since 41.9)

Between writing, executive-producing, and starring on the NBC sitcom she created, *30 Rock* (2006–2013), Fey returned to *SNL* as host and made numerous cameo appearances during the 2008 election as Republican vice presidential candidate Sarah Palin. For her fifth stint as host (41.9), she shared the stage with her former castmate and frequent collaborator Amy Poehler. They also shared the Emmy for Outstanding Guest Actress in a Comedy Series. When she returned in 2015 (43.21), she once again donned her Palin power suit and joined a group of Trump's sycophants in a rendition of "What I Did for Trump."

## John Goodman (Thirteen-time host, member since 19.19)

Goodman auditioned to be a cast member for season 6 and wasn't chosen (but that turned out to be a good thing as he landed a role on *Roseanne* [1988–1997]). When he hosts the show, he always seems like he's up for anything, like putting on a dress to play the Church Lady's mother (16.7) and Linda Tripp (23.13, 24.1, 24.7, 24.13), who snitched on President Clinton and Monica Lewinsky. *On hosting* SNL *(again)*: "If they asked, I wouldn't turn it down. But I don't know if I'd be that much of an asset anymore," Goodman told *Entertainment Weekly*'s Jeff Labrecque, "I mean, I love it. It used to be the absolute highlight of my year when I hosted the show. I just loved doing that above anything else. I don't know, I'm probably a little rusty."

## Elliott Gould (Six-time host, member since 5.11)

Gould was a unique host—a comic actor and a Broadway musical veteran who during his monologue sang a rendition of "Anything Goes" (1.22), the comically perverse "Castration Walk" (2.19), and "Christmas Night in Harlem" (with Garrett Morris) (4.9). Having hosted five times during the first five seasons, he seemed like an unofficial cast member. He also gets points for hosting the season 6 opener, though his only appearance since has been a cameo in a Five-Timers Club sketch (16.8) welcoming its newest member, Tom Hanks.

## Tom Hanks (Ten-time host, member since 16.8)

The two-time Oscar winner, who is usually cast as the "good guy" and certainly doesn't need the work, likes to occasionally return to his comedy roots

(remember *Bosom Buddies* [1980–1982]?) and take a leave of absence from his wholesome image. *Hanks's Most Memorable Moments*: Girl Watcher (with Jon Lovitz) (13.12, 14.1, 15.13), a roadie for Aerosmith who hooks them up with *Wayne's World* (15.13), and Jeff Morrow, a.k.a. Mr. Short Term Memory (14.1, 15.13, 16.8). *On hosting* SNL: In 1993, Hanks wrote a column in the February 1993 issue of *Spin* magazine: "The reason I keep coming back is that, in all honesty, it's the only experience like it on the planet Earth. Certainly because it's live, but that's really the smallest part of it. The fact that it's 90 minutes long is another big part—you're not just showing up and doing one thing. In the course of the show, a lot is expected of everybody, particularly the host. There's no other workout like that in show business, especially one that's disposable."

### Woody Harrelson (Five-time host, member since 48.13)

There is a thirty-three-year time span between Harrelson's stint as host (in 1989 [15.6]), when he was on *Cheers*, and his fifth time. But the versatile actor has maintained his laid-back persona and "up-for-anything" attitude, making him a perfect fit for hosting *SNL*. When Scarlett Johansson presented a Five-Timer's jacket to Harrelson, musical guest Jack White, who was making his fifth appearance on the show, also received a robe.

## Buck Henry (Ten-time host, member since 3.6)

Prior to his appearances on *Saturday Night Live*, Henry was best known in Hollywood as a screenwriter (*The Graduate* [1967], *Catch-22* [1970], *What's Up, Doc?* [1972]) and the cocreator (with Mel Brooks) of *Get Smart* (1976–1970). He was also a staff writer on the American version of *That Was the Week That Was* (1964–1965), the British television series that took a satirical look at current events that is considered a predecessor to *SNL* (see chapter 5). During seasons 1–5, Henry, the first to qualify as a member of the Five-Timers Club, hosted the show so often (twice a season, including the final shows for seasons 2–5) that people thought he was a regular on the series. He also made several cameos, which, like Steve Martin and Alec Baldwin, gave the impression he spent most of his Saturday nights hanging out in Studio 8H. Capitalizing on the fact that he looked like an ordinary fellow, Henry's recurring roles included Mr. Dantley (1.10, 1.21, 2.6, 3.6, 3.20, 4.5, 4.20), the meek customer in the samurai sketches; Todd the nerd's equally nerdy father, Marshall DiLaMuca (3.20, 5.4); and Uncle Roy (4.5, 4.20, 5.20), the creepy babysitter with a penchant for taking Polaroids of the little girls, Terri (Laraine Newman) and Tracy (Gilda Radner), in his care. Henry also appeared in the disastrous *SNL* Mardi Gras special, where he sat next to Jane Curtin. Together they were going to provide the commentary for the Bacchus Parade—but it never arrived. *On hosting SNL*: In the February 1993 issue of *Spin* magazine, Henry explained why he found hosting the show such a pleasurable experience: "Where else could I have offered members of a studio audience an intimate on-air tryst with me, a whip, some handcuffs, and a vat of cottage cheese? Where else could I have publicly insulted several presidents, their immediate staffs, and families? . . . Those were the days, my friend."

## Jonah Hill (Five-time host, member since 44.4)

Jonah Hill hosted *SNL* five times over a ten-year period, during which he graduated from playing teenagers to adult roles (and scoring Oscar nominations for Best Supporting Actor for *Money Ball* [2011] and *The Wolf of Wall Street* [2013]). For *SNL*, he is one of the few hosts, ex–cast members aside, who has his own recurring character: precocious six-year-old Adam Grossman, who sounds like a Borscht Belt comedian (with his own catchphrase: "I'm six!") when he accompanies his father (Bill Hader) and his father's girlfriend (Vanessa Bayer) to Benihana's.

## Scarlett Johansson (Six-time host, member since 42.16)

Tony Award–winning actress Scarlett Johansson became *SNL*'s resident Ivanka Trump for several sketches and fell in love (and married) one of the show's head writers, Colin Jost, in 2020. In a 2017 interview with Howard Stern, she explained why she loves to host the show: "It's a well-oiled machine. It can be a little intimidating. . . . It's a crazy environment. It's an amazing environment." One of her best moments: A commercial for Ivanka Trump's fragrance, aptly named Complicit (42.16).

## Dwayne Johnson (Five-time host, member since 42.21)

Sometimes comedic talent emerges from the unlikeliest of places. Dwayne Johnson, known in the world of wrestling as the Rock, accepted an invitation to host *SNL* in 2000.

After his opening monologue, which featured other wrestlers from the WWE and its president, Vince McMahon, Johnson proved he was fearless out of the ring as an undercover cop in drag who the Ladies' Man Leon Phelps (Tim Meadows) thinks is a real woman; as Papa Peepers, the father of the half-monkey/half-human, Mr. Peepers (Chris Kattan), who is as frenetic as his primate son; and as newspaper reporter Clark Kent who doesn't do a very good job of hiding his Superman identity. A year after hosting *SNL*, Johnson played the Scorpion King in *The Mummy Returns* (2001) and repeated the role in the prequel to the *Mummy* franchise, *The Scorpion King* (2002). His $5.5 million salary landed him in the *Guinness Book of World Records* for the highest salary for a first-time leading man. He starred in the HBO series *Ballers* (2015–2019) and the biographical sitcom, *Young Rock* (2021–2023). Johnson hosted four more times over the next seventeen years. His most memorable recurring character is President Barack Obama's alter ego, the Rock Obama (34.17, 35.4, 40.16).

## Steve Martin (Sixteen-time host, member since 12.6)

In a March 1992 interview with *Playboy* magazine, Lorne Michaels admitted that back in the beginning, he was "incredibly judgmental about who I would let on the show." One of the people he actually stopped from appearing would be one of the most successful hosts, comedian Steve Martin. Michaels recalled that he "didn't take his act seriously. Here was this guy with an arrow on his head and doing balloon animals. It wasn't my definition of the show. I wanted to distance us from that—for fear of not being taken seriously." Fortunately, Michaels recognized that Martin's unconventional brand of humor—a blend of wit, sarcasm, and absurdity—appealed to *SNL*'s demographic. Martin became an unofficial "Not Ready for Prime Time Player," hosting eight times during seasons 1–5. Perhaps the reason why many viewers thought he was a cast member because unlike other hosts, he created memorable recurring characters, like Georg

Festrunk (3.1, 3.9, 3.18, 4.4, 24.1, 38.16), who, along with his brother Yortuk (Dan Aykroyd), were two "wild and crazy guys," and Theodoric of York, Medieval Barber (3.18, 4.4), who treated the sick yet had no idea what he was doing. The best part is that when he hosts the show, he still gets to be Steve Martin. *Martin's best moments*: "King Tut" (3.18), "Dancing in the Dark" with Gilda Radner (3.18) (also shown as part of Martin's tribute to her on 14.20), "A Holiday Wish" (12.6), and "The Tonight Song," a.k.a. "I'm Not Going to Phone It In Tonight" (17.9). *On hosting* SNL: In his 2008 autobiography, *Born Standing Up: A Comic's Life*, Martin shared what made his time at *SNL* so special: "My appearances on *SNL*, whether I was dancing with Gilda Radner, clowning with Danny, pitching show ideas with Lorne and the writers, simply admiring Bill Murray, were community comic efforts that made me feel like I had been off at a playground rather than an office. Watching the gleam in your partner's eye, acting on impulses that had been nurtured over thousands of shows, working with edgy comics—some so edgy they died from it—was thrilling. We were all united in one, single goal, which was using the comedian's parlance, to kill."

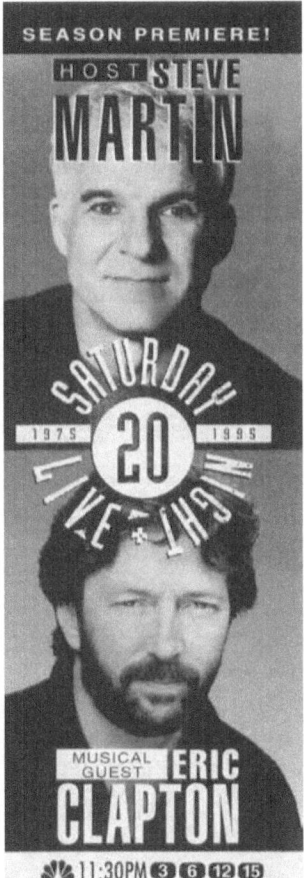

Melissa McCarthy is unrecognizable as hostile White House press secretary Sean Spicer.

## Melissa McCarthy (Five-time host, member since 42.20)

McCarthy is an A-list comedian who, like Carol Burnett and Lucille Ball, completely immerses herself in the characters and, enjoys physical comedy.

The characters she plays are mostly society's outsiders, whose personalities range from the downright mean (abusive girls' basketball coach [38.17], Congresswoman Sheila Kelly [39.13], and White House press secretary Sean Spicer [42.13, 42.14, 42.18, 42.20]) to disruptive (Nanelle, who turns the wrong letters on a game show [38.17]; Linda, a taste tester who can't contain her enthusiasm for Hidden Valley Ranch dressing [37.2]; and P.J., who discusses killing her father in her women's support group [39.13]).

## John Mulaney (Five-time host, member since 47.13)

As a member of the Five-Timers Club, the talented John Mulaney is only one of four *SNL* writers/non–cast members to host the show (Conan O'Brien [26.14]; Louis C.K. [38.6, 39.16, 40.21, 42.17]; and Larry David [41.12, 43.4]). For his first hosting stint, Mulaney dusted off an old, unproduced sketch—a musical tribute to *Les Misérables* that begins with a guy who does the unthinkable and orders a lobster dinner at a New York City diner, which evolves into a major musical number (43.18). Mulaney's subsequent productions, which incorporate a mixture of Broadway show tunes, also begin with someone making a questionable decision, like using a bathroom in a bodega ("Bodega Bathroom" [44.14]), buying sushi at an airport ("Airport Sushi" [45.14]), buying underwear at a souvenir shop ("Souvenir Underwear" [46.6]), and buying a churro in a subway ("Subway Churro" [47.3]).

John Mulaney (second from left) is initiated into the Five-Timers Club by Tina Fey (far left), Candice Bergen (second from right), and Steve Martin (far right) (47.13).

## "No Comedy Experience Required"

### Bill Murray (Five-time host, member since 24.14)

Murray is the one cast member who should not be such a stranger to the show; his last appearance was a cameo playing Steve Bannon in a parody of *Morning Joe* (43.10). His first hosting gig was at the end of the disastrous season 6 when he bravely tried to help producer Jean Doumanian salvage the show. It turned out to be the best episode of the season (and the last one for Doumanian), but at the same time it reminded us how much we missed the old cast. Murray has always been willing to revisit characters he played back in the early days, like Honker (12.14) and Nick the Lounge Singer (6.12, 12.14), who opened *Saturday Night Live 25* live from an Indian casino.

### Paul Rudd (Five-time host, member since 47.9)

Paul Rudd was the perfect candidate for the Five-Timers Club. He is a talented, versatile actor who never ages—and when he hosts he seems to genuinely enjoy being part of an ensemble cast. In her piece on Rudd in *Primetimer*, Christine Persaud notes what is impressive about Rudd is the "sheer number of sketches in which he's ably performed the role of a seasoned repertory player, helping to tee up standout performances from others." He has played the director of Beyoncé's "Single Ladies" video (with male backup dancers [34.8]), the straight man to Andy Samberg's Nicolas Cage on *Weekend Update* (39.21), and a member of the overly affectionate Vogelcheck family.

### Paul Simon (Four-time host, nine musical guest appearances, member since 16.6)

Simon qualifies for the Five-Timers Club because he has been the musical guest nine times (plus five additional cameo appearances). Prior to his *SNL* appearances, Simon was known mostly as a serious songwriter and performer. He appears in the occasional sketch, but the highlights of his appearances have always been musical, like his reunion with Art Garfunkel (1.2), duets with

## ★ ★ ★ ★ Monologues

Steve Martin (2.5) plays the banjo and wears an arrow through his head . . . Paul Simon (2.8) comes onstage for the Thanksgiving show dressed as a turkey and sings "Still Crazy After All These Years" . . . The Reverend Jesse Jackson (10.3) is under the illusion that *SNL* hires many black people, so when he heads into the control room to check on a problem, the all-white crew scurries out and black men take their places . . . Norm Macdonald (25.3), who was fired back in 1998 for not being funny, wonders why he is funny enough now to host the show . . . *Brokeback Mountain* star Jake Gyllenhaal (32.10) honors his gay fan base by wearing a wig and a dress and performing Effie's big number from *Dreamgirls*, "And I'm Telling You I'm Not Going" . . . Zach Braff (32.20) sings about his home state of New Jersey to the tune of Billy Joel's "New York State of Mind" . . . Tina Fey (33.5) hosts the first show after *SNL*'s twelve-week hiatus during the Writers Guild strike. After expressing how she felt bad for the crew who were laid off during that time, she's hit in the head with a boom microphone . . . Comically bizarre actor John Malkovich (34.10) continually interrupts his reading of "'Twas the Night Before Christmas" to a group of children to share some inappropriate facts ("True or False: During the holiday season the suicide rate increases significantly?") . . . With her security guards behind her, Taylor Swift (35.5) sings the "Monologue Song (La La La)," which lists the things she won't talk about in her monologue . . . Actor Joseph Gordon-Levitt (35.7) brings down the house singing and dancing his rendition of "Make 'Em Laugh" from *Singin' in the Rain* (1952) . . . Zach Galifianakis (35.16) tickles the ivories and unleashes an endless stream of non sequiturs . . . Eighty-eight-year-old Betty White (35.21), who hosted the show as a result of a Facebook campaign, tells the audience that Facebook "sounds like a huge waste of time. I would never say that people on it are losers, but that's only because I'm polite." . . . Jeff Bridges sings "Silver Bells" with the Cookie Monster (36.10) . . . Justin Timberlake (36.22), who is only hosting this time around (Lady Gaga was the musical guest), sings a song about not singing tonight.

George Harrison ("Here Comes the Sun," "Homeward Bound") (2.8) and Linda Ronstadt ("Under African Skies") (13.8), and his performance of "Graceland" and "Homeless" with Ladysmith Black Mambazo (11.16). Simon also proved to be a good sport when he allowed the Sweeney Sisters (Jan Hooks, Nora Dunn) to serenade him with a medley of his songs (13.8).

## Emma Stone (Five-time host, member since 49.6)

Two-time Oscar winner Stone was excited to receive her jacket from Tina Fey and Candice Bergen during her monologue. The youngest member of the club, Stone shared how *SNL* has become a "huge part" of her life because it is where she met her husband (segment director Jim McCary). On a *Tonight Show* appearance after her induction, Stone revealed to host Jimmy Fallon that *SNL* told her she needed to return her Five-Timers Club jacket after the show. But

Stone was non-compliant. She wore it to the after-party and took it home. "And now it's in my closet!" Stone confessed.

## Justin Timberlake (Five-time host, member since 38.16)

Timberlake took everyone by surprise when he first hosted the show (and doubled as the musical guest) back in 2003 (29.2) and let the rest of us know that he was talented and very funny. The first time around he impersonated *Punk'd* (2003–2012) host Ashton Kutcher (Timberlake was punk'd on the first episode), donned drag as Jessica Simpson, dressed up like an omelet and competed in a sing and dance-off ("Hurry on down to Omelet-ville!"), and appeared as Bee Gee Robin Gibb as the cohost of *The Barry Gibb Talk Show* (with Jimmy Fallon as Barry). If Timberlake did not already have a successful acting and recording career, in addition to his many ventures as an entrepreneur, he would probably be a regular player on *SNL*. He won two Emmys for hosting *SNL* (as Outstanding Guest Actor in a Comedy Series) in 2009 (34.21) and 2011 (36.22) and two additional Emmys as cowriter of the song "Dick in a Box" (32.9) and for his 2011 musical monologue (36.22).

## Christopher Walken (Seven-time host, member since 26.20)

Academy Award–winning actor Christopher Walken is best known for playing odd, intense, unbalanced characters, who are often borderline or full-blown psychotics. Viewers who saw his first stint as host of *SNL* in 1990 were probably surprised to learn that Walken is a trained dancer when he tap-danced and sang "Throwin' a Ball Tonight" (15.11). Walken proved that despite the dark roles he plays in indie films, he has a sense of humor. One of his recurring characters, "The Continental," is based on a CBS program of the same title that aired in 1952–1953. The show's host, Renzo Cesana, was a suave playboy who spoke into the camera at his presumably female audience, about love and romance. But in Walken's version, he's creepy, and whenever a woman is in his apartment—even if it's just to retrieve a lost glove (18.4) or get her mail (25.16)—he begins to pour on the charm, and she tries to make a quick getaway. Walken's most memorable contribution to *SNL* history will be his role as music producer Bruce Dickinson ("Yes, *the* Bruce Dickinson"), who introduced the catchphrase "More cowbell!" (25.16) in a sketch that is supposedly behind-the-scenes footage of Blue Öyster Cult's recording "(Don't Fear) The Reaper." (See chapter 21.)

## Kristen Wiig (Five-time host, member since 49.16)

Avid viewers were most likely surprised when Wiig was inducted into the Five-Timers Club on August 6, 2024. Since her exit at the end of season 37, Wiig has made ten cameos in episodes hosted by former cast members (she appeared earlier in the season when Kate McKinnon returned to *SNL* to host the show).

Expecting to be inducted during her monologue, she was surprised to see several *non*-Five-Timer club members, like Fred Armisen, Matt Damon, Jon Hamm, Will Forte, and Martin Short, wearing club jackets. During the "Goodnights," Wiig wore her Five-Timers robe, along with everyone else on the stage, including all the cast members.

## Four Unusual Hosts

In the 1970s and 1980s, *SNL* occasionally made some unconventional choices when selecting a host and at times even experimented with the host's role. Here are four such examples.

### Ron Nessen, Press Secretary to President Gerald Ford (1.17)

Among the list of comedians, singers, film and television stars, and characters actors who guest hosted *SNL* during its freshman season, there is one name that was unfamiliar at the time to most Americans. Ron Nessen, a former NBC reporter, was President Gerald Ford's press secretary from 1974 to 1977, replacing Jerald terHorst, who resigned after one month in protest of Ford pardoning ex-President Richard Nixon for his involvement in the Watergate scandal.

According to Nessen's autobiography, *Making the News, Taking the News*, he was first approached by Al Franken about hosting. "I was intrigued but leery," Nessen recalled—and rightfully so. The show—and Chase in particular—had perpetuated Ford's public image as an idiot and a klutz. But Nessen changed his mind when he saw how Ford responded at the correspondents' banquet to Chase's routine by making fun of himself by pretending to pull his placemat off the table and knock his speech off the podium. "The audience roared," Nessen recalled. "They got the joke. Ford was making fun of himself. It was self-deprecating humor at the highest level. It won over the audience and made Chase's harsh put-downs seem unfriendly and out of place." Nessen also revealed that Ford and Chase "hit it off" and even played a game of tennis the next day.

Prior to Nessen's show, which aired on Easter Eve (1.17), Chase, Lorne Michaels, Dan Aykroyd, and John Belushi traveled to Washington, D.C., where they filmed the president, who makes two filmed cameos on the show. In the opening, after Chevy, as a member of the "Dead String Quartet," falls to the ground, there's a cut to footage of Ford, who, looks into the camera and says, "Live from New York, it's *Saturday Night!*" At the start of *Weekend Update*, Chevy Chase says, "I'm Chevy Chase, and you're not." Cut to Ford again, who says, "I'm Gerald Ford, and you're not."

Chase appeared as Ford in an Oval Office sketch in which Nessen (playing himself) asks President Ford for permission to host *Saturday Night*. He explains that he thinks "it would be a good idea to show that you can take a joke" and "demonstrate that this administration has a sense of humor." For the remainder of the sketch, Chase does his usual bumbling President Ford routine—he thinks his stuffed dog Liberty is alive, confuses Easter with Christmas, and reviews his daily schedule (7:05: break the water glass by the sink and Mrs. Ford's shampoo bottle by mistake. 7:12: tumble down the stairs). The fact that Nessen (and to a certain extent, President Ford) was a willing participant in all of this and the audience knew the president and First Lady were most likely watching took some of the show's satirical edge off. Michaels claimed in a 1977 *Playboy* magazine piece on the show that the episode's content was dictated more by the technicians' strike at NBC, which limited them to sketches that were "stand-up presentations—such as ad parodies—because the cameras couldn't move." Writer Rosie Shuster told Hill and Weingrad a different story, admitting that the general attitude was "The President's watching. Let's make him cringe and squirm."

The writers certainly give the President and the First Lady plenty of opportunity. Compared to the first sixteen episodes, the humor of episode 1.17 was more in the style of *National Lampoon* magazine—a bit grosser, raunchier, and certainly more provocative than what is typically included in a single episode. Nessen did not appear in any of the commercial parodies, which included a repeat of the Berkeley Wallpaper collection from earlier in the season (1.2) with Yippie leader Jerry Rubin; a parody of a current commercial for Smucker's Jam with the slogan "With a name like Smucker's, it has to be good" in which Aykroyd, Belushi, Curtin, Chase, and Morris try to outdo each other with the most disgusting name for a jam ("Fluckers," "Death Camp," "Painful Rectal Itch," etc.); and an ad for "Autumn Fizz," a carbonated douche. On *Weekend Update*, the pretaped footage of President Ford is followed by several jokes at the president's expense and Emily Litella's editorial about the upcoming 1976 presidential "erection."

## Charles Grodin, Actor/Director/Writer (3.4)

On a rare occasion, an entire *SNL* episode will be built around a running gag, like "Who Shot Charles Rocket?" (6.11), which ended with Rocket inadvertently dropping the f-bomb. Another example is an episode in the fall of 1977 when Charles Grodin hosted the show with musical guest Paul Simon and a cameo by Art Garfunkel, both of whom Grodin directed in their 1969 CBS special, *Simon and Garfunkel: Songs of America*. During the cold open, it's established that everyone on the show is upset with Grodin, who spent the week sightseeing, visiting his friends, and buying gifts for the cast instead of rehearsing. In fact, he didn't know that there was a studio audience or that the show was live. In his monologue he confesses that he's never seen the show and wishes he had more time to rehearse. When he does appear in a sketch, he reads Belushi's lines off the cue card in the "Samurai Dry Cleaners"; doesn't understand why they are dressed like bees in "The Killer Bees" sketch, which also pisses off Belushi; and wears an Art Garfunkel wig and tries to sing "The Sound of Silence" with Paul Simon, only he doesn't know the words. At the end of the show, he does a PSA for "Hire the Incompetent," which marks the first appearance of Roseanne Roseannadanna.

Grodin's name often mistakenly appears on the list of "banned hosts" from the show. First of all, "banned" means to prohibit someone from doing something (like smoking on a plane). There is a difference between being "banned" from doing something and not being asked back (over the course of forty-nine seasons, that list is very long). Grodin set the record straight in an interview with AV Club, saying that they had asked him to host again, but he chose not to. "I can do two things," he explained. "I can learn a script, or I can improvise. But you can't improvise there, because it's all done to time, and you can't learn a script, because they're changing it, changing it, changing it, so you're pretty much forced to read teleprompters, and I just didn't want to do it again."

## Miskel Spillman, Winner, "Anyone Can Host" Contest (3.8)

On October 8, 1977, Lorne Michaels announced *Saturday Night Live*'s first and only "Anyone Can Host" contest (3.2). Viewers were invited to send a postcard by November 1 on which they state in twenty-five words or less why they want to host *Saturday Night Live*. "You need no theatrical experience—just talent and a strong belief in yourself," Michaels explained. "If your postcard is funny, in the opinion of the staff, you might be one of the five finalists who will be flown to New York in November to read your postcard live on the show." The viewers at home will decide the winner, who will be paid $3,000 (the same amount they paid any other host at the time), to host the Christmas show on December 17. Michaels warned viewers to mail their postcard in and not hand it to anyone affiliated with the show.

In the shows that followed, viewers were reminded about the contest. Garrett Morris (3.3) repeated all the essential information and added that he couldn't host because, as announcer Don Pardo reminds viewers, NBC employees and their relatives were not eligible. The following week Bill Murray and Michael O'Donoghue are rummaging through entries (3.4), and as Murray explains the rules, O'Donoghue is ripping them up one by one for various reasons: poor penmanship, smudge on the corner, uneven margins, typing error, one word over the twenty-five word limit.

On November 19, 1977 (3.6), Buck Henry introduced America to the five finalists, who shared their reasons for wanting to host the show (they were also given the opportunity to give the official "Live from New York" greeting in the cold open).

- **Dave Lewis**, from Oregon, recently lost his job, for which he was grossly underpaid as an interior decorator in a turkey farm. He went into his boss's office to ask for a raise: "I looked him straight in the eye and I said, 'Look you're gonna give me a raise or I'm gonna host *Saturday Night!*' And he gets up from his desk, and I was scared, he looks at me and says, 'Gobble, gobble.'"

- **Deb Blair**, a mother of three from Peoria, Illinois, said her children only listen to people on television, so she thought if she hosted the show, she could tell them something.
- **Connie Crawford**, a freshman at Vassar College, who describes herself as a "groupie" of the show for the past two years: "I'm one of those nauseatingly enthusiastic-type people, you know, go for all the gusto you can get, that sort of thing."
- **Dick Knelp**, governor of South Dakota, has nine good reasons why he'd like to host the show: his eight sons and his lovely wife, Nancy.
- **Miskel Spillman**, age eighty: "Well, I love everyone in the cast. I watch it every Saturday night. And I thought, as I am eighty years old, I want a lot of old, old people all over the world to watch it, to get the thrill that I have every Saturday night watching it."

Miskel Spillman—the winner—returned to host the Christmas episode (3.8) with Buck Henry serving as her guide. Unfortunately, John Belushi gives the octogenarian one of his killer joints before the start of the show, which is the reason why a stoned Mrs. Spillman appears during the monologue clutching a bowl of fruit. Over the course of the show, she appears in a few sketches: "Sartresky & Hutch," a parody of *Starsky & Hutch*; "The Gift of the Magi," a modern-day version of the classic story, which is read by Jane Curtin to Mrs. Spillman; and a holiday sketch in which John Belushi brings home his much older girlfriend (Spillman) to meet his parents.

Mrs. Spillman may have been the perfect contest winner, but the episode is probably best remembered for the last-minute, on-air switcheroo Elvis Costello did when he started to play "Less Than Zero," then stopped the band, and began playing "Radio, Radio" (see chapter 19).

## Francis Ford Coppola Directs (11.13)

The highlight of the 1985–1986 season was an appearance by Francis Ford Coppola, director of such film classics as *The Godfather* (1972), *The Godfather II* (1974), and *Apocalypse Now* (1979). *Cheers* star George Wendt was the host, while Coppola was the guest director, who, as Lorne Michaels explains to the cast in the opening, has been given complete control of the episode. Cut to the opening credits: "Francis Ford Coppola Presents Francis Ford Coppola's *Saturday Night Live*." Throughout the episode, Coppola makes fun of his reputation as a "control freak." Sitting on a dolly, he interrupts host George Wendt's monologue to get the audience to laugh more (and encourages them to use "sense memory" if they don't think it's funny). He also takes over for director Dave Wilson and calls the shots for a sketch, and even makes a last-minute cut during *Weekend Update*. In a parody of the 1960s television series *That Girl* (1966–1971), "*That Black Girl*" (with the talented Danitra Vance as the perky "LaToya Marie"), he questions why there are no black female writers and decides he wants more grit and realism out of the sketch, forcing the scenic designers to transform LaToya

*SNL* cast member Jon Lovitz (left), directed by special guest Francis Ford Coppola.

Marie's apartment into a tenement. In a spoof of *Apocalypse Now*, the cast starts to rebel when cast member Anthony Michael Hall gets shot with real ammo. Coppola decides he can't handle live television, but Michaels convinces him to stay for the grand finale in which he pans around the studio and all the characters that appeared in the sketches throughout the evening. It is a truly unique and highly experimental episode of *SNL*—something Michaels unfortunately never tried to repeat.

# Keeping Live Music Alive

## SNL's Musical Guests

For nearly four decades, *Saturday Night Live* has been a showcase for musical talent, ranging from living legends to up-and-coming artists, one-hit wonders, and singers and bands of whom you've never heard. No matter how many gold albums hang on their wall or Grammy statues sit on their shelf, at approximately 12:10 a.m. and 12:50 a.m. they will all stand front and center on the same stage in Studio 8H and perform in front of a live audience.

In a special issue of *Spin* magazine (February 1993) guest edited by the folks at *SNL*, John Zonars, the show's musical coordinator, emphasized the significant role *Saturday Night Live* has played in keeping live music alive: "*SNL* is perhaps the most accurate barometer of what's hot and what's not in music. It doesn't matter if you're a three-piece band such as Nirvana or a forty-two-piece orchestra backing Sinéad O'Connor—when you get that cue from the stage manager, you're going live in front of millions of Americans. There's no chance to remix, no opportunities for a second take."

When *SNL* debuted in 1975, live musical performances were a thing of the past. Variety shows were taped in front of a live audience. The last "really big show" to feature live performances, *The Ed Sullivan Show* (1948–1971), had been off the air for four years. In the 1960s, Sullivan hosted big names like the Beatles, Elvis Presley, the Doors, the Rolling Stones, the Band, the Mamas and the Papas, and Janis Joplin. Unfortunately, the Beatles did not take Lorne Michaels up on his offer of $3,000 to reunite on SNL (1.18). According to Lennon's biographer Philip Norman, Lennon and McCartney were uptown in Lennon's apartment in the Dakota watching the show that night and considered taking a cab to 30 Rock and making a surprise appearance, but decided against it. The Rolling Stones did perform live from 30 Rock in 1978 (4.1), along with the Band (2.6), the Grateful Dead (4.5, 5.15), and Bob Dylan (5.2), who walked off *The Ed Sullivan Show* during rehearsals when, as the legend goes, CBS Standards and Practices refused to allow him to sing "Talkin' John Birch Paranoid Blues" because it equated the right-wing group to Hitler.

According to Hill and Weingrad's backstage history of the show, in the beginning Lorne Michaels had the "sole responsibility" of choosing the host and the musical guest. One of the show's talent coordinators characterizes Michaels's

The Blues Brothers perform "Soul Man" (4.6).

selection process back then as "unbelievably arbitrary" and not based on if they had recently released a studio or "Best of" album and, if they did, where it ranked on the *Billboard* Chart. In the February 1993 issue of Spin magazine, Michaels explained to editor Bob Guccione Jr., "In '75, when we were starting, it was rare to have this kind of music on television, so it was enough that people who didn't perform on television came on.... We weren't booking from the charts.... By presenting music in a very straightforward way, people began to trust us and certain people volunteering to come on gave us a certain credibility." This explains the eclectic lineup of artists who appeared in season 1: jazz singer Betty Carter, Canadian country/pop singer Anne Murray, ABBA, Rita Coolidge, Patti Smith Group, Neil Sedaka, Leon Redbone, Al Jarreau, Janis Ian, John Sebastian, Loudon Wainwright III, Gil Scott-Heron, and Carly Simon. Still, many of these artists did perform songs off of their most recent studio or "Best of" album, and some of them also had a single on the *Billboard* Chart.

There's no question the national exposure *SNL* gives an artist or band can help boost album sales. Many artists have seen significant jumps in their album and singles sales immediately after their performance on *SNL*. According to a 2010 study by Terry Tompkins published in the *Journal of the Music & Entertainment Industry Educators Association*, artists performing on *SNL* experience a 35 percent increase in sales. Tompkins cites as a test case study the appearance of British singer Adele on *SNL* on October 18, 2008 (34.5). She sang two songs from her album *19*: "Chasing Pavements" and "Cold Shoulder." Also appearing on the same show, hosted by Josh Brolin, was Republican vice presidential candidate Sarah Palin. Approximately seventeen million viewers tuned in, making it the most watched episode of the season. According to the *Hollywood Reporter*, the show's overnight ratings (10.7/24 in metered markets) were the highest since Nancy Kerrigan hosted in 1994 (19.15). After her appearance, Adele's album sales increased by 132 percent in the United States. During the week after her performance, her album *19* sold 24,926 units, an increase of 14,000 from her previous top-selling week of 11,850. Tompkins points out that in addition to having higher ratings than the daily weeknight talk shows like *The Late Show with David Letterman* (1993–present) and *Jimmy Kimmel Live!* (2003–present), *SNL* guests get to sing two numbers and benefit from the on-air promotion leading up to their appearance.

Kate Pierson performs "Cosmic Thing" during the 1990 appearance by the B-52's (15.18).

Some artists have pulled double duty as both the musical guest and the host. Although they were billed as the show's host, three performers—Paul Simon (1.2), Lily Tomlin (1.6), and Desi Arnaz (1.14)—did this during the show's first season. Paul Simon was the first in the show's history (1.2), with Randy Newman and Phoebe Snow as his musical guests and Art Garfunkel as his "special guest." Except for a filmed segment in which he plays a game of one-on-one with NBA star Connie Hawkins, Simon spends most of his airtime behind a microphone singing (alone, with Garfunkel, and then Snow). When he returned to host the show, he performed with George Harrison (2.8), Ladysmith Black Mambazo (11.16), and Linda Ronstadt (13.8). In addition, Simon has been a musical guest eight times between the years 1977 and 2011 and has made numerous cameo appearances. Additional hosts who've worn both hats include Justin Bieber (38.13), Garth Brooks (23.14, 25.5) (his musical guest was his alter ego,

Chris Gaines), Ray Charles (3.5), Hammer (17.8), Janet Jackson (29.17), Mick Jagger (37.22), Elton John (36.18), Jon Bon Jovi (33.3) (who also featured the Foo Fighters), Jennifer Lopez (26.11, 35.15), Ludacris (32.6), Bruno Mars (38.5), Willie Nelson (12.12), Olivia Newton-John (7.20), Dolly Parton (14.17), Queen Latifah (30.2), the Rolling Stones (4.1), Britney Spears (25.19, 27.12), Sting (16.11), Taylor Swift (35.5), Justin Timberlake (29.2, 32.9, 38.16), Stevie Wonder (8.19), and Frank Zappa (4.3). Interestingly, most, but not all, of them had previous acting experience on television and in feature films.

## Why God Created Live Television

### Simon & Garfunkel, "The Boxer," "Scarborough Fair," and "My Little Town" (1.2)

In a promo on the premiere episode of *SNL*, next week's host Paul Simon invites everyone to tune in to see Phoebe Snow, Randy Newman, and his "ex-partner, Art Garfunkel, for a little Simon & Garfunkel reunion." When Garfunkel joins Simon onstage the following week, they get a standing ovation. After Simon kids Garfunkel about "crawling back" and his movie career, they sing—in perfect harmony—"The Boxer," "Scarborough Fair," and their new single, "My Little Town," which appears on their respective solo releases, Simon's *Still Crazy After All These Years*, and Garfunkel's *Breakaway*, which were both released that month. There was so much press surrounding their breakup, no one imagined we would ever see them sharing a stage again. Considering this was show 1.2, it was a major coup for *SNL*.

Between 1977 and 2018, Paul Simon was a musical guest on SNL nine times.

## Patti Smith Group, "Gloria" and "My Generation" (1.17)

In season 1, when *SNL* was still a little raw and rough around the edges, "Godmother of Punk" Patti Smith traveled uptown to make her television debut and introduce punk rock into America's living rooms. Unless they frequented CBGB, the East Village club that at the time was the center of the New York underground music scene, they probably never heard anything like Smith's rendition of Van Morrison's "Gloria" and the Who's "My Generation," which were on her 1975 album *Horses*. Hosting the show that evening was Ron Nessen, the press secretary to President Gerald Ford, which means there's a chance he was tuning in that evening also (see also chapter 18). Smith was the inspiration for Gilda Radner's punk rocker Candy Slice, who made her debut in season 4 (4.8).

## Elvis Costello and the Attractions, "Radio, Radio" (3.8)

Elvis Costello stole some of the limelight away from the week's guest host, eighty-year-old Miskel Spillman, winner of the first and only "Anyone Can Host" contest, when thirty seconds into his second number, "Less Than Zero," he stopped the band and said, "I'm sorry, ladies and gentlemen, there's no reason to do this song here." He then launched into "Radio, Radio" from his forthcoming album, *This Year's Model*, which is critical of the radio and music industries. In a 1989 Rolling Stone article commemorating the show's fifteenth anniversary, Costello explained he and his band knew they were not the first choice as the evening's musical guests (the Sex Pistols had visa problems and couldn't travel to the United States), and he was not impressed with the atmosphere around

After reportedly being banned from the show, Costello returned in 1989 to sing "Veronica" and "Let Him Dangle" (14.15).

the show. They decided to do what Jimi Hendrix did when he was a guest on a British television series and switch songs at the last minute. Considering this a form of improvising (as songs are rehearsed for the camera), Michaels was reportedly furious and banned Costello from the show, though he was invited back in March 1989 (14.15) and again in 1991 (16.20). Costello also appeared on *Saturday Night Live 25* in which he interrupted the Beastie Boys' number, and together they sang "Radio, Radio."

## Fear, "I Don't Care About You," "Beef Bologna," "New York's Alright If You Like Saxophones," and "Let's Have a War" (7.4)

The punk band Fear were the musical guests on the 1981 Halloween show. The host was British actor Donald Pleasence, best known to young audiences as Dr. Sam Loomis in *Halloween* (1978) and the sequel, *Halloween II* (1981), which was released in theaters the previous night. Unlike the performers and bands that appear on *SNL*, Fear had not yet released an album (their first, *The Record*, was released in 1982). But they had a loyal fan base within the punk rock world and gained national exposure when they appeared in Penelope Spheeris's documentary about the Los Angeles–based punk rock scene, *The Decline of Western Civilization*, which was released in the summer of 1981. John Belushi was a fan, and he had lobbied to use their music for the soundtrack of what would be his last film, the black comedy *Neighbors*, costarring Dan Aykroyd. But the studio didn't go for it, so to make it up to the band he convinced Dick Ebersol, with the support of Michael O'Donoghue, to feature them on *SNL*. Only they didn't come alone.

Fear's fans from Washington, D.C., described by the press as "Skinheads" (rockers with shaved heads), were bused to New York to appear on the show so they could "stage dive" (literally running up to the stage and diving off into the crowd) and slam dance, a style of dance in which the participants push and slam into each other with their bodies. Despite how it looks on camera, slam dancing is not intentionally violent, though it has resulted in serious injuries and even some fatalities. As a result, slam dancing (or as it is known today, "moshing") is prohibited today in some venues.

Their first set, in which they sing "I Don't Care About You," is like any other *SNL* musical performance. It's during their second set, in which they sing "Beef Bologna," "New York's Alright If You Like Saxophones," and "Let's Have a War," that the stage is surrounded by mostly white teenage boys who slam dance and dive off the stage. Someone yells out, "New York Sucks," and by the time they get to the third song, the crowd is even more unruly. Ebersol tells director Dave Wilson to cut to a film ("Prose and Cons" from the season opener).

"'Fear' Riot Leaves Saturday Night Glad to Be Alive" read the *New York Post* headline the following Tuesday. According to *Billboard* magazine, the *Post* reported that the band and their fans caused "an estimated $200,000" in damages to a Mini-cam camera, two viewers, a viewing room, and the greenroom. They described Fear's performance as a "total out of control free-for-all" in which the band's fans "jumped up and started slamdancing—a new punk craze that involves dancing, biting, and kicking." The *Post* article also said that "all hell was breaking loose with the affiliates" because of obscenities shouted during the performance. The *Billboard* story included a quote from *Saturday Night Live* spokesman Pete Hamilton, who claimed that the *New York Post* "did not check its facts, and . . . chose to print an erroneous story. As far as we can tell there has been no $200,000 in damages. We had to pay $40 in labor penalties."

*Billboard* interviewed the band's frontman, Lee Ving, and Robert Biggs, president of Slash Records, who said there was a problem during dress rehearsal when one of the kids tripped over a camera cable. The cameraman refused to work under these conditions, but Ebersol convinced him to return to work. Ving also explained that "the band wanted their audience so they wouldn't be playing to a bunch of blockheads, so they called down to Washington. In New York there really isn't the scene, but it remains viable in suburban areas. So they went to Washington and imported a bunch of skinheads."

One aspect of the performance *Billboard* doesn't mention is the tension in Studio 8H between the punk rock fans and *SNL*'s studio audience. In an interview with PUNKHOuseTV, "John Belushi Was a Punk Rocker," John Joseph, of the punk rock band ProMags, was part of the slam-dancing crowd that night. He described how the crowd bused in from Washington, D.C., tore up the greenroom (and pulled the strings right out of the piano). When it was time for them to appear on camera, they were not only slamming into one another, but were diving on top of the audience members. A fight broke out between the D.C. and New York people. When Fear was finished, the fighting continued, and when the head of security stood on the stage and tried to clear everyone out, someone hit him in the head with a pumpkin.

In exchange for allowing the slam-dancing fans to participate, Belushi agreed to do a cameo on the show. He appears in the cold open, in which a nervous Pleasence gets advice from Eddie Murphy, who shares with him what all the cast members do before each show—vomit. When Eddie leaves, Pleasence puts his finger down his mouth and rushes into a stall. Out of the next stall comes John Belushi, who lifts his hat and fixes his hair in the mirror. The audience goes wild. Acting as if he suddenly realized where he is, Belushi exits. It would be Belushi's last appearance on *SNL*.

## The Red Hot Chili Peppers Perform "Under the Bridge" (17.14)

The Red Hot Chili Peppers sounded like a wasted garage band performing their hit single "Under the Bridge." In his autobiography, *Scar Tissue*, Anthony Kiedis admits singing the song live is a challenge and that he depends on guitarist John Frusciante for the music cues in the introduction to the song. "I had no idea what song he was playing or what key he was in. He looked like he was in a different world," Kiedis writes. "I felt like I was getting stabbed in the back and hung out to dry in front of all of America. . . ."

## Sinéad O'Connor's Declaration of "War" (18.2)

Irish singer Sinéad O'Connor was scheduled to make her first appearance on *Saturday Night Live* on the second-to-last show of the fifteenth season (15.19). When controversial comedian Andrew Dice Clay was announced as the guest host, O'Connor, along with cast member Nora Dunn, boycotted the show because of the sexist and derogatory nature of Clay's comedy. *Variety* reported that O'Connor made her decision after watching some of his routines on video. Through her publicist, she explained, "I feel it shows disrespect of women that 'Saturday Night Live' expected me to perform on the same show as Andrew Dice Clay." O'Connor finally did appear on the season 16 opener with a non-controversial host, actor Kyle MacLachlan. She performed "Three Babies" and "The Last Day of Our Acquaintance" from her 1990 album *I Do Not Want What I Haven't Got.*

Two years later, O'Connor made her second and last appearance on *SNL.* On October 3, 1992, hosted by Tim Robbins (18.2), she sang "Success Has Made a Failure of Our Home" from her new album, *Am I Not Your Girl?* For her second song of the night, O'Connor sang a haunting a cappella version of "War," by Jamaican singer/songwriter Bob Marley.

Marley was a follower of the Rastafari movement, which hailed Ethiopian minister Haile Selassie I (1892–1975) as the Messiah. The lyrics to Marley's song were excerpted from a famous speech delivered by Selassie to the United Nations on October 6, 1961. Selassie, an advocate for peace, call for the disarmament of nations "because of the immense destructive capacity of which men

To protest child abuse in the Catholic Church, Irish singer Sinead O'Connor created a storm of controversy by ending her a cappella rendition of Bob Marley's "War" by ripping up a photo of Pope John Paul II, tossing the pieces into camera, and declaring, "Fight the real enemy!"

dispose." Marley immortalized a part of the same speech in which he talks about how the "African continent will not know peace" until racial inequality is "finally and permanently discredited and abandoned . . . until there are no longer first class and second class citizens of any nation . . . until the color of a man's skin is of no more significance that the color of his eyes . . . until the basic human rights are equally guaranteed to all without regard to race . . . We Africans will fight, if necessary, and we know that we shall win, as we are confident in the victory of good over evil."

Marley's song and Selassie's words were used by O'Connor to wage a different kind of war—against child abuse. She substituted the line "fight racial injustice" with "fight sexual abuse," and in the dress rehearsal she held up a photograph of a child. But on the live, East Coast broadcast, at the end of the song, on the word "evil," O'Connor, in a medium close-up, holds up a picture of Pope John Paul II, tears it up in several pieces, and says, "Fight the real enemy." She then throws the pieces directly into the camera. The studio is silent (because the Applause signs were not turned on). There is a cut to a long shot of her standing on the stage. She takes off the earphones she's wearing and blows out the candles in front of her.

The NBC switchboard immediately lit up. According to *Variety*, NBC logged more than 900 calls from people who did not like the show and seven who did. "It goes without saying that NBC does not condone what Ms. O'Connor did," network vice president Curt Block told the Associated Press. "We would never authorize something like that. . . . I was offended; the executive producer, Lorne Michaels, likewise was offended and surprised."

In Shales and Miller's *Live from New York*, Michaels explains what he was focusing on that evening was not O'Connor, but what host Tim Robbins was wearing, namely an anti–General Electric T-shirt (GE was NBC's parent company) he was planning to wear to protest GE's pollution of the Hudson River. According to Michaels, he had even written a sketch about it, but it was never done. Instead, Robbins begins his monologue by telling the audience that GE doesn't just make kitchen appliances and lightbulbs but triggering devices for nuclear warheads. Director Dave Wilson asks him to go backstage to talk to Lorne, who then wakes up in bed (with Phil Hartman!) and reveals Robbins's monologue was only a dream.

As for O'Connor's surprise, Lorne told Shales and Miller "it was the bravest possible thing she could do. . . . To her the church symbolized everything that was bad about growing up in Ireland . . . and so she was making a strong political statement."

When asked for a statement, O'Connor's spokesperson, Elaine Shock, said the singer did not plan to offer an explanation for her actions: "The performance makes her own statement. She relates a lot of the ills of the world to the church." Americans who publicly agreed with O'Connor were in the minority. A dozen protestors and free-speech activists stood in front of St. Patrick's Cathedral wearing Sinéad masks and tearing up pictures of the Pope. Those who were offended and outraged by what she did were vocal in their opposition. On *SNL* the following week (18.3), host Joe Pesci tore up a picture of O'Connor. A week later, on October 16, 1992, O'Connor was scheduled to sing in a sold-out concert in Madison Square Garden to celebrate Bob Dylan's thirtieth-year anniversary on the singer/songwriter's career. The list of performers included Eric Clapton, George Harrison, Johnny Cash, Willie Nelson, and Stevie Wonder. O'Connor was slated to sing Dylan's "I Believe in You." As she was being jeered and booed by the crowd, she started to sing Bob Marley's "War," but broke down in the middle. Kris Kristofferson came out onstage to comfort her.

In 2002, in a piece on O'Connor for salon.com, Jake Tapper revisited the controversy and had a chance to sit down with O'Connor, who said, "It's very understandable that the American people did not know what I was going on about. But outside of America, people did really know and it was quite supported and I think very well understood." What Americans were in the dark about back then was how the Catholic Church in Dublin was protecting pedophile priests by reassigning them to other parishes. The irony, of course, is that since then, the sexual abuse scandals involving the Catholic Church did erupt in the United States. O'Connor said she "felt sad for the American people that they have to suffer such a shock." Her feelings toward the Catholic Church and the Pope had also evolved since then. In April 1999, she was ordained the first-ever Latin Tridentine female Catholic Priest and given the name Mother Bernadette Marie. As for the man whose photograph she tore into tiny pieces in front of millions of people, she said, "Ripping up the picture was more about the office than the man. I don't have a particular problem with him as a man or what he's done as pope."

### Rage Against the Machine (Steve Forbes) (21.17)

A musical artist's availability is limited due to his or her touring schedule, which is one of the primary factors when scheduling someone to appear on the show. Consequently, there have been some odd pairings over the years: Don Rickles and Billy Idol (9.11) (what do you think they talked about backstage?), Jeremy Irons and Fishbone (16.16), Sean Hayes and singer/rapper Shaggy (26.12), and Al Gore and Phish (28.8). In each case, the difference within each pair is either generational and/or a difference in their artistic sensibilities.

In the case of host Steve Forbes and Rage Against the Machine, the difference was not simply generational but ideological. Steve Forbes is a publishing magnate (his father was Malcolm Forbes) and a conservative who, at the time, was making his first unsuccessful bid for the Republican presidential nomination for the forthcoming 1996 election. The main plank of his political platform was the establishment of a flat tax, an idea he promoted in his monologue.

On the other end of the ideological spectrum is Rage Against the Machine, a rap metal band from Los Angeles whose music is an explicit expression of their leftist politics. In a flyer distributed by Kenny Moore, the Florida representative for "Rock Out Censorship," RATM guitarist Tom Morello, stated that the band "wanted to stand in sharp juxtaposition to a billionaire telling jokes and promoting his flat tax . . . by making their own statement." Before performing their first song, "Bulls on Parade," *SNL* producers ordered stagehands to remove the upside-down flags hanging on the band's amplifiers. As Morello later explained, the inverted flags represented their "contention that American democracy is inverted when what passes for democracy is an electoral choice between two representatives of the privileged class. America's freedom of expression is inverted when you're free to say anything until it upsets a corporate sponsor."

Once the band headed offstage, they were told they would not be playing again and they needed to leave the building immediately. RATM bassist Timothy Commerford was reportedly so angry he went into Forbes's dressing room and threw shreds of one of the torn flags.

"*SNL* censored Rage, period," Morello concluded. "They could not have sucked up to the billionaire more. The thing that is ironic is *SNL* is supposedly this cutting edge show, but they proved they're bootlickers to their corporate masters when it comes down to it."

Surely this was not one of *SNL*'s proudest hours.

By the way, Forbes was a terrible host, and there was no reason to have him on the show.

# An Unexpected Surprise

## *SNL*'s Late-Night Cameos

A "cameo" is a brief, unbilled appearance by a famous enough individual in a film, TV show, or otherwise in the public eye who is usually instantly recognizable to the audience. One of *Saturday Night Live*'s predecessors, *Rowan & Martin's Laugh-In* (1967–1973), featured weekly cameos by an eclectic roster of movie stars and entertainers. The show's second season opener in September 1968 included cameos by John Wayne, Zsa Zsa Gabor, Jack Lemmon, Bob Hope, and the undisputed king of comedy himself, President Richard Nixon, who uttered the show's most famous catchphrase in the form of a question: "Sock it to *me*?" Check it out on YouTube.

*Saturday Night Live* has featured cameos by actors, models, athletes, and politicians, along with an occasional appearance by a famous person whose name is more recognizable than his or her face.

**ABDUL, Paula** (23.20, 30.18): The former Laker Girl turned Grammy- and Emmy-winning singer/choreographer made her first appearance on *SNL* when Spartan cheerleaders Arianna and Craig (Cheri Oteri and Will Ferrell) attended Paula Abdul's Cheerleading Camp (23.30). Seven years later, she returned (30.18) during her *American Idol* (2002–present) judging days to introduce a sketch about the current relationship scandal involving Abdul (Amy Poehler) and *Idol* contestant Corey Clarke (Finesse Mitchell). At the end of that sketch, Abdul gives Poehler and her costars, Chris Parnell (as Simon Cowell) and Kenan Thompson (as Randy Jackson), a few notes on their performances before opening the show with "Live from New York, it's *Saturday Night!*"

**ANISTON, Jennifer** (42.8): Twelve years after her second stint as *SNL* host in January 2004 (29.9), *Friends* star Jennifer Aniston returned for a cameo appearance (42.8) on *Weekend Update* to confront *SNL* cast member Vanessa Bayer about her impression of Aniston's character on *Friends*, Rachel Green. According to *Entertainment Weekly* reporter Ruth Kinane, Aniston was initially "put off" by her *Office Christmas Party* costar's impression, claiming she initially didn't think Bayer sounded anything like her. Aniston also admitted she needed some time to accept it as a compliment (one wonders if she had

Jennifer Aniston is not impressed by Vanessa Bayer's impersonation of Aniston's *Friends* character, Rachel Green.

seen Casey Wilson's impression of her in a sketch parodying *The View* [34.7]). But in the end Aniston proves she is a good sport in her comical exchange with Bayer and even stuck around to appear in a sketch (as herself) with host Emma Stone.

**ARMANI, Giorgio** (18.12): On January 21, 1993, the day after his inauguration, President Bill Clinton and First Lady Hillary Clinton revived a presidential tradition and greeted two thousand citizens selected by lottery in the Diplomatic Reception Room of the White House. In a cold open (18.12), the Clintons (Phil Hartman and Jan Hooks) meet several crazy visitors, including an Italian, who turns out to be Italian prime minister Giuliano Amato, played by renowned fashion designer Giorgio Armani.

**BARROWS, Sydney Biddle** (13.5): "I ran the wrong kind of business, but I did it with integrity," Sydney Biddle Barrows admitted to journalist Marian Christy in a 1986 interview with the *Boston Globe*. Barrows (under the pseudonym Sheila Devin) ran a high-class Manhattan escort service, which is only illegal if the women are having sex in exchange for money (and they were). When her Cachet Escort service got busted in 1984, Barrows became an overnight celebrity and was dubbed "The Mayflower Madam" (Barrows was from a prominent Philadelphia family whose ancestors came over on the *Mayflower*). Her appearance on *SNL* (13.5) with guest host Candice Bergen coincided with the premiere of the 1987 made-for-TV movie based on her memoir, *Mayflower Madam*, with Bergen in the title role. In this sketch Barrows serves as the narrator of the real story of the first Thanksgiving—a "celebration of whoremongering"—in which the original Mayflower Madam, Priscilla Biddle

Barrows (Candice Bergen), throws a dinner party to introduce the Indians to the female pilgrims.

**BIDEN, Joseph** (48.10): President Biden made a short pretaped cameo appearance in an episode hosted by actress and star of HBO's much-publicized second season of *The White Lotus* (2021–present) Aubrey Plaza. In her monologue Plaza referenced she is from Delaware, the state Biden represented in Congress for decades, and joked that, because of her series, she was recently voted the most famous person from the state, ahead of the president, and that "he was pissed." At that moment, Biden appeared on a video screen to tell the world, "Aubrey, you're the most famous person out of Delaware, and there's no question about that. We're just grateful you made it out of *White Lotus* alive." It was a vintage Biden moment of "empathy," even if it concerned a fictional character she played on TV.

**BURNETT, Carol** (10.13): "One of the reasons why we're in this business is right here," says host Harry Anderson (10.13), who brings a surprised Carol Burnett, who is sitting in the front row, up onstage at the end of the show. The audience applauds wildly as Anderson and the cast say "good night." Burnett also gives her signature tug on her ear, which started as her way of telling her grandmother who raised her that she was well and that she loved her.

**BURROUGHS, William** (7.5): In season 7, *SNL* tried to regain some of its counterculture edge with an appearance by writer William Burroughs (7.5), who, looking like an old-time newscaster, sat behind a metal desk and read excerpts from two of his novels, *Naked Lunch* and *Nova Express*.

**BUTTAFUOCO, Joey** (20.6): Buttafuoco's fifteen minutes of fame were sparked by his affair with a minor, Amy Fisher (dubbed "The Long Island Lolita"), who, in 1992, shot Buttafuoco's wife, Mary Jo, leaving her deaf in one ear and her face partially paralyzed. The story and the subsequent trial of Fisher made headlines around the country. Fisher served seven years in prison; Buttafuoco served several months in jail for statutory rape.

In November 1994, host John Turturro (20.6) was starring at the time in the film *Quiz Show* (1994). Turturro plays Herbert Stempel, a contestant on the NBC quiz show 21, who was fed the answers and then forced to throw the game in favor of a more popular contestant, the handsome Charles Van Doren. Stempel eventually blew the whistle that set the whole scandal in motion. In the *SNL* sketch, to be chosen as host of the show, Turturro is required during his monologue to answer a series of questions (for example, fill in the blank: "It's ____ to be here hosting *Saturday Night Live!*"). Otherwise, it is announced that Buttafuoco, who has been watching backstage, will be allowed to host.

To our relief, Turturro answers the final question (fill in the blank: "Lorne Michaels is a _____") with some help from Michaels, who has been feeding Turturro the answers from the control room. Buttafuoco is certain the game is rigged and storms off. Or maybe he just suddenly remembered that two years earlier, an episode of SNL (18.10) included not one, but three parodies of the Buttafuoco-Fisher scandal: *Aaron Spelling's Amy Fisher 10516*, a made-for-TV movie starring Tori Spelling (Melanie Hutsell) as Fisher and host Danny DeVito as Buttafuoco; *Amy Fisher: One Messed-Up Bitch*, with an all-black cast that included Jackée Harry (Ellen Cleghorne) as Fisher and Tim Meadows as Buttafuoco; and a *Masterpiece Theatre* version, *The House of Buttafuoco*, with Julia Sweeney as Fisher.

**CAGE, Nicolas**: Andy Samberg first impersonated actor Nicolas Cage on a parody of *The View* (35.5) before making recurring appearances on *Weekend Update* in a segment called "In the Cage," in which the actor talks to fellow thespians about their craft and their recent film. Samberg as Cage interviews Jake Gyllenhaal (36.18), Bradley Cooper (36.22), Jude Law (37.10), and Liam Neeson (37.21), and after discussing their latest movie, Samberg as Cage always asks the same question, "How am I not in that movie?" At one point he is joined in the cage by the real Nicholas Cage himself (37.14), who explains that his dream as an actor is to appear in every film ever released, which made it necessary to clone himself. Like all the other actors who stepped "into the cage," he also plugs his latest film, in this case *Ghost Rider: Spirit of Vengeance* (2012). Proving he's a good sport who can laugh at his own on-screen persona, Cage explains that the film has the "two key qualities of a classic Nic Cage action film: All the dialogue is either whispered or screamed and everything in the movie is on fire." Samberg also imitated Cage in an earlier sketch in which he competes against Jude Law for the role of Hamlet (35.17), though Jimmy Fallon was the first to impersonate the action star as a contestant on *Celebrity Jeopardy!* (24.16). Cage hosted the show back in September 1992 (18.1) with his *Moonstruck* (1987) costar Cher making a cameo.

Nicolas Cage joined his impersonator Andy Samberg for his "In the Cage" segment on *Weekend Update*.

**CAMERON, James** (24.10, 35.12): Director James Cameron shows he has a sense of humor about his own work when he introduces (24.10) the "original ending" of his 1997 blockbuster *Titanic*, in which Rose (Cheri Oteri) finishes telling her story to treasure hunter Brock Lovett (guest host Bill Paxton, who played the role in the film) and his crew. Only they've grown impatient and are really only interested in the Heart of the Ocean necklace. When she admits that she was actually never on the ship, they start to rough her up. When his latest blockbuster, *Avatar* (2009), broke box-office records, Cameron returned in 2010 (35.12) to help Bill Hader and Andy Samberg pitch *James Cameron's Laser Cats*, with Sigourney Weaver playing "Ripley," her role in *Alien* (1979), to Lorne Michaels. Once again, Michaels tells them to all get out of his office. In 2012, Michaels had a similar response to Steven Spielberg's pitch for *Laser Cats 7* (37.19).

**CHRISTIE, Chris** (38.8): The governor of New Jersey made a surprise appearance on *Weekend Update* (38.8) to give a status report on the cleanup efforts following Hurricane Sandy. He gives anchor Seth Meyers a little Jersey attitude and jokes about never taking off his signature fleece pullover with his name and title on it, which he wore throughout the hurricane.

**CHUCKY** (24.3): In what is perhaps one of *SNL*'s most unexpected cameos, Chucky, star of the *Child's Play* horror franchise, gives an editorial on *Weekend Update* (24.3) defending President Clinton, who at the time was preparing for his impeachment defense. Chucky also pulls a knife on anchor Colin Quinn and is hauled off the set, only to return at the end of the show when host Lucy Lawless says her good nights. Like the star of any horror film franchise, Chucky returns in a filmed sketch (47.17) in which he is terrorizing his female coworkers (cast member Sarah Sherman supplies the voice).

**CRANSTON, Bryan** (42.9): In this sketch, three years after the cult series *Breaking Bad* (2008–2013) ended, high school chemistry teacher/meth cooker Walter White (Cranston) appeared on CNN's *The Lead with Jake Tapper*, along with guest Kellyanne Conaway (Kate McKinnon). Tapper (Beck Bennett) announces that President Trump has appointed White to be the new head of the federal DEA (Drug Enforcement Agency). Using coded language fans of the show will understand (like "blue" and "Make America Cook Again"), White expresses his support of Trump's policies because they are "good for business." Tapper points out that White is yet another Trump appointee hired to run an agency with the goal of dismantling it.

**DAMON, Matt** (44.1): Matt Damon made a memorable guest appearance as a crying, crazed, and emotionally angry Brett Kavanaugh during *SNL*'s account of the latter's U.S. Supreme Court confirmation hearings. It is another example of a sketch that captured the essence of the larger-than-life "characters" and behaviors the country witnessed during the Trump administration. Three women had accused Kavanaugh of attempted rape or sexual harassment while in high school and at Yale University, in addition to being a blackout drunk. The sketch is based on Kavanaugh's forty-minute opening statement and questioning from the Senate Judiciary Committee, where Kavanaugh (Damon) rages that his "good name" is being smeared, all the while drinking a lot of water, sniffing back tears, and telling snippets of anecdotes from his high school years about friends "P.J., Tobin, and Squee" (some of which he addressed at his actual hearing). The judge is nearly at the end of his rope when Senator Amy Klobuchar (Rachel Dratch) finally questions him about his drinking, and he replies, "I like beer, okay! I like beer!" which once again mirrors when the real senator asked him about blacking out while drinking. He paused nervously, replying to the real Klobuchar, "Have you—I'm curious if you have?" Numerous *SNL* cast members played other senators, the standout being Kate McKinnon as a bloated Lindsey Graham.

Matt Damon appeared as an overly emotional Brett Kavanaugh. defending himself over allegations of sexual assault at his confirmation hearings to be the next Supreme Court Justice.

**GANDOLFINI, James** (30.1): In his only appearance on *SNL*, the late, great star of *The Sopranos* demonstrates why he would have made a terrific guest host. Identified only as a "New Jersey Resident," Gandolfini gives an editorial on *Weekend Update* about then New Jersey governor Jim McGreevey's announcement that he is gay and resigning over his involvement with a male staffer. Gandolfini explains that McGreevey is a *fanook* (a derogatory slang term for "gay" used by wise guys) and had an affair—"big deal"—but the mistake he made was putting him on the payroll. As he continues to make offensive remarks, anchor Tina Fey repeatedly interrupts him, which ticks him off. When he finally finishes, he tells anchor Amy Poehler it was nice to meet her "and the mouthy one [indicating Fey]—I'm not so sure."

**GIBB, Barry** (39.10): This sketch has Bee Gee Barry Gibb (Jimmy Fallon) hosting a political talk show, but he would rather harmonize in falsetto with his brother Robin (Justin Timberlake) than engage with his guests about serious issues. This is the sixth and last time Fallon and Timberlake teamed up for *The Barry Gibb Talk Show*, which was first introduced in 2003 (29.2). Tonight's guests are Fox News host Megyn Kelly (Cecily Strong), Congressman Paul Ryan (Taran Killam), and Madonna (as in the *real* Madonna), who makes the only sound political observation about how politicians should not put their own ideology over doing the right thing. The topper is at the close of the show, when Barry and Robin launch into *The Barry Gibb Talk Show* theme song (to the tune of "Lights on Broadway"), and they are joined by the real Barry Gibb, marking his only appearance on *SNL*. Previously, Barry and Robin appeared with Jimmy Fallon and Justin Timberlake on *The Tonight Show with Jimmy Fallon* on March 16, 2010. Robin died in 2012, the year before the *SNL* sketch aired on December 21, 2013. Barry Gibb returned to *The Tonight Show* on January 27, 2014, to launch his solo tour in the United States.

**HASSELHOFF, David** (20.6): Here's a good example of how far *SNL* would sometimes go for a laugh. When Norm Macdonald hosted *Weekend Update*, one of the running jokes concerned actor/singer David Hasselhoff's popularity in Germany, which would end with the line: "Which once again proves my theory: Germans love David Hasselhoff!" What Macdonald is saying is in fact true. In between his two hit television shows, *Knight Rider* (1982–1986) and *Baywatch* (1989–2001), Hasselhoff's 1988 recording of "Looking for Freedom" held on to the number one spot on the West Germany pop charts for eight weeks from March 31 to May 19, 1989 (the song was originally recorded in 1978 by German singer Marc Seaberg). In fact, Hasselhoff performed the song, about a rich man's son who leaves his hometown and goes off on his own looking for freedom, at the Berlin Wall on New Year's Eve, 1989. In his appearance on *Weekend Update* (20.6), the real Hasselhoff gives an update on his recent world tour and names all of the countries he's been—only Germany is not on the list. When Hasselhoff is asked about how much Germans love him, he's modest, forcing Macdonald to write "Germans love me" on a piece of paper and ask him to read it out loud (which he does). Macdonald thanks him and Hasselhoff bids the audience, "Auf Wiedersehen."

**JEWELL, Richard** (23.1): One of the show's most unusual cameos was an appearance by former security guard Richard Jewell, who discovered the pipe bomb at Centennial Olympic Park during the 1996 Summer Olympic Games in Atlanta and was later suspected of planting it so he would look like a hero. Several newspaper and television news networks reported that Jewell was a "person of interest," and although he was never charged, his home was searched and he was put under surveillance. The real bomber, Eric Robert Rudolph, was caught and eventually took responsibility for the attack along with several others. Meanwhile, Jewell filed lawsuits against the *New York Post*, NBC, and CNN, which settled out of court. After that, Jewell made an *SNL* appearance on *Weekend Update* during which he is questioned by anchor Norm Macdonald, who suspects he was also involved in the deaths of Lady Di and Mother Teresa.

Apparently Macdonald was not happy that he had to share the *Weekend Update* desk with Jewell. "He was creepy," Macdonald told Mark Seliger of *Rolling Stone*. "What the hell did he ever do? Not bomb something?"

**KUHN, Maggie** (1.8): The fight for racial equality that began in the 1950s with the civil rights movement in the United States gave birth to the women's rights movement in the late 1960s and the gay and lesbian rights movement in the 1970s. Another war waged in the early 1970s was against age-ism, and its leader was sixty-seven-year-old Margaret Kuhn, founder of a movement known as the Gray Panthers. As Eleanor Blau reported in a 1972 *New York Times* article on the Panthers, the group's goal is to "liberate the old." Since its inception, the organization has tackled common problems faced by retirees in the areas of health care, civil rights, jobs and economic security, and sustainability. The real Kuhn made a brief appearance on *SNL*'s first Christmas show hosted by Candice Bergen (1.8), who asks Ms. Kuhn, "If she could give us anything for Christmas, what would you choose?" Ms. Kuhn obviously came prepared. Her "give" list includes changing the way people think about old people, and the fear of getting old (Bergen admits she is). She would also like to give everyone who has "copped out" and given up a "big shot in the arm of courage and guts to be involved, to get to work and heal this sick old world of ours." She ends with a "Gray Panther" sign-off—with her fist in the air, she shouts, "Off your asses!"

**LEWINSKY, Monica** (24.18): Lewinsky was the former White House intern whose affair with President Bill Clinton became the biggest political scandal of the decade. Clinton's denial that he engaged in "sexual relations" with Ms. Lewinsky led to his impeachment on two charges (perjury in regard to his testimony on his relationship with Lewinsky and Paula Jones and obstruction of justice in the Jones case). The House of Representatives voted to impeach Clinton, who was acquitted of all charges on February 12, 1999, by a Senate vote (a two-thirds majority was needed to convict). From the moment the story broke to the Senate trial, *SNL* had a field day with the scandal with a series of sketches that reenacted such events as the conversations between Monica (Molly Shannon) and her former confidante, Linda Tripp (played by John Goodman in drag) (23.12, 24.7), who recorded their conversations, which she handed over to independent counsel Kenneth Starr.

So it was only a matter of time before Lewinsky would appear on *SNL*, though Michaels had the good sense to wait until May 8, 1999, about three months after the Senate vote was taken. The episode opens with a dream sequence in which Clinton imagines his postpresidential life in Malibu with his "old lady"—Lewinsky (who opens the show with "Live from New York"). Later in the episode, Lewinsky is a guest on *The Ladies' Man* with Leon Phillips. She answers callers' questions and gives advice about affairs with people at work ("First, people around the office start gossiping, and the next thing you know, your face is all over Arabic newspapers") and phone sex ("If you do it, don't tell anybody about it"). They also take a call from Linda Tripp (John Goodman in a cameo), who asks for Lewinsky's forgiveness. She flatly refuses and seemed to be relishing the opportunity to say it on national television. As for Tripp, she told Larry King in an interview that she "laughed hysterically" at John Goodman's imitation of her, but admitted her feelings were hurt over the most recent sketch (in which NBC's Linda Gangel [Ana Gasteyer] interviews Tripp, "the most hated person in America" [24.13]).

After being in the center of the biggest political scandal of the Clinton presidency, Monica Lewinsky made a cameo on *The Ladies' Man* with Leon Phelps.

A compilation of the sketches aired on February 27, 1999, under the title *Saturday Night Live: Best of the Clinton Scandal*. Excerpts from the sketches were published in book form that same year under the title *SNL Presents: The Clinton Years*.

**LIBERACE** (10.15): For over three decades (1962–1993), talk show host Joe Franklin was a fixture on New York television. *The Joe Franklin Show*, which aired on WWOR-TV (Channel 9), gave its legendary host a chance to share his extensive knowledge of show business and movie trivia while chatting with everyone from the famous to the relatively obscure. Billy Crystal impersonated the legendary talker in parodies of *The Joe Franklin Show*. In one episode (10.15), Franklin is joined by songwriter Irving Cohen (Martin Short), a Hispanic ventriloquist (Christopher Guest), and the real Liberace, who looks a little unsure why he's there. When Liberace died two years later, in 1987, Phil Hartman appeared in a cold open in which Liberace is wearing angel's wings and playing in heaven (12.11). The following week, the cold open once again features Liberace (Hartman), who is being interviewed by Robin Leach on *Afterlife Styles of the Rich and Famous* (12.12). More recently, Fred Armisen portrayed Liberace in a series of parodies of 1950s holidays specials hosted by Vincent Price (Bill Hader) in celebration of Halloween (34.6, 36.5), Valentine's Day (34.16), and Christmas (35.10).

**NICHOLSON, Jack** (23.9, 33.3): Academy Award–winning actor Jack Nicholson's television appearances are limited to awards shows, so it was a genuine surprise when he made two appearances on the main stage of Studio 8H. The first was in 1997 (23.9). During her monologue, guest host Helen Hunt, who was promoting her new film, *As Good as It Gets* (for which she and costar Nicholson won Oscars), is interrupted by cast members, who all come out and do their lousy Jack Nicholson imitations. When the real Jack Nicholson appears, Jim Breuer asks him what he thinks of his imitation, and Nicholson responds with the famous line from *A Few Good Men*: "You want to know the truth? You can't handle the truth!" He later pops up in a sketch as Hunt's husband. Ten seasons later (33.3), Nicholson appeared without warning during the goodnights to introduce Bon Jovi, who closed the show with "Who Says You Can't Go Home?"

**OBAMA, Barack** (33.4): Senator and Democratic presidential candidate Barack Obama made a surprise appearance on *SNL* on November 3, 2007, in the cold open set at a Halloween costume party in the Westchester County home of Bill and Hillary Clinton (Darrell Hammond and Amy Poehler). The guest list includes senators and politicians who are vying to be Hillary Clinton's vice presidential running mate for the 2008 election (Joe Biden and Chris Dodd are dressed like Spongebob Squarepants twins). The guest in a Barack Obama mask turns out to be the future president himself, who gets to open the show with a "Live from New York, it's *Saturday Night!*"

**PELLER, Clara** (9.17): Eighty-two-year-old Clara Peller became one of the most famous faces on television in the 1980s when she asked the question "Where's the beef?" on commercials for the fast-food chain Wendy's (the question was posed to Wendy's competitors, whose burgers were skimpy on the beef). Peller appeared on *SNL* in a commercial parody pitching a line of frozen dinners suited for those living below the poverty line. The commercial begins with Dad (played by host and former Democratic presidential candidate George McGovern) coming home after a long hard day of hopeless job hunting and is disgusted that they have to eat surplus cheese-loaf for the eighteenth day in a row. His wife (Mary Gross) asks how a welfare mother is supposed to plan a menu on $11 a day? Then President Ronald Reagan (Joe Piscopo) appears to introduce America to White House Foods' new collection of "starvation-level cooking from around the Third World." The selections include "Curried Fish Heads and Bread Crusts," "Dead Pigeons with Paint Chips," and "African Dirt Pie." Peller appears at the very end to ask her famous question, "Where the beef?"

**PITT, Brad** (24.5, 45.17): Has Brad Pitt ever been asked to host *Saturday Night Live*? Based on his two cameo appearances, in 1998 and 2020, Pitt demonstrates he has natural comedic timing that many dramatic actors who host often lack. In 1998 (24.5), coinciding with the release of his film *Meet Joe Black*, Pitt appears in the cold open as a therapist to former cast member and this week's host, David Spade. Spade returns to host with an inflated ego, claiming everyone treats him differently because he is an "international film star," a "sex symbol," and on a "hit television series" (*Just Shoot Me!*). "Is it

During the COVID-19 pandemic, Brad Pitt appeared as Dr. Anthony Fauci, who clarifies some of the inaccurate statements President Trump had made about the coronavirus and the vaccine.

*really* a hit? Like *Friends*?" asks Pitt, who exclaims at the end of their therapy session, "Live from New York! . . ."

On April 25, 2020, *SNL* paid respect to Dr. Anthony Fauci, the longtime director of the National Institute of Allergy and Infectious Diseases (NIAID; 1984–2022) and one of the lead members of President Donald Trump's White House Coronavirus Task Force. In the cold open of the second episode of *Saturday Night Live at Home*, Pitt, wearing a white wig and glasses, appears as the gravelly voiced immunologist, who explains what President Trump "was trying to say" when he made inane and/or false statements about the virus ("I'm not sure anyone really knows what it is"), the vaccine (will be available "relatively soon"), and how it can be treated ("injecting disinfectant, ultralight").

Pitt then removes the wig and glasses and thanks the real Dr. Fauci for "your calm and your clarity in this unnerving time . . . and thank you to medical workers and first responders and their families for being on the front line." Pitt then opens the show, "Live, kind of, from all across America, it's *Saturday Night!*" For his three-minute-and-twelve-second appearance, Pitt was nominated for Outstanding Guest Actor in a Comedy Series.

**RENO, Janet** (22.12): Will Ferrell tapped into a small part of his feminine side to play United States attorney general Janet Reno in a sketch, *Janet Reno's Dance Party*, a teenage dance party show broadcast from her basement. In the first *Dance Party* sketch, Ferrell/Reno is joined by Secretary of Health and Human Services Donna Shalala (Kevin Spacey) and President Bill Clinton (Darrell Hammond) (22.12). On January 20, 2001, the day President Clinton's successor, George W. Bush, was sworn in as the 43rd President of the United States, Reno (26.10) appeared alongside her impersonator in the final episode of *Dance Party*. After some reminiscing and a surprise visit from Clinton (Hammond), the real Janet Reno, wearing an identical blue dress and pearls as Ferrell, breaks through the wall and joins her impersonator in a final dance. In a 2001 interview with *Playboy*'s David Rensin, Ferrell credited his wife Viveca for the suggestion that he impersonate Reno because she was around the same height as Ferrell, who is 6'3". "Somebody's always going to do the president and probably the vice president," Ferrell explained, "but there's no reason to do Reno. It's creating something out of nowhere."

**RUBIN, Jerry** (1.2): Former Yippie leader Jerry Rubin was one of the seven anti-war protestors known as "The Chicago Seven," who famously led the large group of demonstrations against President Johnson's policies in the Vietnam War at the 1968 Democratic National Convention. Five of the seven were found guilty of crossing state lines with the intent to incite a riot—a violation of anti-riot provisions of the Civil Rights Act of 1968. Their convictions were reversed by an appeals court and seven years later Rubin appeared in the second episode of *SNL* in a commercial parody for the Berkeley Collection (by Chemstro)—three kinds of vinyl acrylic-coated wallpaper covered with graffiti and slogans from the 1960s: "The Dissident" (it contains slogans like "Legalize Abortion" and "Death to U.S. Imperialist Warmongers"), "The Peacemaker" ("Flower Power," "Get Out of Vietnam," etc.), and "The Digger" ("Free Bobby Seale," "Free Angela Davis"). This commercial was repeated when President Gerald Ford's press secretary, Ron Nessen, hosted the show (1.17), for which the president did a filmed cameo, so it was likely he would be watching (see chapter 18). By the 1980s, Rubin had traded his tie-dyed T-shirts in for a suit and tie and became a successful entrepreneur. The man who once told young people to "never trust anyone under 30" died in 1994 at the age of fifty-six when he was fatally injured while jaywalking in the Westwood section of Los Angeles.

**SCORSESE, Martin**: Even when one of his films ventures into comedic territory, like *The King of Comedy* (1983) and *After Hours* (1985), director Scorsese's dark sensibility still prevails. Scorsese first appeared as a guest (17.6) on *The Chris Farley Show*, though Farley isn't smart enough to ask him any in-depth questions (though to his credit, he does get Scorsese to do a little of De Niro's "You talkin' to me?" speech from *Taxi Driver* [1981]). The following season Scorsese made an appearance backstage with Robert De Niro when their buddy Joe Pesci is hosting (18.3). In his third appearance, Scorsese is taken hostage by Admiral General Aladeen, played by Sacha Baron Cohen, who is promoting his film *The Dictator* (2012). With the help of electroshock, Aladeen gets the director to endorse his movie. The Cohen-Scorsese connection stemmed from Cohen's appearance in Scorsese's latest film, *Hugo* (2011).

**SHEINDLIN, Judge Judy** (24.3): *Judge Judy* is one of the more entertaining TV courtroom shows, and Cheri Oteri's impersonation of TV's most popular judge emphasizes her impatience with the plaintiffs and defendants who appear in her courtroom, especially when they get out of line or, even worse, when she suspects they are lying ("Don't pee on my shoe and tell me it's raining, sir!"). In one sketch, just as Oteri as Judy is about to rule, the real Judge Judy Sheindlin makes a surprise visit, tells Oteri to get her "bony ass" out of her chair, and rules in favor of the plaintiff.

**SISKEL, Gene** and **EBERT, Roger** (8.1, 9.1): Chicago movie critics Gene Siskel (of the *Chicago Tribune*) and Roger Ebert (of the *Chicago Sun-Times*) were television stars themselves with their own weekly review show, *At the Movies* (later retitled *Siskel & Ebert*), when they made their first of three appearances on *SNL* (8.1) at the end of the show to provide their honest reviews of three of the sketches we just watched. Ebert found a televangelist sketch to be a "tired and clichéd reworking on an ancient old satirical target." Siskel thought a sketch about white liberals and angry blacks worked because of Eddie Murphy. The duo also later appeared on one of *SNL*'s early specials, *SNL Film Festival* (3/2/85), a compilation of the best shorts and commercials from past seasons.

**STONE, Oliver** (34.5): Josh Brolin hosted the show in October 2008 to promote his new film, *W* (2008), Oliver Stone's biopic of President George W. Bush. During his monologue, while Brolin talks about how he prepared for the role, Stone stands up from the audience and reminds him to tell people it opened this weekend and give the name of the film. The same show marked the appearance of Republican vice presidential nominee Sarah Palin, who, in her book *Going Rogue*, revealed she is not a fan of the director: "Unbelievably, he is a supporter of Communist dictator Hugo Chávez [President of Venezuela] who in a 2006 speech to the United Nations referred to the president of the United States [George W. Bush] as 'the devil himself.'" Knowing where Stone stands, one wonders if he even extended his hand to her.

**STREISAND, Barbra** (17.14): In February 1992, *Coffee Talk* hostess Linda Richman (Mike Myers in drag), joined by her mother (guest host Roseanne) and Liz Rosenberg (surprise guest Madonna), were all verklempt when they received a surprise visit from Barbra Joan Streisand (17.14). Linda Richman repaid the favor when Myers appeared onstage as the Richman character in the second act of the opening of Streisand's 1994 tour on New Year's Eve, December 31, 1993, at the opening of the MGM Grand in Las Vegas. Myers brought along his then-wife Robin and her mother, on whom the character of Linda Richman was based, to meet Streisand in person. In between *SNL* and Vegas, Myers did an impersonation of Streisand singing a few bars of

"People" at Clinton's 1992 Inaugural Gala (18.11) and again later that year on *SNL* as one of a long line of artists recording a song with Frank Sinatra (Joe Piscopo) for his album *Duets* (19.6).

**WAHLBERG, Mark** (34.5): Actor Mark Wahlberg is another good sport because they don't just go after *him*, they also go after his mom. Although October 18, 2008 (34.5) is best remembered for an appearance by the real Sarah Palin (or better yet, Adele, who sang "Chasing Pavements" and "Cold Shoulders"), it also featured a cameo by Mark Wahlberg. His appearance was prompted by Andy Samberg's previous impression of him in the sketch "Mark Wahlberg Talks to the Animals." This was not the first time an *SNL* cast member imitated the actor with the heavy Boston accent. Adam Sandler played him as one of Sassy magazine's "Sassiest Boys" (18.12), as well as his brother Donnie as one of the New Kids on the Block in a spoof of *The Arsenio Hall Show* (17.13). As played by Jim Breuer, Mark Wahlberg later turned up as a guest on *The Robin Byrd Show* (23.5), with Cheri Oteri as the porn star turned cable access host.

Samberg's rendition of Wahlberg is less conventional. He walks through a farm set in the studio and stops to talk to a dog ("I like your fur, that looks great"), a donkey ("You eat apples, right? I produce *Entourage*"), a chicken ("How's it hangin'?"), and a goat ("I like your beard. I had a beard like that in *The Perfect Storm*"). He punctuates each conversation with a heavily accented: "Say hi to your mom for me, all right?" The following week (34.5), Wahlberg confronts a nervous Samberg. Their conversation gets interrupted by Amy Poehler, host Josh Brolin, and a donkey—and he talks to each one just like Samberg in the sketch (including "Say hi to your mom for me, all right?," though he includes "stepmom" for Brolin [his dad is married to Barbra Streisand]). Samberg promises not to do it again, and the two even "hug it out" à la *Entourage*.

But Samberg breaks his promise later in the season when Samberg's Wahlberg is sitting in the audience during *How I Met Your Mother* star Neil Patrick Harris's monologue (34.12), which gives him the opportunity to make "Hey, you know how I met your mother?" jokes, and again in "Mark Wahlberg Talks to the Christmas Animals" (and a snowman) (35.10) ("Hey partridge. How's it hanging? How's your pear tree?").

When asked about how he really felt about the sketch by Nadine Rajabi on nationallampoon.com's *The Zazz*, the actor admitted, "Once they do that kind of thing, it's very flattering . . . I never say that. Now I have a new catch phrase, so I will."

**WALTERS, Barbara** (39.20): *Weekend Update* anchor Cecily Strong announces May 17, 2014, would be Barbara Walters's last appearance on *The View*, marking the end of her five-decade career as a broadcast journalist. As a tribute, we see video clips of cast members Gilda Radner, Cheri Oteri, Nassim Pedrad, and Rachel Dratch impersonating Walters. When Walters appears, she dismisses the tribute and points out that Strong is not a real journalist

(Strong implies neither is Walters by reminding her she hosts *The View*). Demonstrating that she does have a sense of humor about herself, Walters offers Strong some advice she has learned over the course of her career: Develop a signature voice ("Hello, I'm Barbara Wawa"); the softer the news, the softer the focus on the lens (President Obama warrants a softer lens than a Kardashian); don't be afraid to ask the tough question ("If you are a tree, what kind of tree would you be?"); and it's fine to make people smile, but the real money is in making a celebrity cry ("Kerching, kerching").

**ZUCKERBERG, Mark** (36.13): The cofounder of Facebook was given the chance to confront host Jesse Eisenberg, who just scored an Oscar nomination for his portrayal of him in *The Social Network* (2010), and Andy Samberg, who had done his impression of the young billionaire earlier in the season (36.3, 36.10). Samberg interrupts Eisenberg's monologue, claiming to be the real Zuckerberg, who we see backstage with Lorne Michaels, who tells him he's better off backstage. When Zuckerberg appears onstage, Samberg makes a hasty exit. Eisenberg asks him if saw *The Social Network*—he did and said it was "interesting." Eisenberg accepts the compliment and graciously asks Zuckerberg to announce the name of the musical guest (Nicki Minaj). Eisensberg invites the audience to "stick around, we'll be right back."

# "A Nonexistent Problem with an Inadequate Solution"

## SNL's Commercial Parodies

One of *Saturday Night Live*'s many major contributions to the annals of American comedy are its commercial parodies. In between the monologue, the comedy sketches, and the musical performances (and, in the early days, during *Weekend Update*), *SNL* will feature parodies of current commercials, phony ads for fictional products and services, and fake political campaign ads and PSAs. Some parodies, like the classic commercials for Super Bass-O-Matic '76 (1.17) (see chapter 6) and the Velvet Jones School of Technology (7.3), are performed live in Studio 8H, but most of them are shot on film or video in the style of actual commercials. That's the reason why they can be easily mistaken for the real thing, particularly in the early years when they used writers and bit players as actors. Nowadays cast members appear in most commericial parodies, and NBC insists on keeping its peacock logo on the bottom left of the screen throughout the show (just in case you forget which network you are watching).

When *SNL* debuted in October 1975, critics singled out the commercials as one of the show's highlights. Benjamin Stein of the *Wall Street Journal* felt they were "done with great imagination." "It is possible," he wrote, "that the reason the best parts are commercials is that commercials themselves come so close to self parody that they need only a small shove to push them into comedy." In his review, *Times-Picayune* critic David Cuthbert admitted, "The best of these [commercials] were so close to the originals, it took several moments before you were aware they were parodies." One television critic, the *New York Times*' John O'Connor, was not amused. He found a commercial parody that used senior citizens' pacemakers to demonstrate the longevity of the Try-Hard 1-11 Battery vs. other leading brands (1.2) "thoroughly tasteless and insensitive." O'Connor also admitted it took some time to realize the next commercial for an antidiarrheal medication was a "genuine commercial." "Going from the objectionable to the ridiculous in a matter of seconds," observed O'Connor, "may be one of the unique experiences in watching television."

Director James Signorelli would agree albeit for different reasons. Over the course of four decades (minus Lorne Michaels's five-year absence), he was a film segment producer on SNL and the creative force behind the show's filmed commercial parodies. In the early 1970s, Signorelli was a cinematographer on blaxploitation films (*Super Fly* [1972], *Super Fly T.N.T.* [1973]) and later directed feature films (*Easy Money* [1983], *Elvira: Mistress of the Dark* [1988]) and produced prime-time specials for *SNL* and *Simon and Garfunkel: The Concert in Central Park* (1982) for HBO. In the *Directors Guild of America Quarterly*, Signorelli explained to Tarvis Watson how the *SNL* commercial parodies developed over the years: "At first the parodies were casual and improvisational. As time went on, we tried to refine the parody commercial so that it really reflected the excesses of commercial production, and at the same time have at least four or five good laughs in them." In a 1989 interview with *Backstage*, Signorelli emphasized the important role irony plays in a successful commercial parody: "We're pretty hip to irony, and that's a winner in real commercials, as well as here. We're able to take the mock sincerity that you see in some real commercials and turn it into irony." He also described the process of producing commercials for *SNL* "very collaborative," beginning with working with the writers who, over a three-day period, create the product, storyline and ad copy. The commercial would be shot the following week at a budget 20–25 percent of a real commercial and be ready to air on the next show.

Signorelli would eventually transfer the skills he developed directing ad parodies to actual commercials, including spots for Ameritech and Budweiser. His director's demo reel includes such classic *SNL* commercials as Little Chocolate Donuts (3.6), Swill (the mineral water "dredged from Lake Erie") (3.2), Angora Bouquet ("Washes your brain, as well as your face") (3.3), and Jewess Jeans (5.11) ("Guaranteed to ride up.").

According to Signorelli, what has stayed consistent over the years is the philosophy behind *SNL*'s commercial parodies, which the director credits in *Shoot* magazine to longtime head writer Jim Downey, who "coined the idea that our joke spots are addressing a nonexistent problem with an inadequate solution. That's been the thing we've sailed on ever since."

## "Live from New York: The Polaroid Deluxe SX-70 Camera"

Adding to viewers' confusion surrounding ad parodies during season 1 was the inclusion of four actual, live, in-studio commercials for the new Polaroid Deluxe SX-70 Camera, two of which featured guest host Candice Bergen, who at the time was the company's real spokesperson.

Live commercials were hardly new to television. Big-name television hosts like Ed Sullivan, Jack Paar, and Johnny Carson often doubled as pitchmen for everything from Fab Detergent to Polaroid cameras to Jell-O pudding. But their series didn't include fake commercials, which is why adding an actual commercial for a real product into the mix on *SNL* no doubt confused members of its studio audience not to mention viewers at home.

"A Nonexistent Problem with an Inadequate Solution"

The first Polaroid commercial (1.4), which paired Bergen and Chevy Chase, is particularly awkward because it is preceded by a comedy bit in which Chase, dressed in Elizabethan garb, is playing Hamlet. Holding the skull of his court jester, Yorick, Chase recites a soliloquy mourning his death ("Alas, poor Yorick!"). The joke is that he has not memorized his lines, but is reading them off of Yorick's skull. When Chase drops the skull, breaking it into little pieces, he tries to improvise his lines as he reads words off of the remaining fragments, which contain the segue to the commercial: "Looks like it's time for a Polaroid commercial." Bergen appears dressed as a Bee, and while Chase takes her picture, she points out the special features of the Polaroid Deluxe SX-70 Camera. As there is not enough time to wait for the Polaroid to develop, we are shown photos of Bergen taken earlier that evening. The remaining three commercials, which paired John Belushi (as Santa) and Bergen (dressed as a reindeer) (1.8), Belushi and Jane Curtin (1.18), and Garrett Morris and Gilda Radner (1.21), followed a similar script.

When Polaroid dropped the spots after the first season, *SNL* couldn't resist parodying one of Bergen's Polaroid commercials in which she shoots pictures at the Grand Canyon with the FX-70 Cheese Slicer, out of which comes a piece of cheese instead of a photo. "And I certainly heard from Polaroid on that one," Bergen recalled in Saturday Night Live: *The First Twenty Years*. "They weren't thrilled. I was their spokesperson. I wasn't supposed to be shooting Velveeta out of their camera."

In a live commercial for one of *SNL*'s sponsors, Polaroid, Chevy Chase takes a photo of Candice Bergen (in a bee costume).

SNL's library contains over 450 commercial parodies, the best of which have been showcased in three specials: Saturday Night Live *Goes Commercial* (1991); Saturday Night Live: *The Best of Commercial Parodies* (2005), hosted by Will Ferrell; and Saturday Night Live: *Just Commercials* (2009). Here is a small sampling of the some of *SNL*'s most memorable commercial parodies.

## Little Chocolate Donuts: "The Donuts of Champions" (3.6)

Before he became known as Kim Kardashian's stepfather (and later, Caitlyn Jenner), Bruce Jenner was the "World's Greatest Athlete"—winner of the gold medal in the decathlon at the 1976 Montreal Summer Olympics, where he set a new world record of 8,616 points. One of the many endorsements Jenner, with his All-American good looks, received in his post-Olympic career was for Wheaties cereal—"The Breakfast of Champions"—with his picture on the box.

Jenner's Wheaties commercial begins with Olympic footage of Jenner throwing the shot put, doing the long jump, and waving an American flag as the announcer declares, "Bruce Jenner has won the Olympic decathlon and set a new world record!" We then cut to Jenner in his kitchen. He grabs milk from his fridge and sits down to enjoy a bowl of Wheaties, while telling us, "I really worked hard getting ready for that day. I put in a lot of years, and put away a lot of Wheaties, because a complete breakfast with Wheaties is good tasting and good for you."

Apparently everyone did not believe that America's golden boy actually "put away a lot of Wheaties." In 1977, the San Francisco District Attorney's office, which clearly thought it had nothing better to do, charged Jenner and General Mills, the maker of Wheaties, with false and misleading advertising. According to the New York Times, Jenner held a news conference and confirmed that he does eat Wheaties. "I don't like people thinking I don't tell the truth," Jenner explained. The athlete claimed he had Wheaties "maybe two or three times a week as a kid," but also included them in his diet through the years. District Attorney Joseph Freitas withdrew the advertising suit, which he admitted was "a case of overzealousness" on the part of his staff.

*SNL*'s parody of Jenner's Wheaties commercial begins with footage of decathlon champion John Belushi winning the high jump and a long-distance run, setting a new world record. Sports announcer Marv Albert shouts over a screaming crowd, "A spectacular time! A new world's record! Unbelievable! What a day for John Belushi." Cut to Belushi, with a burning cigarette in his hand, at his breakfast table with a bowl and a box of "Little Chocolate Donuts." He testifies that they taste good, and give him the sugar he needs to get going in the morning—"That's why Little Chocolate Donuts have been on my training table since I was a kid."

The commercial was written by Al Franken and Tom Davis and directed by Signorelli, who recalled in Shales and Miller's backstage history that Belushi, who was a high school athlete, really didn't want to do the parody. When he

"A Nonexistent Problem with an Inadequate Solution"

Instead of Wheaties, Olympic athlete John Belushi starts his day with Little Chocolate Donuts (and a cigarette).

was practicing the jump, he acted as if he really hurt himself and wanted an ambulance to take him to the hospital—but he was okay, and they managed to finish the shoot. Still, the end result was certainly one of the funniest moments in season 3 and one of the rare times that a cast member played himself in a commercial parody and, in this case, made fun of his own persona.

Over the years, hosts have also been in on the joke, making fun of themselves and celebrity endorsements in commercial parodies for numerous products, some of which bear their name:

- **Martin Sheen Hairspray** (5.7): Afro Sheen was a hair product for African Americans formulated to make their hair softer and more manageable. In a personal testimonial, actress Jane Curtin uses "Martin Sheen Hairspray," which is essentially Sheen (this week's host) taking a sip of water and spitting into her hair.
- **Steve Martin's All-Natural Penis Beauty Cream (New Formula)** (20.1): Martin is proud to put his name on a new beauty cream that will make your penis "looking smoother and softer, the way women like it."
- **Kelly Ripa for Tressant Suprême** (29.4): At the time, Ripa was doing double duty as cohost of *Live! With Regis and Kelly* (2001–2011) and the star of the ABC sitcom *Hope & Faith* (2003–2006). She was also a spokesperson for Pantene Shampoo. She explains in this parody that her active lifestyle is the reason why she uses Tressant Suprême hair coloring. It's gentle on her hair,

keeps it silky—and contains crack cocaine. That's why she highlights her hair three or four times a day.

- **Mary-Kate & Ashley Perfume** (29.20): In 2003, Mary-Kate and Ashley Olsen introduced their own fragrance line, Mary-Kate & Ashley Perfume. When hosting *SNL*, the former child stars showed America they have a sense of humor by appearing in a commercial parody for their perfume designed for the "complex lady." We're told it's one perfume, yet it's "two fragrances, both completely unique, yet remarkably similar" because sometimes you're an "Ashley" and other times you're a "Mary-Kate." The twins pose on a chaise lounge and listen to an unseen male announcer rattle off a list of things you might be in the mood for and a female voice respond with either "Ashley" or "Mary-Kate": "A drive in a Rolls-Royce? Ashley. Or a Maserati? Mary-Kate." But as the commercial goes on, the list gets more and more absurd ("Coal mining? Tornados? Spearfishing?"), while the wind machine blowing their hair gets stronger and stronger.

Sometimes the writers like to have fun with a guest host's last name.

- Former power forward for the Houston Rockets Charles Barkley, whose name sounds like the British bank "Barclays," advertises his own bank bearing his name, **Barkley's Bank** (35.11). Barkley is a major gambler, so his bank makes a simple promise: "I'm either going to double it or lose it all. And that's a promise." Sports analyst Barkley also has his own app, the **Charles Barkley's Post Game Translator** (37.11), which is recommended for sports fans while watching postgame interviews with coaches and athletes. Using real clips, he shows you there's a difference between what they're saying and what they really mean.
- **Jon Hamm's John Ham** (34.6) looks like a toilet roll dispenser, but instead of tissue, it dispenses ham. Hamm also teams up with singer Michael Bublé to lend their last names to **Hamm & Bublé** (35.13), a restaurant that specializes in pork dishes and "bubbly" (champagne). Only Michael's last name is not pronounced "Bubb-ly," and he clearly only agreed to do the commercial because Hamm threatened him.
- In his monologue, the great Michael Jordan (17.1) agrees with critics who have called him out for doing one too many product endorsements. He then shares two commercials he shot that never aired. In the first, an ad for a female hygiene product, a teenager (Julia Sweeney) takes a walk with Mr. Jordan and confides to him that sometimes she gets that "not so fresh feeling" ("That's why there's **Feminine Secret**," he assures). The second is for hardcore pornography videos that carry his name on the label because "It's not really pornography unless it says 'Michael Jordan.'"
- Athletes who have hosted have also done commercials for ethnic restaurants bearing their name, even if it's a cultural mismatch, like **Derek Jeter's Taco Hole** (27.7) and **Tom Brady's Falafel City** (30.17).

"A Nonexistent Problem with an Inadequate Solution"

In this parody of a public service announcement for the United Way, legendary quarterback Peyton Manning is a verbally abusive mentor to a bunch of kids.

Two of the cleverest—and funniest—commercials featuring athletes were a pair of PSAs, each of which starred one of the Manning brothers, Peyton and Eli. Denver Broncos quarterback Peyton Manning is a spokesman for the NFL in a spot for the United Way (32.16), in which we see him volunteering his time to work with kids. Only Manning acts like a complete asshole, throwing the ball too hard and shaming and swearing at them when they don't catch it. His mentoring skills are not limited to football. He also teaches them how to break into a car and get a tattoo (of the quarterback) on his arm. He even uses a little girl to help him pick up women.

When Peyton's younger brother Eli, quarterback for the New York Giants, hosted five years later (37.20), he did a PSA on behalf of the "Little Brothers" program. "Our organization helps kids build confidence, reach their goals, and overcome their adversity—especially when that adversity is an older sibling." He demonstrates how he helps little bros overcome adversity by helping them get revenge on their older siblings by using bullying tactics—like holding the older brother's head over a toilet, giving him a wedgie, and chasing him with a bow and arrow.

## Bad Idea Jeans: "Well, he's an ex-freebase addict . . ." (16.1)

In 1987, Levi Strauss & Company ran a series of national commercials for Dockers, their new brand of khaki pants. The twenty-seven television spots featured a group of men sitting in a bar, office, and living room. The handheld camera moves so fast and the editing is so quick that you barely see their faces—just their pants. According to a 1997 article by Malcolm Gladwell published in the *New Yorker* about the campaign, the conversations between the men were not scripted. The producers asked a group of men to talk about certain topics and the conversations were taped. The footage was added later. As a result of the campaign, Dockers grew into a $600 million business for Levi Strauss. "It is no exaggeration," Gladwell writes, "to call the original Dockers ad one of the most successful fashion-advertising campaigns in history." The advertising and fashion worlds were especially surprised because no company had ever achieved that much success marketing fashion directly to male consumers.

The "Bad Idea Jeans" ad essentially uses the same concept. A group of men are sitting on bleachers throwing around a basketball, and the camera moves around freely with intermittent shots of the seat of their jeans and the "bad idea" tag. We hear snippets of their conversations; all of their statements sound like bad ideas: remodeling a house you're renting, letting a former freebase addict stay with you, feeling safer with a gun in the house now that you have children, not using protection when having sex in Haiti. Between each statement, the words "Bad Idea" appear on the screen. At the very end, the all-white group goes to play a pickup game of basketball with a group of very tall African Americans.

Over the years, *SNL* has featured commercials for many different brands of jeans: Jewess Jeans (5.11), featuring Rhonda Weiss (Gilda Radner); Clovin Hind Jeans, a parody of Brooke Shield's Calvin Klein commercials with Gail Matthius (6.4); Ronald Reagan Jeans (10.13), which incorporate real footage of the president on his ranch; Leevi's 3 Legged Jeans (17.6); and Mom Jeans (28.19), which, with their nine-inch zipper and casual front pleats, say "I'm not a woman anymore, I'm a mom." Then there's Wrangler Open Fly Jeans (36.4) with spokesperson, New York Jet Brett Favre, who was accused of sexting and sending inappropriate voice messages to an in-house sideline reporter, Jenn Sterger. He prefers jeans with no fly because "it's always out and camera-ready."

## First CityWide Change Bank: "Our business is making change." (14.1)

Banks love to sell themselves as people-friendly, service-oriented institutions that exist for one reason—to serve their customers. This idea is taken to the point of absurdity in a pair of ads for First CityWide Change Bank (14.1), which does only one thing—make change. In two separate spots, satisfied customers (Jan Hooks/Kevin Nealon, Nora Dunn/Phil Hartman) give testimonials of what happened when they needed change in a hurry. The "mock sincerity" of real commercials, as Signorelli explained, is turned into irony by the bank's self-satisfied service representative Paul McElroy (writer Jim Downey), who talks about how they are willing to work with their customers in meeting their change needs. He begins to list the various combinations the bank can give if a customer needs change, which are punctuated by on-screen graphics ("We can give you fifty singles." "We can give you twenty-five twos."). Then, to show how it's all about you, McElroy states that they will not give you change you don't want (for a $100 bill, "we are not going to give you two thousand nickels"). His final statement says it all: "We will give you the change equal to the amount of money that you want change for! That's what we do."

Another commercial parody that puts a twist on the same idea is for a credit card company, Metrocard, that provides its customers with a twenty-four-hour helpline (16.13). A customer (Phil Hartman) provides a testimonial of how he called the helpline when he lost his card while traveling and attests to how helpful the customer rep was over the phone. His story is intercut with the operator's (Roseanne) testimonial—and how she had no patience listening to this loser's story and had no trouble telling him so.

## Colon Blow: "How many bowls of your oat bran would it take . . . ?" (15.5)

In the 1980s, Total Cereal launched a campaign comparing its nutritional content with other leading brands of cereal. In one spot, comedian Richard Lewis is told by the disembodied voice of the male announcer he may have to eat four bowls of Grape-Nuts to get all the vitamins in Total. In another commercial, Sherman Hemsley, star of the sitcom *The Jeffersons* (1975–1985), is told four bowls of Post Raisin Bran equals one bowl of Total. Other commercials make a similar comparison between Total and All-Bran Cereal and Fruit & Fiber.

In the *SNL* spoof, when Phil Hartman sits down to enjoy his bowl of oat bran cereal, an unseen announcer begins to question him about the fiber content of his cereal. He invites him to try Colon Blow and to take a guess: "How many bowls of your oat bran would it take to equal the fiber content of one bowl of Colon Blow?" Hartman's guesses ("Two? . . . Five? . . . Nine?") are not even close. "It would take 30,000 bowls!" Suddenly, a giant stack of cereal bowls appears underneath Hartman, lifting him high in the air. He goes even higher when the announcer tells him about Super Colon Blow ("It would take over two and a half million bowls of your oat bran").

## Schmitt's Gay: "If you've got a big thirst, and you're gay . . ." (17.1)

This commercial is a smart reversal of all those fantasy ads that use scantily clad women to sell beer to a presumably heterosexual male consumer. Adam Sandler is house-sitting, but Chris Farley is not impressed by the dumpy house or the empty pool. But once Sandler turns on the water, the backyard pool turns into a gay paradise complete with muscular guys in skimpy bathing suits. Then there's a montage of point-of-view shots as an excited Farley and Sandler ogle and react to the hunky men, looking at their crotches and butts, the way heterosexual men in beer commercials ogle women. Then we see Sandler horsing around with the guys in the water and Farley leading a conga around the pool. An announcer (Phil Hartman) says, "If you've got a big thirst, and you're gay, reach for a cold, tall bottle of Schmitt's Gay."

Over the years, *SNL* has featured other commercials for alcoholic beverages:

- **Buddweiser Light** (9.12): A face-off between two hockey players (Joe Piscopo and Robin Williams) erupts into a full-out brawl, after which the two players sit together on the side of the rink and enjoy a cold Buddweiser Light. "The best. You found it inside. Now you'll fit it in the beer you drink."
- **Coldcock Malt Liquor** (17.4): At a fancy cocktail party, African Americans sing the praises of Coldcock Malt Liquor. Take a sip and an animated muscular arm and hand that appears on the can punches you in the face and knocks you unconscious. "Coldcock. You never see it coming."
- **A.M. Ale** (21.1): Here is ale to help you take on the challenge of a brand-new day. "Because you can't wait until afternoon."

## Happy Fun Ball: "The toy sensation that's sweeping the nation!" (16.13)

Three kids (Jan Hooks, Dana Carvey, and Mike Myers) are all excited about "Happy Fun Ball—the toy sensation that's sweeping the nation!" While we see the happy tykes playing with their ball, the announcer reads a long list of warnings, including how prolonged exposure should be avoided by pregnant women, the elderly, and children under ten, especially to its liquid core if it ruptures. Like a warning on a pharmaceutical label, you are advised to discontinue use if any of the following occur: itching, vertigo, temporary blindness, etc. The warnings get even more outrageous. The ball contains substance that fell to earth and is being used by our warplanes to drop on Iraq. But hey, it's fun.

## "Oops! I Crapped My Pants": "Just visit your pharmacy and say 'Oops! I crapped my pants.'" (24.1)

There is nothing more depressing than commercials targeting senior citizens. Whether it's for an alert system in case they fall and can't get up, or a laxative to relieve "irregularity," their tone is often condescending, treating older consumers like helpless children. This commercial for adult diapers ("Depends" is the brand name that comes to mind) is funny because instead of talking around the issue, as most commercials do, it uses explicit language.

Grandma wants to play tennis with her granddaughter, but she changes her mind. Grandpa knows why ("You still having control problems, aren't you?"). Grandpa lets her in on a little secret—Oops! I Crapped My Pants. If the name of the product is not explicit enough, there's his demonstration. While most commercials cut to someone in a lab coat who can demonstrate the product,

# "A Nonexistent Problem with an Inadequate Solution"

Grandpa takes it upon himself to pour a pitcher of iced tea into a pair to show their absorbency ("Imagine the pitcher of tea is really a gallon of your feces"). She's impressed ("Oops! I Crapped My Pants can hold a lot of dung."). But having these sweet, old, lovable old folks using words like "dung" and "feces" wasn't the end. Grandpa admits "he just did" (crap in his pants), and Grandma is later seen playing tennis carrying what is obviously a major load under her tennis skirt.

## Chantix: "Chantix. Just keep smoking." (37.11)

Once upon a time pharmaceutical companies only marketed their products to physicians through mail order and the occasional visit from the company sales rep (the person you see in your doctor's waiting room with a suitcase full of brochures and free samples). Sales reps are still making the rounds, but pharmaceutical companies have found a more lucrative way to sell their wares to potential patients: direct-to-consumer drug advertising, which started with print ads in magazines and newspapers and expanded to include radio and television commercials, billboards, the internet, and direct mailings. According to a 2011 article by C. Lee Ventola published in the *Pharmacy and Therapeutics Journal*, the shift from print ads to broadcast media occurred due to changes in the Food and Drug Administration's policies that now require pharmaceutical companies to include only "major risks" in their ads and direct viewers to a place where they can access a "brief summary" of information (a toll-free number, a website, etc.).

In one of many pharmaceutical commercial parodies, we're told Chantix will help you stop smoking—but there's a long list of potentially lethal side effects (37.11).

At the time, the *New York Times* reported that drug companies were spending nearly $5 billion a year on television ads.

As with ads for any product, drug ads promise consumers they will live a happier, more fulfilling life if they buy their product. But unlike other commercials, they also have to list the downsides to using their product, namely the possible side effects, the severity of which range from mild to life-threatening.

An *SNL* commercial for Chantix features a testimonial from a husband and wife (Bill Hader and Kristen Wiig) who explain that she had to quit smoking for her son and her husband because it wasn't a habit, but an addiction. The voice of the unseen announcer tells consumers that they need to talk to their doctor about any history of depression or other mental health problems, which can get worse while using Chantix. More specifically, there may be behavioral changes, such as hostility, depression, and "a powerful, overwhelming desire to kill the person you love most." The husband (Hader) looks worried, and although the wife assures him it's not the case, she starts to exhibit the list of symptoms, which grows increasingly absurd (droopy lip, jazz hands, Robert De Niro face, Incredible Hulk strength, etc.). In the end, the wife chases the husband out of the room, and the announcer says: "Chantix. Just keep smoking."

*SNL* has also featured commercials for pharmaceuticals that are either parodies of existing drug commercials or ads for drugs for conditions that don't exist or can't be treated by taking a pill.

### Homicil: "Until you come around. Because it's your problem, not theirs." (26.12)

In this "gay-friendly" commercial, moms and dads suffering from "Parental Anxiety Disorder" due to certain behaviors exhibited by their son indicating he might be gay (like making a fabulous dress or crème brûlée or twirling a baton) can dramatically decrease their anxiety by taking Homocil.

### Gaystrogen: "Get back to your old self." (29.3)

When the sons of the parents who take Homocil become adults themselves and begin to notice some changes in their tastes and mood, there's Gaystrogen, which works "to replenish your natural gayness and boost your fabu."

### Dr. Porkenheimer's Boner Juice: "A thicker, longer sexual experience." (30.1)

Ads for erectile dysfunction (ED) medication usually go for the soft sell by depicting couples sharing a romantic moment that the commercial implies is a prelude to something that can't be shown on television—like hot and heavy sex. Like its name, Dr. Porkenheimer's Boner Juice uses the more direct approach by basically stating exactly what you have to gain by taking it—"Bigger, and stronger, and more meaty . . . It's boners when you feel right. Giant ones that are thick and sturdy."

## Annuale: "Annuale. Once a year. Period." (33.5)

There's a new female hygiene product on the market that alters a woman's menstrual cycle so she will only have her period once a year. When it's that time of the year, watch out—hold on to your f–kin' hat! We see a woman swinging an axe at her coworkers, destroying a kid's birthday cake, and slugging her husband in the crotch.

This commercial is one of those brilliant feminist-infused parodies, which have advertised such products as Chess for Girls (23.8); Woomba (30.8), the first completely robotic feminine hygiene product ("It's a robot and it cleans my business, my lady business. And I like that"); and Lil Poundcake (37.2), the doll that has a needle in one hand that gives little girls a shot for the HPV (human papillomavirus). The latter was in response to Texas governor Rick Perry's mandating that little girls receive the vaccine against a sexual transmitted virus that can cause cervical cancer. The Texas legislature overturned the mandate, which Perry admitted was a mistake.

## "You're a Rat Bastard, Charlie Brown": "A new twist on an old classic" (38.10)

Just in time for the holidays, the New York Actors Studio presents a "new twist on an old classic": a *Peanuts* stage show for the whole family. This commercial showcases the talents of the *SNL* cast members (and one host) doing their best impressions of characters actors playing iconic Charles Schulz characters: Al Pacino (Bill Hader) as Charlie Brown, Philip Seymour Hoffman (Jason Sudeikis) as Pig-Pen, Edie Falco (Kate McKinnon) as Lucy, Larry David (guest host Martin Short) as Linus, and more. Hader as Pacino is hilarious as he chews up the scenery with his R-rated rants, which are intercut with shots of children sitting in the audience looking confused and horrified.

## "Xanax for Summer Gay Weddings" (38.21): "Because your friends have it all figured out—and you don't."

Two years before the U.S. Supreme Court legalized same-sex marriage, *SNL* closed out its thirty-eighth season with another faux pharmaceutical commercial for "Xanax for Summer Gay Weddings." This special brand of the popular tranquilizer is recommended for heterosexuals who feel anxious or stressed out about attending a "flawlessly executed" gay summer wedding—complete with

Commercial parodies with a queer sensibility: (top left, clockwise) Schmitt's Gay Beer (17.1); Homocil, to suppress parents' homophobia (26.12); Wells for Boys, part of Fisher-Price's toy line for sensitive boys (42.8); and Xanax for Gay Summer Weddings (38.21), to alleviate your anxiety when you attend the perfect gay wedding.

handsome men in pastel suits, released doves, choreographed dance moves, and a phone call from President Obama.

## "Wells for Boys" (42.8): "To wish upon, confide in, and reflect."

One of the more original *SNL* ads is for "Wells for Boys," a Fisher-Price toy line for sensitive little boys. As the narrator (Cecily Strong) explains, "Some boys live unexamined lives. But this one's heart is full of questions." Then there are little boys, like Spencer, who we are told will "grow up to have a widely passionate and successful, creative life, but not just yet." In the meantime, he can sit by his plastic well "to wish upon, confide in, and reflect." There is also a balcony for when they are ready to announce something and a shattered mirror they can look into to "examine the complex contradictions of their being." Daniel Reynolds, writing in *The Advocate*, commended the commercial's writers, Julio Torres and Jeremy Beiler, for nailing the "loneliness of queer kids" and tapping into the "cultural conversation over how many items for young people are needlessly gendered, in ways that can pressure kids to conform to the gender binary."

# Real Products, Fake Commercials

Since its debut in 1975, *Saturday Night Live* has included parodies of television commercials for fake products. Over the past decade, *SNL* has started to include commercial parodies for actual products and services, yet the producers claim there is no product placement, a common practice in both films and on television that involves a company paying producers for their product to be seen or mentioned in dialogued. *SNL* can use actual trademarks, brand names, and intellectual property because parody is protected under the First Amendment and the Fair Use Doctrine. Writers still need to clear their script through NBC's legal department to ensure there are no grounds for a lawsuit.

## Calvin Klein (40.11)

In a series of ads with blonde model Lara Stone (Cecily Strong), an impish Justin Bieber (Kate McKinnon) acts more like an overgrown kid than an adult.

## Totino's: Pizza rolls for "my hungry guys." (40.13, 41.12, 42.13)

*SNL* managed to turn a commercial about Totino's Pizza Rolls into a trilogy that aired over three consecutive seasons (40, 41, 42) the night before Super Bowl Sunday (2015, 2016, 2017). All three commercials feature Vanessa Bayer as a dim yet happy housewife who is relegated to the kitchen during the Super Bowl to prepare Totino's Pizza Rolls for her "hungry guys" (a phrase she uses repeatedly in all three commercials).

The 2015 spot (40.13) doubles as a commercial for Totino's Pizza Rolls and the Totino's Super Bowl Activity Pack, which contains little games and puzzles "for grown women five and up" to keep them busy while the men watch the "big game."

In the 2016 commercial (41.12), Bayer is once again back in the kitchen making Totino's for her "hungry guys," while the men's eyes are glued to the television set. Their enthusiastic cheers turn into repeated chants ("Go, go, go, go, touchdown!" "No, no, no, aww, fumble!"), which breaks Bayer's concentration—only to discover the television set is not even on and all the men's eyeballs are all black. It turns out this is not a Totino's commercial but a promo for a forthcoming episode of the sci-fi series *The X-Files*.

The following year, everything is back to normal (42.13). Bayer is busy feeding her "hungry guys" when her husband's friend arrives with his sister, Sabine (Kristen Stewart). They exchange looks, and suddenly we are in a French lesbian film (aptly titled *Tostino* with the tagline "This spring, find your Tostino."). As the women make love, the housewife admits she has no name, tells Sabine (in

French), "My husband, he has his Tostinos. And you, you are my Tostino." At last, she has been liberated from the confines of her kitchen.

## Lexus (46.8)

In a parody of Lexus's annual holiday commercial, Nathan (Beck Bennett) surprises his wife Cathy (Heidi Gardner) with a new Lexus on Christmas morning, and she is—horrified. "Are you f–king kidding me, Nathan?" she shouts. The couple start to argue in front of their son (Timothée Chalamet), and all the family secrets are revealed: Dad has been unemployed for more than a year, and he borrowed money from his neighbor (Mikey Day), who is having an affair with Cathy. The family gets into the car to return it to the dealership.

## It Gets Better (46.11)

This ad for the nonprofit organization understands that it can be tough being young and queer and assures young people their lives will get better. But the testimonials by queer adults, played by *SNL*'s gay and lesbian cast members (Kate McKinnon, Punkie Johnson, Bowen Yang) and guest host Dan Levy, reveal that it may get better as they get older, but adulthood is not necessarily all smooth sailing.

## AMC Theatres (46.20, 48.1)

In a parody of an extended post-COVID-19 ad in 2021 (46.20) inviting us back to the AMC Theatres chain, an inarticulate Vin Diesel (Beck Bennett) explains in painstaking detail the reasons you should come back to the movies—until he finds out that he is required to wear a mask.

Chloe Fineman does a spot-on impression of Nicole Kidman in her iconic 2022 commercial (48.1), explaining the power of the movies—a force so powerful it has a cultlike effect on theatergoers, who stand and salute the screen.

## State Farm Insurance (48.11)

Host Michael B. Jordan plays Jake, the State Farm spokesman who is literally available 24/7 to answer all your insurance questions. He turns out to be a not-so-good neighbor when he advises a young couple (Mikey Day, Heidi Gardner) about their insurance policy and inserts himself into their daily lives and marriage—to the point where he is sleeping with her (Gardner) and spending time with the couple's children.

## Mario Kart (48.12)

After the success of the TV version of the apocalyptic video game *The Last of Us*, HBO has adapted another popular video game into a dramatic series, with Pedro Pascal as Mario, Mikey Day as Luigi, and Chloe Fineman as Peach. The mock trailer scored an Emmy nomination for Ryan Spears and Christopher Salerno for Outstanding Picture Editing for Variety Programming.

# 22

# "And Here's a Short Film By . . ."

## SNL's Original Shorts

Since its debut in 1975, *Saturday Night Live* has showcased an eclectic mixture of over three hundred narrative, nonfiction, and animated film and video shorts. The majority of shorts were produced specifically for *SNL* by a series of filmmakers, some of whom were also staff writers on the show.

- **Albert Brooks**, who was based in Los Angeles, contributed six films during season 1.
- **Gary Weis**, who specialized in comedy shorts and documentary pieces, many of which focused on New York City and some of its more eccentric inhabitants, helmed over forty shorts that aired during seasons 1–5.
- **Tom Schiller**, a member of the show's original writing staff, directed shorts for seasons 3–5 and 14–18 under the segment title "Schiller's Reel" (plus the occasional film during other seasons). Schiller's oeuvre includes some of SNL's funniest and artiest films, including mockumentaries that incorporate archival footage, and parodies and pastiches of European art and Hollywood genre films.
- **Walter Williams** directed over twenty episodes of *The Mr. Bill Show*, which aired during seasons 1–5.
- **Adam McKay**, who was a head writer for three of six of his seasons on *SNL* (21–26), and later cofounded Funny or Die with Will Ferrell. He directed nine feature films and won an Oscar for co-writing *The Big Short* (2015).
- **T. Sean Shannon** wrote and directed a series of bizarre (in a good way) digital shorts in season 30, *Bear City*, which are set—you guessed it—in a city inhabited by bears (actually actors in bear costumes).
- **Robert Smigel**, a longtime staff writer on *SNL*, created a series of hilarious animated shorts presented under the segment title "Saturday TV Funhouse," several of which were recurring: *The Ambiguously Gay Duo*, *Fun with Real Audio*, *The X-Presidents*, and *The Anatominals*. Smigel and his team are masters at imitating iconic animation styles, like the cartoons of Hanna-Barbera and Ruby-Spears, and the stop-motion animation of Rankin/Bass, makers of such

holiday classics as *Rudolph the Red-Nosed Reindeer* (1964) and *The Little Drummer Boy* (1968).
- **The Lonely Island**, a comedy trio comprised of Akiva Schaffer, Jorma Taccone, and *SNL* cast member Andy Samberg, wrote, directed, and performed in over one hundred shorts under the segment title "An *SNL* Digital Short." Many of their most memorable shorts featured original songs that showcased the musical talents of such stars as Adam Levine, Justin Timberlake, Michael Bolton, Lady Gaga, and Nicki Minaj. Schaffer and Taccone also directed other *SNL* shorts not presented under the "*SNL* Digital Short" banner, including episodes of *MacGruber*, which was adapted into a feature film in 2010 (see chapter 26).

The best of *SNL*'s film short library has been showcased on two specials. The first, SNL *Film Festival*, which aired on March 2, 1985, featured the best film shorts and commercial parodies since season 1. The special was hosted by Billy Crystal and featured reviews of the shorts by critics Gene Siskel and Roger Ebert. Twenty-four years later, on May 17, 2009, Andy Samberg hosted Saturday Night Live: *Just Shorts*, which was comprised of shorts from seasons 1–34.

Here, in chronological order, are some of *SNL*'s more memorable, entertaining, and provocative film shorts:

## *Homeward Bound*, directed by Gary Weis (1.8)

*SNL* has never been much for sentiment, but considering it was the show's first holiday episode, they were willing to let their guard down—if only for a few minutes. Set to the classic Simon & Garfunkel tune "Homeward Bound," Weis's film is a slow-motion montage consisting of a series of emotional reunions in an airport between recent arrivals and their friends and family waiting for them at the gate.

## *A Home Movie*, directed by Howard Grunwald (1.13)

In addition to films by Albert Brooks, Gary Weis, and Tom Schiller, *SNL* also invited amateur filmmakers to send in their Super 8 and 16mm shorts. Selected films were screened in the segment "Home Movies." The filmmakers did not receive any monetary compensation—only the satisfaction of knowing their work would air on national television and be seen by millions of people. A viewer named Howard Grunwald submitted this forty-five second comedy short, which, according to the opening titles, he produced, conceived, and shot with some assistance from a pair of technical advisors. The opening credits of *A Home Movie* are twice as long as the film itself, which consists of a single, sixteen-second shot of the outside of a house (presumably Grunwald's home). The End.

## The Mr. Bill Show (1.15)

Oh noooooooooo!

In the first episode of this parody of a children's show, we are introduced to three clay figures: a little guy named Mr. Bill; his dog, Spot; and Mr. Bill's nemesis, the evil Mr. Sluggo. The narrator is Mr. Hands (a pair of human hands), who doesn't think twice about putting poor Mr. Bill in harm's way. Over the course of three and a half minutes, Mr. Bill is stabbed by Mr. Sluggo, who, now pretending to be a doctor, amputates his leg. Mr. Hands next suggests Mr. Bill go on a "deep sea mission" and drops him in a pot of water. Then it's time for Mr. Hands to brush Mr. Bill's teeth, but the human size toothbrush wipes off his entire face. Finally, it's time to skydive, but Mr. Bill's parachute doesn't work. Oh nooooooooo!

Mr. Bill was originally submitted by Walter Williams for the "Home Movie" segment. It's purposely crudely made (the clay figures don't actually move), completely original, and very unexpected, which is why it was followed by twenty more adventures in which Mr. Bill goes to the circus (3.15), to New York (4.2), fishing (4.6), to the movies (4.19), and to Los Angeles (7.3)—and runs into Mr. Sluggo every time.

Mr. Bill's creator ran into another kind of trouble when Williams was slapped with a lawsuit by the original Mr. Hands, Vance DeGeneres (Ellen's brother), claiming he was entitled to artistic credit and 50 percent of all profits. "I want to be able to put Mr. Bill on my resume," DeGeneres told the *New York Times* in 1979. In the same article, Williams confirmed that "definitely and obviously, I feel myself the sole creator."

In 1980, DeGeneres told *People* magazine that when he and Williams lived together, they were working on an 8mm film for a comedy act. "We were sitting around the table one night and I started making a head out of Play-Doh and Walter started making a body for the head," Williams explained. "Then we put it together and were just playing around—and somehow we started mutilating it. Then it hit us: If we did this right, it might make a film."

"Oh noooooooooo!": Mr. Bill and his dog Spot pose with his nemesis, Mr. Sluggo.

They moved to New York together, but their friendship ended over creative differences. In the same interview, DeGeneres said that he phoned Williams to give him a chance to settle the suit, but his former friend and roommate refused.

In November 1981, the *Sarasota Journal* reported that a New Orleans judge awarded Williams total control over the characters of Mr. Bill, Spot, Sluggo, and Mr. Hands and declared that Williams was responsible for "the basic idea in concept," yet DeGeneres "participated in bringing that idea." According to the judgment, Williams had to refile copyrights on all four characters and add DeGeneres's name as cocreator. DeGeneres would also receive 25 percent of all net proceeds produced around the four characters. In exchange, DeGeneres relinquished all claims to copyright and trademark. David Derickson, who replaced DeGeneres as Mr. Hands, also joined the suit and was granted 5 percent of the proceeds from Mr. Bill records and books on the market and 20 percent of the past, present, and future revenues derived from the eleven shorts he coproduced with Williams.

## "Crackerbox Palace" and "This Song" (2.8)

In the 1970s, music videos became a popular form of entertainment on television in both Australia (on shows like *Countdown* [1974–1987] and *Sounds Unlimited/Sounds* [1974–1987]) and the United Kingdom on the long-running *Top of the Pops* (1964–2006). Prior to the debut of MTV in 1981 and the USA Cable Network show *Night Flight* (1981–1996), music videos on American television were a rarity.

On November 20, 1977, *Saturday Night Live* debuted two music videos by George Harrison: "Crackerbox Palace" and "This Song," both directed by Harrison's close friend, Monty Python's Eric Idle.

In his memoir, *I, Me, Mine*, Harrison recalled how the song "Crackerbox Palace" was inspired by the name a comedian named Lord Buckley gave his "beaten-up house in Los Angeles." Harrison thought the name "sounds like a song" and wrote it down on a cigarette pack. The result is a playful little ditty sung by Harrison in the video as he welcomes us to Crackerbox Palace, which is home to an odd assortment of inhabitants, who look like they wandered over from a *Monty Python* sketch—gnomes in raincoats, British military officers, women clad in leather, clowns, drag queens, and a dummy of the Queen. The video was shot in Harrison's home, Friar Park, a 120-room Victorian neo-Gothic mansion in Henley-on-Thames in South Oxfordshire that he purchased in 1970. In 1999, a thirty-three-year-old Liverpool man, who according to a *New York Times* story was mentally ill and obsessed with the Beatles, broke into Friar Park and stabbed Harrison in the chest, puncturing his lung.

Harrison's "This Song" is a self-referential tune from his 1976 album *Thirty Three & 1/3*. It was written after he spent a week in a New York courtroom defending himself and his 1970 hit song "My Sweet Lord" against accusations of plagiarism. A suit was filed against Harrison claiming he plagiarized the song

"He's So Fine," written by Ronald Mack and recorded by the Chiffons in 1963. In *I, Me, Mine,* Harrison describes "This Song" as "a bit of light comedy relief—and a way to exorcize the paranoia about song writing that had started to build up in me. I still don't understand how the courts aren't filled with similar cases—as 99 percent of the popular music that can be heard is reminiscent of something or other." "This Song" opens with a policeman dragging Harrison into a courtroom, where he testifies that the very song that he is singing doesn't infringe on any copyright and has no point (I won't quote any lyrics for fear of infringing on Harrison's copyright. You can watch for yourself on YouTube). As for *Bright Tunes Music v. Harrisongs Music,* Harrison was found guilty of subconsciously plagiarizing "He's So Fine" and was ordered to pay damages.

Harrison's connection to Eric Idle didn't end here. When *Monty Python's Life of Brian* (1979) lost one of its financial backers right before it was going into production, Harrison and his business partner Denis O'Brien agreed to invest in the film. They formed Handmade Films, which continued to produce and distribute films throughout the 1980s, including Terry Gilliam's *Time Bandits* (1981) and *Monty Python Live at the Hollywood Bowl* (1982), and several British art house films, including *Mona Lisa* (1986), *Withnail and I* (1987), and *The Lonely Passion of Judith Hearne* (1987).

## Three Films by Tom Schiller

### Don't Look Back in Anger (3.13)

Writer/director Tom Schiller produced a pair of shorts, airing a few weeks apart in 1978, that were self-referential films about two of *SNL*'s most popular cast members, John Belushi and Gilda Radner, whose careers tragically ended far too soon.

In *Don't Look Back in Anger,* John Belushi, who is now an elderly, white-haired old man who walks with a cane, takes us on a tour through a snowy graveyard, which he says is the Not Ready for Prime Time Cemetery, where all of his castmates are buried. "I was one of those 'Live Fast, Die Young, Leave a Good-Looking Corpse' types," he confesses, "but I guess they were wrong." He tells us they all died young; Bill Murray, who lived the longest, was thirty-eight. He points out each of their graves and share a little about what they did after the show (Gilda had her own show in Canada, Laraine had a pecan farm in the San Fernando Valley) and how some of them died (Jane Curtin from complications during cosmetic surgery, Garrett Morris of a heroin overdose, and Dan Aykroyd in a motorcycle crash).

"Why me, why did I live so long?" he asks. "They're all dead. I'll tell you why. Because I'm a dancer." He begins to dance to the Yiddish song "Roumania, Roumania," by Aaron Lebedeff. Ironically, Belushi would be the first to go. He died of a drug overdose on March 5, 1982, and was laid to rest on Martha's Vineyard on March 11, 1982, exactly four years after the film first aired on *SNL*.

Schiller's decision to shoot in black and white adds to the film's haunting quality. As Michael Streeter observes in *Nothing Lasts Forever: The Films of Tom Schiller*, the film is about the future, yet it has the look and feel of the past: "The manner in which Schiller manipulates time. The manner in which it is shot, the film scratches, Belushi's old-fashioned mustache and garb, the fact that he travels by train—all make this film that is set in the future look as if it were produced in the thirties and forties."

In this eerie, ironic short directed by Tom Schiller, an aged John Belushi visits the graves of his *SNL* castmates, who he tells us all died young.

In Judith Belushi Pisano and Tanner Colby's *Belushi: A Biography*, Schiller explained that the title was a combination of the 1967 Bob Dylan documentary *Don't Look Back* and the 1956 British "angry young man" drama *Look Back in Anger* by John Osborne, which was adapted into a film in 1958 starring Richard Burton and Claire Bloom. Pisano told Streeter that she had considered using the title for her own heartfelt 1990 autobiography about coping with her loss, but she instead decided to go with *Samurai Widow*.

## *La Dolce Gilda* (3.17)

One of Schiller's talents as a filmmaker is his ability to pastiche cinematic styles of the past. He succeeds once again in *La Dolce Gilda*, a homage to famed Italian director Federico Fellini and two of his cinematic masterpieces: *La Dolce Vita* (1960), starring Marcello Mastroianni as a journalist who has an identity crisis while covering the jet set in Rome; and *8½* (1963), in which Mastroianni plays an Italian director who struggles to reconcile his past with the present and his fantasies with reality as he prepares for his next film. In *La Dolce Gilda*, Gilda is struggling with her newfound fame. She arrives at a party with an unnamed woman who bears a slight resemblance to Italian film director Lina Wertmüller (Laraine Newman) and "Marcello" (Dan Aykroyd), who, like Mastroianni in the orgy sequence in *La Dolce Vita*, climbs onto a woman's back and begins to ride her. Once inside, she is overwhelmed by the attention (even her mother is there, telling her to eat something) and leaves the party. Outside, she walks along a dock as the sun comes out. Accordion music, from Nino Rota's score for Fellini's *Amarcord*, plays in the background. She turns and, addressing the camera, tells us to leave her alone. She walks away, but turns around and tells us to come closer. "You know I love you, my little monkeys," she says, "but leave me my dreams. Dreams are like paper, they tear so easily. I love to play. Every time I play . . . you win. Ciao." As Gilda walks away, the camera pans to a mime holding a balloon. He opens his jacket to reveal a paper heart on his chest. He releases the balloon.

Schiller's visual design, black-and-white cinematography, and frenetic editing and camerawork, complete with close-ups of mouths speaking what is obviously postdubbed English, brilliantly capture the milieu of a Fellini movie. The Italian director himself agreed. Schiller had the opportunity to meet Fellini and show him the film while he was vacationing in Rome. According to Streeter, Fellini was amused by *La Dolce Gilda*. The director told Schiller it was carina ("pretty" or "sweet") and "had the atmosphere of some of his films."

## *Java Junkie* (5.8)

One of Schiller's most original films is this pastiche of a 1940s film noir, specifically *The Lost Weekend,* a 1945 drama starring Ray Milland as an alcoholic that won four Oscars including Best Picture, Actor (Milland), Direction (Billy Wilder), and Screenplay (Wilder and cowriter, Charles Brackett). In *Java Junkie,* Peter Aykroyd plays a guy named Joe who is feeling low after losing his job and his girl, Betty. Every morning he orders breakfast at the same diner, only on this one particular morning he decides to skip breakfast and just have a cup of coffee. But one cup isn't enough, and Joe keeps drinking and drinking until he becomes a "java junkie." He starts wandering the streets looking for that next cup and is picked up by the police. After seven weeks of rehab in "Maxwell House," where he's treated for caffeine addiction, he is ready to resume his life with that "java monkey" off his back.

## *A Day in the Life of a Hostage* (6.9)

The Iranian hostage crisis, which started on November 4, 1979, with the storming of the United States Embassy in Tehran, lasted one year, two months, two weeks, and two days, until the fifty-two remaining American hostages were released by Iran to U.S. custody on January 20, 1981. All during that time, the hostage crisis, including the failed negotiations for their release and the failed rescue attempts, were front-page news. *CBS Evening News* anchor Walter Cronkite ended his broadcast by stating the number of days the hostages had been held in captivity. Backlash against Iranians living in the United States was on the rise as many Americans, in a display of national solidarity and support for the hostages, tied yellow ribbons around trees in their front yards. The yellow ribbon, a cultural symbol for remembrance, was popularized by the 1973 song "Tie a Yellow Ribbon Round the Ole Oak Tree," the top-selling single in the United States recorded by Tony Orlando and Dawn.

The song is heard over the radio in the beginning of this haunting film shot entirely from the point of view of one of the hostages, David Posner, who is trying to resume a normal life—but he is bombarded by people who recognize him (a crowd in a piano bar start singing "Tie a Yellow Ribbon" to him) or want him to sell them his story or endorse their cologne. At the end, he is welcomed back by Uncle Sam himself, who strangles him with a yellow ribbon. It is a haunting image—and quite a radical statement for a network television show.

The same episode featured three other segments devoted to the Iranian hostage crisis. In *The Rocket Report*, Charles Rocket is at the ticker-tape parade held in New York City on January 30, 1981, where he sees one of the hostages, Barry Rosen. The mental cruelty of the Iranian militants toward the American hostages (all of which was made public after their release) was the target of a commercial parody in which a hostage is about to be executed, only to find out it's a joke—one of many, according to pitchman Charles Rocket, that can be found in the *Iranian Joke Book*. A third sketch is a meeting of the Iranian Student Council, at Tehran University, who are jubilant over their successful year (they raised over $8 billion thanks to the hostage crisis). They try to figure out what they will do next year. The audience is quiet, probably thinking that maybe all this Iranian humor is, as they say, "too soon."

## Andy Warhol's TV, by Don Munroe, Vincent Fremont, Sue Etkin (7.1, 7.2, 7.4)

The King of Pop Art appeared on *SNL* in three video shorts in the early 1980s (7.1, 7.2, 7.4), and like his underground films of the 1960s, they are plotless and all talk about subjects like makeup, death, and stardom ("Death means a lot of money, honey. Death can really make you look like a star. But then it can be all wrong because if your makeup isn't right when you're dead then you won't look really right."). Warhol was certainly right about the money part. In 2022, thirty-five years after his death, "The Shot Blue Marilyn," (a painting of Marilyn Monroe with a bullet hole through it) sold for $195.4 million.

The most entertaining was the first video in the series, in which Warhol candidly gives his opinion about *SNL*: "In the first place, I never thought I'd ever be on *Saturday Night Live* because I hate the show. I never watched it. I don't think it was great and if you're home on Saturday night, why ARE you home on a Saturday night and I think all the comedians should be beautiful and not funny." It's hard to take anything Warhol ever said publicly very seriously, yet in his diaries, published two years after his death in 1987, he expressed how surprised he was that people watched *SNL*: "So many people must see *Saturday Night Live*, because instead of people on the street saying, 'There's Andy Warhol the artist,' I heard, 'There's Andy Warhol from *Saturday Night Live*.' They'd seen my first segment on it the night before." Two days later he wrote: "So many people keep saying they saw me on *Saturday Night Live*. I guess people do stay in. I don't know. I'm surprised." Warhol's venture into television continued with his cable series *Andy Warhol's TV*, which was shown on Manhattan Cable in 1983–1984, followed by *Andy Warhol's Fifteen Minutes* (1985–1987) on MTV.

In addition to the shorts featuring Warhol, season 7 attempted to raise the show's hip factor by featuring a music video, "Goodbye Sadness," (7.1) directed by Yoko Ono. The song appears on *Season of Glass*, Ono's solo album released six months after the fatal shooting of John Lennon. The video includes footage of both Ono and Lennon. There was also a short by artist William Wegman (7.6), who made his *SNL* debut back in 1976 (1.15) when he and his Weimaraner, Man Ray, appeared in the first of several shorts by Gary Weis (1.16, 2.5).

## Synchronized Swimming, directed by Claude Kerven (10.1)

Season 10 got off to a great start with the addition of some stellar new cast members (Martin Short, Christopher Guest, and Billy Crystal), characters (Ed Grimley, Fernando), and this hilarious short profiling Gerald (Harry Shearer) and Lawrence (Martin Short), two brothers with a dream—to win a gold medal in synchronized swimming in the 1992 Olympics (they will need the extra time to practice because as Lawrence admits, "I'm not that strong a swimmer.").

Christopher Guest plays their fey director, who was most likely the inspiration for Corky St. Clair, the theater director Guest played in his 1996 mockumentary *Waiting for Guffman*. The short was directed by Claude Kerven, who had directed other segments for *SNL* and several ABC Afterschool Specials, including *High School Narc* (1985).

## White Like Me, directed by Andy Breckman (10.9)

The inspiration for one of the best *SNL* shorts of the 1980s was *Black Like Me*, white author John Howard Griffin's 1961 autobiographical account of the racism he experienced traveling as a black man for six weeks through the segregated South on a Greyhound bus. The tables are turned in this version in which Eddie Murphy, with the help of makeup artists, decides to go underground and experience America as a white man. The results of his experiment are hilarious. As "Mr. White," he discovers that white people don't have to pay for anything (as long as there are no black people around), the New York City bus turns into a party, and banks will loan you all the money you want (with no obligation to pay it back). "So, what did I learn from all of this?" Murphy asks. "Well, I learned that we still have a very long way to go in this country before all men are truly equal. But I'll tell you something. I've got a lot of friends and we've got a lot of makeup."

The short was directed by Andy Breckman, who wrote for *SNL* in the mid-1980s and later created the long-running detective series *Monk* (2002–2009).

## The Narrator That Ruined Christmas (27.9)

In this parody of Rankin/Bass's annual television special *Rudolph the Red-Nosed Reindeer* (1964), the snowman who serves as the narrator begins the story—then stops suddenly during his introduction. In the post-9/11 world, it just seems so trivial. So he invites the two confused children watching to meet him down at Ground Zero for a reality check. Fortunately, Santa comes by to set the narrator straight, explaining that now is exactly the time that he should be bringing happiness to children. He also chastises the narrator for being one of those "show business types" that shifts the focus away from the crisis onto himself. The narrator sees the light, only to be interrupted by Tom Brokaw with a special NBC News report that the FBI has placed the nation on a forty-five-minute alert.

For anyone who grew up watching *Rudolph* every year, it's amazing how Robert Smigel, who cowrote the script with Louis C.K., Michael Gordon, and Stephen Colbert, and his collaborators are able to capture the look of the original puppets with such precision.

## "Christmastime for the Jews" (31.9)

Robert Smigel uncovers the mystery of what Jews do at Christmastime in this music video directed by David Brooks. Shot in black and white using stop-motion Claymation, the title song is sung by Darlene Love, who also appears in the video in Claymation form (when it first aired on the 2005 Christmas show, Love was also live in the studio singing "White Christmas"). On Christmas Eve—the night the Jews take over the town—they go to the movies, eat Chinese food, crank up Barbra Streisand, have bar fights, and see *Fiddler on the Roof* with Jewish actors.

"Christmastime for the Jews": Claymation music video produced by Robert Smigel's "TV Funhouse" studio reveals what Jews do on Christmas Day (with vocals by Darlene Love).

The song, written by Smigel, Scott Jacobson, Eric Drysdale, and Julie Klausner, should be added to everyone's holiday playlist. Between 1985 and 2014, Love appeared around the holidays on David Letterman's late-night shows to sing "Christmas (Baby Please Come Home)," which was first recorded in 1963 by Love for Phil Spector's legendary Christmas album, *A Christmas Gift for You from Philles Records*.

## "Lazy Sunday" (31.9)

The second "*SNL* Digital Short," which aired on the same holiday episode as "Christmastime for the Jews," is a music video for the rap song "Lazy Sunday." The song is performed by Andy Samberg and Chris Parnell in true rap style with plenty of attitude as they shout and gesture into the camera. The joke is what they are rapping about—going to the Magnolia Bakery for cupcakes, getting directions on MapQuest, buying snacks to bring into the movie theater, and going to see the film *Chronicles of Narnia* (2005). Within twenty-four hours after it first aired, the video, which was made with Samberg's collaborators, Lonely Islanders Schaffer and Taccone, became a viral hit, and the song was soon reportedly being played on the radio and in bars. In a *New York Times* article on the video's popularity, David Itzkoff reported that approximately a week after it aired, it was downloaded 1.2 million times from YouTube and was popular on both nbc.com and iTunes. The video was not only a turning point in the careers of Samberg and his collaborators, but it broadened the appeal of *SNL*, which is regarded by millennials as their parents' comedy show. "Lazy Sunday" may have aired on a national television show on a major network, but it has the look and feel of a YouTube video, along with the same ironic playfulness that permeates contemporary youth culture, particularly comedy shows like *The Daily Show with Jon Stewart* (1996–present) and *The Colbert Report* (2005–2014).

"Lazy Sunday": This absurd rap music video, performed by Andy Samberg and Chris Parnell, recounts how the duo spent a lazy Sunday buying snacks and going to see the *Chronicles of Narnia*.

## *Journey to the Disney Vault* (31.16)

Robert Smigel's "TV Funhouse" uncovers some of Walt Disney's dirty little secrets in this classic commercial parody. When Disney rereleases one of their classic animated films on DVD, we are encouraged to go out and buy our copy now because it's only available for a limited time. After a certain date, the film will go back into to the "Disney vault," a magical underground storage unit. This parody of an ad for Walt Disney Home Entertainment starts off with a warning that some of Disney's recent releases, with titles like *Bambi II, Cinderella II, Bambi 2002, Hunchback 6: Air Dog Quasi,* and *Jungle Book 3.0,* will soon be going back into the Disney vault for ten years. When a boy and girl are watching it on television, they wish they could go into the Disney vault. Mickey Mouse appears and grants their wish. They go on a magical journey to the Disney vault, where they learn the truth about Uncle Walt—how he was a friendly House Un-American Activities Committee witness, was planning a Civil War theme park, and had his own personal copy of the racist animated musical, *Song of the South* (1946) that he played only at parties.

## "Dick in a Box" (32.9)

The Lonely Island scored again with another music video that aired on the holiday show in 2006, and like "Lazy Sunday" it became a viral hit. This R&B ballad is sung by Andy Samberg and Justin Timberlake, who collaborated with

"Dick in a Box": Two guys (Andy Samberg, left; Justin Timberlake) reveal the very special gift they give their girlfriends. The song received a Creative Arts Emmy for Outstanding Original Music and Lyrics.

Akiva Schaffer, Jorma Taccone, Asa Taccone, and Katreese Barnes, all of whom won a Creative Arts Emmy for Outstanding Original Music and Lyrics. Both men are singing to their respective girlfriends (Kristen Wiig, Maya Rudolph), about the very special package they have for them this Christmas—their junk, which they've inserted in a hole in a gift-wrapped box. The word "dick" is bleeped out sixteen times, but NBC did agree to post it uncensored on their website.

## "Iran So Far" (33.1)

Mahmoud Ahmadinejad, former president of Iran, made some outrageous statements while he was in office in 2005–2013. He called the Holocaust a "myth," accused America of creating HIV to loot African nations, said Israel should be "wiped off the map," the "mysterious September 11 incident" was a pretext for wars against Afghanistan and Iraq (the U.S. delegation at the United Nations walked out the door when they heard that one), and in Iran, there are no gay people. The latter statement was the inspiration for this music video in which Andy Samberg sings a love song to Mahmoud (played by Fred Armisen) with vocals by Maroon 5's Adam Levine. It was the perfect response to the rantings of a lunatic.

## *Japanese Office* (33.12)

Ricky Gervais, cocreator (with Stephen Merchant) and star of the original British version of *The Office* (2001–2003), introduces a clip from the Japanese show that he claims he used as the jumping-off point. Shot in documentary style, it all looks very familiar as we meet the characters who bear a close resemblance to their American counterparts, except they speak in faux Japanese and bow to each other: Steve Carell as "the boss," Jason Sudeikis as the "Jim" character, Kristen Wiig as "Pam," Bill Hader as "Dwight," and Kenan Thompson as "Stanley."

The idea of a Japanese version of *The Office* is not so far-fetched, considering versions of the show were produced in France (*Le Bureau* [2006]), Germany (*Stromberg* [five seasons aired between 2004 and 2012 plus a 2014 feature film]), Quebec (*La Job* [2006–2007]), Chile (*La Ofis* [2008]), Israel (*HaMisrad* [2010–2013]), and Sweden (*Kontoret* [2012–2013]).

## "3-Way (The Golden Rule)" (36.22)

The "Dick-in-a-Box" guys (Andy Samberg and Justin Timberlake) are back and surprised to find each other at the same girl's door ready for a hookup. But that's okay because she (Lady Gaga) wanted them both. And that's okay, for as the boys explain, according to "the Golden Rule" a three-way is okay (and not gay) as long as there is a "honey" in the middle.

## A Mike O'Brien Picture (2014–2016)

Comedian Mike O'Brien wrote for *SNL* for seven seasons and appeared as a featured player in season 39. One of his major contributions to the show was a series of absurdist shorts he wrote and starred in under the banner "A Mike O'Brien Picture."

## "Prom Queen" (40.17)

The basic premise is straight out of a teen movie: O'Brien is an overaged high school student who has been crowned prom king six years in a row. He bets his classmate he can take anyone to the prom and they will be crowned king and queen. O'Brien mistakenly thinks the person his classmate chooses is their married heterosexual math teacher Mr. Osterberg (Michael Keaton). The two become close—until Mr. Osterberg finds out about the bet.

## "The Jay-Z Story" (40.13) and "Oprah Winfrey: A Life of Love" (41.17)

O'Brien skewers the artificiality of biopics by casting himself as two Black icons—Jay-Z and Oprah Winfrey—with other White actors in Black roles, including J. K. Simmons as Nas, Jason Sudeikis as Kanye West, and Kyle Mooney as Michael Jackson.

## Please Don't Destroy (2021–present)

This comedy troupe consisting of Ben Marshall (red hair), Martin Herlihy (glasses), and John Higgins (the third guy) joined the *SNL* writing staff in 2021 (season 47) to produce video shorts in which they play themselves.

Many sketches feature other cast members and the guest host. In 2023, the trio wrote and starred in their first feature film, *Please Don't Destroy: The Legend of Foggy Mountain*, for Peacock. Their shorts include:

- **"Hard Seltzers" (47.2):** John can't believe companies like JCPenney and Jiffy Lube make hard seltzer.
- **"Three Sad Virgins" (47.6):** Pete Davidson convinces the trio to appear in a Taylor Swift music video.
- **"Martin's Friend" (47.12):** Martin's new best friend, a ten-year-old, causes tension between the trio.
- **"Self-Defense" (48.14):** Tired of being bullied, the guys take a self-defense class taught by an overly aggressive instructor (Travis Kelce).

*SNL*'s current resident short filmmakers, the comedy trio known as Please Don't Destroy—(left to right) John Higgins, Ben Marshall, and Martin Herlihy—are the reluctant stars of Taylor Swift's music video, "Three Sad Virgins."

- **"The Original Princes of Comedy" (49.1):** Pete Davidson learns the guys were successful stand-up comics when they were children.
- **"Bad Bunny Is Shrek" (49.2):** Host Bad Bunny, dressed as Shrek, pitches his idea for a script.
- **"Roast" (49.10):** Host Dakota Johnson swaps insults with the trio.
- **Best moment:** Johnson, Higgins, and Herlihy agree on a "nepo-truce." Johnson is the daughter of Don Johnson and Melanie Griffith, Higgins's dad is longtime *SNL* writer/producer Steve Higgins, and Herlihy's dad is former *SNL* writer Tim Herlihy.

# Weekend Update

## "Our Top Story Tonight..."

Weekend Update is the centerpiece of *Saturday Night Live*. A fake newscast that comments on current events and stories keeps the show timely and provides writers and performers the opportunity to address topics ranging from Washington politics to international news to the latest celebrity scandal. *Weekend Update*'s format also gives performers who might otherwise not get any "me time" to be in the spotlight and show the audience what they can do, whether it's impersonating a politician, playing an original character, or doing material from their stand-up act. *Weekend Update* also advanced the comedy careers of several anchors—Dennis Miller, Norm Macdonald, Colin Quinn, Jimmy Fallon, and Seth Meyers—all of whom moved on to hosting a talk show.

## The 1970s (Seasons 1-5)

### Weekend Update, Seasons 1-2 (1975-1976)

Chevy Chase,* anchor (1.1-2.6)
Greeting: "Good evening, I'm Chevy Chase, and you're not."
Sign-off: "Good night and have a pleasant tomorrow."

*When Chase suffered a groin injury while taking a fall at the start of season 2 (2.1), Jane Curtin filled in until his return (2.4).

### Weekend Update, Seasons 2-5 (1976-1980)

Jane Curtin, anchor (2.7–Season 5)
Dan Aykroyd, coanchor (season 3), station manager (season 4)
Bill Murray, coanchor (seasons 4-5)
*Greeting:* "I'm Jane Curtin. Here now the news. Our top story tonight . . ."
*Sign-off:* "That's the news. Good night and have a pleasant tomorrow."

*Major Correspondents/Contributors/Editorial Respondents*
- John Belushi, whose editorials on various topics turned into rants.
- Chico Escuela (Garrett Morris), sports reporter and a former All-Star second baseman on the New York Mets. Escuela is from the Dominican Republic and has a limited command of the English language.

- Emily Litella (Gilda Radner), correspondent, who repeatedly delivered editorial responses on the wrong subject due to her hearing problem.
- Garrett Morris, headmaster for the New York School of the Hard of Hearing, who shouted the headline of the week's top major story.
- Stargazer Bill Murray, entertainment reporter and critic.
- Laraine Newman, *Weekend Update*'s on-the-scene reporter.
- Roseanne Roseannadanna (Gilda Radner), correspondent, who would go off on a tangent and start discussing something irrelevant and gross.
- Father Guido Sarducci (Don Novello), gossip columnist for the Vatican newspaper, *L'Osservatore Romano*.

Taking a cue from the British comedy series *That Was the Week That Was* (1962–1963), *Weekend Update* initially focused on national and international political news and current issues. As the show's first anchor, Chevy Chase delivered the news like a handsome frat boy who didn't take the news or his job very seriously. He begins each broadcast talking on the telephone with his girlfriend—unaware that he's on the air. We hear a snippet of their conversation, which is clearly sexual in nature ("No, I love it when you make noise . . .").

In addition to repeatedly announcing the death of Spanish dictator Francisco Franco (see chapter 24), Chase liked to repeat certain comedy bits. When reporting on the trials of Lynette "Squeaky" Fromme, who tried to assassinate U.S. President Gerald Ford in 1975 (1.13), and Patty Hearst (1.16), we see an artist's renderings of inside the courtroom that look like children's drawings or footage from an old cartoon with Chase pretending to be the voice of the correspondent by holding his nose. He also liked to read the first few words of a major story—and then suddenly stop. Sometimes he made funny faces behind the backs of Jane Curtin, Dan Aykroyd, and Buck Henry while they delivered an editorial commentary—and would never get caught. Correspondent Laraine Newman often reported live on the scene from the Blaine Hotel, where terrorists were holding someone hostage (1.3) or there was an outbreak of Legionnaires' disease (2.1). Newman also had a tendency to arrive early to a place where a major news event was scheduled to happen, like Times Square on December 20 instead of New Year's Eve (1.8), or had already taken place, like the New Hampshire Primary (1.15). Sometimes it was just the wrong place altogether, like Nassau in the Bahamas instead of NASA (1.24).

When Chase was hospitalized due to injuries from an on-screen fall in the season 2 opener (2.1), Jane Curtin filled in as anchor for the next episodes (2.2, 2.3) and was Chase's permanent replacement when he departed the show (2.7). Curtin did appear on his last *Weekend Update* telecast to report on "People in the News," which included a story on a departing Chase replacing Johnny Carson on *The Tonight Show* where he is looking forward to "interviewing self-indulgent Las Vegas performers and meaningless personalities every single day for the next ten years."

Curtin is not a stand-up comic, but she is a brilliant comedic actress with great timing and a sarcastic tone that borders on the sardonic. She also looked the part of a network news anchor. Curtin approached *Weekend Update* as if she was a serious journalist doing a professional newscast. She delivered stories and jokes "straight," never laughing at the punch line. Over time Curtin grew increasingly impatient with on-camera contributors like Emily Litella (for her malapropisms) and Roseanne Roseannadanna (for grossing her out). Litella always apologized to "Miss Curtin"—and then called her a "bitch." After a while, Curtin told Litella she didn't find her mistakes cute anymore. Roseannadanna just ignored her and delivered her catchphrase, "Well, Jane, it just goes to show you. It's always something."

Curtin also made it known to her *Weekend Update* audience that she was not pleased that viewers preferred Chevy over her. In the middle of season 2 (2.13), she opens *Weekend Update* with a letter from "Margie Kaufman," who tells her she "can't hold a candle" to "sexy Chevy Chase." Apparently similar letters were coming in complaining about how the show is going downhill and how much they miss Chevy. "You see, I just assumed it was responsible journalism you want, not sex," Curtin explained. "I gave you more credit than that. But I was wrong. What can I say, besides [she rips off her blouse to reveal her black bra underneath]—try these on for size, Connie Chung! If it's raw news you want, it's

The running joke was Jane Curtin took her role as *Weekend Update* anchor too seriously, so she didn't hide her frustration when guest host Chevy Chase anchored the news with support from the terminally confused Emily Litella (Gilda Radner, right).

raw news you get!" After losing her temper once too often at Emily Litella and Roseanne Roseannadanna, she makes a pledge on air not to lose her dignity by overreacting to any of her fellow correspondents—"no matter how feeble they may be" (3.19). Of course she goes back on her promise and loses it when Roseannadanna asks her if her breasts are the same size.

Curtin was paired with Dan Aykroyd for season 3, though he never seemed entirely comfortable in the anchor role. When Bill Murray took his seat at the anchor desk, Aykroyd was introduced as the station manager and appeared in a segment that was a parody of the Point/Counterpoint segment on *60 Minutes* (1968–present), in which liberal Shana Alexander and conservative James J. Kirkpatrick took opposing views on an issue. Aykroyd began his response to Curtin's comments with "Jane, you ignorant slut" (see chapter 24). Bill Murray's best moments behind the desk were his Stargazer entertainment reports in season 3, including reviews of films he hadn't seen and his analysis of the Oscar race and why nominating this week's host, Richard Dreyfuss, for Best Actor for *The Goodbye Girl* was a mistake. But he was (probably) only kidding, or as he would say kiddingly, "*Now get outta here, I mean it.*"

## The 1980s (Seasons 6–15)

### Weekend Update, Season 6 (1980–1981)

> Charles Rocket, anchor (6.1–6.11)
> Gail Matthius, coanchor (6.6–6.10)
> *Greeting:* "Good evening, I'm Charles Rocket. Here now the news."
> *Sign-off:* "This is Charles Rocket saying, 'Good night and watch out.'"

*Major Correspondents/Contributors/Editorial Respondents*
> Joe Piscopo, sports reporter
> Raheem Abdul Muhammed (Eddie Murphy), film/TV critic
> Gilbert Gottfried, various characters
> Ann Risley, herself/various characters

### Saturday Night Newsline, Season 6 (6.12)

> Charles Rocket, news anchor (6.12)
> Dr. Jonathan Lear (Mark King), science reporter
> Bill Murray, arts & leisure reporter
> Joe Piscopo, sports reporter

### Weekend Update, Season 6 (6.13)

> Chevy Chase, anchor (6.13)
> Raheem Abdul Muhammed (Eddie Murphy)
> Al Franken, correspondent
> Laurie Metcalf, reporter

In season 6, Charles Rocket, who, in an earlier life, was a local news anchor in Pueblo, Colorado (under his real name, Charles Claverie), and Nashville, Tennessee (as Charles Kennedy), was assigned to the *Weekend Update* desk. The jokes covered the same general topics as the first five seasons—politics and current events—but the writing was not as strong. Rocket, who certainly looked the part, didn't help the situation. He had a tendency to smile and let out a small laugh after delivering the punch line, even when there was little or no reaction from the audience.

The highlight of season 6 were the contributions of the only cast members who returned for season 7, Eddie Murphy and Joe Piscopo. Before he was even officially a featured player, Murphy delivered an editorial as Raheem Abdul Muhammed on a recent ruling by a Cleveland judge that all basketball teams in the city had to have at least two white players (6.3). The character made numerous appearances as a film/TV critic on *Weekend Update* and in a sketch segment, "Focus on Film." Murphy's appearances on *Weekend Update* (appearing as himself or Raheem) showcased his comedic talents and, in the process, advanced his status from a feature player (6.4) to a regular three months later (6.9).

A former television news anchor, Charles Rocket looked very much the part delivering the news behind the *Weekend Update* desk in season 6.

But the real star was sportscaster Joe Piscopo, who delivered his reports in a series of single words and short phrases ("Joe Piscopo! Live! Saturday Night Sports! The big story! Superbowl! Tickets! Scalping! Owner! Players!" [6.7]). In the spirit of the old *Weekend Update*, he responded to NBC sports executive producer Don Ohlmeyer's decision to broadcast a football game (Jets vs. Dolphins on 12/18/80) without a play-by-play announcer or an instant analysis color commentator. In protest, Piscopo silently stared into the camera while his own stats appear on the screen and then asked, "Innovative? Exciting? Revolutionary? Boring!"

Toward the end of season 6, *Weekend Update* was renamed *Saturday Night Newsline* (6.12) and presented in three segments, including one devoted to Piscopo's sports report and another to Bill Murray's Oscar picks. For the final episode of the season (6.13), the show's new producer, Dick Ebersol, changed

*Newsline* back to *Weekend Update* with its traditional format and the episode's unofficial host, Chevy Chase, as anchor.

## SNL Newsbreak, Season 7 (1981–1982)

Brian Doyle-Murray, anchor
Mary Gross, coanchor/reporter (7.1–7.4, 7.7–7.20)
Christine Ebersole, coanchor (7.15–7.20)
*Greeting*: "Good evening, I'm Brian Doyle-Murray. Our top story tonight . . ."
*Sign-off*: "Good night and good news."

**Major Correspondents/Contributors/Editorial Respondents**
Dr. Jack Badofsky (Tim Kazurinsky), science editor
Raheem Abdul Muhammed (Eddie Murphy), correspondent
Joe Piscopo, sports reporter

When *SNL* returned in season 7, *Weekend Update* was now *SNL Newsbreak* with Brian Doyle-Murray, who initially anchored the news solo and coanchored with Mary Gross and, in the second half of the season, Christine Ebersole. Doyle-Murray has the voice and the demeanor of a news anchor, though the banter between him and Gross, with whom it's suggested he had an affair, falls flat. The highlights of the segment continue to be Joe Piscopo's sports reports and Raheem Abdul Muhammed's (Eddie Murphy) editorials. One popular new character is Dr. Jack Badofsky (Tim Kazurinsky), the science editor, who uses flash cards and clever wordplay to discuss new developments in science and medicine.

## Saturday Night News, Seasons 8–9 (1982–1984)

Brad Hall, anchor (8.1–9.8)
Guest hosts and various cast members anchor/coanchored the news (9.9–9.19).
*Greeting*: "Good evening, I'm Brad Hall. Our top story tonight . . ."
*Sign-off*: "That's all for tonight. For *SNL* News, I'm Brad Hall. Good night."

**Major Correspondents/Contributors/Editorial Respondents**
Dr. Jack Badofsky (Tim Kazurinsky), science editor
Raheem Abdul Muhammed (Eddie Murphy), editorials
Joe Piscopo, sports reporter
Patti Lynn Hunnsacker (Julia Louis-Dreyfus), teenage correspondent
Havnagootiim Vishnuuerheer (Tim Kazurinsky), a Hindu "Enlightened Master." His name is pronounced "Having a good time, wish you were here."
Dr. Ruth Westheimer (Mary Gross), sex therapist

## Saturday Night News, Season 10 (1984–1985)

Guest hosts and various cast members anchor/coanchor the news (10.1–10.6)).
Christopher Guest, anchor (10.7–10.17)
*Greeting:* Thank you, Don Pardo. Our top story tonight.
*Sign-off:* "That's the news. Good night."

### Major Correspondents/Contributors/Editorial Respondents
Lew Goldman (Billy Crystal), an elderly Jewish man
Fernando (Billy Crystal), a parody of Argentine American actor Fernando Lamas, who interviewed celebrities, which always included his catchphrase, "You look mahvelous."
Paul Harvey (Rich Hall), radio broadcaster for ABC News Radio
Nathan Thurm (Martin Short), a shady lawyer who chain-smokes and defensively denies and contradicts accusations made against him

For the remainder of Dick Ebersol's tenure as producer, the news underwent another title change and got a new anchor, Brad Hall, for two seasons. During the second half of season 9, the news was anchored mostly by guest anchors, including hosts Don Rickles (9.11), Robin Williams (9.12), recently retired NBC news anchor Edwin Newman (9.14, 9.19), former senator George McGovern (9.17), George Carlin (10.5), and Ed Asner (10.6). This continued for the first six episodes of season 10 (Newman even returned just to do the news [10.4]) until Christopher Guest took over as the permanent anchor for the remainder of the season. Guest, a character actor, delivered the news in a very straightforward, deadpan fashion, only occasionally flashing a smile after a punch line.

## Weekend Update, Seasons 11–16 (1985–1991)

Dennis Miller, anchor
*Greeting:* "Good evening. What can I tell you?"
*Sign-off:* "That's the news, and I am outta here."

### Major Correspondents/Contributors/Editorial Respondents
Father Guido Sarducci (Don Novello)
Annoying Man (Jon Lovitz)
A. Whitney Brown, commentator, "The Big Picture"
Babette (Nora Dunn, foreign correspondent/sex kitten)
Grumpy Old Man (Dana Carvey), whose complaints about the modern world compared to the past begin with the phrase, "In my day, we didn't need . . ."
Mr. Subliminal (Kevin Nealon), who inserts single judgmental words into his editorials

Comedian Dennis Miller enjoyed the longest tenure to date of any news anchor. Starting each newscast with the question "What can I tell you?," he delivered the news in a conversational style, laughing at his own jokes, going off on a rant, and peppering his remarks with arcane references to pop culture. *Playboy* dubbed him the "thinking man's smart aleck."

Miller's high-pitched laugh is key to any Dennis Miller impersonation. In fact, during his tenure behind the anchor desk, he was frequently joined by Dana Carvey doing his impersonation of him. In one episode, the anchor was outnumbered when Carvey was joined by another Miller impersonator, Tom Hanks (16.8). Miller proved to be a good sport who can just laugh it off.

## The 1990s (Seasons 17–25)

### Weekend Update, Seasons 17–19 (1991–1994)

>Kevin Nealon, anchor (1991–1994)
>*Greeting*: "I'm Kevin Nealon, and I'm . . ."
>*Sign-off*: "I'm Kevin Nealon, and that's news to me."

### Weekend Update, Seasons 20–23 (1994–1998)

>Norm Macdonald, anchor (20.1–23.9)
>*Greeting*: "I'm Norm Macdonald, and this is the fake news."
>*Sign-off*: "And that's the way it is folks. Good night."

### Weekend Update, Seasons 24–25 (1998–2000)

>Colin Quinn, anchor (23.10–25.20)
>*Sign-off*: "That's my story and I'm stickin' to it."

***Major Correspondents/Contributors/Editorial Respondents***

>Grumpy Old Man (Dana Carvey)
>Joe Blow (Colin Quinn), working-class guy who gives the "local" news about his family and his changing neighborhood
>Jan Brady (Melanie Hutsell), the middle girl from *The Brady Bunch* who always complains about her older sister, Marcia. Her catchphrase is "Marcia, Marcia, Marcia."
>Bennett Brauer (Chris Farley), commentator, who devotes his airtime to expressing his own insecurities and resentment toward the viewers because he knows he is not "the norm," "camera ready," "no style," and "don't own a toothbrush." He emphasizes each fault with "air quotes."
>Harry Caray (Will Ferrell), legendary Chicago baseball sportscaster who has trouble staying on topic
>Lenny the Lion (Colin Quinn), who talks about living in the Bronx Zoo
>Cajun Man (Adam Sandler), a guy from Louisiana with a Cajun accent who answers questions with one- or two-word answers

Opera Man (Adam Sandler), who, with a handkerchief in his hand, sings about the current events and people in the news, but his lyrics only sound like Italian words

Queen Shenequa (Ellen Cleghorne), an Afrocentric social critic who comments on racial matters

David Spade, "Hollywood Minute," who offers his snide take on celebrities and Hollywood

Kevin Nealon took over *Weekend Update* when Dennis Miller departed the show at the end of season 16. Unlike his predecessor, he was the "straight man" who delivered the news in a straightforward and somewhat low-key style. When Nealon stepped down, he was replaced by the sardonic Norm Macdonald, who never hesitated to editorialize or ad-lib when reading a news story, particularly those involving celebrities. But it was his continuous jokes about O. J. Simpson being a murderer that led to his removal from *Weekend Update*. According to a 1999 *Rolling Stone* profile by David Wild, the O. J. jokes offended NBC West Coast president Don Ohlmeyer. Wild states that Macdonald's subsequent firing from the show may have also been due to the fact that "Ohlmeyer just didn't find Macdonald funny."

When Macdonald was fired from *SNL*, along with *Weekend Update* writer Jim Downey, *Time* magazine came to his defense and published a postcard that

Like a real network news anchor, Macdonald was fired by NBC president Don Ohlmeyer. As Bill Carter reported in the *New York Times* (6/3/98), Macdonald claimed it was due to Ohlmeyer's objections to the anchor's jokes about his friend, O.J. Simpson.

could as well have been written by an *SNL* writer. *Time* instructed readers to clip the postcard out and mail to Don Ohlmeyer, President, NBC West Coast. The postcard read:

> Dear Mr. Ohlmeyer:
>
> I'm writing to express my support for Norm Macdonald, who, as anchor of "Weekend Update," was the only funny part of the otherwise lifeless *Saturday Night Live.* I am asking you to reinstate Norm. Until that time, I will watch *Mad TV,* which I've never seen but doesn't look real good.
>
> Sincerely,
> [Sign here]

Macdonald's replacement was Colin Quinn, who, aware that his predecessor was popular with viewers, started his first newscast with a joke: "You know how you go to your favorite bar, and your local bartender isn't there? You ask, 'Where's Jeff?' 'Jeff no longer works here, I'm Steve.'"

"Well, I'm Steve," Quinn tells his viewers. "What can I get you?"

## 2000–2013 (Seasons 26–38)

### Weekend Update, Seasons 26–31 (2000–2006)

> Tina Fey,* coanchor (2000–2006)
> *Greeting:* "And here are tonight's top stories."
> *Sign-off:* "Good night and have a pleasant tomorrow."
> Coanchors: Jimmy Fallon (2000–2004), Amy Poehler (2004–2006)

*Horatio Sanz substituted for Tina Fey while she was on maternity leave at the start of the 2005–2006 season (31.1 and 31.2).

### Weekend Update, Seasons 32–34 (2006–2008)

> Seth Meyers, coanchor
> Amy Poehler, coanchor (2006–2008 [34.1]).
> *Greeting:*
>   MEYERS: "I'm Seth Meyers."
>   POEHLER: "And I'm Amy Poehler. And here are tonight's top stories."
> *Sign-off:*
>   MEYERS: "For *Weekend Update,* I'm Seth Meyers."
>   POEHLER: "I'm Amy Poehler."
>   MEYERS AND POEHLER: "Good night."

## Weekend Update, Seasons 34–38 (2008–2013)

Seth Meyers, anchor
*Greeting:* "Good evening, I'm Seth Meyers. Here are tonight's top stories."
*Sign-off:* "For *Weekend Update* I'm Seth Meyers. Good night."

*Major Correspondents/Contributors/Editorial Respondents*
- Aunt Linda (Kristen Wiig), film critic who is an angry, sarcastic, middle-aged woman whose inability to understand a film results in a negative review
- Tim Calhoun (Will Forte), political candidate with a criminal record whose speeches, delivered slowly and quietly, are written on index cards
- Jeanine Darcy (Molly Shannon), a stand-up comedian whose jokes fall flat
- Drunk Girl (Jeff Richards), a drunken hot mess with an attitude
- Jasper Hahn (Horatio Sanz), a children's books illustrator whose drawings tend to be phallic
- Jacob Silj (Will Ferrell), who suffers from "voice immodulation syndrome" and is unable to control the volume and inflection of his voice
- Patrick Kelly (Will Forte) and Gunther Kelly (Fred Armisen), who address complex topics through nonsensical songs
- Best friends from growing up (Fred Armisen, Vanessa Bayer), who defend—and criticize in hushed tones—political leaders, like Libyan ruler Muammar Gaddafi (37.2), Syrian politician Bashar al-Assad (38.2), King Richard III (38.13), and Russian president Vladimir Putin (42.10)
- Anthony Crispino (Bobby Moynihan), an Italian American "secondhand" news reporter from New Jersey who shares totally inaccurate information obtained from unreliable sources
- Drunk Uncle (Bobby Moynihan), a drunk, racist, working-class guy who delivers incoherent rants on subjects like the holidays, technology, and "kids today." Moynihan recounted in a 2021 interview with the *Daily Beast*'s Matt Wilstein that, when Donald Trump hosted *SNL* in 2015, he didn't understand that the character and his racist remarks were meant to be offensive:

    > And I remember thinking, this is one of the only things in the show that's actually really bad-mouthing him and pointing out how racist and terrible he is. And he walked up to me afterwards and I'm like, oh no. And he shook my hand. And he was like, "Thank you so much. That was so nice to hear such nice things being said." And I was like, you moron.

- The Devil (Jason Sudeikis), who shares his latest accomplishments
- The Girl You Wish You Hadn't Started a Conversation with at a Party (Cecily Strong), whose name says it all
- Stefon (Bill Hader), a gay city correspondent who recommends the "hottest new club"

- Gay Guys from Jersey (Fred Armisen and Bill Hader), two stereotypical Italian guys from New Jersey who happen to be gay
- Judy Grimes (Kristen Wiig), a travel expert who is nervous about appearing on camera, causing her to speak quickly and repeat her catchphrase, "Just kidding."
- Nicholas Fenn (Fred Armisen), a political comedian whose material is neither satirical nor funny
- Garth and Kat (Fred Armisen and Kristen Wiig), a song duo whose lack of preparation (they forgot they were scheduled to appear) is obvious when they try to improvise duets. As Wiig told *Movieline*, "We don't rehearse. The first time we do it that week is literally at the dress rehearsal." Armisen starts the songs, and she just follows his lead.
- Nicole "Snooki" Polizzi (Bobby Moynihan), the orange-tanned party girl from MTV's *Jersey Shore*

For the first time since season 3, *Weekend Update* had coanchors—and for the first time in *Weekend Update* history, they were two women. Fey was the smart, more serious anchor, as opposed to Fallon and Poehler, who were the jokesters.

As for Seth Meyers, he falls somewhere in between. He seems like a guy who is simply too nice to take a swipe at anyone. He is also very much the writer who likes to wait and see how the audience will react to a joke so he, in turn, can react to their groans or lack of laughter. In recent years, most of *Weekend Update* was devoted to guest correspondents. Some characters, like the Devil (Jason Sudeikis), Stefon (Bill Hader), and The Girl You Wish You Hadn't Started a Conversation with at a Party (Cecily Strong), are original and funny. But there is a tendency for others, especially those that rely on one-joke shtick, like Tim Calhoun (Will Forte), Garth and Kat (Fred Armisen and Kristen Wiig), and Judy Grimes (Kristen Wiig), who overstayed their welcome.

In a podcast with fellow *SNL* writer Neal Brennan, Seth Meyers recounted how landing the anchor position was a game changer. Hired as a writer/

A *Weekend Update* anchor reunion (left to right): Tina Fey, Jimmy Fallon, Seth Meyers, and Amy Poehler.

featured player in 2001 (season 27), Meyers was promoted to a head writer, a title he held on to until his exit from the show in season 39. He also wanted to anchor *Weekend Update*, but he lost out to his friend Amy Poehler, who took over for Jimmy Fallon, who departed to host *The Tonight Show* at the end of season 29 (2003–2004). When Tina Fey exited at the end of season 31 (2005–2006), Meyers auditioned for the anchor job, competing against seven other cast members and writers. Meyers told Brennan that, because his five-year contract as a cast member was up, *SNL* told him that, if he didn't get *Weekend Update*, he would be dropped from the cast and rehired as head writer only. Meyers refused to sign—he was willing to walk away from the show. Fortunately, he was chosen as the new coanchor with Amy Poehler and stayed until his departure during season 39.

When Seth Meyers entered the afterhours talk show arena with *Late Night with Seth Meyers*, he incorporated a segment in the spirit of *Weekend Update*, "A Closer Look," which takes a brief deep dive into a current events or political news story three or four times a week. His former coanchor Poehler has also made multiple appearances that often included another edition of "Really?! With Seth and Amy," in which the duo pick apart a news story on topics like billionaires going into outer space, Trump protestors interrupting a production of *Julius Caesar*, and sexist attitudes toward women's sports, with each joke punctuated by the question—"Really?!"

## 2014–2024 (Seasons 39–49)

### *Weekend Update*, Season 39 (2014–2015)

Seth Meyers, coanchor through February 1, 2014 (39.13)
Cecily Strong, coanchor (season 39)
Colin Jost, coanchor beginning March 1, 2014 (39.14)
*Greeting* (Meyers and Strong):
    MEYERS: "Good evening, I'm Seth Meyers."
    STRONG: "And I'm Cecily Strong."
    MEYERS: "And here are tonight's stories."
*Sign-off*:
    MEYERS: "For *Weekend Update*, I'm Seth Meyers."
    STRONG: "And I'm Cecily Strong. Good night."
[Meyers and Strong fist-bump.]

*Greeting* (Jost and Strong):
    JOST: "Good evening, I'm Colin Jost."
    STRONG: "I'm Cecily Strong, and here are tonight's stories."
*Sign-off*:
    STRONG: "For *Weekend Update*, I'm Cecily Strong."
    JOST: "And I'm Colin Jost. Good night."

*Major Correspondents/Contributors/Editorial Respondents*

    Drunk Uncle (Bobby Moynihan)

    Jacob, the Bar Mitzvah Boy (Vanessa Bayer), the son of Seth Meyers's podiatrist, who explains Jewish traditions and tells corny jokes

    Jebediah Atkinson (Taran Killam), an 1860s newspaper critic who hates everything. He was inspired by a newspaper editor who wrote a negative review of Abraham Lincoln's "Gettysburg Address."

    Olya Porlatsky (Kate McKinnon), a Russian correspondent who hates her life in a remote mountainous village

    Charles Barkley (Kenan Thompson), former professional basketball player and commentator

    Shaquille O'Neal (Jay Pharoah), a.k.a. Shaq, former professional basketball player and sports analyst

    Stephen A. Smith (Jay Pharoah), sports journalist/talk show host

    Angela Merkel (Kate McKinnon), Chancellor of Germany, 2005–2021

## Weekend Update, Seasons 40–48

Colin Jost, coanchor
Michael Che, coanchor

*Greeting:*

    JOST: "Good evening, everyone."

    CHE: "Welcome to *Weekend Update*. I'm Michael Che."

    JOST: "And I'm Colin Jost."

*Sign-off:*

    CHE: "For *Weekend Update*, I'm Michael Che."

    JOST: "I'm Colin Jost. Good night."

*Major Correspondents/Contributors/Editorial Respondents*

    The Girl You Wish You Hadn't Started a Conversation with at a Party (Cecily Strong)

    Drunk Uncle (Bobby Moynihan)

    Angela Merkel (Kate McKinnon), chancellor of Germany (2005–2021)

    Ruth Bader Ginsburg (Kate McKinnon), associate justice of the U.S. Supreme Court (1993–2020), who had her own catchphrase, "You've been Ginsburned!" After her death, she was memorialized by McKinnon, who, dressed as Ginsburg, is seen sitting in the audience after *Weekend Update* (46.1). She looks into the camera, puts her hand on her heart and bows her head, followed by a graphic that reads, "Rest in Power."

    Heather (Cecily Strong), a one-dimensional female character from a male-driven comedy

    Willie (Kenan Thompson), Michael Che's overly optimistic neighbor

    Laura Parsons (Vanessa Bayer), an enthusiastic kid actress and future newscaster who is too young to understand the news stories she is reading

    Riblet (Bobby Moynihan), Michael Che's friend from high school

Fan favorite *WU* commentators: cultural reporter Stefon (Bill Hader), Supreme Court Justice Ruth Bader Ginsburg (Kate McKinnon), and the outspoken, uninhibited Cathy Anne (Cecily Strong).

- David Ortiz (Kenan Thompson), former Red Sox first baseman from the Dominican Republic
- Cathy Anne Vanderbilt (Cecily Strong), an opinionated, working-class woman who chain-smokes
- The Guy Who Just Bought a Boat (Alex Moffat), who bought a big boat to make up for his small penis
- Cecilia Giminez (Kate McKinnon), an elderly Spanish woman whose botched restoration of a fresco of Jesus created controversy
- Eric Trump and Donald Trump Jr. (Alex Moffat and Mikey Day), the president's sons
- Angel (Heidi Gardner), Every Boxer's Girlfriend from Every Movie about Boxing Ever
- LaVar Ball (Kenan Thompson), American businessman and cofounder of Big Baller Brand, a sports apparel company
- Bailey Gismert (Heidi Gardner), an overly emotional teenage film critic
- Carrie Krum (Aidy Bryant), seventh-grader and travel expert
- Terry Fink (Alex Moffat), a film critic who drops LSD before watching a film
- Trend Forecasters (Aidy Bryant and Bowen Yang), a trendy duo who reveal the trends of the future
- Baby Yoda (Kyle Mooney), from *The Mandalorian*

Season 39 was a transition year for *Weekend Update*, with the addition of Cecily Strong as coanchor and Meyers's departure on February 1, 2014. The following week Meyers's chair was assigned to co–head writer and new featured player Colin Jost. At the start of the next season (40), Strong returned to appearing in sketches, and Jost was joined by writer Michael Che, marking the start of their long-term partnership as coanchors.

Unlike most previous *Weekend Update* anchors, Jost and Che don't just read the "news"—they each have their own distinct comic personas and frequently interact with the guest commentators and correspondents. Che has a laid-back quality, yet he is eager to see how a joke is going to be received by the studio audience. Jost is more serious when he reads the news, though he usually cracks

Colin Jost and Michael Che have coanchored *Weekend Update* since season 40.

a smile after each punch line. He is also a more vulnerable target for correspondents like Sarah Sherman, who enjoys twisting Jost's words around and making false accusations about his character.

In addition to *Weekend Update*'s long list of commentators, featured players like Sherman and James Austin Johnson, who graduated to repertory players in season 49, and new cast members Marcello Hernandez, Molly Kearney, Michael Longfellow, and Devon Walker have all appeared on *Weekend Update* and, in some instances, incorporated material from their stand-up into their commentary. Bowen Yang, who frequently appears in a costume, snagged an Emmy nomination for his appearance as the Iceberg That Sank the *Titanic* back in 1912, who is more interested in discussing his new album (46.17). Longfellow, dressed as Michaelangelo's *Statue of David*, addressed the recent resignation of a Florida principal over parents' complaints their children were exposed to pornography when they were shown a photo of the statue (46.3). Dressed as Goober the Clown, Cecily Strong (47.5) effectively used *Weekend Update* as a platform to

Featured players get a chance to showcase their talents on *WU*: (left to right) Bowen Yang as the iceberg that sunk the *Titanic* (46.17); Sarah Sherman, who gives Colin Jost a hard time (47.6); and Michael Longfellow as Michaelangelo's *David* (48.16).

address the U.S. Supreme Court's overturning of *Roe v. Wade* and revealed in the process she had an abortion, which she calls her own "personal clown business": "I know I wouldn't be a clown on TV here today if it weren't for the abortion I had the day before my twenty-third birthday," she explains. "Abortions are gonna happen, so it ought to be safe, legal, and accessible."

# "Yeah, That's the Ticket!"

## *SNL*'s Catchphrases

A catchphrase is a word or phrase that is widely recognized because it is repeated so often that its usage is no longer limited to its original source. For a catchphrase to catch on, it needs to generate laughs the first few times it's said. It then needs to be repeated often enough to the point that the audience is expecting and waiting to hear it—until its expiration date and another popular catchphrase has taken its place.

On situation comedies, a catchphrase becomes a character's trademark. The audience expects to hear Fred Flintstone shout, "Yabba, dabba, do!"; *Friends*' Joey Tribbiani (Matt LeBlanc) to enter a room a room and ask, "How you doin'?"; and for *Big Bang Theory*'s Sheldon Cooper (Jim Parsons) to top off a joke or prank only he thinks is funny with "Bazinga!" What makes the audience laugh is not only the phrase itself but who says it, the context in which it's said, and the actor's delivery.

Stand-up comics use catchphrases for essentially the same purpose. For example, a catchphrase like, "I get no respect. No respect," defined Rodney Dangerfield in the 1980s. *No Respect* is the title of his 1981 Grammy-winning comedy album. Two years later, Dangerfield turned it into a rap song and music video, "Rappin' Rodney." On October 9, 2004, five days after his death, *SNL* paid homage to the legendary comedian in a short sketch (30.2) in which Dangerfield (Darrell Hammond) gets to do his stand-up one last time at the Gates of Heaven before St. Peter invites him in. "Finally," Dangerfield says. "A little respect."

*SNL* poked fun at catchphrase comedy not once but twice, in promos for "The Original Kings of Catchphrase Comedy" (36.17) and its sequel, "The Original Kings of Catchphrase Comedy, Volume 2" (37.5), which feature a host of catchphrase comedians like Mike "Insert Joke Here" Henry (Fred Armisen), Goran "Funky Boy" Bogdan (Paul Brittain), Slappy Pappy (Bobby Moynihan), David "Beef Jelly" Winfield (Kenan Thompson), and Bonnie "My Vagina" Carolina (Nasim Pedrad)—all of whom appear to have built a career by running a catchphrase into the ground. Ironically, a parody of catchphrase comedians is airing on a sketch comedy show that is the birthplace of dozens of catchphrases and opens each week with the catchphrase "Live from New York, it's *Saturday Night*!"

This very issue was addressed in a hilarious, self-reflexive Robert Smigel cartoon that aired toward the end of *SNL*'s twenty-fifth season (25.18). In "The Life of a Catch Phrase," an animated Lorne Michaels responds to complaints he has received from viewers about beating s–t into the ground and hearing the same catchphrases over and over again. Michaels explains that the life of a catchphrase is tenuous— "Even the ones you love today can't last forever." To illustrate his point, he screens *The Life of a Catch Phrase*, which begins with the creation of the catchphrase "Yeah, that's the ticket" by men in lab coats. It's implanted into Jon Lovitz's brain and then repeated over and over on the show, in his bedroom, and on *The Tonight Show with Johnny Carson*. Lovitz is

"Candygram!": The Land Shark lures innocent women to their door by posing as a delivery man.

*Photo by Travis Rainey*

soon sitting in a throne on top of piles of money. But when Lorne Michaels walks in carrying Dana Carvey, sets him down, and Carvey says the Church Lady's catchphrase "Isn't that special?," Lovitz loses the money and the fame and ends up doing appearances in shopping malls. Cut to 2019, when Lovitz is transported in a flying saucer to a planet inhabited by little green men, who are a whole new generation of fans who laugh hysterically at Lovitz and his catchphrase "That's the ticket!"

Here are some of *Saturday Night Live*'s top catchphrases, who said them and why, and the episode in which you heard them first.

## Land Shark (Chevy Chase): "Candygram." (1.4)

One of the many ways the land shark tries to get unsuspecting females to answer the door is to pretend he is delivering a Candygram, which is a box of candy delivered to a person's door with a personal message (1.4). For more on the land shark, played by Chevy Chase, see chapter 6.

**Chevy Chase, anchor, *Weekend Update*: "I'm Chevy Chase and you're not." (1.4) and "Generalissimo Francisco Franco is still dead." (1.7)**

"I'm Chevy Chase and you're not" was Chase's most popular catchphrase, which he used to open his *Weekend Update* newscasts. To understand the significance of the catchphrase regarding Franco, you need to understand the context in which it was repeatedly delivered.

After leading the Nationalists to victory in the Spanish Civil War (1936–1939), General Francisco Franco's fascist regime ruled Spain for thirty-six years. Beginning in October 1975 and continuing through his death from heart failure on November 20, 1975, the media reported on the status of the dictator's health. He was sick, and then he was feeling better, then his condition worsened, and eventually, on October 30, he fell into a coma.

On November 22, 1975 (1.6), *Weekend Update* anchor Chevy Chase reported that Franco had died and read an actual quote from President Richard Nixon on his passing, which could have been easily misinterpreted as a joke: "General Franco was a loyal friend and ally of the United States. He earned worldwide respect for Spain through firmness and fairness." Behind Chase there's a photo of Franco standing next to Hitler and giving the fascist salute. Chase added that despite his death and burial tomorrow, "the doctors say the dictator's health has taken a turn for the worse."

In a comedic exercise in how long can you milk a joke and continue to generate laughs, Chase continued to report on Franco's health, despite the fact that he was pushing up daisies. On next week's show (1.7), the top story was "Generalissimo Francisco Franco is still dead." In the weeks that followed, Franco stayed in the news. On January 10, 1976 (1.9), Chase reported that Franco and Chinese premier Zhou Enlai, who died on January 8, had "high level talks" about Spanish rice (1.9). Two weeks later (1.11), Chase reported that Franco was critically dead, but doctors won't speculate on how long his current condition could last. Over the following weeks, Franco is the reason why Teddy, a koala bear, committed suicide (1.14); and the focus of a live report (1.17) in which Franco's secretary (played by White House press secretary Ron Nessen) tells reporter Laraine Newman that Franco is dead but stable. He even scores 10 out of 10 in cadaver diving at the Montreal Olympics (1.24). Finally, on his last telecast (2.6), Chase gets a collect phone call from the generalissimo himself to say goodbye.

**Emily Litella: "Never mind." (1.7)**

Litella's first appearance was as a guest on a talk show, *Looks at Books* (1.5), in which she discusses her book *Tiny Kingdom* with host Jane Curtin. Two shows later (1.7), she gives her first editorial reply on *Weekend Update* on the subject of "busting" (busing) schoolchildren. Once anchor Chevy Chase points out her mistake, she apologizes and says, "Never mind." Chase is more patient with her than anchor Jane Curtin. For more about Litella, see chapter 6.

## Beldar and Prymaat Conehead: "We come from France." (2.11)

In the first installment of "The Coneheads at Home," Connie Conehead (Laraine Newman) complains to her parental units, Beldar and Prymaat Conehead (Dan Aykroyd and Jane Curtin), that the kids at school know she is different and keep asking her where she is from. Beldar and Prymaat tell her to give the same standard response they give to earthlings—that they come from France. For more about the Coneheads, see chapters 6 and 26.

## John Belushi: "But nooooooooo!" (2.19)

John Belushi's favorite catchphrase whenever he would go off on a rant, usually when he was giving a commentary on *Weekend Update*, was "But nooooooooo!" It was incorporated into his explanation on the different kinds of weather to shut-ins and people too paranoid to go outside (2.19). As was always the case, he was soon off the topic and started to talk about India ("You can't eat the cows because nooooo! They won't eat the cow!") and Japanese eating raw fish ("I mean, didn't they invent the hibachi? But, nooooooo! They won't do that! . . . They want to eat it raw."). His later editorials turn into rants about bar fights (3.11), the demolition of Radio City Music Hall (3.16), and the government wasting money on the U.S. space program (4.19). Belushi also delivered one of his more memorable rants when he interrupts host Art Garfunkel's rendition of "(What a) Wonderful World" (3.13). Garfunkel stops the song when he starts to get feedback from his microphone, prompting Belushi to appear on the stage and start complaining about the inferior equipment the network forces them to use because they are a late-night show. When Garfunkel sheepishly tells Belushi that the sound is okay and maybe he was a little off-key (Art Garfunkel off-key?), Belushi accuses "Mr. LP" of turning on him "like a shark!"

In Pisano and Colby's biography *Belushi*, writer Alan Zweibel recalled watching Belushi doing his weatherman character on the monitor with Lorne

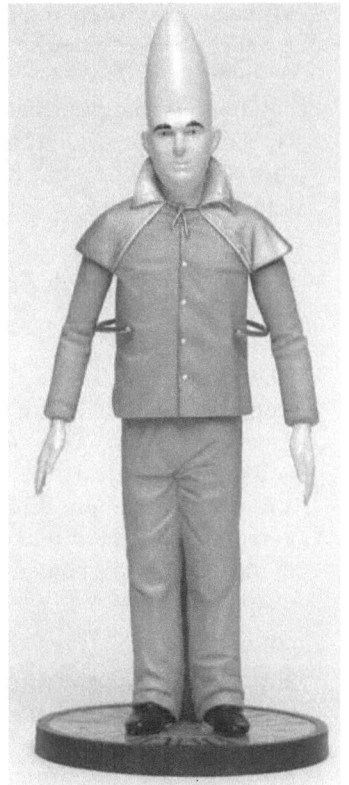

"We come from France" is Beldar Conehead's standard response when someone asks him where he's from.   *Photo by Travis Rainey*

Michaels, who compared the comedian with Jackie Gleason. "And he was right," Zweibel agrees. "When you think about it there was a lot of Jackie Gleason, a lot of Ralph Kramden." Zweibel also observed how, unlike most Jewish and ethnic entertainers that came before him, John never assimilated. "He didn't blend in. He did it on his own terms," Zweibel added. "He was the angry, rebellious voice they all identified with. It's a little wonder a nation of immigrants embraced him."

## Georg and Yortuk Festrunk: "We're two wild and crazy guys." (3.1)

Georg and Yortuk Festrunk (Steve Martin and Dan Aykroyd), two brothers from Czechoslovakia, are wannabe playboys who want to "swing" with a pair of American "foxes." They are totally clueless that the way they dress and behave and the catchphrases they use (like "You and what army?") are neither hip nor a turn-on to women. But they still consider themselves to be "wild and crazy guys," an expression that comes from a catchphrase Steve Martin popularized in the 1970s in his comedy routine. For more about the Festrunk Brothers, see chapter 6.

## Roseanne Roseannadanna: "It just goes to show you, it's always something." (3.9)

Although she first appeared in the sketch "Hire the Incompetent" (3.4), Roseanne Roseannadanna began using her catchphrase until she joined the *Weekend Update* team as a correspondent. When responding to a letter from Mr. Richard Feder from Fort Lee, New Jersey, Roseannadanna had a tendency to go off on a tangent and start describing something irrelevant and unpleasant (like a "teeny tiny ball o' sweat" hanging off Dr. Joyce Brothers's nose [4.6]). When anchorwoman Jane Curtin couldn't bear it anymore and told her to stop, Roseanne would tell her, "Well, Jane. It just goes to show you. It's always something." (For more on Roseanne Roseannadanna, see chapter 6.)

## Pete Dionasopolis, Olympia Café Owner: "Cheezburger, cheezburger, cheezburger." (3.10)

This is what you hear Pete Dionasopolis (John Belushi) and his staff shouting back and forth to each other behind the counter of the Olympia Café when an order comes in, because "cheezburgers" are the only thing on their menu (along with chips and Pepsi) (3.10). For more about Pete and the Olympia Café, see chapter 6.

## Dan Aykroyd, *Weekend Update* Anchor: "Jane, you ignorant slut." (4.3)

In 1971, *60 Minutes* added the segment "Point/Counterpoint," in which conservative editorial columnist and former segregationist James J. Kilpatrick and a liberal commentator faced off in a three-minute debate on a current issue. In his historical study of *60 Minutes,* David Blum recounts how the first liberal commentator, Nicholas von Hoffman, who wrote for the *Washington Post,* was fired in 1974 by *60 Minutes* producer Don Hewitt for calling President Nixon "a dead mouse on the kitchen floor that everyone was afraid to touch and throw in the garbage."

In 1975, von Hoffman was replaced by Shana Alexander, who was the first female staff writer and columnist for *Life* magazine. Kilpatrick and Alexander were satirized on *Weekend Update* by anchor Jane Curtin and *Weekend Update* station manager Dan Aykroyd. In the first installment, a debate over "test tube babies," Curtin takes the liberal position and Aykroyd the conservative. She calls him a "cold pompous ass" for denying a woman the opportunity to conceive a child. He begins his short rant with "Jane, you ignorant slut."

In future broadcasts they debated the Shah of Iran (4.5), U.S.–China diplomatic relations (4.9), the rise of cocaine use/drug laws (4.12), palimony (4.15), and nuclear power ("Jane, you *magnificently* ignorant slut"). Aykroyd always started with the same line, to which Curtin has no reaction at all. For the record, Curtin managed to get some good potshots in also, calling Dan a "reactionary ass," "self-important swine ass," and a "miserable failure." But Aykroyd calling Curtin an "ignorant slut" is what America wanted and waited to hear.

## Paulie Herman: "Are you from Jersey?" (6.3)

The annoying, clueless guy from Jersey who coined the catchphrase "Are you from Jersey? I'm from Jersey" tries video dating (6.3); is hustled in a game of three-card monte by Eddie Murphy (6.4); visits the Turnpike Diner, where he charms a customer (Karen Black, who recreates the scene in which she appeared in *Five Easy Pieces* [1970] in which Jack Nicholson orders wheat toast) (6.10); and falls for another Jerseyite (Deborah Harry) on Valentine's Day (6.10). In the next season, Paulie returned (7.9) alongside pimp Velvet Jones (Eddie Murphy) to announce that both of their characters won't be seen again as they've died—from overexposure.

The highlight of the Paulie Herman sketches was a parody of an industrial film, "Formula for the Good Life," in which we see Paulie Herman in his natural habitat—working at the United Chemical Company plant in Piscataway, New Jersey. He takes the audience on a tour of the plant and doesn't seem to mind that everything is covered with white powder, which, at one point, falls into the sandwich he's eating. Afterward, he visits one of New Jersey's landmarks, the Paramus Mall. Apparently, the mayor of Piscataway, Robert G. Smith, was not amused by the depiction of his city as the toxic chemical waste dump capital of the nation. According to a March 1981 UPI story, NBC regretted that he was offended, but they "did not believe a public apology is appropriate."

### Buckwheat: "O-tay!" (7.2)

In the 1980s, Eddie Murphy resurrected Buckwheat, one of the Little Rascals, whose command of the English language was severely limited and coupled with a speech impediment. "O-tay" was his way of saying, "Okay." Murphy's Buckwheat, who is now all grown up, can't even pronounce his own name. It sounds more like "Buh-Weet," which is how it is spelled on the cover of his album, *Buh-Weet Sings* (7.1). For more about Buckwheat, see chapter 8.

### Gumby: "I'm Gumby, damnit!" (7.15)

Gumby is a green Claymation figure created by Art Clokey who made his television debut in the 1950s on *The Howdy Doody Show* (1947–1960) before getting his own television series, which aired from 1957 to 1968. With his best friend, a red

"That's the ticket" is a favorite catchphrase of pathological liar Tommy Flanagan (Jon Lovitz).

pony named Pokey, Gumby was a kind and considerate fellow who was always willing to help others.

As he had done with Buckwheat, Eddie Murphy resurrected Gumby for 1980s television audiences who grew up watching the little green guy on television. But Gumby is no longer a sweet, kindhearted, heroic kid but a cantankerous, old, cigar-smoking Jewish entertainer who is very bitter about the way the industry treats cartoon characters. He writes two exposés on the industry: *I'm Gumby, Damnit*, which he plugs on *The Uncle Tom Show*, a children's show hosted by Tom Snyder (Joe Piscopo) (7.15); and *I Am Show Business, Damnit*, which he promotes on *Late Night with David Letterman* (1982–1993) (8.1) along with dishing some dirt on the Keebler Elves and Poppin' Fresh. Gumby resurfaces again to reunite with Pokey (Joe Piscopo), who complains of chest pains to a less-than-sympathetic Gumby, who tells him, "You are not working with me, you are working *for* me." Gumby also writes and directs *The Gumby Story* (9.4), only to have a movie executive close down the production. When Murphy returned to *SNL* as host (10.9), Gumby appears in a parody of Woody Allen's *Broadway Danny Rose* (1984) in which he has lunch at Fishman's Deli with other aging Jewish comedians.

In a 1985 *People* magazine article, Jack Friedman reported on the renaissance of Gumby, who had a whole new generation of fans thanks to videocassettes and reruns in the major television markets. Gumby returned in a new show, *Gumby Adventures* (1988–2002), and a feature-length film, *Gumby: The Movie*, was released in 1995. Sixty-three-year-old Clokey did not attribute Gumby's newfound popularity to Eddie Murphy, but to a swami who sprinkled "generated sacred ash" over a Gumby action figure. "Ever since then," Clokey admits, "Gumby has been doing amazing things."

"We're going to pump you up!" is a promise bodybuilders Hans and Franz make to their viewers.  *Photo by Travis Rainey*

## Fernando: "You look mahvelous!"

Billy Crystal based the character "Fernando" on Fernando Lamas (1915–1982), a handsome Argentine actor and singer who played romantic leads and Latin lover roles in MGM films in the 1950s, starring opposite Lana Turner (*The Merry Widow* [1952]), Elizabeth Taylor (*The Girl Who Had Everything* [1953]), and his fourth wife, Esther Williams (*Dangerous When Wet* [1953]). In a 1985 interview for *Playboy*, Crystal recalled watching Lamas when he would appear as Carson's guest on *The Tonight Show*. "He used to have him on there, because he would say, 'You look marvelous, John. That was really marvelous'—but not the way I do it. He would just say it, and that seemed to be the thrust of his in-depth conversation." During one appearance, Carson told Lamas that he looked great too. Fernando replied, "I'd rather look good than feel good." Crystal found this line to be hysterically funny and wrote it down.

Crystal also made it very clear in the interview that he was not doing Fernando Lamas. "The late Mr. Lamas [who died in 1982] was a nice, intelligent man," Crystal added. "My guy is an idiot. But he means well." When Fernando first appeared on *SNL* (and was introduced as Fernando Lamas), he sat behind the *Saturday Night News* desk and offered his assessment of who looks *mahvelous* among the presidential candidates and Oscar contenders. The audience wasn't sure what to make of him (and some were no doubt wondering, "Who is Fernando Lamas?"). He was back again toward the end of the season (9.19), upset that retired NBC newscaster Edwin Newman is the one anchoring the news instead of him (but assures Newman that he looks mahvelous). When Crystal joined the cast the following season (1984–1985), he was eventually given his own recurring sketch, *Fernando's Hideaway*, where he's visited by Ringo Starr and his wife, Barbara Bach (10.8); Mr. T and Hulk Hogan (10.15); and Howard Cosell (10.17). Fernando's last *SNL* appearance was on *Saturday Night Live 25*, in which he marvels over the celebrities in the audience, mistaking Steve Martin for Phil Donahue and Chris Rock for Eddie Murphy.

Crystal's impression of Lamas was not the first on *SNL*. He was imitated by Bill Murray in season 2 in a sketch (2.21) in which he, Ricardo Montalban (Aykroyd), and Cesar Romero (Belushi) approach women in a restaurant and ask the women to tell them apart because they have been best friends who do everything together for so long and they can no longer tell themselves apart.

## Tommy Flanagan: "That's the ticket!" (11.2)

The idiom, which means "Yes, that's it! That's right!," dates back to the nineteenth century, though its exact origins are the subject of debate. Some believe it was derived from the French phrase *c'est l'etiquette*, which translates as "that's the proper thing or course of action" with the word "etiquette" having been twisted into the word "ticket." Some believe it's more likely that "ticket" refers to "political ticket" (as in "that's the right party or candidate").

The phrase was popularized on *SNL* by pathological liar Tommy Flanagan, played by Jon Lovitz. Prior to joining the cast of *SNL* in the fall of 1985, the comedian appeared as Flanagan on *The Tonight Show Starring Johnny Carson* (1962–1992), introducing himself as the President of Pathological Liars Anonymous. Lovitz did a variation of the same routine when he first appeared as Flanagan on *SNL* in a PSA on behalf of the same group, and claimed to have joined the army at the age of thirteen and served in Vietnam, where he caught a mortar shell in his teeth and was made a three-star general. He also said that he killed himself over the death of his cousin, boxer Joe Louis, and was medically dead for a week until he was brought back to life by Indian prime minister Indira Gandhi. One more lie that he liked to tell—he's married to Morgan Fairchild. Between 1985 and 1989, Flanagan pops up over a dozen times, hitting on guest host Jerry Hall (11.10) and appearing in Rosanna Arquette's dressing room (12.3) and in the middle of Oprah Winfrey's monologue (11.14). He's even the self-appointed official spokesman for NBC who responds to *SNL*'s decline in the ratings by telling everyone the ratings are "through the roof! . . . Neck and neck with *The Cosby Show!*"

"Isn't that special?" asks the Church Lady. *Photo by Travis Rainey*

## The Church Lady: "Well, isn't that special?"

A rhetorical question used by Enid Strict, a.k.a. the Church Lady, whenever she hears something that is objectionable. To read more about the Church Lady, see chapter 9.

## Hans (Dana Carvey) and Franz (Kevin Nealon), hosts of *Pumping Up with Hans & Franz*: "We are here to pump [clap] you up!" (13.1)

This was a promise made by Hans and Franz, a pair of Austrian bodybuilders and cousins of Arnold Schwarzenegger, on their television show, *Pumping Up with Hans and Franz*. But they never kept their word because they spent most of the show flexing their muscles for their viewers when they weren't insulting them and calling them "girlie men." Read more about Hans and Franz in chapter 9.

## *Wayne's World*'s Wayne Campbell (Mike Myers) and Garth Algar (Dana Carvey): "Excellent," ". . . Not!," "Party on!," "Schhhhhhhwinnnng," "We're not worthy," "Way. (No way.) Way." (14.13)

Wayne and Garth, hosts of the local access television show *Wayne's World*, are the undisputed kings of the *SNL* catchphrases. Here is how urbandictionary.com defines the words and phrases used and popularized by Wayne and Garth, who in some instances, are also identified as the source. To read more about *Wayne's World*, see chapters 9 and 26.

"Party on! Schwing! We're not worthy!": One of the kings of *SNL* catchphrases, Wayne Campbell. *Photo by Travis Rainey*

*Babe*: An attractive young woman.

*Babelicious*: Babe + Delicious, often applied to supermodels and certain actresses and singers.

*. . . Not!*: Attributed to *Wayne's World*, the addition of "not" at the end of the sentence is a way to make sarcasm more blatant.

*Party on!*: An exclamation to express that you are excited about something ("Party on, Wayne!" "Party on, Garth!")

*Schwing!*: An exclamation used when a guy sees a babe and gets an erection. Urbandictionary.com defines the term as "when Garth or Wayne (*Wayne's World*) pop a boner."

*Way!*: The proper way to respond to someone when they say, "No way." When Aerosmith's Joe Perry tells Wayne they don't do drugs and alcohol any more, Wayne says, "No way!" Perry replies, "Way!" (15.13)

*We're not worthy!*: Exclamation used when one meets someone who is highly distinguished. When Garth sees on the "nook cam" that Aerosmith is upstairs in Wayne's kitchen, he says, "I'm not worthy! I'm not worthy!" (15.13)

## Dieter: "Vould you like to touch my monkey?" "Touch him! Touch my monkey!" (14.16)

Dieter, the pretentious host of a German talk show, *Sprockets*, usually asks his guests, who are equally bizarre and avant-garde, if they would like to "touch his monkey." It sounds like a sexual innuendo—except there is an actual live monkey sitting next to him on the top of a column. Dieter has several other expressions he likes to use while interviewing a guest. When he gets excited, he pulls the front of his black turtleneck out as if he has small breasts and says, "Now I am as happy as a little girl." If he gets bored, he tells the guest, "Your story has become tiresome." He closes the show by declaring, "Now is the time on Sprockets when we dance." And they do.

## *Bill Swerski's Super Fans*: "Da Bears!" (16.10)

It's the mantra of the men who appear on *Bill Swerski's Super Fans*, a television show broadcast from Ditka's restaurant in Chicago. Smigel told Doug Elfman of the *Chicago Sun-Times* that the sketch was first performed on stage in Chicago as part of the revue *The Happy Happy Good Show* (the cast included another *SNL* writer, Conan O'Brien). "That was the first place where I ever tried the Chicago Superfans sketch—the 'Da Bears' thing. They would just have conversations about anything. . . . In the script, I didn't even write 'Da.' That was something that was invented in Chicago." (See also chapter 10.)

## Rich Laymer: "Makin' copies." (16.11)

Rich Laymer, a.k.a. the Richmeister (Rob Schneider), is that guy in your office whose desk is closest to the photocopier. Every time you go to use it, you say hello and he responds by calling you playful variations of your first name followed by "Makin' copies." Schneider admitted in a *Chicago Tribune* story that he did the same thing to Adam Sandler when he would walk by his desk at *SNL* to go to the water cooler ("Adam, Adam-meister. Going to get some water.").

## Stuart Smalley: "I'm good enough, I'm smart enough, and doggone it, people like me!" (16.12)

This is the mantra of Stuart Smalley (Al Franken), "a caring nurturer, a member of several twelve-step programs, but not a licensed therapist," who hosts *Daily Affirmation with Stuart Smalley*. It's also the title of a book of daily affirmations penned by Franken, who wrote and stars in the 1995 feature film *Stuart Saves His Family* (1995). (Read more about Stuart in chapter 26.)

## Linda Richman: "I'm a little verklempt."

Linda Richman, host of *Coffee Talk*, would sometimes get a little verklempt, a Yiddish word for excited. It was one of the many Yiddish words and expressions Richman used, some of which were real and others there was no way to be sure. (Read more about Linda Richman in chapter 10.)

## Matt Foley, Motivational Speaker (Chris Farley): "[L]iving in a van down by the river!" (18.19)

A popular character on *SNL* in the early 1990s, Matt Foley was developed on the Second City stage in Chicago by Chris Farley and writer Bob Odenkirk. Overbearing and hyperactive, Foley had a big, loud, presence whose strategy for motivating people was to mock them and tell them to shut up when they tried to get a word in. He also wallowed in his own self-pity, which was meant to serve as a warning that if they don't wise up, they might end up like him—"thirty-five years old, eating a steady diet of government cheese, thrice divorced, and living in a van down by the river!" Some of his other favorite expressions were "Well, la-dee-frickin-da!" and "Whoop-dee-frickin-do!" Read more about Matt Foley in chapter 10.

"... living in a van down by the river!": Motivational speaker Matt Foley doesn't like to soft-pedal his message.

*Photo by Travis Rainey*

## Flight Attendants, Total Bastard Airlines: "Buh-bye." (19.16)

If you saw these two sketches, it's hard not to get off an airplane these days and think of this catchphrase, repeated over and over by the flight attendants on Total Bastard Airlines. As passengers get ready to deplane, a voice on the intercom thanks them for "flying the blue skies of Total Bastard" and explains that "we at Total Bastard Airlines are bitter about the career paths we have taken, and we do tend to take that out on our passengers." Any questions the passengers may have get answered with repeated "Buh-byes," along with the occasional rude comment or insult. David Spade, who specialized in playing snide characters, is the steward, along with guest host Helen Hunt in the first sketch (19.16) and Ellen Cleghorne in the second (20.1).

In March 1995, Chris Smith did a very critical behind-the-scenes story for *New York* magazine on *SNL*, "Comedy Isn't Funny," with the subheading "*Saturday Night Live* at Twenty—How the Show That Transformed TV Became a Grim Joke." The story does indeed paint a rather grim picture of the creative dissatisfaction among some of the cast and writers on a show that Michaels himself admits is "fighting for its life." Smith claims the inclusion of the second Total Bastard Airlines sketch in a "prime spot" on the twentieth-season opener was a way for Michaels to reward David Spade for the work he had done that summer on the film *Tommy Boy* (1995), which costarred Chris Farley and was produced by Michaels. Smith wrote that the second sketch was "*SNL*'s biggest blunder this season" (*Really?* The *biggest* blunder of season 20?) because it gave critics a chance to "bludgeon *SNL*" and accuse them of "trying to flog another marketable catchphrase." Michaels reportedly thought the sketch was funny and was planning to do another until he read that it was judged by some viewers on the internet the "most hated" sketch in memory.

## Bruce Dickinson (Christopher Walken): "More cowbell!" (25.16)

On April 8, 2000, *SNL* did a parody of *VH1: Behind the Music* that focused on Blue Öyster Cult, the band best known for songs such as "Burnin' for You" and "Dancing in the Ruins." The parody includes footage supposedly shot during a 1976 recording session of the song "(Don't Fear) The Reaper" supervised by "famed producer" Bruce Dickinson (Christopher Walken) (there was a music producer named Bruce Dickinson, but he was not involved with BÖC until many years later). The *SNL* regulars impersonate members of the band, though the sketch is not historically accurate in regard to the band members who were around at the time of the recording. In the sketch, Eric Bloom (Chris Parnell) sings the lead vocals, yet Donald "Buck Dharma" Roeser (Chris Kattan) actually sang lead vocals on the song. The other band members—bass guitarist Danny Miranda (Horatio Sanz) and drummer Bobby Rondinelli (Jimmy Fallon)—were not BÖC members until the 1990s. The fifth band member, Gene Frenkle (Will Ferrell), the overly enthusiastic cowbell player, is a figment of Ferrell's fertile imagination (he wrote the sketch).

Initially, Gene's cowbell proves to be a distraction to the rest of the band, which creates tension, especially between him and Bloom. But Dickinson (or, as he refers to himself, "*the* Bruce Dickinson") insists on more cowbell: "I got a fever and the only prescription is more cowbell." He tells Frenkle to "really explore the studio space," which he does—jumping around all over the studio while hitting the bell.

The whole thing is absurd and completely unexpected. Walken is serious, intense, and, as always, a bit bizarre as he lectures the band about the importance of the cowbell.

Fallon, who developed a reputation for cracking up on camera, told Eric Spitznagel in an interview with *Playboy* magazine that it really started with the cowbell sketch and Will Ferrell trying to make him laugh: "I was just about to do my line when I looked over at Will—his gut was hanging out of his shirt, his glasses were flying off, he was sweating, and his eyes were nuts, and I just lost it."

It's difficult to know why this sketch and the catchphrase it introduced—"More cowbell"—caught on. When E! Entertainment did a countdown of the *101 Most Unforgettable SNL Moments* in 2004, "More cowbell" came in at number five. In 2012, Walken told film critic Peter Travers at abcnews.com, "It follows me around." He also thought enough was enough when he did a play in New York and people would clang cowbells during his curtain calls.

Roeser, BÖC's lead guitarist and cofounder, loved the sketch. "We all thought it was phenomenal," he told the *Washington Post*'s Paul Farhi in 2005. "We're huge Christopher Walken fans. I've probably seen it 20 times and I'm still not tired of it."

"More cowbell!" insists music producer Bruce Dickinson (Christopher Walken, far right) to members of Blue Öyster Cult (left to right) Chris Kattan, Will Ferrell, Chris Parnell, and Horatio Sanz (25.16). *NBCU Photo Bank via Getty Images*

Roeser also set the record straight that there was no Gene Frenkle, whose image appears at the end of the sketch along with the words "In Memoriam. 1950–2000."

So was there actually a cowbell on BÖC's recording of "Reaper"? According to bassist Joe Bouchard, the cowbell was "overdubbed" (meaning "added") to the final track. In a 2000 interview with Mark Voger of the *Asbury Park Press*, Bouchard explained that the producer told Bouchard's brother, drummer Albert, to put tape around a cowbell and go in the recording studio and play it. Joe Bouchard said you can't hear it on the original album, but if you listen carefully to the remastered CD, you can hear a cowbell in the background.

# "Well, Isn't That Special?"

## SNL's Objectionable, Offensive, and Controversial Moments

One of the joys of watching live television is that on occasion we are taken by surprise when someone does or says something totally unexpected. At the same time, in the minds of some viewers, the unexpected can be deemed "objectionable." Granted, what qualifies as "objectionable" in regard to television content has changed over time. For example, the occasional utterance of profanity (bleeped or nonbleeped) on a live awards show or in lyrics sung by a musical guest on *Saturday Night Live* has lost some of its shock value. But today's audiences are less likely to approve the use of the "N-word" in a sketch today as it was uttered by Chevy Chase back in 1975 in the classic "Word Association Sketch" (1.7) with Richard Pryor. Ironically, the Pryor episode was put on a five-second delay so NBC censors could cut two words from the comedian's routine (one of which was "ass"). According to the *Washington Post*, NBC's Standards and Practices Department was also concerned a parody of the horror film *The Exorcist* (1973) would offend Catholics. Producer Lorne Michaels said that "ultimately they [the censors] came around on everything" except for two words in Pryor's routine, which the *Washington Post* article doesn't identify.

You would think that a television show airing at 11:30 p.m. on a Saturday night would not be held to the same standards as a program airing in prime time. But NBC is a commercial broadcast network (not a pay cable station like HBO) under the jurisdiction of the Federal Communications Commission (FCC). Tina Fey poked fun at NBC's Standards and Practices Department in a 2012 episode of *30 Rock* in which Kenneth, the naive NBC page, is appointed the new head of late-night television standards and goes on a mission to clean up *TGS with Tracy Jordan*, the sketch comedy show produced by her character, Liz Lemon.

Lorne Michaels's battle with the censors started with season 1, but when he returned in 1985, the censors, like most of America in the Reagan era, had become increasingly conservative. "It used to be more of a fight," Michaels admitted in 1987. "Now it's just a flat 'no.' . . . There isn't a week in which four or five things aren't suggested that we think would be funny, and the best thing on that subject, and we can't do them." Michaels was speaking to the *Washington Post*'s Tom Shales, who reported how the network censors took a new approach last year by banning comedy after the fact. In other words, a sketch that was approved and broadcast live could then be banned from future broadcasts. Two episodes from season 12—one hosted by Steven Guttenberg (12.7) and the other by Paul Shaffer (12.10) were not shown in reruns because they contained sketches the censor demanded be removed and Michaels refused.

*Saturday Night Live*'s most controversial moments did not all involve a minor slip of the tongue. It might have been a deliberate action (like Sinéad O'Connor ripping up the Pope's photograph), or a scripted sketch approved by the censors that viewers found objectionable. In some instances, such a moment can be easily edited out before *SNL* airs three hours later on the West Coast. But with a click of a button, it's likely that whatever was said and done has already been posted on the internet and word has spread via social media before the host has said "good night" on the live show.

## Controversial Sketches

### *SNL*'s On-Air Apology: Claudine Longet Invitational Ski Championship (1.18)

Claudine Longet is a French recording artist, actress, and the former wife of singer Andy Williams. The Paris-born chanteuse with a soft, sweet singing voice appeared on American television in the 1960s and early 1970s and was a frequent guest on her husband's variety show. In 1968, she starred opposite Peter Sellers in Blake Edwards's 1968 comedy *The Party*. Longet made headlines in 1976 when she accidentally shot her lover, thirty-one-year-old champion skier Vladimir Peter "Spider" Sabich in his Aspen home. Longet claimed that the .22-caliber gun accidentally went off when Sabich was showing her how to use it (the only witness, her daughter Noelle, never took the stand). Longet was arrested and charged with manslaughter. Many questioned her story as rumors about the couple's supposedly tumultuous relationship swirled around Aspen during the months leading up to her high-profile trial, which ended with her devoted ex-husband Williams at her side as the jury found her guilty of a lesser charge ("criminally negligent homicide"). On January 31, 1976, the judge sentenced Longet to thirty days in jail "at the time of her own choosing" and two years' probation. Longet did not have the public's sympathy on her side. Whether it was an accident or not, many people believed she should have received a harsher sentence.

Three months later, Longet's crime was lampooned on *SNL* in a sketch (1.18) written by Michael O'Donoghue in which sportscasters Tom Tryman (Chevy Chase) and Jessica Antlerdance (Jane Curtin) welcome viewers to a skiing competition, "The Claudine Longet Invitational." The pair provides the play-by-play as we see footage of competitive skiers making their way down a hill.

Suddenly, there's a series of gunshots and one by one, each skier falls. "Uh-oh!" says Tom. "He seems to have been accidentally shot by Claudine Longet." The sketch concludes with a montage of skiers falling to the sounds of gunshots while Tom and Jessica explain what happened ("I think she was just cleaning her gun here, wasn't she?" "Here, she mistakenly dropped her gun and it went off," etc.).

It's doubtful Longet saw the broadcast as she was in jail at the time. Apparently Andy Williams saw it and threatened to sue, forcing *SNL* to broadcast its first and only on-air apology. According to Beatts and Heads's *Saturday Night Live* book, the apology appeared over a "Saturday Night" slide and was not heard by the studio audience:

> On April 24th, 1976, "Saturday Night" included a sketch about a Claudine Longet Invitational Ski Championship in Vail, Colorado, as part of the program's topical humor. It is desirable to correct any misunderstanding that a suggestion was made that, in fact, a crime had been committed. The satire was fictitious and its intent only humorous. This is a statement of apology if the material was misinterpreted.

Was Longet a fair target? Jane Curtin, the most private and least outspoken member of the *SNL* company, seemed to think so when she told *Playboy* magazine in a May 1977 interview with the writers and cast that Longet was "a fair target in that situation . . . Why should she be any different from Richard Speck?" (As *Weekend Update*'s Seth and Amy would ask, "*Really, Jane? Richard Speck? You are equating Longet with a serial killer who tortured, raped and murdered eight student nurses? Really?*")

In that same interview, Lorne Michaels clarified his position in regard to humor that is potentially offensive: "What I do is look at a piece and say, 'I think that's funny. I think it's offensive, but I think it's funny.' That becomes the criterion. It might not be what I would create, but it deserves an airing—it either works or it doesn't. Taste is just another word for discrimination. I wouldn't cut something because I thought it was offensive. I decided to suspend that judgment. For example, with the Claudine Longet piece. I thought it was very funny. I also thought it was very offensive."

As for Longet, she disappeared from public life after the trial.

In season 3 (3.14), Gilda Radner played Longet in a sketch, the talk show parody *Celebrity Crack-Up*, in which she is joined by Tony Orlando (Bill Murray), Robert Blake (John Belushi), and Richard Pryor (Garrett Morris), all of whom share their intimate problems in front of millions of people for the benefit of other celebrities who hopefully won't ruin their lives.

## "Nude Beach": Penis, Penis, Penis, etc. (14.2)

How many times can you utter the word "penis" in a single sketch? *SNL* certainly pushed the envelope with a sketch set on a nude beach in St. Martin in the French West Indies. Bob (Dana Carvey) introduces newcomer Doug (Matthew

Broderick) to his friends (Kevin Nealon, Dennis Miller), who comment on Doug's small penis. Doug agrees and is introduced to Bill (Jon Lovitz), who also has a small penis. They are joined by their female friends, one of whom also comments on the size of Doug's penis. The men agree to catch up to the women later, but first they sing the club anthem, "The Penis Song," bringing the grand total of penises to forty-three (seventeen spoken, twenty-six sung). Kevin Nealon then steps out of character and addresses the audience:

> Hi. I'm Kevin Nealon. What you just saw was an attempt to make an important point—that wherever you go, not matter how you look on the outside, we're all pretty much the same. You know, when the Standards Department was dissolved at NBC, we welcomed it as an opportunity to deal with issues like this in a frank way. And to be honest, we're a little disheartened by the snickering we heard during this presentation. It kind of makes us wonder if there's room for serious discussion of these subjects on television. So to those of you who missed the point—grow up.

There are actually two versions of the "Nude Beach" sketch. In the first version, which was cut after dress rehearsal, Jon Lovitz plays the new penis on the beach, and host Tom Hanks is one of the friends. The sketch ends with "The Penis Song." The point of the sketch is evident even without Nealon's speech—that all men have a penis and therefore it is acceptable to say the word "penis" (even more than once). Nealon mentions the "Standards Department" at NBC being "dissolved," but that doesn't mean there was no censor at the network. In his book Saturday Night Live: *Equal Opportunity Offender*, former NBC censor William G. Clotworthy recalled how the network received forty-six thousand postcards condemning the sketch from "the self-appointed guardian of American's morals" Reverend Donald Wildmon and his American Family Association. Clotworthy defended his decision to approve the sketch because the manner in which "penis" is spoken is "casual, conversational and matter-of-fact." Thus the word was "spoken in a non-sexual, harmless, clinical way—which was the point of the sketch."

This was not the first time "penis" was used in a sketch. In December 1979, Al Franken and Tom Davis appeared in the talk show parody *Revisions of Freudian Theory*, in which nasal-voiced Davis proposes a fifth stage in Freud's four-stage model of personality—the nasal stage. The host (Franken) previews next week's topic—"Penis Shame" presented by Dr. Sonya *Kuntmuller.* The word "penis" is uttered six times, and according to Clotworthy, NBC received twenty-four negative phone calls complaining about the sketch.

Apparently "penis" is acceptable, but "dick" is not. NBC bleeped the word "dick" sixteen times from Andy Samberg and Justin Timberlake's music video for their Emmy-winning song "D\*\*k in a Box." After the 1:00 a.m. broadcast, NBC posted the video on their website, nbc.com, and YouTube under the headings "Special Treat in a Box" or "Special Christmas Box," because the web is not under the jurisdiction of the FCC. The *New York Times* reported that Kevin Reilly, president of NBC Entertainment, and Jeff Zucker, chief executive of NBC Universal Television Group, had to approve the video before it was posted.

Other words that have made it on the air are "douchebag" (uttered twelve times in the "Lord and Lady Douchebag" sketch [5.20]), "Vagina/'gina" (twenty times in "Talkin' 'bout 'Ginas," a parody of Eve Ensler's *The Vagina Monologues* [26.12]); and although it is just a play on words, Tina Fey's sketch set in the Civil War era in which a family on a southern plantation, the Shady Thicket, awaits the arrival of the beloved Colonel Angus (pronounced *cunnilingus*) (28.13). His name is mentioned thirty-one times, though at the end of the sketch he mentions he was stripped of his rank due to an incident at Big Beaver in which he lost ten men and suffered an injury to his jaw. So now he goes by his given name—Anal Angus.

## SNL's Off-Air Apology: Wayne's World's "Top 10 List" (18.8)

After the 1992 election, *Wayne's World* featured a Top 10 List of "The Things We Like About Bill Clinton." The list includes such items as Universal Healthcare (#10), his huge head (#8), "Don't Stop Thinking About Tomorrow" ("Fleetwood Mac? Hello, it's the '90s!") (#6), and #2: Chelsea Clinton. There is a pause, and then Wayne explains that while "adolescence has been thus far unkind," Chelsea is "going to be a future fox." Garth agrees, suggesting that "under the right clinical conditions, she could turn into a babe-in-waiting." What made the joke even more cruel was item #3, "The Gore Daughters," who Wayne and Garth both honored with a "Schwing!" "Finally, there's some talent in the White House," Wayne adds, comparing it to an episode of *Petticoat Junction*. At the time, the ages of the Gore daughters were nineteen (Karenna), fifteen (Kristin), and thirteen (Sarah). Ironically, Kristin would grow up to be a staff writer on *Saturday Night Live*.

In an interview with *Redbook* magazine in March 1993, First Lady Hillary Clinton made it clear that she was not pleased with the skit. "I think it's sad that people don't have anything better to do than be mean to a child. . . . I'm going to do everything I can to help Chelsea be strong enough not to let what other people say about her affect her. In her particular situation it's obviously much bigger, but it happens to children all the time. . . . Unkind and mean things are said by people who are either insecure or going for the laugh or going for the nasty remark—whether it's on a playground or on a television set."

Apparently the First Lady's words did not fall on deaf ears. Lorne Michaels issued a public apology in the press, stating, "We felt, upon reflection, that if it was in any way hurtful, it wasn't worth it. She's a kid, a kid who didn't choose to be in a public life." Michaels also pointed out that no one protested in the 1970s when they treated nine-year-old Amy Carter "a little rougher." Mike Myers also wrote a private letter of apology to the Clintons as well.

The joke about Chelsea was edited out of future broadcasts and does not appear in online versions of the episode. Wayne and Garth jump from reason #3 ("The Gore Daughters") to reason #1 ("Live from New York . . .").

Hillary and Chelsea Clinton obviously don't harbor a grudge. Mrs. Clinton made an appearance on *SNL* (something her husband Bill has never done) when she was running to be the Democratic presidential candidate in the 2008 election. As for the former First Daughter, in 2011 she became a part-time NBC employee when she was hired as a special correspondent for the prime-time news show *Rock Center with Brian Williams* (2011–2013).

## Canteen Boy (19.13, 20.8)

Canteen Boy is one of Adam Sandler's twenty-year-old adolescent characters who wears a Boy Scout uniform and a canteen around his neck, though in his first appearance he tells his neighbors that he is no longer in the Scouts because he is too old (18.15). He is susceptible to bullying because he also has no social skills and lives in his own world, where he is preoccupied with snakes (he seems to have the power to summon them).

On February 12, 1994, guest host Alec Baldwin appeared in a sketch as Scoutmaster Armstrong, who is camping in the woods with a group of scouts that includes Canteen Boy. They tell ghost stories, and the other guys make fun of him, so the scoutmaster asks him to stay behind when the other boys go to sleep. Depending on your point of view, what follows is either hilariously creepy, highly offensive, or a combination of both. Armstrong proceeds to try to seduce Canteen Boy by serving him some wine, getting him to share his sleeping bag and rub bug repellent on his bare chest, and play a little game of Truth or Dare. Armstrong falls asleep before anything can happen, and while he goes to make breakfast, Canteen Boy summons some snakes and takes off.

NBC received over fifty complaints, including one from the Boy Scouts of America. In his memoir, *Gasping for Airtime,* Jay Mohr, who played one of the scouts in the sketch, recalled that the Boy Scouts objected to the portrayal of a scoutmaster as a pedophile and that the wardrobe department dressed them in actual Boy Scout uniforms. The original sketch is shocking, even by *SNL* standards, but it is also so absurd it is difficult to believe that anyone is going to think less of the Boy Scouts of America after watching that sketch or conclude that scoutmasters are pedophiles. But *SNL* and NBC didn't want to take any chances, so they added the following statement at the beginning of the sketch whenever it re-aired and on the *Best of Adam Sandler* and *Best of Alec Baldwin* DVDs. The suggestion that it is based on "actual events" is their attempt to show they have a sense of humor, yet the title of the sketch sounds like the title of a young adult storybook from the 1950s:

> The following sketch, "Canteen Boy and the Scout Master," is based on actual events. It tells the story of Canteen Boy, a highly intelligent

though quite eccentric 27-year-old who lives with his mother, and who, despite his age, remains active in scouting. Certain elements of Canteen Boy's story, such as his ability to summon snakes, have been added for dramatic effect.

When Baldwin returned to host the following season (20.13), he appeared onstage with Sandler dressed as Canteen Boy. Baldwin claims that when the sketch aired, "all hell broke loose" because people didn't understand that Canteen Boy is "a grown man, a perfectly intelligent twenty-seven-year-old." Baldwin claims the NBC switchboard received three hundred thousand calls and that he received a letter signed jointly by Clarence Thomas and Anita Hill. He announces that he and Sandler will be touring schools, churches, and community centers "to foster healing and tolerance." They then give a preview of their multimedia presentation "Out of the Tent & Proud: The Politically Correct Version of Canteen Boy," in which Scoutmaster Armstrong asks "consenting bisexual canteen person" if he can stick his hand up the front of his shirt.

If the original sketch aired today, it would most likely receive more public attention. On May 23, 2013, 61 percent of the fourteen hundred members of the Boy Scouts of America National Council voted to remove, effective January 1, 2014, the restriction that denied membership to youth on the basis of sexual orientation. The ban on "open and avowed homosexual" scoutmasters remains in effect. The sketch could be criticized by those who are fighting to remove the ban as well as those who are convinced there *is* a left-wing homosexual conspiracy to infiltrate the Boy Scouts.

## Conspiracy Theory Rock (23.16)

*Schoolhouse Rock* was a series of educational three-minute shorts that combined animation with original rock and pop songs to teach kids about grammar, science, civics, math, economics, and history. The original episodes aired on Saturday mornings on ABC from 1973 to 1985. The series was revived in 1993–1999, with the series *Money Rock*, which included episodes on Taxes ("Tax Man Max"), the Stock Exchange ("Walkin' on Wall Street"), and the budget deficit and the U.S. national debt ("Tyrannosaurus Debt"). Many of the classic episodes were written and, in some instances, performed by bebop and cool jazz pianist Bob Dorough. Tony Award–winning composer Lynn Ahrens, whose credits include *Ragtime, Once on This Island, Seussical,* and the musical version of *Rocky,* was another major contributor to the series.

Robert Smigel's *Conspiracy Theory Rock* (23.16) is not a parody of *Schoolhouse Rock*, but borrows its format to teach kids a lesson about corporate America, namely the large corporations—Disney, Fox, Westinghouse, and General Electric—that form the oligopoly that control the media. Using their corporate logos (Mickey Mouse for Disney, the Peacock for NBC, etc.), Smigel tells you everything you don't know about media conglomerates: the major news outlets that they control don't report on their own business dealings and holdings in controversial industries, such as the electric power plants built by GE and Westinghouse and the link between the PCPs used in their production and cancer and how they receive billions in subsidies from the government for job creation, which they use for PACs and to support politicians who will vote to favor their corporations. Smigel even throws in the firing of Norm Macdonald by NBC/GE for making too many O. J. jokes. The song itself is even censored when a "Please Stand By" with the NBC logo appears on the screen during the song.

The cartoon is shocking because it is so honest and accurate and it is being broadcast on a network owned by one of the conglomerates it is targeting (GE). The piece was obviously approved by the powers that be as it aired on March 14, 1998 (23.16). But when the episode, hosted by Julianne Moore, was repeated in late June, *Conspiracy Theory Rock* was edited out. It also doesn't appear in episode 23.16 on Netflix (but you can watch it for yourself on YouTube). *The Nation*'s David Corn reported that Lorne Michaels "concedes that it's unusual to excise portions of a rerun" and claims that he did it because, in his words, "I didn't think [the cartoon] worked comedically." Michaels explained that no one at NBC or GE talked to him about the segment. An NBC spokesman said, "I don't think the network has an official reaction," but a network source told him that NBC President Robert Wright was upset by the cartoon and that GE had a negative reaction.

Sounds like a conspiracy.

## Bailout Video (34.4)

A joint press conference broadcast on C-SPAN is held by President Bush (Jason Sudeikis), Nancy Pelosi (Kristen Wiig), Barney Frank (Fred Armisen), and hedge fund billionaire and Democratic donor George Soros (Will Forte) to announce the Democratic-controlled Congress has passed a $700 billion bailout package. According to DeadlineHollywood.com, Republicans liked the sketch because it actually blamed the Wall Street crisis on the Democrats (President Bush tells Pelosi that his administration warned them about the problem six years ago and it was the Democrats who refused to listen).

To emphasize that government intervention in the housing markets will help "real Americans who played by the rules," she introduces people who lost their homes to tell their story. What we get instead are people who abused the system. Two deadbeats (Bobby Moynihan, Kenan Thompson) explain they met all the requirements for a subprime mortgage: no credit history, no job, minor criminal record, drug and alcohol problems, etc. Next is a pair of greedy house-flippers (Bill Hader and Anne Hathaway) who bought two dozen time-share condos, which were heavily mortgaged and then the real estate market tanked. Now they'll have to sell their boat or put off cosmetic surgery to pay for them. Finally, there's billionaire philanthropists Herbert and Marion Sandler (Darrell Hammond and Casey Wilson), the former owners of the Golden West Financial

Corporation, which aggressively marketed subprime mortgages, bundled them as securities, and sold them to Wachovia Bank. The corporation made $24 billion, and as 10 percent owners of the company, they made approximately $2.4 billion. When the housing market collapsed, so did Wachovia Bank. The Sandlers are confused as to why they are even there today. "So, in that sense, you're not here to speak as victims." "No, no, no," Sandler replies. "That would be Wachovia Bank! . . . And thank you, Congressman Frank, as well as many Republicans, for helping block congressional oversight of our corrupt activity." While the Sandlers are speaking, they are identified as "Herbert & Marion Sandler." Underneath their names, it reads: *People who should be shot.*

NBC put the video online the following morning, and then it magically disappeared, causing speculation as to who made a phone call to NBC to get them to take it down.

DeadlineHollywood.com suggests that NBC pulled the video because it was "a lawsuit waiting to happen" due to the "People who should be shot" graphic and the accusation that their lending policies were responsible for the collapse of Wachovia Bank (for which no charges were ever filed). The network released this statement: "Upon review, we caught certain elements in the sketch that didn't meet our standards. We took it down and made some minor changes and it will be back online soon." NBC said it edited it out the graphic and the "allegations of corruption" that are made against the Sandlers. There are different versions circulating: the original version, which you will have to hunt down; a slightly edited one (posted on Hulu.com) minus the graphic and Sandler's "thank you" to Congressman Frank and the Republicans for making corrupt activity possible; and the one available on Netflix in which the Sandlers are completely cut out of the sketch.

## Drugs, Religion, and "Pilly-Packers": Sam Kinison and Martin Lawrence (19.14)

Prior to hosting the show in season 12, Sam Kinison, the acerbic, controversial comedian, made five guest appearances on *SNL*. During his stand-up routine, he talked about two topics that make censors very nervous—drugs and religion. Kinison talked about the government's war on drugs. "They've taken the pot, there is no more pot," Kinison said. "You can't get any more pot. If you give us back the pot, we'll forget about the crack." When the show aired later that night on the West Coast, the NBC censors interrupted the broadcast by cutting the sound and putting a slide of last year's *SNL* cast on the screen. Lorne Michaels explained to David T. Friendly at the *New York Times* that Kinison's joke violated NBC's new policy on drugs, which required that all references to drugs be negative. Michaels had mixed feelings about censoring the joke because he did not perform it at dress rehearsal, so everyone was taken by surprise. "But I disagreed with the decision to cut it," Michaels added. "It seems foolish to me to say all comments about drugs are pro-drug. I thought his comment was very smart . . .

What I really resent is the assumption that I or the show are somehow pro-drug, which we certainly are not."

The other touchy subject was religion, of which Kinison, who was trained to be a minister before he became a shock comic, is not a fan. He does a bit about television preachers, followed by an imitation of Jesus screaming as he is nailed to the cross, which no one on the West Coast heard because the sound suddenly went dead.

Apparently, there were no hard feelings, because Kinison hosted the show a month later (12.4).

The same can't be said for comedian Martin Lawrence (19.14), who at the time he hosted *SNL* was starring on his own Fox sitcom, *Martin* (1992–1997). On February 19, 1994, he starts off his monologue by saying that the censors have been following him all week and "[I] wish they'd get off my ass." He then shares with the audience something that concerns him deeply: white women now have the license to cut off men's "pilly-packers." What Lawrence was referring was the recent Lorena Bobbitt case in which she was found not guilty on the grounds of temporary insanity of severing her husband John Wayne Bobbitt's penis and throwing it on the side of the road. He then goes into a whole routine about what it would be like to be the one to find it. Lawrence then moves on to another subject that concerns him—women and their lack of hygiene. He accuses women of not washing their asses properly and suggests they put a Tic-Tac or a Cert or a Stick-Up in their ass.

According to NBC, Lawrence was told he needed to clean up his act between the dress rehearsal and the live show. In Jay Martel's 1994 profile of him in *Rolling Stone*, the comedian denied the charge, insisting, "All they told me was 'This is late night; have a good time, as long as you don't use cuss words.' And that's what I did." There was some fallout. The network canceled a scheduled appearance on *The Tonight Show*, though Lawrence said that Jay Leno phoned him to say that it was the network's decision, not his.

In reruns of the episode, Lawrence's monologue is cut in half. As he switches to the topic of women's hygiene, text appears on the screen, which is read by a voiceover announcer:

> At this point in his monologue, Martin begins a commentary on what he considers the decline in standards of feminine hygiene in this country. Although we at *Saturday Night Live* take no stand on the issue one way or the other, network policy prevents us from re-broadcasting this portion of his remarks.
>
> In summary, Martin feels, or felt at the time, that the failure of many young women to bathe thoroughly is a serious problem that demands our attention. He explores the problem, citing numerous examples from his own experience, and ends proposing several imaginative solutions.
>
> It was a frank and lively presentation, and nearly cost us all our jobs. We now return to the conclusion of Martin's monologue.

Lawrence either underestimated what is permissible on late-night television or knew exactly what he was doing.

## Dropping the "F-Bomb"

The f-bomb has been dropped numerous times on *SNL*—sometimes by mistake, other times deliberately, and, in some instances, the f-bombers' intentions were not entirely clear.

## Paul Shaffer's "Floggin'" Timing (5.14)

The first time it was uttered live on the air was in season 5 (5.14) by composer Paul Shaffer, and while it was in a musical context, everyone's favorite late-night bandleader was not behind his keyboards at the time. Shaffer was in a medieval sketch set in Middlesex, England, in 1267 playing one of the Minstrels of Newcastle, who are about to perform at Gaunt Manor for the lady of house, Elenour of Gaunt (played by John Belushi in drag). But they are having trouble because their drummer, Schwanken (Bill Murray), can't stay on the beat (instead of four successive beats, he would pause between beats two and three). So the group's flutist (Shaffer) keeps berating Schwanken with every other word out of his mouth being "floggin'" this and "floggin'" that: "Where's the fourth beat? It's so floggin' simple! Look! We're in the floggin' Gaunt Manor, floggin' Elenour of Gaunt is gonna come through that floggin' door any minutes, listen to us play this floggin' song. . . ." According to Shaffer's autobiography, *We'll Be Here for the Rest of Our Lives*, the scene was based on an underground rehearsal tape of the 1960s British rock band the Troggs, whose big hits included the 1966 single "Wild Thing." "The tape revealed them unsuccessfully trying to explain a simple beat to their drummer," Shaffer explained. "The problem was their only means of musical communication was to say 'fuckin'' this and 'fuckin'' that, as in 'You had the fuckin' beat. Now you've fuckin' lost it.'"

In the sketch, the expletive was replaced by the word "floggin'," and Shaffer said it over a dozen times. Then at one point, Shaffer turned to Murray and said, "You just think you play better, but you don't play better. It throws the *fuckin'* timing off."

Shaffer immediately realized what he said and turned away from the camera. He later admitted to Lorne Michaels that he "fucked up." Michaels said he should have "flogged up." "You just broke down the last barrier," Michaels added. "Anyway, no one noticed."

The flub occurred on another milestone: *SNL*'s one-hundredth episode. It was the perfect birthday gift.

## Charles Rocket and Prince (6.11)

The f-bomb was dropped not once but twice in one evening (6.11). The first is by Prince while performing his song "Party Up," in which he used the phrase "fuckin' bore." though it is possible viewers not familiar with the song may not have noticed it. The same can't be said for the expletive unleashed by cast member Charles Rocket in the show's final moment. *Dallas* cast member Charlene Tilton was the host, and in a parody of the famous "Who shot J.R.?" cliff-hanger, an unknown assailant shoots cast member Rocket during the show. When it was time to say "good night," Tilton asks Rocket, who is sitting in a chair smoking a cigarette, how he is feeling after being shot. "It's the first time I've ever been shot in my life," Rocket mutters. "I'd like to know who the *fuck* did it." Tilton is taken aback and squeals. The cast is shocked; some of them laugh, while others cover their own mouth. Everyone waves goodbye—except Rocket, who looks like he is clueless about what he just said.

In his book Saturday Night Live: *Equal Opportunity Offender*, William G. Clotworthy, from NBC's Standards and Practices, recounts the reaction in the control room: "I'll never forget that moment. The control room went absolutely silent, then, as on swivels, every head turned to look at me! I saw this through my fingers, mind you, as my hands were covering my face, just before I beat my head against the console." Clotworthy warned the staff to "expect calls" and made sure the word was bleeped from the West Coast broadcast. They did receive calls and letters. Rocket claimed it was not premeditated—and NBC publicly backed him up by confirming that it was "unintended and inexcusable." Rocket appeared in one more episode (6.12), after which he, along with most of the cast and producer Jean Doumanian, was replaced, but Rocket's indiscretion was not necessarily the reason.

## Norm Macdonald, Weekend Update (22.17)

During *Weekend Update*, anchor Macdonald says, "What the fuck was that?" when he stumbles reading over a news story—and then says, "My farewell performance."

## "Biker Chick Chat" (35.1)

In the 2009–2010 season, *SNL* added two new feature players—Nasim Pedrad and Jenny Slate. In a sketch she wrote on her first show (35.1), Slate played Dawn, a tough-talking biker chick in a talk show parody, "Biker Chick Chat." Kristen Wiig plays her equally tough cohost Beth, and host Megan Fox is their guest. Every other word out of their mouths is either "frickin'" or "friggin'" (I counted around fifty-two total). As with Paul Shaffer, she accidentally said the word "f**kin'" instead: "You frickin' just threw an ashtray full of butts at my head. You know what? You stood up for yourself and I fuckin' love you for that." Realizing what she said, Slate closes her mouth and puffs out her cheeks—and the sketch continues. Slate's contract was not renewed for the next season, but it's doubtful that an accidental f-bomb had anything to do with the producers' decision.

## Samuel L. Jackson says "Fuh" and "Bull***t?" (38.10)

Samuel Jackson gave viewers (and the censors) an early Christmas present during this holiday episode in which he appeared as a guest on the recurring sketch *What Up with That?* Kenan Thompson plays DeAndre Cole, the host of this BET talk show parody, who spends more time singing than allowing his three guests to talk. One of the three guests is always Bill Hader as Fleetwood Mac's Lindsey Buckingham, though the real Buckingham appeared as a guest on 36.21. When DeAndre said they were out of time, Samuel Jackson said "Man, Fuh" (not f**k), followed by "That's bullshit!" A startled Thompson replied, "C'mon Sam, that cost money" (referring to the fines the FCC issues for obscenity). As done in the past, "That's bulls**t!" was bleeped from the West Coast airing, which made the exchange all the more confusing to viewers.

Jackson immediately explained what was going on via Twitter (@SamuelLJackson): "I only said FUH not FUCK! K [Kenan] was sposed to cut off da BULLSHIT, blew it!!"

## Musical F-Bombs

The f-bomb is a popular word in rock lyrics, so if songs have to be approved ahead of time, one has to wonder: Was anyone familiar with the artist's music? Was anyone listening during rehearsals? Or did the singer manage to slip a naughty word in at the last minute? In most instances the f-bomb or any other objectionable word would be bleeped out by the time the episode aired on the West Coast (and in reruns as well).

The distinguished list of musical f-bombers has included:

- **Steven Tyler**, lead singer of Aerosmith, singing "Monkey on My Back" from their album *Pump*. The "fucking monkey" on his back refers to the band's battle with alcohol and drugs (15.13).
- **Morris Day and the Time** ended their performance of "Chocolate" (from their 1990 album *Pandemonium*) by sitting down at a table and asking, "Where the fuck this chicken come from? I thought I ordered ribs!" (16.3).
- **Janet Jackson** added the word "fuck" to her live performance of "Throb," from her fifth studio album, *Janet* (1993) (19.20).
- R.E.M.'s lead singer, **Michael Stipe**, said "fuck" in the final line of the song "What's the Frequency, Kenneth?" but he had his back to the camera at the time (20.5).
- The Beastie Boys' **Ad-Rock** joined the list during the performance of "Sure Shot" (20.8).
- System of a Down, an Armenian American heavy metal band, won the Grammy in 2006 for Best Hard Rock Performance for their song "B.Y.O.B." The title of the song is an acronym, but the second *B* refers to *bombs*, not *booze*. The song protests the U.S. invasion of Iraq and how the nation celebrates the horrors of war. The five-second delay allowed co-lead vocalist

Daron Malakian, who cowrote the song with bandmate Serj Tankian, to ask the question, "Where the f–k were you?" so the f-bomb could be bleeped out, though Malakian managed to bypass the censors by yelling one final "F–k yeah!" into his microphone.

## Not-Ready-for-Prime-Time Singer: Ashlee Simpson (30.3)

Simpson was the victim of bad timing on several fronts. First, the week she appeared on the show, *60 Minutes*' Lesley Stahl and her film crew were spending time at 30 Rock doing a piece on how the show is put together. The first sign that there is a problem is at rehearsal when Simpson leaves the stage in tears worried, as Lorne Michaels tells Stahl, about losing her voice, and they weren't sure if she should perform at the dress rehearsal before the show but instead save her voice for the broadcast.

During the live show, Simpson sang her first number, her hit single "Pieces of Me" without any problems. When it was time to do her second number, "Autobiography," the vocal track for "Pieces of Me" was mistakenly played again. At the time, she was holding her microphone at her waist, so it was obvious the vocals were not coming from her lips. Uncertain what to do, a confused Simpson did a few dance steps, and walked off the stage. Her band continued to play "Pieces of Me." According to Michaels, it was the first time in *SNL* history that a guest walked offstage during a live show. An additional episode of the comedy short *Bear City* aired, though Simpson did reappear at the end of the show with host Jude Law.

> Jude Law: "What can I say, it's live TV."
>
> Ashlee Simpson: "Exactly, I feel so bad, my band started to play the wrong song, and I didn't know what to do, so I thought I'd do a hoe-down. I'm sorry. I didn't mean for it to happen."

Michaels later confirmed that no one had discussed Simpson's plans to lip-synch her performance. He explained that the only time he's been aware of lip-synching "is during dance breaks where if it was all about dance, and that's a relatively recent phenomenon." Simpson's father, Joe Simpson, later told the *New York Times* that he had made a call to Ashlee's physician, Dr. Joe Sugerman, who confirmed that Ms. Simpson suffered from acid reflux and had woken with severe laryngitis last week. "I told her that she could really damage her vocal cords if she tried to sing." But because SNL is a national show, Mr. Simpson insisted that she go on and use a recorded backing track. Unfortunately, the drummer accidentally started up the one for "Pieces of Me."

If anyone benefited from the mishap, it was probably Simpson, who received the kind of national publicity you can't buy. She even joked about it during a performance in Las Vegas when her band started to play "Pieces of Me" instead of "Autobiography."

During the "good nights," Ashlee Simpson blamed the gaffe at the start of her second set on the band for playing the "wrong song." What we heard was a recording of her first song, "Pieces of Me," which exposed that she had been lip-synching.

Simpson did return to the show the following season (31.2), singing "Catch Me When I Fall" and "Boyfriend" without incident.

The Ashlee Simpson debacle didn't seem to put the kibosh on live lip-synching, as Eminem took to the stage the following week (30.4) and performed "Just Lose It," which sounded as if it was recorded at another time and place, as the movement of his lips don't correspond directly with the words coming out of his mouth.

To be fair, Simpson and Eminem are not isolated cases. Since the Simpson incident, viewers have been vigilant and continually report any suspicious on-air behavior online.

# From the Small Screen to the Big Screen

## *SNL* Goes to Hollywood

Since the 1950s, Hollywood has been turning television series into motion pictures with limited success. For every *M\*A\*S\*H* (1972–1983), *Buffy the Vampire Slayer* (1997–2003), and *Friday Night Lights* (2006–2011), there are countless unsold pilots and bomb television shows based on popular films. There is simply no guarantee a television series based on a classic Hollywood movie, a box-office hit, or a cult film will garner high ratings, particularly if you subtract one of the major elements that contributed to its popularity. Who wants to see a TV version of *Casablanca* (1983) starring David Soul in the Humphrey Bogart role? Or *Ferris Bueller* (1990) without Matthew Broderick? Or *Delta House* (1979), the short-lived TV version of the box-office hit *Animal House* (1978), minus John Belushi?

The reverse is also true. Some television series simply don't translate to the big screen. The ones that do score at the box office (and, in some instances, with the critics), like *The Addams Family* (1991), *Get Smart* (2008), and the *Mission Impossible* (1996) and *Star Trek* (1979–2013) franchises, are updated and/or retooled to broaden their appeal to contemporary audiences. Still, that doesn't stop some studio executives from overestimating the ticket-buying public's interest in certain old television shows and "greenlighting" television-to-film adaptations, which is exactly what happened with the film versions of *Car 54, Where Are You?* (1994), *My Favorite Martian* (1999), *The Mod Squad* (1999), *The Honeymooners* (2005), and *Land of the Lost* (2009).

The adaptation of a comedy sketch with one or more recurring characters into a feature-length film poses even greater challenges. Recurring characters on sketch comedy shows are thinly drawn and certainly not as developed as sitcom characters because there simply isn't time in a five- to eight-minute sketch. On *SNL*, the character(s) and comedic premise are introduced in the first sketch, so by the third or fourth sketch the audience's expectations are firmly established, which is why recurring sketches are fueled by repetition.

When it's time for characters to make the leap to the big screen, screenwriters face the difficult task of expanding a five- to eight-minute sketch into a ninety-minute film. In most instances, a backstory is developed for the main characters, additional characters are added into the mix, and the characters' "universe" is expanded beyond the sketch's main setting. The audience sees where Pat Riley lives, discovers what the Roxbury Guys do during their daylight hours, and meets Mary Katherine Gallagher's guardian, who was mentioned but never shown on *SNL*.

All of the following films feature characters that first appeared on *SNL*. With the exception of the two Blues Brothers films and *It's Pat* (1994), they were all produced by Lorne Michaels. Most of the films were released in the 1990s, beginning with the box-office hit *Wayne's World* (1992), though none of the subsequent films came close to repeating its success. As the list below illustrates, few of the *SNL* films turned a substantial profit if any at all, and two in particular—*It's Pat* and *Stuart Saves His Family* (1995)—were major financial disasters.

| SNL Sketch Films (1980–2010) | Budget/Box Office (worldwide) |
| --- | --- |
| *Gilda Live* (1980) | None/$2.2 million |
| *The Blues Brothers* (1980) | $27.5 million/$115.2 million |
| *Wayne's World* (1992) | $20 million/$183 million |
| *Coneheads* (1993) | $33 million/$21.1 million |
| *Wayne's World 2* (1993) | $40 million/$48.1 million |
| *It's Pat* (1994) | $8 million/$60,822 |
| *Stuart Saves His Family* (1995) | $6.3 million/$912,082 |
| *Blues Brothers 2000* (1998) | $28 million/$14 million |
| *A Night at the Roxbury* (1998) | $17 million/$30.3 million |
| *Superstar* (1999) | $34 million/$30.6 million |
| *The Ladies Man* (2000) | $24 million/$13.7 million |
| *MacGruber* (2010) | $10 million/$9.3 million |

## *The Blues Brothers* (1980): "They never got caught. They are on a mission from God."

Directed by John Landis. Written by Dan Aykroyd and John Landis. Producer: Robert K. Weiss. Executive Producer: Bernie Brillstein. Cinematography: Stephen M. Katz. Editor: George Folsey Jr.

**Cast:** John Belushi (Jake Blues), Dan Aykroyd (Elwood Blues), James Brown (Reverend Cleophus James), Cab Calloway (Curtis), Ray Charles (Ray), Aretha Franklin (Mrs. Murphy, Carrie Fisher (Mystery Woman), Henry Gibson (Head Nazi), John Freeman (Burton Mercer), Kathleen Freeman (Sister Mary Stigmata), Steve Lawrence (Maury Sline), Twiggy (Chic Lady), Frank Oz (Corrections Officer), Judith Jacklin (Cocktail Waitress), Rosie Shuster (Cocktail Waitress), Steven Spielberg (Cook County Assessor's Office Clerk).

Distributed by Universal. Running time: 133 mins. Rated R.

## Blues Brothers 2000 (1998): "The Blues Are Back."

Directed by John Landis. Written by Dan Aykroyd and John Landis. Producers: Dan Aykroyd, Leslie Belzberg, and John Landis. Cinematography: David Herrington. Editor: Dale Beldin. Original Music: Paul Shaffer.

**Cast:** Dan Aykroyd (Elwood Blues), John Goodman (Mighty Mack McTeer), Kathleen Freeman (Mother Mary Stigmata), B. B. King (Malvern Gasperon), Nia Peeples (Lt. Elizondo), Aretha Franklin (Mrs. Murphy), Steve Lawrence (Maury Sline), Darrell Hammond (Robertson), Paul Shaffer (Marco), James Brown (Cleophus James).

Distributed by Universal. Running time: 123 mins. Rated PG-13.

The Blues Brothers—"Joliet" Jake (John Belushi) and Elwood (Dan Aykroyd)—made their first of three appearances on *SNL* on January 17, 1976 (1.10). Host Buck Henry introduced them as "Howard Shore and the All-Bee Band," and instead of their signature black suits, white shirts, and skinny black ties, Jake and Elwood, along with the rest of the band, wore bee costumes, which was part of a running gag in season 1 (bandleader Shore was dressed as a beekeeper). Jake sang "I'm a King Bee," a swamp blues song written and first recorded by Slim Harpo, accompanied by Elwood on the harmonica. At the time, viewers didn't know what they were watching was not just another *SNL* Bee gag, or even a gag at all, but the birth of a legitimate revivalist rhythm and blues band. This was also not their first public performance. They had played around New York City and warmed up *SNL* audiences before the show. More importantly, Belushi and Aykroyd did not think of themselves as actors playing characters as one does in a sketch. Their alter egos, Elwood and Jake, were serious bluesmen, and their band included members of the *SNL* house band along with other recruits, all of whom appear in the film under their real names.

Over the next four years, the Blues Brothers' debut album, *Briefcase Full of Blues* (1978), would go double platinum, reaching #1 on the *Billboard* 200 in January 1979. During that time, the Brothers appeared twice on *SNL* (minus the bee costumes). On April 22, 1978, they were the musical guests with host Steve Martin (3.18), for whom they opened at the Universal Amphitheatre. They returned on November 18, 1978, with host Carrie Fisher (4.6), who also appears in the film, and opened the show with "Soul Man," which reached #14 on the *Billboard* Hot 100 chart. In the summer of 1980, Universal Studios released *The Blues Brothers*, a big-budget screen comedy that reunited Belushi with *National Lampoon's Animal House* director John Landis.

In the thinly plotted film, Jake and Elwood try to raise the $5,000 that's needed to prevent the foreclosure of the Catholic orphanage where they were raised. They manage to reassemble their old band, but their first gig, for which they pose as a country-western band, the Good Ol' Boys, is a bust. They blackmail their old booking agent to get them a gig at the Palace Hotel Ballroom, where a record executive comes backstage and offers them an advance for a recording contract. With the money they need, the brothers rush to the assessor's office in downtown Chicago to pay the tax bill and save the orphanage.

*The Blues Brothers* is part musical, part action comedy, though most of the film's 133 minutes are devoted to car chases and crashes shot in and around Chicago. Some of the stunts are impressive, such as when Jake and Elwood's car, an old police car dubbed the Bluesmobile, jumps the 95th Street drawbridge. But the car chases, particularly a long sequence inside a shopping mall, and the resulting car crashes and pileups are excessive, and by the second hour, repetitive.

The action sequences were a successful strategy to attract young ticket buyers who Aykroyd, Belushi, and Landis probably assumed have little or no interest in what *The Blues Brothers* was really selling—rhythm and blues music. The film's real high points are the musical performances by living legends James Brown, Cab Calloway, Ray Charles, and Aretha Franklin, who, in between all the chases and wreckage, get to do their thing.

According to a 2013 *Vanity Fair* article by Ned Zeman chronicling the making of the film (including Belushi's heavy drug use that reportedly slowed the production down), Universal Pictures executives were not pleased with the film's rising budget, which did not go unnoticed by the critics. *Variety* (6/18/80) called *The Blues Brothers* a "diverting, but not hilarious, farce [that] has enough to offer to draw sizable crowds but, as always with such inflated enterprises, extent of ultimate payoff is questionable." For *Time* magazine's Richard Corliss (7/7/80), "The most impressive thing about *The Blues Brothers* is its numbers: a budget in the $30 million–$38 million range, a cast of 91, a crew of 191, a stunt team of 78, and the cooperation of nearly every able-bodied Chicagoan except Dave Kingman [a slugger for the Chicago Cubs]." Roger Ebert, film critic for the *Chicago Sun-Times*, was surprised how much he enjoyed what he described as "the Sherman tank of musicals . . . a big, raucous powerhouse that proves against all odds that if you're loud enough, vulgar enough, and have enough raw energy, you can make a steamroller into a musical, and vice versa."

The Blues Brothers didn't die with John Belushi. The band continued to play and even did a world tour in 1988. Ten years later, they reunited for the film sequel, *Blues Brothers 2000*, directed by John Landis, who once again cowrote the screenplay with Dan Aykroyd. Set eighteen years later, the film opens on a somber note. Elwood is released from prison and learns that his brother Jake is dead (the film is dedicated to the late John Belushi, John Candy, and Cab Calloway). Unfortunately, it rehashes the plot of the first film, with Jake reassembling the old band plus two new members—Mighty Mack McTeer (John Goodman) and an orphan, Buster Blues (J. Evan Bonifant). The action extends beyond Chicago's city limits as the band heads to New Orleans with the police, white supremacists, and the Russian mafia on their tail. All roads lead to a mansion, the home of a voodoo queen (Erykah Badu), where the Blues Brothers participate in a battle of the bands against the "the Louisiana Gator Boys," which includes an impressive lineup of musical greats like B. B. King, Eric Clapton, Clarence Clemons, Bo Diddley, Isaac Hayes, Billy Preston, Lou Rawls, and Steve Winwood. The film also features performances by Aretha Franklin and James Brown, reprising their roles from the first film.

The critics gave thumbs-up to the music, but found the film as a whole to be a "lame comedy" (Roger Ebert, 2/6/98), a "wildly uneven sequel" (Joe Leydon, *Variety*, 2/5/98), with a "disposable plot" (Lawrence Van Gelder, *New York Times*, 2/6/98).

## *Coneheads* (1993): "Young ones! Parental units! We summon you!"

Directed by Steve Barron. Written by Tom Davis, Dan Aykroyd, Bonnie Turner, and Terry Turner. Producer: Lorne Michaels. Executive Producer: Michael I. Rachmil. Cinematography: Francis Kenny. Editor: Paul Trejo. Original Music: David Newman.

**Cast:** Dan Aykroyd (Beldar Conehead/Donald R. DeCicco), Jane Curtin (Prymaat Conehead/Mary Margaret DeCicco), Michelle Burke (Connie Conehead), Laraine Newman (Laarta), Phil Hartman (Marlax), Chris Farley (Ronnie the Mechanic), Kevin Nealon (Senator), Jan Hooks (Gladys Johnson), Michael McKean (Gorman Seedling), Jason Alexander (Larry Farber), Lisa Jane Persky (Lisa Farber).

Distributed by Paramount Pictures. Running time: 109 mins. Rated PG.

Fourteen years after we first watched them from our "living chambers," the Coneheads were the subject of a feature-length "celluloid fantasy" (that's Conehead-speak for "film"). The screenplay was written by Coneheads creators Tom Davis and Dan Aykroyd, who cowrote the screenplay with Bonnie and Terry Turner, *SNL* writers and creators of the aliens-on-earth situation comedy *3rd Rock from the Sun* (1996–2001) starring Jane Curtin. *Coneheads* recounts the story of Fuel Survey Underlord Beldar Clorhone ("Conehead" is the Americanized version of their last name) (Aykroyd); his wife, Prymaat (Curtin); and their teenage daughter, Conjaab (known as "Connie" on earth) (Michelle Burke) and their assimilation to suburban life on earth (Laraine Newman, who originated the part of Connie on *SNL*, has a cameo). All the while they are being pursued by an INS agent, Gorman Seedling (Michael McKean) and his equally sleazy assistant (David Spade). As in the sketches, the initial jokes revolve mostly around the Conehead family's assimilation to suburban life on earth. The second half of the film is set on the planet Remulak, where Beldar is forced to fight a *garthok*, a fierce six-legged beast, to the death.

In addition to McKean and Spade, *Coneheads* doubles as an *SNL* cast reunion with Chris Farley in a featured role as Connie's insecure lovestruck beau, Ronnie,

*The Coneheads*: The feature-length comedy based on the popular sketch recounts the backstory of the Conehead family—(left to right) Connie (Michelle Burke), Beldar (Dan Aykroyd) and Prymaat (Jane Curtin)—and their early days on earth.

and smaller bit parts played by former and current cast members including Phil Hartman, Jan Hooks, Tim Meadows, Jon Lovitz, Peter Aykroyd, Tom Davis, Garrett Morris, Kevin Nealon, Julia Sweeney, and Adam Sandler.

Critics were not impressed by the film. "Not much is really funny," complained Roger Ebert. "The story is without purpose; there nothing for us to care about, even in a comedic way." In her review for the *New York Times*, Janet Maslin wrote that the film "has its dopey charms," but "falls flat about as often as it turns funny, and displays more amiability than style." On a more positive note, *Variety* critic Leonard Klady called *Coneheads* "a sweet, funny anarchic pastiche that should find broad based popularity. Its sly combination of the outrageous and the mundane is surprisingly appealing screen entertainment that transcends the one-joke territory it inhabited on television." But Klady was wrong. The film did not find "broad based popularity," and the box-office returns were disappointing.

### *Gilda Live* (1980): "Things like this only happen in the movies."

Directed by Mike Nichols. Written by Anne Beatts, Lorne Michaels, Marilyn Suzanne Miller, Don Novello, Michael O'Donoghue, Gilda Radner, Paul Shaffer, Rosie Shuster, and Alan Zweibel. Producer: Lorne Michaels. Directors of Photography: Ted Churchill, James Contner, Alan Metzger, Peter Norman.

# From the Small Screen to the Big Screen

Editors: Ellen Hovde, Lynzee Klingman, Muffie Meyer. Musical Director: Howard Shore. Musical Consultation: Paul Shaffer. Original Broadway production produced and directed by Lorne Michaels.

**Cast:** Gilda Radner (various characters), Don Novello (Father Guido Sarducci), Rouge (Diana Grasselli, Myriam Valle, Maria Vidal), Paul Shaffer (Don Kirshner/The Candy Slice Group), Howard Shore (The Candy Slice Group).

Distributed by Warner Bros. Running time: 90 mins. Rated R.

In 1979, between seasons 4 and 5 of *SNL*, Gilda Radner spent her summer vacation onstage at the Winter Garden Theatre, where she starred in her own Broadway musical comedy revue, *Gilda Radner—Live from New York*. Produced and directed by Lorne Michaels and written by Radner and members of the *SNL* writing staff, Radner entertained New York audiences with a mixture of songs and sketches. *Gilda Live*, a film version of the concert, was released the following year.

The film, directed by Mike Nichols, is like watching a "Best of Gilda Radner" DVD. All of the characters that made Radner a household name are showcased in this ninety-minute stage show filmed in front of a live audience. Roseanne Roseannadanna gives the commencement speech at the Columbia School of Journalism. Emily Litella is substituting at P.S. 164 in Bedford-Stuyvesant for a teacher recovering from his recent "stubbing" (stabbing). Little Judy Miller bounces around her bedroom as she entertains herself with "The Judy Miller Show." At her piano recital, Lisa Loopner performs "The Way We Were" in honor of her idol, composer Marvin Hamlisch. Zonked-out punk rocker Candy Slice honors Mick Jagger with "Gimme Mick." Former 1960s girl group Rhonda Weiss and the Rhondettes reunite to mourn the loss of a sugar substitute with "Goodbye, Saccharin" (which Radner sang on *SNL* in episode 2.16). Ironically, the film's highlight is the closing number in which Gilda is just being herself. She sings "Honey (Touch Me with My Clothes On)," an original song she wrote with Paul Shaffer. In between we catch glimpses of Radner getting in and out of her costumes backstage and some comedic bits from Paul Shaffer (doing his Don Kirshner impression) and Father Guido Sarducci (Don Novello).

It's all very familiar—and that's the problem. Is it worth the price of a Broadway show admission (average cost back then was around $20) or a movie ticket to see someone perform in person or on film what you have been watching for free on television? The film critics agreed: Radner is funny and talented, but the material lacks the depth one expects for the stage or big screen. As *Herald Examiner* critic Michael Sragow points out, "What's [*sic*] we miss most in "Gilda Live" is Gilda *live* . . . In the night-by-night, rehearsed revue format, the satire loses its spontaneity, its air of luck." It's also not surprising that many critics felt that as Father Guido Sarducci, Novello's talents were better suited for the revue format because he is a solo performer, unlike some of Radner's characters, like Roseannadanna, Litella, and Loopner, who are paired on *SNL* with other characters like *Weekend Update* cranky anchor Jane Curtin and Lisa's equally nerdy boyfriend, Todd (Bill Murray).

*Gilda Live* may have been a critical and box-office failure—but Gilda's fans are grateful that her performance has been preserved. Radner did return to Broadway in 1980 to star in *Lunch Hour*, a comedy written by Jean Kerr and directed by Mike Nichols.

## *It's Pat* (1994): "A comedy that proves love is a many gendered thing."

Directed by Adam Bernstein. Written by Jim Emerson, Stephen Hibbert, and Julia Sweeney. Based on characters by Julia Sweeney. Producer: Charles B. Wessler. Coproducers: Richard S. Wright and Cyrus Yavneh. Cinematography: Jeff Jur. Editor: Norman Hollyn. Original Music: Mark Mothersbaugh.

**Cast:** Julia Sweeney (Pat Riley), Dave Foley (Chris), Charles Rocket (Kyle Jacobsen), Kathy Griffin (Herself), Julie Hayden (Stacy Jacobsen), Kathy Najimy (Tippy), Camille Paglia (Herself), Tim Meadows (KVIB-FM Station Manager).

Distributed by Touchstone Pictures. Running time: 77 mins. Rated PG-13.

Born on the stage of the Groundlings Theatre in Los Angeles, the androgynous Pat Riley made his-her *SNL* debut in a graveyard sketch (the last sketch of the night) in December 1990 (16.7). Bill (Kevin Nealon) gets a new job in an office, but he can't seem to figure out the gender of his new boss, Pat (Julia Sweeney). Donning a black wig, large framed glasses, mannish clothes, and a body suit that makes it impossible to determine what Pat has above or below the waist, Julia Sweeney's androgynous creation only manages to add to the confusion whenever Bill or anyone else asks Pat a question that aims to figure out if Pat is a he or a she. Pat tells Bill his-her ex-fiancé is named "Chris." By the next sketch (16.13), they've apparently reconciled because Pat introduces coworker Sue (Roseanne Barr) to Chris (Dana Carvey), another human question mark with long blonde hair who wears a purple silk shirt (or is it a blouse?) and pants. Pat's coworkers even resort to playing strip poker—but Pat doesn't lose a hand (17.10). At one point it seemed our questions would finally be answered when Pat joins a health club and has to enter the locker room. At that very moment, the sketch is interrupted by *Weekend Update* anchor Kevin Nealon with breaking news (17.6). In later sketches, Pat appears in parodies of *Basic Instinct* (17.17), *Single White Female* (18.3) (the ad for a roommate reads "Single White Person"), and *The Crying Game* (18.16), featuring the film's stars, Miranda Richardson and Stephen Rea. In the final sketch, he-she is about to reveal his-her gender, but an audience member, played by Adam Sandler, pleads with Pat not to reveal the truth (18.11).

As in the sketches, there is a character in *It's Pat*, a neighbor named Kyle (*SNL* alum Charles Rocket), who is trying to solve the mystery surrounding

*It's Pat*: A one-joke sketch was expanded to a seventy-seven-minute feature film without solving the mystery surrounding Pat's (Julia Sweeney) gender.

Pat's true gender. Kyle's quest turns into an obsession to the point that he starts stalking Pat and invading his-her privacy. Of course, the mystery is never solved. But the film's central plotline focuses on Pat's personal problems surrounding his-her inability to hold a job and choose a career, which affects his-her relationship with Chris. What's surprising about the film is how screenwriters Sweeney, Stephen Hibbert, and Jim Emerson made Pat into such an unlikable character. In an interview with *Variety* in 1999, Sweeney explained the origins of Pat: "We all had someone that's like Pat: it has nothing to do with gender. It's just someone who's annoying, who's oblivious, who's always getting in people's way." But does an audience want to spend seventy-seven minutes with a character who is designed to be annoying? More importantly, the film seems to be a missed opportunity—it could have used the character of Pat to make a larger statement about sexual and gender-related issues, such as stereotyping or the acceptance of differences. Instead, it's just silly.

Disney clearly didn't have any faith in the film. *It's Pat* was released in "limited regional engagements" (three cities, actually) and grossed around $60,000.

The critics used adjectives like "shockingly unfunny" (*Variety*) and "truly terrible" (Kevin Thomas, *Los Angeles Times*). *It's Pat* received five Razzie nominations, but thankfully didn't take home any awards, losing to bad films seen by more people, like *Showgirls* (1995) and *The Scarlet Letter* (1995).

## *The Ladies Man* (2000): "He's cool. He's clean. He's a love machine."

Directed by Reginald Hudlin. Written by Tim Meadows, Dennis McNicholas, and Andrew Steele. Producer: Lorne Michaels. Executive Producers: Erin Fraser, Thomas Levine, Robert K. Weiss. Cinematography: Johnny E. Jensen. Editor: Earl Watson. Original Music: Marcus Miller.

**Cast:** Tim Meadows (Leon Phelps), Karyn Parsons (Julie Simmons), Billy Dee Williams (Lester), John Witherspoon (Scrap Iron), Jilly Talley (Candy), Lee Evans (Barney), Will Ferrell (Lance DeLune), Sofia Milos (Cheryl), Eugene Levy (Bucky Kent), Julianne Moore (Audrey), Tiffani Thiessen (Honey DeLune), Rocky Carroll (Cyrus Cunningham), Chris Parnell (Phil Swanson), Mark McKinney (Mr. White).

Distributed by Paramount Pictures. Release date: October 13, 2000.

Leon Phelps (Tim Meadows), better known as "The Ladies' Man," was a popular *SNL* character that made frequent appearances between 1997 and 2000. Phelps hosts his own call-in television show in which he dispenses advice about love, sex, and the art of seduction. But like his waterbed and scented candles, the bottle of Courvoisier cognac he keeps nearby, his oversized Afro, and his affinity for 1970s fashion (tight pants, polyester shirt, and leather vest), Phelps's sexist attitude toward women is outdated. According to the press notes for the film, Meadows modeled Leon on the kind of men he encountered as a teenager while working in a Detroit liquor store: "They were the sort of guys who played the lottery every day and always wore outfits which, though they were cheap, were completely matching. . . . None of these guys had girlfriends, but they had lots of women, and they thought they were pretty cool."

Phelps occasionally featured women on his show, like local actresses Deborah Hogan (Julianne Moore, who has a cameo in the film), who helps him demonstrate how to sweet-talk a lady (23.16), and Julie (Cameron Diaz) (24.1), who plays Monica Lewinsky opposite Leon's Bill Clinton in a reenactment of their sexual encounter detailed in *The Starr Report*. The real Monica Lewinsky even joined Leon (24.18) and answered some of the callers' questions. Based on her own experiences, she strongly advised against getting involved with people at work or telling other people, including your best friend, that you ever have phone sex.

It's not entirely clear why someone thought expanding the sketch into a feature-length film was a good idea. Like Pat Riley, Phelps is essentially a one-joke character in a one-joke sketch. When he's not giving his listeners questionable advice, he's bedding women—actually any woman who is willing and weighs under 250 pounds. There is something innocent about Phelps's sexist ignorance, but it's not enough to make him endearing, making it difficult to believe that his smart, good-natured producer and eventual romantic interest, Julie (Karyn Parsons), would remain loyal to him when he gets canned from a Chicago radio station.

The second plotline focuses on a band of desperate husbands whose wives all cheated on them with the same man. They spend the entire film trying to track down Phelps, and in the film's climactic scene, the men, led by Lance DeLune (Will Ferrell), finally corner Phelps, which is his cue to show his human side and convince the men it's all their fault that he slept with their wives. If they were more attentive husbands, their women would not have been going after him.

The critics were not amused. Roger Ebert gave it one star and called it "desperately unfunny." *New York Times* critic A. O. Scott was kinder than Ebert, but only because *Ladies Man* is better than *Stuart, Pat, Roxbury*, and *Superstar*. Some other choice adjectives used by critics included "slapped-together" (Kirk Honeycutt, *Hollywood Reporter*) and "disconcertingly bland" (Robert Koehler, *Variety*). Boxofficemojo.com reported the film's domestic and foreign total gross at $13.7 million, a little more than half its $24 million budget.

## *MacGruber* (2010): "The Ultimate Tool."

Directed by Jorma Taccone. Written by Will Forte, John Solomon, and Jorma Taccone. Producers: John Goldwyn and Lorne Michaels. Executive Producers: Erin David, Ryan Kavanaugh, Seth Meyers, Akiva Schaffer, Tucker Tooley. Coexecutive producers: Kenneth Halsband and Ben Silverman. Cinematography: Brandon Trost. Editor: Jamie Gross. Original Music: Matthew Compton.

**Cast:** Will Forte (MacGruber), Kristen Wiig (Vicki St. Elmo), Ryan Phillippe (Lt. Dixon Piper), Val Kilmer (Dieter Von Cunth), Powers Boothe (Col. James Faith), Maya Rudolph (Casey Fitzpatrick).

Distributed by Universal. Running time: 95 mins. Rated R.

*MacGruber* is a parody of the television series *MacGyver* (1985–1992), starring Richard Dean Anderson as Angus MacGyver, a low-key secret agent who refuses to carry a gun, choosing instead to defend himself by using his resourcefulness and knowledge of science. Between 2007 and 2010, Will Forte starred in nine shorts (usually shown in three parts over the course of an *SNL* episode) that basically revolve around the same plot. MacGruber and Casey (Maya Rudolph), who was later replaced by Kristen Wiig as Vicki, are in trouble, and he must beat the clock and defuse a bomb using a combination of objects, such as a paper clip, twine, a gum wrapper, and dog turd (32.11) or a paper cup, pine needles, and pubic hair (32.11). With only seconds left, MacGruber gets easily distracted by matters that seem trivial by comparison, like his receding hairline (33.2), the plummeting stock market (34.5), and his son Merrill's (Shia LaBeouf) homosexual tendencies (33.11). MacGruber sketches were also used as part of a Pepsi campaign in a series of three commercials that aired during the January 31, 2009, episode of *SNL*. In the spots, which featured Forte, Wiig, and *MacGyver*'s Richard Dean Anderson, MacGruber has become a pitchman for Pepsi. In one ad, MacGyver accuses MacGruber of "selling out" (because if you acknowledge that you are doing so, maybe you won't get criticized). Another ad, in which MacGruber changes his name to Pepsuber, aired during Super Bowl XLIII. Not since season 1, when host Candice Bergen and cast members did live commercials for Polaroid, has *SNL* been in partnership with Madison Avenue. Commercial parodies are a hallmark of *SNL*'s special brand of satire, so it's ironic that they would be joining forces with an industry they have been targeting since the very first episode.

*MacGruber* appears to die at the end of every sketch, but that didn't stop Forte and his co-screenwriters John Solomon and Jorma Taccone (who also directed) to give the '80s action hero big-screen treatment in what is certainly one of the better sketch-to-screen *SNL* films in recent years. Set in the 1980s, the film shows mullet-haired MacGruber, the former Green Beret, Navy Seal, and Army Ranger, coming out of retirement to battle the villainous Dieter von Cunth (Val Kilmer), who has seized control of the X-5 nuclear missile with a nuclear warhead. MacGruber's mission to stop von Cunth is also personal because he killed MacGruber's wife, Casey (Maya Rudolph). When his entire team of experts is killed, MacGruber assembles a new team consisting of his old friend Vicki St. Elmo (Kristen Wiig) and Lt. Dixon Piper (Ryan Phillippe), who has difficulty adapting to MacGruber's unorthodox methods.

In an interview with *New York* magazine, director Taccone described the film as "an affectionate homage to eighties-era action films like *Commando* and *Die Hard* with an idiot in the middle of it." He added that it is "so dirty it's hard to show things from the movie in the trailer. Ninety percent of it you can't show." The R-rated humor is not entirely surprising considering Taccone is one of the Lonely Island trio (with Akiva Schaffer and Andy Samberg).

Some critics found the film's comic sensibility challenging and even objectionable. In her review for the *Washington Post*, Ruth McCann thought MacGruber was too much of a "schmuck" and found "the whole package . . . often lamentably unsubtle. Like a kid banging pots in a kitchen, it's a little bit funny, until it's not." *New York Times* critic A. O. Scott was puzzled by the "scatology and sexual immaturity of the humor," which indicated that the film's purpose was to "amuse teenagers," yet it's clear the filmmakers were aiming for an R rating. On a more positive note, *Rolling Stone*'s Peter Travers, who had not been a fan of past *SNL* films, commended Jorma Taccone for "spoofing the school of Stallone-Segal-Schwarzenegger with a sense of style and unabashed affection."

## *A Night at the Roxbury* (1998): "Score!"

Directed by John Fortenberry. Written by Steve Koren, Will Ferrell, and Chris Kattan. Producers: Amy Heckerling and Lorne Michaels. Executive Producer: Robert K. Weiss. Cinematography: Francis Kenny. Editor: Jay Kamen. Original Music: Dave Kitay.

**Cast:** Will Ferrell (Steve Butabi), Chris Kattan (Doug Butabi), Dan Hedaya (Kamehl Butabi), Loni Anderson (Barbara Butabi), Molly Shannon (Emily Sanderson), Dwayne Hickman (Fred Sanderson), Lochlyn Munro (Craig), Maree Cheatham (Mabel Sanderson), Colin Quinn (Dooey), Richard Grieco (Himself), Chazz Palminteri (Benny Zadir), Gigi Rice (Vivica), Elisa Donovan (Cambi), Michael Clarke Duncan (Roxbury Bouncer), Jennifer Coolidge (Hottie Cop), Meredith Scott Lynn (Credit Vixen).

Distributed by Paramount Pictures. Running time: 82 mins. Rated PG-13.

According to the press kit for *A Night at the Roxbury*, the film's stars, Chris Kattan and Will Ferrell, recalled the inspiration for the Butabi Brothers. They were in a club in Los Angeles, and they observed a guy leaning against the bar who really wanted to dance. "He was sort of pathetic," recalled Kattan. "We kept checking him out and started picking up on his expressions and mannerisms. Something about this out-of-it guy intrigued us." Ferrell added that the guy "was dying to be a part of the scene, but he'd try and try, and come up with nothing. He was really out of his element—a dorky fish in glitzy water."

The Roxbury Guys, Steve and Doug Butabi (Will Ferrell and Chris Kattan), made their *Saturday Night Live* debut on March 1996 (21.16). In the first sketch, they're standing at the bar of the China Club moving to the beat of Captain Hollywood Project's "More & More" and repeatedly mistakenly thinking someone is signaling them from across the room to dance. They trap an unsuspecting woman (Cheri Oteri) between them and start bouncing her between their chests. Once she gets free, they high-five each other and shout, "Score!" A few weeks later (21.20), the clueless duo are at it again with one major change—for the first time we hear what will become their official theme song, "What Is Love" by Haddaway. They are also joined by a third Roxbury guy (Jim Carrey), and together they bop their heads to the music as they try their luck at a few other venues, like a high school prom, a wedding in a catering hall, and a retirement home. Other hosts seen clubbing with the Butabi brothers include Tom Hanks (22.1), Martin Short (22.8), Alec Baldwin (22.14), and Sylvester Stallone (as Rocky Balboa) (23.1). On the flip side, host Pamela Lee (22.18) can't seem to shake the brothers, who follow her to her gym where they pop up in the sauna and Jacuzzi.

So little was known about the duo beyond their favorite song, so veteran *SNL* writer Steve Koren, who penned the screenplay with Ferrell and Kattan, moved the location to Los Angeles and gave the Roxbury Guys a life outside of the clubs. Steve (Ferrell) and Doug (Kattan) Butabi are brothers and best friends who still live with their parents in Beverly Hills and work in their father's florist shop. They dream of one day owning their own club, but they need to be able to get inside the Roxbury, which is for A-listers only. Their prayers are answered when they get into a fender bender with 1980s television actor Richard Grieco of *21 Jump Street* (1987–1991) and *Booker* (1989–1990) fame (playing himself), who gets them into the club and brings them closer to their dream.

What follows is a short (eighty-two minute) but strained comedy. You suspect that Ferrell and Kattan had more fun making the film than the audience had watching it. With a glut of *SNL* films coming and going in theaters, the critics began to rank them with *Wayne's World* at the top of the list as the best and several others competing for the bottom spot. *Variety* critic Dennis Harvey writes that as "an amiable, if flyweight diversion," *A Night at the Roxbury* "stands just a peg higher" than *It's Pat, Stuart Saves His Family*, and *Blues Brothers 2000*. *New York Times* critic Anita Gates observed that the film is "a lot like the brothers themselves: undeniably pathetic but strangely lovable. Still, do you really want to spend an hour and a half with them in a dark room?"

## *Stuart Saves His Family* (1995): "You'll laugh because it's not your family. You'll cry because it is."

Directed by Harold Ramis. Written by Al Franken, based on his book. Producers: Lorne Michaels and Trevor Albert. Executive Producers: C. O. Erickson, Dinah Minot, Whitney White. Cinematography: Lauro Escorel. Editors: Craig Herring and Pembroke J. Herring. Original Music: Marc Shaiman.

**Cast:** Al Franken (Stuart Smalley), Laura San Giacomo (Julia), Vincent D'Onofrio (Donnie), Shirley Knight (Stuart's Mom), Harris Yulin (Stuart's Dad), Lesley Boone (Jodie), John Link Graney (Kyle), Julia Sweeney (Mea C.), Joe Flaherty (Cousin Ray), Robin Duke (Cousin Denise).

Distributed by Paramount Pictures. Running time: 95 mins. Rated PG-13.

Stuart Smalley (Al Franken) is a "caring nurturer" (but not a licensed therapist) who hosts his own cable access show in Chicago, *Daily Affirmation with Stuart Smalley*. He is also a member of several twelve-step programs, including Adult Children of Alcoholics, Overeaters Anonymous, Debtors Anonymous, and Al-Anon, a support group for friends and relatives of alcoholics. Julie (Laura San Giacomo) is his best friend, confidante, and Al-Anon sponsor who is there for him when his life is on a downward spiral. His show gets canceled, and then he gets sucked into Smalley family drama triggered by an inheritance left by Stuart's recently departed Aunt Paula. Stuart's family is a bastion of dysfunction. His dad (Harris Yulin) is a mentally and emotionally abusive alcoholic, while his mother

(Shirley Knight) is his enabler. His sister Jodie (Lesley Boone) is addicted to food and abusive men, and her unemployed brother Donnie (Vincent D'Onofrio) drinks and smokes pot. Stuart does his best to keep his distance, but his efforts to help settle a family legal matter lands the Smalley family in court. While Stuart has newfound success when his *Daily Affirmation* show is picked up by a cable network, his family back in Minnesota continues to fall apart. When his drunken father accidentally shoots Donnie, the Smalley family plans an intervention in hopes that Dad will agree to go to rehab.

Stuart Smalley's first *Daily Affirmation* episode aired on *SNL* in February 1991 (16.12). Over the next four seasons, Stuart dispensed words of wisdom to *SNL* viewers, usually in the form of twelve-step platitudes ("Denial ain't just a river in Egypt," "It's just stinking thinking," etc.). He has also welcomed some very special guests on his show, like basketball great Michael J. (no last name to protect his anonymity), who encourages him to repeat the affirmation, "I don't have to be a great basketball player." Stuart helps another basketball great, Charles B. (19.1), with some help from Muggsy B., to own the fact that despite all his success, he still feels empty inside because it's not coming from (pointing to his heart) here. Franken's character could easily be misperceived as a parody of twelve-step, new age, self-help types, which it is not. If you read Franken's book of daily affirmations, *I'm Good Enough, I'm Smart Enough, and Doggone It, People Like Me*, it's actually firmly rooted in the philosophy of twelve-step programs.

Stuart Smalley was inspired by Al Franken's experiences in Al-Anon, a twelve-step program for family members and friends of alcoholics. In a 1995 interview with Nancy Spiller, Entertainment News Services, Harvard-educated Franken explained that one of the things he learned in Al-Anon is that "you can learn from people who aren't necessarily smarter than you. I'd hear somebody say something and I'd be very judgmental and say, 'Oh, that person's an idiot,' and a month later the same person would say something that would touch me deeply." Although he won't discuss his own family, he does reveal that his father was not an alcoholic, and the dysfunctional Smalleys were not modeled after his own family.

What distinguishes *Stuart Saves His Family* from the other *SNL* sketch film is that it is genuinely trying to say something about family, human relationships, and self-esteem. Roger Ebert found the film to be "a genuine surprise. A movie as funny as the *SNL* stuff, and yet with convincing characters, a compelling story and a sunny, sweet sincerity shining down on the humor." But other critics were not convinced. Peter Rainer, critic for the *Los Angeles Times*, found Franken's "deep-down commitment to Stuart's dumpy self-love" on *SNL* to be "funny" and "touching" but accused Franken of "starting to take Stuart altogether too seriously. It's kind of creepy." *New York Times* critic Janet Maslin was even more dismissive, calling *Stuart Saves His Family* "little more than a set of intermittently funny skits strung together by a sketchy nonplot about Stuart's relatives."

Hopefully, no one showed the reviews to Stuart, who would probably end up curled up in bed with a box of Oreos and the covers over his head.

### *Superstar* (1999): "Dare to dream."

Directed by Bruce McCulloch. Written by Steve Koren. Based on characters created by Molly Shannon. Producer: Lorne Michaels. Executive Producers: Robert K. Weiss and Susan Cavan. Cinematography: Walt Lloyd. Editor: Malcolm Campbell. Original Music: Michael Gore.

**Cast:** Molly Shannon (Mary Katherine Gallagher), Will Ferrell (Sky Corrigan/Jesus), Elaine Hendrix (Evian), Mark McKinney (Father Ritley), Harland Williams (Slater), Glynis Johns (Grandma).

Distributed by Paramount Pictures. Running time: 81 mins. Rated PG-13.

According to the film's production notes, Shannon created Mary Katherine Gallagher when she was a student at New York University during an improvisation exercise in which actors were required to enter and introduce themselves as a character. Mary is a "combination of herself, her childhood friend Ann Ranft, and 'no one in particular.'" The character was refined in a show she cowrote after college with Rob Muir and later through her collaboration with *SNL* writer Steve Wayne Koren, who wrote the screenplay for *Superstar*. Shannon explains her appeal: "I think people identify with her adolescent struggles because she's hopeful. It's not like she's just a loser that's not going to succeed, but she has hope and she's a fighter. She gets hurt and put down but she never lets that defeat her. She just keeps going after what she wants. She's a character with a lot of heart and passion."

Like her creator, there is something genuinely appealing about the awkward and geeky Gallagher. Although the film is short on plot, the gag-driven story centers around Gallagher's two goals in life: win a school talent contest and get a first kiss, preferably from the school's star football player, Sky Corrigan (Will Ferrell), who unfortunately is hot and heavy with her blonde (and bulimic) nemesis, Evian (Elaine Hendrix). We learn more about Mary Katherine's background and meet her wheelchair-bound guardian/grandmother (Glynis Johns), a former Broadway hoofer, who is against her granddaughter pursuing a career in show business. As one would expect, the humor is a bit sophomoric and the jokes are very hit-and-miss, but under the direction of Bruce McCulloch, the film is fueled by the performers' high energy level, especially Shannon and Ferrell, and some enjoyable musical moments, like a robot-dance number in the cafeteria. *Variety*'s Dennis Harvey was pleasantly surprised by "this amusing, if uneven, comedy," but other critics were not, like the *New York Times*' Anita Gates, who remarked that Shannon is "in fine form as the heroine" but couldn't get past the fact that "the majority of the jokes fall flat, and in the end Mary Katherine

*Superstar*. One of the more successful adaptations of an *SNL* sketch, *Superstar* showcased the comedic talents of Molly Shannon as Mary Catherine Gallagher, the Catholic school girl with big dreams of being a musical superstar.

has proved (and she would have trouble accepting this) that she's a joy only for five minutes or so at a time."

## Wayne's World (1992): "You'll laugh. You'll cry. You'll hurl."

Directed by Penelope Spheeris. Written by Mike Myers, Bonnie Turner, and Terry Turner. Based on characters created by Mike Myers. Producer: Lorne Michaels. Executive Producer: Howard W. Koch Jr. Cinematography: Theo van de Sande. Editor: Malcolm Campbell. Original Music: J. Peter Robinson.

**Cast:** Mike Myers (Wayne Campbell), Dana Carvey (Garth Algar), Rob Lowe (Benjamin Kane), Tia Carrere (Cassandra), Lara Flynn Boyle (Stacy), Michael DeLuise (Alan), Dan Bell (Neil), Lee Tergesen (Terry), Kurt Fuller (Russell Finley), Chris Farley (Security Guard), Meat Loaf (Tiny), Colleen Camp (Mrs. Vanderhoff), Ione Skye (Elyse).

Distributed by Paramount Pictures. Running time: 94 mins. Rated PG-13.

## *Wayne's World 2* (1993): "You'll Laugh Again! You'll Cry Again! You'll Hurl Again!"

Directed by Stephen Surjik. Written by Mike Myers, Bonnie Turner, and Terry Turner. Based on characters created by Mike Myers. Producer: Lorne Michaels. Coproducers: Dinah Minot and Barnaby Thompson. Executive Producer: Howard W. Koch Jr. Cinematographer: Francis Kenny. Editor: Malcolm Campbell. Music: Carter Burwell.

**Cast:** Mike Myers (Wayne Campbell), Dana Carvey (Garth Algar), Christopher Walken (Bobby Cahn), Tia Carrere (Cassandra Wong), Kim Basinger (Honey Hornée), Kevin Pollack (Jerry Segel), Chris Farley (Milton), Lee Tergesen (Terry), Dan Bell (Neil), Rip Taylor (Himself), Aerosmith (Steven Tyler, Joe Perry, Brad Whitford, Tom Hamilton, Joey Kramer), Ralph Brown (Del Preston), James Hong (Jeff Wong).

Distributed by Paramount Pictures. Running time: 95 mins. Rated PG-13.

In a *Wayne's World* reunion celebrating the film's twenty-first anniversary, Mike Myers explained that *Wayne's World* grew out of his years as a "heavy metal kid in the suburbs of Toronto" and his fascination with Manhattan Cable, which aired cable access programs like *The Robin Byrd Show*. Wayne's first appearance was on the segment entitled "Wayne's Power Minute," which aired on *It's Only Rock 'n' Roll*, a 1987 summer series on CBC Television. In his first segment, he points out the misspellings in the names of heavy metal bands (there should be an "a" in "Led Zepplin" and "Ratt" shouldn't have two "t's").

*Wayne's World* debuted on February 19, 1989 (14.13), as a graveyard sketch (the last sketch of the night, between the last musical performance and the "good nights"), which usually means one of two things: comedy wise it's not up to par with the rest of the show, or it's so far out there that only the die-hard *SNL* fans will still be tuned in. The latter may have been true, but the former was certainly—to quote Wayne and Garth—"not!" *Wayne's World* is a cable access television show broadcast from Garth's house over Cable 10, a community access channel in Aurora, Illinois. Their guests that night were Garth's father, Beev (Phil Hartman), who owns the Wishing Well convenience store, and an excellent babe from school, Nancy (Jan Hooks). In a 1990 interview for *The Floridian*,

## From the Small Screen to the Big Screen

Myers told Eric Snider that *Wayne's World* is a spoof of "the adolescent suburban heavy metal experience" and Wayne was much like the guys he grew up with in the suburbs of Toronto. Although Wayne Campbell is Myers's creation, he also gives credit to his four collaborators on the *SNL* writing staff—Greg Daniels, Conan O'Brien, Robert Smigel, and Bob Odenkirk. Much of the sketch's humor is rooted in the language, namely the exchanges between Wayne and Garth, whose catchphrases consist of teen jargon. *Wayne's World* has the distinction of contributing to the teen lexicon of the late 1980s/early 1990s—words and phrases like "babelicious," "schwing!," and "we're not worthy!" (see chapter 24 for a complete list).

*Wayne's World* and its sequel, *Wayne's World 2*, are the *SNL* films that got it right. The central characters—Wayne and Garth—are not only from the same demographic that the film is targeting (teenagers, particularly males), but they share the same cheeky, postmodern comic sensibility. Its style is reminiscent of a Marx Brothers movie in which the plot merely functions as a device to hold a string of gags together, most of which involve references to pop culture. *Wayne's World* even has a "Scooby-Do" ending, while one of the endings of *Wayne's World 2* has Wayne and Garth driving over a cliff à la *Thelma & Louise* (1991). The sequel also references kung-fu movies, *The Graduate* (1967), and *The Doors* (1991). The humor is also highly self-reflexive. Two decades before *30 Rock*, *Wayne's World* featured a hysterical sequence that points out the use of product placement within the film.

The plots (a term I use loosely here) of both films revolve around Wayne's battle against the establishment in the form of a network that takes over his cable show and a handsome TV executive (Rob Lowe) who causes problems for a jealous Wayne and his girlfriend Cassandra (Tia Carrere), a rock singer from Hong Kong. It's an ironic premise considering the filmmakers can also be accused of taking a television sketch and turning it into a feature-length film to make some cash (but hey, that's Hollywood). In *Wayne's World 2*, Wayne is jealous of a sleazy music executive (Christopher Walken), who is trying to break up him and Cassandra so he can make her a star. With the help of the spirit of Jim Morrison, Wayne is on a mission to do something with his life, so he organizes Waynestock, a music festival. If only he could get Aerosmith to play.

*Wayne's World* took many critics by surprise. Roger Ebert admitted he walked in expecting a "dumb, vulgar comedy," but was surprised by the film's "genuinely amusing, sometimes even intelligent undercurrent." *New York Times* critic Janet Maslin observed that the reason the film succeeds is that Wayne and Garth's "mock-moronic attitudes are intentional and the viewer is let in on the joke." Not everyone appreciated the film. Kenneth Turan of the *Los Angeles Times* felt it was "unimaginatively padded" as "there is not nearly enough satisfactory plot and incident to film's bare bones 95 minutes."

It sounds like the movie made him hurl.

*Wayne's World* posed a challenge for its distributor, Paramount Pictures, as every other word of dialogue is an expression to which there needs to be an equivalent in non-English-speaking countries. The solution was to create and distribute pocket-sized dictionaries in German, French, Italian, and Spanish that contained translations of some of the more popular phrases.

# Appendix A
# Episode Guide

**Note:** "★ ★ ★ ★ Four-Star" indicates a memorable sketch, monologue, or moment.

## Season I (1975–1976)

**Airdate:** 10/11/75
**Episode:** 1.1
**Host:** George Carlin
**Musical Guest:** Janis Ian, Billy Preston
**Musical and Guest Performances/Cameo(s)/Program Notes:**
- "Live from New York": Chevy Chase, who appears onstage at the end of the cold open with John Belushi and Michael O'Donoghue.
- Preston performs "Nothing from Nothing" and "Fancy Lady."
- Ian performs "At Seventeen" and "In the Winter."
- Guest comic performances by Andy Kaufman and Valri Bromfield.
- "A Film by Albert Brooks": *The Impossible Truth*.
- *Weekend Update*: Chevy Chase is the first anchor.
- Debut of the Not Ready for Prime Time Players, who announcer Don Pardo mistakenly refers to as "Not for Ready Prime Time Players" in the opening credits: Dan Aykroyd, John Belushi, Chevy Chase, Jane Curtin, Garrett Morris, Laraine Newman, and Gilda Radner. For the first episode only, the cast also included George Coe, who was dropped after the first show but would make uncredited appearances in the future, and head writer Michael O'Donoghue, who would continue to appear in sketches and as his alter ego Mr. Mike.
- According to the *Washington Post*, Carlin, who doesn't appear in any sketches, was put on a five-second delay because he was known for using "vivid language" in his stand-up.
- This episode was repeated on June 28, 2008, in memory of Carlin, who died on June 22.

**Airdate:** 10/18/75
**Episode:** 1.2
**Host:** Paul Simon
**Musical Guest:** Art Garfunkel, Randy Newman, Phoebe Snow
**Musical and Guest Performances/Cameo(s)/Program Notes:**
- "Live from New York": Chevy Chase, who does his first pratfall after Simon sings "Still Crazy After All These Years."
- The show consists mostly of musical numbers. The cast appears as the bees, only to be told by Simon their number was cut because it didn't work last week.
- Simon performs "Marie," "American Tune," and, with the Jesse Dixon Singers, "Loves Me Like a Rock."
- Simon and Garfunkel perform "The Boxer," "Scarborough Fair," and "My Little Town."

- Garfunkel performs "I Only Have Eyes for You."
- Newman performs "Sail Away."
- Snow performs "No Regrets" and "Gone at Last" with Simon and the Jesse Dixon Singers.
- "A Film by Albert Brooks": *Home Movies.*
- Cameos by former political activist Jerry Rubin, former NBA star Connie Hawkins, sportscaster Marv Albert, and New York Knicks star Bill Bradley.
- Director Dave Wilson won an Emmy for this episode.

**Airdate:** 10/25/75
**Episode:** 1.3
**Host:** Rob Reiner
**Musical and Guest Performances/Cameo(s)/ Program Notes:**
- "Live from New York": An injured man (Chevy Chase) in a wheelchair miraculously walks, but falls to the ground on his second attempt.
- No musical guest. John Belushi impersonates Joe Cocker singing "With a Little Help from My Friends."
- Guest appearances by Andy Kaufman, Denny Dillon & Mark Hampton, and the Lockers. Dillon returns as a regular in season 6.
- Special guest Penny Marshall (Mrs. Rob Reiner) appears in three sketches.
- "A Film by Albert Brooks": Brooks performs open-heart surgery.

**Airdate:** 11/8/75
**Episode:** 1.4
**Host:** Candice Bergen
**Musical Guest:** Esther Phillips
**Musical and Guest Performances/Cameo(s)/ Program Notes:**
- "Live from New York": President Gerald Ford (Chevy Chase), who takes a fall during his speech.
- Phillips performs "What a Difference a Day Makes" and "I Can Stand a Little Rain."
- Chase and Bergen do a real commercial for Polaroid.
- "A Film by Albert Brooks": A parody of a "sneak peek" at three new NBC television series.

**Airdate:** 11/15/75
**Episode:** 1.5
**Host:** Robert Klein
**Musical Guest:** ABBA, Loudon Wainwright III
**Musical and Guest Performances/Cameo(s)/ Program Notes:**
- "Live from New York": A beauty pageant emcee (Chevy Chase), who stumbles down the runway.
- ABBA performs "S.O.S." and "Waterloo."
- Wainwright performs "Bicentennial" and "Unrequited to the Nth Degree."
- Klein performs "I Can't Stop My Leg."
- Character Debut: Emily Litella (Gilda Radner).

**Airdate:** 11/22/75
**Episode:** 1.6
**Host:** Lily Tomlin
**Musical and Guest Performances/Cameo(s)/ Program Notes:**
- "Live from New York": President Ford (Chevy Chase), who takes a tumble during a televised speech.
- Tomlin performs "St. James Infirmary Blues" and "I Got You Babe" (with Muppet Scred), and is joined by the bees in a little "Bee Bop." The music is by the *SNL* house band, who wear nurses' uniforms and are billed as "Howard Shore and His All Nurse Band."

**Airdate:** 12/13/75
**Episode:** 1.7
**Host:** Richard Pryor
**Musical Guest:** Gil Scott-Heron

**Musical and Guest Performances/Cameo(s)/ Program Notes:**
- "Live from New York": Garrett Morris, who explains to Chevy Chase that Pryor wants him to open the show. Chase takes the fall and Morris says the line.
- Scott-Heron performs "Johannesburg" and "A Lovely Day."
- Guest appearances by Pryor's ex-wife, Shelley Pryor, and his girlfriend, Kathrine McKee.
- The *Washington Post* reported Pryor was put on a five-second delay.
- Character Debut: Samurai Futaba (John Belushi) in "Samurai Hotel."
- "A Film by Albert Brooks": The director is sick in bed.
- ★ ★ ★ ★ Four-Star Sketch: "Word Association Test."

**Airdate:** 12/20/75
**Episode:** 1.8
**Host:** Candice Bergen
**Musical Guest:** Martha Reeves, the Stylistics
**Musical and Guest Performances/Cameo(s)/ Program Notes:**
- "Live from New York": President Ford (Chevy Chase) falls on the White House Christmas tree.
- Reeves performs "Higher and Higher" and "Silver Bells."
- The Stylistics perform "You Make Me Feel Brand New."
- Bergen performs "Winter Wonderland" with the cast and "Have Yourself a Merry Little Christmas" with Muppets King Ploobis and Scred.
- Special appearance by Margaret Kuhn, founder of the Gray Panthers.
- "A Film by Gary Weis": *Homeward Bound*.

**Airdate:** 1/10/76
**Episode:** 1.9
**Host:** Elliott Gould
**Musical Guest:** Anne Murray

**Musical and Guest Performances/Cameo(s)/ Program Notes:**
- "Live from New York": The Dead String Quartet topple over one by one ending with the cellist (Chevy Chase), who falls to the ground and opens the show.
- Murray performs "The Call" and "Blue Finger Lou."
- Producer Lorne Michaels and director Dave Wilson make their first on-camera appearance during the Killer Bees sketch.
- Guest performance by Franken and Davis.
- "A Film by Albert Brooks": *Audience Research*, with a cameo by director James L. Brooks (no relation).
- "A Film by Gary Weis": *Play Misty for Me*.
- This episode won an Emmy for Outstanding Writing in a Comedy-Variety or Music Series.

**Airdate:** 1/17/76
**Episode:** 1.10
**Host:** Buck Henry
**Musical Guest:** Bill Withers, Toni Basil
**Musical and Guest Performances/Cameo(s)/ Program Notes:**
- "Live from New York": An operator at a suicide prevention center (Chevy Chase) stumbles as he tries to answer the phone.
- Withers performs "Ain't No Sunshine."
- Basil sings "Wham Re-Bop Boom Bam."
- Characters Debut: The Blues Brothers (Dan Aykroyd and John Belushi), dressed as bees, sing "I'm a King Bee."
- "A Film by Gary Weis": *Who's Funny?*
- Chase won an Emmy for Outstanding Continuing or Single Performance by a Supporting Actor in Variety or Music Series for this episode.

**Airdate:** 1/24/76
**Episode:** 1.11

**Host:** Peter Cook and Dudley Moore
**Musical Guest:** Neil Sedaka
**Musical and Guest Performances/Cameo(s)/Program Notes:**
- "Live from New York": A bomb expert (Chevy Chase) gets a cream pie in the face when he deactivates a bomb.
- Sedaka performs "Breaking Up Is Hard to Do" and "Lonely Night."
- "A Film by Gary Weis": *The Paramount Novelty Store*.
- ★★★★ Four-Star Sketch: "Lifer Follies."

**Airdate:** 1/31/76
**Episode:** 1.12
**Host:** Dick Cavett
**Musical Guest:** Jimmy Cliff
**Musical and Guest Performances/Cameo(s)/Program Notes:**
- "Live from New York": Chevy Chase, who says he can't do a fall due to a back injury. A jealous Garrett Morris makes him fall by sticking pins in a voodoo doll.
- Cliff performs "The Harder They Come," "Many Rivers to Cross," and "Wahjahka Man."
- Guest performance by Al Alen Petersen.
- Guest appearance by comedian Marshall Efron.
- "A Film by Gary Weis": A clothing designer and plastic surgeon each make recommendations on how the other can improve his appearance.
- "Home Movie": *The Apple Follies*, by Harry McDevitt.

**Airdate:** 2/14/76
**Episode:** 1.13
**Host:** Peter Boyle
**Musical Guest:** Al Jarreau
**Musical and Guest Performances/Cameo(s)/Program Notes:**
- "Live from New York": A Chicago waiter (Chevy Chase), who gets gunned down in the St. Valentine's Day Massacre.
- Jarreau performs "We Got By" and "Somebody's Watching You."
- "A Film by Gary Weis": Schoolchildren recite the Pledge of Allegiance.
- "Home Movie": *A Home Movie*, by Howard Grunwald.

**Airdate:** 2/21/76
**Episode:** 1.14
**Host:** Desi Arnaz
**Musical and Guest Performances/Cameo(s)/Program Notes:**
- "Live from New York": President Ford (Chevy Chase), after walking through a wall.
- Arnaz performs "Cuban Pete" and "Babalu" with his son, Desi Arnaz Jr.
- "A Film by Gary Weis": A profile of poet/underground film star Taylor Mead and his cat.

**Airdate:** 2/28/76
**Episode:** 1.15
**Host:** Jill Clayburgh
**Musical Guest:** Leon Redbone, the Singing Idlers
**Musical and Guest Performances/Cameo(s)/Program Notes:**
- "Live from New York": Chevy Chase, who tells Lorne Michaels he's tired of being a buffoon and refuses to do the fall—and then falls off Michaels's desk.
- Redbone performs "Ain't Misbehavin'" and "Big Time Woman."
- The Singing Idlers of the U.S. Coast Guard Academy perform "Semper Paratus" and sing backup for Clayburgh's rendition of "Sea Cruise."
- "A Film by Gary Weis": Profile of artist William Wegman and his pet Weimaraner.
- "Film Short" Series Debut: *The Mr. Bill Show*.
- Guest performance by Andy Kaufman.

**Airdate:** 3/13/76
**Episode:** 1.16
**Host:** Anthony Perkins
**Musical Guest:** Betty Carter
**Musical and Guest Performances/Cameo(s)/ Program Notes:**
- "Live from New York": While responding to viewers' complaints that *SNL* pads the show to stretch it to ninety minutes, Chevy Chase falls backward in his chair.
- Carter performs "Music, Maestro, Please," "Swing Brother Swing," and "I Can't Help It."
- The network's name is removed from the graphic in the opening title, which now reads *Saturday Night* (instead of *NBC's Saturday Night*).
- "A Film by Gary Weis": Profiles of New Yorkers and their pets, including Warhol superstar Jackie Curtis, designer Constance Abernathy, writer Dan Greenburg, poet Taylor Mead, and restaurateur Elaine Kaufman.
- "Home Movie": *P-Nut*, by Phil Van De Carr.

**Airdate:** 4/17/76
**Episode:** 1.17
**Host:** Ron Nessen
**Musical Guest:** Patti Smith Group
**Musical and Guest Performances/Cameo(s)/ Program Notes:**
- "Live from New York": The real President Gerald Ford, who makes a filmed cameo appearance.
- At the time, Nessen was President Ford's press secretary.
- Patti Smith Group performs "Gloria" and "My Generation."
- Guest performance by Billy Crystal.
- "A Film by Gary Weis": *Garbage*.
- "Home Movie": *Men's Room Urinal*, by David Massar.

**Airdate:** 4/24/76
**Episode:** 1.18
**Host:** Raquel Welch

**Musical Guest:** John Sebastian, Phoebe Snow
**Musical and Guest Performances/Cameo(s)/ Program Notes:**
- "Live from New York": Chevy Chase, who falls while leaving the stage after being told not to stretch out a comedy bit.
- Snow performs "All Over" and "Two-Fisted Love."
- Sebastian performs "Welcome Back" (the theme song from *Welcome Back, Kotter*).
- Welch performs "It Ain't Necessarily So."
- Character Debut: Baba Wawa (Gilda Radner).
- "A Film by Gary Weis": Raquel Welch dances for the camera.
- ★★★★ Four-Star Sketches: "The Claudine Longet Invitational" for which *SNL* gives an on-air apology in a later show; Lorne Michaels offers the Beatles $3,000 to reunite on *SNL*.

**Airdate:** 5/8/76
**Episode:** 1.19
**Host:** Madeline Kahn
**Musical Guest:** Carly Simon
**Musical and Guest Performances/Cameo(s)/ Program Notes:**
- "Live from New York": Ronald Reagan (Chevy Chase), after he insults a black sax player (Garrett Morris), who punches him to the ground.
- Simon, in pretaped performances, performs "Half a Chance" and "You're So Vain" with Chase playing the cowbell.
- Kahn performs "I Feel Pretty" (dressed as the Bride of Frankenstein) and "Lost in the Stars."
- "A Film by Gary Weis": A portrait of New York sports fans.
- ★★★★ Four-Star Sketches: "Slumber Party," in which girls discuss where babies come from, and Richard Nixon's "Final Days."

**Airdate:** 5/15/76
**Episode:** 1.20
**Host:** Dyan Cannon
**Musical Guest:** Leon and Mary Russell
**Musical and Guest Performances/Cameo(s)/ Program Notes:**
- "Live from New York": Chevy Chase, who has to do a fall from a ladder twice because the show wasn't yet on the air when he did it the first time.
- Leon and Mary Russell perform "Satisfy You" and accompany Belushi as Joe Cocker performing "Daylight."
- "A Film by Gary Weis": Interviews with newlyweds and men who investigate marital infidelity.
- "Home Movie": *The Hub-Cap Thief*, a Nugent, Rasero, Fitzgerald Production.

**Airdate:** 5/22/76
**Episode:** 1.21
**Host:** Buck Henry
**Musical Guest:** Gordon Lightfoot
**Musical and Guest Performances/Cameo(s)/ Program Notes:**
- "Live from New York": Chevy Chase, who pretends he broke his leg while accepting his Emmy last week, asks Laraine Newman to fall for him. She yanks his crutch from under him and he falls to the floor.
- Lightfoot performs "Summertime Dream," "Spanish Moss," and "Only Two Songs."
- "A Film by Gary Weis": Henry interviews people shopping for toilet seats.
- ★ ★ ★ ★ Four-Star Sketch: Lorne Michaels ups his offer to the Beatles to reunite on the show to $3,200.

**Airdate:** 5/29/76
**Episode:** 1.22
**Host:** Elliott Gould
**Musical Guest:** Leon Redbone, Harlan Collins and Joyce Everson
**Musical and Guest Performances/Cameo(s)/ Program Notes:**
- "Live from New York": A flasher (Chevy Chase) in a wax museum.
- Redbone performs "Shine On, Harvest Moon."
- Collins and Everson perform "Heaven Only Knows."
- "A Film by Gary Weis": *Uncle Charlie's School*, where kids learn vaudeville routines.
- ★ ★ ★ ★ Four-Star Sketch: "The Last Voyage of the Starship Enterprise."

**Airdate:** 7/24/76
**Episode:** 1.23
**Host:** Louise Lasser
**Musical Guest:** The Preservation Hall Jazz Band
**Musical and Guest Performances/Cameo(s)/ Program Notes:**
- "Live from New York": Rivals John Belushi and Chevy Chase give each other "high-fives," which turn into a fistfight with Chase falling over a folding chair and landing on the ground.
- Preservation Hall Jazz Band performs "Panama."
- Filmed cameo by actor Michael Sarrazin.

**Airdate:** 7/31/76
**Episode:** 1.24
**Host:** Kris Kristofferson
**Musical Guest:** Rita Coolidge
**Musical and Guest Performances/Cameo(s)/ Program Notes:**
- "Live from New York": Chevy Chase, who tries to get a ribbon out of his lover's hair while Kristofferson performs "Help Make It Through the Night."
- Kristofferson performs "I've Got a Life of My Own" and "Eddie the Eunuch" with Coolidge.
- Coolidge sings "Hula Hoop."

## Season 2 (1976-1977)

**Airdate:** 9/18/76
**Episode:** 2.1
**Host:** Lily Tomlin
**Musical Guest:** James Taylor
**Musical and Guest Performances/Cameo(s)/ Program Notes:**
- "Live from New York": Chevy Chase, who is tripped by Lily Tomlin's dwarf chauffeur.
- Taylor performs "Shower the People" and "Sweet Baby James."
- During the presidential debate sketch, Chase (as Gerald Ford) falls over a podium that was not properly padded and suffers a serious groin injury.
- "A Film by Gary Weis": Profile of poet/Warhol superstar Taylor Mead.
- Episode ends with Lily Tomlin leading the cast, writers, and the audience in "The Antler Dance," written by Paul Shaffer and Michael O'Donoghue.

**Airdate:** 9/25/76
**Episode:** 2.2
**Host:** Norman Lear
**Musical Guest:** Boz Scaggs
**Musical and Guest Performances/Cameo(s)/ Program Notes:**
- "Live from New York": Chevy Chase, who injured himself during last week's fall, calls from the hospital and talks Gilda Radner through this week's fall.
- Scaggs performs "Lowdown" and "What Can I Say."
- Filmed cameos by stars of Lear's current sitcoms: Bea Arthur (*Maude*), Richard Crenna and Bernadette Peters (*All's Fair*), Sherman Hemsley and Isabel Sanford (*The Jeffersons*), Jean Stapleton and Carroll O'Connor (*All in the Family*), and Nancy Walker (*The Nancy Walker Show*).
- Cameo by Lear's daughter, Kate.
- "A Film by Gary Weis": Footage of Weis humming "Yankee Doodle Dandy" into a phone is intercut with the cast performing slapstick gags.

- "Home Movie": *Spanish Peanuts*, by John Brister.
- ★ ★ ★ ★ Four-Star Sketch: "Chevy's Girls," sung by Radner, Jane Curtin, and Laraine Newman.

**Airdate:** 10/2/76
**Episode:** 2.3
**Host:** Eric Idle
**Musical Guest:** Joe Cocker, Stuff
**Musical and Guest Performances/Cameo(s)/ Program Notes:**
- "Live from New York": Chevy Chase, who opens the show via the telephone while comedian Richard Belzer pretends to be him.
- Cocker performs "You Are So Beautiful" and, with John Belushi as Cocker, "Feelin' Alright."
- Stuff performs "Foots."
- "Film Short": *The Rutles*, a mockumentary of a British rock group parodying the Beatles.

**Airdate:** 10/16/76
**Episode:** 2.4
**Host:** Karen Black
**Musical Guest:** John Prine
**Musical and Guest Performances/Cameo(s)/ Program Notes:**
- "Live from New York": Chevy Chase, who falls out of a wheelchair.
- Prine performs "Hello in There" and "The Bottomless Lake."
- "A Film by Gary Weis": George Schultz talks about his club, Pip's Comedy Club, which opened in Brooklyn in 1962.

**Airdate:** 10/23/76
**Episode:** 2.5
**Host:** Steve Martin
**Musical Guest:** Kinky Friedman
**Musical and Guest Performances/Cameo(s)/ Program Notes:**
- "Live from New York": A ballplayer (Chevy Chase), who, after losing the

World Series, kicks a stool out from underneath his coach, who hangs himself.
- Friedman performs "Dear Abbie."
- "A Film by Gary Weis": The director and people on the street lip-synch "Autumn in New York."
- ★★★★ Four-Star Monologue: Martin plays the banjo with an arrow through his head ("Excuuuse Meee!").

**Airdate:** 10/30/76
**Episode:** 2.6
**Host:** Buck Henry
**Musical Guest:** The Band
**Musical and Guest Performances/Cameo(s)/ Program Notes:**
- "Live from New York": A Land Shark (Chevy Chase), pretending to be collecting for UNICEF, attacks an unsuspecting woman (Gilda Radner).
- The Band performs "Life Is a Carnival," "The Night They Drove Old Dixie Down," and "Stage Fright."
- "A Film by Gary Weis": Henry transforms into a woman.
- During "Samurai Stockbroker," John Belushi accidentally cuts Henry's head with his sword, forcing the host to wear a bandage on his head for the rest of the show. To show their support, members of the cast wear Band-Aids or bandages on their head.
- Chevy Chase's final episode.

**Airdate:** 11/13/76
**Episode:** 2.7
**Host:** Dick Cavett
**Musical Guest:** Ry Cooder
**Musical and Guest Performances/Cameo(s)/ Program Notes:**
- "Live from New York": Gilda Radner as the Chroma-Trak girl.
- Cooder performs "Tattler" and "He'll Have to Go."
- *Weekend Update*: Jane Curtin replaces Chevy Chase as anchor.

**Airdate:** 11/20/76
**Episode:** 2.8
**Host:** Paul Simon
**Musical Guest:** George Harrison
**Musical and Guest Performances/Cameo(s)/ Program Notes:**
- "Live from New York": George Harrison, who wants to be paid the entire $3,000 Lorne Michaels offered the Beatles to reunite on their show.
- ★★★★ Four-Star Monologue: Paul Simon, dressed as a turkey, performs "Still Crazy After All These Years."
- Simon and Harrison perform "Homeward Bound."
- Music Videos: George Harrison's "Crackerbox Palace" and "This Song."
- Cameo by Chevy Chase, who is seen in the opening playing a guitar for change outside of 30 Rock.

**Airdate:** 11/27/76
**Episode:** 2.9
**Host:** Jodie Foster
**Musical Guest:** Brian Wilson
**Musical and Guest Performances/Cameo(s)/ Program Notes:**
- "Live from New York": Gilda Radner, who explains why she won't be seen very much in this episode.
- Wilson performs "Love Is a Woman" and "Good Vibrations."
- "A Film by Gary Weis": *Kids' Dreams.*

**Airdate:** 12/11/76
**Episode:** 2.10
**Host:** Candice Bergen
**Musical Guest:** Frank Zappa
**Musical and Guest Performances/Cameo(s)/ Program Notes:**
- "Live from New York": Patty Hearst (Gilda Radner).
- Zappa performs "Lagoon"(with Samurai Futaba), "Peaches en Regalia," and "I'm the Slime" (with Don Pardo).
- The cast performs "Let's Kill Gary Gilmore for Christmas."
- "A Film by Gary Weis": Swimmer Diana Nyad.

**Airdate:** 1/15/77
**Episode:** 2.11
**Host:** Ralph Nader
**Musical Guest:** George Benson
**Musical and Guest Performances/Cameo(s)/Program Notes:**
- "Live from New York": Ralph Nader, who objects to wearing makeup containing Red Dye #2.
- Benson performs "Masquerade" and "Gonna Love You More."
- Guest performance by Andy Kaufman.
- Sketch Debut: "The Coneheads."

**Airdate:** 1/22/77
**Episode:** 2.12
**Host:** Ruth Gordon
**Musical Guest:** Chuck Berry
**Musical and Guest Performances/Cameo(s)/Program Notes:**
- "Live from New York": John Belushi, who snaps out of a drugged haze when he hears he might not get paid.
- Berry performs "Marie" and "Carol."
- Guest performance by magician Ricky Jay.
- "A Film by Gary Weis": *Night Moves*.

**Airdate:** 1/29/77
**Episode:** 2.13
**Host:** Fran Tarkenton
**Musical Guest:** Leo Sayer, Donnie Harper and the Voices of Tomorrow
**Musical and Guest Performances/Cameo(s)/Program Notes:**
- "Live from New York": Tarkenton, the cast, and their coach (Belushi), who prepares them for the show.
- Sayer performs "When I Need You" and "You Make Me Feel Like Dancing."
- Harper and the Voices of Tomorrow perform "Sing a Song."
- ★★★★ Four-Star Moment: *Weekend Update* anchor Jane Curtin responds to repeated comparisons to "sexy Chevy Chase" by ripping open her blouse for viewers.
- "A Film by Gary Weis": Small World pet store.

**Airdate:** 2/26/77
**Episode:** 2.14
**Host:** Steve Martin
**Musical Guest:** The Kinks
**Musical and Guest Performances/Cameo(s)/Program Notes:**
- "Live from New York": Steve Martin is forced by John Belushi to say it.
- The Kinks perform "Sleep Walker" and a medley of their hit songs, including "You Really Got Me," "All Day and All of the Night," "Well-Respected Man," and "Lola."
- Guest star Lily Tomlin performs "Broadway Baby" with Jane Curtin, Laraine Newman, and Gilda Radner.
- "A Film by Gary Weis": Buster Holmes's New Orleans restaurant.
- "Home Movie": *From the Big Orange to the Big Apple*, by "Friends of Lily Tomlin."

**Airdate:** 3/12/77
**Episode:** 2.15
**Host:** Sissy Spacek
**Musical Guest:** Richard Baskin
**Musical and Guest Performances/Cameo(s)/Program Notes:**
- "Live from New York": The entire cast and host Sissy Spacek, in order to revive director Dave Wilson, who appears to have died in the control room.
- Baskin, brother of *SNL* photographer Edie Baskin, performs "City of One-Night Stands" and, with Spacek, "One I Love You."
- "A Film by Gary Weis": Spacek twirls her baton for the camera.
- "Home Movie": A short by Robert Altman featuring Spacek and Shelley Duvall.
- This episode won an Emmy for Outstanding Writing in a Comedy-Variety or Music Series.

- ★★★★ Four-Star Sketch: A newlywed couple (Spacek and John Belushi) is having trouble in the bedroom.

**Airdate:** 3/19/77
**Episode:** 2.16
**Host:** Broderick Crawford
**Musical Guest:** Dr. John, Levon Helm, Paul Butterfield, the Meters
**Musical and Guest Performances/Cameo(s)/ Program Notes:**
- "Live from New York": Rhonda Weiss (Gilda Radner) after performing "Goodbye Saccharin" with the Rhondettes (Jane Curtin, Laraine Newman, and, in a cameo appearance, Linda Ronstadt).
- Dr. John, Helm, and Butterfield perform "Sing, Sing, Sing."
- The Meters perform "I Got to Get My Name Up in Lights."
- "A Film by Gary Weis": A visit to Crawford's old neighborhood.
- ★★★★ Four-Star Sketch: Bill Murray, the "new kid" on the show, apologizes for not being funny and promises to do better.

**Airdate:** 3/26/77
**Episode:** 2.17
**Host:** Jack Burns
**Musical Guest:** Santana
**Musical and Guest Performances/Cameo(s)/ Program Notes:**
- "Live from New York": John Belushi, after reading his list of demands to NBC.
- Santana performs "Black Magic Woman" and "Europa."
- "A Film by Gary Weis": Burns trains like Rocky Balboa.
- "Home Movie": *Mirage*, produced by Robert David Crane and Richard Decker.
- The show's new title, *Saturday Night Live*, appears in the opening title sequence for the first time.

**Airdate:** 4/9/77
**Episode:** 2.18
**Host:** Julian Bond
**Musical Guest:** Tom Waits, Brick
**Musical and Guest Performances/Cameo(s)/ Program Notes:**
- "Live from New York": Emily Litella (Gilda Radner), who tells Jane Curtin she's in love with a man who makes her "feel like a 'national' woman."
- Waits performs "Eggs & Sausage."
- Brick performs "Dazz."
- "A Film by Gary Weis": Singer Patti Smith on censorship.

**Airdate:** 4/16/77
**Episode:** 2.19
**Host:** Elliott Gould
**Musical Guest:** The McGarrigle Sisters, Roslyn Kind
**Musical and Guest Performances/Cameo(s)/ Program Notes:**
- "Live from New York": Leonid Brezhnev (John Belushi) wants to appear on NBC in exchange for the rights to the Olympics.
- Kate and Ann McGarrigle perform "Heart Like a Wheel."
- Kind performs "I'm Not Anyone."
- "A Film by Gary Weis": A montage of sports fights.
- "Home Movie": *Clown Doll.*

**Airdate:** 4/23/77
**Episode:** 2.20
**Host:** Eric Idle
**Musical Guest:** Alan Price, Neil Innes
**Musical and Guest Performances/Cameo(s)/ Program Notes:**
- "Live from New York": An Irish prisoner (Bill Murray), in response to three questions posed by his British captors: "Is the bomb live or defused?," "What city was it mailed to?," and "When will it go off?"
- Price performs "Poor People" and "In Times Like These."

- Innes performs "Cheese and Onions" as Ron Nasty, his character from Idle's Beatles parody, *The Rutles*, and "Shangri-La."
- "A Film by Gary Weis": Idle narrates a short about body language.
- ★ ★ ★ ★ Four-Star Commercial: "American Dope Growers Union."

**Airdate:** 5/14/77
**Episode:** 2.21
**Host:** Shelley Duvall
**Musical Guest:** Joan Armatrading
**Musical and Guest Performances/Cameo(s)/ Program Notes:**
- "Live from New York": John Belushi, dressed as a bee.
- Armatrading performs "Love and Affection" and "Down to Zero."
- "Film Short": *Brides* by Sharon Sacks, narrated by Spalding Gray.

**Airdate:** 5/21/77
**Episode:** 2.22
**Host:** Buck Henry
**Musical Guest:** Jennifer Warnes, Kenny Vance
**Musical and Guest Performances/Cameo(s)/ Program Notes:**
- "Live from New York": President Carter's mother, Miss Lillian (Laraine Newman).
- Warnes performs "Right Time of the Night."
- Vance performs "The Performer."
- Cameos by Bella Abzug and Chevy Chase (as a Land Shark).
- "Film Short": Artist William Wegman talks about his Weimaraner, Man Ray, who wakes up by an alarm clock.

## Season 3 (1977–1978)

**Airdate:** 9/24/77
**Episode:** 3.1
**Host:** Steve Martin
**Musical Guest:** Jackson Browne and the Section
**Musical and Guest Performances/Cameo(s)/ Program Notes:**
- "Live from New York": President Jimmy Carter (Dan Aykroyd).
- Browne performs "Runnin' on Empty" and "The Pretender."
- Sketch Debuts: "Two wild and crazy guys," the Festrunk Brothers (Martin and Dan Aykroyd); *The Franken and Davis Show*.
- *Weekend Update*: Dan Aykroyd joins Jane Curtin as coanchor.
- Debut of featured players Tom Davis and Al Franken.

**Airdate:** 10/8/77
**Episode:** 3.2
**Host:** Madeline Kahn
**Musical Guest:** Taj Mahal
**Musical and Guest Performances/Cameo(s)/ Program Notes:**
- "Live from New York": Lee Harvey Oswald (Bill Murray) after getting a pie shoved in his face.
- Lorne Michaels announces the "Anyone Can Host" Contest.
- Taj Mahal performs "Queen Bee."
- Cameo by Barry Humphries as Dame Edna Everage.
- "Schiller's Reel": *The Acid Generation: Where Are They Now?*

**Airdate:** 10/15/77
**Episode:** 3.3
**Host:** Hugh Hefner
**Musical Guest:** Libby Titus
**Musical and Guest Performances/Cameo(s)/ Program Notes:**
- "Live from New York": A Playboy bunny (Laraine Newman).
- Titus performs "Fool That I Am."

- Guest performance by Andy Kaufman.

**Airdate:** 10/29/77
**Episode:** 3.4
**Host:** Charles Grodin
**Musical Guest:** Paul Simon, the Persuasions
**Musical and Guest Performances/Cameo(s)/ Program Notes:**
- "Live from New York": John Belushi, who, along with the cast, are frustrated with host Grodin, who has missed rehearsals and was unaware the show was live. Grodin's lack of preparedness is a running joke throughout the episode.
- Simon performs "Slip Sliding Away" (with the Persuasions) and "You're Kind."
- Character Debuts: Hyperactive Judy Miller (Gilda Radner) and Roseanne Roseannadanna (Radner).
- Art Garfunkel has a cameo.

**Airdate:** 11/12/77
**Episode:** 3.5
**Host/Musical Guest:** Ray Charles
**Musical and Guest Performances/Cameo(s)/ Program Notes:**
- "Live from New York": Don Vito Corleone (John Belushi), who talks to Tom Hagen (Bill Murray) about improving his image on television.
- Charles performs "I Can See Clearly Now," "What'd I Say," "Oh! What a Beautiful Morning," and "I Can't Stop Loving You."
- Guest performance by comedian Franklyn Ajaye.

**Airdate:** 11/19/77
**Episode:** 3.6
**Host:** Buck Henry
**Musical Guest:** Leon Redbone
**Musical and Guest Performances/Cameo(s)/ Program Notes:**
- "Live from New York": The five finalists of the "Anyone Can Host" contest, who are introduced by host Buck Henry.
- Redbone performs "Champagne Charlie" and "Please Don't Talk About Me When I'm Gone."
- "A Film by Gary Weis": A hidden camera catches each of the finalists chatting with Henry and trying to influence his decision.
- "Schiller's Reel": *Life After Death*.

**Airdate:** 12/10/77
**Episode:** 3.7
**Host:** Mary Kay Place
**Musical Guest:** Willie Nelson
**Musical and Guest Performances/Cameo(s)/ Program Notes:**
- "Live from New York": Place and the cast dressed as cheerleaders hold a pep rally before the show.
- Nelson performs "Whiskey River," "Blue Eyes Crying in the Rain," and, with Place, "Something to Brag About."
- Guest performance by Andy Kaufman.

**Airdate:** 12/17/77
**Episode:** 3.8
**Host:** Miskel Spillman
**Musical Guest:** Elvis Costello
**Musical and Guest Performances/Cameo(s)/ Program Notes:**
- "Live from New York": John Belushi, after getting eighty-year-old Miskel Spillman, winner of the "Anyone Can Host" contest, stoned.
- Buck Henry serves as Spillman's escort throughout the show.
- Costello performs "Watching the Detectives" and "Radio, Radio," though for the second song he was scheduled to perform "Less Than Zero" but stopped a few seconds in and switched songs.

**Airdate:** 1/21/78
**Episode:** 3.9
**Host:** Steve Martin

Episode Guide · 423

**Musical Guest:** The Dirt Band, Randy Newman
**Musical and Guest Performances/Cameo(s)/ Program Notes:**
- "Live from New York": Jimmy Carter (Dan Aykroyd) in his State of the Union Address.
- The Dirt Band performs "On the Loose with the Blues" and "White Russia" (with Steve Martin on banjo).
- Randy Newman performs "Short People" and "Rider in the Brain."
- Cameo by singer Andrew Gold ("Lonely Boy").
- "A Film by Gary Weis": *Hollywood Homes.*
- ★★★★ Four-Star Sketch: "The Coneheads" on *Family Feud.*

**Airdate:** 1/28/78
**Episode:** 3.10
**Host:** Robert Klein
**Musical Guest:** Bonnie Raitt
**Musical and Guest Performances/Cameo(s)/ Program Notes:**
- "Live from New York": Don Kirshner (Paul Shaffer), who introduces Mr. Mike (Michael O'Donoghue) and Tina Turner (Garrett Morris), who perform "Proud Mary."
- Bonnie Raitt performs "Runaway" and "Give It All Up or Let Me Go."
- Sketch Debuts: The Olympia Café ("Cheezburger, cheezburger"), and the nerds, Todd (Bill Murray) and Lisa (Gilda Radner).
- At the end of the episode, atomic lobsters take over Studio 8H.

**Airdate:** 2/18/78
**Episode:** 3.11
**Host:** Chevy Chase
**Musical Guest:** Billy Joel
**Musical and Guest Performances/Cameo(s)/ Program Notes:**
- "Live from New York": Former president Gerald Ford (Chevy Chase).
- Joel performs "Only the Good Die Young" and "Just the Way You Are."

- "A Film by Gary Weis": *The Voice* with Valri Bromfield.

**Airdate:** 2/25/78
**Episode:** 3.12
**Host:** O. J. Simpson
**Musical Guest:** Ashford & Simpson
**Musical and Guest Performances/Cameo(s)/ Program Notes:**
- "Live from New York": Gilda Radner, taking questions from the audience.
- Ashford & Simpson perform "So, So Satisfied" and "Don't Cost You Nothing."

**Airdate:** 3/11/78
**Episode:** 3.13
**Host:** Art Garfunkel
**Musical Guest:** Stephen Bishop
**Musical and Guest Performances/Cameo(s)/ Program Notes:**
- "Live from New York": Charlie Chaplin (Gilda Radner), who mouths the phrase.
- Garfunkel sings "All I Know," "Scarborough Fair," "Crying in My Sleep," and, with Bishop, "Wonderful World."
- Bishop performs "On and On."
- "Schiller's Reel": *Don't Look Back in Anger.*

**Airdate:** 3/18/78
**Episode:** 3.14
**Host:** Jill Clayburgh
**Musical Guest:** Eddie Money
**Musical and Guest Performances/Cameo(s)/ Program Notes:**
- "Live from New York": Garrett Morris, after singing "Danny Boy."
- Money performs "Baby Hold On" and "Two Tickets to Paradise."

**Airdate:** 3/25/78
**Episode:** 3.15
**Host:** Christopher Lee
**Musical Guest:** Meat Loaf
**Musical and Guest Performances/Cameo(s)/ Program Notes:**

- "Live from New York": John Belushi, who is being forced by NBC to change his name to Kevin Scott and play Grizzly Adams. He is introduced in the opening credits as Kevin Scott.
- Meat Loaf performs "All Revved Up with No Place to Go" and "Two out of Three Ain't Bad."
- "A Film by Gary Weis": *Cold as Ice* with Stacy Keach.
- Cameos (in the audience) by Cheetah Chrome, guitarist of the punk rock band the Dead Boys, and actor Rick Overton.
- ★★★★ Four-Star Sketch: Mr. Death (Lee) apologizes to a little girl (Laraine Newman) for taking her dog away.

**Airdate:** 4/8/78
**Episode:** 3.16
**Host:** Michael Palin
**Musical Guest:** Eugene Record
**Musical and Guest Performances/Cameo(s)/ Program Notes:**
- "Live from New York": Jimmy Carter (Dan Aykroyd) at the Oscars.
- Record performs "Have You Seen Her?" and "Trying to Get to You."

**Airdate:** 4/15/78
**Episode:** 3.17
**Host:** Michael Sarrazin
**Musical Guest:** Keith Jarrett, Gravity
**Musical and Guest Performances/Cameo(s)/ Program Notes:**
- "Live from New York": President Carter's daughter, Amy (Laraine Newman).
- Jarrett performs "Country."
- Gravity performs "Tuba City Gitback."
- "Schiller's Reel": *La Dolce Gilda*.

**Airdate:** 4/22/78
**Episode:** 3.18
**Host:** Steve Martin
**Musical Guest:** The Blues Brothers
**Musical and Guest Performances/Cameo(s)/ Program Notes:**
- "Live from New York": Don Kirshner (Paul Shaffer), who introduces the Blues Brothers.
- The Blues Brothers perform "Hey, Bartender" and "I Don't Know."
- "A Film by Gary Weis": *Swan Lake* with a voice-over by Toni Basil and Weis.
- ★★★★ Four-Star Sketches: "King Tut," sung by Martin; Martin and Gilda Radner play two strangers in a nightclub whose eyes meet and engage in a romantic dance routine. The sketch was repeated when Martin paid tribute to the late Radner in his monologue in episode 14.20.

**Airdate:** 5/13/78
**Episode:** 3.19
**Host:** Richard Dreyfuss
**Musical Guest:** Jimmy Buffett, Gary Tigerman
**Musical and Guest Performances/Cameo(s)/ Program Notes:**
- "Live from New York": Bill Murray, who is about to light up a marijuana joint given to him by an *SNL* band member, bass player Buddy Williams, which may contain the herbicide paraquat.
- Buffett, with his leg in a cast, performs "Son of a Son of a Sailor."
- Tigerman performs "White Oaxacan Moon."
- Character Debut: Father Guido Sarducci (Don Novello).

**Airdate:** 5/20/78
**Episode:** 3.20
**Host:** Buck Henry
**Musical Guest:** Sun Ra
**Musical and Guest Performances/Cameo(s)/ Program Notes:**
- "Live from New York": Richard Nixon (Dan Aykroyd), promoting his memoir, *RN*.
- Sun Ra performs "Space Is the Place" and "Space Loneliness."

Episode Guide

# Season 4 (1978–1979)

**Airdate:** 10/7/78
**Episode:** 4.1
**Host/Musical Guest:** The Rolling Stones
**Musical and Guest Performances/Cameo(s)/ Program Notes:**
- "Live from New York": A 1930s NBC radio announcer (Dan Aykroyd).
- The Rolling Stones perform "Beast of Burden," "Respectable," and "Shattered."
- *Weekend Update*: Bill Murray coanchors with Jane Curtin; Aykroyd appears as the station manager.
- "Schiller's Reel": *Sushi by the Pool*, with Carrie Fisher, Hal Holbrook, and Desi Arnaz Jr.

**Airdate:** 10/14/78
**Episode:** 4.2
**Host:** Fred Willard
**Musical Guest:** Devo
**Musical and Guest Performances/Cameo(s)/ Program Notes:**
- "Live from New York": Honker (Bill Murray) sits in the audience thinking he's at a Yankees game.
- Devo performs "Satisfaction" and "Jocko Homo."

**Airdate:** 10/21/78
**Episode:** 4.3
**Host/Musical Guest:** Frank Zappa
**Musical and Guest Performances/Cameo(s)/ Program Notes:**
- "Live from New York": NBC President Fred Silverman (John Belushi) promotes the network's new star, Frank Zappa.
- Zappa performs "Dancing Fool," "Meek," and, with Samurai Futaba, "Rollo."
- In the sketches Zappa continually breaks character and makes it clear he is reading his lines off cue cards.

**Airdate:** 11/4/78
**Episode:** 4.4

**Host:** Steve Martin
**Musical Guest:** Van Morrison
**Musical and Guest Performances/Cameo(s)/ Program Notes:**
- "Live from New York": President Carter (Dan Aykroyd) addresses the nation about the economy.
- Van Morrison performs "Wavelength" and "Kingdom Hall."

**Airdate:** 11/11/78
**Episode:** 4.5
**Host:** Buck Henry
**Musical Guest:** The Grateful Dead
**Musical and Guest Performances/Cameo(s)/ Program Notes:**
- "Live from New York": Reporter Laraine Newman from the headquarters of congressional candidate Dennis V. Hunkler (Bill Murray).
- Grateful Dead performs "Casey Jones," "I Need a Miracle," and "Good Lovin'."
- Character Debut: Baseball player Chico Escuela (Garrett Morris).

**Airdate:** 11/18/78
**Episode:** 4.6
**Host:** Carrie Fisher
**Musical Guest:** The Blues Brothers
**Musical and Guest Performances/Cameo(s)/ Program Notes:**
- "Live from New York": Monty (Garrett Morris), the emcee at the Black Rhino Club, where the Blues Brothers perform "Soul Man."
- Blues Brothers also perform "Got Everything I Need, Almost" and "B Movie Boxcar Blues."
- "Schiller's Reel": *Roman Holiday*.

**Airdate:** 12/2/78
**Episode:** 4.7
**Host:** Walter Matthau
**Musical and Guest Performances/Cameo(s)/ Program Notes:**

- "Live from New York": Barbara (Gilda Radner), assistant to NBC president Fred Silverman (John Belushi).
- Garrett Morris performs "Dalla Sua Pace" at Matthau's request.

**Airdate:** 12/9/78
**Episode:** 4.8
**Host:** Eric Idle
**Musical Guest:** Kate Bush
**Musical and Guest Performances/Cameo(s)/ Program Notes:**
- "Live from New York": Telepsychic Ray (Dan Aykroyd).
- Bush performs "The Man with the Child in His Eyes."
- ★★★★ Four-Star Sketches: The French Chef (Dan Aykroyd) cuts her finger, Candy Slice's (Gilda Radner) recording session, and *Consumer Probe* with Irwin Mainway (Aykroyd).

**Airdate:** 12/16/78
**Episode:** 4.9
**Host:** Elliott Gould
**Musical Guest:** Peter Tosh
**Musical and Guest Performances/Cameo(s)/ Program Notes:**
- "Live from New York": President Carter's daughter, Amy (Laraine Newman).
- Tosh sings "Bush Doctor" and, with special guest Mick Jagger, "Don't Look Back."
- Guest appearance by comedians Bob (Elliott) and Ray (Goulding). Elliott is the father of future regular Chris Elliott (1994–1995), whose daughter, Abby, was a regular from 2008 to 2012. Bob and Ray also starred in a 1979 NBC special, *Bob & Ray, Jane, Laraine & Gilda*, costarring the three female Not Ready for Prime Time Players.

**Airdate:** 1/27/79
**Episode:** 4.10
**Host:** Michael Palin
**Musical Guest:** The Doobie Brothers
**Musical and Guest Performances/Cameo(s)/ Program Notes:**
- "Live from New York": President Jimmy Carter (Dan Aykroyd).
- The Doobie Brothers sing "What a Fool Believes" and "Taking It to the Streets."

**Airdate:** 2/10/79
**Episode:** 4.11
**Host:** Cicely Tyson
**Musical Guest:** Talking Heads
**Musical and Guest Performances/Cameo(s)/ Program Notes:**
- "Live from New York": John Belushi, who is upset one of his sketches was cut.
- Talking Heads perform "Take Me to the River" and "Artists Only."

**Airdate:** 2/17/79
**Episode:** 4.12
**Host:** Rick Nelson
**Musical Guest:** Judy Collins
**Musical and Guest Performances/Cameo(s)/ Program Notes:**
- "Live from New York": A deliveryman (John Belushi), who brings lobsters to a radio station.
- Collins performs "Hard Times for Lovers."
- Nelson performs "Dream Lover."
- "Schiller's Reel": *Picasso: The New York Years.*

**Airdate:** 2/24/79
**Episode:** 4.13
**Host:** Kate Jackson
**Musical Guest:** Delbert McClinton
**Musical and Guest Performances/Cameo(s)/ Program Notes:**
- "Live from New York": NBC president Fred Silverman (John Belushi), who tells Charlie's Angels (Jackson, Jane Curtin, and Gilda Radner) he is working undercover for ABC to destroy NBC.
- McClinton performs "B Movie Boxcar Blues" and "Talkin' About You."

Episode Guide

**Airdate:** 3/10/79
**Episode:** 4.14
**Host:** Gary Busey
**Musical Guest:** Eubie Blake and Gregory Hines
**Musical and Guest Performances/Cameo(s)/ Program Notes:**
- "Live from New York": John Belushi, who is jealous of Gary Busey's Oscar nomination for *The Buddy Holly Story*.
- Blake and Hines perform "Low Down Blues," "I'm Just Simply Full of Jazz," and "I'm Just Wild About Harry."
- Busey and special guests Paul Butterfield and Rick Danko perform "Stay All Night."
- "Schiller's Reel": *Perchance to Dream*.

**Airdate:** 3/17/79
**Episode:** 4.15
**Host:** Margot Kidder
**Musical Guest:** The Chieftains
**Musical and Guest Performances/Cameo(s)/ Program Notes:**
- "Live from New York": The Ghost of Jimmy Hoffa (John Belushi).
- The Chieftains perform "If I Had Maggie in the Woods" and "Morning Dew."

**Airdate:** 4/7/79
**Episode:** 4.16
**Host:** Richard Benjamin
**Musical Guest:** Rickie Lee Jones
**Musical and Guest Performances/Cameo(s)/ Program Notes:**
- "Live from New York": Dan Aykroyd, after giving instructions to John Belushi's understudy (Marvin Goldhar).
- Jones performs "Chuck E's in Love" and "Coolsville."

**Airdate:** 4/14/79
**Episode:** 4.17
**Host:** Milton Berle
**Musical Guest:** Ornette Coleman, Prime Time
**Musical and Guest Performances/Cameo(s)/ Program Notes:**
- "Live from New York": The Men from Texaco (Bill Murray, John Belushi, Dan Aykroyd, Garrett Morris).
- Coleman and Prime Time perform "Times Square."

**Airdate:** 5/12/79
**Episode:** 4.18
**Host:** Michael Palin
**Musical Guest:** James Taylor
**Musical and Guest Performances/Cameo(s)/ Program Notes:**
- "Live from New York": NBC president Fred Silverman (John Belushi) hires *Diff'rent Strokes* star Gary Coleman, who shares his taste in programming, as an executive vice president at NBC.
- Taylor performs "Up on the Roof" and "Millworker."

**Airdate:** 5/19/79
**Episode:** 4.19
**Host:** Maureen Stapleton
**Musical Guest:** Linda Ronstadt and Phoebe Snow
**Musical and Guest Performances/Cameo(s)/ Program Notes:**
- "Live from New York": Telepsychic Ray (Dan Aykroyd).
- Ronstadt and Snow perform "The Shoop Shoop Song (It's in His Kiss)" and "The Married Man."

**Airdate:** 5/26/79
**Episode:** 4.20
**Host:** Buck Henry
**Musical Guest:** Bette Midler
**Musical and Guest Performances/Cameo(s)/ Program Notes:**
- "Live from New York": John Belushi, despite Jane Curtin's complaint that she's never opened the show.
- Midler performs "Married Men" and "Martha."
- "Schiller's Reel": *Clones Exist Now*.
- Final episode for Belushi and Dan Aykroyd.

# Season 5 (1979-1980)

**Airdate:** 10/13/79
**Episode:** 5.1
**Host:** Steve Martin
**Musical Guest:** Blondie
**Musical and Guest Performances/Cameo(s)/ Program Notes:**
- "Live from New York": The Pope (Steve Martin), who visits New York.
- Blondie sings "Dreaming" and "The Hardest Part."
- Special report from Father Guido Sarducci (Don Novello).

**Airdate:** 10/20/79
**Episode:** 5.2
**Host:** Eric Idle
**Musical Guest:** Bob Dylan
**Musical and Guest Performances/Cameo(s)/ Program Notes:**
- "Live from New York": Buck Henry, who offers to go on for an ailing Eric Idle.
- Dylan performs "Gotta Serve Somebody" and "I Believe in Youth" (with Fred Tackett).
- Guest performance by Andy Kaufman.
- Guest appearance by Harry Shearer.

**Airdate:** 11/3/79
**Episode:** 5.3
**Host:** Bill Russell
**Musical Guest:** Chicago
**Musical and Guest Performances/Cameo(s)/ Program Notes:**
- "Live from New York": Ted Kennedy (Bill Murray), who is announcing his run for the presidency.
- Chicago performs "I'm a Man" and "Street Player."

**Airdate:** 11/10/79
**Episode:** 5.4
**Host:** Buck Henry
**Musical Guest:** Tom Petty and the Heartbreakers

**Musical and Guest Performances/Cameo(s)/ Program Notes:**
- "Live from New York": Jane Curtin, who, after hearing from Bill Murray how Henry saved NBC president Fred Silverman's life during the war, feels bad she opposed him hosting the show again.
- Tom Petty and the Heartbreakers perform "Refugee" and "Don't Do Me Like That."

**Airdate:** 11/17/79
**Episode:** 5.5
**Host:** Bea Arthur
**Musical Guest:** The Roches
**Musical and Guest Performances/Cameo(s)/ Program Notes:**
- "Live from New York": Makeup girl (Laraine Newman), taking Governor Reagan's makeup off after his speech.
- The Roches perform "Bobby's Song" and "Hallelujah."
- Tom Davis, Paul Shaffer, and Harry Shearer are credited as featured players. Although not featured in the credits, writers Tom Schiller and Alan Zweibel also appear in this episode.

**Airdate:** 12/8/79
**Episode:** 5.6
**Host:** Howard Hesseman
**Musical Guest:** Randy Newman
**Musical and Guest Performances/Cameo(s)/ Program Notes:**
- "Live from New York": Don Kirshner (Paul Shaffer).
- Newman performs "It's Money That I Love," "I'm Gonna Take Off My Pants," and "The Story of a Rock & Roll Band."
- Debut of Don Novello as a featured player.

Episode Guide | 429

**Airdate:** 12/15/79
**Episode:** 5.7
**Host:** Martin Sheen
**Musical Guest:** David Bowie
**Musical and Guest Performances/Cameo(s)/ Program Notes:**
- "Live from New York": Bill Murray, after undergoing a sex-change operation.
- Bowie performs "The Man Who Sold the World" and "TVC-15."
- Debut of Al Franken as a featured player.

**Airdate:** 12/22/79
**Episode:** 5.8
**Host:** Ted Knight
**Musical Guest:** Desmond Child and Rouge
**Musical and Guest Performances/Cameo(s)/ Program Notes:**
- "Live from New York": Mohammad Reza Pahlavi (Bill Murray), the Shah of Iran.
- Desmond Child and Rouge perform "Tumble in the Night" and "Goodbye Baby."
- "Schiller's Reel": *Java Junkie.*

**Airdate:** 1/26/80
**Episode:** 5.9
**Host:** Teri Garr
**Musical Guest:** The B-52's
**Musical and Guest Performances/Cameo(s)/ Program Notes:**
- "Live from New York": Father Guido Sarducci (Don Novello) reporting from Tokyo.
- The B-52's sing "Rock Lobster" and "Dance This Mess Around."
- Debut of Peter Aykroyd, Jim Downey, and Brian Doyle-Murray as featured players.

**Airdate:** 2/9/80
**Episode:** 5.10
**Host:** Chevy Chase
**Musical Guest:** Marianne Faithfull, Tom Scott
**Musical and Guest Performances/Cameo(s)/ Program Notes:**
- "Live from New York": Former president Gerald Ford (Chevy Chase) after taking a tumble.
- Faithfull performs "Broken English" and "Guilt."
- Chase and Scott perform "16 Tons."
- "Schiller's Reel": *Linden Palmer, Hollywood's Forgotten Director.*
- Harry Shearer is bumped up to a regular.

**Airdate:** 2/16/80
**Episode:** 5.11
**Host:** Elliott Gould
**Musical Guest:** Gary Numan
**Musical and Guest Performances/Cameo(s)/ Program Notes:**
- "Live from New York": Father Guido Sarducci (Don Novello) reporting on Nixon in New York.
- Numan performs "Cars" and "Praying to the Aliens."

**Airdate:** 2/23/80
**Episode:** 5.12
**Host:** Kirk Douglas
**Musical Guest:** Sam and Dave
**Musical and Guest Performances/Cameo(s)/ Program Notes:**
- "Live from New York": Gilda Radner, who brings her Aunt Margie to meet Kirk Douglas.
- Sam and Dave perform "You Don't Know Like I Know" and "Soul Man."
- "Schiller's Reel": *Mask of Fear.*

**Airdate:** 3/8/80
**Episode:** 5.13
**Host:** Rodney Dangerfield
**Musical Guest:** The J. Geils Band
**Musical and Guest Performances/Cameo(s)/ Program Notes:**

- "Live from New York": Rodney Dangerfield from his overcrowded dressing room.
- The J. Geils Band performs "Love Stinks" and "Sanctuary."
- Cameos by Jerry Mathers and Tony Dow (TV's Beaver and Wally Cleaver).
- Actor Rob Morrow, who will host the show in 1992 (17.10), is an extra in the courtroom sketch.

**Airdate:** 3/15/80
**Episode:** 5.14
**Host:** No host
**Musical Guest:** James Taylor, Paul Simon, David Sanborn
**Musical and Guest Performances/Cameo(s)/Program Notes:**
- The 100th Show!
- "Live from New York": John Belushi, from inside a crystal ball.
- Cameos by Michael O'Donoghue, Michael Palin, Steve Jordan, Senator Daniel P. Moynihan, and Ralph Nader.
- Taylor, Simon, and Sanborn perform "Cathy's Clown," "Sunny Skies," and "Take Me to the Mardi Gras."
- Sanborn performs "Anything You Want."
- F-bomb!: In the Medieval Band sketch, Paul Shaffer accidentally says "fucking" instead of "flogging."

**Airdate:** 4/5/80
**Episode:** 5.15
**Host:** Richard Benjamin and Paula Prentiss
**Musical Guest:** The Grateful Dead
**Musical and Guest Performances/Cameo(s)/Program Notes:**
- "Live from New York": ABC News anchor Frank Reynolds (Harry Shearer).
- The Grateful Dead performs "Alabama Getaway" and "Saint of Circumstances."

**Airdate:** 4/12/80
**Episode:** 5.16
**Host:** Burt Reynolds
**Musical Guest:** Anne Murray
**Musical and Guest Performances/Cameo(s)/Program Notes:**
- "Live from New York": Gilda Radner, from inside a locker she was shoved into backstage by Reynolds, who was tired of being reminded he didn't get an Oscar nomination for *Starting Over*.
- Murray performs "Lucky Me" and "Why Don't You Stick Around."

**Airdate:** 4/19/80
**Episode:** 5.17
**Host:** Strother Martin
**Musical Guest:** The Specials
**Musical and Guest Performances/Cameo(s)/Program Notes:**
- "Live from New York": Rosa Santangelo (Gilda Radner), in Spanish.
- The Specials perform "Gangsters" and "Too Much, Too Young."

**Airdate:** 5/10/80
**Episode:** 5.18
**Host:** Bob Newhart
**Musical Guest:** The Amazing Rhythm Aces, Bruce Cockburn
**Musical and Guest Performances/Cameo(s)/Program Notes:**
- "Live from New York": Singing duo Mie (Laraine Newman) and Kei (Gilda Radner), stars of the bomb NBC variety show *Pink Lady and Jeff*.
- The Amazing Rhythm Aces perform "Who Will the Next Fool Be" and "Third-Rate Romance."
- Cockburn performs "Wondering Where the Lions Are."

**Airdate:** 5/17/80
**Episode:** 5.19
**Host:** Steve Martin
**Musical Guest:** Paul and Linda McCartney, 3-D
**Musical and Guest Performances/Cameo(s)/Program Notes:**

- "Live from New York": An unidentified English milkman (in London), who is asked by Father Guido Sarducci to open the show.
- Music Video: "Coming Up," starring Paul and Linda McCartney, who do not appear in the studio.
- 3-D performs "All Night Television."

**Airdate:** 5/24/80
**Episode:** 5.20
**Host:** Buck Henry
**Musical Guest:** Andrew Gold, Andrae Crouch and the Voices of Unity
**Musical and Guest Performances/Cameo(s)/Program Notes:**
- "Live from New York": ABC News anchor Frank Reynolds (Harry Shearer), reporting on the 1980 election that is still a year and a half away.
- Andrew Gold performs "Kiss This One Goodbye."
- Andrae Crouch and the Voices of Unity perform "Can't Nobody Do Me Like Jesus."
- ★★★★ Four-Star Sketch: "Lord & Lady Douchebag."
- Final episode for Peter Aykroyd, Jane Curtin, Tom Davis, Jim Downey, Al Franken, Garrett Morris, Bill Murray, Laraine Newman, Don Novello, Gilda Radner, Tom Schiller, Paul Shaffer, and Harry Shearer (who will return in 1984).
- Last episode produced by Lorne Michaels until season 11.
- Final shot is a flashing "On Air" sign that turns off.

## Season 6 (1980–1981)

**Airdate:** 11/15/80
**Episode:** 6.1
**Host:** Elliott Gould
**Musical Guest:** King Creole and the Coconuts
**Musical and Guest Performances/Cameo(s)/Program Notes:**
- "Live from New York": Denny Dillon, who wakes up in bed with Gould and new regulars Gilbert Gottfried, Gail Matthius, Joe Piscopo, Ann Risley, and Charles Rocket.
- First episode produced by Jean Doumanian.
- Kid Creole and the Coconuts perform "Mister Softee" and "There But for the Grace of God Go I."
- "Film Shorts": *Foot Fetish*, directed by Randal Kleiser; "Gidgette Goes to Hell," a music video directed by Jonathan Demme and Jack Cummins, featuring punk band Suburban Lawns singing the title song; and *Heart to Heart*, a short by filmmaker/staff writer Mitchell Kriegman.
- Charles Rocket, a former newscaster, anchors *Weekend Update*.

**Airdate:** 11/22/80
**Episode:** 6.2
**Host:** Malcolm McDowell
**Musical Guest:** Captain Beefheart and His Magic Band
**Musical and Guest Performances/Cameo(s)/Program Notes:**
- "Live from New York": A prisoner (Gilbert Gottfried), who gets the electric chair.
- Captain Beefheart and His Magic Band sing "Hot Head" and "Ashtray Heart."
- Eddie Murphy's first appearance on *SNL* as an unbilled extra.
- According to UPI, NBC received more than 150 complaints over a sketch about the first day of "Commie Hunting Season" in Greensboro, North Carolina.

Appendix A

**Airdate:** 12/6/80
**Episode:** 6.3
**Host:** Ellen Burstyn
**Musical Guest:** Aretha Franklin, Keith Sykes
**Musical and Guest Performances/Cameo(s)/Program Notes:**
- "Live from New York": David Rockefeller (Charles Rocket).
- Franklin sings "United Together" and "Can't Turn You Loose."
- Sykes, who is introduced as "New Talent," sings "B.I.G.T.I.M.E." during the opening credits.
- "Music Video": "Fish Heads," directed by Bill Paxton.

**Airdate:** 12/13/80
**Episode:** 6.4
**Host:** Jamie Lee Curtis
**Musical Guest:** James Brown, Ellen Shipley
**Musical and Guest Performances/Cameo(s)/Program Notes:**
- "Live from New York": Denny Dillon, Gail Matthius, and Charles Rocket, on behalf of "The Mean Majority."
- Debut of featured players Matthew Laurance, Eddie Murphy and Patrick Weathers.
- Brown sings "Rapp Payback."
- Shipley sings "Fotogenic."
- "Film Shorts": *Who Is Gilbert Gottfried?* by Linda Lee, and a shortened version of director Martin Brest's NYU student film *Hot Dogs for Gauguin*, starring Danny DeVito and Rhea Perlman.

**Airdate:** 12/20/80
**Episode:** 6.5
**Host:** David Carradine
**Musical Guest:** Linda Ronstadt, George Rose, Rex Smith, and the Broadway cast of *The Pirates of Penzance*
**Musical and Guest Performances/Cameo(s)/Program Notes:**
- "Live from New York": Joe Piscopo, after getting caught practicing to be the show's announcer by Don Pardo.
- Debut of featured player Yvonne Hudson, who had occasionally appeared uncredited since 1978.
- Ronstadt, Rose, Smith, and chorus sing selections from the Broadway production of *The Pirates of Penzance* and a medley of Christmas carols.
- "Film Shorts": *The Dancing Man*, directed by Mitchell Kriegman and starring Bill Irwin; Mr. Bill recalls his first Christmas.

**Airdate:** 1/10/81
**Episode:** 6.6
**Host:** Ray Sharkey
**Musical Guest:** Jack Bruce and Friends
**Musical and Guest Performances/Cameo(s)/Program Notes:**
- "Live from New York": Joe Piscopo as the announcer in a parody of *To Tell the Truth* with mobsters.
- Bruce and Friends sing "Dancing on Air" and "Livin' Without Ja."
- Gail Matthius joins Charles Rocket as coanchor of *Weekend Update*.

**Airdate:** 1/17/81
**Episode:** 6.7
**Host:** Karen Black
**Musical Guest:** Cheap Trick, Stanley Clarke Trio
**Musical and Guest Performances/Cameo(s)/Program Notes:**
- "Live from New York": Rosalynn Carter (Ann Risley).
- Cheap Trick performs "Baby Loves to Rock" and "Can't Stop but I'm Gonna Try."
- Stanley Clarke Trio performs "Wild Dog."
- "Film Short": *The Tragically Hip*, a scene from Michael Nesmith's 1981 video *Elephant Parts*.

**Airdate:** 1/24/81
**Episode:** 6.8

**Host:** Robert Hays
**Musical Guest:** Joe "King" Carrasco and the Crowns, 14 Karat Soul
**Musical and Guest Performances/Cameo(s)/ Program Notes:**
- "Live from New York": Ted Koppel (Joe Piscopo) reporting on Day 4 of noncaptivity for the Iranian hostages.
- Carrasco and the Crowns sing "Don't Bug Me Baby."
- 14 Karat Soul sing "I Wish That We Were Married" and "This Time It's for Real."

**Airdate:** 2/7/81
**Episode:** 6.9
**Host:** Sally Kellerman
**Musical Guest:** Jimmy Cliff
**Musical and Guest Performances/Cameo(s)/ Program Notes:**
- "Live from New York": President Ronald Reagan (Charles Rocket).
- Cliff performs "I Am the Living" and "Gone Clear."
- Eddie Murphy is bumped up to regular.
- Terry Sweeney, a staff writer on the show who appears as an extra in the opening, will portray Nancy Reagan when he returns as a regular in season 11.

**Airdate:** 2/14/81
**Episode:** 6.10
**Host:** Deborah Harry
**Musical Guest:** Funky 4 + 1
**Musical and Guest Performances/Cameo(s)/ Program Notes:**
- "Live from New York": President Ronald Reagan (Charles Rocket), who talks to Frank Sinatra (Piscopo) and answers the question "Is Frank Sinatra a Hoodlum?"
- Harry sings "Love TKO" and "Come Back Jonee."
- Funky 4 + 1 sings "That's the Joint."

**Airdate:** 2/21/81
**Episode:** 6.11
**Host:** Charlene Tilton
**Musical Guest:** Todd Rundgren, Prince
**Musical and Guest Performances/Cameo(s)/ Program Notes:**
- "Live from New York": Sportscaster Joe Piscopo.
- Rundgren performs "Healer" and "Time Heals."
- F-bombs! (two of them): The first is by Prince during his performance of "Party Up." The second is by Rocket during the "good nights," when, as part of a running gag, he is in a wheelchair after being gunned down by an unknown assailant in a parody of prime-time soap *Dallas*'s "Who shot J. R.?" cliff-hanger. When *Dallas* star Tilton asks Rocket, "Charlie, how are you feeling after you've been shot?," he replies, "It's the first time I've ever been shot in my life. I'd like to know who the fuck did it."
- Sketch Debut: *Mister Robinson's Neighborhood*, hosted by Mr. Robinson (Eddie Murphy).

**Airdate:** 3/7/81
**Episode:** 6.12
**Host:** Bill Murray
**Musical Guest:** Delbert McClinton
**Musical and Guest Performances/Cameo(s)/ Program Notes:**
- "Live from New York": Host Murray and the cast after giving them a pep talk.
- McClinton performs "Givin' It Up for Your Love" and "Shotgun Rider."
- *Weekend Update* is renamed *Saturday Night Newsline*.
- Final episode for producer Jean Doumanian.
- Final episode for Gilbert Gottfried, Matthew Laurance, Ann Risley, Charles Rocket, and Patrick Weathers.

**Airdate:** 4/11/81
**Episode:** 6.13
**Host:** No host
**Musical Guest:** Jr. Walker & the All-Stars

Appendix A

**Musical and Guest Performances/Cameo(s)/ Program Notes:**
- "Live from New York": Chevy Chase, who reunites with Mr. Bill and his dog Spot in a storage room backstage.
- Jr. Walker & the All-Stars perform "Road Runner," "Shotgun," "How Sweet It Is," and "What Does It Take."
- Dick Ebersol's first episode as producer. This was the last episode of season 6 due to the Writers Guild of America strike.
- Final episode for Denny Dillon, Gail Matthius, and Yvonne Hudson, though Hudson will occasionally appear in unbilled bit roles in seasons 7–10.
- Debut of Robin Duke, Tim Kazurinsky, and Tony Rosato as regulars.
- Sketch Debut: *I Married a Monkey*, featuring Tim Kazurinsky.
- Laurie Metcalf, best known for playing Jackie on *Roseanne*, is a new featured player who appears in a "woman on the street" filmed segment during *Weekend Update* in which she asks New Yorkers, "Would you take a bullet for the President?" Eight seasons later (14.2), she appeared on *SNL* in a short film with Catherine O'Hara.
- The name of a second featured player, Emily Prager, appears in the opening credits, but she does not appear in any of the sketches, which were cut after the dress rehearsal.

## Season 7 (1981–1982)

**Airdate:** 10/3/81
**Episode:** 7.1
**Host:** No host
**Musical Guest:** Rod Stewart
**Musical and Guest Performances/Cameo(s)/ Program Notes:**
- "Live from New York" intro is eliminated from the opening.
- Stewart performs "Young Turks."
- Special guest Tina Turner, who performs "Dance with Me" and "Hot Legs" with Rod Stewart.
- Guest performance by Michael Davis.
- "Film Short": *Andy Warhol's TV*.
- "Music Video": Yoko Ono's "Goodbye Sadness" with footage of Yoko and the late John Lennon.
- Debut of regulars Christine Ebersole and Mary Gross, who coanchors *SNL Newsbreak* with Brian Doyle-Murray.

**Airdate:** 10/10/81
**Episode:** 7.2
**Host:** Susan Saint James
**Musical Guest:** The Kinks
**Musical and Guest Performances/Cameo(s)/ Program Notes:**
- The Kinks perform "Destroyer" and "Art Lover."
- "Film Short": *Andy Warhol's TV* and an untitled short, directed by John Fox, about the assassination of Anwar Sadat.

**Airdate:** 10/17/81
**Episode:** 7.3
**Host:** George Kennedy
**Musical Guest:** Miles Davis
**Musical and Guest Performances/Cameo(s)/ Program Notes:**
- Davis performs "Jean Pierre."
- Guest performance by Harry Anderson.
- Cameos by John Candy, Ron Howard, and Regis Philbin.

**Airdate:** 10/31/81
**Episode:** 7.4
**Host:** Donald Pleasence
**Musical Guest:** Fear
**Musical and Guest Performances/Cameo(s)/ Program Notes:**
- Fear performs "I Don't Care About You," "Beef Bologna," "New York's

Alright If You Like Saxophones," and "Let's Have a War" as slam dancers jump onto the stage.
- Guest performance by Michael Davis.
- Cameo by John Belushi, in his last *SNL* appearance.
- "Film Short": *Andy Warhol's TV.*

**Airdate:** 11/7/81
**Episode:** 7.5
**Host:** Lauren Hutton
**Musical Guest:** Rick James
**Musical and Guest Performances/Cameo(s)/ Program Notes:**
- James (with Stone City Band) performs "Give It to Me Baby" and "Superfreak."
- Guest performance by author William Burroughs, who reads from *Naked Lunch* and "Twilight's Last Gleaming" from *Nova Express*.
- "Schiller's Reel": *Art Is Ficial.*

**Airdate:** 11/14/81
**Episode:** 7.6
**Host:** Bernadette Peters
**Musical Guest:** The Go-Go's, Billy Joel
**Musical and Guest Performances/Cameo(s)/ Program Notes:**
- Peters performs "Making Love Alone."
- The Go-Go's perform "We Got the Beat."
- Joel performs "Miami 2017" and "She's Got a Way."
- "Film Short": William Wegman and his Weimaraner Man Ray.

**Airdate:** 12/5/81
**Episode:** 7.7
**Host:** Tim Curry
**Musical Guest:** Meat Loaf
**Musical and Guest Performances/Cameo(s)/ Program Notes:**
- Meat Loaf performs "Promised Land" and "Bat out of Hell."
- Cameos by Bryant Gumbel and Frank Nelson.
- Curry and Meat Loaf both appeared in *Rocky Horror Picture Show* (1975).

**Airdate:** 12/12/81
**Episode:** 7.8
**Host:** Bill Murray
**Musical Guest:** The Spinners, the Yale Whiffenpoofs
**Musical and Guest Performances/Cameo(s)/ Program Notes:**
- The Spinners perform "Then Came You," "I'll Be Around," and "Working My Way Back to You."
- The Yale Whiffenpoofs perform "The Whiffenpoof Song," "The Boar's Head Carol," "God Rest Ye Merry Gentlemen," and "Jingle Bells." They are joined by the cast at the end.
- Guest appearance by Michael Davis.

**Airdate:** 1/23/82
**Episode:** 7.9
**Host:** Robert Conrad
**Musical Guest:** The Allman Brothers Band
**Musical and Guest Performances/Cameo(s)/ Program Notes:**
- The Allman Brothers perform "Midnight Rider " and "Southbound."

**Airdate:** 1/30/82
**Episode:** 7.10
**Host:** John Madden
**Musical Guest:** Jennifer Holliday
**Musical and Guest Performances/Cameo(s)/ Program Notes:**
- Holliday performs "And I Am Telling You I'm Not Going" and "One Night Only" (from *Dreamgirls*).
- Guest appearance by Andy Kaufman.
- Cameos by Brent Musburger, Marv Throneberry, and Bob Zmuda.

**Airdate:** 2/6/82
**Episode:** 7.11
**Host:** James Coburn
**Musical Guest:** Lindsey Buckingham, the Cholos
**Musical and Guest Performances/Cameo(s)/ Program Notes:**
- Buckingham and the Cholos perform "Bwana" and "Trouble."

Appendix A

- Guest performance by Marc Weiner.

**Airdate:** 2/20/82
**Episode:** 7.12
**Host:** Bruce Dern
**Musical Guest:** Luther Vandross
**Musical and Guest Performances/Cameo(s)/Program Notes:**
- Vandross performs "Never Too Much" and "A House Is Not a Home."

**Airdate:** 2/27/82
**Episode:** 7.13
**Host:** Elizabeth Ashley
**Musical Guest:** Hall & Oates
**Musical and Guest Performances/Cameo(s)/Program Notes:**
- Hall & Oates perform "You Make My Dreams" and "You've Lost That Lovin' Feeling."
- Guest performance by Harry Anderson.
- Cameo by theater producer and founder of the Public Theater, Joseph Papp.
- Character Debut: Dr. Jack Badofsky (Tim Kazurinsky) on SNL *Newsbreak*.

**Airdate:** 3/20/82
**Episode:** 7.14
**Host:** Robert Urich
**Musical Guest:** Mink DeVille
**Musical and Guest Performances/Cameo(s)/Program Notes:**
- Mink DeVille performs "Maybe Tomorrow" and "Love and Emotion."

**Airdate:** 3/27/82
**Episode:** 7.15
**Host:** Blythe Danner
**Musical Guest:** Rickie Lee Jones
**Musical and Guest Performances/Cameo(s)/Program Notes:**
- Jones performs "Pirates," "Lush Life," and "Woody and Dutch."
- Guest performance by Michael Davis.

**Airdate:** 4/10/82
**Episode:** 7.16
**Host:** Daniel J. Travanti
**Musical Guest:** John Cougar
**Musical and Guest Performances/Cameo(s)/Program Notes:**
- Cougar performs "Hurts So Good" and "Ain't Even Done with the Night."
- Cameos by Susan Saint James, Barry Mitchell, and Bruce Weitz.
- Viewers are asked to call a 900 number to decide the fate of Larry the Lobster. The final results: Save Larry: 239,096 votes; Kill Larry: 227,452 votes.

**Airdate:** 4/17/82
**Episode:** 7.17
**Host:** Johnny Cash
**Musical Guest:** Elton John
**Musical and Guest Performances/Cameo(s)/Program Notes:**
- Cash performs "I Walk the Line," "Folsom Prison Blues," "Ring of Fire," and "Sunday Morning Coming Down."
- Elton John performs "Empty Garden" and "Ball and Chain."

**Airdate:** 4/24/82
**Episode:** 7.18
**Host:** Robert Culp
**Musical Guest:** The Charlie Daniels Band
**Musical and Guest Performances/Cameo(s)/Program Notes:**
- The Charlie Daniels Band performs "Still in Saigon" and "The Devil Went Down to Georgia."

**Airdate:** 5/15/82
**Episode:** 7.19
**Host:** Danny DeVito
**Musical Guest:** Sparks
**Musical and Guest Performances/Cameo(s)/Program Notes:**
- Sparks performs "Mickey Mouse" and "I Predict."
- Cameos by DeVito's fellow *Taxi* cast members Tony Danza, Marilu Henner, Judd Hirsch, Christopher Lloyd, and his mother, Julia DeVito.

- Guest appearance by Andy Kaufman (in a neck brace) with wrestler Jerry Lawler.

**Airdate:** 5/22/82
**Episode:** 7.20
**Host/Musical Guest:** Olivia Newton-John
**Musical and Guest Performances/Cameo(s)/ Program Notes:**
- Newton-John performs "Physical" and "Landslide."
- Cameo by Graham Chapman in the "Hitler in Heaven" sketch.
- Guest performance by Michael Davis.
- Final episode for Brian Doyle-Murray, Christine Ebersole, and Tony Rosato.

## Season 8 (1982–1983)

**Airdate:** 9/25/82
**Episode:** 8.1
**Host:** Chevy Chase
**Musical Guest:** Queen
**Musical and Guest Performances/Cameo(s)/ Program Notes:**
- "Live from New York": Chevy Chase, who missed his flight from Los Angeles, via a monitor from Burbank.
- Queen performs "Crazy Little Thing Called Love" and "Under Pressure."
- Cameos by Danny DeVito, Roger Ebert, Gene Siskel, and John Zacherle.
- Debut of Brad Hall, Julia Louis-Dreyfus, and Gary Kroeger as regulars.
- *Saturday Night News*: Hall takes over as anchor.

**Airdate:** 10/2/82
**Episode:** 8.2
**Host:** Louis Gossett Jr.
**Musical Guest:** George Thorogood and the Destroyers
**Musical and Guest Performances/Cameo(s)/ Program Notes:**
- George Thorogood and the Destroyers perform "Bad to the Bone" and "Back in Wentzville."
- Cameo by Mr. T.

**Airdate:** 10/9/82
**Episode:** 8.3
**Host:** Ron Howard
**Musical Guest:** The Clash
**Musical and Guest Performances/Cameo(s)/ Program Notes:**
- The Clash performs "Straight to Hell" and "Should I Stay or Should I Go."
- Guest performance by Harry Anderson.
- Cameos by Andy Griffith and film critic Rex Reed.

**Airdate:** 10/23/82
**Episode:** 8.4
**Host:** Howard Hesseman
**Musical Guest:** Men at Work
**Musical and Guest Performances/Cameo(s)/ Program Notes:**
- "Live from New York": A drunken Howard Hesseman, who arrives to the studio on the back of a motorcycle.
- Men at Work perform "Who Can It Be Now?" and "Down Under."
- Cameos by Susan Saint James and music producer Milan Melvin.
- Guest performance by Bill Irwin.

**Airdate:** 10/30/82
**Episode:** 8.5
**Host:** Michael Keaton
**Musical Guest:** The New Joe Jackson Band
**Musical and Guest Performances/Cameo(s)/ Program Notes:**
- "Live from New York": Eddie Murphy, backstage, with a nervous Keaton.
- The New Joe Jackson Band performs "Steppin' Out" and "Another World."
- Monty Python's Michael Palin appears in several sketches.

## Appendix A

**Airdate:** 11/13/82
**Episode:** 8.6
**Host:** Robert Blake
**Musical Guest:** Kenny Loggins
**Musical and Guest Performances/Cameo(s)/Program Notes:**
- "Live from New York": Merv Griffin (in a cameo), hosting his show from Studio 8H, via a video monitor.
- Loggins sings "Heart to Heart" and "I Gotta Try."

**Airdate:** 11/20/82
**Episode:** 8.7
**Host:** Drew Barrymore
**Musical Guest:** Squeeze
**Musical and Guest Performances/Cameo(s)/Program Notes:**
- "Live from New York": Drew Barrymore, backstage in her dressing room.
- Squeeze performs "Annie Get Your Gun" and "Pulling Mussels from a Shell."
- Cameo by Ed Asner.
- Viewers vote by telephone to dump Andy Kaufman from *SNL* (final count is 195,544 votes to dump him vs. 169,186 votes to save him).
- Seven-year-old Drew Barrymore is *SNL*'s youngest host to date.

**Airdate:** 12/4/82
**Episode:** 8.8
**Host:** The Smothers Brothers
**Musical Guest:** Laura Branigan
**Musical and Guest Performances/Cameo(s)/Program Notes:**
- "Live from New York": The Smothers Brothers, in a *Tonight Show* parody.
- Branigan performs "Gloria" and "Living a Lie."
- Cameo by Lawrence K. Grossman.

**Airdate:** 12/11/82
**Episode:** 8.9
**Host:** Eddie Murphy
**Musical Guest:** Lionel Richie
**Musical and Guest Performances/Cameo(s)/Program Notes:**
- "Live from New York": Eddie Murphy, who says, "Live from New York, it's *The Eddie Murphy Show!*"
- Richie sings "You Are" and "Truly."
- Eddie Murphy is the only cast member to host the show.
- Cameo appearance by Steve Martin.
- Eight-year-old Seth Green appears in a Christmas sketch.

**Airdate:** 1/22/83
**Episode:** 8.10
**Host:** Lily Tomlin
**Musical and Guest Performances/Cameo(s)/Program Notes:**
- "Live from New York": Lily Tomlin.
- Cameos by Rick Moranis and Dave Thomas, who host next week.
- In his last appearance on *SNL*, Andy Kaufman, in a filmed spot, thanks everyone who voted for him (see 8.7).
- Cameo by Barry Mitchell, who impersonates Woody Allen.

**Airdate:** 1/29/83
**Episode:** 8.11
**Host:** Rick Moranis and Dave Thomas
**Musical Guest:** The Bus Boys
**Musical and Guest Performances/Cameo(s)/Program Notes:**
- "Live from New York": Woody Allen (Rick Moranis).
- The Bus Boys perform "The Boys Are Back in Town" (with Eddie Murphy) and "New Shoes."

**Airdate:** 2/5/83
**Episode:** 8.12
**Host:** Sid Caesar
**Musical Guest:** Joe Cocker, Jennifer Warnes
**Musical and Guest Performances/Cameo(s)/Program Notes:**
- Cocker and Warnes sing "Up Where We Belong."
- Cocker performs "Seven Days."
- Guest performance by Harry Anderson.

Episode Guide

**Airdate:** 2/19/83
**Episode:** 8.13
**Host:** Howard Hesseman
**Musical Guest:** Tom Petty and the Heartbreakers
**Musical and Guest Performances/Cameo(s)/ Program Notes:**
- "Live from New York": Howard Hesseman, backstage in his dressing room.
- Tom Petty and the Heartbreakers perform "Change of Heart" and "The Waiting."
- Cameo by Milan Melvin.

**Airdate:** 2/26/83
**Episode:** 8.14
**Host:** Beau and Jeff Bridges
**Musical Guest:** Randy Newman
**Musical and Guest Performances/Cameo(s)/ Program Notes:**
- Newman performs "I Love L.A." and "Real Emotional Girl."
- Cameos by Beau and Jeff's father, Lloyd Bridges.

**Airdate:** 3/12/83
**Episode:** 8.15
**Host:** Bruce Dern
**Musical Guest:** Leon Redbone
**Musical and Guest Performances/Cameo(s)/ Program Notes:**
- "Live from New York": A drunken Gary Kroeger.
- Redbone performs "Sweet Sue," "When You Wish Upon a Star," and "I Ain't Got Nobody."

**Airdate:** 3/19/83
**Episode:** 8.16
**Host:** Robert Guillaume
**Musical Guest:** Duran Duran
**Musical and Guest Performances/Cameo(s)/ Program Notes:**
- Duran Duran performs "Hungry Like the Wolf" and "Girls on Film."

**Airdate:** 4/9/83
**Episode:** 8.17
**Host:** Joan Rivers

**Musical Guest:** Musical Youth
**Musical and Guest Performances/Cameo(s)/ Program Notes:**
- "Live from New York": Doug and Wendy Whiner (Joe Piscopo and Robin Duke).
- Musical Youth performs "Pass the Dutchie" and "Never Gonna Give You Up."
- Cameo by David Susskind.

**Airdate:** 4/16/83
**Episode:** 8.18
**Host:** Susan Saint James
**Musical Guest:** Michael McDonald
**Musical and Guest Performances/Cameo(s)/ Program Notes:**
- McDonald performs "If That's What It Takes," "I Can't Let Go Now," and "Go Home."
- Guest performance by Steven Wright.
- Cameo by Edgar Winter.

**Airdate:** 5/7/83
**Episode:** 8.19
**Host/Musical Guest:** Stevie Wonder
**Musical and Guest Performances/Cameo(s)/ Program Notes:**
- Wonder performs "Fingertips" and "Overjoyed."
- Guest performance by Greg Dean and Michael Davis.

**Airdate:** 5/14/83
**Episode:** 8.20
**Host:** Ed Koch
**Musical Guest:** Kevin Rowland and Dexy's Midnight Runners
**Musical and Guest Performances/Cameo(s)/ Program Notes:**
- Kevin Rowland and Dexy's Midnight Runners perform "Come On, Eileen" and "The Celtic Soul Brothers."
- Guest performance by Harry Anderson (with Leslie Pollack).
- Cameos by Don King and Marv Albert.

## Season 9 (1983–1984)

**Airdate:** 10/8/83
**Episode:** 9.1
**Host:** Brandon Tartikoff
**Musical Guest:** John Cougar
**Musical and Guest Performances/Cameo(s)/ Program Notes:**
- "Live from New York": Eddie Murphy, who breaks into the office of President of NBC's Entertainment Division Brandon Tartikoff with Mary Gross and Tim Kazurinsky to figure out why he's hosting.
- Cougar performs "Pink Houses" and "Crumblin' Down."
- Cameos by film critics Roger Ebert and Gene Siskel, who review the show.

**Airdate:** 10/15/83
**Episode:** 9.2
**Host:** Danny DeVito and Rhea Perlman
**Musical Guest:** Eddy Grant
**Musical and Guest Performances/Cameo(s)/ Program Notes:**
- "Live from New York": Julia Louis-Dreyfus, in a parody of a Calvin Klein Jeans commercial.
- Eddy Grant performs "I Don't Wanna Dance," "Electric Avenue," and "Living on the Front Line."
- Cameo by Dick Cavett.

**Airdate:** 10/22/83
**Episode:** 9.3
**Host:** John Candy
**Musical Guest:** Men at Work
**Musical and Guest Performances/Cameo(s)/ Program Notes:**
- "Live from New York": Jim Belushi and John Candy (as Mr. Mambo) backstage.
- Men at Work perform "Doctor Heckyll and Mr. Jive" and "It's a Mistake."
- Debut of regular Jim Belushi.

**Airdate:** 11/5/83
**Episode:** 9.4
**Host:** Betty Thomas
**Musical Guest:** Stray Cats
**Musical and Guest Performances/Cameo(s)/ Program Notes:**
- "Live from New York": Democratic presidential candidate Jesse Jackson (Joe Piscopo).
- Stray Cats perform "She's Sexy + 17," and "I Won't Stand in Your Way" (with 14 Karat Soul).

**Airdate:** 11/12/83
**Episode:** 9.5
**Host:** Teri Garr
**Musical Guest:** Mick Fleetwood's Zoo
**Musical and Guest Performances/Cameo(s)/ Program Notes:**
- "Live from New York": Garr as a cheerleader.
- Mick Fleetwood's Zoo performs "Tonight" and "Way Down."
- Guest performance by Joel Hodgson, future creator and star of *Mystery Science Theater 3000*.

**Airdate:** 11/19/83
**Episode:** 9.6
**Host:** Jerry Lewis
**Musical Guest:** Loverboy
**Musical and Guest Performances/Cameo(s)/ Program Notes:**
- "Live from New York": Lewis, who dreams Dean Martin is the surgeon performing his bypass operation.
- Loverboy performs "Working for the Weekend."
- Florence Henderson has a cameo in a filmed segment in which people on the street are asked, "What famous person do you look like?"

**Airdate:** 12/3/83
**Episode:** 9.7
**Host:** Tom and Dick Smothers
**Musical Guest:** Big Country
**Musical and Guest Performances/Cameo(s)/ Program Notes:**

- "Live from New York": Ron Luciano, a baseball umpire who signals the start of the show following a rain delay.
- Big Country performs "In a Big Country" and "Fields of Fire."
- Cameos by Tom Seaver and Larry Holmes.

**Airdate:** 12/10/83
**Episode:** 9.8
**Host:** Flip Wilson
**Musical Guest:** Stevie Nicks
**Musical and Guest Performances/Cameo(s)/ Program Notes:**
- "Live from New York": Geraldine (Wilson), who visits her son Dion (Eddie Murphy) at his salon.
- Nicks performs "Stand Back" and "Nightbird."
- Guest performance by Joel Hodgson.

**Airdate:** 1/14/84
**Episode:** 9.9
**Host:** Father Guido Sarducci
**Musical Guest:** Huey Lewis and the News
**Musical and Guest Performances/Cameo(s)/ Program Notes:**
- "Live from New York": Joe Piscopo, who, in a National Phone-In Democratic primary, invites viewers to call a 900 number and vote for their favorite Democratic presidential candidate.
- Huey Lewis and the News perform "Heart and Soul" and "I Want a New Drug."
- Guest performance by Steven Wright.
- Rock band ZZ Top wins the Democratic runoff with Rev. Jesse Jackson coming in second with 66,968 votes.

**Airdate:** 1/21/84
**Episode:** 9.10
**Host:** Michael Palin and Mary Palin
**Musical Guest:** The Motels
**Musical and Guest Performances/Cameo(s)/ Program Notes:**
- "Live from New York": Joe Piscopo, who opens the show with a parody of Phil Donahue's talk show, only to be told by an audience member that he was mistakenly made up to look like Chinese detective Charlie Chan.
- The Motels perform "Suddenly Last Summer" and "Remember the Nights."
- *Saturday Night News*: Brad Hall's final appearance as permanent anchor. Subsequent anchors are mostly guest hosts.

**Airdate:** 1/28/84
**Episode:** 9.11
**Host:** Don Rickles
**Musical Guest:** Billy Idol
**Musical and Guest Performances/Cameo(s)/ Program Notes:**
- "Live from New York": President Ronald Reagan (Joe Piscopo) in a campaign commercial in the style of a Ronco commercial (he offers voters a set of Ginsu knives).
- Idol performs "White Wedding" and "Rebel Yell."
- Cameo appearances by Dr. Joyce Brothers, John Madden, Brandon Tartikoff, and Stevie Wonder.

**Airdate:** 2/11/84
**Episode:** 9.12
**Host:** Robin Williams
**Musical Guest:** Adam Ant
**Musical and Guest Performances/Cameo(s)/ Program Notes:**
- "Live from New York": Joe Piscopo, reporting on the U.S. bobsledding team at the Winter Olympics.
- Adam Ant performs "Strip" and "Goody Two Shoes."
- Guest performance by comedian Paula Poundstone.

**Airdate:** 2/18/84
**Episode:** 9.13
**Host:** Jamie Lee Curtis
**Musical Guest:** The Fixx
**Musical and Guest Performances/Cameo(s)/ Program Notes:**

Appendix A

- "Live from New York": A rap by Jimmy B (Jim Belushi).
- The Fixx performs "One Thing Leads to Another" and "Red Skies at Night."

**Airdate:** 2/25/84
**Episode:** 9.14
**Host:** Edwin Newman
**Musical Guest:** Kool and the Gang
**Musical and Guest Performances/Cameo(s)/ Program Notes:**
- "Live from New York": Dion (Eddie Murphy) and his assistant Blaire (Joe Piscopo) are the new official *SNL* hairdressers.
- Kool and the Gang sings "Joanna" and "Celebration."
- Special guest appearance by Harry Anderson.
- Cameo by Robin Williams.

**Airdate:** 3/17/84
**Episode:** 9.15
**Host:** Billy Crystal
**Musical Guest:** Al Jarreau
**Musical and Guest Performances/Cameo(s)/ Program Notes:**
- "Live from New York": Irish reporter Siobhan Cahill (Mary Gross), reporting on St. Patrick's Day festivities.
- Jarreau performs "Mornin'" and "Trouble in Paradise."
- Cameo by Ed Koch.

**Airdate:** 4/7/84
**Episode:** 9.16
**Host:** Michael Douglas
**Musical Guest:** Deniece Williams
**Musical and Guest Performances/Cameo(s)/ Program Notes:**
- "Live from New York": Douglas, who has lost his script, is given a replacement by Karl Malden in a parody of the American Express commercial.
- Williams performs "Let's Hear It for the Boy" and "Wrapped Up."

**Airdate:** 4/14/84
**Episode:** 9.17
**Host:** George McGovern
**Musical Guest:** Madness
**Musical and Guest Performances/Cameo(s)/ Program Notes:**
- "Live from New York": Richard Nixon (Joe Piscopo), interviewed on *60 Minutes*.
- Madness performs "Our House" and "Keep Moving."
- Cameos by Eleanor McGovern, Frankie Pace, and Clara Peller ("Where's the beef?").

**Airdate:** 5/5/84
**Episode:** 9.18
**Host:** Barry Bostwick
**Musical Guest:** Spinal Tap
**Musical and Guest Performances/Cameo(s)/ Program Notes:**
- "Live from New York": Mary Gross and Julia Louis-Dreyfus after a simulated catfight.
- Spinal Tap performs "Christmas with the Devil" and "Big Bottom."
- Special guest appearance by Billy Crystal.
- Cameos by A. Whitney Brown and Soupy Sales.

**Airdate:** 5/12/84
**Episode:** 9.19
**Host:** Billy Crystal, Ed Koch, Edwin Newman, Betty Thomas, Father Guido Sarducci
**Musical Guest:** The Cars
**Musical and Guest Performances/Cameo(s)/ Program Notes:**
- "Live from New York": Frank Sinatra (Joe Piscopo) and Sammy Davis Jr. (Crystal).
- The Cars perform "Magic" and "Drive."
- Final episode for Robin Duke, Brad Hall, Tim Kazurinsky, and Joe Piscopo.

# Season 10 (1984–1985)

**Airdate:** 10/6/84
**Episode:** 10.1
**Host:** No host
**Musical Guest:** Thompson Twins
**Musical and Guest Performances/Cameo(s)/ Program Notes:**
- Thompson Twins perform "Hold Me Now" and "The Gap."
- Debut of regulars Billy Crystal, Christopher Guest, Rich Hall, Martin Short, Pamela Stephenson, and the return of Harry Shearer.

**Airdate:** 10/13/84
**Episode:** 10.2
**Host:** Bob Uecker
**Musical Guest:** Peter Wolf
**Musical and Guest Performances/Cameo(s)/ Program Notes:**
- "Live from New York": Robin Williams (Martin Short) on *Password*.
- Wolf performs "Lights Out" and "I Need You Tonight."

**Airdate:** 10/20/84
**Episode:** 10.3
**Host:** Jesse Jackson
**Musical Guest:** Andrae Crouch, Wintley Phipps
**Musical and Guest Performances/Cameo(s)/ Program Notes:**
- "Live from New York": Sammy Davis Jr. (Billy Crystal), who coaches Reverend Jesse Jackson for his hosting gig.
- Crouch performs "Right Now."
- Phipps performs "Tell Me Again."

**Airdate:** 11/3/84
**Episode:** 10.4
**Host:** Michael McKean
**Musical Guest:** Chaka Khan
**Musical and Guest Performances/Cameo(s)/ Program Notes:**
- Chaka Khan performs "I Feel for You" and "This Is My Night."
- The Folksmen, a musical group featuring Mark Shubb (Harry Shearer), Alan Barrows (Christopher Guest), and Jerry Palter (McKean) perform "Old Joe's Place." The musical trio are featured in Guest's 2003 mockumentary *A Mighty Wind*.

**Airdate:** 11/10/84
**Episode:** 10.5
**Host:** George Carlin
**Musical Guest:** Frankie Goes to Hollywood
**Musical and Guest Performances/Cameo(s)/ Program Notes:**
- "Live from New York": Gary Kroeger, who, after the 1984 election, realizes his Walter Mondale imitation was a waste of time.
- Frankie Goes to Hollywood performs "Two Tribes" and "Born to Run."

**Airdate:** 11/17/84
**Episode:** 10.6
**Host:** Ed Asner
**Musical Guest:** The Kinks
**Musical and Guest Performances/Cameo(s)/ Program Notes:**
- "Live from New York": Ted Baxter (Billy Crystal) in a *Mary Tyler Moore Show* sketch.
- The Kinks perform "Do It Again" and "Word of Mouth."

**Airdate:** 12/1/84
**Episode:** 10.7
**Host:** Ed Begley, Jr.
**Musical Guest:** Billy Squier
**Musical and Guest Performances/Cameo(s)/ Program Notes:**
- "Live from New York": Michael Reagan (Jim Belushi).
- Squier performs "Rock Me Tonight" and "All Night Long."
- *Saturday Night News*: Christopher Guest's debut as anchor.

**Airdate:** 12/8/84
**Episode:** 10.8

**Host:** Ringo Starr
**Musical Guest:** Herbie Hancock
**Musical and Guest Performances/Cameo(s)/Program Notes:**
- "Live from New York": Ringo Starr, who is for sale at a Beatles memorabilia auction.
- Hancock performs "Junku" and "Rockit."

**Airdate:** 12/15/84
**Episode:** 10.9
**Host:** Eddie Murphy
**Musical Guest:** Robert Plant and the Honeydrippers
**Musical and Guest Performances/Cameo(s)/Program Notes:**
- Plant and the Honeydrippers perform "Rockin' at Midnight" and "Santa Claus Is Back in Town."

**Airdate:** 1/12/85
**Episode:** 10.10
**Host:** Kathleen Turner
**Musical Guest:** John Waite
**Musical and Guest Performances/Cameo(s)/Program Notes:**
- "Live from New York": Fernando (Billy Crystal), backstage in Phil Donahue's greenroom.
- Waite performs "Saturday Night."
- Harry Shearer's final episode.

**Airdate:** 1/19/85
**Episode:** 10.11
**Host:** Roy Scheider
**Musical Guest:** Billy Ocean
**Musical and Guest Performances/Cameo(s)/Program Notes:**
- Ocean performs "Caribbean Queen" and "Loverboy."
- Guest performance by comedian Steven Wright.

**Airdate:** 2/2/85
**Episode:** 10.12
**Host:** Alex Karras
**Musical Guest:** Tina Turner
**Musical and Guest Performances/Cameo(s)/Program Notes:**
- "Live from New York": Prince (Billy Crystal).
- Turner performs "What's Love Got to Do with It," "Better Be Good to Me," and "Private Dancer."

**Airdate:** 2/9/85
**Episode:** 10.13
**Host:** Harry Anderson
**Musical Guest:** Bryan Adams
**Musical and Guest Performances/Cameo(s)/Program Notes:**
- "Live from New York": Robert Latta (Rich Hall), a water meter reader who unlawfully entered the executive residence of the White House on the day of Reagan's inauguration.
- Adams performs "Somebody" and "Run to You."
- Cameos by Johnny Cash, June Carter Cash, Waylon Jennings, and Christopher Reeve.
- At the end of the show, Harry Anderson invites Carol Burnett, who is sitting in the audience, onstage.

**Airdate:** 2/16/85
**Episode:** 10.14
**Host:** Pamela Sue Martin
**Musical Guest:** Power Station
**Musical and Guest Performances/Cameo(s)/Program Notes:**
- Power Station performs "Some Like It Hot" and "Get It On (Bang a Gong)."

**Airdate:** 3/30/85
**Episode:** 10.15
**Host:** Mr. T and Hulk Hogan
**Musical Guest:** The Commodores
**Musical and Guest Performances/Cameo(s)/Program Notes:**
- "Live from New York": Mr. T, Hulk Hogan, and Prince (Billy Crystal).
- The Commodores perform "Night Shift" and "Animal Instinct."

Episode Guide

**Airdate:** 4/6/85
**Episode:** 10.16
**Host:** Christopher Reeve
**Musical Guest:** Santana
**Musical and Guest Performances/Cameo(s)/ Program Notes:**
- "Live from New York": Pope John Paul II (Jim Belushi).
- Santana performs "Say It Again" and "Right Now."
- Guest performance by comedian Steven Wright.

**Airdate:** 4/13/85
**Episode:** 10.17
**Host:** Howard Cosell
**Musical Guest:** Greg Kihn
**Musical and Guest Performances/Cameo(s)/ Program Notes:**
- "Live from New York": Willie (Billy Crystal) and Frankie (Christopher Guest).
- Kihn performs "Boys Won't" and "Lucky."
- Final episode for Billy Crystal, Mary Gross, Christopher Guest, Gary Kroeger, Julia Louis-Dreyfus, Martin Short, and Pamela Stephenson.

## Season II (1985–1986)

**Airdate:** 11/9/85
**Episode:** 11.1
**Host:** Madonna
**Musical Guest:** Simple Minds
**Musical and Guest Performances/Cameo(s)/ Program Notes:**
- "Live from New York": Anthony Michael Hall, after taking a mandatory blood test and the NBC pledge to remain drug free, which is administered by Brandon Tartikoff.
- Simple Minds perform "Alive and Kicking."
- Guest performance by Penn & Teller. Teller almost drowns during a water tank trick.
- Debut of regulars Joan Cusack, Robert Downey Jr., Nora Dunn, Anthony Michael Hall, Jon Lovitz, Dennis Miller, Randy Quaid, Terry Sweeney, and Danitra Vance.
- Debut of featured players Dan Vitale and Damon Wayans; Don Novello, who appeared as a featured player in season 4, returns.
- *Weekend Update*: Miller takes over as anchor.

**Airdate:** 11/16/85
**Episode:** 11.2

**Host:** Chevy Chase
**Musical Guest:** Sheila E.
**Musical and Guest Performances/Cameo(s)/ Program Notes:**
- "Live from New York": Chevy Chase as a fire chief, who faints after ordering his men to check every door during a fire.
- Sheila E. performs "Hollyrock" and "A Love Bizarre."
- Sketch Debut: *The Pat Stevens Show*, hosted by Pat Stevens (Nora Dunn).
- Character Debut: Pathological liar Tommy Flanagan.

**Airdate:** 11/23/85
**Episode:** 11.3
**Host:** Pee-wee Herman
**Musical Guest:** Queen Ida and the Bon Temps Zydeco Band
**Musical and Guest Performances/Cameo(s)/ Program Notes:**
- "Live from New York": Pee-wee Herman, who walks a tightrope between the Twin Towers.
- Queen Ida performs "La Louisiane" and "Frisco Zydeco."

**Airdate:** 12/7/85
**Episode:** 11.4

Appendix A

**Host:** John Lithgow
**Musical Guest:** Mr. Mister
**Musical and Guest Performances/Cameo(s)/ Program Notes:**
- "Live from New York": Dr. Federico (John Lithgow), a mad scientist, warns President Reagan (Randy Quaid) about Halley's Comet heading toward Earth.
- Mr. Mister perform "Broken Wings" and "Kyrie."

**Airdate:** 12/14/85
**Episode:** 11.5
**Host:** Tom Hanks
**Musical Guest:** Sade
**Musical and Guest Performances/Cameo(s)/ Program Notes:**
- "Live from New York": Robb Weller (Tom Hanks).
- Sade performs "Is It a Crime" and "The Sweetest Taboo."
- Guest performance by comic Steven Wright.

**Airdate:** 12/21/85
**Episode:** 11.6
**Host:** Teri Garr
**Musical Guest:** Dream Academy, the Cult
**Musical and Guest Performances/Cameo(s)/ Program Notes:**
- "Live from New York": Sung by teenager Cabrini Green (Danitra Vance) and a rapping department store gift wrapper named "The Gifted Wrapper" (Damon Wayans).
- Dream Academy perform "Life in a Northern Town."
- The Cult performs "She Sells Sanctuary."
- Guest performance by Penn & Teller.

**Airdate:** 1/18/86
**Episode:** 11.7
**Host:** Harry Dean Stanton
**Musical Guest:** The Replacements
**Musical and Guest Performances/Cameo(s)/ Program Notes:**
- "Live from New York": Dennis Miller, reporting from a press conference for Burger King spokesman Herb (Randy Quaid), the only man in America to never have a Whopper.
- The Replacements perform "Bastards of the Young" and "Kiss Me on the Bus." The band appeared to be heavily intoxicated when performing their second song.
- Guest performance by comic Sam Kinison.

**Airdate:** 1/25/86
**Episode:** 11.8
**Host:** Dudley Moore
**Musical Guest:** Al Green
**Musical and Guest Performances/Cameo(s)/ Program Notes:**
- "Live from New York": Brother Kenny (Robert Downey Jr.), a monk.
- Green performs "Going Away" and "True Love."

**Airdate:** 2/8/86
**Episode:** 11.9
**Host:** Ron Reagan
**Musical Guest:** The Nelsons
**Musical and Guest Performances/Cameo(s)/ Program Notes:**
- "Live from New York": Ron Reagan, who has fun *Risky Business*-style in the White House.
- The Nelsons perform "Walk Away" and "Do You Know What I Mean."
- Guest performance by Penn & Teller.

**Airdate:** 2/15/86
**Episode:** 11.10
**Host:** Jerry Hall
**Musical Guest:** Stevie Ray Vaughan and Double Trouble
**Musical and Guest Performances/Cameo(s)/ Program Notes:**
- "Live from New York": Mick Jagger, who interrupts pathological liar Tommy Flanagan (Jon Lovitz) trying to pick up Jerry Hall.

Episode Guide   447

- Vaughan and Double Trouble perform "Say What" and, with Jimmie Vaughn, "Change It."
- Guest performance by comedian Sam Kinison.

**Airdate:** 2/22/86
**Episode:** 11.11
**Host:** Jay Leno
**Musical Guest:** The Neville Brothers
**Musical and Guest Performances/Cameo(s)/ Program Notes:**
- "Live from New York": Jay Leno, who gets a backstage tour from Tommy Flanagan (Jon Lovitz).
- The Neville Brothers perform "Studio Tour," "The Big Chief," and "The Midnight Key."
- Debut of featured player A. Whitney Brown.

**Airdate:** 3/15/86
**Episode:** 11.12
**Host:** Griffin Dunne
**Musical Guest:** Rosanne Cash
**Musical and Guest Performances/Cameo(s)/ Program Notes:**
- "Live from New York": Tommy Flanagan (Jon Lovitz) comments on *SNL*'s big ratings.
- Cash performs "Hold On" and "I Don't Know Why."
- Guest performance by Penn & Teller.
- In the "Mr. Monopoly" sketch, Damon Wayans plays the part of a police officer as a gay stereotype, which is different from how he played it in dress rehearsal. He is fired by Lorne Michaels for improvising.

**Airdate:** 3/22/86
**Episode:** 11.13
**Host:** George Wendt, Francis Ford Coppola
**Musical Guest:** Phillip Glass
**Musical and Guest Performances/Cameo(s)/ Program Notes:**
- Glass performs "Lightning," "Rubric," and during the Grand Finale.
- In a parody of himself, Coppola is seen throughout the episode directing Wendt and the cast.
- Al Franken returns as a featured player.

**Airdate:** 4/12/86
**Episode:** 11.14
**Host:** Oprah Winfrey
**Musical Guest:** Joe Jackson
**Musical and Guest Performances/Cameo(s)/ Program Notes:**
- "Live from New York": Oprah Winfrey, who refuses to wear her Aunt Jemima outfit for the first sketch.
- Jackson performs "Right and Wrong" and "Soul Kiss."

**Airdate:** 4/19/86
**Episode:** 11.15
**Host:** Tony Danza
**Musical Guest:** Laurie Anderson
**Musical and Guest Performances/Cameo(s)/ Program Notes:**
- "Live from New York": Soldiers (Robert Downey Jr., Anthony Michael Hall) and Randy Quaid.
- Anderson performs "Baby Doll" and "Day the Devil."
- Guest performance by Penn & Teller.

**Airdate:** 5/10/86
**Episode:** 11.16
**Host:** Catherine Oxenberg, Paul Simon
**Musical Guest:** Ladysmith Black Mambazo
**Musical and Guest Performances/Cameo(s)/ Program Notes:**
- "Live from New York": Paul Simon, after performing "You Can Call Me Al."
- Simon performs "Graceland" and, with Ladysmith Black Mambazo, "Homeless."
- Guest performance by Penn & Teller.
- Oxenberg's mother, Princess Elizabeth of Yugoslavia, has a cameo.

**Airdate:** 5/17/86
**Episode:** 11.17

**Host:** Jimmy Breslin
**Musical Guest:** Level 42, E. G. Daily
**Musical and Guest Performances/Cameo(s)/ Program Notes:**
- "Live from New York": Middleweight champion of the world, boxer Marvelous Marvin Hagler.
- Level 42 performs "Something About You."
- E. G. Daily performs "Say It, Say It."
- Guest performance by comedian Sam Kinison.

**Airdate:** 5/24/86
**Episode:** 11.18
**Host:** Anjelica Huston, Billy Martin
**Musical Guest:** George Clinton and Parliament-Funkadelic
**Musical and Guest Performances/Cameo(s)/ Program Notes:**
- "Live from New York": Kevin Brennan (Randy Quaid), a one-legged runner, can't convince the people participating in "Hands Across America" to break the chain to let him through.
- Clinton and Parliament-Funkadelic perform "Let's Take It to the Stage" (with Thomas Dolby) and "Do Fries Go with That Shake."
- In the final cliff-hanger, the cast, except for Jon Lovitz, are trapped in a burning room.
- Guest performance by Damon Wayans, who was fired after episode 11.12.
- Final episode for Al Franken, Joan Cusack, Robert Downey Jr., Anthony Michael Hall, Randy Quaid, Terry Sweeney, and Danitra Vance.

## Season 12 (1986–1987)

**Airdate:** 10/11/86
**Episode:** 12.1
**Host:** Sigourney Weaver
**Musical Guest:** Buster Poindexter
**Musical and Guest Performances/Cameo(s)/ Program Notes:**
- "Live from New York": Madonna, who reads a statement informing viewers that last season was a horrible dream (like season 8 of *Dallas*).
- Buster Poindexter performs "Smack Dab in the Middle" and, with Sigourney Weaver, "Baby, It's Cold Outside."
- Special guest appearance by playwright Christopher Durang.
- Debut of regulars Dana Carvey, Phil Hartman, Jan Hooks, Victoria Jackson, and Dennis Miller, who anchors *Weekend Update*, and featured player Kevin Nealon.
- Sketch Debut: *Church Chat*, hosted by the Church Lady (Dana Carvey).
- Character Debut: Mr. Subliminal (Kevin Nealon).

**Airdate:** 10/18/86
**Episode:** 12.2
**Host:** Malcolm-Jamal Warner
**Musical Guest:** Run-DMC
**Musical and Guest Performances/Cameo(s)/ Program Notes:**
- "Live from New York": Ed Jaymes (A. Whitney Brown) of Bartles & Jaymes.
- Run-DMC perform "Walk This Way" and "Hit It, Run."
- Special guest Buster Poindexter performs "Hit the Road Jack" with Soozie Tyrell.
- Guest performance from comedian Sam Kinison.
- Cameo by director Spike Lee.

**Airdate:** 11/8/86
**Episode:** 12.3
**Host:** Rosanna Arquette
**Musical Guest:** Ric Ocasek
**Musical and Guest Performances/Cameo(s)/ Program Notes:**

- "Live from New York": Rosanna Arquette opens the show, though the cold open is preceded by a fake newsreel in which New York Mets pitcher Ron Darling publicly apologizes on behalf of the Mets for preempting the show when Game 6 of the World Series ran overtime (ten innings) on October 25, 1986. The Mets won the game and the series. The show was taped that evening between 1 a.m. and 3:30 a.m. It was the first time the show was pretaped for a later broadcast.
- Ric Ocasek performs "Emotion in Motion" and "Keep on Laughin'" and is a guest on *Church Chat*.

**Airdate:** 11/15/86
**Episode:** 12.4
**Host:** Sam Kinison
**Musical Guest:** Lou Reed
**Musical and Guest Performances/Cameo(s)/ Program Notes:**
- "Live from New York": Sam Kinison, after planting a kiss on the Church Lady (Dana Carvey).
- Reed performs "I Love You, Suzanne" and "Original Wrapper."

**Airdate:** 11/22/86
**Episode:** 12.5
**Host:** Robin Williams
**Musical Guest:** Paul Simon
**Musical and Guest Performances/Cameo(s)/ Program Notes:**
- "Live from New York": President Ronald Reagan (Robin Williams).
- Simon sings "Diamonds on the Soles of Her Shoes," "The Boy in the Bubble," and "The Late Great Johnny Ace."
- Cameos by Art Garfunkel and Whoopi Goldberg.

**Airdate:** 12/6/86
**Episode:** 12.6
**Host:** Chevy Chase, Steve Martin, and Martin Short
**Musical Guest:** Randy Newman
**Musical and Guest Performances/Cameo(s)/ Program Notes:**
- "Live from New York": Chevy Chase, after taking a fall.
- Randy Newman sings "Longest Night" and "Roll with the Punches."
- Chevy Chase's fifth time hosting.
- Cameo by Eric Idle.

**Airdate:** 12/13/86
**Episode:** 12.7
**Host:** Steve Guttenberg
**Musical Guest:** The Pretenders
**Musical and Guest Performances/Cameo(s)/ Program Notes:**
- "Live from New York": Mr. Rafsan-Jani (Jon Lovitz), of the Iranian National Assembly.
- The Pretenders sing "Don't Get me Wrong," "How Much Did You Get for Your Soul?," and, with Buster Poindexter, "Rockin' Good Way."
- "Film Short": *Bob Roberts*, which was the basis for the 1992 mockumentary written by, directed by, and starring Tim Robbins.
- Guest performance by Penn & Teller.

**Airdate:** 12/20/86
**Episode:** 12.8
**Host:** William Shatner
**Musical Guest:** Lone Justice
**Musical and Guest Performances/Cameo(s)/ Program Notes:**
- "Live from New York": Oliver North (William Shatner).
- Lone Justice performs "Shelter" and "I Found Love."
- Guest performance by Buster Poindexter, who sings "Zat You, Santa?"
- ★★★★ Four-Star Sketches: "16th Annual *Star Trek* Convention," in which Shatner tells Trekkies to get a life; parody of *It's a Wonderful Life*.

**Airdate:** 1/24/87
**Episode:** 12.9
**Host:** Joe Montana, Walter Payton
**Musical Guest:** Debbie Harry

Appendix A

**Musical and Guest Performances/Cameo(s)/ Program Notes:**
- "Live from New York": Hotsni (Jon Lovitz), on the "NFL Video Countdown."
- Harry performs "French Kissin' in the USA" (with Chris Stein) and "In Love with Love."

**Airdate:** 1/31/87
**Episode:** 12.10
**Host:** Paul Shaffer
**Musical Guest:** Bruce Hornsby and the Range
**Musical and Guest Performances/Cameo(s)/ Program Notes:**
- "Live from New York": Paul Shaffer, his dressing room.
- Bruce Hornsby and the Range perform "The Way It Is" and "Mandolin Rain."

**Airdate:** 2/14/87
**Episode:** 12.11
**Host:** Bronson Pinchot
**Musical Guest:** Paul Young
**Musical and Guest Performances/Cameo(s)/ Program Notes:**
- "Live from New York": The recently deceased Liberace (Phil Hartman).
- Paul Young performs "War Games" and "The Long Run."
- Special guest Buster Poindexter sings "Heart of Gold" (with Soozie Tyrell).
- Cameo appearance by Paulina Porizkova.

**Airdate:** 2/21/87
**Episode:** 12.12
**Host/Musical Guest:** Willie Nelson
**Musical and Guest Performances/Cameo(s)/ Program Notes:**
- "Live from New York": Liberace (Phil Hartman) in *Afterlife Styles of the Rich and Famous*.
- Guest appearance by Danny DeVito.
- Nelson sings "Nightlife," "Partners After All," "Blue Eyes," and "The Boyfriend Song" (with Victoria Jackson).

**Airdate:** 2/28/87
**Episode:** 12.13
**Host:** Valerie Bertinelli
**Musical Guest:** Robert Cray Band
**Musical and Guest Performances/Cameo(s)/ Program Notes:**
- "Live from New York": Ronald Reagan (Phil Hartman).
- Robert Cray Band performs "Smoking Gun" and "Right Next Door."
- Cameos by Edwin Newman and Bertinelli's husband, Eddie Van Halen.

**Airdate:** 3/21/87
**Episode:** 12.14
**Host:** Bill Murray
**Musical Guest:** Percy Sledge
**Musical and Guest Performances/Cameo(s)/ Program Notes:**
- "Live from New York": Bill Murray, backstage at the show.
- Sledge performs "When a Man Loves a Woman."

**Airdate:** 3/28/87
**Episode:** 12.15
**Host:** Charlton Heston
**Musical Guest:** Wynton Marsalis
**Musical and Guest Performances/Cameo(s)/ Program Notes:**
- "Live from New York": God (Charlton Heston), who pays Oral Roberts (Phil Hartman) a visit.
- Wynton Marsalis performs "J Mood" and "Juan (E. Mustard)."
- "Film Short": A parody of *The Color of Money* features Ben Stiller as Tom Cruise, John Mahoney as Paul Newman, and appearances by Anne Meara, Jerry Stiller, Danny Aiello, Julie Hagerty, and Nina Tremblay.

**Airdate:** 4/11/87
**Episode:** 12.16
**Host:** John Lithgow
**Musical Guest:** Anita Baker
**Musical and Guest Performances/Cameo(s)/ Program Notes:**

- "Live from New York": A Marine commander (John Lithgow) in the American embassy in Moscow.
- Baker performs "Sweet Love" and "Same Ole Love."

**Airdate:** 4/18/87
**Episode:** 12.17
**Host:** John Larroquette
**Musical Guest:** Timbuk 3
**Musical and Guest Performances/Cameo(s)/ Program Notes:**
- "Live from New York": Casey Kasem (Dana Carvey), appearing in the *Pagan Easter Special.*
- Timbuk 3 performs "Just Another Movie" and "Hairstyles and Attitudes."

**Airdate:** 5/9/87
**Episode:** 12.18
**Host:** Mark Harmon
**Musical Guest:** Suzanne Vega
**Musical and Guest Performances/Cameo(s)/ Program Notes:**
- "Live from New York": Chase Steele (Mark Harmon), in a political parody of *Charlie's Angels.*
- Vega performs "Luka" and "Marlene on the Wall."

**Airdate:** 5/16/87
**Episode:** 12.19
**Host:** Garry Shandling
**Musical Guest:** Los Lobos
**Musical and Guest Performances/Cameo(s)/ Program Notes:**
- "Live from New York": Robert McFarlane (Phil Hartman), during the Iran-Contra Hearings.
- Los Lobos perform "Is That All There Is" and "One Time, One Night."
- Cameos by Nell Campbell and Tracey Ullman.

**Airdate:** 5/23/87
**Episode:** 12.20
**Host:** Dennis Hopper
**Musical Guest:** Roy Orbison
**Musical and Guest Performances/Cameo(s)/ Program Notes:**
- "Live from New York": Billy (Dennis Hopper) from *Easy Rider.*
- Orbison performs "Crying," "Pretty Woman," and "In Dreams."

## Season 13 (1987–1988)

**Airdate:** 10/17/87
**Episode:** 13.1
**Host:** Steve Martin
**Musical Guest:** Sting
**Musical and Guest Performances/Cameo(s)/ Program Notes:**
- "Live from New York": Judge Robert Bork (Jon Lovitz).
- Sting performs "We'll Be Together" and "Little Wing" (with special guest Branford Marsalis).
- Cameo by Bruce Babbitt.
- Sketch Debut: *Pumping Up with Hans & Franz,* hosted by Hans (Dana Carvey) and Franz (Kevin Nealon).

**Airdate:** 10/24/87
**Episode:** 13.2
**Host:** Sean Penn
**Musical Guest:** LL Cool J, Michael Penn and the Pull
**Musical and Guest Performances/Cameo(s)/ Program Notes:**
- "Live from New York": Sean Penn in *Fatal Attraction II* with LL Cool J as Alex Forrest, who Penn was involved with when he was in prison.
- LL Cool J performs "Go Cut Creator Go."
- The Pull performs "This & That."

**Airdate:** 10/31/87
**Episode:** 13.3
**Host:** Dabney Coleman
**Musical Guest:** The Cars

**Musical and Guest Performances/Cameo(s)/ Program Notes:**
- "Live from New York": Robin Leach (Dana Carvey), host of *Lifestyles of the Rich, Famous and Scary*.
- The Cars perform "Strap Me In" and "Double Trouble."
- Guest appearance by Elvira.

**Airdate:** 11/14/87
**Episode:** 13.4
**Host:** Robert Mitchum
**Musical Guest:** Simply Red
**Musical and Guest Performances/Cameo(s)/ Program Notes:**
- "Live from New York": Jeffrey Bell (Phil Hartman), political operative.
- Simply Red performs "The Right Thing" and "Suffer."
- Cameos by Jane Greer, Mitchum's costar from the film *Out of the Past* (1947), and his grandson, Bentley Mitchum.

**Airdate:** 11/21/87
**Episode:** 13.5
**Host:** Candice Bergen
**Musical Guest:** Cher
**Musical and Guest Performances/Cameo(s)/ Program Notes:**
- "Live from New York": President George H. W. Bush (Dana Carvey).
- Cher performs "We All Sleep Alone" and "I Found Someone."
- Cameos by the Mayflower Madam, Sydney Biddle Barrows, who Bergen played in a 1987 made-for-TV movie, and Paul Shaffer.

**Airdate:** 12/5/87
**Episode:** 13.6
**Host:** Danny DeVito
**Musical Guest:** Bryan Ferry
**Musical and Guest Performances/Cameo(s)/ Program Notes:**
- "Live from New York": Mikhail Gorbachev (Danny DeVito).
- Ferry performs "The Right Stuff" and "Kiss and Tell."

**Airdate:** 12/12/87
**Episode:** 13.7
**Host:** Angie Dickinson
**Musical Guest:** Buster Poindexter, David Gilmour
**Musical and Guest Performances/Cameo(s)/ Program Notes:**
- "Live from New York": Gorbachev's translator (Kevin Nealon), who says, "Live, outta New York, it's night, this Saturday!"
- Poindexter performs "Hot Hot Hot" with Soozie Tyrell, the Banshees of Blue, and the Uptown Horns.
- Gilmour performs "Song for My Sara."

**Airdate:** 12/19/87
**Episode:** 13.8
**Host:** Paul Simon
**Musical Guest:** Linda Ronstadt and the Mariachi Vargas de Tecalitlán
**Musical and Guest Performances/Cameo(s)/ Program Notes:**
- "Live from New York": Mary Magdalene (Jan Hooks).
- Ronstadt performs "Los Laureles" and "La Cigarra" with the Mariachi Vargas de Tecatitlán.
- Simon and Ronstadt perform "Under African Skies."

**Airdate:** 1/23/88
**Episode:** 13.9
**Host:** Robin Williams
**Musical Guest:** James Taylor
**Musical and Guest Performances/Cameo(s)/ Program Notes:**
- "Live from New York": Hans (Dana Carvey) and Franz (Kevin Nealon).
- Taylor performs "Never Die Young," "Sweet Potato Pie," and "Lonesome Road."

**Airdate:** 1/30/88
**Episode:** 13.10
**Host:** Carl Weathers
**Musical Guest:** Robbie Robertson

**Musical and Guest Performances/Cameo(s)/ Program Notes:**
- "Live from New York": President George H. W. Bush (Dana Carvey).
- Robertson performs "Testimony" and "Somewhere down the Crazy River."

**Airdate:** 2/13/88
**Episode:** 13.11
**Host:** Justine Bateman
**Musical Guest:** Terence Trent D'Arby
**Musical and Guest Performances/Cameo(s)/ Program Notes:**
- "Live from New York": Republican presidential candidate Bob Dole (Dan Aykroyd) at the Republican debate.
- D'Arby performs "Wishing Well" and "Under My Thumb."

**Airdate:** 2/20/88
**Episode:** 13.12
**Host:** Tom Hanks

**Musical Guest:** Randy Travis
**Musical and Guest Performances/Cameo(s)/ Program Notes:**
- "Live from New York": Mark Mossano (Tom Hanks), a terrible American figure skater at the '88 Calgary Olympics.
- Travis performs "Forever and Ever, Amen" and "What'll You Do."

**Airdate:** 2/27/88
**Episode:** 13.13
**Host:** Judge Reinhold
**Musical Guest:** 10,000 Maniacs
**Musical and Guest Performances/Cameo(s)/ Program Notes:**
- "Live from New York": Hans (Dana Carvey) and Franz (Kevin Nealon).
- 10,000 Maniacs perform "Like the Weather" and "What's the Matter Here."

## Season 14 (1988–1989)

**Airdate:** 10/8/88
**Episode:** 14.1
**Host:** Tom Hanks
**Musical Guest:** Keith Richards
**Musical and Guest Performances/Cameo(s)/ Program Notes:**
- "Live from New York": Hans (Dana Carvey) and Franz (Kevin Nealon).
- Richards performs "Take It So Hard" and "Struggle" (with Steve Jordan and Ivan Neville).
- Al Franken returns (again) as a featured player.

**Airdate:** 10/15/88
**Episode:** 14.2
**Host:** Matthew Broderick
**Musical Guest:** The Sugarcubes
**Musical and Guest Performances/Cameo(s)/ Program Notes:**
- "Live from New York": Dan Quayle (Matthew Broderick).
- The Sugarcubes perform "Birthday" and "Motorcrash."
- Cameos by Douglas McGrath, Laurie Metcalf, Fred Newman, and Catherine O'Hara.
- ★ ★ ★ ★ Four-Star Sketch: "Nude Beach."

**Airdate:** 10/22/88
**Episode:** 14.3
**Host:** John Larroquette
**Musical Guest:** Randy Newman, Mark Knopfler
**Musical and Guest Performances/Cameo(s)/ Program Notes:**
- "Live from New York": Michael Dukakis (Jon Lovitz).
- Randy Newman and Mark Knopfler sing "It's Money That Matters" and "Dixie Flyer."

**Airdate:** 11/5/88
**Episode:** 14.4

**Host:** Matthew Modine
**Musical Guest:** Edie Brickell and New Bohemians
**Musical and Guest Performances/Cameo(s)/ Program Notes:**
- "Live from New York": Drill Sergeant McCarthy (Phil Hartman).
- Edie Brickell and New Bohemians perform "What I Am" and "Little Miss S."
- Cameo by Morton Downey Jr.

**Airdate:** 11/12/88
**Episode:** 14.5
**Host:** Demi Moore
**Musical Guest:** Johnny Clegg and Savuka
**Musical and Guest Performances/Cameo(s)/ Program Notes:**
- "Live from New York": George H. W. Bush (Dana Carvey) and his grandchildren (one of whom is played by six-year-old Kirsten Dunst, who would host *SNL* in 2002 [27.19]).
- Johnny Clegg and Savuka perform "I Call Your Name" and "Take My Heart Away."
- Cameo by Bruce Willis.

**Airdate:** 11/19/88
**Episode:** 14.6
**Host:** John Lithgow
**Musical Guest:** Tracy Chapman
**Musical and Guest Performances/Cameo(s)/ Program Notes:**
- "Live from New York": Director of *The Oprah Winfrey Show* (voice of Dana Carvey).
- Chapman performs "Mountains O' Things," "Freedom Now," and "Baby, Can I Hold You."

**Airdate:** 12/3/88
**Episode:** 14.7
**Host:** Danny DeVito
**Musical Guest:** The Bangles
**Musical and Guest Performances/Cameo(s)/ Program Notes:**
- "Live from New York": Arnold Schwarzenegger, who appears with Hans and Franz (Dana Carvey, Kevin Nealon).
- The Bangles perform "In Your Room" and "Hazy Shade of Winter."

**Airdate:** 12/10/88
**Episode:** 14.8
**Host:** Kevin Kline
**Musical Guest:** Bobby McFerrin
**Musical and Guest Performances/Cameo(s)/ Program Notes:**
- "Live from New York": Donald and Ivana Trump (Phil Hartman and Jan Hooks).
- McFerrin sings "Drive" and "The Star-Spangled Banner."

**Airdate:** 12/17/88
**Episode:** 14.9
**Host:** Melanie Griffith
**Musical Guest:** Little Feat
**Musical and Guest Performances/Cameo(s)/ Program Notes:**
- "Live from New York": The Church Lady (Dana Carvey), who is visited by Mephistopheles (Jon Lovitz).
- Little Feat sings "Let It Roll" and "Hate to Lose Your Lovin'."
- Cameo by Don Johnson.
- "Schiller's Reel": *Love Is a Dream*.

**Airdate:** 1/21/89
**Episode:** 14.10
**Host:** John Malkovich
**Musical Guest:** Anita Baker
**Musical and Guest Performances/Cameo(s)/ Program Notes:**
- "Live from New York": The voice of Ronald Reagan (Phil Hartman).
- Baker sings "Giving You the Best That I Got" and "Just Because."
- Debut of featured player Mike Myers.

**Airdate:** 1/28/89
**Episode:** 14.11
**Host:** Tony Danza
**Musical Guest:** John Hiatt and the Goners

**Musical and Guest Performances/Cameo(s)/ Program Notes:**
- "Live from New York": Serial killer Ted Bundy (Dana Carvey), who was electrocuted on January 24, 1989.
- John Hiatt and the Goners sing "Paper Thin" and "Slow Turning."

**Airdate:** 2/11/89
**Episode:** 14.12
**Host:** Ted Danson
**Musical Guest:** Luther Vandross
**Musical and Guest Performances/Cameo(s)/ Program Notes:**
- "Live from New York": Michael Dukakis (Jon Lovitz) and John Tower (Phil Hartman) visit the Boston bar Cheers.
- Vandross performs "She Won't Talk to Me" and "For You to Love."

**Airdate:** 2/18/89
**Episode:** 14.13
**Host:** Leslie Nielsen
**Musical Guest:** Cowboy Junkies
**Musical and Guest Performances/Cameo(s)/ Program Notes:**
- "Live from New York": Steve Amad Ben Bazir (Phil Hartman).
- Cowboy Junkies perform "Sweet Jane" and "Misguided Angels."
- Cameos by models Beverly Johnson, Cheryl Tiegs, and Kim Alexis, who appear as themselves on *The Pat Stevens Show*.
- Sketch Debut: *Wayne's World*, hosted by Wayne Campbell (Mike Myers) and Garth Algar (Dana Carvey).

**Airdate:** 2/25/89
**Episode:** 14.14
**Host:** Glenn Close
**Musical Guest:** Gipsy Kings
**Musical and Guest Performances/Cameo(s)/ Program Notes:**
- "Live from New York": Phil Hartman.
- Gipsy Kings perform "Bamboleo" and "Djobi Djoba."
- Cameo by William Hurt, who appears in the monologue.

**Airdate:** 3/25/89
**Episode:** 14.15
**Host:** Mary Tyler Moore
**Musical Guest:** Elvis Costello
**Musical and Guest Performances/Cameo(s)/ Program Notes:**
- "Live from New York": Mephistopheles (Jon Lovitz).
- Costello sings "Veronica" and "Let Him Dangle."
- Debut of featured player Ben Stiller.
- "Schiller's Reel": *Broadway Story*.

**Airdate:** 4/1/89
**Episode:** 14.16
**Host:** Mel Gibson
**Musical Guest:** Living Colour
**Musical and Guest Performances/Cameo(s)/ Program Notes:**
- "Live from New York": Raymond Babbit (Dana Carvey) in a parody of *Rain Man* with Pete Rose (Phil Hartman).
- Living Colour sings "Cult of Personality" and "Open Letter to a Landlord."
- Cameo by Gibson's *Lethal Weapon* costar Danny Glover.

**Airdate:** 4/15/89
**Episode:** 14.17
**Host/Musical Guest:** Dolly Parton
**Musical and Guest Performances/Cameo(s)/ Program Notes:**
- "Live from New York": Joseph Hazelwood (Kevin Nealon), captain of the *Exxon Valdez* during the 1989 oil spill.
- Parton sings "Why'd You Come in Here Lookin' Like That" and "White Limozeen."
- *Planet of the Enormous Hooters* was a sketch written by Franken and Davis for host Raquel Welch (1.18).
- Sketch Debut: *Sprockets*, hosted by Dieter (Mike Myers).

**Airdate:** 4/22/89
**Episode:** 14.18
**Host:** Geena Davis
**Musical Guest:** John Mellencamp

**Musical and Guest Performances/Cameo(s)/ Program Notes:**
- "Live from New York": President George H. W. Bush (Dana Carvey).
- Mellencamp sings "Pop Singer" and "Jackie Brown."

**Airdate:** 5/13/89
**Episode:** 14.19
**Host:** Wayne Gretzky
**Musical Guest:** Fine Young Cannibals
**Musical and Guest Performances/Cameo(s)/ Program Notes:**
- "Live from New York": Former president Jimmy Carter (Dana Carvey) in Panama.
- Fine Young Cannibals sing "She Drives Me Crazy" and "Good Thing."

**Airdate:** 5/20/89
**Episode:** 14.20
**Host:** Steve Martin
**Musical Guest:** Tom Petty and the Heartbreakers
**Musical and Guest Performances/Cameo(s)/ Program Notes:**
- "Live from New York": President George H. W. Bush (Dana Carvey).
- Tom Petty and the Heartbreakers sing "Runnin' Down a Dream" and "Free Fallin'."
- Sketch Debut: *Toonces, the Cat Who Could Drive a Car.*
- Ben Stiller's final episode.
- Steve Martin pays tribute to the late Gilda Radner.

## Season 15 (1989–1990)

**Airdate:** 9/30/89
**Episode:** 15.1
**Host:** Bruce Willis
**Musical Guest:** Neil Young
**Musical and Guest Performances/Cameo(s)/ Program Notes:**
- "Live from New York": President George H. W. Bush (Dana Carvey).
- Young performs "Rockin' in the Free World," "Needle and the Damage Done," and "No More."

**Airdate:** 10/7/89
**Episode:** 15.2
**Host:** Rick Moranis
**Musical Guest:** Rickie Lee Jones
**Musical and Guest Performances/Cameo(s)/ Program Notes:**
- "Live from New York": Comedian Jackie Mason (Rick Moranis).
- Jones performs "Satellites" and "Ghetto of My Mind."

**Airdate:** 10/21/89
**Episode:** 15.3
**Host:** Kathleen Turner
**Musical Guest:** Billy Joel
**Musical and Guest Performances/Cameo(s)/ Program Notes:**
- "Live from New York": Kevin Nealon, voice of the American flag.
- Joel performs "We Didn't Start the Fire" and "Downeaster Alexa."

**Airdate:** 10/28/89
**Episode:** 15.4
**Host:** James Woods
**Musical Guest:** Don Henley
**Musical and Guest Performances/Cameo(s)/ Program Notes:**
- "Live from New York": Nancy Reagan (Jan Hooks).
- Henley performs "The Last Worthless Evening" and "The Boys of Summer."
- "Schiller's Reel": *Falling in Love.*

**Airdate:** 11/11/89
**Episode:** 15.5
**Host:** Chris Evert
**Musical Guest:** Eurythmics
**Musical and Guest Performances/Cameo(s)/ Program Notes:**
- "Live from New York": Chris Evert, at Wimbledon.

- Eurythmics perform "Angel" and "Baby's Gonna Cry."

**Airdate:** 11/18/89
**Episode:** 15.6
**Host:** Woody Harrelson
**Musical Guest:** David Byrne
**Musical and Guest Performances/Cameo(s)/ Program Notes:**
- "Live from New York": Jack Nicholson (Phil Hartman) in *Five Easy Pieces '89*.
- Byrne performs "Dirty Old Town" and "Loco de Amor."

**Airdate:** 12/2/89
**Episode:** 15.7
**Host:** John Goodman
**Musical Guest:** k.d. lang and the Reclines
**Musical and Guest Performances/Cameo(s)/ Program Notes:**
- "Live from New York": George Bailey/ Jimmy Stewart (Dana Carvey) in *It Used to Be a Wonderful Night*.
- k.d. lang and the Reclines perform "Pullin' Back the Reins" and "Johnny Get Angry."

**Airdate:** 12/9/89
**Episode:** 15.8
**Host:** Robert Wagner
**Musical Guest:** Linda Ronstadt and Aaron Neville
**Musical and Guest Performances/Cameo(s)/ Program Notes:**
- "Live from New York": President George H. W. Bush (Dana Carvey).
- Ronstadt and Neville perform "Don't Know Much" and "When Something Is Wrong."

**Airdate:** 12/16/89
**Episode:** 15.9
**Host:** Andie MacDowell
**Musical Guest:** Tracy Chapman
**Musical and Guest Performances/Cameo(s)/ Program Notes:**
- "Live from New York": Kevin Nealon, in an Energizer Bunny commercial.
- Chapman performs "Gimme One Reason" and "All That You Have."
- "Schiller's Reel": *Dieter in Space*.

**Airdate:** 1/13/90
**Episode:** 15.10
**Host:** Ed O'Neill
**Musical Guest:** Harry Connick Jr.
**Musical and Guest Performances/Cameo(s)/ Program Notes:**
- "Live from New York": President George H. W. Bush (Dana Carvey), who visits Manuel Noriega (Jon Lovitz) in prison.
- Connick performs "It Had to Be You" and "It's Alright with Me."
- Cameo by Maury Povich.

**Airdate:** 1/20/90
**Episode:** 15.11
**Host:** Christopher Walken
**Musical Guest:** Bonnie Raitt
**Musical and Guest Performances/Cameo(s)/ Program Notes:**
- "Live from New York": Ed McMahon (Phil Hartman).
- Raitt performs "Have a Heart" and "Thing Called Love."

**Airdate:** 2/10/90
**Episode:** 15.12
**Host:** Quincy Jones
**Musical Guest:** Tevin Campbell, Andrae and Sandra Crouch, Kool Moe Dee, Big Daddy Kane, Melle Mel, Quincy D III, Siedah Garrett, Al Jarreau, Take 6
**Musical and Guest Performances/Cameo(s)/ Program Notes:**
- "Live from New York": Hans (Dana Carvey) and Franz (Kevin Nealon).
- The musical guests perform "Back on the Block" and "We Be Doin' It."

**Airdate:** 2/17/90
**Episode:** 15.13
**Host:** Tom Hanks
**Musical Guest:** Aerosmith
**Musical and Guest Performances/Cameo(s)/ Program Notes:**

Appendix A

- "Live from New York": Donald Trump (Phil Hartman).
- Aerosmith performs "Janie's Got a Gun" and "Monkey on My Back."

**Airdate:** 2/24/90
**Episode:** 15.14
**Host:** Fred Savage
**Musical Guest:** Technotronic
**Musical and Guest Performances/Cameo(s)/ Program Notes:**
- "Live from New York": The Church Lady (Dana Carvey) and her niece, Enid (Fred Savage).
- Technotronic performs "Pump Up the Jam" and "Get Up!"
- "Schiller's Reel": *Hooked on Sushi*.

**Airdate:** 3/17/90
**Episode:** 15.15
**Host:** Rob Lowe
**Musical Guest:** The Pogues
**Musical and Guest Performances/Cameo(s)/ Program Notes:**
- "Live from New York": George H. W. Bush (Dana Carvey), who won't gloat over the fall of the Berlin Wall.
- The Pogues perform "White City" and "Body."
- Cameo by Chevy Chase.

**Airdate:** 3/24/90
**Episode:** 15.16
**Host:** Debra Winger
**Musical Guest:** Eric Clapton
**Musical and Guest Performances/Cameo(s)/ Program Notes:**
- "Live from New York": Former president Ronald Reagan (Phil Hartman) has difficulty answering questions from a census-taker (Victoria Jackson).
- Clapton performs "No Alibis," "Pretending," and "Wonderful Tonight."

**Airdate:** 4/14/90
**Episode:** 15.17
**Host:** Corbin Bernsen
**Musical Guest:** The Smithereens
**Musical and Guest Performances/Cameo(s)/ Program Notes:**
- "Live from New York": Recently fired CBS sportscaster Brent Musburger (Kevin Nealon), who is now a host on the Cable Shopping Network with Jimmy the Greek (Phil Hartman).
- The Smithereens perform "A Girl Like You" and "Blue Before & After."

**Airdate:** 4/21/90
**Episode:** 15.18
**Host:** Alec Baldwin
**Musical Guest:** The B-52's
**Musical and Guest Performances/Cameo(s)/ Program Notes:**
- "Live from New York": President George H. W. Bush (Dana Carvey) on Earth Day.
- The B-52's perform "Cosmic Thing" and "Channel Z."

**Airdate:** 5/12/90
**Episode:** 15.19
**Host:** Andrew Dice Clay
**Musical Guest:** The Spanic Boys, Julee Cruise
**Musical and Guest Performances/Cameo(s)/ Program Notes:**
- "Live from New York": Mephistopheles (Jon Lovitz) consoles Clay over the negative publicity surrounding Nora Dunn's refusal to appear on the show with him due to his sexist humor.
- The Spanic Boys perform "Keep on Walking."
- Julee Cruise performs "Falling."
- Sinéad O'Connor was originally scheduled to appear but reportedly pulled out due to Clay.

**Airdate:** 5/19/90
**Episode:** 15.20
**Host:** Candice Bergen
**Musical Guest:** The Notting Hillbillies
**Musical and Guest Performances/Cameo(s)/ Program Notes:**

Episode Guide

- "Live from New York": President George H. W. Bush (Dana Carvey) promises "No huge new taxes."
- Candice Bergen's fifth time hosting.

- The Notting Hillbillies perform "Railroad Worksong" and "Love You Too Much."
- Nora Dunn and Jon Lovitz's last episode.

## Season 16 (1990–1991)

**Airdate:** 9/29/90
**Episode:** 16.1
**Host:** Kyle MacLachlan
**Musical Guest:** Sinéad O'Connor
**Musical and Guest Performances/Cameo(s)/Program Notes:**
- "Live from New York": The moderator (Phil Hartman) of a panel discussion show on Iraqi State Television.
- O'Connor performs "Three Babies" and "The Last Day of Our Acquaintance."
- Debut of featured players Chris Farley and Chris Rock.

**Airdate:** 10/6/90
**Episode:** 16.2
**Host:** Susan Lucci
**Musical Guest:** Hothouse Flowers
**Musical and Guest Performances/Cameo(s)/Program Notes:**
- "Live from New York": New England Patriots and Remington Shaver owner Victor Kiam (Phil Hartman), who advertises the new "Remington Classic Bitch" and "Lezbo" Electric Shavers. (When a female reporter sued Kiam after being sexually harassed in the Patriots' locker room, he called her a "classic bitch.")
- Hothouse Flowers perform "Give It Up" and "I Can See Clearly Now."
- Cameo by game show host Gene Rayburn.

**Airdate:** 10/20/90
**Episode:** 16.3
**Host:** George Steinbrenner
**Musical Guest:** The Time
**Musical and Guest Performances/Cameo(s)/Program Notes:**
- "Live from New York": George Steinbrenner, who awakens from a dream in which he plays every position on the Yankees.
- The Time performs "Jerk Out" and "Chocolate."
- "Schiller's Reel": *The Vision of Van Gogh.*

**Airdate:** 10/27/90
**Episode:** 16.4
**Host:** Patrick Swayze
**Musical Guest:** Mariah Carey
**Musical and Guest Performances/Cameo(s)/Program Notes:**
- "Live from New York": Johnny (Patrick Swayze) in *Dirty Square Dancing.*
- Mariah Carey performs "Vision of Love" and "Vanishing."
- Lisa Niemi, Swayze's wife, dances with her husband in the monologue.
- ★★★★ Four-Star Sketch: Swayze and Chris Farley compete at a Chippendales dancer audition.
- Debut of featured player Rob Schneider.

**Airdate:** 11/10/90
**Episode:** 16.5
**Host:** Jimmy Smits
**Musical Guest:** World Party
**Musical and Guest Performances/Cameo(s)/Program Notes:**
- "Live from New York": Vice President Dan Quayle (child actor Jeff Renaudo).
- World Party performs "Way Down Now" and "Ship of Fools."

Appendix A

- Cameo by Bob Costas.
- Character Debut: Simon (Mike Myers), the little British boy who hosts a show from his bathtub.
- Debut of featured players David Spade and Julia Sweeney.

**Airdate:** 11/17/90
**Episode:** 16.6
**Host:** Dennis Hopper
**Musical Guest:** Paul Simon
**Musical and Guest Performances/Cameo(s)/Program Notes:**
- "Live from New York": Regis Philbin (Dana Carvey) and Kathie Lee Gifford (Jan Hooks).
- Simon performs "The Obvious Child" (with Olodum), "Proof," and "Late in the Evening."
- Cameo by Bert Parks.
- "Schiller's Reel": *Sudden Pressure.*

**Airdate:** 12/1/90
**Episode:** 16.7
**Host:** John Goodman
**Musical Guest:** Faith No More
**Musical and Guest Performances/Cameo(s)/Program Notes:**
- "Live from New York": Saddam Hussein (Phil Hartman), who is a guest on *Church Chat.*
- Faith No More performs "Epic" and "From Out of Nowhere."
- Character Debut: Pat (Julia Sweeney).

**Airdate:** 12/8/90
**Episode:** 16.8
**Host:** Tom Hanks
**Musical Guest:** Edie Brickell and New Bohemians
**Musical and Guest Performances/Cameo(s)/Program Notes:**
- "Live from New York": Mr. Subliminal (Kevin Nealon).
- Edie Brickell and New Bohemians perform "Woyaho" and "He Said."
- Hanks is inducted into the "Five-Timers Club" by Paul Simon, Steve Martin, and Elliott Gould. Jon Lovitz plays the waiter and then-unknown *SNL* writer Conan O'Brien is Sean the Doorman.

**Airdate:** 12/15/90
**Episode:** 16.9
**Host:** Dennis Quaid
**Musical Guest:** The Neville Brothers
**Musical and Guest Performances/Cameo(s)/Program Notes:**
- "Live from New York": President George H. W. Bush (Dana Carvey).
- The Neville Brothers perform "Brother Jake" and "River of Life."
- Cameo by Jon Lovitz on *Weekend Update* as "Annoying Man."
- "Schiller's Reel": *Schillervision Theatre.*

**Airdate:** 1/12/91
**Episode:** 16.10
**Host:** Joe Mantegna
**Musical Guest:** Vanilla Ice
**Musical and Guest Performances/Cameo(s)/Program Notes:**
- "Live from New York": Joe Mantegna as a Mafia don, who tries to negotiate a deal between President Bush (Dana Carvey) and Saddam Hussein (Phil Hartman).
- Vanilla Ice performs "Ice Ice Baby" and "Play That Funky Music."
- Sketch Debut: *Bill Swerski's Super Fans.*

**Airdate:** 1/19/91
**Episode:** 16.11
**Host/Musical Guest:** Sting
**Musical and Guest Performances/Cameo(s)/Program Notes:**
- "Live from New York": Wayne Campbell (Mike Myers).
- Sting performs "All This Time" and "Purple Haze."
- Character Debut: Richard Laymer (Rob Schneider) ("Makin' copies").

**Airdate:** 2/9/91
**Episode:** 16.12
**Host:** Kevin Bacon
**Musical Guest:** INXS
**Musical and Guest Performances/Cameo(s)/Program Notes:**

- "Live from New York": Lt. Colonel William Pierson (Kevin Nealon).
- INXS performs "Bitter Tears" and "Suicide Blonde."
- Debut of featured players Tim Meadows and Adam Sandler.
- Sketch Debut: *Daily Affirmation with Stuart Smalley* (Al Franken).

**Airdate:** 2/16/91
**Episode:** 16.13
**Host:** Roseanne Barr
**Musical Guest:** Deee-Lite
**Musical and Guest Performances/Cameo(s)/Program Notes:**
- "Live from New York": Lt. Colonel William Pierson (Kevin Nealon) at a press conference about the Iraq Invasion.
- Deee-Lite performs "World Clique" and "The Power of Love."
- Cameos by Jon Lovitz and Tom Arnold.

**Airdate:** 2/23/91
**Episode:** 16.14
**Host:** Alec Baldwin
**Musical Guest:** Whitney Houston
**Musical and Guest Performances/Cameo(s)/Program Notes:**
- "Live from New York": John McLaughlin (Dana Carvey), who opens with "Show, show, show—here we go!"
- Houston performs "I'm Your Baby Tonight" and "All the Man I Need."

**Airdate:** 3/16/91
**Episode:** 16.15
**Host:** Michael J. Fox
**Musical Guest:** The Black Crowes
**Musical and Guest Performances/Cameo(s)/Program Notes:**
- "Live from New York": George H. W. Bush (Dana Carvey) in his second post-Iraq address to a joint session of the Senate and the House.
- The Black Crowes perform "Thick and Thin" and "She Talks to Angels."

**Airdate:** 3/23/91
**Episode:** 16.16
**Host:** Jeremy Irons
**Musical Guest:** Fishbone
**Musical and Guest Performances/Cameo(s)/Program Notes:**
- "Live from New York": Hans (Dana Carvey) and Franz (Kevin Nealon).
- Fishbone performs "Sunless Saturday" and "Everyday Sunshine."
- Cameo by Razor Ruddock.

**Airdate:** 4/13/91
**Episode:** 16.17
**Host:** Catherine O'Hara
**Musical Guest:** R.E.M.
**Musical and Guest Performances/Cameo(s)/Program Notes:**
- "Live from New York": Former president Ronald Reagan (Phil Hartman).
- R.E.M. performs "Losing My Religion" and "Shiny Happy People."

**Airdate:** 4/20/91
**Episode:** 16.18
**Host:** Steven Seagal
**Musical Guest:** Michael Bolton
**Musical and Guest Performances/Cameo(s)/Program Notes:**
- "Live from New York": Hans (Dana Carvey) and Franz (Kevin Nealon).
- Bolton performs "Love Is a Wonderful Thing" and "Time, Love and Tenderness."

**Airdate:** 5/11/91
**Episode:** 16.19
**Host:** Delta Burke
**Musical Guest:** Chris Isaak and Silvertone
**Musical and Guest Performances/Cameo(s)/Program Notes:**
- "Live from New York": President George H. W. Bush (Dana Carvey).
- Isaak and Silvertone perform "Wicked Game" and "Diddley Daddy."

**Airdate:** 5/18/91
**Episode:** 16.20
**Host:** George Wendt
**Musical Guest:** Elvis Costello

**Musical and Guest Performances/Cameo(s)/ Program Notes:**
- "Live from New York": Lorne Michaels, who offers Dennis Miller the chance to open the show—only it doesn't start until Michaels says, "Live from New York."
- Costello performs "The Other Side of Summer" and "So Like Candy."
- Final episode for A. Whitney Brown, Jan Hooks, and Dennis Miller.

## Season 17 (1991–1992)

**Airdate:** 9/28/91
**Episode:** 17.1
**Host:** Michael Jordan
**Musical Guest:** Public Enemy
**Musical and Guest Performances/Cameo(s)/ Program Notes:**
- "Live from New York": Wayne Campbell (Mike Myers) and Garth Algar (Dana Carvey).
- Public Enemy performs "Can't Truss It" and "Bring Tha Noize."
- Debut of Ellen Cleghorne, Siobhan Fallon, and Robert Smigel as featured players.
- Chris Farley and Chris Rock are bumped up to regulars.
- *Weekend Update*: Kevin Nealon takes over as anchor.

**Airdate:** 10/5/91
**Episode:** 17.2
**Host:** Jeff Daniels
**Musical Guest:** Color Me Badd
**Musical and Guest Performances/Cameo(s)/ Program Notes:**
- "Live from New York": Johnny Carson (Dana Carvey).
- Color Me Badd performs "I Wanna Sex You Up" and "I Adore Mi Amor."

**Airdate:** 10/12/91
**Episode:** 17.3
**Host:** Kirstie Alley
**Musical Guest:** Tom Petty and the Heartbreakers
**Musical and Guest Performances/Cameo(s)/ Program Notes:**
- "Live from New York": Long Dong Silver (Chris Rock) testifying at the Clarence Thomas hearings.
- Tom Petty and the Heartbreakers perform "Into the Great Wide Open" and "King's Highway."
- Cameos by Alley's *Cheers* costars Ted Danson, Woody Harrelson, Kelsey Grammer, and George Wendt.
- Sketch Debut: *Coffee Talk*, hosted by Linda Richman (Mike Myers).

**Airdate:** 10/26/91
**Episode:** 17.4
**Host:** Christian Slater
**Musical Guest:** Bonnie Raitt
**Musical and Guest Performances/Cameo(s)/ Program Notes:**
- "Live from New York": John McLaughlin, who makes a cameo in a parody of *The McLaughlin Group*.
- Raitt performs "Something to Talk About" and "I Can't Make You Love Me."

**Airdate:** 11/2/91
**Episode:** 17.5
**Host:** Kiefer Sutherland
**Musical Guest:** Skid Row
**Musical and Guest Performances/Cameo(s)/ Program Notes:**
- "Live from New York": Mark Strobel (Chris Farley), during jury selection for the William Kennedy Smith trial.
- Skid Row performs "Piece of Me" and "Kiddie Metal."

**Airdate:** 11/16/91
**Episode:** 17.6

**Host:** Linda Hamilton
**Musical Guest:** Mariah Carey
**Musical and Guest Performances/Cameo(s)/ Program Notes:**
- "Live from New York": David Duke (Dana Carvey).
- Carey performs "Can't Let Go" and "If It's Over."
- Debut of Beth Cahill and Melanie Hutsell as featured players.
- "Schiller's Reel": *Hidden Camera Commercials*.

**Airdate:** 11/23/91
**Episode:** 17.7
**Host:** Macaulay Culkin
**Musical Guest:** Tin Machine
**Musical and Guest Performances/Cameo(s)/ Program Notes:**
- "Live from New York": Macaulay Culkin, alone in the studio, in a parody of *Home Alone*.
- Tin Machine performs "Baby Universal" and "If There Is Something."
- Sketch Debut: *Unfrozen Cave Man Lawyer*.

**Airdate:** 12/7/91
**Episode:** 17.8
**Host/Musical Guest:** Hammer
**Musical and Guest Performances/Cameo(s)/ Program Notes:**
- "Live from New York": President George H. W. Bush (Dana Carvey).
- Hammer performs "Too Legit to Quit" and "Addams Groove."
- Cameos by Christina Ricci and Jimmy Workman, who play Wednesday and Pugsley Adams in *The Addams Family* (1991).

**Airdate:** 12/14/91
**Episode:** 17.9
**Host:** Steve Martin
**Musical Guest:** James Taylor
**Musical and Guest Performances/Cameo(s)/ Program Notes:**
- "Live from New York": Steve Martin and the cast, who open the show with the rousing musical number "Tonight."
- Taylor performs "Stop Thinkin' About That," "Shed a Little Light" (with Don Grolnick), and "Sweet Baby James."

**Airdate:** 1/11/92
**Episode:** 17.10
**Host:** Rob Morrow
**Musical Guest:** Nirvana
**Musical and Guest Performances/Cameo(s)/ Program Notes:**
- "Live from New York": Elliot Rifkin (Kevin Nealon), a Warner Bros. executive who meets with conspiracy theory–crazed Oliver Stone (Phil Hartman).
- Nirvana performs "Smells Like Teen Spirit" and "Territorial Pissing."

**Airdate:** 1/18/92
**Episode:** 17.11
**Host:** Chevy Chase
**Musical Guest:** Robbie Robertson
**Musical and Guest Performances/Cameo(s)/ Program Notes:**
- "Live from New York": Wayne (Mike Myers) and Garth (Dana Carvey).
- Robertson performs "Go Back to Your Woods" and "The Weight" (with Bruce Hornsby, Ivan Neville, and Monk Boudreaux).
- Cameo by George Wendt.

**Airdate:** 2/8/92
**Episode:** 17.12
**Host:** Susan Dey
**Musical Guest:** C+C Music Factory
**Musical and Guest Performances/Cameo(s)/ Program Notes:**
- "Live from New York": Richard Laymer (Rob Schneider) working at the copier at *L.A. Law*'s McKenzie, Brackman, Chaney, and Kuzak.
- C+C Music Factory perform "Here We Go Let's Rock and Roll," "Gonna Make You Sweat," and "A Deeper Love."

Appendix A

**Airdate:** 2/15/92
**Episode:** 17.13
**Host:** Jason Priestley
**Musical Guest:** Teenage Fanclub
**Musical and Guest Performances/Cameo(s)/Program Notes:**
- "Live from New York": Brian Deming (Jason Priestley), a terrible skater competing in the Olympics.
- Teenage Fanclub performs "The Concept," "What You Do to Me," and "Pet Rock."

**Airdate:** 2/22/92
**Episode:** 17.14
**Host:** Roseanne and Tom Arnold
**Musical Guest:** Red Hot Chili Peppers
**Musical and Guest Performances/Cameo(s)/Program Notes:**
- "Live from New York": President George H. W. Bush (Dana Carvey) on the New Hampshire Republican presidential primary.
- Red Hot Chili Peppers perform "Stone Cold Bush" and "Under the Bridge."
- ★ ★ ★ ★ Four-Star Sketch: David Spade as Dick Clark's receptionist.

**Airdate:** 3/14/92
**Episode:** 17.15
**Host:** John Goodman
**Musical Guest:** Garth Brooks
**Musical and Guest Performances/Cameo(s)/Program Notes:**
- "Live from New York": C-SPAN announcer (Jim Downey).
- Brooks performs "Rodeo" and "The River."

**Airdate:** 3/21/92
**Episode:** 17.16
**Host:** Mary Stuart Masterson
**Musical Guest:** En Vogue
**Musical and Guest Performances/Cameo(s)/Program Notes:**
- "Live from New York": John McLaughlin (Dana Carvey).
- En Vogue performs "Never Gonna Get It," "Hold On," and "Free Your Mind."
- "Schiller's Reel": *Million Dollar Zombie.*

**Airdate:** 4/11/92
**Episode:** 17.17
**Host:** Sharon Stone
**Musical Guest:** Pearl Jam
**Musical and Guest Performances/Cameo(s)/Program Notes:**
- "Live from New York": Wayne Campbell (Mike Myers) and Garth Algar (Dana Carvey).
- Pearl Jam performs "Alive" and "Porch."

**Airdate:** 4/18/92
**Episode:** 17.18
**Host:** Jerry Seinfeld
**Musical Guest:** Annie Lennox
**Musical and Guest Performances/Cameo(s)/Program Notes:**
- "Live from New York": Paul Tsongas (Al Franken).
- Lennox performs "Why" and "Legend in My Living Room."

**Airdate:** 5/9/92
**Episode:** 17.19
**Host:** Tom Hanks
**Musical Guest:** Bruce Springsteen
**Musical and Guest Performances/Cameo(s)/Program Notes:**
- "Live from New York": Presidential candidate Ross Perot (Dana Carvey) on the Los Angeles riots.
- Springsteen performs "Lucky Town," "57 Channels," and "Living Proof."

**Airdate:** 5/16/92
**Episode:** 17.20
**Host:** Woody Harrelson
**Musical Guest:** Vanessa Williams
**Musical and Guest Performances/Cameo(s)/Program Notes:**
- "Live from New York": Johnny Carson (Dana Carvey).

Williams performs "Save the Best for Last" and "The Comfort Zone."

## Season 18 (1992–1993)

**Airdate:** 9/26/92
**Episode:** 18.1
**Host:** Nicolas Cage
**Musical Guest:** Bobby Brown
**Musical and Guest Performances/Cameo(s)/ Program Notes:**
- "Live from New York": Frank Sinatra (Phil Hartman).
- Brown performs "Humpin' Around" and "Good Enough."
- Cameos by Cher and Jan Hooks.
- Rob Schneider is bumped up to a regular.

**Airdate:** 10/3/92
**Episode:** 18.2
**Host:** Tim Robbins
**Musical Guest:** Sinéad O'Connor
**Musical and Guest Performances/Cameo(s)/ Program Notes:**
- "Live from New York": Ross Perot (Dana Carvey).
- Cameo by Susan Sarandon.
- O'Connor performs "Success Has Made a Failure of Our Home." During her second song, "War," she tears up a picture of the pope, which causes a storm of controversy.

**Airdate:** 10/10/92
**Episode:** 18.3
**Host:** Joe Pesci
**Musical Guest:** Spin Doctors
**Musical and Guest Performances/Cameo(s)/ Program Notes:**
- "Live from New York": President George H. W. Bush (Dana Carvey) in the '92 Presidential debate.
- Spin Doctors perform "Little Miss Can't Be Wrong" and "Jimmy Olsen's Blues."

- Beth Cahill, Siobhan Fallon, and Victoria Jackson's final episode.

- In his monologue, Pesci tears up a picture of Sinéad O'Connor in retaliation for last week.

**Airdate:** 10/24/92
**Episode:** 18.4
**Host:** Christopher Walken
**Musical Guest:** Arrested Development
**Musical and Guest Performances/Cameo(s)/ Program Notes:**
- "Live from New York": Vice presidential candidate James Stockdale (Phil Hartman).
- Arrested Development performs "Tennessee" and "People Everyday."
- Special guest appearance by Jan Hooks.

**Airdate:** 10/31/92
**Episode:** 18.5
**Host:** Catherine O'Hara
**Musical Guest:** 10,000 Maniacs
**Musical and Guest Performances/Cameo(s)/ Program Notes:**
- "Live from New York": Ross Perot (Dana Carvey).
- 10,000 Maniacs perform "These Are Our Days" and "Candy Everybody Wants."

**Airdate:** 11/14/92
**Episode:** 18.6
**Host:** Michael Keaton
**Musical Guest:** Morrissey
**Musical and Guest Performances/Cameo(s)/ Program Notes:**
- "Live from New York": President George H. W. Bush (Phil Hartman).
- Morrissey performs "Glamorous Glue" and "Suedehead."

**Airdate:** 11/21/92
**Episode:** 18.7

**Host:** Sinbad
**Musical Guest:** Sade
**Musical and Guest Performances/Cameo(s)/ Program Notes:**
- "Live from New York": President George H. W. Bush (Dana Carvey) and President-Elect Bill Clinton (Phil Hartman).
- Sade performs "No Ordinary Love" and "Cherish the Day."

**Airdate:** 12/5/92
**Episode:** 18.8
**Host:** Tom Arnold
**Musical Guest:** Neil Young
**Musical and Guest Performances/Cameo(s)/ Program Notes:**
- "Live from New York": Garth Algar (Dana Carvey) and Wayne Campbell (Mike Myers).
- Young performs "From Hank to Hendrix" and "Harvest Moon."
- Cameos by Roseanne Arnold, George Wendt, and Dick Butkus.

**Airdate:** 12/12/92
**Episode:** 18.9
**Host:** Glenn Close
**Musical Guest:** The Black Crowes
**Musical and Guest Performances/Cameo(s)/ Program Notes:**
- "Live from New York": Queen Elizabeth (Mike Myers).
- The Black Crowes perform "Sometimes Salvation" and "Non-Fiction."

**Airdate:** 1/9/93
**Episode:** 18.10
**Host:** Danny DeVito
**Musical Guest:** Bon Jovi
**Musical and Guest Performances/Cameo(s)/ Program Notes:**
- "Live from New York": Chicago Bears coach Mike Ditka.
- Bon Jovi performs "Bed of Roses" and "Wanted Dead or Alive."

**Airdate:** 1/16/93
**Episode:** 18.11
**Host:** Harvey Keitel
**Musical Guest:** Madonna
**Musical and Guest Performances/Cameo(s)/ Program Notes:**
- "Live from New York": Madonna, singing at Clinton's inauguration.
- Madonna performs "Fever" and "Bad Girl."

**Airdate:** 2/6/93
**Episode:** 18.12
**Host:** Luke Perry
**Musical Guest:** Mick Jagger
**Musical and Guest Performances/Cameo(s)/ Program Notes:**
- "Live from New York": Jim Downey (Voice).
- Jagger performs "Sweet Thing" and "Don't Tear Me Up."
- Dana Carvey's final episode.

**Airdate:** 2/13/93
**Episode:** 18.13
**Host:** Alec Baldwin
**Musical Guest:** Paul McCartney
**Musical and Guest Performances/Cameo(s)/ Program Notes:**
- "Live from New York": Toonces, the Cat Who Can Drive a Car.
- McCartney performs "Get Out of My Way" and "Hey Jude."

**Airdate:** 2/20/93
**Episode:** 18.14
**Host:** Bill Murray
**Musical Guest:** Sting
**Musical and Guest Performances/Cameo(s)/ Program Notes:**
- "Live from New York": Bill Clinton (Phil Hartman), at a town hall meeting.
- Sting performs "If I Ever Lose My Faith in You," "Love Is Stranger Than Justice," and "Every Breath You Take."

Episode Guide    467

**Airdate:** 3/13/93
**Episode:** 18.15
**Host:** John Goodman
**Musical Guest:** Mary J. Blige
**Musical and Guest Performances/Cameo(s)/ Program Notes:**
- "Live from New York": Richard Laymer (Rob Schneider), who works at the Branch Davidian compound.
- Blige performs "Reminisce" and "Sweet Thing."
- "Schiller's Reel": *Dexter's Dream*.

**Airdate:** 3/20/93
**Episode:** 18.16
**Host:** Miranda Richardson
**Musical Guest:** Soul Asylum
**Musical and Guest Performances/Cameo(s)/ Program Notes:**
- "Live from New York": Pat (Julia Sweeney), in a parody of *The Crying Game*.
- Soul Asylum performs "Somebody to Shove" and "Black Gold."
- Cameo by Stephen Rea.

**Airdate:** 4/10/93
**Episode:** 18.17
**Host:** Jason Alexander
**Musical Guest:** Peter Gabriel
**Musical and Guest Performances/Cameo(s)/ Program Notes:**
- "Live from New York": Naina Yeltsin (Julia Sweeney).
- Gabriel performs "Steam" and "In Your Eyes."

**Airdate:** 4/17/93
**Episode:** 18.18
**Host:** Kirstie Alley
**Musical Guest:** Lenny Kravitz
**Musical and Guest Performances/Cameo(s)/ Program Notes:**
- "Live from New York": Tim Meadows, speaking for "Recurring Characters for Unity."
- Kravitz performs "Are You Gonna Go My Way" and "Always on the Run."
- "Schiller's Reel": *While the City Sleeps*.

**Airdate:** 5/8/93
**Episode:** 18.19
**Host:** Christina Applegate
**Musical Guest:** Midnight Oil
**Musical and Guest Performances/Cameo(s)/ Program Notes:**
- "Live from New York": Linda Richman (Mike Myers).
- Midnight Oil performs "Truganini" and "My Country."

**Airdate:** 5/15/93
**Episode:** 18.20
**Host:** Kevin Kline
**Musical Guest:** Willie Nelson and Paul Simon
**Musical and Guest Performances/Cameo(s)/ Program Notes:**
- "Live from New York": Bob Dole (Dan Aykroyd).
- Nelson and Simon perform "Graceland" and "Still Is Still Moving to Me."
- "Schiller's Reel": *Criminal Encounter*.

## Season 19 (1993–1994)

**Airdate:** 9/25/93
**Episode:** 19.1
**Host:** Charles Barkley
**Musical Guest:** Nirvana
**Musical and Guest Performances/Cameo(s)/ Program Notes:**
- "Live from New York": President Bill Clinton (Phil Hartman).
- Nirvana performs "Heart-Shaped Box" and "Rape Me."
- Cameos by RuPaul and Muggsy Bogues.
- "Film Short": *Office Space*.

- Melanie Hutsell and Tim Meadows are bumped up to regulars.
- Chris Rock and Robert Smigel's final episode.

**Airdate:** 10/2/93
**Episode:** 19.2
**Host:** Shannen Doherty
**Musical Guest:** Cypress Hill
**Musical and Guest Performances/Cameo(s)/ Program Notes:**
- "Live from New York": Phil Hartman, after Operaman (Adam Sandler) plays the Scratch Lottery.
- Cypress Hill performs "Insane in the Brain" and "I Ain't Goin' Out Like That."
- Cameo by Doherty's husband, Ashley Hamilton.
- Debut of featured player Norm Macdonald.

**Airdate:** 10/9/93
**Episode:** 19.3
**Host:** Jeff Goldblum
**Musical Guest:** Aerosmith
**Musical and Guest Performances/Cameo(s)/ Program Notes:**
- "Live from New York": Joe Perry and Steven Tyler, performing at "Rock for Michael," where singers and musicians protest Michael Jordan's retirement.
- Aerosmith performs "Cryin'" and "Bad Dancer."
- Cameo by Laura Dern.
- Debut of featured players Jay Mohr and Sarah Silverman.

**Airdate:** 10/23/93
**Episode:** 19.4
**Host:** John Malkovich
**Musical Guest:** Billy Joel
**Musical and Guest Performances/Cameo(s)/ Program Notes:**
- "Live from New York": Anne Murray (Melanie Hutsell), after singing "O Canada" at the World Series.
- Joel performs "River of Dreams" and "All About Soul."
- Guest appearance by Jan Hooks.

**Airdate:** 10/30/93
**Episode:** 19.5
**Host:** Christian Slater
**Musical Guest:** The Smashing Pumpkins
**Musical and Guest Performances/Cameo(s)/ Program Notes:**
- "Live from New York": Linda Richman (Mike Myers).
- The Smashing Pumpkins perform "Cherub Rock" and "Today."

**Airdate:** 11/13/93
**Episode:** 19.6
**Host:** Rosie O'Donnell
**Musical Guest:** James Taylor
**Musical and Guest Performances/Cameo(s)/ Program Notes:**
- "Live from New York": Senator Bob Packwood (Phil Hartman) recounts in his audio diaries the women he sexually harassed that day.
- Taylor performs "Memphis," "Slap Leather," and "Secret of Life."
- Cameo by Casey Kasem.
- "Schiller's Reel": *Will Work for Food.*

**Airdate:** 11/20/93
**Episode:** 19.7
**Host:** Nicole Kidman
**Musical Guest:** Stone Temple Pilots
**Musical and Guest Performances/Cameo(s)/ Program Notes:**
- "Live from New York": Wayne Campbell (Mike Myers) and Garth Algar (Dana Carvey).
- Stone Temple Pilots perform "Creep" and "Naked Sunday."
- Cameo appearances by Dana Carvey, Christina Ricci, and Jimmy Workman.

**Airdate:** 12/4/93
**Episode:** 19.8
**Host:** Charlton Heston
**Musical Guest:** Paul Westerberg

**Musical and Guest Performances/Cameo(s)/ Program Notes:**
- "Live from New York": Charlton Heston, who dreams the show has been taken over by apes.
- Westerberg performs "Knockin' on Mine" and "Can't Hardly Wait."

**Airdate:** 12/11/93
**Episode:** 19.9
**Host:** Sally Field
**Musical Guest:** Tony! Toni! Toné!
**Musical and Guest Performances/Cameo(s)/ Program Notes:**
- "Live from New York": Adam Sandler sings his apology to Santa Claus for being a bad boy.
- Tony! Toni! Toné! perform "If I Had No Loot" and "Tell Me Mama."

**Airdate:** 1/8/94
**Episode:** 19.10
**Host:** Jason Patric
**Musical Guest:** Blind Melon
**Musical and Guest Performances/Cameo(s)/ Program Notes:**
- "Live from New York": Chris Farley as Mayor Giuliani's son, Andrew Giuliani, who upstages his father during the mayor's inaugural speech.
- Blind Melon performs "No Rain" and "Paper Scratcher."
- Cameo by Richard Simmons.

**Airdate:** 1/15/94
**Episode:** 19.11
**Host:** Sara Gilbert
**Musical Guest:** Counting Crows
**Musical and Guest Performances/Cameo(s)/ Program Notes:**
- "Live from New York": Court TV's Cynthia McFadden (Julia Sweeney), covering the John Bobbitt trial.
- Counting Crows perform "Round Here" and "Mr. Jones."

**Airdate:** 2/5/94
**Episode:** 19.12
**Host:** Patrick Stewart
**Musical Guest:** Salt-N-Pepa
**Musical and Guest Performances/Cameo(s)/ Program Notes:**
- "Live from New York": Michael Jackson (Tim Meadows), whose bodyguards take him out to a club to make over his image.
- Salt-N-Pepa performs "Shoop" and "Whatta Man."

**Airdate:** 2/12/94
**Episode:** 19.13
**Host:** Alec Baldwin and Kim Basinger
**Musical Guest:** UB40
**Musical and Guest Performances/Cameo(s)/ Program Notes:**
- "Live from New York": Alec Baldwin, in a *Goodfellas* parody, recalls the "wise guys" from his old Long Island neighborhood.
- UB40 perform "C'est la Vie" and "Can't Help Falling in Love."
- Cameos by Billy and Stephen Baldwin, who appear in a *Family Feud* parody.

**Airdate:** 2/19/94
**Episode:** 19.14
**Host:** Martin Lawrence
**Musical Guest:** Crash Test Dummies
**Musical and Guest Performances/Cameo(s)/ Program Notes:**
- "Live from New York": Tonya Harding's boyfriend, Jeff Gillooly (Rob Schneider).
- Crash Test Dummies perform "Mmm Mmm Mmm Mmm" and "Afternoons & Coffeespoons."

**Airdate:** 3/12/94
**Episode:** 19.15
**Host:** Nancy Kerrigan
**Musical Guest:** Aretha Franklin
**Musical and Guest Performances/Cameo(s)/ Program Notes:**
- "Live from New York": President Bill Clinton (Phil Hartman).
- Franklin performs "A Deeper Love," Willing to Forgive," and "Chain of Fools."

- Debut of Michael McKean as a regular.

**Airdate:** 3/19/94
**Episode:** 19.16
**Host:** Helen Hunt
**Musical Guest:** Snoop Doggy Dogg
**Musical and Guest Performances/Cameo(s)/Program Notes:**
- "Live from New York": Cindy Crawford, in a cameo, introduces "Rockers to Help Explain Whitewater."
- Snoop Doggy Dogg performs "Gin & Juice" and "Lodi Dodi."

**Airdate:** 4/9/94
**Episode:** 19.17
**Host:** Kelsey Grammer
**Musical Guest:** Dwight Yoakam
**Musical and Guest Performances/Cameo(s)/Program Notes:**
- "Live from New York": Hillary Clinton (Jan Hooks, in a cameo) offers investment tips.
- Yoakam performs "Pocket of a Clown" and "Fast as You."
- Cameos by Sy Sperling and Manute Bol.

**Airdate:** 4/16/94
**Episode:** 19.18
**Host:** Emilio Estevez
**Musical Guest:** Pearl Jam
**Musical and Guest Performances/Cameo(s)/Program Notes:**
- "Live from New York": A warden (Rob Schneider) in a Singapore prison.
- Pearl Jam performs "Not for You," "Rearview Mirror," and "Daughter."

**Airdate:** 5/7/94
**Episode:** 19.19
**Host:** John Goodman
**Musical Guest:** The Pretenders
**Musical and Guest Performances/Cameo(s)/Program Notes:**
- "Live from New York": Howard Stern (Michael McKean).
- The Pretenders perform "Night in My Veins" and "I'll Stand by You."
- Guest appearance by Jan Hooks.

**Airdate:** 5/14/94
**Episode:** 19.20
**Host:** Heather Locklear
**Musical Guest:** Janet Jackson
**Musical and Guest Performances/Cameo(s)/Program Notes:**
- "Live from New York": Linda Richman (Mike Myers).
- Jackson performs "Throb" and "Any Time, Any Place."
- Cameos by Jay Leno and Rafael Fuchs.
- ★★★★ Four-Star Sketch: The cast, most of them appearing as the recurring characters they play, sing a parody of "So Long, Farewell" from *The Sound of Music*.
- Final episode for Phil Hartman, Melanie Hutsell, Rob Schneider, Sarah Silverman, and Julia Sweeney.

## Season 20 (1994–1995)

**Airdate:** 9/24/94
**Episode:** 20.1
**Host:** Steve Martin
**Musical Guest:** Eric Clapton
**Musical and Guest Performances/Cameo(s)/Program Notes:**
- "Live from New York": Tim Meadows, who is one of several cast members auditioning to play Bill Clinton.
- Eric Clapton performs "I'm Tore Down" and "Five Long Years."
- Cameos by Brian Austin Green and Bobby Bonilla, Jack McDowell, Lenny Dykstra, Mo Vaughn, and Roger Clemens.
- Debuts of featured player Laura Kightlinger and Chris Elliott as a regular;

Norm Macdonald is bumped up to a regular.
- *Weekend Update*: Norm Macdonald's debut as anchor.

**Airdate:** 10/1/94
**Episode:** 20.2
**Host:** Marisa Tomei
**Musical Guest:** Bonnie Raitt
**Musical and Guest Performances/Cameo(s)/Program Notes:**
- "Live from New York": A recorded telephone voice that is part of President Clinton's demonstration of how his proposed Universal Health Care system will work.
- Raitt performs "Love Sneaking Up on You" and "Storm Warning."

**Airdate:** 10/15/94
**Episode:** 20.3
**Host:** John Travolta
**Musical Guest:** Seal
**Musical and Guest Performances/Cameo(s)/Program Notes:**
- "Live from New York": John Travolta as he tours backstage to the *Saturday Night Fever* soundtrack.
- Seal performs "Prayer for the Dying" and "Crazy."
- Cameos by David Lander (as Squiggy) and Steve Buscemi (as *Reservoir Dogs*' Mr. Pink).

**Airdate:** 10/22/94
**Episode:** 20.4
**Host:** Dana Carvey
**Musical Guest:** Edie Brickell, Paul Simon
**Musical and Guest Performances/Cameo(s)/Program Notes:**
- "Live from New York": Former president of the United States George H. W. Bush, who introduces the show at the request of guest host Dana Carvey, who imitated the elder Bush in seasons 13–18.
- Brickell performs "Green" (with Paul Simon) and "Tomorrow Comes."

**Airdate:** 11/12/94
**Episode:** 20.5
**Host:** Sarah Jessica Parker
**Musical Guest:** R.E.M.
**Musical and Guest Performances/Cameo(s)/Program Notes:**
- "Live from New York": Bob Hudnut (Chris Elliott), a Democratic candidate in the Montana 2nd Congressional Race.
- R.E.M. performs "What's the Frequency, Kenneth?," "Bang & Blame," and "I Don't Sleep, I Dream."
- Cameo by Bill Murray, who pays tribute to the show's first head writer and performer, Michael O'Donoghue, who died suddenly of a cerebral hemorrhage on November 8, 1994.

**Airdate:** 11/19/94
**Episode:** 20.6
**Host:** John Turturro
**Musical Guest:** Tom Petty and the Heartbreakers
**Musical and Guest Performances/Cameo(s)/Program Notes:**
- "Live from New York": Newt Gingrich (Chris Farley), who is visited by the ghost of Richard Nixon (Turturro).
- Tom Petty and the Heartbreakers perform "You Don't Know How It Feels" and "Honey Bee" (with Dave Grohl).
- Cameos by Joey Buttafuoco and David Hasselhoff.

**Airdate:** 12/3/94
**Episode:** 20.7
**Host:** Roseanne
**Musical Guest:** Green Day
**Musical and Guest Performances/Cameo(s)/Program Notes:**
- "Live from New York": Sen. Jesse Helms (Mike Myers).
- Green Day performs "When I Come Around" and "Geek Stink Breath."
- Cameo by comedian Rip Taylor.

**Airdate:** 12/10/94
**Episode:** 20.8

## Appendix A

**Host:** Alec Baldwin
**Musical Guest:** Beastie Boys
**Musical and Guest Performances/Cameo(s)/ Program Notes:**
- "Live from New York": Surgeon General Joycelyn Elders (Ellen Cleghorne), who was forced to resign by President Clinton over her statement in an address on United Nations World AIDS Day that masturbation should be taught in schools "as a natural part of human sexuality."
- Beastie Boys perform "Sure Shot," "Ricky's Theme," and "Heart Attack Man."
- Cameo by Christian Slater.

**Airdate:** 12/17/94
**Episode:** 20.9
**Host:** George Foreman
**Musical Guest:** Hole
**Musical and Guest Performances/Cameo(s)/ Program Notes:**
- "Live from New York": President Bill Clinton (Michael McKean) in his Christmas address.
- Hole performs "Doll Parts" and "Violet."
- Cameo by professional boxing ring announcer Michael Buffer.

**Airdate:** 1/14/95
**Episode:** 20.10
**Host:** Jeff Daniels
**Musical Guest:** Luscious Jackson
**Musical and Guest Performances/Cameo(s)/ Program Notes:**
- "Live from New York": Newt Gingrich (Chris Farley).
- Luscious Jackson performs "Citysong" and "Here."
- Debut of Mark McKinney as a regular.

**Airdate:** 1/21/95
**Episode:** 20.11
**Host:** David Hyde Pierce
**Musical Guest:** Live
**Musical and Guest Performances/Cameo(s)/ Program Notes:**
- "Live from New York": Judge Lance Ito (Mike Myers).
- Live performs "I Alone" and "Selling the Drama."

**Airdate:** 2/11/95
**Episode:** 20.12
**Host:** Bob Newhart
**Musical Guest:** Des'ree
**Musical and Guest Performances/Cameo(s)/ Program Notes:**
- "Live from New York": Court TV's Terry Moran (Kevin Nealon).
- Des'ree performs "You Gotta Be" and "Feels So High."
- Mike Myers's final episode.
- At the end of the show, Newhart (as Bob Hartley, his character on *The Bob Newhart Show*) wakes up in bed with his wife, Emily (Suzanne Pleshette), to tell her he had a dream he hosted *SNL*.

**Airdate:** 2/18/95
**Episode:** 20.13
**Host:** Deion Sanders
**Musical Guest:** Bon Jovi
**Musical and Guest Performances/Cameo(s)/ Program Notes:**
- "Live from New York": O. J. Simpson (Tim Meadows).
- Bon Jovi performs "Always" and "Someday I'll Be Saturday Night."
- Cameo by 7'7" Sudanese basketball player Manute Bol.

**Airdate:** 2/25/95
**Episode:** 20.14
**Host:** George Clooney
**Musical Guest:** The Cranberries
**Musical and Guest Performances/Cameo(s)/ Program Notes:**
- "Live from New York": Ellen Cleghorne and Tim Meadows, in a tribute to Black History month.
- The Cranberries perform "Zombie" and "Ode to My Family."
- Janeane Garofalo's final episode.

- Debut of featured player Molly Shannon.

**Airdate:** 3/18/95
**Episode:** 20.15
**Host:** Paul Reiser
**Musical Guest:** Annie Lennox
**Musical and Guest Performances/Cameo(s)/ Program Notes:**
- "Live from New York": Newt Gingrich (Chris Farley).
- Lennox performs "No More I Love You's" and "Train in Vain."
- Cameo by TV writer and producer Bill Grundfest.
- In the final sketch, Michael McKean and Jay Mohr play pub owners O'Callahan & Son. In his memoir, *Gasping for Airtime*, Jay Mohr admitted he stole the sketch from a routine by comedian Rick Shapiro, who sued. As part of the settlement, the sketch was cut from future broadcasts.

**Airdate:** 3/25/95
**Episode:** 20.16
**Host:** John Goodman
**Musical Guest:** The Tragically Hip
**Musical and Guest Performances/Cameo(s)/ Program Notes:**
- "Live from New York": Bob Dole (Dan Aykroyd).
- The Tragically Hip perform "Grace, Too" and "Nautical Disaster."
- Special guest Dan Aykroyd impersonates Bob Dole, Tom Snyder, and Rush Limbaugh and appears as Elwood Blues alongside Mighty Mack Blues (Goodman) during the monologue.
- *Bob Swerski's Super Fans* sketch features actor Brian Dennehy, George Wendt (as Bob Swerski), and Dan Aykroyd as Irwin Mainway.

**Airdate:** 4/8/95
**Episode:** 20.17
**Host:** Damon Wayans
**Musical Guest:** Dionne Farris
**Musical and Guest Performances/Cameo(s)/ Program Notes:**
- "Live from New York": Judge Lance Ito (Mark McKinney).
- Wayans and David Alan Grier play gay film critics Blaine Edwards and Antoine Merriweather, characters they played on *In Living Color* (1990–1994).
- Farris performs "I Know" and "Blackbird."
- Debut of Morwenna Banks as a regular.

**Airdate:** 4/15/95
**Episode:** 20.18
**Host:** Courteney Cox
**Musical Guest:** Dave Matthews Band
**Musical and Guest Performances/Cameo(s)/ Program Notes:**
- "Live from New York": Motivational speaker Matt Foley (Chris Farley) (in Spanish): "Viva de Neuva York, es Sabado noche!"
- Dave Matthews Band performs "What Would You Say" and "Ants Marching."

**Airdate:** 5/6/95
**Episode:** 20.19
**Host:** Bob Saget
**Musical Guest:** TLC
**Musical and Guest Performances/Cameo(s)/ Program Notes:**
- "Live from New York": Celtics fan Tony Vallencourt (Adam Sandler).
- TLC performs "Creep" and "Red Light Special."

**Airdate:** 5/13/95
**Episode:** 20.20
**Host:** David Duchovny
**Musical Guest:** Rod Stewart
**Musical and Guest Performances/Cameo(s)/ Program Notes:**
- "Live from New York": Michael McKean, backstage, in a spoof of *The X-Files*.
- Stewart performs "Leave Virginia Alone" and "Maggie May."
- Cameo by model Naomi Campbell.

- Final episode for Morwenna Banks, Ellen Cleghorne, Chris Elliott, Chris Farley, Al Franken, Laura Kightlinger, Jay Mohr, and Adam Sandler.

## Season 21 (1995–1996)

**Airdate:** 9/30/95
**Episode:** 21.1
**Host:** Mariel Hemingway
**Musical Guest:** Blues Traveler
**Musical and Guest Performances/Cameo(s)/ Program Notes:**
- "Live from New York": Lawyer Johnnie Cochran (Tim Meadows).
- Blues Traveler performs "Run-Around" and "Hook."
- Sketch Debut: *Leg Up!*, hosted by Debbie Reynolds (Cheri Oteri) and Ann Miller (Molly Shannon).
- Debut of regulars Jim Breuer, Will Ferrell, Darrell Hammond, David Koechner, Cheri Oteri, and Nancy Walls.
- Debut of featured players Colin Quinn and Fred Wolf.

**Airdate:** 10/7/95
**Episode:** 21.2
**Host:** Chevy Chase
**Musical Guest:** Lisa Loeb
**Musical and Guest Performances/Cameo(s)/ Program Notes:**
- "Live from New York": O. J. Simpson (Tim Meadows).
- Loeb performs "Do You Sleep?" and "Stay."
- Cameos by Mariel Hemingway and Don Novello.

**Airdate:** 10/21/95
**Episode:** 21.3
**Host:** David Schwimmer
**Musical Guest:** Natalie Merchant
**Musical and Guest Performances/Cameo(s)/ Program Notes:**
- "Live from New York": Frat boy Darius Rucker (Tim Meadows).
- Merchant performs "Wonder" (with Jennifer Turner) and "Carnival" (with Turner and Katell Keineg).
- Cameos by Jennifer Aniston, Gary Coleman, Lisa Kudrow, Jimmie Walker, and Barry Williams.

**Airdate:** 10/28/95
**Episode:** 21.4
**Host:** Gabriel Byrne
**Musical Guest:** Alanis Morissette
**Musical and Guest Performances/Cameo(s)/ Program Notes:**
- "Live from New York": Bob Dole (Norm Macdonald).
- Morissette performs "Hand in My Pocket" and "All I Really Want."
- Cameos by Lamar Alexander, Bill Bradley, Tom Glavine, Chrissie Hynde, Chipper Jones, and Mark Wohlers.
- Character Debut: Mary Katherine Gallagher (Molly Shannon).

**Airdate:** 11/11/95
**Episode:** 21.5
**Host:** Quentin Tarantino
**Musical Guest:** The Smashing Pumpkins
**Musical and Guest Performances/Cameo(s)/ Program Notes:**
- "Live from New York": George (Tim Meadows), who delivers a pizza to the White House kitchen, where President Clinton (Darrell Hammond) is stuffing his face.
- The Smashing Pumpkins perform "Bullet with Butterfly Wings."
- Cameo by Robert Hegyes (Epstein from *Welcome Back, Kotter*).
- Sketch Debut: The Spartan cheerleaders Arianna (Cheri Oteri) and Craig Buchanan (Will Ferrell).

## Episode Guide

**Airdate:** 11/18/95
**Episode:** 21.6
**Host:** Laura Leighton
**Musical Guest:** Rancid
**Musical and Guest Performances/Cameo(s)/ Program Notes:**
- "Live from New York": Bob Dole (Norm Macdonald).
- Rancid performs "Roots Radical" and "Ruby Soho."
- Cameos by Sean Penn, Grant Show, and Sam Waterston.

**Airdate:** 12/2/95
**Episode:** 21.7
**Host:** Anthony Edwards
**Musical Guest:** Foo Fighters
**Musical and Guest Performances/Cameo(s)/ Program Notes:**
- "Live from New York": Jesse Helms (Darrell Hammond).
- Foo Fighters perform "I'll Stick Around" and "For All the Cows."
- Sketch Debut: *The Joe Pesci Show*, hosted by Joe Pesci (Jim Breuer).

**Airdate:** 12/9/95
**Episode:** 21.8
**Host:** David Alan Grier
**Musical Guest:** Silverchair
**Musical and Guest Performances/Cameo(s)/ Program Notes:**
- "Live from New York": Michael Jackson (Tim Meadows).
- Silverchair performs "Tomorrow" and "Pure Massacre."

**Airdate:** 12/16/95
**Episode:** 21.9
**Host:** Madeline Kahn
**Musical Guest:** Bush
**Musical and Guest Performances/Cameo(s)/ Program Notes:**
- "Live from New York": George Burns (Norm Macdonald).
- Bush performs "Comedown" and "Glycerine."

**Airdate:** 1/13/96
**Episode:** 21.10
**Host:** Christopher Walken
**Musical Guest:** Joan Osborne
**Musical and Guest Performances/Cameo(s)/ Program Notes:**
- "Live from New York": Governor George Pataki and New York City mayor Rudy Giuliani: "Live from New York, from the greatest city in the world, in the greatest city in the world, it's *Saturday Night!*"
- Osborne performs "One of Us."

**Airdate:** 1/20/96
**Episode:** 21.11
**Host:** Alec Baldwin
**Musical Guest:** Tori Amos
**Musical and Guest Performances/Cameo(s)/ Program Notes:**
- "Live from New York": Michael Jackson (Tim Meadows).
- Amos performs "Caught a Lite Sneeze" and "Hey Jupiter."

**Airdate:** 2/10/96
**Episode:** 21.12
**Host:** Danny Aiello
**Musical Guest:** Coolio
**Musical and Guest Performances/Cameo(s)/ Program Notes:**
- "Live from New York": Bob Dole (Norm Macdonald).
- Coolio performs "1, 2, 3, 4" and "Gangsta's Paradise" (with guest L.V.).
- Cameos by Larry Brown and Chris Farley (as Newt Gingrich).

**Airdate:** 2/17/96
**Episode:** 21.13
**Host:** Tom Arnold
**Musical Guest:** Tupac Shakur
**Musical and Guest Performances/Cameo(s)/ Program Notes:**
- "Live from New York": Judy Woodruff (Nancy Walls).
- Shakur performs "California Love" (with Danny Boy and Roger Troutman)

and "I Ain't Mad at Cha"(with Danny Boy).
- Cameo by Adam Sandler.

**Airdate:** 2/24/96
**Episode:** 21.14
**Host:** Elle Macpherson
**Musical Guest:** Sting
**Musical and Guest Performances/Cameo(s)/ Program Notes:**
- "Live from New York": Steve Forbes (Mark McKinney).
- Sting performs "Let Your Soul Be Your Pilot" and "You Still Touch Me."
- Darrell Hammond imitates absent announcer Don Pardo during the opening title sequence.

**Airdate:** 3/16/96
**Episode:** 21.15
**Host:** John Goodman
**Musical Guest:** Everclear
**Musical and Guest Performances/Cameo(s)/ Program Notes:**
- "Live from New York": *20/20*'s Hugh Downs (Darrell Hammond) and Barbara Walters (Cheri Oteri).
- Everclear performs "Santa Monica."
- Cameos by Elle MacPherson and Kurt Loder.
- Debut of featured player Chris Kattan.

**Airdate:** 3/23/96
**Episode:** 21.16
**Host:** Phil Hartman
**Musical Guest:** Gin Blossoms
**Musical and Guest Performances/Cameo(s)/ Program Notes:**
- "Live from New York": Charlton Heston (Phil Hartman).
- Gin Blossoms perform "Follow You Down" and "Memphis Time."

**Airdate:** 4/13/96
**Episode:** 21.17
**Host:** Steve Forbes
**Musical Guest:** Rage Against the Machine
**Musical and Guest Performances/Cameo(s)/ Program Notes:**
- "Live from New York": Ted Kaczynski (Will Ferrell).
- Rage Against the Machine performs "Bulls on Parade."
- Cameos by Forbes's wife, Sabina Beekman, and the couple's five daughters—Catherine, Elizabeth, Moira, Roberta, and Sabina.

**Airdate:** 4/20/96
**Episode:** 21.18
**Host:** Teri Hatcher
**Musical Guest:** Dave Matthews Band
**Musical and Guest Performances/Cameo(s)/ Program Notes:**
- "Live from New York": Ted Kaczynski (Will Ferrell).
- Dave Matthews Band performs "Too Much" and "So Much to Say."

**Airdate:** 5/11/96
**Episode:** 21.19
**Host:** Christine Baranski
**Musical Guest:** The Cure
**Musical and Guest Performances/Cameo(s)/ Program Notes:**
- "Live from New York": Tom Brokaw (Darrell Hammond).
- The Cure performs "Mint Car" and "Inbetween Days."
- Cameos by Dennis Rodman and Jim Gaffigan.

**Airdate:** 5/18/96
**Episode:** 21.20
**Host:** Jim Carrey
**Musical Guest:** Soundgarden
**Musical and Guest Performances/Cameo(s)/ Program Notes:**
- "Live from New York": Bob Dole (Norm Macdonald).
- Soundgarden performs "Pretty Noose" and "Burden in My Heart."
- Final episode for David Koechner, David Spade, and Nancy Walls.

## Season 22 (1996–1997)

**Airdate:** 9/28/96
**Episode:** 22.1
**Host:** Tom Hanks
**Musical Guest:** Tom Petty and the Heartbreakers
**Musical and Guest Performances/Cameo(s)/ Program Notes:**
- "Live from New York": President Bill Clinton (Darrell Hammond) during a 1996 presidential debate.
- Tom Petty and the Heartbreakers perform "Walls" and "Angel Dream."
- Cameo by Olympic gymnast Kerri Strug.
- Debut of regulars Ana Gasteyer and Tracy Morgan; Chris Kattan is bumped up to a regular.
- "TV Funhouse": Debut of *Ambiguously Gay Duo* ("It Takes Two to Tango").
- Sketch Debut: *Hey, Remember the '80s*, hosted by Goat Boy (Jim Breuer).

**Airdate:** 10/5/96
**Episode:** 22.2
**Host:** Lisa Kudrow
**Musical Guest:** Sheryl Crow
**Musical and Guest Performances/Cameo(s)/ Program Notes:**
- "Live from New York": Republican presidential candidate Bob Dole (Norm Macdonald) as he prepares for the next debate.
- Crow performs "If It Makes You Happy" and "Love Is a Good Thing."
- Cameo by David Lander (Squiggy from *Laverne and Shirley*).
- "TV Funhouse": *Fun with Real Audio* ("Ross Perot & Larry King").
- Character Debut: Joyologist Helen Madden (Molly Shannon).

**Airdate:** 10/19/96
**Episode:** 22.3
**Host:** Bill Pullman
**Musical Guest:** New Edition

**Musical and Guest Performances/Cameo(s)/ Program Notes:**
- "Live from New York": Don Pardo (voice).
- New Edition performs "Hit Me Off" and "I'm Still in Love with You."
- "TV Funhouse": *Fun with Real Audio* ("Bill Clinton and Bob Dole").
- Fred Wolf's final episode.

**Airdate:** 10/26/96
**Episode:** 22.4
**Host:** Dana Carvey
**Musical Guest:** Dr. Dre
**Musical and Guest Performances/Cameo(s)/ Program Notes:**
- "Live from New York": Dana Carvey: "Live from New York, home of the Yankees, it's *Saturday Night!*"
- Dr. Dre performs "Been There Done That."

**Airdate:** 11/2/96
**Episode:** 22.5
**Host:** Chris Rock
**Musical Guest:** The Wallflowers
**Musical and Guest Performances/Cameo(s)/ Program Notes:**
- "Live from New York": George H. W. Bush (Dana Carvey) and Bob Dole (Norm Macdonald).
- The Wallflowers perform "One Headlight."
- Special guest appearance by Dana Carvey.
- Cameo by Abe Vigoda.
- "TV Funhouse": *Ambiguously Gay Duo* ("Queen of Terror").
- Sketch Debut: Musical duo Marty Culp (Will Ferrell) and Bobbi Mohan-Culp (Ana Gasteyer).

**Airdate:** 11/16/96
**Episode:** 22.6
**Host:** Robert Downey Jr.
**Musical Guest:** Fiona Apple

**Musical and Guest Performances/Cameo(s)/ Program Notes:**
- "Live from New York": Senator Bob Dole.
- Apple performs "Shadowboxer."
- Cameos by Elizabeth Dole and boxer Evander Holyfield.
- "TV Funhouse": *Fun with Real Audio* ("Diane Sawyer and Mark Fuhrman"; "Barbara Walters and Robert Kardashian"; "Katie Couric and Johnnie Cochran").
- Sketch Debut: *The Delicious Dish*, hosted by Terry Rialto (Molly Shannon) and Margaret Jo McCullin (Ana Gasteyer).

**Airdate:** 11/23/96
**Episode:** 22.7
**Host:** Phil Hartman
**Musical Guest:** Bush
**Musical and Guest Performances/Cameo(s)/ Program Notes:**
- "Live from New York": Will Ferrell, an anchor on OJ-TV.
- Bush performs "Swallowed" and "Insect Kin."
- Cameos by Rodney Dangerfield and Cliff Robertson.
- "TV Funhouse": *Michael Jackson*.

**Airdate:** 12/7/96
**Episode:** 22.8
**Host:** Martin Short
**Musical Guest:** No Doubt
**Musical and Guest Performances/Cameo(s)/ Program Notes:**
- "Live from New York": O. J. Simpson (Tim Meadows).
- No Doubt performs "Don't Speak" and "Excuse Me Mr."
- Sketch Debut: Parody of *Jeopardy!*, hosted by Alex Trebek (Will Ferrell).

**Airdate:** 12/14/96
**Episode:** 22.9
**Host:** Rosie O'Donnell
**Musical Guest:** Whitney Houston

**Musical and Guest Performances/Cameo(s)/ Program Notes:**
- "Live from New York": Michael Jackson (Tim Meadows).
- Houston performs "I Believe in You and Me" and "I Go to the Rock" (with the Georgia Mass Singers).
- Cameo by Penny Marshall.
- "TV Funhouse": *Ambiguously Gay Duo* ("Don We Now or Never").

**Airdate:** 1/11/97
**Episode:** 22.10
**Host:** Kevin Spacey
**Musical Guest:** Beck
**Musical and Guest Performances/Cameo(s)/ Program Notes:**
- "Live from New York": Monty Pythoners John Cleese and Michael Palin, who explain the new television ratings system.
- Beck perform "Where It's At" and "Devil's Haircut."
- Sketch Debut: *Janet Reno's Dance Party*, hosted by Janet Reno (Will Ferrell).
- "TV Funhouse": *The X-Presidents* ("North Korea").

**Airdate:** 1/18/97
**Episode:** 22.11
**Host:** David Alan Grier
**Musical Guest:** Snoop Doggy Dogg
**Musical and Guest Performances/Cameo(s)/ Program Notes:**
- "Live from New York": Bill Clinton (Darrell Hammond).
- Snoop Doggy Dog performs (with Daz Dillinger and Charlie Wilson) "Snoops Upside Ya Head" and "Vapors."
- "TV Funhouse": *Wheaty, the Wheaten Terrier.*

**Airdate:** 2/8/97
**Episode:** 22.12
**Host:** Neve Campbell
**Musical Guest:** David Bowie
**Musical and Guest Performances/Cameo(s)/ Program Notes:**

- "Live from New York": O. J. Simpson (Tim Meadows).
- Bowie performs "Little Wonder" and "Scary Monsters."
- "TV Funhouse": *Fun with Real Audio* ("State of the Union").
- Cameo by David Spade.

**Airdate:** 2/15/97
**Episode:** 22.13
**Host:** Chevy Chase
**Musical Guest:** Live
**Musical and Guest Performances/Cameo(s)/ Program Notes:**
- "Live from New York": Courtney Love (Molly Shannon).
- Live performs "Lakini's Juice" and "Heropsychodreamer."

**Airdate:** 2/22/97
**Episode:** 22.14
**Host:** Alec Baldwin
**Musical Guest:** Tina Turner
**Musical and Guest Performances/Cameo(s)/ Program Notes:**
- "Live from New York": Robert De Niro (Alec Baldwin).
- Turner performs "In Your Wildest Dreams" and "Proud Mary."
- Cameo by Howard Stern.
- "TV Funhouse": *Fun with Real Audio* ("Tom Snyder and Dolly Parton").

**Airdate:** 3/15/97
**Episode:** 22.15
**Host:** Sting
**Musical Guest:** Veruca Salt
**Musical and Guest Performances/Cameo(s)/ Program Notes:**
- "Live from New York": Bill Clinton (Darrell Hammond).
- Veruca Salt performs "Shutterbug."
- Sting performs "My One and Only Love."
- Cameos by Mark Hamill and Trudie Styler.

**Airdate:** 3/22/97
**Episode:** 22.16
**Host:** Mike Myers
**Musical Guest:** Aerosmith
**Musical and Guest Performances/Cameo(s)/ Program Notes:**
- "Live from New York": Billy Bob Thornton (Darrell Hammond).
- Aerosmith performs "Falling in Love" and "Nine Lives."

**Airdate:** 4/12/97
**Episode:** 22.17
**Host:** Rob Lowe
**Musical Guest:** Spice Girls
**Musical and Guest Performances/Cameo(s)/ Program Notes:**
- "Live from New York": Zantar (Mark McKinney).
- Spice Girls perform "Wannabe" and "Say You'll Be There."
- *Weekend Update* anchor Norm Macdonald drops the f-bomb and then jokes, "My farewell performance."
- Sketch Debut: *Goth Talk* with Chris Kattan as Azrael Abyss and Molly Shannon as Circe Nightshade.
- "TV Funhouse": *The X-Presidents* ("Brazilian Environmental Summit").
- Robert De Niro and Joe Pesci visit *The Joe Pesci Show* and confront their respective impersonators, Jim Breuer and Colin Quinn.

**Airdate:** 4/19/97
**Episode:** 22.18
**Host:** Pamela Lee
**Musical Guest:** Rollins Band
**Musical and Guest Performances/Cameo(s)/ Program Notes:**
- "Live from New York": Janet Reno (Will Ferrell).
- Rollins Band performs "Starve."
- Cameo by Tommy Lee.
- "TV Funhouse": *Ambiguously Gay Duo* ("Safety Tips").

**Airdate:** 5/10/97
**Episode:** 22.19
**Host:** John Goodman
**Musical Guest:** Jewel

Appendix A

**Musical and Guest Performances/Cameo(s)/ Program Notes:**
- "Live from New York": Anne Heche (Chris Kattan).
- Jewel performs "Who Will Save Your Soul" and "You Were Meant for Me."
- Cameo by Mike Myers.

**Airdate:** 5/17/97
**Episode:** 22.20

## Season 23 (1997–1998)

**Airdate:** 9/27/97
**Episode:** 23.1
**Host:** Sylvester Stallone
**Musical Guest:** Jamiroquai
**Musical and Guest Performances/Cameo(s)/ Program Notes:**
- "Live from New York": Marv Albert (Norm Macdonald) on *Oprah*.
- Jamiroquai performs "Alright."
- Cameo by Richard Jewell, who discovered the pipe bomb at Centennial Olympic Park during the 1996 Summer Olympics in Atlanta and was later (falsely) suspected of planting it (see chapter 20).
- "TV Funhouse": *Fun with Real Audio* ("*Casablanca* Outtakes").

**Airdate:** 10/4/97
**Episode:** 23.2
**Host:** Matthew Perry
**Musical Guest:** Oasis
**Musical and Guest Performances/Cameo(s)/ Program Notes:**
- "Live from New York": Spartan Cheerleaders Craig and Arianna (Will Ferrell, Cheri Oteri).
- Oasis performs "Don't Go Away," and "Acquiesce."
- Sketch Debut: *The Ladies' Man*, hosted by Leon Phelps (Tim Meadows).

**Airdate:** 10/18/97
**Episode:** 23.3

**Host:** Jeff Goldblum
**Musical Guest:** En Vogue
**Musical and Guest Performances/Cameo(s)/ Program Notes:**
- "Live from New York": Ted Koppel (Darrell Hammond).
- En Vogue performs "Don't Let Go (Love)."
- "TV Funhouse": *Fun with Real Audio* ("Sally Jessy Raphael").

**Host:** Brendan Fraser
**Musical Guest:** Björk
**Musical and Guest Performances/Cameo(s)/ Program Notes:**
- "Live from New York": Janet Reno (Will Ferrell).
- Björk performs "Bachelorette."
- Character Debut: Mango (Chris Kattan).
- Cameo by Eric Dickerson.

**Airdate:** 10/25/97
**Episode:** 23.4
**Host:** Chris Farley
**Musical Guest:** The Mighty Mighty Bosstones
**Musical and Guest Performances/Cameo(s)/ Program Notes:**
- "Live from New York": Chris Farley, asking Lorne Michaels's permission to host the show. Farley says he's been sober for six weeks with Chevy Chase as his AA sponsor.
- The Mighty Mighty Bosstones perform "The Impression That I Get."
- Cameos by Chevy Chase, Chris Rock, Mike Ditka, Bill Kurtis, and George Wendt.
- Sketch Debut: *Morning Latte*, hosted by Tom Wilkins (Will Ferrell) and Cass Van Rye (Cheri Oteri).
- Farley's final appearance on the show. He died less than two months later

from a drug overdose at the age of thirty-three.

**Airdate:** 11/8/97
**Episode:** 23.5
**Host:** Jon Lovitz
**Musical Guest:** Jane's Addiction
**Musical and Guest Performances/Cameo(s)/ Program Notes:**
- "Live from New York": Bill Gates (Chris Kattan).
- Jane's Addiction performs "Jane Says" (with Flea).
- Cameo by Dana Carvey (as Ross Perot and George Michael).
- "TV Funhouse": *Fun with Real Audio* ("Clinton Press Conference").

**Airdate:** 11/15/97
**Episode:** 23.6
**Host:** Claire Danes
**Musical Guest:** Mariah Carey
**Musical and Guest Performances/Cameo(s)/ Program Notes:**
- "Live from New York": Hillary Clinton (Ana Gasteyer).
- Carey performs "Butterfly" and "My All."
- "TV Funhouse": *Ambiguously Gay Duo* ("Blow Hot, Blow Cold").

**Airdate:** 11/22/97
**Episode:** 23.7
**Host:** Rudy Giuliani
**Musical Guest:** Sarah McLachlan
**Musical and Guest Performances/Cameo(s)/ Program Notes:**
- "Live from New York": Mayor Rudy Giuliani ("Live from the capital of the world, it's *Saturday Night!*")
- McLachlan performs "Sweet Surrender."

**Airdate:** 12/6/97
**Episode:** 23.8
**Host:** Nathan Lane
**Musical Guest:** Metallica

**Musical and Guest Performances/Cameo(s)/ Program Notes:**
- "Live from New York": Bobbi McCaughey (Molly Shannon), whose septuplets have fallen down a well.
- Metallica performs "Fuel" and "The Memory Remains" (with guest Marianne Faithfull).
- Cameos by Ernie Sabella and the Dallas Cowboy Cheerleaders.

**Airdate:** 12/13/97
**Episode:** 23.9
**Host:** Helen Hunt
**Musical Guest:** Hanson
**Musical and Guest Performances/Cameo(s)/ Program Notes:**
- "Live from New York": Connie Davenport (Helen Hunt), who is out caroling with Marty Culp and Bobbi Mohan-Culp (Will Ferrell and Ana Gasteyer).
- Hanson performs "MMMBop" and "Merry Christmas Baby."
- Cameos by Jack Nicholson and Major League Baseball players: Pedro Borbón Jr., Marty Cordova, Russ Davis, Jeff Fassero, Cliff Floyd, Mark Grudzielanek, David Howard, Todd Hundley, Gregg Jefferies, Scott Rolen, Mike Sweeney, Rondell White, Gerald Williams, Mark Wohlers, and Todd Zeile.
- "TV Funhouse": *Fun with Real Audio* (Jesus tackles the commercialization of Christmas).

**Airdate:** 1/10/98
**Episode:** 23.10
**Host:** Samuel L. Jackson
**Musical Guest:** Ben Folds Five
**Musical and Guest Performances/Cameo(s)/ Program Notes:**
- "Live from New York": President Clinton (Darrell Hammond).
- Ben Folds Five performs "Brick."

- Sketch Debut: Parody of *Judge Judy*, with Judge Judy Sheindlin (Cheri Oteri).
- "TV Funhouse": *George Clooney in the Sexiest Car Alive.*
- *Weekend Update*: Colin Quinn replaces Norm Macdonald as anchor.

**Airdate:** 1/17/98
**Episode:** 23.11
**Host:** Sarah Michelle Gellar
**Musical Guest:** Portishead
**Musical and Guest Performances/Cameo(s)/ Program Notes:**
- "Live from New York": Unabomber Ted Kaczynski (Will Ferrell).
- Portishead performs "Only You."

**Airdate:** 2/7/98
**Episode:** 23.12
**Host:** John Goodman
**Musical Guest:** Paula Cole
**Musical and Guest Performances/Cameo(s)/ Program Notes:**
- "Live from New York": Monica Lewinsky (Molly Shannon), lunching with Linda Tripp (Goodman).
- Cole performs "I Don't Wanna Wait."
- Special guest Dan Aykroyd (as Elwood Blues) and John Goodman (Mighty Mack Blues) perform "Lookin' for a Fox."
- "TV Funhouse": *The X-Presidents* ("X-First Ladies").

**Airdate:** 2/14/98
**Episode:** 23.13
**Host:** Roma Downey
**Musical Guest:** Missy "Misdemeanor" Elliott
**Musical and Guest Performances/Cameo(s)/ Program Notes:**
- "Live from New York": Ted Koppel (Darrell Hammond).
- Elliott performs "Sock It 2 Me" and "Beep Me 911" (with Timbaland & Magoo).
- "TV Funhouse": *Ah Lin the Skater Man.*

**Airdate:** 2/28/98
**Episode:** 23.14
**Host/Musical Guest:** Garth Brooks
**Musical and Guest Performances/Cameo(s)/ Program Notes:**
- "Live from New York": Saddam Hussein (Will Ferrell).
- Brooks performs "Two Piña Coladas."
- Cameo by Robert Duvall.
- "TV Funhouse": *Fun with Real Audio* ("Interviewing David Brenner").

**Airdate:** 3/7/98
**Episode:** 23.15
**Host:** Scott Wolf
**Musical Guest:** Natalie Imbruglia
**Musical and Guest Performances/Cameo(s)/ Program Notes:**
- "Live from New York": President Clinton (Darrell Hammond) and his sixteen accusers on *Larry King Live*.
- Imbruglia performs "Torn."

**Airdate:** 3/14/98
**Episode:** 23.16
**Host:** Julianne Moore
**Musical Guest:** Backstreet Boys
**Musical and Guest Performances/Cameo(s)/ Program Notes:**
- "Live from New York": Kenneth Starr (Will Ferrell).
- Backstreet Boys perform "As Long as You Love Me."
- "TV Funhouse": *Conspiracy Theory Rock*, which targets the unscrupulous practices of the major media conglomerates, including NBC's parent company, General Electric. The cartoon was pulled from subsequent airings.
- Norm Macdonald's final episode.

**Airdate:** 4/4/98
**Episode:** 23.17
**Host:** Steve Buscemi
**Musical Guest:** Third Eye Blind
**Musical and Guest Performances/Cameo(s)/ Program Notes:**
- "Live from New York": President Clinton (Darrell Hammond), Janet Reno

(Will Ferrell), Oprah Winfrey (Tim Meadows), and Monica Lewinsky (Molly Shannon).
- Third Eye Blind performs "How's It Gonna Be."
- Cameos by Didi Conn, John Hurt, Lewis Lapham, and Natasha Henstridge.
- "TV Funhouse": *Titey*, Disney's animated version of *Titanic*.

**Airdate:** 4/11/98
**Episode:** 23.18
**Host:** Greg Kinnear
**Musical Guest:** All Saints
**Musical and Guest Performances/Cameo(s)/ Program Notes:**
- "Live from New York": Martha Stewart (Ana Gasteyer) in a promo for her Easter show.
- All Saints performs "Never End."
- Cameo by Bob Hoskins.

**Airdate:** 5/2/98
**Episode:** 23.19
**Host:** Matthew Broderick
**Musical Guest:** Natalie Merchant
**Musical and Guest Performances/Cameo(s)/ Program Notes:**
- "Live from New York": Leon Phelps (Tim Meadows).
- Merchant performs "Kind & Generous."
- Guest performance by Tenacious D (Kyle Gass and Jack Black).
- Cameo by Regis Philbin.

**Airdate:** 5/9/98
**Episode:** 23.20
**Host:** David Duchovny
**Musical Guest:** Puff Daddy
**Musical and Guest Performances/Cameo(s)/ Program Notes:**
- "Live from New York": Janet Reno (Will Ferrell), who has the hots for *X-Files*' Agent Mulder (David Duchovny).
- Puff Daddy performs "Come with Me" (with special guest Jimmy Page).
- Cameos by Paula Abdul, John Goodman, Matt Lauer, Nicolas Lea, and Al Roker.
- "TV Funhouse": *Ambiguously Gay Duo* ("A Hard One to Swallow").

## Season 24 (1998–1999)

**Airdate:** 9/26/98
**Episode:** 24.1
**Host:** Cameron Diaz
**Musical Guest:** The Smashing Pumpkins
**Musical and Guest Performances/Cameo(s)/ Program Notes:**
- "Live from New York": Oprah Winfrey (Tim Meadows).
- The Smashing Pumpkins perform "Perfect."
- Cameos by John Goodman (as Linda Tripp), Dan Aykroyd, and Steve Martin (as Yortuk and Georg Festrunk), and musical performers Jonathan Richman and Tommy Larkins.
- "TV Funhouse": *Fun with Real Audio* ("Presidential Address Outtakes").
- Debut of featured players Jimmy Fallon, Chris Parnell, and Horatio Sanz.

**Airdate:** 10/3/98
**Episode:** 24.2
**Host:** Kelsey Grammer
**Musical Guest:** Sheryl Crow
**Musical and Guest Performances/Cameo(s)/ Program Notes:**
- "Live from New York": Bill Clinton (Darrell Hammond).
- Crow performs "My Favorite Mistake" (with Wendy Melvoin).
- Cameos by Christine Baranski, Hal Linden, and Patti Lupone.

Appendix A

**Airdate:** 10/17/98
**Episode:** 24.3
**Host:** Lucy Lawless
**Musical Guest:** Elliott Smith
**Musical and Guest Performances/Cameo(s)/ Program Notes:**
- "Live from New York": Jesse Helms (Darrell Hammond).
- Smith performs "Waltz #2."
- Cameos by Chucky (from the horror film *Child's Play*) and Judge Judy Sheindlin.
- "TV Funhouse": *Fun with Real Audio* ("Howard Stern Dishes *SNL*").

**Airdate:** 10/24/98
**Episode:** 24.4
**Host:** Ben Stiller
**Musical Guest:** Alanis Morissette
**Musical and Guest Performances/Cameo(s)/ Program Notes:**
- "Live from New York": Ben Stiller, as he's thrown off the roof of 30 Rock by Lorne Michaels.
- Morissette performs "Thank U" and "Baba."
- Cameos by members of the New York Yankees: David Cone, Chili Davis, Graeme Lloyd, Tino Martinez, and David Wells.
- "TV Funhouse": *Heteroy*, a Biblical superhero who turns gay men straight.

**Airdate:** 11/7/98
**Episode:** 24.5
**Host:** David Spade
**Musical Guest:** Eagle-Eye Cherry
**Musical and Guest Performances/Cameo(s)/ Program Notes:**
- "Live from New York": Brad Pitt (in a cameo) as David Spade's therapist.
- Eagle-Eye Cherry performs "Save Tonight."
- Cameo by Chris Rock.

**Airdate:** 11/14/98
**Episode:** 24.6
**Host:** Joan Allen
**Musical Guest:** Jewel
**Musical and Guest Performances/Cameo(s)/ Program Notes:**
- "Live from New York": President Clinton (Hammond) and Newt Gingrich (Chris Parnell).
- Jewel performs "Hands" and "Down So Long."
- Cameo by John Goodman.

**Airdate:** 11/21/98
**Episode:** 24.7
**Host:** Jennifer Love Hewitt
**Musical Guest:** Beastie Boys
**Musical and Guest Performances/Cameo(s)/ Program Notes:**
- "Live from New York": Monica Lewinsky (Molly Shannon).
- Beastie Boys perform "3 MC's and One DJ" and "Sabotage."
- Cameos by John Goodman and Muse Watson.
- "TV Funhouse": *Ambiguously Gay Duo* ("Ace and Gary's Fan Club").

**Airdate:** 12/5/98
**Episode:** 24.8
**Host:** Vince Vaughn
**Musical Guest:** Lauryn Hill
**Musical and Guest Performances/Cameo(s)/ Program Notes:**
- "Live from New York": Rep. Maxine Waters (Tracy Morgan).
- Hill performs "Doo Wop (That Thing)" and "Ex-Factor."
- Sketch Debut: *Dog Show*, with David Larry (Will Ferrell) and Miss Colleen (Molly Shannon).

**Airdate:** 12/12/98
**Episode:** 24.9
**Host:** Alec Baldwin
**Musical Guest:** Luciano Pavarotti, Vanessa Williams
**Musical and Guest Performances/Cameo(s)/ Program Notes:**
- "Live from New York": Bill Clinton (Darrell Hammond).
- Pavarotti and Williams sing "Adeste Fideles."

- Cameos by John Goodman and Janice Pendarvis.
- "TV Funhouse": *The Harlem Globetrotters First Christmas*.
- ★ ★ ★ ★ Four-Star Sketch: Pete Schweddy (Alec Baldwin) appears on *The Delicious Dish* and shares his Schweddy Balls with hosts Terry Rialto (Molly Shannon) and Margaret Jo McCullin (Ana Gasteyer).

**Airdate:** 1/9/99
**Episode:** 24.10
**Host:** Bill Paxton
**Musical Guest:** Beck
**Musical and Guest Performances/Cameo(s)/ Program Notes:**
- "Live from New York": Newt Gingrich (Chris Parnell).
- Beck performs "Nobody's Fault but My Own" and "Tropicalia."
- Cameos by Debbie Matenopoulos and James Cameron.

**Airdate:** 1/16/99
**Episode:** 24.11
**Host:** James Van Der Beek
**Musical Guest:** Everlast
**Musical and Guest Performances/Cameo(s)/ Program Notes:**
- "Live from New York": Larry Flynt (Horatio Sanz), who pays a visit to President Clinton (Hammond).
- Everlast performs "What It's Like."

**Airdate:** 2/6/99
**Episode:** 24.12
**Host:** Gwyneth Paltrow
**Musical Guest:** Barenaked Ladies
**Musical and Guest Performances/Cameo(s)/ Program Notes:**
- "Live from New York": President Clinton (Darrell Hammond).
- Barenaked Ladies performs "It's All Been Done."
- "TV Funhouse": *The X-Presidents*.
- Cameo by Ben Affleck.

**Airdate:** 2/13/99
**Episode:** 24.13
**Host:** Brendan Fraser
**Musical Guest:** Busta Rhymes
**Musical and Guest Performances/Cameo(s)/ Program Notes:**
- "Live from New York": Linda Tripp (John Goodman).
- Busta Rhymes performs "Gimme Some More" and "Tear Da Roof Off" (with the Roots).
- Cameos by Tom Davis, John Goodman, and George Plimpton.
- "TV Funhouse": *Fun with Real Audio* ("The Poetry of Jewel").

**Airdate:** 2/20/99
**Episode:** 24.14
**Host:** Bill Murray
**Musical Guest:** Lucinda Williams
**Musical and Guest Performances/Cameo(s)/ Program Notes:**
- "Live from New York": Leon Phelps (Tim Meadows) and supermodel Stephanie Seymour.
- Williams performs "Can't Let Go" and "2 Kool 2 Be 4-Gotten."
- Cameos by Chevy Chase and Stephanie Seymour.

**Airdate:** 3/13/99
**Episode:** 24.15
**Host:** Ray Romano
**Musical Guest:** The Corrs
**Musical and Guest Performances/Cameo(s)/ Program Notes:**
- "Live from New York": Hillary Clinton (Ana Gasteyer).
- The Corrs perform "What Can I Do" and "So Young."
- Cameos by Peter Boyle and Doris Roberts.

**Airdate:** 3/20/99
**Episode:** 24.16
**Host:** Drew Barrymore
**Musical Guest:** Garbage
**Musical and Guest Performances/Cameo(s)/ Program Notes:**

- "Live from New York": Joan Rivers (Ana Gasteyer).
- Garbage performs "Special" and "When I Grow Up."
- Cameo by Edward Norton (as Captain and Tennille's Daryl Dragon).
- "TV Funhouse": *Fun with Real Audio* ("Oscar's Greatest Moments").

**Airdate:** 4/10/99
**Episode:** 24.17
**Host:** John Goodman
**Musical Guest:** Tom Petty and the Heartbreakers
**Musical and Guest Performances/Cameo(s)/ Program Notes:**
- "Live from New York": President Clinton (Darrell Hammond).
- Petty and the Heartbreakers perform "Swingin'" and "Room at the Top."

**Airdate:** 5/8/99
**Episode:** 24.18
**Host:** Cuba Gooding Jr.
**Musical Guest:** Ricky Martin
**Musical and Guest Performances/Cameo(s)/ Program Notes:**

- "Live from New York": Monica Lewinsky.
- Martin performs "Livin' la Vida Loca."
- Cameos by Monica Lewinsky and John Goodman, who provides the voice of Linda Tripp.
- "TV Funhouse": *Ambiguously Gay Duo* ("AmbiguoBoys").

**Airdate:** 5/15/99
**Episode:** 24.19
**Host:** Sarah Michelle Gellar
**Musical Guest:** Backstreet Boys
**Musical and Guest Performances/Cameo(s)/ Program Notes:**
- "Live from New York": Marty Culp (Will Ferrell) and Bobbie Mohan-Culp (Ana Gasteyer).
- Backstreet Boys perform "I Want It That Way" and "All I Have to Give."
- Cameos by David Boreanaz and Seth Green.
- "TV Funhouse": *The Ginsburg Gang*.
- Sketch Debut: *Brian Fellow's Safari Planet*, featuring Tracy Morgan as Brian Fellow, a character who first appeared on *Weekend Update* on 24.11.

## Season 25 (1999–2000)

**Airdate:** 10/2/99
**Episode:** 25.1
**Host:** Jerry Seinfeld
**Musical Guest:** David Bowie
**Musical and Guest Performances/Cameo(s)/ Program Notes:**
- "Live from New York": Jesse Ventura (Will Ferrell).
- Bowie performs "Thursday's Child" and "Rebel Rebel."
- Cameos by characters from the TV show *Oz*: Ryan O'Reily (Dean Winters), Vern Schillinger (J. K. Simmons), and Tobias Beecher (Lee Tergesen).
- Cameos by A. J. Benza and Rick Ludwin.

- Jimmy Fallon, Chris Parnell, and Horatio Sanz are bumped up to regulars.

**Airdate:** 10/16/99
**Episode:** 25.2
**Host:** Heather Graham
**Musical Guest:** Marc Anthony
**Musical and Guest Performances/Cameo(s)/ Program Notes:**
- "Live from New York": Al W. Bush-Gore (Horatio Sanz).
- Anthony performs "I Need to Know" and "That's Okay."
- Cameos by Dana Carvey and Kevin Nealon.

**Airdate:** 10/23/99
**Episode:** 25.3
**Host:** Norm Macdonald
**Musical Guest:** Dr. Dre, Snoop Dogg, Eminem
**Musical and Guest Performances/Cameo(s)/ Program Notes:**
- "Live from New York": Rudolph Giuliani (Darrell Hammond).
- Dr. Dre and Snoop Dogg perform "Still D.R.E.," and Dr. Dre and Eminem perform "Forgot About Dre."
- Episode was delayed fourteen minutes due to Game 1 of the World Series (the Yankees beat the Atlanta Braves 4–1).
- Cameo by Savion Glover.
- "TV Funhouse": *Fun with Real Audio* ("House Judiciary Committee").
- Sketch Debut: Parody of *Inside the Actors Studio*, hosted by James Lipton (Will Ferrell).
- Debut of featured player Rachel Dratch.

**Airdate:** 11/6/99
**Episode:** 25.4
**Host:** Dylan McDermott
**Musical Guest:** Foo Fighters
**Musical and Guest Performances/Cameo(s)/ Program Notes:**
- "Live from New York": Ellenor (Horatio Sanz as Camryn Manheim) from *The Practice*.
- Foo Fighters perform "Learn to Fly" and "Stacked Actors."

**Airdate:** 11/13/99
**Episode:** 25.5
**Host:** Garth Brooks
**Musical Guest:** Garth Brooks (as Chris Gaines)
**Musical and Guest Performances/Cameo(s)/ Program Notes:**
- "Live from New York": Spartan cheerleaders Craig (Will Ferrell) and Arianna (Cheri Oteri).
- Brooks (as Chris Gaines) performs "Way of the Girl."

**Airdate:** 11/20/99
**Episode:** 25.6
**Host:** Jennifer Aniston
**Musical Guest:** Sting
**Musical and Guest Performances/Cameo(s)/ Program Notes:**
- "Live from New York": Director John Carpenter.
- Sting performs "Brand New Day" and "Desert Rose" (with Cheb Mami).
- Sketch Debut: *Nick Burns, Your Company's Computer Guy*, with Nick Burns (Jimmy Fallon).

**Airdate:** 12/4/99
**Episode:** 25.7
**Host:** Christina Ricci
**Musical Guest:** Beck
**Musical and Guest Performances/Cameo(s)/ Program Notes:**
- "Live from New York": Bill Clinton (Darrell Hammond).
- Beck performs "Mixed Bizness" and "Sexx Laws."
- "TV Funhouse": *Millennium Fun with Real Audio* ("Friends Apocalypse").

**Airdate:** 12/11/99
**Episode:** 25.8
**Host:** Danny DeVito
**Musical Guest:** R.E.M.
**Musical and Guest Performances/Cameo(s)/ Program Notes:**
- "Live from New York": Arnold Schwarzenegger (Darrell Hammond) and Tom Brokaw (Chris Parnell).
- R.E.M. performs "Great Beyond" and "Man on the Moon" (the title song of the 1999 biopic of Andy Kaufman starring Jim Carrey).
- Cameos by the Rockettes and Al Franken and his son, Joe Franken.
- "TV Funhouse": *Fun with Real Audio* ("1999: The Year in Journalism").
- Character Debut: Sally O'Malley (Molly Shannon).

**Airdate:** 1/8/00
**Episode:** 25.9
**Host:** Jamie Foxx
**Musical Guest:** Blink-182
**Musical and Guest Performances/Cameo(s)/ Program Notes:**
- "Live from New York": Bill Clinton (Darrell Hammond).
- Blink-182 performs "All the Small Things" and "What's My Age Again?"
- Cameo by John Goodman.

**Airdate:** 1/15/00
**Episode:** 25.10
**Host:** Freddie Prinze Jr.
**Musical Guest:** Macy Gray
**Musical and Guest Performances/Cameo(s)/ Program Notes:**
- "Live from New York": Elián González (Chris Kattan).
- Gray performs "I Try" and "Why Didn't You Call Me."
- Cameo by Angie Everhart.

**Airdate:** 2/5/00
**Episode:** 25.11
**Host:** Alan Cumming
**Musical Guest:** Jennifer Lopez
**Musical and Guest Performances/Cameo(s)/ Program Notes:**
- "Live from New York": John McCain (Chris Parnell).
- Lopez performs "Feelin' So Good" and "Waiting for Tonight" (with Fat Joe).
- Cameo by Ben Stiller.
- "A Short Film by Adam McKay": *The Heat Is On.*

**Airdate:** 2/12/00
**Episode:** 25.12
**Host:** Julianna Margulies
**Musical Guest:** DMX
**Musical and Guest Performances/Cameo(s)/ Program Notes:**
- "Live from New York": Bill Clinton (Darrell Hammond).
- DMX performs "Party Up" and "What's My Name."
- Cameo by Noah Wyle.

**Airdate:** 2/19/00
**Episode:** 25.13
**Host:** Ben Affleck
**Musical Guest:** Fiona Apple
**Musical and Guest Performances/Cameo(s)/ Program Notes:**
- "Live from New York": *Peanuts* characters Marcy (Rachel Dratch), Franklin (Tim Meadows), and Pigpen (Horatio Sanz).
- Apple performs "Limp."
- Cameos by Gwyneth Paltrow and G. E. Smith.
- "TV Funhouse": *The All-New Adventures of Mr. T* ("A Doll's House").

**Airdate:** 3/11/00
**Episode:** 25.14
**Host:** Joshua Jackson
**Musical Guest:** 'NSYNC
**Musical and Guest Performances/Cameo(s)/ Program Notes:**
- "Live from New York": News anchors Ted Koppel (Darrell Hammond), Bernard Shaw (Tim Meadows), Tom Brokaw (Chris Parnell), and Shaw's girlfriend (Molly Shannon).
- 'NSYNC performs "On the Road with the Boys," "Bye Bye Bye," and "I Thought She Knew."
- Cameos by the Statler Brothers and Badal Roy.
- "A Short Film by Adam McKay": *Neil Armstrong: The Ohio Years.*

**Airdate:** 3/18/00
**Episode:** 25.15
**Host:** The Rock
**Musical Guest:** AC/DC
**Musical and Guest Performances/Cameo(s)/ Program Notes:**
- "Live from New York": Vince McMahon.
- AC/DC performs "Stiff Upper Lip" and "Shook Me All Night Long."
- Cameos by wrestlers Big Show, Mick Foley, Triple H, and Vince McMahon.

**Airdate:** 4/8/00
**Episode:** 25.16
**Host:** Christopher Walken
**Musical Guest:** Christina Aguilera
**Musical and Guest Performances/Cameo(s)/ Program Notes:**
- "Live from New York": George H. W. Bush (Dana Carvey).
- Aguilera performs "I Turn to You," "At Last," and "What a Girl Wants."
- Cameo by Dana Carvey (as George H. W. Bush).
- ★ ★ ★ ★ Four-Star Sketch: "More cowbell!" A parody of *VH1: Behind the Music* focuses on Blue Öyster Cult recording "(Don't Fear) The Reaper."

**Airdate:** 4/15/00
**Episode:** 25.17
**Host:** Tobey Maguire
**Musical Guest:** Sisqó
**Musical and Guest Performances/Cameo(s)/ Program Notes:**
- "Live from New York": Tobey Maguire.
- Sisqó performs "The Thong Song."
- "A Short Film by Adam McKay": *Stavenhagens Pawn Shop*, with a cameo by Steve Buscemi.
- "TV Funhouse": *Fun with Real Audio* ("Up Close with Geppetto").

**Airdate:** 5/6/00
**Episode:** 25.18
**Host:** John Goodman
**Musical Guest:** Neil Young
**Musical and Guest Performances/Cameo(s)/ Program Notes:**
- "Live from New York": Regis Philbin (Darrell Hammond).
- Young performs "Razor Love" and "Silver & Gold."
- Debut of featured player Maya Rudolph.
- "TV Funhouse": *The Life of a Catch Phrase*.

**Airdate:** 5/13/00
**Episode:** 25.19
**Host/Musical Guest:** Britney Spears
**Musical and Guest Performances/Cameo(s)/ Program Notes:**
- "Live from New York": Hillary Clinton (Ana Gasteyer).
- Spears performs "Oops! . . . I Did It Again" and "Don't Let Me Be the Last to Know."
- "TV Funhouse": *Ambiguously Gay Duo* ("Trouble Coming Twice").

**Airdate:** 5/20/00
**Episode:** 25.20
**Host:** Jackie Chan
**Musical Guest:** Kid Rock
**Musical and Guest Performances/Cameo(s)/ Program Notes:**
- "Live from New York": *The Ladies' Man*'s Leon Phelps (Tim Meadows) and his guests Florence Henderson, Wilma Slossen (Gina Gershon), and Brandy Lane (Sarah Michelle Gellar).
- Kid Rock performed "American Bad Ass" and "Only God Knows Why" (with Trey Anastasio).
- Cameos by Trey Anastasio and G. E. Smith.
- "TV Funhouse": *Fun with Real Audio* ("Madonna").
- Final episode for Cheri Oteri and Colin Quinn.

## Season 26 (2000–2001)

**Airdate:** 10/7/00
**Episode:** 26.1
**Host:** Rob Lowe
**Musical Guest:** Eminem
**Musical and Guest Performances/Cameo(s)/ Program Notes:**
- "Live from New York": Jim Lehrer (Chris Parnell), moderating the Gore

- (Darrell Hammond)–Bush (Will Ferrell) debate.
- Eminem performs "Stan" (with Dido) and "The Real Slim Shady."
- Cameos by Brendan Fraser, Tim Meadows, and Ralph Nader.
- Debut of featured players Jerry Minor and Tina Fey.
- *Weekend Update*: Jimmy Fallon and Tina Fey take over as coanchors.

**Airdate:** 10/14/00
**Episode:** 26.2
**Host:** Kate Hudson
**Musical Guest:** Radiohead
**Musical and Guest Performances/Cameo(s)/ Program Notes:**
- "Live from New York": Jim Lehrer (Chris Parnell).
- Radiohead performs "The National Anthem" and "Idioteque."
- Cameo by Boston Red Sox shortstop Nomar Garciaparra.
- "TV Funhouse": *The X-Presidents* ("Independents").

**Airdate:** 10/21/00
**Episode:** 26.3
**Host:** Dana Carvey
**Musical Guest:** The Wallflowers
**Musical and Guest Performances/Cameo(s)/ Program Notes:**
- "Live from New York": George W. Bush (Will Ferrell), in the third presidential debate.
- The Wallflowers perform "Sleepwalker" and "Hand Me Down."
- Guest performance by Baha Men.
- Cameo by Robert De Niro.

**Airdate:** 11/04/00
**Episode:** 26.4
**Host:** Charlize Theron
**Musical Guest:** Paul Simon
**Musical and Guest Performances/Cameo(s)/ Program Notes:**
- "Live from New York": George W. Bush (Will Ferrell).
- Simon performs "Hurricane Eye" and "Old."
- "TV Funhouse": *The All New Adventures of Mr. T* ("Actors Strike").

**Airdate:** 11/11/00
**Episode:** 26.5
**Host:** Calista Flockhart
**Musical Guest:** Ricky Martin
**Musical and Guest Performances/Cameo(s)/ Program Notes:**
- "Live from New York": George W. Bush (Will Ferrell), who announces he and Gore (Darrell Hammond) will share the presidency.
- Martin performs "She Bangs" and "Loaded."

**Airdate:** 11/18/00
**Episode:** 26.6
**Host:** Tom Green
**Musical Guest:** David Gray
**Musical and Guest Performances/Cameo(s)/ Program Notes:**
- "Live from New York": George W. Bush (Will Ferrell) and Al Gore (Darrell Hammond) sing a parody of "I Got You, Babe."
- Gray performs "Babylon" and "Wedding."
- Cameos by Drew Barrymore, Derek Harvie, Glenn Humplik, Shawn Greenson, Gwyneth Paltrow, and Tom Green's parents, Mary Jane and Richard Green.
- During his monologue, Green proposes to Barrymore and announces they will be married at the end of the episode. In the final moments, the stage is set for a wedding, but Barrymore gets cold feet. The couple eventually did marry on July 7, 2001, but filed for divorce five months later.
- "TV Funhouse": *Fun with Real Audio* ("Sex and the Country").

**Airdate:** 12/9/00
**Episode:** 26.7
**Host:** Val Kilmer

**Musical Guest:** U2
**Musical and Guest Performances/Cameo(s)/ Program Notes:**
- "Live from New York": Vice presidential candidate Senator Joseph Lieberman (Chris Parnell), following the 5–4 Supreme Court ruling that officially made Bush the winner in the 2000 election.
- U2 performs "Beautiful Day" and "Elevation."

**Airdate:** 12/16/00
**Episode:** 26.8
**Host:** Lucy Liu
**Musical Guest:** Jay-Z
**Musical and Guest Performances/Cameo(s)/ Program Notes:**
- "Live from New York": George W. Bush (Will Ferrell).
- Jay-Z performs "I Just Wanna Love U (Give It 2 Me)" and "Is That Your Chick" (with Beanie Sigel and Memphis Bleek).
- Sketch Debut: *Jarret's Room*, featuring Jarret (Jimmy Fallon) and Gobi (Horatio Sanz).

**Airdate:** 1/13/01
**Episode:** 26.9
**Host:** Charlie Sheen
**Musical Guest:** Nelly Furtado
**Musical and Guest Performances/Cameo(s)/ Program Notes:**
- "Live from New York": George W. Bush (Will Ferrell).
- Furtado performs "I'm Like a Bird."
- "A Short Film by Adam McKay": *The Pervert*.

**Airdate:** 1/20/01
**Episode:** 26.10
**Host:** Mena Suvari
**Musical Guest:** Lenny Kravitz
**Musical and Guest Performances/Cameo(s)/ Program Notes:**
- "Live from New York": Citizen President Bill Clinton (Darrell Hammond).
- Kravitz performs "Again" and "Mr. Cab Driver."
- Cameo by Janet Reno.
- "TV Funhouse": *The X-Presidents* ("Clinton Joins the Group").

**Airdate:** 2/10/01
**Episode:** 26.11
**Host/Musical Guest:** Jennifer Lopez
**Musical and Guest Performances/Cameo(s)/ Program Notes:**
- "Live from New York": Will Ferrell, backstage.
- Lopez performs "Play" and "Love Don't Cost a Thing."
- Although the taping began on time, broadcast of the episode was delayed forty-five minutes due to an XFL game running late.
- Cameo by Tom Hanks.
- "A Short Film by Adam McKay": *The Baby & the German Intellectual*.
- "TV Funhouse": *Ray of Light*.

**Airdate:** 2/17/01
**Episode:** 26.12
**Host:** Sean Hayes
**Musical Guest:** Shaggy
**Musical and Guest Performances/Cameo(s)/ Program Notes:**
- "Live from New York": George W. Bush (Will Ferrell).
- Shaggy performs "It Wasn't Me" (with Rikrok) and "Angel" (with Rayvon and Rikrok).
- Molly Shannon's final episode.

**Airdate:** 2/24/01
**Episode:** 26.13
**Host:** Katie Holmes
**Musical Guest:** Dave Matthews Band
**Musical and Guest Performances/Cameo(s)/ Program Notes:**
- "Live from New York": Bill Clinton (Darrell Hammond).
- Dave Matthews Band performs "I Did It" and "The Space Between."
- "TV Funhouse": *Backstreet Boys*.

Appendix A

- Character Debut: Lovers Roger Klarvin (Will Ferrell) and his wife, Virginia (Rachel Dratch).

**Airdate:** 3/10/01
**Episode:** 26.14
**Host:** Conan O'Brien
**Musical Guest:** Don Henley
**Musical and Guest Performances/Cameo(s)/ Program Notes:**
- "Live from New York": George W. Bush (Will Ferrell).
- Henley performs "Everything Is Different Now" and "Heart of the Matter."
- Cameos by Ben Affleck and Max and Becky Weinberg.
- "TV Funhouse": *Find the Black People at the Knicks Game.*

**Airdate:** 3/17/01
**Episode:** 26.15
**Host:** Julia Stiles
**Musical Guest:** Aerosmith
**Musical and Guest Performances/Cameo(s)/ Program Notes:**
- "Live from New York": Martha Stewart (Ana Gasteyer).
- Aerosmith performs "Jaded" and "Big Ten Inch Record."
- Cameo by David Copperfield.
- "A Short Film by Adam McKay": *The Doberman!*

**Airdate:** 4/7/01
**Episode:** 26.16
**Host:** Alec Baldwin
**Musical Guest:** Coldplay
**Musical and Guest Performances/Cameo(s)/ Program Notes:**
- "Live from New York": President George W. Bush (Will Ferrell) and daughter Jenna Bush (Julia Stiles).
- Coldplay performs "Yellow" and "Don't Panic."
- Cameos by Kid Rock and David Spade.

**Airdate:** 4/14/01
**Episode:** 26.17
**Host:** Renée Zellweger
**Musical Guest:** Eve
**Musical and Guest Performances/Cameo(s)/ Program Notes:**
- "Live from New York": Marty Culp and Bobbi Mohan-Culp (Will Ferrell and Ana Gasteyer).
- Eve performs "Let Me Blow Ya Mind" (with Gwen Stefani) and "Who's That Girl?"
- Cameo by Molly Shannon.
- "TV Funhouse": *Fun with Real Audio* ("Bryant Gumbel Interviews *Survivor* Cast").

**Airdate:** 5/5/01
**Episode:** 26.18
**Host:** Pierce Brosnan
**Musical Guest:** Destiny's Child
**Musical and Guest Performances/Cameo(s)/ Program Notes:**
- "Live from New York": Jenna Bush (Julia Stiles) and George W. Bush (Will Ferrell).
- Destiny's Child performs "Survivor" and "Emotion."
- Cameos by Julia Stiles and Molly Shannon.
- "A Short Film by Adam McKay": *Five Finger Discount.*

**Airdate:** 5/12/01
**Episode:** 26.19
**Host:** Lara Flynn Boyle
**Musical Guest:** Bon Jovi
**Musical and Guest Performances/Cameo(s)/ Program Notes:**
- "Live from New York": Vice President Dick Cheney (Darrell Hammond).
- Bon Jovi performs "My Life" and "You Give Love a Bad Name."
- Cameo by Lou Reed, who appears on *Weekend Update* to confirm the rumors that he's dead.

**Airdate:** 5/19/01
**Episode:** 26.20
**Host:** Christopher Walken
**Musical Guest:** Weezer

**Musical and Guest Performances/Cameo(s)/ Program Notes:**
- "Live from New York": New York mayor Rudy Giuliani (Hammond).
- Weezer performs "Hash Pipe" and "Island in the Sun."
- Cameos by Kevin Nealon and Winona Ryder.
- Jerry Minor's final episode; Chris Parnell is temporarily dropped from the cast.
- "TV Funhouse": *The Anatominals* ("Yogi Bear").

## Season 27 (2001–2002)

**Airdate:** 9/29/01
**Episode:** 27.1
**Host:** Reese Witherspoon
**Musical Guest:** Alicia Keys
**Musical and Guest Performances/Cameo(s)/ Program Notes:**
- "Live from New York": Mayor Rudy Giuliani, who opens the show with a tribute to the heroes of September 11. He is joined onstage by representatives of the New York Police Department, the New York Fire Department, the Port Authority Police Department, Fire Commissioner Tom Von Essen, and Police Commissioner Bernard Kerik. Paul Simon sings "The Boxer."
- Keys performs "Fallin'" and "A Woman's Worth."
- Rachel Dratch and Maya Rudolph are bumped up to regulars.
- Debut of featured players Dean Edwards, Seth Meyers, and Amy Poehler.

**Airdate:** 10/6/01
**Episode:** 27.2
**Host:** Seann William Scott
**Musical Guest:** Sum 41
**Musical and Guest Performances/Cameo(s)/ Program Notes:**
- "Live from New York": George W. Bush (Will Ferrell), who tells Osama bin Laden he "screwed up big time."
- Cameo by Chevy Chase as a land shark.
- Seann William Scott substituted for Ben Stiller, who was originally slated as host but pulled out after 9/11.
- Sum 41 performs "In Too Deep."

**Airdate:** 10/13/01
**Episode:** 27.3
**Host:** Drew Barrymore
**Musical Guest:** Macy Gray
**Musical and Guest Performances/Cameo(s)/ Program Notes:**
- "Live from New York": Vice President Dick Cheney (Darrell Hammond) from a cave in Kandahar, Afghanistan.
- In her monologue, Barrymore mentions the discovery of anthrax in 30 Rockefeller Center.
- Gray performs "Sexual Revolution" and "Sweet Baby."
- "TV Funhouse": *Fun with Real Audio* ("NBC Fall Retooling Preview").

**Airdate:** 11/3/01
**Episode:** 27.4
**Host:** John Goodman
**Musical Guest:** Ja Rule
**Musical and Guest Performances/Cameo(s)/ Program Notes:**
- "Live from New York": Attorney General John Ashcroft (Darrell Hammond) answers questions during a press conference concerning the threat of terrorist attack.
- Elwood Blues (Dan Aykroyd) and Mighty Mack (John Goodman) appear on *Weekend Update* to give an editorial comment about the terrorist threat (and to sing "The Letter").
- Leonard Pinth-Garnell introduces "Bad Conceptual Theatre."

Appendix A

- Ja Rule performs "Always on Time" (with Ashanti) and "Livin' It Up."

**Airdate:** 11/10/01
**Episode:** 27.5
**Host:** Gwyneth Paltrow
**Musical Guest:** Ryan Adams
**Musical and Guest Performances/Cameo(s)/ Program Notes:**
- "Live from New York": George W. Bush (Will Ferrell) exposes Islamic myths about America.
- Adams performs "New York, New York."
- A cameo by Matt Damon, who is infatuated with "Mango" (Chris Kattan).
- "TV Funhouse": *Michael Jackson*.

**Airdate:** 11/17/01
**Episode:** 27.6
**Host:** Billy Bob Thornton
**Musical Guest:** Creed
**Musical and Guest Performances/Cameo(s)/ Program Notes:**
- "Live from New York": Donald Rumsfeld (Darrell Hammond).
- Creed performs "My Sacrifice" and "Bullets."
- Cameo by Ashton Kutcher.

**Airdate:** 12/1/01
**Episode:** 27.7
**Host:** Derek Jeter
**Musical Guest:** Bubba Sparxxx, Shakira
**Musical and Guest Performances/Cameo(s)/ Program Notes:**
- "Live from New York": George W. Bush (Will Ferrell).
- Shakira performs "Whenever, Wherever."
- Bubba Sparxxx performs "Ugly" and "Lovely."
- Cameos by two former New York Yankees: Boston Red Sox pitcher David Cone and Chicago White Sox pitcher David Lee Wells.

**Airdate:** 12/8/01
**Episode:** 27.8
**Host:** Hugh Jackman
**Musical Guest:** Mick Jagger
**Musical and Guest Performances/Cameo(s)/ Program Notes:**
- "Live from New York": Al Gore (Darrell Hammond).
- Jagger performs "God Gave Me Everything" and "Visions of Paradise."
- Jagger impersonates designer Karl Lagerfeld in a sketch with Donatella Versace (Maya Rudolph).

**Airdate:** 12/15/01
**Episode:** 27.9
**Host:** Ellen DeGeneres
**Musical Guest:** No Doubt
**Musical and Guest Performances/Cameo(s)/ Program Notes:**
- "Live from New York": Dan Rather (Darrell Hammond).
- No Doubt performs "Hey Baby" and "Hella Good."
- "TV Funhouse": *The Narrator That Ruined Christmas*.
- Cameo by Rudy Giuliani.

**Airdate:** 1/12/02
**Episode:** 27.10
**Host:** Josh Hartnett
**Musical Guest:** Pink
**Musical and Guest Performances/Cameo(s)/ Program Notes:**
- "Live from New York": Bill Clinton (Darrell Hammond).
- Pink performs "Get the Party Started" and "Don't Let Me Get Me."
- "TV Funhouse": *The X-Presidents* ("Hunt for Osama") (with a cameo by the Ambiguously Gay Duo).

**Airdate:** 1/19/02
**Episode:** 27.11
**Host:** Jack Black
**Musical Guest:** The Strokes
**Musical and Guest Performances/Cameo(s)/ Program Notes:**
- "Live from New York": Secret Service agent (Jimmy Fallon).

Episode Guide 495

- The Strokes perform "Last Nite" and "Hard to Explain."
- Kyle Gass, who is the other half of Tenacious D with Black, appears in the monologue.

**Airdate:** 2/2/02
**Episode:** 27.12
**Host/Musical Guest:** Britney Spears
**Musical and Guest Performances/Cameo(s)/ Program Notes:**
- "Live from New York": A Mormon reporter (Seth Meyers) at the Winter Olympics in Utah.
- Spears performs "I'm Not a Girl, Not Yet a Woman" and "Boys."
- Cameos by Dan Aykroyd and Justin Timberlake.

**Airdate:** 3/2/02
**Episode:** 27.13
**Host:** Jonny Moseley
**Musical Guest:** Outkast
**Musical and Guest Performances/Cameo(s)/ Program Notes:**
- "Live from New York": George W. Bush (Will Ferrell).
- Outkast performs "Whole World" and "Ms. Jackson."
- Cameo by comedian Rip Taylor.
- Chris Parnell returns as a regular.

**Airdate:** 3/9/02
**Episode:** 27.14
**Host:** Jon Stewart
**Musical Guest:** India.Arie
**Musical and Guest Performances/Cameo(s)/ Program Notes:**
- "Live from New York": Dick Cheney (Darrell Hammond).
- India.Arie performs "Video" and "Ready for Love."
- Cameo by George Plimpton.
- "TV Funhouse": *Fun with Real Audio* ("Colin Powell on MTV").

**Airdate:** 3/16/02
**Episode:** 27.15
**Host:** Ian McKellen

**Musical Guest:** Kylie Minogue
**Musical and Guest Performances/Cameo(s)/ Program Notes:**
- "Live from New York": Tom Ridge (Darrell Hammond).
- Minogue performs "Can't Get You Out of My Head" and "In Your Eyes."
- "TV Funhouse": *Fun with Real Audio* ("Oscars' Greatest Moments").
- This episode won an Emmy for Outstanding Writing for a Variety, Music or Comedy Program.

**Airdate:** 4/6/02
**Episode:** 27.16
**Host:** Cameron Diaz
**Musical Guest:** Jimmy Eat World
**Musical and Guest Performances/Cameo(s)/ Program Notes:**
- "Live from New York": Marty Culp (Will Ferrell) and Bobbi Mohan-Culp (Ana Gasteyer).
- Jimmy Eat World performs "The Middle" and "Sweetness."

**Airdate:** 4/13/02
**Episode:** 27.17
**Host:** The Rock
**Musical Guest:** Andrew W. K.
**Musical and Guest Performances/Cameo(s)/ Program Notes:**
- "Live from New York": George W. Bush (Will Ferrell).
- Andrew W. K. performs "Party Hard" and "I Get Wet."

**Airdate:** 4/20/02
**Episode:** 27.18
**Host:** Alec Baldwin
**Musical Guest:** P.O.D.
**Musical and Guest Performances/Cameo(s)/ Program Notes:**
- "Live from New York": A cockatoo.
- P.O.D. performs "Youth of the Nation" and "Alive."
- "TV Funhouse": *The Anatominals.*

**Airdate:** 5/11/02
**Episode:** 27.19

**Host:** Kirsten Dunst
**Musical Guest:** Eminem
**Musical and Guest Performances/Cameo(s)/ Program Notes:**
- "Live from New York": George W. Bush (Will Ferrell).
- Eminem performs "Without Me" (with Proof).
- "TV Funhouse": *Bambi 2002*.

**Airdate:** 5/18/02
**Episode:** 27.20

**Host:** Winona Ryder
**Musical Guest:** Moby
**Musical and Guest Performances/Cameo(s)/ Program Notes:**
- "Live from New York": Fidel Castro (Will Ferrell) and his interpreter (Maya Rudolph).
- Moby performs "We Are All Made of Stars" and "South Side."
- Cameos by Alex Trebek and Neil Diamond.

## Season 28 (2002–2003)

**Airdate:** 10/5/02
**Episode:** 28.1
**Host:** Matt Damon
**Musical Guest:** Bruce Springsteen and the E Street Band
**Musical and Guest Performances/Cameo(s)/ Program Notes:**
- "Live from New York": Dick Cheney (Darrell Hammond).
- Springsteen and the E Street Band perform "Lonesome Day" (with Soozie Tyrell) and "You're Missing."
- "TV Funhouse": *The Smurfette Show*, a parody of E!'s *The Anna Nicole Show*.
- Debut of Fred Armisen and Will Forte as featured players.
- Amy Poehler is bumped up to a regular.

**Airdate:** 10/12/02
**Episode:** 28.2
**Host:** Sarah Michelle Gellar
**Musical Guest:** Faith Hill
**Musical and Guest Performances/Cameo(s)/ Program Notes:**
- "Live from New York": George W. Bush (Chris Parnell).
- Hill performs "Cry" and "Free."

**Airdate:** 10/19/02
**Episode:** 28.3
**Host:** Sen. John McCain
**Musical Guest:** The White Stripes
**Musical and Guest Performances/Cameo(s)/ Program Notes:**
- "Live from New York": Saddam Hussein (Horatio Sanz).
- The White Stripes perform "Dead Leaves and the Dirty Ground" and "We're Going to Be Friends."
- "TV Funhouse": *Ambiguously Gay Duo* ("The Third Leg of Justice").

**Airdate:** 11/2/02
**Episode:** 28.4
**Host:** Eric McCormack
**Musical Guest:** Jay-Z
**Musical and Guest Performances/Cameo(s)/ Program Notes:**
- "Live from New York": Rudy Giuliani (Darrell Hammond).
- Jay-Z performs "Guns & Roses" (with special guest Lenny Kravitz) and "'03 Bonnie & Clyde" (with Kravitz and special guest Beyoncé).

**Airdate:** 11/9/02
**Episode:** 28.5
**Host:** Nia Vardalos
**Musical Guest:** Eve
**Musical and Guest Performances/Cameo(s)/ Program Notes:**
- "Live from New York": George W. Bush (Chris Parnell).
- Eve performs "Gangsta Lovin'" and "Satisfaction."

Episode Guide    497

- Cameo by Tina Fey's mother, Jeanne.
- Sketch Debut: *The Falconer*, featuring Will Forte in the title role.

**Airdate:** 11/16/02
**Episode:** 28.6
**Host:** Brittany Murphy
**Musical Guest:** Nelly
**Musical and Guest Performances/Cameo(s)/ Program Notes:**
- "Live from New York": Adam Sandler, who in a cameo appearance performs "The Chanukah Song" (with Rob Schneider, also in a cameo).
- Nelly performs "Dilemma" (with Kelly Rowland) and "Hot in Herre."
- Cameo by Garrett Morris.
- "TV Funhouse": *The Religetables*.

**Airdate:** 12/7/02
**Episode:** 28.7
**Host:** Robert De Niro
**Musical Guest:** Norah Jones
**Musical and Guest Performances/Cameo(s)/ Program Notes:**
- "Live from New York": Craig Fenson (Robert De Niro).
- Jones performs "Don't Know Why" and "Come Away with Me."
- Cameo by Harvey Keitel.

**Airdate:** 12/14/02
**Episode:** 28.8
**Host:** Al Gore
**Musical Guest:** Phish
**Musical and Guest Performances/Cameo(s)/ Program Notes:**
- "Live from New York": Tipper Gore.
- Phish performs "46 Days" and "Chalk Dust Torture."
- Cameos by Al Franken, Tipper Gore, and cast members of *The West Wing*: Allison Janney, Richard Schiff, Martin Sheen, John Spencer, and Bradley Whitford.
- "TV Funhouse": *Charlie Brown Christmas*.

**Airdate:** 1/11/03
**Episode:** 28.9
**Host:** Jeff Gordon
**Musical Guest:** Avril Lavigne
**Musical and Guest Performances/Cameo(s)/ Program Notes:**
- "Live from New York": Kim Jong-Il (Horatio Sanz) and translator (Maya Rudolph).
- Lavigne performs "I'm with You" and "Complicated."

**Airdate:** 1/18/03
**Episode:** 28.10
**Host:** Ray Liotta
**Musical Guest:** The Donnas
**Musical and Guest Performances/Cameo(s)/ Program Notes:**
- "Live from New York": Donald Rumsfeld (Darrell Hammond).
- The Donnas perform "Take It Off" and "Who Invited You."

**Airdate:** 2/8/03
**Episode:** 28.11
**Host:** Matthew McConaughey
**Musical Guest:** The Dixie Chicks
**Musical and Guest Performances/Cameo(s)/ Program Notes:**
- "Live from New York": Translator's voice (Maya Rudolph) for German delegate to the UN Security Council (Chris Parnell).
- The Dixie Chicks perform "Travelin' Soldier" and "Sin Wagon."

**Airdate:** 2/15/03
**Episode:** 28.12
**Host:** Jennifer Garner
**Musical Guest:** Beck
**Musical and Guest Performances/Cameo(s)/ Program Notes:**
- "Live from New York": President George W. Bush (Chris Parnell).
- Beck performs "Lost Cause" and "Guess I'm Doin' Fine."

**Airdate:** 2/22/03
**Episode:** 28.13

Appendix A

**Host:** Christopher Walken
**Musical Guest:** Foo Fighters
**Musical and Guest Performances/Cameo(s)/ Program Notes:**
- "Live from New York": French foreign minister Dominique de Villepin (Christopher Walken).
- Foo Fighters perform "All My Life" and "Times Like These (One-Way Motorway)," which features an appearance by Jim Carrey.
- Cameos by Jim Carrey, Steve Martin, Britney Spears, and Will Ferrell.

**Airdate:** 3/8/03
**Episode:** 28.14
**Host:** Queen Latifah
**Musical Guest:** Ms. Dynamite
**Musical and Guest Performances/Cameo(s)/ Program Notes:**
- "Live from New York": *60 Minutes* announcer (Chris Parnell).
- Ms. Dynamite performs "Dy-Na-Mi-Tee."
- Cameo by Dan Aykroyd (as Bob Dole).
- "TV Funhouse": *The X-Presidents* ("Iraq 2003").

**Airdate:** 3/15/03
**Episode:** 28.15
**Host:** Salma Hayek
**Musical Guest:** Christina Aguilera
**Musical and Guest Performances/Cameo(s)/ Program Notes:**
- "Live from New York": President George W. Bush (Chris Parnell).
- Aguilera performs "Beautiful" and "Fighter."
- Cameo by Edward Norton.
- "TV Funhouse": *Are You Hot?*

**Airdate:** 4/5/03
**Episode:** 28.16
**Host:** Bernie Mac
**Musical Guest:** Good Charlotte
**Musical and Guest Performances/Cameo(s)/ Program Notes:**
- "Live from New York": President George W. Bush (Chris Parnell).
- Good Charlotte performs "Anthem" and "Lifestyles of the Rich and Famous."

**Airdate:** 4/12/03
**Episode:** 28.17
**Host:** Ray Romano
**Musical Guest:** Zwan
**Musical and Guest Performances/Cameo(s)/ Program Notes:**
- "Live from New York": Saddam Hussein (Horatio Sanz).
- Zwan performs "Lyric" and "Settle Down."

**Airdate:** 5/3/03
**Episode:** 28.18
**Host:** Ashton Kutcher
**Musical Guest:** 50 Cent
**Musical and Guest Performances/Cameo(s)/ Program Notes:**
- "Live from New York": George W. Bush (Chris Parnell).
- 50 Cent performs "In Da Club" (with G-Unit) and "21 Questions" (with G-Unit and Nate Dogg).

**Airdate:** 5/10/03
**Episode:** 28.19
**Host:** Adrien Brody
**Musical Guest:** Sean Paul, Wayne Wonder
**Musical and Guest Performances/Cameo(s)/ Program Notes:**
- "Live from New York": Mya (Maya Rudolph) appearing in Coke commercials during *American Idol.*
- Sean Paul performs "Get Busy."
- Wayne Wonder performs "No Letting Go."
- Cameos by Brody's parents, Elliot Brody and photographer Sylvia Plachy.
- "TV Funhouse": *Saddam and Osama.*
- Brody reportedly angered the producers when he improvised his introduction to Wayne Wonder.

**Airdate:** 5/17/03
**Episode:** 28.20
**Host:** Dan Aykroyd
**Musical Guest:** Beyoncé
**Musical and Guest Performances/Cameo(s)/Program Notes:**
- "Live from New York": MSNBC's *Hardball* host Chris Matthews (Darrell Hammond).
- Beyoncé performs "Crazy in Love" (with Jay-Z) and "Dangerously in Love."
- Cameos by Jim Belushi, John Goodman, and actor Kip King, father of Chris Kattan and one of the original Groundlings.
- "TV Funhouse": *Cokee, the Most Expensive Dog in the World*.
- Final episode for Dean Edwards and Tracy Morgan.

## Season 29 (2003–2004)

**Airdate:** 10/4/03
**Episode:** 29.1
**Host:** Jack Black
**Musical Guest:** John Mayer
**Musical and Guest Performances/Cameo(s)/Program Notes:**
- "Live from New York": California governor Arnold Schwarzenegger (Darrell Hammond).
- Mayer performs "Bigger Than My Body" and "Clarity."
- "TV Funhouse": *Yankee Super-Heroes*.
- Seth Meyers and Jeff Richards are bumped up to regulars.
- Debut of featured players Finesse Mitchell and Kenan Thompson.

**Airdate:** 10/11/03
**Episode:** 29.2
**Host/Musical Guest:** Justin Timberlake
**Musical and Guest Performances/Cameo(s)/Program Notes:**
- "Live from New York": Chris Matthews (Darrell Hammond).
- Timberlake performs "Rock Your Body," "Señorita," and, with Kermit the Frog, "The Rainbow Connection."
- Sketch Debut: *The Barry Gibb Talk Show*, featuring Jimmy Fallon as Barry Gibb and Justin Timberlake as Robin Gibb.

**Airdate:** 10/18/03
**Episode:** 29.3
**Host:** Halle Berry
**Musical Guest:** Britney Spears
**Musical and Guest Performances/Cameo(s)/Program Notes:**
- "Live from New York": Vanessa Laine Bryant (Maya Rudolph), wife of basketball player Kobe Bryant (Finesse Mitchell), who has been accused of rape.
- Spears performs "Me Against the Music" and "Everytime."
- Cameo by George Wendt as Bob Swerski.

**Airdate:** 11/1/03
**Episode:** 29.4
**Host:** Kelly Ripa
**Musical Guest:** Outkast
**Musical and Guest Performances/Cameo(s)/Program Notes:**
- "Live from New York": George W. Bush (Darrell Hammond).
- Outkast performs "Hey Ya!" and "The Way You Move."
- Cameo by Chris Kattan as *Live! With Regis and Kelly* producer Michael Gelman.

**Airdate:** 11/8/03
**Episode:** 29.5
**Host:** Andy Roddick
**Musical Guest:** Dave Matthews
**Musical and Guest Performances/Cameo(s)/Program Notes:**

# Appendix A

- "Live from New York": Barbara Walters (Rachel Dratch) interviewing Martha Stewart (Amy Poehler).
- Matthews performs "Save Me" and "So Damn Lucky" (with guest Trey Anastasio).
- Cameo by John McEnroe.

**Airdate:** 11/15/03
**Episode:** 29.6
**Host:** Alec Baldwin
**Musical Guest:** Missy Elliott
**Musical and Guest Performances/Cameo(s)/ Program Notes:**

- "Live from New York": President George W. Bush (Darrell Hammond).
- Elliott performs "Pass That Dutch" and "Work It."
- Cameo by Mike Myers, who plugs his film *Cat in the Hat* (2003).

**Airdate:** 12/6/03
**Episode:** 29.7
**Host:** Rev. Al Sharpton
**Musical Guest:** Pink
**Musical and Guest Performances/Cameo(s)/ Program Notes:**

- "Live from New York": President of NBC Entertainment Jeff Zucker (Jimmy Fallon).
- Pink performs "Trouble" and "God Is a DJ."
- Cameo by Tracy Morgan.

**Airdate:** 12/13/03
**Episode:** 29.8
**Host:** Elijah Wood
**Musical Guest:** Jet
**Musical and Guest Performances/Cameo(s)/ Program Notes:**

- "Live from New York": MSNBC's *Hardball* host Chris Matthews (Darrell Hammond).
- Jet performs "Are You Gonna Be My Girl" and "Look What You've Done."
- "TV Funhouse": *Fun with Real Audio* ("George W. Bush").

**Airdate:** 1/10/04
**Episode:** 29.9
**Host:** Jennifer Aniston
**Musical Guest:** The Black Eyed Peas
**Musical and Guest Performances/Cameo(s)/ Program Notes:**

- "Live from New York": Donald Trump (Darrell Hammond).
- The Black Eyed Peas perform "Where Is the Love" and "Hey Mama."
- Sketch Debut: *Appalachian Emergency Room.*
- Cameo by Al Franken.

**Airdate:** 1/17/04
**Episode:** 29.10
**Host:** Jessica Simpson and Nick Lachey
**Musical Guest:** G-Unit
**Musical and Guest Performances/Cameo(s)/ Program Notes:**

- "Live from New York": Howard Dean (Jeff Richards).
- G-Unit performs "Stunt 101" and "Wanna Get to Know You" (with guest artist Joe).
- Final episode for Jeff Richards.

**Airdate:** 2/7/04
**Episode:** 29.11
**Host:** Megan Mullally
**Musical Guest:** Clay Aiken
**Musical and Guest Performances/Cameo(s)/ Program Notes:**

- "Live from New York": *Nightline* host Ted Koppel (Darrell Hammond).
- Aiken performs "Invisible" and "The Way."
- Cameo by Nick Offerman.

**Airdate:** 2/14/04
**Episode:** 29.12
**Host:** Drew Barrymore
**Musical Guest:** Kelis
**Musical and Guest Performances/Cameo(s)/ Program Notes:**

- "Live from New York": Al Gore (Darrell Hammond).

- Kelis performs "Milkshake" and "Trick Me."
- Sketch Debut: *The Prince Show*, hosted by Prince (Fred Armisen).

**Airdate:** 2/21/04
**Episode:** 29.13
**Host:** Christina Aguilera
**Musical Guest:** Maroon 5
**Musical and Guest Performances/Cameo(s)/ Program Notes:**
- "Live from New York": MSNBC's *Hardball* host Chris Matthews (Darrell Hammond).
- Maroon 5 performs "This Love" and "Harder to Breathe."
- "TV Funhouse": *Fun with Real Audio* ("*Access Hollywood*").

**Airdate:** 3/6/04
**Episode:** 29.14
**Host:** Colin Firth
**Musical Guest:** Norah Jones
**Musical and Guest Performances/Cameo(s)/ Program Notes:**
- "Live from New York": Martha Stewart (Ana Gasteyer).
- Jones performs "Sunrise" and "What Am I to You?"
- "TV Funhouse": *Cartoons and Your Government.*

**Airdate:** 3/13/04
**Episode:** 29.15
**Host:** Ben Affleck
**Musical Guest:** N.E.R.D.
**Musical and Guest Performances/Cameo(s)/ Program Notes:**
- "Live from New York": Sully (Jimmy Fallon), Denise (Rachel Dratch), and Donnie (Ben Affleck), who gets married to Smithy (Seth Meyers).
- N.E.R.D. performs "She Wants to Move" and "Maybe."
- "TV Funhouse": *The Making of* The Passion of the Dumpty (a parody of *The Passion of the Christ*).

**Airdate:** 4/3/04
**Episode:** 29.16
**Host:** Donald Trump
**Musical Guest:** Toots and the Maytals
**Musical and Guest Performances/Cameo(s)/ Program Notes:**
- "Live from New York": *The Apprentice*'s Carolyn Kepcher.
- Toots and the Maytals perform "Love Gonna Walk Out on Me" and "Funky Kingston."

**Airdate:** 4/10/04
**Episode:** 29.17
**Host/Musical Guest:** Janet Jackson
**Musical and Guest Performances/Cameo(s)/ Program Notes:**
- "Live from New York": Condoleezza Rice (Janet Jackson).
- Jackson performs "All Nite (Don't Stop)" and "Strawberry Bounce."

**Airdate:** 5/1/04
**Episode:** 29.18
**Host:** Lindsay Lohan
**Musical Guest:** Usher
**Musical and Guest Performances/Cameo(s)/ Program Notes:**
- "Live from New York": George W. Bush (Will Forte).
- Usher performs "Yeah" (with guest Ludacris) and "Burn."
- ★★★★ Four-Star Sketch: Debut of Debbie Downer (Rachel Dratch). Watch how no one can keep a straight face.
- "TV Funhouse": *Pothead Theatre.*

**Airdate:** 5/8/04
**Episode:** 29.19
**Host:** Snoop Dogg
**Musical Guest:** Avril Lavigne
**Musical and Guest Performances/Cameo(s)/ Program Notes:**
- "Live from New York": Donald Rumsfeld (Darrell Hammond).
- Lavigne performs "Don't Tell Me" and "My Happy Ending."

**Airdate:** 5/15/04
**Episode:** 29.20
**Host:** Mary-Kate and Ashley Olsen
**Musical Guest:** J-Kwon
**Musical and Guest Performances/Cameo(s)/ Program Notes:**
- "Live from New York": MSNBC *Hardball* host Chris Matthews (Darrell Hammond).
- J-Kwon performs "Tipsy."
- Jimmy Fallon's final episode.

## Season 30 (2004–2005)

**Airdate:** 10/2/04
**Episode:** 30.1
**Host:** Ben Affleck
**Musical Guest:** Nelly
**Musical and Guest Performances/Cameo(s)/ Program Notes:**
- "Live from New York": Jim Lehrer (Chris Parnell), moderating the Kerry-Bush presidential debate.
- Nelly sings "My Place" with guest Jaheim and "Na-Nana-Na."
- Cameos by Alec Baldwin and James Gandolfini.
- Debut of featured player Rob Riggle; Fred Armisen is bumped up to a regular.
- *Weekend Update*: Amy Poehler replaces Jimmy Fallon as coanchor with Tina Fey.

**Airdate:** 10/9/04
**Episode:** 30.2
**Host/Musical Guest:** Queen Latifah
**Musical and Guest Performances/Cameo(s)/ Program Notes:**
- "Live from New York": George W. Bush (Will Forte), during the second presidential debate.
- Queen Latifah performs "The Same Love That Made Me Laugh" and "Hard Times."
- Tribute to the late Rodney Dangerfield (Darrell Hammond), who finally finds respect at the Gates of Heaven.
- "TV Funhouse": *The X-Presidents* ("Election Meddling").

**Airdate:** 10/23/04
**Episode:** 30.3
**Host:** Jude Law
**Musical Guest:** Ashlee Simpson
**Musical and Guest Performances/Cameo(s)/ Program Notes:**
- "Live from New York": MSNBC *Hardball* host Chris Matthews (Darrell Hammond), on the Kerry campaign.
- Ashlee Simpson performs "Pieces of Me." When she is about to start her second song, "Autobiography," the vocal track of "Pieces of Me" starts, which reveals she was lip-synching. She leaves the stage. The incident was part of a *60 Minutes* report that was coincidentally shooting during this episode.
- "Film Short" Series Debut: *Bear City*, directed by T. Sean Shannon.

**Airdate:** 10/30/04
**Episode:** 30.4
**Host:** Kate Winslet
**Musical Guest:** Eminem
**Musical and Guest Performances/Cameo(s)/ Program Notes:**
- "Live from New York": Videotaped message from Osama bin Laden (Seth Meyers) via the voice of his translator (Jim Downey).
- Eminem performs "Mosh" and "Just Lose It."
- "TV Funhouse": *Fun with Real Audio* ("John McCain").

**Airdate:** 11/13/04
**Episode:** 30.5
**Host:** Liam Neeson
**Musical Guest:** Modest Mouse

**Musical and Guest Performances/Cameo(s)/ Program Notes:**
- "Live from New York": President George W. Bush (Will Forte), who receives a congratulatory call from John Kerry (Seth Meyers).
- Modest Mouse performs "Float On" and "Ocean Breathes Salty."

**Airdate:** 11/20/04
**Episode:** 30.6
**Host:** Luke Wilson
**Musical Guest:** U2
**Musical and Guest Performances/Cameo(s)/ Program Notes:**
- "Live from New York": George W. Bush (Will Forte), who, in a parody of *The Apprentice*, must decide whether to fire Donald Rumsfeld (Darrell Hammond), Condoleezza Rice (Maya Rudolph), or Colin Powell (Finesse Mitchell) over their handling of "a simple task—start a war, set up a democracy, and get out."
- U2 performs "Vertigo," "Sometimes You Can't Make It On Your Own," and "I Will Follow."
- "TV Funhouse": *The Homocranial Mind Mixer*.

**Airdate:** 12/11/04
**Episode:** 30.7
**Host:** Colin Farrell
**Musical Guest:** Scissor Sisters
**Musical and Guest Performances/Cameo(s)/ Program Notes:**
- "Live from New York": Donald Rumsfeld (Darrell Hammond), addressing the troops in Kuwait, who are in need of basic equipment.
- Scissor Sisters perform "Take Your Mama" and "Comfortably Numb."
- Cameos by Lindsay Lohan and hockey star Brett Hull.

**Airdate:** 12/18/04
**Episode:** 30.8
**Host:** Robert De Niro
**Musical Guest:** Destiny's Child

**Musical and Guest Performances/Cameo(s)/ Program Notes:**
- "Live from New York": Dept. of Homeland Security Craig Fenson (Robert De Niro), who reads names of suspected terrorists obviously sent in by pranksters.
- Destiny's Child performs "Soldier" and "Cater 2 U."
- Guest appearance by Kermit the Frog, who sings "Have Yourself a Merry Little Christmas" with De Niro.
- "TV Funhouse": *Blue Christmas*.

**Airdate:** 1/15/05
**Episode:** 30.9
**Host:** Topher Grace
**Musical Guest:** The Killers
**Musical and Guest Performances/Cameo(s)/ Program Notes:**
- "Live from New York": Bill Clinton (Darrell Hammond), who answers questions at a press conference directed at President George W. Bush (Will Forte).
- The Killers perform "Somebody Told Me" and "Mr. Brightside."
- Character Debuts: Art dealers Nuni Schoener (Fred Armisen) and Nuni Schoener (Maya Rudolph).

**Airdate:** 1/22/05
**Episode:** 30.10
**Host:** Paul Giamatti
**Musical Guest:** Ludacris
**Musical and Guest Performances/Cameo(s)/ Program Notes:**
- "Live from New York": The Bush twins, Barbara (Amy Poehler) and Jenna (Tina Fey).
- Ludacris performs "Number One Spot" and, with special guest Sum 41, sings "Get Back."

**Airdate:** 2/5/05
**Episode:** 30.11
**Host:** Paris Hilton
**Musical Guest:** Keane

# Appendix A

**Musical and Guest Performances/Cameo(s)/Program Notes:**
- "Live from New York": A teenager with a baby's arm growing out of her skull (Rachel Dratch) auditions for *American Idol*.
- Keane sings "Somewhere Only We Know" and "Everybody's Changing."

**Airdate:** 2/12/05
**Episode:** 30.12
**Host:** Jason Bateman
**Musical Guest:** Kelly Clarkson
**Musical and Guest Performances/Cameo(s)/Program Notes:**
- "Live from New York": North Korean leader Kim Jong-Il (Horatio Sanz) answers questions at a press conference.
- Clarkson performs "Since U Been Gone" and "Breakaway."

**Airdate:** 2/19/05
**Episode:** 30.13
**Host:** Hilary Swank
**Musical Guest:** 50 Cent
**Musical and Guest Performances/Cameo(s)/Program Notes:**
- "Live from New York": Michael Jackson (Amy Poehler).
- 50 Cent performs "Disco Inferno" and, with guest Olivia, sings "Candy Shop."

**Airdate:** 3/12/05
**Episode:** 30.14
**Host:** David Spade
**Musical Guest:** Jack Johnson
**Musical and Guest Performances/Cameo(s)/Program Notes:**
- "Live from New York": Martha Stewart (David Spade), who was just released from prison.
- Johnson performs "Sitting, Waiting, Wishing" and, with guest G. Love, sings "Mudfootball."

**Airdate:** 3/19/05
**Episode:** 30.15
**Host:** Ashton Kutcher
**Musical Guest:** Gwen Stefani
**Musical and Guest Performances/Cameo(s)/Program Notes:**
- "Live from New York": MSNBC *Hardball* host Chris Matthews (Darrell Hammond), on steroid use in Major League Baseball.
- Stefani performs "Hollaback Girl" and, with guest Eve, sings "Rich Girl."
- ★ ★ ★ ★ Four-Star Monologue: Kutcher discusses the age difference between him and wife Demi Moore, who joins him onstage looking like a senior citizen.

**Airdate:** 4/9/05
**Episode:** 30.16
**Host:** Cameron Diaz
**Musical Guest:** Green Day
**Musical and Guest Performances/Cameo(s)/Program Notes:**
- "Live from New York": Cardinal DeGiaccomo (Fred Armisen), who is in the running to be pope, and his interpreter (Seth Meyers).
- Green Day performs "Boulevard of Broken Dreams" and "Holiday."
- "TV Funhouse": *Michael Jackson*.

**Airdate:** 4/16/05
**Episode:** 30.17
**Host:** Tom Brady
**Musical Guest:** Beck
**Musical and Guest Performances/Cameo(s)/Program Notes:**
- "Live from New York": House majority leader Tom DeLay (Chris Parnell), who demonstrates he has the means to get even with people who don't toe the Republican Party line.
- Beck performs "E-Pro" and "Girl."
- "TV Funhouse": *Sexual Harassment and You*.
- Martin Short appears during *Weekend Update* as Jiminy Glick, who promotes his latest "Best of" DVD featuring a 1975 interview with Lorne Michaels, played by Will Forte.

**Airdate:** 5/7/05
**Episode:** 30.18
**Host:** Johnny Knoxville
**Musical Guest:** System of a Down
**Musical and Guest Performances/Cameo(s)/Program Notes:**
- "Live from New York": Paula Abdul, who introduces a reenactment of her alleged come-ons to *American Idol* contestants.
- System of a Down performs "B.Y.O.B." and "Aerials."
- Debut of featured player Jason Sudeikis.

**Airdate:** 5/14/05
**Episode:** 30.19
**Host:** Will Ferrell
**Musical Guest:** Queens of the Stone Age
**Musical and Guest Performances/Cameo(s)/Program Notes:**
- "Live from New York": Egocentric Will Ferrell, who has returned to host the show for the first time.
- Queens of the Stone Age perform "Little Sister" and "In My Head."
- "TV Funhouse": *Shazzang!*

**Airdate:** 5/21/05
**Episode:** 30.20
**Host:** Lindsay Lohan
**Musical Guest:** Coldplay
**Musical and Guest Performances/Cameo(s)/Program Notes:**
- "Live from New York": MSNBC *Hardball* host Chris Matthews (Darrell Hammond), on *Newsweek*'s retraction of a story that U.S. forces desecrated the Quran.
- Coldplay performs "Speed of Sound" and "Fix You."
- Rob Riggle's final episode.
- "TV Funhouse": *Divertor.*

## Season 31 (2005–2006)

**Airdate:** 10/1/05
**Episode:** 31.1
**Host:** Steve Carell
**Musical Guest:** Kanye West
**Musical and Guest Performances/Cameo(s)/Program Notes:**
- "Live from New York": President George W. Bush (Will Forte), fielding questions on national and international issues.
- West performs "Gold Digger," "Touch the Sky," and, with Adam Levine, "Heard 'Em Say."
- Cameo by Mike Myers.
- Debut of featured players Bill Hader and Andy Samberg.
- Kenan Thompson is bumped up to a regular.
- "TV Funhouse": *Fun with Real Audio* ("John Roberts").
- First episode broadcast in high definition.

**Airdate:** 10/8/05
**Episode:** 31.2
**Host:** Jon Heder
**Musical Guest:** Ashlee Simpson
**Musical and Guest Performances/Cameo(s)/Program Notes:**
- "Live from New York": Alberto Gonzalez (Horatio Sanz) is upset he was passed over as a Supreme Court nominee.
- Simpson performs "Catch Me When I Fall" and "Boyfriend" (without lip-synching).

**Airdate:** 10/22/05
**Episode:** 31.3
**Host:** Catherine Zeta-Jones
**Musical Guest:** Franz Ferdinand
**Musical and Guest Performances/Cameo(s)/Program Notes:**
- "Live from New York": Fox News's Brit Hume (Darrell Hammond), who moderates an obviously scripted Q&A

between President Bush and U.S. soldiers in Iraq.
- Franz Ferdinand performs "Do You Want To" and "Take Me Out."
- *Weekend Update* ends with a photo of former anchorman Charles Rocket (1949–2005), who committed suicide on October 7, 2005.

**Airdate:** 10/29/05
**Episode:** 31.4
**Host:** Lance Armstrong
**Musical Guest:** Sheryl Crow
**Musical and Guest Performances/Cameo(s)/ Program Notes:**
- "Live from New York": As smoke fills his office, Vice President Dick Cheney (Darrell Hammond) assures the American people the recent indictment of his top aide Scooter Libby is an isolated case.
- Crow performs "Good Is Good" and "Strong Enough."
- Cameo by Chicago White Sox leftfielder Scott Podsednik.

**Airdate:** 11/12/05
**Episode:** 31.5
**Host:** Jason Lee
**Musical Guest:** Foo Fighters
**Musical and Guest Performances/Cameo(s)/ Program Notes:**
- "Live from New York": Former senator and Fox News commentator Zell Miller (Will Forte), who is a guest on *Hardball* discussing the scandals plaguing the GOP.
- Foo Fighters perform "DOA" and "Best of You."
- Debut of featured player Kristen Wiig.

**Airdate:** 11/19/05
**Episode:** 31.6
**Host:** Eva Longoria
**Musical Guest:** Korn
**Musical and Guest Performances/Cameo(s)/ Program Notes:**
- "Live from New York": President George W. Bush (Will Forte), who tries to avoid answering questions about the Iraq War during his visit to China.
- Korn performs "Twisted Transistor" and "Freak on a Leash."

**Airdate:** 12/3/05
**Episode:** 31.7
**Host:** Dane Cook
**Musical Guest:** James Blunt
**Musical and Guest Performances/Cameo(s)/ Program Notes:**
- "Live from New York": Donald Trump (Darrell Hammond), Megan Mullally (Kristen Wiig), Al Roker (Kenan Thompson), Harry Connick Jr. (Jason Sudeikis), and a choir sing "all-inclusive" holiday carols during the "re-lighting" of the Rockefeller Center tree.
- Blunt performs "You're Beautiful" and "Goodbye My Lover."
- "*SNL* Digital Short": *Lettuce*.
- Character Debut: The Target Lady (Kristen Wiig).

**Airdate:** 12/10/05
**Episode:** 31.8
**Host:** Alec Baldwin
**Musical Guest:** Shakira
**Musical and Guest Performances/Cameo(s)/ Program Notes:**
- "Live from New York": An imprisoned Saddam Hussein (Alec Baldwin), who chats up a prison guard (Fred Armisen).
- Shakira performs "Don't Bother" and, with Alejandro Sanz, "La Tortura."
- "TV Funhouse": *Celebrity Mugshot Poker*.

**Airdate:** 12/17/05
**Episode:** 31.9
**Host:** Jack Black
**Musical Guest:** Neil Young
**Musical and Guest Performances/Cameo(s)/ Program Notes:**
- "Live from New York": President George W. Bush (Will Forte), while

sitting on Santa Dick Cheney's (Darrell Hammond) lap.
- Young performs "It's a Dream" and "He Was the King."
- "TV Funhouse": "Christmastime for the Jews," featuring Darlene Love.
- "*SNL* Digital Short": "Lazy Sunday" with Andy Samberg and Chris Parnell.
- Cameos by Johnny Knoxville, Tracy Morgan, and Kyle Gass.

**Airdate:** 1/14/06
**Episode:** 31.10
**Host:** Scarlett Johansson
**Musical Guest:** Death Cab for Cutie
**Musical and Guest Performances/Cameo(s)/ Program Notes:**
- "Live from New York": Robert Smigel (voice), in a "TV Funhouse" short, *Darwin*, a cartoon produced by Pat Robertson's *700 Club*.
- Death Cab for Cutie performs "Soul Meets Body" and "Crooked Teeth."

**Airdate:** 1/21/06
**Episode:** 31.11
**Host:** Peter Sarsgaard
**Musical Guest:** The Strokes
**Musical and Guest Performances/Cameo(s)/ Program Notes:**
- "Live from New York": Anderson Cooper (Seth Meyers).
- The Strokes perform "Juicebox" and "You Only Live Once."
- "*SNL* Digital Short": *Young Chuck Norris*.
- Cameo by Drew Barrymore.

**Airdate:** 2/4/06
**Episode:** 31.12
**Host:** Steve Martin
**Musical Guest:** Prince
**Musical and Guest Performances/Cameo(s)/ Program Notes:**
- "Live from New York": Steve Martin, who is out to stop Alec Baldwin from tying his hosting record.
- Prince performs (with Tamar) "Fury" and "Beautiful, Loved and Blessed."
- "*SNL* Digital Shorts": *Close Talkers* and *The Tangent*, with cameos by Scarlett Johansson, Brian Williams, Gideon Yago, and Conan O'Brien.
- Kelly Ripa has a cameo in the cold open.

**Airdate:** 3/4/06
**Episode:** 31.13
**Host:** Natalie Portman
**Musical Guest:** Fall Out Boy
**Musical and Guest Performances/Cameo(s)/ Program Notes:**
- "Live from New York": Dick Cheney (Darrell Hammond).
- Fall Out Boy performs "Dance, Dance" and "Sugar, We're Goin' Down."
- "*SNL* Digital Short": "Natalie Rap," sung by Portman.
- "TV Funhouse": *Belated Black History Moments*, with Dennis Haysbert.

**Airdate:** 3/11/06
**Episode:** 31.14
**Host:** Matt Dillon
**Musical Guest:** Arctic Monkeys
**Musical and Guest Performances/Cameo(s)/ Program Notes:**
- "Live from New York": College girl Jessica (Maya Rudolph) and her girlfriends (Rachel Dratch, Amy Poehler, Kristen Wiig) on spring break, while waiting for their flight to Cancún, along with Jessica's parents (Chris Parnell and Paula Pell) and the airline attendant (Finesse Mitchell).
- Arctic Monkeys perform "I Bet You Look Good on the Dancefloor" and "A Certain Romance."
- "*SNL* Digital Short": *Doppelganger*.

**Airdate:** 4/8/06
**Episode:** 31.15
**Host:** Antonio Banderas
**Musical Guest:** Mary J. Blige

**Musical and Guest Performances/Cameo(s)/ Program Notes:**
- "Live from New York": Anderson Cooper (Seth Meyers), leading a discussion on immigration.
- Blige performs "Be Without You" and "Enough Cryin'."
- Cameo by Chris Kattan.

**Airdate:** 4/15/06
**Episode:** 31.16
**Host:** Lindsay Lohan
**Musical Guest:** Pearl Jam
**Musical and Guest Performances/Cameo(s)/ Program Notes:**
- "Live from New York": Brittany Doyle (Lindsay Lohan).
- Pearl Jam performs "World Wide Suicide" and "Severed Hand."
- "*SNL* Digital Short": *Laser Cats!*
- ★★★★ Four-Star Short: "TV Funhouse": *Journey to the Disney Vault.*

**Airdate:** 5/6/06
**Episode:** 31.17
**Host:** Tom Hanks
**Musical Guest:** Red Hot Chili Peppers
**Musical and Guest Performances/Cameo(s)/ Program Notes:**
- "Live from New York": George W. Bush (Will Forte).
- Red Hot Chili Peppers perform "Dani California" and "Give It Away."

- "*SNL* Digital Short": *My Testicles.*

**Airdate:** 5/13/06
**Episode:** 31.18
**Host:** Julia Louis-Dreyfus
**Musical Guest:** Paul Simon
**Musical and Guest Performances/Cameo(s)/ Program Notes:**
- "Live from New York": Al Gore.
- Simon performs "How Can You Live in the Northeast" and "Outrageous."
- "*SNL* Digital Short": *Peyote.*
- Louis-Dreyfus is the first former female cast member to host the show.
- Cameos by Jason Alexander and Jerry Seinfeld.

**Airdate:** 5/20/06
**Episode:** 31.19
**Host:** Kevin Spacey
**Musical Guest:** Nelly Furtado
**Musical and Guest Performances/Cameo(s)/ Program Notes:**
- "Live from New York": Pat Danahy (Rachel Dratch).
- Furtado performs "Maneater" and, with Timbaland, "Promiscuous."
- "*SNL* Digital Short": *Andy Walking.*
- "TV Funhouse": *Fun with Real Audio* ("Presidential Outtakes").
- Final episode for Rachel Dratch, Tina Fey, Finesse Mitchell, Chris Parnell, and Horatio Sanz.

## Season 32 (2006–2007)

**Airdate:** 9/30/06
**Episode:** 32.1
**Host:** Dane Cook
**Musical Guest:** The Killers
**Musical and Guest Performances/Cameo(s)/ Program Notes:**
- "Live from New York": Jason Sudeikis as South Carolina comptroller Richard Eckstrom.
- The Killers perform "When You Were Young" and "Bones."

- Cameo by Brian Williams on *Weekend Update.*
- "*SNL* Digital Short": *Cubicle Fight.*
- Jason Sudeikis and Kristen Wiig are bumped up to regulars.

**Airdate:** 10/7/06
**Episode:** 32.2
**Host:** Jaime Pressly
**Musical Guest:** Corinne Bailey Rae
**Musical and Guest Performances/Cameo(s)/ Program Notes:**

- "Live from New York": Speaker of the House Dennis Hastert (Darrell Hammond) on the Mark Foley scandal.
- Corinne Bailey Rae performs "Put Your Records On" and "Like a Star."

**Airdate:** 10/21/06
**Episode:** 32.3
**Host:** John C. Reilly
**Musical Guest:** My Chemical Romance
**Musical and Guest Performances/Cameo(s)/ Program Notes:**
- "Live from New York": President George W. Bush (Will Forte) during an interview with Fox News's Brit Hume (Darrell Hammond).
- My Chemical Romance performs "Welcome to the Black Parade" and "Cancer."
- Cameo by Will Ferrell as *Inside the Actors Studio* host James Lipton.
- "SNL Digital Short": *Harpoon Man.*

**Airdate:** 10/28/06
**Episode:** 32.4
**Host:** Hugh Laurie
**Musical Guest:** Beck
**Musical and Guest Performances/Cameo(s)/ Program Notes:**
- "Live from New York": Borat (Sacha Baron Cohen, in a cameo), who says, "Live from New York, home of the Jew, it's Saturday Night!"
- Beck performs "Nausea" and "Clap Hands."
- "TV Funhouse": *Republican Attack Ads.*

**Airdate:** 11/11/06
**Episode:** 32.5
**Host:** Alec Baldwin
**Musical Guest:** Christina Aguilera
**Musical and Guest Performances/Cameo(s)/ Program Notes:**
- "Live from New York": Speaker-Elect of the House of Representatives Nancy Pelosi (Kristen Wiig).
- Christina Aguilera performs "Hurt," "Ain't No Other Man," and, with special guest Tony Bennett, "Steppin' Out with My Baby."
- Appearances by Tina Fey, Tracy Morgan, Steve Martin, Paul McCartney, and Martin Short.
- Baldwin visits Steve Martin in the Platinum Lounge, where Martin Short is their waiter.
- "TV Funhouse": *Kobayashi*, a parody of *Dragon Ball Z.*

**Airdate:** 11/18/06
**Episode:** 32.6
**Host/Musical Guest:** Ludacris
**Musical and Guest Performances/Cameo(s)/ Program Notes:**
- "Live from New York": President George W. Bush (Jason Sudeikis) announces to the American people that the U.S. is at war with Vietnam due to something he may have done at the Asia-Pacific Economic Cooperation Forum.
- Ludacris performs "Money Maker" and, with guest Mary J. Blige, "Runaway Love."

**Airdate:** 12/2/06
**Episode:** 32.7
**Host:** Matthew Fox
**Musical Guest:** Tenacious D
**Musical and Guest Performances/Cameo(s)/ Program Notes:**
- "Live from New York": Iraqi Prime Minister Nouri al-Maliki (Fred Armisen) and his interpreter (Will Forte), during a press conference with President George W. Bush (Jason Sudeikis).
- Tenacious D performs "Kickapoo" and "The Metal."

**Airdate:** 12/9/06
**Episode:** 32.8
**Host:** Annette Bening
**Musical Guest:** Gwen Stefani, Akon
**Musical and Guest Performances/Cameo(s)/ Program Notes:**

Appendix A

- "Live from New York": President George W. Bush (Jason Sudeikis), who dismisses the recommendations made by *The Iraq Study Group Report* and letters he's received regarding U.S.'s strategy in the Iraq war.
- Gwen Stefani performs "Wind It Up."
- Akon performs "I Wanna Love You."
- "TV Funhouse": *Diddy Kiddies.*
- "*SNL* Digital Shorts": *Apocalypto* and *Pep Talk.*

**Airdate:** 12/16/06
**Episode:** 32.9
**Host/Musical Guest:** Justin Timberlake
**Musical and Guest Performances/Cameo(s)/Program Notes:**
- "Live from New York": Amy Poehler, Maya Rudolph, and Kristen Wiig, who sing "Santa's My Boyfriend."
- Timberlake performs "My Love" and "What Goes Around."
- "*SNL* Digital Short": "Dick in a Box," for which Timberlake, Andy Samberg, Jorma Taccone, Katreese Barnes, and Asa Taccone won an Emmy for Outstanding Original Music and Lyrics.
- Cameo by Jimmy Fallon.

**Airdate:** 1/13/07
**Episode:** 32.10
**Host:** Jake Gyllenhaal
**Musical Guest:** The Shins
**Musical and Guest Performances/Cameo(s)/Program Notes:**
- "Live from New York": George W. Bush (Jason Sudeikis) on drafting more Americans to fight in Iraq.
- The Shins perform "Phantom Limb" and "New Slang."
- Sketch Debut: *Bronx Beat*, hosted by Betty Caruso (Amy Poehler) and Jodi Deitz (Maya Rudolph).
- "*SNL* Digital Short": *Laser Cats! 2.*

**Airdate:** 1/20/07
**Episode:** 32.11
**Host:** Jeremy Piven
**Musical Guest:** AFI

**Musical and Guest Performances/Cameo(s)/Program Notes:**
- "Live from New York": Hillary Clinton (Amy Poehler), who is interviewed on *Hardball* by Chris Matthews (Darrell Hammond).
- AFI performs "Love Like Winter" and "Miss Murder."
- Cameo by hip-hop recording artist/actor Common.
- Sketch Debut: *MacGruber*, featuring Will Forte as MacGruber.
- "TV Funhouse": *Fun with Real Audio* ("Frontline: 2007 in Review").
- "*SNL* Digital Short": *Nurse Nancy.*

**Airdate:** 2/3/07
**Episode:** 32.12
**Host:** Drew Barrymore
**Musical Guest:** Lily Allen
**Musical and Guest Performances/Cameo(s)/Program Notes:**
- "Live from New York": Ryan Seacrest (Seth Meyers), in a parody of *American Idol.*
- Allen performs "Smile" and "LDN."
- Cameo by Horatio Sanz (as Elton John).
- "*SNL* Digital Short": *Body Fuzion.*
- Barrymore is second female to host five times.

**Airdate:** 2/10/07
**Episode:** 32.13
**Host:** Forest Whitaker
**Musical Guest:** Keith Urban
**Musical and Guest Performances/Cameo(s)/Program Notes:**
- "Live from New York": Dick Cheney (Darrell Hammond) shares the Valentine's Day cards he and his wife, Lynne (Kristen Wiig), received.
- Urban sings "Stupid Boy" and "Once in a Lifetime."
- "*SNL* Digital Short": *Andy Popping into Frame.*

**Airdate:** 2/24/07
**Episode:** 32.14

**Host:** Rainn Wilson
**Musical Guest:** Arcade Fire
**Musical and Guest Performances/Cameo(s)/ Program Notes:**
- "Live from New York": Wolf Blitzer (Darrell Hammond), during CNN's endless coverage of the death of Anna Nicole Smith.
- Arcade Fire performs "Intervention" and "Keep the Car Running."
- Cameo by Rashida Jones in a parody of *The Office*.
- "*SNL* Digital Short": *Business Meeting*.

**Airdate:** 3/17/07
**Episode:** 32.15
**Host:** Julia Louis-Dreyfus
**Musical Guest:** Snow Patrol
**Musical and Guest Performances/Cameo(s)/ Program Notes:**
- "Live from New York": Chris Rock, who predicts Barack Obama will be the next President of the United States.
- Snow Patrol performs "You're All I Have" and "Chasing Cars."
- Sketch Debut: *La Rivista Della Televisione*, hosted by Vinny Vedecci (Bill Hader).

**Airdate:** 3/24/07
**Episode:** 32.16
**Host:** Peyton Manning
**Musical Guest:** Carrie Underwood
**Musical and Guest Performances/Cameo(s)/ Program Notes:**
- "Live from New York": George W. Bush (Jason Sudeikis), defending Attorney General Alberto Gonzalez (Fred Armisen).
- Underwood performs "Before He Cheats" and "Wasted."
- "TV Funhouse": *Maraka*, a parody of the bilingual children's animated series *Dora the Explorer*.
- Cameos by Dan Aykroyd and Peyton's brother Eli, who will host in 2012 (37.20), and their parents, Archie and Olivia Manning.

**Airdate:** 4/14/07
**Episode:** 32.17
**Host:** Shia LaBeouf
**Musical Guest:** Avril Lavigne
**Musical and Guest Performances/Cameo(s)/ Program Notes:**
- "Live from New York": Rev. Al Sharpton (Kenan Thompson), who, along with Jesse Jackson (Darrell Hammond), responds to radio talk show host Don Imus's racial slur.
- Lavigne performs "Girlfriend" and "I Can Do Better" and plays Elle Fanning in the sketch *The Dakota Fanning Show*.
- Cameo by Alec Baldwin.
- "*SNL* Digital Short": *Dear Sister*.

**Airdate:** 4/21/07
**Episode:** 32.18
**Host:** Scarlett Johansson
**Musical Guest:** Björk
**Musical and Guest Performances/Cameo(s)/ Program Notes:**
- "Live from New York": Democratic senator from New York Charles Schumer.
- Björk performs "Earth Intruders" and "Wanderlust."
- Cameo by New York senator Charles Schumer.
- "*SNL* Digital Short": "Roy Rules!," performed by Andy Samberg.
- "TV Funhouse": *Torboto* (a parody of *Gigantor*), a robot built by Bush and Cheney to torture prisoners.

**Airdate:** 5/12/07
**Episode:** 32.19
**Host:** Molly Shannon
**Musical Guest:** Linkin Park
**Musical and Guest Performances/Cameo(s)/ Program Notes:**
- "Live from New York": Mary Katherine Gallagher (Molly Shannon), auditioning for *American Idol*.
- Linkin Park performs "What I've Done" and "Bleed It Out."

Appendix A

- "TV Funhouse": *Tales from the Greatest Generation.*

**Airdate:** 5/19/07
**Episode:** 32.20
**Host:** Zach Braff
**Musical Guest:** Maroon 5
**Musical and Guest Performances/Cameo(s)/ Program Notes:**
- "Live from New York": Condoleezza Rice (Maya Rudolph).
- Maroon 5 performs "Makes Me Wonder" and "Won't Go Home Without You."
- "*SNL* Digital Short": *Talking Dog.*
- "TV Funhouse": *Decision '08: Spring '07 Cleaning.*

## Season 33 (2007–2008)

**Airdate:** 9/29/07
**Episode:** 33.1
**Host:** LeBron James
**Musical Guest:** Kanye West
**Musical and Guest Performances/Cameo(s)/ Program Notes:**
- "Live from New York": Hillary Clinton (Amy Poehler).
- West performs "Stronger," "Good Life," "Champion," and "Everything I Am."
- "TV Funhouse": *Ambiguously Gay Duo* ("First Served, First Come").
- "*SNL* Digital Short": "Iran So Far," performed by Andy Samberg and Adam Levine.

**Airdate:** 10/6/07
**Episode:** 33.2
**Host:** Seth Rogen
**Musical Guest:** Spoon
**Musical and Guest Performances/Cameo(s)/ Program Notes:**
- "Live from New York": Kevin Federline (Andy Samberg).
- Spoon performs "The Underdog" and "You Got Yr. Cherry Bomb."
- Cameo by Chevy Chase.

**Airdate:** 10/13/07
**Episode:** 33.3
**Host:** Jon Bon Jovi
**Musical Guest:** Foo Fighters
**Musical and Guest Performances/Cameo(s)/ Program Notes:**
- "Live from New York": Teenager Amy Poehler, who, in 1976, is visited by Jon Bon Jovi in her bedroom.
- Foo Fighters perform "The Pretender."
- Jon Bon Jovi performs "Lost Highway" and "Who Says You Can't Go Home?"
- "*SNL* Digital Short": *People Getting Punched Before Eating.*
- Cameo by Jack Nicholson.

**Airdate:** 11/3/07
**Episode:** 33.4
**Host:** Brian Williams
**Musical Guest:** Feist
**Musical and Guest Performances/Cameo(s)/ Program Notes:**
- "Live from New York": Presidential candidate Barack Obama at the Clintons' Halloween party.
- Feist performs "1234" and "I Feel It All."
- Cameos by Senator Barack Obama, Horatio Sanz, Bono, Matt Lauer, and Al Roker.
- "*SNL* Digital Short": *Brian Diaries,* starring Brian Williams.
- This is the last episode of 2007 due to the Writers Guild of America strike.
- Maya Rudolph's final show.

**Airdate:** 2/23/08
**Episode:** 33.5
**Host:** Tina Fey
**Musical Guest:** Carrie Underwood

**Musical and Guest Performances/Cameo(s)/ Program Notes:**
- "Live from New York": CNN's Campbell Brown (Kristen Wiig), moderating the Obama-Clinton Democratic presidential candidate debate.
- Underwood performs "All-American Girl" and "Flat on the Floor."
- Cameos by "Obama Girl" Amber Lee Ettinger, Mike Huckabee, and Steve Martin.
- "*SNL* Digital Short": *Grandkids in the Movies.*
- Debut of featured player Casey Wilson.

**Airdate:** 3/1/08
**Episode:** 33.6
**Host:** Ellen Page
**Musical Guest:** Wilco
**Musical and Guest Performances/Cameo(s)/ Program Notes:**
- "Live from New York": Hillary Clinton.
- Wilco performs "Hate It Here" and "Walken."
- Cameos by Vincent D'Onofrio and Rudy Giuliani.
- "TV Funhouse": *The Obama Files.*
- "*SNL* Digital Short": *The Mirror.*

**Airdate:** 3/8/08
**Episode:** 33.7
**Host:** Amy Adams
**Musical Guest:** Vampire Weekend
**Musical and Guest Performances/Cameo(s)/ Program Notes:**
- "Live from New York": Hillary Clinton (Amy Poehler).
- Vampire Weekend performs "A-Punk" and "M79."
- "*SNL* Digital Short": "Hero Song," performed by Andy Samberg.

**Airdate:** 3/15/08
**Episode:** 33.8
**Host:** Jonah Hill
**Musical Guest:** Mariah Carey

**Musical and Guest Performances/Cameo(s)/ Program Notes:**
- "Live from New York": Former New York governor Eliot Spitzer (Bill Hader), who advertises his new law firm specializing in legal cases involving embarrassing and shameful behavior.
- Carey performs "Touch My Body" and "Migrate" (with T-Pain).
- Cameo by Tracy Morgan.
- "*SNL* Digital Short": *Andy's Dad.*

**Airdate:** 4/5/08
**Episode:** 33.9
**Host:** Christopher Walken
**Musical Guest:** Panic! at the Disco
**Musical and Guest Performances/Cameo(s)/ Program Notes:**
- "Live from New York": Bill and Hillary Clinton (Darrell Hammond and Amy Poehler).
- Panic! at the Disco performs "Nine in the Afternoon" and "I Write Sins Not Tragedies."
- "*SNL* Digital Short": *Laser Cats! 3D.*

**Airdate:** 4/12/08
**Episode:** 33.10
**Host:** Ashton Kutcher
**Musical Guest:** Gnarls Barkley
**Musical and Guest Performances/Cameo(s)/ Program Notes:**
- "Live from New York": General David Petraeus (Will Forte).
- Gnarls Barkley performs "Run (I'm a Natural Disaster)" and "Who's Gonna Save My Soul."
- "*SNL* Digital Short": "Daiquiri Girl," performed by Clementine (Andy Samberg).

**Airdate:** 5/10/08
**Episode:** 33.11
**Host:** Shia LaBeouf
**Musical Guest:** My Morning Jacket
**Musical and Guest Performances/Cameo(s)/ Program Notes:**

Appendix A

- "Live from New York": Hillary Clinton (Amy Poehler) admits she will be a sore loser if she doesn't get the Democratic Party presidential nomination.
- My Morning Jacket performs "I'm Amazed" and "Evil Urges."
- "*SNL* Digital Short": *The Best Look in the World.*

**Airdate:** 5/17/08
**Episode:** 33.12
**Host:** Steve Carell
**Musical Guest:** Usher
**Musical and Guest Performances/Cameo(s)/ Program Notes:**
- "Live from New York": Professor (Steve Carell) reading off students' sexually suggestive names at a commencement ceremony.
- Usher sings "This Ain't Sex" and, with Young Jeezy, "Love in This Club."
- Cameos by Senator John McCain and former *SNL* cast member (1995–1996) Nancy Walls, who is married to Carell.
- "*SNL* Digital Short": *Japanese Office.*

## Season 34 (2008–2009)

**Airdate:** 9/13/08
**Episode:** 34.1
**Host:** Michael Phelps
**Musical Guest:** Lil Wayne
**Musical and Guest Performances/Cameo(s)/ Program Notes:**
- "Live from New York": Sarah Palin (Tina Fey) and Hillary Clinton (Amy Poehler).
- Lil Wayne performs "Got Money" and "Lollipop."
- Cameos by Tina Fey, Jared Fogel, Debbie Phelps (Michael's mom), and William Shatner.
- "*SNL* Digital Short": *Space Olympics.*

**Airdate:** 9/20/08
**Episode:** 34.2
**Host:** James Franco
**Musical Guest:** Kings of Leon
**Musical and Guest Performances/Cameo(s)/ Program Notes:**
- "Live from New York": John McCain (Darrell Hammond).
- Kings of Leon perform "Sex on Fire" and "Use Somebody."
- Cameos by Blake Lively, Kumail Nanjiani, and Cameron Diaz.
- "*SNL* Digital Short": *Hey! (Murray Hill).*

**Airdate:** 9/27/08
**Episode:** 34.3
**Host:** Anna Faris
**Musical Guest:** Duffy
**Musical and Guest Performances/Cameo(s)/ Program Notes:**
- "Live from New York": Sarah Palin (Tina Fey).
- Duffy performs "Mercy" and "Stepping Stone."
- Cameo by Chris Parnell.

**Airdate:** 10/4/08
**Episode:** 34.4
**Host:** Anne Hathaway
**Musical Guest:** The Killers
**Musical and Guest Performances/Cameo(s)/ Program Notes:**
- "Live from New York": Gwen Ifill (Queen Latifah), moderating the vice-presidential debate.
- The Killers perform "Human" and "Spaceman."
- Sketch Debut: Parody of *The Lawrence Welk Show*, featuring Dooneese (Kristen Wiig).
- "*SNL* Digital Short": *Extreme Challenge.*

**Airdate:** 10/18/08
**Episode:** 34.5
**Host:** Josh Brolin
**Musical Guest:** Adele

Episode Guide

**Musical and Guest Performances/Cameo(s)/ Program Notes:**
- "Live from New York": Sarah Palin.
- Adele performs "Chasing Pavements" and "Cold Shoulder."
- Cameos by Alec Baldwin, Tina Fey, Sarah Palin, Oliver Stone, and Mark Wahlberg.

**Airdate:** 10/25/08
**Episode:** 34.6
**Host:** Jon Hamm
**Musical Guest:** Coldplay
**Musical and Guest Performances/Cameo(s)/ Program Notes:**
- "Live from New York": Vice presidential candidate Joe Biden (Jason Sudeikis).
- Coldplay performs "Viva La Vida," "Lost!," "Yellow," and "Lovers in Japan."
- ★★★★ Four-Star Sketch: *Vincent Price's Halloween Special.*
- Cameos by Elisabeth Moss, Maya Rudolph, and John Slattery.
- "*SNL* Digital Short": "Ras Trent," performed by Andy Samberg.

**Airdate:** 11/1/08
**Episode:** 34.7
**Host:** Ben Affleck
**Musical Guest:** David Cook
**Musical and Guest Performances/Cameo(s)/ Program Notes:**
- "Live from New York": Senator John McCain.
- Cook performs "Light On" and "Declaration."
- Cameos by Tina Fey, Cindy McCain, and Sen. John McCain.

**Airdate:** 11/15/08
**Episode:** 34.8
**Host:** Paul Rudd
**Musical Guest:** Beyoncé
**Musical and Guest Performances/Cameo(s)/ Program Notes:**
- "Live from New York": Vice President–Elect Joe Biden (Jason Sudeikis).
- Beyoncé performs "If I Were a Boy" and "Single Ladies (Put a Ring on It)."
- ★★★★ Four-Star Sketch: Justin Timberlake, in a cameo, along with Andy Samberg and Bobby Moynihan play Beyoncé's backup dancers.
- Debut of featured players Abby Elliott and Michaela Watkins.
- "*SNL* Digital Short": *Everyone's a Critic.*

**Airdate:** 11/22/08
**Episode:** 34.9
**Host:** Tim McGraw
**Musical Guest:** Ludacris and T-Pain
**Musical and Guest Performances/Cameo(s)/ Program Notes:**
- "Live from New York": Congressman Barney Frank (Fred Armisen) during the automaker bailout hearings.
- Ludacris and T-Pain perform "One More Drink" and "Chopped N Skrewed."

**Airdate:** 12/6/08
**Episode:** 34.10
**Host:** John Malkovich
**Musical Guest:** T.I.
**Musical and Guest Performances/Cameo(s)/ Program Notes:**
- "Live from New York": Bill and Hillary Clinton (Darrell Hammond and Amy Poehler).
- T.I. performs "Whatever You Like" and "Swing Ya Rag" (with Swizz Beatz).
- "*SNL* Digital Short": "Jizz in My Pants," performed by Andy Samberg and Jorma Taccone and featuring Jamie-Lynn Sigler, Justin Timberlake, and Molly Sims.

**Airdate:** 12/13/08
**Episode:** 34.11
**Host:** Hugh Laurie
**Musical Guest:** Kanye West
**Musical and Guest Performances/Cameo(s)/ Program Notes:**

Appendix A

- "Live from New York": Illinois governor Rod Blagojevich (Jason Sudeikis).
- West performs "Love Lockdown" and "Heartless."
- Amy Poehler's final show.
- "*SNL* Digital Short": *Cookies*.

**Airdate:** 1/10/09
**Episode:** 34.12
**Host:** Neil Patrick Harris
**Musical Guest:** Taylor Swift
**Musical and Guest Performances/Cameo(s)/ Program Notes:**
- "Live from New York": Rachel Maddow (Abby Elliott).
- Swift performs "Love Story" and "Forever & Always."
- Cameo by Liza Minnelli.
- "*SNL* Digital Short": "Doogie Howser Theme."

**Airdate:** 1/17/09
**Episode:** 34.13
**Host:** Rosario Dawson
**Musical Guest:** Fleet Foxes
**Musical and Guest Performances/Cameo(s)/ Program Notes:**
- "Live from New York": Diane Sawyer (Kristen Wiig).
- Fleet Foxes perform "Mykonos" and "Blue Ridge Mountains."
- Sketch Debut: *Gilly*, with Kristen Wiig in the title role.
- "*SNL* Digital Short": *A Couple of Homies*.

**Airdate:** 1/31/09
**Episode:** 34.14
**Host:** Steve Martin
**Musical Guest:** Jason Mraz
**Musical and Guest Performances/Cameo(s)/ Program Notes:**
- "Live from New York": President Barack Obama (Fred Armisen).
- Mraz performs "I'm Yours" and "Lucky" (with Colbie Caillat).
- Martin performs "Late for School" (with Britney Haas, Craig Eastman, Michael Daves, and Skip Ward).
- "*SNL* Digital Short": *Laser Cats! 4-Ever!*

**Airdate:** 2/7/09
**Episode:** 34.15
**Host:** Bradley Cooper
**Musical Guest:** TV on the Radio
**Musical and Guest Performances/Cameo(s)/ Program Notes:**
- "Live from New York": Nancy Pelosi (Kristen Wiig).
- TV on the Radio performs "Golden Age" and "Dancing Choose."
- Cameo by James Lipton.
- "*SNL* Digital Short": "I'm on a Boat," performed by Andy Samberg, Akiva Schaffer, and T-Pain.

**Airdate:** 2/14/09
**Episode:** 34.16
**Host:** Alec Baldwin
**Musical Guest:** Jonas Brothers
**Musical and Guest Performances/Cameo(s)/ Program Notes:**
- "Live from New York": Senate Minority Leader Mitch McConnell (Darrell Hammond).
- Jonas Brothers perform "Tonight" and "Video Girl."
- Cameos by Dan Aykroyd, Alia Baldwin, Hailey Baldwin, Cameron Diaz, and Jack McBrayer.
- "*SNL* Digital Short": "Property of the Queen" featuring the Jonas Brothers.

**Airdate:** 3/7/09
**Episode:** 34.17
**Host:** Dwayne Johnson
**Musical Guest:** Ray LaMontagne
**Musical and Guest Performances/Cameo(s)/ Program Notes:**
- "Live from New York": U.S. Secretary of the Treasury Timothy Geithner (Will Forte).
- LaMontagne performs "You Are the Best Thing" and "Trouble."
- Cameos by Jessica Biel, Justin Timberlake, and Richard Dean Anderson (in a *MacGruber* segment).

**Airdate:** 3/14/09
**Episode:** 34.18

**Host:** Tracy Morgan
**Musical Guest:** Kelly Clarkson
**Musical and Guest Performances/Cameo(s)/ Program Notes:**
- "Live from New York": Tracy Morgan, who knocks out anyone who gets in his way as he heads up to Studio 8H.
- Clarkson performs "My Life Would Suck Without You" and "I Do Not Hook Up."
- Cameos by Tina Fey and John Cena.
- "*SNL* Digital Short": *Party Guys.*

**Airdate:** 4/4/09
**Episode:** 34.19
**Host:** Seth Rogen
**Musical Guest:** Phoenix
**Musical and Guest Performances/Cameo(s)/ Program Notes:**
- "Live from New York": President Barack Obama (Fred Armisen).
- Phoenix performs "Lisztomania," "1901," and "Too Young."
- "*SNL* Digital Short": "Like a Boss," performed by Andy Samberg.

**Airdate:** 4/11/09
**Episode:** 34.20
**Host:** Zac Efron
**Musical Guest:** Yeah Yeah Yeahs
**Musical and Guest Performances/Cameo(s)/ Program Notes:**
- "Live from New York": Vice President Joe Biden (Jason Sudeikis).
- Yeah Yeah Yeahs perform "Zero" and "Maps."

**Airdate:** 5/9/09
**Episode:** 34.21
**Host:** Justin Timberlake
**Musical Guest:** Ciara
**Musical and Guest Performances/Cameo(s)/ Program Notes:**
- "Live from New York": U.S. Secretary of the Treasury Timothy Geithner (Will Forte).
- Ciara performs "Love Sex Magic" and "Never Ever."
- Cameos by Jessica Biel, Jimmy Fallon, Leonard Nimoy, Chris Pine, and Zachary Quinto.
- "*SNL* Digital Short": "Mother Lover," performed by Andy Samberg and Justin Timberlake and featuring Patricia Clarkson and Susan Sarandon.

**Airdate:** 5/16/09
**Episode:** 34.22
**Host:** Will Ferrell
**Musical Guest:** Green Day
**Musical and Guest Performances/Cameo(s)/ Program Notes:**
- "Live from New York": Former vice president Dick Cheney (Darrell Hammond).
- Green Day performs "Know Your Enemy," "21 Guns," and "Goodnight Saigon."
- Cameos by Tom Hanks, Anne Hathaway, Artie Lange, Norm Macdonald, Elisabeth Moss, Amy Poehler, Paul Rudd, and Maya Rudolph.
- Final episode for Darrell Hammond, Michaela Watkins, and Casey Wilson.

## Season 35 (2009–2010)

**Airdate:** 9/26/09
**Episode:** 35.1
**Host:** Megan Fox
**Musical Guest:** U2
**Musical and Guest Performances/Cameo(s)/ Program Notes:**
- "Live from New York": Muammar al-Gaddafi (Fred Armisen) and voice of translator (Bill Hader).
- U2 performs "Breathe," "Moment of Surrender," and "Ultraviolet."
- Cameo by Brian Austin Green.
- "*SNL* Digital Shorts": *The Date* and *Megan's Roommate.*

Appendix A

- Debut of featured players Nasim Pedrad and Jenny Slate.

**Airdate:** 10/3/09
**Episode:** 35.2
**Host:** Ryan Reynolds
**Musical Guest:** Lady Gaga
**Musical and Guest Performances/Cameo(s)/ Program Notes:**
- "Live from New York": President Barack Obama (Fred Armisen)
- Lady Gaga performs "Paparazzi" and a medley of her hits.
- Cameos by Darrell Hammond, Scarlett Johansson, Madonna, and Elijah Wood.
- "*SNL* Digital Short": "On the Ground," performed by Andy Samberg.

**Airdate:** 10/10/09
**Episode:** 35.3
**Host:** Drew Barrymore
**Musical Guest:** Regina Spektor
**Musical and Guest Performances/Cameo(s)/ Program Notes:**
- "Live from New York": President Obama (Fred Armisen), on winning the Nobel Peace Prize.
- Spektor performs "Eet" and "The Calculation."
- Cameo by Justin Long.
- "*SNL* Digital Short": *Brenda & Shaun*.

**Airdate:** 10/17/09
**Episode:** 35.4
**Host:** Gerard Butler
**Musical Guest:** Shakira
**Musical and Guest Performances/Cameo(s)/ Program Notes:**
- "Live from New York": The Rock Obama (Dwayne Johnson).
- Shakira performs "She Wolf" and "Did It Again."
- Cameos by James Franco and Dwayne Johnson.
- Sketch Debut: *What Up with That?*

**Airdate:** 11/7/09
**Episode:** 35.5
**Host/Musical Guest:** Taylor Swift
**Musical and Guest Performances/Cameo(s)/ Program Notes:**
- "Live from New York": Fox News anchor Greta Van Susteren (Kristen Wiig).
- Swift performs "You Belong with Me" and "Untouchable."
- Cameo by Amy Poehler.
- "*SNL* Digital Short": *Firelight*, a parody of *Twilight*, in which Swift falls in love with Philip Frank(enstein) (Bill Hader).

**Airdate:** 11/14/09
**Episode:** 35.6
**Host:** January Jones
**Musical Guest:** The Black Eyed Peas
**Musical and Guest Performances/Cameo(s)/ Program Notes:**
- "Live from New York": Vice President Joe Biden (Jason Sudeikis), who reveals his plan to fix health care while the president is away.
- The Black Eyed Peas perform "I Gotta Feeling," "Meet Me Halfway," and "Boom Boom Pow."
- Cameo by Darrell Hammond.
- "*SNL* Digital Short": *Get Out!*

**Airdate:** 11/21/09
**Episode:** 35.7
**Host:** Joseph Gordon-Levitt
**Musical Guest:** Dave Matthews Band
**Musical and Guest Performances/Cameo(s)/ Program Notes:**
- "Live from New York": Chinese president Hu Jintao (Will Forte).
- Dave Matthews Band performs "You & Me" and "Shake Me Like a Monkey."
- Cameos by Al Gore and Mindy Kaling.
- "*SNL* Digital Short": "Two Worlds Collide."
- ★★★★ Four-Star Monologue: Gordon-Levitt sings "Make 'em Laugh."

**Airdate:** 12/5/09
**Episode:** 35.8
**Host:** Blake Lively

Episode Guide 519

**Musical Guest:** Rihanna
**Musical and Guest Performances/Cameo(s)/ Program Notes:**
- "Live from New York": President Obama (Fred Armisen) and party crashers Tareq and Michaele Salahi (Bobby Moynihan and Kristen Wiig).
- Rihanna performs "Russian Roulette" and "Hard."
- "*SNL* Digital Short": "Shy Ronnie," featuring Rihanna.

**Airdate:** 12/12/09
**Episode:** 35.9
**Host:** Taylor Lautner
**Musical Guest:** Bon Jovi
**Musical and Guest Performances/Cameo(s)/ Program Notes:**
- "Live from New York": South Carolina governor Mark Sanford (Jason Sudeikis), in an "Adulterers Press Conference" with John Edwards (Will Forte) and John Ensign (Bill Hader).
- Bon Jovi performs "Superman Tonight" and "When We Were Beautiful."

**Airdate:** 12/19/09
**Episode:** 35.10
**Host:** James Franco
**Musical Guest:** Muse
**Musical and Guest Performances/Cameo(s)/ Program Notes:**
- "Live from New York": Lawrence Welk (Fred Armisen) and Dooneese (Kristen Wiig).
- Muse performs "Uprising" and "Starlight."
- Cameos by Jack McBrayer and Mike Tyson.
- Sketch Debut: *The Manuel Ortiz Show*, hosted by Manuel Ortiz (Fred Armisen).
- "*SNL* Digital Short": *Tizzle Wizzle Show.*

**Airdate:** 1/9/10
**Episode:** 35.11
**Host:** Charles Barkley
**Musical Guest:** Alicia Keys

**Musical and Guest Performances/Cameo(s)/ Program Notes:**
- "Live from New York": Yemen president Ali Abdullah Saleh (Fred Armisen).
- Keys performs "Try Sleeping with a Broken Heart" and "Empire State of Mind."
- "*SNL* Digital Short": "Booty Call" with Alicia Keys.

**Airdate:** 1/16/10
**Episode:** 35.12
**Host:** Sigourney Weaver
**Musical Guest:** The Ting Tings
**Musical and Guest Performances/Cameo(s)/ Program Notes:**
- "Live from New York": Larry King (Fred Armisen).
- The Ting Tings perform "That's Not My Name" and "Shut Up and Let Me Go."
- Cameos by Darrell Hammond and James Cameron.
- "*SNL* Digital Short": *James Cameron's Laser Cats 5.*

**Airdate:** 1/30/10
**Episode:** 35.13
**Host:** Jon Hamm
**Musical Guest:** Michael Bublé
**Musical and Guest Performances/Cameo(s)/ Program Notes:**
- "Live from New York": President Obama's (Fred Armisen) State of the Union Address.
- Bublé performs "Haven't Met You Yet" and "Baby (You've Got What It Takes)" (with Sharon Jones).
- "*SNL* Digital Short": *The Curse.*

**Airdate:** 2/6/10
**Episode:** 35.14
**Host:** Ashton Kutcher
**Musical Guest:** Them Crooked Vultures
**Musical and Guest Performances/Cameo(s)/ Program Notes:**
- "Live from New York": Greta Van Susteren (Kristen Wiig).

- Them Crooked Vultures performs "Mind Eraser, No Chaser" and "New Fang."

**Airdate:** 2/27/10
**Episode:** 35.15
**Host/Musical Guest:** Jennifer Lopez
**Musical and Guest Performances/Cameo(s)/Program Notes:**
- "Live from New York": Quincy Jones (Kenan Thompson), who presents "We Are the World 3."
- Lopez performs "Until It Beats No More" and "Starting Over."
- "*SNL* Digital Short": "Flags of the World."

**Airdate:** 3/6/10
**Episode:** 35.16
**Host:** Zach Galifianakis
**Musical Guest:** Vampire Weekend
**Musical and Guest Performances/Cameo(s)/Program Notes:**
- "Live from New York": President Barack Obama (Fred Armisen).
- Vampire Weekend performs "Cousins" and "Giving Up the Gun."
- Cameos by Anthony Anderson, Jane Krakowski, Jack McBrayer, Dr. Mehmet Oz, Frank Rich, Paul Rudd, Jeremy Sisto, and Brian Williams.
- "*SNL* Digital Short": *Zach Drops by the Set.*

**Airdate:** 3/13/10
**Episode:** 35.17
**Host:** Jude Law
**Musical Guest:** Pearl Jam
**Musical and Guest Performances/Cameo(s)/Program Notes:**
- "Live from New York": U.S. Representative Eric Massa (D-NY) (Bobby Moynihan), who resigned due to pending House Ethics Committee investigation into allegations of sexual misconduct.
- Pearl Jam performs "Just Breathe" and "Unthought Known."
- "*SNL* Digital Short": "Boombox," featuring Julian Casablancas.

**Airdate:** 4/10/10
**Episode:** 35.18
**Host:** Tina Fey
**Musical Guest:** Justin Bieber
**Musical and Guest Performances/Cameo(s)/Program Notes:**
- "Live from New York": President Barack Obama (Fred Armisen).
- Bieber performs "Baby" and "U Smile."
- Cameos by Steve Martin and Mark Sanchez.

**Airdate:** 4/17/10
**Episode:** 35.19
**Host:** Ryan Phillippe
**Musical Guest:** Ke$ha
**Musical and Guest Performances/Cameo(s)/Program Notes:**
- "Live from New York": Larry King (Fred Armisen).
- Ke$ha performs "Tik Tok" and "Your Love Is My Drug."
- "*SNL* Digital Short": *The Other Man.*

**Airdate:** 4/24/10
**Episode:** 35.20
**Host:** Gabourey Sidibe
**Musical Guest:** MGMT
**Musical and Guest Performances/Cameo(s)/Program Notes:**
- "Live from New York": President Barack Obama (Fred Armisen).
- MGMT performs "Flash Delirium" and "Brian Eno."
- "*SNL* Digital Short": *Cherry Battle.*

**Airdate:** 5/8/10
**Episode:** 35.21
**Host:** Betty White
**Musical Guest:** Jay-Z
**Musical and Guest Performances/Cameo(s)/Program Notes:**
- "Live from New York": Performers on *The Lawrence Welk Show*, including Betty White, Amy Poehler, Ana

Gasteyer, Maya Rudolph, Molly Shannon, and Rachel Dratch.
- Jay-Z performs "Real as It Gets," "99 Problems," "Empire State of Mind" (with Bridget Kelly), and "Young Forever" (with Mr. Hudson).
- "*SNL* Digital Short": "'Thank You for Being a Friend' (*Golden Girls* Theme)."
- Cameos by Rachel Dratch, Tina Fey, Ana Gasteyer, Amy Poehler, Maya Rudolph, and Molly Shannon.

**Airdate:** 5/15/10
**Episode:** 35.22

**Host:** Alec Baldwin
**Musical Guest:** Tom Petty and the Heartbreakers
**Musical and Guest Performances/Cameo(s)/Program Notes:**
- "Live from New York": Tony Hayward (Bill Hader), chief executive of oil and energy for British Petroleum.
- Petty and the Heartbreakers sing "I Should Have Known It" and "Jefferson Jericho Blues."
- Cameo by Steve Martin.
- "*SNL* Digital Short": "Great Day."
- Final episode for Will Forte and Jenny Slate.

## Season 36 (2010–2011)

**Airdate:** 9/25/10
**Episode:** 36.1
**Host:** Amy Poehler
**Musical Guest:** Katy Perry
**Musical and Guest Performances/Cameo(s)/Program Notes:**
- "Live from New York": Republican Delaware Senate candidate Christine O'Donnell (Kristen Wiig).
- Perry performs "California Girls" and "Teenage Dream."
- Cameos by Rachel Dratch, Jimmy Fallon, Tina Fey, Maya Rudolph, Justin Timberlake, and New York governor David Paterson.
- "*SNL* Digital Short": "Boogerman," featuring Perry and Peter Sarsgaard.
- Debut of Vanessa Bayer, Paul Brittain, and Jay Pharoah as featured players.
- Abby Elliott is bumped up to a regular.

**Airdate:** 10/2/10
**Episode:** 36.2
**Host:** Bryan Cranston
**Musical Guest:** Kanye West
**Musical and Guest Performances/Cameo(s)/Program Notes:**

- "Live from New York": Rahm Emanuel (Andy Samberg) resigns as White House chief of staff.
- West performs "Power" and "Runaway" (with Pusha T).
- Cameos by Ernest Borgnine, Morgan Freeman, and Helen Mirren.
- "*SNL* Digital Short": *Rescue Dogs 3D*, featuring Helen Mirren.
- Sketch Debut: *The Miley Cyrus Show*, hosted by Miley Cyrus (Vanessa Bayer).

**Airdate:** 10/9/10
**Episode:** 36.3
**Host:** Jane Lynch
**Musical Guest:** Bruno Mars
**Musical and Guest Performances/Cameo(s)/Program Notes:**
- "Live from New York": Self-promoting attorney Gloria Allred (Nasim Pedrad).
- Mars performs "Just the Way You Are" and "Grenade."
- "*SNL* Digital Short": "Relaxation Therapy."

**Airdate:** 10/23/10
**Episode:** 36.4
**Host:** Emma Stone

Appendix A

**Musical Guest:** Kings of Leon
**Musical and Guest Performances/Cameo(s)/ Program Notes:**
- "Live from New York": Nevada senator Harry Reid (Paul Brittain), who tries to distance himself from President Obama (Fred Armisen) during his reelection campaign.
- Kings of Leon perform "Radioactive" and "Pyro."
- "*SNL* Digital Short": "I Broke My Arm."

**Airdate:** 10/30/10
**Episode:** 36.5
**Host:** Jon Hamm
**Musical Guest:** Rihanna
**Musical and Guest Performances/Cameo(s)/ Program Notes:**
- "Live from New York": Joe Biden (Jason Sudeikis).
- Rihanna performs "What's My Name?" and "Only Girl (in the World)."
- "*SNL* Digital Short": "Ronnie and Clyde," performed by Andy Samberg and Rihanna.

**Airdate:** 11/13/10
**Episode:** 36.6
**Host:** Scarlett Johansson
**Musical Guest:** Arcade Fire
**Musical and Guest Performances/Cameo(s)/ Program Notes:**
- "Live from New York": Chinese leader Hu Jintao (Bill Hader) and his translator (Nasim Pedrad).
- Arcade Fire performs "We Used to Wait" and "Sprawl II (Mountains Beyond Mountains)."
- "*SNL* Digital Short": "What Was That?"

**Airdate:** 11/20/10
**Episode:** 36.7
**Host:** Anne Hathaway
**Musical Guest:** Florence + the Machine
**Musical and Guest Performances/Cameo(s)/ Program Notes:**
- "Live from New York": Rachel Maddow (Abby Elliott).
- Florence + the Machine perform "Dog Days Are Over" and "You've Got the Love."
- Cameos by Ben Stiller and Robin Williams.

**Airdate:** 12/4/10
**Episode:** 36.8
**Host:** Robert De Niro
**Musical Guest:** Diddy-Dirty Money
**Musical and Guest Performances/Cameo(s)/ Program Notes:**
- "Live from New York": Wikileaks founder Julian Assange (Bill Hader), who interrupts President Obama's (Fred Armisen) address to the American people.
- Diddy-Dirty Money performs "Coming Home," "Blizzard Man," and "Ass on the Floor" (with Swizz Beatz).
- Cameos by Ben Stiller and Robin Williams.
- "*SNL* Digital Short": *Party at Mr. Bernard's.*
- Film Short: *American America*, "I, Hippie."

**Airdate:** 12/11/10
**Episode:** 36.9
**Host:** Paul Rudd
**Musical Guest:** Paul McCartney
**Musical and Guest Performances/Cameo(s)/ Program Notes:**
- "Live from New York": President Obama (Fred Armisen) explaining his support for tax cuts for the rich.
- McCartney performs "Jet," "Band on the Run," "A Day in the Life," "Give Peace a Chance," and "Get Back."
- "*SNL* Digital Short": "Stumblin'," featuring Mario Batali, Paul McCartney, and Paul Rudd.

**Airdate:** 12/18/10
**Episode:** 36.10
**Host:** Jeff Bridges
**Musical Guest:** Eminem, Lil Wayne

**Musical and Guest Performances/Cameo(s)/ Program Notes:**
- "Live from New York": Frosty the Snowman (Kenan Thompson).
- Eminem and Lil Wayne perform "No Love," "Won't Back Down," and "6'7'."
- Cameo by Jim Henson's Muppets.
- "*SNL* Digital Short": "I Just Had Sex," performed by Andy Samberg, Jorma Taccone, and Akon, and featuring Akiva Schaffer, Blake Lively, Jessica Alba, and John McEnroe.

**Airdate:** 1/8/11
**Episode:** 36.11
**Host:** Jim Carrey
**Musical Guest:** The Black Keys
**Musical and Guest Performances/Cameo(s)/ Program Notes:**
- "Live from New York": New York City mayor Michael Bloomberg (Fred Armisen) on the Great Blizzard of 2010.
- The Black Keys perform "Howlin' for You" and "Tighten Up."

**Airdate:** 1/15/11
**Episode:** 36.12
**Host:** Gwyneth Paltrow
**Musical Guest:** CeeLo Green
**Musical and Guest Performances/Cameo(s)/ Program Notes:**
- "Live from New York": Fox News anchor Greta Van Susteren (Kristen Wiig).
- CeeLo Green performs "Forget You" and "Bright Lights Bigger City."
- "*SNL* Digital Short": "Andy and Pee-wee's Night Out," featuring Pee-wee Herman and Anderson Cooper.

**Airdate:** 1/29/11
**Episode:** 36.13
**Host:** Jesse Eisenberg
**Musical Guest:** Nicki Minaj
**Musical and Guest Performances/Cameo(s)/ Program Notes:**
- "Live from New York": Congresswoman Michele Bachmann's (Kristen Wiig) response to President Obama's State of the Union Address.
- Minaj performs "Right Thru Me" and "Moment 4 Life."
- Cameo by Mark Zuckerberg.
- "*SNL* Digital Short": "The Creep," performed by Andy Samberg, Akiva Schaffer, Jorma Taccone, and Nicki Minaj, and featuring John Waters.

**Airdate:** 2/5/11
**Episode:** 36.14
**Host:** Dana Carvey
**Musical Guest:** Linkin Park
**Musical and Guest Performances/Cameo(s)/ Program Notes:**
- "Live from New York": Wayne (Mike Myers) and Garth (Dana Carvey).
- Linkin Park performs "Waiting for the End" and "When They Come Back for Me."
- Cameos by Dana Carvey, Justin Bieber, Jon Lovitz, Mike Myers, and Carvey's sons, Dex and Tom.

**Airdate:** 2/12/11
**Episode:** 36.15
**Host:** Russell Brand
**Musical Guest:** Chris Brown
**Musical and Guest Performances/Cameo(s)/ Program Notes:**
- "Live from New York": Bill O'Reilly (Jason Sudeikis), who interviews President Obama (Fred Armisen).
- Brown performs "Yeah 3x" and "No Bullshit."

**Airdate:** 3/5/11
**Episode:** 36.16
**Host:** Miley Cyrus
**Musical Guest:** The Strokes
**Musical and Guest Performances/Cameo(s)/ Program Notes:**
- "Live from New York": Charlie Sheen (Bill Hader), host of *Duh! Winning!*
- The Strokes perform "Under Cover of Darkness" and "Life Is Simple in the Moonlight."
- "*SNL* Digital Short": *Beastly*.

**Airdate:** 3/12/11
**Episode:** 36.17
**Host:** Zach Galifianakis
**Musical Guest:** Jessie J
**Musical and Guest Performances/Cameo(s)/ Program Notes:**
- "Live from New York": March Madness with *CBS Sports* anchor Jim Nantz (Jason Sudeikis) and Greg Gumbel (Kenan Thompson), who take a look at the tournament to determine the craziest person in the world.
- Jessie J performs "Price Tag" (with B.o.B.) and "Mamma Knows Best."
- "*SNL* Digital Short": *Zack Looks for a New Assistant.*

**Airdate:** 4/2/11
**Episode:** 36.18
**Host/Musical Guest:** Elton John
**Musical and Guest Performances/Cameo(s)/ Program Notes:**
- "Live from New York": Lawrence Welk (Fred Armisen) and Dooneese (Kristen Wiig), the fourth singing sister with the doll hands.
- John performs "Hey Ahab" (with Leon Russell) and "Monkey Suit."
- Cameos by Will Forte and Jake Gyllenhaal.
- "*SNL* Digital Short": *Laser Cats the Musical!* featuring Tom Hanks and Carmelo Anthony.

**Airdate:** 4/9/11
**Episode:** 36.19
**Host:** Helen Mirren
**Musical Guest:** Foo Fighters
**Musical and Guest Performances/Cameo(s)/ Program Notes:**
- "Live from New York": President Obama (Fred Armisen) on averting the government shutdown.
- Foo Fighters perform "Rope" and "Walk."
- "*SNL* Digital Short": *Helen Mirren's Magical Bosom.*

**Airdate:** 5/7/11
**Episode:** 36.20
**Host:** Tina Fey
**Musical Guest:** Ellie Goulding
**Musical and Guest Performances/Cameo(s)/ Program Notes:**
- "Live from New York": Osama bin Laden (Fred Armisen), reading his last will and testament with the help of a translator (voice-over by Jim Downey).
- Goulding performs "Lights" and "Your Song."
- Cameos by Darrell Hammond and Maya Rudolph.
- "*SNL* Digital Short": "Jack Sparrow," sung by Michael Bolton and featuring Robin Wright.

**Airdate:** 5/14/11
**Episode:** 36.21
**Host:** Ed Helms
**Musical Guest:** Paul Simon
**Musical and Guest Performances/Cameo(s)/ Program Notes:**
- "Live from New York": CNN's Wolf Blitzer (Jason Sudeikis).
- Simon performs "Rewrite" and "So Beautiful or So What?"
- Cameos by Lindsey Buckingham, Chris Colfer, Jon Hamm, Steve Carell, and Stephen Colbert.
- "TV Funhouse": *Ambiguously Gay Duo* ("The Dark, Clenched Hole of Evil").

**Airdate:** 5/21/11
**Episode:** 36.22
**Host:** Justin Timberlake
**Musical Guest:** Lady Gaga
**Musical and Guest Performances/Cameo(s)/ Program Notes:**
- "Live from New York": French politician Dominique Strauss-Kahn (Taran Killam) and his cellmates (Jay Pharoah, Kenan Thompson) on Riker's Island.
- Lady Gaga performs "The Edge of Glory," "Judas," and "Born This Way."

- Cameos by Bradley Cooper and Jimmy Fallon.
- "*SNL* Digital Short": "3-Way (The Golden Rule)," sung by Timberlake, Lady Gaga, and Andy Samberg.

## Season 37 (2011–2012)

**Airdate:** 9/24/11
**Episode:** 37.1
**Host:** Alec Baldwin
**Musical Guest:** Radiohead
**Musical and Guest Performances/Cameo(s)/ Program Notes:**
- "Live from New York": Fox News's Shepard Smith (Bill Hader) hosting the "7th or 8th GOP Debate."
- This is Baldwin's sixteenth time hosting, putting him one ahead of Steve Martin, who has a cameo along with Seth Rogen.
- Radiohead performs "Lotus Flower" and "Staircase."
- Nasim Pedrad is bumped up to a regular.

**Airdate:** 10/1/11
**Episode:** 37.2
**Host:** Melissa McCarthy
**Musical Guest:** Lady Antebellum
**Musical and Guest Performances/Cameo(s)/ Program Notes:**
- "Live from New York": Dooneese (Kristen Wiig), the musical sister with the tiny hands, and her cousin Gert (Melissa McCarthy) on *The Lawrence Welk Show*.
- Lady Antebellum performs "We Owned the Night" and "Just a Kiss."

**Airdate:** 10/8/11
**Episode:** 37.3
**Host:** Ben Stiller
**Musical Guest:** Foster the People
**Musical and Guest Performances/Cameo(s)/ Program Notes:**
- "Live from New York": New Jersey governor Chris Christie (Bobby Moynihan) at Mitt Romney's (Jason Sudeikis) press conference.
- Foster the People sing "Pumped Up Kicks" and, with Kenny G, "Houdini."
- "*SNL* Digital Short": *V-Necks*.
- Cameo by Hugh Jackman.

**Airdate:** 10/15/11
**Episode:** 37.4
**Host:** Anna Faris
**Musical Guest:** Drake
**Musical and Guest Performances/Cameo(s)/ Program Notes:**
- "Live from New York": Mayor Michael Bloomberg (Fred Armisen) on "Occupy Wall Street."
- Drake performs "Headlines" and "Make Me Proud" (with Nicki Minaj).

**Airdate:** 11/5/11
**Episode:** 37.5
**Host:** Charlie Day
**Musical Guest:** Maroon 5
**Musical and Guest Performances/Cameo(s)/ Program Notes:**
- "Live from New York": The Ghost of Muammar al-Gaddafi (Fred Armisen) reporting from hell.
- Maroon 5 performs "Moves Like Jagger" and, with Travie McCoy, "Stereo Hearts."
- Cameo by Danny DeVito, Day's costar on *It's Always Sunny in Philadelphia*.

**Airdate:** 11/12/11
**Episode:** 37.6
**Host:** Emma Stone
**Musical Guest:** Coldplay
**Musical and Guest Performances/Cameo(s)/ Program Notes:**
- "Live from New York": Republican presidential candidate Rick Perry (Bill Hader), who struggles to remember

the third federal department he would cut if elected.
- Coldplay performs "Paradise" and "Every Teardrop Is a Waterfall."
- Cameo by Andrew Garfield.

**Airdate:** 11/19/11
**Episode:** 37.7
**Host:** Jason Segel
**Musical Guest:** Florence + the Machine
**Musical and Guest Performances/Cameo(s)/ Program Notes:**
- "Live from New York": Republican presidential candidate Mitt Romney (Jason Sudeikis) trying to prove he's not boring.
- Florence + the Machine perform "Shake It Out" and "No Light, No Light."
- Cameos by Jon Huntsman, Jim Henson's Muppets, Paul Rudd, and Olivia Wilde.
- "*SNL* Digital Short": *Seducing Women Through Chess.*

**Airdate:** 12/3/11
**Episode:** 37.8
**Host:** Steve Buscemi
**Musical Guest:** The Black Keys
**Musical and Guest Performances/Cameo(s)/ Program Notes:**
- "Live from New York": President Barack Obama (Fred Armisen), listing who in the government is more powerful than him.
- The Black Keys perform "Lonely Boy" and "Gold on the Ceiling."
- Cameo by Maya Rudolph.

**Airdate:** 12/10/11
**Episode:** 37.9
**Host:** Katy Perry
**Musical Guest:** Robyn
**Musical and Guest Performances/Cameo(s)/ Program Notes:**
- "Live from New York": Donald Trump (Darrell Hammond) appearing on *On the Record with Greta Van Susteren.*
- Robyn performs "Call Your Girlfriend" and "Dancing on My Own."

- Cameos by Alec Baldwin and Darrell Hammond.
- "*SNL* Digital Short": "Best Friends," featuring Katy Perry, Matt Damon, and Val Kilmer.

**Airdate:** 12/17/11
**Episode:** 37.10
**Host:** Jimmy Fallon
**Musical Guest:** Michael Bublé
**Musical and Guest Performances/Cameo(s)/ Program Notes:**
- "Live from New York": Pat Sullivan (Jimmy Fallon), who is now married to Denise (Rachel Dratch), tries to capture the magic of their second date by crashing a holiday formal.
- Michael Bublé performs "Holly Jolly Christmas" and "Have Yourself a Merry Little Christmas."
- Cameos by Rachel Dratch, Tina Fey, Chris Kattan, Jude Law, Tracy Morgan, Amy Poehler, and Horatio Sanz.
- Fallon won a Prime Time Emmy for Outstanding Guest Actor in a Comedy Series for this episode.

**Airdate:** 1/7/12
**Episode:** 37.11
**Host:** Charles Barkley
**Musical Guest:** Kelly Clarkson
**Musical and Guest Performances/Cameo(s)/ Program Notes:**
- "Live from New York": Republican presidential candidate Rick Santorum (Andy Samberg).
- Clarkson performs "Stronger" and "Mr. Know It All."

**Airdate:** 1/14/12
**Episode:** 37.12
**Host:** Daniel Radcliffe
**Musical Guest:** Lana Del Rey
**Musical and Guest Performances/Cameo(s)/ Program Notes:**
- "Live from New York": Republican presidential candidate Mitt Romney (Jason Sudeikis) trying to prove he's a regular guy.

# Episode Guide

- Lana Del Rey performs "Video Games" and "Blue Jeans."
- Paul Brittain's final show.

**Airdate:** 2/4/12
**Episode:** 37.13
**Host:** Channing Tatum
**Musical Guest:** Bon Iver
**Musical and Guest Performances/Cameo(s)/ Program Notes:**
- "Live from New York": Newt Gingrich (Bobby Moynihan), President of the Moon.
- Bon Iver performs "Holocene" and "Beth/Rest."

**Airdate:** 2/11/12
**Episode:** 37.14
**Host:** Zooey Deschanel
**Musical Guest:** Karmin
**Musical and Guest Performances/Cameo(s)/ Program Notes:**
- "Live from New York": Republican presidential candidate Mitt Romney (Jason Sudeikis) on his decline in the recent primaries.
- Karmin performs "Broken Hearted" and "I Told You So."
- Cameo by Jean Dujardin.

**Airdate:** 2/18/12
**Episode:** 37.15
**Host:** Maya Rudolph
**Musical Guest:** Sleigh Bells
**Musical and Guest Performances/Cameo(s)/ Program Notes:**
- "Live from New York": Sportscaster Dan Mardell (Bill Hader) on the "Linsanity" surrounding New York Knicks guard Jeremy Lin.
- Sleigh Bells perform "Comeback Kid" and "End of the Line."
- Cameos by Bill O'Reilly, Amy Poehler, Paul Simon, Justin Timberlake, and Kate Upton.

**Airdate:** 3/3/12
**Episode:** 37.16
**Host:** Lindsay Lohan
**Musical Guest:** Jack White
**Musical and Guest Performances/Cameo(s)/ Program Notes:**
- "Live from New York": Fox News anchor Shepard Smith (Bill Hader) interviews Mitt Romney and his five sons.
- Jack White performs "Love Interruption" (with Ruby Amanfu) and "Sixteen Saltines."
- Cameos by Jimmy Fallon and Joe Hamm.
- *SNL* Digital Short": "Afros," sung by Andy Samberg and Kristen Wiig.

**Airdate:** 3/10/12
**Episode:** 37.17
**Host:** Jonah Hill
**Musical Guest:** The Shins
**Musical and Guest Performances/Cameo(s)/ Program Notes:**
- "Live from New York": Rush Limbaugh (Taran Killam).
- The Shins perform "Simple Song" and "It's Only Life."
- Cameo by Tom Hanks.
- "*SNL* Digital Short": *Science Finders*, featuring John McEnroe.

**Airdate:** 4/7/12
**Episode:** 37.18
**Host:** Sofia Vergara
**Musical Guest:** One Direction
**Musical and Guest Performances/Cameo(s)/ Program Notes:**
- "Live from New York": Audience member (voice of Bill Hader) when Mitt Romney hosts *SNL*.
- One Direction performs "What Makes You Beautiful" and "One Thing."
- Kate McKinnon's debut as a featured player.
- Cameo by Vergara's son, Manolo Gonzalez.

**Airdate:** 4/14/12
**Episode:** 37.19
**Host:** Josh Brolin
**Musical Guest:** Gotye
**Musical and Guest Performances/Cameo(s)/ Program Notes:**

Appendix A

- "Live from New York": Republican presidential candidates Rick Perry (Bill Hader), Newt Gingrich (Bobby Moynihan), Rick Santorum (Andy Samberg), Mitt Romney (Jason Sudeikis), Herman Cain (Kenan Thompson), and Michele Bachmann (Kristen Wiig).
- Gotye performs "Somebody I Used to Know" (with Kimbra) and "Eyes Wide Open."
- "SNL Digital Short": *Laser Cats 7*, with a cameo by Steven Spielberg.
- Sketch Debut: *The Californians*.

**Airdate:** 5/5/12
**Episode:** 37.20
**Host:** Eli Manning
**Musical Guest:** Rihanna
**Musical and Guest Performances/Cameo(s)/ Program Notes:**

- "Live from New York": *Fox & Friends* hosts Steve Doocy (Taran Killam), Gretchen Carlson (Vanessa Bayer), and Brian Kilmeade (Bobby Moynihan).
- Rihanna performs "Talk That Talk" and "Where Have You Been."
- Cameos by Sacha Baron Cohen; Martin Scorsese; Manning's wife, Abby McGrew; and Manning's New York Giants teammates David Baas, David Diehl, Shaun O'Hara, and Chris Snee.

**Airdate:** 5/12/12
**Episode:** 37.21
**Host:** Will Ferrell
**Musical Guest:** Usher
**Musical and Guest Performances/Cameo(s)/ Program Notes:**

- "Live from New York": George W. Bush (Will Ferrell).
- Usher performs "Scream" and "Climax."
- Cameos by Will Forte, Ana Gasteyer, Liam Neeson, and Ferrell's mom, Kay.
- "*SNL* Digital Short": "The 100th *SNL* Digital Short" featuring Jon Hamm, Julian Casablancas, Justin Bieber, Justin Timberlake, Michael Bolton, and Natalie Portman.

**Airdate:** 5/19/12
**Episode:** 37.22
**Host/Musical Guest:** Mick Jagger
**Musical and Guest Performances/Cameo(s)/ Program Notes:**

- "Live from New York": Johnny Prosciutto (Jon Hamm), Lawrence Welk (Fred Armisen), and Dooneese (Kristen Wiig).
- Jagger performs "The Last Time," "19th Nervous Breakdown," and "It's Only Rock 'n' Roll."
- Mick Jagger wishes 2012 graduate Kristen Wiig goodbye after seven seasons. Arcade Fire and Andy Samberg sing "She's a Rainbow" and "Ruby Tuesday." Wiig dances with the cast members and Lorne Michaels and is joined onstage by *SNL* alums Chris Kattan, Amy Poehler, Rachel Dratch, Chris Parnell, and Will Forte, along with Steve Martin, Jon Hamm, Foo Fighters, and Jeff Beck.
- Abby Elliott and Andy Samberg's last show.
- "*SNL* Digital Short": "Lazy Sunday 2," performed by Chris Parnell and Andy Samberg.

## Season 38 (2012–2013)

**Airdate:** 9/15/12
**Episode:** 38.1
**Host:** Seth MacFarlane
**Musical Guest:** Frank Ocean
**Musical and Guest Performances/Cameo(s)/ Program Notes:**

- "Live from New York": President Barack Obama (Jay Pharoah) at a Democratic rally in Ohio.

- Ocean and special guest John Mayer perform "Thinkin Bout You" and "Pyramids."
- Debut of featured players Aidy Bryant, Tim Robinson, and Cecily Strong.
- Vanessa Bayer and Jay Pharoah are bumped up to regulars.

**Airdate:** 9/22/12
**Episode:** 38.2
**Host:** Joseph Gordon-Levitt
**Musical Guest:** Mumford & Sons
**Musical and Guest Performances/Cameo(s)/ Program Notes:**
- "Live from New York": Kelly Ripa (Nasim Pedrad) and cohost Michael Strahan (Jay Pharoah).
- Mumford & Sons sing "I Will Wait" and "Below My Feet."

**Airdate:** 10/6/12
**Episode:** 38.3
**Host:** Daniel Craig
**Musical Guest:** Muse
**Musical and Guest Performances/Cameo(s)/ Program Notes:**
- "Live from New York": Jim Lehrer (Chris Parnell), moderator of the first 2012 presidential debate.
- Muse performs "Madness" and "Panic Station."
- Cameo by Big Bird.

**Airdate:** 10/13/12
**Episode:** 38.4
**Host:** Christina Applegate
**Musical Guest:** Passion Pit
**Musical and Guest Performances/Cameo(s)/ Program Notes:**
- "Live from New York": Martha Raddatz (Kate McKinnon), ABC News, moderator of 2012 vice presidential debate.
- Passion Pit performs "Take a Walk" and "Carried Away."
- Cameo by Usain Bolt.

**Airdate:** 10/20/12
**Episode:** 38.5
**Host/Musical Guest:** Bruno Mars
**Musical and Guest Performances/Cameo(s)/ Program Notes:**
- "Live from New York": CNN's Candy Crowley (Aidy Bryant), host of second 2012 presidential debate.
- Mars performs "Locked Out of Heaven" and "Young Girls."
- Cameo by Tom Hanks.

**Airdate:** 11/3/12
**Episode:** 38.6
**Host:** Louis C.K.
**Musical Guest:** Fun.
**Musical and Guest Performances/Cameo(s)/ Program Notes:**
- "Live from New York": New York City mayor Michael Bloomberg (Fred Armisen) addressing New Yorkers six days after Hurricane Sandy.
- Fun. performs "Some Nights" and "Carry On."

**Airdate:** 11/10/12
**Episode:** 38.7
**Host:** Anne Hathaway
**Musical Guest:** Rihanna
**Musical and Guest Performances/Cameo(s)/ Program Notes:**
- "Live from New York": Mitt and Ann Romney (Jason Sudeikis and Kate McKinnon).
- Rihanna performs "Diamonds" and "Stay."
- Short: "The Legend of Mokiki and the Sloppy Swish," performed by Kenan Thompson.

**Airdate:** 11/17/12
**Episode:** 38.8
**Host:** Jeremy Renner
**Musical Guest:** Maroon 5
**Musical and Guest Performances/Cameo(s)/ Program Notes:**
- "Live from New York": Voice of C-SPAN (Jim Downey).
- Maroon 5 perform "One More Night" and "Daylight."

- Cameo by New Jersey governor Chris Christie.

**Airdate:** 12/8/12
**Episode:** 38.9
**Host:** Jamie Foxx
**Musical Guest:** Ne-Yo
**Musical and Guest Performances/Cameo(s)/ Program Notes:**
- "Live from New York": President Barack Obama (Jay Pharoah).
- Ne-Yo performs "Let Me Love You" and "She Is."
- Cameos by 2 Chainz, Charlie Day, and Dermot Mulroney in game show sketch *Dylan McDermott or Dermot Mulroney?*

**Airdate:** 12/15/12
**Episode:** 38.10
**Host:** Martin Short
**Musical Guest:** Paul McCartney
**Musical and Guest Performances/Cameo(s)/ Program Notes:**
- "Live from New York": In memoriam for the twenty children and six adults tragically killed at the Sandy Hook Elementary School in Newtown, Connecticut, on December 14, 2012, the New York City Children's Chorus sings "Silent Night."
- McCartney performs "My Valentine," "Cut Me Some Slack," and "Wonderful Christmastime" with the New York City Children's Chorus.
- Cameo appearances by Alec Baldwin, Carrie Brownstein, Jimmy Fallon, Tina Fey, David Grohl, Tom Hanks, Samuel L. Jackson, Krist Novoselic, Paul Shaffer, Pat Smear, Joe Walsh, and Kristen Wiig.
- F-bomb: Samuel Jackson, who appears in a *What Up with That?* sketch, sent a message out on Twitter saying he did not drop the f-bomb but said "Fuh," but he may have said "Bull—."

**Airdate:** 1/19/13
**Episode:** 38.11
**Host:** Jennifer Lawrence
**Musical Guest:** The Lumineers
**Musical and Guest Performances/Cameo(s)/ Program Notes:**
- "Live from New York": CNN's Piers Morgan (Taran Killam).
- The Lumineers perform "Ho Hey" and "Stubborn Love."

**Airdate:** 1/26/13
**Episode:** 38.12
**Host:** Adam Levine
**Musical Guest:** Kendrick Lamar
**Musical and Guest Performances/Cameo(s)/ Program Notes:**
- "Live from New York": President Obama (Jay Pharoah) and the ghost of Martin Luther King Jr. (Kenan Thompson).
- Lamar performs "Swimming Pools" and "Poetic Justice."
- Cameos by Cameron Diaz, Andy Samberg, Jerry Seinfeld, Mickey Madden, and Danny McBride.
- "*SNL* Digital Short": "YOLO (You Only Live Once)," sung by Levine and the Lonely Island.

**Airdate:** 2/9/13
**Episode:** 38.13
**Host/Musical Guest:** Justin Bieber
**Musical and Guest Performances/Cameo(s)/ Program Notes:**
- "Live from New York": Sportscaster James Brown (Kenan Thompson) and his fellow sportscasters try to fill the time when the lights go out during the Super Bowl.
- Bieber sings "As Long as You Love Me" and "Nothing Like Us."
- Cameo by Whoopi Goldberg.

**Airdate:** 2/16/13
**Episode:** 38.14
**Host:** Christoph Waltz
**Musical Guest:** Alabama Shakes
**Musical and Guest Performances/Cameo(s)/ Program Notes:**

- "Live from New York": Carnival Triumph cruise directors (Jason Sudeikis and Cecily Strong) try to entertain the passengers who are stuck on the ship with no working toilets.
- Alabama Shakes perform "Hold On" and "Always Alright."
- Waltz was the third host this season to win an Academy Award at the 2013 Oscars (best supporting actor for *Django Unchained*). Anne Hathaway won best supporting actress for *Les Misérables*, and Jennifer Lawrence won best actress for *Silver Linings Playbook*.

**Airdate:** 3/2/13
**Episode:** 38.15
**Host:** Kevin Hart
**Musical Guest:** Macklemore, Ryan Lewis
**Musical and Guest Performances/Cameo(s)/Program Notes:**
- "Live from New York": President Barack Obama (Jay Pharoah) on the financial crisis.
- Macklemore and Ryan Lewis perform "Thrift Shop" (with, in a cameo, singer Wanz) and "Can't Hold Us" (with Ray Dalton).

**Airdate:** 3/9/13
**Episode:** 38.16
**Host/Musical Guest:** Justin Timberlake
**Musical and Guest Performances/Cameo(s)/Program Notes:**
- "Live from New York": Elton John (Timberlake), singing a version of "Candle in the Wind" at Hugo Chávez's memorial service.
- Timberlake performs "Suit & Tie" (with Jay-Z) and "Mirrors."
- Timberlake joins the "Five-Timers Club," where he meets Paul Simon, Steve Martin, Alec Baldwin, Chevy Chase, Tom Hanks, and Candice Bergen. Dan Aykroyd is the bartender and Martin Short is the waiter.
- Cameo by Andy Samberg.

**Airdate:** 4/6/13
**Episode:** 38.17
**Host:** Melissa McCarthy
**Musical Guest:** Phoenix
**Musical and Guest Performances/Cameo(s)/Program Notes:**
- "Live from New York": Dennis Rodman (in a cameo), who is visiting North Korean dictator Kim Jong-Un (Bobby Moynihan).
- Phoenix performs "Entertainment," "Trying to Be Cool," and "Drakkar Noir."
- Cameo by Peter Dinklage.

**Airdate:** 4/13/13
**Episode:** 38.18
**Host:** Vince Vaughn
**Musical Guest:** Miguel
**Musical and Guest Performances/Cameo(s)/Program Notes:**
- "Live from New York": President Barack Obama (Jay Pharoah).
- Miguel performs "Adorn" and "How Many Drinks?"
- ★★★★ Four-Star Film Short: "History of Punk" profiles Ian Rubbish (Fred Armisen), a punk rocker who was a staunch supporter of conservative prime minister Margaret Thatcher. The short features a cameo by Steve Jones, founder of the punk rock group the Sex Pistols.

**Airdate:** 5/4/13
**Episode:** 38.19
**Host:** Zach Galifianakis
**Musical Guest:** Of Monsters and Men
**Musical and Guest Performances/Cameo(s)/Program Notes:**
- "Live from New York": *Fox and Friends* hosts Steve Doocy (Taran Killam), Gretchen Carlson (Vanessa Bayer), and Brian Kilmeade (Bobby Moynihan).
- Of Monsters and Men perform "Little Talks" and "Mountain Sound."

Appendix A

- Cameos by Bradley Cooper, Nikolaj Coster-Waldau, Jon Hamm, and Ed Helms.

**Airdate:** 5/11/13
**Episode:** 38.20
**Host:** Kristen Wiig
**Musical Guest:** Vampire Weekend
**Musical and Guest Performances/Cameo(s)/Program Notes:**
- "Live from New York": Darrell Issa (Bill Hader), leading the Benghazi hearings.
- Vampire Weekend performs "Diane Young" and "Unbelievers."
- Cameos by Jonah Hill and Maya Rudolph.

**Airdate:** 5/18/13
**Episode:** 38.21
**Host:** Ben Affleck
**Musical Guest:** Kanye West
**Musical and Guest Performances/Cameo(s)/Program Notes:**
- "Live from New York": *Politics Nation* with Rev. Al Sharpton (Kenan Thompson).
- West performs "Black Skinhead" and "New Slaves."
- Cameos by Anderson Cooper, Carrie Brownstein, Jennifer Garner, Kim Gordon, Steve Jones, Aimee Mann, J. Mascis, Michael Penn, and Amy Poehler.
- Final episode for Bill Hader, Fred Armisen, and Jason Sudeikis.

## Season 39 (2013–2014)

**Airdate:** 9/28/13
**Episode:** 39.1
**Host:** Tina Fey
**Musical Guest:** Arcade Fire
**Musical and Guest Performances/Cameo(s)/Program Notes:**
- "Live from New York": Barack Obama (Jay Pharoah) on the Affordable Care Act.
- Arcade Fire performs "Reflektor" and "Afterlife."
- Cameo by Aaron Paul, who appears as his *Breaking Bad* character, Jesse Pinkman, in the cold open; in a commercial for "emeth," electronic meth cigarettes; and as Drunk Uncle's (Bobby Moynihan) Meth Nephew on *Weekend Update*.
- Cecily Strong's debut as *Weekend Update* coanchor with Seth Meyers.
- In her monologue, Tina Fey declares, "It's a rebuilding year!" and leads the six new featured players (Beck Bennett, John Milhiser, Kyle Mooney, Mike O'Brien, Noël Wells, and Brooks Wheelan) in an "embarrassing dance number."

**Airdate:** 10/5/13
**Episode:** 39.2
**Host:** Miley Cyrus
**Musical Guest:** Miley Cyrus
**Musical and Guest Performances/Cameo(s)/Program Notes:**
- "Live from New York": Backstage at the Video Music Awards, Cyrus meets an older version of herself (Vanessa Bayer).
- Cyrus performs "Wrecking Ball" and "We Can't Stop."
- Music Video: "We Did Stop."

**Airdate:** 10/12/13
**Episode:** 39.3
**Host:** Bruce Willis
**Musical Guest:** Katy Perry
**Musical and Guest Performances/Cameo(s)/Program Notes:**
- "Live from New York": "NASA Shutdown" with astronauts Kazanski (Taran Killam) and Dr. Janet Stone (Cecily Strong) floating in space.
- Perry performs "Roar" and "Walking on Air."
- Music Video: "Boy Dance Party."

Episode Guide 533

**Airdate:** 10/26/13
**Episode:** 39.4
**Host:** Edward Norton
**Musical Guest:** Janelle Monáe
**Musical and Guest Performances/Cameo(s)/ Program Notes:**
- "Live from New York": U.S. Secretary of Health and Human Services Kathleen Sebelius (Kate McKinnon), who oversaw the implementation of Obamacare.
- Monáe performs "Dance Apocalyptic" and "Electric Lady."
- Cameos by Alec Baldwin and Miley Cyrus.
- ★★★★ Four-Star Commercial: *The Midnight Coterie of Sinister Intruders*, a horror movie trailer parodying the films of director Wes Anderson.

**Airdate:** 11/2/13
**Episode:** 39.5
**Host:** Kerry Washington
**Musical Guest:** Eminem
**Musical and Guest Performances/Cameo(s)/ Program Notes:**
- "Live from New York": Reverend Al Sharpton in a sketch addressing the lack of Black cast members, featuring Washington as Michelle Obama and Oprah Winfrey.
- Eminem performs "Berzerk" and "Survival."
- Music Video: "My Girl."
- In Memoriam: Singer Lou Reed (1942–2013).

**Airdate:** 11/16/13
**Episode:** 39.6
**Host:** Lady Gaga
**Musical Guest:** Lady Gaga
**Musical and Guest Performances/Cameo(s)/ Program Notes:**
- "Live from New York": Disgraced Toronto Mayor Rob Ford (Bobby Moynihan).
- Lady Gaga performs "Do What You Want" (with R. Kelly) and "Gypsy."

**Airdate:** 11/23/13
**Episode:** 39.7
**Host:** Josh Hutcherson
**Musical Guest:** HAIM
**Musical and Guest Performances/Cameo(s)/ Program Notes:**
- "Live from New York": Piers Morgan (Taran Killam) discusses George Zimmerman, who was acquitted of the second-degree murder of teenager Trayvon Martin and recently charged with felony aggravated assault.
- HAIM performs "The Wire" and "Don't Save Me."

**Airdate:** 12/7/13
**Episode:** 39.8
**Host:** Paul Rudd
**Musical Guest:** One Direction
**Musical and Guest Performances/Cameo(s)/ Program Notes:**
- "Live from New York": Lawrence Welk (Fred Armisen) and Dooneese (Kristen Wiig), who plays one of the von Trapp children in *The Sound of Music Live*.
- One Direction performs "Story of My Life" and "Through the Dark."
- Cameos by Fred Armisen, Steve Carell, Will Ferrell, David Koechner, and Kristen Wiig.
- ★★★★ Four-Star Sketch: Paul Rudd as One Direction's #1 Fan.

**Airdate:** 12/14/13
**Episode:** 39.9
**Host:** John Goodman
**Musical Guest:** Kings of Leon
**Musical and Guest Performances/Cameo(s)/ Program Notes:**
- "Live from New York": President Barack Obama (Jay Pharoah) and Thamsanqa Jantjie (Keenan Thompson), the fake sign interpreter at Nelson Mandela's funeral.
- Kings of Leon perform "Temple" and "Wait for Me."
- Cameos by Robert De Niro and Sylvester Stallone.

Appendix A

**Airdate:** 12/21/13
**Episode:** 39.10
**Host:** Jimmy Fallon
**Musical Guest:** Justin Timberlake
**Musical and Guest Performances/Cameo(s)/ Program Notes:**
- "Live from New York": Dressed as Christmas wrapping paper, Jimmy Fallon and Justin Timberlake urge shoppers to "Hurry on down to Wrappinville."
- Timberlake performs "Only When I Walk Away" and "Pair of Wings."
- ★★★★ Music Video: "(Do It on My) Twin Bed." Emmy-nominated song by Eli Brueggemann (music) and lyrics by Chris Kelly, Sarah Schneider, Aidy Bryant, and Kate McKinnon.
- Cameos by Barry Gibb, Madonna, Paul McCartney, Michael Bloomberg, and Chris Rock.

**Airdate:** 1/18/14
**Episode:** 39.11
**Host:** Drake
**Musical Guest:** Drake
**Musical and Guest Performances/Cameo(s)/ Program Notes:**
- "Live from New York": Justin Bieber (Kate McKinnon).
- Drake performs "Started from the Bottom" and "Trophies"; "Hold On We're Going Home" and "From Time" (with Jhené Aiko).
- Music Video: "Resolution Revolution."

**Airdate:** 1/25/14
**Episode:** 39.12
**Host:** Jonah Hill
**Musical Guest:** Bastille
**Musical and Guest Performances/Cameo(s)/ Program Notes:**
- "Live from New York": U.S. Men's Heterosexual Figure Skating Championships with ice skating champions and Olympic announcers Scott Hamilton (Taran Killam) and Tara Lipinski (Cecily Strong).
- Bastille performs "Pompeii" and "Oblivion."
- Cameos by Leonardo DiCaprio and Michael Cera.

**Airdate:** 2/1/14
**Episode:** 39.13
**Host:** Melissa McCarthy
**Musical Guest:** Imagine Dragons
**Musical and Guest Performances/Cameo(s)/ Program Notes:**
- "Live from New York": "Halftime Spectacular": football broadcasters Howie Long (Beck Bennett) and Michael Strahan (Jay Pharoah).
- Imagine Dragons perform "Radioactive" and "Demons."
- Cameos by Fred Armisen, Bill Hader, Amy Poehler, and Andy Samberg.
- Seth Meyers's final episode.
- In Memoriam: Singer Pete Seeger (1919–2014).

**Airdate:** 3/1/14
**Episode:** 39.14
**Host:** Jim Parsons
**Musical Guest:** Beck
**Musical and Guest Performances/Cameo(s)/ Program Notes:**
- "Live from New York": Talk show host Ellen DeGeneres (Kate McKinnon).
- Beck performs "Blue Moon" and "Wave" (with Father John Misty).
- Colin Jost's debut as *Weekend Update* anchor.

**Airdate:** 3/8/14
**Episode:** 39.15
**Host:** Lena Dunham
**Musical Guest:** The National
**Musical and Guest Performances/Cameo(s)/ Program Notes:**
- "Live from New York": Presidential address by Barack Obama (Jay Pharoah).
- The National performs "Graceless" and "I Need My Girl."
- Cameos by Fred Armisen, Jon Hamm, and Liam Neeson.

**Airdate:** 3/29/14
**Episode:** 39.16
**Host:** Louis C.K.
**Musical Guest:** Sam Smith
**Musical and Guest Performances/Cameo(s)/ Program Notes:**
- "Live from New York": HealthCare.gov strategy meeting with President Barack Obama (Jay Pharoah) and online media consultants Mike (Taran Killam) and Mara (Noël Wells), who convince a reluctant Obama to pose for photos to post on social media with Justin Bieber (Kate McKinnon), Kim Kardashian (Nasim Pedrad), Harry Styles (Brooks Whelan), and Pope Francis (Kyle Mooney).
- Sam Smith performs "Stay with Me" and "Lay Me Down."

**Airdate:** 4/5/14
**Episode:** 39.17
**Host:** Anna Kendrick
**Musical Guest:** Pharrell Williams
**Musical and Guest Performances/Cameo(s)/ Program Notes:**
- "Live from New York": Pennsylvania congressman Tim Murphy (Taran Killam) chairs a congressional hearing on General Motors' ignition-switch recall with new GM CEO Mary Barra (Kate McKinnon), who is clueless and dodges the committee's questions.
- Williams performs "Happy" and "Marilyn Monroe" (with Hans Zimmer).
- Music Video: "Dongs All Over the World."

**Airdate:** 4/12/14
**Episode:** 39.18
**Host:** Seth Rogan
**Musical Guest:** Ed Sheeran
**Musical and Guest Performances/Cameo(s)/ Program Notes:**
- "Live from New York": Jeb Bush (Beck Bennett), Paul Ryan (Taran Killam), Bobby Jindal (Nassim Pedrad), and Paul Rand (Brooks Whelan) at Coachella Valley Music and Arts Festival.
- Sheeran performs "Sing" and "Don't."
- Cameos by James Franco, Taylor Swift, and Zooey Deschanel.
- *Weekend Update*: In her on-camera debut, *SNL* writer Leslie Jones delivers a commentary on "how we view Black beauty has changed."

**Airdate:** 5/3/14
**Episode:** 39.19
**Host:** Andrew Garfield
**Musical Guest:** Coldplay
**Musical and Guest Performances/Cameo(s)/ Program Notes:**
- "Live from New York": Los Angeles Clippers owner Donald Sterling (Bobby Moynihan) responds to his recorded racist remarks with support from Dennis Rodman (Jay Pharoah), outgoing Los Angeles NAACP president Leon Jenkins (Kenan Thompson), and his mistress Kayla (Sasheer Zamata).
- Coldplay performs "Magic" and "A Sky Full of Stars."
- Cameos by Emma Stone, Mary Lynn Rajskub, and Kiefer Sutherland.

**Airdate:** 5/10/14
**Episode:** 39.20
**Host:** Charlize Theron
**Musical Guest:** The Black Keys
**Musical and Guest Performances/Cameo(s)/ Program Notes:**
- "Live from New York": "A Mother's Day Message" from Michelle Obama (Sasheer Zamata) and Hillary Clinton (Vanessa Bayer).
- The Black Keys perform "Fever" and "Bullet in the Brain."
- Cameo by Barbara Walters on *Weekend Update*.

**Airdate:** 5/17/14
**Episode:** 39.21
**Host:** Andy Samberg
**Musical Guest:** St. Vincent

Appendix A

**Musical and Guest Performances/Cameo(s)/ Program Notes:**
- "Live from New York": "And Now a Message from Solange and Jay-Z": Jay-Z (Jay Pharoah) and his sister-in-law, Solange Knowles (Sasheer Zamata), assure the public they are friends despite the security-camera footage leaked to the press that shows Solange attacking Jay-Z. A guard (Kenan Thompson) stands between them, and Beyoncé (Maya Rudolph) appears to explain what happened.
- St. Vincent performs "Digital Witness" and "Birth in Reverse."
- Cameos by 2Chainz, Fred Armisen, Bill Hader, Seth Meyers, Paul Rudd, Maya Rudolph, Martin Short, and Kristen Wiig.
- Cecily Strong's final episode as *Weekend Update* anchor.
- Filmed cameos by Lil Jon, Tatiana Maslany, and Pharrell Williams.
- *SNL* Digital Shorts: "When Will the Bass Drop?" and "Hugs."

## Season 40 (2014–2015)

**Airdate:** 9/27/14
**Episode:** 40.1
**Host:** Chris Pratt
**Musical Guest:** Ariana Grande
**Musical and Guest Performances/Cameo(s)/ Program Notes:**
- "Live from New York": CNN's *State of the Union* on "NFL in Crisis," hosted by Candy Crowley (Aidy Bryant) with NFL commissioner Roger Goodell (Chris Pratt) and veterans Shannon Sharpe (Jay Pharoah) and Ray Lewis (Kenan Thompson).
- Grande performs "Break Free" and "Love Me Harder" (with The Weeknd).
- Cameo by Anna Faris.
- In Memoriam: Veteran *SNL* announcer Don Pardo (1918–2014).

**Airdate:** 10/4/14
**Episode:** 40.2
**Host:** Sarah Silverman
**Musical Guest:** Maroon 5
**Musical and Guest Performances/Cameo(s)/ Program Notes:**
- "Live from New York": Barack Obama (Jay Pharoah), who is interviewed by *60 Minutes* cohost Steve Kroft (Beck Bennett).
- Maroon 5 performs "Animals" and "Maps."
- In Memoriam: Joan Rivers (1933–2014).
- Sarah Silverman plays Rivers, who arrives in Heaven, where she roasts an eclectic list of residents that includes Freddie Mercury (Maroon 5 front man Adam Levine), Lucille Ball (Kate McKinnon), Richard Pryor (Jay Pharoah), Benjamin Franklin (Bobby Moynihan), Steve Jobs (Kyle Mooney), Ava Gardner (Cecily Strong), and Eartha Kitt (Sasheer Zamata).

**Airdate:** 10/11/14
**Episode:** 40.3
**Host:** Bill Hader
**Musical Guest:** Hozier
**Musical and Guest Performances/Cameo(s)/ Program Notes:**
- "Live from New York": North Korea leader Kim Jong-un (Bobby Moynihan).
- Hozier performs "Take Me to Church" and "Angel of Small Death and the Codeine Scene."
- Cameos by Harvey Fierstein and Kristen Wiig.
- In Memoriam: Former *SNL* cast member Jan Hooks (1957–2014; seasons 12–16), who is seen in a 1988

sketch, "Love Is a Dream" (14.9), with the late Phil Hartman.

**Airdate:** 10/25/14
**Episode:** 40.4
**Host:** Jim Carrey
**Musical Guest:** Iggy Azalea
**Musical and Guest Performances/Cameo(s)/ Program Notes:**
- "Live from New York": "Ebola Press Conference" with Ron Klain (Taran Killam), Barack Obama (Jay Pharoah), and Al Sharpton (Kenan Thompson).
- Azelea performs "Fancy" and "Black Widow" (with Rita Ora); "Beg for It" (with MØ).
- Cameo by Carrey's *Dumb and Dumber* costar Jeff Daniels.
- Writer Leslie Jones's first episode as a featured player.

**Airdate:** 11/1/14
**Episode:** 40.5
**Host:** Chris Rock
**Musical Guest:** Prince
**Musical and Guest Performances/Cameo(s)/ Program Notes:**
- "Live from New York": *The Kelly File* with Megyn Kelly (Cecily Strong), Kaci Hickox (Kate McKinnon), and Chris Christie (Bobby Moynihan).
- Prince and 3RDEYEGIRL perform a medley of songs, including "Clouds" (with Lianne La Havas), "Plectrumelectrum," "Marz," and "Anotherlove."

**Airdate:** 11/15/14
**Episode:** 40.6
**Host:** Woody Harrelson
**Musical Guest:** Kendrick Lamar
**Musical and Guest Performances/Cameo(s)/ Program Notes:**
- "Live from New York": "Drinks at the White House" with Taran Killam (Mitch McConnell), Barack Obama (Jay Pharoah), and Michelle Obama (Sasheer Zamata).
- Lamar performs "I" and "Pay for It" (with Chantal Kreviazuk and Jay Rock).
- Cameo by Uzo Aduba (as Crazy Eyes, her character from *Orange Is the New Black*).
- Cameos by Harrelson's *Hunger Games* costars Liam Hemsworth, Josh Hutcherson, and Jennifer Lawrence.

**Airdate:** 11/22/14
**Episode:** 40.7
**Host:** Cameron Diaz
**Musical Guest:** Bruno Mars and Mark Ronson
**Musical and Guest Performances/Cameo(s)/ Program Notes:**
- "Live from New York": "Schoolhouse Rock!" parody in which a kid (Kyle Mooney) learns from President Barack Obama (Jay Pharoah) about the difference between a Bill (Kenan Thompson) and an Executive Order (Bobby Moynihan).
- Mars and Ronson perform "Uptown Funk" and "Feel Right" (with Mystikal).
- Music Video: "Back Home Ballers."
- In Memoriam: Director Mike Nichols (1931–2014).

**Airdate:** 12/6/14
**Episode:** 40.8
**Host:** James Franco
**Musical Guest:** Nicki Minaj
**Musical and Guest Performances/Cameo(s)/ Program Notes:**
- "Live from New York": *Politics Nation* with Reverend Al Sharpton (Kenan Thompson), who speaks about police brutality.
- Minaj performs "Bed of Lies" (with Skylar Grey) and a medley of "Only" and "All Things Go."
- Cameo by Seth Rogen in the monologue and a sketch, "Sunseeker Yachts."
- Film short: A Mike O'Brien Picture: "Grow-a-Guy."

**Airdate:** 12/13/14
**Episode:** 40.9
**Host:** Martin Freeman
**Musical Guest:** Charli XCX
**Musical and Guest Performances/Cameo(s)/ Program Notes:**
- "Live from New York": Charlie Rose (Taran Killam) on the Democratic report on the CIA's torture program.
- Charli XCX performs "Boom Clap" and "Break the Rules."
- Music Video: "Sump'n Claus."
- ★★★★ Sketch: *The Office* parody: *The Office: Middle Earth* with Freeman as Bilbo Baggins.

**Airdate:** 12/20/14
**Episode:** 40.10
**Host:** Amy Adams
**Musical Guest:** One Direction
**Musical and Guest Performances/Cameo(s)/ Program Notes:**
- "Live from New York": Singer Sam Smith's (Taran Killam) holiday special is interrupted by Dr. Evil (Mike Myers).
- One Direction performs "Night Changes" and "Ready to Run."
- Music Video: "Office Christmas Party."
- Cameos by Mike Myers, Kristen Wiig, and Fred Armisen.

**Airdate:** 1/17/15
**Episode:** 40.11
**Host:** Kevin Hart
**Musical Guest:** Sia
**Musical and Guest Performances/Cameo(s)/ Program Notes:**
- "Live from New York": The ghost of Martin Luther King Jr. (Kenan Thompson) appears to help a teenager (Pete Davidson) write his paper about King's legacy.
- Sia performs "Elastic Heart" and "Chandelier."

**Airdate:** 1/24/15
**Episode:** 40.12
**Host:** Blake Shelton
**Musical Guest:** Blake Shelton
**Musical and Guest Performances/Cameo(s)/ Program Notes:**
- "Live from New York": *Inside the NFL* hosted by Greg Gumbel (Kenan Thompson).
- Shelton performs "Neon Light" and "Boys 'round Here."
- "Wishin' Boot."

**Airdate:** 1/31/2015
**Episode:** 40.13
**Host:** J. K. Simmons
**Musical Guest:** D'Angelo
**Musical and Guest Performances/Cameo(s)/ Program Notes:**
- "Live from New York": "Super Bowl Shut Down" with Richard Sherman (Jay Pharoah) and Marshawn Lynch (Kenan Thompson).
- D'Angelo performs "Really Love" and "The Charade" (with Pino Palladino).
- Music Video: "Teacher Snow Day."
- Cameo by Fred Armisen.
- Film short: A Mike O'Brien Picture: "The Jay-Z Story" with a cameo by Jason Sudeikis as Kanye West.

**Airdate:** 2/28/15
**Episode:** 40.14
**Host:** Dakota Johnson
**Musical Guest:** Alabama Shakes
**Musical and Guest Performances/Cameo(s)/ Program Notes:**
- "Live from New York": "Giuliani Birdman" with Rudy Giuliani (Taran Killam), Carol Giuliani (Dakota Johnson), Gretchen Carlson (Vanessa Bayer), and Birdman (Beck Bennett).
- Alabama Shakes perform "Don't Wanna Fight" and "Gimme All Your Love."
- Cameos by Dakota Johnson's parents, Melanie Griffith and Don Johnson.
- Music Video: "Say What You Wanna Say."
- In Memoriam: Leonard Nimoy (1931–2015), who is seen in a photo as *Star Trek*'s Dr. Spock giving the Vulcan salute with the photo caption "Live Long and Prosper."

**Airdate:** 3/7/15
**Episode:** 40.15
**Host:** Chris Hemsworth
**Musical Guest:** Zac Brown Band
**Musical and Guest Performances/Cameo(s)/ Program Notes:**
- "Live from New York": "A Message from Hillary Clinton": The secretary of state (Kate McKinnon) discusses her use of nongovernment emails.
- Zac Brown Band performs "Homegrown" and "Heavy Is the Head" (with Chris Cornell).
- Cameos by Liam Hemsworth and Luke Hemsworth.

**Airdate:** 3/28/15
**Episode:** 40.16
**Host:** Dwayne Johnson
**Musical Guest:** George Ezra
**Musical and Guest Performances/Cameo(s)/ Program Notes:**
- "Live from New York": Dwayne Johnson as "The Rock Obama."
- Ezra performs "Budapest" and "Blame It on Me."

**Airdate:** 4/4/15
**Episode:** 40.17
**Host:** Michael Keaton
**Musical Guest:** Carly Rae Jepsen
**Musical and Guest Performances/Cameo(s)/ Program Notes:**
- "Live from New York": "Road to the Final Four" with Ernie Johnson Jr. (Beck Bennett), Kenny Smith (Jay Pharoah), and Charles Barkley (Kenan Thompson).
- Jepsen performs "I Really Like You" and "All That."
- Cameo by Norman Reedus as his *Walking Dead* character, Daryl Dixon.
- Film short: A Mike O'Brien Picture: "Prom Queen."

**Airdate:** 4/11/15
**Episode:** 40.18
**Host:** Taraji P. Henson
**Musical Guest:** Mumford & Sons
**Musical and Guest Performances/Cameo(s)/ Program Notes:**
- "Live from New York": Election video with Bill Clinton (Darrell Hammond) and Hillary Clinton (Kate McKinnon).
- Mumford & Sons perform "The Wolf" and "Believe."
- Cameos by Nikolaj Coster-Waldau, Billy Crystal, and Jim Henson's Muppets.

**Airdate:** 5/2/15
**Episode:** 40.19
**Host:** Scarlett Johansson
**Musical Guest:** Wiz Khalifa
**Musical and Guest Performances/Cameo(s)/ Program Notes:**
- "Live from New York": Floyd Mayweather (Jay Pharoah)–Manny Pacquiao (Aidy Bryant) fight.
- Wiz Khalifa performs "See You Again" with Charlie Puth and "We Dem Boyz."

**Airdate:** 5/9/15
**Episode:** 40.20
**Host:** Reese Witherspoon
**Musical Guest:** Florence + the Machine
**Musical and Guest Performances/Cameo(s)/ Program Notes:**
- "Live from New York": "The Southern Republican Leadership Conference!" with Mike Huckabee (Beck Bennett), Carly Fiorina (Kate McKinnon), Ben Carson (Kenan Thompson), Marco Rubio (Taran Killam), Rand Paul (Kyle Mooney), and Ted Cruz (Bobby Moynihan).
- Florence + the Machine perform "Ship to Wreck" and "What Kind of Man."
- To commemorate Mother's Day, Reese Witherspoon and the cast are joined onstage during the cold open with their mothers.

**Airdate:** 5/16/15
**Episode:** 40.21

**Host:** Louis C.K.
**Musical Guest:** Rihanna
**Musical and Guest Performances/Cameo(s)/ Program Notes:**
- "Live from New York": A musical tribute to "Summertime" is interrupted by presidential candidate Hillary Clinton (Kate McKinnon) and former President Bill Clinton (Darrell Hammond).
- Rihanna performs "Bitch Better Have My Money" and "American Oxygen."

## Season 41 (2015–2016)

**Airdate:** 10/3/15
**Episode:** 41.1
**Host:** Miley Cyrus
**Musical Guest:** Miley Cyrus
**Musical and Guest Performances/Cameo(s)/ Program Notes:**
- "Live from New York": A Message from Donald and Melania Trump (Taran Killam and Cecily Strong).
- Cyrus performs "Karen Don't Be Sad" and "Twinkle Song."
- Cameo by Hillary Clinton as Val, a bartender in "Hillary Clinton Bar Talk," with Kate McKinnon as Hillary Clinton and Darrell Hammond as Bill Clinton.
- Debut of new featured player Jon Rudnitsky.

**Airdate:** 10/10/15
**Episode:** 41.2
**Host:** Amy Schumer
**Musical Guest:** The Weeknd
**Musical and Guest Performances/Cameo(s)/ Program Notes:**
- "Live from New York": *Fox and Friends* with Elisabeth Hasselbeck (Vanessa Bayer), Steve Doocy (Taran Killam), and Brian Kilmeade (Bobby Moynihan).
- The Weeknd performs "The Hills" with Nicki Minaj and "Can't Feel My Face."

**Airdate:** 10/17/15
**Episode:** 41.3
**Host:** Tracy Morgan
**Musical Guest:** Demi Lovato
**Musical and Guest Performances/Cameo(s)/ Program Notes:**
- "Live from New York": "Presidential Democratic Debate" with Hillary Clinton (Kate McKinnon) and Bernie Sanders (Larry David, in a cameo).
- Lovato performs "Cool for the Summer" and "Confident" and, for her second set, "Stone Cold."
- Cameos by Morgan's *30 Rock* castmates Alec Baldwin, Tina Fey, Jane Krakowski, and Jack McBrayer.

**Airdate:** 11/7/15
**Episode:** 41.4
**Host:** Donald Trump
**Musical Guest:** Sia
**Musical and Guest Performances/Cameo(s)/ Program Notes:**
- "Live from New York": "Democratic Candidates Forum" feature Senator Bernie Sanders (Larry David), Hillary Clinton (Kate McKinnon), and Rachel Maddow (Cecily Strong).
- Sia performs "Alive" and "Bird Set Free."
- During his monologue, future U.S. president Donald Trump is joined by Trump impressionists Taran Killam and Darrell Hammond.
- A sketch set in the White House in 2018 includes a cameo by Ivanka Trump, Cecily Strong as Melania Trump, and Sasheer Zamata as Omarosa Manigault.
- Music Videos: "Bad Girls" and "Hotline Bling."
- Cameo by Martin Short as Ed Grimley in the music video "Hotline Bling."

**Airdate:** 11/14/15
**Episode:** 41.5
**Host:** Elizabeth Banks
**Musical Guest:** Disclosure
**Musical and Guest Performances/Cameo(s)/ Program Notes:**
- "Live from New York": The show opens with Cecily Strong, speaking in English and French, paying tribute to the 130 people who lost their lives in the terrorist attacks in Paris on Friday, November 13, 2015. Throughout the show, the colors of the French flag (blue, white, and red) appear on the *SNL* logo and in the lighting during the musical performances.
- Disclosure performs "Magnets" with Lorde and "Omen" with Sam Smith.
- Film short: A Mike O'Brien Picture: "Uber for Jen."
- Music Video: "First Got Horny 2 U."

**Airdate:** 11/21/15
**Episode:** 41.6
**Host:** Matthew McConaughey
**Musical Guest:** Adele
**Musical and Guest Performances/Cameo(s)/ Program Notes:**
- "Live from New York": *Fox and Friends* with Elisabeth Hasselbeck (Vanessa Bayer), Steve Doocy (Taran Killam), and Brian Kilmeade (Bobby Moynihan).
- Adele performs "Hello" and "When We Were Young."
- In "A Thanksgiving Miracle," a little girl stops bickering family members by turning on a recording of Adele's hit song "Hello."
- *Star Wars* auditions parody includes cameos by J. J. Abrams, John Boyega, Michael Bublé, Jon Hamm, Daisy Ridley, and Emma Stone.

**Airdate:** 12/5/15
**Episode:** 41.7
**Host:** Ryan Gosling
**Musical Guest:** Leon Bridges
**Musical and Guest Performances/Cameo(s)/ Program Notes:**
- "Live from New York": A Christmas message from Donald (Taran Killam) and Melania (Cecily Strong) Trump.
- Leon Bridges performs "Smooth Sailin'" and "River."
- Cameo by Mike Myers.
- ★ ★ ★ ★ Four-Star Sketch debut: "Close Encounter" with UFO abductees Colleen Rafferty (Kate McKinnon), Sharon (Cecily Strong), and Todd (Ryan Gosling).
- In Memoriam: Jenna Krempel (1955–2015), *SNL* Wardrobe Department.

**Airdate:** 12/12/15
**Episode:** 41.8
**Host:** Chris Hemsworth
**Musical Guest:** Chance the Rapper
**Musical and Guest Performances/Cameo(s)/ Program Notes:**
- "Live from New York": Presidential address by George W. Bush (Will Ferrell).
- Chance the Rapper performs "Somewhere in Paradise" with Jeremih and "Sunday Candy" with Jamila Woods.

**Airdate:** 12/19/15
**Episode:** 41.9
**Hosts:** Tina Fey and Amy Poehler
**Musical Guest:** Bruce Springsteen and the E Street Band
**Musical and Guest Performances/Cameo(s)/ Program Notes:**
- "Live from New York": "CNN Republican Debate" hosted by Wolf Blitzer (Jon Rudnitsky), with Donald Trump (Darrell Hammond), Jeb Bush (Beck Bennett), Marco Rubio (Pete Davidson), John Kasich (Colin Jost), Ted Cruz (Taran Killam), Rand Paul (Kyle Mooney), Chris Christie (Bobby Moynihan), Ben Carson (Jay Pharoah), and Carly Fiorina (Cecily Strong).
- Springsteen and the E Street Band perform "Meet Me in the City"; "The Ties That Bind"; and, with the *SNL*

cast, hosts, and guests, "Santa Claus Is Comin' to Town."
- In-studio cameos by Paul McCartney and Maya Rudolph.
- Filmed cameos by Gayle King and Amy Schumer.

**Airdate:** 1/16/16
**Episode:** 41.10
**Host:** Adam Driver
**Musical Guest:** Chris Stapleton
**Musical and Guest Performances/Cameo(s)/ Program Notes:**
- "Live from New York": "FOX Business Republican Debate" hosted by Maria Bartiromo (Cecily Strong) and Neil Cavuto (Kyle Mooney), with Donald Trump (Darrell Hammond), Jeb Bush (Beck Bennett), Marco Rubio (Pete Davidson), Ted Cruz (Taran Killam), Lindsey Graham (Kate McKinnon), Chris Christie (Bobby Moynihan), and Ben Carson (Jay Pharoah).
- Stapleton performs "Parachute" and "Nobody to Blame."
- In Memoriam: David Bowie (1947–2016), with Fred Armisen, who introduces a clip of Bowie singing "The Man Who Sold the World" from 1979 (5.7).
- Filmed cameo by Liev Schreiber.
- Live airing on the East Coast delayed by forty-five minutes due to the Green Bay Packers vs. Arizona Cardinals NFC Division Playoff game running into overtime.

**Airdate:** 1/23/16
**Episode:** 41.11
**Host:** Ronda Rousey
**Musical Guest:** Selena Gomez
**Musical and Guest Performances/Cameo(s)/ Program Notes:**
- "Live from New York": Trump rally with cameos by Tina Fey as Sarah Palin and Darrell Hammond as Donald Trump.
- Gomez performs a medley of "Good for You" and "Same Old Love" and, for her second set, "Hands to Myself."
- Music Video: "At the Club."

**Airdate:** 2/6/16
**Episode:** 41.12
**Host:** Larry David
**Musical Guest:** The 1975
**Musical and Guest Performances/Cameo(s)/ Program Notes:**
- "Live from New York": "A Message from Ted Cruz" (Taran Killam) with Catherine Cruz (Kate McKinnon).
- The 1975 performs "The Sound" and "Love Me."
- Cameos by Bernie Sanders, who, with Larry David, appears in a sketch as immigrants on a steamship, and, on *Weekend Update*, Ben Stiller as Derek Zoolander and Owen Wilson as Hansel.

**Airdate:** 2/13/16
**Episode:** 41.13
**Host:** Melissa McCarthy
**Musical Guest:** Kanye West
**Musical and Guest Performances/Cameo(s)/ Program Notes:**
- "Live from New York": "Hillary for President" with Hillary Clinton (Kate McKinnon), Bill Clinton (Darrell Hammond), and Jeb Bush (Beck Bennett).
- West performs "Highlights" with El DeBarge, Kelly Price, Kirk Franklin, The-Dream, and Young Thug and "UltralightBeam" with Chance the Rapper, Kelly Price, Kirk Franklin, and The-Dream.
- Cameo by Buffalo Bills linebacker Von Miller, meteorologists Al Roker and Dylan Dreyer, and Natalie Morales.

**Airdate:** 3/5/16
**Episode:** 41.14
**Host:** Jonah Hill
**Musical Guest:** Future
**Musical and Guest Performances/Cameo(s)/ Program Notes:**

Episode Guide  543

- "Live from New York": "CNN Election Center" with Mitt Romney (Jason Sudeikis, in a cameo), Jake Tapper (Beck Bennett), Donald Trump (Darrell Hammond, in a cameo), Ted Cruz (Taran Killam), Hillary Clinton (Kate McKinnon), and Chris Christie (Bobby Moynihan).
- Future performs "Low Life" with The Weeknd and "March Madness."

**Airdate:** 3/12/16
**Episode:** 41.15
**Host:** Ariana Grande
**Musical Guest:** Ariana Grande
**Musical and Guest Performances/Cameo(s)/Program Notes:**
- "Live from New York": "CNN Election Center" with host Jake Tapper (Beck Bennett) and his guests Bernie Sanders (Larry David, in a cameo), Donald Trump (Darrell Hammond), and Ben Carson (Jay Pharoah).
- Grande performs "Dangerous Woman" and "Be Alright."
- Music video: "This Is Not a Feminist Song."

**Airdate:** 4/2/16
**Episode:** 41.16
**Host:** Peter Dinklage
**Musical Guest:** Gwen Stefani
**Musical and Guest Performances/Cameo(s)/Program Notes:**
- "Live from New York": "CNN's *At this Hour*" with Kate Bolduan (Kate McKinnon), pro-Trump CNN commentator Scottie Nell Hughes (Cecily Strong), and guest Donald Trump (Darrell Hammond).
- Stefani performs "Make Me Like You" and "Misery."

**Airdate:** 4/9/16
**Episode:** 41.17
**Host:** Russell Crowe
**Musical Guest:** Margo Price
**Musical and Guest Performances/Cameo(s)/Program Notes:**

- "Live from New York": "A Message from Hillary Clinton" (Kate McKinnon).
- Margo Price performs "Hurtin' (On the Bottle)" and "Since You Put Me Down."
- In Memoriam: Country singer Merle Haggard (1937–2016).
- Cameos by Al Sharpton, Jason Sudeikis, and Mike O'Brien.
- Film short: A Mike O'Brien Picture: "Oprah Winfrey: A Life of Love."

**Airdate:** 4/16/16
**Episode:** 41.18
**Host:** Julia Louis-Dreyfus
**Musical Guest:** Nick Jonas
**Musical and Guest Performances/Cameo(s)/Program Notes:**
- "Live from New York": "Democratic Presidential Debate" with Bernie Sanders (Larry David in a cameo), Hillary Clinton (Kate McKinnon), and *Seinfeld*'s Elaine Benes (Julia Louis-Dreyfus).
- Nick Jonas performs "Close" with Tove Lo and "Champagne Problems."
- Cameo by Louis-Dreyfus's *Veep* costar Tony Hale.

**Airdate:** 5/7/16
**Episode:** 41.19
**Host:** Brie Larson
**Musical Guest:** Alicia Keys
**Musical and Guest Performances/Cameo(s)/Program Notes:**
- "Live from New York": "Church Chat" with the Church Lady (Dana Carvey) and her guests Donald Trump (Darrell Hammond), Ivanka Trump (Vanessa Bayer), Melania Trump (Cecile Strong), and Ted Cruz (Taran Killam).
- Keys performs "In Common" and "Hallelujah."
- Cameos by Dana Carvey, Darrell Hammond, Amy Davidson (Pete Davidson's mom), Laura Campbell (Kate McKinnon's mom), and Heather Desaulniers (Brie Larson's mom).

**Airdate:** 5/14/16
**Episode:** 41.20
**Host:** Drake
**Musical Guest:** Drake
**Musical and Guest Performances/Cameo(s)/ Program Notes:**
- "Live from New York": Trump Tower with Donald Trump (Darrell Hammond), Chris Christie (Bobby Moynihan), Ben Carson (Jay Pharoah), and Ivanka Trump (Vanessa Bayer).
- Drake performs "One Dance" and "Hype."
- Cameos by Darrell Hammond and Chris Rock.

**Airdate:** 5/21/16
**Episode:** 41.21
**Host:** Fred Armisen
**Musical Guest:** Courtney Barnett
**Musical and Guest Performances/Cameo(s)/ Program Notes:**
- "Live from New York": Hillary Clinton (Kate McKinnon), Senator Bernie Sanders (Larry David), Bill Clinton (Darrell Hammond), and the cast.
- Courtney Barnett performs "Nobody Really Cares If You Don't Go to the Party" and "Pedestrian at Best."
- *SNL* Digital Short: "Finest Girl" with Andy Samberg.
- Cameos by Carrie Brownstein, Larry David, Darrell Hammond, Maya Rudolph, Andy Samberg, and Jason Sudeikis.
- Final show for Taran Killam, Jay Pharoah, and Jon Rudnitsky.

## Season 42 (2016–2017)

**Airdate:** 10/1/16
**Episode:** 42.1
**Host:** Margot Robbie
**Musical Guest:** The Weeknd
**Musical and Guest Performances/Cameo(s)/ Program Notes:**
- "Live from New York": The presidential debate with Donald Trump (Alec Baldwin) and Hillary Clinton (Kate McKinnon).
- The Weeknd performs "Starboy" and "False Alarm."
- First episode for new featured players Mikey Day, Alex Moffat, and Melissa Villaseñor.
- Cameos by Darrell Hammond (as Bill Clinton) and Larry David (as Bernie Sanders) in a game show parody "Family Feud: Political Edition."
- This episode marks Alec Baldwin's first of more than fifty appearances as GOP candidate/president Donald Trump.

**Airdate:** 10/8/16
**Episode:** 42.2
**Host:** Lin-Manuel Miranda
**Musical Guest:** Twenty One Pilots
**Musical and Guest Performances/Cameo(s)/ Program Notes:**
- "Live from New York": CNN vice-presidential debate with Mike Pence (Beck Bennett), Tim Kane (Mikey Day), Donald Trump (Alec Baldwin), Hillary Clinton (Kate McKinnon), and CNN's Brooke Baldwin (Cecily Strong) and Elaine Quijano (Melissa Villaseñor).
- Twenty One Pilots performs "Heathens" and "Ride."
- Music Video: "Crucible Cast Party."
- Cameos by Tina Fey and Jimmy Fallon on *Weekend Update*.

**Airdate:** 10/15/16
**Episode:** 42.3
**Host:** Emily Blunt
**Musical Guest:** Bruno Mars
**Musical and Guest Performances/Cameo(s)/ Program Notes:**
- "Live from New York": The presidential debate with Hillary Clinton (Kate

Episode Guide

McKinnon) and Donald Trump (Alec Baldwin).
• Mars performs "24K Magic" and "Chunky."

**Airdate:** 10/22/16
**Episode:** 42.4
**Host:** Tom Hanks
**Musical Guest:** Lady Gaga
**Musical and Guest Performances/Cameo(s)/ Program Notes:**
• "Live from New York": The presidential debate with Donald Trump (Alec Baldwin) and Hillary Clinton (Kate McKinnon).
• Lady Gaga performs "A-YO" (with Mark Ronson on guitar) and "Million Reasons."
• ★★★★ Four-Star Sketches: "Haunted Elevator": Tom Hanks's debut as David S. Pumpkins, and *Black Jeopardy!*

**Airdate:** 11/5/16
**Episode:** 42.5
**Host:** Benedict Cumberbatch
**Musical Guest:** Solange
**Musical and Guest Performances/Cameo(s)/ Program Notes:**
• "Live from New York": *Erin Burnett OutFront* with CNN's Erin Burnett (Cecily Strong), Hillary Clinton (Kate McKinnon), and Donald Trump (Alec Baldwin).
• Solange performs "Cranes in the Sky" and "Don't Touch My Hair" with Sampha.
• Cameos by Dana Carvey as the Church Lady, Bill Murray, and Chicago Cubs David Ross, Dexter Fowler, and Anthony Rizzo.
• In Memoriam: Former *SNL* stagehand John Homer.
• In Memoriam: When a repeat of the episode aired on December 31, an image of Carrie Fisher (1956–2016) was added.

**Airdate:** 11/12/16
**Episode:** 42.6
**Host:** Dave Chappelle
**Musical Guest:** A Tribe Called Quest
**Musical and Guest Performances/Cameo(s)/ Program Notes:**
• "Live from New York": Post-2016 election show with Hillary Clinton (Kate McKinnon) at the piano singing "Hallelujah" by Leonard Cohen, who died on November 7, 2016.
• A Tribe Called Quest performs "We the People" and "The Space Program" (with Busta Rhymes and Consequence).
• ★★★★ Four-Star Sketch: "Election Night" with a cameo by Chris Rock.

**Airdate:** 11/19/16
**Episode:** 42.7
**Host:** Kristen Wiig
**Musical Guest:** The xx
**Musical and Guest Performances/Cameo(s)/ Program Notes:**
• "Live from New York": Trump National Golf Club with Donald Trump (Alec Baldwin) and Mike Pence (Beck Bennett).
• The xx performs "On Hold" and "I Dare You."
• Cameos by Jason Sudeikis as Mitt Romney in the cold open and Steve Martin and Will Forte in Kristen Wiig's monologue.

**Airdate:** 12/3/16
**Episode:** 42.8
**Host:** Emma Stone
**Musical Guest:** Shawn Mendes
**Musical and Guest Performances/Cameo(s)/ Program Notes:**
• "Live from New York": President-elect Trump (Alec Baldwin) prefers to re-Tweet than listen to a security briefing.
• Mendes performs "Mercy" and "Treat You Better."
• Music Video: "The Christmas Candle."
• Cameo by Jennifer Aniston, who confronts Vanessa Bayer about her impersonation of her *Friends* character, Rachel Green, on *Weekend Update*.

Aniston also appears as herself in a sketch, "Paley Center Event," a round table featuring elderly veteran actress Debette Goldry (Kate McKinnon).
- ★ ★ ★ ★ TV Commercial: Fisher Price's "Wells for Boys," a toy line for sensitive boys.

**Airdate:** 12/10/16
**Episode:** 42.9
**Host:** John Cena
**Musical Guest:** Maren Morris
**Musical and Guest Performances/Cameo(s)/ Program Notes:**
- "Live from New York": *The Lead* with Jake Tapper (Beck Bennett) with his guests Kellyanne Conway (Kate McKinnon) and *Breaking Bad*'s Walter White (cameo by Bryan Cranston).
- Maren Morris performs "My Church" and "80s Mercedes."

**Airdate:** 12/17/16
**Episode:** 42.10
**Host:** Casey Affleck
**Musical Guest:** Chance the Rapper
**Musical and Guest Performances/Cameo(s)/ Program Notes:**
- "Live from New York": Trump Christmas with Donald Trump (Alec Baldwin), Rex Tillerson (John Goodman in a cameo), and Vladimir Putin (Beck Bennett).
- Chance the Rapper performs "Finish Line/Drown" with Noname and "Same Drugs" with Francis Farewell Starlite.
- Music Video: "Jingle Barack" (with Darryl McDaniels in a cameo)
- Cameos by Fred Armisen and Darryl McDaniels, who appears in the music video "Jingle Barack."

**Airdate:** 1/14/17
**Episode:** 42.11
**Host:** Felicity Jones
**Musical Guest:** Sturgill Simpson
**Musical and Guest Performances/Cameo(s)/ Program Notes:**
- "Live from New York": Donald Trump's (Alec Baldwin) press conference.
- Simpson performs "Keep It Between the Lines" and "Call to Arms."
- In Memoriam: *SNL* cast member Tony Rosato (1954–2017; season 6 [4/11/1981]–Season 7).

**Airdate:** 1/21/17
**Episode:** 42.12
**Host:** Aziz Ansari
**Musical Guest:** Big Sean
**Musical and Guest Performances/Cameo(s)/ Program Notes:**
- "Live from New York": "A Paid Message from the Russian Federation" by Vladimir Putin (Beck Bennett) with Olya Povlatsky (Kate McKinnon).
- Big Sean performs "Bounce Back" and "Sunday Morning Jetpack."

**Airdate:** 2/4/17
**Episode:** 42.13
**Host:** Kristen Stewart
**Musical Guest:** Alessia Cara
**Musical and Guest Performances/Cameo(s)/ Program Notes:**
- "Live from New York": The Oval Office with Donald Trump (Alec Baldwin) and Steve Bannon (Mikey Day).
- Cara sings "Scars to Your Beautiful" and "River of Tears."
- ★ ★ ★ ★ Four-Star Sketch: Melissa McCarthy in a cameo appearance as White House press secretary Sean Spicer.

**Airdate:** 2/11/17
**Episode:** 42.14
**Host:** Alec Baldwin
**Musical Guest:** Ed Sheeran
**Musical and Guest Performances/Cameo(s)/ Program Notes:**
- "Live from New York": Cameo by Melissa McCarthy as White House press secretary Sean Spicer in another White House briefing.
- Sheeran performs "Shape of You" and "Castle on the Hill."
- Cameo by Tracey Morgan.

Episode Guide

**Airdate:** 3/4/17
**Episode:** 42.15
**Host:** Octavia Spencer
**Musical Guest:** Father John Misty
**Musical and Guest Performances/Cameo(s)/ Program Notes:**
- "Live from New York": "Jeff Sessions Gump," a parody of *Forrest Gump* with Jeff Sessions (Kate McKinnon).
- Father John Misty performs "Total Entertainment Forever" and "Pure Comedy."

**Airdate:** 3/11/17
**Episode:** 42.16
**Host:** Scarlett Johansson
**Musical Guest:** Lorde
**Musical and Guest Performances/Cameo(s)/ Program Notes:**
- "Live from New York": "Alien Attack" with Donald Trump (Alec Baldwin).
- Lorde performs "Green Light" and "Liability" with Jack Antonoff.

**Airdate:** 4/8/17
**Episode:** 42.17
**Host:** Louis C.K.
**Musical Guest:** The Chainsmokers
**Musical and Guest Performances/Cameo(s)/ Program Notes:**
- "Live from New York": "Trump's People"—Donald Trump (Alec Baldwin) talks to his supporters.
- The Chainsmokers perform "Paris" with Emily Warren and "Break Up Every Night."

**Airdate:** 4/15/17
**Episode:** 42.18
**Host:** Jimmy Fallon
**Musical Guest:** Harry Styles
**Musical and Guest Performances/Cameo(s)/ Program Notes:**
- "Live from New York": The Oval Office with Donald Trump (Alec Baldwin), Jared Kushner (Jimmy Fallon), Mike Pence (Beck Bennett), and Steve Bannon (Mikey Day).
- Styles performs "Sign of the Times" and "Ever since New York."

- Cameos by Rachel Dratch, Melissa McCarthy (as Sean Spicer), and record producer Nile Rodgers.

**Airdate:** 5/6/17
**Episode:** 42.19
**Host:** Chris Pine
**Musical Guest:** LCD Soundsystem
**Musical and Guest Performances/Cameo(s)/ Program Notes:**
- "Live from New York": MSNBC's *Morning Joe* with Joe Scarborough (Alex Moffat) and Mika Brzezinski (Kate McKinnon).
- LCD Soundsystem performs "Call the Police" and "American Dream."
- Music Video: "Song for Peace."

**Airdate:** 5/13/17
**Episode:** 42.20
**Host:** Melissa McCarthy
**Musical Guest:** HAIM
**Musical and Guest Performances/Cameo(s)/ Program Notes:**
- "Live from New York": NBC's Lester Holt (Michael Che) interviews Donald Trump (Alec Baldwin).
- HAIM performs "Want You Back" and "Little of Your Love."
- Melissa McCarthy won an Emmy as Outstanding Guest Actress in a Comedy Series for this episode.
- Cameos by Ryan Reynolds, Blake Lively, and Steve Martin.
- "Good Night": Martin inducts McCarthy into the Five-Timers Club.

**Airdate:** 5/20/17
**Episode:** 42.21
**Host:** Dwayne Johnson
**Musical Guest:** Katy Perry
**Musical and Guest Performances/Cameo(s)/ Program Notes:**
- "Live from New York": Donald Trump (Alec Baldwin) and family, Mike Pence (Beck Bennett), Sarah Huckabee Sanders (Aidy Bryant), and Kellyanne Conaway (Kate McKinnon) sing Leonard Cohen's "Hallelujah" to reflect on their current scandals.

- Perry sings "Swish Swish" and "Bon Appétit" with Migos.
- In Memoriam: Television/film producer Brad Grey (1957–2017).
- Alec Baldwin and Tom Hanks induct Dwayne Johnson into the Five-Timers club.
- Cameo by Scarlett Johansson.
- Final episode for Vanessa Bayer, Bobby Moynihan, and Sasheer Zamata.
- Music Video: "One Voice."

## Season 43 (2017–2018)

**Airdate:** 9/30/17
**Episode:** 43.1
**Host:** Ryan Gosling
**Musical Guest:** Jay-Z
**Musical and Guest Performances/Cameo(s)/ Program Notes:**
- "Live from New York": "The Chaos President" with Donald Trump (Alec Baldwin); Sara Huckabee Sanders (Aidy Bryant); Jeff Sessions (Kate McKinnon); Senator Chuck Schumer (Alex Moffat); and the mayor of San Juan, Puerto Rico, Carmen Yulín Cruz (Melissa Villaseñor).
- Jay-Z performs "Bam" with Damian Marley and "4:44."
- First episode for new featured players Heidi Gardner, Luke Null, and Chris Redd.
- The episode marks cast member Kenan Thompson's fifteenth season, surpassing Darrell Hammond's previous fourteen-season record.
- Cameo by Gosling's *La La Land* costar Emma Stone.
- In Memoriam: Hugh Hefner (1926–2017).

**Airdate:** 10/7/17
**Episode:** 43.2
**Host:** Gal Gadot
**Musical Guest:** Sam Smith
**Musical and Guest Performances/Cameo(s)/ Program Notes:**
- "Live from New York": As a tribute to the victims of the Las Vegas shooting on October 1, 2017, at the Route 91 Harvest Music Festival and in memory of Tom Petty on October 2, Jason Aldean sings "I Won't Back Down."
- Smith performs "Too Good at Goodbyes" and "Pray."
- In her monologue, Israel-born Gal Gadot states that this was the first *SNL* episode to air live in Israel. Gadot tells the audience in Hebrew (with English subtitles): "This might be a big mistake. In every sketch they have me eating hummus."
- In Memoriam: Aretha Franklin (1942–2018), whose photo was added when the show re-aired on August 18, 2018.

**Airdate:** 10/14/17
**Episode:** 43.3
**Host:** Kumail Nanjiani
**Musical Guest:** Pink
**Musical and Guest Performances/Cameo(s)/ Program Notes:**
- "Live from New York": Trucker rally with Donald Trump (Alec Baldwin), Mike Pence (Beck Bennett), and Karen Pence (Aidy Bryant).
- Pink performs "What about Us" and "Beautiful Trauma."

**Airdate:** 11/4/17
**Episode:** 43.4
**Host:** Larry David
**Musical Guest:** Miley Cyrus
**Musical and Guest Performances/Cameo(s)/ Program Notes:**
- "Live from New York": "Paul Manafort's Apartment" with Donald Trump (Alec Baldwin), Paul Manafort

(Alex Moffat), Jeff Sessions (Kate McKinnon), and Mike Pence (Beck Bennett).
- Cyrus performs "Bad Mood" and "I Would Die for You."
- Cameos by Houston Astros' George Springer, Alex Bregman, and José Altuve.
- Larry David's monologue was criticized for a joke about checking out and dating women if he was in a Nazi concentration camp.

**Airdate:** 11/11/17
**Episode:** 43.5
**Host:** Tiffany Haddish
**Musical Guest:** Taylor Swift
**Musical and Guest Performances/Cameo(s)/ Program Notes:**
- "Live from New York": Vice president's office with Mike Pence (Beck Bennett); Jeff Sessions (Kate McKinnon); and Roy Moore (Mikey Day), the former chief justice of the Supreme Court of Alabama who was removed twice for misconduct and lost his bid for the U.S. Senate due to allegations of sexual misconduct with underage girls.
- Swift performs "... Ready for It?" and "Call It What You Want."
- Cameos by Jason Sudeikis (as Joe Biden) and Larry David (as Bernie Sanders).
- Tiffany Haddish won an Emmy for Outstanding Guest Actress in a Comedy Series for this episode.
- In Memoriam: George Corrado (1942–2017), member of *SNL*'s sound department.

**Airdate:** 11/18/17
**Episode:** 43.6
**Host:** Chance the Rapper
**Musical Guest:** Eminem
**Musical and Guest Performances/Cameo(s)/ Program Notes:**
- "Live from New York": "The Mueller Files" with Donald Trump Jr. (Mikey Day), Julian Assange (Kate McKinnon), and Eric Trump (Alex Moffat).
- In a single musical segment, Eminem performs a medley of "Walk on Water," "Stan," and "Love the Way You Lie" with Skylar Grey.
- Cameos by Questlove and Common in "Rap History."
- Music Video: "Come Back Barack."
- Kenan Thompson, Chris Redd, Will Stephen, and Eli Brueggemann won an Emmy for Outstanding Original Music and Lyrics for "Come Back, Barack."

**Airdate:** 12/2/17
**Episode:** 43.7
**Host:** Saoirse Ronan
**Musical Guest:** U2
**Musical and Guest Performances/Cameo(s)/ Program Notes:**
- "Live from New York": "Spirits of Trump's Past" with Donald Trump (Alec Baldwin), Vladimir Putin (Beck Bennett), Michael Flynn (Mikey Day), Hillary Clinton (Kate McKinnon), Kellyanne Conway (Kate McKinnon), Billy Bush (Alex Moffat), and Melania Trump (Cecily Strong).
- U2 performs "American Girl" and "Get Out of Your Own Way."
- Music Video: "Welcome to Hell."
- Cameo by actor/director Greta Gerwig in "Office Race" and John McEnroe in "Bachelor Auction."

**Airdate:** 12/9/17
**Episode:** 43.8
**Host:** James Franco
**Musical Guest:** SZA
**Musical and Guest Performances/Cameo(s)/ Program Notes:**
- "Live from New York": Department store Santa Claus (Kenan Thompson) and his elf Amy (Kate McKinnon) field kids' politically charged questions.
- SZA performs "The Weekend" and "Love Galore."

Cameos by Jonah Hill, Steve Martin, and Seth Rogan in the monologue and Dave Franco in "Reunion."

**Airdate:** 12/16/17
**Episode:** 43.9
**Host:** Kevin Hart
**Musical Guest:** Foo Fighters
**Musical and Guest Performances/Cameo(s)/ Program Notes:**
- "Live from New York": A Christmas message from the White House with Donald Trump (Alec Baldwin) and family.
- Foo Fighters perform "The Sky Is a Neighborhood" and, in their second set, a medley of "Everlong," "Christmas (Baby Please Come Home)," and "Linus and Lucy."

**Airdate:** 1/13/18
**Episode:** 43.10
**Host:** Sam Rockwell
**Musical Guest:** Halsey
**Musical and Guest Performances/Cameo(s)/ Program Notes:**
- "Live from New York": MSNBC's *Morning Joe* with hosts Mika Brzezinski (Kate McKinnon) and Joe Scarborough (Alex Moffat) and guests Steve Bannon (Bill Murray) and Michael Wolff (Fred Armisen).
- Halsey sings "Bad at Love" and "Him & I" with G-Eazy.
- Cameo by Stanley Tucci in music video "Tucci Time."
- In "Science Room," the frustrated host Mr. Science (Sam Rockwell) drops an f-bomb when he yells at the dumb kids, Josh (Mikey Day) and Lonnie (Cecily Strong), on the show: "You can't be this f–king stupid!" The word was bleeped out in the West Coast broadcast due to the two-second delay.
- On *Weekend Update*, anchors Colin Jost and Michael Che defy NBC and quote President Trump, who remarked that African nations are "shithole countries."

**Airdate:** 1/20/18
**Episode:** 43.11
**Host:** Jessica Chastain
**Musical Guest:** Troye Sivan
**Musical and Guest Performances/Cameo(s)/ Program Notes:**
- "Live from New York": White House press secretary Sarah Huckabee Sanders (Aidy Bryant) and Surgeon General Ronny Jackson (Beck Bennett) give a health update about President Trump.
- Sivan performs "My My My" and "The Good Side."
- Cameo by Method Man in a parody of *The Fresh Prince of Bel Air* theme song with Chris Redd.

**Airdate:** 1/27/18
**Episode:** 43.12
**Host:** Will Ferrell
**Musical Guest:** Chris Stapleton
**Musical and Guest Performances/Cameo(s)/ Program Notes:**
- "Live from New York": George W. Bush (Will Ferrell) returns.
- Stapleton performs "Midnight Train to Memphis" and "Hard Livin'" with Sturgill Simpson.
- Cameo by Tracy Morgan.

**Airdate:** 2/3/18
**Episode:** 43.13
**Host:** Natalie Portman
**Musical Guest:** Dua Lipa
**Musical and Guest Performances/Cameo(s)/ Program Notes:**
- "Live from New York": *Fox and Friends* with hosts Brian Kilmeade (Beck Bennett), Ainsley Earhardt (Heidi Gardner), and Steve Doocy (Alex Moffat) and guests Donald Trump (Alec Baldwin), Hope Hicks (Cecily Strong), and Louis Farrakhan (Chris Redd).
- Dua Lipa performs "New Rules" and "Homesick."

- Cameos by Andy Samberg in the music video "Natalie Raps II" and Tina Fey and Rachel Dratch in "New England Patriots vs. Philadelphia Eagles."

**Airdate:** 3/3/18
**Episode:** 43.14
**Host:** Charles Barkley
**Musical Guest:** Migos
**Musical and Guest Performances/Cameo(s)/ Program Notes:**
- "Live from New York": *Anderson Cooper 360* hosted by Anderson Cooper (Alex Moffat), with President Donald Trump (Alec Baldwin), Mike Pence (Beck Bennett), Jeff Sessions (Kate McKinnon), and Senator Dianne Feinstein (Cecily Strong).
- Migos performs "Stir Fry" and Narcos."
- Cameos by Alex Rodriguez and Hilary Knight.

**Airdate:** 3/10/18
**Episode:** 43.15
**Host:** Sterling K. Brown
**Musical Guest:** James Bay
**Musical and Guest Performances/Cameo(s)/ Program Notes:**
- "Live from New York": Parody of *The Bachelor* with Rebecca Kufrin (Cecily Strong), Robert Mueller (Kate McKinnon), and host Chris Harrison (Alex Moffat).
- Bay performs "Pink Lemonade" and "Wild Love."
- Cameo by Vanessa Bayer on *Weekend Update* as weather girl Dawn Lazarus.

**Airdate:** 3/17/18
**Episode:** 43.16
**Host:** Bill Hader
**Musical Guest:** Arcade Fire
**Musical and Guest Performances/Cameo(s)/ Program Notes:**
- "Live from New York": *Anderson Cooper 360* with host Anderson Cooper (Alex Moffat) and guests Anthony Scaramucci (Bill Hader), Michael Wolff (Fred Armisen), Rex Tillerson (John Goodman), and Jeff Sessions (Kate McKinnon).
- Arcade Fire performs "Creature Comfort' and "Put Your Money on Me."
- Cameos by John Mulaney on *Weekend Update* as Stefon's lawyer Shy; director Spike Jonze during Arcade Fire's "Put Your Money on Me"; and Jon Hamm in the "Good Nights."

**Airdate:** 4/7/18
**Episode:** 43.17
**Host:** Chadwick Boseman
**Musical Guest:** Cardi B
**Musical and Guest Performances/Cameo(s)/ Program Notes:**
- "Live from New York":
- Cardi B performs a medley of "Bodak Yellow" and "Bartier Cardi" and, for her second set, "Be Careful."
- ★★★★ Four-Star Sketch: *Black Jeopardy!* featuring Boseman as his Black Panther character, T'Challa.

**Airdate:** 4/14/18
**Episode:** 43.18
**Host:** John Mulaney
**Musical Guest:** Jack White
**Musical and Guest Performances/Cameo(s)/ Program Notes:**
- "Live from New York": "Mueller and Cohen" with Robert Mueller (Robert De Niro), Michael Cohen (Ben Stiller), Mike Pence (Beck Bennett), and Jeff Sessions (Kate McKinnon).
- White performs "Over and Over and Over" and "Connected by Love" with the McCrary Sisters.
- Cameo by Nasim Pedrad as Ma Anand Sheela in "Wild Wild Country."
- Musical Sketch: "Diner Lobster."
- De Niro's first of seven cameos as FBI director Robert Mueller.
- Stiller's first of six cameos as President Trump's former lawyer Michael Cohen.

**Airdate:** 5/5/18
**Episode:** 43.19
**Host:** Donald Glover

**Musical Guest:** Childish Gambino
**Musical and Guest Performances/Cameo(s)/ Program Notes:**
- "Live from New York": "Michael Cohen Wiretap" with Donald Trump (Alec Baldwin) and cameos by Ben Stiller (as Michael Cohen), Jimmy Fallon (Jared Kushner), Martin Short (Harold Bonstein), Scarlett Johansson (Ivanka Trump), and Stormy Daniels (as herself).
- Childish Gambino (Glover's alter ego) performs "Saturday" and premieres his video, "This Is America."
- Cameos by ASAP Rocky (in "FRIEN-DOS"), Zoë Kravitz, and Daniel Kaluuya.

**Airdate:** 5/12/18
**Episode:** 43.20
**Host:** Amy Schumer
**Musical Guest:** Kasey Musgraves
**Musical and Guest Performances/Cameo(s)/ Program Notes:**
- "Live from New York": In honor of Mother's Day, the cast appears with their mothers.
- Musgraves performs "High Horse" and "Slow Burn."
- Cameo by Melissa McCarthy

**Airdate:** 5/19/18
**Episode:** 43.21
**Host:** Tina Fey
**Musical Guest:** Nicki Minaj
**Musical and Guest Performances/Cameo(s)/ Program Notes:**
- "Live from New York": "Holsten's Restaurant" with Donald Trump (Alec Baldwin), Michael Cohen (Ben Stiller), Robert Mueller (Robert De Niro), Donald Trump Jr. (Mikey Day), Rudy Giuliani (Kate McKinnon), Eric Trump (Alex Moffat), and Heidi Gardner as their waitress.
- Minaj performs "Chun-Li" and "Poke It Out" with Playboi Carti.
- Cameos by Anne Hathaway, Benedict Cumberbatch, Chris Rock, Donald Glover, Fred Armisen, Jerry Seinfeld, Robert De Niro, Ben Stiller, and Tracy Morgan.
- Filmed segment on the musical version of *Mean Girls* with book's writer Tina Fey, director/choreographer Casey Nicholaw, composer Jeff Richmond, producer Lorne Michaels, and Lin-Manuel Miranda.
- In Memoriam: Actress Margot Kidder (1948–2018)

## Season 44 (2018–2019)

**Airdate:** 9/29/18
**Episode:** 44.1
**Host:** Adam Driver
**Musical Guest:** Kanye West
**Musical and Guest Performances/Cameo(s)/ Program Notes:**
- "Live from New York": Supreme Court judicial hearing for justice nominee Brett Kavanaugh (Matt Damon).
- West performs "I Love It" (with Lil Pump and Adele Givens), "We Got Love" (with Teyana Taylor), and "Ghost Town" (with Kid Cudi, 070 Shake, and Ty Dolla Sign on guitar).
- Cameos by Matt Damon and Rachel Dratch.
- After the broadcast, West, wearing a "Make America Great Again" hat, delivered a pro-Trump rant that was recorded and posted on Instagram.
- Debut of featured player Ego Nwodim.

**Airdate:** 10/6/18
**Episode:** 44.2
**Host:** Awkwafina
**Musical Guest:** Travis Scott
**Musical and Guest Performances/Cameo(s)/ Program Notes:**

- "Live from New York": CNN's "Brett Kavanaugh Hearings—Post-Game" with hosts Dana Bash (Heidi Gardner), Don Lemon (Kenan Thompson), and Kate Bennett (Melissa Villaseñor), with Mitch McConnell (Beck Bennett), Rachel Mitchell (Aidy Bryant), Jeff Flakes (Pete Davidson), Joe Manchin (Mikey Day), Lindsey Graham (Kate McKinnon), Charles Schumer (Alex Moffat), John Kennedy (Kyle Mooney), and Susan Collins (Cecily Strong).
- Scott performs a medley of "Skeletons" and "Astrothunder" with John Mayer on guitar and Kevin Parker on bass and, for the second set, "Sicko Mondo."

**Airdate:** 10/13/18
**Episode:** 44.3
**Host:** Seth Meyers
**Musical Guest:** Paul Simon
**Musical and Guest Performances/Cameo(s)/ Program Notes:**
- "Live from New York": Kanye West's (Chris Redd) meeting with Donald Trump (Alec Baldwin) in the Oval Office.
- Simon and yMusic perform "Can't Run But" and "Bridge over Troubled Water."
- "Good Night": Simon, who turns seventy-seven today, is presented with a birthday cake.

**Airdate:** 11/3/18
**Episode:** 44.4
**Host:** Jonah Hill
**Musical Guest:** Maggie Rogers
**Musical and Guest Performances/Cameo(s)/ Program Notes:**
- "Live from New York": Fox News' *The Ingraham Angle* with host Laura Ingraham (Kate McKinnon), Judge Jeanine Pirro (Cecily Strong), and Sheriff David Clarke (Keenan Thompson).
- Rogers performs "Light On" and "Fallingwater."
- Hill is inducted into the Five-Timers Club by Drew Barrymore, Candice Bergen, and Tina Fey.

**Airdate:** 11/10/18
**Episode:** 44.5
**Host:** Liev Schreiber
**Musical Guest:** Lil Wayne
**Musical and Guest Performances/Cameo(s)/ Program Notes:**
- "Live from New York": Farewell to Attorney General Jeff Sessions (Kate McKinnon) with Robert Mueller (Robert De Niro), Mike Pence (Beck Bennett), Sarah Huckabee Sanders (Aidy Bryant), Donald Trump Jr. (Mikey Day), and Eric Trump (Alex Moffat).
- Lil Wayne performs "Can't Be Broken" with Halsey and "Uproar" with Swizz Beatz. He also appears with Future in the music video "Booty Kings."
- Music Video: "Unity Song" and "Booty Kings."

**Airdate:** 11/17/18
**Episode:** 44.6
**Host:** Steve Carell
**Musical Guest:** Ella Mai
**Musical and Guest Performances/Cameo(s)/ Program Notes:**
- "Live from New York": *The Ingraham Angle* with host Laura Ingraham (Kate McKinnon), Jeanine Pirro (Cecily Strong), U.S. secretary of housing and urban development Marcia Fudge (Leslie Jones), Tom Scibelli (Pete Davidson), and Mark Zuckerberg (Alex Moffat).
- Mai performs "Boo'd Up" and "Trip."
- Music Video: "RBG."
- Cameos by Steve Carell's family—former *SNL* cast member Nancy Walls, Annie Carell, and Johnny Carell—and his *Office* castmates Ellie Kemper, Ed Helms, and Jenna Fischer.

**Airdate:** 12/1/18
**Episode:** 44.7

# Appendix A

**Host:** Claire Foy
**Musical Guest:** Anderson .Paak
**Musical and Guest Performances/Cameo(s)/ Program Notes:**
- "Live from New York": "Trump in Argentina" with Donald Trump (Alec Baldwin); Michael Cohen (Ben Stiller); Mohammad bin Salman (Fred Armisen); Vladimir Putin (Beck Bennett); Rudy Giuliani (Kate McKinnon); and Melania Trump (Cecily Strong).
- Anderson .Paak performs "Tints" with Kendrick Lamar and "Who R U?"
- Cameos by Alec Baldwin, Ben Stiller, and Fred Armisen.
- In Memoriam: President George H. W. Bush (1924–2018).

**Airdate:** 12/8/18
**Episode:** 44.8
**Host:** Jason Momoa
**Musical Guest:** Mumford & Sons
**Musical and Guest Performances/Cameo(s)/ Program Notes:**
- "Live from New York": "Trump Brothers Bedtime" with Robert Mueller (Robert De Niro, in a cameo); Donald Trump Jr. (Mikey Day); and Eric Trump (Alex Moffat).
- Mumford & Sons perform "Guiding Light" and "Delta."

**Airdate:** 12/15/18
**Episode:** 44.9
**Host:** Matt Damon
**Musical Guest:** Mark Ronson and Miley Cyrus
**Musical and Guest Performances/Cameo(s)/ Program Notes:**
- "Live from New York": "It's a Wonderful Trump," a parody of *It's a Wonderful Life*, with Donald Trump (Alec Baldwin) and cameos by Robert De Niro (Robert Mueller) and Ben Stiller (Michael Cohen).
- Ronson and Cyrus perform "Nothing Breaks like a Heart" and "Happy Xmas (War Is Over)" with Sean Lennon.

**Airdate:** 1/19/19
**Episode:** 44.10
**Host:** Rachel Brosnahan
**Musical Guest:** Greta Van Fleet
**Musical and Guest Performances/Cameo(s)/ Program Notes:**
- "Live from New York": *Deal or No Deal: Government Shutdown Edition* hosted by Steve Harvey (Kenan Thompson) with Donald Trump (Alec Baldwin).
- Van Fleet performs "Black Smoke Rising" and "You're the One."
- Cameo by John Mulaney on *Weekend Update*.

**Airdate:** 1/26/19
**Episode:** 44.11
**Host:** James McAvoy
**Musical Guest:** Meek Mill
**Musical and Guest Performances/Cameo(s)/ Program Notes:**
- "Live from New York": *Tucker Carlson Tonight* hosted by Tucker Carlson (Alex Moffat), with Roger Stone (Steve Martin, in a cameo); Wilbur Ross (Kate McKinnon); and Jeanine Pirro (Cecily Strong).
- Meek Mill performs "Going Bad" and "Uptown Vibes" with Fabolous and, for his second set, "Championships."
- Music Video: "I Love My Dog."

**Airdate:** 2/9/19
**Episode:** 44.12
**Host:** Halsey
**Musical Guest:** Halsey
**Musical and Guest Performances/Cameo(s)/ Program Notes:**
- "Live from New York": *Meet the Press* hosted by Chuck Todd (Kyle Mooney), with guests Matt Whitaker (Aidy Bryant), Donna Brazile (Leslie Jones), Wilbur Ross (Kate McKinnon), Peggy Noonan (Cecily Strong), and Eugene Robinson (Kenan Thompson).
- Halsey performs "Without Me" and "Eastside."

Episode Guide

- Music Video: "Valentine's Day" with Halsey.

**Airdate:** 2/16/19
**Episode:** 44.13
**Host:** Don Cheadle
**Musical Guest:** Gary Clark Jr.
**Musical and Guest Performances/Cameo(s)/ Program Notes:**
- "Live from New York": Press conference with Donald Trump (Alec Baldwin).
- Clark Jr. performs "Pearl Cadillac" and "This Land."
- In Memoriam: *SNL* stage manager Joe Dicso (1929–2019).

**Airdate:** 3/2/19
**Episode:** 44.14
**Host:** John Mulaney
**Musical Guest:** Thomas Rhett
**Musical and Guest Performances/Cameo(s)/ Program Notes:**
- "Live from New York": "Michael Cohen Hearing" with cameos by Bill Hader (Jim Jordan) and Ben Stiller (Michael Cohen).
- Thomas Rhett performs "Look What God Gave Her" and "Don't Threaten Me with a Good Time."
- Musical Sketch: "Bodega Bathroom."
- In Memoriam: Margaret Karolyi, *SNL* costume and wardrobe department from 1978 to 2013.

**Airdate:** 3/9/19
**Episode:** 44.15
**Host:** Idris Elba
**Musical Guest:** Khalid
**Musical and Guest Performances/Cameo(s)/ Program Notes:**
- "Live from New York": The Gayle King (Leslie Jones) interview with R. Kelly (Kenan Thompson).
- Khalid performs "Talk" and "Better."
- Cameo by Gwyneth Paltrow on *Weekend Update*.

**Airdate:** 3/30/19
**Episode:** 44.16
**Host:** Sandra Oh
**Musical Guest:** Tame Impala
**Musical and Guest Performances/Cameo(s)/ Program Notes:**
- "Live from New York": "The Mueller Report" with Robert Mueller (Robert De Niro, in a cameo) and Donald Trump (Alec Baldwin).
- Tame Impala performs "Patience" and "Borderline."
- *SNL* writer Bowen Yang, who will join the cast next season as a featured player, appears in a sketch as North Korean leader Kim Jong-un.

**Airdate:** 4/6/19
**Episode:** 44.17
**Host:** Kit Harington
**Musical Guest:** Sara Bareilles
**Musical and Guest Performances/Cameo(s)/ Program Notes:**
- "Live from New York": "Biden Headquarters" with Joe Biden (Jason Sudeikis, in a cameo).
- Bareilles performs "Fire" and "Saint Honesty."
- Cameos by Harington's *Game of Thrones* costars Emilia Clarke and John Bradley and his spouse, Rose Leslie, and *Law & Order: Special Victims Unit* stars Mariska Hargitay and Ice-T.

**Airdate:** 4/13/19
**Episode:** 44.18
**Host:** Emma Stone
**Musical Guest:** BTS
**Musical and Guest Performances/Cameo(s)/ Program Notes:**
- "Live from New York": "Jail Cell": Julian Assange (Michael Keaton, in a cameo) is joined by lawyer Michael Avenatti (Pete Davidson), actress Lori Loughlin (Kate McKinnon), and other inmates.
- BTS perform "Boy with Luv" and "Mic Drop."

- In a filmed sketch, "Actress," Stone plays an actress with a walk-on role in a gay porn film that features adult performer Ty Mitchell.

**Airdate:** 5/4/19
**Episode:** 44.19
**Host:** Adam Sandler
**Musical Guest:** Shawn Mendes
**Musical and Guest Performances/Cameo(s)/ Program Notes:**
- "Live from New York": *Family Feud* parody hosted by Steve Harvey (Kenan Thompson): *Game of Thrones* vs. *The Avengers*.
- Mendes performs "If I Can't Have You" and "In My Blood."
- Sandler performs a moving musical tribute to his friend and former *SNL* castmate the late Chris Farley from his 2018 special, *Adam Sandler 100% Fresh*.
- Cameos by Allen Covert, Jimmy Fallon, Chris Rock, and Kristen Wiig.

**Airdate:** 5/11/19
**Episode:** 44.20
**Host:** Emma Thompson
**Musical Guest:** Jonas Brothers
**Musical and Guest Performances/Cameo(s)/ Program Notes:**
- "Live from New York": *Meet the Press* with host Chuck Todd (Kyle Mooney) and guests Mitch McConnell (Beck Bennett), Lindsey Graham (Kate McKinnon), and Susan Collins (Cecily Strong).
- Jonas Brothers sing "Sucker" and, for their second set, a medley of "Cool" and "Burnin' Up."
- In honor of Mother's Day, Pete Davidson's mom, Amy, appears with her son on *Weekend Update*.
- Cameos by Tina Fey, Amy Poehler, and Jon Hamm.

**Airdate:** 5/18/19
**Episode:** 44.21
**Host:** Paul Rudd
**Musical Guest:** DJ Khaled
**Musical and Guest Performances/Cameo(s)/ Program Notes:**
- "Live from New York": "Don't Stop Me Now" with Donald Trump (Alec Baldwin), Robert Mueller (Robert De Niro), and the Trump White House staff and family.
- DJ Khalid performs a medley of "Jealous" (with Lil Wayne and Big Sean) and "You Stay" (with Jeremih, Meek Mill, Lil Baby, and J Balvin). For his second set, he performs a medley consisting of "Just Us" (with SZA), "Weather and Storm" (with Meek Mill), and "Higher" (with John Legend), which was dedicated to the late Nipsey Hussle.
- Music Video: "Grace and Frankie Rap," with cameos by Jane Fonda, Lily Tomlin, and Jacob Anderson.

## Season 45 (2019–2020)

**Airdate:** 9/28/19
**Episode:** 45.1
**Host:** Woody Harrelson
**Musical Guest:** Billie Eilish
**Musical and Guest Performances/Cameo(s)/ Program Notes:**
- "Live from New York": "Impeachment" with Donald Trump (Alec Baldwin) and others, including a cameo by Liev Schreiber.
- Eilish, accompanied by Finneas O'Connell, performs "Bad Guy," which borrows an effect from the 1951 musical *Royal Wedding* in which Fred Astaire appears to be dancing on the walls and ceiling, and "I Love You."
- Cameos by Larry David (as Bernie Sanders) and Maya Rudolph (as Kamala Harris).

Episode Guide

- Debut of feature players Chloe Fineman and Bowen Yang.
- In Memoriam: Chadwick Boseman (1976–2020; added in rebroadcast on 8/29/2020).

**Airdate:** 10/5/19
**Episode:** 45.2
**Host:** Phoebe Waller-Bridge
**Musical Guest:** Taylor Swift
**Musical and Guest Performances/Cameo(s)/ Program Notes:**
- "Live from New York": "Impeachment Strategy" with Rudy Giuliani (Kate McKinnon); Mike Pence (Beck Bennett); and Mike Pompeo (Matthew Broderick, in a cameo).
- Swift performs "Lover" and "False God" with *SNL* bandleader Lenny Pickett on saxophone.

**Airdate:** 10/12/19
**Episode:** 45.3
**Host:** David Harbour
**Musical Guest:** Camila Cabello
**Musical and Guest Performances/Cameo(s)/ Program Notes:**
- "Live from New York": "Equality Town Hall," with cameos by Billy Porter, Lin-Manuel Miranda (Julián Castro), and Woody Harrelson (Joe Biden).
- Cabello performs "Cry for Me" and "Easy."

**Airdate:** 10/26/19
**Episode:** 45.4
**Host:** Chance the Rapper
**Musical Guest:** Chance the Rapper
**Musical and Guest Performances/Cameo(s)/ Program Notes:**
- "Live from New York": "Trump Rally" with Donald Trump (Alec Baldwin) and Turkish President Recep Tayyip Erdogan (Fred Armisen).
- Chance the Rapper performs "Zanies and Fools" and "Handsome" with Megan Thee Stallion.
- Cameo by Jason Momoa

**Airdate:** 11/2/19
**Episode:** 45.5
**Host:** Kristen Stewart
**Musical Guest:** Coldplay
**Musical and Guest Performances/Cameo(s)/ Program Notes:**
- "Live from New York": Elizabeth Warren (Kate McKinnon) rally.
- Coldplay performs "Orphans" and "Everyday Life."
- During the monologue, writer/future cast member Andrew Dismukes appears as an audience member.

**Airdate:** 11/16/19
**Episode:** 45.6
**Host:** Harry Styles
**Musical Guest:** Harry Styles
**Musical and Guest Performances/Cameo(s)/ Program Notes:**
- "Live from New York": "Days of Our Impeachment" with cameo by Jon Hamm (as Bill Taylor).
- Styles performs "Lights Up" and "Watermelon Sugar."
- In Memoriam: Longtime NBC executive Rick Ludwin (1948–2019).

**Airdate:** 11/23/19
**Episode:** 45.7
**Host:** Will Ferrell
**Musical Guest:** King Princess
**Musical and Guest Performances/Cameo(s)/ Program Notes:**
- "Live from New York": Press conference with Donald Trump (Alec Baldwin) and Gordon Sondland (Will Ferrell), U.S. ambassador to the European Union.
- King Princess performs "1950" and "Hit the Back."
- Music Video: "Party Song."
- Cameos by Fred Armisen, Larry David, Rachel Dratch, Tracy Morgan, Ryan Reynolds, Maya Rudolph, and Woody Harrelson.

**Airdate:** 12/7/19
**Episode:** 45.8

**Host:** Jennifer Lopez
**Musical Guest:** DaBaby
**Musical and Guest Performances/Cameo(s)/ Program Notes:**
- "Live from New York": NATO cafeteria, with cameos by James Corden (as UK prime minister Boris Johnson), Jimmy Fallon (as Canadian prime minister Justin Trudeau), and Paul Rudd (as French president Emmanuel Macron), who won't let Donald Trump (Alec Baldwin) sit at their table.
- DaBaby performs "BOP" and "Suge" with Jabbawockeez.
- Cameo by the Rockettes and Alex Rodriguez.

**Airdate:** 12/14/19
**Episode:** 45.9
**Host:** Scarlett Johansson
**Musical Guest:** Niall Horan
**Musical and Guest Performances/Cameo(s)/ Program Notes:**
- "Live from New York": Sam the Snowman (Aidy Bryant), narrator of the classic holiday special *Rudolph the Red-Nosed Reindeer*, introduces scenes from "American households," where family members on the left and right discuss politics and Trump's presidency over holiday dinner.
- Horan performs "Nice to Meet Ya" and "Put a Little Love on Me."
- Music Video: "I Saw Mommy Kissing Santa Claus."

**Airdate:** 12/21/19
**Episode:** 45.10
**Host:** Eddie Murphy
**Musical Guest:** Lizzo
**Musical and Guest Performances/Cameo(s)/ Program Notes:**
- "Live from New York": Democratic debate with Donald Trump (Alec Baldwin) and cameos by Fred Armisen (Michael Bloomberg), Jason Sudeikis (Joe Biden), Larry David (Bernie Sanders), Maya Rudolph (Kamala Harris), and Rachel Dratch (Amy Klobuchar).
- Lizzo performs "Truth Hurts" and "Good as Hell."
- Cameos by Dave Chappelle, Tracy Morgan, and Chris Rock, who appear during Murphy's monologue.
- Host and former *SNL* cast member Murphy resurrects some of his old characters: Mister Robinson of *Mr. Robinson's Neighborhood*; Buckwheat (as a contestant on *The Masked Singer*); Gumby, who appears on *Weekend Update*; and sleazy author Velvet Jones.
- Winner of Four Emmy Awards, including Eddie Murphy (Outstanding Guest Actor in a Comedy Series), Maya Rudolph (Outstanding Guest Actress in a Comedy Series), and director Don Roy King (Outstanding Directing for a Variety Series).

**Airdate:** 1/25/20
**Episode:** 45.11
**Host:** Adam Driver
**Musical Guest:** Halsey
**Musical and Guest Performances/Cameo(s)/ Program Notes:**
- "Live from New York": Lawyer Alan Dershowitz (Jon Lovitz, in a cameo) in Hell with Satan (Kate McKinnon), Jeffrey Epstein (Adam Driver), Mitch McConnell (Beck Bennett), Mr. Peanut (Mikey Day), Mark Zuckerberg (Alex Moffat), and others.
- Halsey performs "You Should Be Sad" and "Finally//Beautiful Stranger."
- In Memoriam: Actor/screenwriter/director Buck Henry (1930–2020), who hosted *SNL* ten times during the first five seasons (1975–1980).

**Airdate:** 2/1/20
**Episode:** 45.12
**Host:** J. J. Watt
**Musical Guest:** Luke Combs
**Musical and Guest Performances/Cameo(s)/ Program Notes:**

Episode Guide 559

- "Live from New York": "The Trial You Wish Had Happened"—reimagining of Trump's impeachment trial with Judge Mathis (Kenan Thompson); Mitch McConnell (Beck Bennett); Lindsey Graham (Kate McKinnon); John Bolton (Cecily Strong); Hunter Biden (Pete Davidson); Donald Trump (Alec Baldwin); Adam Schiff (Alex Moffat); and Vinny (Kyle Mooney), Joe Pesci's character in *My Cousin Vinny*.
- Luke Combs performs "Lovin' on You" and "Beer Never Broke My Heart."
- "Good Nights": Watt wears a #24 Los Angeles Lakers jersey in honor of Kobe Bryant, who tragically died in a helicopter crash on January 26, 2020.

**Airdate:** 2/8/20
**Episode:** 45.13
**Host:** RuPaul
**Musical Guest:** Justin Bieber
**Musical and Guest Performances/Cameo(s)/ Program Notes:**
- "Live from New York": Democratic debate between Joe Biden (Jason Sudeikis), Bernie Sanders (Larry David), Amy Klobuchar (Rachel Dratch), Tom Steyer (Pete Davidson), Pete Buttigieg (Colin Jost), Elizabeth Warren (Kate McKinnon), and Andrew Yang (Bowen Yang).
- Bieber performs "Yummy" and "Intentions" with Quavo.

**Airdate:** 2/29/20
**Episode:** 45.14
**Host:** John Mulaney
**Musical Guest:** David Byrne

**Musical and Guest Performances/Cameo(s)/ Program Notes:**
- "Live from New York": White House briefing on COVID-19 with Vice President Mike Pence (Beck Bennett), Joe Biden (John Mulaney), Pete Buttigieg (Colin Jost), Elizabeth Warren (Kate McKinnon), and Ben Carson (Kenan Thompson) and cameos by Fred Armisen (Mike Bloomberg), Larry David (Bernie Sanders), and Rachel Dratch (Amy Klobuchar).
- David Byrne and the company from the Broadway musical *American Utopia* perform "Once in a Lifetime" and "Toe Jam."
- Cameos by Justin Theroux and Jake Gyllenhaal.
- Musical Sketch: "Airport Sushi."

**Airdate:** 3/7/20
**Episode:** 45.15
**Host:** Daniel Craig
**Musical Guest:** The Weeknd
**Musical and Guest Performances/Cameo(s)/ Program Notes:**
- "Live from New York": *The Ingraham Angle* with host Laura Ingraham (Kate McKinnon) and her guests Chris Matthews (Darrell Hammond, in a cameo); Senator Elizabeth Warren (in a cameo); and Kate McKinnon's impersonation of Warren.
- The Weeknd performs "Blinding Lights" and "Scared to Live" with Oneohtrix Point Never.
- Music Videos: "On the Couch" and "Overnight Salad."
- Cameo by Rachel Dratch as Debbie Downer.

## Season 45: *Saturday Night Live at Home* (2020)

**Airdate:** 4/11/20
**Episode:** 45.16
**Host:** Tom Hanks
**Musical Guest:** Chris Martin

**Musical and Guest Performances/Cameo(s)/ Program Notes:**
- Due to the stay-at-home order in New York City during the COVID-19

pandemic, the episode consists of remotely produced content.
- Cast appears on Zoom at the start of the show, followed by an intro title sequence.
- Monologue by Tom Hanks, who was one of the first celebrities to go public when he contracted COVID-19. He also introduces musical guest Martin, who sings "Shelter from the Storm."
- Music Videos: Pete Davidson performs "Drake Song" in his mother's basement and "2000."
- Cameos by Larry David (as Bernie Sanders) and Fred Armisen.
- A tribute to *SNL* music producer Hal Willner (1956–2020) who died of COVID-19 on April 7, 2020. Current cast members and *SNL* share their memories, which are intercut with an interview with Willner and a Zoom sing-a-long of Lou Reed's "Perfect Day."

**Airdate:** 4/25/20
**Episode:** 45.17
**Host:** ——
**Musical Guest:** Miley Cyrus
**Musical and Guest Performances/Cameo(s)/Program Notes:**
- Episode does not have a host, a monologue, and the traditional "Good Night."
- "Live from New York": Dr. Anthony Fauci (Brad Pitt, in a cameo), who interprets President Donald Trump's nonsensical quotations about COVID-19. At the end, Pitt thanks the "real Dr. Fauci," medical workers, first responders, and their families "for being on the front line." Pitt then opens the show, "Live, kind of, from all across America, it's *Saturday Night!*"
- Cyrus performs "Wish You Were Here" with Andrew Watt on guitar.
- Music Video: "Stuck in the House."
- Cameos by Fred Armisen, Bad Bunny, Charles Barkley, DJ Khaled, Paul Rudd, Adam Sandler, Rob Schneider, and Jason Sudeikis.

**Airdate:** 5/9/20
**Episode:** 45.18
**Host:** Kristen Wiig
**Musical Guest:** Boyz II Men with Babyface
**Musical and Guest Performances/Cameo(s)/Program Notes:**
- "Live from New York": Donald Trump (Alec Baldwin) delivers a graduation speech via Zoom.
- Boys II Men and Babyface perform "A Song for Mama."
- Music Video: "Danny Trejo."
- Cameos by Amy Davidson, Abbott Day, Tina Fey, Josh Gad, Martin Short, and Danny Trejo.
- In Memoriam: Little Richard (1932–2020).

## Season 46 (2020–2021)

**Airdate:** 10/3/20
**Episode:** 46.1
**Host:** Chris Rock
**Musical Guest:** Megan Thee Stallion
**Musical and Guest Performances/Cameo(s)/Program Notes:**
- "Live from New York": Fox News anchor Chris Wallace (Beck Bennett) moderates the presidential debate between President Donald Trump (Alec Baldwin) and Joe Biden (Jim Carrey), with an appearance by Kamala Harris (Maya Rudolph), who referees.
- Megan Thee Stallion performs "Savage" and "Don't Stop" with Young Thug.
- In honor of the late Supreme Court Justice Ruth Bader Ginsburg, who died on September 18, 2020, Kate McKinnon is seen as Justice Ginsburg silently sitting in the audience at the end of *Weekend Update*. She puts her

hand over her heart, followed by a graphic that reads, "Rest in Power."
- Debut of featured players Andrew Dismukes, Lauren Holt, and Punkie Johnson.
- Cameos by Harry Styles and Maya Rudolph.

**Airdate:** 10/10/20
**Episode:** 46.2
**Host:** Bill Burr
**Musical Guest:** Jack White
**Musical and Guest Performances/Cameo(s)/ Program Notes:**
- "Live from New York": CNN vice presidential debate between Kamala Harris (Maya Rudolph) and Mike Pence (Beck Bennett), with Joe Biden (Jim Carrey) and Herman Cain (Kenan Thompson).
- White performs a medley of "Don't Hurt Yourself," "Ball and Biscuit," and "Jesus Is Coming Soon," and, for the second set, "Lazaretto."
- White replaced singer Morgan Wallen, whose appearance was canceled after a video surfaced showing Wallen violating COVID-19 protocols for social distancing and mask wearing.
- Cameo by Maya Rudolph.
- In Memoriam: Eddie Van Halen (1955–2020), with footage of him playing with the Robert Cray Band (12.13).

**Airdate:** 10/17/20
**Episode:** 46.3
**Host:** Issa Rae
**Musical Guest:** Justin Bieber
**Musical and Guest Performances/Cameo(s)/ Program Notes:**
- "Live from New York": "Dueling Town Halls" with Donald Trump (Alec Baldwin), Joe Biden (Jim Carrey), Kamala Harris (Maya Rudolph), and Savannah Guthrie (Kate McKinnon).
- Bieber performs "Holy" with Chance the Rapper and "Lonely" with Benny Blanco on keyboard.
- Cameos by Jim Carrey and Maya Rudolph.

**Airdate:** 10/24/20
**Episode:** 46.4
**Host:** Adele
**Musical Guest:** H.E.R.
**Musical and Guest Performances/Cameo(s)/ Program Notes:**
- "Live from New York": The presidential debate with Joe Biden (Jim Carrey), Donald Trump (Alec Baldwin), and Kristen Welker (Maya Rudolph).
- H.E.R. performs "Damage" and "Hold On."

**Airdate:** 10/31/20
**Episode:** 46.5
**Host:** John Mulaney
**Musical Guest:** The Strokes
**Musical and Guest Performances/Cameo(s)/ Program Notes:**
- "Live from New York": A holiday message from former vice president Joe Biden (Jim Carrey) and Kamala Harris (Maya Rudolph).
- The Strokes perform "The Adults Are Talking" and "Bad Decisions."
- "Music Video: "Strollin'."
- Musical Sketch: "Souvenir Underwear."

**Airdate:** 11/7/20
**Episode:** 46.6
**Host:** Dave Chappelle
**Musical Guest:** Foo Fighters
**Musical and Guest Performances/Cameo(s)/ Program Notes:**
- "Live from New York": Biden's presidential victory with Joe Biden (Jim Carrey), Kamala Harris (Maya Rudolph), and Donald Trump (Alec Baldwin).
- The Foo Fighters perform "Shame Shame" and "Times like These."

**Airdate:** 12/5/20
**Episode:** 46.7
**Host:** Jason Bateman

**Musical Guest:** Morgan Wallen
**Musical and Guest Performances/Cameo(s)/Program Notes:**
- "Live from New York": "Michigan Election Hearing" with Rudy Giuliani (Kate McKinnon), lawyer Jenna Ellis (Lauren Holt), and election denier Melissa Carone (Cecily Strong).
- Wallen performs "7 Summers" and "Still Goin' Down."
- Wallen was originally slated as the musical guest for 46.2, but his appearance was canceled because he violated COVID-19 protocols. The events that led to his cancellation are parodied in a sketch, "Morgan Wallen Party."

**Airdate:** 12/12/20
**Episode:** 46.8
**Host:** Timothée Chalamet
**Musical Guest:** Bruce Springsteen and the E Street Band
**Musical and Guest Performances/Cameo(s)/Program Notes:**
- "Live from New York": *The Situation Room* with Dr. Anthony Fauci (Kate McKinnon) and Dr. Deborah Birx (Heidi Gardner).
- Springsteen and the E Street Band perform "Ghosts" and "I'll See You in My Dreams."
- Cameos by Questlove and Nicole Flender.

**Airdate:** 12/19/20
**Episode:** 46.9
**Host:** Kristen Wiig
**Musical Guest:** Dua Lipa
**Musical and Guest Performances/Cameo(s)/Program Notes:**
- "Live from New York": A doctor (Mikey Day) gives Mike Pence (Beck Bennett) the COVID-19 vaccine, featuring Karen Pence (Lauren Holt), Joe Biden (Alex Moffat), and Kamala Harris (Maya Rudolph).
- Lipa performs "Don't Start Now" and "Levitating."
- Cameo by Maya Rudolph.

**Airdate:** 1/30/21
**Episode:** 46.10
**Host:** John Krasinski
**Musical Guest:** Machine Gun Kelly
**Musical and Guest Performances/Cameo(s)/Program Notes:**
- "Live from New York": Kate McKinnon, host of *What Still Works?* a talk show that wonders what's still works (the government, stock market, social media, the COVID-19 vaccine, and Tom Brady).
- Machine Gun Kelly performs "My Ex's Best Friend" and "Lonely."
- In Memoriam: Actress Cicely Tyson (1924–2021)

**Airdate:** 2/6/21
**Episode:** 46.11
**Host:** Dan Levy
**Musical Guest:** Phoebe Bridgers
**Musical and Guest Performances/Cameo(s)/Program Notes:**
- "Live from New York": Super Bowl LV pregame show with CBS sportscasters Boomer Esiason (Beck Bennett); Phil Simms (Mikey Day); Bill Cowher (Alex Moffat); Nate Burleson (Chris Redd); and James "No, Not That One" Brown II (Kenan Thompson).
- Bridgers performs "Kyoto" and "I Know the End."

**Airdate:** 2/13/21
**Episode:** 46.12
**Host:** Regina King
**Musical Guest:** Nathaniel Rateliff
**Musical and Guest Performances/Cameo(s)/Program Notes:**
- "Live from New York": On *Tucker Carlson Tonight*, Carlson (Alex Moffat) interviews Congressman Mitch McConnell (Beck Bennett), Senator Ted Cruz (Aidy Bryant), Trump lawyer Michael van der Veen (Pete Davidson), Senator Lindsey Graham (Kate McKinnon), and Pennsylvania attorney general Bruce Castor (Mikey Day).
- Rateliff performs "Redemption" and "A Little Honey" with the Night Sweats.

Episode Guide 563

**Airdate:** 2/20/21
**Episode:** 46.13
**Host:** Regé-Jean Page
**Musical Guest:** Bad Bunny
**Musical and Guest Performances/Cameo(s)/ Program Notes:**
- "Live from New York": "Oops, You Did It Again," Britney Spears's (Chloe Fineman) talk show with Ted Cruz (Aidy Bryant), Andrew Cuomo (Pete Davidson), and actress/mixed martial artist Gina Carano (Cecily Strong).
- Bad Bunny performs "La Noche de Anoche" with Rosalía and "Te Deseo Lo Mejor."
- Music Video: "The Grocery Rap."

**Airdate:** 2/27/21
**Episode:** 46.14
**Host:** Nick Jonas
**Musical Guest:** Nick Jonas
**Musical and Guest Performances/Cameo(s)/ Program Notes:**
- "Live from New York": "So You Think You Can Get the Vaccine," hosted by Dr. Fauci (Kate McKinnon), with panelists California governor Gavin Newsom (Alex Moffat), New York governor Andrew Cuomo (Pete Davidson), and Michigan governor Gretchen Whitmer (Cecily Strong), who decide if guests, including senior citizen Seymour Freeman (Mike Day), are eligible for the COVID-19 vaccine.
- Jonas performs "Spaceman" and "This Is Heaven."
- Jonas's brother Kevin has a cameo in the opening monologue and introduces Nick's second song.

**Airdate:** 3/27/21
**Episode:** 46.15
**Host:** Maya Rudolph
**Musical Guest:** Jack Harlow
**Musical and Guest Performances/Cameo(s)/ Program Notes:**
- "Live from New York": "Snatched! Vaxed! or Waxed!" COVID-19 MTV spring break dating show parody hosted by Cece Vuvuzela (Maya Rudolph).
- Harlow performs "Tyler Herro" and "WHATS POPPIN" and, for his second set, "Same Guy" with Adam Levine.
- Music Video: "Boomers Get the Vax."
- Maya Rudolph won an Emmy for Outstanding Guest Actress in a Comedy Series for hosting this episode.

**Airdate:** 4/3/21
**Episode:** 46.16
**Host:** Daniel Kaluuya
**Musical Guest:** St. Vincent
**Musical and Guest Performances/Cameo(s)/ Program Notes:**
- "Live from New York": "Oops, You Did It Again," Britney Spears's (Chloe Fineman) talk show, with guests Congressman Matt Gaetz (Pete Davidson), French cartoon skunk Pepé Le Pew (Kate McKinnon), and singer Lil Nas X (Chris Redd).
- St. Vincent performs "Pay Your Way in Pain" and "The Melting of the Sun."

**Airdate:** 4/10/21
**Episode:** 46.17
**Host:** Carey Mulligan
**Musical Guest:** Kid Cudi
**Musical and Guest Performances/Cameo(s)/ Program Notes:**
- "Live from New York": On "Eye on Minnesota," Black anchors (Kenan Thompson, Ego Nwodim) and weatherman (Chris Redd) spar with White anchors (Kate McKinnon, Alex Moffat) over racial politics.
- Kid Cudi performs "Tequila Shots" and "Sad People."
- Kid Cudi appears in "Weird Little Flute" music video with a cameo by Timothée Chalamet.
- ★★★★ Character: Bowen Yang as the Iceberg That Sank the *Titanic* on *Weekend Update*.
- In Memoriam: Anne Beatts (1947–2021), one of *SNL*'s original sketch comedy writers (1975–1979).

**Airdate:** 5/8/21
**Episode:** 46.18

**Host:** Elon Musk
**Musical Guest:** Miley Cyrus
**Musical and Guest Performances/Cameo(s)/ Program Notes:**
- "Live from New York": Cast members and their moms celebrate Mother's Day.
- Cyrus performs "WITHOUT YOU" with the Kid Laroi and "Plastic Hearts."
- First episode to be live-streamed internationally on YouTube to more than one hundred countries.

**Airdate:** 5/15/21
**Episode:** 46.19
**Host:** Keegan-Michael Key
**Musical Guest:** Olivia Rodrigo
**Musical and Guest Performances/Cameo(s)/ Program Notes:**
- "Live from New York": Dr. Anthony Fauci (Kate McKinnon) and doctors from the CDC perform sketches to teach the public the new masking rules.
- Rodrigo performs "driver's license" and "good 4 u" accompanied by Dan Nigro on guitar.

**Airdate:** 5/22/21
**Episode:** 46.20
**Host:** Anya Taylor-Joy
**Musical Guest:** Lil Nas X
**Musical and Guest Performances/Cameo(s)/ Program Notes:**
- "Live from New York": "What I Remember about This Year"—Chris Rock and the entire cast.
- Lil Nas X performs "MONTERO (Call Me by Your Name)" and "Son Goes Down."
- Music Video: "Pride Month Song."
- Beck Bennett's and Lauren Holt's final episode.
- In Memoriam: Actor Charles Grodin (1935–2021)

## Season 47 (2021–2022)

**Airdate:** 10/2/21
**Episode:** 47.1
**Host:** Owen Wilson
**Musical Guest:** Kacey Musgraves
**Musical and Guest Performances/Cameo(s)/ Program Notes:**
- "Live from New York": "Biden Unites Democrats"—President Biden (James Austin Johnson), with Senator Kyrsten Sinema (Cecily Strong), Congresswoman Alexandria Ocasio-Cortez (Melissa Villaseñor), Joe Manchin (Aidy Bryant), Senator Chuck Schumer (Alex Moffat), Ilhan Omar (Ego Nwodim), and Governor Andrew Cuomo (Pete Davidson).
- When Kacey Musgraves performs her first song, "Justified," she is naked, with her guitar and guitar strap covering parts of her body. She is fully clothed for her second song, "Camera Roll."
- Debut of feature players Aristotle Athari, James Austin Johnson, and Sarah Sherman.
- Cameos by Owen's brothers, Luke Wilson and Andrew Wilson.
- In Memoriam: As a tribute to former *SNL* cast member and *Weekend Update* anchor Norm Macdonald (1959–2021), a clip of Macdonald anchoring the news is seen at the end of *Weekend Update*. Pete Davidson wears a T-shirt with Macdonald's picture on it.
- In Memoriam: Former NBC president Herbert Schlosser (1926–2021), who was responsible for putting *SNL* on the air in the 1970s.
- "Good Night": Colin Jost holds up a sign—"We'll miss you, Ken"—in tribute to retiring supervising producer Ken Aymong, whose tenure with *SNL* began in 1985.

Episode Guide

**Airdate:** 10/9/21
**Episode:** 47.2
**Host:** Kim Kardashian West
**Musical Guest:** Halsey
**Musical and Guest Performances/Cameo(s)/ Program Notes:**
- "Live from New York": Facebook hearings with Tom Davidson (the MySpace guy); (Pete Davidson).
- Halsey performs "I Am Not a Woman, I'm a God" and "Darling," with Lindsey Buckingham on guitar and singing background vocals.
- Cameos by Kris Jenner and Khloé Kardashian in a parody of *People's Court*.
- Cameos by Tyler Cameron, John Cena, Chace Crawford, Blake Griffin, Chris Rock, Amy Schumer, and Jesse Williams in "The Dream Guy" sketch.
- Music Video: "Grown Ass Women in the Club."
- Debut of Please Don't Destroy (writers Martin Herlihy, John Higgins, and Ben Marshall) in a prerecorded segment, "Hard Seltzer."
- In Memoriam: Actor Ray Liotta (1954–1922).

**Airdate:** 10/16/21
**Episode:** 47.3
**Host:** Rami Malek
**Musical Guest:** Young Thug
**Musical and Guest Performances/Cameo(s)/ Program Notes:**
- "Live from New York": NFL press conference addressing Las Vegas Raiders coach Jon Gruden's (James Austin Johnson) racist and homophobic emails that includes NFL commissioner Roger Goodell (Colin Jost), Raiders owner Mark Davis (Alex Moffat), Colin Kaepernick (Chris Redd), and others.
- Young Thug performs "Tick Tock" (with Travis Barker on drums), and "Love You More" (with Barker, Nate Ruess, Gunna, and Jeff Bhasker).
- Cameo by Daniel Craig, who appears in the "Prince Audition" and "Angelo" sketches.

**Airdate:** 10/23/21
**Episode:** 47.4
**Host:** Jason Sudeikis
**Musical Guest:** Brandi Carlile
**Musical and Guest Performances/Cameo(s)/ Program Notes:**
- "Live from New York": "The Ghost of Biden Past" with three Joe Bidens (Jason Sudeikis, Alex Moffat, and James Austin Johnson).
- Carlile performs "Broken Horses" and "Right on Time."
- Cameos by Fred Armisen, Nicholas Braun, Oscar Isaac, and Emily Ratajkowski

**Airdate:** 11/6/21
**Episode:** 47.5
**Host:** Kieran Culkin
**Musical Guest:** Ed Sheeran
**Musical and Guest Performances/Cameo(s)/ Program Notes:**
- "Live from New York": "Justice with Judge Jeanine [Pirro]" (Cecily Strong).
- Sheeran performs "Shivers" and "Overpass Graffiti."
- Please Don't Destroy: "Calling Angie."
- *Weekend Update*: Cecily Strong as Goober the Clown, who had an abortion, speaks out against the recent Supreme Court ruling overturning *Roe v. Wade*.
- Cameos by Dionne Warwick and Tracy Morgan

**Airdate:** 11/13/21
**Episode:** 47.6
**Host:** Jonathan Majors
**Musical Guest:** Taylor Swift
**Musical and Guest Performances/Cameo(s)/ Program Notes:**
- "Live from New York": "Cruz Street," a *Sesame Street* parody with Ted Cruz (Aidy Bryant).
- Taylor Swift sings "All Two Well" as the same-titled short film starring Sadie Sink and Dylan O'Brien plays in the background.
- Please Don't Destroy: "Three Sad Virgins," a music video with Taylor Swift;

Pete Davidson; and, in the title roles, Please Don't Destroy's Martin Herlihy, John Higgins, and Ben Marshall.

**Airdate:** 11/20/21
**Episode:** 47.7
**Host:** Simu Liu
**Musical Guest:** Saweetie
**Musical and Guest Performances/Cameo(s)/Program Notes:**
- "Live from New York": *Justice with Judge Jeanine* [Pirro] (Cecily Strong).
- Saweetie performs "Tap In" and "Best Friend" and, in her second set, "Icy Chain."
- In Memoriam: Former *SNL* writer/featured player, Peter Aykroyd (1955–2021), brother of Dan Aykroyd.

**Airdate:** 12/11/21
**Episode:** 47.8
**Host:** Billie Eilish
**Musical Guest:** Billie Eilish
**Musical and Guest Performances/Cameo(s)/Program Notes:**
- "Live from New York": A holiday message from Dr. Anthony Fauci (Kate McKinnon).
- Eilish performs "Happier than Ever" and "Male Fantasy" with her brother Finneas O'Connell.
- Return of Kate McKinnon after a seven-episode absence.
- Cameos by Billie Eilish and Finneas O'Connell's parents, Maggie Baird and Patrick O'Connell.

**Airdate:** 12/18/21
**Episode:** 47.9
**Host:** Paul Rudd
**Musical and Guest Performances/Cameo(s)/Program Notes:**
- Due to the Omicron variant, the show has no audience, a limited crew, and only two cast members in the studio, Keenan Thompson and Michael Che.
- Tina Fey, Tom Hanks, and Steve Martin and Martin Short on video induct Paul Rudd into the Five-Timers Club.
- Charli XCX appears in a holiday music video spoof "The Christmas Socks."
- Tina Fey fills in for *Weekend Update*'s Colin Jost, who contracted COVID-19.
- The list of past Christmas sketches includes "A Holiday Wish from Steve Martin" (12.6), the Claymation music video "Christmastime for the Jews" (31.9), and "Dick in the Box" (32.9) sung by Justin Timberlake and Andy Samberg.
- After fifteen and a half seasons and eleven Emmy wins, Don Roy King directs his final episode.

**Airdate:** 1/15/22
**Episode:** 47.10
**Host:** Ariana DeBose
**Musical Guest:** Bleachers
**Musical and Guest Performances/Cameo(s)/Program Notes:**
- "Live from New York": Presidential address by Joe Biden (James Austin Johnson) blames Omicron on Americans going to see *Spiderman: No Way Home*.
- Bleachers performs "How Dare You Want More" and "Chinatown."
- Director Liz Patrick's first episode.

**Airdate:** 1/22/22
**Episode:** 47.11
**Host:** Will Forte
**Musical Guest:** Måneskin
**Musical and Guest Performances/Cameo(s)/Program Notes:**
- "Live from New York": *The Ingraham Angle* with Laura Ingraham (Kate McKinnon), who interviews Senator Ted Cruz (Aidy Bryant); tennis player Novak Djokovic (Pete Davidson), who was deported from Australia for refusing to be vaccinated; Donald Trump (James Austin Johnson); and Candace Owens (Ego Nwodim).
- Måneskin performs "Beggin" and "I Wanna Be Your Slave."

- Cameos by Willem Dafoe, Kristen Wiig, and Ryan Phillippe.
- In Memoriam: *SNL* writer John Bowman (1957–2021).

**Airdate:** 1/29/22
**Episode:** 47.12
**Host:** Willem Dafoe
**Musical Guest:** Katy Perry
**Musical and Guest Performances/Cameo(s)/ Program Notes:**
- "Live from New York": A presentation on "Russian disinformation" on the impending invasion of Ukraine to President Biden (James Austin Johnson).
- Perry performs "When I'm Gone" with Alesso and "Never Really Over."
- Please Don't Destroy: "Martin's Friend."
- Cameo by Peyton Manning on *Weekend Update*, who shares his perspective on *Emily in Paris*, season 2.
- Music Video: "Now I'm Up."

**Airdate:** 2/26/22
**Episode:** 47.13
**Host:** John Mulaney
**Musical Guest:** LCD Soundsystem
**Musical and Guest Performances/Cameo(s)/ Program Notes:**
- "Live from New York": In response to the Russian invasion of Ukraine, the Ukrainian Chorus Dumka of New York perform "Prayer for Ukraine."
- LCD Soundsystem performs "Thrills" and "Yr City's a Sucker."
- Musical Sketch: "Subway Churra."
- Please Don't Destroy: "Good Variant" with cameos by Paul Rudd and Al Roker.
- Mulaney is inducted into the Five-Timers Club by Candice Bergen, Tina Fey, Elliott Gould, Steve Martin, Paul Rudd, with a cameo by Conan O'Brien.

**Airdate:** 3/5/22
**Episode:** 47.14
**Host:** Oscar Isaac
**Musical Guest:** Charli XCX

**Musical and Guest Performances/Cameo(s)/ Program Notes:**
- "Live from New York": "Fox News Ukrainian Invasion Celebration Spectacular" with Laura Ingraham (Kate McKinnon), Tucker Carlson (Alex Moffat), and Donald Trump (James Austin Johnson).
- Charli XCX performs "Beg for You" and "Baby."

**Airdate:** 3/12/22
**Episode:** 47.15
**Host:** Zoë Kravitz
**Musical Guest:** Rosalía
**Musical and Guest Performances/Cameo(s)/ Program Notes:**
- "Live from New York": White House TikTok meeting with President Biden (James Austin Johnson).
- Rosalia performs "Chicken Teriyaki" and "La Fama."
- Please Don't Destroy: "We Got Her a Cat," with cameo by Paul Dano.

**Airdate:** 4/2/22
**Episode:** 47.16
**Host:** Jerrod Carmichael
**Musical Guest:** Gunna
**Musical and Guest Performances/Cameo(s)/ Program Notes:**
- "Live from New York": *Fox and Friends* with hosts Brian Kilmeade (Mikey Day), Ainsley Earhardt (Heidi Gardner), and Steve Doocy (Alex Moffat) and guests Supreme Court Justice Clarence Thomas (Kenan Thompson), Ginni Thomas (Kate McKinnon), Donald Trump (James Austin Johnson), and Jeanine Pirro (Cecily Strong).
- Gunna performs "Banking on Me" and "Pushin P" with Future.
- Cameo by Simon Rex.
- In Memoriam: Foo Fighters drummer Taylor Hawkins (1972–2022).
- Carmichael's stand-up special *Rothaniel*, in which he came out as a gay man, debuted on HBO the previous evening (April 1, 2022).

**Airdate:** 4/9/22
**Episode:** 47.17
**Host:** Jake Gyllenhaal
**Musical Guest:** Camila Cabello
**Musical and Guest Performances/Cameo(s)/ Program Notes:**
- "Live from New York": President Joe Biden (James Austin Johnson) welcomes Supreme Court Justice Ketanji Brown Jackson (Ego Nwodim), who is visited in the Oval Office by late justices Ruth Bader Ginsburg (Kate McKinnon) and Thurgood Marshall (Kenan Thompson), Harriet Tubman (Punkie Johnson), and Jackie Robinson (Chris Redd).
- Camila Cabello sings "Bam Bam" and "Psychofreak" with Willow.

**Airdate:** 4/16/22
**Episode:** 47.18
**Host:** Lizzo
**Musical Guest:** Lizzo
**Musical and Guest Performances/Cameo(s)/ Program Notes:**
- "Live from New York": A message from the Easter Bunny (Bowen Yang) with Elon Musk (Mikey Day), Britney Spears (Chloe Fineman), Donald Trump (James Austin Johnson), Dr. Anthony Fauci (Kate McKinnon), Jared Leto (Kyle Mooney), Eric Adams (Chris Redd), and Marjorie Taylor Greene (Cecily Strong).
- Lizzo performs "About Damn Time" and "Special."
- Cameo by Lizzo's mom, Shari Johnson-Jefferson, who introduces her daughter's second musical performance.
- Please Don't Destroy: "Lizzo Has Writers' Block."
- In Memoriam: *SNL* cast member Gilbert Gottfried (1955–2022).

**Airdate:** 5/7/22
**Episode:** 47.19
**Host:** Benedict Cumberbatch
**Musical Guest:** Arcade Fire
**Musical and Guest Performances/Cameo(s)/ Program Notes:**
- "Live from New York": In response to the leaked decision overturning *Roe v. Wade*, in which Judge Alito references thirteenth-century British law, British male lawmakers (Benedict Cumberbatch, Andrew Dismukes, and James Austin Johnson) in the year 1235 contemplate outlawing abortion.
- Arcade Fire performs "Unconditional I (Lookout Kid)"; "The Lightning I, II"; and, during the closing credits, "End of the Empire II."
- Filmed cameo by Elizabeth Olsen.
- "Good Night": Benedict Cumberbatch and cast members wear shirts that read "1973" (the year *Roe v. Wade* legalized abortion) in protest of the leaked Supreme Court decision that recriminalized abortion.

**Airdate:** 5/14/22
**Episode:** 47.20
**Host:** Selena Gomez
**Musical Guest:** Post Malone
**Musical and Guest Performances/Cameo(s)/ Program Notes:**
- "Live from New York": *MSNBC Special Report* with Nicole Wallace (Kate McKinnon) on the *Johnny Depp vs. Amber Heard* trial.
- Post Malone performs "Cooped Up" with Roddy Ricch and "Love/Hate Letter to Alcohol" with Fleet Foxes.
- Cameo by Steve Martin.

**Airdate:** 5/21/22
**Episode:** 47.21
**Host:** Natasha Lyonne
**Musical Guest:** Japanese Breakfast
**Musical and Guest Performances/Cameo(s)/ Program Notes:**
- "Live from New York": "Final Encounter," where UFO abductees Sharon (Cecily Strong), Carla (Natasha Lyonne), and Colleen Rafferty (Kate McKinnon) are questioned about their experience.

- Japanese Breakfast performs "Be Sweet" and "Paprika" with Luna Li.
- Final episode for Kate McKinnon, Aidy Bryant, Melissa Villaseñor, Alex Moffat, and Chris Redd.

## Season 48 (2022–2023)

**Airdate:** 10/1/22
**Episode:** 48.1
**Host:** Miles Teller
**Musical Guest:** Kendrick Lamar
**Musical and Guest Performances/Cameo(s)/ Program Notes:**
- "Live from New York": "ManningCast," where NFL legends Peyton Manning (Miles Teller) and his younger brother Eli Manning (Andrew Dismukes), with the assistance of Jon Hamm (in a cameo), provide the offscreen play-by-play criticism of the cold open, with President Donald Trump (James Austin Johnson), most of the cast, and a gratuitous cameo by professional snowboarder Shaun White.
- Lamar sings "Rich Spirit" and "N95" and, in his second set, "Father Time" with Sampha.
- Debut of featured players Marcello Hernandez, Molly Kearney, Michael Longfellow, and Devon Walker.

**Airdate:** 10/8/22
**Episode:** 48.2
**Host:** Brendan Gleeson
**Musical Guest:** Willow
**Musical and Guest Performances/Cameo(s)/ Program Notes:**
- "Live from New York": "So You Think You Won't Snap!" a game show parody hosted by Morgan Freegirl (Bowen Yang).
- Willow performs "Curious/Furious" and "Ur a Stranger."
- Please Don't Destroy: "Tommy."
- Cameo by Colin Farrell.

**Airdate:** 10/15/22
**Episode:** 48.3
**Host:** Megan Thee Stallion
**Musical Guest:** Megan Thee Stallion
**Musical and Guest Performances/Cameo(s)/ Program Notes:**
- "Live from New York": January 6 Committee hearings, which includes footage of Speaker of the House Nancy Pelosi (Chloe Fineman) and Senate Majority Leader Chuck Schumer (Sarah Sherman) during the insurrection.
- Megan Thee Stallion performs "Anxiety" and, for her second set, a medley of "NDA" and "Plan B."
- Please Don't Destroy: "Wellness."
- Music Video: "We Got Brought."

**Airdate:** 10/29/22
**Episode:** 48.4
**Host:** Jack Harlow
**Musical Guest:** Jack Harlow
**Musical and Guest Performances/Cameo(s)/ Program Notes:**
- "Live from New York": *PBS Newshour* host Judy Woodruff (Heidi Gardner) interviews Republican Senate candidates Dr. Mehmet Oz (Mikey Day), Kari Lake (Cecily Strong), and Herschel Walker (Keenan Thompson).
- Harlow performs "Lil Secret" and "First Class" and, for his second set, "State Fair."
- Cameos by Jeff Probst ("Joker Wedding"), Bobby Moynihan as Drunk Uncle, and Tom Hanks as David S. Pumpkins.

**Airdate:** 11/5/22
**Episode:** 48.5
**Host:** Amy Schumer
**Musical Guest:** Steve Lacy

Appendix A

**Musical and Guest Performances/Cameo(s)/ Program Notes:**
- "Live from New York": President Joe Biden (James Austin Johnson) introduces some of the Democratic candidates running in the midterm elections: Tekashi 6ix9ine (Marcello Hernández), Guy Fieri (Molly Kearney), Azealia Banks (Ego Nwodim), Stormy Daniels (Cecily Strong), and Tracy Morgan (Kenan Thompson).
- Steve Lacy performs "Bad Habit" and "Helmet."
- In Memoriam: Rapper Kirsnick "Take Off" Khari Ball (1994–2002).

**Airdate:** 11/12/22
**Episode:** 48.6
**Host:** Dave Chappelle
**Musical Guest:** Black Star
**Musical and Guest Performances/Cameo(s)/ Program Notes:**
- "Live from New York": *Fox & Friends* hosts interview Donald Trump (James Austin Johnson) with Republican Arizona governor candidate/election denier Kari Lake (Cecily Strong) about the midterm elections.
- Black Star (with Madlib) perform "So Be It" and "The Main Thing Is to Keep the Main Thing The Main Thing."
- Cameos by Ice-T and Donnell Rawlings.
- Please Don't Destroy: "Election Night," with a cameo by MSNBC's Steve Kornacki.

**Airdate:** 12/3/22
**Episode:** 48.7
**Host:** Keke Palmer
**Musical Guest:** SZA
**Musical and Guest Performances/Cameo(s)/ Program Notes:**
- "Live from New York": Mitch McConnell (James Austin Johnson), John Cornyn (Mikey Day), and Marsha Blackburn (Cecily Strong) talk to clueless Georgia senatorial candidate Herschel Walker (Kenan Thompson) about the upcoming Georgia runoffs.
- SZA performs "Shirt" and "Blind."
- Product Sketch Integration: "Hello Kitty" and "Arby's."
- Music Video: "Big Boys."
- Cameo by Natasha Lyonne in the "Hello Kitty" sketch and Kenan Thompson's former *All That* costar Kel Mitchell.

**Airdate:** 12/10/22
**Episode:** 48.8
**HOSTS:** Steve Martin and Martin Short
**Musical Guest:** Brandi Carlile
**Musical and Guest Performances/Cameo(s)/ Program Notes:**
- "Live from New York": Cast members sing "Blocking It Out for Christmas."
- Brandi Carlile performs "The Story" and, for her second set, "You and Me on the Rock" with Lucius.
- Please Don't Destroy: "Chelsea."
- Cameo by Selena Gomez, who appears with her *Only Murders in the Building* costars in *Father of the Bride—Part 8*, Martin and Short reprise their roles from parts 1 and 2. Martin is the father, George; Short is the wedding planner, Franck; and in a cameo, Kieran Culkin is George's son Matty.

**Airdate:** 12/17/22
**Episode:** 48.9
**Host:** Austin Butler
**Musical Guest:** Lizzo
**Musical and Guest Performances/Cameo(s)/ Program Notes:**
- "Live from New York": Donald Trump (James Austin Johnson) advertises his digital Trump cards with appearances by Donald Jr. (Mikey Day) and his fiancée, Kimberly Guilfoyle (Cecily Strong).
- Lizzo performs "Break Up Twice" and "Someday at Christmas."
- *Weekend Update*: In her final appearance, Cecily Strong appears as her

chain-smoking character Cathy Ann, who is heading to prison.
- Please Don't Destroy: "Plirts."
- Cecily Strong's last episode: Austin Butler, Strong, and the cast sing "Blue Christmas."

**Airdate:** 1/21/23
**Episode:** 48.10
**Host:** Aubrey Plaza
**Musical Guest:** Sam Smith
**Musical and Guest Performances/Cameo(s)/ Program Notes:**
- "Live from New York": *NFL on Fox* with Howie Long (Mikey Day); Curt Menefee (Kenan Thompson); Jimmy Johnson (James Austin Johnson); Michael Strahan (Devon Walker); Terry Bradshaw (Molly Kearney); Pam Oliver (Ego Nwodim); and New York congressman George Santos (Bowen Yang), who, in an interview, spouts a string of lies.
- Sam Smith sings "Unholy" with Kim Petras and "Gloria" with a cameo by Sharon Stone.
- Filmed cameo by President (and Delaware native) Joe Biden, who confirms that Plaza is the most famous person from Delaware. Plaza, a former NBC page, gives a tour backstage, which includes cameos by her *Parks & Recreation* costar Amy Poehler; talent coordinator Jeff Blake; and set designers Akira Yoshimura, Joe DeTullio, and Keith Raywood.
- *Weekend Update*: Plaza appears as her *Parks & Recreation* character, April Ludgate, alongside Poehler as Leslie Knope.
- Additional cameos by the *Property Brothers* Drew and Jonathan Scott, Tony Hawk, and Alison Williams in a horror-film parody, "M3GAN 2.0."

**Airdate:** 1/28/23
**Episode:** 48.11
**Host:** Michael B. Jordan
**Musical Guest:** Lil Baby
**Musical and Guest Performances/Cameo(s)/ Program Notes:**
- "Live from New York": Justice Department press conference on the search for more classified documents with Merrick Garland (Mikey Day) and agents Conrad Nance (Kenan Thompson), Casey Combs (Ego Nwodim), and Derek Kaye (Bowen Yang).
- Lil Baby performs "California Breeze" and "Forever."
- Product Sketch Integration: Southwest Airlines and State Farm.

**Airdate:** 2/4/23
**Episode:** 48.12
**Host:** Pedro Pascal
**Musical Guest:** Coldplay
**Musical and Guest Performances/Cameo(s)/ Program Notes:**
- "Live from New York": MSNBC's Katy Tur (Chloe Fineman) with General William Hamilton (Kenan Thompson) and Bowen Yang as the Spy Balloon Recently Shot Down over the Ocean.
- Coldplay performs "The Astronaut" and a medley of "Human Heart" and "Fix You" (with Jacob Collier and the Jason Max Ferdinand Singers). ASL interpretation of "The Astronaut" is provided by Natasha Ofili, who is wearing an alien mask.
- Product Sketch Integration: *Mario Kart*.
- Cameo by Sarah Paulson as a teacher in "Fancam Assembly."

**Airdate:** 2/25/23
**Episode:** 48.13
**Host:** Woody Harrelson
**Musical Guest:** Jack White
**Musical and Guest Performances/Cameo(s)/ Program Notes:**
- "Live from New York": C-SPAN coverage of Donald Trump's (James Austin John) visit to East Palestine, Ohio, after the recent tragic train accident.
- Jack White performs "Taking Me Back" and "Fear of the Dawn" and,

for his second set, "A Tip from You to Me."
- Product Integration: Cologuard.
- Please Don't Destroy: "The Stakeout."
- In Memoriam: Comedian/actor Richard Belzer (1944–2023) and longtime *SNL* production designer Eugene Lee (1939–2023).
- Cameos by Scarlett Johansson, who inducts Woody Harrelson into the Five-Timers Club. Kenan Thompson also presents Jack White a Five-Timers jacket to commemorate his fifth appearance.

**Airdate:** 3/4/23
**Episode:** 48.14
**Host:** Travis Kelce
**Musical Guest:** Kelsea Ballerini
**Musical and Guest Performances/Cameo(s)/ Program Notes:**
- "Live from New York": *Fox and Friends* with Steve Doocy (Mikey Day), Ainsley Earhardt (Heidi Gardner), and Brian Kilmeade (Bowen Yang) and guests Mike Lindell (James Austin Johnson) and O. J. Simpson (Kenan Thompson).
- Ballerini performs "Blindside" and "Penthouse."
- Cameo by Travis's brother Jason Kelce, a center for the Philadelphia Eagles.
- Please Don't Destroy: "Self-Defense."
- In Memoriam: John Head, *SNL* talent acquisitions.

**Airdate:** 3/11/23
**Episode:** 48.15
**Host:** Jenna Ortega
**Musical Guest:** The 1975
**Musical and Guest Performances/Cameo(s)/ Program Notes:**
- "Live from New York": On the Oscars' red carpet, Mario Lopez (Marcello Hernandez) and Maria Menounos (Heidi Gardner) interview Mike Tyson (Kenan Thompson), Jamie Lee Curtis (Chloe Fineman), Colin Farrell and Brendan Gleeson (Mikey Day, Molly Kearny), and New York congressman George Santos (Bowen Yang).
- The 1975 performs "I'm in Love with You" and "Oh Caroline."
- Cameo by Fred Armisen.
- Please Don't Destroy: "Road Trip."
- In Memoriam: Former writer Erin Moroney Fraser (1969–2023).

**Airdate:** 4/1/23
**Episode:** 48.16
**Host:** Quinta Brunson
**Musical Guest:** Lil Yachty
**Musical and Guest Performances/Cameo(s)/ Program Notes:**
- "Live from New York": Donald Trump (James Austin Johnson) promotes his new album, *Now That's What I Call My Legal Defense Fund*.
- Lil Yachty performs "the BLACK seminole" and "drive ME crazy!" with Diana Gordon.
- Please Don't Destroy: "Street Eats."

**Airdate:** 4/8/23
**Episode:** 48.17
**Host:** Molly Shannon
**Musical Guest:** Jonas Brothers
**Musical and Guest Performances/Cameo(s)/ Program Notes:**
- "Live from New York": A reenactment of the Last Supper interrupted by Donald Trump (James Austin Johnson), who compares himself to Jesus.
- Jonas Brothers perform "Waffle House" and "Walls" (with Jon Bellion and Kirk Franklin).
- Cameos by Martin Short and Lorne Michaels.
- Molly Shannon reprises her characters Jeannie Darcy ("Jeannie Darcy: Selective Startage") and Sally O'Malley ("New Choreographer").
- Please Don't Destroy: "Molly Shannon 2K23."

**Airdate:** 4/15/23
**Episode:** 48.18
**Host:** Ana de Armas
**Musical Guest:** Karol G.
**Musical and Guest Performances/Cameo(s)/Program Notes:**
- "Live from New York": "First Warm Day of the Year Arrival Show—Live from Central Park" hosted by Dana Barnes (Heidi Gardner) and Jace L. Rio (Bowen Yang), who introduce the "characters" who populate Central Park when it gets warm.
- Karol G performs "Mientras Me Curo del Cora" and "Tus Gafitas."
- Please Don't Destroy: "Hangxiety."

## Season 49 (2023–2024)

**Airdate:** 10/14/23
**Episode:** 49.1
**Host:** Pete Davidson
**Musical Guest:** Ice Spice
**Musical and Guest Performances/Cameo(s)/Program Notes:**
- "Live from New York": Pete Davidson addresses Hamas's surprise attack on Israel on October 7, 2023. Speaking directly into the camera, he pays tribute to the victims, which he relates to the loss of his father, a firefighter, who died during 9/11.
- Ice Spice performs "In Ha Mood" and Pretty Girl" with Rema.
- James Austin Johnson and Sarah Sherman are promoted to regular cast members.
- The trio billed as Please Don't Destroy appear in the opening title sequence.
- Debut of featured player Chloe Troast.
- On "Fox NFL Sunday," the sportscasters can't stop talking about quarterback Travis Kelce's relationship with Taylor Swift. Kelce appears in a cameo at the end of the sketch.
- In a cameo, Taylor Swift introduces Ice Spice's second set.

**Airdate:** 10/21/23
**Episode:** 49.2
**Host:** Bad Bunny
**Musical Guest:** Bad Bunny
**Musical and Guest Performances/Cameo(s)/Program Notes:**
- "Live from New York": "House of Representatives": Donald Trump (James Austin Johnson) visits Jim Jordan (Mikey Day), who fails to get elected Speaker of the House.
- Bad Bunny sings "Un Preview" and "Monaco."
- Cameos by Fred Armisen, Lady Gaga, Mick Jagger, and Pablo Pascal.
- Please Don't Destroy: "Bad Bunny Is Shrek."

**Airdate:** 10/28/23
**Episode:** 49.3
**Host:** Nate Bargatze
**Musical Guest:** Foo Fighters
**Musical and Guest Performances/Cameo(s)/Program Notes:**
- "Live from New York": While celebrating Halloween, President Joe Biden (James Austin Johnson) is visited by the Spirit of Halloween (Christopher Walken) and the new Speaker of the House, Mike Johnson (Michael Longfellow).
- In their ninth appearance, Foo Fighters perform "Rescued" and "The Glass" with H.E.R.
- Dave Grohl's fifteenth appearance as a music performer on *SNL*.
- Music Video: "Lake Beach."
- Cameos by Christopher Walken and Padma Lakshmi.
- Please Don't Destroy: "Dog Food."
- In Memoriam: Matthew Perry (1969–2023).

**Airdate:** 10/28/23
**Episode:** 49.4
**Host:** Timothée Chalamet
**Musical Guest:** boygenius
**Musical and Guest Performances/Cameo(s)/ Program Notes:**
- "Live from New York": Republican Debate with Nikki Haley (Heidi Gardner), Donald Trump (James Austin Johnson), Chris Christie (Molly Kearney), Vivek Ramaswamy (Ego Nwodim), Tim Scott (Devon Walker), Ron DeSantis (John Higgins), and moderator Lester Holt (Kenan Thompson).
- Boygenius performs "Not Strong Enough" and "Satanist."
- Cameo by Alec Baldwin.
- Please Don't Destroy: "Jumper."

**Airdate:** 11/18/23
**Episode:** 49.5
**Host:** Jason Momoa
**Musical Guest:** Tate McRae
**Musical and Guest Performances/Cameo(s)/ Program Notes:**
- "Live from New York": President Joe Biden (Mikey Day) and Tian Tian, the panda leaving the National Zoo to live on a panda preserve in China.
- McRae performs "Greedy" and "Grave."
- Cameo by Alec Baldwin.
- Please Don't Destroy: "Ramen Order."

**Airdate:** 12/2/23
**Episode:** 49.6
**Musical Guest:** Noah Kahan
**Musical and Guest Performances/Cameo(s)/ Program Notes:**
- "Live from New York": *The Situation Room* with Wolf Blitzer (Sarah Sherman) and Congressman George Santos (Bowen Yang), who was expelled from the House of Representatives on December 1, 2023.
- Kahan performs "Dial Drunk" and "Stick Season."

- Cameos by Candice Bergen and Tina Fey, who induct Emma Stone into the Five-Timers Club.
- Please Don't Destroy: "AI."

**Airdate:** 12/9/23
**Episode:** 49.7
**Host:** Adam Driver
**Musical Guest:** Olivia Rodrigo
**Musical and Guest Performances/Cameo(s)/ Program Notes:**
- "Live from New York": Congressional hearing on anti-Semitism with congresswomen Elise Stefanik (Chloe Troast) and Virginia Foxx (Molly Kearney).
- Rodrigo performs "vampire" and "all-american bitch."
- Cameo by Julia Stiles.
- In Memoriam: Norman Lear (1922–2023).

**Airdate:** 12/16/2023
**Episode:** 49.8
**Host:** Kate McKinnon
**Musical Guest:** Billie Eilish
**Musical and Guest Performances/Cameo(s)/ Program Notes:**
- "Live from New York": Ninety-Fifth Annual Christmas Awards hosted by Tina Cabrini (Heidi Gardner) and John Parker-Lee (Bowen Yang).
- Eilish and Finneas perform "What Was I Made For?" and "Have Yourself a Merry Little Christmas."
- Cameos by Greta Gerwig, Paula Pell, Maya Rudolph, Daphne Skeeter, and Kristen Wiig.
- Music Video: "Tampon Farm."

**Airdate:** 1/20/24
**Episode:** 49.9
**Host:** Jacob Elordi
**Musical Guest:** Reneé Rapp
**Musical and Guest Performances/Cameo(s)/ Program Notes:**
- "Live from New York": Donald Trump (James Austin Johnson) addresses

Episode Guide

America from the U.S. District Courthouse, Lower Manhattan.
- Reneé Rapp performs "Snow Angel" and "Not My Fault" (with Megan Thee Stallion).
- Cameo by Rachel McAdams.

**Airdate:** 1/27/24
**Episode:** 49.10
**Host:** Dakota Johnson
**Musical Guest:** Justin Timberlake
**Musical and Guest Performances/Cameo(s)/ Program Notes:**
- "Live from New York": The NFL on CBS: Sportscasters upset about the end of the football season.
- Timberlake performs "Sanctified" and "Selfish."
- Cameos by Dave Chappelle, Barbara Corcoran, Mark Cuban, and Jimmy Fallon.
- Please Don't Destroy: "Roast."

**Airdate:** 2/3/24
**Episode:** 49.11
**Host:** Ayo Edebiri
**Musical Guest:** Jennifer Lopez
**Musical and Guest Performances/Cameo(s)/ Program Notes:**
- "Live from New York": Trump town hall with Donald Trump (James Austin Johnson) and Nikki Haley (in a cameo).
- Lopez performs "Can't Get Enough" with Latto and Redman and "This Is Me . . . Now."
- Music Video: "Dune Popcorn Bucket."

**Airdate:** 2/24/24
**Episode:** 49.12
**Host:** Shane Gillis
**Musical Guest:** 21 Savage
**Musical and Guest Performances/Cameo(s)/ Program Notes:**
- "Live from New York": Trump victory party with James Risch (Mikey Day), Marco Rubio (Marcello Hernández), Lindsey Graham (James Austin Johnson), and Tim Scott (Devon Walker).

- 21 Savage performs "Redrum" and "Should've Wore a Bonner" (with Brent Faiyaz and Summer Walker).
- Host Gillis was hired as a cast member in 2019 but was fired five days later when a podcast in which he used ethnic slurs surfaced.

**Airdate:** 3/2/24
**Episode:** 49.13
**Host:** Sydney Sweeney
**Musical Guest:** Kacey Musgraves
**Musical and Guest Performances/Cameo(s)/ Program Notes:**
- "Live from New York": *Inside Politics* with Dana Bash (Heidi Gardner).
- Musgraves performs "Deeper Well" and "Too Good to Be True."
- Cameos by Glen Powell and Gina Gershon.
- Please Don't Destroy: "Gone Too Soon."

**Airdate:** 3/9/24
**Episode:** 49.14
**Host:** Josh Brolin
**Musical Guest:** Ariana Grande
**Musical and Guest Performances/Cameo(s)/ Program Notes:**
- "Live from New York": State of the Union with President Joe Biden (Mikey Day) and the GOP response delivered by Congresswoman Katie Britt (Scarlett Johansson in a cameo).
- Grande performs "we can't be friends (wait for your love)" and "imperfect for you."
- Music Video: "Airplane Song."

**Airdate:** 3/30/24
**Episode:** 49.15
**Host:** Ramy Youssef
**Musical Guest:** Travis Scott
**Musical and Guest Performances/Cameo(s)/ Program Notes:**
- "Live from New York": Donald Trump celebrates Easter by selling Bibles.
- Scott performs "MY EYES" and "FE!N" (with Playboi Carti).

## Appendix A

- Please Don't Destroy: "We Got Too High."

**Airdate:** 4/6/24
**Episode:** 49.16
**Host:** Kristen Wiig
**Musical Guest:** RAYE
**Musical and Guest Performances/Cameo(s)/ Program Notes:**
- "Live from New York": March Madness postgame.
- RAYE performs "Escapism" and "Worth It."
- Wiig is inducted into the Five-Timers Club.
- Cameos by Fred Armisen, Matt Damon, Will Forte, Ryan Gosling, Jon Hamm, Paula Pell, Paul Rudd, Martin Short, and Kaia Gerber.

**Airdate:** 4/13/24
**Episode:** 49.17
**Host:** Ryan Gosling
**Musical Guest:** Chris Stapleton
**Musical and Guest Performances/Cameo(s)/ Program Notes:**
- "Live from New York": "Close Encounter" with abductees Colleen Rafferty (Kate McKinnon, in a cameo) and Todd (Ryan Gosling).
- Stapleton performs "White Horse" and "Mountains of My Mind."
- Music Video: "Get That Boy Back."
- Cameo by Emily Blunt.

**Airdate:** 5/4/24
**Episode:** 49.18
**Host:** Dua Lipa
**Musical Guest:** Dua Lipa
**Musical and Guest Performances/Cameo(s)/ Program Notes:**
- "Live from New York": *Community Affairs* with host Ryan Abernathy (Michael Longfellow), who interviews parents of college students about the current protests happening on campus.
- Lipa performs "Illusion" and "Happy for You."
- Cameos by Jerry Seinfeld and Troye Sivan.

**Airdate:** 5/11/24
**Episode:** 49.19
**Host:** Maya Rudolph
**Musical Guest:** Vampire Weekend
**Musical and Guest Performances/Cameo(s)/ Program Notes:**
- "Live from New York": Cast members and their moms celebrate Mother's Day.
- Vampire Weekend performs "Gen-X Cops" and "Capricorn."

**Airdate:** 5/18/24
**Episode:** 49.20
**Host:** Jake Gyllenhaal
**Musical Guest:** Sabrina Carpenter
**Musical and Guest Performances/Cameo(s)/ Program Notes:**
- "Live from New York": Donald Trump holds a press conference outside of the courthouse and introduces some of his supporters, including Tim Scott (Devon Walker), Governor Kristi Noem (Heidi Gardner), and Hannibal Lecter (Michael Longfellow).
- Carpenter performs "Espresso" and, in her second set, "Feather" and "Nonsense."
- In Memoriam: Dabney Coleman (1932–2024).

# Appendix B
# Awards

## Directors Guild of America, USA

### 2024
*Outstanding Directorial Achievement in Variety/Talk/News/Sports—Regularly Scheduled Programming*
Michael Mancini and Liz Patrick
For episode: Pedro Pascal/Coldplay (48.12)

### 2023
*Outstanding Directorial Achievement in Variety/Talk/News/Sports—Regularly Scheduled Programming*
Liz Patrick, director
For episode: Jack Harlow (48.4)

### 2022
*Outstanding Directorial Achievement in Variety/Talk/News/Sports—Regularly Scheduled Programming*
Don Roy King, director; Michael Mancini, associate director; Michael Poole, associate director; Laura Ouziel-Mack, associate director; Gena Rositano, stage manager; Chris Kelly, stage manager; Eddie Valk, stage manager
For episode: Keegan-Michael Key/Olivia Rodrigo (46.19)

### 2021
*Outstanding Directorial Achievement in Variety/Talk/News/Sports—Regularly Scheduled Programming*
Don Roy King, director; Michael Mancini, associate director; Michael Poole, associate director; Laura Ouziel-Mack, associate director; Gena Rositano, stage manager; Chris Kelly, stage manager; Eddie Valk, stage manager
For episode: Dave Chappelle/Foo Fighters (46.6)

## 2020
*Outstanding Directorial Achievement in Variety/Talk/News/Sports—Regularly Scheduled Programming*
Don Roy King, director; Michael Mancini, associate director; Michael Poole, associate director; Laura Ouziel-Mack, associate director; Gena Rositano, stage manager; Chris Kelly, stage manager
For episode: Eddie Murphy/Lizzo (45.10)

## 2019
*Outstanding Directorial Achievement in Variety/Talk/News/Sports—Regularly Scheduled Programming*
Don Roy King, director; Michael Mancini, associate director; Michael Poole, associate director; Rob Caminiti, associate director; Gena Rositano, stage manager; Chris Kelly, stage manager
For episode: Adam Driver/Kanye West (44.1)

## 2018
*Outstanding Directorial Achievement in Variety/Talk/News/Sports—Regularly Scheduled Programming*
Don Roy King, director; Michael Mancini, associate director; Michael Poole, associate director; Robert Caminiti, associate director; Gena Rositano, stage manager; Chris Kelly, stage manager
For episode: Jimmy Fallon/Harry Styles (42.18)

## 2017
*Outstanding Directorial Achievement in Variety/Talk/News/Sports—Regularly Scheduled Programming*
Don Roy King, director; Michael Mancini, associate director; Michael Poole, associate director; Robert Caminiti, associate director; Gena Rositano, stage manager; Chris Kelly, stage manager
For episode: Dave Chappelle/A Tribe Called West (42.6)

*Outstanding Directorial Achievement in Variety/Talk/News/Sports - Specials*
Saturday Night Live: 40th Anniversary Special
Don Roy King, director; Michael Mancini, associate director; Michael Poole, associate director; Robert Caminiti, associate director; Dan Dome, associate director; Gena Rositano, stage manager; Chris Kelly, stage manager; Joey Despenzero, stage manager; Lynn Finkel, stage manager; Eddie Falk, stage manager

## 2014
*Outstanding Directorial Achievement in Variety/Talk/News/Sports—Regularly Scheduled Programming*
Don Roy King, director; Michael Mancini, associate director; Michael Poole, associate director; Matt Yonks, associate director; Robert Caminiti, associate director; Gena Rositano, stage manager; Chris Kelly, stage manager
For episode: Justin Timberlake (38.16)

## 2001
*Outstanding Directorial Achievement in Musical/Variety*
Beth McCarthy-Miller, director; Stefani Cohen, associate director; Robert Caminiti, associate director; Mark Jankeloff, associate director; Gena Rositano, stage manager; Chris Kelly, stage manager
For episode: Val Kilmer/U2 (26.7)

# Primetime Emmy Awards
Presented by the Academy of Television Arts and Sciences.

## 2023
*Outstanding Directing for a Variety Series*
Liz Patrick
For episode: Steve Martin and Martin Short (48.8)

*Outstanding Production Design for a Variety or Reality Series*
Akira Yoshimura, Keith Raywood, Danielle Webb, and Andrea Purcigliotti
For episodes: Steve Martin and Martin Short (48.8) and Jenna Ortega (48.15)

## 2022
*Outstanding Variety Sketch Series*
Lorne Michaels, executive producer; Erik Kenward, producer; Steve Higgins, producer; Caroline Maroney, producer; Tom Broecker, producer; Erin Doyle, producer; Lindsay Shookus, producer; Javier Winnik, supervising producer

## 2021
*Outstanding Guest Actor in a Comedy Series*
Dave Chappelle, host
For episode: Dave Chappelle/Foo Fighters (46.6)

*Outstanding Guest Actress in a Comedy Series*
Maya Rudolph, host
For episode: Maya Rudolph/Jack Harlow (46.15)

*Outstanding Production Design for a Variety, Reality, or Competition Series*
Eugene Lee, production designer; Akira Yoshimura, production designer; Keith Raywood, production designer; Joe DeTullio, production designer; Melissa Shakun, art director
For episode: Kristen Wiig/Dua Lipa (46.9)

*Outstanding Directing for a Variety Series*
Don Roy King
For episode: Dave Chappelle/Foo Fighters (46.6)

*Outstanding Variety Sketch Series*
Lorne Michaels, executive producer; Ken Aymong, supervising producer; Erik Kenward, producer; Steve Higgins, producer; Caroline Maroney, producer; Tom Broecker, producer; Erin Doyle, producer; Lindsay Shookus, producer

*Outstanding Contemporary Hairstyling for a Variety, Nonfiction, or Reality Programming*
Jodi Mancuso, department head hairstylist; Cara Hannah, key hairstylist; Inga Thrasher, hairstylist; Joseph Whitmeyer, hairstylist; Amanda Duffy Evans, hairstylist; Gina Ferrucci, hairstylist
For episode: Maya Rudolph/Jack Harlow (46.15)

*Outstanding Contemporary Makeup for a Variety, Nonfiction, or Reality Program (Non-Prosthetic)*
Louie Zakarian, department head makeup artist; Amy Tagliamonti, key makeup artist; Christopher Milone, makeup artist; Jason Milani, key makeup artist; Kim Weber, makeup artist; Joanna Pisani, key makeup artist; Young Bek, key makeup artist
For episode: Elon Musk/Miley Cyrus (46.18)

*Outstanding Lighting Design/Lighting Direction for a Variety Series*
Geoff Amoral, lighting director; Rick McGuinness, lighting director; William McGuinness, lighting director; Trevor Brown, lighting director; Tim Stasse, lighting director
For episode: Adele/H.E.R. (46.4)

## 2020

*Outstanding Guest Actor in a Comedy Series*
Eddie Murphy
For episode: Eddie Murphy/Lizzo (45.10)

*Outstanding Variety Sketch Series*
Lorne Michaels, executive producer; Ken Aymong, supervising producer; Lindsay Shookus, producer; Erin Doyle, producer; Tom Broecker, producer; Steve Higgins, producer; Erik Kenward, producer

*Outstanding Guest Actress in a Comedy Series*
Maya Rudolph
For playing: "Senator Kamala Harris"
For episode: Eddie Murphy/Lizzo (45.10)

*Outstanding Directing for a Variety Series*
Don Roy King, director
For episode: Eddie Murphy/Lizzo (45.10)

*Outstanding Production Design for a Variety, Reality, or Competition Series*
Eugene Lee, production designer; Akira Yoshimura, production designer; Keith Raywood, production designer; Joe DeTullio, production designer
For episodes: Eddie Murphy/Lizzo (45.10) and John Mulaney/David Byrne (45.14)

*Outstanding Lighting Design/Lighting Direction for a Variety Series*
Geoff Amoral, lighting director; Rick McGuinness, lighting director; William McGuinness, lighting director; Trevor Brown, lighting director; Tim Stasse, lighting director
For episode: John Mulaney/David Byrne (45.14)

## 2019

*Outstanding Variety Sketch Series*
Lorne Michaels, executive producer; Ken Aymong, supervising producer; Lindsay Shookus, producer; Erin Doyle, producer; Tom Broecker, producer; Steve Higgins, producer; Erik Kenward, producer

*Outstanding Directing for a Variety Series*
Don Roy King
For episode: Adam Sandler/Shawn Mendes (44.19)

*Outstanding Lighting Design/Lighting Direction for a Variety Series*
Geoff Amoral, lighting director; Rick McGuinness, lighting director; William McGuinness, lighting director; Trevor Brown, lighting director; Tim Stasse, lighting director
For episode: John Mulaney/Jack White (43.18)

*Outstanding Makeup for a Multi-Camera Series or Special (Non-Prosthetic)*
Louie Zakarian, department head makeup artist; Amy Tagliamonti, key makeup artist; Jason Milani, key makeup artist; Rachel Pagani, additional makeup artist; Sarah Egan, makeup artists; Young Bek, makeup artist
For episode: Adam Sandler/Shawn Mendes (44.19)

*Outstanding Production Design for a Variety, Reality, or Competition Series*
Eugene Lee, production designer; Akira Yoshimura, production designer; Keith Raywood, production designer; Joe DeTullio, production designer
For episodes: John Mulaney/Jack White (43.18) and Emma Stone/BTS (44.13)

*Outstanding Short-Form Nonfiction or Reality Series*
*Creating* Saturday Night Live
Lorne Michaels, executive producer; Oz Rodriguez, co–executive producer; Chris Voss, co–executive producer; Matt Yonks, co–executive producer; Michael Scogin, supervising producer; Erin Doyle, producer

## 2018

*Outstanding Directing for a Variety Series*
Don Roy King, director
For episode: Donald Glover/Childish Gambino (43.19)

*Outstanding Guest Actress in a Comedy Series*
Tiffany Haddish
For episode: Tiffany Haddish/Taylor Swift (43.5)

Appendix B

*Outstanding Variety Sketch Series*
Lorne Michaels, executive producer; Ken Aymong, supervising producer; Lindsay Shookus, producer; Erin Doyle, producer; Tom Broecker, producer; Steve Higgins, producer; Erik Kenward, producer

*Outstanding Original Music and Lyrics*
"Come Back, Barack"
Chris Redd, lyrics; Kenan Thompson, lyrics; Will Stephen, lyrics; Eli Brueggemann, music
For episode: Chance the Rapper/Eminem (43.6)

*Outstanding Production Design for Variety, Nonfiction, Reality, or Reality-Competition Series*
Eugene Lee, production designer; Akira Yoshimura, production designer; Keith Raywood, production designer; Joe DeTullio, production designer
For episode: Bill Hader/Arcade Fire (43.16)

*Outstanding Lighting Design/Lighting Direction for a Variety Series*
Phil Hymes, lighting designer; Geoff Amoral, lighting designer; Rick McGuinness, lighting director
For episode: Kevin Hart/Foo Fighters (43.9)

*Outstanding Makeup for a Multi-Camera Series or Special (Non-Prosthetic)*
Louie Zakarian, department head makeup artists; Amy Tagliamonti, key makeup artist; Jason Milani, key makeup artist; Rachel Pagani, makeup artist; Sarah Egan, makeup artist; Daniela Zivkovic, makeup artist
For episode: Tina Fey/Nicki Minaj (43.21)

*Outstanding Technical Direction, Camerawork, Video Control for a Series*
Steven Cimino, technical director; Susan Noll, video control; Frank Grisanti, video control; John Pinto, camera; Paul Cangialosi, camera; Len Wechsler, camera; Dave Driscoll, camera; Eric Eisenstein, camera; Joseph DeBonis, camera
For episode: Donald Glover/Childish Gambino (43.19)

## 2017

*Outstanding Supporting Actor in a Comedy Series*
Alec Baldwin
For playing "Donald Trump"

*Outstanding Supporting Actress in a Comedy*
Kate McKinnon

*Outstanding Directing for a Variety Series*
Don Roy King, director
For episode: Jimmy Fallon/Harry Styles (42.18)

*Outstanding Guest Actress in a Comedy Series*
Melissa McCarthy
For episode: Melissa McCarthy/HAIM (42.20)

# Awards

*Outstanding Guest Actor in a Comedy Series*
Dave Chappelle
For episode: Dave Chappelle/A Tribe Called Quest (42.6)

*Outstanding Makeup for a Multi-Camera Series or Special (Non-Prosthetic)*
Louie Zakarian, department head makeup artists; Amy Tagliamonti, key makeup artist; Jason Milani, key makeup artist; Rachel Pagani, makeup artist; Andrew Sotomayor, makeup artists; Daniela Zivkovic, makeup artist
For episode: Alec Baldwin/Ed Sheeran (42.14)

*Outstanding Production Design for Variety, Nonfiction, Reality or Reality-Competition Programming*
Eugene Lee, production designer; Akira Yoshimura, production designer; Keith Raywood, production desiger; Joe DeTullio, production designer.
For episode: Alec Baldwin/Ed Sheeran (42.14)

*Outstanding Variety Sketch Series*
Lorne Michaels, executive producer; Ken Aymong, supervising producer; Lindsay Shookus, producer; Erin Doyle, producer; Tom Broecker, producer; Steve Higgins, producer; Erik Kenward, producer

*Outstanding Technical Direction, Camerawork, Video Control for a Series*
Steven Cimino, technical director; John Pinto, camera; Paul Cangialosi, camera; Len Wechsler, camera; Eric Eisenstein, camera; Dave Driscoll, camera; Susan Noll, video control; Frank Grisanti, video control; Jeff Latonero, camera; Ann Bergstrom, camera, Randy Brittle, camera
For episode: Jimmy Fallon/Harry Styles (42.18)

## 2016

*Outstanding Supporting Actress in a Comedy Series*
Kate McKinnon

*Outstanding Guest Actress in a Comedy Series*
Tina Fey and Amy Poehler
For episode: Tina Fey and Amy Poehler/Bruce Springsteen and the E Street Band (41.9)

*Outstanding Hairstyling for a Multi-Camera Series or Special*
Bettie O. Rogers, department head hairstylist; Jodi Mancuso, key hairstylist; Inga Thrasher, hairstylist; Jennifer Serio, hairstylist; Cara Hannah, hairstylist; Joseph Whitmeyer, hairstylist
For episode: Fred Armisen/Courtney Barnett (41.21)

## 2015

*Outstanding Hairstyling*
Bettie O. Rogers, department head hairstylist; Jodi Mancuso, key hairstylist; Inga Thrasher, hairstylist; Jennifer Serio, hairstylist; Cara Hannah, hairstylist; Joseph Whitmeyer, hairstylist
For episode: Martin Freeman/Charli XCX (40.9)

Appendix B

*Outstanding Technical Direction, Camerawork, Video Control for a Series*
Steven Cimino, technical director; Paul Cangialosi, camera; Mike Cimino, camera; Carl Eckett, camera; Eric Eisenstein, camera; John Pinto, camera; Len Wechsler, camera; Frank Grisanti, video control; Susan Noll, video control
For episode: Taraji P. Henson/Mumford & Sons (40.18)

*Outstanding Directing for a Variety Special*
*Saturday Night Live 40th Anniversary Special*
Don Roy King

*Outstanding Sound Mixing for a Variety Series or Special*
*Saturday Night Live 40th Anniversary Special*
Robert Palladino (production sound mixer), Bill Taylor (production sound mixer), Marty Brumbach (production sound mixer), Ezra Matychak (production sound mixer), Robert Selitto (foh mixer), Chris Costello (monitor mixer), Devin Emke (film audio mixer), Josiah Gluck (music mixer), Bob Clearmountain (music mixer)

*Outstanding Variety Special*
*Saturday Night Live 40th Anniversary Special*
Lorne Michaels (executive producer), Ken Aymong (supervising producer), Lindsay Shookus (producer), Erin Doyle (producer), Rhys Thomas (producer), Steve Higgins (produced by), Erik Kenward (produced by)

*Outstanding Makeup for a Multi-Camera Series or Special (Non-Prosthetic)*
*Saturday Night Live 40th Anniversary Special*
Louie Zakarian (department head makeup artist), Amy Tagliamonti (makeup artist), Jason Milani (makeup artist), Sarah Egan (makeup artist), Daniela Zivkovic (makeup artist), Melanie Demetri (makeup artist)

## 2014

*Outstanding Costumes for a Variety Program or Special*
Tom Broecker, costume designer; Eric Justian, costume designer
For episode: Jimmy Fallon/Justin Timberlake (39.10)

*Outstanding Directing for a Variety Series*
Don Roy King, director
For episode: Jimmy Fallon/Justin Timberlake (39.10).

*Outstanding Guest Actor in a Comedy Series*
Jimmy Fallon, host (39.10)

*Outstanding Hairstyling for a Multi-Camera Series or Special*
Bettie O. Rogers, department head hairstylist; Jodi Mancuso, key hairstylist; Inga Thrasher, hairstylist; Jennifer Serio, hairstylist; Cara Hannah, hairstylist; Joseph Whitmeyer, hairstylist
For episode: Anna Kendrick/Pharrell Williams (39.17)

Awards 585

*Outstanding Makeup for a Multi-Camera Series or Special (Non-Prosthetic)*
Louie Zakarian, department head makeup artist; Amy Tagliamonti, additional makeup artist; Sarah Egan, additional makeup artist; Daniela Zivkovic, additional makeup artist; Melanie Demetri, additional makeup artist
For episode: Jimmy Fallon/Justin Timberlake (39.10)

## 2013

*Outstanding Art Direction for Variety and Nonfiction Programming*
[tied with London 2012 Olympic Opening Ceremony]
Eugene Lee, production designer; Akira Yoshimura, production designer; Keith Raywood, production designer
For episodes: Justin Timberlake (38.16) and Ben Affleck/Kanye West (38.21)

*Outstanding Directing for a Variety Series*
Don Roy King, director
For episode: Justin Timberlake (38.16)

*Outstanding Hairstyling for a Multi-Camera Series or Special*
Bettie O. Rogers, department head hairstylist; Jodi Mancuso, key hairstylist; Inga Thrasher, key hairstylist; Jennifer Serio, hairstylist; Cara Hannah, hairstylist
For episode: Jennifer Lawrence/The Lumineers (38.11)

*Outstanding Makeup for a Multi-Camera Series or Special (Non-Prosthetic)*
Louie Zakarian, department head makeup artist; Josh Turi, makeup artist; Amy Tagliamonti makeup artist; Daniela Zivkovic, additional makeup artist; Melanie Demetri, additional makeup artist
For episode: Justin Timberlake (38.16)

## 2012

*Outstanding Director for a Variety Series*
Don Roy King, director
For episode hosted by Mick Jagger (37.22)

*Outstanding Guest Actor in a Comedy Series*
Jimmy Fallon, host (37.10)

*Outstanding Hairstyling for a Multi-Camera Series or Special*
Bettie O. Rogers, department head hairstylist; Jodi Mancuso, key hairstylist; Inga Thrasher, hairstylist; Jennifer Stauffer, hairstylist; Cara Hannah Sullivan, hairstylist; Christal Schanes, hairstylist
For episode hosted by Zooey Deschanel (37.14)

*Outstanding Technical Direction, Camerawork, Video Control for a Series*
Steven Cimino, technical director; John Pinto, camera; Paul Cangialosi, camera
For episode hosted by Mick Jagger (37.22)

## 2011
*Outstanding Directing for a Variety, Music or Comedy Series*
Don Roy King
For episode hosted by Justin Timberlake (36.22)

*Outstanding Guest Actor in a Comedy Series*
Justin Timberlake (36.22)

*Outstanding Makeup for a Multi-Camera Series or a Special (Non-Prosthetic)*
Louie Zakarian, department head makeup artist; Josh Turi, additional makeup artist; Amy Tagliamonti, additional makeup artist; Katherine O'Donnell, additional makeup artist
For episode hosted by Jon Hamm (36.5)

*Outstanding Original Music and Lyrics*
"Justin Timberlake Monologue"
Katreese Barnes (music), Justin Timberlake (lyrics), John Mulaney (lyrics), and Seth Meyers (lyrics)

## 2010
*Outstanding Direction for a Variety, Music or Comedy Series*
Don Roy King
For episode hosted by Betty White (35.21)

*Outstanding Guest Actress in a Comedy Series*
Betty White, host (35.21)

*Outstanding Makeup for a Multi-Camera Series or Special (Non-prosthetic)*
Louie Zakarian, department head makeup artist; Josh Turi, makeup artist; Amy Tagliamonti, makeup artist
For episode hosted by Betty White (35.21)

## 2009
*Outstanding Guest Actor in a Comedy Series*
Justin Timberlake (34.21)

*Outstanding Guest Actress in a Comedy Series*
Tina Fey, *SNL Presidential Bash 2008*

## 2008
*Outstanding Hairstyling for a Multi-Camera Series or a Special*
Bettie O. Rogers, department head hairstylist; AnneMichelle Radcliffe, key hairstylist; Jodi Mancuso, additional hairstylist
For episode hosted by Tina Fey (33.5)

## 2007
*Outstanding Original Music and Lyrics*
"Dick in a Box"
Justin Timberlake (music/lyrics), Jorma Taccone (music/lyrics), Katreese Barnes (music), Asa Taccone (music), Akiva Schaffer (lyrics), Andy Samberg (lyrics)

*Outstanding Technical Direction, Camerawork, Video for a Series*
Steven Cimino, technical director; Johnny Pinto, camera; Richard B. Fox, camera; Brian Phraner, camera; Barry Frisher, camera; Eric Eisenstein, camera; Susan Noll, senior video; Frank Grisanti, senior video
For episode hosted by Alec Baldwin (32.5)

## 2006
*Outstanding Directing for a Variety, Music or Comedy Program*
Beth McCarthy-Miller, director
For episode hosted by Steve Martin (31.12)

*Outstanding Technical Direction, Camerawork, Video for a Series*
Steven Cimino, technical director; Johnny Pinto, camera operator; Richard B. Fox, camera operator; Brian Phraner, camera operator; Michael Bennett, camera operator; Eric Eisenstein, camera operator; John Rosenblatt, camera operator; Eugene Huelsman, camera operator; Susan Noll, senior video control; Frank Grisanti, senior video control
For episode hosted by Jack Black (31.9)

## 2004
*Outstanding Technical Direction, Camerawork, Video for a Series*
Steven Cimino, technical director; Johnny Pinto, camera; Richard B. Fox, camera; Brian Phraner, camera; Michael Bennett, camera; Eric Eisenstein, camera; Susan Noll, camera; Frank Grisanti, senior video control
For episode hosted by Janet Jackson (29.17)

## 2003
*Outstanding Technical Direction, Camerawork, Video for a Series*
Steven Cimino, technical director; Johnny Pinto, camera; Richard B. Fox, camera; Brian Phraner, camera; Michael Bennett, camera; James Mott, camera; Susan Noll, senior video control; Frank Grisanti, senior video control
For episode hosted by Christopher Walken (28.13)

## 2002
*Outstanding Technical Direction, Camerawork, Video for a Series*
Steven Cimino, technical director; Jan Kasoff, camera operator; Michael Bennett, camera operator; Richard B. Fox, camera operator; Carl Eckett, camera

Appendix B

operator; Johnny Pinto, camera operator; Susan Noll, senior video control; Frank Grisanti, senior video control
For episode hosted by Britney Spears (27.12)

*Outstanding Writing for a Variety, Music or Comedy Program*
Tina Fey, head writer; Dennis McNicholas, head writer; writers: Doug Abeles, James Anderson, Max Brooks, James Downey, Hugh Fink, Charlie Grandy, Jack Handey, Steve Higgins, Erik Kenward, Lorne Michaels, Matt Murray, Paula Pell, Matt Piedmont, Ken Scarborough, Michael Schur, Frank Sebastiano, T. Sean Shannon, Robert Smigel, Emily Spivey, Andrew Steele, Scott Wainio

## 2000

*Outstanding Hairstyling for a Series*
Bobby Grayson
For episode hosted by Alan Cumming (25.11)

*Outstanding Technical Direction, Camerawork, Video for a Series*
(Tied with *Politically Incorrect*)
Steven Cimino, technical director; Carl Eckett, camera operator; Jan Kasoff, camera operator; Johnny Pinto, camera operator; Michael Bennett, camera operator; Richard B. Fox, camera operator; Susan Noll, video control; Frank Grisanti, video control
For episode hosted by Christopher Walken (25.16)

*Outstanding Variety, Music or Comedy Special*
*Saturday Night Live 25*
Lorne Michaels, executive producer; Ken Aymong, supervising producer; Marci Klein, producer; Michael Shoemaker, producer

## 1995

*Outstanding Technical Direction, Camerawork, Video for a Series*
Steven Cimino, technical director; Michael Bennett, electronic camera operator; Carl Eckett, electronic camera operator; Jan Kasoff, electronic camera operator; Johnny Pinto, electronic camera operator; Robert Reese, electronic camera operator; Gregory Aull, senior video control; William Vaccaro, senior video control

## 1994

*Outstanding Technical Direction, Camerawork, Video for a Series*
Steven Cimino, technical director; Jan Kasoff, camera; Michael Bennett, camera; Carl Eckett, camera; Johnny Pinto, camera; Robert Reese, camera; William Vaccaro, video control
For episode hosted by Alec Baldwin and Kim Basinger (19.13)

Awards 589

## 1993
*Outstanding Individual Performance in a Variety or Music Program*
Dana Carvey
For Saturday Night Live's *Presidential Bash.*

*Outstanding Variety, Music or Comedy Series*
Lorne Michaels, executive producer; James Downey, producer; Al Franken, producer

## 1990
*Outstanding Technical Direction, Camera, Video for a Series*
Terry Rohnke, technical director; Steve Jambeck, camera operator; Joe De Bonis, camera operator; Jan Kasoff, camera operator; Johnny Pinto, camera operator; Robert Reese, camera operator; Bruce Shapiro, senior video control
For episode hosted by Christopher Walken (15.11)

## 1989
*Outstanding Writing in a Variety or Music Program*
James Downey, head writer; writers: John Bowman, A. Whitney Brown, Greg Daniels, Too Davis, Al Franken, Shannon Gaughan, Jack Handey, Phil Hartman, Lorne Michaels, Mike Myers, Conan O'Brien, Bob Odenkirk, Herbert Sargent, Tom Schiller, Robert Smigel, Bonnie Turner, Terry Turner, Christine Zander; George Meyer (additional sketches)

## 1985
*Outstanding Graphic and Title Design*
Alex Weil, title sequence creator; Charles Levi, title sequence creator

## 1983
*Outstanding Technical Direction and Electronic Camerawork for a Series*
Heino Ripp, technical director; Michael Bennett, cameraperson, Al Camoin, cameraperson; Jan Kasoff, cameraperson; Johnny Pinto, cameraperson; Maury Verschoore, cameraperson
For episode hosted by Sid Caesar (8.12)

## 1978
*Outstanding Continuing or Single Performance by a Supporting Actress in Variety or Music*
Gilda Radner

## 1977
*Outstanding Writing in a Comedy-Variety or Music Series*
Dan Aykroyd, Al Franken, Tom Davis, James Downey, Lorne Michaels, Marilyn Suzanne Miller, Michael O'Donoghue, Herbert Sargent, Tom Schiller, Rosie Shuster, Alan Zweibel, John Belushi, Bill Murray
For episode hosted by Sissy Spacek (2.15)

## 1976

*Outstanding Comedy-Variety or Music Series*
Lorne Michaels, producer

*Outstanding Continuing or Single Performance by a Supporting Actor in Variety or Music*
Chevy Chase
For episode hosted by Buck Henry (1.10)

*Outstanding Directing in a Comedy-Variety or Music Series*
Dave Wilson
For episode hosted by Paul Simon (1.2)

*Outstanding Writing in a Comedy-Variety or Music Series*
Anne Beatts, Chevy Chase, Al Franken, Tom Davis, Lorne Michaels, Marilyn Suzanne Miller, Michael O'Donoghue, Herbert Sargent, Tom Schiller, Rosie Shuster, Alan Zweibel
For episode hosted by Elliott Gould (1.9)

## Writers Guild of America

### 2018

*Comedy/Variety Sketch Series*
Chris Kelly, Sarah Schneider, Bryan H. Tucker, James Anderson, Kristen Bartlett, Jeremy Beiler, Neal Brennan, Zack Bornstein, Joanna Bradley, Megan Callahan-Shah, Michael Che, Anna Drezen, Fran Gillespie, Sudi Green, Steve Higgins, Colin Jost, Erik Kenward, Rob Klein, Nick Kocher, Michael Koman, Dave McCary, Brian McElhaney, Dennis McNicholas, Drew Michael, Lorne Michaels, Josh Patten, Katie Rich, Pete Schultz, Streeter Seidell, Will Stephen, Kent Sublette, and Julio Torres

### 2017

*Comedy/Variety Sketch Series*
Rob Klein, Bryan H. Tucker, James Anderson, Fred Armisen, Jeremy Beiler, Chris Belair, Megan Callahan-Shah, Michael Che, Mikey Day, James Downey, Tina Fey, Fran Gillespie, Sudi Green, Tom Herlihy, Steve Higgins, Colin Jost, Zach Kanin, Chris Kelly, Erik Kenward, Paul Masella, Dave McCary, Dennis McNicholas, Seth Meyers, Lorne Michaels, Josh Patten, Paula Pell, Katie Rich, Tim Robinson, Sarah Schneider, Pete Schultz, Streeter Seidell, Dave Sirus, Emily Spivey, Harper Steele, Will Stephen, and Kent Sublette

## 2010
*Comedy/Variety (including Talk) Series*
Seth Meyers, head writer; writers: Doug Abeles, James Anderson, Alex Baze, Jessica Conrad, James Downey, Steve Higgins, Colin Jost, Erik Kenward, Rob Klein, John Lutz, Lorne Michaels, John Mulaney, Paula Pell, Simon Rich, Marika Sawyer, Akiva Schaffer, John Solomon, Emily Spivey, Kent Sublette, Jorma Taccone, Bryan H. Tucker; Adam McKay, additional sketch; Andrew Steele, additional sketch
Tied with *The Daily Show with Jon Stewart.*

## 2009
*Comedy/Variety (including Talk) Series*
Seth Meyers, head writer/writer; Andrew Steele, head writer/writer; Paula Pell, head writer; Doug Abeles, James Anderson, Alex Baze, Jessica Conrad, James Downey, Charlie Grandy, Steve Higgins, Colin Jost, Erik Kenward, Rob Klein, John Lutz, Lorne Michaels, John Mulaney, Paula Pell, Simon Rich, Marika Sawyer, Akiva Schaffer, Robert Smigel, John Solomon, Emily Spivey, Kent Sublette, Jorma Taccone, Bryan H. Tucker; Robert Carlock, additional sketches

## 2007
*Comedy/Variety (including Talk) Series*
Tina Fey, head writer; Seth Meyers, head writer; Andrew Steele, head writer; writers: Doug Abeles, James Anderson, Alex Baze, Liz Cackowski, Charlie Grandy, Steve Higgins, Colin Jost, Erik Kenward, John Lutz, Lorne Michaels, Matt Murray, Paula Pell, Akiva Schaffer, Frank Sebastiano, T. Sean Shannon, Robert Smigel, J. B. Smoove, Emily Spivey, Jorma Taccone, Bryan H. Tucker; Michael Schwartz, additional sketches; Kristin Gore, additional sketches

## 2001
*Comedy/Variety—Music, Awards, Tributes—Specials—Any Length*
Saturday Night Live 25
Tina Fey, supervising writer; writers: Anne Beatts, Tom Davis, Steve Higgins, Lorne Michaels, Marilyn Suzanne Miller, Paul Pell, Paul Shaffer, T. Sean Shannon, Michael Shoemaker, Robert Smigel

# Selected Bibliography

Adalian, Josef. "How Each Era of *SNL* Has Ridiculed American Presidents." Vulture, June 2, 2017. https://www.vulture.com/2017/06/snl-how-each-era-has-ridiculed-american-presidents.html.

Adalian, Josef, and Megh Wright. "Will NBC Finally Do Justice to the *SNL* Library?" Vulture, July 17, 2020. https://www.vulture.com/2020/07/snl-library-nbc-streaming-peacock.html.

Adler, Dick. "Saturday Is for Laughing." *Los Angeles Times*, December 12, 1975.

Alvarez, Priscilla. "Hillary Clinton Shows a Sense of Humor on 'Saturday Night Live.'" *Atlantic*, October 5, 2015. https://www.theatlantic.com/politics/archive/2015/10/val-the-bartender-meets-hillary-clinton-on-saturday-night-live/408859/.

Andreeva, Nellie. "'Saturday Night Live' Draws 8.3 Million Viewers in Strongest Season Opener since 2008—Update." Deadline, October 4, 2016. https://www.yahoo.com/entertainment/saturday-night-live-biggest-season-151624528.html.

Baker, Rachel. "Live from New York." *New York*, September 5, 2011.

Barbier, Sandra. "Some Aren't Laughing." *Times-Picayune*, February 21, 1977.

Beatts, Anne P., John Head, and Edie Baskin. *Saturday Night Live*. New York: Avon Books, 1977.

Belushi, Judith Jacklin. *Samurai Widow*. New York: Carroll & Graf, 1990.

Bennetts, Leslie. "Struggles at the New 'Saturday Night.'" *New York Times*, December 12, 1985.

Berger, Phil. *The Last Laugh: The World of Stand-Up Comics*. Updated ed. Lanham, MD: Cooper Square Press, 2000.

Bianco, Robert. "*SNL* Writer Creates a Carbon Copy of the Ultimate Office Bore." *Chicago Tribune*, March 23, 1991.

Bierbaum, Tom. "Ebersol Tabbed New Producer of 'Sat. Night Live.'" *Variety*, March 10, 1981.

Bierly, Mandi. "'Come Back, Barack': The Oral History of 'SNL' and Chance the Rapper's Emmy-Nominated '90s R&B Parody." *Billboard*, August 23, 2018. https://www.billboard.com/music/awards/snl-come-back-barack-oral-history-chance-the-rapper-8471871/.

"Big 'SNL' Leap from Kerrigan." *Hollywood Reporter*, March 15, 1994.

Blau, Eleanor. "Gray Panthers Out to Liberate Aged." *New York Times*, May 21, 1972.

Blount, Roy, Jr. "Gilda Radner." In Partridge, Rolling Stone *Visits* Saturday Night Live, 48–61.

Blum, David. *Tick–Tick–Tick–: The Long Life and Turbulent Times of* 60 *Minutes*. New York: HarperCollins Publishers, 2004.

Blumenthal, John, and Lindsay Maracotta. "Playboy Interview: NBC's 'Saturday Night.'" *Playboy*, May 1977.

Bogdanovich, Peter. "*SNL*'s Killer Contract." *New York Observer*, August 16, 1999.

Bogle, Donald. "Black Beginnings: From *Uncle Tom's Cabin* to *The Birth of a Nation*." In *Toms, Coons, Mulattoes, Mammies, and Bucks: An Interpretive History of Blacks in American Films*. 1973. Reprint, New York: Viking Press, 2001. 3–18.

Boyer, Peter J. "Johnny Says No to Another Half-Hour." Associated Press, March 12, 1981. LexisNexis Academic.

Breuer, Jim. *I'm Not High: (But I've Got a Lot of Crazy Stories About Life as a Goat Boy, a Dad, and a Spiritual Warrior)*. New York: Gotham Books, 2010.

Brown, Les. "Carson's Salary Nears $3 Million." *New York Times*, December 22, 1977.

Burgheim, Richard. "Television: Viewable Alternatives." *Time*, February 8, 1971.

Burros, Marian. "Bill Clinton and Food: Jack Sprat He's Not." *New York Times*, December 23, 1992.

Busis, Hillary. "Eli Manning and Lorne Michaels Talk Chris Farley, Living Up to Peyton, and Why Athletes Make Good 'SNL' Hosts." *Entertainment Weekly*, May 2, 2012. http://insidetv.ew.com/2012/05/02/eli-manning-and-lorne-michaels-talk-chris-farley-living-up-to-peyton-and-why-athletes-make-good-snl-hosts.

Cader, Michael, and Edie Baskin. Saturday Night Live: *The First Twenty Years*. Boston: Houghton Mifflin, 1994.

Capoot, Ashley. "Biden Makes Surprise Video Appearance on 'SNL,' Joining Host Aubrey Plaza." CNBC, January 22, 2023. https://www.cnbc.com/2023/01/22/bidcn-makes-surprise-video-appearance-on-snl-joining-host-aubrey-plaza-.html Carlin, George, and Tony Hendra. *Last Words*. New York: Free Press, 2009.

Carmody, John. "The TV Column." *Washington Post*, November 14, 1985.

Carter, Bill. "'Saturday Night' Lives for Now, but Then What?" *New York Times*, March 8, 1995.

Clotworthy, William G. Saturday Night Live: *Equal Opportunity Offender: The Uncensored Censor*. New York: 1st Books Library, 2001.

Coe, Steve. "NBC to Retool *Saturday Night Live*." *Broadcasting & Cable*, March 6, 1995.

Cohen, Brian Tyler, and Tommy Vietor. "The Best of *SNL* Political Sketches." *Pod Save America*, September 25, 2023. Video, 19:36. https://www.youtube.com/watch?v=OstIEF9DOEw.

Connelly, Christopher. "Attorneys Had Word for 'Silverman's Bunker': Libelous." *Anchorage Daily News*, January 2, 1982.

Corliss, Richard. "Cinema: A Rock 'n' Roll Caravan." *Time*, July 7, 1980.

Corn, David. "Saturday Night Censored." *The Nation*, July 13, 1998.

"Curtin Finds New Horizon." *Zanesville Times Recorder* (Zanesville, OH), May 2, 1976.

Cuthbert, David. Review of *Saturday Night Live*. *Times-Picayune*, October 13, 1975.

Davis, Tom. *Thirty-Nine Years of Short-Term Memory Loss*. New York: Grove Press, 2009.

Davis, Tom, and Dan Aykroyd. *Coneheads: The Life and Times of Beldar Conehead, as Told to Gorman Seedling, INS Commissioner, Retired*. New York: Hyperion, 1993.

Deeb, Gary. "New 'Saturday Night' Embarrassing to NBC." *Syracuse Post-Standard*, December 15, 1990.

Deggans, Eric. "Here's the Deal, Folks: A POTUS Impression Is Harder than It Looks." *Weekend Edition Saturday*, National Public Radio, November 14, 2020.

Delay, Brittany. "The Best *SNL* Music Videos of All Time." Looper, February 11, 2023. https://www.looper.com/1188025/the-best-snl-music-videos-of-all-time/.

Demaret, Kent. "A *Saturday Night Live* Writer and a Deejay Fight Over the Battered Body of 'Oh No, Mr. Bill.'" *People*, January 14, 1980.

Desmon, Stephanie. "Skip the Grades, Just Play the Tape." *Baltimore Sun*, May 23, 2001.

Director, Roger. "Fear and Laughing at *Saturday Night Live*." *New York*, November 23, 1981.

Dratch, Rachel. *Girl Walks into a Bar—: Comedy Calamities, Dating Disasters, and a Midlife Miracle*. New York: Gotham Books, 2012.

Dunn, Nora. *Nobody's Rib: Pat Stevens, Liz Sweeney, Babette and Some Other Women You Know*. New York: HarperPerennial, 1991.

Ebersol, Dick. Interview by Dan Pasternack. Archive of American Television video, June 23 and 24, 2009. http://www.emmytvlegends.org/interviews/people/dick-ebersol.

Ebert, Roger. Review of *The Blues Brothers*. Rogerebert.com, January 1, 1980. http://www.rogerebert.com/reviews/the-blues-brothers-1980.

———. Review of *Blues Brothers 2000*. Rogerebert.com, February 6, 1998. http://www.rogerebert.com/reviews/blues-brothers-2000-1998.

———. Review of *Stuart Saves His Family*. *Chicago Sun-Times*, April 12, 1995.

———. Review of *The Ladies Man*. Rogerebert.com, October 13, 2000. http://www.rogerebert.com/reviews/the-ladies-man-2000.

———. Review of *Wayne's World*. *Chicago-Sun Times*, February 14, 1992.

Eggen, Dan. "Rick Perry Backs Away from HPV Vaccine Decision During Presidential Run." *Washington Post*, August 16, 2011.

Falk, Karen. *Imagination Illustrated: The Jim Henson Journal*. San Francisco: Chronicle Books, 2012.

Farhi, Paul. "Blue Oyster Cult, Playing Along with 'More Cowbell.'" *Washington Post*, January 29, 2005.

Farley, Tom, and Tanner Colby. *The Chris Farley Show: A Biography in Three Acts*. New York: Viking, 2008.

Ferretti, Fred. "TV: Great American Dream Machine." *New York Times*, January 7, 1971.
Fey, Tina. *Bossypants*. New York: Little, Brown, 2011.
Fleming, Michael. "'Sprocket' Man." *Variety*, April 7, 1998.
Fox, Jesse David. "Live from New York Once Again: Lorne Michaels Reveals Everything about *SNL*'s 46th Season, Including the Show's New Biden." Vulture, September 16, 2020. https://www.vulture.com/2020/09/snl-lorne-michaels-season-46-interview.html.
Franken, Al, and Melody Beattie. *I'm Good Enough, I'm Smart Enough, and Doggone It, People Like Me! Daily Affirmations by Stuart Smalley*. New York: Dell, 1992.
Friedman, Jack. "Gumby's on a Roll and There's an Art (Clokey) Behind It." *People*, February 4, 1985.
Fruchter, Rena. *I'm Chevy Chase—and You're Not*. London: Virgin, 2007.
Gardella, Kay. "Andy Kaufman vs. *SNL* Producer: Real or Fantasy?" *Chronicle-Telegram*, November 24, 1982.
Gates, Anita. "A Lucky Break for the Terminally Uncool" (review of *A Night at the Roxbury*). *New York Times*, October 2, 1998.
———. "The Things She'll Do for Fame and a Date." *New York Times*, October 8, 1999.
Gelbart, Larry. *Laughing Matters: On Writing M*A*S*H, Tootsie, Oh, God!, and a Few Other Funny Things*. New York: Random House, 1998.
Gendel, Morgan. "Lorne Michaels: Live from New York—Again." *Los Angeles Times*, September 7, 1985.
"Geritol Ads Result in Fines of $812,000." *New York Times*, January 23, 1973.
Gladwell, Malcolm. "Listening to Khakis." *New Yorker*, July 28, 1997.
Gran, Ben. "Why the Tom Hanks *SNL* Sketch 'Black Jeopardy' Matters." *Paste Magazine*, October 25, 2016. https://www.pastemagazine.com/politics/snl/why-the-tom-hanks-snl-sketch-black-jeopardy-matter.
Greenfield, Jeff. "He's Chevy Chase and You're Not, and He's TV's Hot New Comedy Star." *New York*, December 22, 1975.
Greppi, Michele. "'*SNL*' Ratings at Six-Year High; 'Rugrats' Rules." *Hollywood Reporter*, May 30, 2000.
Gstalter, Morgan. "Ex-*SNL* Actor: Lorne Michaels Told Cast Not to Vilify Trump, Find a Way to Make Him Likable." The Hill, October 12, 2018. https://thehill.com/blogs/blog-briefing-room/news/411117-ex-snl-actor-lorne-michaels-told-cast-not-to-vilify-trump-find/.
Hammond, Darrell. *God, If You're Not Up There, I'm F*cked: Tales of Stand-Up, Saturday Night Live, and Other Mind-Altering Mayhem*. New York: Harper, 2011.
Hanks, Tom. "Top Spin." *Spin*, February 1993.
Harris, Judy. "Muppet Master: An Interview with Jim Henson." Muppet Central, September 21, 1998. http://www.muppetcentral.com/articles/interviews/jim1.shtml.
Harris, Mark. "Entertainers of the Year: 1. The Cast of 'Saturday Night Live.'" *Entertainment Weekly*, December 25, 1992.

Harrison, George. *I, Me, Mine.* New York: Simon and Schuster, 1980.
Harvey, Dennis. Review of *Superstar. Variety*, October 7, 1999.
———. Review of *A Night at the Roxbury. Variety*, October 2, 1998.
Hay, Carla. "Alec Baldwin Sounds Off on Acting, Politics, and Controversial Issues," Part One. Examiner.com, July 6, 2010. http://www.examiner.com/article/alec-baldwin-sounds-off-on-acting-politics-and-controversial-issues-part-one.
"Here Comes Mr. Bill's Lawsuit." *New York Times*, December 18, 1979.
Hibberd, James. "Donald Trump Gives 'SNL' Biggest Ratings in Years." *Entertainment Weekly*, November 8, 2015.
Hill, Doug. "Can 'Saturday Night' Regain Its Bite?'" *New York Times*, October 2, 1994.
Hill, Doug, and Jeff Weingrad. *Saturday Night: A Backstage History of* Saturday Night Live. San Francisco: Untreed Reads, 2011.
"The Impact of Late Night Television Musical Performances on the Sale of Recorded Music." *Journal of the Music & Entertainment Industry Educators Association* 10, no. 1 (2010): 39–58.
Izadi, Elahe. "How Janet Reno Came to Embrace Will Ferrell's Absurd *SNL* Impression." *Washington Post*, November 7, 2016.
Jacklin, Judith Victoria. *Blues Brothers: Private.* New York: Putnam, 1980.
James, Caryn. "Where Politics and Comedy Intermingle, the Punch Lines Can Draw Blood." *New York Times*, November 4, 2000.
Jillette, Penn, and Teller. *Penn & Teller's How to Play with Your Food.* New York: Villard Books, 1992.
Jones, Jeffrey P. "Politics and the Brand: Saturday Night Live's Campaign Season Humor." In Saturday Night Live *and American TV*, edited by Ron Becker, Nick Marx, and Matt Sienkiewicz, 77–92. Bloomington: Indiana University Press, 2013.
Jory, Tom. "Second Producer Takes Over." *Cedar Rapids Gazette*, November 15, 1980.
"Judge Sluggo Ends Dispute in Mr. Bill Copyright Suit." *Sarasota Journal*, November 11, 1981.
Kahn, Eve. "Television, Women in the Locker Room at 'Saturday Night Live.'" *New York Times*, February 16, 1992.
Kaylan, Wayne. "20 Questions: Dennis Miller." *Playboy*, September 1, 1992.
Keefe, Terry. "Anthony Michael Hall: The Hollywood Interview." *The Hollywood Interview*, November 30, 2012. http://thehollywoodinterview.blogspot.com/2008/11/anthony-michael-hall-hollywood.html.
Kiedis, Anthony, and Larry Solomon. *Scar Tissue.* New York: Hyperion, 2004.
Knoedelseder, William K., Jr. "Trying to Resurrect 'Saturday Night Live.'" *Los Angeles Times*, March 29, 1981.
Krebs, Albin, and Robert McG. Thomas Jr. "Mailer Feels Responsibility for Slaying." *New York Times*, February 22, 1982.
Kronke, David. "Sweeney's Got It Down Pat." *Variety*, July 24, 1994.

Larnick, Eric. "Adrien Brody, 'Detachment' Star, on the Education System, 'The Pianist' & Being Banned from 'SNL.'" *Huffington Post*, March 16, 2012. http://www.huffingtonpost.com/2012/03/16/adrien-brody-interview-detachment-pianist-snl_n_1354090.html.

"Leak Dampens NBC Splash for 'Sat. Night Live.'" *Variety*, October 22, 1980.

Lee, Michelle Ye Hee. "Donald Trump's False Comments Connecting Mexican Immigrants and Crime." *Washington Post*, July 8, 2015.

Leeds, Jeff. "Ailing Singer Needed Lip-Sync, Father Says." *New York Times*, October 26, 2004.

Leibovich, Mark. "Chevy Chase as the Klutz in Chief and a President Who Was In on the Joke." *New York Times*, December 29, 2006.

Lewyn, Mark. "Thousands Ring Up 900 Each Day." *USA Today*, August 29, 1988.

Leydon, Joe. Review of *It's Pat*. *Variety*, August 26, 1994.

———. Review of *Blues Brothers 2000*. *Variety*, February 5, 1998.

Lorando, Mark. "Live! From New Orleans! It's the 'Saturday Night Live' Mardi Gras Episode!'" *Times-Picayune*, January 26, 2008.

Love, Matthew. "The 10 Best *Saturday Night Live* Sketches about Hillary Clinton." Vulture, October 27, 2016. https://www.vulture.com/2016/10/hillary-clinton-best-snl-sketches.html.

Lyall, Sarah. "George Harrison Stabbed in Chest by an Intruder." *New York Times*, December 31, 1999.

Margulies, Lynn. *Dear Andy Kaufman, I Hate Your Guts!* Port Townsend, WA: Process Media, 2009.

Marin, Rich. "Dear 'Saturday Night Live': It's Over. Please Die." *Newsweek*, October 17, 1994.

Martel, Jay. "Martin Lawrence: He's Super, Fly, Black and Blue. So Why Is He Getting the Shaft?" *Rolling Stone*, April 21, 1994.

Martin, Steve. *Born Standing Up: A Comic's Life*. New York: Scribner, 2007.

Maslin, Janet. "They're from Another Planet (Another Medium, Actually)." *New York Times*, July 23, 1993.

———. "Playing Dumb Isn't a Job for Nitwits." *New York Times*, March 8, 1992.

McCann, Ruth. "*MacGruber*: Defuse This Bomb at Will." *Washington Post*, May 21, 2010.

McCarthy, Todd. Review of *The Blues Brothers*. *Variety*, June 18, 1980.

McGee, Ryan, Noel Murray, and David Fear. "20 Best 'Saturday Night Live' Political Sketches." *Rolling Stone*, August 22, 2017.

"Michaels Again to Head 'Saturday Night Live.'" *New York Times*, August 7, 1985.

Miller, Richard. "From Parodies to the Real Thing: 'SNL' Veteran Signorelli Directs." *Backstage*, June 16, 1989.

Mischer, Don. Interview by Beth Cochran. Archive of American Television video, November 7, 2008. http://www.emmytvlegends.org/interviews/people/don-mischer.

Mohr, Jay. *Gasping for Airtime: Two Years in the Trenches of* Saturday Night Live. New York: Hyperion, 2004.

Mooney, Paul. *Black Is the New White*. New York: Gallery Books, 2009.

Morgan, Tracy. *I Am the New Black*. New York: Spiegel & Grau, 2009.

Morris, Garrett. Interview by Amy Harrington. Archive of American Television video, April 13, 2013. http://www.emmytvlegends.org/interviews/people/garrett-morris.

Murphy, Ryan. "Well, Isn't He Special? *SNL*'s Dana Carvey, Turning 'Church Lady' into a National Heroine." *Washington Post*, July 25, 1987.

Myers, Mike, and Robin Ruzan. *Wayne's World: Extreme Close-Up*. New York: Hyperion, 1991.

Nessen, Ron. *Making the News, Taking the News*. Middletown, CT: Wesleyan University Press, 2011.

Norman, Philip. *John Lennon: The Life*. New York: HarperCollins, 2008.

Oberlag, Reginald. "Live from New York: *Saturday Night Live* Ad Spoofs." *Shoot*, October 3, 1997.

O'Connor, John J. "After Two Decades, How Much Longer?" *New York Times*, October 20, 1994.

———. "The '75 Season—A Few Nuggets amid the Dross." *New York Times*, December 28, 1975.

———. "Spring Mix Brightens NBC's 'Saturday Night.'" *New York Times*, November 30, 1975, sec. Arts & Leisure.

———. "TV: Simon and Garfunkel Reunion on NBC's 'Saturday Night'." *New York Times*, October 20, 1975.

Orlean, Susan. "Saturday Night Alive." *Rolling Stone*, June 19, 1986.

The Paley Center for Media. *She Made It*. http://shemadeit.org.

Palin, Sarah. *Going Rogue: An American Life*. New York: Harper, 2009.

Partridge, Marianne, editor. Rolling Stone *Visits* Saturday Night Live. Garden City, NY: Dolphin Books, 1979.

Partridge, Marianne. *Saturday Night Live*. New York: Doubleday, 1979.

Patinkin, Sheldon, and Robert Klein. *The Second City: Backstage at the World's Greatest Comedy Theater*. Naperville, IL: Sourcebooks, 2000.

Perrin, Dennis. *Mr. Mike: The Life and Work of Michael O'Donoghue*. New York: Avon Books, 1998.

"Phelps, Fey Help 'SNL' to Strong Start." *Hollywood Reporter*, September 15, 2008.

Pisano, Judith Belushi, and Tanner Colby. *Belushi: A Biography*. New York: Rugged Land, 2005.

Plasketes, George M. "The Invisible Artist." *Journal of Popular Film & Television* 16, no. 1 (Spring 1988): 22–31.

"Pryor Restraint." *Washington Post*, December 18, 1975.

Purdum, Todd S. "'Saturday Night Live' Mocks Politics with Bipartisan Gusto." *Politico*, April 29, 2011. http://www.politico.com/news/stories/0411/53754.html.

———. "*S.N.L.*: The Skyscraper of Satire." *Vanity Fair*, April 29, 2001.

Rabin, Nathan. "Interview: Charles Grodin." *The A.V. Club*, May 20, 2009. http://www.avclub.com/articles/charles-grodin,28125/.

Radner, Gilda, and Alan Zweibel. *Roseanne Roseannadanna's "Hey, Get Back to Work!" Book.* New York: Pocket Books, 1983.

———. *It's Always Something.* 1989. Reprint, New York: Simon and Schuster, 2009.

"Rage Against the Machine Censored on *Saturday Night Live.*" The Flag Burning Page. http://www.esquilax.com/flag/ratm.shtml.

Rainer, Peter. "Stuart: The Joke Gets Lost in the Mix." *Los Angeles Times*, April 12, 1995.

Rein, Richard K. "Charlie Rocket Blasts Off Amid the Turmoil of the 'Saturday Night Live' Massacres." *People*, March 23, 1981.

Reincheld, Aaron. "*Saturday Night Live* and Weekend Update: The Formative Years of Comedy News Dissemination." *Journalism History* 31, no. 4 (Winter 2006): 190–197.

Rensin, David. "20 Questions: Jon Lovitz." *Playboy*, July 1, 1997.

———. "Playboy Interview: Lorne Michaels." *Playboy*, March 1, 1992.

———. "20Q: Will Ferrell." *Playboy*, November 1, 2001.

Rose, Frank. "Building the Fun Bomb." *Wired* 13, no. 2 (February 2005).

Rosenberg, Howard. "New 'Saturday Night' Is as Funny as a Crutch." *Los Angeles Times*, November 13, 1985.

Rothenberg, Fred. "New 'Saturday Night Live' Has Weak Debut." Associated Press, November 10, 1985. LexisNexis Academic.

Ryfle, Steve. "War of the Funnymen: Jim Carrey vs. Will Ferrell." Netscape Celebrity. http://webcenters.netscape.compuserve.com/celebrity/package.jsp?name=celebrity/content/bsf_carreyvsfarrell (accessed July 11, 2013).

Safire, William. "Nixon on His Knees." *New York Times*, March 29, 1976.

Saltman, David. *Gilda: An Intimate Portrait.* Chicago: Contemporary Books, 1992.

*Saturday Night Live* Transcripts. http://snltranscripts.jt.org.

Schindehette, Susan, Jeanne Park, Victoria Balfour, Alan Carter, Leslie Strauss, Mark Zwonitzer, Michael Alexander, Tom Cunneff, and Vicki Sheff. "*Saturday Night Live*'s 15th Anniversary." *People*, September 25, 1989.

Schlosser, Herbert S. Interview by Karen Herman. Archive of American Television video, May 10, 2007. http://www.emmytvlegends.org/interviews/people/herbert-s-schlosser.

Schwab, Nikki. "Will Ferrell Explains How He Became George W. Bush." *U.S. News & World Report*, December 4, 2013.

Schwartz, Tony. "'Saturday Night Live' Loses Cast and Producer." *New York Times*, June 17, 1980.

———. "'Saturday Night Live' Is Back in Third Incarnation." *New York Times*, October 3, 1981.

———. "'Saturday Night Live' Gets New Cast." *New York Times*, October 17, 1980.

Scott, A. O. "One Flew Over the Cuckold's Nest." *New York Times*, October 13, 2000.

Sellers, John. "A Vulture Study: Which *SNL* Season Reused the Most Characters?" Vulture.com, November 21, 2011. http://www.vulture.com/2011/11/saturday-night-live-most-recurring-characters.html.

Shaffer, Paul, and David Ritz. *We'll Be Here for the Rest of Our Lives: A Swingin' Show-Biz Saga.* New York: Doubleday/Flying Dolphin Press, 2009.
Shales, Tom. "Barely Alive, It's *Saturday Night!*; Can Lorne Michaels Revive *SNL* Before It's Too Late?" *Washington Post*, August 20, 1995.
———. "The Ghost of 'Saturday Night Live.'" *Los Angeles Times*, April 18, 1985.
———. "'SNL' and the Censors: NBC Holds the Line Against Controversy." *Washington Post*, October 7, 1987.
———. "Zingers on *Saturday Night.*" *Washington Post*, November 8, 1975.
Shales, Tom, and James A. Miller. *Live from New York: An Uncensored History of Saturday Night Live as told by Its Stars, Writers, and Guests.* Boston: Little, Brown, 2002.
Shoemaker, Mike, and Scott Weinstein. SNL *Presents: The Clinton Years.* New York: TV Books, 1999.
"Show Business: Mr. Ear-Laffs." *Time*, August 4, 1975.
Smith, Chris. "Comedy Isn't Funny." *New York*, March 1995, 31–41.
The *SNL* Archives. http://snl.jt.org.
Spitznagel, Eric. "Jimmy Fallon—20Q." *Playboy*, October 1, 2004.
Stein, Joel. "Save Norm!" *Time*, January 19, 1998.
Steinberg, Jacques. "Censored 'SNL' Sketch Jumps Bleepless onto the Internet." *New York Times*, December 21, 2006.
Sternbergh, Adam. "Jizzy with It." *New York Magazine*, May 24, 2010.
Streeter, Michael. *Nothing Lost Forever: The Films of Tom Schiller.* Boalsburg, PA: BearManor Media, 2005.
Sweeney, Julia, and Christine Zander. *It's Pat! My Life Exposed.* New York: Hyperion, 1992.
Talorico, Patricia. "'SNL' Producer Lorne Michaels Talks Comedy, Politics at UD, but Not Its Most Famous Alumnus." *Delaware News Journal*, October 22, 2021.
Tapper, Jake. "Sin." Salon.com, October 12, 2002. http://www.salon.com/2002/10/12/sinead_3/.
Taylor, Clarke. "The New 'Saturday Night Live' Team." *Los Angeles Times*, October 21, 1985.
Thomas, Kevin. "'It's Pat' Takes Ambiguous Look at Life." *Los Angeles Times*, February 3, 1995.
Thompson, Robert J., and Gary Burns. *Making Television: Authorship and the Production Process.* New York: Praeger, 1990.
Turan, Kenneth. "*Wayne's World*: Awesome . . . Not." *Los Angeles Times*, February 14, 1992.
"TV Clips." *The Hollywood Reporter*, September 15, 2008.
Urban Dictionary. http://www.urbandictionary.com/.
Van Gelder, Lawrence. "*Blues Brothers 2000*: A Brotherly Reprise: Wrecks and All." *New York Times*, February 6, 1998.
Ventola, C. Lee. "Direct-to-Consumer Pharmaceutical Advertising: Therapeutic or Toxic?" *Pharmacy and Therapeutics* 36, no. 10 (October 2011): 681–684.

Voger, Mark. "Hey Joe—Founding B.O.C. Bassist Is Rarin' to Go." *Asbury Park Press*, May 12, 2000.

Walters, Barbara. *Audition: A Memoir.* New York: Vintage Books, 2008.

Warner, Jay. *On This Day in Music History.* New York: Hal Leonard, 2004.

Watson, Tarvis. "On Directing *SNL.*" *Directors Guild America Quarterly (Television)*, July 2004.

Whalley, Jim. Saturday Night Live, *Hollywood Comedy, and American Culture: From Chevy Chase to Tina Fey.* New York: Palgrave Macmillan, 2010.

White, Timothy. "An Interview with Lorne Michaels." In Partridge, Rolling Stone *Visits* Saturday Night Live. 175–191.

Wild, David. "Looking for the Heart of 'Saturday Night.'" *Rolling Stone*, November 27, 1997.

———. "Mr. Wrong." *Rolling Stone*, April 15, 1999.

Wolcott, James. "Amateur Hours." *New Yorker*, December 13, 1993.

Yasharoff, Hannah. "Tina Fey Talks *SNL*'s Political Impact: 'I Don't Think That Show Can Really Sway People." *USA Today*, April 18, 2019.

Zaslow, Jeffrey. "Staying in Character." *USA Weekend Magazine*, August 26, 2001.

Zeman, Ned. "Soul Men: The Making of *The Blues Brothers.*" *Vanity Fair*, January 2013.

Zito, Tom. "'Saturday Night' at Georgetown." *Washington Post*, September 10, 1976.

Zmuda, Bob, and Matthew Scott Hensen. *Andy Kaufman Revealed!* New York: Hachette Digital, 1999.

Zonars, John. "Got Live If You Want It." *Spin*, February 1993.

Zweibel, Alan. *Bunny, Bunny: Gilda Radner: A Sort of Love Story.* New York: Villard Books, 1994.

# Index

2 Chainz, 530, 536
3-D, 430, 431
3RDEYEGIRL, 166, 537
8G Band, the, 228
10,000 Maniacs, 453, 465
14 Karat Soul, 432, 433, 440
21 Savage, 575
50 Cent, 92, 153, 498, 504
070 Shake, 552
1975, the, 542, 572

A Tribe Called Quest, 545, 583
A Tribe Called West, 578
ABBA, 286, 412
Abdul, Paula, 151, 296, 483, 505
Abeles, Doug, 587, 590
Abernathy, Constance, 415
Abrams, J. J., 541
AC/DC, 488
Adalian, Josef, 160
Adams, Amy, 513, 538
Adams, Bryan, 444
Adams, Ryan, 494
Adele, 138, 153, 165, 166, 230, 286, 287, 309, 514–515, 541, 561, 580
Adler, Dick, 38
Aduba, Uzo, 537
Aerosmith, 117–118, 270, 370, 388, 408, 409, 457, 458, 468, 479, 492
Affleck, Ben, 155, 206, 267–269, 485, 488, 492, 501, 502, 515, 532, 585
Affleck, Casey, 546
AFI, 510
Aguilera, Christina, 489, 498, 501, 509
Ahmadinejad, Mahmoud, 340
Ahrens, Lynn, 382
Aiello, Danny, 450, 475
Aiken, Clay, 500
Aiko, Jhené, 534
Ailes, Roger, 179
Akon, 509, 510, 523
Alabama Shakes, 530, 531, 538

Alba, Jessica, 523
Albert, Marv, 314, 412, 439, 480
Albert, Trevor, 404
Alda, Alan, 237
Aldean, Jason, 548
Alexander, Jason, 395, 467, 508
Alexander, Lamar, 474
Alexander, Shana, 346, 365
Alexis, Kim, 455
Ali, Asif, 228
Ali, Muhammad, 16, 99
Alito, Judge, 568
All Saints, 483
Allen, Joan, 484
Allen, Lily, 510
Allen, Steve, 11
Allen, Woody, 39, 79, 84, 252, 438
Alley, Kirstie, 462, 467
Allman Brothers Band, the, 184, 435
Alter, Rebecca, 167
Altman, Robert, 419
Altuve, José, 549
Amanfu, Ruby, 527
Amazing Rhythm Aces, the, 430
Amoral, Geoff, 580–582
Amos, Tori, 475
Amwar, Fahi, 228
Anastasio, Trey, 489, 500
Anderson, Anthony, 520
Anderson, Dana, 115
Anderson, Harry, 298, 434, 436, 438, 439, 442, 444
Anderson, Jacob, 556
Anderson, James, 587, 590
Anderson, Laurie, 447
Anderson, Loni, 403
Anderson, Richard Dean, 40, 159, 401, 516
Anderson, Wes, 22, 533
Aniston, Jennifer, 137, 296–297, 474, 487, 500, 545, 546

Anka, Paul, 4
Ansari, Aziz, 261, 546
Ant, Adam, 441
Anthony, Carmelo, 524
Anthony, Marc, 486
Antonoff, Jack, 547
Apatow, Judd, 11, 115, 119
Apple, Fiona, 477, 478, 488
Applegate, Christina, 130, 467, 529
Arcade Fire, 153, 511, 522, 528, 532, 551, 568, 582
Arctic Monkeys, 507
Arledge, Roone, 2, 4
Armani, Giorgio, 297
Armatrading, Joan, 421
Armisen, Fred, 144, 148, 176, 206–208, 210, 211, 228, 237, 245, 250, 274, 280, 304, 353, 354, 360, 383, 496, 501–504, 506, 509, 511, 515–520, 522–526, 528, 529, 531–534, 536, 538, 542, 544, 546, 550–552, 554, 557–560, 572, 573, 576, 584
Armstrong, Lance, 264, 506
Arnaz, Desi, 4, 70, 287, 414
Arnaz, Desi, Jr., 425
Arnold, Roseanne, 127, 466. *See also*, Rosanne Barr
Arnold, Tom, 464, 466, 475
Aronson, Letty, 84
Arquette, Rosanna, 114, 369, 448
Arthur, Bea, 417, 428
Ashley, Elizabeth, 436
Asner, Ed, 438, 443
al-Assad, Bashar, 353
Assange, Julian, 237, 522, 549, 555
Astaire, Fred, 116, 556
Athari, Aristotle, 158, 228, 564
Attractions, the, 289
Aull, Gregory, 588
Awkwafina, 552

Index

Aykroyd, Dan, ix, xvii, 8–10, 12, 14–16, 18, 22, 24–26, 41, 43, 44, 52, 58, 60–65, 67, 68, 70–72, 74, 80, 117, 138, 175, 176, 184, 186, 187, 267, 275, 280, 290, 332, 343, 344, 346, 363–365, 392–396, 411, 421, 425–427, 453, 467, 473, 482, 483, 493, 495, 498, 499, 511, 516, 531, 566, 589
Aykroyd, Peter, 25–26, 334, 396, 429, 431, 566
Aymong, Ken, 564, 580–583, 588
Azalea, Iggy, 537

B-52s, the, 287, 429, 458
Baas, David, 528
Babbitt, Bruce, 451
Baby, Lil, 556, 571
Babyface, 560
Bach, Barbara, 368
Backstreet Boys, 125, 482, 486
Bacon, Kevin, 124, 460
Bunny, Bad, 166, 342, 560, 563, 573
Badu, Erykah, 394
Baez, Joan, 53, 172
Baha Men, 490
Baird, Maggie, 566
Baker, Anita, 231, 450, 454
Bakker, Jim, 111
Bakker, Tammy Faye, 111
Baldwin, Alec, 133, 135, 141, 145, 173, 176, 177, 200, 206, 208, 217–219, 221, 223, 224, 267, 268, 271, 273, 381, 382, 403, 458, 461, 466, 469, 472, 475, 479, 484, 485, 492, 495, 500, 502, 506, 509, 511, 515, 516, 521, 525, 526, 530, 531, 533, 540, 544–548, 550–561, 574, 583, 587–588
Baldwin, Alia, 516
Baldwin, Billy, 469
Baldwin, Brooke, 544
Baldwin, Hailey, 516
Baldwin, Stephen, 469
Ballerini, Kelsea, 572
Balvin, J, 556
Band, the, 70, 285, 418
Banderas, Antonio, 507

Bangles, the, 454
Banks, Elizabeth, 163, 541
Banks, Morwenna, 132, 228–229, 473, 474
Banshees of Blue, the, 452
Baranski, Christine, 476, 483
Barbier, Sandra, 64
Bareilles, Sara, 555
Barenaked Ladies, 485
Bargatze, Nate, 573
Barker, Travis, 565
Barkley, Charles, 259, 264, 316, 356, 467, 519, 526, 539, 551, 560
Barnes, Clive, 20
Barnes, Katreese, 163, 340, 510, 586
Barnett, Courtney, 544, 584
Barr, Roseanne, 239, 461. See also, Rosanne Arnold
Barron, Steve, 395
Barrows, Sydney Biddle, 297, 452
Barrymore, Drew, 94, 151–153, 268, 438, 485, 490, 493, 500, 507, 510, 518, 553
Basil, Toni, 413, 424
Basinger, Kim, 408, 469, 588
Baskin, Burt, 29
Baskin, Edie, xv, 3, 29, 419
Baskin, Richard, 419
Bassey, Shirley, 4
Bastille, 534
Batali, Mario, 522
Bateman, Jason, 504, 562
Bateman, Justine, 453
Battaglio, Stephen, 159
Battista, Bobbie, 260
Bay, James, 551
Bayer, Vanessa, 68, 111, 154, 161, 165, 229, 255, 272, 296, 297, 325, 353, 356, 521, 528, 529, 531, 532, 535, 538, 540, 541, 543–545, 548, 551
Baze, Alex, 590
Beastie Boys, 125, 142, 290, 388, 472, 484
Beatles, the, 50, 52, 126, 285, 331, 415–418
Beatts, Anne, 8, 9, 29, 67, 378, 396, 563, 590, 591
Beck, 153, 478, 485, 497, 504, 509, 534
Beck, Jeff, 528
Bee, Samantha, 180

Beekman, Sabina, 476
Begley, Ed, Jr., 443
Behar, Joy, 228
Beiler, Jeremy, 324
Bek, Young, 580, 581
Belafonte, Harry, 50
Beldin, Dale, 393
Bell, Dan, 408
Bellafante, Ginia, 132
Bellion, Jon, 572
Belushi, Jim, 99, 100, 229, 440, 499
Belushi, John, ix, xvii, 7–10, 14–18, 24, 25, 27–28, 32, 34, 40–42, 44, 52, 56–60, 62, 63, 65–68, 70, 72, 73, 78, 80, 87, 117, 142, 149, 186, 279, 282–283, 290, 291, 313–315, 332, 333, 343, 363, 364, 378, 386, 391–394, 411, 412, 417–422, 424, 426, 427, 430, 435, 589
Belzberg, Leslie, 393
Belzer, Richard, 417, 572
Ben Folds Five, 481
Bening, Annette, 509
Benjamin, Richard, 72, 427, 430
Bennett, Beck, 193, 218, 220, 223, 224, 229, 300, 326, 532, 534–536, 538, 539, 541–551, 553, 554, 556–562, 564
Bennett, Michael, 589–589
Bennett, Tony, 268, 509
Bennetts, Leslie, 106
Benson, George, 419
Benza, A. J., 486
Bergen, Candice, x, 38, 41, 46, 61, 89, 119, 142, 145, 148, 269, 274, 278, 297, 303, 312–313, 402, 412, 413, 418, 452, 458, 459, 531, 553, 567, 574
Bergstrom, Ann, 583
Berle, Milton, 4, 264, 427
Bernsen, Corbin, 458
Bernstein, Adam, 398
Bernstein, Carl, 181, 182, 186
Berry, Chuck, 419
Berry, Halle, 499
Bertinelli, Valerie, 450
Beyoncé, 151, 157, 253, 496, 499, 515, 536. See also Knowles, Beyoncé

Bhasker, Jeff, 565
Biden, Hunter, 559
Biden, Joseph (Joe), 170, 176, 199, 206, 220, 223–227, 240, 246, 258, 298, 305, 515, 517, 518, 522, 549, 555, 557–562, 564–568, 570, 571, 573–575
Bieber, Justin, 138, 153, 167, 212, 287, 325, 520, 523, 528, 530, 534, 535, 559, 561
Biel, Jessica, 516, 517
Bierly, Mandi, 166
Big Country, 440, 441
Big Daddy Kane, 457
Big Sean, 546, 556
Biggs, Robert, 291
bin Laden, Osama, 493, 502
Birch, Patricia, 116
Bishop, Stephen, 423
Björk, 139, 480, 511
Black, Jack, 483, 494, 499, 506, 587
Black, Karen, 365, 417, 432
Black Crowes, the, 461, 466
Black Eyed Peas, the, 500, 518
Black Keys, the, 523, 526, 535
Black Star, 570
Blair, Deb, 283
Blake, Eubie, 53, 427
Blake, Jeff, 571
Blake, Robert, 378, 438
Blanco, Benny, 561
Blau, Eleanor, 303
Bleachers, 566
Blige, Mary J., 231, 467, 507–509
Blind Melon, 469
Blink-182, 488
Blitzer, Wolf, 179, 229, 258, 511, 524, 541, 574
Block, Curt, 293
Blondie, 428
Bloom, Claire, 333
Bloomberg, Michael, 523, 525, 529, 534, 558
Blount, Roy, Jr., 24, 70
Blue Man Group, 228
Blue Öyster Cult (BOC), 279, 373–375, 489
Blues Brothers, the, 15, 41, 68, 70, 286, 393, 394, 424, 425
Blues Traveler, 474
Blum, David, 365
Blumenthal, John, 38

Blunt, Emily, 544
Blunt, James, 506
B.o.B, 524
Bobbitt, Lorena, 385
Bogdanovich, Peter, 251
Bogues, Muggsy, 405, 467
Bol, Manute, 470, 472
Bolt, Usain, 529
Bolton, Michael, 164, 329, 461, 524, 528
Bon Iver, 527
Bon Jovi, Jon, 153, 288, 512
Bon Temps Zydeco Band, the, 445
Bond, Julian, 420
Bonifant, J. Evan, 394
Bonilla, Bobby, 470
Bono, 512
Booker, Cory, 227, 251
Boone, Lesley, 404, 405
Boothe, Powers, 401
Borbón, Pedro, Jr., 481
Boreanaz, David, 486
Borgnine, Ernest, 154, 521
Bornstein, Harold, 218, 223, 552
Boseman, Chadwick, 163, 551, 557
Bostwick, Barry, 442
Bouchard, Joe, 375
Boudreaux, Monk, 463
Bowie, David, 70, 429, 478, 479, 486, 542
Bowman, John, 567, 589
Boyega, John, 541
Boyer, Peter J., 86
boygenius, 573, 574
Boyle, Lara Flynn, 408, 492
Boyle, Peter, 42, 59, 414, 485
Boys II Men, 560
Brackett, Charles, 334
Bradley, Bill, 412, 474
Bradley, John, 555
Bradshaw, Terry, 571
Brady, Tom, 264, 316, 504, 562
Braff, Zach, 153, 218, 278, 512
Brand, Russell, 523
Brando, Marlon, 16, 59, 63, 139
Brandt, Mel, 11, 88, 93
Branigan, Laura, 438
Branson, Richard, 237
Breckman, Andy, 336
Bregman, Alex, 549
Brennan, Neal, 354
Brenner, David, 482

Breslin, Jimmy, 448
Brest, Martin, 83, 269, 432
Breuer, Jim, 133–136, 140, 229, 305, 309, 474, 475, 477, 479
Brick, 420
Brickell, Edie, 454, 460, 471
Bridgers, Phoebe, 562
Bridges, Beau, 439
Bridges, Jeff, 154, 278, 439, 522
Bridges, Leon, 541
Brill, Fran, 38
Brillstein, Bernie, 8, 392
Britt, Katie, 225, 575
Brittain, Paul, 154, 208, 229, 360, 521, 522, 527
Brittle, Randy, 583
Broderick, Matthew, 218, 379–380, 391, 453, 483, 557
Brody, Adrien, 264–265, 498
Brody, Elliot, 498
Broecker, Tom, 579–584
Brokaw, Tom, 80, 203, 337, 476, 488
Brolin, Josh, 286, 308, 309, 514, 527, 550, 575
Bromfield, Valri, 14, 43, 411
Brooks, Albert, 8, 39, 53, 328, 329, 411–413
Brooks, David, 337
Brooks, Garth, 141, 287, 464, 482, 487
Brooks, James L., 10, 11, 39, 413
Brooks, Max, 587
Brooks, Mel, 47, 271
Brooks, Tim, 49
Brosnahan, Rachel, 554
Brosnan, Pierce, 492
Brothers, Dr. Joyce, 441
Brown, A. Whitney, 119, 229, 349, 442, 447, 448, 462, 589
Brown, Bobby, 465
Brown, Campbell, 207, 208
Brown, Chris, 523
Brown, James, 109, 392–395, 432, 530
Brown, Jerry, 128
Brown, Larry, 475
Brown, Les, 1
Brown, Sterling K., 551
Brown, Trevor, 580, 581
Brown, Zac, 539

# Index

Browne, Jackson, 421
Brownstein, Carrie, 530, 532, 544
Bruce, Jack, 432
Bruce, Lenny, 38, 39
Bruce Hornsby and the Range, 450
Brueggemann, Eli, 165, 166, 534, 549, 582
Brunson, Quinta, 572
Bryant, Aidy, 158, 164, 165, 218, 223, 230, 252, 262, 357, 529, 534, 536, 539, 548, 550, 553, 554, 558, 562–566, 569
Bryant, Anita, 20, 77
Bryant, Kobe, 499, 559
BTS, 555, 581
Bubba Sparxxx, 494
Bublé, Michael, 316, 519, 526, 541
Buckingham, Lindsey, 388, 435, 524, 565
Buffer, Michael, 472
Buffett, Jimmy, 424
Bundy, Ted, 455
Burgheim, Richard, 53
Burke, Delta, 461
Burke, Michelle, 395, 396
Burnett, Carol, 50, 138, 261, 273, 298, 444
Burns, George, 4, 50, 475
Burns, Jack, 420
Burns, Nick, 143, 487
Burr, Bill, 537, 561
Burroughs, William S., 90, 298, 435
Burstyn, Ellen, 84, 431
Burton, Richard, 60, 90, 333
Burwell, Carter, 408
Bus Boys, the, 438
Buscemi, Steve, 471, 482, 526
Busey, Gary, 427
Bush, 475, 478
Bush, Barbara, 191, 192
Bush, Billy, 549
Bush, George H. W., 113, 128, 171, 176, 188–193, 230, 383, 452–454, 456–461, 463–466, 477, 489, 554
Bush, George W., 26, 174–176, 199–203, 206, 234, 269, 307, 308, 489–503, 505, 506, 508–511, 528, 541, 550
Bush, Jeb, 193, 197, 200–201, 535, 541, 542

Bush, Jenna, 492
Bush, Kate, 426
Bush, Neil, 193
Busta Rhymes, 485, 545
Butkus, Dick, 466
Butler, Austin, 160, 570
Butler, Gerard, 518
Butler, Win, 153
Buttafuoco, Joey, 298–299, 471
Buttafuoco, Mary Jo, 298
Butterfield, Paul, 420, 427
Buttigieg, Pete, 559
Buzzi, Ruth, 51
Byrne, David, 457, 559, 581
Byrne, Gabriel, 474

Cabello, Camila, 557, 568
Cackowski, Liz, 590
Cader, Michael, xv
Caesar, Sid, 47–48, 94, 438, 589
Cage, Nicolas, 277, 299, 465
Cahill, Beth, 120, 121, 230, 463, 465
Cahill, Siobhan, 442
Caillat, Colbie, 516
Cain, Herman, 208, 528, 561
Calloway, Cab, 392, 394
Cameron, James, 300, 485, 519
Cameron, Tyler, 565
Caminiti, Rob, 578, 579
Camoin, Al, 589
Camp, Colleen, 408
Campbell, Laura, 543
Campbell, Malcolm, 406–408
Campbell, Naomi, 473
Campbell, Nell, 451
Campbell, Neve, 478
Campbell, Tevin, 457
Candy, John, 434, 440
Cangialosi, Paul, 582–585
Cannon, Dyan, 416
Captain Beefheart and His Magic Band, 431
Cara, Alessia, 546
Cardi B, 551
Carell, Steve, 235, 260, 340, 505, 514, 524, 533, 553
Carey, Mariah, 459, 463, 481, 513
Carlile, Brandi, 565, 570
Carlin, George, x, 2, 3, 8, 27, 29–31, 34, 39, 43–45, 263, 349, 411, 443
Carlin, Jacqueline, 31

Carlock, Robert, 12, 590
Carlson, Gretchen, 528, 531, 538
Carlson, Tucker, 554, 567
Carmichael, Jerrod, 567
Carmody, John, 105
Carne, Judy, 51
Carney, Jay, 156, 157
Carpenter, John, 487
Carpenter, Sabrina, 576
Carradine, David, 84, 432
Carrasco, Joe "King" and the Crowns, 432
Carrere, Tia, 408, 409
Carrey, Jim, 176, 223–225, 246, 403, 476, 498, 523, 537, 560, 561
Carroll, Rocky, 400
Cars, the, 109, 442, 451, 452
Carson, Ben, 539, 541–544, 559
Carson, Johnny, 1–2, 18, 39, 86, 312, 344, 368, 464
Carter, Amy, 380
Carter, Betty, 286, 415
Carter, Bill, 122, 207, 351
Carter, Jimmy, 15, 58, 63, 77, 80, 91, 151, 174–176, 181, 183–184, 187, 188, 421, 423, 424, 426, 456
Carter, Rosalynn, 60, 63, 80–81, 184, 432
Carvey, Dana, 8, 109–111, 113, 114, 116, 117, 119, 121, 127, 128, 133, 148, 149, 171, 176, 189, 190, 193, 194, 200, 230, 248, 257, 265, 269, 320, 340, 349–350, 361, 369, 370, 379, 398, 408, 448, 449, 451–466, 468, 471, 477, 481, 486, 489, 490, 523, 543, 545, 588
Carvey, Dex, 523
Carvey, Tom, 523
Carville, James, 177, 178, 237, 267
Casablancas, Julian, 520, 528
Casey, William, 190
Cash, Johnny, 294, 436, 444
Cash, June Carter, 444
Cash, Rosanne, 447
Castor, Bruce, 562
Castro, Fidel, 496
Castro, Julián, 557
Cavan, Susan, 406

## Index

Cavett, Dick, 89, 90, 414, 418, 440
Cavuto, Neil, 542
C+C Music Factory, 463
Cena, John, 176, 517, 546, 565
Cera, Michael, 534
Cesana, Renzo, 279
Chainsmokers, the, 547
Chalamet, Timothée, 326, 562, 563, 574
Chan, Jackie, 133, 489
Chance the Rapper, 164–166, 251, 259, 541, 542, 546, 549, 557, 561, 582
Chapman, Graham, 48, 52, 172
Chapman, Tracy, 454, 457
Chappelle, Dave, 221, 545, 558, 561, 570, 575, 577–579, 583
Charles, Ray, 70, 288, 392, 394, 422
Charles B., 405
Charli XCX, 538, 567, 584
Charlie Daniels Band, the, 436
Chase, Chevy, ix, xi, xvii, 3, 5, 8, 11, 14–19, 21, 22, 28, 29, 31, 35–36, 38, 41, 44, 47, 53–58, 60, 78, 80–82, 84, 85, 87, 103, 138, 170, 171, 175, 176, 182–183, 185, 230, 237, 269, 270, 280, 313, 344, 346, 348, 361–363, 376, 377, 411, 413–419, 423, 429, 434, 437, 445, 449, 458, 463, 474, 479, 480, 485, 493, 512, 531, 589, 590
Chase, Cornelius Crane. *See* Chase, Chevy
Chastain, Jessica, 550
Chavez, Hugo, 308, 531
Che, Michael, 158, 230, 241, 356–358, 547, 550, 566
Cheadle, Don, 555
Cheap Trick, 432
Cheatham, Maree, 403
Cheney, Dick, 201, 203, 204, 238, 492, 493, 495, 496, 506, 507, 510, 511, 517
Cheney, Lynne, 150
Cher, 268, 299, 452, 465
Cherry, Eagle-Eye, 484
Chicago, 428

Chieftains, the, 427
Child, Desmond, 429
Child, Julia, 74
Childish Gambino, 552, 582
Cholos, the, 435
Christie, Chris, 300, 525, 530, 537, 541–544, 574
Chrome, Cheetah, 424
Chucky, 300
Chung, Connie, 345
Churchill, Ted, 396
Ciara, 517
Cimino, Mike, 584
Cimino, Steven, 582–585, 587–588
C.K., Louis, 163, 274, 337, 529, 535, 540, 547
Clapton, Eric, 275, 294, 395, 458, 470
Clark, Dick, 464
Clark, Gary, Jr., 555
Clarke, Emilia, 555
Clarkson, Kelly, 504, 517, 526
Clarkson, Patricia, 517
Clash, the, 109, 437
Clay, Andrew Dice, 114, 119, 292, 458
Clayburgh, Jill, 414, 423
Cleese, John, 48, 52, 172, 478
Clegg, Johnny, and Savuka, 454
Cleghorne, Ellen, 120, 121, 127, 132, 157, 230–231, 236, 299, 351, 373, 462, 472, 474
Clemens, Roger, 470
Clemons, Clarence, 395
Cliff, Jimmy, 414, 433
Clinton, Bill, 122, 127–129, 133, 140, 175, 177, 178, 193–199, 213, 214, 220, 221, 238, 270, 297, 300, 303–305, 307, 400, 466, 467, 469, 472, 477, 478, 481–488, 491, 494, 503, 513, 515, 539, 540, 542, 544
Clinton, Chelsea, 128–129, 380, 381
Clinton, George, 448
Clinton, Hillary, 167, 172, 175, 194, 195, 198–199, 205, 207–210, 212–215, 217, 220, 221, 227, 239, 245, 250, 251, 297, 305, 380, 381, 470, 481, 485, 489,

510, 512–515, 535, 539, 540, 542–545, 549
Clokey, Art, 366, 367
Clooney, George, 472
Close, Glenn, 455, 466
Clotworthy, William G., 67, 379, 387
Coburn, James, 435
Coburn, Tom, 211
Coca, Imogene, 47
Cochran, Johnnie, 474, 478
Cockburn, Bruce, 430
Cocker, Joe, 16, 412, 417, 438
Coe, George, 24, 35, 411
Cohen, Irving, 99
Cohen, Leonard, 221, 545, 548
Cohen, Michael, 218, 223, 257, 551, 552, 554, 555
Cohen, Sacha Baron, 307–308, 509, 528
Cohen, Stefani, 577, 579
Colbert, Stephen, 180, 337, 524
Colby, Tanner, 15, 41, 58, 73, 127, 234, 333, 363
Coldplay, 492, 505, 515, 525, 526, 535, 557, 571, 577
Cole, Monica, 142
Cole, Natalie, 231
Cole, Paula, 482
Coleman, Dabney, 451, 576
Coleman, Gary, 427, 474
Colman, Olivia, 229
Coleman, Ornette, 427
Colfer, Chris, 154, 524
Collier, Jacob, 571
Collins, Harlan, 416
Collins, Joan, 257, 259
Collins, Judy, 426
Collins, Susan, 553, 556
Color Me Badd, 462
Combs, Luke, 558, 559
Commodores, the, 444
Common, 510, 549
Compton, Matthew, 401
Cone, David, 484
Conn, Didi, 483
Connelly, Christopher, 92
Connery, Sean, 139, 238
Connick, Harry, Jr., 457, 506
Connolly, Billy, 257
Conrad, Jessica, 590
Conrad, Robert, 435
Consequence, 545
Contner, James, 396

# Index

Conway, Kellyanne, 167, 177, 218, 220, 300, 546, 548, 549
Cooder, Ry, 418
Cook, Dane, 258, 506, 508
Cook, David, 515
Cook, Peter, 48, 414
Cooke, Cardinal, 43
Coolidge, Jennifer, 235, 403
Coolidge, Rita, 286, 416
Coolio, 475
Cooper, Anderson, 155, 220, 221, 507, 508, 523, 532, 551
Cooper, Bradley, 299, 516, 525, 532
Copperfield, David, 492
Coppola, Francis Ford, 283–284
Coppola, Sofia, 22
Corcoran, Barbara, 575
Corden, James, 558
Cordova, Marty, 481
Corliss, Richard, 394
Corn, David, 383
Cornell, Chris, 539
Cornyn, John, 570
Corrado, George, 549
Corrs, the, 485
Cosby, Bill, 4, 248, 259
Cosell, Howard, 4–6, 21, 99, 368, 445
Costas, Bob, 460
Costello, Elvis, 70, 125, 142, 283, 289–290, 422, 455, 461, 462
Coster-Waldau, Nikolaj, 532, 539
Cougar, John, 436, 440
Coulter, Ann, 151
Counting Crows, 469
Couric, Katie, 205, 478
Covert, Allen, 556
Cowboy Junkies, 455
Cowell, Simon, 249, 296
Cowher, Bill, 562
Craig, Daniel, 529, 559, 565
Cranberries, the, 472
Crane, Robert David, 420
Cranston, Bryan, 154, 300, 521, 546
Crash Test Dummies, 469
Crawford, Broderick, 4, 420
Crawford, Chace, 565
Crawford, Cindy, 470
Crawford, Connie, 283

Crawford, Joan, 20
Crawford, Phyllis, 34
Creed, 494
Crenna, Richard, 417
Cronenberg, David, 12
Cronkite, Walter, 77, 187, 334
Crouch, Andrae, 431, 443, 457
Crouch, Sandra, 457
Crow, Sheryl, 477, 483, 506
Crowe, Russell, 543
Crowns, the, 432, 433
Cruise, Julee, 458
Cruise, Tom, 107, 139, 257, 450
Cruz, Carmen Yulín, 548
Cruz, Catherine, 542
Cruz, Ted, 230, 539, 541–543, 562, 563, 565, 566
Crystal, Billy, xvii, 13, 31, 87, 99–101, 231, 237, 244, 303, 329, 336, 349, 368, 415, 442, 443, 445, 539
Cuban, Mark, 575
Culkin, Kieran, 565, 570
Culkin, Macaulay, 123, 124, 135, 463
Culp, Robert, 436
Cult, the, 446
Cumberbatch, Benedict, 545, 552, 568
Cumming, Alan, 488, 588
Cummins, Jack, 431
Cuomo, Andrew, 563, 564
Cure, the, 476
Curry, Tim, 98, 435
Curtin, Jane, xvii, 9, 10, 14, 19–20, 25, 32, 34, 35, 40, 41, 55, 58, 60–64, 68, 70, 74, 78, 80–82, 116, 138, 271, 279, 282, 313, 315, 332, 343–346, 362–365, 377, 378, 395, 396, 398, 411, 418–421, 425, 427, 428, 431
Curtis, Jackie, 415
Curtis, Jamie Lee, 82, 84, 432, 441, 572
Cusack, Joan, 103, 104, 108, 110, 231, 445, 448
Cuthbert, David, 45, 311
Cypress Hill, 468
Cyrus, Billy Ray, 154
Cyrus, Miley, 152–154, 166, 229, 521, 523, 532, 533, 540, 548, 554, 560, 564, 580

DaBaby, 558
Dafoe, Willem, 567
Dahl, Roald, 48, 172
Daily, E. G., 448
Dalton, Ray, 531
Damon, Matt, 218, 280, 300–301, 494, 496, 526, 552, 554, 576
Danahy, Pat, 508
Danes, Claire, 481
D'Angelo, 538
Dangerfield, Rodney, 188, 360, 429, 430, 478, 502
Daniels, Greg, xvii, 409, 589
Daniels, Jeff, 127, 462, 537
Daniels, Stormy, 218, 223, 552, 570
Danko, Rick, 427
Danner, Blythe, 436
Dano, Paul, 567
Danson, Ted, 455, 462
Danza, Tony, 90, 436, 447, 454
D'Arby, Terence Trent, 453
Darcy, Jeannie, 572
Darling, Ron, 449
Dave Matthews Band, 473, 476, 491, 518
Davenport, Connie, 481
Daves, Michael, 516
David, Erin, 401
David, Larry, xvii, 168, 214–215, 243, 274, 323, 540, 542–544, 548, 549, 556–560
Davidson, Amy, 543, 560
Davidson, Pete, 158, 176, 231, 341, 538, 541–543, 553, 555, 556, 559, 560, 562–566, 573
Davidson, Tom, 565
Davies, Marion, 235
Davis, Bette, 50, 239
Davis, Chili, 484
Davis, Ed, 51
Davis, Geena, 455
Davis, Mark, 565
Davis, Michael, 434–436, 439
Davis, Miles, 434
Davis, Russ, 481
Davis, Sammy, Jr., 99, 185, 442, 443
Davis, Tom, 9–10, 25, 38, 43, 44, 52, 61, 74, 102, 108, 109, 185, 314, 379, 395, 396, 413, 421, 428, 431, 485, 589–591

# Index

Dawson, Richard, 62
Dawson, Rosario, 516
Day, Abbott, 560
Day, Charlie, 525, 530
Day, Doris, 105
Day, Mikey, 176, 218, 219, 223, 224, 227, 231–232, 326, 327, 357, 544, 546, 547, 549, 550, 552–554, 558, 562, 567–575
de Armas, Ana, 573
De Bonis, Joe, 589
De Niro, Robert, 135, 218, 307, 322, 479, 490, 497, 503, 522, 533, 551–556
de Sande, Theo van, 407
de Villepin, Dominique, 498
Dead Boys, the, 424
Dean, Greg, 439
Dean, Howard, 252, 500
Death Cab for Cutie, 507
DeBarge, El, 542
DeBonis, Joseph, 582
DeBose, Ariana, 566
Decker, Richard, 420
Dee, Billy, 400
Deeb, Gary, 76
Deee-Lite, 461
DeGeneres, Ellen, 141, 245, 494, 534
DeGeneres, Vance, 330, 331
Del Rey, Lana, 526, 527
Delay, Brittany, 165
DeLay, Tom, 504
DeLuise, Michael, 408
DeLune, Lance, 401
Demetri, Melanie, 584, 585
Demme, Jonathan, 83, 431
Dempsey, John, 84
Dennehy, Brian, 473
Denver, John, 4
Depp, Johnny, 154
Derickson, David, 331
Dern, Bruce, 436, 439
Dern, Laura, 468
Dershowitz, Alan, 558
DeSantis, Ron, 574
Desaulniers, Heather, 543
Deschanel, Zooey, 527, 535, 585
Desmon, Stephanie, 94
Desmond Child and Rouge, 429
Des'ree, 472
Destiny's Child, 492, 503
DeTullio, Joe, 571, 580–583

DeVito, Danny, 83, 123, 269, 298, 432, 436, 437, 440, 450, 452, 454, 466, 487, 525
DeVito, Julia, 436
DeVito, Tommy, 134, 135
Devo, 425
DeVos, Betsy, 218
Dexy's Midnight Runners, 439
Dey, Susan, 265, 463
Diamond, Neil, 496
Diaz, Cameron, 151, 165, 483, 495, 504, 514, 516, 530, 537
DiCaprio, Leonardo, 534
Dick, Andy, 119
Dickerson, Eric, 480
Dickinson, Angie, 452
Dickinson, Bruce, 279, 373
Dickman, Audrey Peart, 11
Diddley, Bo, 395
Diddy-Dirty Money, 522
Diehl, David, 528
Diesel, Vin, 326
Dietrich, Marlena, 60
Dillinger, Daz, 478
Dillon, Denny, 75, 77, 79–82, 85, 232, 412, 431, 432, 434
Dillon, Matt, 507
Dinklage, Peter, 531, 543
Director, Roger, 91
Dirt Band, the, 423
Disclosure, 541
Dismukes, Andrew, 232, 557, 561, 568, 569
Disney, Walt, 339
Ditka, Mike, 124, 480
Dixie Chicks, the, 497
Dixon, Jesse, 412
DJ Khaled, 556, 560
Djokovic, Novak, 566
DMX, 138, 488
Dobyns, Lloyd, 3
Dodd, Chris, 305
Doherty, Shannen, 468
Dolby, Thomas, 448
Dole, Bob, 15, 196–197, 244, 453, 467, 473–478, 498
Dole, Elizabeth, 478
Dominus, Susan, 149
Donahue, Phil, 368
Donaldson, Sam, 248
Donnas, the, 497
D'Onofrio, Vincent, 404, 405, 513
Donovan, Elisa, 403

Doobie Brothers, the, 426
Doocy, Steve, 179, 528, 531, 540, 541, 550, 567, 572
Doors, the, 50, 285
Dorough, Bob, 382
Double Trouble, 109, 446, 447
Douglas, Kirk, 429
Douglas, Michael, 442
Doumanian, Jean, 76, 78–80, 83–85, 102, 274, 387, 431
Dow, Tony, 430
Downey, James, 587–590
Downey, Jim, 25, 26, 74, 102, 103, 122, 126, 127, 132, 176, 189, 199, 207, 232, 312, 318, 351, 429, 431, 464, 466, 524, 529
Downey, Morton, Jr., 454
Downey, Robert, Jr., 103, 104, 108, 232, 445, 447, 477
Downey, Roma, 482
Downs, Hugh, 476
Doyle, Brittany, 508
Doyle, Erin, 579–583
Doyle-Murray, Brian, 5, 8, 14, 16, 25, 26, 43, 73, 93, 232, 348, 429, 434
Dr. Demento, 83
Dr. Dre, 477, 487
Dr. John, 420
Drake, 163, 166, 525, 534, 544, 560
Dratch, Rachel, 133, 144, 147, 149, 152, 232–233, 235, 267, 268, 301, 309, 487, 488, 492, 493, 500, 501, 504, 507, 508, 521, 526, 528, 547, 551, 552, 557–559
Dream Academy, 446
Dreyer, Dylan, 542
Dreyfuss, Richard, 62, 346, 424
Driscoll, Dave, 582, 583
Driver, Adam, 542, 552, 558, 574, 578
Driver, Minnie, 139
Drysdale, Eric, 338
Duchovny, David, 136, 139, 141, 473, 483
Duffy, 514
Duffy, Patrick, 110
Duggan, Larry, 71
Dujardin, Jean, 527
Dukakis, Michael, 191, 243, 453, 455

Duke, David, 463
Duke, Robin, 85, 87, 94, 99, 233, 404, 434, 442
Duncan, Michael Clarke, 403
Dunham, Lena, 534
Dunn, Nora, 103, 104, 108–110, 112, 114, 116, 117, 119, 133, 233, 239, 278, 292, 318, 349, 445, 459
Dunne, Griffin, 107–108, 447
Dunst, Kirsten, 495
Duran Duran, 109, 439
Durang, Christopher, 448
Duvall, Robert, 482
Duvall, Shelley, 42, 419, 421
Dykstra, Lenny, 470
Dylan, Bob, 285, 294, 333, 428

E Street Band, the, 166, 496, 541, 562, 584
Earhardt, Ainsley, 550, 567, 572
Eastman, Craig, 516
Eastwood, Clint, 237
Ebersol, Dick, 2, 4, 7, 8, 10, 11, 17, 19, 31, 43–45, 85–88, 90, 91, 95, 96, 99, 101, 102, 188, 290, 291, 347, 349, 434
Ebersole, Christine, 90, 93, 233, 348, 434
Ebert, Roger, 308, 329, 394, 396, 401, 405, 409, 437, 440
Eckett, Carl, 584, 587, 588
Eckstrom, Richard, 508
Edebiri, Ayo, 575
Edie Brickell and New Bohemians, 454, 460
Edwards, Anthony, 135, 475
Edwards, Blaine, 473
Edwards, Blake, 377
Edwards, Dean, 233, 493, 499
Edwards, John, 519
Efron, Marshall, 53, 414
Efron, Zac, 517
Egan, Sarah, 581, 582, 584
Eilish, Billie, 166, 556, 566, 574
Eisenberg, Jesse, 310, 523
Eisenstein, Eric, 582, 584, 587
Elba, Idris, 555
Elders, Joycelyn, 472
Elliot, Mama Cass, 259
Elliott, Abby, 111, 149, 233, 515, 516, 521, 522, 528

Elliott, Chris, 122, 129, 132, 233–234, 426, 470, 471, 474
Elliott, Missy, 482, 500
Ellis, Jenna, 562
Elordi, Jacob, 574
Elvira, 452
Emanuel, Rahm, 211, 212, 521
Emerson, Jim, 398, 399
Eminem, 153, 390, 487, 489, 490, 496, 502, 522, 523, 533, 549, 582
En Vogue, 464, 480
Ensign, John, 519
Ensler, Eve, 380
Epstein, Jeffrey, 558
Erickson, C. O., 404
Erickson, Hal, 51
Escorel, Lauro, 404
Esiason, Boomer, 562
Essen, Tom Von, 145
Essman, Susie, 215
Estevez, Emilio, 470
Ettinger, Amber Lee, 513
Eurythmics, the, 109, 142, 456, 457
Evans, Amanda Duffy, 580
Evans, Lee, 400
Evans, Linda, 105
Eve, 492, 496, 504
Everclear, 476
Everlast, 485
Everson, Joyce, 416
Evert, Chris, 456
Ezra, George, 539

Fairchild, Morgan, 369
Faith No More, 460
Faithfull, Marianne, 429
Faiyaz, Brent, 575
Falco, Edie, 245, 323
Fall Out Boy, 507
Fallon, Jimmy, xvii, 42, 139, 143, 144, 147–149, 151, 161, 162, 166, 218, 223, 234, 245, 256, 267, 279, 299, 301, 302, 343, 352, 354, 355, 373, 374, 483, 486, 490, 491, 494, 500–502, 510, 517, 521, 525–527, 530, 534, 544, 547, 552, 556, 558, 575, 578, 583–585
Fallon (Hogan), Siobhan, 120, 121, 234, 462, 465
Fanning, Dakota, 152

Fanning, Elle, 511
Farhi, Paul, 374
Faris, Anna, 514, 525, 536
Farley, Chris, 119–122, 124–130, 132, 142, 148, 234, 245, 257, 307, 319–320, 350, 372, 373, 395, 408, 459, 462, 469, 471–475, 480, 556
Farley, Tom, Jr., 234
Farrakhan, Louis, 550
Farrell, Colin, 503, 569, 572
Farris, Dionne, 473
Fassero, Jeff, 481
Father John Misty, 534, 547
Fauci, Anthony, 167, 218, 306, 560, 562–564, 566, 568
Fear, 91, 109, 290–291, 434
Feder, Richard, 69, 70
Federline, Kevin, 512
Feely, Ariel, 90
Feinstein, Dianne, 220, 551
Feist, 512
Fellini, Federico, 333, 334
Fenson, Craig, 497, 503
Ferdinand, Jason Max, 571
Ferguson, Turd. *See* Reynolds, Burt
Ferrell, Will, xvii, 9, 26, 68, 132–142, 144, 146–149, 161, 162, 174, 176, 177, 197–203, 206, 234–235, 265, 269, 296, 307, 314, 328, 350, 353, 374, 400, 401, 403, 404, 406, 474, 476–480, 482–484, 486, 487, 490–496, 498, 505, 509, 517, 528, 533, 541, 550, 557
Ferretti, Fred, 53
Ferrucci, Gina, 580
Ferry, Bryan, 452
Fey, Tina, xvii, 3, 12, 54, 144, 149, 170, 175, 180, 200, 201, 205–210, 217, 232, 235, 245, 250, 251, 264, 270, 274, 278, 301, 352, 354, 355, 376, 380, 490, 496, 503, 508, 509, 512, 514, 515, 517, 520, 521, 524, 526, 530, 532, 540–542, 544, 551–553, 556, 560, 566, 567, 574, 582, 584, 586, 587, 590, 591
Field, Sally, 469
Fieri, Guy, 247, 570

# Index

Fierstein, Harvey, 536
Fine Young Cannibals, 456
Fineman, Chloe, 226–227, 235, 326, 327, 557, 563, 568, 569, 571, 572
Fink, Hugh, 587
Fiorina, Carly, 539, 541
Firth, Colin, 501
Fischbacher, Siegfried, 4
Fischer, Jenna, 553
Fishbone, 294, 461
Fisher, Amy, 298, 299
Fisher, Carrie, 393, 425, 545
Fixx, the, 441, 442
Flack, Roberta, 4
Flaherty, Joe, 14, 404
Flakes, Jeff, 553
Fleet Foxes, 516, 568
Fleetwood, Mick, 440
Flockhart, Calista, 139, 268, 490
Florence + the Machine, 522, 526, 539
Floyd, Cliff, 481
Flynn, Michael, 218, 549
Flynt, Larry, 485
Fogel, Jared, 514
Foley, Dave, 398
Foley, Mark, 509
Folksmen, the, 443
Folsey, George, Jr., 392
Fonda, Jane, 556
Foo Fighters, 153, 166, 288, 475, 487, 497, 498, 506, 512, 524, 528, 550, 561, 567, 573, 577, 578, 582
Forbes, Malcolm, 294, 295
Forbes, Steve, 294–295, 476
Ford, Betty, 20, 60, 239
Ford, Gerald R., 16, 18, 29, 35, 58, 80, 170, 171, 175, 176, 181–185, 280, 289, 307, 344, 412, 413, 415, 423, 429
Ford, Rob, 533
Foreman, George, 472
Forte, Will, xvii, 9, 159, 176, 201, 202, 211, 235–236, 261, 280, 353, 354, 401, 402, 496, 497, 502–506, 508–510, 513, 516–519, 521, 528, 545, 566, 576
Fortenberry, John, 403
Foster, Jodie, 11, 239, 245, 418
Foster the People, 525
Fowler, Dexter, 545

Fowler, Jim, 83
Fox, John, 434
Fox, Matthew, 509
Fox, Megan, 517
Fox, Michael J., 461
Fox, Richard B., 587, 588
Foxx, Jamie, 488, 530
Foxx, Virginia, 574
Foy, Claire, 553
Franco, Dave, 550
Franco, Francisco, 344, 362
Franco, James, 514, 518, 519, 535, 537, 549
Frank, Barney, 383, 515
Frank, Philip, 518
Franken, Al, 9, 25, 38, 44, 52, 61, 102, 108, 109, 119, 125, 128, 132, 185, 186, 189–191, 194, 280, 314, 346, 371, 379, 404, 405, 413, 421, 429, 431, 447, 448, 453, 461, 464, 474, 487, 497, 500, 588–590
Frankie Goes to Hollywood, 443
Franklin, Aretha, 109, 259, 392–395, 431, 432, 469, 548
Franklin, Benjamin, 536
Franklin, Joe, 99, 231, 304
Franklin, Kirk, 542, 572
Franz Ferdinand, 505, 506
Fraser, Brendan, 480, 485, 490
Fraser, Erin, 400
Frazier, Walt, 4
Freeman, John, 392
Freeman, Kathleen, 392, 393
Freeman, Martin, 538, 584
Freeman, Morgan, 521
Freeman, Seymour, 563
Freitas, Joseph, 314
French, Leigh, 50
Fretts, Bruce, 121
Freud, 379
Friedman, Jack, 367
Friedman, Kinky, 417
Friendly, David T., 384
Frisher, Barry, 587
Frith, Michael, 37
Frost, David, 47, 49
Fruchter, Rena, 5
Frusciante, John, 291
Fuchs, Rafael, 470
Fuhrman, Mark, 478
Fuller, Kurt, 408
Fun, 529

Funky 4 + 1, 433
Furtado, Nelly, 491, 508
Future, 542, 543, 553, 567

G. Love, 504
Gable, Clark, 15
Gabor, Zsa Zsa, 239, 296
Gabriel, Peter, 467
Gad, Josh, 560
Gaddafi, Muammar, 353
al-Gaddafi, Muammar, 517, 525
Gadot, Gal, 548
Gadsby, Hannah, 230
Gaetz, Matt, 563
Gaffigan, Jim, 476
Gaines, Chris, 288, 487
Galifianakis, Zach, 212, 278, 520, 524, 531
Galligan, Zach, 12
Galtieri, Leopoldo, 91
Gandhi, Indira, 60, 369
Gandolfini, James, 301, 502
Gangel, Linda, 303
Garbage, 485, 486
Garber, Victor, 24
Garciaparra, Nomar, 490
Gardella, Kay, 95
Gardner, Heidi, 227, 236, 326, 357, 548, 550, 552, 553, 562, 567, 569, 572–576
Garfield, Andrew, 526, 535
Garfunkel, Art, 35, 45, 70, 277, 281, 287, 288, 329, 363, 411, 412, 423, 449
Garner, Jennifer, 268, 497, 532
Garofalo, Janeane, 119, 122–123, 129, 132, 236, 472
Garr, Teri, 429, 440, 446
Garrett, Siedah, 457
Gass, Kyle, 483, 495, 507
Gasteyer, Ana, 9, 133, 137, 141, 142, 195, 198, 236, 269, 303, 477, 478, 481, 483, 485, 486, 489, 492, 495, 501, 520–521, 528
Gates, Anita, 404, 406
Gates, Bill, 481
Gaughan, Shannon, 589
G-Eazy, 550
Geithner, Timothy, 516, 517
Gelbart, Larry, 47
Gellar, Sarah Michelle, 140, 482, 486, 489, 496
Gelman, Michael, 499
Gendel, Morgan, 103

Index

George Thorogood and the Destroyers, 437
Gershon, Gina, 489, 575
Gertz, Jami, 24
Gervais, Ricky, 340
Gerwig, Greta, 549, 574
Giamatti, Paul, 503
Gianas, Tom, 136
Gibb, Barry, 301–302, 499, 534
Gibb, Robin, 279, 301, 302, 499
Gibbs, Marla, 127
Gibson, Henry, 51, 392
Gibson, Mel, 115, 455
Gifford, Kathie Lee, 239, 256, 261, 460
Gilbert, Sara, 123, 469
Gilliam, Terry, 52, 332
Gillis, Shane, 575
Gilmore, Gary, 89
Gilmour, David, 452
Gin Blossoms, 476
Gingrich, Callista, 150
Gingrich, Newt, 208, 471–473, 475, 484, 485, 527, 528
Ginsberg, Allen, 90
Ginsburg, Ruth Bader, 167, 177, 245, 356, 357, 560, 568
Gipsy Kings, 455
Giuliani, Andrew, 469
Giuliani, Carol, 538
Giuliani, Rudolph (Rudy), 140, 145–146, 167, 170, 177, 197, 218, 223, 245, 475, 481, 487, 493, 494, 496, 513, 538, 552, 554, 557, 562
Givens, Adele, 552
Gladwell, Malcolm, 318
Glaser, Paul Michael, 90
Glass, Phillip, 447
Glavine, Tom, 474
Glazer, Mitch, 11
Gleason, Jackie, 364
Gleeson, Brendan, 569, 572
Glick, Jiminy, 504
Glover, Danny, 455
Glover, Donald, 166, 551, 552, 582
Glover, Savion, 487
Gnarls Barkley, 513
Goetz, Bernhard, 238
Go-Go's, the, 435
Gold, Andrew, 431

Goldberg, Whoopi, 231, 259, 449, 530
Goldblum, Jeff, 139, 468, 480
Goldman, Lew, 349
Goldry, Debette, 546
Goldwyn, John, 401
Gomez, Selena, 542, 568, 570
González, Elián, 197, 488
Gonzalez, Alberto, 505, 511
Gonzalez, Manolo, 527
Good Charlotte, 498
Goodell, Roger, 536, 565
Gooding, Cuba, Jr., 141, 246, 486
Goodman, Herb, 60
Goodman, John, 133, 135, 139, 168, 179, 218, 271, 303, 393, 394, 457, 460, 464, 467, 470, 473, 476, 479, 482–486, 488, 489, 493, 499, 533, 546, 551
Gorbachev, Mikhail, 114, 452
Gordon, Diana, 572
Gordon, Jeff, 497
Gordon, Kim, 532
Gordon, Michael, 337
Gordon, Ruth, 55, 419
Gordon-Levitt, Joseph, 278, 518, 529
Gore, Al, 174, 194, 199–200, 202, 203, 238, 244, 264, 294, 490, 494, 497, 500, 508, 518
Gore, Kristin, 590
Gore, Michael, 406
Gore, Tipper, 239, 497
Gosling, Ryan, 169, 541, 548, 576
Gossett, Louis, Jr., 437
Gottfried, Gilbert, 75, 77, 79, 80, 85, 236–237, 346, 431, 433, 568
Gotye, 527, 528
Gould, Elliott, 41, 59–61, 77, 79–81, 83, 84, 145, 263, 267, 270, 413, 416, 420, 426, 429, 431, 460, 567, 590
Goulding, Ellie, 524
Goulet, Robert, 269
Gourley, Matt, 217
Grace, Topher, 503
Graham, Heather, 486
Graham, Lindsey, 167, 542, 553, 556, 559, 562, 575
Grammer, Kelsey, 462, 470, 483

Gran, Ben, 163
Grande, Ariana, 164–166, 536, 543, 575
Grandy, Charlie, 587, 590
Graney, John Link, 404
Grant, Eddy, 440
Grateful Dead, 70, 285, 425, 430
Gravity, 424
Gray, David, 490
Gray, Macy, 488, 493
Gray, Spalding, 421
Grayson, Bobby, 588
Green, Al, 446
Green, Brian Austin, 517
Green, CeeLo, 259, 523
Green, Seth, 486
Green, Tom, 490
Green Day, 471, 504, 517
Greenblatt, Robert, 159
Greenburg, Dan, 415
Greene, Marjorie Taylor, 179, 568
Greenfield, Jeff, 18
Greenson, Shawn, 490
Greer, Jane, 452
Greta Van Fleet, 554
Gretzky, Wayne, 456
Grey, Brad, 548
Grey, Skylar, 537, 549
Grieco, Richard, 403, 404
Grier, David Alan, 473, 475, 478
Griffin, Blake, 565
Griffin, John Howard, 336
Griffin, Kathy, 398
Griffin, Merv, 138, 438
Griffith, Andy, 437
Griffith, Melanie, 454, 538
Grisanti, Frank, 582–587, 588
Grodin, Charles, 279–281, 422
Grohl, Dave, 153, 166, 530, 573
Gross, Jamie, 401
Gross, Mary, 87, 90, 91, 99, 100, 237, 305, 348, 434, 440, 442, 445
Gross, Michael, 237
Grossman, Adam, 272
Grossman, Lawrence K., 438
Gruden, Jon, 565
Grudzielanek, Mark, 481
Grundfest, Bill, 473
Grunwald, Howard, 329, 414

# Index

Guccione, Bob, Jr., 109, 264, 286
Guest, Christopher, xvii, 5, 31, 87, 99, 100, 234, 237, 304, 336, 349, 443, 445
Guilfoyle, Kimberly, 218, 570
Guillaume, Robert, 439
Gumbel, Bryant, 435
Gumbel, Greg, 524, 538
G-Unit, 498, 500
Gunna, 565, 567
Gussow, Mel, 16
Guthrie, Savannah, 561
Guttenberg, Steve, 377, 449
Gyllenhaal, Jake, 152, 278, 299, 510, 559, 568, 576
Gzowski, Peter, 59

Haas, Britney, 516
Hack, Shelley, 90
Haddaway, 136
Haddish, Tiffany, 549, 582
Hader, Bill, xvii, 144, 148, 151, 152, 154, 155, 161, 177, 178, 208, 218, 237, 245, 272, 300, 304, 322, 323, 353, 354, 357, 383, 388, 505, 513, 517–519, 521–523, 525, 527, 528, 532, 534, 536, 551, 555, 582
Hagerty, Julie, 450
Haggard, Merle, 543
Hagler, Marvin, 448
Hahn, Jessica, 111
HAIM, 533, 547, 583
Haimer, Robert, 83
Hale, Tony, 543
Halen, Eddie Van, 450
Haley, Nikki, 574, 575
Hall, Anthony Michael, 103–105, 108, 237–238, 283, 445, 447
Hall, Brad, 87, 99, 238, 242, 348, 349, 437, 441, 442
Hall, Daryl, 436
Hall, Jerry, 113, 369, 446
Hall, Rich, 87, 99, 100, 238, 349, 443
Halsband, Kenneth, 401
Halsey, 166, 550, 553–555, 558, 565
Hamill, Mark, 479
Hamilton, Ashley, 468
Hamilton, Linda, 148, 463
Hamilton, Pete, 291
Hamilton, Scott, 534

Hamilton, Tom, 118
Hamilton, William, 571
Hamlisch, Marvin, 71, 397
Hamm, Jon, 145, 267, 268, 280, 515, 519, 522, 524, 527, 528, 532, 534, 541, 551, 556, 557, 569, 576, 586
Hammer, 127, 288, 463
Hammond, Darrell, 122, 129, 133, 134, 139, 140, 144, 151, 174, 176, 177, 193, 195, 197, 198, 201–203, 206, 211, 213, 214, 216, 238, 245, 274, 305, 307, 360, 383, 393, 474–497, 499–507, 509–511, 513–519, 524, 526, 539–544, 548, 559
Hampton, Mark, 412
Hancock, Herbie, 444
Hanks, Tom, 117, 133, 136, 142, 145, 163, 191, 267, 271–272, 379, 403, 446, 453, 457, 460, 464, 477, 491, 508, 517, 524, 527, 529–531, 545, 559, 560, 566, 569
Hannah, Cara, 580, 584, 585
Hanrahan, Bill, 11
Hansome, Rhonda, 38
Hanson, 265, 481
Harbour, David, 557
Harding, Tonya, 239, 469
Hardwick, Cheryl, 109
Hargitay, Mariska, 555
Harlow, Jack, 166, 563, 569, 577, 579, 580
Harmon, Mark, 451
Harper, Donnie, 419
Harpo, Slim, 41, 393
Harrelson, Woody, 176, 271, 457, 462, 464, 537, 556, 557, 571, 572
Harington, Kit, 555
Harris, Judy, 38
Harris, Kamala, 218, 225, 227, 253, 556, 558, 560–562, 581
Harris, Mark, 121
Harris, Neil Patrick, 309, 516
Harrison, Chris, 551
Harrison, George, 278, 287, 294, 331, 332, 418
Harry, Deborah, 82, 84, 433, 449

Harry, Jackée, 299
Hart, Kevin, 531, 538, 550, 582
Hartley, Bob, 472
Hartman, Phil, 9, 109, 111, 113, 114, 116, 119, 121, 122, 124, 127–130, 133, 135, 142, 148, 176, 189–193, 195, 196, 238–239, 243, 293, 297, 304, 318–320, 395, 396, 448, 450–452, 454, 455, 457–461, 463, 465–470, 476, 478, 537, 589
Hartnett, Josh, 494
Harvey, Dennis, 404, 406
Harvey, Paul, 238, 349
Harvey, Steve, 259, 554, 556
Harvie, Derek, 490
Hasselbeck, Elisabeth, 150, 261, 540, 541
Hasselhoff, David, 302, 471
Hastert, Dennis, 509
Hatcher, Teri, 476
Hathaway, Anne, 154, 383, 514, 517, 522, 529, 531, 552
Havas, Lianne La, 537
Hawk, Tony, 571
Hawkins, Connie, 287
Hawkins, Taylor, 567
Hawn, Goldie, 51
Hay, Carla, 568
Hayden, Julie, 398
Hayek, Salma, 498
Hayes, Isaac, 395
Hayes, Sean, 148, 294, 491
Hays, Robert, 84, 432
Haysbert, Dennis, 507
Hayward, Tony, 521
Hazelwood, Joseph, 455
Hearst, Patty, 16, 344
Heartbreakers, the, 125, 153, 428, 439, 456, 462, 471, 477, 486, 521
Heche, Anne, 139, 480
Heckerling, Amy, 403
Hedaya, Dan, 403
Heder, Jon, 505
Hefner, Hugh, 4, 421, 548
Hegyes, Robert, 474
Heimeau, Henri, 65
Helm, Levon, 420
Helms, Ed, 524, 532, 553
Helms, Jesse, 471, 475, 484
Helmsley, Leona, 111, 233
Hemingway, Mariel, 474

Hemsley, Sherman, 319, 417
Hemsworth, Chris, 539, 541
Hemsworth, Liam, 537, 539
Hemsworth, Luke, 539
Henderson, Florence, 440, 489
Hendrix, Elaine, 406
Hendrix, Jimi, 246, 290
Henley, Don, 456, 492
Henner, Marilu, 436
Henning, Doug, 238
Henry, Buck, 9, 24, 29, 54, 57–58, 63, 64, 74, 79, 145, 271, 282, 344, 393, 413, 416, 418, 421–422, 424, 425, 427, 428, 431, 558, 589
Henson, Jim, 8, 37, 523, 526, 539
Henson, Taraji P., 539, 584
Henstridge, Natasha, 483
Hepburn, Katharine, 99, 256
H.E.R., 561, 573, 580
Herlihy, Martin, 341, 342, 565, 566
Herman, Pee-wee (Paul Reubens), 238, 445, 523
Hernández, Marcello, 158, 239, 358, 569, 570, 572, 575
Herring, Craig, 404
Herring, Pembroke J., 404
Herrington, David, 393
Hessoman, Howard, 428, 437, 439
Heston, Charlton, 116, 127, 450, 468, 469, 476
Hewitt, Don, 365
Hewitt, Jennifer Love, 134, 484
Hiatt, John, 454, 455
Hibbert, Stephen, 398, 399
Hickman, Dwayne, 403
Hickox, Kaci, 537
Hicks, Hope, 550
Higgins, John, 341, 342, 565, 566, 574
Higgins, Steve, 579–583, 587, 590, 591
Hill, Anita, 382
Hill, Doug, xv, 4, 6, 66, 122, 285
Hill, Faith, 496
Hill, Jonah, 272, 513, 527, 532, 534, 542, 550, 553
Hill, Lauryn, 484

Hilton, Paris, 503
Hines, Gregory, 427
Hirsch, Judd, 436
Hitchcock, Alfred, 265
Hodgson, Joel, 440, 441
Hoffa, Jimmy, 35
Hoffman, Philip Seymour, 323
Hogan, Deborah, 400
Hogan, Hulk, 368, 444
Holbrook, Hal, 425
Hole, 316, 472
Holliday, Jennifer, 435
Hollyn, Norman, 398
Holmes, Buster, 419
Holmes, Katie, 137, 154, 268, 491
Holmes, Larry, 441
Holt, Lauren, 239, 561, 562, 564
Holt, Lester, 574
Holyfield, Evander, 478
Homer, John, 545
Honeycutt, Kirk, 401
Honeydrippers, the, 444
Hong, James, 408
Hooks, Jan, 109, 111, 112, 114, 119–121, 133, 144, 178, 191–192, 239, 268, 278, 297, 318, 320, 395, 396, 408, 448, 452, 454, 456, 460, 462, 465, 468, 470, 536
Hope, Bob, 4, 296
Hopper, Dennis, 451, 460
Horan, Niall, 558
Horn, Roy, 4
Hornsby, Bruce, 450, 463
Hoskins, Allen, 97
Hoskins, Bob, 483
Hothouse Flowers, 459
Houston, Whitney, 154, 253, 478
Hovde, Ellen, 397
Howard, David, 481
Howard, Robert T., 2
Howard, Ron, 434, 437
Hozier, 536
Huckabee, Mike, 513, 539
Hudlin, Reginald, 400
Hudnut, Bob, 471
Hudson, Kate, 268, 490
Hudson, Rock, 105
Hudson, Yvonne, 79, 85, 157, 239, 432, 434
Huelsman, Eugene, 587
Huey Lewis and the News, 441

Huffington, Arianna, 250, 260
Hughes, John, 103, 237
Hughes, Scottie Nell, 543
Hull, Brett, 503
Hume, Brit, 505, 509
Humphries, Barry, 421
Humplik, Glenn, 490
Hundley, Todd, 481
Hunt, Helen, 265, 305, 373, 470, 481
Hunt, Richard, 37
Huntsman, Jon, 208, 526
Hurt, John, 483
Hurt, William, 455
Hussein, Saddam, 111, 197, 198, 203, 506
Huston, Anjelica, 108, 448
Hutcherson, Josh, 533, 537
Hutchinson, Kay Bailey, 211
Hutsell, Melanie, 120–122, 230, 239, 298, 350, 463, 468, 470
Hutton, Lauren, 435
Hymes, Phil, 582
Hynde, Chrissie, 474

Ian, Janis, 27, 32, 34, 44, 286, 411
Ice Spice, 573
Ice-T, 555, 570
Idle, Eric, 41, 52, 63, 67, 332, 417, 420, 426, 428
Idol, Billy, 257, 294, 441
Ifill, Gwen, 514
Imagine Dragons, 534
Imbruglia, Natalie, 482
Imus, Don, 511
Ingraham, Laura, 167, 179, 553, 559, 567
Innes, Neil, 420, 421
INXS, 460, 461
Irons, Jeremy, 294, 461
Irwin, Bill, 437
Isaac, Oscar, 567
Isaak, Chris, 461
Issa, Darrell, 532
Ito, Lance, 248, 472, 473

J. Geils Band, the, 429, 430
Jacklin, Judith, 392
Jackman, Hugh, 494, 525
Jackson, Janet, 148, 151, 288, 388, 470, 501, 587
Jackson, Jesse, 278, 440, 441, 443, 511
Jackson, Joe, 447

Jackson, Joshua, 488
Jackson, Kate, 426
Jackson, Ketanji Brown, 568
Jackson, Luscious, 472
Jackson, Michael, 233, 245, 341, 469, 475, 478, 504
Jackson, Peter, 12
Jackson, Randy, 296
Jackson, Reggie, 42
Jackson, Ronny, 550
Jackson, Samuel L., 141, 154, 388, 481, 530
Jackson, Sheila, 231
Jackson, Victoria, 109–110, 114, 115, 119, 120, 133, 239–240, 448, 450, 458, 465
Jacobson, Scott, 338
Jagger, Mick, 98, 125, 288, 397, 426, 446, 466, 494, 528, 573, 585
Jambeck, Steve, 589
James, Caryn, 199, 200
James, LeBron, 512
James, Rick, 435
James, Susan Saint, 101, 434, 436, 437, 439
Jamiroquai, 480
Jane's Addiction, 481
Jankeloff, Mark, 579
Janney, Allison, 497
Jantjie, Thamsanqa, 533
Japanese Breakfast, 568, 569
Jarreau, Al, 286, 414, 442, 457
Jarrett, Keith, 424
Jay, Ricky, 419
Jaymes, Ed, 448
Jay-Z, 250, 341, 491, 496, 499, 520, 521, 531, 536, 538, 548
Jefferies, Gregg, 481
Jenner, Bruce, 314
Jenner, Kris, 565
Jennings, Peter, 191
Jennings, Waylon, 444
Jensen, Heidi, ix
Jensen, Johnny E., 400
Jepsen, Carly Rae, 539
Jeremih, 541, 556
Jessie J, 524
Jet, 500
Jeter, Derek, 316, 494
Jewel, 479, 480, 484
Jewell, Richard, 302, 480
Jindal, Bobby, 535
Jintao, Hu, 518, 522

J-Kwon, 502
Jobs, Steve, 536
Joel, Billy, 70, 125, 255, 423, 456, 468
Johansson, Scarlett, 218, 219, 223, 225, 245, 271, 272, 507, 511, 518, 522, 539, 547, 552, 558, 572, 575
John, Elton, 254, 255, 288, 436, 510, 524, 531
John Hiatt and the Goners, 454, 455
Johnny Clegg and Savuka, 454
Johns, Glynis, 406
Johnson, Arte, 51
Johnson, Austin, 568
Johnson, Beverly, 455
Johnson, Boris, 558
Johnson, Dakota, 342, 538, 575
Johnson, Don, 454, 538
Johnson, Dwayne ("The Rock"), 137, 210–211, 272, 488, 495, 516, 518, 539, 547
Johnson, Ernie, Jr., 539
Johnson, Jack, 504
Johnson, James Austin, 176, 223, 224, 226, 240, 358, 562, 564–575
Johnson, Jimmy, 571
Johnson, Mike, 225, 573
Johnson, Punkie, 158, 166, 167, 227, 240, 326, 561, 568
Johnson-Jefferson, Shari, 568
Jonas, Nick, 166, 543, 563
Jonas Brothers, 516, 556, 572
Jones, Chipper, 474
Jones, Felicity, 546
Jones, January, 518
Jones, Leslie, xvii, 157, 165, 218, 223, 240, 247, 252–253, 537, 553–555
Jones, Norah, 497, 501
Jones, Paula, 193, 303
Jones, Quincy, 457, 520
Jones, Rashida, 511
Jones, Rickie Lee, 427, 436, 456
Jones, Sharon, 519, 541, 568
Jones, Steve, 531, 532
Jones, Terry, 52
Jong-un, Kim, 531, 536, 555
Jonze, Spike, 551
Joplin, Janis, 285
Jordan, Jim, 555, 573

Jordan, Michael, 124, 264, 405, 462, 468
Jordan, Michael B., 316, 326, 571
Jordan, Steve, 430, 453
Jory, Tom, 80
Joseph, John, 291
Jost, Colin, 230, 240–241, 255, 272, 355–358, 541, 550, 559, 565, 566, 590
Jr. Walker & the All Stars, 433, 434
Jur, Jeff, 398
Justian, Eric, 584

Kaczynski, Ted, 476, 482
Kaepernick, Colin, 565
Kahan, Noah, 574
Kahn, Eve, 121
Kahn, Madeline, 10, 38, 60, 65, 185, 415, 421, 475
Kaling, Mindy, 154, 518
Kaluuya, Daniel, 552, 563
Kamen, Jay, 403
Kane, Benjamin, 408
Kane, Tim, 544
Kardashian, Khloé, 111, 229, 565
Kardashian, Kim, 111, 212, 250, 314, 535, 565
Kardashian, Kourtney, 111
Kardashian, Robert, 478
Karmin, 527
Karol G, 573
Karras, Alex, 444
Kasem, Casey, 451, 468
Kasich, John, 541
Kasoff, Jan, 587–589
Kattan, Chris, 9, 65, 68, 132, 133, 135, 136, 140, 141, 144, 161, 234, 241, 267, 272, 373, 374, 403, 404, 476, 477, 479–481, 488, 494, 499, 508, 526, 528
Katz, Stephen M., 392
Kaufman, Andy, xvii, 32–33, 94–96, 411, 412, 414, 419, 422, 428, 435, 437, 438, 487
Kaufman, Elaine, 415
Kavanaugh, Brett, 218, 300–301, 552
Kavanaugh, Ryan, 401
Kazurinsky, Tim, 85, 87, 99, 241, 348, 434, 436, 440, 442

# Index

k.d. lang and the Reclines, 457
Keach, Stacy, 424
Keane, 503, 504
Kearney, Molly, 158, 241–242, 358, 569–572, 574
Keaton, Michael, 139, 437, 465, 539, 555
Keefe, Terry, 103
Ke$ha, 520
Keineg, Katell, 474
Keitel, Harvey, 466, 497
Kelce, Jason, 572
Kelce, Travis, 341, 572, 573
Kelis, 500, 501
Kellerman, Sally, 433
Kelly, Bridget, 521
Kelly, Chris, 165, 255, 534, 577–579
Kelly, Megyn, 301, 537
Kelly, Michael, 218
Kelly, R., 533, 555
Kelly, Sheila, 273
Kemper, Ellie, 553
Kendrick, Anna, 535, 584
Kennedy, Bobby, 105
Kennedy, Charles, 347
Kennedy, George, 434
Kennedy, John F., 49, 105, 106, 185, 553
Kennedy, Ted, 428
Kenny, Francis, 395, 403, 408
Kenny G, 525
Kenward, Erik, 579–583, 587, 590
Kepcher, Carolyn, 501
Kerik, Bernard, 145, 493
Kerouac, Jack, 90
Kerr, Jean, 398
Kerrigan, Nancy, 264, 287, 469
Kerry, John, 201–202, 503
Kerven, Claude, 336
Key, Keegan-Michael, 564, 577
Keyes, Paul, 51, 173
Keys, Alicia, 493, 519, 543
Khalid, 555
Khalifa, Wiz, 539
Khan, Chaka, 443
Kiam, Victor, 459
Kid Creole and the Coconuts, 431
Kid Cudi, 552, 563
Kid Laroi, 564
Kid Rock, 133, 489, 492
Kidder, Margot, ix, 427
Kidman, Nicole, 235, 326, 468
Kiedis, Anthony, 291, 292

Kightlinger, Laura, 132, 242, 470, 474
Kihn, Greg, 445
Killam, Taran, 9, 156, 161, 176, 208, 212, 217, 242, 301, 356, 524, 527, 528, 530–535, 537–544
Killers, the, 503, 508, 514
Kilmeade, Brian, 179, 247, 528, 531, 540, 541, 550, 567, 572
Kilmer, Val, 401, 490, 526, 579
Kilpatrick, James J., 365
Kim Jong-Il, 497, 504
Kimbra, 528
Kimmel, Jimmy, 256, 287
Kinane, Ruth, 296
King, B. B., 393, 395
King, Don, 97, 439
King, Don Roy, 558, 566, 577–586
King, Gayle, 542, 555
King, John, 207
King, Kip, 499
King, Larry, 19, 179, 303, 519, 520
King, Martin Luther, Jr., 138, 530, 538
King, Regina, 562
King Princess, 557
Kingman, Dave, 394
Kings, Gipsy, 455
Kings of Leon, 514, 522, 533
Kinison, Sam, 384, 385, 446, 447, 449
Kinks, the, 419, 434, 443
Kinnear, Greg, 483
Kirkpatrick, James J., 346
Kirshner, Don, 423, 424, 428
Kirsnick, Rapper, 570
Kissinger, Henry, 16, 60, 185, 186
Kitay, Dave, 403
Kitman, Marvin, 75
Klady, Leonard, 396
Klain, Ron, 537
Klausner, Julie, 338
Klein, Marci, 588
Klein, Rob, 590, 591
Klein, Robert, ix, 46, 71, 263, 412, 423
Kleiser, Randal, 83, 431
Kline, Kevin, 454, 467
Klingman, Lynzee, 397
Klobuchar, Amy, 301, 558, 559

Knabel, Friedrich, 65
Knelp, Dick, 283
Knight, Shirley, 404, 405
Knight, Ted, 429
Knoedelseder, William K., Jr., 85
Knopfler, Mark, 453
Knowles, Beyoncé, 151
Knowles, Solange, 536, 545
Knoxville, Johnny, 505, 507
Koch, Ed, 439, 442
Koch, Howard W. Jr., 407, 408
Koechner, Dave, 132
Koechner, David, 242, 474, 476, 533
Koehler, Robert, 401
Kool and the Gang, 442
Kool Moe Dee, 457
Koppel, Ted, 98, 178, 238, 250, 433, 480, 482, 488, 500
Koren, Steve, 135, 403, 406
Korn, 506
Kornacki, Steve, 570
Kotb, Hoda, 256, 260
Krakowski, Jane, 520, 540
Krasinski, John, 562
Kravitz, Lenny, 467, 491, 496
Kravitz, Zoë, 552, 567
Krempel, Jenna, 541
Kreviazuk, Chantal, 537
Kriegman, Mitchell, 431, 432
Kristofferson, Kris, 294, 416
Kroeger, Gary, 87, 94, 97, 99, 100, 238, 242–243, 437, 439, 443, 445
Kroft, Steve, 536
Kucinich, Dennis, 250
Kudrow, Lisa, 474, 477
Kufrin, Rebecca, 551
Kuhn, Maggie, 302–303, 413
Kurosawa, Akira, 56, 57
Kurtis, Bill, 480
Kushner, Jared, 218, 223, 547, 552
Kutcher, Ashton, 279, 494, 498, 504, 513, 519

LaBelle, Patti, 231, 259
LaBeouf, Shia, 151, 153, 402, 511, 513
Labrecque, Jeff, 270
Lachey, Nick, 500
Lacy, Steve, 569
Lady, Church, 543
Lady Antebellum, 525

# Index

Lady Gaga, 152–153, 164, 166, 278, 329, 340, 518, 524, 525, 533, 545, 573
Ladysmith Black Mambazo, 278, 287, 447
Lagerfeld, Karl, 494
Lahti, Christine, 90
Lake, Kari, 569, 570
Lakshmi, Padma, 573
Lamar, Kendrick, 530, 537, 554, 569
Lamas, Fernando, 99, 349, 368
LaMontagne, Ray, 516
Lander, David, 471, 477
Landis, John, 392–394
Lane, Brandy, 489
Lane, Nathan, 481
lang, k.d., 457
Lange, Artie, 517
Lapham, Lewis, 483
Larkins, Tommy, 483
Larnick, Eric, 265
Larroquette, John, 451, 453
Larry, David, 133, 484
Larry the Cable Guy, 252
Larson, Brie, 543
Lasser, Louise, 54, 416
Latonero, Jeff, 583
Latta, Robert, 444
Latto, 575
Lauer, Matt, 483, 512
Lauper, Cyndi, 257
Laurance, Matthew, 79, 85, 243, 432, 433
Laurie, Hugh, 509, 515
Lautner, Taylor, 519
Lavigne, Avril, 497, 501, 511
Law, Jude, 299, 502, 520, 526
Lawler, Jerry, 437
Lawless, Lucy, 140, 484
Lawrence, Jennifer, 247, 530, 531, 537, 585
Lawrence, Martin, 385, 469
Lawrence, Steve, 392, 393
Laymer, Richard, 460, 463, 467
Lazar, Swifty, 88
Lazarus, Dawn, 551
LCD Soundsystem, 547, 567
Lea, Nicolas, 483
Leach, Robin, 99, 304, 452
Lear, Jonathan, 346
Lear, Norman, 4, 417
Lebedeff, Aaron, 332
LeBlanc, Matt, 360
Lecter, Hannibal, 576

Lee, Christopher, 22, 60, 423
Lee, Eugene, 3, 10, 102, 572, 580–583, 585
Lee, Franne, 3, 10, 41
Lee, Jason, 506
Lee, Linda, 432
Lee, Pamela, 403, 479
Lee, Spike, 448
Lee, Stan, 58
Lee, Tommy, 479
Legend, John, 556
Lehrer, Jim, 199, 249, 489, 490, 502, 529
Leighton, Laura, 475
Lemmon, Jack, 296
Lemon, Don, 553
Lennon, John, 285, 336, 434
Lennon, Sean, 554
Lennox, Annie, 12, 464, 473
Leno, Jay, 234, 385, 447, 470
Leslie, Rose, 555
Leto, Jared, 568
Letterman, David, 244, 338
Level 42, 448
Levi, Charles, 589
Levine, Adam, 329, 505, 512, 530, 536, 563
Levine, Thomas, 400
Levy, Dan, 326, 562
Levy, Eugene, 23, 400
Levy, Neil, 83
Lewinsky, Monica, 134, 179, 193, 195, 197–199, 255, 270, 303–304, 400, 482–484, 486
Lewis, Dave, 282
Lewis, Huey, 441
Lewis, Jerry, 256, 440
Lewis, Ray, 536
Lewis, Richard, 319
Lewis, Ryan, 531
Lewyn, Mark, 92
Libby, Scooter, 506
Liberace, 304, 450
Lieberman, Joseph, 491
Lightfoot, Gordon, 58, 416
Lil Jon, 536
Lil Nas X, 166, 563, 564
Lil Pump, 552
Lil Yachty, 572
Limbaugh, Rush, 252, 473, 527
Lin, Jeremy, 527
Lindbergh, Charles, 54
Lindell, Mike, 572
Linden, Hal, 483

Linkin Park, 511, 523
Liotta, Ray, 497, 565
Lipa, Dua, 550, 562, 576, 580
Lipinski, Tara, 534
Lipowitz, Florence, 7
Lipowitz, Henry, 7
Lipowitz, Lorne. *See* Michaels, Lorne
Lipton, James, 234, 487, 509, 516
Lithgow, John, 446, 450, 454
Little, Rich, 3, 4
Little Feat, 454
Littlefield, Warren, 122
Liu, Lucy, 139, 491
Liu, Simu, 566
Live, 472, 479
Lively, Blake, 514, 518, 523, 547
Living Colour, 455
Lizzo, 166, 558, 568, 570, 578, 580
LL Cool J, 451
Lloyd, Christopher, 436
Lloyd, Graeme, 484
Lloyd, Walt, 406
Loaf, Meat, 408, 423–424, 435
Lobos, Los, 451
Locklear, Heather, 470
Loder, Kurt, 476
Loeb, Lisa, 474
Loggins, Kenny, 438
Lohan, Lindsay, 151, 267, 501, 503, 505, 508, 527
Lone Justice, 449
Long, Howie, 534
Long, Justin, 518
Longet, Claudine, 377, 378
Longfellow, Michael, 243, 358, 569, 573, 576
Longoria, Eva, 506
Lopez, Jennifer, 268, 288, 488, 491, 520, 557, 575
Lopez, Mario, 572
Lorando, Mark, 63, 64
Lorde, 541, 547
Loughlin, Lori, 555
Louis, Joe, 369
Louis-Dreyfus, Julia, xvii, 87, 94, 97, 99, 100, 153, 238, 242, 243, 260, 348, 437, 440, 442, 445, 508, 511, 543
Lovato, Demi, 540
Love, Courtney, 268
Love, Darlene, 337, 338, 507

## Index

Loverboy, 126, 440, 444
Lovitz, Jon, 9, 103, 104, 107–110, 113, 114, 119, 133, 144, 148, 190, 191, 243, 267, 270, 349, 361, 366, 369, 379, 396, 445, 447–449, 451, 453–455, 457, 459–460, 481, 523, 558
Lowe, Rob, 111, 140, 266, 408, 409, 458, 479, 489
Lucci, Susan, 459
Luciano, Ron, 441
Lucius, 570
Ludacris, 288, 501, 503, 509, 515
Ludwin, Rick, 486, 557
Lumineers, the, 530, 585
Luna Li, 569
Lupone, Patti, 483
Lutz, John, 590
Lynch, Jane, 167, 521
Lynch, Marshawn, 538
Lynn, Meredith Scott, 403
Lyonne, Natasha, 253, 568, 570

Mac, Bernie, 498
Macdonald, Norm, 26, 133, 139, 162, 196, 242–244, 278, 302, 343, 350–352, 383, 387, 468, 471, 474–477, 479, 480, 482, 487, 517, 564
MacDowell, Andie, 457
MacFarlane, Seth, 528
Machine Gun Kelly, 562
Mack, Ronald, 332
Macklemore, 531
MacLachlan, Kyle, 292, 459
Macmillan, Harold, 48
MacPherson, Elle, 476
Macron, Emmanuel, 558
Macy, W. H., 113
Madden, Helen, 255, 477
Madden, John, 435, 441
Madden, Mickey, 530
Maddow, Rachel, 179, 260, 516, 522, 540
Madlib, 570
Madness, 442
Madonna, xi, 104–105, 110, 111, 152, 257, 265, 266, 301, 308, 445, 448, 466, 518, 534
Magic Band, 431

Maguire, Tobey, 139, 151, 489
Mahal, Taj, 421
Mahoney, John, 450
Mai, Ella, 553
Mailer, Norman, 88, 89
Majors, Jonathan, 565
Malakian, Daron, 389
Malden, Karl, 442
Malek, Rami, 565
al-Maliki, Nouri, 509
Malkovich, John, 278, 454, 468, 515
Malone, Post, 568
Malone, Tom, 109
Mamas and the Papas, the, 285
Manafort, Paul, 218, 548
Manchin, Joe, 553, 564
Mancini, Michael, 577–579
Måneskin, 566
Manheim, Camryn, 487
Mann, Aimee, 532
Manning, Eli, 264, 317, 528, 569
Manning, Peyton, 152, 264, 317, 511, 567, 569
Mantegna, Joe, 124, 460
Maracotta, Lindsay, 38
Mardell, Dan, 527
Margulies, Julianna, 488
Mariachi Vargas de Tecalitlán, the, 452
Marie, Rose, 20
Marin, Cheech, 138
Marin, Rich, 122
Marley, Bob, 292–293
Marley, Damian, 548
Maroney, Caroline, 579–580
Maroon 5, 340, 501, 512, 525, 529, 536
Mars, Bruno, 288, 521, 529, 537, 544, 545
Marsalis, Branford, 451
Marsalis, Wynton, 450
Marsh, Earle, 49
Marshall, Ben, 341, 342, 565, 566
Marshall, Penny, 16, 41, 63, 127, 412, 478
Marshall, Thurgood, 568
Martel, Jay, 385
Martin, Andrea, 23
Martin, Billy, 108, 448
Martin, Chris, 559, 560
Martin, Dean, 440
Martin, Dick, 51

Martin, George, 570
Martin, Millicent, 49
Martin, Pamela Sue, 444
Martin, Ricky, 486, 490
Martin, Steve, 38, 50, 62, 67, 68, 84, 116, 127–128, 138, 145, 162, 172, 256, 267, 271–275, 278, 315, 364, 368, 385, 393, 417, 419, 421, 423–425, 428, 430, 438, 449, 451, 456, 460, 463, 483, 498, 507, 509, 513, 516, 520, 521, 525, 528, 531, 545, 547, 550, 554, 566–568, 570, 579, 587
Martin, Strother, 4, 430
Martin, Trayvon, 533
Martinez, Tino, 484
Mascis, J., 532
Maslany, Tatiana, 536
Maslin, Janet, 396, 405
Mason, Jackie, 456
Massa, Eric, 520
Massar, David, 415
Masterson, Mary Stuart, 464
Mastroianni, Marcello, 333
Matenopoulos, Debbie, 485
Mathers, Jerry, 430
Matthau, Walter, 21, 42, 73, 425
Matthews, Chris, 177, 179, 238, 499–502, 504, 505, 510, 559
Matthews, Dave, 499, 500, 518
Matthius, Gail, 75, 77, 79–83, 85, 244, 318, 346, 431, 432, 434
Mayer, John, 499, 529, 553
Mays, Willie, 4
Mayweather, Floyd, 539
McAdams, Rachel, 575
McAvoy, James, 554
McBrayer, Jack, 516, 519, 520, 540
McBride, Danny, 530
McCain, Cindy, 515
McCain, John, 171, 205–207, 211, 212, 274, 488, 496, 514, 515
McCann, Ruth, 402
McCarthy, Melissa, 167, 177, 217, 218, 222, 240, 273, 525, 531, 534, 542, 546, 547, 583
McCarthy-Miller, Beth, 579

Index 621

McCartney, Linda, 430, 431
McCartney, Paul, 127, 153, 154, 166, 285, 430, 431, 466, 509, 522, 530, 534, 542
McCary, Dave, 247
McCary, Jim, 278
McClinton, Delbert, 426, 433
McConaughey, Matthew, 157, 497, 541
McConnell, Mitch, 212, 516, 537, 553, 556, 558, 559, 562, 570
McCormack, Eric, 496
McCoy, Travie, 525
McCulloch, Bruce, 406
McDaniels, Darryl, 165, 546
McDermott, Dylan, 487
McDevitt, Harry, 414
McDonald, Michael, 439
McDonell, Terry, 88
McDormand, Frances, 167
McDowell, Jack, 470
McDowell, Malcolm, 82, 431
McEnany, Kayleigh, 167
McEnroe, John, 500, 523, 527, 549
McFerrin, Bobby, 454
McGarrigle, Ann, 420
McGarrigle, Kate, 420
McGovern, Eleanor, 442
McGovern, George, 305, 349, 442
McGraw, Tim, 515
McGreevey, Jim, 301
McGrew, Abby, 528
McGuiness, Rick, 580, 581
McGuiness, William, 580, 581
McGuinness, Rick, 582
McIlroy, Randal, 81
McKay, Adam, xvii, 145, 232, 234, 242, 328, 488, 491, 492, 590
McKean, Michael, 122, 129, 132, 138, 176, 244, 395, 443, 470, 472, 473
McKee, Kathrine, 413
McKellen, Ian, 495
McKinney, Mark, 122, 136, 242, 244, 400, 406, 472, 473, 476, 479
McKinnon, Kate, 158, 164–169, 172, 177, 212–214, 218, 219, 221, 223, 230, 240, 244–245, 258, 279, 300, 323,
325, 326, 356–357, 527, 529, 533–537, 539–564, 566–569, 574, 576, 583
McLachlan, Sarah, 481
McLaughlin, John, 461, 462, 464
McLean, Don, 53
McMahon, Ed, 457
McMahon, Vince, 272, 488
McNicholas, Dennis, 201, 400, 587
McRae, Tate, 574
Mead, Taylor, 415, 417
Meadows, Tim, 119, 125, 129, 133, 136, 198, 245, 272, 299, 396, 398, 400, 461, 467–469, 472, 474, 475, 478–480, 483, 485, 488–490
Meara, Anne, 450
Medved, Michael, 71
Meese, Ed, 91, 188
Mel, Melle, 457
Mellencamp, John Cougar, 93, 455, 456
Melvin, Milan, 437, 439
Melvoin, Wendy, 483
Men at Work, 109, 437, 440
Mendes, Shawn, 545, 556, 581
Menefee, Curt, 571
Merchant, Natalie, 474, 483
Merchant, Stephen, 340
Mercury, Freddie, 536
Merkel, Angela, 356
Merriweather, Antoine, 473
Metallica, 481
Metcalf, Laurie, 85, 245, 251, 346, 434
Meters, the, 420
Metzger, Alan, 396
Meyer, George, 190, 589
Meyer, Muffie, 397
Meyers, Mike, 114–116
Meyers, Seth, xvii, 144, 154, 155, 161, 178, 180, 195, 201, 202, 208, 212, 237, 241, 245, 247, 250, 300, 343, 352–355, 357, 401, 493, 495, 499, 501, 503, 504, 507, 508, 510, 532, 534, 536, 553, 586, 590
MGMT, 520
Michael, George, 481
Michaels, Lorne, xvii, 4, 6–15, 17, 20, 22, 23, 28–30, 33, 35–38, 40, 41, 43, 45, 49, 51, 52, 57, 59, 61, 63,
78, 79, 88, 101–110, 119, 121, 122, 128, 131–132, 144, 146, 156, 159, 160, 162, 166, 170, 173, 177, 183, 189, 199, 207, 217, 218, 230, 240, 246, 257, 263–267, 272–273, 280, 282–286, 293, 298, 300, 303, 310, 361, 363–364, 373, 376–378, 380, 383, 384, 386, 389, 392, 395–397, 400, 401, 403, 404, 406–408, 413–416, 418, 421, 447, 462, 480, 504, 528, 552, 572, 570–583, 587–591
Mick Fleetwood's Zoo, 440
Midler, Bette, 427
Midnight Oil, 467
Mifune, Toshiro, 56, 57
Mighty Mighty Bosstones, the, 480
Migos, 548, 551
Miguel, 531
Milani, Jason, 580–583
Milhiser, John, 245–246, 532
Mill, Meek, 554, 556
Milland, Ray, 334
Miller, Ann, 93, 255, 474
Miller, Dennis, 103, 104, 109, 114, 119, 133, 246, 254, 257, 314, 343, 349–351, 379, 445, 446, 448, 462
Miller, James Andrew, xv, 6, 28, 29, 38–40, 75, 78, 107, 108, 189, 293
Miller, Judy, 397, 422
Miller, Marcus, 400
Miller, Marilyn Suzanne, 10, 67, 86, 396, 589–591
Miller, Stephen, 218
Miller, Von, 542
Miller, Zell, 506
Mills, Donna, 138
Milone, Christopher, 580
Milos, Sofia, 400
Minaj, Nicki, 310, 329, 523, 525, 537, 540, 552, 582
Minhaj, Hasan, 228
Mink DeVille, 436
Minnelli, Liza, 261, 516
Minogue, Kylie, 495
Minor, Jerry, 246, 490, 493
Minot, Dinah, 404, 408
Miranda, Lin-Manuel, 544, 552, 557

Mirren, Helen, 521, 524
Mischer, Don, 5, 53
Mitchell, Barry, 436, 438
Mitchell, Finesse, 246, 296, 499, 503, 507, 508
Mitchell, Kel, 570
Mitchell, Rachel, 553
Mitchell, Ty, 556
Mitchum, Bentley, 452
Mitchum, Robert, 452
MØ, 537
Moby, 496
Modest Mouse, 502, 503
Modine, Matthew, 454
Moffat, Alex, 158, 176, 218–221, 227, 246, 357, 544, 547–554, 558, 559, 562–565, 567, 569
Mohr, Jay, 127, 132, 246–247, 381, 468, 473, 474
Momoa, Jason, 554, 574
Monáe, Janelle, 533
Money, Eddie, 423
Monroe, Marilyn, 105, 106
Montalban, Ricardo, 368
Montana, Joe, 264, 449
Monty Python, 331, 437
Mooney, Kyle, 158, 161, 215, 229, 247, 341, 357, 532, 535–537, 539, 541, 542, 553, 554, 556, 559, 568
Mooney, Paul, 56
Moore, Demi, 454, 504
Moore, Dudley, 414, 446
Moore, Julianne, 383, 400, 482
Moore, Kenny, 294
Moore, Mary Tyler, 112, 116, 117, 455
Moore, Roy, 549
Morales, Natalie, 542
Moran, Terry, 472
Moranis, Rick, 90, 438, 456
Morello, Tom, 294, 295
Morgan, Piers, 530, 533
Morgan, Tracy, 133, 142, 161, 247, 477, 484, 486, 499, 500, 507, 509, 513, 517, 526, 540, 547, 550, 552, 557, 558, 570
Morissette, Alanis, 125, 474, 484
Moroney, Erin, 572
Morris, Garrett, 20–21, 24, 25, 41, 44, 63, 65, 68, 73, 74, 78, 96, 270, 281, 282, 313, 332, 343, 344, 378, 396, 411, 413, 423, 425, 426, 431, 497
Morris, Howard, 47
Morris, Maren, 546
Morrison, Jim, 409
Morrison, Keith, 237
Morrison, Van, 289, 425
Morrissey, 465
Morrow, Jeff, 270
Morrow, Rob, 430, 463
Moseley, Jonny, 495
Moss, Elisabeth, 515, 517
Mossano, Mark, 453
Mota, Manny, 73, 81
Motels, the, 441
Mother Teresa, 302
Mothersbaugh, Mark, 398
Mott, James, 587
Moynihan, Bobby, 68, 111, 206, 208, 247–248, 353, 354, 356, 357, 360, 383, 515, 519, 520, 525, 527, 528, 531–533, 535–537, 539–544, 548, 569
Moynihan, Daniel P., 430
Mr. Mister, 446
Mr. T, 96, 268, 368, 437, 444
Mraz, Jason, 516
Ms. Dynamite, 498
Mudd, Roger, 80
Mueller, Robert, 218, 551–556
Muhammed, Raheem Abdul, 346–348
Muir, Rob, 406
Mulaney, John, xvii, 148, 155, 274, 551, 554, 555, 559, 561, 567, 581, 586, 590
Mullally, Megan, 500, 506
Mulligan, Carey, 563
Mulroney, Dermot, 530
Mumford & Sons, 529, 539, 554, 584
Mumolo, Annie, 261
Mumy, Billy, 83
Munro, Lochlyn, 403
Murdoch, Rupert, 179
Murphy, Brittany, 497
Murphy, Eddie, xvii, 75, 77, 79, 83, 85, 87–89, 92, 93, 96–99, 117, 148, 156, 233, 248, 250, 252, 268, 291, 308, 336, 347, 348, 365–368, 431–433, 438, 440, 444, 558, 578, 580, 581
Murphy, Ryan, 110

Murphy, Tim, 535
Murray, Anne, 286, 413, 430, 468
Murray, Bill, ix, xvii, 5, 8, 9, 12, 14, 16, 18, 21–22, 24, 25, 52, 60, 62, 64, 65, 68, 71, 72, 74–78, 80, 84, 97, 148, 162, 187, 188, 218, 232, 273, 275, 277, 282, 332, 343, 344, 346, 347, 368, 378, 386, 398, 420, 424, 425, 428, 429, 431, 433, 435, 450, 466, 471, 485, 545, 550, 591
Murray, Matt, 587–588, 590
Musburger, Brent, 435, 458
Muse, 519, 529
Musgraves, Kacey, 552, 564, 575
Musical Youth, 439
Musk, Elon, 563, 568, 580
My Chemical Romance, 509
My Morning Jacket, 513, 514
Myers, Mike, xvii, 110, 117, 119, 120, 123–125, 127, 128, 130, 132, 133, 149, 230, 248, 308, 320, 370, 380, 407–409, 454, 455, 460, 462–464, 466, 468, 470, 471, 479, 480, 500, 505, 523, 538, 541, 589
Mystikal, 537

Nader, Ralph, 4, 419, 430
Najimy, Kathy, 398
Namath, Joe, 3, 4
Nanjiani, Kumail, 514, 548
Nate Dogg, 498
National, the, 534
Nealon, Kevin, 109, 113, 114, 119, 121, 126, 133, 148, 176, 248, 318, 349–351, 369, 379, 395, 396, 398, 448, 451–455, 457, 458, 460–463, 472, 486, 493
Neeson, Liam, 299, 502, 528, 534
Nelly, 497, 502
Nelson, Frank, 435
Nelson, Jerry, 38
Nelson, Rick, 426
Nelson, Willie, 111, 288, 294, 422, 450, 467
Nelsons, the, 446
N.E.R.D., 501
Nesmith, Michael, 432

Nessen, Ron, 4, 170, 171, 183, 280–281, 289, 307, 415
Netanyahu, Benjamin, 177
Neville, Aaron, 457
Neville, Ivan, 453, 463
Neville Brothers, the, 447, 460
New Edition, 477
New Joe Jackson Band, the, 437
Newhart, Bob, 229, 430, 472
Newman, David, 395
Newman, Edwin, 80, 349, 368, 442, 450
Newman, Laraine, 3, 8–10, 22–23, 25, 35, 40, 42, 59–63, 65, 68, 72, 78, 80, 116, 138, 271, 344, 362, 363, 395, 411, 416, 419, 420, 430, 431
Newman, Paul, 450
Newman, Randy, 35, 63, 287, 288, 411, 412, 423, 428, 439, 449, 453
Newsom, Gavin, 563
Newton-John, Olivia, 288, 437
Ne-Yo, 530
Nicholaw, Casey, 552
Nichols, Mike, 396–398, 537
Nicholson, Jack, 304–305, 365, 457, 481, 512
Nicks, Stevie, 441
Nielsen, Leslie, 455
Niemi, Lisa, 459
Night Sweats, the, 562
Nigro, Dan, 564
Nimoy, Leonard, 517
Nirvana, 125, 153, 285, 463, 467
Nixon, Pat, 20, 185, 186
Nixon, Richard, 15, 51, 53, 172, 173, 181–182, 185–187, 280, 296, 362, 365, 415, 424, 442, 471
No Doubt, 478, 494
Noah, Trevor, 180
Noem, Governor Kristi, 576
Noll, Susan, 582–584, 587, 588
Nolte, Nick, 96, 154, 156
Noname, 546
Noriega, Manuel, 457
Norman, Peter, 396
Norman, Philip, 285
Norton, Edward, 486, 498, 533
Norton, Ken, 42
Notting Hillbillies, the, 458, 459

Novello, Don, 25, 26, 68, 73, 108, 349, 396, 397, 428, 429, 431, 445, 474
Novoselic, Krist, 153, 530
NSYNC, 488
Null, Luke, 248–249, 548
Numan, Gary, 429
Nwodim, Ego, 158, 167, 249, 552, 563, 564, 566, 568, 570, 571, 574
Nyad, Diana, 418

Oasis, 480
Oates, John, 436
Obama, Barack, 156, 165, 166, 171, 174–176, 184, 189, 207–214, 223, 226, 228, 250, 251, 272, 274, 305, 310, 324, 356, 511, 512, 516–520, 522–524, 526, 528, 530–537
Obama, Michelle, 156, 157, 533, 535, 537
O'Brien, Conan, xvii, 110, 132, 178, 191, 267, 274, 371, 409, 460, 492, 507, 567, 589
O'Brien, Dylan, 565
O'Brien, Mike, 249, 341, 532, 543
Ocasek, Ric, 448, 449
Ocasio-Cortez, Alexandria, 260, 564
Ocean, Billy, 444
Ocean, Frank, 528
O'Connell, Finneas, 556, 566, 574
O'Connell, Patrick, 566
O'Connor, Carroll, 417
O'Connor, John J., 45, 46, 122, 311
O'Connor, Johnny, 238
O'Connor, Sandra Day, 151
O'Connor, Sinéad, 121, 285, 292–294, 376, 377, 458, 459, 465
Odenkirk, Bob, xvii, 115, 119, 129, 372, 409, 589
O'Donnell, Christine, 150, 521
O'Donnell, Katherine, 586
O'Donnell, Rosie, 125, 127, 468, 478
O'Donnell, Steve, 11
O'Donoghue, Michael, ix, 8, 10–11, 15, 16, 22, 24,

27–29, 35, 38, 84–86, 89–92, 106, 282, 290, 377, 396, 411, 417, 430, 471, 589, 591
Of Monsters and Men, 531
Offerman, Nick, 500
Ofili, Natasha, 571
Oh, Sandra, 555
O'Hara, Catherine, 434, 461, 465
O'Hara, Shaun, 528
Ohlmeyer, Don, 26, 131, 132, 244, 347, 351, 352
Olbermann, Keith, 267
Oliver, John, 180
Oliver, Pam, 571
Olsen, Ashley, 256, 316, 502
Olsen, Elizabeth, 568
Olsen, Mary-Kate, 316, 502
One Direction, 527, 533, 538
O'Neal, Shaquille, 356
O'Neill, Ed, 457
Oneohtrix Point Never, 559
Ora, Rita, 537
Orbison, Roy, 451
O'Reilly, Bill, 154, 179, 180, 252, 523, 527
Orlando, Tony, 334, 378
Orlean, Susan, 102, 106, 108
Ortega, Jenna, 572, 579
Osborne, Joan, 475
Osborne, John, 333
Osbourne, Ozzy, 254, 255
Osbourne, Sharon, 139, 250
Osmond, Donny, 97, 242
Osmond, Marie, 97
Oteri, Cheri, 9, 132–136, 234, 249, 296, 300, 308, 309, 474, 476, 480, 482, 487, 489
Outkast, 495, 499
Ouziel-Mack, Laura, 577, 578
Overton, Rick, 424
Owens, Candace, 566
Owens, Valerie Biden, 170
Oxenberg, Catherine, 447
Oz, Frank, 38, 392
Oz, Mehmet, 520, 569

Paak, Anderson, 553, 554
Paar, Jack, 312
Pace, Frankie, 442
Pacino, Al, 135, 237
Pagani, Rachel, 581–583
Page, Ellen, 513
Page, Jimmy, 483

## Index

Page, Regé-Jean, 563
Paglia, Camille, 398
Palin, Mary, 441
Palin, Michael, 52, 424, 426, 427, 430, 441, 478
Palin, Sarah, 153, 170, 175, 200, 205–210, 217, 235, 270, 287, 308, 309, 514, 515, 542
Palin, Todd, 206
Palladino, Pino, 538
Palmer, Keke, 570
Palminteri, Chazz, 403
Paltrow, Gwyneth, 485, 488, 490, 494, 523, 555
Panic! at the Disco, 513
Papp, Joseph, 436
Pardo, Don, 11, 29, 35, 58, 88, 138, 238, 282, 411, 432, 477, 536
Parker, Kevin, 553
Parker, Sarah Jessica, 9, 471
Parker-Lee, John, 574
Parks, Bert, 460
Parliament-Funkadelic, 448
Parnell, Chris, 9, 144, 146, 163, 176, 199, 201, 203, 236, 249, 254, 255, 296, 338, 373, 374, 400, 483, 485, 486, 488–491, 493, 495–498, 502, 504, 507, 508, 514, 528, 529
Parsons, Jim, 360, 534
Parsons, Karyn, 400, 401
Parton, Dolly, 20, 90, 264, 288, 455, 479
Pascal, Pablo, 573
Pascal, Pedro, 327, 571, 577
Passion Pit, 529
Pataki, George, 475
Paterson, David, 521
Patric, Jason, 469
Patrick, Butch, 115
Patrick, Liz, 566, 577, 579
Patti Smith Group, 286, 289, 415
Paul, Aaron, 532
Paul, Rand, 539, 541
Paul, Ron, 208
Paul, Sean, 265, 267, 498
Paulin, Viveca, 307
Paulsen, Pat, 172
Paulson, Sarah, 571
Pavarotti, Luciano, 484
Paxton, Bill, 83, 300, 432, 485
Payton, Walter, 449

Pearl Jam, 464, 470, 508, 520
Peckham, Diana, 94
Peckham, James, 94–95
Pedrad, Nasim, 111, 212, 228, 250, 309, 360, 387, 518, 521, 522, 525, 529, 535, 551
Peeples, Nia, 393
Pell, Paula, 12, 175, 507, 574, 576, 588, 590, 591
Peller, Clara, 305, 442
Pelosi, Nancy, 151, 167, 261, 383, 509, 516, 569
Pence, Karen, 548, 562
Pence, Mike, 218, 220, 223, 544, 545, 547–549, 551, 553, 557, 559, 561, 562
Pendarvis, Janice, 485
Penn, Michael, 451, 532
Penn, Sean, xi, 104, 111, 127, 265, 266, 451, 475
Penn & Teller, 445–447, 449
Perkins, Anthony, 38, 42, 265, 415
Perkins, Marlin, 83
Perlman, Rhea, 269, 432, 440
Perot, Ross, 128, 194, 199, 464–465, 481
Perrin, Dennis, 10, 90, 91
Perry, Joe, 370, 468
Perry, Katy, 152, 521, 526, 532, 547, 567
Perry, Luke, 466
Perry, Matthew, 139, 234, 480, 573
Perry, Rick, 208, 323, 525, 528
Persky, Lisa Jane, 395
Persuasions, the, 422
Pesci, Joe, 134–136, 229, 294, 307, 465, 475, 479, 559
Peters, Bernadette, 417, 435
Petersen, Al Alen, 414
Petski, Denise, 159
Petty, Tom, 125, 153, 428, 439, 456, 462, 471, 477, 486, 521, 548
Pharoah, Jay, 156, 175, 176, 212, 250, 356, 521, 524, 528–539, 541–544
Phelps, Leon, 480, 483, 485, 489
Phelps, Michael, 264, 514
Philbin, Regis, 138, 238, 434, 460, 483, 489
Phillippe, Ryan, 401, 402, 520, 567

Phillips, Esther, 412
Phipps, Wintley, 443
Phish, 294, 497
Phoenix, 517, 531
Phraner, Brian, 587
Pickett, Lenny, 557
Piedmont, Matt, 588
Pierce, David Hyde, 472
Pierson, Kate, 287
Pinchot, Bronson, 450
Pine, Chris, 517, 547
Pink, 494, 500, 548
Pinto, John, 582–585, 587, 589
Pirro, Jeanine, 177, 218, 258, 553, 554, 565–567
Pisano, Judith Belushi, 15, 41, 56, 58, 73, 333, 363
Piscopo, Joe, 75, 77, 79–83, 85, 87, 88, 91, 94, 96–99, 176, 188, 250, 305, 320, 346–348, 431–433, 441, 442
Pitt, Brad, 135, 218, 305–307, 484, 560
Piven, Jeremy, 510
Place, Mary Kay, 422
Plachy, Sylvia, 498
Plant, Robert, 444
Plasketes, George, 51
Playboi Carti, 575
Plaza, Aubrey, 298, 571
Pleasence, Donald, 17, 91, 290, 434
Pleshette, Suzanne, 472
Plimpton, George, 485, 495
P.O.D, 495
Podsednik, Scott, 506
Poehler, Amy, xvii, 139, 144, 149, 151, 152, 180, 205, 207–209, 221, 235, 245, 250–251, 270, 296, 301, 305, 309, 352, 354, 355, 493, 496, 500, 502–504, 507, 510, 512–518, 520, 521, 526–528, 532, 534, 541, 556, 571, 584
Pogues, the, 458
Poindexter, Buster, 448–450, 452
Polizzi, Nicole "Snooki," 48, 111, 247
Pollack, Kevin, 408
Pomerantz, Hart, 7, 51
Pompeo, Mike, 218, 557
Pook, Bob, 29
Poole, Michael, 577–579

Pope John Paul II, 292, 293
Porizkova, Paulina, 450
Porter, Billy, 557
Portishead, 482
Portman, Natalie, 507, 528, 550
Posner, David, 334
Potter, Dennis, 48
Poundstone, Paula, 441
Povich, Maury, 457
Powell, Colin, 233, 495, 503
Powell, Glen, 575
Power Station, 444
Prager, Emily, 85, 251, 434
Pratt, Chris, 536
Prentiss, Paula, 430
Preservation Hall Jazz Band, 416
Presley, Elvis, 160, 285
Pressly, Jaime, 508
Preston, Billy, 27, 32, 44, 395, 411
Pretenders, the, 109, 449, 470
Price, Alan, 420
Price, Kelly, 542
Price, Margo, 543
Price, Vincent, 237, 304
Priestley, Jason, 116, 464
Prime Time, 427
Prince, 166, 241, 386, 433, 444, 501, 507, 537
Prince Charles, 104
Princess Diana, 104
Principal, Victoria, 110
Prine, John, 417
Prinze, Freddie, Jr., 488
Probst, Jeff, 569
ProMags, 291
Pryor, Richard, 2, 3, 8, 56, 57, 82, 263, 376, 378, 412, 536
Pryor, Shelley, 413
Psaki, Jen, 226
Public Enemy, 125, 462
Puff Daddy, 483
Pull, the, 451
Pullman, Bill, 477
Purcigliotti, Andrea, 579
Purdham, Todd, 170
Pusha T, 521
Puth, Charlie, 539
Putin, Vladimir, 218, 220, 229, 353, 546, 549, 554

Quaid, Dennis, 460
Quaid, Randy, 103–105, 107, 108, 110, 176, 188, 251, 445, 448

Quavo, 559
Quayle, Dan, 191, 453, 459
Queen, 109, 437
Queen Ida, 445
Queen Elizabeth, 228
Queen Latifah, 288, 498, 502, 514
Queens of the Stone Age, 505
Questlove, 549
Quincy D III, 457
Quinn, Colin, 133, 135, 251, 252, 300, 343, 350, 403, 474, 479, 482, 489
Quinto, Zachary, 517

Rachmil, Michael I., 395
Radcliffe, AnneMichelle, 586
Radcliffe, Daniel, 152, 265, 526
Radiohead, 153, 490, 525
Radner, Gilda, ix, xvii, 8–10, 12–14, 16, 20, 22–25, 32, 38, 40–44, 52, 55, 59, 61, 63, 65–66, 68–74, 78, 80, 116, 117, 142, 148, 149, 230, 269, 271, 273, 289, 309, 313, 318, 332–334, 344, 345, 378, 396–398, 411, 415, 417–420, 423, 424, 426, 429–431, 456, 589
Radner, Martin, 424
Rae, Corinne Bailey, 508, 509
Rae, Issa, 561
Rafferty, Colleen, 541, 568, 576
Rage Against the Machine (RATM), 294–295, 476
Rainer, Peter, 405
Raitt, Bonnie, ix, 125, 423, 457, 462, 471
Raitt, John, ix
Rajskub, Mary Lynn, 535
Ramis, Harold, 16, 404
Rancid, 475
Rand, Paul, 535
Raphael, June Diane, 261
Rapp, Reneé, 574
Rateliff, Nathaniel, 562
Rathbone, Basil, 47
Rather, Dan, 250, 494
Rawlings, Donnell, 570
Rawls, Lou, 395
Rayburn, Gene, 459
RAYE, 575, 576
Raywood, Keith, 571, 579–583, 585

Rea, Stephen, 398, 467
Reagan, Nancy, 20, 80, 81, 104, 106, 107, 191–192, 237, 239, 259, 433, 456
Reagan, Ronald, 51, 80, 81, 91, 98, 103, 106, 107, 114, 174, 176, 184, 188–190, 305, 415, 433, 441, 446, 449, 450, 454, 458, 461
Reagan, Ronald Prescott, 106–107
Record, Eugene, 424
Red Hot Chili Peppers, 291–292, 464, 508
Redbone, Leon, 414, 416, 422, 439
Redd, Chris, 158, 164, 165, 167, 176, 251, 548–550, 553, 562, 563, 565, 568, 569, 582
Reddy, Helen, 3
Redman, 575
Reece, Daniel, 105
Reed, Lou, 449, 492, 533, 560
Reed, Rex, 437
Reedus, Norman, 539
Reese, Robert, 590, 589
Reeve, Christopher, 444, 445
Reeves, Keanu, 139
Reeves, Martha, 413
Regan, Don, 190
Reilly, Charles Nelson, 268
Reilly, John C., 509
Rein, Richard K., 79
Reincheld, Aaron, 36
Reiner, Carl, 47, 50
Reiner, Rob, 16, 17, 39, 41, 263, 412
Reinhold, Judge, 453
Reiser, Paul, 473
Reitz, Stephanie, 142
R.E.M., 125, 388, 461, 471, 487
Renaudo, Jeff, 191, 459
Renner, Jeremy, 529
Reno, Janet, 140, 177, 197, 234, 307, 478–480, 482, 483, 491
Rensin, David, 307
Replacements, the, 446
Rex, Simon, 567
Reynolds, Burt, 98, 139, 162, 244, 269, 430
Reynolds, Daniel, 324
Reynolds, Debbie, 249, 474
Reynolds, Ryan, 518, 547, 557
Rhett, Thomas, 555

Ricch, Roddy, 568
Ricci, Christina, 140, 463, 468, 487
Rice, Condoleezza, 501, 503, 512
Rice, Gigi, 403
Rich, Frank, 154, 520
Rich, Simon, 590
Richards, Jeff, 251–252, 353, 499, 500
Richards, Keith, 453
Richards, Michael, 95
Richardson, Miranda, 398, 467
Richie, Lionel, 438
Richman, Jonathan, 483
Richmond, Jeff, 552
Rickles, Don, 294, 349, 441
Ridley, Daisy, 541
Riggle, Rob, 252, 502, 505
Riggs, Dudley, 9
Rihanna, 164, 519, 522, 528–529, 540
Riley, Pat, 392, 398, 399, 401
Ripa, Kelly, 315, 499, 507, 529
Riperton, Minnie, 253
Ripp, Heino, 589
Risley, Ann, 75, 77, 79, 80, 85, 252, 346, 431, 433
Rivera, Geraldo, 238
Rivers, Joan, 94, 439, 486, 536
Rizzo, Anthony, 545
Roach, Hal, 97
Robbie, Margot, 218, 544
Robbins, Tim, 292, 293, 449, 465
Robert Cray Band, 450, 561
Roberts, Cokie, 233, 260
Roberts, Doris, 485
Roberts, John, 505
Roberts, Oral, 450
Robertson, Cliff, 478
Robertson, Pat, 507
Robertson, Robbie, 452, 463
Robinson, Doug, 126
Robinson, J. Peter, 407
Robinson, Jackie, 568
Robinson, Tim, 252, 529
Robyn, 526
Roches, the, 428
Rock, Chris, xvii, 120, 123, 222, 250, 252–253, 257, 368, 459, 462, 468, 477, 480, 484, 511, 534, 537, 544, 545, 552, 556, 558, 560, 564, 565
Rock, Jay, 537

Rockefeller, David, 432
Rocket, Charles, 75, 77, 79–83, 85, 176, 188, 244, 253, 279, 335, 346, 347, 387, 398, 431–433, 506
Rockettes, the, 487, 558
Rockwell, Sam, 550
Roddenberry, Gene, 61
Roddick, Andy, 499
Rodgers, Nile, 547
Rodman, Dennis, 476, 531, 535
Rodrigo, Olivia, 564, 574, 577
Rodriguez, Alex, 558
Rodriguez, Oz, 582
Rogen, Seth, 512, 517, 525, 535, 537, 550
Rogers, Bettie O., 584–586
Rogers, Jackie, Jr., 99
Rogers, Maggie, 553
Rohnke, Terry, 589
Roker, Al, 483, 506, 512, 542, 567
Rolen, Scott, 481
Rolling Stones, the, 70, 285, 288, 289, 425
Rollins Band, 479
Romano, Ray, 485, 498
Romero, Cesar, 368
Romney, Mitt, 208, 258, 525–529, 542, 545
Ronan, Saoirse, 164, 166, 549
Ronson, Mark, 537, 545, 554
Ronstadt, Linda, 128, 278, 287, 427, 432, 452, 457
Rooney, Andy, 250
Rooney, Mickey, 50, 93
Rooney, Tom, 24
Roosevelt, Eleanor, 20
Roosevelt, Franklin, 185, 186
Rosalía, 563, 567
Rosato, Tony, 85, 87, 91, 92, 253, 434, 546
Rose, Charlie, 136, 538
Rose, Frank, 120
Rose, George, 432
Rose, Pete, 455
Rosen, Barry, 335
Rosenberg, Howard, 77, 105, 106
Rosenblatt, John, 587
Rositano, Gena, 577–579
Ross, David, 545
Ross, Diana, 259
Rota, Nino, 333
Rothenberg, Fred, 106

Rousey, Ronda, 542
Rove, Karl, 252
Rowan, Dan, 51
Rowland, Kelly, 497
Rowland, Kevin, 439
Roy, Badal, 488
Rubin, Jerry, 281, 307, 412
Rubio, Marco, 539, 541, 542, 575
Rucker, Darius, 474
Rudd, Paul, 235, 277, 515, 517, 520, 522, 526, 533, 536, 556, 558, 560, 566, 567, 576
Ruddock, Razor, 461
Rudnitsky, Jon, 253, 540, 541, 544
Rudolph, Dick, 253
Rudolph, Eric Robert, 302
Rudolph, Maya, xvii, 9, 144, 149, 151, 152, 154, 157, 218, 225, 235, 239, 253–254, 340, 401, 402, 489, 493, 494, 497–499, 503, 507, 510, 512, 515, 517, 521, 524, 526, 527, 532, 536, 542, 544, 556–558, 560–563, 574, 576, 579, 581
Ruess, Nate, 565
Rule, Ja, 493
Rumsfeld, Donald, 494, 497, 501, 503
Rundgren, Todd, 433
Run-DMC, 109, 165, 448
RuPaul, 467, 559
Russell, Bill, 4, 428
Russell, Leon, 416, 524
Russell, Mary, 416
Russert, Tim, 207
Ryan, Paul, 301, 535
Ryder, Winona, 139, 267, 493, 496
Ryfle, Steve, 201

Sabella, Ernie, 481
Sacks, Sharon, 421
Sadat, Anwar, 185, 434
Saddam Hussein, 460, 482, 496
Sade, 446, 466
Sagan, Carl, 242
Saget, Bob, 473
Sajak, Pat, 99
Salerno, Christopher, 327
Sales, Soupy, 442

# Index

Saltman, David, 59
Salt-N-Pepa, 469
Sam and Dave, 429
Samberg, Andy, xvii, 68, 144, 145, 152, 163, 206, 208, 211, 249, 254, 299, 300, 309, 310, 329, 338–340, 379, 505, 507, 510–513, 515–518, 521–523, 525–528, 530, 531, 534, 535, 544, 551, 566, 586
Sampha, 545, 569
San Giacomo, Laura, 404
Sanborn, David, 430
Sanchez, Mark, 520
Sanders, Bernie, 214–215, 540, 542–544, 549, 556, 558–560
Sanders, Deion, 472
Sanders, Sarah Huckabee, 218, 223, 548, 550, 553
Sandler, Adam, xvii, 8, 26, 120, 121, 132, 139, 254–257, 268, 309, 319, 350, 351, 371, 381, 382, 396, 398, 461, 468, 469, 473, 474, 476, 497, 556, 560, 581
Sandler, Herbert and Marion, 383, 384
Sanford, Isabel, 417
Santana, 420, 445
Santorum, Rick, 208, 526, 528
Santos, George, 571, 572, 574
Sanz, Alejandro, 506
Sanz, Horatio, 144, 147–149, 241, 254–255, 352, 353, 373, 374, 483, 485–488, 491, 496–498, 504, 505, 508, 510, 512, 526
Sarandon, Susan, 465, 517
Sargent, Herbert, 11, 29, 589, 590
Sarrazin, Michael, 416, 424
Sarsgaard, Peter, 507, 521
Savage, Fred, 458
Saweetie, 566
Sawyer, Diane, 191, 260, 478, 516
Sawyer, Marika, 590
Sayer, Leo, 419
Scaggs, Boz, 417
Scamardella, Rose Ann, 70
Scaramucci, Anthony, 218, 551
Scarborough, Joe, 550
Scarborough, Ken, 588

Schaffer, Akiva, 145, 163, 254, 329, 339–340, 401, 516, 523, 586, 590
Schanes, Christal, 585
Scheider, Roy, 444
Schiff, Richard, 497
Schiller, Bob, 12
Schiller, Tom, 12, 25, 36, 57, 328, 329, 332–334, 428, 431, 589, 590
Schlatter, George, 51
Schlosser, Herb, 7, 8
Schlosser, Herbert S., 1, 2, 4, 6, 564
Schneider, Rob, 120, 124, 196, 255, 257, 371, 460, 463, 467, 469–470, 497, 560
Schneider, Sarah, 165, 534
Schreiber, Liev, 542, 553, 556
Schroeder, Pat, 233
Schulz, Charles, 323
Schumer, Amy, 168, 540, 542, 552, 565, 569
Schumer, Chuck, 511, 548, 553, 564, 569
Schur, Michael, xvii, 588
Schwartz, Michael, 590
Schwartz, Tony, 78, 79, 84, 89
Schwarzenegger, Arnold, 113, 238, 242, 248, 369, 454, 487, 499
Schwimmer, David, 474
Scissor Sisters, 503
Scogin, Michael, 582
Scorsese, Martin, 12, 70, 127, 135, 307–308, 528
Scott, A. O., 401, 402
Scott, Drew, 571
Scott, Jonathan, 571
Scott, Seann William, 493
Scott, Tom, 429
Scott, Travis, 552, 575
Scott-Heron, Gil, 286, 412
Seaberg, Marc, 302
Seacrest, Ryan, 510
Seagal, Steven, 461
Seal, 471
Seaver, Tom, 441
Sebastian, John, 286, 415
Sebastiano, Frank, 588, 590
Section, the, 421
Sedaka, Neil, 38, 286, 414
Seeger, Pete, 172, 534
Segel, Jason, 526
Seger, Bob, 107

Seinfeld, Jerry, xvii, 247, 251, 464, 486, 508, 530, 552, 576
Selassie I, Haile, 292, 293
Seliger, Mark, 302
Sellers, Peter, 377
Serio, Jennifer, 584, 585
Serling, Rod, xvii, 15
Sessions, Jeff, 167, 218, 219, 548, 549, 551, 553
Sex Pistols, the, 289, 531
Seymour, Stephanie, 485
Shaffer, Paul, 25, 63, 242, 377, 386, 387, 393, 396, 397, 417, 428, 430, 431, 450, 452, 530, 591
Shaggy, 294, 491
Shaiman, Marc, 404
Shakira, 167, 196, 494, 506, 518
Shakun, Melissa, 580
Shakur, Tupac, 475
Shalala, Donna, 140, 307
Shales, Tom, xv, 6, 28, 29, 38–40, 45, 75, 77, 78, 81, 100, 101, 107, 108, 132, 189, 293, 314, 377
Shandling, Garry, 451
Shannon, Molly, 111, 133, 139–141, 144, 198, 255, 303, 353, 403, 406, 407, 474, 477–479, 481–485, 487, 488, 491, 511, 521, 572
Shannon, T. Sean, 328, 502, 588, 590, 591
Shapiro, Bruce, 589
Shapiro, Ken, 53
Sharkey, Nancy, 100
Sharkey, Ray, 82, 432
Sharpton, Al, 157, 179, 246, 259, 500, 511, 532, 537, 543
Shatner, William, 16, 115, 449, 514
Shearer, Harry, 25, 26, 31, 74, 80, 87, 99, 100, 176, 188, 237, 336, 428, 429, 431, 443, 444
Sheen, Charlie, 491, 523
Sheen, Martin, 429, 497
Sheeran, Ed, 535, 546, 547, 565, 583
Sheila E., 445
Sheindlin, Judge Judy, 308, 482, 484

Shelton, Blake, 166, 538
Sherman, Sarah, 254–256, 300, 358, 564, 569, 573, 574
Shield, Brooke, 318
Shins, the, 510, 527
Shipley, Ellen, 432
Shock, Elaine, 293
Shoemaker, Michael, 588, 591
Shookus, Lindsay, 579–583
Shore, Howard, 3, 12, 42, 102, 397
Short, Martin, xvii, 8, 13, 23–24, 87, 99–101, 218, 223, 233, 237, 256, 267, 280, 304, 323, 336, 403, 443, 445, 449, 478, 504, 509, 530, 536, 540, 552, 560, 570, 572, 576, 579
Show, Grant, 475
Shuster, Frank, 12
Shuster, Rosie, 9, 12, 40, 67, 86, 281, 392, 396, 589–590
Sia, 166, 538, 540
Sidibe, Gabourey, 520
Sigler, Jamie-Lynn, 515
Signorelli, James, 312, 314, 318
Silverchair, 475
Silverman, Ben, 401
Silverman, Fred, 75, 79, 92, 425–428
Silverman, Sarah, xvii, 120, 256, 260, 468, 470, 536
Silvertone, 461
Simmons, J. K., 341, 486, 538
Simmons, Richard, 469
Simms, Paul, 12, 29, 35
Simms, Phil, 562
Simon, Carly, 53, 70, 286, 415
Simon, Danny, 47, 78
Simon, Neil, 47, 91
Simon, Paul, x, 12, 29, 38, 41, 45, 70, 112, 125, 142, 145, 146, 158, 166, 267, 277, 278, 287, 288, 329, 411, 418, 422, 430, 447, 449, 452, 460, 467, 471, 490, 493, 508, 524, 527, 531, 553, 590
Simple Minds, 109, 445
Simply Red, 452
Simpson, Ashlee, 389, 390, 502, 505
Simpson, Jessica, 151, 279, 500

Simpson, O. J., 4, 26, 111, 116–117, 351, 423, 472, 474, 478, 479, 572
Simpson, Sturgill, 546, 550
Sims, Molly, 515
Sinatra, Frank, 4, 81, 97, 127, 135, 192, 250, 309, 433, 442, 465
Singing Idlers, the, 414
Sink, Sadie, 565
Siskel, Gene, 308, 329, 437, 440
Sisqó, 138, 489
Sisto, Jeremy, 520
Sivan, Troye, 550, 576
Sizz Beatz, 553
Skeeter, Daphne, 574
Skid Row, 462
Skye, Ione, 408
Slate, Jenny, 149, 256, 387, 518, 521
Slater, Christian, 462, 468, 472
Slattery, John, 515
Sledge, Percy, 450
Sleigh Bells, 527
Smashing Pumpkins, the, 468, 474, 483
Smear, Pat, 153, 530
Smigel, Robert, 124, 145, 190, 233, 257, 328, 337–339, 361, 371, 382, 383, 409, 462, 468, 507, 588–591
Smith, Anna Nicole, 511
Smith, Chris, 122, 373
Smith, David F., 59
Smith, Elliott, 484
Smith, G. E., 109, 488, 489
Smith, Kate, 50
Smith, Kenny, 539
Smith, Patti, 286, 289, 420
Smith, Rex, 432
Smith, Robert G., 366
Smith, Sam, 535, 538, 541, 548, 571
Smith, Shepard, 525, 527
Smith, Stephen A., 356
Smith, Will, 250
Smithereens, the, 458
Smits, Jimmy, 459
Smoove, J. B., 590
Smothers, Dick, 49–50, 440
Smothers, Tom, 49–50, 440
Snee, Chris, 528
Snider, Eric, 409
Snoop Dogg, 470, 478, 487, 501

Snow, Phoebe, 35, 287, 288, 411, 415, 427
Snow Patrol, 511
Snyder, Tom, 2, 14, 15, 63, 80, 98, 367, 473, 479
Solomon, John, 401, 402, 590
Sotomayor, Andrew, 583
Soul, David, 391
Soul Asylum, 467
Soundgarden, 476
Spacek, Sissy, 10, 419, 591
Spacey, Kevin, 135, 140, 307, 478, 508
Spade, David, 8, 120, 121, 127, 129, 130, 132, 135, 142, 194, 230, 234, 257, 305, 351, 373, 395, 460, 464, 476, 479, 484, 492, 504
Spanic Boys, the, 458
Sparks, 436
Spears, Britney, 288, 489, 495, 498, 499, 568, 587
Spears, Ryan, 327
Specials, the, 430
Speck, Richard, 378
Spector, Phil, 338
Spektor, Regina, 518
Spelling, Tori, 239, 298
Spencer, John, 497
Spencer, Octavia, 547
Sperling, Sy, 470
Spheeris, Penelope, 290, 407
Spice Girls, 125, 479
Spicer, Sean, 177, 217, 218, 222, 273, 546, 547
Spielberg, Steven, 16, 54, 300, 392, 528
Spiller, Nancy, 405
Spillman, Miskel, 67, 282–283, 289, 422
Spin Doctors, 465
Spinal Tap, 26, 99, 237, 442
Spinks, Leon, 16
Spinners, the, 435
Spitzer, Eliot, 513
Spitznagel, Eric, 143, 374
Spivey, Emily, 588, 590
Spoon, 512
Springer, George, 549
Springsteen, Bruce, 166, 464, 496, 541, 562, 584
Squeeze, 438
Squier, Billy, 443
Sragow, Michael, 397
St. Vincent, 535, 536, 563
Stahl, Lesley, 389

# Index

Stallion, Megan Thee, 166, 557, 560, 569, 575
Stallone, Sylvester, 403, 480, 533
Stanley Clarke Trio, 432
Stanton, Harry Dean, 446
Stapleton, Chris, 542, 550, 576
Stapleton, Jean, 417
Stapleton, Maureen, 427
Starlite, Francis Farewell, 546
Starr, Kenneth, 303, 482
Starr, Ringo, 368, 444
Stasse, Tim, 580, 581
Statler Brothers, the, 488
Stauffer, Jennifer, 585
Steele, Andrew, 245, 400, 588, 590
Stefani, Gwen, 260, 492, 504, 509, 510, 543
Stefanik, Elise, 574
Stein, Benjamin, 311
Steinberg, Brian, 159
Steinbrenner, George, 459
Steinem, Gloria, 172
Stempel, Herbert, 298
Stephen, Will, 165, 549, 582
Stephenson, Pamela, 99, 100, 257, 443, 445
Sterger, Jenn, 318
Sterling, Donald, 535
Stern, Howard, 132–133, 264, 272, 470, 479
Sternberg, Brian, 145
Stewart, French, 139
Stewart, Jimmy, 116, 190, 457
Stewart, Jon, 180, 495
Stewart, Kristen, 256, 325, 546, 557
Stewart, Martha, 236, 483, 492, 500, 501, 504
Stewart, Patrick, 469
Stewart, Rod, 434, 473
Stiles, Julia, 492, 574
Stiller, Ben, 116, 119, 139, 218, 223, 257–258, 450, 455, 484, 488, 522, 525, 551, 552, 554, 555
Stiller, Jerry, 450
Sting, 277, 288, 451, 460, 466, 476, 479, 487
Stipe, Michael, 388
Stockdale, James, 128
Stone, Emma, 259, 278, 297, 521, 525, 535, 541, 545, 548, 555, 574, 581
Stone, Oliver, 308, 463, 515

Stone, Roger, 554
Stone, Sharon, 135, 464
Stone Temple Pilots, 468
Strahan, Michael, 529, 534, 571
Stray Cats, 440
Streeter, Michael, 56, 333, 334
Streisand, Barbra Joan, 121, 127, 236, 308–309, 337
Stritch, Elaine, 53
Strokes, the, 494, 507, 523, 561
Strong, Cecily, 158–161, 164, 165, 168, 177, 215, 218, 220, 221, 223, 241, 245, 252, 258, 301, 309–310, 324, 325, 353, 354, 356–358, 529, 531, 532, 534, 536, 537, 540–545, 549–551, 553, 554, 556, 559, 562–570
Strug, Kerri, 477
Stuff, 417
Styler, Trudie, 479
Styles, Harry, 212, 535, 547, 557, 561, 578, 583
Stylistics, the, 413
Sublette, Kent, 592
Suburban Lawns, 83, 431
Sudeikis, Jason, xvii, 144, 152, 154, 176, 201, 206–208, 223, 226, 227, 258, 323, 341, 353, 354, 383, 505, 506, 508–511, 515–519, 522–529, 531, 532, 538, 542–545, 549, 555, 558–560, 565
Sugarcubes, the, 453
Sullivan, Ed, 5, 49, 312
Sullivan, Pat, 526
Sum 41, 493, 503
Sun Ra, 424
Surjik, Stephen, 408
Susskind, David, 439
Sutherland, Kiefer, 462, 535
Suvari, Mena, 491
Swaggart, Jimmy, 111
Swank, Hilary, 139, 504
Swayze, Patrick, 125, 126, 459
Sweeney, Julia, 9, 119–121, 124, 130, 258, 299, 316, 396, 398, 399, 404, 460, 467, 469, 470
Sweeney, Mike, 481
Sweeney, Sydney, 575
Sweeney, Terry, 103–107, 110, 191, 245, 259, 433, 445, 448

Swerski, Bob, 473, 499
Swift, Taylor, 153, 278, 288, 516, 518, 535, 549, 557, 565, 573, 582
Swinton, Tilda, 167
Swizz Beatz, 515, 522
Sykes, Keith, 431
Sykes, Wanda, 12
System of a Down, 388, 505
SZA, 549, 556, 570

Taccone, Asa, 340, 510, 586
Taccone, Jorma, 145, 163, 254, 329, 340, 401, 402, 510, 515, 523, 586, 590
Tagliamonti, Amy, 580–586
Take 6, 457
Talking Heads, 426
Talley, Jilly, 400
Tamar, 507
Tame Impala, 555
Tankian, Serj, 389
Tapper, Jake, 294, 300, 543, 546
Tarantino, Quentin, 474
Tarkenton, Fran, 67, 419
Tartikoff, Brandon, 102, 440, 441, 445
Tatum, Channing, 527
Taylor, Bill, 557
Taylor, Clarke, 103
Taylor, Elizabeth, 368
Taylor, James, 70, 125, 417, 427, 430, 452, 463, 468
Taylor, Rip, 408, 471, 495
Taylor, Teyana, 552
Taylor-Joy, Anya, 166, 564
Technotronic, 458
Teenage Fanclub, 464
Teller, Miles, 569
Tenacious D, 483, 495, 509
Tergesen, Lee, 408, 486
terHorst, Jerald, 280
Terkel, Studs, 53
Thatcher, Margaret, 91, 531
The-Dream, 542
Them Crooked Vultures, 153, 519, 520
Theron, Charlize, 167, 490, 535
Theroux, Justin, 559
Thiessen, Tiffani, 400
Third Eye Blind, 482, 483
Thomas, Betty, 440, 442
Thomas, Clarence, 177, 382, 462, 567

Thomas, Dave, 438
Thomas, Ginni, 567
Thomas, William "Billie," 97
Thompson, Barnaby, 408
Thompson, Emma, 556
Thompson, Kenan, 144, 152, 153, 156, 158, 160–162, 164, 165, 167, 168, 208, 243, 245, 259, 296, 356–357, 360, 383, 388, 499, 505, 506, 511, 520, 523, 524, 528–530, 532, 533, 535–539, 548, 549, 553–556, 559, 561–563, 566–572, 574, 582
Thompson Twins, the, 109, 443
Thornton, Billy Bob, 143, 479, 494
Thorogood, George, 437
Thrasher, Inga, 580, 584, 585
Throneberry, Marv, 435
T.I., 515
Tiegs, Cheryl, 455
Tigerman, Gary, 424
Tillerson, Rex, 218, 546, 551
Tilton, Charlene, 84, 387, 433
Timberlake, Justin, 68, 145, 151, 162, 164, 254, 279, 278, 288, 301, 302, 329, 339, 340, 379, 495, 499, 510, 515–517, 521, 524, 525, 527, 528, 531, 534, 566, 575, 579, 584–586
Timbuk 3, 451
Time, the, 388, 459
Tin Machine, 463
Ting Tings, the, 519
Tinker, Grant, 101
Tischler, Bob, 86
Titus, Libby, 421
TLC, 473
Tolkin, Mel, 47
Tom Petty and the Heartbreakers, 125, 153, 428, 439, 456, 462, 471, 477, 486, 521
Tomashoff, Craig, 122
Tomei, Marisa, 125, 471
Tomlin, Lily, x–xi, 2, 3, 7, 8, 12, 22, 38, 41, 46, 51, 79, 97, 142, 263, 287, 412, 417, 419, 438, 556
Tompkins, Terry, 286, 287
Tony! Toni! Toné!, 469
Tooley, Tucker, 401

Toots and the Maytals, 501
Torres, Julio, 324
Tosh, Peter, 426
Tower, John, 455
T-Pain, 513, 515, 516
Tragically Hip, the, 473
Travanti, Daniel J., 93, 436
Travers, Peter, 374, 402
Travis, Randy, 453
Travolta, John, 238, 471
Trebek, Alex, 138, 139, 162, 234–235, 269, 478, 496
Trejo, Danny, 560
Trejo, Paul, 395
Tremblay, Nina, 450
Trenchmouth, 228
Trillin, Calvin, 172
Tripp, Linda, 179, 303, 482, 483, 485, 486
Troast, Chloe, 259, 573, 574
Troggs, the, 386
Trost, Brandon, 401
Troutman, Roger, 475
Trouva, Helen, 65
Trudeau, Justin, 558
Trump, Donald, Jr., 218, 219, 232, 357, 549, 552–554
Trump, Donald J., 111, 170, 175–177, 200, 213, 216–226, 238, 240, 257, 270, 300, 306, 353, 454, 458, 500, 501, 506, 526, 540–561, 566–576, 583
Trump, Eric, 218, 219, 246, 357, 549, 552–554
Trump, Ivana, 454
Trump, Ivanka, 217–219, 223, 272, 540, 543, 544, 552
Trump, Melania, 218, 223, 258, 540, 541, 543, 549, 554
Tsongas, Paul, 128, 464
Tubman, Harriet, 568
Tucci, Stanley, 550
Tucker, Bryan H., 590
Tucker, Chris, 233
Tur, Katy, 571
Turan, Kenneth, 409
Turi, Josh, 585, 586
Turner, Bonnie, 110, 395, 407, 408, 589
Turner, Jennifer, 474
Turner, Kathleen, 444, 456
Turner, Lana, 368
Turner, Terry, 110, 395, 407, 408, 589

Turner, Tina, 231, 423, 434, 444, 479
Turturro, John, 298, 471
TV on the Radio, 516
Tweedie, Alice, 37
Twenty One Pilots, 544
Ty Dolla Sign, 552
Tyler, Steven, 118, 388, 468
Tyrell, Soozie, 450, 452
Tyson, Cicely, 426
Tyson, Mike, 519, 572

U2, 491, 503, 517, 579
UB40, 469
Uecker, Bob, 443
Ullman, Tracey, 451
Underwood, Carrie, 511–513
Upton, Kate, 527
Uptown Horns, 452
Urban, Keith, 510
Urich, Robert, 98, 436
US, 549
Usher, 153, 501, 514, 528

Vaccaro, William, 588
Valk, Eddie, 577, 578
Vampire Weekend, 513, 520, 532, 576
Van Der Beek, James, 485
Van der Scheinen, Hans, 65
van der Veen, Michael, 562
Van Doren, Charles, 298
Van Halen, Eddie, 561
van Leeuwenhoek, Antonie Philips, 65
Van Rye, Cass, 480
Van Susteren, Greta, 150, 179, 518, 519, 523
Vance, Danitra, 103, 104, 108, 110, 157, 240, 259, 283, 445, 448
Vance, Kenny, 421
Vandross, Luther, 436, 455
Vanilla Ice, 124, 460
Vardalos, Nia, 496
Vaughan, Stevie Ray, 446, 447
Vaughn, Mo, 470
Vaughn, Vince, 137, 484, 531
Vega, Suzanne, 451
Ventura, Jesse, 486
Vergara, Sofia, 527
Versace, Donatella, 494
Verschoore, Maury, 589
Veruca Salt, 479
Vic Mensa, 166
Vietor, Tommy, 184, 203

# Index

Vigoda, Abe, 477
Villaseñor, Melissa, 158, 259–260, 544, 548, 553, 564, 569
Ving, Lee, 291
Vitale, Dan, 260, 445
Voger, Mark, 375
Voices of Tomorrow, the, 419
Voices of Unity, 431
Vollers, Maryanne, 22
Von Essen, Tom, 493
von Hoffman, Nicholas, 365
Von Trier, Lars, 234
Vonnegut, Kurt, 53
Voss, Chris, 582

W. K., Andrew, 495
Wagner, Jane, 258
Wagner, Robert, 457
Wahlberg, Mark, 309, 515
Wainio, Scott, 197, 588
Wainwright III, Loudon, 286, 412
Waite, John, 109, 444
Waits, Tom, 420
Walken, Christopher, 247, 279, 373, 374, 408, 409, 457, 465, 475, 489, 492, 497, 513, 573, 587–589
Walker, Devon, 158, 260, 358, 569, 571, 574–576
Walker, Herschel, 569
Walker, Jimmie, 474
Walker, Nancy, 417
Walker, Summer, 575
Wallace, Chris, 224, 560
Wallace, Nicole, 568
Wallechinsky, David, 71
Wallen, Morgan, 561, 562
Waller-Bridge, Phoebe, 557
Wallflowers, the, 477, 490
Walls, Nancy, 132, 135, 242, 260, 474–476, 514, 553
Walsh, Fran, 12
Walsh, Joe, 530
Walters, Barbara, 59, 249, 260, 309–310, 476, 478, 500, 535
Waltz, Christoph, 530, 531
Wanz, 531
Ward, Skip, 516
Warhol, Andy, 335–336
Warner, Malcolm-Jamal, 448
Warnes, Jennifer, 421, 438
Warren, Elizabeth, 167, 557, 559

Warren, Emily, 547
Warwick, Dionne, 249
Washington, Denzel, 233, 250
Washington, Kerry, 156, 157, 533
Waters, John, 523
Waters, Maxine, 484
Waterston, Sam, 475
Watkins, Michaela, 149, 260, 515, 517
Watson, Earl, 400
Watson, Muse, 484
Watson, Tarvis, 312
Watt, Andrew, 560
Watt, J. J., 558
Wayans, Damon, 107, 108, 260, 445, 447, 448, 473
Wayans, Keenen Ivory, 260
Wayne, John, 35, 296, 385
Wayne, Johnny, 12
Wayne, Lil, 153, 514, 522, 523, 553, 556
Wayne, Steve, 406
Weathers, Carl, 452
Weathers, Patrick, 260–261, 432, 433
Weaver, Sigourney, 300, 448, 519
Webb, Danielle, 579
Weber, Kim, 580
Wechsler, Len, 582–584
Weeknd, the, 536, 540, 543, 544, 559
Weezer, 492, 493
Wegman, William, 336, 414, 421, 435
Weil, Alex, 591
Weinberg, Becky, 492
Weinberg, Mark, 107
Weinberg, Max, 492
Weiner, Marc, 436
Weingrad, Jeff, xv, 4, 6, 66, 281, 285
Weinstein, Harvey, 166
Weis, Gary, 52, 63, 68, 328, 329, 336, 413–424
Weis, Toni, 424
Weiss, Robert K., 392, 400, 403, 406
Weitz, Bruce, 436
Welch, Raquel, 38, 42, 415, 455
Welk, Lawrence, 519, 524, 528, 533
Welker, Kristen, 561
Weller, Robb, 94, 446

Welles, Orson, 15
Wells, David, 484
Wells, Noël, 261, 532, 535
Wendt, George, 124, 283, 447, 461–463, 466, 473, 480, 499
Wertmüller, Lina, 60, 333
Wessler, Charles B., 398
West, Kanye, 166, 250, 341, 505, 512, 515, 521, 532, 538, 542, 552, 553, 578, 585
Westerberg, Paul, 468
Westheimer, Ruth, 237, 348
Weston, Clint, 105
Whalley, Jim, 98
Wheelan, Brooks, 212, 261, 532, 535
Whitaker, Forest, 510
White, Betty, 142, 278, 520, 586
White, Jack, 271, 527, 551, 561, 571, 572, 581
White, Rondell, 481
White, Shaun, 569
White, Timothy, 8, 14
White, Walter, 546
White, Whitney, 404
White Stripes, the, 496
Whitehead, Clay, 53
Whitford, Bradley, 497
Whitmer, Gretchen, 563
Whitmeyer, Joseph, 580, 584
Whitson, Ed, 108
Wiig, Kristen, 9, 144, 149, 151, 167, 168, 207–208, 211, 237, 239, 240, 256, 261, 268, 280, 322, 340, 353, 354, 383, 401, 402, 506–510, 513, 514, 516, 518, 519, 521, 523–525, 527, 528, 530, 532, 533, 536, 538, 545, 556, 560, 562, 567, 574–576, 580
Wilco, 513
Wild, David, 351
Wilde, Olivia, 526
Wilder, Billy, 334
Wilder, Gene, 24
Wildmon, Donald, 379
Wilkins, Tom, 133, 480
Willard, Fred, 425
Williams, Alison, 571
Williams, Andy, 377, 378
Williams, Barry, 474
Williams, Billy Dee, 400

# Index

Williams, Brian, 152, 207, 265, 507, 508, 512, 520
Williams, Buddy, 424
Williams, Cindy, 63
Williams, Deniece, 442
Williams, Esther, 368
Williams, Gerald, 481
Williams, Harland, 406
Williams, Jesse, 565
Williams, Lucinda, 485
Williams, Pharrell, 212, 535, 536, 584
Williams, Robin, 113, 117, 176, 188, 320, 349, 441–443, 449, 452, 522
Williams, Vanessa, 464, 465, 484
Williams, Walter, 328, 330–332
Willis, Bruce, 253, 454, 456, 532
Willner, Hal, 560
Willow, 568, 569
Wilson, Andrew, 564
Wilson, Brian, 418
Wilson, Casey, 149, 261–262, 296, 383, 513, 517
Wilson, Charlie, 478
Wilson, Darren, 161
Wilson, Dave, 11, 12, 41, 78, 283, 293, 412, 413, 590
Wilson, Flip, 441
Wilson, Irv, 84
Wilson, Luke, 503, 564
Wilson, Owen, 260, 564
Wilson, Rainn, 511
Wilstein, Matt, 353
Winfrey, Oprah, 136, 156, 157, 245, 253, 341, 369, 447, 483, 533, 543
Winger, Debra, 458
Winkler, Henry, 63
Winnik, Javier, 579
Winslet, Kate, 502
Winstead, Lizz, 180
Winter, Edgar, 439

Winters, Dean, 486
Winwood, Steve, 395
Withers, Bill, 413
Witherspoon, John, 400
Witherspoon, Reese, 139, 146, 167, 253, 493, 539
Wohlers, Mark, 474, 481
Wolcott, James, 120
Wolf, Dick, xvii
Wolf, Fred, 262, 474, 477
Wolf, Peter, 443
Wolf, Scott, 482
Wolfe, George C., 259
Wolff, Michael, 550, 551
Wonder, Stevie, 96, 248, 288, 294, 439, 441
Wonder, Wayne, 498
Wood, Elijah, 500, 518
Woodruff, Judy, 260, 475, 569
Woods, James, 456
Woods, Jamila, 541
Woods, Tiger, 245
Woodward, Bob, 117, 181, 182, 186
Workman, Jimmy, 463, 468
World Party, 459
Worley, Joanne, 51
Worstraad, Jan, 64
Wright, Megh, 160
Wright, Richard S., 398
Wright, Robert, 383
Wright, Steven, 441, 444–446

xx, the, 545

Yago, Gideon, 507
Yale Whiffenpoofs, the, 435
Yang, Andrew, 559
Yang, Bowen, 158, 166, 227, 262, 326, 357, 358, 555, 557, 559, 563, 568, 569, 571–574
Yavneh, Cyrus, 398
Yeah Yeah Yeahs, 517
Yeltsin, Naina, 467

Yoakam, Dwight, 470
Yonks, Matt, 579–582
Yoshimura, Akira, 102, 571, 579–585
Yothers, Tina, 136
Young, Charles M., 92
Young, Neil, 456, 466, 489, 506, 507
Young, Paul, 450
Young Jeezy, 514
Young Thug, 542, 560, 565
Youssef, Ramy, 575
Yulin, Harris, 404

Zac Brown Band, 539
Zacherle, John, 437
Zakarian, Louie, 580–586
Zamata, Sasheer, 157, 158, 165, 262, 535–537, 540, 548
Zander, Christine, 591
Zannella, Michael, 84
Zappa, Frank, 11, 58, 288, 418, 425
Zaslow, Jeffrey, 140
Zeile, Todd, 481
Zellweger, Renée, 492
Zeman, Ned, 394
Zeta-Jones, Catherine, 139, 505
Ziegler, Maddie, 538
Zimmer, Hans, 535
Zimmerman, George, 533
Zito, Tom, 63
Zivkovic, Daniela, 582–585
Zmuda, Bob, 94, 435
Zonars, John, 285
Zoomont, Melinda, 105
Zucker, Jeff, 380, 500
Zuckerberg, Mark, 310, 523, 553, 558
Zwan, 498
Zweibel, Alan, 12–13, 25, 38, 57, 70, 363, 364, 396, 428, 591, 590
ZZ Top, 441

www.ingramcontent.com/pod-product-compliance
Lightning Source LLC
Chambersburg PA
CBHW031659230426
43668CB00006B/50